FIFTH EDITION

WORLDS TOGETHER,
WORLDS APART

Volume 2

NORTH POLAR REGION

NORTH AMERICA

ARCTIC OCEAN

ASIA

GREENLAND

ARCTIC CIRCLE

North Pole

North Magnetic Pole

New Siberian Islands

Laptev Sea

Novaya Zemlya

Svalbard

Greenland Sea

Baffin Bay

Iceland

ARCTIC

QUEEN ELIZABETH ISLANDS

GREENLAND

Baffin Bay

Iceland

Great Bear Lake

Great Slave Lake

Hudson Bay

NORTH AMERICA

Lake Winnipeg

Lake Superior

Lake Michigan

L. Huron

L. Ontario

L. Erie

GULF OF MEXICO

WEST INDIES

CARIBBEAN SEA

CENTRAL AMERICA

NORTH PACIFIC OCEAN

TROPIC OF CANCER

Hawaii

EQUATOR

POLYNESIA

Samoa Islands

Tahiti

Tuamotu Archipelago

NORTH ATLANTIC OCEAN

MID ATLANTIC RIDGE

Amazon Basin

ANDES

SOUTH AMERICA

PERU-CHILE TRENCH

SOUTH ATLANTIC OCEAN

SOUTH PACIFIC OCEAN

TROPIC OF CAPRICORN

Falkland Islands

Cape Horn

Drake Passage

ANTARCTIC PENINSULA

WEDDELL SEA

ANTARCTIC CIRCLE

ELLSWORTH LAND

Marie Byrd Land

ANTARCTICA

Ross Ice Shelf

GLOBAL SATELLITE MOSAIC

The beauty and complexity of Earth's landscapes/above and below the oceans/is revealed with the Global Satellite Mosaic. The mosaic was produced for the National Geographic Society by NASA's Jet Propulsion Laboratory, using more than 600 satellite images from the National Oceanic and Atmospheric Administration. The cloud-free images show Earth in its natural colors as it would be seen from space. One can easily identify the world's major glaciers, deserts, mountain ranges, and rain forests. For example, follow the green ribbon of lush vegetation along the Nile into the stark, dry Sahara. The mountain ranges seem to rise off the map thanks to digital elevation databases from the Department of Defense. The deepest areas of the ocean realm are colored dark blue in contrast to the light blue areas highlighting continental shelves, submarine ridges, and underwater mountains.

BIOSPHERE

Thousands of satellite images are combined to show a picture of biological productivity. In the oceans, red, yellow, and green indicate waters rich in phytoplankton. On land, green areas show high potential plant productivity; tan areas suffer from productivity limitations due to aridity and temperature.

THE W

SATELLI

SOUTH POLAR
REGION

ARCTIC CIRCLE

SIBERIA

EUROPE

ASIA

Lake
Baikal

Aral
Sea

Black Sea

Plateau of Tibet

HIMALAYA

ARABIAN
PENINSULA

ARABIAN
SEA

INDIA

BAY
OF
BENGAL

SAHARA

AFRICA

Congo
Basin

Lake
Tanganyika

Lake
Malawi

Madagascar

Kalahari
Desert

Cape of Good Hope

INDONESIA

INDIAN

OCEAN

SOUTHWEST INDIAN RIDGE

SOUTHEAST INDIAN RIDGE

KERGUELEN
PLATEAU

NORTH

PACIFIC

OCEAN

TROPIC OF CANCER

PHILIPPINE SEA

Kamchatka
Peninsula

MICRONESIA

EQUATOR

MELANESIA

New Guinea

AUSTRALIA

CORAL
SEA

New Caledonia

SOUTH

PACIFIC

OCEAN

TROPIC OF CAPRICORN

Fiji
Islands

TASMANIA

NEW
ZEALAND

North Island

South Island

Wilkes
Land

ANTARCTICA

Weddell
Sea

Queen Maud Land

Antarctic
Peninsula

Alexander I.

Bellingshausen
Sea

WEST
ANTARCTICA

South Pole

EAST
ANTARCTICA

Ross
Sea

ANTARCTIC CIRCLE

South
Magnetic Pole

Transantarctic Mountains

Marie Byrd Land

Wilkes Land

THE NEED FOR SATELLITES

The Global Satellite Mosaic along with the biosphere image (lower left) and the temperature image (lower right) provides an integrated view of our world. In very high elevations of the Himalaya and Tibet show up as a cold area (blue, temperature image) and as a plant-poor area (tan, biosphere image). Temperature, plant life, and landscape are interrelated. The need to understand the forces shaping environmental change has led to a space race among various countries. In 1997 alone some 85 rockets launched more than 140 satellites—mostly from China, Europe, Japan, Russia, and the United States. Some satellites provide vital communication links propelling economic development; other satellites supply data on patterns and trends associated with agricultural productivity, pollution monitoring, weather forecasting, and many other environmental concerns.

WINKEL TRIPEL PROJECTION, CENTRAL MERIDIAN 0°
SCALE 1:39,931,000

SURFACE TEMPERATURE
Reddish colors vividly show average high temperatures on the two largest continents, Africa and Asia, from the Sahara to Central Asia. Latitude, mountains, and oceans influence land temperatures.

ORLD
E MAP

Political World

NORTH POLAR REGION

WINKEL TRIPEL PROJECTION, CENTRAL MERIDIAN 0°

KILOMETERS
0 500 1000 1500 2000 2500

STATUTE MILES
0 500 1000 1500 2000 2500

International boundaries and disputed territories, where scale permits, reflect de facto status at the time of publication.

SOUTH POLAR REGION

AZIMUTHAL EQUIDISTANT PROJECTION
⦿ Research station

FIFTH EDITION

WORLDS TOGETHER,
WORLDS APART

Volume 2: From 1000 CE to the Present

Robert **Tignor** · Jeremy **Adelman** · Stephen **Aron** · Stephen **Kotkin**

Suzanne **Marchand** · Gyan **Prakash** · Michael **Tsin**

W. W. Norton & Company, Inc.

New York · London

W. W. Norton & Company has been independent since its founding in 1923, when William Warder Norton and Mary D. Herter Norton first published lectures delivered at the People's Institute, the adult education division of New York City's Cooper Union. The firm soon expanded its program beyond the Institute, publishing books by celebrated academics from America and abroad. By midcentury, the two major pillars of Norton's publishing program—trade books and college texts—were firmly established. In the 1950s, the Norton family transferred control of the company to its employees, and today—with a staff of four hundred and a comparable number of trade, college, and professional titles published each year— W. W. Norton & Company stands as the largest and oldest publishing house owned wholly by its employees.

Editor: Jon Durbin
Associate Editor: Scott Sugarmann
Project Editor: Jennifer Barnhardt
Editorial Assistant: Kelly Rafey
Managing Editor, College: Marian Johnson
Managing Editor, College Digital Media: Kim Yi
Production Manager: Andy Ensor
Media Editor: Laura Wilk
Associate Media Editor: Michelle Smith
Media Project Editor: Rachel Mayer
Assistant Media Editor: Chris Hillyer
Marketing Manager, History: Sarah England Bartley
Design Director: Rubina Yeh
Book Design: Jillian Burr
Photo Editor: Travis Carr
Permissions Manager: Megan Schindel
Permissions Associate: Elizabeth Trammell
Composition: Cenveo® Publisher Services
Illustrations: Mapping Specialists, Ltd.
Manufacturing: Quad Graphics—Versailles

Permission to use copyrighted material is included on page C-1.

The Library of Congress has cataloged the one-volume edition as follows:

Names: Tignor, Robert L., author.
Title: World together, worlds apart : a history of the world from the beginnings
    of humankind to the present / Robert Tignor ... [and eleven others].
Description: Fifth edition. | New York : W. W. Norton & Company, [2018] |
    Includes bibliographical references and index.
Identifiers: LCCN 2017032085 | **ISBN 9780393624786 (hardcover)**
Subject: LCSH: World history—Textbooks. | World
    history—Examinations—Study guides. | Advanced placement programs
    (Education)—Examinations—Study guides
Classification: LCC D21 .T53 2018 | DDC 909—dc23 LC record available at https://lccn.loc.gov/2017032085

ISBN this edition: 978-0-393-62483-0 (pbk.)

W. W. Norton & Company, Inc., 500 Fifth Avenue, New York, NY 10110-0017
wwnorton.com

W. W. Norton & Company Ltd., 15 Carlisle Street, London W1D 3BS
2 3 4 5 6 7 8 9 0

CONTENTS IN BRIEF

CONTENTS

Chapter 10
BECOMING "THE WORLD," 1000–1300 CE   356

Chapter 11
CRISES AND RECOVERY IN AFRO-EURASIA, 1300–1500 402

Chapter 12
CONTACT, COMMERCE, AND COLONIZATION, 1450–1600 **438**

Chapter 13
WORLDS ENTANGLED, 1600–1750 476

Chapter 14

CULTURES OF SPLENDOR AND POWER, 1500–1780   **518**

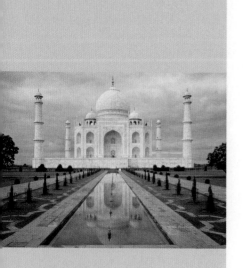

Chapter 15
REORDERING THE WORLD, 1750–1850 **554**

Chapter 17
NATIONS AND EMPIRES, 1850–1914   **628**

Chapter 18
AN UNSETTLED WORLD, 1890–1914 **668**

Chapter 19
OF MASSES AND VISIONS OF THE MODERN, 1910–1939 **706**

Chapter 20
THE THREE-WORLD ORDER, 1940–1975 **748**

Chapter 21
GLOBALIZATION, 1970–2000   **788**

Epilogue
2001–THE PRESENT   **828**

CURRENT TRENDS IN WORLD HISTORY

ANALYZING GLOBAL DEVELOPMENTS

PRIMARY SOURCES

MAPS

PREFACE

Worlds Together, Worlds Apart has set the standard for four editions for those who want to teach a globally integrated world history survey course. Just as the dynamic field of world history evolves, so, too, has *Worlds Together, Worlds Apart*. Building on the success of the first four editions, the Fifth Edition continues to offer a highly coherent, cutting-edge survey of the field built around world history stories of significance that make it possible for students to readily make connections and comparisons across time and place and make the teaching of the course more manageable for instructors (for example, the building of the Silk Road, the spread of the Black Death across Afro-Eurasia, the impact of New World silver on global trade, and alternative ways to organize societies during the rise of nineteenth-century capitalism). The Fifth Edition is the most accessible to date. Many of the chapters were substantially reorganized and streamlined to place greater emphasis on the main chapter ideas and amplify comparisons and connections—the book's greatest strength. The new edition will be the most relevant yet for students. They will find increased coverage on numerous topics, but in particular a topic students care a lot about: the environment's role in world history. The Fifth Edition pays considerable attention to the role of climate in producing radical changes in the lives of humans. For example, a long-term warming of the globe facilitated the domestication of plants and animals and led to an agricultural revolution and the emergence of settled societies. In the seventeenth century, the dramatic drop in global temperatures, now known as the Little Ice Age, produced political and social havoc and led to civil wars, population decline, and regime change all around the globe. These are the new focuses of Chapters 1 and 13. Indeed, all chapters have been substantially revised, not because they were inadequate when originally written, but because the recent studies of comparative and global historians have transformed our understanding of the history of the world.

The Fifth Edition is also the most interactive to date. Lead media author Alan Karras (University of California, Berkeley) has brought together an outstanding media team to develop the comprehensive ancillary package for the Fifth Edition, substantially increasing the learning and teaching support available to students and instructors.

- New **InQuizitive**, Norton's adaptive quizzing platform, uses interactive questions and guided feedback to support students' understanding of each chapter's focus questions.
- New **History Skills Tutorials** combine video and interactive activities to provide students with a framework for analyzing a variety of sources.
- New **Primary Source Exercises** in the Coursepack provide ready-made quizzes to assess students' ability to analyze images and documents tied to each chapter.
- New **Story Maps** break complex maps into a sequence of five annotated screens that focus on the story behind the geography.

Since work began on *Worlds Together, Worlds Apart*, world history has gained even more prominence in college classrooms and historical studies. Courses in the history of the world now abound, often replacing the standard surveys of European history and western civilization overviews. Graduate history students receive training in world history, and journals routinely publish studies in this field. A new generation of textbooks was needed to help students and instructors make sense of this vast, complex, and rapidly evolving field. We believe that *Worlds Together, Worlds Apart* remains the most current, cutting-edge, engaging, readable, interactive, and useful text available for all students of world history. We also believe that this text, one that has advanced the teaching of this field, could only have grown out of the highly collaborative effort of a team of scholars and teachers rather than the more typical single- or two-author efforts. Indeed, the idea to build each chapter around stories of world history significance and the execution of this model grew out of our monthly team meetings and our joint writing efforts during the development stage. As a team-driven text, *Worlds Together, Worlds Apart* also has the advantage of area experts to make sure the material is presented accurately, which is always a challenge for the single- or two-author texts, especially in world history. Finally, our book reads with a single voice, due to the extraordinary efforts of our general editor and leader, Robert Tignor, who with every edition makes the final major sweep through the text to make sure that the voice, style, and level of detail are consistent throughout. Building on these distinctive strengths, we have worked hard and thoughtfully to make the Fifth Edition of *Worlds Together, Worlds Apart* the best edition so far. While there are many exciting additions to the main text and support package, we have made every effort to remain true to our original vision.

OUR GUIDING PRINCIPLES

Five principles inform this book, guiding its framework and the organization of its individual chapters. The first is that **world history is global history**. There are many fine histories of the individual regions of the world, which we have endeavored to make good use of. But unlike the authors of many other so-called world histories, we have chosen not to deal with the great regions and cultures of the world as separate units, reserving individual chapters to East Asia, South Asia, Southwest Asia, Europe, Africa, and the Americas. Our goal is to place each of these regions in its largest geographical context. Accordingly, we have written chapters that are truly global in that most major regions of the world are discussed in each one. We achieved these globally integrated chapters by building each around a significant world history story or theme. There are a number of wonderful examples throughout the book: the peopling of the earth (Chapter 1), the building of the Silk Road (Chapter 6), the rise of universal religions (Chapters 8 and 9), the Black Death (Chapter 11), the Little Ice Age and its far-reaching impact on political systems globally as well as the effects of New World silver on the economies of the world (Chapter 13), alternative visions to nineteenth-century capitalism (Chapter 15), the rise of nation-states and empires (Chapter 16), and so on. It would be misleading, of course, to say that the context is the world, because none of these regions, even the most highly developed commercially, enjoyed commercial or cultural contact with peoples all over the globe before Columbus's voyage to the Americas and later expeditions of the sixteenth century. But the peoples living in the Afro-Eurasian landmass, probably the single most important building block for our study, were deeply influenced by one another, as were the more scattered peoples living in the Americas and in Africa below the Sahara. Products, ideas, and persons traveled widely across the large land units of Eurasia, Africa, and the Americas. Indeed, Afro-Eurasia was not divided or thought of as divided into separate landmasses until recent times. It is in this sense that our world history is global.

The second principle informing this work is **the importance of chronology in framing world history**. Rather than telling the story of world history by analyzing separate geographical areas, we have elected to frame the chapters around significant world history themes and periods that transcended regional and cultural boundaries—moments or periods of meaningful change in the way that human beings organized their lives. Some of these changes were dramatic and affected many people. Environments changed; the earth became drier and warmer; humans learned to domesticate plants and animals; technological innovations in warfare, political organization, and commercial activities occurred; diseases crossed political and cultural borders, as did dramatic changes in the world's climate; and new religious and cultural beliefs spread far and wide. These changes swept across large landmasses, paying scant heed to preexisting cultural and geographical unity. They affected peoples living in widely dispersed societies, and they often led to radically varied cultural responses in different regions of the world. In other cases, changes occurred in only one locality while other places retained their traditions or took alternative routes. Chronology helps us understand the ways in which the world has, and has not, shared a common history.

The third principle is **historical and geographical balance**. Ours is not a history focused on the rise of the west. We seek to pay attention to the global histories of all peoples and not to privilege those developments that led directly into European history as if the rest of the history of the world was but a prelude to the rise of the West. We deal with peoples living outside Europe on their own terms and try to see world history from their perspective. Even more significantly, while we describe societies that obviously influenced Europe's historical development, we do so in a context very different from that which western historians have stressed. Rather than simply viewing these cultures in terms of their role in western development, we seek to understand them in their own right and to illuminate the ways they influenced other parts of the world. From our perspective, it is historically inaccurate to annex Mesopotamia and Egypt to the West because these territories lay well outside Europe and had a large influence on Africa, South Asia, and East Asia as well as on Europe. Indeed, our presentation of Europe in the period leading up to and including the founding of the Roman Empire is different from many of the standard treatments. The Europeans we describe are rather rough, wild-living, warring peoples living on the fringes of the settled parts of the world and looked down on by more politically stable communities. They hardly seem to be made of the stuff that will catapult Europeans to world leadership a millennium later—indeed, they were very different people from those who, as the result of myriad intervening and contingent events, founded the nineteenth- and twentieth-century empires whose ruins are still all around us.

Our fourth principle is **an emphasis on connections and what we call disconnections across societal and cultural boundaries.** World history is not the history of separate regions of the world at different periods of time. It is the history of the connections among peoples living often at great distances from one another, and it is also the history of the resistance of peoples living within and outside societies to connections that threatened to put them in subordinate positions or to rob them of their independence.

A stress on connections inevitably foregrounds those elements within societies that promoted long-distance ties. Merchants are important, as are military men and political potentates seeking to expand their polities. So are scholars and religious leaders, particularly those who believed that they had universalistic messages with which to convert others to their visions. Perhaps most important of all in premodern world history, certainly the most understudied, are the nomadic pastoral peoples, who were often the agents for the transmission of products, peoples, and ideas across long and harsh distances. They exploded onto the scene of settled societies at critical junctures, erasing old cultural and geographical barriers and producing new unities, as the Arabs did in the seventh century CE and the Mongols did in the thirteenth century. *Worlds Together, Worlds Apart* is not intended to convey the message that the history of the world is a story of increasing integration. What for one ruling group brought benefits in the form of increased workforces, material prosperity, and political stability often meant enslavement, political subordination, and loss of territory for other groups. The historian's task, then, is not only to represent the different experiences of increased connectedness, describing worlds that came together, but also to be attentive to the opposite trends, describing peoples and communities that remained apart.

The fifth and final principle is that **world history is a narrative of big themes and high-level comparisons.** *Worlds Together, Worlds Apart* is not a book of record. Indeed, in a work that tells the story of humankind from the beginnings of history to the present, the notion that no event or individual worthy of attention would be excluded is the height of folly. We have sought to offer clear themes and interpretations in order to synthesize the vast body of data that often overwhelms histories of the world. Our aspiration is to identify the main historical forces that have moved history, to highlight those monumental innovations that have changed the way humans lived, and to describe the creation and evolution of those bedrock institutions, many of which, of course, endure. In this regard, self-conscious cross-cultural comparisons of developments, institutions, and even founding figures receive attention to make students aware that some common institutions, such as slavery, did not have the same features in every society. But conversely, the seemingly diverse terms that were used, say, to describe learned and religious men in different parts of the world—monks in Europe, *ulama* in Islam, Brahmans in India, and scholar-gentries in China—often meant much the same thing in very different settings. We have constructed *Worlds Together, Worlds Apart* around big ideas, stories, and themes rather than filling the book with names and dates that encourage students only to memorize rather than understand world history concepts.

OUR MAJOR THEMES

The primary organizing framework of *Worlds Together, Worlds Apart*—one that runs through the chapters and connects the different parts of the narrative—is the theme of **interconnection and divergence.** While describing movements that facilitated global connectedness, this book also shows how different regions developed their own ways of handling or resisting connections and change. Throughout history, different regions and different population groups often stood apart from the rest of the world until touched by traders or explorers or missionaries or soldiers. Some of these regions welcomed global connections; others sought to change the nature of their connections with the outside world; and yet others resisted efforts to bring them into the larger world. All, however, were somehow affected by their experience of connection. Thus, the history of the world is not simply one of increasing globalization, in which all societies eventually join a common path to the present. Rather, it is a history of the ways in which, as people became linked, their experience of these global connections diverged.

Besides the central theme of interconnection and divergence, other themes also stand out in *Worlds Together, Worlds Apart*. First, the book discusses **how the recurring efforts of people to cross religious, political, and cultural borders brought the world together**. Merchants and educated men and women traded goods and ideas. Whole communities, in addition to select groups, moved to safer or more promising environments. **The transregional crossings of ideas, goods, and peoples produced transformations and conflicts**—a second important theme. Finally, the movement of ideas, peoples, products, climates, and germs over long distances upset the balance of power across the world and within individual societies. Such movements changed the relationship of different population groups with other peoples and areas of the world and led over time to dramatic shifts in the ascendancy of regions. **Changes in power arrangements within and between regions explain which parts of the world and regional groups benefited from integration and which resisted it.** These three themes (exchange and migration, conflict and resistance, and alterations in the balance of power) weave themselves through every chapter of this work. While we highlight major themes throughout, we tell the stories of the people caught in these currents of exchange, conflict, and changing power relations, paying particular attention to the role that gender and the environment play in shaping the evolution of societies. The history of the world is not a single, sweeping narrative. On the contrary, the last 5,000 years have produced multiple histories, moving along many paths and trajectories. Sometimes these histories merge, intertwining themselves in substantial ways. Sometimes they disentangle themselves and simply stand apart. Much of the time, however, they are simultaneously together and apart. In place of a single narrative, the usual one being the rise of the west, this book maps the many forks in the road that confronted the world's societies at different times and the surprising turns and unintended consequences that marked the choices that peoples and societies made, including the unanticipated and dramatic rise of the west in the nineteenth century. Formulated in this way, world history is the unfolding of many possible histories, and readers of this book should come away with a reinforced sense of the unpredictability of the past, the instability of the present, and the uncertainty of the future.

OVERVIEW OF VOLUME ONE

Volume One of *Worlds Together, Worlds Apart* deals with the period from the beginnings of human history through the Mongol invasions of the thirteenth century and the spread of the Black Death across Afro-Eurasia. It is divided into eleven chapters, each of which marks a distinct historical period. Hence, each chapter has an overarching theme or small set of themes that holds otherwise highly diverse material together.

Chapter 1, "Becoming Human," presents biological and cultural perspectives on the way that early hominins became truly human. This chapter incorporates much new research, largely the result of new techniques and methods employed by climatologists, biologists specializing in DNA analysis, linguists, and paleoanthropologists in the tradition of Mary and Louis Leakey. These scientists have transformed our understanding of the evolution of human beings. So much of this work is now being incorporated into the history profession and history courses that it has acquired its own name, big history. We believe that this chapter is important in establishing the global context of world history. We believe, too, that our chapter is unique in its focus on how hominins became humans—how early hominins became bipedal and how they developed complex cognitive processes such as language and artistic abilities. We have incorporated a new understanding of evolution, which now appears to have taken place not in a steady and gradual way as was once thought, but in punctuated bursts, often in response to major climate and environmental challenges. In addition, our findings about the evolution of hominins from *Austrolopithecus* to *Homo sapiens* are based on more precise information than was available in earlier editions. Research indicates that *Homo sapiens* originated in Africa, probably no more than 200,000 years ago. These early men and women walked out of the African landmass sometime between 100,000 and 50,000 years ago, gradually populating all regions of the world. What is significant in this story is that the different population groups around the world, the so-called races of humankind, have only recently broken off from one another. Also in this chapter, we emphasize the role of climate in human evolution; indeed, the first group of *Homo sapiens* nearly went extinct because of severe freezing temperatures, produced by an eruption of vast quantities of lava into the atmosphere. This critical phase in human evolution was followed almost immediately by a strong warming trend that occurred 10,000 years ago and that has remained with us ever since, despite some significant drops in global temperatures. This warming trend led humans to domesticate plants and animals and to found the first village settlements, beginning in Southwest Asia.

Chapter 2, "Rivers, Cities, and First States, 3500–2000 BCE," covers the period during which five of the great river basins experienced extraordinary breakthroughs in human activity. On the floodplains of the Tigris and Euphrates in Mesopotamia, the Nile in Egypt, the Indus Valley in modern-day northern India and Pakistan, and the Yellow and Yangzi Rivers in China, men and women mastered annual floods and became expert in seeding and cultivating foodstuffs. In these areas, populations became dense. River-basin cultures had much in common. They had highly developed hierarchical political, social, and cultural systems, priestly and bureaucratic classes, and organized religious and cultural systems. But they also differed greatly, and these differences were passed from generation to generation. The development of these major complex societies certainly is a turning point in world history. We include in this chapter an expanded discussion on the rise of city-states and provide a greater emphasis on the political aspects leading to the emergence of city-states.

Extensive climatic and technological changes serve as major turning points for **Chapter 3, "Nomads, Chariots, Territorial States, and Microsocieties, 2000–1200 BCE."** Drought, environmental degradation, and political instability brought the first river-basin societies to a crashing end around 2000 BCE. When aridity forced tribal and nomadic peoples living on the fringes of the settled populations to move closer to settled areas, they brought with them an insurmountable military advantage. They had become adept at yoking horses to war chariots and hence were in a position to subjugate and later intermarry with the peoples in the settled polities in the river basins. Around 2000 BCE, these peoples established new territorial kingdoms in Mesopotamia, Egypt, the Indus Valley, and China, which gave way a millennium later (1000 BCE) to even larger and more militarily and politically powerful states. The section on China features a major rewriting and reorganization of the Shang territorial states in East Asia with a new section on Shang writing. In the Americas, the Mediterranean, sub-Saharan Africa, and the Pacific worlds, microsocieties arose as an alternative form of a political system in which peoples lived in much smaller-scale societies that showcased their own unique and compelling features.

Chapter 4, "First Empires and Common Cultures in Afro-Eurasia, 1250–325 BCE," describes the different ways in which larger-scale societies grew and became unified. In the case of the world's first empires, the neo-Assyrian and Persian, political power was the main unifying element. Both states established different models that future empires would emulate. The Assyrians used brute force to intimidate and subjugate different groups within their societies and neighboring states. The Persians followed a pattern that relied less on coercion and more on tributary relationships, while reveling in cultural diversity.

The Zhou state in China offered yet a third way of political unity, basing its rule on the doctrine of the mandate of heaven, which legitimated its rulers' succession as long as they were able to maintain stability and order. Vedic society in South Asia offers a dramatically different model in which religion and culture rather than centralizing monarchies were the main unifying forces. Religion moves to the forefront of the narrative in other ways in this chapter. The birth of monotheism occurred in the Zoroastrian and Hebrew faiths and the beginnings of Buddhism. All three religions endure today.

The last millennium before the Common Era witnessed some of the most monumental developments in human history. In the six and a half centuries discussed in **Chapter 5, "Worlds Turned Inside Out, 1000–350 BCE,"** teachers and thinkers, rather than kings, priests, and warriors, came to the fore. Men like Confucius, the Buddha, Plato, and Aristotle, to name only the best known of this brilliant group, offered new insights into the natural world and provided new guidelines for how to govern justly and live ethically. Drawing on the work of sociologist Karl Jaspars, we call this era the Axial Age, during which Greek, Chinese, and South Asian thinkers elaborated political, religious, and philosophical ideas that informed the societies in which they lived and that have been central to the lives of these societies ever since. In this era, small-scale societies, benefiting from more intimate relationships, took the place of the first great empires, now in decline. These highly individualistic cultures developed new strategies for political organization, even experimenting with a democratic polity. In Africa, the Bantu peoples spread across sub-Saharan Africa, and the Sudanic peoples of Meroe created a society that blended Egyptian and sub-Saharan influences. These were all dynamic hybrid societies building on existing knowledge. Equally dramatic transformations occurred in the Americas, where the Olmec and Chavin peoples were creating hierarchical societies of the like never before seen in their part of the world.

Chapter 6, "Shrinking the Afro-Eurasian World, 350 BCE–250 CE," describes three major forces that simultaneously integrated large segments of the Afro-Eurasian landmass culturally and economically. First, Alexander and his armies changed the political and cultural landscape of North Africa and Southwest and South Asia. Culturally, Alexander spread Hellenism through North Africa and Southwest and central Asia, making it the first cultural system to achieve a transregional scope. Second, it was in the post-Alexander world that long-distance trade was intensified and stabilized. For the first time, a trading network, known as the Silk Road, stretching from Palmyra in the west to central Asia in the east, came into being. This chapter incorporates new research on the origins of the Silk Road and its Afro-Eurasian political, commercial, and cultural importance. Despite the fact that the Silk Road was actually made up of many different roads and was not always accessible, and despite the fact that trade took place mainly over short distances, its reputation was well known to merchants, military adventurers, travelers, religious leaders, and political elites. Buddhism was the first religion to seize on the Silk Road's more formal existence as its followers moved quickly with the support of the Mauryan Empire to spread their ideas into central Asia. Finally, we witness the growth of a "silk road of the seas" as new technologies and bigger ships allowed for a dramatic expansion in maritime trade from South Asia all the way to Egypt and East Africa.

Chapter 7, "Han Dynasty China and Imperial Rome, 300 BCE–300 CE," builds on our comparison of the Neo-Assyrian and Persian Empires in Chapter 4 by comparing in great detail the Han dynasty and Roman Empire, the two political, economic, and cultural powerhouses that dominated much of the Afro-Eurasian landmass from 200 BCE to 200 CE. Both the Han dynasty and the Roman Empire ruled effectively in their own way, providing an instructive comparative case study. Both left their imprint on Afro-Eurasia; rulers for centuries afterward tried to revive these glorious imperial systems and use them as models of greatness. Only the Chinese were successful in restoring imperial rule and did so for more than two millennia. European efforts to re-create the Roman Empire, at least in western Europe, failed. This chapter also discusses the effect of state sponsorship on religion, as Christianity came into existence in the context of the late Roman Empire and Buddhism was introduced to China during the decline of the Han.

Out of the crumbling Roman Empire new political systems and a new religion emerged, the major topic of Chapter 8, "The Rise of Universal Religions, 300–600 CE." The Byzantine Empire, claiming to be the successor state to the Roman Empire, embraced Christianity as its state religion. The Tang rulers patronized Buddhism to such a degree that Confucian statesmen feared it had become the state religion. This chapter has new information on the Sogdians, a pastoral peoples who inhabited central Asia and were vital in spreading Buddhism and supporting Silk Road trade. Both Buddhism and Christianity enjoyed spectacular success in the politically fragmented post-Han era in China and in the feudal world of western Europe. These dynamic religions represent a decisive transformation in world history. Christianity enjoyed its eventual successes through state sponsorship via the Roman and Byzantine Empires and by providing spiritual comfort and hope during the chaotic years of Rome's decline. Buddhism grew through imperial sponsorship and significant changes to its fundamental beliefs, when adherents to the faith deified Buddha and created notions of an afterlife. In Africa, a wide range of significant developments and myriad cultural practices existed; yet large common cultures also arose. The Bantu peoples spread throughout the southern half of the landmass, spoke closely related languages, and developed similar political institutions based on the prestige of individuals of high achievement. In the Americas, the Olmecs established their own form of the city-state, while the Maya owed their success to a decentralized common culture built around a strong religious belief system and a series of spiritual centers.

In Chapter 9, "New Empires and Common Cultures, 600–1000 CE," we see another world religion, Islam, explode with world-changing consequences in a relatively remote corner of the Arabian Peninsula. The rise of Islam provides a contrast to the way universalizing religions and political empires interacted. Islam and empire arose in a fashion quite different from Christianity and the Roman Empire. Christianity took over an already existing empire—the Roman—after suffering persecution at its hands for several centuries. In contrast, Islam created an empire almost at the moment of its emergence. There is much new scholarship on early Islam, the life of Muhammad, and the creation of the Quran, based mainly on the writings of non-Muslim observers and scholars. Although these texts are often critical of Muhammad and early Islam, they must be used (albeit very carefully) because of the dearth of information on the beginnings of Islam found in the few Muslim and Arabic sources that remain to us. We have added this important perspective to our discussion of the birth of Islam. By the time the Abbasid Empire came into being in the middle of the eighth century, Islamic armies, political leaders, and clerics exercised power over much of the Afro-Eurasian landmass from southern Spain, across North Africa, all the way to central Asia. The Tang Empire in China, however, served as a counterweight to Islam's power both politically and intellectually. Confucianism enjoyed a spectacular recovery in this period. With the Tang rulers, Confucianism slowed the spread of Buddhism and further reinforced China's development along different, more secular pathways. Japan and Korea also enter world history at this time as tributary states to Tang China and as hybrid cultures that mixed Chinese customs and practices with their own. The Christian world split in this period between the western Latin church and the eastern Byzantine church. Both branches of Christianity played a role in unifying societies, especially in western Europe, which lacked strong political rule at a time when all of Europe experienced a profound and disabling drop in temperature.

In the three centuries from 1000 to 1300 (**Chapter 10, "Becoming 'The World,' 1000–1300 CE"**), Afro-Eurasia experienced an unprecedented rise in prosperity and population that even spread into West and East Africa. Just as importantly, the world in this period divided into regional zones that are recognizable today. And trade grew rapidly.

A view of the major trading cities of this time demonstrates how commerce transformed cultures. Sub-Saharan Africa also underwent intense regional integration via the spread of the Mande-speaking peoples and the Mali Empire. The Americas witnessed their first empire in the form of the Chimu peoples in the Andes. This chapter ends with the Mongol conquests of the twelfth and thirteenth centuries, which brought massive destruction. The Mongol Empire, however, once in place, promoted long-distance commerce, scholarly exchange, and travel on an unprecedented scale. The Mongols brought Eurasia, North Africa, and many parts of sub-Saharan Africa into a new connectedness. The Mongol story also underscores the important role that nomads played throughout the history of the early world. Just as much of Europe had suffered through a drop in temperature in the ninth and tenth centuries, as described in Chapter 9, now a radical fall in temperature in combination with drought troubled the eastern Mediterreanean and the Islamic world. Here the result was a steep decline in standards of living, leading to riots and political fragmentation. Even so, Islamic science flourished, and China became the most urbanized part of the world.

The Black Death brought Afro-Eurasia's prosperity and population growth to a catastrophic end, as discussed in **Chapter 11, "Crises and Recovery in Afro-Eurasia, 1300–1500."** The death and destruction of the fourteenth century saw traditional institutions give way, forcing peoples to rebuild their cultures. The political systems that came into being at this time and the intense religious experimentation that took place effected a sharp break with the past. The bubonic plague wiped out as much as two-thirds of the population in many of the densely settled locations of Afro-Eurasia. Societies once brought to their knees by the Mongols' depredations now suffered grievously from biological pathogens. In the face of one of humanity's grimmest periods, peoples and societies demonstrated tremendous resilience as they looked for new ways to rebuild their communities, some turning inward and others seeking inspiration, conquests, and riches elsewhere.

New dynasties emerged all across Afro-Eurasia. The Ming replaced the Mongol Yuan dynasty in China. A small band of Muslim warriors in Anatolia became sophisticated military tacticians and administrators and created an empire that would last as the Ottoman Empire until the end of World War I. New Muslim dynasts also took over South Asia (the Mughals) and the Iranian plateau (Safavids). Nor was Europe left behind, for here, too, new dynamic rulers came to the thrones in England, France, Spain, and Portugal, ready to project their power overseas. Volume One concludes on the eve of the Columbian Exchange, the moment when "old" worlds discovered "new" ones and a vast series of global interconnections and divergences commenced.

OVERVIEW OF VOLUME TWO

The organizational structure for Volume Two reaffirms the commitment to write a decentered, global history of the world. Christopher Columbus is not the starting point, as he is in so many modern world histories. Rather, we begin in the eleventh and twelfth centuries with two major developments in world history: the Mongols and the Black Death. The first, set forth in **Chapter 10, "Becoming 'The World,' 1000–1300 CE,"** describes a world that was divided for the first time into regions that are recognizable today. This world experienced rapid population growth, as is shown by a simple look at the major trading cities from Asia in the east to the Mediterranean in the west. Yet nomadic peoples remained a force, as revealed in the Mongol invasions of Afro-Eurasia.

Chapter 11, "Crises and Recovery in Afro-Eurasia, 1300–1500," describes how the Mongol warriors, through their conquests and the integration of the Afro-Eurasian world, unwittingly spread the bubonic plague, which brought death and depopulation to much of Afro-Eurasia. Both these stories set the stage for the modern world and are clear-cut turning points in world history. The primary agents of world connection described in this chapter were dynasts, soldiers, clerics, merchants, and adventurers who rebuilt the societies that disease and political collapse had destroyed.

The Mongols joined the two hemispheres, as we describe in **Chapter 12, "Contact, Commerce, and Colonization, 1450–1600,"** bringing the peoples and products of the Western Hemisphere into contact and conflict with Eurasia and Africa. It is the collision between the Eastern and Western Hemispheres that sets in motion modern world history and marks a distinct divide or turning point between the premodern and the modern. Here, too, disease and increasing trade linkages were vital. Unprepared for the advanced military technology and the disease pool of European and African peoples, the Amerindian population experienced a population decline even more devastating than that caused by the Black Death.

Europeans sailed across the Atlantic Ocean to find a more direct, less encumbered route to Asia and came upon lands, peoples, and products that they had not expected. One item, however, that they had sought in every part of the world and that they found in abundance in the Americas was precious metal. Although historians rightly emphasize the European intrusion into the Indian Ocean and their discovery of the Americas, we remind readers that the Europeans were not alone in expanding their influence through the oceans. The Ottomans made gains in the Red Sea and ventured into the Indian Ocean as rivals to the Portuguese.

In **Chapter 13, "Worlds Entangled, 1600–1750,"** we discuss how New World silver from Mexico and Peru became the major currency of global commerce, oiling the long-distance trading networks that had been revived after the Black Death. The effect of New World silver on the world economy was so great that it, even more than the Iberian explorations of the New World, brought the hemispheres together and marks the true genesis of modern world history. Sugar also linked the economies and political systems of western Europe, Africa, and the Americas and was a powerful force in a triangular trade centered on the Atlantic Ocean. This trade involved the shipment of vast numbers of African captives to the Americas, where they toiled as slaves on sugar, tobacco, cotton, and rice plantations.

For Europe and the rest of the world, the sudden dip in temperature in the seventeenth century, which historians now call the Little Ice Age, brought immense suffering not seen around the world since the Black Death. Wars broke out, and regimes were overthrown in China and Iran. Much of the new research into the Little Ice Age is based on a better understanding of the climate through the studies of climatologists, research that has transformed the way historians now look at the seventeenth century.

Chapter 14, "Cultures of Splendor and Power, 1500–1780," discusses the Ottoman scientists, Safavid and Mughal artists, Chinese literati, and European thinkers, whose notable achievements were rooted in their own cultures but tempered by awareness of the intellectual activities of others. In this chapter, we look closely at how culture is created as a historical process and describe how the massive increase in wealth during this period, growing out of global trade, led to one of the great periods of cultural flourishing in world history. In our discussion of Europe's scientific revolution, which got under way at the end of the sixteenth century and came to full fruition in the seventeenth century through the studies of Isaac Newton, we tackle the vexed question of why the scientific breakthrough occurred in Europe and not in China, India, and the Muslim world, which had been in the lead up to then. It was a turn to quantification that catapulted Europe ahead of the rest of the world, coupled with the fact that the Chinese had their exposure to European science through the Jesuits.

Around 1800, transformations reverberated outward from the Atlantic world and altered economic and political relationships in the rest of the world. In **Chapter 15, "Reordering the World, 1750–1850,"** we discuss how political revolutions in the Americas and Europe, new ideas about how to trade and organize labor, and a powerful rhetoric of freedom and universal rights underlay the beginning of "a great divide" between peoples of European descent and those who were not. These forces of laissez-faire capitalism, industrialization, the nation-state, and republicanism not only attracted diverse groups around the world; they also threatened groups that put forth alternative visions. Ideas of freedom, as manifested in trading relations, labor, and political activities, clashed with a traditional world based on inherited rights and statuses and further challenged the way men and women had lived in earlier times. These political, intellectual, and economic reorderings changed the way people around the world saw themselves and thus represent something quite novel in world history.

Much new comparative work has been done on the industrial revolution in the same way that historians have placed Europe's scientific revolution within a global context.

These new ways of envisioning the world did not go unchallenged, as **Chapter 16, "Alternative Visions of the Nineteenth Century,"** makes clear. Here, intense resistance to evolving modernity reflected the diversity of peoples and their hopes for the future. Wahabbism in Islam, the strongman movement in Africa, Indian resistance in America and Mexico, socialism and communism in Europe, the Taiping Rebellion in China, and the Indian mutiny in South Asia catapulted to historical prominence prophets and leaders whose visions often drew on earlier traditions and led these individuals to resist rapid change.

Chapter 17, "Nations and Empires, 1850–1914," discusses the political, economic, military, and ideological power that thrust Europe and North America to the fore of global events and led to an era of nationalism and modern imperialism, new forces in world history. Yet this period of seeming European supremacy was to prove short-lived. This chapter has new material on the Irish potato famine and an in-depth analysis of European colonialism.

As **Chapter 18, "An Unsettled World, 1890–1914,"** demonstrates, even before World War I shattered Europe's moral certitude, many groups at home (feminists, Marxists, and unfulfilled nationalists) and abroad (anticolonial nationalists) had raised a chorus of complaints about European and North American dominance. As in Chapter 14, we look at the processes by which specific cultural movements rose and reflected the concerns of individual societies. Yet here, too, syncretistic movements emerged in many cultures and reflected the sway of global imperialism, which by then had become a dominant force.

In keeping with our stress on the environment, this chapter discusses Teddy Roosevelt's promotion of the conservation of nature and other efforts by Europeans to be stewards of the earth. There is also a new environmentally oriented Current Trends in World History about the felt need for sustainable agricultural methods on the Russian steppe lands.

Chapter 19, "Of Masses and Visions of the Modern, 1910–1939," briefly covers World War I and then discusses how, from the end of World War I until World War II, different visions of being modern competed around the world. It is the development of modernism and its effects on multiple cultures that integrate the diverse developments discussed in this chapter. In the decades between the world wars, proponents of liberal democracy struggled to defend their views and often to impose their will on authoritarian rulers and anticolonial nationalists.

The chapter presents a number of revisionist views on the origins of World War I, the Armenian genocide, the Sykes-Picot agreement that was reached by Britain and France during World War I to partition the Ottoman Middle Eastern lands once the war was over, and the secularizing and modernizing ideas that animated Mustafa Kemal, later known as Ataturk, to create a new nation in Turkey.

Chapter 20, "The Three-World Order, 1940–1975," covers World War II and describes how new adversaries arose after the war. A three-world order came into being—the First World, led by the United States and extolling capitalism, the nation-state, and democratic government; the Second World, led by the Soviet Union and favoring authoritarian polities and economies; and the Third World, made up of former colonies seeking an independent status for themselves in world affairs. The rise of this three-world order dominated the second half of the twentieth century and constitutes another major theme of world history.

In **Chapter 21, "Globalization, 1970–2000,"** we explain that at the end of the cold war, the modern world, while clearly more unified than before, still had profound cultural differences and political divisions. At the beginning of the twenty-first century, capital, commodities, peoples, and ideas moved rapidly over long distances. But cultural tensions and political impasses continued to exist. The rise of this form of globalism represented a vital new element as humankind headed into a new century and millennium. This chapter contains an expanded discussion of the role of international and supranational financial organizations; the environmental crisis, brought on by the release of carbon emissions into the atmosphere and the resulting global warming; and the end of white rule in South Africa.

We close with the **Epilogue, "2001–The Present,"** which tracks developments since the turn of the millennium. These last few years have brought profound changes to the world order, yet we hope readers of *Worlds Together, Worlds Apart* will see more clearly how this most recent history is, in fact, entwined with trends of much longer duration that are the chief focus of this book.

We see the last half decade as pointing the peoples and countries of the world in more populist, ethnic nationalist, and violent directions. Britain's vote to withdraw from the European Union, known as Brexit; the election of Donald Trump to the American presidency; the rise of ethnic and religious consciousness in Turkey and India most notably and throughout the world in general; and the emergence of militant Islam in al-Qaeda and then in ISIS (the Islamic State in Iraq and Syria) all seem to us to be the consequence of various groups believing themselves to be disenfranchised and demanding to be heard.

MEDIA & PRINT ANCILLARIES

The Fifth Edition of *Worlds Together, Worlds Apart* is supported by an array of digital resources to help faculty meet their course goals—in the classroom and online—and activities for students to develop core skills in reading comprehension, historical analysis, and writing.

FOR STUDENTS

- InQuizitive (Shane Carter, Siobhan McGurk) is an adaptive quizzing tool that improves students' understanding of the themes and objectives of each chapter while honing their critical analysis skills with primary source, image, and map analysis questions. Students receive personalized quiz questions with detailed, guiding feedback on the topics in which they need the most help, while the engaging, gamelike elements motivate them as they learn.

- The **History Skills Tutorials** feature three modules—Images, Documents, and Maps—to support students' development of the key skills needed for the history course. These tutorials feature author videos modeling the analysis process, followed by interactive questions that will challenge students to apply what they have learned.

- The free and easy-to-use **Student Site** offers additional resources for students to use outside of class. Resources include interactive iMaps, author videos, and a comprehensive Online Reader featuring 100 additional sources.

- Free and included with new copies of the text, the **Norton Ebook Reader** provides an enhanced reading experience that works on all computers and mobile devices. Features include intuitive highlighting, note-taking, and book-marking, as well as pop-up definitions and enlargeable maps and images. Author videos are embedded throughout to create an engaging reading environment.

FOR INSTRUCTORS

- **Norton Coursepacks** allow instructors to bring strong assessment and lecture tools directly into their Learning Management System (LMS). Available at no cost to professors or students, Norton Coursepacks include chapter-based assignments, including Guided Reading Exercises, Primary Source Exercises, Chapter Review Quizzes, author videos, interactive iMaps, forum prompts, and more.

- **Story Maps** (Ruth Mostern) break complex maps into a sequence of five annotated screens that focus on the story behind the geography. Twelve maps, including two new maps, cover such topics as "The Silk Road," "The Spread of the Black Death," and "Population Growth and the Economy."

- The **Instructor's Manual** (Sharon Cohen) has everything instructors need to prepare lectures and classroom activities: lecture outlines, lecture ideas, classroom activities, and lists of recommended books, films, and Web sites.

- The **Test Bank** (Ryba Epstein, Derek O'Leary) contains approximately 1,400 multiple-choice, true/false, and essay questions. All test questions are now aligned with Bloom's Taxonomy for greater ease of assessment (available in print, PDF, Word, and Examview formats).

- **Lecture PowerPoints and Art PowerPoints** feature lecture outlines, key talking points, and the photographs and maps from the book to support in-class presentations.

ACKNOWLEDGMENTS

Worlds Together, Worlds Apart would never have happened without the full support of Princeton University. In a highly unusual move, and one for which we are truly grateful, the university helped underwrite this project with financial support from its 250th Anniversary Fund for undergraduate teaching and by allowing released time for the authors from campus commitments.

The history department's support of the effort over many years has been exceptional. Four chairs made funds and departmental support available, including the department's incomparable administrative talents. We would be remiss if we did not single out the department manager, Judith Hanson, who provided us with assistance whenever we needed it. We also thank Eileen Kane, who tracked down references and illustrations and merged changes into the manuscript. We also would like to thank Pamela Long, who made all of the complicated arrangements for ensuring that we were able to discuss matters in a leisurely and attractive setting. Sometimes that meant arranging for long-distance conference calls. She went even further and proofread the entire manuscript, finding errors that we had all overlooked.

We drew shamelessly on the expertise of the departmental faculty, and although it might be wise simply to include a roster of the Princeton history department, that would do an injustice to those of whom we took most advantage. So here they are: Mariana Candido, Robert Darnton, Sheldon Garon, Anthony Grafton, Molly Greene, David Howell, Harold James, William Jordan, Emmanuel Kreike, Michael Mahoney, Arno Mayer, Kenneth Mills, John Murrin, Susan Naquin, Willard Peterson, Theodore Rabb, Bhavani Raman, Stanley Stein, and Richard Turits. When necessary, we went outside the history department, getting help from Michael L. Bender, L. Carl Brown, Michael Cook, Norman Itzkowitz, Martin Kern, Thomas Leisten, Heath Lowry, and Peter Schaefer. Two departmental colleagues—Natalie Z. Davis and Elizabeth Lunbeck—were part of the original team but had to withdraw because of other commitments. Their contributions were vital, and we want to express our thanks to them. David Gordon, now at Bowdoin College, used portions of the text while teaching an undergraduate course at the University of Durban in South Africa and shared comments with us. Shamil Jeppie, like David Gordon a graduate of the Princeton history department, now teaching at the University of Cape Town in South Africa, read and commented on various chapters.

Beyond Princeton, we have also benefited from exceptionally gifted and giving colleagues who have assisted this book in many ways. Colleagues at Louisiana State

University, the University of North Carolina, the University of Pennsylvania, and the University of California at Los Angeles, where Suzanne Marchand, Michael Tsin, Holly Pittman, and Stephen Aron, respectively, are now teaching, pitched in whenever we turned to them. Especially helpful have been the contributions of Joyce Appleby, James Gelvin, Naomi Lamoreaux, and Gary Nash at UCLA; Michael Bernstein at Tulane University; and Maribel Dietz, John Henderson, Christine Kooi, David Lindenfeld, Reza Pirbhai, and Victor Stater at Louisiana State University. It goes without saying that none of these individuals bears any responsibility for factual or interpretive errors that the text may contain. Xinru Liu would like to thank her Indian mentor, Romila Thapar, who changed the way we think about Indian history.

The quality and range of reviews on this project were truly exceptional. The final version of the manuscript was greatly influenced by the thoughts and ideas of numerous instructors. We wish to particularly thank our consulting reviewers, who read multiple versions of the manuscript from start to finish.

First Edition Consultants

Hugh Clark, Ursinus College
Jonathan Lee, San Antonio College
Pamela McVay, Ursuline College
Tom Sanders, United States Naval Academy

Second Edition Consultants

Jonathan Lee, San Antonio College
Pamela McVay, Ursuline College
Steve Rapp, Georgia State University
Cliff Rosenberg, City University of New York

First Edition Reviewers

Lauren Benton, New Jersey Institute of Technology
Ida Blom, University of Bergen, Norway
Ricardo Duchesne, University of New Brunswick
Major Bradley T. Gericke, United States Military Academy
John Gillis, Rutgers University
David Kenley, Marshall University
John Kicza, Washington State University
Matthew Levinger, Lewis and Clark College
James Long, Colorado State University
Adam McKeown, Columbia University
Mark McLeod, University of Delaware
John Mears, Southern Methodist University
Michael Murdock, Brigham Young University
David Newberry, University of North Carolina, Chapel Hill

Tom Pearcy, Slippery Rock State University
Oliver B. Pollak, University of Nebraska, Omaha
Ken Pomeranz, University of California, Irvine
Major David L. Ruffley, United States Air Force Academy
William Schell, Murray State University
Major Deborah Schmitt, United States Air Force Academy
Sarah Shields, University of North Carolina, Chapel Hill
Mary Watrous-Schlesinger, Washington State University

Second Edition Reviewers

William Atwell, Hobart and William Smith Colleges
Susan Besse, City University of New York
Tithi Bhattacharya, Purdue University
Mauricio Borrerero, St. John's University
Charlie Briggs, Georgia Southern University
Antoinne Burton, University of Illinois, Urbana-Champaign
Jim Cameron, St. Francis Xavier University
Kathleen Comerford, Georgia Southern University
Duane Corpis, Georgia State University
Denise Davidson, Georgia State University
Ross Doughty, Ursinus College
Alison Fletcher, Kent State University
Phillip Gavitt, Saint Louis University
Brent Geary, Ohio University
Henda Gilli-Elewy, California State Polytechnic University, Pomona
Fritz Gumbach, John Jay College
William Hagen, University of California, Davis
Laura Hilton, Muskingum College
Jeff Johnson, Villanova University
David Kammerling-Smith, Eastern Illinois University
Jonathan Lee, San Antonio College
Dorothea Martin, Appalachian State University
Don McGuire, State University of New York, Buffalo
Pamela McVay, Ursuline College
Joel Migdal, University of Washington
Anthony Parent, Wake Forest University
Sandra Peacock, Georgia Southern University
David Pietz, Washington State University
Jared Poley, Georgia State University
John Quist, Shippensburg State University
Steve Rapp, Georgia State University
Paul Rodell, Georgia Southern University
Ariel Salzman, Queen's University
Bill Schell, Murray State University
Claire Schen, University at Buffalo
Jonathan Skaff, Shippensburg State University
David Smith, California State Polytechnic University, Pomona

Neva Specht, Appalachian State University
Ramya Sreeniva, State University of New York, Buffalo
Charles Stewart, University of Illinois, Urbana-Champaign
Rachel Stocking, Southern Illinois University, Carbondale
Heather Streets, Washington State University
Tim Teeter, Georgia Southern University
Charlie Wheeler, University of California, Irvine
Owen White, University of Delaware
James Wilson, Wake Forest University

Third Edition Reviewers

Henry Antkiewicz, Eastern Tennessee State University
Anthony Barbieri-Low, University of California, Santa Barbara
Andrea Becksvoort, University of Tennessee, Chattanooga
Hayden Bellonoit, United States Naval Academy
John Bloom, Shippensburg University
Kathryn Braund, Auburn University
Catherine Candy, University of New Orleans
Karen Carter, Brigham Young University
Stephen Chappell, James Madison University
Jessey Choo, University of Missouri, Kansas City
Timothy Coates, College of Charleston
Gregory Crider, Wingate University
Denise Davidson, Georgia State University
Jessica Davidson, James Madison University
Sal Diaz, Santa Rosa Junior College
Todd Dozier, Baton Rouge Community College
Richard Eaton, University of Arizona
Lee Farrow, Auburn University, Montgomery
Bei Gao, College of Charleston
Behrooz Ghamari-Tabrizi, University of Illinois, Urbana-Champaign
Steven Gish, Auburn University, Montgomery
Jeffrey Hamilton, Baylor University
Barry Hankins, Baylor University
Brian Harding, Mott Community College
Tim Henderson, Auburn University, Montgomery
Marjorie Hilton, University of Redlands
Richard Hines, Washington State University
Lisa Holliday, Appalachian State University
Jonathan Lee, San Antonio College
David Kalivas, University of Massachusetts, Lowell
Christopher Kelley, Miami University, Ohio
Kenneth Koons, Virginia Military Institute
Michael Kulikowski, Pennsylvania State University
Benjamin Lawrence, University of California, Davis
Lu Liu, University of Tennessee, Knoxville

David Longfellow, Baylor University
Harold Marcuse, University of California, Santa Barbara
Dorothea Martin, Appalachian State University
David Mayes, Sam Houston State University
James Mokhiber, University of New Orleans
Mark Munzinger, Radford College
David Murphree, Virginia Tech University
Joshua Nadel, North Carolina Central University
Wing Chung Ng, University of Texas, San Antonio
Robert Norrell, University of Tennessee, Knoxville
Chandrika Paul, Shippensburg University
Beth Pollard, San Diego State University
Timothy Pytell, California State University, San Bernardino
Stephen Rapp, professional historian
Alice Roberti, Santa Rosa Junior College
Aviel Roshwald, Georgetown University
James Sanders, Utah State University
Lynn Sargeant, California State University, Fullerton
William Schell, Murray State University
Michael Seth, James Madison University
Barry Stentiford, Grambling State University
Gabrielle Sutherland, Baylor University
Lisa Tran, California State University, Fullerton
Michael Vann, California State University, Sacramento
Peter Von Sivers, University of Utah
Andrew Wackerfuss, Georgetown University
Ted Weeks, Southern Illinois University, Carbondale
Angela White, Indiana University of Pennsylvania
Jennifer Williams, Nichols State University
Andrew Wise, State University of New York, Buffalo
Eloy Zarate, Pasadena City College
William Zogby, Mohawk Valley Community College

Fourth Edition Reviewers

Andrea Becksvoort, University of Tennessee, Chattanooga
Hayden Bellenoit, United States Naval Academy
Volker Benkert, Arizona State University
Gayle Brunelle, California State University, Fullerton
Jessica Clark, California State University, Chico
Brian Harding, Mott Community College
Emily Hill, Queen's University at Kingston
Laura Hilton, Muskingum University
Dennis Laumann, University of Memphis
Elaine MacKinnon, University of West Georgia
Ronald Mellor, University of California, Los Angeles
Carol Miller, Tallahassee Community College
Greg O'Malley, University of California, Santa Cruz
David Ortiz Jr., University of Arizona

Charles Parker, Saint Louis University

Juanjuan Peng, Georgia Southern University

Dana Rabin, University of Illinois, Urbana-Champaign

Matthew Rothwell, University of Southern Indiana

Teo Ruiz, University of California, Los Angeles

Jeffrey Shumway, Brigham Young University

Lisa Tran, California State University, Fullerton

Lela Urquhart, Georgia State University

Fifth Edition Reviewers

Andreas Agocs, University of the Pacific

Anthony Barbieri-Low, University of California, Santa Barbara

Michelle Benson-Saxton, University at Buffalo

Brett Berliner, Morgan State University

Carolyn Noelle Biltoft, Georgia State University

Edward Bond, Alabama A&M University

Gayle Brunelle, California State University, Fullerton

Grace Chee, West Los Angeles College

Stephen Colston, San Diego State University

Paula Devos, San Diego State University

Paul Hudson, Georgia Perimeter College

Alan Karras, University of California, Berkeley

Elaine MacKinnon, University of West Georgia

Harold Marcuse, University of California, Santa Barbara

Jeff McEwen, Chattanooga State Community College

Thomas McKenna, Concord University

Eva Moe, Modesto Junior College

Alice Pate, Kennesaw State University

Chandrika Paul, Shippensburg University

Jared Poley, Georgia State University

Dana Rabin, University of Illinois, Urbana-Champaign

Masako Racel, Kennesaw State University

Charles Reed, Elizabeth City State University

Alice Roberti, Santa Rosa Junior College

Steven Rowe, Chicago State University

Ariel Salzmann, Queen's University

Lynn Sargeant, California State University, Fullerton

Robert Saunders, Farmingdale State College

Sharlene Sayegh-Canada, California State University, Long Beach

Claire Schen, University at Buffalo

Jeffrey Shumway, Brigham Young University

Greg Smay, University of California, Berkeley

Margaret Stevens, Essex County College

Lisa Tran, California State University, Fullerton

Michael Vann, California State University, Sacramento

Theodore Weeks, Southern Illinois University

Krzysztof Ziarek, University of Buffalo

For the Fifth Edition, we also had a mix of new and returning authors who helped create the best support materials to accompany *Worlds Together, Worlds Apart*. Alan Karras served as the lead media author, directing the development of our ancillary author team. For their tremendous efforts, we would like to thank Sharon Cohen for authoring the Instructor's Manual, Ryba Epstein and Derek O'Leary for creating the test bank, and Shane Carter and Siobhan McGurk for developing InQuizitive.

For the Fifth Edition, we have some familiar and new friends at Norton to thank. Chief among them is Jon Durbin, who once again played a major role in bringing this edition to publication. Laura Wilk, our new media editor, has put together a fabulous package of support materials for students and instructors. Sarah England has put together a creative marketing plan for the book. Jillian Burr is responsible for the book's beautiful and effective design. Jennifer Barnhardt has done an amazingly efficient job as our project editor. Andy Ensor has shepherded the project through production beautifully. Kelly Rafey has done a masterful job compiling the manuscript with a special focus on photos, primary sources, and permissions. Michelle Smith and Chris Hillyer have done a fine job lending their support in strengthening the media support materials to meet the ever more complex classroom and assessment needs of instructors. Alice Vigliani did a spectacular job working on the manuscript, paying particular attention to our efforts to reorganize and streamline many of the chapters in both volumes. Janet Greenblatt did a superb job with the copyediting, turning the chapters around quickly to meet our schedule. A special shout-out goes to Debra Morton-Hoyt and her team of cover designers. *Worlds Together, Worlds Apart* has always been incredibly creative and distinctive looking, and the Fifth Edition covers are even more eye-catching and memorable than the first four editions. Bravo!

Finally, we must recognize that while this project often kept us apart from family members, their support held our personal worlds together.

ABOUT THE AUTHORS

ROBERT TIGNOR (*Ph.D. Yale University*) is professor emeritus and the Rosengarten Professor of Modern and Contemporary History at Princeton University and the three-time chair of the history department. With Gyan Prakash, he introduced Princeton's first course in world history nearly thirty years ago. Professor Tignor has taught graduate and undergraduate courses in African history and world history and written extensively on the history of twentieth-century Egypt, Nigeria, and Kenya. Besides his many research trips to Africa, Professor Tignor has taught at the University of Ibadan in Nigeria and the University of Nairobi in Kenya.

JEREMY ADELMAN (*D.Phil. Oxford University*) has lived and worked in seven countries and four continents. A graduate of the University of Toronto, he earned a master's degree in economic history at the London School of Economics (1985) and a doctorate in modern history at Oxford University (1989). He is the author or editor of ten books, including *Sovereignty and Revolution in the Iberian Atlantic* (2006) and *Worldly Philosopher: The Odyssey of Albert O. Hirschman* (2013), a chronicle of one of the twentieth century's most original thinkers. He has been awarded fellowships by the British Council, the Social Science and Humanities Research Council of Canada, the Guggenheim Memorial Foundation, and the American Council Learned Societies (the Frederick Burkhardt Fellowship). He is currently the Henry Charles Lea Professor of History and the director of the Global History Lab at Princeton University. His next book is called *Earth Hunger: Markets, Resources and the Need for Strangers.*

STEPHEN ARON (*Ph.D. University of California, Berkeley*) is professor of history and Robert N. Burr Chair at the University of California, Los Angeles and president of the Western History Association (2016–2017). Professor Aron is the author of *How the West Was Lost: The Transformation of Kentucky from Daniel Boone to Henry Clay*; *American Confluence: The Missouri Frontier from Borderland to Border State*; and *The American West: A Very Short Introduction.*

He is currently writing a book with the tentative title *Can We All Get Along: An Alternative History of the American West.*

ALAN KARRAS (*Ph.D. University of Pennsylvania*) is the Associate Director of International & Area Studies at the University of California, Berkeley, and has served as chair of the College Board's test development committee for world history and as co-chair of the College Board's commission on AP history course revisions. He studies the eighteenth-century Atlantic world and global interactions more broadly concerning illegal activities like smuggling and corruption.

STEPHEN KOTKIN (*Ph.D. University of California, Berkeley*) is Birkelund Professor of History and International Affairs at Princeton University and director of the Princeton Institute for International and Regional Studies. His books include *Stalin: Waiting for Hitler, 1929–1941*; *Stalin: Paradoxes of Power, 1878–1928*; *Magnetic Mountain: Stalinism as a Civilization*; *Uncivil Society: 1989 and the Implosion of the Communist Establishment*; and *Armageddon Averted: The Soviet Collapse, 1970–2000*. He has coedited many works, including *Mongolia in the Twentieth Century: Landlocked Cosmopolitan.*

SUZANNE MARCHAND (*Ph.D. University of Chicago*) is Boyd Professor of European and Intellectual History at Louisiana State University, Baton Rouge. Professor Marchand also spent a number of years teaching at Princeton University. She is the author of *Down from Olympus: Archaeology and Philhellenism in Germany, 1750–1970* and *German Orientalism in the Age of Empire: Religion, Race and Scholarship.*

GYAN PRAKASH (*Ph.D. University of Pennsylvania*) is the Dayton-Stockton Professor of History at Princeton University, specializing in South Asian history. A member of the Subaltern Studies Collective until its dissolution in 2006, he directed the Shelby Cullom Davis Center for Historical Studies (2003–2008) and was awarded fellowships by the National Science Foundation, the Guggenheim Foundation, and the National Endowment of Humanities. He is the author of *Bonded Histories* (1990) and *Another Reason* (1999) and has edited several volumes of essays, including *After Colonialism* (1994), *The Spaces of the Modern City* (2009), *Utopia/Dystopia* (2010), and *Noir Urbanisms* (2010). His latest book is *Mumbai Fables*, and he wrote the script for the film *Bombay Velvet* (2015). He is currently writing a book on the history of Indira Gandhi's Emergency rule in India. With Robert Tignor, he introduced the modern world history course at Princeton University.

MICHAEL TSIN (*Ph.D. Princeton*) is associate professor of history and global studies at the University of North Carolina at Chapel Hill. He previously taught at the University of Illinois at Chicago, Princeton University, Columbia University, and the University of Florida. Professor Tsin's primary interests include the histories of modern China and colonialism. He is the author of *Nation, Governance, and Modernity in China: Canton, 1900–1927*. He is currently writing a cultural history of the reconfiguration of Chinese identity in the twentieth century.

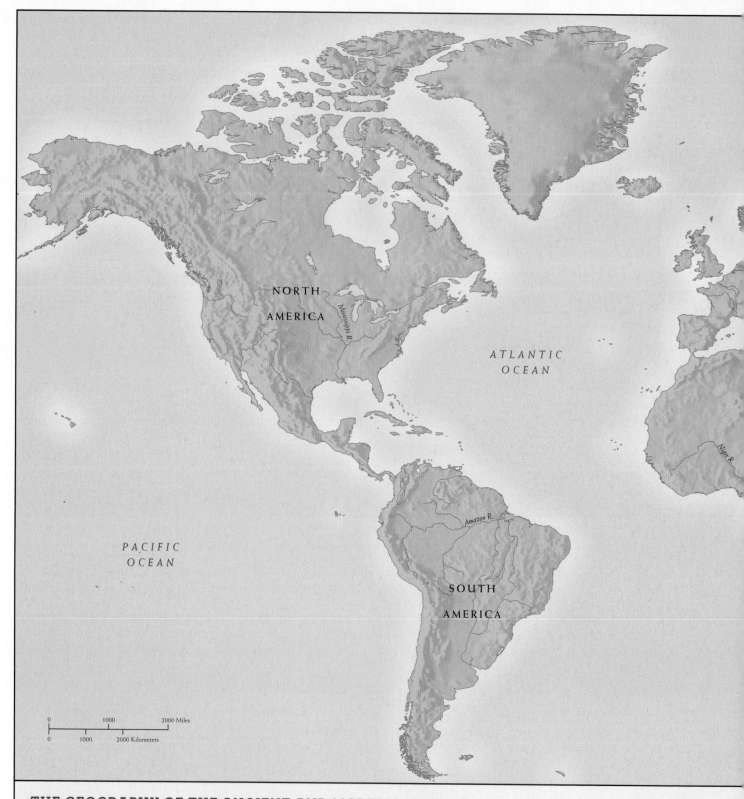

THE GEOGRAPHY OF THE ANCIENT AND MODERN WORLDS

Today, we believe the world to be divided into continents, and most of us think that it was always so. Geographers usually identify six inhabited continents: Africa, North America, South America, Europe, Asia, and Australia. Inside these continents they locate a vast number of subcontinental units, such as East Asia, South Asia, Southeast Asia, the Middle East, North Africa, and sub-Saharan Africa. Yet this geographical understanding would have been completely alien to premodern men and women, who did not think that they inhabited continents bounded by large bodies of water. Lacking a firm command of the seas, they

saw themselves living on contiguous landmasses, and they thought these territorial bodies were the main geographical units of their lives. Hence, in this volume we have chosen to use a set of geographical terms, the main one being Afro-Eurasia, that more accurately reflect the world that the premoderns believed that they inhabited.

The most interconnected and populous landmass of premodern times was Afro-Eurasia. The term Eurasia is widely used in general histories, but we think it is in its own ways inadequate. The preferred term from our perspective must be Afro-Eurasia, for the interconnected

ARCTIC OCEAN

AFRO-EURASIA

EUROPE

Danube R.

BLACK SEA

CASPIAN SEA

AEGEAN SEA

TAURUS MTS.

MEDITERRANEAN SEA

Tigris R.

Euphrates R.

ARAL SEA

CENTRAL ASIA

SOUTHWEST ASIA

Indus R.

HIMALAYA MTS.

Yellow R.

Yangzi R.

EAST ASIA

YELLOW SEA

Pearl R.

AFRICA

RED SEA

ARABIAN SEA

SOUTH ASIA

SOUTHEAST ASIA

SOUTH CHINA SEA

PACIFIC OCEAN

Nile R.

Lake Chad

Congo R.

Lake Victoria

SUB-SAHARAN AFRICA

INDIAN OCEAN

AUSTRALIA

landmass of premodern and indeed much of modern times included large parts of Europe and Asia and significant regions in Africa. The major African territories that were regularly joined to Europe and Asia were Egypt, North Africa, and even parts of sub-Saharan Africa.

Only gradually and fitfully did the divisions of the world that we take for granted today take shape. The peoples inhabiting the northwestern part of the Afro-Eurasian landmass did not see themselves as European Christians, and hence as a distinctive cultural entity, until the Middle Ages drew to a close in the twelfth and thirteenth centuries. Islam did not arise and extend its influence throughout the middle zone of the Afro-Eurasian landmass until the eighth and ninth centuries. And, finally, the peoples living in what we today term the Indian subcontinent did not feel a strong sense of their own cultural and political unity until the Delhi Sultanate of the thirteenth and fourteenth centuries and the Mughal Empire, which emerged at the beginning of the sixteenth century, brought political unity to that vast region. As a result, we use the terms South Asia, Vedic society, and India in place of Indian subcontinent for the premodern part of our narrative, and we use Southwest Asia and North Africa to refer to what today is designated as the Middle East. In fact, it is only in the period from 1000 to 1300 that some of the major cultural areas that are familiar to us today truly crystallized.

WORLDS TOGETHER,
WORLDS APART

FIFTH EDITION

guinea
sudam
tenbuch
ciutatdomelli
tagaza

Before You Read This Chapter

Go to INQUIZITIVE to see what you know & learn what you've missed.

GLOBAL STORYLINES

- Advances in maritime technology lead to increased sea trade, transforming coastal cities into global trading hubs and elevating Afro-Eurasian trade to unprecedented levels.

- Intensified trade and religious and linguistic integration shape four major cultural "spheres": the Islamic world, India, China, and Europe.

- Sub-Saharan Africa is drawn into Eurasian exchange, resulting in a true Afro-Eurasia–wide network. Meanwhile, the Americas experience more limited political, economic, and cultural integration.

- The Mongol Empire integrates many of the world's major cultural spheres.

10

Becoming "The World," 1000–1300 CE

FOCUS QUESTIONS

- What technological advances occurred during this period, especially in ship design and navigation, and how did they facilitate the expansion of Afro-Eurasian trade?

- What types of social and political forces shaped the Islamic world, India, China, and Europe at this time? To what degree did these forces integrate cultures and geographical areas?

- How did sub-Saharan Africa compare with the Americas in terms of internal integration and external interactions?

- In what ways did the Mongol Empire influence peoples and places within Afro-Eurasia?

In the late 1270s, two Christian monks, Bar Sāwmā and Markōs, voyaged into the heart of Islam. They were not Europeans. They were Uighurs, a Turkish people of central Asia, many of whom had converted to Christianity centuries earlier. Sent by the mighty Mongol ruler Kubilai Khan as he prepared to become the first formally recognized emperor of China's Yuan dynasty, the monks were supposed to worship at the temple in Jerusalem. But the Great Khan also had political ambitions. He was eager to conquer Jerusalem, held by the Muslims. Accordingly, he dispatched the monks as agents to make alliances with Christian kings in the area and to gather intelligence about his potential enemy in Palestine.

By 1280, conflict and conquest had transformed many parts of the world. But friction was simply one manifestation of cultures brushing up against one another. More important was trade. Indeed, Bar Sāwmā and Markōs lingered at the magnificent trading hub of Kashgar in what is now western China, where caravan routes converged in a market for jade, exotic spices, and precious silks. Later, at Baghdad, the monks parted ways. Bar Sāwmā visited Constantinople (where the king gave him gold and silver), Rome (where he met with the pope at the shrine of Saint Peter), and Paris (where he saw that city's vibrant university) before deciding to return to China, where the Christians of the east awaited his reports. In the end, neither monk ever returned. Yet their voyages exemplified the crisscrossing of people, money, and goods along the trade routes and sea-lanes that connected the world's regions. For just as religious conflict was a hallmark of this age, so was a surge in trade, migration, and global exchange.

The period brought to a climax many centuries of human development, and it ushered in a new, very long cycle of cultural interaction from which emerge three interrelated themes. First, trade was shifting from land-based routes to sea-based routes. Coastal trading cities began to dramatically expand. Second, intensified trade and linguistic and religious integration generated the world's four major cultural "spheres," whose inhabitants were linked by shared institutions and beliefs: the Islamic world, India, China, and Europe. Not all cultures turned into "spheres," though. In the Americas and sub-Saharan Africa, there was not the same impulse to integrate regions, which remained more fragmented but thrived nonetheless. Third, the rise of the Mongol Empire represented the peak in the long history of ties and tensions between settled and mobile peoples. From China to Persia and as far as eastern Europe, the Mongols ruled over much land in the world's major cultural spheres. Each of these three themes contributes to an understanding of how Afro-Eurasia became a "world" unified through trade, migration, and even religious conflict.

DEVELOPMENT OF MARITIME TRADE

Innovations at Sea

By the tenth century CE, sea routes were eclipsing land networks for long-distance trade. Improved navigational aids, refinements in shipbuilding, better mapmaking, and new legal arrangements and accounting practices made shipping easier and slashed the costs of seaborne trade. The numbers testify to the maritime revolution: while a porter could carry about 10 pounds over long distances, and animal-drawn wagons could move 100 pounds over small distances, the Arab dhows plying the Indian Ocean were capable of transporting up to 5 tons of cargo. (Dhows are ships with triangle-shaped sails, called lateens, that allow the best use of the monsoon trade winds on the Arabian Sea and the Indian Ocean.) As a result, some coastal ports, like Mogadishu in eastern Africa, became vast transshipment centers for a thriving trade across the Indian Ocean.

A new navigational instrument spurred this boom: the needle compass. This Chinese invention initially identified promising locations for houses and tombs, but eleventh-century sailors from Guangzhou (anglicized as Canton) used it to find their way on the high seas. The device spread rapidly. Not only did it allow sailing under cloudy skies, but it also improved mapmaking. And it made all the oceans, including the Atlantic, easier to navigate.

Dhow. *This modern dhow in the harbor of Zanzibar displays the characteristic triangle sail. The triangle sail can make good use of the trade wind monsoon and thus has guided dhows on the Arabian Sea since ancient times.*

Antique Chinese Compass. *Chinese sailors from Canton started to use needle compasses in the eleventh century. By the thirteenth century, needle compasses were widely used on ships in the Indian Ocean and were starting to appear in the Mediterranean.*

Now shipping became less dangerous. Navigators relied on lateen-rigged dhows between the Indian Ocean and the Red Sea, heavy junks in the South China Sea, and Atlantic "cogs," which linked Genoa to locations as distant as the Azores and Iceland. They also enjoyed the protection of political authorities, such as the Song dynasts in China, in guiding the trading fleets in and out of harbors. The Fatimid caliphate in Egypt, for instance, profited from maritime trade and defended merchant fleets from pirates. Armed convoys of ships escorted commercial fleets and regularized the ocean traffic. The system soon spread to North Africa and southern Spain. Most of these shipping firms were family based, and they sent young men of the family, sometimes servants or slaves, to work in India. Wives in Cairo could expect gifts from their husbands to arrive with the fleet.

Changes in navigation ushered in the demise of overland routes. Silk Road merchants eventually gave up using camel trains, caravansaries (inns for travelers), and oasis hubs as they switched to the sea-lanes. The shift took centuries, but overland routes and camels were no match for multiple-masted cargo ships.

Global Commercial Hubs

Long-distance trade spawned the growth of commercial cities. (See Map 10.1.) These cosmopolitan **entrepôts** served as transshipment centers where ships could drop anchor and merchants

could find lodging, exchange commodities, and replenish supplies. Their locations between borders or in ports enabled merchants to link diverse peoples commercially. Beginning in the late tenth century CE, regional centers became major anchorages of the maritime trade: in the west, the Egyptian port cities of Alexandria and Cairo; in the east, the Chinese city of Quanzhou; in the Malaysian Archipelago, the city of Melaka; and near the tip of the Indian Peninsula, the port of Kollam (often anglicized as Quilon). These hubs thrived under the political stability of dynasts who recognized that the free-for-all of trade and market life would generate wealth for them through taxes collected on cargoes.

Cairo and Alexandria were the Mediterranean's main maritime commercial centers. Cairo was home to numerous Muslim and Jewish trading firms, and Alexandria was their lookout post on the Mediterranean. It was through Alexandria that Europeans acquired silks from China and Spanish silks headed to eastern Mediterranean markets along with olive oil, glassware, flax, corals, and metals. Gemstones and aromatic perfumes poured in from India. Also changing hands were minerals and chemicals for dyeing or tanning and raw materials such as timber and bamboo. The real novelties were paper and books. Hand-copied Bibles, Talmuds, Qurans, legal and moral works, grammars in various languages, and Arabic books became the first best-sellers of the Mediterranean.

The Islamic legal system prevalent in Egypt promoted a favorable business environment. Legal specialists got around the rule that might have brought commerce to a halt—the *sharia*'s (see Chapter 9) prohibition against earning interest on loans. With the clerics' blessing, Muslim traders formed partnerships between those who had capital to lend and those who needed money to expand their businesses: owners of capital entrusted their money or commodities to agents who, after completing their work, returned the investment and a share of the profits to the owners—and kept the rest as their reward. The English word *risk* derives from the Arabic *rizq,* the extra allowance paid to merchants in lieu of interest.

In China, the Song government set up offices of Seafaring Affairs in three major ports: Canton, Quanzhou, and an area near present-day Shanghai in the Yangzi Delta. In return for a portion of the taxes, these offices registered cargoes, sailors, and traders, while guards kept a keen eye on the traffic. Arabs, Persians, Jews, and Indians, as well as Chinese, traded at Quanzhou, and some stayed on to manage their businesses. Perhaps as many as 100,000 Muslims lived there during the Song dynasty. A mosque from this period is still standing. Hindu traders living in Quanzhou worshiped in a Buddhist shrine where statues of Hindu deities stood alongside those of Buddhist gods.

Because of its strategic location and proximity to Malayan tropical produce, Melaka became a key cosmopolitan city.

MAP 10.1 | **Afro-Eurasian Trade, 1000–1300**

During the early second millennium, Afro-Eurasian merchants increasingly turned to the Indian Ocean to transport their goods.

- Locate the global hubs of Kollam, Alexandria, Cairo, Melaka, and Quanzhou on this map.
- What regions do each of these global hubs represent?
- Based on the map, why would sea travel have been preferable to overland travel?
- According to the text, what revolutions in maritime travel facilitated this development?

During peak season, Southeast Asian ports teemed with colorfully dressed Indian, Javanese, and Chinese merchants and sailors selling their goods, purchasing return cargo, and waiting for the winds to change so they could reach their next destination. Local artisans hawked batik handicrafts, and money-grubbing traders converged from all over Asia to flood the markets with their merchandise and to search for pungent herbs, aromatic spices, and agrarian staples to ship out.

In the tenth century CE, South India likewise supported a nerve center of maritime trade. Many Muslim traders settled in Malabar, on the southwest coast of the Indian Peninsula, and Kollam became a cosmopolitan hub. Dhows delivered goods from the Red Sea and Africa. Chinese junks unloaded silks and porcelain and picked up passengers and commodities for East Asian markets. Muslim traders shipped horses from Arab countries to India and the southeast islands, where kings viewed them as symbols of royalty. There was even trade in elephants and cattle from tropical countries, though most goods were spices, perfumes, and textiles. Personal relationships were key. When striking a deal with a local merchant, a Chinese trader would mention his Indian neighbor in Quanzhou and that family's residence in Kollam.

Global commercial hubs relied on friendship and family to keep their businesses thriving across religious and regional divides. Whether in India, Melaka, China, or Egypt, each bustling port teemed with a cosmopolitan mix of peoples,

Mazu. *As much as sailors used compasses, they could still appeal for divine help—as these Quanzhou sailors did in seeking protection at the shrine of Mazu, the goddess of seafarers. According to legend, before assuming godhood Mazu had performed many miracles. Her temple became prominent after 1123, when Quanzhou's governor survived a storm at sea while returning from Korea. After that, sailors and their families burned incense for the goddess and prayed for her aid in keeping them safe at sea.*

goods, and ideas that flowed through the growing maritime networks, thanks to improved ships and better navigational tools.

THE ISLAMIC WORLD IN A TIME OF POLITICAL FRAGMENTATION

While the number of Muslim traders began to increase in commercial hubs from the Mediterranean to the South China Sea, it was not until the ninth and tenth centuries CE that Muslims became a majority within their own Abbasid Empire (see Chapter 9). From the outset, Muslim rulers and clerics dealt with large non-Muslim populations, even as these groups were converting to Islam. Rulers accorded non-Muslims religious toleration as long as the non-Muslims accepted Islam's political dominion. Jewish, Christian, and Zoroastrian communities were free to choose their own religious leaders and to settle internal disputes in their own religious courts. They did, however, have to pay a special tax, the *jizya*, and defer to their rulers. While tolerant, Islam was an expansionist, universalizing faith. Intense proselytizing—especially by Sufi merchants—carried the sacred word to new frontiers and, in the process, reinforced the spread of Islamic institutions that supported commercial exchange. (See Primary Source: The Merchants of Egypt.)

Environmental Challenges and Fragmentation

Whereas western Europe experienced a climatic dark age between 500 and 900 CE (see Chapter 9), severe conditions—freezing temperatures and lack of rainfall—afflicted the eastern Mediterranean and the Islamic lands of Mesopotamia, the Iranian plateau, and the steppe region of central Asia in the late eleventh and early twelfth centuries. The Nile's low water levels devastated Egypt, the breadbasket for much of the area. No less than one-quarter of the summer floods that normally brought sediment-enriching deposits to Egypt's soils and guaranteed abundant harvests were utter failures in this period. Turkish nomadic pastoralists poured out of the steppe lands of central Asia, driven by drought, in search of better lands, wreaking political and economic havoc everywhere they invaded.

The Seljuk Turks entered the Iranian plateau in 1029, bringing an end to the magnificent cultural flourishing of the first half of the eleventh century (see Chapter 9). Seljuk warriors invaded Baghdad in 1055, establishing a nomadic state in Mesopotamia over a once powerful Abbasid state that now lacked the resources to defend its lands and its peoples, weakened by famines and pestilence. The invaders destroyed institutions of learning and public libraries and looted the region's antiquities. Nor was the Byzantine Empire spared.

PRIMARY SOURCE

The Merchants of Egypt

The most comprehensive collection of eleventh- and twelfth-century commercial materials from the Islamic world comes from a repository, known as a geniza, connected to the Jewish synagogue in Cairo. (It was the custom of the Jewish community to preserve, in a special storeroom, all texts that mention God.) These papers, a rich source of information about the Jewish community in Egypt at that time, touch on all manner of activities: cultural, religious, judicial, political, and commercial. The following letter is addressed to Joseph ibn 'Awkal, one of Egypt's leading merchants in the eleventh century.

Dear and beloved elder and leader, may God prolong your life, never take away your rank, and increase his favors and benefactions to you.

I inform you, my elder, that I have arrived safely. I have written you a letter before, but have seen no answer. Happy preoccupations—I hope. In that letter I provided you with all the necessary information.

I loaded nine pieces of antimony (kohl), five in baskets and four in complete pieces, on the boat of Ibn Jubār—may God keep it; these are for you personally, sent by Mūsā Ibn al-Majjānī. On this boat, I have in partnership with you—may God keep you—a load of cast copper, a basket with (copper) fragments, and two pieces of antimony. I hope God will grant their safe arrival. Kindly take delivery of everything, my lord.

I have also sent with Banāna a camel load for you from Ibn al-Majjānī and a camel load for me in partnership with you—may God keep you. He also carries another partnership of mine, namely, with 'Ammār Ibn Yijū, four small jugs (of oil).

With Abū Zayd I have a shipload of tin in partnership with Salāma al-Mahdawī. Your share in this partnership with him is fifty pounds. I also have seventeen small jugs of s[oap]. I hope they arrive safely. They belong to a man [called . . .] r b. Salmūn, who entrusted them to me at his own risk. Also a bundle of hammered copper, belonging to [a Muslim] man from the Maghreb, called Abū Bakr Ibn Rizq Allah. Two other bundles, on one is written Abraham, on the other M[. . .]. I agreed with the shipowner that he would transport the goods to their destination. I wish my brother Abū Nasr—may God preserve him—to take care of all the goods and carry them to his place until I shall arrive, if God wills.

Please sell the tin for me at whatever price God may grant and leave its "purse" (the money received for it) until my arrival. I am ready to travel, but must stay until I can unload the tar and oil from the ships.

Please take care of this matter and take from him the price of five skins (filled with oil). The account is with Salāma.

Al-Sabbāgh of Tripoli has bribed Bu 'l-'Al ā the agent, and I shall unload my goods soon.

Kindest regards to your noble self and to my master [. . . and] Abu 'l-Fadl, may God keep them.

QUESTIONS FOR ANALYSIS

- List all the different kinds of commodities that the letter talks about.
- How many different people are named as owners, partners, dealers, and agents?
- What does the letter reveal about the ties among merchants and about how they conducted their business?

Source: Letters of Medieval Jewish Traders, translated with introductions and notes by S. D. Goitein (Princeton, NJ: Princeton University Press, 1973), pp. 85–87.

Constantinople, once with a population of 1 million, saw its numbers dwindle to 200,000 by the late eleventh century; yet it was still Europe's largest city.

Political Divisions

These environmental challenges also caused Islam's political institutions to fragment just when it appeared that Shiism would be the vehicle for uniting the Islamic world. The Fatimid Shiites had established their authority over Egypt and much of North Africa (see Chapter 9), and the Abbasid state in Baghdad was controlled by a Shiite family, the Buyids. Each group created universities, in Cairo and Baghdad, respectively, ensuring that leading centers of higher learning were Shiite. But divisions also sapped Shiism, as Sunni Muslims began to challenge Shiite power and establish their own strongholds. In Baghdad, the Buyid family surrendered to a group of Sunni strongmen in 1055. A century later, the last of the Shiite Fatimid rulers gave way to a new Sunni regime in Egypt (see Map 10.2).

The new strongmen were mainly Turks. Their people had been migrating into the Islamic heartland from the Asian

10.2 | Islam between 900 and 1200

The Muslim world experienced political disintegration in the first centuries of the second millennium.

- According to the map key, what were the two major types of Muslim states in this period and what were the two major empires?
- What were the sources of instability in this period according to the map?
- As Islam continued to expand in this period, what challenges did it face?

steppes since the eighth century CE, bringing superior military skills and an intense devotion to Sunni Islam. Once established in Baghdad, they founded outposts in Syria and Palestine and then moved into Anatolia after defeating Byzantine forces in 1071. But this Turkish state also crumbled, as tribesmen quarreled for preeminence.

By the thirteenth century, the Islamic heartland had fractured into three regions. In the east (central Asia, Iran, and eastern Iraq), the remnants of the old Abbasid state persevered. Caliphs succeeded one another, still claiming to speak for all of Islam yet deferring to their Turkish military commanders. In the core of the Islamic world—Egypt, Syria, and the Arabian Peninsula—where Arabic was the primary tongue, military men of non-Arab origin held the reins of power. Farther west in North Africa, Arab rulers prevailed, but the influence of Berbers, some from the northern Sahara, was extensive. Islam was a vibrant faith, but its political systems were splintered.

The Spread of Sufism

Even in the face of political splintering, Islam's spread was facilitated by a popular form of the religion, highly mystical and communal, called **Sufism**. The term *Sufi* comes from the Arabic word for wool (*suf*), which many of the early mystics wrapped themselves in to mark their penitence. Seeking closer union with God, they also performed ecstatic rituals, such as repeating over and over again the name of God. In time, groups of devotees gathered to read aloud the Quran and other religious tracts. Sufi mystics' desire to experience God's love found ready expression in poetry. Most admired of Islam's mystic poets was Jalal al-Din Rumi (1207–1273), spiritual founder of the Mevlevi Sufi order that became famous for the ceremonial dancing of its whirling devotees, known as dervishes.

Although many *ulama* (scholars) despised the Sufis and loathed their seeming lack of theological rigor, the movement

Dervishes. *Today, the whirling dance of dervishes is a tourist attraction, as shown in this picture from the Jerash Cultural Festival in Jordan. Though Sufis in the early second millennium were not this neatly dressed, the whirling dance was an important means of reaching union with God.*

spread with astonishing speed and offered a unifying force within Islam. Sufism's emotional content and strong social bonds, sustained in Sufi brotherhoods, added to its appeal. Sufi missionaries carried the universalizing faith to India, to Southeast Asia, across the Sahara Desert, and to many other distant regions. It was from these brotherhoods that Islam became truly a religion of the people. As trade increased and more converts appeared in the Islamic lands, urban and peasant populations came to understand the faith practiced by the political, commercial, and scholarly upper classes even while they remained attached to their Sufi brotherhood ways. Over time, Islam became even more accommodating, embracing Persian literature, Turkish ruling skills, and Arabic-language contributions in law, religion, literature, and science.

What Was Islam?

Buoyed by Arab dhows on the high seas and carried on the backs of camels following commercial networks, Islam had been transformed from Muhammad's original goal of creating a religion for Arab peoples. By 1300, its influence spanned Afro-Eurasia and enjoyed multitudes of non-Arab converts. (See Map 10.3.) It attracted urbanites and rural peasants alike, as well as its original audience of desert nomads. Its extraordinary universal appeal generated an intense Islamic cultural flowering around 1000 CE.

Some people worried about the preservation of Islam's true nature as, for example, Arabic ceased to be the language of many Islamic believers. True, the devout read and recited the Quran in its original tongue, as the religion mandated. But Persian was now the language of Muslim philosophy and art, and Turkish

was the language of law and administration. Moreover, Jerusalem and Baghdad no longer stood alone as Islamic cultural capitals. Other cities, housing universities and other centers of learning, promoted alternative versions of Islam. In fact, some of the most dynamic thought came from Islam's fringes.

At the same time, diversity fostered cultural blossoming in all fields of high learning. Indicative of the prominence of the Islamic faith and the Arabic language in thought was the legendary Ibn Rushd (1126–1198). Known as Averroës in the west, where scholars pored over his writings, he wrestled with the same theological issues that troubled western scholars. Steeped in the writings of Aristotle, Ibn Rushd became Islam's most thoroughgoing advocate for the use of reason in understanding the universe. His knowledge of Aristotle was so great that it influenced the thinking of the Christian world's leading philosopher and theologian, Thomas Aquinas (1225–1274). Above all, Ibn Rushd believed that faith and reason could be compatible. He also argued for a social hierarchy in which learned men would command influence akin to Confucian scholars in China or Greek philosophers in Athens. Ibn Rushd believed that the proper forms of reasoning had to be entrusted to the educated class—in the case of Islam, the *ulama*—who would serve the common people.

Equally powerful works appeared in Persian, which by now was expressing the most sophisticated ideas of culture and religion. Best representing the new Persian ethnic pride was Abu al-Qasim Firdawsi (920–1020), a devout Muslim who believed in the importance of pre-Islamic Sasanian traditions. In the epic poem *Shah Namah,* or *Book of Kings,* he celebrated the origins of Persian culture and narrated the history of the Iranian highland peoples from the dawn of time to the Muslim conquest. As part of his effort to extol a pure Persian culture, Firdawsi attempted to compose his entire poem in Persian, unblemished by other languages and even avoiding Arabic words.

The Islamic world's achievements in science were truly remarkable. Its scholars were at the pinnacle of scientific knowledge throughout the world in this era. In truth, the "Islamic sciences"—law, study of the Quran, traditions of the Prophet (*hadith*), theology, poetry, and the Arabic language—held primacy among the learned classes. In contrast, "foreign sciences" (later called the natural sciences in Europe) were held in lower esteem. Even so, Ibn al-Shatir (1304–1375), working on his own in Damascus, produced non-Ptolemaic models of the universe that later researchers noted were mathematically equivalent to those of Copernicus. Even earlier, the Maragha school of astronomers (1259 and later) in western Iran had produced a non-Ptolemaic model of the planets. Some historians of science believe that Copernicus must have seen an Arabic manuscript written by a thirteenth-century Persian astronomer that contained a table of the movements of the planets. In addition,

MAP 10.3 | Islamic and Hindu States and the Byzantine Empire between 1200 and 1300

Islam continued to expand after the thirteenth century.

- Where were its largest and most important gains according to the map?
- How did other religions fare under Islamic rule in this period?
- How was Islam able to continue to expand in this period?

scholars in the Islamic world produced works in medicine, optics, and mathematics as well as astronomy that were in advance of the achievements of Greek and Roman scholars.

By the fourteenth century, Islam had achieved what early converts would have considered unthinkable. No longer a religion of a minority of peoples living among Christian, Zoroastrian, and Jewish communities, it had become the people's faith. The agents of conversion were mainly Sufi saints and Sufi brotherhoods—not the *ulama*, whose exhortations had little impact on common people. The Sufis had carried their faith far and wide to North African Berbers, to Anatolian villagers, and to West African animists who believed that things in nature have souls. Ibn Rushd worried about the growing appeal of what he considered an "irrational" piety. But his message failed, because he did not appreciate that Islam's expansionist powers rested on its appeal to common folk. While the *sharia* was the core of Islam for the educated and scholarly classes, Sufism spoke to ordinary men and women.

During this period, Islam became one of the four cultural spheres that would play a major role in world history. Islam

became the majority religion of most of the inhabitants of Southwest Asia and North Africa, Arabic became the everyday language for most people, and the Turks began to establish themselves as the dominant rulership force, ultimately creating the Ottoman Empire, which would last into the twentieth century. The Islamic world became integral in transregional trade and the creation and maintenance of knowledge.

INDIA AS A CULTURAL MOSAIC

Trade and migration affected India, just as it did the rest of Asia and Africa. As in the case of Islam, India's growing cultural interconnections and increasing prosperity produced little political integration. Under the canopy of Hinduism it remained a cultural mosaic; Islamic faith now joined others to make the region even more diverse. (See Map 10.4.) India illustrates how cross-cultural integration can just as easily preserve diversity as promote internal unity.

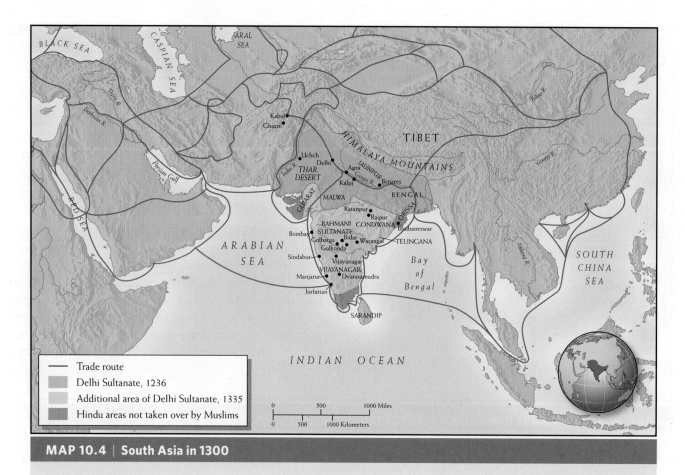

MAP 10.4 | South Asia in 1300

As the fourteenth century began, India was a blend of many cultures. Politically, the Turkish Muslim regime of the Delhi Sultanate dominated the region.

- Use the key to the map to identify the areas dominated by the Delhi Sultanate.
- How do you suppose the trade routes helped to spread the Muslims' influence in India?
- Now use the key to find the Hindu areas. Based on your reading, what factors accounted for Hinduism's continued appeal despite the Muslims' political power?

With its pivotal location along land- and sea-based routes, India became an intersection for the trade, migration, and culture of Afro-Eurasian peoples. With 80 million inhabitants in 1000 CE, it had the second-largest population in the region, not far behind China's 120 million. (See Analyzing Global Developments: Growth in the World Population to 1340.) Turks ultimately spilled into India as they had the Islamic heartlands, bringing their newfound Islamic beliefs. But the Turkish newcomers encountered an ethnic and religious mix of which they were just one part.

Before the Turks arrived, India had been splintered among rival chiefs called *rajas*. These leaders gained support from high-caste Brahmans by doling out land grants to them. Since much of the land was uncultivated, the Brahmans first built temples, then converted the indigenous hunter-gatherer peoples to the Hindu faith, and finally taught the converts how to cultivate the land. In this way the Brahmans simultaneously spread their faith and expanded the agrarian tax base for themselves and the rajas. They also repaid the rajas' support by compiling elaborate genealogies for them and endowing them with legitimizing ancestries. In return, the rajas demonstrated that they, too, were well versed in Sanskrit culture and were prepared to patronize artists and poets. Ultimately, many of the warriors and their heirs became Indian rajas.

Invasions and Consolidations

When the Turkish warlords began entering India, South Asia's rulers, the rajas, had neither the will nor the resources to resist them after centuries of fighting off invaders. The most powerful and enduring of the Turkish Muslim regimes of northern India was the **Delhi Sultanate** (1206–1526), whose rulers brought political integration but also strengthened the cultural

Hindu Temple. *When Buddhism started to decline in India, Hinduism was on the rise. Numerous Hindu temples were built, many of them adorned with ornate carvings like this small tenth-century temple in Bhubaneshwar, in eastern India.*

diversity and tolerance that were a hallmark of the Indian social order. Sultans recruited local artisans for building projects, and palaces and mosques became displays of Indian architectural tastes adopted by Turkish newcomers. But the sultans did not force their subjects to convert, so South Asia never became an Islamic-dominant region. Nor did they display much interest in the flourishing commercial life along the Indian coast, permitting these areas to develop on their own and allowing Persian Zoroastrian traders to settle around modern-day Mumbai (Bombay). Farther south, the Malabar coast became the preserve

of Arab traders. The Delhi Sultanate was a rich and powerful regime that brought political integration but did not enforce cultural homogeneity.

What Was India?

During the eleventh, twelfth, and thirteenth centuries, India became the most diverse and, in some respects, most tolerant region in Afro-Eurasia. India in this era arose as an impressive but fragile mosaic of cultures, religions, and ethnicities.

When the Turks arrived, the local Hindu population, having had much experience with foreign invaders and immigrants, assimilated these intruders as they had done earlier peoples. Before long, the newcomers thought of themselves as Indians who, however, retained their Islamic beliefs and steppe ways. They continued to wear their distinctive trousers and robes and flaunted their horse-riding skills. At the same time, the local population embraced some of their conquerors' ways, donning the tunics and trousers that characterized central Asian peoples.

Diversity and cultural mixing became most visible in the multiple languages that flourished in India. Although the sultans spoke Turkish languages, they regarded Persian literature as a high cultural achievement and made Persian their courtly and administrative language. Meanwhile, most Hindu subjects spoke local languages, followed their caste regulations, and practiced diverse forms of Hindu worship. The rulers did what Muslim rulers in Southwest Asia and the

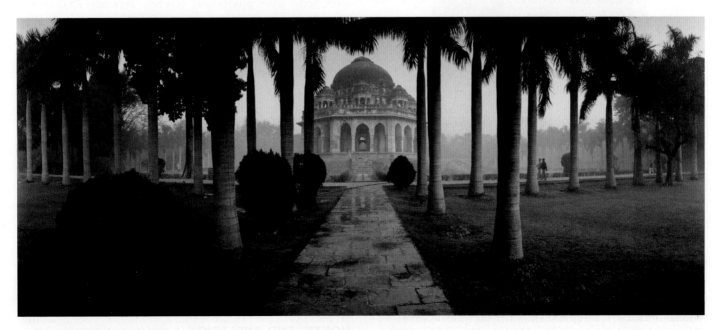

Lodi Gardens. *The Lodi dynasty was the last dynasty of the Delhi Sultanate. Lodi Gardens, the cemetery of Lodi sultans, placed central Asian Islamic architecture in an Indian landscape, thereby creating a scene of "heaven on the earth."*

Mediterranean did with Christian and Jewish communities living in their midst: they collected the *jizya* tax and permitted communities to worship as they saw fit and to administer their own communal law.

Ultimately, Islam in India proved that it did not have to be a conquering religion to prosper. Although Buddhism had been in decline there for centuries, it, too, became part of the cultural intermixing of these centuries. As Vedic Brahmanism evolved into Hinduism (see Chapter 8), it absorbed many Buddhist doctrines and practices, such as *ahimsa* (nonkilling) and vegetarianism. The two religions became so similar that Hindus simply considered the Buddha to be one of their deities—an incarnation of the great god Vishnu. Many Buddhist moral teachings mixed with and became Hindu stories.

Once the initial disruptive effects of the Turkish invasions were absorbed, India remained a highly diverse and tolerant region during this period. Most important, it emerged as one of the four major cultural spheres, enjoying a tremendous level of integration as Turkish-Muslim rulership and their traditions and practices successfully blended into the native Hindu society, leading to a more integrated and peaceful India.

Vishnu. *In addition to the Buddha, the four-armed Vishnu has nine other avatars, some of whom are portrayed at his feet in this tenth-century sandstone sculpture.*

SONG CHINA: INSIDERS VERSUS OUTSIDERS

The preeminent world power in 1000 CE was still China, despite its recent turmoil. Once dampened, the turbulence yielded to a long era of stability and splendor that made China a regional engine of Afro-Eurasian prosperity. In 907 CE, the Tang dynasty splintered into regional kingdoms, mostly led by military generals. In 960 CE, one of these generals ended the fragmentation, reunified China, and assumed the mandate of heaven for the Song dynasty (960–1279). (See Maps 10.5 and 10.6.) Ultimately, a nomadic group, the Jurchen (ancestors of the Manchu, who would rule China from the seventeenth until the twentieth century), would bring the Song dynasty to an end, but not before Song influence had fanned out into Southeast Asia, helping to create new identities in the political systems there.

Economic Progress

China, like India and the Islamic world, participated in Afro-Eurasia's powerful long-distance trade. Chinese merchants were as energetic as their Muslim and Indian counterparts. Yet China's commercial successes could not have occurred without the country's strong agrarian base—especially its vast wheat, millet, and rice fields, which fed a population that reached 120 million. Agriculture benefited from breakthroughs in metalworking that produced stronger iron plows, which the Song harnessed to sturdy water buffalo to extend the agricultural frontier.

Manufacturing also flourished. In 1078, for example, total Song iron production reached between 75,000 and 150,000 tons, roughly the equivalent of European iron production in the early eighteenth century. The Chinese piston-driven bellows that provided forced air for furnaces were of a size unsurpassed until the nineteenth century. Also, in the early tenth century, Chinese alchemists mixed saltpeter with sulfur and charcoal to produce a product that would burn and that could be deployed on the battlefield: gunpowder. Song entrepreneurs were soon inventing a remarkable array of incendiary devices that flowed from their mastery of techniques for controlling explosions and high heat. Moreover, artisans produced increasingly light, durable, and exquisitely beautiful porcelains. Before long, their porcelain (now called "china") was the envy of all Afro-Eurasia. Also unspooling from the artisans' hands were vast amounts of clothing and handicrafts, made from the fibers grown by Song farmers. In effect, the Song Chinese oversaw the world's first manufacturing revolution, producing finished goods on a large scale for consumption far and wide.

MONEY AND INFLATION Expanding commerce transformed the role of money and its wide circulation. By now the

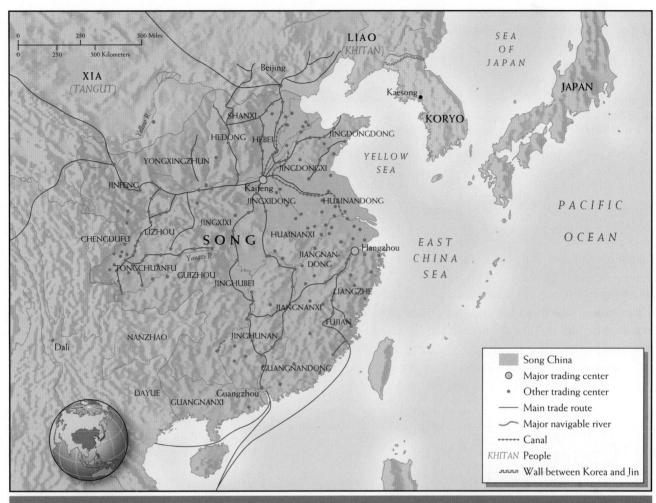

MAP 10.5 | East Asia in 1000

Several states emerged in East Asia between 1000 and 1300, but none were as strong as the Song dynasty in China.

- Using the key to the map, try to identify the factors that contributed to the Song state's economic dynamism.
- What external factors kept the Song dynasty from completely securing its reign?
- What factors drove the Chinese commercial revolution in this period?

Song government was annually minting nearly 2 million strings of currency, each containing 1,000 copper coins. In fact, as the economy grew, the supply of metal currency could not match the demand. One result was East Asia's thirst for gold from East Africa. At the same time, merchant guilds in northwestern Shanxi developed the first letters of exchange, called **flying cash**. These letters linked northern traders with their colleagues in the south. Before long, printed money had eclipsed coins. Even the government collected more than half its tax revenues in cash rather than grain and cloth. The government also issued more notes to pay its bills—a practice that ultimately contributed to the world's first case of runaway inflation.

New Elites

Song emperors ushered in a period of social and cultural vitality. They built on Tang institutions by expanding a central bureaucracy of scholar-officials chosen through competitive civil service examinations. Zhao Kuangyin, or Emperor Taizu (r. 960–976 CE), himself administered the final test for all who had passed the highest-level palace examination. In subsequent dynasties, the emperor was the nation's premier examiner, symbolically demanding oaths of allegiance from successful candidates. By 1100, these ranks of learned men had accumulated sufficient power to become China's new ruling elite.

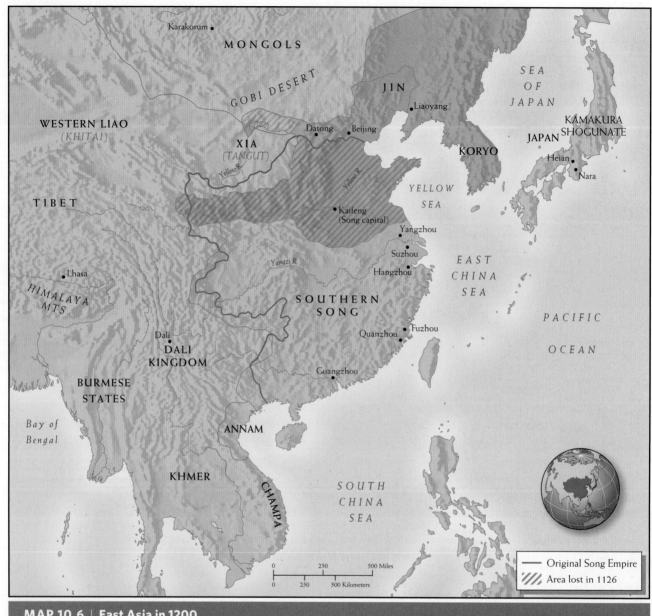

MAP 10.6 | East Asia in 1200

The Song dynasty regularly dealt with "barbarian" neighbors.

- What were the major "barbarian" tribes during this period?
- Approximately what percentage of Song China was lost to the Jin in 1126?
- How did the "barbarian" tribes affect the Han Chinese identity in this period?

Expansion of the civil service examination system was crucial to a shift in power from the still powerful hereditary aristocracy to a less wealthy but more highly schooled class of scholar-officials. Consider the career of the Northern Song reformer Wang Anshi (1021–1086), who ascended to power from a commoner family outside of Hangzhou in the east. He owed his success to gaining high marks in Song state examinations—a not insignificant achievement, for in nearby Fujian Province alone, of the roughly 18,000 candidates who gathered triennially to take the provincial examination, over 90 percent failed! After gaining the emperor's ear, Wang eventually challenged the political and cultural influence of the old Tang dynasty elites from the northwest.

Song Dynasty Coin. *The Song dynasty's rapid economic development led to the use of vast amounts of metal currency, including many copper coins like this one. The hole in the center meant that the coins could be strung together in groups.*

Negotiating with Nomads on the Borderlands

As the Song flourished, nomads on the outskirts eyed the Chinese successes closely. To the north, Khitan, Tungusic, Tangut, and Jurchen nomadic societies formed their own dynasties and adopted Chinese institutions. Located within the "greater China," as defined by the Han and Tang dynasties, these non-Chinese nomads saw China proper as an object of both conquest and emulation.

In military power the Song dynasts were relatively weak. Despite their sophisticated weapons, they could not match their enemies on the steppe when the latter united against them. Steel tips improved the arrows that the Song soldiers shot from their crossbows, and flamethrowers and "crouching tiger catapults" sent incendiary bombs streaking into their enemies' ranks. But none of these breakthroughs was secret. Warrior neighbors on the steppe mastered the new arts of war more fully than did the Song dynasts themselves.

China's strength as a manufacturing powerhouse made economic diplomacy an option, so the Song relied on "gifts" and generous trade agreements with the borderlanders. For example, after losing North China to the Khitan Liao dynasty, the Song agreed to make annual payments of 100,000 ounces of silver and 200,000 bolts of silk. The treaty allowed them to live in relative peace for more than a century. Securing peace meant emptying the state coffers and then printing more paper money. The resulting inflation added economic instability to military weakness, making the Song an easy target when Jurchen invaders made their final assault.

What Was China?

Paradoxically, the increasing exchange between outsiders and insiders within China hardened the lines that divided them and gave residents of China's interior a highly developed sense of themselves as a distinctive people possessing a superior culture. Exchanges with outsiders nurtured a "Chinese" identity among those who considered themselves true insiders and referred to themselves as Han. Driven south from their ancient homeland in the eleventh century, they grew increasingly suspicious and resentful toward the outsiders living in their midst. They called these outsiders "barbarians" and treated them accordingly.

Vital in crystallizing this sense of a distinct Chinese identity was print culture. Of all Afro-Eurasian societies in 1300, the Chinese were the most advanced in their use of printing and book publishing and circulation. Moreover, their books established classical Chinese as the common language of educated classes in East Asia. The Song government used its plentiful supply of paper to print books, especially medical texts, and to distribute calendars. The private publishing industry also expanded. Printing houses throughout the country produced Confucian classics, works on history, philosophical treatises, and literature—all of which figured in the civil examinations. Buddhist publications, too, were available everywhere.

Wang Anshi. *He owed his rise from a commoner family to a powerful position as a reformer to the Song state examinations.*

Chinese and Barbarian. *After losing the north, the Han Chinese grew resentful of outsiders. They drew a dividing line between their own agrarian society and the nomadic warriors, calling them "barbarians." Such identities were not fixed, however. Chinese and so-called barbarians were mutually dependent.*

In many respects, the Song period represented China's greatest age. China's resources, its huge population base coupled with a strong agrarian economy, and its strong foreign trade and diplomatic relations made it the most wealthy among the four major cultural spheres; its common language and its transfer of power to nonhereditary Confucian scholars made it the most unified. The country's bureaucracy was the largest in the world, totaling between 200,000 and 300,000 civil servants during the Song period, of whom 20,000 were high officials. No society had larger cities or a more urbanized population. In mid-Song times, an estimated 5 percent of its people lived in cities. The capital, Kaifeng, had a population of 1 million; 30 cities varied in size from 40,000 to 100,000 or more; 60 cities had about 15,000 residents; and 400 cities, mainly county seats and smaller prefectural centers, had populations ranging between 4,000 and 5,000.

Yet in spite of its great wealth, immense population, highly developed bureaucracy, and powerful military forces, the Han Chinese never felt secure from the strong nomadic pastoralists who inhabited the western and northern frontiers. The construction of walls in the north and military outposts along the frontiers never seemed to afford complete protection. Especially when dynastic regimes weakened, China was vulnerable to invasion and conquest by these well-armed tribal confederacies. They moved south into China proper whenever the Chinese dynasty faltered and environmental conditions drove the militarily skilled nomads in search of better lives.

CHINA'S NEIGHBORS ADAPT TO CHANGE

Feeling the pull of China's economic and political gravity, cultures around China consolidated their own internal political authority and defined their own identities in order to keep from being swallowed up. At the same time, they increased their commercial transactions.

The Rise of Warriors in Japan

Japan, like China, laid many political and cultural foundations for its later development in the three centuries between 1000 and 1300. Not only did its leaders distance themselves from Chinese influences, but they also developed a strong sense of their islands' distinctive identity. Even so, the long-standing dominance of Chinese ways remained apparent at virtually every level of Japanese society and was most pronounced at the imperial court in the capital city of Heian, present-day Kyoto. (See Primary Source: The Tale of Genji.) The city itself, founded in 795 CE, was modeled after the former Tang Chinese capital city of Chang'an.

Outside Kyoto, however, a less China-centered way of life existed and began to impose itself on the center. Here, local notables, mainly military leaders and large landowners, began to challenge the imperial court for dominance. These military adventurers nevertheless elected to keep the Japanese emperors and their court at Kyoto in office even while stripping them of real power; Japan continued to have an emperor residing at the imperial city of Kyoto right down to 1868, when the Meiji restoration took place (see Chapter 17).

The emergence of these military men marked the arrival of an important new social group in Japanese society—the warriors, or samurai. In lightweight leather armor, these expert horsemen defended their private estates with remarkable long-range bowmanship and superbly crafted single-edged long steel swords, lethal for close combat in warfare. The warriors also brought an idealization of their martial ethics, with an emphasis on loyalty, self-discipline, and a simple life tied to the land, which helped to shape Japanese society until recent times.

By the beginning of the fourteenth century, Japan had multiple sources of political and cultural power: an endangered and declining aristocracy; an imperial family with prestige but little authority; powerful landowning notables based in the provinces; and a rising and increasingly ambitious class of samurai. This yielded a combustible mix of refined high culture in the capital versus a warrior ethos in the provinces. Such a mix produced social intrigue in politics and led different provincial factions to vie with one another for preeminence.

The Tale of Genji

Lacking a written language of their own, Heian aristocrats adopted classical Chinese as the official written language while continuing to speak Japanese. Men at the court took great pains to master the Chinese literary forms, but Japanese court ladies were not expected to do so. Lady Murasaki Shikibu, the author of **The Tale of Genji,** *hid her knowledge of Chinese, fearing that she would be criticized. In the meantime, the Japanese developed a native syllabary (a table of syllables) based on Chinese written graphs. Using this syllabary, Murasaki kept a diary in Japanese that gave vivid accounts of Heian court life. Her story— possibly the world's first novel—relates the adventures of a dashing young courtier named Genji. In the passage below, Genji evidently speaks for Murasaki in explaining why fiction can be as truthful as a work of history in capturing human life and its historical significance.*

Genji . . . smiled, and went on: "But I have a theory of my own about what this art of the novel is, and how it came into being. To begin with, it does not simply consist in the author's telling a story about the adventures of some other person. On the contrary, it happens because the storyteller's own experience of men and things, whether for good or ill—not only what he has passed through himself, but even events which he has only witnessed or been told of—has moved him to an emotion so passionate that he can no longer keep it shut up in his heart. Again and again something in his own life or in that around him will seem to the writer so important that he cannot bear to let it pass into oblivion. There must never come a time, he feels, when men do not know about it. That is my view of how this art arose.

"Clearly then, it is no part of the story-teller's craft to describe only what is good or beautiful. Sometimes, of course, virtue will be his theme, and he may then make such play with it as he will. But he is just as likely to have been struck by numerous examples of vice and folly in the world around him, and about them he has exactly the same feelings as about the pre-eminently good deeds which he encounters: they are more important and must all be garnered in. Thus anything whatsoever may become the subject of a novel, provided only that it happens in this mundane life and not in some fairyland beyond our human ken.

"The outward forms of this art will not of course be everywhere the same. At the court of China and in other foreign lands both the genius of the writers and their actual methods of composition are necessarily very different from ours; and even here in Japan the art of storytelling has in course of time undergone great changes. There will, too, always be a distinction between the lighter and the more serious forms of fiction. . . . So too, I think, may it be said that the art of fiction must not lose our allegiance because, in the pursuit of the main purpose to which I have alluded above, it sets virtue by the side of vice, or mingles wisdom with folly. Viewed in this light the novel is seen to be not, as is usually supposed, a mixture of useful truth with idle invention, but something which at every stage and in every part has a definite and serious purpose."

QUESTIONS FOR ANALYSIS

- According to this passage, what motivates an author to write a story (that is, fiction)?
- Genji feels it is appropriate for a writer to address not only "what is good or beautiful" but also "vice and folly." What explanation does he give? Do you agree?

Source: Sources of Japanese Tradition, compiled by Ryūsaku Tsunoda, William Theodore de Bary, and Donald Keene (New York: Columbia University Press, 1964), vol. 1, pp. 177–79.

Southeast Asia: A Maritime Mosaic

Southeast Asia, like India, now became a crossroads of Afro-Eurasian influences. Its sparse population of probably around 10 million in 1000 CE—tiny compared with that of China and India—was not immune to the foreign influences riding the sea-lanes into the archipelago. The Malay Peninsula became home to many trading ports and stopovers for traders shuttling between India and China, because it connected the Bay of Bengal and the Indian Ocean with the South China Sea. (See Map 10.7.)

Indian influence had been prominent both on the Asian mainland and in island portions of Southeast Asia since 800 CE, but Islamic expansion into the islands after 1200 gradually superseded these influences. Only Bali and a few other islands far to the east of Malaya preserved their Brahmanic-Vedic religious

Heiji Rebellion. *This illustration from the Kamakura Shogunate (1185–1333) depicts a battle during the Heiji Rebellion, which was fought between rival subjects of the cloistered emperor Go-Shirakawa in 1159. Riding in full armor on horseback, the fighters on both sides are armed with devastating long bows.*

origins. Elsewhere in Java and Sumatra, Islam became the dominant religion. In Vietnam and northern portions of mainland Southeast Asia, Chinese cultural influences and northern schools of Mahayana Buddhism were especially prominent.

During this period, Cambodian, Burmese, and Thai peoples founded powerful mixed polities along the Mekong, Salween, Chao Phraya, and Irrawaddy River basins of the Asian mainland. Important Vedic and Buddhist kingdoms emerged here as political buffers between the strong states in China and India and brought stability and further commercial prosperity to the region.

Consider the kingdom that ruled Angkor in present-day Cambodia. With their capital in Angkor, the Khmers (889–1431) created the most powerful and wealthy empire in Southeast Asia. Countless water reservoirs enabled them to flourish on the great plain to the west of the Mekong River after the loss of eastern territories. Public works and magnificent temples dedicated to the revived Vedic gods from India went hand in hand with the earlier influence of Indian Buddhism. Eventually, the Khmer kings united adjacent kingdoms and extended Khmer influence to the Thai and Burmese states along the Chao Phraya and Irrawaddy Rivers.

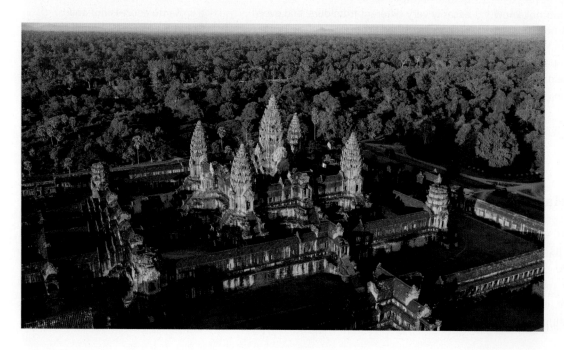

Angkor Wat. *Mistaken by later European explorers as a remnant of Alexander the Great's conquests, the enormous temple complexes built by the Khmer people in Angkor borrowed their intricate layout and stupa architecture from the Brahmanist Indian temples of the time. (A stupa is a moundlike structure containing religious relics.) As the capital, Angkor was a microcosm of the world for the Khmer, who aspired to represent the macrocosm of the universe in the magnificence of Angkor's buildings and their geometric layout.*

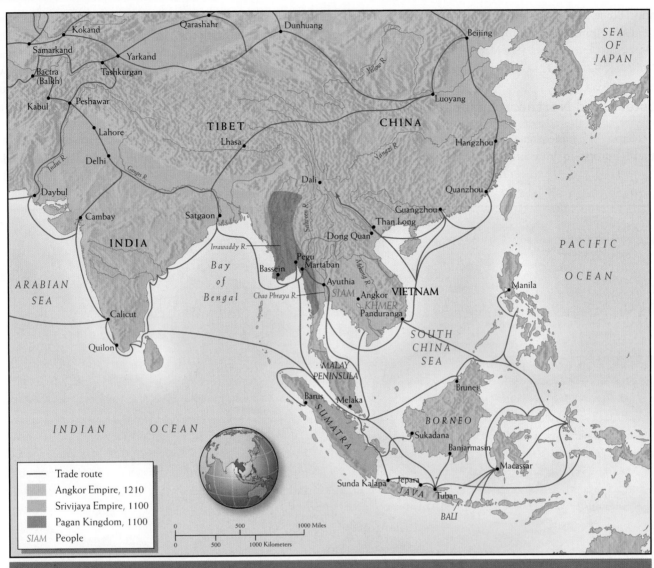

MAP 10.7 | Southeast Asia, 1000–1300

Cross-cultural influences affected Southeast Asian societies during this period.

- What makes Southeast Asia unique geographically compared with other regions of the world?
- Based on the map, why were the kingdoms of Southeast Asia exposed to so many cross-cultural influences?
- In this chapter, the term *mosaic* describes both South and Southeast Asia. Compare Map 10.4 with this map, and explain how the mosaic of Southeast Asia differed from the mosaic of India.

One of the greatest temple complexes in Angkor exemplified the Khmers' heavy borrowing from Vedic Indian architecture. Angkor aspired to represent the universe in the magnificence of its buildings. As signs of the ruler's power, the pagodas, pyramids, and terra-cotta friezes (ornamented walls) presented the life of the gods on earth. The crowning structure of the royal palace was the magnificent temple of Angkor Wat, possibly the largest religious structure ever built. In ornate detail and with great artistry, its buildings and statues represented the revival of the Hindu pantheon within the Khmer royal state.

CHRISTIAN EUROPE

Europe from 1000 to 1300 was a region of strong contrasts. Intensely localized power was balanced by a shared sense of Europe's place in the world, especially with respect to Christian identity. Some inhabitants even began to believe in the existence of something called "Europe" and increasingly referred to themselves as "Europeans." (See Map 10.8.)

Western and Northern Europe

The collapse of Charlemagne's empire had exposed much of northern Europe to invasion, principally from the Vikings, and left the peasantry with no central authority to protect them from local warlords. Armed with deadly weapons, these strongmen collected taxes, imposed forced labor, and became the unchallenged rulers of society. Within this growing warrior aristocracy, northern France led the way. The Franks (later called Frenchmen) were the trendsetters of eleventh- and twelfth-century western Europe.

The most important change was the peasantry's subjugation to these strongmen, many of whom became large landholders.

MAP 10.8 | Latin Christendom in 1300

Catholic Europe expanded geographically and integrated culturally during this era.

- According to this map, into what areas did western Christendom successfully expand?
- What factors contributed to the growth of a widespread common culture and shared ideas?
- How did long-distance trade shape the history of the region during this time?

Previously, well-to-do peasants had carried arms as "free" men. The moment the farmers lost the right to carry arms, they were no longer free. They slipped back to being mere agricultural laborers. Each peasant toiled under the authority of a landholding lord, who controlled every detail of his or her life. This was the basis of a system now called **manorialism**.

This landholding manorial class emerged around the Mediterranean basin as the Roman Empire declined in the west and the Byzantine Empire rose in the east. In both regions, important individuals in the imperial bureaucracies were granted land in payment for their service. Many turned the imperial system's large supply of slaves as well as free peasants into dependent workers serving on their estates. Estates valued self-sufficiency, and most became bipartite: the land, owned by the lord, was divided into two units. The lord held one unit, a demesne, on which the peasants had labor, tax, and other service obligations to the lord. The other consisted of small holdings farmed by peasant families for themselves. Estates also had fisheries, mills, and mineral rights. Lords constructed their homes or manors in the villages. Some were large and ornate, though the majority were modest. Many of the wealthy owners preferred to reside in large cities and turned the management of the estate over to administrators.

In lands distant from the Mediterranean, notably England, France, and Germany, manorial villages emerged out of tribal lands. These lands, originally held by chiefs, were distributed to churches and important officials. Here, too, the bipartite division of the land occurred, and here, too, though some estates were huge, nearly two-thirds of the estates were 500 acres or less.

The manorial system provided the economic and territorial foundations of this era. Political and social ties, which formed the basis of what we call **feudalism**, also bound different classes of peoples together. Feudal societies essentially had three orders: those who prayed (the clergy), those who fought (the lords), and those who toiled (the peasants). Each had obligations to the others. Lords were expected to provide protection for peasants and clerics, while clerics promoted an ethical and holy life for all. Peasants provided society's sustenance. What we might call the classic form of feudalism existed only in England, Sicily, and the Holy Land, those lands conquered by Norman warriors in the tenth century CE from their base in Normandy, France. Here, powerful landholding lords, including kings, gave some of their lands to other freemen, called vassals, in return for fealty, or loyalty, and military service. The grant of land was called a fief, and over time these lands, held by the vassals, became private estates that could be passed on to heirs. Elsewhere in Europe, feudal arrangements were not so clear-cut. The handing over of lands from nobles to subordinates, the so-called vassals, was not accompanied by formal ceremonies, the taking of oaths, and the swearing of fealty, as was the case in regions under Norman authority. Nor were the lands held by vassals always known as fiefs, and even the nobles' ownership of these lands was often disputed.

Assured of control of the peasantry, feudal lords and their vassals watched over an agrarian breakthrough—which fueled a commercial transformation that drew Europe into the rest of the global trading networks. Lordly protection and more advanced metal tools like axes and plows, combined with heavier livestock to pull plows through the root-infested sods of northern Europe, led to massive deforestation. Above this clearing activity stood castles, built by powerful lords and sometimes by strong vassals to ensure their regional autonomy. Their threatening presence also enabled lords to collect rents and tithes (shares of crops, earmarked as "donations" for the church) from the peasantry. In this blunt way, the feudal and manorial systems harnessed agrarian energy to their own needs. The population of western

The Bayeux Tapestry. *This tapestry was allegedly prepared by Queen Matilda, wife of William the Conqueror, and her ladies to celebrate the successful invasion of England in 1066. It shows the fascination of the entire "feudal" class, even women, with war. Great horses, tightly meshed chain mail, long shields, and stirrups all made such cavalry warfare possible.*

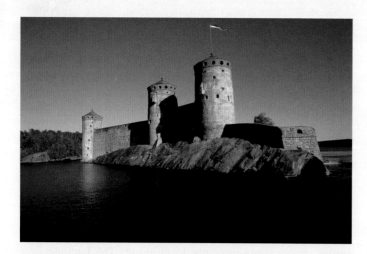

Olavinilinna Castle. *This castle in Finland was the easternmost extension of a "western" feudal style of rule through great castles. It was built at the very end of the Baltic, to keep away the Russians of Novgorod.*

Europe as a whole leaped forward, most spectacularly in the north. As a result, northern Europe, from England to Poland, ceased to be an underdeveloped "barbarian" appendage of the Mediterranean.

Eastern Europe

Nowhere did pioneering peasants develop more land than in the wide-open spaces of eastern Europe, the region's land of opportunity. Between 1100 and 1200, some 200,000 farmers emigrated from Flanders (in modern Belgium), Holland, and northern Germany to eastern frontiers. Well-watered landscapes covered with vast forests filled up what are now Poland,

the Czech Republic, Hungary, and the Baltic states. "Little Europes," whose castles, churches, and towns echoed the landscape of France, now replaced economies that had been based on gathering honey, hunting, and the slave trade. For 1,000 miles along the Baltic Sea, forest clearings dotted with new farmsteads and small towns edged inward from the coast up the river valleys.

The social structure here was a marriage of convenience between migrating peasants and local elites. The area offered the promise of freedom from the feudal lords' arbitrary justice and imposition of forced labor. Even the harsh landscape of the eastern Baltic (where the sea froze every year and impenetrable forests blocked settlers from the coast) was preferable to life in the feudal west. For their part, the elites of eastern Europe— the nobility of Poland, Bohemia, and Hungary and the princes of the Baltic—wished to live well, in the "French" style. But they could do so only if they attracted workers to their lands by offering newcomers a liberty that they had no hope of enjoying in the west.

The Russian Lands

In Russian lands, western settlers and knights met an eastern brand of Christian devotion. This world looked toward Byzantium, not Rome or western Europe. Russia was a giant borderland between the steppes of Eurasia and the booming centers of Europe. Its cities lay at the crossroads of overland trade and migration, and Kiev became one of the region's greatest cities. Standing on a bluff above the Dnieper River, it straddled newly opened trade routes. With a population exceeding 20,000, including merchants from eastern and western Europe

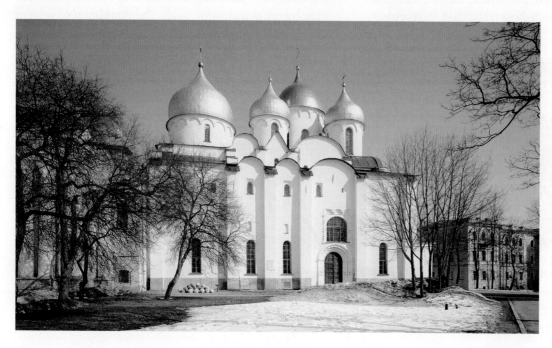

Saint Sophia Cathedral, Novgorod. *The cathedral of Novgorod (like that of Kiev) was called Hagia Sophia. It was a deliberate imitation of the Hagia Sophia of Constantinople, showing Russia's roots in a glorious Roman/Byzantine past that had nothing to do with western Europe.*

The Birch Bark Letters of Novgorod

The city of Novgorod was a vibrant trading center with a diverse population. From 1951 onward, Russian archaeologists in Novgorod have excavated almost 1,000 letters and accounts scratched on birch bark and preserved in the sodden, frequently frozen ground. Reading them, we realize how timeless people's basic concerns can be.

First, we meet the merchants. Many letters are notes by creditors of the debts owed to them by trading partners. The sums are often expressed in precious animal furs. They contain advice to relatives or to partners in other cities:

> Giorgii sends his respects to his father and mother: Sell the house and come here to Smolensk or to Kiev: for the bread is cheap there.

Then we meet neighborhood disputes:

> From Anna to Klemiata: Help me, my lord brother, in my matter with Konstantin. . . . [For I asked him,] "Why have you been so angry with my sister and her daughter. You called her a cow and her daughter a whore. And now Fedor has thrown them both out of the house."

There are even glimpses of real love. A secret marriage is planned:

> Mikiti to Ulianitza: Come to me. I love you, and you me. Ignato will act as witness.

And a poignant note from a woman was discovered in 1993:

> I have written to you three times. What is it that you hold against me, that you did not come to see me this Sunday? I regarded you as I would my own brother. Did I really offend you by that which I sent to you? If you had been pleased you would have torn yourself away from company and come to me. Write to me. If in my clumsiness I have offended you and you should spurn me, then let God be my judge. I love you.

QUESTIONS FOR ANALYSIS

- What does the range of people writing on birch bark tell us about these people?
- Think of the messages you send to friends and relatives today. Even if texting and e-mailing seem centuries distant from writing on birch bark, can you relate in any way to these ancient letter writers?

Source: A. V. Artsikhovskii and V. I. Borkovski, Novgorodskie Gramoty na Bereste, 11 vols. (Moscow: Izd-vo Akademii nauk SSSR, 1951–2004), document nos. 424, 531, 377, and 752.

and Southwest Asia, South Asia, Egypt, and North Africa, Kiev was larger than Paris—larger even than the much-diminished city of Rome.

Kiev looked south to the Black Sea and to Constantinople. Under Iaroslav the Wise (1016–1054), it became a small-scale Constantinople on the Dnieper. A stone church called St. Sophia stood (as in Constantinople) beside the imperial palace. With its distinctive "Byzantine" domes, it was a miniature Hagia Sophia (see Chapter 8). Its highest dome towered 100 feet above the floor, and its splendid mosaics depicting Byzantine saints echoed the religious art of Constantinople. But the message was political as well, for the ruler of Kiev was cast in the mold of the emperor of Constantinople. He now took the title *tsar* from the ancient Roman name given to the emperor, Caesar. From this time onward, *tsar* was the title of rulers in Russia.

The Russian form of Christianity replicated the Byzantine style of churches all along the great rivers leading to the trading cities of the north and northeast. These were not agrarian centers, but hubs of expanding long-distance trade. (See Primary Source: The Birch Bark Letters of Novgorod.) Each city became a small-scale Kiev and a smaller-scale echo of Constantinople. The Orthodox religion looked to Byzantium's Hagia Sophia rather than the Catholic faith associated with the popes in Rome. Russian Christianity remained the Christianity of a borderland—vivid oases of high culture set against the backdrop of vast forests and widely scattered settlements. Like the agricultural manors of western Europe, these Russian cities demonstrated the highly localized nature of power in Europe during this period.

What Was Christian Europe?

Christianity in this era—primarily the Roman Catholicism of the west, but also the Orthodoxy of the east—became a universalizing faith that transformed the region that was becoming known as "Europe." The Christianity of post-Roman Europe had been a religion of monks, and its most dynamic centers were great monasteries. Members of the laity were expected to revere and support their monks, nuns, and clergy, but not to imitate them. By 1200, all this had changed. The internal colonization of western Europe—the clearing of woods and founding of villages—ensured that parish churches arose in all but the wildest landscapes. Their spires were visible and their bells were audible from one valley to the next. Church graveyards were the only places where good Christians could be buried; criminals' and outlaws' bodies piled up in "heathen" graves outside the cemetery walls.

Now the clergy reached more deeply into the private lives of the laity. Marriage and divorce, previously considered family matters, became a full-time preoccupation of the church. And sin was no longer an offense that just "happened"; it was a matter that every person could do something about. Regular confession to a priest became obligatory for all Catholic, western Christians. The followers of Francis of Assisi (1182–1226) emerged as

Saint Francis of Assisi. *In this fresco by the Renaissance artist Giotto, Saint Frances of Assisi is seen renouncing his earthly wealth and embarking on a life of poverty. Saint Francis founded the order that took his name, the Franciscan Order, and promoted his principles of a life of poverty, devotion to the teachings of Jesus Christ, and concern for the poor.*

an order of preachers who brought a message of repentance. Their listeners were to weep, confess their sins to local priests, and strive to be better Christians. Franciscans instilled in the hearts of all believers a Europe-wide Catholicism based on daily remorse and daily contemplation of the sufferings of Christ and his mother, Mary. From Ireland to Riga and Budapest, Catholic Christians came to share a common piety.

UNIVERSITIES AND INTELLECTUALS Vital to the creation of Europe's Christian identity was the emergence of universities, for it was during this era that Europe acquired its first class of intellectuals. Since the late twelfth century, scholars had gathered in Paris, where they formed a *universitas*—a term borrowed from merchant communities, where it denoted a type of union. Those who belonged to the *universitas* enjoyed protection by their fellows and freedom to continue their trade. Similarly protected by their own "union," the scholars of Paris began wrestling with the new learning from Arab lands. When the bishop of Paris forbade this undertaking, they simply moved to the Left Bank of the Seine, so as to place the river between themselves and the bishop's officials, who lived around the Notre Dame Cathedral.

Those scholars were called schoolmen because of the halls—*scholae* in Latin—in which they taught. Their philosophy, scholasticism, sought to render the Christian tradition totally intelligible: God and his creation were penetrable by human reason; they made sense; so did the Bible and the traditions of the church. Teaching took the form of commentaries on the Bible and on the laws of the church (canon law). The aim was to explain every passage in the Bible so that its message could be preached with confidence. The day's teaching began with theology and the Bible—for the mind was freshest in the morning! But this community now involved rational discussions of science, astronomy, and medicine. The greatest poet of the age, the Italian Dante Alighieri (1265–1321), reflects this new expansive view of the universe. In his *Divine Comedy* (1307), he imagined a journey to heaven through hell and purgatory in which every stage—from the punishments of hell through purgatory to the fullness of joy in heaven—reflected the supreme wisdom of God, which human reason could understand and enjoy.

The scholars' ability to organize themselves gave them an advantage that their Arab contemporaries lacked. For all his genius, Ibn Rushd had to spend his life courting the favor of individual monarchs to protect him from conservative fellow Muslims, who frequently burned his books. Ironically, European scholars congregating in Paris could quietly absorb the most persuasive elements of Arabic thought, like Ibn Rushd's. Yet they endeavored to prove that Christianity was the only religion that fully met the aspirations of all rational human beings. Such was the message of many scholars, including the great intellectual Thomas Aquinas, who wrote *Summa contra Gentiles* (Summary of Christian Belief against Non-Christians) in 1264.

The Europe of 1300 was more culturally unified than in previous centuries. It was permeated by Catholicism, and its leading intellectuals extolled the virtues of Christian learning. Such a confident region was not, however, a tolerant place for heretics, Jews, or Muslims.

Christian Europe on the Move: The Crusades and Iberia

By the tenth and eleventh centuries CE, western Christianity was on the move, spreading into Scandinavia, southern Italy, the Baltic, and eastern Europe. Its ambitions to reconquer Spain and Portugal (which had been under Islamic control since the eighth century CE) demonstrated one of the effects of feudal power: the lords' self-confidence, their belief in their military capability, and their pious sense of destiny were all inflated. Besides, the wealth of the east was irresistible to those whose piety entwined with an appetite for plunder. Yet the two Christendoms formed an uneasy alliance to roll back the expanding frontiers of Islam. Europeans zealously took war outside their own borders.

CRUSADES In the late eleventh century, western Europeans launched a wave of attacks known as the Crusades. The First Crusade began in 1095, when Pope Urban II appealed to the warrior nobility of France to put their violence to good use: they should combine their role as pilgrims to Jerusalem with that of soldiers and free Jerusalem from Muslim rule. What the clergy proposed was a novel kind of war. Whereas previously war had been a dirty business and a source of sin, now the clergy told the knights that good and just wars were possible. Such wars could cancel out the sins of those who waged them.

Starting in 1097, an armed host of around 60,000 men moved all the way from northwestern Europe to Jerusalem. This was a huge crowd. But it was divided. Knights in heavy armor led, as they did in Europe. But in the eastern Mediterranean they depended on poor masses who joined the movement to help besiege cities and construct a network of castles as the Christian knights drove their frontier forward. Later Crusaders brought their wives, especially those from the upper class. As in many colonial societies away from the homeland, these women felt freer. Eleanor of Aquitaine, for example, led her own army. Also, queens were crucial in identifying with the problems of local populations. Consider the Armenian queen, Melisende (r. 1131–1152): regarded as wise and experienced in affairs of the state, she was popular with local Christians. As a result, the society of the Crusader states remained more open to women and the lower classes than in Europe. Above all, the Crusades could not have happened without the sailors and merchants of

Crusader. *Kneeling, this Crusader promises to serve God (as he would serve a feudal lord) by going to fight on a Crusade (as he would fight for any lord to whom he had sworn loyalty). The two kinds of loyalty—to God and to one's lord—were deliberately intertwined in promoting the Crusades. Both were about war. But fighting for God was unambiguously good, while fighting for a lord was not always so clear-cut.*

Italy. It was the fleets of Venice, Genoa, and Pisa that transported the later Crusaders and supplied their kingdom.

No fewer than nine crusades were fought in the two centuries that followed Urban II's call, but none ultimately created permanent Christian kingdoms in the lands they "reconquered." Only a small proportion of Crusaders remained in Southwest Asia, and those who did met their match in Muslim armies. (See Current Trends in World History: The Crusades from Dual Perspectives.) Part of the problem was that few Crusaders had any intention of becoming colonists. Only a small number remained to defend the Kingdom of Jerusalem after the First Crusade. Most knights returned home, their epic pilgrimage completed. The remaining fragile network of Crusader lordships could barely threaten the Islamic heartlands.

The Crusades from Dual Perspectives

World history promotes comparative historical study, and when two cultures come together, as they did in the European crusades, their meeting offers a unique opportunity to see how the two societies view each other, as well as providing a sense of each culture's self-identity. Such a confrontation took place during the crusades between European Christians and Muslims between 1095 and 1272 CE

In 1095, Pope Urban II called for the First Crusade with the following words:

"Oh, race of Franks, race from across the mountains, race chosen and beloved by God, as shines forth in very many of your works, set apart from all nations by the situation of your country, as well as by your Catholic faith and the honor of the Holy Church! To you our discourse is addressed, and for you our exhortation is intended. We wish you to know what a grievous cause has led us to your country, what peril, threatening you and all the faithful, has brought us."

The "grievous cause" was the occupation of the Holy City of Jerusalem by the Islamic empire. Formed within the complex relationship between the Byzantine Empire and the western Christian papacy and kingdoms of Europe, the religious motivation behind the Crusades became the subject of many literary renditions of the tumultuous events. It also generated emotionally stirring and polemical (argumentative) writing, depicting either a Muslim or Christian enemy (depending on the work's author).

Polemics are often passionate, harsh, and emotional. They also inspire and reinforce the conviction of fellow believers, with little concern for accuracy. Thus, authors of polemics in the time of the Crusades were usually too biased or too misinformed to present accurate portraits of their enemies. But occasionally, first-hand accounts in the form of chronicles and histories offer us unique glimpses into Christian-Muslim relations in the age of the Crusades.

Consider Usāmah ibn Munqidh (1095-1188), the learned ruler of the city

of Shaizar in western Syria. Skirmishes, truces, and the ransoming of prisoners were part of his daily life, and Usāmah socialized with his Frankish neighbors as much as he fought with them. He offers a dismissive opinion of his enemies. Basically, they struck him as "animals possessing the virtues of courage and fighting, but nothing else." In particular, their medical practice appalled him. More strange, the Franks allowed their wives to walk about freely and to talk to strangers unaccompanied by male guardians. How could men be at once so brave and yet so lacking in a proper, Arab sense of honor, which would lead a man to protect his women? Unlike other Muslim authors of his time, however, Usāmah does not refer to the Franks in derogatory terms such as "infidels" or "devils." In fact, he occasionally refers to some of them as his companions and writes of a Frank who called him "my brother" (Hitti, p. 16).

Christian authors had similar interests in documenting the customs of their enemies in battle. Jean de Joinville (1224/1225-1317) was a chronicler of

---

Muslim leaders, however, did not see the Frankish knights as a threat. For them, the Crusades were irrelevant. And as far as the average Muslim of the region was concerned, the Crusaders hardly mattered at all. Jerusalem and Palestine had always been fringe areas in Southwest Asia. Real prosperity and the capital cities of Muslim kingdoms lay inland, away from the coast—at Cairo, Damascus, and Baghdad. The assaults' long-term effect was to harden Muslim feelings against the Franks and the millions of nonwestern Christians who had previously lived peacefully in Egypt and Syria. Muslims viewed the Crusaders as brave but uncivilized warriors. A neighboring Muslim wrote: "The Franks possess none of the virtues of men except courage. . . . Nobody counts for them except knights." (See again Current Trends in World History: The Crusades from Dual Perspectives.) Their lack of medical knowledge shocked this observer. He noted that they would rather chop off a man's leg than administer ointments, as Muslim doctors would have advised.

IBERIA Other campaigns of Christian expansion, like the Iberian efforts to drive out the Muslims, were more successful. Beginning with the capture of Toledo in 1061 CE, the Christian kings of northern Spain slowly pushed back the Muslims. Eventually, they reached the heart of Andalusia in southern Iberia and conquered Seville, adding more than 100,000 square miles of territory to Christian Europe. Another force from northern France crossed Italy to conquer Muslim-held Sicily, ensuring Christian rule in the strategically located mid-Mediterranean island. Unlike the Crusaders' fragile foothold at the edge of Southwest Asia, these two conquests turned the tide in relations between Christian and Muslim power.

Christianity—in particular the rise of the Roman Catholic Church, the spread of universities, and the fight against the Muslims in their native and spiritual homelands—would be the force that would create the fourth cultural sphere known as medieval France. During one crusade, while in the service of the king, Joinville had occasion to note the Muslims' social behavior:

> "Whenever the Sultan was in the camp, the men of the personal Guard were quartered all round his lodging, and appointed to guard his person. At the door of the Sultan's lodging there was a little tent for the Sultan's door-keepers, and for his musicians, who had Arabian horns and drums and kettledrums; and they used to make such a din at daybreak and at nightfall that people near them could not hear one another speak, and that they could be heard plainly all through the camp. The musicians never dared sound their instruments in the daytime unless by the order of the Chief of the Guard. Thus it was, that whenever the Sultan had a proclamation to make he used to send for the Chief of the Guard, and give him the order; and then the Chief would cause all the Sultan's instruments to be sounded; and thereupon all the host would come to hear the Sultan's commands."

Jeane de Joinville. *Joinville dictating his memoir of St. Louis, in which he described the Seventh Crusade.*

Although scholars regard such literary renditions with caution, they are useful for gleaning personal details that other types of works omit. The colorful accounts by authors such as Usāmah ibn Munqidh and Joinville are invaluable resources for the social history of the Crusaders.

QUESTIONS FOR ANALYSIS

- What customs or practices of their opponents did the Muslim and Christian writers select to write about? Why?
- What aspects of the other side's customs does each writer seem to see as unusual or praiseworthy? What does that tell us about their perceptions of the strangers they encountered?
- If a historian is to use polemical written sources like this to analyze societies in the past, what can he or she say is trustworthy about them?

Explore Further

Hodgson, Natasha. *Women, Crusading and the Holy Land in Historical Narrative* (2007).

Maalouf, Amin. *The Crusades through Arab Eyes,* translated by Jon Rothschild (1984).

Peters, Edward (ed.). *The First Crusade: The Chronicle of Fulcher of Chartres and Other Source Materials* (1971).

Europe, whose peoples would become known as European, at the western end of the Afro-Eurasian landmass.

SUB-SAHARAN AFRICA COMES TOGETHER

During this period, sub-Saharan Africa's relationship to the rest of the world changed dramatically. Before 1000 CE, sub-Saharan Africa had never been a world entirely apart, but now its integration became much stronger. Africans and outsiders were determined to overcome the sea, river, and desert barriers that had blocked sub-Saharan peoples from participating in long-distance trade and intellectual exchanges (see Map 10.9). Increasingly, interior hinterlands found themselves touched by the commercial and migratory impulses emanating from the Indian Ocean and Arabian Sea transformations.

West Africa and the Mande-Speaking Peoples

Once trade routes bridged the Sahara Desert (see Chapter 9), the flow of commodities and ideas linked sub-Saharan Africa to North Africa and Southwest Asia. As the savanna region became increasingly connected to developments in Afro-Eurasia, Mande-speaking peoples emerged as the primary agents for integration within and beyond West Africa. Exploiting their expertise in commerce and political organization, the Mande edged out rivals.

The Mande, or Mandinka, homeland was a vast area, 1,000 miles wide, between the bend in the Senegal River to the west and the bend of the Niger River to the east, stretching more than 2,000 miles from the Senegal River in the north to the Bandama River in the south. This was where the kingdom of Ghana had arisen (see Chapter 9) and where Ghana's successor state—the Mandinka state of Mali, discussed shortly—emerged around 1100 CE.

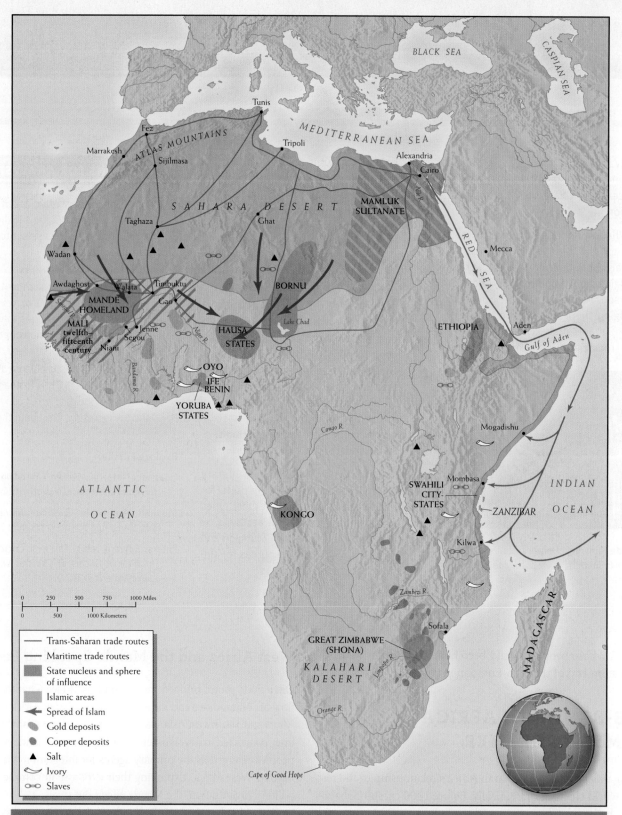

MAP 10.9 | Sub-Saharan Africa in 1300

Increased commercial contacts influenced the religious and political dimensions of sub-Saharan Africa at this time. Compare this map with Map 9.3 (p. 329).

- Where had strong Islamic communities emerged by 1300?
- According to this map, what types of activity were affecting the Mande homeland?
- To what extent had sub-Saharan Africa "come together"?

Legend:
- Trans-Saharan trade routes
- Maritime trade routes
- State nucleus and sphere of influence
- Islamic areas
- Spread of Islam
- Gold deposits
- Copper deposits
- ▲ Salt
- Ivory
- Slaves

Map labels: BLACK SEA, CASPIAN SEA, MEDITERRANEAN SEA, Tunis, Fez, Marrakesh, ATLAS MOUNTAINS, Sijilmasa, Tripoli, Alexandria, Cairo, Nile R., SAHARA DESERT, MAMLUK SULTANATE, Ghat, Taghaza, RED SEA, Mecca, Wadan, BORNU, Aden, Awdaghost, Walata, Timbuktu, MANDE HOMELAND, Gao, Lake Chad, ETHIOPIA, Gulf of Aden, MALI twelfth–fifteenth century, Jenne, Segou, HAUSA STATES, Niger R., Niani, Bandama R., OYO, IFE, BENIN, YORUBA STATES, Mogadishu, Congo R., INDIAN OCEAN, Mombasa, SWAHILI CITY-STATES, ZANZIBAR, KONGO, Kilwa, ATLANTIC OCEAN, Zambezi R., MADAGASCAR, Sofala, GREAT ZIMBABWE (SHONA), KALAHARI DESERT, Limpopo R., Orange R., Cape of Good Hope

PRIMARY SOURCE

An African Epic

The traditional story of the founding of the kingdom of Mali was passed down orally from generation to generation by griots, counselors, and other official historians to the royal family. Only in 1960 was it finally written down in French. The narrative recounts the life of Sundiata, the heroic founder of the Mali state. The following passage provides insight into the role of the narrator (the griot) in the Malian kingdom, as well as some of the qualities of good and bad rulers.

Griots know the history of kings and kingdoms and that is why they are the best counsellors of kings. Every king wants to have a singer to perpetuate his memory, for it is the griot who rescues the memories of kings from oblivion, as men have short memories.

Kings have prescribed destinies just like men, and seers who probe the future know it. They have knowledge of the future, whereas we griots are depositories of the knowledge of the past. But whoever knows the history of a country can read its future.

Other peoples use writing to record the past, but this invention has killed the faculty of memory among them. They do not feel the past any more, for writing lacks the warmth of the human voice. . . .

I, Djeli Mamoudou Kouyaté, am the result of a long tradition. For generations we have passed on the history of kings from father to son. The narrative was passed on to me without alteration and I deliver it without alteration, for I received it free from all untruth.

Listen now to the story of Sundiata, the Na'Kamma, the man who had a mission to accomplish.

At the time when Sundiata was preparing to assert his claim over the kingdom of his fathers, Soumaoro was the king of kings, the most powerful king in all the lands of the setting sun. The fortified town of Sosso was the bulwark of fetishism against the word of Allah. For a long time Soumaoro defied the whole world. Since his accession to the throne of Sosso he had defeated nine kings whose heads served him as fetishes in his macabre chamber. Their skins served as seats and he cut his footwear from human skin. Soumaoro was not like other men, for the jinn had revealed themselves to him and his power was beyond measure. So his countless sofas [soldiers] were very brave since they believed their king to be invincible. But Soumaoro was an evil demon and his reign had produced nothing but bloodshed. Nothing was taboo for him.

His greatest pleasure was publicly to flog venerable old men. He had defiled every family and everywhere in his vast empire there were villages populated by girls whom he had forcibly abducted from their families without marrying them.

QUESTIONS FOR ANALYSIS

- What are you able to understand about the function of the griot after reading this passage?
- What makes this kind of oral history reliable? What makes it unreliable?
- Soumaoro, the adversary of Sundiata, exemplified the characteristics of a bad ruler. What were they? Can you tell, indirectly, what the characteristics of a good ruler (like Sundiata) were?

Source: *Sundiata: An Epic of Old Mali*, compiled by D. T. Niane (Harlow, UK: Longman Group, 1965), pp. 40–41.

The Mande-speaking peoples were constantly on the go and marvelously adaptable. By the eleventh century, they were spreading their cultural, commercial, and political hegemony from the high savanna grasslands southward into the woodlands and tropical rain forests stretching to the Atlantic Ocean. Those dwelling in the rain forests organized small-scale societies led by local councils, while those in the savanna lands developed centralized forms of government under sacred kingships. These peoples believed that their kings had descended from the gods and that they enjoyed the gods' blessing.

As the Mande broadened their territory to the Atlantic coast, they gained access to tradable items that residents of the interior were eager to have—notably kola nuts and malaguetta peppers, for which the Mande exchanged iron products and manufactured textiles.

From the eleventh century to the late fifteenth century, the most vigorous businesses were those that spanned the Sahara Desert. The Mande-speaking peoples, with their far-flung commercial networks and highly dispersed populations, dominated this trade as well. Here one of the most prized commodities was salt, mined in the northern Sahel around the city of Taghaza; it was in demand on both sides of the Sahara. Another valuable commodity was gold, mined within the Mande homeland and borne by camel caravans to the far northern side of the Sahara, where traders exchanged it for various manufactures. Equally important in West African commerce were slaves, who were shipped to the settled Muslim communities of North Africa and Egypt. By 1300, the Mandinka merchants had followed the Senegal River to its outlet on the coast and then pushed their commercial frontiers farther inland and down the coast. Thus, even before European explorers and traders arrived in the mid-fifteenth century, West African peoples had created dynamic networks linking the hinterlands with coastal trading hubs.

The Empire of Mali

As booming trade spawned new political organizations, the **Mali Empire** became the Mande successor state to the kingdom of Ghana. Founded in the twelfth century, it exercised political sway over a vast area for three centuries.

The Mali Empire represented the triumph of horse warriors, and its origins are enshrined in the epic poem *The Epic of Sundiata,* which tells the story of the dynasty's founder, the legendary Sundiata. Sundiata might well have actually existed. Arab historian Ibn Khaldun referred to him by name and reported that he was "their [Mali's] greatest king" (Levtzion and Pouwels, p. 64). His triumph, which occurred in the thirteenth century, marked the victory of new cavalry forces over traditional foot soldiers. Horses—which had always existed in some parts of Africa— now became prestige objects of the savanna peoples, symbols of state power. (See Primary Source: An African Epic.)

Under the Mali Empire, commerce was in full swing. With Mande trade routes extending to the Atlantic Ocean and spanning the Sahara Desert, West Africa was no longer an isolated periphery of the central Muslim lands. Mali's most famous sovereign, Mansa Musa (r. 1312–1332), made a celebrated hajj, or pilgrimage to Mecca, in 1325–1326, traveling through Cairo

West African Gold. *This 1375 picture shows the king of Mali, head of West Africa's largest empire, known for its great wealth based on supplies of gold.*

and impressing crowds with the size of his retinue and his displays of wealth, especially many dazzling items made of gold.

Mansa Musa's visit to Cairo was a sensation in its time. The stopover in one of Islam's primary cities astonished the Egyptian elite and awakened much of the world to the fact that Islam had spread far below the Sahara and that a sub-Saharan state could mount such an ostentatious display of power and wealth. Mansa Musa spared no expense to impress his hosts. He sent ahead an enormous gift of 50,000 dinars (a unit of money widely used in the Islamic world at this time), and his entourage included soldiers, wives, consorts, and as many as 12,000 slaves, many wearing rich brocades woven of Persian silks. And there was gold—a lot of it. He brought immense quantities and distributed it lavishly during his three-month stay. Preceding his retinue as it crossed the desert were 500 slaves, each carrying a golden staff. The caravan also included around 100 camels, each bearing two 300-pound sacks of gold.

The Mali Empire boasted two of West Africa's largest cities. Jenne, an ancient entrepôt, was a vital assembly point for caravans laden with salt, gold, and slaves preparing for journeys west to the Atlantic coast and north over the Sahara. The city had originated as an urban settlement around 200 BCE; by 1000 CE, most substantial structures were made of brick. Around the city ran an impressive wall over 11 feet thick at its base and extending over a mile in length. More spectacular was the city of Timbuktu; founded around 1100 CE as a seasonal camp for nomads, it grew in size and importance under the patronage of various Malian kings. By the fourteenth century, it was a thriving commercial and religious center famed for its two large mosques, which are still standing. Timbuktu was also renowned for its intellectual vitality. Here, West African Muslim scholars congregated to debate the tenets of Islam and to ensure that the faithful, even when distant from the Muslim heartland, practiced their religion with no taint of pagan observances. These clerics acquired treatises on Islam from all over the world for their personal libraries, remnants of which remain to this day.

Trade between East Africa and the Indian Ocean

Africa's eastern and southern regions were also integrated into long-distance trading systems. Because of monsoon winds, East Africa was a logical end point for much of the Indian Ocean trade. Swahili peoples living along that coast became brokers for trade from the Arabian Peninsula, the Persian Gulf territories, and the western coast of India. Merchants in the city of Kilwa on the coast of present-day Tanzania brought ivory, slaves, gold, and other items from the interior and shipped them to destinations around the Indian Ocean.

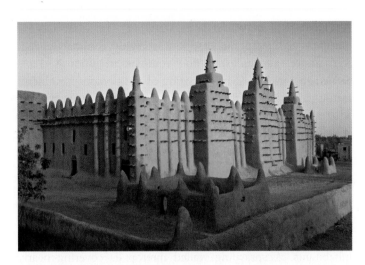

Jenne Mosque. *This fabulous mosque arose in the kingdom of Mali when that kingdom was at the height of its power. The mosque speaks to the depth and importance of Islam's roots in the Malian kingdom and well before. Jenne had originated in 200 CE and soon became an important trade city for all of West Africa, facilitating trade between West Africa and North Africa. The mosque viewed here was modernized at the beginning of the twentieth century.*

The most valued commodity being traded was gold. Shona-speaking peoples grew rich by mining the ore in the highlands between the Limpopo and Zambezi Rivers. By the year 1000 CE, the Shona had founded up to fifty small religious and political centers, each one erected from stone to display its power over the peasant villages surrounding it. Around 1100 CE, one of these centers, Great Zimbabwe, stood supreme among the Shona. Built on the fortunes made from gold, its most impressive landmark was a massive elliptical building made of stone fitted so expertly that it needed no grouting. The buildings of Great Zimbabwe probably housed the king and may also have contained smelters for melting down gold.

THE SLAVE TRADE African slaves were as valuable as African gold in shipments to the Mediterranean and Indian Ocean markets. There had been a lively trade in African slaves (mainly from Nubia) into pharaonic Egypt well before the Common Era. After Islam spread into Africa and sailing techniques improved, the slave trade across the Sahara Desert and Indian Ocean boomed. Although the Quran attempted to mitigate the severity of slavery, requiring Muslim slave owners to treat their slaves kindly and praising manumission as an act of piety, nonetheless the African slave trade flourished under Islam.

Africans became slaves during this period much as they had before: some were prisoners of war; others were considered criminals and sold into slavery as punishment. Their duties were varied. Some slaves were pressed into military service; others with seafaring skills worked as crewmen on dhows or as dockworkers. Still others, mainly women, were domestic

servants, and many became concubines of Muslim political figures and businessmen. Slaves also did forced labor on plantations, the most oppressive being the agricultural estates of lower Iraq. There, slaves endured fearsome discipline and revolted in the ninth century CE in one of the great slave wars documented in world history (the Zanj Rebellion). Yet in this era, plantation slave labor, like that which later became prominent in the Americas, was the exception, not the rule. Slaves were more prized as additions to family labor or as status symbols for their owners.

Unlike the Americas, sub-Saharan Africa no longer remained a people and a territory apart. The desert that had shielded Africans living beneath the Sahara desert was bridged, and commodities like salt, gold, and captive human beings that became slaves in North Africa and Indian Ocean countries were exchanged for textiles, horses, and other products of the north.

Great Zimbabwe. *These walls surrounded the city of Great Zimbabwe, which was a center of the gold trade between the East African coastal peoples and traders sailing on the Indian Ocean. Great Zimbabwe flourished during the thirteenth, fourteenth, and fifteenth centuries.*

Slave Market. *Slaves were a common commodity in the marketplaces of the Islamic world. Turkish conquests during the years from 1000 to 1300 put many prisoners on the slave market.*

THE AMERICAS EXPAND REGIONAL CONTACTS

During this period, the Americas were untouched by the connections reverberating across Afro-Eurasia. Apart from limited Viking contacts in North America (see Chapter 9), navigators still could not cross the large oceans that separated the Americas from other lands. Yet, here, too, commercial and expansionist impulses fostered closer contact among the peoples who lived there.

Andean States

Growth and prosperity in the Andean region gave rise to South America's first empire. Known as the **Chimú Empire**, it developed early in the second millennium in the fertile Moche Valley, bordering the Pacific Ocean. (See Map 10.10.) Ultimately, the Moche people expanded their influence across numerous valleys and ecological zones, from pastoral highlands to rich valley floodplains to the fecund fishing grounds of the Pacific coast. As their geographical reach grew, so did their wealth.

A THRIVING LOWLAND ECONOMY The Chimú economy was successful because it was highly commercialized. Agriculture was its base, and complex irrigation systems turned the arid coast into a string of fertile oases capable of feeding an increasingly dispersed population. Cotton became a lucrative export to distant markets along the Andes. Parades of llamas and porters lugged these commodities up and down the steep mountain chains that are the spine of South America. As in China, a well-trained bureaucracy oversaw the construction and maintenance of canals, with a hierarchy of provincial administrators watching over commercial hinterlands.

Between 850 and 900 CE, the Moche peoples founded their biggest city, Chan Chan, with a core population of 30,000 inhabitants. A sprawling walled metropolis covering nearly 10 square miles, with extensive roads circulating through neighborhoods, it boasted ten huge palaces at its center. Protected by thick walls 30 feet high, the opulent residence halls bespoke the rulers' power. Within the compound, emperors erected mortuary monuments for storing their accumulated riches: fine cloth, gold and silver objects, splendid *Spondylus* shells, and other luxury goods. Around the compound spread neighborhoods for nobles and artisans; farther out stood rows of commoners' houses. The Chimú regime, centered at Chan Chan, lasted until Incan armies invaded in the 1460s and incorporated the Pacific state into their own immense empire.

AN INVENTIVE HIGHLAND STATE The Andes also saw its first highland empires during this period. On the shores of the Lake Titicaca, the people of Tiahuanaco forged a high-altitude state. Though neither as large nor as wealthy as the Chimú Empire, its residents converted the inhospitable highlands to an environment where farmers and herders thrived. There is evidence of long-distance trade with neighbors in semitropical valleys and even signs of highlanders migrating to the lowlands to produce agrarian staples for their kin in the mountains. Dried fish and cotton came from the coast; fruits and vegetables came from lowland valleys. Trade sustained an enormous urban population of up to 115,000 people. Looming over the skyline of Tiahuanaco was an imposing pyramid of massive sandstone blocks. Its advanced engineering system conveyed water to the summit, from which an imitation rainfall coursed down the carefully carved sides—an awesome spectacle of engineering prowess in such an arid region.

Connections to the North

Additional hubs of regional trade developed farther north, showing once again that even in areas of relative geographical isolation, cultures could flourish and interact within expanding regional spheres. The Toltecs and the Cahokians are superb examples.

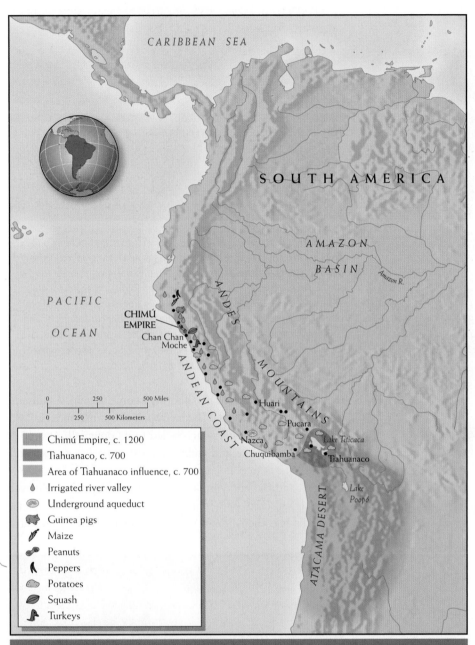

(See Map 10.11.)

of Central America to the arid regions of modern Texas. The region's heartland was the rich valley of central Mexico. Here the **Toltecs** filled the political vacuum left by the decline of Teotihuacán (see Chapter 8) and tapped into the commercial network radiating from the valley.

The Toltecs were a combination of migrant groups, refugees from the south, and farmers from the north. They settled northwest of Teotihuacán as the city waned, making their capital at Tula. They relied on a maize-based economy supplemented by beans, squash, and dog, deer, and rabbit meat. Their rulers made sure that enterprising merchants provided them with status goods such as ornamental pottery, rare shells and stones, and precious skins and feathers.

Tula was a commercial hub, a political capital, and a ceremonial center. While its layout differed from Teotihuacán's, many features revealed borrowings from other Mesoamerican peoples. Temples consisted of giant pyramids topped by colossal stone soldiers, and ball courts where subjects and conquered peoples alike played their ritual sport were found everywhere. The architecture and monumental art reflected the mixed and migratory origins of the Toltecs: a combination of Maya and Teotihuacáno influences. At its height, the Toltec capital teemed with 60,000 people, a huge metropolis by contemporary European standards (if small by Song and Abbasid Islamic standards).

THE CAHOKIANS IN NORTH AMERICA As in South America (Chan Chan of the Chimú) and Mesoamerica (Tula of the Toltecs), cities took shape at the hubs of trading networks all across North America. The largest was **Cahokia**, along the Mississippi River near modern-day East St. Louis, Illinois. A city of about 15,000, it approximated the size of London at the time. Farmers and hunters settled in the region around 600 CE, attracted by its rich soil, its woodlands for fuel and game, and its access to the

MAP 10.10 | Andean States

Although the Andes region of South America was isolated from Afro-Eurasian developments before 1500, it was not stagnant. Indeed, political and cultural integration brought the peoples of this region closer together.

- Where are the areas of the Chimú Empire and Tiahuanaco influence on the map?
- What kinds of ecological niches did they govern?
- According to your reading, how did each political system encourage greater cultural and economic integration?

THE TOLTECS IN MESOAMERICA By 1000 CE, Mesoamerica had seen the rise and fall of several complex societies. Caravans of porters worked the intricate roads that connected the coast of the Gulf of Mexico to the Pacific and the southern lowlands

Andean States. Left: *This photo shows what remains of Chan Chan. The city covered 15 square miles and was divided into neighborhoods for nobles, artisans, and commoners, with the elites living closest to the hub of governmental and spiritual power. Right: The buildings of Tiahuanaco were made of giant, hand-hewn stones assembled without mortar. Engineers had not discovered the principle of curved arches and keystones and instead relied on massive slabs atop gateways. Gateways were important symbolic features, for they were places where people acknowledged the importance of sun and moon gods.*

trading artery of the Mississippi. Eventually, fields of maize and other crops fanned out toward the horizon. The hoe replaced the trusty digging stick, and satellite towns erected granaries to hold the increased yields.

Now Cahokia became a commercial center for regional and long-distance trade. The hinterlands produced staples for Cahokia's urban consumers, and in return Cahokia's crafts rode inland on the backs of porters and to distant markets in canoes. The city's woven fabrics and ceramics were especially desirable. In exchange, traders brought mica from the Appalachian Mountains, seashells and sharks' teeth from the Gulf of Mexico, and copper from the upper Great Lakes. Cahokia became more than an importer and exporter: it was the exchange hub for an entire regional network trading in salt, tools, pottery, woven stuffs, jewelry, and ceremonial goods.

Dominating Cahokia's urban landscape were enormous mounds (thus the Cahokians' nickname, "mound people"). These earthen monuments reveal a sophisticated design and careful maintenance: their builders applied layers of sand and clay to prevent the foundations from drying and cracking. It was from these artificial hills that the people paid homage to spiritual forces. Building this kind of infrastructure without draft animals, hydraulic tools, or even wheels was labor-intensive, so

the Cahokians recruited neighboring people to help. A palisade around the city protected the metropolis from marauders.

Ultimately, Cahokia's success led to its downfall. As woodlands fell to the axe and arable soil lost nutrients, timber and food became scarce. In contrast to the sturdy dhows of the Arabian Sea and the bulky junks of the China Sea, Cahokia's river canoes could carry only limited cargoes. Cahokia's commercial networks met their limits. When the creeks that fed its water

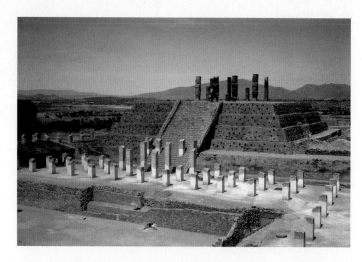

Toltec Temple. *Tula, the capital of the Toltec Empire, carried on the Mesoamerican tradition of locating ceremonial architecture at the center of the city. The Pyramid of the Morning Star cast its shadow over all other buildings. And above them stood columns of the Atlantes, carved Toltec god-warriors, the figurative pillars of the empire itself. The walls of this pyramid were likely embellished with images of snakes and skulls. The north face of the pyramid has the image of a snake devouring a human.*

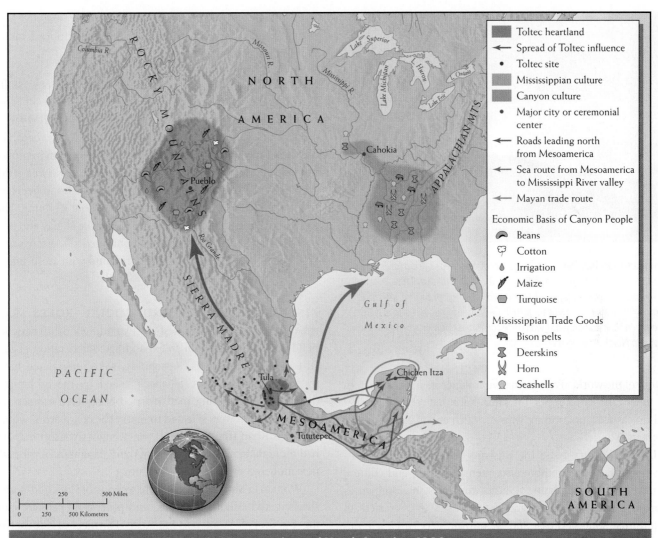

MAP 10.11 | Commercial Hubs in Mesoamerica and North America, 1000 CE

Both Cahokia and Tula were commercial hubs of vibrant regional trade networks.

- Where are Cahokia and Tula on the map?
- According to the map, what kinds of goods circulated through these cities?
- How much political influence on the surrounding region do you think each city had?

system could not keep up with demand, engineers changed their course, but to no avail. By 1350, the city was practically empty. Nevertheless, Cahokia was a remarkable center of exchange while it lasted. It represented the growing networks of trade and migration and the ability of North Americans to organize vibrant commercial societies.

Two forces contributed to a growing integration in sub-Saharan Africa and the Americas—trade and urbanization. The commodities differed: salt, gold, and slaves in as well as out of sub-Saharan Africa; and pottery, shells, textiles, and metals in the Americas. The new urban areas were Jenne, Timbuktu, and Great Zimbabwe in sub-Saharan Africa and Chan Chan,

Tula, and Cahokia in the Americas. But while Sub-Saharan Africa experienced contact with the North African, European, and Asian worlds, the Americas had to wait until the sixteenth century to be drawn into this larger community of peoples.

THE MONGOL TRANSFORMATION OF AFRO-EURASIA

The world's sea-lanes grew crowded with ships; ports buzzed with activity. Commercial networks were clearly one way to integrate the world. But just as long-distance trade connected people, so could conquerors—as we have seen throughout the

Cahokia Mounds. *This is all that is left of what was once a large city organized around temple mounds in what today is Illinois. The largest of the temples, known as Monks Mound, was likely a burial site, with four separate terraces for crowds to gather. Centuries of neglect and erosion have taken their toll on what was once the largest human-made earthen mound in North America.*

history of the world. Transformative conquerors now came from the Inner Eurasian steppes, the same place that centuries earlier had unleashed horse-riding warriors such as the Xiongnu (see Chapters 6 and 7).

Like the Xiongnu and the Kushans before them, the Mongols not only conquered but also intensified trade and cultural exchange. By consolidating a latticework of states (known as khanates) across northern and central Asia, they created an empire that straddled east and west. (See Map 10.12.) It was unstable and not as durable as other dynasties. It did not even have a shared faith; the mother of the conquering emperors Hulagu and Kubilai Khan was a devout Christian, reflecting Nestorian missionaries' (see Chapter 8) centuries-long efforts to convert the nomads. Many Europeans prayed that the entire empire would convert. But it did not; the Mongols were a religious patchwork of Afro-Eurasian belief systems. Yet they brought far-flung parts of the world together as they conquered territories much larger than their own.

Who Were the Mongols?

The Mongols were a combination of forest and prairie peoples, dwelling in Inner China in a region that today is known as Mongolia. Residing in circular, felt-covered tents, which they shared with some of their animals, they lived by hunting and livestock herding. They changed campgrounds with the seasons. Life on the steppes was such a constant struggle that only the strong survived. Their food, primarily animal products, provided high levels of protein, which built up their muscle mass and their

strength. Always on the march, their society resembled a perpetual standing army with bands of well-disciplined military units led by commanders chosen for their skill.

MILITARY SKILLS Mongol archers were uniquely skilled. Wielding heavy recurved compound bows made of sinew, wood, and horns, they were deadly accurate at over 200 yards—even at full gallop. Their small but sturdy horses, capable of withstanding extreme cold, bore saddles with high supports in front and back, enabling the warriors to maneuver at high speeds. With their feet secure in iron stirrups, the archers could rise in their saddles to aim their arrows without stopping. These expert horsemen often remained in the saddle all day and night, even sleeping while their horses continued on. Each warrior kept many horses, replacing tired mounts with fresh ones so that the armies could cover up to 70 miles per day.

KINSHIP NETWORKS AND SOCIAL ROLES Mongol tribes solidified their conquests by extending kinship networks, building an empire out of an expanding confederation of familial tribes. The tents, or households, were interrelated mostly by marriage: they were alliances sealed by the exchange of daughters. Conquering men married conquered women, and conquered men were selected to marry the conquerors' women. Chinggis Khan (the founder of the Mongol dynasty) may have had more than 500 wives, most of them daughters of tribes that he conquered or that allied with him.

Women in Mongol society were responsible for child-rearing, shearing and milking livestock, and processing pelts for clothing. But they also took part in battles. The niece of Kubilai Khan (the first official Mongol ruler of China), Khutulun, became famous for besting men in wrestling matches and claiming their horses as spoils. Although women were often bought and sold, Mongol wives had the right to own property and to divorce. Elite women even played important political roles. Consider Sorghaghtani Beki, Kubilai Khan's mother, who helped to engineer her sons' rule. Illiterate herself, she made sure that each son acquired a second language to aid in administering conquered lands. She gathered Confucian scholars to prepare Kubilai Khan to rule China. Chabi, Kubilai's senior wife, followed a similar pattern, offering patronage to Tibetan monks who set about converting the Mongol elite in China to Tibetan Buddhism.

Conquest and Empire

The Mongols' need for grazing lands contributed to their desire to conquer the splendors of distant fertile belts and rich cities. As they acquired new lands, they increasingly craved control of richer agricultural and urban areas nearby to increase their wealth and power through tribute. The Mongols depended on

Mongol Warriors. *This miniature painting is one of the illustrations for* History *by Rashid al Din, the most outstanding scholar under the Mongol regimes. Note the relatively small horses and strong bows used by the Mongol soldiers.*

settled peoples for grain and manufactured goods—including iron for tools, wagons, weapons, bridles, and stirrups—and their first expansionist forays followed caravan routes.

The expansionist thrust began in 1206 under a united cluster of tribes. A gathering of clan heads acclaimed one of those present as Chinggis (Genghis) Khan, or Supreme Ruler. Chinggis (c. 1155–1227) launched a series of conquests southward across the Great Wall of China and westward to Afghanistan, Persia, and Russia and created a series of interconnected imperial states. The Mongols even invaded Korea (Koryo) in 1231. The armies of Chinggis's son reached both the Pacific Ocean and the Adriatic Sea. His grandsons founded dynasties in China, in Persia, and on the southern Eurasian steppes. One of them, Kubilai Khan, enlisted thousands of Koryo men and ships for ill-fated invasions of Japan. Thus, a realm took shape that touched all four of Afro-Eurasia's main worlds.

Mongol raiders ultimately built a permanent empire, incorporating conquered peoples and some of their ways and also at the same time absorbing the learning and institutions of these settled societies. Their feat of unification was far more surprising and sudden than the ties developed incrementally by traders and travelers on ships. Now, Afro-Eurasian regions were connected by land and by sea in historically unparalleled ways.

MONGOLS IN CHINA In the east, Mongol forces under Chinggis Khan entered northern China at the beginning of the thirteenth century, defeating the Jin army, which was no match for the Mongols' superior cavalry, on the North China plain. But below the Yangzi River, where the climate and weather changed, the Mongol horsemen fell ill from diseases such as malaria, and their horses perished from the heat. To conquer the semitropical south, the Mongols took to boats and fought along rivers and canals. Kubilai Khan (1215–1294) seized the grandest prize of all—southern China—after 1260. His cavalry penetrated the higher plateaus of southwest China and then attacked South China's economic heartland from the west. The Southern Song army fell before his warriors brandishing the latest gunpowder-based weapons (which the Mongols had borrowed from Chinese inventors only to be used against them).

Hangzhou, the last Song capital, succumbed in 1276. Rather than see the invaders pillage the city and their emperors' tombs, the Southern Song bowed to the inevitable. Kubilai Khan's most able commander, Bayan, led his crack Mongol forces in seizing town after town, ever closer to the capital. The empress dowager tried to buy them off, proposing substantial tribute payments, but Bayan kept his eye on the prize: Hangzhou, which fell under Mongol control but survived reasonably intact. Bayan escorted the emperor and the empress dowager to Dadu (present-day Beijing), where Kubilai treated them with honor. Within three years, Song China's defeat was complete. With all of South China in their grip, the Mongols established the Yuan dynasty with a new capital at Dadu, "Great Capital."

Although it fell to Mongol control, Hangzhou was still one of the greatest cities in the world when it was visited by the Venetian traveler Marco Polo in the 1280s and by the Muslim traveler Ibn Battuta in the 1340s. Both men agreed that neither Europe nor the Islamic world had anything like it. (See Current Trends in World History: The Travels of Marco Polo and Ibn Battuta.)

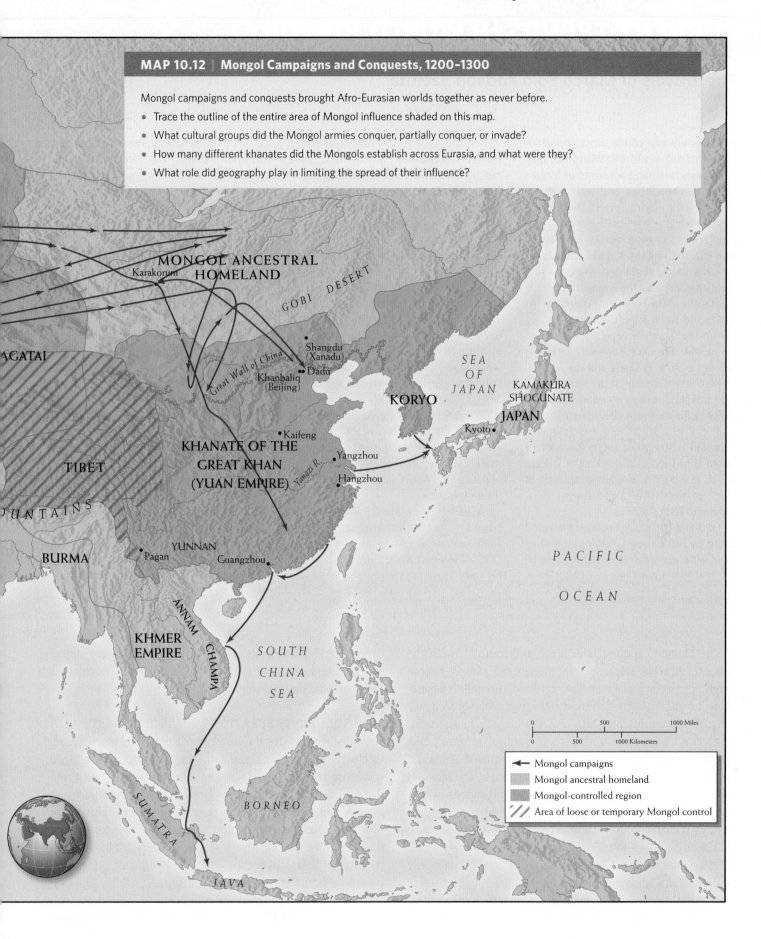

MAP 10.12 | Mongol Campaigns and Conquests, 1200–1300

Mongol campaigns and conquests brought Afro-Eurasian worlds together as never before.

- Trace the outline of the entire area of Mongol influence shaded on this map.
- What cultural groups did the Mongol armies conquer, partially conquer, or invade?
- How many different khanates did the Mongols establish across Eurasia, and what were they?
- What role did geography play in limiting the spread of their influence?

Mongol campaigns
Mongol ancestral homeland
Mongol-controlled region
Area of loose or temporary Mongol control

The Travels of Marco Polo and Ibn Battuta

Travelers are one of the most important resources for world historians because they create firsthand accounts of foreign rulers, their societies, and their cultures through their diaries, letters, and books. Recall from the start of the chapter our two Turkish Christian monks, Bar Sāwmā and Markōs, whom Kubilai Khan sent to learn more about the Muslims and Europeans prior to the Mongol invasions across the Afro-Eurasian landmass. At nearly the same time they were setting out on their travels, Marco Polo, one of the most famous European travelers, was setting out to visit China and the Mongol emperor, creating one of the most widely read travel narratives in world history. It also helped motivate the search for the most direct route to China and Southeast Asia. Only fifty years later, Ibn Battuta would travel most of the known Islamic world, leaving an invaluable portrait of much of North Africa, Southwest Asia, and South Asia.

Polo and Battuta encountered a world linked by trade routes that often had as their ultimate destination the imperial court of the Great Khan in China. These two men, as well as less celebrated travelers, observed worlds that were highly localized and yet culturally unified.

In 1271, Marco Polo (1254–1324), the son of an enterprising Venetian merchant, set out with his father and uncle on a journey to East Asia. Making their way along the fabled Silk Road across central Asia, after a three-and-a-half-year journey the Polos arrived in Xanadu, the summer capital of the Mongol Empire. There they remained for more than two decades. When they returned to Venice in 1295, fellow townsmen greeted them with astonishment, believing that the Polos had perished years before. So, too, Marco Polo's published account of his travels generated an incredulous reaction. Some of his European readers considered his tales of eastern wonders to be mere fantasy; yet others found their appetites for Asian splendor whetted by his descriptions.

A half-century after Polo began his travels, the Moroccan-born scholar Muhammad ibn Abdullah ibn Battuta (1304–1369) embarked on a journey of his own. Then just twenty-one, he vowed to visit the whole of the Islamic world without traveling the same road twice. It was an ambitious goal, for Islam's domain extended from one end of the Afro-Eurasian landmass to the other and far into Africa as well. On his journey, Ibn Battuta eventually covered some 75,000 miles. Along his way, he claimed to have met at least sixty rulers, and in his book he recorded the names of more than 2,000 persons whom he knew personally.

The writings of Marco Polo and Ibn Battuta provide a wealth of information on the well-traversed lands of Africa, Europe, and Asia. What they and other travelers observed was the extreme diversity of Afro-Eurasian peoples, reflecting numerous ethnicities, political formations, and religious faiths. In addition, they observed that the vast majority of people lived deeply localized lives, primarily seeking to obtain the basic necessities of everyday life. Yet, they were also aware that the same societies welcomed trade and cultural exchange. In fact, they wrote most eloquently about how each of the four major cultural systems of the landmass—Christian, Muslim, Indian, and

---

The Mongol conquest both north and south changed the political and social landscape. But Mongol rule did not impose rough steppe-land ways on the "civilized" urbanite Chinese. Non-Chinese outsiders—a mixed and varied group of Mongols, Tanguts, Khitan, Jurchen, Muslims, Tibetans, Persians, Turks, Nestorians, Jews, Armenians—took political control. Like earlier nomadic pastoral groups who had conquered China and established their authority over the Han Chinese, the Mongols embraced Chinese cultural and political institutions within China proper while retaining their own political and cultural ways in the original homeland. The result was a dual set of political institutions in China proper and Mongolia, such that the Mongols allowed Chinese elites considerable autonomy in local affairs while employing non-Mongol subordinates to manage the central dynastic political system and to collect taxes for the Mongols. In China, the Mongols' rule employed the same dynastic and bureaucratic institutions that previous Chinese dynasties had used, but in their steppe lands they maintained their nomadic pastoral ways.

MONGOL REVERBERATIONS IN SOUTHEAST ASIA

Southeast Asia also felt the whiplash of Kubilai Khan's conquest. Circling Song defenses in southern China, the Mongols galloped southwest and conquered states in Yunnan and in Burma. From there, in the 1270s, the armies headed directly back east into the soft underbelly of the Song state. In this sweep, portions of mainland Southeast Asia became annexed to China for the first time. Even the distant Khmer regime felt repercussions when the Mongol fleet, which grew out of the conquered Song navy, passed by on its way to attack Java (unsuccessfully) in 1293. Kubilai Khan amalgamated the conquered Chinese fleets with the remnants of the Korya navy to push his expansionism onto

Chinese—struggled to define itself. Interestingly, if Ibn Battuta and Marco Polo had been able to travel in the "unknown" worlds—the African hinterlands, the Americas, and Oceania—they would have witnessed to varying degrees similar phenomena and challenges.

Marco Polo. *This medieval painting shows the caravan of Marco Polo's father and uncle crossing Asia.*

Explore Further

Battuta. *The Travels of Ibn Battuta,* translated by H. A. R. Gibb (2002).

Polo, Marco. *The Travels of Marco Polo,* edited by Manuel Komroff, translated by William Marsden (1926).

the high seas. He also used improved navigation technology to enable his ships to sail into deep waters; yet his invasions of Japan from Korea failed in 1274 and 1281. The ill-fated Javanese expedition was his last.

MONGOLS IN THE ISLAMIC WORLD In the thirteenth century, Mongol tribesmen streamed out of the steppes, crossing the whole of Asia and entering the eastern parts of Europe. Möngke Khan, a grandson of Chinggis, made clear the Mongol aspiration for world domination: he appointed his brother Kubilai to rule over China, Tibet, and the northern parts of India; and he commanded another brother, Hulagu, to conquer Iran, Syria, Egypt, Byzantium, and Armenia.

When Hulagu reached Baghdad in 1258, he encountered a feeble foe and a city that was a shadow of its former glorious self. Merely 10,000 horsemen faced his army of 200,000 soldiers, who were eager to acquire the booty of a wealthy city. Even before the battle had taken place, Baghdadi poets were composing elegies for their dead and mourning the defeat of Islam.

The slaughter was vast. Hulagu himself boasted of taking the lives of at least 200,000 people. The Mongols pursued their adversaries everywhere. They hunted them in wells, latrines, and sewers and followed them into the upper floors of buildings, killing them on rooftops until, as an Iraqi historian observed, "blood poured from the gutters into the streets. . . . The same happened in the mosques" (Lewis, pp. 82–83). In a few weeks of sheer terror, the venerable Abbasid caliphate was demolished. Hulagu's forces showed no mercy to the caliph himself, who was rolled up in a carpet and trampled to death by horses, his blood soaked up by the rug so it would leave no mark on the ground. With Baghdad crushed, the Mongol armies pushed on to Syria, slaughtering Muslims along the way.

The world experienced considerable human population growth during the first millennium of the Common Era in spite of occasional downturns, such as in Asia and Europe between 200 CE and 600 CE that were the result of climate change, movement of peoples, and the decline of the Roman and Han Empires. Overall, however, an upward trajectory occurred, though it averaged out to a mere 0.06 percent per year. For the period from 1750 to 1950, that percentage increased to a little more than 0.5 percent per year, and since 1950, the number has risen to 1.75 percent per year. Even so, as we will see in the next chapter, the major populations in the Afro-Eurasian landmass were terrified by the loss of life that accompanied the spread of the Black Death across this immense area. Since the Afro-Eurasian recovery from the Black Death, the world's population has been on a steady increase, spectacularly so in the twentieth century, the result of more abundant food supplies, more accurate knowledge of the spread of diseases and a resulting control of epidemic diseases, and a general rise in the standards of living.

QUESTIONS FOR ANALYSIS

- Why was the rate of population growth so limited in premodern times?
- Comparing the population size of the regions in 1340, what do the numbers tell us about where the largest share of wealth and power resided? How does this compare with earlier eras in the chart?
- Why was the population of the Americas in 1340 so small considering its large territorial size?
- Why were the peoples living in the Afro-Eurasian landmass so vulnerable to epidemic diseases in the fourteenth century?
- How do changes in global population relate to the developments tracked in this chapter: a maritime revolution; a more integrally connected Africa; a thriving Abbasid caliphate; and an expanding Mongol Empire?

Regional Human Population (in millions)						
Year	Asia	Europe	Africa	Americas	Oceania	World
400 BCE	97	30	17	8	1	**153**
1 CE	172	41	26	12	1	**252**
200	160	55	30	11	1	**257**
600	136	31	24	16	1	**208**
1000	154	41	39	18	1	**253**
1200	260	64	48	26	2	**400**
1340	240	88	80	32	2	**442**

Source: **Massimo Livi-Bacci**, *A Concise History of World Population* (Malden, MA: Wiley-Blackwell, 2012), p. 25.

The Collapse of Mongol Rule

In the end, the Mongol Empire reached its outer limits. In the west, the Egyptian Mamluks stemmed the advancing Mongol armies and prevented Egypt from falling into their hands. In the east, the waters of the South China Sea and the Sea of Japan foiled Mongol expansion into Java and Japan. And in the northwest, Mongol armies moved through Ukraine and went to the border of Poland. Yet they proved better at conquering than governing. They struggled to rule their vast possessions in makeshift states. Bit by bit, they yielded control to local administrators and dynasts who governed as their surrogates. There was also chronic feuding among the Mongol dynasts themselves. In China and Persia, Mongol rule collapsed in the fourteenth century. Ultimately, the Mongols would meet a deadly adversary more brutal than they were—the plague of the fourteenth century (see Chapter 11).

Mongol conquest reshaped Afro-Eurasia's social landscape. Islam would never again have a unifying authority like the caliphate or a powerful center like Baghdad. China, too, was divided and changed, but in other ways. The Mongols introduced Persian, Islamic, and Byzantine influences on China's architecture, art, science, and medicine. The Yuan policy of benign tolerance also brought elements from Christianity, Judaism, Zoroastrianism, and Islam into the Chinese mix. The Mongol thrust led to a great opening, as fine goods, traders, and technology flowed from China to the rest of the world in ensuing centuries. Finally, the Mongol conquests, somewhat like those of Alexander the Great in an earlier age (see Chapter 5), encouraged an Afro-Eurasian interconnectedness, but on a scale that the huge landmass had not known before and would not experience again for hundreds of years. Out of conquest and warfare would come centuries of trade, migration, and increasing contact between Africa, Europe, and Asia.

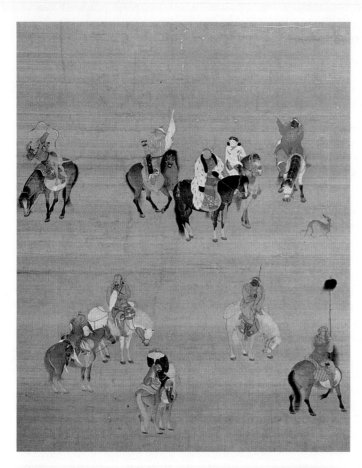

Mongols on Horseback. *Even after the Mongols became the rulers of China, the emperors remembered their steppe origin and maintained the skills of horse-riding nomads. This detail from a thirteenth/fourteenth-century silk painting shows Kubilai Khan hunting.*

CONCLUSION

Between 1000 and 1300 CE, Afro-Eurasia was forming large cultural spheres. As trade and migration spanned longer distances, these spheres prospered and became more integrated. In central Afro-Eurasia, Islam was firmly established, its merchants, scholars, and travelers acting as commercial and cultural intermediaries as they spread their universalizing faith. As seaborne trade expanded, India, too, became a commercial crossroads. Merchants in its port cities welcomed traders arriving from Arab lands to the west, from China, and from Southeast Asia. China also boomed, pouring its manufactures into trading

networks that reached throughout Eurasia and North Africa and even Sub-Saharan Africa. Christian Europe had two centers, both of which were at war with Islam. In the east, Byzantium was a formidable empire with a resplendent and unconquerable capital city, Constantinople, in many ways the pride of Christianity. In the west, the Catholic papacy had risen from the ashes of the Roman Empire and sought to extend its ecclesiastical authority over Rome's territories in western Europe.

Neither the Americas nor sub-Saharan Africa saw the same degree of integration, but trade and migration in these areas had profound effects. Certain African cultures flourished as they encountered the commercial energy of trade on the Indian Ocean. Africans' trade with one another linked coastal and interior regions in an ever more integrated world. American peoples also built cities that dominated cultural areas and thrived through trade. American cultures shared significant features: reliance on trade, maize, and the exchange of goods such as shells and precious feathers. And larger areas honored the same spiritual centers.

By 1300, trade, migration, and conflict were connecting Afro-Eurasian worlds in unprecedented ways. When Mongol armies swept into China, into Southeast Asia, and into the heart of Islam, they applied a thin coating of political integration to these widespread regions and built on existing trade links. At the same time, most people's lives remained quite local, driven by the need for subsistence and governed by spiritual and governmental representatives acting at the behest of distant authorities.

Still, locals noticed the evidence of cross-cultural exchanges everywhere—in the clothing styles of provincial elites, such as Chinese silks in Paris or Quetzal plumes in northern Mexico; in enticements to move (and forced removals) to new frontiers; in the news of faraway conquests or advancing armies. Worlds were coming together within themselves and across territorial boundaries, while remaining apart as they sought to maintain their own identity and traditions. In Afro-Eurasia especially, as the movement of goods and peoples shifted from ancient land routes to sea-lanes, these contacts were more frequent and far-reaching. Never before had the world seen so much activity connecting its parts. Nor within them had there been so much shared cultural similarity—linguistic, religious, legal, and military. By the time the Mongol Empire arose, the regions composing the globe were those that we now recognize as the cultural spheres of today's world.

After You Read This Chapter

Go to iNQUIZITIVE to see what you know & learn what you've missed.

FOCUS ON: *Foundational Cultural Spheres*

The Islamic World

- Islam undergoes a burst of expansion, prosperity, and cultural diversification but remains politically fractured.

- Arab merchants and Sufi mystics spread Islam over great distances and make it more appealing to other cultures, helping to transform Islam into a foundational world.

- Islam travels across the Sahara Desert; the powerful gold- and slave-supplying empire of Mali arises in West Africa.

China

- The Song dynasty reunites China after three centuries of fragmented rulership, reaching into the past to reestablish a sense of a "true" Chinese identity as the Han through a widespread print culture and denigration of outsiders.

- Agrarian success and advances in manufacturing—including the production of both iron and porcelain—fuel an expanding economy, complete with paper money.

India

- India remains a mosaic under the canopy of Hinduism despite cultural interconnections and increasing prosperity.

- The invasion of Turkish Muslims leads to the Delhi Sultanate, which rules over India for three centuries, strengthening cultural diversity and tolerance.

Christian Europe

- Catholicism becomes a "mass" faith and helps to create a common European cultural identity.

- Feudalism organizes the elite-peasant relationship, while manorialism forms the basis of the economy.

- Europe's growing confidence is manifest in the Crusades and the reconquering of Iberia, an effort to drive Islam out of Christian lands.

CHRONOLOGY

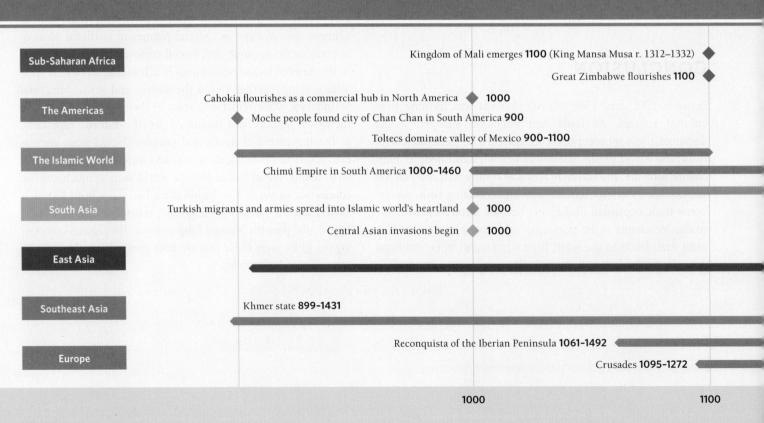

Sub-Saharan Africa		Kingdom of Mali emerges **1100** (King Mansa Musa r. 1312–1332) ◆
		Great Zimbabwe flourishes **1100** ◆
The Americas	Cahokia flourishes as a commercial hub in North America ◆ **1000**	
	◆ Moche people found city of Chan Chan in South America **900**	
	Toltecs dominate valley of Mexico **900–1100**	
The Islamic World	Chimú Empire in South America **1000–1460**	
South Asia	Turkish migrants and armies spread into Islamic world's heartland ◆ **1000**	
	Central Asian invasions begin ◆ **1000**	
East Asia		
Southeast Asia	Khmer state **899–1431**	
Europe	Reconquista of the Iberian Peninsula **1061–1492**	
	Crusades **1095–1272**	

1000   1100

KEY TERMS

STUDY QUESTIONS

1. **Explain** how specific technological advances, especially in ship design and navigation, facilitated the expansion of Afro-Eurasian trade. In what ways did global commercial hubs in Egypt, China, Melaka, and India reflect revolutions in maritime transportation and foster commercial contact regionwide?

2. **Analyze** the social and political forces that shaped the Islamic world, India, China, and Europe at this time. **Evaluate** the degree to which these forces integrated cultures and geographical areas.

3. **Identify** environmental and political forces that contributed to fragmentation within the Islamic world. **Describe** the cultural forces that enabled diverse Islamic communities to achieve a uniform regional identity.

4. **Discuss** the impact of Muslim Turkish invaders on India. To what extent did India remain distinct from the Islamic world in this era?

5. **Explain** how economic and manufacturing developments, coupled with political developments, cemented the power of the Song dynasty. How did Song interactions with nomads and neighbors lead to distinctive identities for both the Song and their neighbors?

6. **Compare and contrast** cultural and political developments in Korea, Japan, and Southeast Asia during this era. **Analyze** the influence of other regional cultures on these societies.

7. **Describe** how Christianity expanded its geographical reach during this era; **evaluate** the roles of manorialism and feudalism, universities, and the Crusades in contributing to Europe's identity as a fragmented yet distinctive cultural sphere.

8. **Identify** the areas of sub-Saharan Africa that were parts of the larger Afro-Eurasian world by 1300. **Explain** how contact with other regions shaped political and cultural developments in sub-Saharan Africa.

9. **Analyze** the extent to which American peoples established closer contact with each other. How extensive were these contacts compared with those in the Afro-Eurasian world? Compared with those in sub-Saharan Africa?

10. **Describe** the empire that the Mongols created in the thirteenth century. How did their policies promote greater contact among the various regions and peoples of Afro-Eurasia? **Contrast** the expansion of Hulagu into the west with that of Kubilai Khan into the east.

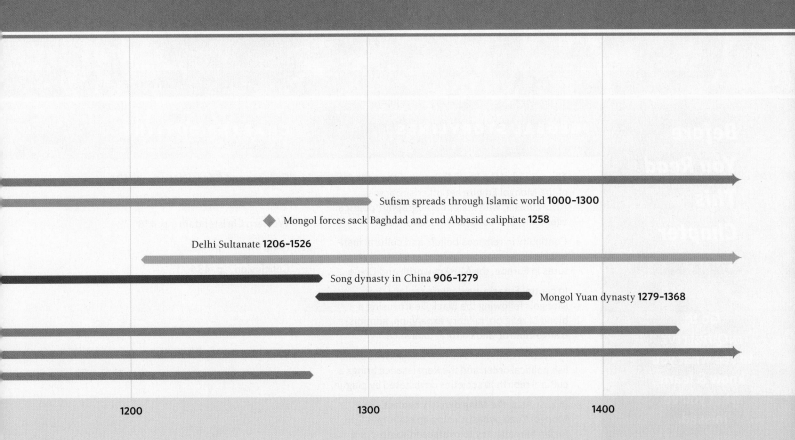

Sufism spreads through Islamic world **1000–1300**

Mongol forces sack Baghdad and end Abbasid caliphate **1258**

Delhi Sultanate **1206–1526**

Song dynasty in China **906–1279**

Mongol Yuan dynasty **1279–1368**

| 1200 | 1300 | 1400 |

Crises and Recovery in Afro-Eurasia, 1300–1500

FOCUS QUESTIONS

- What were the nature and origins of the crises that spanned Afro-Eurasia during the fourteenth century? How extensive were their effects, locally and transregionally?

- In what ways did religious belief systems maintain continuity from the fourteenth through the fifteenth centuries?

- How similar and different were the ways in which regional rulers in postplague Afro-Eurasia attempted to construct unified states? What were their greatest successes?

- How did the art and architecture of different regions reflect political realities, and what themes communicate these messages to viewers?

- In what different ways did the Iberian kingdoms, the Ottoman, Safavid, and Mughal Empires, the Ming dynasty, and European political systems extend their territory and regional influence?

When Mongol armies besieged the Genoese trading outpost of Caffa on the Black Sea in 1346, they not only damaged trading links between East Asia and the Mediterranean but also unleashed a devastating disease: the bubonic plague. Defeated Genoese merchants and soldiers withdrew, inadvertently taking the germs with them aboard their ships. By the time they arrived in Messina, Sicily, half the passengers were dead. The rest were dying. People waiting on shore for the ships' trade goods were horrified at the sight and turned the ships away. Desperately, the captains went to the next port, only to face the same fate. Despite these efforts at isolation, Europeans could not keep the plague (called the Black Death) from reaching their shores. As it spread from port to port, it eventually contaminated all of Europe, killing nearly two-thirds of the population.

This story illustrates the disruptive effects of the Mongol invasion from which the bubonic plague originated and the long-distance trade routes the Mongol Empire imposed on societies. The invasions left behind a series of khanates ruled by local warlords, rather than a centralized state. But they also ushered in an age of intensified cultural and political contact, and the channels of exchange—the land trails and sea-lanes of human voyagers—became accidental conduits for deadly microbes. These germs devastated societies far more decisively than did Mongol warfare. They were the real "murderous hordes" of world history, infecting people from every community, class, and culture. So staggering was the Black Death's toll that population densities did not recover for 200 years. Most severely affected were regions that the Mongols had brought together: settlements and commercial hubs along the old Silk Road and around the Mediterranean and South China Seas. While segments of the Indian Ocean trading world experienced death and disruption, South Asian societies, which had escaped the Mongol conquest, also escaped the great loss of life and political disruptions associated with the Black Death.

This chapter explores the ways in which Afro-Eurasian peoples restored what they thought was valuable from the old while discarding what they felt had failed them in favor of radically new institutions and ideas. The recovery had striking similarities across Afro-Eurasia. Societies reaffirmed their most deeply held and long-standing beliefs, though in a modified form. Chinese elites relied on Confucian tenets and dynastic institutions to revive their devastated communities. In the societies of India, Iran, and Turkey, new rulers turned to Islam for solace in peoples' suffering and hope for the future. Europeans also looked to their traditions. New monarchies, the forerunners of European nation-states, rose to provide leadership, while scholars looked to the Greek and Roman past for cultural and political inspiration.

Radically new political institutions and ideas appeared all across Afro-Eurasia in the aftermath of the Black Death. What historians have called the "Renaissance" captivated the European learned elite and sent its practitioners in search of the scholarship of the Greeks and Romans. They used this inspiration to produce a cultural flourishing in the arts, literature, architecture, and political and financial institutions. While recognizing the new mindsets that appeared in these centuries, this chapter also stresses continuity. Considering how grievously people suffered and how many had died, it is surprising that so much of the old—particularly religious beliefs and institutions—survived the aftermath of the Black Death. Rulers altered but did not transform inherited traditions. What was truly new and would prove enduring was a group of imperial dynasties that emerged all across Afro-Eurasia.

COLLAPSE AND CONSOLIDATION

Although the Mongol invasions overturned political systems, the plague devastated society itself. The pandemic killed millions, disrupted economies, and threw communities into chaos. Rulers could explain to their people the assaults of "barbarians," but it was much harder to make sense of an invisible enemy. Many concluded that mass death was God's wish and humankind's punishment. However, the upheaval gave ruling groups the opportunity to consolidate power by making dynastic matches through marriage, establishing new armies and taxes, and creating new systems to administer their states.

The Black Death

The spread of the **Black Death** was the fourteenth century's most significant historical development. (See Map 11.1.) Originating in Inner Asia, the disease stemmed from a combination of bubonic, pneumonic, and septicemic plague strains, and it caused a staggering loss of life. Among infected populations, death rates ranged from 25 to 65 percent.

How did the Black Death spread so far? One explanation may lie in climate changes. A cooler climate—what scholars refer to as the "Little Ice Age"—may have weakened populations and left them vulnerable to disease. In Europe, for instance, beginning around 1310, harsh winters and rainy summers shortened the growing season and ruined harvests. Here, exhausted soils no longer supplied the resources required by growing urban and rural populations, while nobles squeezed the peasantry in an effort to maintain their luxurious lifestyle. The ensuing European famine lasted from 1315 to 1322, during which time millions died of starvation or of diseases against which the malnourished population had little resistance. This climate change and famine was a factor in the Black Death that soon followed. Another climate-related factor in the spread of the plague occurred in East Asia: here, the drying up of the central Asian steppe borderlands, where bubonic plague had existed for centuries, forced rodents out of their usual dwelling places and pressed pastoral peoples, who carried the strains, to move closer to settled agricultural communities. So, it is thought, began the migration of microbes.

What spread the germs across Afro-Eurasia was the Mongols' trading network. The first outbreak in a heavily populated region occurred in the 1320s in southwestern China. From there, the disease spread through China and then took its death march along the major trade routes. The main avenue of transmission was across central Asia to the Crimea and the Black Sea and from there by ship to the Mediterranean Sea and the Italian city-states. Secondary routes were by sea: one from China to the Red Sea, and another across the Indian Ocean, through the Persian Gulf, and into the Fertile Crescent and Iraq. All routes terminated at the Italian port cities, where ships with dead and dying men aboard arrived in 1347. From there, what Europeans called the Pestilence or the Great Mortality engulfed the western end of the landmass.

The Black Death struck an expanding Afro-Eurasian population, made vulnerable because its members had no immunity to the disease and because its major realms were thoroughly

Plague Victim. *The plague was highly contagious and after a series of grotesque symptoms quickly resulted in death. Here the physician and his helper cover their noses, most likely in attempt to block out the unbearable stench emanating from the patient's boils.*

connected through trading networks. Rodents, mainly rats, carried the plague bacilli that caused the disease. Fleas transmitted the bacilli from rodent to rodent, as well as to humans. The epidemic was terrifying, for its causes were unknown at the time. Infected victims died quickly—sometimes overnight—and in great agony, coughing up blood and oozing pus and blood from ugly black sores the size of eggs. Some European sages attributed the ravaging of their societies to an unusual alignment of Saturn, Jupiter, and Mars. Many believed that God was angry with humankind. One Florentine historian compared the plague to the biblical Flood and believed that the end of humankind was imminent. Everywhere in Afro-Eurasia peoples of all classes had no explanation for the dying and often acted in ways that would be considered reprehensible or outrageous in normal times.

PLAGUE IN CHINA China was ripe for the plague's pandemic. Its population had increased significantly under the Song dynasty (960–1279) and subsequent Mongol rule. But by 1300, hunger and scarcity began to spread as resources stretched thin. A weakened population was especially vulnerable to plague. For seventy years, the Black Death ravaged China and shattered the Mongols' claim to a mandate from heaven. In 1331, plague may have killed 90 percent of the population in Bei Zhili (modern Hebei) Province. From there it spread throughout other provinces, reaching Fujian and the coast at Shandong. By the 1350s, most of China's large cities suffered severe outbreaks.

The reign of the last Yuan Mongol rulers was a time of utter chaos. Even as the Black Death was engulfing large parts of China, bandit groups and dissident religious sects were undercutting the state's power. As in other realms devastated by the plague, popular religious movements foretold impending doom. Most prominent was the **Red Turban Movement**, which took its name from its soldiers' red headbands. This movement blended China's diverse cultural and religious traditions, including Buddhism, Daoism, and other faiths. Its leaders emphasized strict dietary restrictions, penance, and ceremonial rituals in which the sexes freely mixed, and made proclamations that the world was drawing to an end.

PLAGUE IN THE ISLAMIC WORLD The plague devastated parts of the Muslim world as well. The Black Death reached Baghdad by 1347, perhaps carried there by an Azerbaijani army that besieged the city. By the next year, the plague had overtaken Egypt, Syria, and Cyprus; one report from Tunis records the death of more than 1,000 people a day in that North African city. Animals, too, were afflicted. One Egyptian writer commented: "The country was not far from being ruined. . . . One found in the desert the bodies of savage animals with the bubos under their arms. It was the same with horses, camels, asses, and all the beasts in general, including birds, even the ostriches" (Dols, p. 156). In the eastern Mediterranean, the plague left much of the Islamic world in a state of near political and economic collapse. The great Arab historian Ibn Khaldun (1332–1406), who lost his mother and father and a number of his teachers to the Black Death in Tunis, underscored the sense of desolation: "Cities and buildings were laid waste, roads and way signs were obliterated, settlements and mansions became empty, dynasties and tribes grew weak," he wrote. "The entire world changed" (p. 67). (See Primary Source: Qalandar Dervishes in the Islamic World.)

PLAGUE IN EUROPE In Europe, the Black Death first ravaged the Italian Peninsula; then it seized France, the Low Countries (present-day Netherlands, Belgium, and Luxembourg), the Holy Roman Empire, and Britain in its deathly grip. The overcrowded and unsanitary cities were particularly vulnerable. Bremen lost at least 8,000 souls, perhaps two-thirds of its population; Hamburg, another port city, at least as

SCANDINAVIA
• 1349

NORTH SEA

BALTIC SEA

Novgorod

Edinburgh
(1350)
BRITAIN

Dublin
(1349)

Oxford
(1348)
London
(1348)

Amiens
(1348)
Paris
(1348)

EUROPE

Moscow
MUSCOVY
• 1351

KHANATE OF THE
GOLDEN HORDE

Bremen
(1349)
Cologne
(1349)

Lübeck
(1349)

Danzig

Cracow

Kiev

ARAL
SEA

Bordeaux
(1348)

Avignon
(1347)

Genoa
(1347)

Venice
(1347)

Buda
(1349)

Rostov

New Sarai

CASPIAN
SEA

Florence
(1347)

Pisa
(1347)

Siena
(1347)

BLACK
SEA

Caffa
(1346)

Bukhara

Barcelona
(1348)

Marseille

Naples

Constantinople
(1347)

Trebizond

Tabriz

Silk route

Madrid

Palermo
(1347)

Messina
(1347)

Athens
(1347)

ANATOLIA

Maraghah

IL-KHANAT

Lisbon
(1349)

SPAIN
• 1348

Ceuta

Fez

Algiers

Tunis

MEDITERRANEAN

SEA

CYPRUS

SYRIA

Aleppo
(1347)

Damascus
(1347)

Baghdad
(1347)

Isfahan

PERSIA

Shiraz

Alexandria
(1347)

Jerusalem
(1347)

Basra

Hormuz

Marrakesh
(1349)

Tripoli
(1348)

Cairo
(1347)

EGYPT

Persian Gulf

AFRICA

RED SEA

Medina

Mecca
(1348)

ARABIA

Aden
(1351)

ARABIA

ATLANTIC

OCEAN

Mogadishu

INDIA

Progress of bubonic plague

Trade routes

• Known areas of major outbreaks

* Modern Chinese provincial names for
regions affected by outbreak of plague

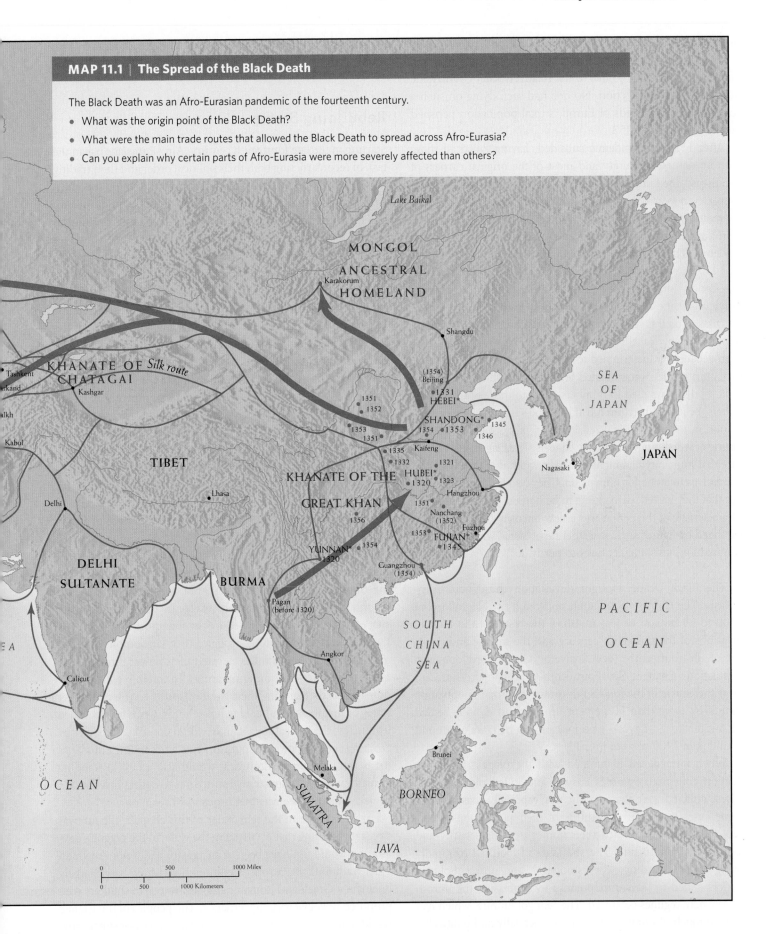

MAP 11.1 | The Spread of the Black Death

The Black Death was an Afro-Eurasian pandemic of the fourteenth century.

- What was the origin point of the Black Death?
- What were the main trade routes that allowed the Black Death to spread across Afro-Eurasia?
- Can you explain why certain parts of Afro-Eurasia were more severely affected than others?

many. The poor, sleeping in crowded quarters, were especially at risk. But master bakers, bankers, and aristocrats died too, unless they were able to flee to the relatively safer countryside in time to escape infection. No one had seen dying on such a scale. Nearly two-thirds of Europe's total population perished between 1346 and 1353.

After 1353, the epidemic subsided, having killed all those with no natural immunity and most of the original carriers of the disease, the European black rat. But the plague would return every seven years or so for the rest of the century, as well as sporadically through the entire fifteenth century, killing the young and those who had managed to escape exposure in the first epidemic. The European population continued to decline, until by 1450 many areas had only one-quarter the number of a century earlier. Indeed, it took three centuries to return to population levels that existed prior to the Black Death.

Disaster on this scale had enduring psychological, social, economic, and political effects. Many individuals turned to pleasure, even debauchery, determined to enjoy themselves before it came their turn to die. Some blamed Jews for unleashing the plague, even though Jews died in numbers equal to those of Christians. Others, believing the church had lost God's favor, sought consolidation in more individualized forms of piety, such as extreme fasting or worshiping in private chapels. The Flagellants were so sure that humanity had incurred God's wrath that they whipped themselves to atone for human sin. They also bullied communities that they visited, demanding to be housed, clothed, and fed. Characteristic of the period was a new intensity of private piety, exhibited by figures such as Catherine of Siena, who was widely admired for punishing her body to purify her soul.

The Black Death wrought devastation throughout Afro-Eurasia. The Chinese population plunged from 115 million in 1200 to 75 million or less in 1400, the result of the Mongol invasions of the thirteenth century and the disease and disorder of the fourteenth. (See Analyzing Global Developments: Population Changes in Fourteenth-Century Afro-Eurasia.) Over the course of the fourteenth century, Europe's population shrank by more than 50 percent. In the most densely settled Islamic territory—Egypt—a population that had totaled around 6 million in 1400 was cut in half.

When farmers fell ill or died with the plague, food production collapsed. Famines ensued and killed off survivors. Worse afflicted were the coastal cities, especially coastal ports. Some cities lost up to two-thirds of their populations. Refugees from urban areas fled their homes, seeking security and food in the countryside. The shortages of food led to rapidly rising prices, hoarding, work stoppages, and unrest. Political leaders added to their unpopularity by repressing the unrest. Everywhere regimes collapsed. The Mongol Empire, which had held so much of Eurasia together commercially and politically, collapsed. Thus, the way was prepared for experiments in state building, religious beliefs, and cultural achievements.

Rebuilding States

Starting in the late fourteenth century, Afro-Eurasians began the task of reconstructing both their political order and their trading networks. (By then the plague had subsided, though it continued to afflict peoples for centuries.) The rebuilding of military and civil administrations—no easy task—also required political legitimacy. Rulers needed to revive confidence in themselves and their political systems, which they did by fostering beliefs and rituals that confirmed their legitimacy and by increasing their control over subjects.

The form that power took in most places was a political institution well known to Afro-Eurasians for centuries: the **dynasty**, the hereditary ruling family that passed control from one generation to the next. Dynasties sought to establish their legitimacy in three ways. First, ruling families insisted that their power derived from a divine calling: Ming emperors in China claimed for themselves what previous dynasts had asserted—the "mandate of heaven"—while European monarchs claimed to rule by "divine right." From their base in Anatolia, Ottoman warrior-princes asserted that they now carried the banner of Islam. In these ways, ruling households affirmed that God or the heavens intended for them to hold power. The new Safavid regime on the Iranian plateau embraced a Shiite form of governance. Second, leaders squelched squabbling among potential heirs by establishing clear rules about succession to the throne. Many European states tried to standardize succession by passing titles to the eldest male heir, but in practice there were countless complications and quarrels. In the Islamic world, successors could be designated by the incumbent or elected by the community; here, too, struggles over succession were frequent. Third, ruling families elevated their power through conquest or alliance—by ordering armies to forcibly extend their domains or by marrying their royal offspring to rulers of other states or members of other elite households. Once it established legitimacy, the typical royal family would consolidate power by enacting coercive laws and punishments and sending emissaries to govern far-flung territories. It would also establish standing armies and new administrative structures to collect taxes and to oversee building projects that proclaimed royal power.

As we will see in the remainder of this chapter, the innovative state building that occurred in the wake of the plague's devastation would not have been as successful had it not drawn on older traditions. In Europe, a cultural flourishing based largely on ancient Greek and Roman models gave rise to thinkers who proposed novel views of governance. The peoples of the Islamic world held fiercely to their religion as two successor states—the

ANALYZING GLOBAL DEVELOPMENTS

Population Changes in Fourteenth-Century Afro-Eurasia

Famine, warfare, and disease led to vast population declines all across Afro-Eurasia in the fourteenth century. The Mongols were instrumental players in spreading disease across the landmass, starting in China and moving westward along land- and sea-based trading routes toward the Mediterranean World and ultimately northern Europe. (See Map 11.1.) While the effects of these destructive forces were felt across the Afro-Eurasian landmass, some states and regions were less affected than others. The population data in the table come from the best historical studies of the last forty years and are based on painstaking archival research. They serve as one of the best ways for us to gain historical insight into this tumultuous century.

QUESTIONS FOR ANALYSIS

- In what regions or cities does population loss seem to have been lower? Higher? What might account for those variations in the death rate?

- How do the losses in urban areas compare with the losses in the region where those urban areas are located? What might that comparison suggest about the impact of fourteenth-century disasters on urban versus other populations?

- Why do you think the population decline was more severe and widespread in Europe than in Asia?

- In what ways was the great loss of population in Europe and China a turning point in their histories?

Location	Earlier Population Figures	Later Population Figures	Percent Change
By Region			
Europe	80 mᵃ in 1346	30 m in 1353	−60%
Asia	230 m in 1300	235 m in 1400	+2%
Islam	(regional data are not available)		
By Country			
Spain	6 m in 1346	2.5 m in 1353	−60%
Italy	10 m in 1346	4.5 m in 1363	−55%
France	18 m in 1346	7.2 m in 1353	−60%
England	6 m in 1346	2.25 m in 1353	−62.5%
China	115 m in 1200	75 m in 1400	−35%
Japan	9.75 m in 1300	12.5 m in 1400	+28%
Korea	3 m in 1300	3.5 m in 1400	+17%
India	91 m in 1300	97 m in 1400	+6.5%
By City			
London	100,000 in 1346	37,000 in 1353	−62.5%
Florence	92,000 in 1346	37,250 in 1353	−59.5%
Siena	50,000 in 1346	20,000 in 1353	−60%
Bologna	50,000 in 1346	27,500 in 1353	−45%
Cairo	500,000 in 1300	300,000 in 1400	−40%
Damascus	80,000 in 1300	50,000 in 1400	−37%

ᵃm = millions

Sources: Ole J. Benedictow, *The Black Death, 1346–1353: The Complete History* (2004); Michael Dols, *The Black Death in the Middle East* (1974); Colin McEvedy and Richard Jones, *Atlas of World Population History* (1978). Ping-ti Ho, *Studies on the Population of China, 1368–1953* (1959).

Ottoman Empire and the Safavid state—absorbed numerous Turkish-speaking groups. A third Islamic state—the Mughal Empire—drew on local traditions of religious and cultural tolerance as its rulers built a new regime on the foundations of the weakened Delhi Sultanate (see Chapter 10). The Ming, having failed in their attempts to control northern Vietnam and Korea, renounced the expansionist Mongol legacy and emphasized a return to Han rulership, consolidating control of Chinese lands and concentrating on internal markets rather than overseas trade. Many of these regimes lasted for centuries, promoting political institutions and cultural values that became deeply embedded in the fabric of their societies.

ISLAMIC DYNASTIES

The devastation of the Black Death followed hard on the heels of the Mongol destruction of Islam's most important city, Baghdad (see Chapter 10), and eliminated Islam's old political order. Nonetheless, these two catastrophes prepared the way for new Islamic states to emerge. Although the Arabic-speaking peoples remained vital, still at the heart of Islam geographically, they now had to cede authority to Persian and Turkish political leaders. Persians and Turks had embraced Islam and had made their cultural, intellectual, and military influence felt well before the Mongol invasions and the Black Death. Now they became

PRIMARY SOURCE

Qalandar Dervishes in the Islamic World

The Qalandar dervish order sprang up in Damascus, Syria, and Egypt in the thirteenth century and spread rapidly throughout the Islamic world. In reaction to the period's widespread unrest, its members renounced the world and engaged in highly individualistic practices as they moved from place to place. The educated elite, however, criticized them as ignorant hypocrites living on alms obtained from gullible common folk. One of their practices was chiromancy, or palm reading. In this excerpt, Giovan Antonio Manavino, a European observer of Ottoman society, gives an obviously biased account of the Qalandars, whom he called the torlaks.

Dressed in sheepskins, the *torlaks* [Qalandars] are otherwise naked, with no headgear. Their scalps are always clean-shaven and well rubbed with oil as a precaution against the cold. They burn their temples with an old rag so that their faces will not be damaged by sweat. Illiterate and unable to do anything manly, they live like beasts, surviving on alms only. For this reason, they are to be found around taverns and public kitchens in cities. If, while roaming the countryside, they come across a well-dressed person, they try to make him one of their own, stripping him naked. Like Gypsies in Europe, they practice chiromancy, especially for women who then provide them with bread, eggs, cheese, and other foods in return for their services.

Amongst them there is usually an old man whom they revere and worship like God. When they enter a town, they gather around the best house of the town and listen in great humility to the words of this old man, who, after a spell of ecstasy, foretells the descent of a great evil upon the town. His disciples then implore him to fend off the disaster through his good services. The old man accepts the plea of his followers, though not without an initial show of reluctance, and prays to God, asking him to spare the town the imminent danger awaiting it. This time-honored trick earns them considerable sums of alms from ignorant and credulous people.

QUESTIONS FOR ANALYSIS

- Describe the way the Qalandar dervishes dressed, where they congregated, and how they obtained food. How did their lifestyle reflect the turmoil of the times?
- Why do you think the Qalandars chose individualistic practices rather than communal living?
- Why do you think Manavino is so critical of the Qalandars?

Source: Ahmet T. Karamustafa, "Dervish Groups in the Ottoman Empire, 1450–1550," from *God's Unruly Friends: Dervish Groups in the Islamic Later Middle Period, 1200–1550* (Salt Lake City: University of Utah Press, 1994), pp. 6–7.

Islam's most effective rulers. The world that they dominated occupied a vast geographical triangle. It stretched from Anatolia in the west to Khurasan in the east and to the southern apex at Baghdad.

The Ottomans, the Safavids, and the Mughals emerged as the dominant states in the Islamic world in the early sixteenth century. They exploited the rich agrarian resources of the Indian Ocean regions and the Mediterranean Sea basin, and they benefited from a brisk seaborne and overland trade. By the mid-sixteenth century, the Mughals controlled the northern Indus River valley; the Safavids occupied Persia; and the Ottomans ruled Anatolia, the Arab world, and much of southern and eastern Europe.

Despite sharing core Islamic beliefs, each empire had unique political features. The most powerful, the **Ottoman Empire**, occupied the pivotal area between Europe and Asia. The Ottomans embraced a Sunni view of Islam, while adopting traditional Byzantine ways of governance and trying new ways of integrating the diverse peoples of their expanding territories. The Safavids, though adherents of the Shiite vision of Islam, were at the same time ardently devoted to the pre-Islamic traditions of Persia (present-day Iran). Unlike the Ottomans, their rulers were not so effective at expanding beyond their Persian base. The Mughals ruled over the wealthy but divided realm that is much of today's India, Pakistan, and Bangladesh; here they carried even further the region's religious and political traditions of assimilating Islamic and pre-Islamic Indian ways. Their wealth and the decentralization of their domain made the Mughals constant targets for internal dissent and eventually for external aggression.

The Ottoman Empire

The rise of the Ottoman Empire owed as much to innovative administrative techniques and religious tolerance as to military strength. Although the Mongols considered Anatolia to be a borderland region of little economic importance, their military forays against the Anatolian Seljuk Turkish state in the late thirteenth century brought political turmoil bordering on chaos, but opened up the region to new political forces. The ultimate victors here were the Ottoman Turks. They transformed themselves from warrior bands roaming the borderlands between Islamic and Christian worlds into rulers of a settled state and, finally, into sovereigns of a far-flung, highly bureaucratic empire. (See Map 11.2.)

Many modern Western-trained historians have portrayed the early Ottoman state as a plundering regime, engaged in rape and slaughter and carrying out campaigns of massive devastation by galvanizing their zealous warriors to terrorize local populations. They did indeed have stern and disciplined warriors, known as *ghazis*, whose commitment to Islam and their leaders was boundless. Even so, what enabled the Ottoman leaders to triumph in a region of widespread disorder was their ability to form alliances with previously hostile divergent ethnic and religious communities. Their first chief, Osman (r. 1299–1326), and his son Orhan (r. 1326–1362) were Sunni Muslims but proved skilled at working with those who held different religious beliefs, such as Byzantine leaders, Kurds, Sufi dervish orders, and Shiites. By constructing eclectic political institutions possessing enormous elasticity, they succeeded in offering not merely toleration to diverse populations but opportunities to exercise power and gain wealth. Theirs was a hybrid state, which welcomed Christian supporters as fervently as Muslims. Hence, they prevailed over other Turkic competitors and transformed their small principality in northwestern Anatolia during the fourteenth century into the preeminent state in Anatolia. The principal characteristics of the early Ottoman state were inclusivity, resilience, and syncretism. Their takeover of the city of Bursa in 1404 marked an ascendancy in Anatolia that now threatened the very existence of the once powerful, now greatly weakened Byzantine Empire. Other Turkic warrior bands, which like the Ottomans lived off the land and fought for booty under charismatic military leaders, ultimately failed in their quest for power because they had little regard for other groups such as artisans, merchants, bureaucrats, and clerics, whose support was essential in the Ottoman rise.

THE CONQUEST OF CONSTANTINOPLE The empire's spectacular territorial expansion into Europe and eventually the Arab world was at heart a military affair. To recruit followers, the Ottomans promised wealth and glory to new subjects. This was an expensive undertaking, but territorial expansion generated financial and administrative rewards. Moreover, by spreading the spoils of conquest and lucrative administrative positions, rulers bought off potentially discontented subordinates. Still, without military might, the Ottomans would not have enjoyed the successes associated with the brilliant reigns of Murad II (r. 1421–1451) and his aptly named successor, Mehmed the Conqueror (r. 1451–1481).

Mehmed's most stunning triumph was the conquest of Constantinople, an ambition for Muslim rulers ever since the birth of Islam. Mehmed left no doubt that this was his primary goal. Indeed, shortly after his coronation, he vowed to capture the capital of the Byzantine Empire, a city of immense strategic and commercial importance. He exclaimed early in his reign that Constantinople was "an island in the midst of an Ottoman ocean." His desire to take the city "never left his tongue" (Faroqhi, p. 23). Mehmed knew this feat would require a large and well-armed fighting force, for the heavily fortified city had kept Muslims at bay for almost a century. First he built a fortress of his own, on the European bank of the Bosporus Strait,

The Fall of Constantinople. *The use of heavy artillery in the fifty-three-day siege of Constantinople was instrumental to the Ottoman victory. At the center of this Turkish miniature is one such cannon, possibly of Hungarian origin, which required hundreds of men and oxen to transport and secure outside the city walls.*

MAP 11.2 | The Ottoman Empire, 1300–1566

This map charts the expansion of the Ottoman state from the time of its founder, Osman, through the reign of Suleiman, the empire's most illustrious ruler.

- Identify the earliest part of the empire under Osman. Then identify all the areas of conquest under Suleiman. Against whom did the Ottomans fight between the years 1326 and 1566?
- What were the geographical limits of the empire?
- According to your reading, how did Ottoman rulers promote unity among such a diverse population?

to prevent European vessels from reaching the capital. Then, by promising his soldiers free access to booty and portraying the city's conquest as a holy cause, he amassed a huge army that outnumbered the defending force of 7,000 by more than tenfold. For forty days his troops bombarded Constantinople's massive walls with artillery that included enormous cannons built by Hungarian and Italian engineers. On May 29, 1453, Ottoman troops overwhelmed the surviving soldiers and took the ancient Roman and Christian capital of Byzantium—which Mehmed promptly renamed Istanbul.

Although Christians generally portrayed the "fall" of Constantinople as an insult and a disaster, in fact the Muslim conquest had cultural benefits for western Europe. Many Christian survivors fled to ports in the west, bringing with them classical and Arabic manuscripts previously unknown in Europe. The well-educated, Greek-speaking émigrés generally became teachers and translators, thereby helping to revive Europeans' interest in classical antiquity and spreading knowledge of ancient Greek (which had virtually died out in medieval times). These manuscripts and teachers would play a vital role in Europe's Renaissance.

THE TOOLS OF EMPIRE BUILDING Mehmed made Istanbul the Ottoman capital, adopting Byzantine administrative practices to unify his enlarged state and incorporating many of Byzantium's powerful families into it. From Istanbul, Mehmed and his successors would continue their expansion, eventually seizing all of Greece and the Balkan region. As a result, Ottoman navies increasingly controlled sea-lanes in the eastern Mediterranean, curtailing European access to the rich ports that handled the lucrative caravan trade. By the late fifteenth century, Ottoman forces menaced another of Christendom's great capitals, Vienna, and European merchants feared that never again would they obtain the riches of Asia via the traditional overland route.

Having penetrated the heartland of Christian Byzantium, under Selim (r. 1512–1520) and Suleiman (r. 1520–1566), the Ottomans turned their expansionist designs to the Arab world. During the latter's reign, the Ottomans reached the height of their territorial expansion, with Suleiman himself leading thirteen major military campaigns and many minor engagements. An exceptional military leader, Suleiman was an equally gifted administrator. His subjects called him "the Lawgiver" and "the Magnificent" in recognition of his attention to civil bureaucratic efficiency and justice for his people. His fame spread to Europe, where he was known as "the Great Turk." Under Suleiman's administration, the Ottoman state ruled over 20 to 30 million people. By the time Suleiman died, the Ottoman Empire bridged Europe and the Arab world. Istanbul by then was a dynamic imperial hub, dispatching bureaucrats and military men to oversee a vast domain.

Ottoman dynastic power was, however, not only military; it also rested on a firm religious foundation. The sultans combined a warrior ethos with an unwavering devotion to Islam. Describing themselves as the "shadow of God" on earth, they claimed to be caretakers for the welfare of the Islamic faith and assumed the role of protectors of the holy cities on the Arabian Peninsula and in Jerusalem after the conquests in the Arab world. They devoted substantial resources to the construction of elaborate mosques and to the support of Islamic schools throughout the empire and to extend the borders of Islam. Thus, the Islamic faith helped to unite a diverse and sprawling imperial populace, with the sultan's power fusing the sacred and the secular.

ISTANBUL AND THE TOPKAPI PALACE Istanbul reflected the splendor of this awesome empire. After the Ottoman

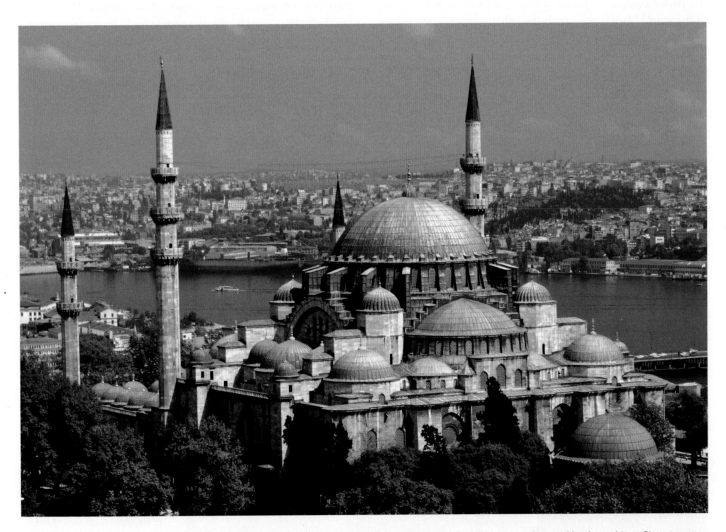

The Suleymaniye Mosque. *Built by Sultan Suleiman to crown his achievements, the Suleymaniye Mosque was designed by the architect Sinan to dominate the city. Four tall minarets called the faithful to prayer.*

conquest, the sultans' engineers rebuilt the city's crumbling walls, while their architects redesigned homes, public buildings, baths, inns, and marketplaces to display the majesty of Islam's new imperial center. To crown his achievements, Suleiman ordered the construction of the Suleymaniye Mosque, which sat opposite the Hagia Sophia. The latter, a domed Byzantine cathedral, was formerly the most sacred of Christian cathedrals, the largest house of worship in all of Christendom, but Suleiman had it turned into a mosque. Moreover, the Ottoman dynasts welcomed (indeed, forcibly transported) thousands of Muslims and non-Muslims to the city and revived Istanbul as a major trading center. Within twenty-five years of its conquest, its population more than tripled; by the end of the sixteenth century, 400,000 people regularly swarmed through its streets and knelt in its mosques, making it the world's largest city outside China.

Istanbul's **Topkapi Palace** reflected the Ottomans' view of governance, the sultans' emphasis on religion, and the continuing influence of Ottoman familial traditions—even in the administration of a far-flung empire. Laid out by Mehmed II, the palace complex reflected a vision of Istanbul as the center of the world. As a way to exalt the sultan's magnificent power, architects designed the complex so that the buildings containing the imperial household nestled behind layers of outer courtyards in a mosaic of mosques, courts, and special dwellings for the sultan's harem.

The growing importance of Topkapi Palace as the command post of the empire represented a crucial transition in the history of Ottoman rulers. Not only was the palace the place where future bureaucrats received their training; it was also the place where the chief bureaucrat, the grand vizier, carried out the day-to-day running of the empire. Whereas the early sultans had led their soldiers into battle personally and had met face-to-face with their kinsmen, the later rulers withdrew into the sanctity of the palace, venturing out only occasionally for grand ceremonies. Still, every Friday, subjects queued up outside the palace to introduce their petitions, ask for favors, and seek justice. If they were lucky, the sultans would be there to greet them—but they did so behind grated glass, issuing their decisions by tapping on the window. The palace thus projected a sense of majestic, distant wonder, a home fit for commanders of the faithful.

And Topkapi was indeed a home for the increasingly sedentary sultan and his harem. Among his most cherished quarters were those set aside for women. At first, women's influence in the Ottoman polity was slight. But as the realm consolidated, women became a powerful political force. The harem, like the rest of Ottoman society, had its own hierarchy of rank and prestige. At the bottom were slave women; at the top were the sultan's mother and his favorite consorts. As many as 10,000 to 12,000 women inhabited the palace, often in cramped quarters. Those who had the ruler's ear conspired to have him favor their own children, which made for widespread intrigue. When a sultan died, the entire retinue of women would be sent to a distant palace poignantly called the Palace of Tears, because the women who occupied it wept at the loss of the sultan and their own banishment from power.

DIVERSITY AND CONTROL The fact that the Ottoman Empire endured into the twentieth century owed much to the ruling elite's ability to gain the support and employ the talents of exceedingly diverse populations. After all, neither conquest nor conversion eliminated cultural differences in the empire's distant provinces. Thus, for example, the Ottomans' language policy was one of flexibility and tolerance. Although Ottoman

The Topkapi Palace. *A view of the inner courtyard of the seraglio, where the sultan and his harem lived.*

Turkish was the official language of administration, Arabic was the primary language of the Arab provinces, the common tongue of street life. Within the empire's European corner, the sounds and cadences of various languages continued to prevail. From the fifteenth century onward, the Ottoman Empire was more multilingual than any of its rivals.

In politics, as in language, the Ottomans showed flexibility and tolerance. The imperial bureaucracy permitted extensive regional and religious autonomy. In fact, Ottoman military cadres perfected a technique for absorbing newly conquered territories into the empire by parceling them out as revenue-producing units among loyal followers and kin. Regional appointees could collect local taxes, part of which they earmarked for Istanbul and part of which they pocketed for themselves. (This was a common administrative device for many world dynasties ruling extensive domains.)

Like other empires, the Ottoman state was always in danger of losing control over its provincial rulers. Local rulers—the group that the imperial center allowed to rule locally—found that great distances enabled them to operate independently from central authority. These local authorities kept larger amounts of tax revenues than Istanbul deemed proper. So, to clip local autonomy, the Ottomans established a corps of infantry soldiers and bureaucrats (called janissaries) who owed direct allegiance to the sultan. The system at its high point involved a conscription of Christian youths from the empire's European lands. This conscription, called the ***devshirme***, required each village to hand over a certain number of males between the ages of eight and eighteen. Uprooted from their families and villages, selected for their fine physiques and good looks, these young men were converted to Islam and sent to farms to build up their bodies and learn Turkish. A select few were moved on to Topkapi Palace to learn Ottoman military, religious, and administrative techniques. Some of these men—such as the architect Sinan, who designed the Suleymaniye Mosque—later enjoyed exceptional careers in the arts and sciences. Recipients of the best education available in the Islamic world, trained in Ottoman ways, instructed in the use of modern weaponry, and shorn of all family connections, the ***devshirme*** recruits were prepared to serve the sultan (and the empire as a whole) rather than the interests of any particular locality or ethnic group.

Thus, the Ottomans established their legitimacy via military skills, religious backing, and a loyal bureaucracy. They artfully balanced the decentralizing tendencies of the outlying regions with the centralizing forces of the imperial capital. Relying on a careful mixture of faith, patronage, and tolerance, the sultans curried loyalty and secured political stability. Indeed, so strong and stable was the political system that the Ottoman Empire dominated the coveted and highly contested crossroads between Europe and Asia for many centuries.

The *Devshirme*. *A miniature painting from 1558 depicts the* devshirme *system of taking non-Muslim children from their families in the Balkan Peninsula as a human tribute in place of cash taxes, which the poor region could not pay. The children were educated in Ottoman Muslim ways and prepared for service in the sultan's civil and military bureaucracy.*

The Safavid Empire in Iran

The Ottoman dynasts were not the only rulers to extend Islam's political domain. In Persia, too, a new empire arose in the aftermath of the Mongols. The legitimacy of the Safavid Empire, like that of the Ottoman, rested on an Islamic foundation. But the Shiism espoused by Safavid rulers was quite different from the Sunni faith of the Ottomans, and these contrasting religious visions shaped distinct political systems.

In the western part of central Asia, the khanate of Chagatai, one of four governments created by the Mongols (see again Map 11.1), slipped into decline at the end of the thirteenth century. With no power dominating the area, the region fell into disorder, with warrior chieftains squabbling for preeminence. Adding to the volatility were various populist Islamic movements, some of which urged followers to withdraw from society or to parade around without clothing. Among the more prominent movements was a Sufi brotherhood led by Safi al-Din (1252–1334), which gained the backing of religious adherents and Turkish-speaking warrior bands. However, his successors, known as Safaviyeh or Safavids, embraced Shiism.

A RELIGIOUS SHIITE STATE The Safavid aspirants to power had their origins among Turkic Sufi groups in eastern Anatolia and Azerbaijan. The Ottoman takeover of most of Anatolia turned these regions into conflict zones between the Ottomans and the Safavids, but Ottoman power also forced the communities living there to find a new location. This they did in the Iranian plateau, rallying support from tribal groups in badly devastated parts of Persia and promising good governance. Forsaking their Sufi origins in this new land, they also steeped themselves in the separatist sacred tradition of Shiism. As a result, of the three great Islamic empires, the Safavid state became the most single-mindedly religious, persecuting those who did not follow its Shiite form of Islam. The most dynamic of Safi al-Din's successors, Ismail (r. 1501–1524), required that the call to prayer announce that there is no God but Allah, that Muhammad is His prophet, and that Ali is the successor of Muhammad. Rejecting his advisers' counsel to tolerate the Sunni creed of the majority of the city's population, Ismail made Shiism the official state religion. He offered the people a choice between conversion to Shiism or death, exclaiming at the moment of conquest that "with God's help, if the people utter one word of protest, I will draw the sword and leave not one of them alive" (Savory, p. 29). In 1502, Ismail proclaimed himself the first shah of the Safavid Empire. (*Shah* is the Persian word for king or leader, a title that many other cultures adopted as well.) Under Ismail and his successors, the Safavid shahs restored Persian sovereignty over the entire region traditionally regarded as the homeland of Persian speakers. (See Map 11.3.)

In the hands of the Safavids, Islam assumed an extreme and often militant form. The Safavids revived the traditional Persian idea that rulers

were ordained by God, believing the shahs to be divinely chosen. Some Shiites even went so far as to affirm that there was no God but the shah. Moreover, Persian Shiism fostered an activist clergy who (in contrast to Sunni clerics) saw themselves as political and religious enforcers against any heretical authority. They compelled Safavid leaders to rule with a sacred purpose. Because the Safavids did not tolerate diversity, unlike the Ottomans, they never had as expansive an empire. Whatever territories they conquered, the Safavids ruled much more directly, based on central—and theocratic—authority. They also succeeded in transforming Iran, once a Sunni area, into a Shiite stronghold, a change that has endured down to the present.

MAP 11.3 | **The Safavid Empire, 1500–1722**

The Safavid Empire rose to prominence alongside the Ottoman state.

- Locate the area where it originated. With which empire did the Safavids fight the most battles?
- Why were most of the battles limited to the regions of Azerbaijan, Kurdistan, and Mesopotamia?
- What were the geographical and political limits on the growth of the Safavid Empire?

The Delhi Sultanate and the Early Mughal Empire

A quarter century after the Safavids seized power in Persia, another Islamic dynasty, the Mughals, emerged in South Asia. Like the Ottomans and Safavids, the Mughals created a regime destined to last for many centuries. But unlike those other empires, the Mughals did not replace a Mongol regime. Instead, they erected their state on the foundations of the old Delhi Sultanate, which had come into existence in 1206. Although spared the devastating effects of the Mongols and the Black Death, nonetheless the peoples of India had to deal with an invading nomadic force every bit as destructive as the Mongols: the warriors of Timur, or Tamerlane. His military forays crushed the Delhi Sultanate

Raid on Delhi. *Timur's swift raid on Delhi in 1398 was notable for the death and destruction it caused. This sixteenth-century miniature captures the plunder and violence.*

and opened the way for a new, even more powerful regime. (See Chapter 10 for more on the Delhi Sultanate.)

RIVALRIES, RELIGIOUS REVIVAL, AND THE FIRST MUGHAL EMPEROR A wave of religious revival followed in the wake of Timur's conquests. Bengal broke away from Delhi and soon embraced a Sufi form of mystical Islam, emphasizing personal union with God. Here, too, a special form of Hinduism, called Bhakti Hinduism, put down deep roots. Its devotees preached the doctrine of divine love. In the Punjab, previously a core area of the Delhi Sultanate, a new religion known as Sikhism came into being. Sikhism largely followed the teachings of Nanak (1469–1539). Although born a Hindu, he was inspired by Islamic ideals and called on his followers to renounce the caste system and to treat all believers as equal before God. (See Primary Source: Nanak's Teachings in India.)

Following Timur's attack, rival kingdoms and sultanates asserted their independence. The Delhi Sultanate became a mere shadow of its former self, just one of several competing powers in northern India. Out of this political chaos emerged a Turkish prince, Babur (the "Tiger"), invited in 1526 by the governor of the Punjab to restore order. A great-grandson of Timur, Babur traced his lineage to both the Turks and the Mongols (he was said to be a descendant of Chinggis Khan). For years, Babur had longed to conquer India. Massing an army of Turks and Afghans armed with matchlock cannons, he easily breached the wall of elephants put together by defenders of the sultan. Delhi fell, and the Delhi Sultanate came to an end. Babur proclaimed himself emperor and spent the next few years snuffing out the remaining resistance to his rule. (See Map 11.4.) Thus, he laid the foundation of the Mughal Empire, the third great Islamic dynasty (discussed in detail in Chapter 12).

By the sixteenth century, then, the Islamic heartland had seen the emergence of three new empires. Their differences were obvious, especially in the religious sphere. The Ottomans were Sunni Islam's most fervent champions, determined to eradicate the Shiite heresy on their border, where an equally determined Persian Safavid dynasty sought to expand the realm of Shiism. In contrast to these dynasties' sectarian religious commitments, the Mughals of India, drawing on well-established Indian traditions of religious and cultural tolerance, were open-minded toward non-Muslim believers and sectarian groups within the Muslim community. Yet, the political similarities of these imperial dynasties were equally clear-cut. Although these states did not hesitate to go to war against each other, they shared similar styles of rule. All established their legitimacy via military prowess, religious backing, and a loyal bureaucracy. This combination of spiritual and military weaponry enabled emperors, espousing Muhammad's preachings, to claim vast domains. Moreover, their religious differences did not prevent the movement of

Nanak's Teachings in India

Nanak (1469–1539), generally recognized as the founder of Sikhism, lived in northern India and participated in the religious discussions that were prominent at the time. As in western Europe and Islamic Southwest Asia, this was a period of political turmoil and intense personal introspection. The following excerpts demonstrate Nanak's views on the failings of the age and his use of Islamic and Hindu ideas to elaborate a unique spiritual perspective. Nanak stressed the unity of God, an emphasis that reflected Islamic influences. Nonetheless, his insistence on the comparative unimportance of prophets ran counter to Islam, and his belief in rebirth was strictly Hindu.

There is but one God, whose name is true, the Creator, devoid of fear and enmity, immortal, unborn, self-existent; God the great and bountiful. Repeat His Name.

Numberless are the fools appallingly blind;
Numberless are the thieves and devourers of others' property;
Numberless are those who establish their sovereignty by force;
Numberless the cutthroats and murderers;
Numberless the liars who roam about lying;
Numberless the filthy who enjoy filthy gain;
Numberless the slandered who carry loads of calumny on their heads;
Nanak thus described the degraded.
So lowly am I, I cannot even once be a sacrifice unto Thee. Whatever pleaseth Thee is good.
O Formless One, Thou art ever secure.

The Hindus have forgotten God, and are going the wrong way.

They worship according to the instruction of Narad.
They are blind and dumb, the blindest of the blind.
The ignorant fools take stones and worship them.
O Hindus, how shall the stone which itself sinketh carry you across?

What power hath caste? It is the reality that is tested.
Poison may be held in the hand, but man dieth if he eat it.
The sovereignty of the True One is known in every age. He who obeyeth God's order shall become a noble in His court.

Those who have meditated on God as the truest of the true have done real worship and are contented;
They have refrained from evil, done good deeds, and practiced honesty;

They have lived on a little corn and water, and burst the entanglements of the world.
Thou art the great Bestower; ever Thou givest gifts which increase a quarterfold.
Those who have magnified the great God have found Him.

QUESTIONS FOR ANALYSIS

- Identify all the "numberless" groups that Nanak lists. What range of social classes do they represent? How does this enumeration reflect the tumultuous times?
- What criticisms of Hindu worship does Nanak raise?
- What lines reveal his belief in rebirth?
- How does Nanak expect true believers to behave?

Source: "Nanak's Teachings in India." In William Theodore de Bary, Sources of Indian Tradition (New York: Columbia University Press, 1958), pp. 536–38.

goods, ideas, merchants, and scholars across political and religious boundaries—even across the most divisive boundary of all, that between Sunni Iraq and Shiite Persia.

WESTERN CHRISTENDOM

No region suffered more from the Black Death than western Christendom, and no region made a more spectacular comeback. From 1100 to 1300, Europe had enjoyed a surge in population, economic growth, and significant technological and intellectual progress, only to see these achievements halted in the fourteenth century by famine and the Black Death. Europeans responded by creating new political and cultural forms. New dynasties arose, and a cultural flourishing called the Renaissance revived Europe's connections with its Greek and Roman past and produced masterpieces in art, architecture, and other forms of thought.

Reactions and Revolts

The Black Death brought with it social and economic disorder that challenged the political order. The massive death toll and

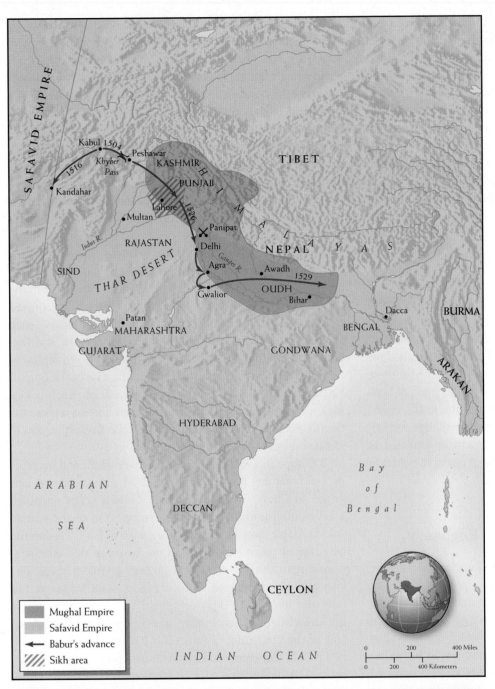

MAP 11.4 | The Mughal Empire, 1530

Compare the Mughal state with the other major Asian empires of this period, notably the Ottoman, Safavid, and Ming states (see Maps 11.2, 11.3, and 11.6).

- What geographical characteristic distinguished the Mughal state at this time from the others?

- Where in the landmass did the new state arise, and what effect do you think its place of origin had on the nature of Mughal rule?

- Based on its geographical location, to what religious traditions did the Mughals need to be sensitive?

the suddenness with which the disease struck also prompted survivors to ask questions about the major institution uniting Christendom, the Catholic Church. Even before the plague arrived, the late medieval western Church had found itself divided at the top (at one point there were three popes) and challenged from below, both by individuals critical of the extravagant lifestyles of some clergymen and by increasing demands on the clergy and church administration. Now the Black Death raised questions about God's relationship to humankind and the Catholic Church's role as God's appointed mediator on earth: Could sinful mortals ever find mercy from a vengeful God, and could an already overstretched and self-interested Church lead them to salvation? Facing challenges to its right to define religious doctrine and practices, the Church responded by demanding strict obedience to the true faith. This entailed the persecution of heretics, Jews, Muslims, homosexuals, prostitutes, and "witches." But the Church also reacted to society's suffering during this period, expanding its charitable and bureaucratic functions, providing alms to the urban poor, and registering births, deaths, and economic transactions. Its responses reassured many that God—and the church—had not abandoned true Christians and shored up the power of religious authorities.

Persecution and administration, however, cost money. Indeed, the needs as well as the extravagances of the clergy spurred certain questionable money-making tactics. One was the selling of indulgences (certificates that reduced one's time in purgatory, where souls continued the repentance that would eventually make them fit for heaven). This sort of unconventional fund-raising, and the growing gap between the church's promises and its ability to bring Christianity into people's everyday lives, more than the persecutions, eventually sparked the Protestant Reformation (see Chapter 12).

At the same time, the high death toll of the fourteenth and fifteenth centuries emboldened those who survived to seek higher wages or reductions in their feudal obligations. When landlords resisted or kings tried to impose new taxes, there were uprisings, including a 1358 peasant revolt in France that was dubbed the Jacquerie (the term derived from "Jacques Bonhomme," a name that contemptuous masters used for all peasants). Armed with only knives and staves, the peasantry went on a rampage, killing hated nobles and clergy and burning and looting all the property they could get their hands on. At issue was the peasants' insistence that they should no longer be tied to their land or have to pay for the tools they used in farming.

A better-organized uprising took place in England in 1381. Although the English Peasants' Revolt began as a protest against a tax levied to raise money for a war on France, it was also fueled by postplague labor shortages: serfs demanded the freedom to move about, and free farmworkers called for higher wages and lower rents. When landlords balked at these demands, aggrieved peasants assembled at the gates of London. The protesters demanded abolition of the feudal order, but the king ruthlessly suppressed them. Nonetheless, in both France and England, a free peasantry gradually emerged as labor shortages made it impossible to keep peasants bound to the soil.

State Building and Economic Recovery

Out of the chaos of famine, disease, and warfare, the diverse peoples of Europe found a political way forward. This path involved the formation of centralized monarchies, much as the Ottomans, Safavids, Mughals, and Ming were accomplishing in Asia. (A **monarchy** is a political system in which one individual holds supreme power and passes that power on to his or her next of kin.) Consolidation of these political systems occurred sometimes through strategic marriages but more often through warfare, both between local princely families and with local aristocratic allies and foreign mercenaries. Many of these dynasties fell as a result of civil war or conquest, but some, like the Tudors in England and the Valois in France, consolidated considerable power. In central Europe, one family, the Habsburgs, established a powerful and long-lasting dynasty. This family provided emperors for the Holy Roman Empire from 1440 to 1806. The Holy Roman Empire included territory that would later be divided into separate states such as the Netherlands, Germany, Austria, Belgium, and Croatia, and it also incorporated parts of present-day Italy, Poland, and Switzerland. Yet the Habsburg monarchs never succeeded in restoring an integrated

empire to western Europe (as Chinese dynasts had done by claiming the mandate of heaven). Indeed, although hereditary monarchy was Europe's dominant form of governance, there were also a number of oligarchic republics in which a handful of wealthy and influential voters selected their leaders, a sprinkling of political systems ruled by archbishops or other clergymen, and many "free" towns, surrounded by walls and protective of their special privileges.

Those who sought to rule the emerging states faced numerous obstacles. For example, rival claimants to the throne financed private armies. Also, the clergy demanded and received privileges and often meddled in politics themselves. The church's huge landholdings and exemptions from taxation made it, too, a formidable economic powerhouse. Towns—many of which had the right to rule themselves—refused to submit to rulers' demands. And once the printing press became available in the 1460s, printers circulated anonymous pamphlets criticizing the court and the clergy. Some states had consultative bodies—such as the Estates General in France, the Cortes in Spain, and Parliament in England—in which princes formally asked representatives of their people for advice and, in the case of the English Parliament, for consent to new forms of taxation. Such bodies gave no voice to most nonaristocratic men and no representation to women. But they did allow the collective expression of grievances against high-handed policies.

If Europe in 1450 had no central government and no prospect of obtaining political unity, it also had no common language. In China, the written literary Chinese script remained a key administrative tool for the dynasts. And in the Islamic world, Arabic was the common language of faith, Persian the language of poetry, and Turkish the language of administration. But in Europe, Latin lost ground as rulers chose various regional dialects to be their official state language. For centuries afterward, Latin continued to be the language of the church and of scholarship. Poets, however, took advantage of the upgrading of vernacular languages such as Italian or English and composed sophisticated poetic masterpieces, such as Dante Alighieri's *The Divine Comedy* or, later, Edmund Spenser's *The Faerie Queen*.

Despite, or perhaps because of, Europe's political fragmentation, new economic initiatives began to take hold, as the English and Flemish competed to expand cloth production and German and Dutch merchants extended their trading networks in the North Sea. Economic recovery was swiftest in southern Europe, where trade with Southwest Asia enriched merchants and subsidized the flourishing of luxury industries, such as glass-making in Venice. Although they remained small compared with Asian cities such as Istanbul or Beijing, Europe's towns rebounded quickly from the Black Death, particularly in Italy, the Netherlands, and along the North Sea coast. (See Map 11.5.) New prosperity and the influx of Christian

MAP 11.5 | Europe, 1400–1500

Europe was a region divided by dynastic rivalries during the fifteenth century.

- Locate the most powerful regional dynasties on the map: Portugal, Castile, Aragon, France, England, and the Holy Roman Empire. Where did the heaviest fighting occur?

- Why do you think one state was the scene for so many battles?

- On the basis of this map, predict which European territories and political systems would become powerful in subsequent centuries and which would not.

exiles from Istanbul into Italian city-states such as Venice and Florence led to a cultural flowering known as the Renaissance (discussed shortly). In northern and western Europe, the process took longer. In England and France, in particular, internal feuding, regional warfare, and religious fragmentation delayed recovery for decades (see Chapter 12).

Political Consolidation and Trade in Portugal

Portugal's fortunes demonstrate how political stabilization and the emergence of a stronger state could be useful in the revival of trade. After the chaos of the fourteenth century, Spain,

England, and France followed the Portuguese example and established national monarchies. In Spain and Portugal, warfare against Muslims would help unite Christian territories, and Mediterranean trade would add valuable income to state coffers.

Through the fourteenth century, Portuguese Christians devoted themselves to fighting the Moors, who were Muslim occupants of North Africa, the western Sahara, and the Iberian Peninsula. Decisive in this struggle was the Portuguese decision to cross the Strait of Gibraltar and seize the Moorish Moroccan fortresses at Ceuta, in North Africa: their ships could now sail between the Mediterranean and the Atlantic without Muslim interference. With that threat diminished, the Portuguese perceived their neighbor, Castile (part of what is now Spain), as their chief foe. Under João I (r. 1385–1433) the Castilians were defeated, and the monarchy could seek new territories and trading opportunities in the North Atlantic and along the West African coasts. João's son Prince Henrique, known later as Henry the Navigator, further expanded the family's domain by supporting expeditions down the coast of Africa and offshore to the Atlantic islands of the Madeiras and the Azores. The west and central coasts of Africa and the islands of the North and South Atlantic, including the Cape Verde Islands, São Tomé, Principe, and Fernando Po, soon became Portuguese ports of call.

The Portuguese monarchs granted the Atlantic islands to nobles as hereditary possessions on condition that the grantees colonize them, and soon the colonizers were establishing lucrative sugar plantations. In gratitude, noble families and merchants threw their political weight behind the king. Subsequent monarchs continued to reduce local elites' authority and

to ensure smooth succession for members of the royal family. This political consolidation enabled Portugal to thrive in the wake of the Black Death.

Dynasty Building and Reconquest in Spain

The road to dynasty in Spain was arduous. Medieval Spain comprised rival kingdoms that quarreled ceaselessly. Also, Spain lacked religious uniformity: Muslims, Jews, and Christians lived side by side in relative harmony, and Muslim armies still occupied strategic areas in the south. Over time, however, marriages and the formation of kinship ties among nobles and between royal lineages yielded a new political order. One by one, the major houses of the Spanish kingdoms intermarried, culminating in the fateful wedding of Isabella of Castile and Ferdinand of Aragon. Thus, Spain's two most important provinces were joined, and Spain became a state to be reckoned with.

THE UNION OF CASTILE AND ARAGON By the time Isabella and Ferdinand married in 1469, Spain was recovering from the miseries of the fourteenth century. This was more than a marriage of convenience. Castile was wealthy and populous; Aragon enjoyed an extended trading network in the Mediterranean. Together, the monarchs brought unruly nobles and distant towns under their domain. They topped off their achievements by marrying their children into other European royal families—especially the Habsburgs, central Europe's most powerful dynasty.

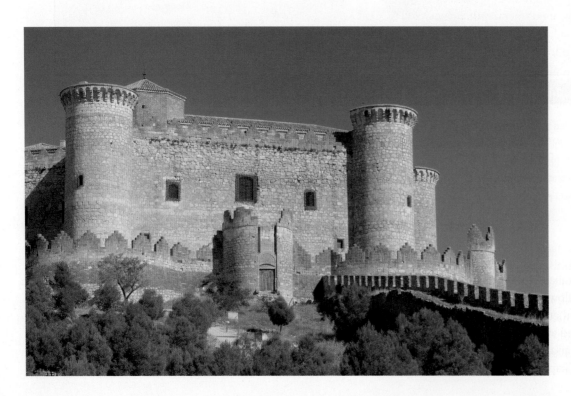

Renaissance Fortifications. *This image of Belmonte Castle in Castile, Spain, built by Don Juan de Pacheco in 1456, shows just how much money and material European nobles were willing to invest to protect their centers of power.*

The new rulers also sent Christian armies south to push Muslim forces out of the Iberian Peninsula. By the mid-fifteenth century, only Granada, a strategic lynchpin overlooking the straits between the Mediterranean and the Atlantic, remained in Muslim hands. After a long and costly siege, Christian forces captured the fortress there in January 1492. This was a victory of enormous symbolic importance, as joyous, to Christians, as the fall of Constantinople was depressing. Many people in Spain thumped their chests in pride, unaware or unconcerned that at the same time Ottoman armies were conquering large sections of southeastern Europe.

THE INQUISITION AND WESTWARD EXPLORATION
Just as the Safavid rulers had tried to stamp out all non-Shiite forms of Islam within their domains, so Isabella and Ferdinand sought to drive all non-Catholics out of Spain. Terrified by Ottoman incursions into Europe, in 1481 they launched the **Inquisition**, taking aim especially against *conversos*—converted Jews and Muslims—whom they suspected were Christians only in name. When Granada fell, the crown ordered the expulsion of all Jews from Spain; after 1499, a more tolerant attempt to convert the Moors by persuasion gave way to forced conversion—or emigration. This lack of tolerance meant that Spain, like other European states in this era, became increasingly homogenous. With fewer groups vying for influence within their territories, rulers turned their attention outward, fueling rivalries among the various European states.

Confident in the stability of their state, by late 1491 the Spanish monarchs were willing to listen to a Genoese navigator whose pleas for patronage they had previously rejected. Christopher Columbus promised them unimaginable riches that could finance their military campaigns and bankroll a crusade to liberate Jerusalem from Muslim hands. Off he sailed with a royal patent that guaranteed the monarchs a share of all he discovered. Soon the Spanish economy was reorienting itself toward the Atlantic, and Spain's merchants, missionaries, and soldiers were preparing for conquest and profiteering in what had been, just a few years before, a blank space on the map.

The Struggles of France and England and the Success of Small States

Warfare and strategic marriages allowed the Portuguese and Spanish monarchies to consolidate state power and to lay the foundations for revived commerce. But by no means were all states immediately successful. In France and England, the great age of European monarchy had yet to dawn.

When French forces finally pushed the English back across the English Channel in the Hundred Years' War (1337–1453), the French House of Valois began a slow process of consolidating royal power. Although diplomatic marriages helped the French crown expand its domain, two more centuries of royal initiatives and civil war were required to tame the powerful nobility. In England, even thirty years of civil war between the houses of Lancaster and York did not settle which one would take the throne. Both families in this War of the Roses ultimately lost out to the Tudors, who seized the throne in 1485.

Even where stable states did arise, they were fairly small compared with the Ottoman and Ming Empires. In the mid-sixteenth century, Portugal and Spain, Europe's two most expansionist states, had populations of 1 million and 9 million, respectively. England, excluding Wales, was a mere 3 million in 1550. Only France, with 17 million, had a population close to the Ottoman Empire's 20 to 30 million. And these numbers paled in comparison with Ming China's population of nearly 200 million in 1550 and Mughal India's 110 million in 1600.

But in Europe, small was advantageous. Portugal's relatively small population meant that the crown had fewer groups to instill with loyalty. Also, in the world of finance, the most successful merchants were those inhabiting the smaller Italian city-states and, a bit later, the cities of the northern Netherlands. The Florentines developed sophisticated banking techniques, created extensive networks of agents throughout Europe and the Mediterranean, and served as bankers to the popes. Venetian merchants enjoyed a unique role in the exchange of silks and spices from the eastern Mediterranean. It was in these prosperous city-states that the Renaissance began.

The Renaissance

Just as the Ming harkened back to Han Chinese traditions and the Ottomans looked to Sunni Islam to point the way forward, so European elites looked to their own traditions for guidance as they rebuilt after the devastation of the plague. They found inspiration in ancient Greek and Roman ideas. Europe's political and economic revival also included a powerful outpouring of cultural achievements, led by Italian scholars and artists and financed by bankers, churchmen, and nobles. Much later, scholars coined the word **Renaissance** ("rebirth") to characterize the expanded cultural production of the Italian city-states, France, the Low Countries, England, and the Holy Roman Empire in the period 1430–1550. What was being "reborn" was ancient Greek and Roman art and learning— knowledge that could illuminate a world of expanding horizons and support the rights of people other than clergymen or kings to exert power in it. Although the Renaissance was largely funded by popes and Christian monarchs, it broke the medieval church's monopoly on answers to the big questions and opened the way for secular forms of learning and a more human-centered understanding of the cosmos.

THE ITALIAN RENAISSANCE The Renaissance, ironically, was all about the new—new exposure, that is, to the old classical texts and ancient art and architectural forms. Although some Greek and Roman texts were known in Europe and the Islamic world, the fall of Constantinople and the invention of the printing press made others accessible to western scholars for the first time. Scholars now realized that the pre-Christian Greeks and Romans had known more: more about how to represent and care for the human body; more about geography, astronomy, and architecture; more about how to properly govern states and armies. It was no longer enough to understand Christian doctrine and to trust medieval authorities; one had to accurately retranslate the original sources, which required the learning of languages and of history. This dive backward into ancient Greece and Rome became known as **humanism**, the aspiration to know more about the human experience beyond what the Christian scriptures offered. Humanism was a powerful tool in the hands of those who knew how to use it. Several women, including the celebrated Italian humanist Laura Cereta (1469–1499), used their learning and rhetorical skills to defend the equality of male and female intellects at a time in which both the church and society as a whole believed women scholars to be freaks of nature. (See Primary Source: A Renaissance Defense of Human Equality.)

Wealthy families, powerful rulers, and the Catholic Church were the sponsors of Renaissance achievement. For example, by the 1480s, the Medici family had been patronizing art based on ancient models for three generations. The Medicis were bankers but also influential political players in Florence and Rome. The family contributed greatly to making Florence one of the showplaces of Renaissance art and architecture as well as the center stage for early Renaissance philosophy. Cosimo de' Medici (1389–1464) funded the completion of the sumptuous duomo (cathedral) of Florence, topped by the architect Brunelleschi's masterful dome, the largest built since antiquity. Cosimo's grandson, Lorenzo the Magnificent, supported many of the great Renaissance artists, including Leonardo da Vinci, Sandro Botticelli, and Michelangelo Buonarroti.

The artists who flourished in Florence, Rome, and Venice embraced their own form of humanism. For them, the return to ancient sources meant reviving the principles of the Roman architect Vitruvius and the imitation of nude classical sculpture. Their masterpieces, like Leonardo's *Last Supper* or Michelangelo's *David*, used the technique of perspective and classical treatments of the body to give vivacity and three-dimensionality to paintings and sculptures—even religious ones. Raphael's madonnas portrayed the Virgin Mary as a beautiful individual and not just as a symbol of chastity; similarly, Michelangelo's Sistine Chapel ceiling gave Adam the beautiful body of a Greek god so that viewers could appreciate the glory of the Creation. Of course, these artists also hoped to draw attention to their own achievements, and they were not disappointed. For soon northern European princes, too, sought out both ancient artifacts and the modern artists and humanists who could bring this inspiring new style to their courts.

THE RENAISSANCE SPREADS In the sixteenth century, a series of crises on the Italian Peninsula—including the sacking

Renaissance Masterpieces. Left: *Leonardo da Vinci's* The Last Supper *depicts Christ's disciples reacting to his announcement that one of them will betray him.* Right: *Michelangelo's* David *stands over 13 feet high and was conceived as an expression of Florentine civic ideals.*

A Renaissance Defense of Human Equality

Laura Cereta (1469-1499) was fortunate to have been the daughter of well-educated parents, her father a highly placed lawyer and her mother a successful businesswoman. But it was Laura who devoted herself at a young age to obtaining a deeply human-ist education, provided at first at the convent in her home town of Brescia, Italy, and then pursued by intense self-discipline once she had become her father's assistant (at age 12) and after her early marriage (at age 15). As a young woman she became widely known among Renaissance scholars for her learning. This achievement, however, embroiled her in a controversy that had been raging for decades about whether or not intelligent women were freaks of nature. Cereta responded to this line of thought with anger and disdain.

In the following letter to a fictional correspondent—but meant to denounce men such as the medieval writer Boccaccio, who had ridiculed women's intellects—Cereta uses her extensive knowledge of the ancient world and her rhetorical brilliance to denounce those who, in praising her exceptional talents, showed contempt for others of her "race." She invokes figures from Near Eastern and classical antiquity to show that there have always been women who were learned and wise. Notice, too, that the pursuit of the good that Cereta recommends does not involve the church; although she was a pious Christian, Cereta here recommends that individuals pursue secular knowledge rather than devote themselves to religious duties or to prayer.

To Bibolo Semproni
January 13, 1488

Your complaints are hurting my ears, for you say publicly and quite openly that you are not only surprised but pained that I am said to show this extraordinary intellect of the sort one would have thought nature would give to the most learned of men—as if you had reached the conclusion, on the facts of the case, that a similar girl had seldom been seen among peoples of the world. You are wrong on both counts, Semproni, and now that you've abandoned the truth, you are going to spread information abroad that is clearly false.

. . . My cause itself is worthy; I am impelled to show what great glory that noble lineage which I carry in my own breast has won for virtue and literature—a lineage that knowledge, the bearer of honors, has exalted in every age. For the possession of this lineage is legitimate and sure, and it has come all the way down to me from the continuance of a more enduring race.

We have read that the breast of Ethiopian Sabba, imbued with divinity, solved the prophetic riddles of the Egyptian king Solomon. . . . The enduring fame of Inachan Isis will flourish, for she alone of the Argive goddesses revealed to the Egyptians her own alphabet for reading. But Zenobia, an Egyptian woman of noble erudition, became so learned not only in Egyptian but also in Latin and Greek literature that she wrote the histories of barbarian and foreign peoples. . . . Those little Greek women Phyliasia and Lasthenia were wonderful sources of light in the world of letters and they filled me with new life because they ridiculed the students of Plato, who frequently tied themselves in knots over the snare-filled sophistries of their arguments.

All history is full of such examples. My point is that your mouth has grown foul because you keep it sealed so that no arguments can come out of it that might enable you to admit that nature imparts one freedom to all human beings equally—to learn. But the question of my exceptionality remains. And here choice alone, since it is the arbiter of characters, is the distinguishing factor. For some women worry about the styling of their hair, the elegance of their clothes, and the pearls and other jewelry they wear on their fingers. Others love to say cute little things, to hide their feeling behind a mask of tranquility, to indulge in dancing, and lead pet dogs around on a leash. But those women for whom the quest for the good represents a higher value restrain their young spirits and ponder better plains. They harden their bodies with sobriety and toil, they control their tongues, they carefully monitor what they hear, they ready their minds for all-night vigils. . . . For knowledge is not given as a gift but by study. For a mind free, keen, and unyielding in the face of hard work always rises to the good, and desire for learning grows in depth and breadth.

QUESTIONS FOR ANALYSIS

- Why is Cereta upset that she is seen as exceptional?
- How does she counter claims that women are not equal to men in intelligence?
- What recommendations does she have for women who want to pursue "the quest for the good"?

Source: Laura Cereta, *Collected Letters of a Renaissance Feminist*, transcribed, translated and edited by Diana Robin (Chicago: University of Chicago Press, 1997), pp. 76–79.

of Rome in 1527 by troops under the control of the Holy Roman Empire—and increasing economic prosperity in other parts of Europe helped to spread Renaissance culture throughout Europe. Philip II of Spain, for example, purchased more than 1,000 paintings during his reign; Henry IV of France and his queen, Marie de' Medici, invested a fortune in renovating the Louvre, building a new royal residence at Fontainebleau, and hiring Peter Paul Rubens to paint grand canvases. Courtiers built up-to-date palaces and invited scholars to live on their estates; Dutch, German, and French merchants also patronized the arts. All wanted their sons to be educated in the humanistic manner. Some families and religious institutions offered women access to the new learning, and some men encouraged their sisters, daughters, and wives to expand their horizons. The well-educated nun Caritas Pirckheimer (1467–1532), for example, exchanged learned letters and books with male humanists in the German states. Studying Greek, Latin, and ancient rhetoric did not make the commercial elite equal to the aristocrats, or women equal to men, but this sort of education did enable some non-nobles to obtain social influence and to criticize the ruling elites.

THE REPUBLIC OF LETTERS Since political and religious powers were not united in Europe (as they were in China and the Islamic world), scholars and artists could play one side against the other or, alternatively, could suffer both clerical and political persecution. Michelangelo completed commissions for the Medicis, for the Florentine Wool Guild, and for Pope Julius II. Peter Paul Rubens painted for the courts of France, Spain, England, and the Netherlands, as well as selling paintings on the open market. These two painters, renowned for showing a great deal of flesh, frequently offended conservative church officials, but their secular patrons kept them in oils. The Dutch scholar Desiderius Erasmus was able to ridicule the church because he had the patronage of English, Dutch, and French supporters. Other scholars used their learning to defend the older elites: for example, numerous lawyers and scholars continued to work for the popes, defending the papacy.

The search for patrons and the flight from persecution, especially after the Reformation, made Europe's educated elite increasingly cosmopolitan (as it had in China and the Islamic empires). Scholars met one another in royal palaces and cultural centers such as Florence, Antwerp, and Amsterdam. Seeking specialized information or rare books, they formed what was known as "the republic of letters"—a network of correspondents who were more interested in individual knowledge or talent than in noble titles or clerical rank. In this way, the Renaissance knitted together the European elite. This did not mean, however, that a consensus emerged about who should rule.

POWER AND THE RENAISSANCE THEORIZING ABOUT WAR The Renaissance was not only an embrace of the arts and

sciences of this world, but also a vehicle that enabled the more direct study of worldly power. Close reading of the ancient histories of Sallust, Livy, and Caesar emboldened scholars to address more forthrightly the conditions under which power could be maintained or undermined. New forms of governance were invented—and older forms buttressed. The Florentines pioneered a form of civic humanism under which all citizens were to devote themselves to defending the state against tyrants and foreign invaders; according to this view, the state would reward their civic virtue by ensuring their liberty. Yet it was also a Florentine, Niccolò Machiavelli, who wrote the most famous treatise on authoritarian power, *The Prince* (1513). Machiavelli argued that political leadership was not about obeying God's rules but about mastering the amoral means of modern statecraft. Holding and exercising power were ends in themselves, he claimed; civic virtue was merely a pretense on the part of those (like the Medici family he knew so well) who simply wanted to keep the upper hand.

In his own lifetime, Machiavelli was even more renowned for his essay *The Art of War* (1521). Here, the Florentine humanist argued that Roman military tactics, including the deploying of trained, armed citizens, would make for a more trustworthy army than the use of mercenary soldiers. The enrollment of a broadly based citizenry in the defense of the state, he insisted, would also make for political stability. His advice was hardly practicable in a Europe in which monarchs put little trust in their fellow nobles and even less in their subjects, but his ideas circulated widely and would gradually catch on and inspire military reforms in the Dutch Republic and during the Thirty Years' War (see Chapter 13). And he made little of the use of artillery, although the cannon had been used in European siege warfare since at least the 1420s; the Portuguese had already mounted them on oceangoing ships and had begun to use them to blast open South Asian ports. Machiavelli's fellow humanist Niccolò Tartaglia noticed the upsurge in cannon usage and produced an important treatise on ballistics, in which mathematics was first applied to the trajectory of projectiles. But neither of these was as influential as a wave of publications devoted to proper fortification designs, written by specialized military engineers who, for the first time, advocated the construction of defenses not to be pleasing to the eye but to best absorb the force of modern cannons. Thus began a long-lasting battle between military architects seeking to construct invincible defenseworks and artillery makers seeking to destroy them.

Like artistic and early manufacturing techniques, European military technologies diffused across the continent through conflict between states. Europeans learned much by observing one another at close range, especially during the many wars that marked the fifteenth and sixteenth centuries. As princes began to orient themselves more and more to obtaining and preserving power in this world, they began to value subjects who could build sturdy fortifications or more effectively mix gunpowder (a Chinese invention in widespread use in Europe by 1400). By the sixteenth century, many had also formed what were essentially standing armies and had begun to invest heavily in improved fortifications, not only for their castles but for their cities of residence as well. But like the church's new worldly activities, these princely activities also cost a great deal of money and demanded an expansion of state operations. In orienting the elite toward both ancient ideas and this-worldly power, in this way, too, the Renaissance revolutionized both European culture and politics—even if it could not unify the states and peoples who cultivated it.

MING CHINA

Like the Europeans, the Chinese saw their stable worldview and political order crumble under the cataclysms of human and bacterial invasions. Moreover, like the Europeans, people in China had long regarded outsiders as "barbarians." Together, the Mongols and the Black Death upended the political and intellectual foundations of what had appeared to be the world's most integrated society. The Mongols brought the Yuan dynasty to power; then the plague devastated China and prepared the way for the emergence of the Ming dynasty.

Ruled by ethnically Han Chinese, the Ming dynasty defined itself against its foreign predecessors. Ming emperors sought to reinforce everything Chinese. In particular, they supported China's vast internal agricultural markets in an attempt to minimize dependence on merchants and foreign trade.

Restoring Order

In the chaotic fourteenth century, as plague and famine ravaged China and as the Mongol Yuan dynasty collapsed, only a strong military movement capable of overpowering other groups could restore order. That intervention began at the hands of a poor young man who had trained in the Red Turban Movement: Zhu Yuanzhang. He was an orphan from a peasant household in an area devastated by disease and famine and a former novice at a Buddhist monastery. At age twenty-four, Zhu joined the Red Turbans, after which he rose quickly to become a distinguished commander. Eventually, his forces defeated the Yuan and drove the Mongols from China.

It soon became clear that Zhu had a much grander design for all of China than the ambitions of most warlords. When he took the important city of Nanjing in 1356, he renamed it Yingtian ("In response to Heaven"). Buoyed by subsequent successful military campaigns, twelve years later Zhu (r. 1368–1398) proclaimed the founding of the Ming ("brilliant") dynasty. Soon thereafter, his troops met little resistance when they seized the Yuan capital of Beijing, causing the Mongol emperor to flee to his homeland in the steppe. It would, however, take Zhu almost another twenty years to reunify the entire country.

Centralization under the Ming

Zhu and successive Ming emperors had to rebuild a devastated society from the ground up. Although in the past China had experienced natural catastrophes, wars, and social dislocation,

The Forbidden City. *The Yongle Emperor relocated the capital to Beijing, where he began the construction of the Forbidden City, or imperial palace. The palace was designed to inspire awe in all who saw it.*

the plague's legacy was devastation on an unprecedented scale. It left the new rulers with the formidable challenge of rebuilding the great cities, restoring respect for ruling elites, and reconstructing the bureaucracy.

IMPERIAL GRANDEUR AND KINSHIP The rebuilding began under Zhu, the Hongwu ("expansive and martial") Emperor, whose extravagant capital at Nanjing reflected imperial grandeur. When the dynasty's third emperor, the Yongle ("perpetual happiness") Emperor, relocated the capital to Beijing, he flaunted an even more grandiose style. Construction here mobilized around 100,000 artisans and 1 million laborers. The city had three separate walled enclosures. Inside the outer city walls sprawled the imperial city; within its walls lay the palace city, the Forbidden City. Traffic within the walled sections navigated through boulevards leading to the different gates, above which imposing towers soared. The palace compound, where the imperial family resided, had more than 9,000 rooms. Anyone standing in the front courts, which measured more than 400 yards on a side and boasted marble terraces and carved railings, would gasp at the sense of awesome power. That was precisely the effect the Ming emperors wanted (just as the Ottoman sultans did in building Topkapi Palace).

Marriage and kinship buttressed the power of the Ming imperial household. The dynasty's founder married the adopted daughter of a leading Red Turban rebel (her father, according to

legend, was a convicted murderer), thereby consolidating his power and eliminating a threat. Empress Ma, as she was known, became the Hongwu Emperor's principal wife and was praised for her compassion. Emerging as the kinder face of the regime, she tempered the harsh and sometimes cruel disposition of her spouse. He had numerous other consorts as well, including Korean and Mongol women, who bore him twenty-six sons and sixteen daughters (similar to, although on smaller scale than, the sultan's harem at Topkapi Palace).

BUILDING A BUREAUCRACY Faced with the challenge of reestablishing order out of turmoil, the Hongwu Emperor initially sought to rule through his many kinsmen by giving imperial princes generous stipends, command of large garrisons, and significant autonomy in running their domains. However, when the princes' power began to threaten the court, the emperor slashed their stipends, reduced their privileges, and took control of their garrisons. No longer dependent on these men, he established an imperial bureaucracy beholden only to him and to his successors. These officials won appointments through their outstanding performance on a reinstated civil service examination.

In addition, the Hongwu Emperor took other steps to install a centralized system of rule. He assigned bureaucrats to oversee the manufacture of porcelain, cotton, and silk products as well as tax collection. He reestablished the Confucian school system as a means of selecting a cadre of loyal officials (not

Chinese Irrigation. *Farmers in imperial China used sophisticated devices to extract water for irrigation, as depicted in this illustration from the Yuan Mongol period.*

PRIMARY SOURCE

The Hongwu Emperor's Proclamation

This proclamation by the founder of the Ming dynasty, the Hongwu Emperor (r. 1368–1398), reveals how he envisioned recon-structing the devastated country as his own personal project. He sought a return to austerity by denouncing the morally corro-sive effect of money and material possessions, and he especially distrusted his officials. Although frustrated in his efforts, the Hongwu Emperor nonetheless set the tone for the centralization of power in the person of the emperor.

To all civil and military officials:

I have told you to refrain from evil. Doing so would enable you to bring glory to your ancestors, your wives and chil-dren, and yourselves. With your virtue, you then could assist me in my endeavors to bring good fortune and prosperity to the people. You would establish names for yourselves in Heaven and on earth, and for thousands and thousands of years, you would be praised as worthy men.

However, after assuming your posts, how many of you really followed my instructions? Those of you in charge of money and grain have stolen them your-selves; those of you in charge of criminal laws and punishments have neglected the regulations. In this way grievances are not redressed and false charges are ignored. Those with genuine grievances have nowhere to turn; even when they merely wish to state their complaints, their words never reach the higher officials. Occa-sionally these unjust matters come to my attention. After I discover the truth, I cap-ture and imprison the corrupt, villainous,

and oppressive officials involved. I punish them with the death penalty or forced labor or have them flogged with bamboo sticks in order to make manifest the con-sequences of good or evil actions. . . .

Alas, how easily money and profit can bewitch a person! With the exception of the righteous person, the true gentleman, and the sage, no one is able to avoid the temptation of money. But is it really so difficult to reject the temptation of profit? The truth is people have not really tried.

Previously, during the final years of the Yuan dynasty, there were many ambi-tious men competing for power who did not treasure their sons and daughters but prized jade and silk, coveted fine horses and beautiful clothes, relished drunken singing and unrestrained pleasure, and enjoyed separating people from their par-ents, wives, and children. I also lived in that chaotic period. How did I avoid such snares? I was able to do so because I val-ued my reputation and wanted to preserve my life. Therefore I did not dare to do these evil things. . . .

In order to protect my reputation and to preserve my life, I have done away with music, beautiful girls, and valuable objects. Those who love such things are usually "a success in the morning, a failure in the evening." Being aware of the fallacy of such behavior, I will not indulge such foolish fancies. It is not really that hard to do away with these tempting things.

QUESTIONS FOR ANALYSIS

- What criticisms does the Hongwu Emperor level against the Mongol Yuan, whose rule he overthrew?
- What crimes does he accuse his own officials of committing, and what punishments does he carry out?
- Why would this Chinese emperor issue a decree that focuses on defining moral behavior?

Source: Patricia Buckley Ebrey (ed.), *Chinese Civilization: A Sourcebook,* Second Edition, revised and expanded (New York: The Free Press, 1993), pp. 205–6.

unlike the Ottoman janissaries and administrators). He also set up local networks of villages to rebuild irrigation systems and to supervise reforestation projects to prevent flooding—with the astonishing result that the amount of land reclaimed nearly tripled within eight years. Historians estimate that the Hongwu Emperor's reign oversaw the planting of about 1 billion trees, including 50 million sterculia, palm, and varnish trees around Nanjing. Their products served in building a maritime expedition fleet in the early fifteenth century. For water control, 40,987 reservoirs underwent repairs or new construction.

Now the imperial palace not only projected the image of a power center; it *was* the center of power. Every official received his appointment by the emperor through the Ministry of Per-sonnel. The Hongwu Emperor also eliminated the post of prime minister (he executed the man who held the post) and hence-forth ruled directly. Ming bureaucrats literally lost their seats and had to kneel before the emperor. In one eight-day period, the Hongwu Emperor reputedly reviewed over 1,600 petitions dealing with 3,392 separate matters. The drawback, of course, was that he had to keep tabs on this immense system, and his bureaucrats were not always up to the task. Indeed, the Hongwu Emperor constantly juggled personal and impersonal forms of authority, sometimes fortifying the administration, sometimes undermining it lest it become too autonomous. In due course, he nurtured a bureaucracy far more extensive than those of the Islamic empires. The Ming thus established the most highly centralized system of government of all the monarchies of this period. (See Primary Source: The Hongwu Emperor's Proclamation.)

Religion under the Ming

Just as the Ottoman sultans projected themselves as Muslim rulers, calling themselves the shadow of God, and European monarchs claimed to rule by divine right, so the Ming emperors enhanced their legitimacy by drawing on ancient Chinese religious traditions. Citing the mandate of heaven, the emperor revised and strengthened the elaborate protocol of rites and ceremonies that had undergirded dynastic power for centuries. As well as underscoring the emperor's centrality, official rituals (such as those related to the gods of soil and grain) reinforced political and social hierarchies.

Under the guise of "community" gatherings, rites and sacrifices solidified the Ming order by portraying the rulers as the moral and spiritual benefactors of their subjects. On at least ninety occasions each year, the emperor engaged in sacrificial rites, providing symbolic communion between the human and the spiritual worlds. These lavish festivities reinforced the ruler's image as mediator between otherworldly affairs of the gods and worldly concerns of the empire's subjects. The message was clear: the gods were on the side of the Ming household.

As an example of religious rituals reinforcing hierarchies, the emperor sanctioned official cults that were either civil or military and further distinguished as great, middle, or minor as well as celestial, terrestrial, or human categories. Official cults, however, often conflicted with local faiths. In this regard, they revealed the limits of Ming centralism. Consider Dongyang, a hilly interior region. As was common in Ming China, the people of Dongyang supported Buddhist institutions. Guan Yu, a legendary martial hero killed centuries earlier, was enshrined in a local Buddhist monastery there. But he was also worshipped as part of a state cult. Herein lay the problem: the state cult and the Buddhist monastery were separate entities, and imperial law held that the demands of the state cult prevailed over those of the local monastery. So the state-appointed magistrates in Dongyang kept a watchful eye on local religious leaders, although the magistrates refrained from tampering directly in the monastery's affairs. Although the imperial government insisted that people honor their contributions to the state, Dongyang's residents delivered most of their funds to the Buddhist monks. So strong were local sentiments that even the officials siphoned revenues to the monastery.

Ming Deities. *A pantheon of deities worshipped during the Ming, demonstrating the rich religious culture of the period.*

Ming Rulership

Religious sources of political power were less essential for the Ming dynasty than for the Islamic dynasties. Conquest and defense helped establish the realm, and bureaucracy kept it functioning. The empire's large scale (see Map 11.6) required a remarkably complex administration. To many outsiders (especially Europeans, whose region was in a state of constant war), Ming stability and centralization appeared to be political wizardry.

In terms of the structures underlying Ming power, the usual dynastic dilemmas were present. The emperor wished to be seen as the special guardian of his subjects. He wanted their

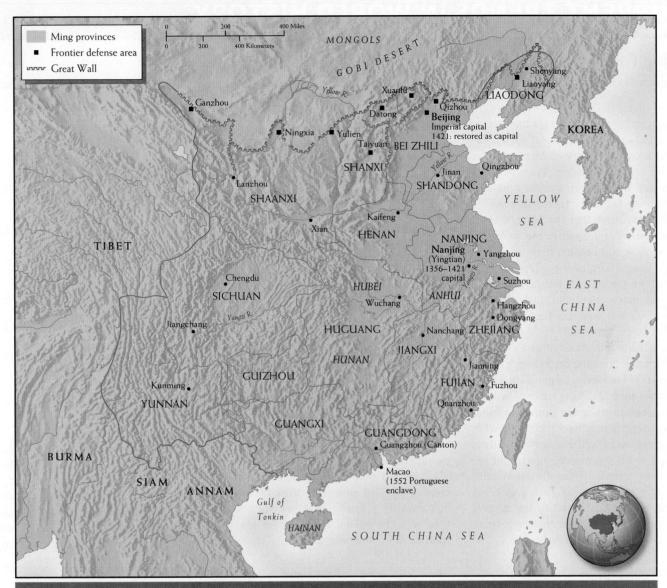

MAP 11.6 | Ming China, 1500s

The Ming state was one of the largest empires at this time—and the most populous. It had a long seacoast and even longer internal borders.

• What were the two Ming capitals, and what were the three main seaport trading cities?

• According to the map, where did the Ming rulers expect the greatest threat to their security?

• From your reading, how did the Ming rulers view foreign contact and exchange during this period?

allegiance as well as their taxes and labor. But during hard times, poor farmers were reluctant to provide resources—taxes or services—to distant officials. For these reasons alone, the Hongwu Emperor preferred to entrust management of the rural world to local leaders, whom he appointed as village chiefs, village elders, or tax captains. (In fact, a popular Chinese proverb was "The mountain is high and the emperor is far away.") Within these communities, the dynasty created a social hierarchy based on age, sex, and kinship. While women's labor remained critical for the village economy, the government reinforced a

gender hierarchy by promoting women's chastity and constructing commemorative arches for widows who refrained from remarrying. The Ming thus produced a more elaborate system for classifying and controlling its subjects than did the other Afro-Eurasian dynasties. But individuals also sought to define themselves by dressing in ways that expressed their own view of their place in the social order. (See Current Trends in World History: Ming Fashion.)

The Ming Empire, like the European and Islamic states, also faced periodic unrest and rebellion. Rebels often proclaimed

CURRENT TRENDS IN WORLD HISTORY

Ming Fashion

Ming rulers liked to represent themselves as custodians of the "civilized" Han traditions, in contrast to the "barbarian" ways of the previous Mongol Yuan dynasty. However, from governmental practices to clothing fashions, there were visible signs everywhere that the Ming, despite their rhetoric, followed in the footsteps of the Yuan and became more and more linked to an ever-growing, interconnected world. As trade with neighboring and faraway lands continued unabated and merchants and travelers kept moving, it proved to be impossible for the Ming to keep outside influences at arm's length. At the same time, the rhetoric of a return to the Han traditions did generate moves to invoke antiquity in the realm of fashion. Status-conscious elites with newfound wealth eagerly purchased clothes in what they believed to be the ancient Han style, hoping to set themselves apart from the common people. Their flirtation with antiquity, however, often ended up being more reinvention to satisfy the surging demands of the market than a genuine return to earlier conventions.

Founder Zhu Yuanzhang set the tone of the Ming by trying to rid the country of the close-fitting tunics worn by the Mongols. He advocated instead the wearing of the reputedly Tang-style garment of earlier times. While this measure did meet with some success, the vibrant clothing sector was hardly free of its fascination with the "exotic," such as horsehair skirts from Korea for men. A rare commodity when they first arrived, probably via trade missions, by the late fifteenth century, local weavers had become so skilled in making these skirts and consumers so eager to obtain them that craftsworkers were caught stealing the tails of horses to satisfy the soaring demand for the raw materials. Indeed, undoubtedly to the chagrin of the first Ming emperor and his descendants, much of the Yuan style and even terminology in both male and female clothing persisted during the Ming era.

The retro movement in fashion, as mentioned, had more to do with the demands of a changing Ming society than with the official advocacy for restorationism. Nowhere was this more

An example of headwear used by Ming officials, reputedly following the style of earlier dynasties. The beams attached to the crown of the cap indicate the official's rank, so the cap is known as a "beamed cap."

apparent than in the myriad styles of hats for men—a convenient yet highly visible way to make a statement in social standing. Invoking the names of earlier dynasties, there were the Han cap, the Jin cap, the Tang cap, and so on. The most interesting, however, was the Chunyang hat,

their own brand of religious beliefs, just as local elites resented central authority. Outright terror helped stymie threats to central authority. In a massive wave of carnage, the Hongwu Emperor slaughtered anyone who posed a threat to his authority, from the highest of ministers to the lowliest of scribes. From 1376 to 1393, four of his purges condemned close to 100,000 subjects to execution.

Yet, despite the emperor's immense power, the Ming Empire remained undergoverned. Indeed, as the population multiplied, there were too few loyal officials to handle local affairs. By the sixteenth and early seventeenth centuries, for example, some 10,000 to 15,000 officials shouldered the responsibility of managing a population exceeding 200 million people. Nonetheless, the Hongwu Emperor bequeathed to his descendants a set of tools for ruling that drew on subjects' direct loyalty to the emperor and on the intricate workings of an extensive bureaucracy. His legacy enabled his successors to balance local sources of power with the needs of dynastic rulership.

Trade and Exploration

In the fourteenth century, China began its economic recovery from the devastation of disease and political turmoil. Gradually, political stability allowed trade to revive. Now the new dynasty's merchants reestablished China's preeminence in long-distance commercial exchange. Chinese silk and cotton textiles, as well as fine porcelains, ranked among the world's most coveted luxuries. Wealthy families from Lisbon to Kalabar loved to wash their hands in delicate Chinese bowls and to flaunt fine wardrobes made from bolts of Chinese dyed linens and smoothly spun silk. When a Chinese merchant ship sailed into port, trading partners and onlookers crowded the docks to watch the unloading of precious cargoes. Although Ming rulers' support for overseas ventures wavered and eventually declined, this period saw important developments in Chinese trade and exploration.

During the Ming period, Chinese traders based in ports such as Hangzhou, Quanzhou, and Guangzhou (Canton) were

The "paddy-field gown" for women might have had its origins in Buddhist robes.

Nor was the rage for fashion reserved for men only or even for just the privileged. As one Ming writer lamented, perhaps with a hint of exaggeration: "Nowadays the very servant girls dress in silk gauze, and the singsong girls look down on brocaded silks and embroidered gowns." Respectable women, we are told, looked to the clothing and style of the courtesans of the prosperous southern region of the country for ideas and inspiration for fashion. Indeed, much of our visual knowledge of Ming womens' clothing comes from paintings likely of highly trained courtesans or those female "entertainers" ubiquitous in Ming urban centers. These paintings reveal the different and consistently evolving styles of clothing for Ming women, including the "paddy-field gown"—which might have owed its origins to Buddhist robes—that were the focus of much criticism from those who frowned on the growing penchant for the exotic, the strange, the outrageous, and the irreverent in the realm of fashion. If nothing else, this debate about clothing certainly tells us that despite the often conservative

which allegedly drew upon both Han and Tang styles in its design but had actually become a symbol of the so-called new and strange fashion that so often attracted commentary in Ming writings. In fact, it was favored by the young, who had nothing but disdain for ancient styles!

stance and policies of the Ming regime, the everyday life of many Ming subjects was a constant exercise in negotiating the multiple impacts of both the old and the new as well as the familiar and the foreign in different arenas of their rapidly changing society.

Explore Further

Finnane, Antonia. *Changing Clothes in China: Fashion, History, Nation* (2008).

as energetic as their Muslim counterparts in the Indian Ocean. These ports were home to prosperous merchants and the point of convergence for vast sea-lanes. Leaving the mainland ports, Chinese vessels carried precious wares to offshore islands, the Pescadores, and Taiwan. From there they sailed on to the ports of Kyūshū, the Ryūkyūs, Luzon, and maritime Southeast Asia. As entrepôts for global goods, East Asian ports flourished. Former fishing villages developed into major urban centers.

The Ming dynasty viewed overseas expansion with suspicion, however. The Hongwu Emperor feared that too much contact with the outside world would cause instability and undermine his rule. In fact, he banned private maritime commerce in 1371. But enforcement was lax, and by the late fifteenth century, maritime trade once again surged. Because much of the thriving business took place in defiance of official edicts, it led to constant friction between government officials and maritime traders. Although the Ming government ultimately agreed to issue licenses for overseas trade in the mid-sixteenth century, its

policies continued to vacillate. To Ming officials, the sea represented problems of order and control rather than opportunities.

THE EXPEDITIONS OF ZHENG HE One spectacular exception to the Ming's attitude toward maritime trade was a series of officially sponsored expeditions in the early fifteenth century. It was the ambitious Yongle Emperor who took the initiative. One of his loyal followers was a Muslim whom the Ming army had captured as a boy. The youth was castrated and sent to serve at the court (as a eunuch, he could not continue his family line and so theoretically owed sole allegiance to the emperor). Given the name **Zheng He** (1371–1433), he grew up to be an important military leader. The emperor entrusted him with venturing out to trade, collect tribute, and display China's power to the world.

From 1405 to 1433, Zheng He commanded the world's greatest armada and led seven naval expeditions. His larger ships stretched 400 feet in length (Columbus's *Santa Maria* was 85 feet), carried hundreds of sailors on four tiers of decks, and

Zheng He's Ship. *A testament to centuries of experience in shipbuilding and maritime activities, the largest ship in Zheng He's armada in the early fifteenth century was about five times the length of Columbus's Santa Maria (pictured next to Zheng's ship) and had nine times the capacity in terms of tonnage. It had nine staggered masts and twelve silk sails, all designed to demonstrate the grandeur of the Ming Empire.*

maneuvered with sophisticated rudders, nine masts, and water-tight compartments. The first expedition set sail with a flotilla of 62 large ships and over 200 lesser ones. All 28,000 men aboard pledged to promote Ming glory.

Zheng He and his entourage aimed to establish tributary relations with far-flung territories—from Southeast Asia to the Indian Ocean ports, to the Persian Gulf, and to the east coast of Africa. (See Map 11.7.) These expeditions did not seek territorial expansion, but rather control of trade and tribute. Zheng traded for ivory, spices, ointments, exotic woods, and even some wildlife, including giraffes, zebras, and ostriches. He also used his considerable force to intervene in local affairs, exhibiting China's might in the process. If a community refused to pay tribute, Zheng's fleet would attack it. He encouraged rulers or envoys from Southeast Asia, India, Southwest Asia, and Africa to visit his homeland. When local rulers were uncooperative, Zheng might seize them and drag them all the way to China to face the emperor, as he did the rulers of Sumatra and Ceylon.

As spectacular as they were, Zheng's accomplishments could not survive the changing tides of events at home. Although many items gathered on his voyages delighted the court, most were not the stuff of everyday commerce. The expeditions were glamorous but expensive, and in 1424, when the Yongle Emperor died, they lost their most enthusiastic patron. Moreover, by the mid-fifteenth century, there was a revival of military threats from the north. At that time, the Ming court was shocked to discover that during a tour of the frontiers, the emperor had been captured and held hostage by the Mongols. Recalling how the maritime-oriented Song dynasty had been overrun by invaders from the north (see Chapter 10), Ming officials withdrew imperial support for seagoing ventures and instead devoted their energies to overland

ventures and defense. Thus, Zheng's expeditions came to a complete halt in 1433. Never again did the Ming undertake such large-scale maritime ventures, although individual merchants, of course, returned to their profitable coastal trade routes.

The Chinese decision to forgo overseas ventures after 1433 was momentous. Although China remained the wealthiest, most densely settled region of the world with the most fully developed state structure and thriving market, the empire's wariness of overseas projects deprived merchants and would-be explorers of vital support in an age when others were beginning to look outward and across the oceans.

CONCLUSION

How could all the dying and devastation that came with the Black Death not have transformed the peoples of Afro-Eurasia? Much did change, but certain underlying ideals and institutions endured. What changed were mainly the political regimes, which took the blame for the catastrophes. The Delhi Sultanate, the Abbasid Empire, and the Yuan dynasty collapsed. In contrast, universal religions and wide-ranging cultural systems persisted even though they underwent vast transformations. The Ming dynasts in China set the stage for a long tenure by claiming, as had previous rulers, the mandate of heaven and stressing China's place at the center of their universe. A strict Shiite version of Islam emerged in Iran, while a fervent form of Sunni Islam found its champion in the Ottoman Empire. In Europe, national monarchies appeared in Spain, Portugal, France, and England. Debilitated by death and disorder, the Catholic Church recovered its centrality, though some Europeans, too, began to

MAP 11.7 | Voyages of Zheng He, 1405–1433

Zheng He's voyages are some of the most famous in world history. Many historians have speculated about how history might have been different if the Chinese emperors had allowed the voyages to continue.

• For how many years did Zheng's voyages last?

• How far did Zheng's voyages take him?

• Why did Chinese expeditions not have the same impact as European voyages of exploration toward the end of the fifteenth century?

satisfy their spiritual longings in ways that went beyond traditional practices.

The new states and empires had notable differences. These were evident in the ambition of a Ming warlord who established a new dynasty, the military expansionism of Turkish households bordering the Byzantine Empire, the unifying vision of Mughal rulers in northern India, and the desire of various European rulers to consolidate power. But interactions among peoples also mattered: an eagerness to reestablish and expand trade networks and a desire to convert unbelievers to "the true faith"—be it a form of Islam, a variant of Hinduism, an exclusive Christianity, or a local type of Buddhism.

The dynasties all faced similar problems. They had to establish legitimacy, ensure smooth succession, deal with religious groups, and forge working relationships with nobles, townspeople, merchants, and peasants. Yet each state developed distinctive traits as a result of political innovation, traditional ways of ruling, and borrowing from neighbors. European monarchies achieved significant internal unity, often through warfare and in the context of a cultural Renaissance. Ottoman rulers perfected techniques for ruling an ethnically and religiously diverse empire: they moved military forces swiftly, allowed local communities a degree of political and religious autonomy, and trained a

bureaucracy dedicated to the Ottoman and Sunni Islamic way of life. The Ming dynasty fashioned an imperial system based on a Confucian-trained bureaucracy and intense subordination to the emperor so that it could manage a mammoth population. The rising monarchies of Europe, the Shiite regime of the Safavids in Persia, and the Ottoman state all blazed with religious fervor and sought to eradicate or subordinate the beliefs of other groups.

The new states displayed unprecedented political and economic powers. All demonstrated military prowess, a desire for stable hierarchies and secure borders, and a drive to expand. Each legitimized its rule via dynastic marriage and succession, state-sanctioned religion, and administrative bureaucracies. Each supported vigorous commercial activity. The Islamic regimes, especially, engaged in long-distance commerce and, by conquest and conversion, extended their holdings.

For western Christendom, the Ottoman conquests were decisive. They provoked Europeans to establish commercial connections to the east, south, and west. The consequences of their new toeholds would be momentous—just as the Chinese decision to turn *away* from overseas exploration and commerce marked a turning point in world history. Both decisions were instrumental in determining which worlds would come together and which would remain apart.

After You Read This Chapter

Go to **INQUIZITIVE** to see what you know & learn what you've missed.

FOCUS ON: *Crisis and Recovery in Afro-Eurasia*

Collapse and Consolidation

- Bubonic plague originates in Inner Asia and afflicts people from China to Europe.
- Climate change and famine leave people vulnerable, while commerce facilitates the spread of disease.
- The plague kills 25 to 65 percent of infected populations and leaves societies in turmoil.

Islamic Dynasties

- Ottoman, Safavid, and Mughal Empires replace the Mongols.
- Ottomans overrun Constantinople and become the primary Sunni regime in the Islamic world.
- The Ottomans establish their legitimacy with military prowess, religious backing, and a loyal bureaucracy.
- Sultans manage decentralizing tendencies of outlying provinces with flexibility and tolerance, relying on religious faith, patronage, and bureaucracy.
- Safavid and Mughal regimes arise in Iran and South Asia.

Western Christendom

- New dynastic monarchies that claim to rule by divine right appear in Portugal, Spain, France, and England.
- The Inquisition takes aim against *conversos*—converted Jews and Muslims.
- A rebirth of classical learning, known as the Renaissance, originates in Italian city-states and spreads throughout western Europe.
- War making becomes more scientific, expensive, and deadly.

Ming China

- The Ming dynasty replaces the Mongol Yuan dynasty and rebuilds a strong state from the ground up, claiming a mandate from heaven.
- An elaborate, centralized bureaucracy oversees the revival of infrastructure and long-distance trade.
- The emperor and bureaucracy concentrate on developing internal markets and overland trade at the expense of overseas commerce.

CHRONOLOGY

Islamic World

Osman begins Ottoman Empire **1299**

The Black Death arrives in Baghdad **1347**

Western Christendom

Black Death reaches Italian port cities ◆ **1347**

Peasant revolts in England and France **1358–1381**

East Asia

Black Death reaches China **1320**

The Hongwu Emperor founds Ming dynasty **1368**

1300   1350

1. **Explain** how the Black Death, or bubonic plague, spread throughout Afro-Eurasia. What human activity facilitated its diffusion?

2. **Describe** the long-term consequences of bubonic plague for the Afro-Eurasian world. What were the plague's social, political, and economic ramifications in various parts of the landmass?

3. **Identify** the three main Islamic dynasties that emerged after the bubonic plague. How were they similar, and how were they different?

4. **Analyze** the ways in which the Ming dynasty centralized its power in China in the fourteenth and fifteenth centuries. What political innovations did it pursue, and what traditions did it sustain? **Compare** Chinese efforts at bureaucratic centralization with those of the Ottomans.

5. **Describe** the goals of the Ming dynasty's maritime exhibitions. Why did the government later abandon them?

6. **Compare and contrast** the ways in which regional rulers in post-plague Afro-Eurasia attempted to construct unified states. **Identify** their greatest successes.

7. **Explain** why the bubonic plague undermined the feudal order of the Catholic Church. How did regional monarchs in Europe capitalize on this development?

8. **Identify** the ways in which religious belief systems maintained continuity from the fourteenth through the fifteenth centuries.

9. **Describe** the key features of the Renaissance in Europe. How did the Renaissance spread and change?

10. **Discuss** how the art and architecture of different regions reflected the political realities of this period. **Identify** themes that communicated these messages to viewers.

11. **Analyze** the role of philosophical and religious developments—both elite movements, like humanism in Europe, and popular movements, like the Red Turban Movement in China—in politics from 1300 to 1500, and **explain** how they provided both continuity and change in each society.

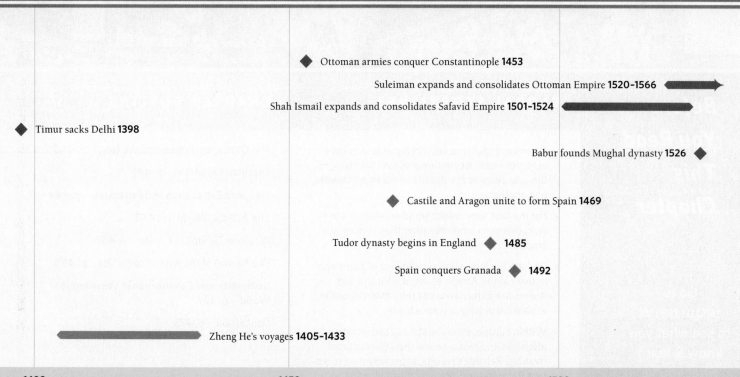

Ottoman armies conquer Constantinople **1453**

Suleiman expands and consolidates Ottoman Empire **1520-1566**

Shah Ismail expands and consolidates Safavid Empire **1501-1524**

Timur sacks Delhi **1398**

Babur founds Mughal dynasty **1526**

Castile and Aragon unite to form Spain **1469**

Tudor dynasty begins in England **1485**

Spain conquers Granada **1492**

Zheng He's voyages **1405-1433**

1400   1450   1500

Before You Read This Chapter

Go to
INQUIZITIVE
to see what you
know & learn
what you've
missed.

GLOBAL STORYLINES

- Ottoman expansion and Portuguese overseas ventures begin a complex process that changes the way peoples around the world interact with one another.

- For the first time, major world empires are oceanic, overseas empires rather than continental empires.

- Despite the long-term significance of European activity in the Americas, most Africans and Asians are barely aware of the Americas or the expansion of long-distance trade.

- Within Europe, dynastic states concentrate attention and resources on their own internal rivalries. Religious revolts, especially the Protestant Reformation, intensify those rivalries.

- Asian empires thrive in the sixteenth century, thanks to commercial expansion and political consolidation.

CHAPTER OUTLINE

12

Contact, Commerce, and Colonization, 1450–1600

FOCUS QUESTIONS

- What were the broad patterns in world trade after 1450? How were the major features of world trade in Asia, the Americas, Africa, and Europe alike and different?

- What factors enabled Europeans to increase their trade relationships with Asian empires in the fifteenth and sixteenth centuries? How significant was each factor?

- How similar and different were the practices and the impact of European explorers in Asia and the Americas?

- Within the Afro-Eurasian polities, what types of social and political relationships developed during this period? What were the sources of conflict?

- In what ways did European colonization of the Americas affect African and Amerindian peoples? How did those groups respond?

At the time of Christopher Columbus's birth in 1451, the great world power on the rise was neither Spain nor Portugal, but the Ottoman Empire. For the Ottomans, unlike the other major Asian empires, the fifteenth and sixteenth centuries marked a period of frenzied territorial expansion in the Mediterranean as well as the Indian Ocean. The Ottomans were eager to fulfill what they considered to be Islam's primary mission: world dominion. Sultans Bayezid II (r. 1481–1512), Selim I (r. 1512–1520), and Suleiman the Magnificent (r. 1520–1566) continued the conquests of Mehmed the Conqueror and led the thrust into Arab lands and the Indian Ocean even while pressing ahead in Europe. Indeed, Selim I boasted that "he was the ruler of the east and the west" (Ozbaran, p. 64).

The sultans drew on the talents of two high officials, Ibrahim Pasha, grand vizier and briefly governor of Egypt, and Piri Reis, an Ottoman admiral and arguably the age's most accomplished cartographer. Piri Reis's researches into the Indian Ocean, an area previously unknown to the Ottomans, were vital to the Ottoman entry into this region. Not only did he produce a map of the world, but in 1526 he presented to Sultan Suleiman a masterpiece of geography and cartography known as

The Book of the Sea. The book was compendious in its research, drawing on ten Arab sources as well as four Indian maps obtained from Portuguese sources and offering full information on the geography of the world. This learned cartographer had consulted one of Columbus's maps and included a chart outlining Ferdinand Magellan's circumnavigation of the globe, completed in 1522, and information on the travels of Vasco da Gama. The Ottomans by now had become a world power, and a worldly one, and their armada dwarfed that of all others at the time. It consisted of seventy-four ships, including twenty-seven large and small galleys and munitions ships, mounted with cannons. The fleet transported 20,000 men, including 6,500 janissaries.

As they turned their attention to conquest of the Red Sea, the Arabian Peninsula, and North Africa, reestablishing under their own control trade routes disrupted by the Mongols and the Black Death, the Ottomans forced others seeking shares in South and East Asian luxuries to seek new sea passages. One of these was a pesky European state known as Portugal, which was also making inroads into South Asia. Entering the Indian Ocean essentially as well-armed pirates, the Portuguese gave the Ottomans no cause for alarm. After all, it was not Ottoman territory the Portuguese were contesting, and the Ottomans, looking westward, had bigger fish to fry.

Vasco da Gama's rounding of the Cape of Good Hope in 1498 nonetheless marked a turning point in world history. His entrance into the Indian Ocean and the subsequent Portuguese attempt to establish domination over the region's strategically located port cities gave Europeans their first toeholds in Asia. When the Portuguese pulled off a major naval victory against an Ottoman attempt to take the South Asian Portuguese-controlled port city of Diu in 1538, the Ottomans lost interest in the region, leaving it to the Portuguese—and later the Spanish, Dutch, English, and French—to exploit. No one could have predicted, in 1538, that European conquests of a few South Asian trading cities were particularly significant, compared with the Ottomans' relentless annexations of large territories, including great stretches of southeastern Europe.

Even more unpredictable, though nonetheless consequential, was an accidental discovery made by the Genoese ship captain Christopher Columbus. Seeking to circumvent Ottoman power in the eastern Mediterranean, Columbus opened up a "New World" about which Afro-Eurasians had no previous knowledge. In his wake, for the first time since the Ice Age migrations, peoples again moved from Afro-Eurasian landmasses to the Americas. So did animals, plants, commercial products, and—most momentous—deadly germs. Again, the Ottomans or Chinese might have been the ones to stumble on the Americas, but they were occupied with their own massive and prosperous empires. It was the Europeans who became empire builders of a different kind, creating overseas empires that disrupted the cultures and economies of millions and transformed their own cultures and societies in the process.

Despite the significance of Europeans' activity in the Americas, most Africans and Asians, and even most peoples indigenous to the Americas, remained, for decades or even centuries, barely aware of the importance of Columbus's discovery. As the chapter demonstrates, Asian empires in Ottoman-controlled lands and in India and China continued to flourish after recovering from the Black Death, and the Ottomans continued to focus on their own conquests. Nor did most Europeans pay much attention to events in the Americas, for they were grappling with a religious revolt—the Protestant Reformation—in their own backyard. Imperial conquests, whether Ottoman or European, reshaped old worlds. But trade, both along its older Asian routes and in its linking of Europe and the Americas, was also crucial in generating both productive and volatile new cultural syntheses.

THE OLD EXPANSIONISM AND THE NEW

Ottoman expansion overland continued as European expansion overseas began. Both caused important global shifts in the organization of polities as well as in patterns of trade. The two were interconnected, as increasing Ottoman control in the eastern Mediterranean motivated Portuguese and Spanish explorers to turn toward the Atlantic in hopes of reaching the rich trading posts of China and the Indian Ocean by another route. Ottoman expansion was made possible by the Ottomans' domination of Afro-Eurasian trade routes as they recovered in the wake of the Black Death, and it was marked by the sultanate's cooptation of local elites and a relatively tolerant attitude toward other peoples and religions. It was so successful that by 1529, the Ottomans had conquered Egypt and were knocking on the doors of Vienna. But their expansionism was not endless, running up against the powerful resistance of the Shiite Safavid regime in Persia. Nor, though they were now unquestionably *the* great power in Mediterranean shipping and the Afro-Eurasian caravan trades, did Ottoman trading methods or goods change all that much. Older forms of imperial expansion and long-distance trade worked well for them, and they stuck to them.

For the Europeans, in contrast, expansion overseas was quite new and experimental. Born from a position of weakness, Portuguese and Spanish exploration and expansion benefited greatly from unexpected accidents: first, that Columbus found a "New World" rather than the "Old World" he hoped to reach, and second, tragically, that European pathogens killed or greatly weakened Amerindian populations, making conquest and settlement possible. Expansion across the Atlantic entailed, first, the military conquest of the rich empires of the Aztecs

Chinese Porcelain Bowl. *This Dutch still-life painting features an imported Chinese porcelain bowl, demonstrating Europeans' appreciation for East Asian craftsmanship as well as their dependence on long-distance trade for the acquisition of such coveted luxury goods.*

and the Incas and the scramble to locate and exploit gold and silver deposits. But the Europeans stayed, coopting some local elites but also inventing new forms of landholding and resource extraction. The importation of thousands, and then millions, of African slaves to form a new, fully subservient labor force was also a tragic and inhumane innovation that transformed both global commerce and the Atlantic ecosystem.

Both the new expansionism and the old knitted worlds together that had previously been apart or only loosely interconnected. Together they laid the foundations for a new chapter in world history. But we must not forget that even in the midst of this global transformation, the peoples of each continent continued to focus on local, and often religious, struggles closer to their everyday lives.

OTTOMAN EXPANSION

Having built the period's most powerful military forces and armed with the latest maps and scientific instruments, the Ottomans began the sixteenth century in possession of Constantinople and great swaths of southeastern Europe and Anatolia. During the sultanate of Suleiman the Magnificent (r. 1520–1566), Ottoman forces carried the empire southward into Egypt, eastward to the Iranian borderlands, and westward into Europe. By 1550, the Ottoman Empire stretched from Hungary and the Crimea in the north to the Arabian Peninsula in the south, from Morocco in the west to the contested border with Safavid Iran in the east. (See Map 12.1.)

The Multiethnic Ottoman Elite

The institutions that early sultans had established in the fifteenth century—the devshirme system involving the seizing of young recruits for service in the Ottoman military and civil bureaucracies, the rise of the janissaries in the military's front ranks, and the replacement of powerful landholding families in Anatolia with individuals of proven loyalty to the state—became more pronounced during the sixteenth, seventeenth, and eighteenth centuries. As it spread, the Ottoman Empire encountered more and more ethnic and religious groups, incorporating them into the Ottoman hierarchy. Those who were willing to serve could rise high. Of the fifteen grand viziers who held that position between 1453 and 1515, eight were drawn from Byzantine and Balkan nobility, four were from the devshirme system, and only three were of Muslim Turkish descent. Others were not forced to convert but left largely to govern their own communities, as well as to pay hefty taxes to their Turkish overlords.

Ottoman Conquests in Egypt

The conquest of Syria and Egypt in 1516–1517 was decisive in allowing Ottoman leaders to regard their Sunni state as the preeminent Muslim empire from that moment forward, even enabling some sultans to call themselves caliphs. Egypt became

The Catalan Atlas. *This 1375 map shows the world as it was then known. Not only does it depict the location of continents and islands, but it also includes information on ancient and medieval tales, regional politics, astronomy, and astrology.*

MAP 12.1 | The Ottoman Empire at the Middle of the Sixteenth Century

This map shows the expansive area controlled by the Ottoman Empire by the middle of the sixteenth century. Note the very close proximity of the Ottoman borders to the Habsburg capital of Vienna.

- What territories did the Ottomans add to their empire in the sixteenth century?
- Why did they aspire to take over Vienna, and why did they fail?
- Was the Ottoman Empire reaching its outermost limits?
- Why did the Ottomans venture so aggressively into the Red Sea and the Indian Ocean in the sixteenth century?

the Ottomans' most lucrative and important acquisition, the breadbasket of the empire and the province that provided Istanbul with the largest revenue stream. But the conquest was no easy matter. The Mamluk rulers resisted mightily, losing a bloody battle in 1516 at Marj Dabiq, north of Aleppo, after which, according to Ibn Iyas, the Arab chronicler of the age, "the battlefield was strewn with corpses and headless bodies and faces covered with dust and grown hideous." Nor did the conquest of Egypt prove any easier, for the Mamluks were determined to hold on to their most precious possession. Emotions ran high, for both sides prided themselves on being warrior states. Decapitation of enemies was common practice. In revenge for the Mamluk beheading of their fallen soldiers, the Ottoman troops plundered, raped, and killed an estimated 10,000 residents of

Cairo. The destruction, wrote Ibn Iyas, was such as "to strike terror into the hearts of man and its horrors to unhinge their reason" (Salmon, pp. 45, 111).

Ottoman Expansionism Stalls in Iran

The conquest of Constantinople and the Arab lands transformed the Ottoman Empire, creating a Muslim majority in an empire once mainly populated by conquered Christians and enabling Ottoman sultans to see themselves as heirs of a long line of empires that had ruled over these regions.

Yet on the eastern front, in conflicts with the Safavid Empire, the Ottomans encountered their earliest military failures and their most determined foe, an enemy state that plagued the Ottoman Empire until its collapse early in the eighteenth century (see Chapter 13). The Safavid state had arisen as a result of Turkic tribesmen migrating from eastern Anatolia and Azerbaijan to the Iranian plateau, where they established a zealous Shiite state (see Chapter 11). Their leaders continued to seek support and to spread their faith among the dispossessed in Ottoman-ruled Syria and Anatolia, near to the Safavid borders, and even sent agents into these areas to stir up discontent against the Ottomans. Selim II sought to defeat the Safavids, mustering a powerful force of 100,000 armed with muskets, which the Safavid force of 80,000 did not have. Selim's victory at the Battle of Chaldiran in 1514 was entirely predictable, and he had his forces sack the Safavid capital at Tabriz. His victory was short lived, however, for he could not persuade his troops to bivouac there through the harsh winter. After his troops withdrew, the Safavid rulers returned. Similar conflicts proved equally unsuccessful, failing to unseat a politically and religiously antagonist state.

In reality, the bitter conflict between Safavids and Ottomans intensified the religious commitments of both sides. The Ottomans, who had begun as a flexible ethnic and religious state dealing openly with Christian and Jewish groups and heterodox Muslims, now became the champions of Sunni Islam. By the same token, the Safavids, who had been Sufis and had migrated from eastern Anatolia, now embraced their Shiite commitments even more firmly.

The Ottomans in Europe

Blocked from further eastward expansion by the Safavids, the Ottomans were on the march westward, into Europe. Having taken Constantinople in 1453, Sultan Mehmed II took Athens in 1458 and set in motion plans to conquer Italy, though that project lapsed after his death. The Ottomans also added large swaths of Balkan territory, cutting into the Venetians' empire, and coveted commercial and naval regions in the Black Sea. The Turks then turned to North Africa and Egypt, succeeding in bringing coastal areas as well as Egypt under their dominion by 1550. This allowed them to exert more control than ever over commerce in the Mediterranean and to capture many European ships, often turning their crews into slaves or hostages for ransom, and spreading fear of "the Turk" across Christendom.

The Ottomans' encroachment into central Europe was equally terrifying for Europeans. Just at the time Martin Luther's reformers were stirring up trouble inside the Holy Roman Empire, the Turks were slicing off large sections of its easternmost territories. In the 1520s, the Ottomans seized what is today Serbia, as well as sections of Hungary, and in 1529 they threatened the Habsburg capital, Vienna. Although winter weather forced Suleiman to retreat, he ultimately took Budapest in 1541, and Turkish armies marched on into Transylvania. With little success, a series of popes sought to unite a Christendom now divided by the Reformation against the Turkish "infidels." In 1571, in a moment of rare unity, a coalition of European princes destroyed much of the Ottoman navy in the Battle of Lepanto, near the western coast of Greece. This weakened the Turkish striking force in the Mediterranean, but the Ottomans continued to dominate the area and exert control over most of southeastern Europe for centuries.

Ottoman conquests in southeastern and central Europe resulted in the subordination of Christians and Jews to Muslim rule. The Ottomans allowed minority religious communities in their provincial borderlands a large measure of self-administration. Some Turks moved into these areas, and some Christians converted to Islam, but little economic

Ottoman Attack. *In 1480, at the height of their naval strength, a huge Ottoman army besieged the island of Rhodes, one of the most prized territories held by the Venetian Republic. After a brutal battle, the Christian Hospitaller Knights, whose ships are pictured in the foreground, narrowly managed to defeat the Turkish invaders (whose tent-camp is pictured here, outside the walls of the port city of Otrano). But the Ottomans would return in 1521-1522, and this time would conquer the island.*

development occurred and most people remained poor peasants. Ottoman control, which lasted for centuries in places like Bosnia, left a multiethnic legacy, including large populations of Muslims in areas reconquered by the Habsburg Empire. Thus, the Ottomans, too, from the eastern end of the Mediterranean, became key players in the transformation of Europe's religious as well as economic and political history in the age of Da Gama and Columbus.

EUROPEAN EXPLORATION AND EXPANSION

The Muslim conquest of Constantinople and the Ottoman expansion into the Mediterranean sent shock waves through Christendom and prompted Europeans to probe unexplored links to the east. That entailed looking south and west—and venturing across the seas. (See Map 12.2.) Taking the lead were the Portuguese, whose search for new routes to Asia led them first to Africa, then the Canary Islands, and then into the Indian Ocean. Using New World silver and new military and maritime technology as their tickets to entry, the Portuguese in the fifteenth and sixteenth centuries broke into lucrative Indian Ocean networks, although they remained minor go-betweens or irksome pirates in a world still dominated by Arab, Persian, Indian, and Chinese merchants. It would be a century or more before their toeholds were firmly established.

The Portuguese in Africa and Asia

Europeans had long believed that Africa was a storehouse of precious metals. In fact, a fourteenth-century map, the Catalan Atlas, depicted a single black ruler controlling a vast quantity of gold in the interior of Africa. Thus, as the price of gold skyrocketed during and after the Black Death, ambitious men ventured southward in search of this commodity and its twin, silver. The first Portuguese sailors expected to find giants and Amazons, savages and cannibals. Sailors' stories and myths, indeed, would continue to shape their view of the places and peoples they would encounter. But the first intrepid adventurers did not allow their fears of the world they anticipated encountering to overcome their ambitions.

NAVIGATION AND MILITARY ADVANCES Innovations in maritime technology and information from Arab mariners and ancient Greek texts helped Portuguese sailors navigate the treacherous waters along the African coast. The carrack, a three- or four-masted ship, worked well on bodies of water like the Mediterranean; the caravel, with specially designed triangular sails, could nose in and out of estuaries and navigate

Caravel. *Caravels became the classic vessel for European exploration. They had many decks and plenty of portholes for cannons, could house a large crew, and had lots of storage for provisions, cargo, and booty.*

unpredictable currents and winds. By using highly maneuverable caravels and perfecting the technique of tacking (sailing into the wind rather than before it), the Portuguese advanced far along the West African coast. In addition, newfound expertise with the compass and the astrolabe helped them determine latitude. And they participated eagerly in the development of the Renaissance arts of war (see Chapter 11), adapting the new artillery technologies so that smaller cannons could be mounted on ships and used to bombard ports and rival navies—or merchant vessels.

SUGAR AND SLAVES Africa and the islands along its coast soon proved to be far more than a stop-off en route to India or a source of precious metals. Africa became a valued trading area, and its islands were prime locations for growing sugarcane—a crop that had exhausted the soils of Mediterranean islands, where it had been cultivated since the twelfth century. Along what they called the Gold Coast, the Portuguese established many fortresses and ports of call.

After seizing islands along the West African coast, the Portuguese introduced sugarcane cultivation on large plantations and exploited slave labor from the African mainland. The Madeira, Canary, and Cape Verde archipelagoes became laboratories for plantation agriculture, for their rainfall and fertile soils made them ideally suited for growing sugarcane. And because it took droves of workers to cultivate, harvest, and process sugarcane, a ready supply of slave labor enabled Portugal and Spain to build sizable plantations in their first formal colonies (regions under the political control of another country). In the 1400s, these islands saw the beginnings of a system of plantation agriculture built on slavery that would travel across the Atlantic in the following century.

COMMERCE AND CONQUEST IN THE INDIAN OCEAN

Having established plantation colonies on West Africa's outlying islands, Portuguese seafarers ventured into the Indian Ocean and inserted themselves into its thriving commerce. In Asia, Portugal never wanted to rule directly or to establish colonies. Rather, its seaborne empire adapted to local circumstances in order to exploit Asian commercial networks and trading systems.

The first Portuguese mariner to reach the Indian Ocean was Vasco da Gama (1469–1524). Like Columbus, da Gama was relatively unknown before his extraordinary voyage commanding four ships around the Cape of Good Hope at the southern tip of Africa. He explored Africa's eastern coast, and found neither savages nor impoverished lands in need of European assistance, but instead a network of commercial ties spanning the Indian Ocean, as well as skilled Muslim mariners who knew the currents, winds, and ports of call. Da Gama took on board a Muslim pilot at Malindi for instruction in navigating the Indian Ocean's winds and currents. He then sailed for the Malabar coast in southern India, one of the region's most important trading areas, arriving in 1498. Da Gama was briefly taken hostage near Calicut but was eventually allowed to leave India with a valuable cargo of spices and silks.

To the Portuguese, who traded in the name of their crown, commercial access was worth fighting for. Although da Gama lost more than half his crew on the difficult voyage back to Lisbon, he had proved the feasibility—and profitability—of trade via the Indian Ocean. When he returned to Calicut in 1502 with a larger crew, he asserted Portuguese supremacy by acting the pirate, boarding all twenty ships in the harbor and cutting off the noses, ears, and hands of their sailors. Then he burned the ships with the mutilated sailors on board. The Portuguese repeated their show of force in strategic locations, especially the three naval choke points: Aden, at the base of the Red Sea; Hormuz, in the Persian Gulf; and Melaka, at the tip of the Malay Peninsula. Once established in key ports, the Portuguese attempted to take over the trade or, failing this, to tax local merchants. Although they did not hold Aden for long, they solidified control in Sofala, Kilwa, and other important ports on the East African coast; in Goa and Calicut, in India; and in Macao, in southern China. From these strongholds, the Portuguese soon commanded the most active sea-lanes of the Indian Ocean. (See again Map 12.2; see also Primary Source: Portuguese Views of the Chinese.)

The Portuguese did not seek to interrupt the flow of luxuries among Asian and African elites in the Indian Ocean; rather, their naval captains simply kept a portion of the profits for themselves. The Portuguese introduced a pass system that required ships to pay for *cartazes*—documents identifying the ship's captain, size of the ship and crew, and its cargo. The Portuguese were unable to impose this system on Indian Ocean rulers and powerful merchants, but minor players and outsiders calculated it was cheaper to pay what were essentially bribes rather than risk losses at sea from the Portuguese fleet. The Portuguese were also active in the spice trade, and Lisbon gradually eclipsed Italian ports, such as Venice, that had previously been prime entrepôts (commercial hubs for long-distance trade) for Asian goods. But they found it even more lucrative to enter the spice trade *within* the Indian Ocean world, where there were wealthier customers to serve. Only with the discovery of the Americas and the conquest of Brazil did Portugal become an empire with large overseas colonies. For this to transpire, mariners would have to traverse the Atlantic Ocean itself.

THE ATLANTIC WORLD

Crossing the Atlantic was a feat of monumental importance in world history. It did not occur, however, with an aim to discover new lands. Columbus had wanted to voyage into the "Ocean Sea" so as to open a more direct—and more lucrative—route to Japan and China. Fired by their victory at Granada, Ferdinand and Isabella had agreed to finance his trip, hoping for riches to bankroll a crusade to liberate Jerusalem from Muslim hands. Just as Columbus had no idea he would find a "New World," Spain's monarchs (not to mention its merchants, missionaries, and soldiers) never dreamed that soon they would be preparing for conquest and profiteering in what had been, just a few years before, a blank space on their maps. (Thus the term *New World*, as applied to the Americas, reflects the Europeans' view that anything previously unknown to them was "new," even if it had existed and supported societies long before European explorers arrived on its shores.)

Columbus's voyages, in opening new sea-lanes in the Atlantic, set the stage for an epochal transformation in world history. As news of his voyages spread through Europe, ambitious mariners prepared to sail west. European rivalries, for trade and prestige, sharpened. By 1550, many of Europe's powers were scrambling, not just for a share of Indian Ocean action but also for spoils from the Atlantic.

But the opening of new trade routes for Europeans was less important for world history than the biological consequences of the first contacts between Europeans and Amerindians. In Africa and Asia, long-standing patterns of trade had yielded the development of shared immunities. But Amerindian populations, in

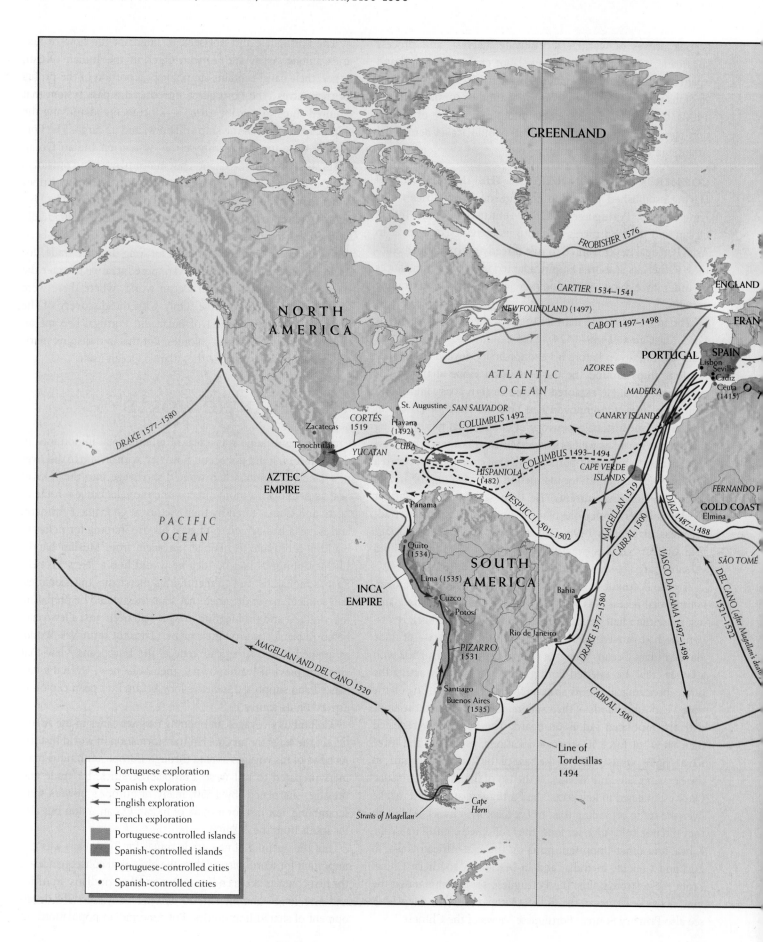

GREENLAND

FROBISHER 1576

CARTIER 1534–1541

NEWFOUNDLAND (1497)

CABOT 1497–1498

ENGLAND

FRAN

NORTH AMERICA

PORTUGAL SPAIN

Lisbon
Seville
Cadiz
Ceuta (1415)

ATLANTIC OCEAN

AZORES

MADEIRA

CANARY ISLANDS

COLUMBUS 1492

St. Augustine SAN SALVADOR

CORTÉS 1519

Zacatecas

Havana (1492)

Tenochtitlán

YUCATAN CUBA

AZTEC EMPIRE

HISPANIOLA (1482)

COLUMBUS 1493–1494

CAPE VERDE ISLANDS

FERNANDO P

GOLD COAST

Elmina

DRAKE 1577–1580

PACIFIC OCEAN

Panama

VESPUCCI 1501–1502

MAGELLAN 1519

CABRAL 1500

DÍAZ 1487–1488

VASCO DA GAMA 1497–1498

SÃO TOMÉ

DEL CANO 1521–1522 (after Magellan's death)

Quito (1534)

SOUTH AMERICA

Lima (1535)

INCA EMPIRE

Cuzco

Potosí

Bahia

Rio de Janeiro

DRAKE 1577–1580

MAGELLAN AND DEL CANO 1520

PIZARRO 1531

CABRAL 1500

Santiago

Buenos Aires (1535)

Line of Tordesillas 1494

Cape Horn

Straits of Magellan

→ Portuguese exploration
→ Spanish exploration
→ English exploration
→ French exploration
▇ Portuguese-controlled islands
▇ Spanish-controlled islands
• Portuguese-controlled cities
• Spanish-controlled cities

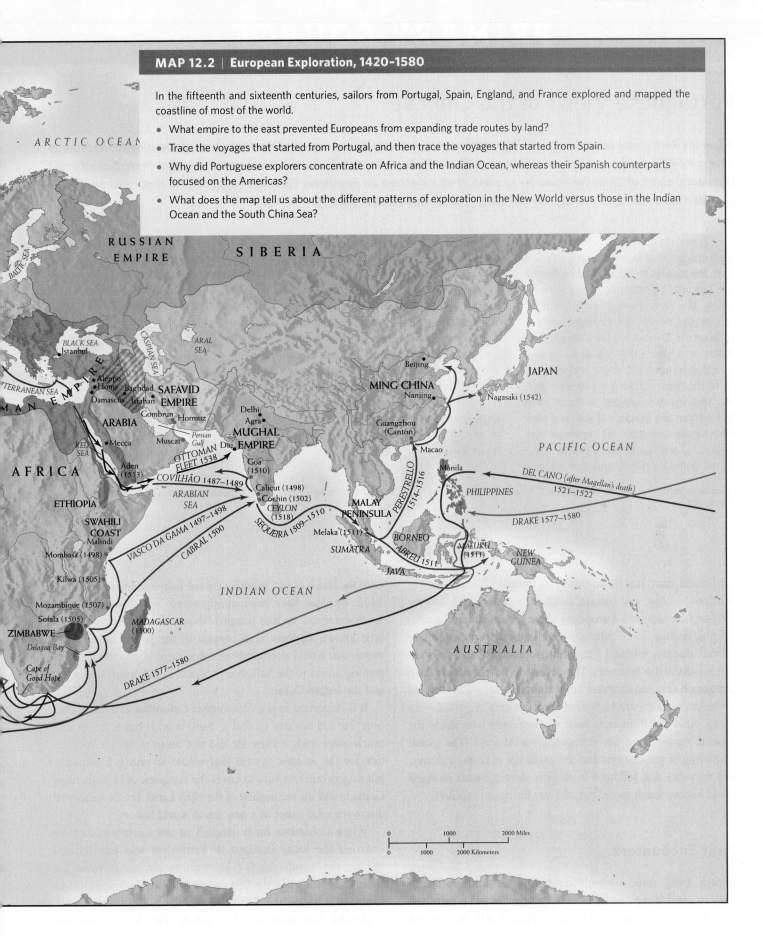

MAP 12.2 | European Exploration, 1420–1580

In the fifteenth and sixteenth centuries, sailors from Portugal, Spain, England, and France explored and mapped the coastline of most of the world.

- What empire to the east prevented Europeans from expanding trade routes by land?
- Trace the voyages that started from Portugal, and then trace the voyages that started from Spain.
- Why did Portuguese explorers concentrate on Africa and the Indian Ocean, whereas their Spanish counterparts focused on the Americas?
- What does the map tell us about the different patterns of exploration in the New World versus those in the Indian Ocean and the South China Sea?

PRIMARY SOURCE

Portuguese Views of the Chinese

When the Portuguese arrived in China, they encountered an empire whose organizational structure and ideological orientation were quite different from their own. Written in 1517, this Portuguese report reflects misrepresentations that characterized many Europeans' views of China for centuries to come. It also signaled an aggressive European expansionism that celebrated brute force as a legitimate means to destroy and conquer those who stood in the way.

God grant that these Chinese may be fools enough to lose the country; because up to the present they have had no dominion, but little by little they have gone on taking the land from their neighbors; and for this reason the kingdom is great, because the Chinese are full of much cowardice, and hence they come to be presumptuous, arrogant, cruel; and because up to the present, being a cowardly people, they have managed without arms and without any practice of war, and have always gone on getting the land from their neighbors, and not by force but by stratagems and deceptions; and they imagine that no one can do them harm. They call every foreigner a savage; and their country they call the kingdom of God.

Whoever shall come now, let it be a captain with a fleet of ten or fifteen sail. The first thing will be to destroy the fleet if they should have one, which I believe they have not; let it be by fire and blood and cruel fear for this day, without sparing the life of a single person, every junk being burnt, and no one being taken prisoner, in order not to waste the provisions, because at all times a hundred Chinese will be found for one Portuguese.

Source: *Letters from Canton,* translated and edited by D. Ferguson, *The Indian Antiquary* 31 (January 1902), in J. H. Parry, *European Reconnaissance: Selected Documents* (New York: Walker, 1968), p. 140.

QUESTIONS FOR ANALYSIS

- What do you think was the main purpose of this report?
- How could this observer's views be so inaccurate?
- What is the irony in the comment "They call every foreigner a savage," followed by instructions to destroy, burn, and not spare "the life of a single person"?

---

their world apart, had no immunity for Eurasian diseases such as smallpox, typhus, and cholera; in a few short decades following their first contact with Europeans, these groups suffered a catastrophic decline. More than any other factor, the spread of "Old World" diseases allowed Europeans to conquer and colonize vast swaths of the Americas. The devastation of the Amerindian population resulted in severe labor shortages, which in turn led to the large-scale introduction of slave laborers imported from Africa. After 1500, in fact, most of the people who made the Atlantic voyage were not Europeans but Africans. The global reordering of populations and the exchange of crops, cultures, and microbes that followed from these developments changed world history much more than did any European explorer.

First Encounters

In early 1492, three modestly sized ships set sail from Spain. They stopped in the Canary Islands for supplies and repairs and cast off into the unknown. When the expedition leader stepped onto the beach of San Salvador (in the Bahamas) on October 12, 1492, he must have been disappointed: where were the rich Asian entrepôts he had sought? This leader, an ambitious but little-known Genoese ship captain in the pay of the Spanish monarchs, would attempt three subsequent voyages in hopes of gaining access to the valuable products of the South China Sea and the Indian Ocean.

It is important to see Christopher Columbus as a man of his time. He did not aim to find a "New World" but to break into much older trade routes. He did not mean to lay the foundation for the Atlantic system that would so enrich Europeans, but to generate revenues to cover the conquest of Muslim-ruled Granada and the reconquest of the Holy Land. Yet his accidental discoveries did usher in a new era in world history.

When Columbus made landfall in the Caribbean Sea, he unfurled the royal standard of Ferdinand and Isabella and claimed the "many islands filled with people innumerable" for Spain. It is fitting that the first encounter with Caribbean inhabitants, in this case the Tainos, drew blood. Columbus noted, "I showed them swords and they took them by the edge and

Columbus. *As Columbus made landfall and encountered Indians, he planted a cross to indicate the spiritual purpose of the voyage and read aloud a document proclaiming the sovereign authority of the king and queen of Spain. Quickly, he learned that the Spanish could barter for precious stones and metals.*

through ignorance cut themselves." The Tainos had their own weapons but did not forge steel and thus had no knowledge of such sharp edges.

For Columbus, the Tainos' naivety in grabbing his sword symbolized the childlike primitivism of these people, whom he would mislabel "Indians" because he thought he had arrived off the coast of Asia. In Columbus's view, the Tainos had no religion, but they did have at least some gold (found initially hanging as pendants from their noses). Likewise, Pedro Alvares Cabral, a Portuguese mariner whose trip down the coast of Africa in 1500 was blown off course across the Atlantic, wrote that the people of Brazil had all "the innocence of Adam." He also noted that they were ripe for conversion and that the soils "if rightly cultivated would yield everything." But, as with Africans and Asians, Europeans also developed a contradictory view of the peoples of the Americas. From the Tainos, Columbus learned of another people, the Caribs, who (according to his informants) were savage, warlike cannibals. For centuries, these contrasting images—innocents and savages—structured European (mis)understandings of the native peoples of the Americas.

We know less about what the Indians thought of Columbus or other Europeans on their first encounters. Certainly, the Europeans' appearance and technologies inspired awe. The Tainos fled into the forest at the approach of European ships, which they thought were giant monsters; others thought they were floating islands. European metal goods, especially weaponry, struck them as otherworldly. The strangely dressed white

men seemed godlike to some, although many Indians soon abandoned this view. The Amerindians found the newcomers different not for their skin color (only Europeans drew the distinction based on skin pigmentation) but for their hairiness. Indeed, the Europeans' beards, breath, and bad manners repulsed their Indian hosts. The newcomers' inability to live off the land also stood out.

In due course, the Indians realized that the strange, hairy people bearing metal weapons meant to stay and force the Amerindian population to labor for them. But by then it was too late. The explorers had become **conquistadors** (conquerors).

First Conquests

First contacts between peoples gave way to dramatic conquests in the Americas. After his first voyage, Columbus claimed that on Hispaniola (present-day Haiti and the Dominican Republic) "he had found what he was looking for"—gold. That was sufficient to persuade the Spanish crown to invest in larger expeditions and to seek to conquer this promising new territory. Whereas Columbus first sailed with three small ships and 87 men, ten years later the Spanish outfitted an expedition with 2,500 men. Exploration now yielded to warfare and exploitation.

Between 1492 and 1519, the Spanish conquerors of Hispaniola experimented with institutions of colonial rule over local populations. Ultimately, they created a model that the rest of the New World colonies would adapt. But the Spaniards faced Indian resistance. As early as 1494, starving Spaniards raided and pillaged Indian villages. When the Indians revolted, Spanish soldiers replied with punitive expeditions and began enslaving them to work in mines extracting gold. As the crown systematized grants (*encomiendas*) to the conquistadors for control over Indian labor, a rich class of **encomenderos** arose who enjoyed the fruits of the system. Although the placer gold mines soon ran dry, the model of granting favored settlers the right to coerce Indian labor endured. In return, those who received the labor rights paid special taxes on the precious metals that were extracted. Thus, both the crown and the *encomenderos* benefited from the extractive economy. The same cannot be said of the Amerindians, who perished in great numbers from disease, dislocation, malnutrition, and overwork.

Not all Europeans celebrated the pillaging. Dominican friars protested the abuse of the Indians, seeing them as potential converts who were equal to the Spaniards in the eyes of God. In 1511, Father Antonio Montesinos accused the settlers of barbarity: "By what right and with what justice do you keep these poor Indians in such cruel and horrible servitude?" Dissent and debate would be a permanent feature of Spanish colonialism in the New World.

The Aztec Empire and the Spanish Conquest

As Spanish colonists saw the bounty of Hispaniola dry up, they set out to discover and conquer new territories. Finding their way to the mainlands of the American landmasses, they encountered larger, more complex, and more militarized societies than those they had overrun in the Caribbean.

On the mainland, great civilizations had arisen centuries before, boasting large cities, monumental buildings, and riches based on wealthy agrarian societies. In both Mesoamerica, starting with the Olmecs (see Chapter 5), and the Andes, starting with the Chimú (see Chapter 10), large polities had laid the foundations for subsequent Aztec and Inca Empires. These empires were powerful. But they also represented the evolution of states and commercial systems untouched by Afro-Eurasian developments; as worlds apart, they were unprepared for the kind of assaults that European invaders had perfected. In pre-Columbian Mesoamerica and then the Andes, warfare was more ceremonial, less inclined to wipe out enemies than to make them tributary subjects. As a result, the wealth of these empires made them irresistible to outside conquerors, whose habits of war they could never have foreseen.

AZTEC SOCIETY In Mesoamerica, the ascendant Mexicas had created an empire known to us as Aztec. Around Lake Texcoco, Mexica cities grew and formed a three-city league in 1430, which then expanded through the valley of central Mexico to incorporate neighboring peoples. Gradually, the **Aztec Empire** united numerous small, independent states under a single monarch who ruled with the help of counselors, military leaders, and priests. By the late fifteenth century, the Aztec realm may have embraced 25 million people. Tenochtitlán, the primary city, situated on an immense island in Lake Texcoco, ranked among the world's largest.

Tenochtitlán spread in concentric circles, with the main religious and political buildings in the center and residences radiating outward. The city's outskirts connected a mosaic of floating gardens producing food for urban markets. As the city grew, clan-like networks evolved, and powerful families married their children to each other or found nuptial partners among the prominent families of other important cities. (Certain ruling houses in Europe were solidifying alliances in much the same way at this time; see Chapter 11.) Not only did this practice concentrate power in the great city, but it also ensured a pool of potential successors to the throne. Soon a lineage emerged to create a corps of "natural" rulers.

Holding this stratified order together was a shared understanding of the cosmos. But unlike European and most Asian cosmologies, Aztecs saw the natural order as intrinsically unstable. They believed that the universe was prone to recurring

Tenochtitlán. *At its height, the Aztec capital, Tenochtitlán, was as populous as Europe's largest city. As can be seen from this map, it spread in concentric circles, with the main religious and political buildings in the center and residences radiating outward.*

cycles of disaster that would eventually end in apocalypse. Such an unstable cosmos exposed mortals to repeated creations and destructions of their world. It was the priesthood's job to balance a belief that history was destined to run in cycles with a faith that mortals could influence the gods, and their own fate, through religious rituals. These rituals also legitimized the Aztec power structure by portraying the emperor and the elite as closer to the gods than the lower orders.

Ultimately, Aztec power spread through much of Mesoamerica, but the empire's constant wars and conquests deprived it of stability. In successive military campaigns, the Aztecs subjugated their neighbors, feeding off plunder and then forcing subject peoples to pay tribute of crops, gold, silver, textiles, and other goods that financed Aztec grandeur. Such conquests also provided a constant supply of humans for sacrifice, because the Aztecs believed that the great god of the sun required human hearts to keep on burning and blood to replace that given by the gods to moisten the earth through rain. Priests escorted captured warriors up the temple steps and tore out their hearts, offering their lives and blood as a sacrifice to the sun god. Allegedly, between 20,000 and 80,000 men, women, and children were slaughtered in a single ceremony in 1487, with the four-person-wide line of victims stretching for over two miles. In this marathon of bloodletting, knife-wielding priests collapsed from exhaustion and surrendered their places to fresh executioners.

Those whom the Aztecs sought to dominate did not submit peacefully. From 1440, the empire faced constant turmoil as subject peoples resented Aztec domination, and independent peoples—such as the Tlaxcalans to the east and Tarascans (or Purépecha) to the west—waged war to preserve their independence and fiercely resisted incorporation into the Aztec's tributary empire. To pacify the realm, the Aztecs diverted more and more men and money into a mushrooming military. By the time the electoral committee chose Moctezuma II as emperor in 1502, divisions among elites and pressures from the periphery placed the Aztec Empire under extreme stress.

CORTÉS AND CONQUEST Not long after Moctezuma became emperor, news arrived from the coast of strange

sightings of floating mountains (ships) bearing pale, bearded men and monsters (horses and dogs). Moctezuma consulted with his ministers and soothsayers, wondering if these men were the god Quetzalcóatl and his entourage. The people of Tenochtitlán saw omens of impending disaster. Moctezuma sank into despair, hesitating over what to do. He sent emissaries bearing jewels and prized feathers; later he sent sorcerers to confuse and bewitch the newcomers. But he did not prepare for any military engagement. After all, Mesoamericans had no idea of the interlopers' destructive potential in weaponry and germs.

Aboard one of the ships was Hernán Cortés (1485–1547), a former law student from one of the Spanish provinces. He would become the conquistador that all subsequent conquerors tried to emulate, just as Columbus was the model explorer. For a brief time, Cortés was an *encomendero* in Hispaniola; but when news arrived of a potentially wealthier land to the west, he set sail with over 500 men, eleven ships, sixteen horses, and artillery.

When the expedition arrived near present-day Veracruz, Cortés acquired two translators, including the daughter of a local Indian noble family. The daughter, who became known as Doña Marina, was a "gift" to the triumphant Spaniards from the ruler of the Tabasco region (a rival to the Aztecs). Fluent in several languages, Doña Marina displayed such linguistic skills and personal charm that she soon became Cortés's lover and

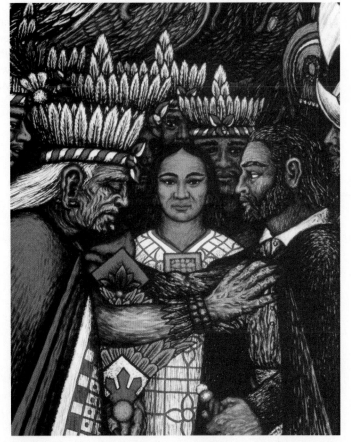

Cortés Meets Mesoamerican Rulers. Left: *This colonial image depicts the meeting of Cortés (second from right) and Moctezuma (seated on the left), with Doña Marina serving as an interpreter and informer for the Spanish conquistador. Notice at the bottom what are likely Aztec offerings for the newcomer.* Right: *This detail from a twentieth-century Mexican mural depicts the meeting of Cortés and the king of Tlaxcala (enemy of the Aztecs). As Mexicans began to celebrate their mixed-blood heritage, Doña Marina (in the middle) became the symbolic mother of the first mestizos.*

Cortés Approaches Tenochtitlán

When the Spanish conquered the Aztec Empire, they defeated a mighty power. The capital, Tenochtitlán, was probably the same size as Europe's biggest city. Glimpsing Tenochtitlán in 1521, Hernán Cortés marveled at its magnificence. But to justify his acts, he claimed to be bringing civilization and Christianity to the Aztecs. Note the contrast between Cortés's admiration for Tenochtitlán and his condemnation of Indian beliefs and practices—as well as his claim that he abolished cannibalism, something the Aztecs did not practice (although they did sacrifice humans).

This great city of Tenochtitlán is built on the salt lake. . . . It has four approaches by means of artificial causeways. . . . The city is as large as Seville or Cordoba. Its streets . . . are very broad and straight, some of these, and all the others, are one half land, and the other half water on which they go about in canoes. . . . There are bridges, very large, strong, and well constructed, so that, over many, ten horsemen can ride abreast. . . . The city has many squares where markets are held. . . . There is one square, twice as large as that of Salamanca, all surrounded by arcades, where there are daily more than sixty thousand souls, buying and selling. . . . [I]n the service and manners of its people, their fashion of living was almost the same as in Spain, with just as much harmony and order; and considering that these people were barbarous, so cut

off from the knowledge of God and other civilized peoples, it is admirable to see to what they attained in every respect. . . .

It happened . . . that a Spaniard saw an Indian . . . eating a piece of flesh taken from the body of an Indian who had been killed. . . . I had the culprit burned, explaining that the cause was his having killed that Indian and eaten him, which was prohibited by Your Majesty, and by me in Your Royal name. I further made the chief understand that all the people . . . must abstain from this custom. . . . I came . . . to protect their lives as well as their property, and to teach them that they were to adore but one God . . . that they must turn from their idols, and the rites they had practised until then, for these were lies and deceptions which the devil . . . had invented. . . . I, likewise, had come to teach them that Your Majesty, by the will of

Divine Providence, rules the universe, and that they also must submit themselves to the imperial yoke, and do all that we who are Your Majesty's ministers here might order them. . . .

QUESTIONS FOR ANALYSIS

- What does Cortés's report tell us about the city of Tenochtitlán?
- Why does Cortés justify his actions to the degree that he does?
- Cortés writes, "I came . . . to protect their lives as well as their property." Based on your reading of the chapter text, would you say he accomplished these objectives?

Source: Letters of Cortés, translated by Francis A. MacNutt (New York: G. P. Putnam, 1908), pp. 244, 256–57.

ultimately revealed several Aztec plots against the tiny Spanish force. Doña Marina subsequently bore Cortés a son, who is considered one of the first mixed-blooded Mexicans (mestizos).

With the assistance of Doña Marina and other native allies, Cortés marched his troops to Tenochtitlán. Upon entering, he gasped in wonder that "this city is so big and so remarkable" that it was "almost unbelievable." In a letter home, one of his soldiers wrote, "It was all so wonderful that I do not know how to describe this first glimpse of things never heard of, seen or dreamed of before."

How was this tiny force to overcome an empire of many millions with an elaborate warring tradition? Crucial to Spanish conquest was their alliance, negotiated through translators, with Moctezuma's enemies—especially the Tlaxcalans. After decades of yearning for release from the Aztec yoke, the Tlaxcalans and

other Mesoamerican peoples embraced Cortés's promise of help. The Spaniards' second advantage was their method of warfare. The Aztecs were seasoned fighters, but they fought to capture, not to kill. Nor were they familiar with gunpowder or sharp steel swords. Although outnumbered, the Spaniards killed their foe with abandon, using superior weaponry, horses, and war dogs. The Aztecs, still unsure who these strange men were, allowed Cortés to enter their city. With the aid of the Tlaxcalans and a handful of his own men, in 1519 Cortés captured Moctezuma, who became a puppet of the Spanish conqueror. (See Primary Source: Cortés Approaches Tenochtitlán.)

Within two years, the Aztecs realized that the newcomers were not gods, and they staged an uprising that forced Cortés to retreat and regroup. This time, with the Tlaxcalans' help, he chose to defeat the Aztecs completely. He ordered the building

The Conquest of the Aztecs. *Diego Rivera's twentieth-century representation of the fall of Tenochtitlán (left) emphasizes the helplessness of the Aztecs to the ruthless and technologically superior Spanish soldiers. Though the Aztecs outnumber the Spanish in this portrayal, their faces are obscured in postures of grief and suffering, unlike their counterparts in the sixteenth-century illustration of the same event (right). Painted by a converted Indian and based on indigenous oral histories, it shows the Aztec warriors in a glory of their own, as well as the cruel fact that they were forced to fight other Indians who had sided with the Spanish.*

of boats to sail across Lake Texcoco to bombard the capital with artillery. Even more devastating was the spread of smallpox, brought by the Spanish, which ran through the soldiers and commoners like wildfire. The total number of Aztec casualties may have reached 240,000. As Spanish troops retook the capital, they found it in ruins, with a population too weak to resist. The last emperor, Cuauhtémoc, himself faced execution, thereby ending the royal Mexica lineage. The Aztecs lamented their defeat in verse: "We have pounded our hands in despair against the adobe walls, for our inheritance, our city, is lost and dead." Cortés became governor of the new Spanish colony, renamed "New Spain." He promptly allocated *encomiendas* to his loyal followers and dispatched expeditions to conquer the more distant Mesoamerican provinces.

The Mexica experience taught the Spanish an important lesson: an effective conquest had to be swift—and it had to remove completely the symbols of legitimate authority. Their winning advantage, however, was disease. The Spaniards unintentionally introduced germs that made their subsequent efforts at military conquest much easier.

The Incas

The other great Spanish conquest occurred in the Andes, where Quechua-speaking rulers, called Incas, had established an impressive polity. By the mid-fifteenth century, the **Inca Empire**

controlled a vast domain incorporating 4 to 6 million people and running from what is now Chile to southern Colombia. At its center was the capital, Cuzco, with the magnificent fortress of Sacsayhuaman as its head. Built of huge boulders, the citadel was the nerve center of a complex network of strongholds that held the empire together.

Disease and Decimation of Indians. *The real conqueror of Native Americans was not so much guns as germs. Even before Spanish soldiers seized the Aztec capital, germs had begun decimating the population. The first big killer was smallpox, recorded here by an Indian artist.*

Pizarro and the Incas. *This illustration is by the Andean native Guaman Poma, whose circa 1587 epic of the conquest of Peru depicted many of the barbarities of the Spanish. Here we see the conquistador Pizarro and a Catholic priest appealing to Atahualpa—before betraying and then killing him.*

But the Incas were internally split. Lacking a clear inheritance system, the empire suffered repeated convulsions. In the early sixteenth century, the struggle over who would succeed Huayna Capac, the ruler, was especially fierce. Huáscar, his "official" son, took Cuzco (the capital), while Atahualpa, his favored son, governed the province of present-day Ecuador. Open conflict might have been averted were it not for Huayna's premature death. His killer was probably smallpox, which swept down the trade routes from Mesoamerica into the Andes (much as the bubonic plague had earlier spread through Afro-Eurasian trade routes; see Chapter 11). With the father gone, Atahualpa declared war on his brother, crushed him, forced him to witness the execution of all his supporters, and then killed him and used his skull as a vessel for maize beer.

When the Spaniards arrived in 1532, they wandered into an internally divided empire, a situation they quickly learned to exploit. Francisco Pizarro, who led the Spanish campaign, had been inspired by Cortés's victory and yearned for his own glory. Commanding a force of about 600 men, he invited Atahualpa to confer at the town of Cajamarca. There he laid a trap.

As columns of Inca warriors and servants covered with colorful plumage and plates of silver and gold entered the main square, the Spanish soldiers were awed. Writing home, one recalled, "many of us urinated without noticing it, out of sheer terror." But Pizarro's plan worked. His guns and horses shocked the Inca forces. Atahualpa himself fell into Spanish hands, later to be decapitated. Pizarro's conquistadors overran Cuzco in 1533 and then vanquished the rest of the Inca forces, a process that took decades in some areas.

Silver

For the first Europeans in the Americas, the foremost measure of success was the gold and silver that they could hoard for themselves and their monarchs. But in plundering massive amounts of silver, the conquistadors introduced it to the world's commercial systems, an act that electrified them. In the twenty years after the fall of Tenochtitlán, conquistadors took more precious metals from Mexico and the Andes than all the gold accumulated by Europeans over the previous centuries. (See Map 12.6 on p. 469.)

Having looted Indian coffers, the Spanish entered the business of mining directly, opening the Andean Potosí mines in 1545. Between 1560 and 1685, Spanish America sent 25,000 to 35,000 tons of silver annually to Spain. From 1685 to 1810, this sum doubled. The two mother lodes were Potosí, in present-day Bolivia, and Zacatecas, in northern Mexico. Silver brought bounty not only to the crown but also to privileged families based in Spain's colonial capitals; thus, private wealth funded the formation of local aristocracies.

Silver. *Silver was an important discovery for Spanish conquerors in Mesoamerica and the Andes. Conquerors expanded the custom of Inca and Aztec labor drafts to force the natives to work in mines, often in brutal conditions.*

PRIMARY SOURCE

Silver, the Devil, and Coca Leaf in the Andes

When Spanish colonists forced thousands of Andean Indians to work in the silver mines of Potosí, they permitted the chewing of coca leaves (which are now used to extract cocaine). Chewing the leaves gave Indians a mild "high," alleviated their hunger, and blunted the pain of hard work and deteriorating lungs. The habit also spread to some Spaniards. In this document, Bartolomé Arzáns de Orsúa y Vela, a Spaniard born in Potosí in 1676, expresses how important coca was to Indian miners and how harmful it was for Spaniards who fell under its spell. By the time the author wrote his observations in the late seventeenth century, the use of the coca leaf had become widespread.

I wish to declare the unhappiness and great evil that, among so many felicities, this kingdom of Peru experiences in possessing the coca herb. . . . No Indian will go into the mines or to any other labor, be it building houses or working in the fields, without taking it in his mouth, even if his life depends on it. . . .

Among the Indians (and even the Spaniards by now) the custom of not entering the mines without placing this herb in the mouth is so well established that there is a superstition that the richness of the metal will be lost if they do not do so. . . .

The Indians being accustomed to taking this herb into their mouths, there is no doubt that as long as they have it there they lose all desire to sleep, and since it is extremely warming, they say that when the weather is cold they do not feel it if they have the herb in their mouths. In addition, they also say that it increases their strength and that they feel neither hunger nor thirst; hence these Indians cannot work without it.

When the herb is ground and placed in boiling water and if a person then takes a few swallows, it opens the pores, warms the body, and shortens labor in women; and this coca herb has many other virtues besides. But human perversity has caused it to become a vice, so that the devil (that inventor of vices) has made a notable harvest of souls with it, for there are many women who have taken it—and still take it—for the sin of witchcraft, invoking the devil and using it to summon him for their evil deeds. . . .

With such ferocity has the devil seized on this coca herb that—there is no doubt about it—when it becomes an addiction it impairs or destroys the judgment of its users just as if they had drunk wine to excess and makes them see terrible visions; demons appear before their eyes in frightful forms. In this city of Potosí it is sold publicly by the Indians who work in the mines, and so the harm arising from its continued abundance cannot be corrected; but neither is that harm remediable in other large cities of this realm, where the use and sale of coca have been banned under penalties as severe as that of excommunication and yet it is secretly bought and sold and used for casting spells and other like evils.

Would that our lord the king had ordered this noxious herb pulled up by the roots wherever it is found. . . . Great good would follow were it to be extirpated from this realm: the devil would be bereft of the great harvest of souls he reaps, God would be done a great service, and vast numbers of men and women would not perish (I refer to Spaniards, for no harm comes to the Indians from it).

QUESTIONS FOR ANALYSIS

- Why would the Spaniards ban the sale of the coca herb everywhere except Potosí?
- Why would Bartolomé believe that no harm would come to the Indians for taking the coca herb?
- How does this document reveal the central role of the Catholic Church in Spanish colonial thinking? Find several words and phrases that express this outlook.

Source: Bartolomé Arzáns de Orsúa y Vela, "Claudia the Witch," in *Tales of Potosí,* edited by R. C. Padden. Trans. Morillas F. M. López (Providence, NH: Brown University Press, 1975), pp. 117–121.

Colonial mines epitomized the Atlantic world's new economy. They relied on an extensive network of Indian labor, at first enslaved, subsequently drafted. Here again, the Spanish adopted Inca and Aztec practices of requiring labor from subjugated villages: each year, village elders selected a stipulated number of men to toil in the shafts, refineries, and smelters. Under the Spanish, the digging, hauling, and smelting taxed human limits to their capacity—and beyond. Those unfortunate enough to be sent underground pounded the rock walls with chisels and hammers, releasing silicon dust. Miners could not help but breathe in the toxic dust, which created lesions and made simply inhaling seem like swallowing broken glass. (See Primary Source: Silver, the Devil, and Coca Leaf in the Andes.) Mortality rates were appalling. But the miners' sufferings reaped huge profits and significant consequences for the Europeans. The Spanish pumped so much New World silver into global commercial networks that they caused painful price inflation in Europe and transformed Europe's relationship to all its trading partners, especially those in China and India. (For more on Spain's tributary empire in the New World, see p. 468.)

The defeat of the New World's two great empires gave Europeans the means to extract human and material wealth from the Americas. In time, as Europeans settled in to stay, it also gave Europeans a market for their own products—goods that found little favor in Afro-Eurasia—and opened a new frontier that the Europeans could colonize as staple-producing provinces. At first, however, most Europeans took little notice of the Atlantic frontiers opening before them. They were, after all, embroiled in a continent-wide series of religious and political conflicts that would divide Christendom itself, as it turns out, forever.

RELIGIOUS TURMOIL IN EUROPE

In the sixteenth century, most European rulers and their subjects were focused on Europe or on Ottoman threats to the east, and not on the New World to their west. Their lives and belief systems were being turned upside down by the religious split within the Catholic Church known as the Reformation and by the wars that followed it. Religious fragmentation exacerbated already-existing dynastic rivalries and encouraged states to further centralize their bureaucracies and build up their military forces. Some of those military forces had to be used to keep the Ottomans at bay, for in this period, as we have seen, the Ottomans were making significant inroads into eastern and southern Europe.

The Reformation

Like the Renaissance, the **Protestant Reformation** in Europe began as a movement devoted to returning to ancient sources—in this case, to biblical scriptures. But it was also provoked by long-simmering dissatisfaction with the Catholic Church that came from below. Long before Martin Luther came on the scene, some scholars and believers had despaired of the church's ability to satisfy their longings for deeper, more individualized religious experience. In the fourteenth and fifteenth centuries, the church hierarchy continued to oppose reforms such as allowing laypersons to read the scriptures for themselves, as it feared heresies and challenges to its authority would arise. The church was right: for when political circumstances and the arrival of the printing press permitted Luther to avoid a heretic's death and to expand the campaign for

reform, he paved the way for a "Protestant" Reformation that split Christendom for good.

MARTIN LUTHER CHALLENGES THE CHURCH The opening challenge to the authority of the pope and the Catholic Church originated in the **Holy Roman Empire**, the sprawling, loosely centralized, multiethnic empire that covered much of central and eastern Europe. When the Reformation commenced, the Holy Roman Empire was under the rule of the Habsburg prince Charles V, who inherited three great kingdoms: that of Spanish monarchs Isabella and Ferdinand (including their New World holdings), that of Holy Roman Emperor Maximilian I (in central Europe), and that of Burgundy and the Netherlands. Charles's transatlantic empire, although larger than any before or since, was not destined to last. By the time of his death (1556), it had been shattered, largely by the ideas of a stubborn and rhetorically gifted professor of theology named **Martin Luther** (1483–1546).

Initially a pious Catholic believer, Luther nonetheless believed that mortals were so given to sin that none would ever be worthy of salvation. In 1516, Luther found an answer to his quest for salvation in reading Paul's Letters to the Romans: since no human acts could be sufficient to earn admittance to heaven, individuals could only be saved by their faith in God's grace. God's free gift of forgiveness, Luther believed, did not depend on taking sacraments or performing good deeds. This faith, moreover, was something Christians could obtain just from reading the Bible—rather than by having a priest tell them what to believe. Finally, Luther concluded that Christians did not need mediators to speak to God for them; all were, in his eyes, priests, equally bound by God's laws and obliged to minister to one another's spiritual needs.

These became the three main principles that launched Luther's reforming efforts: (1) belief that faith alone saves, (2) belief that the scriptures alone hold the key to Christian truth, and (3) belief in the priesthood of all believers. But other things motivated Luther as well: corrupt practices in the church, such as the keeping of mistresses by monks, priests, and even popes; and the selling of indulgences, certificates that would supposedly shorten the buyer's time in purgatory. In the 1510s, clerics were hawking indulgences across Europe in an effort to raise money for the sumptuous new Saint Peter's Basilica in Rome.

In 1517, Luther formulated ninety-five statements, or theses, and posted them on the doors to the Wittenberg cathedral, hoping to stir up his colleagues in debate. Before long, his theses made him famous—and bolder in his criticisms. In a widely circulated pamphlet called *On the Freedom of the Christian Man* (1520), he upbraided "the Roman Church, which in past ages was the holiest of all" for having "become a den of murderers beyond all other dens of murderers, a thieves' castle beyond all other thieves' castles, the head and empire of every sin, as well as of death and damnation." As Luther's ideas spread, Pope Leo X and the Habsburg emperor, Charles V, demanded that Luther take back his criticisms and theological claims. When he refused, he was declared a heretic and avoided being burned at the stake only by the intervention of a powerful German prince who let Luther hole up in his castle.

Luther wrote many more pamphlets attacking the church and the pope, whom he now described as the anti-Christ. In 1525, he attacked another aspect of Catholic doctrine by marrying a former nun, Katharina von Bora. In Luther's view, God approved of human sexuality within the bonds of marriage, and encouraging marriage for both the clergy and the laity was the only way to prevent illicit forms of sexual behavior. Luther also translated the New Testament from Latin into German so that laypersons could have direct access, without the clergy, to the word of God. This act spurred many other daring scholars across Europe to undertake translations of their own, and it encouraged the Protestant clergy to teach children (and adults) to read their local languages.

OTHER "PROTESTANT" REFORMERS Luther's doctrines won widespread support. The renewed Christian creed appealed to commoners as well as elites, especially in communities that resented rule by Catholic "outsiders" (like the Dutch, who resented being ruled by Philip II, a Habsburg prince who lived in Spain). Thus, the reformed ideas took particularly firm hold in the German states, France, Switzerland, Scandinavia, the Low Countries, and England.

Some zealous reformers, like **Jean Calvin** (1509–1564), in France, modified Luther's ideas. To Luther's emphasis on the individual's relationship to God, Calvin added a focus on preaching and moral discipline, which he believed was best applied by autonomous religious communities. In Geneva, Switzerland, he became the leading force in a city-state republic governed by Calvinist clergymen, who banned entertainments such as the theater and gambling and saw to it that all citizens attended church and learned to read. Calvin's belief that morally righteous persons should be free to govern themselves emboldened political and religious dissenters to challenge the church and to seek more religious and political independence for their followers, who were known as Puritans in England, Presbyterians in Scotland, and Huguenots in France, the places where (in addition to Switzerland and the Netherlands) Calvinism was most popular. In contrast, those who remained loyal to the original Protestant cause now described themselves as Lutherans.

In England, Henry VIII (r. 1509–1547) and his daughter Elizabeth (r. 1558–1603) crafted a moderate reformed religion—a "middle way"—called Anglicanism, which retained many Catholic practices and a hierarchy topped by bishops. (American followers later called themselves Episcopalians, from the Latin word for bishop, *episcopus*.) Although Anglican rule was imposed on Ireland, most nonelite Irish remained Catholic. The Scots maintained a fierce devotion to their Presbyterian Church, ensuring a measure of religious diversity within the British Isles. In England, as with the rest of Europe, more radical Protestant sects, such as the Anabaptists and Quakers, also developed. While all Protestants were opposed to Catholicism and distrustful of the papal hierarchy, these different

Protestant Reformation.
Following Luther's lead, many reformers created inexpensive pamphlets to increase the circulation of their message. Pictured here is a woodcut from one such pamphlet, which shows Luther and his followers fending off the corrupt Pope Leo X.

MAP 12.3 | Religious Divisions in Europe after the Reformation, 1590

In the sixteenth century, the Protestant Reformation divided western Europe. In eastern Europe, the Ottomans controlled territories inhabited by Eastern Orthodox Christians as well as some Jewish communities.

- Within the formerly all-Catholic Holy Roman Empire, what Protestant groups took hold?
- Looking at the map, can you identify any geographical patterns in the distribution of Protestant communities?
- In what regions would you expect Protestant-Catholic tensions to be the most intense?

communities sometimes developed animosities toward one another as well. (See Map 12.3.)

COUNTER-REFORMATION AND PERSECUTION The Catholic Church responded to Luther and Calvin by embarking on its own renovation, which became known as the **Counter-Reformation**. At the Council of Trent in northern Italy, whose twenty-five sessions stretched from 1545 to 1563, Catholic leaders reaffirmed most church doctrines, including papal supremacy, the holiness of all seven sacraments, the clergy's distinctive role, and the insistence that priests, monks, and nuns remain celibate. But the council also enacted reforms and adopted some of the Protestants' tactics in an effort to win back European believers and to spread the Church's message abroad. The reformed Catholics carried their message overseas—especially through an order established by Ignatius Loyola (1491–1556). Loyola founded a brotherhood of priests, the Society of Jesus, or **Jesuits**, dedicated to the revival of the Catholic Church. From bases in Lisbon, Rome, Paris, and elsewhere in Europe, the Jesuits opened missions as far as South and North America, India, Japan, and China.

Yet the Vatican continued to use repression and persecution to combat what it regarded as heretical beliefs. Priests in Augsburg performed public exorcisms, seeking to free Protestant parishioners from possession by "demons." The Index of Prohibited Books (a list of books and theological treatises banned by the Catholic Church) and the medieval Inquisition (which began around 1184 CE) were weapons against those deemed the church's enemies. But the proliferation of printing presses and the spread of Protestantism made it impossible for the Catholic Counter-Reformation to turn back the tide leading toward increased autonomy from the papacy.

Both Catholics and Protestants persecuted witches. Between about 1500 and 1700, up to 100,000 people, mostly women, were accused of being witches. Many were tried, tortured, burned at the stake, or hanged. Older women, widows, and nurses were vulnerable to charges of cursing or poisoning babies. Other charges included killing livestock, causing hailstorms, and scotching marriage arrangements. People also believed that weak and susceptible women might have sex with the devil or be tempted to do his bidding. Clearly, neither the Reformation—nor the Catholic response to it—made Europe a more tolerant society. Indeed, the Reformation split European society deeply as both Catholics and Protestants promoted their faiths.

Religious Warfare in Europe

Religious reform led Europe into another round of ferocious wars. Their ultimate effect was to weaken the Holy Roman Empire and strengthen the English, French, and Dutch. Already in the 1520s, the circulation of books presenting Luther's ideas sparked peasant revolts across central Europe. Some peasants, hoping that Luther's assault on the church's authority would help liberate them, rose up against repressive feudal landlords. In contrast to earlier wars, in which one noble's retinue fought a rival's, the defense of the Catholic mass and the Protestant Bible brought crowds of simple folk to arms. Now wars between and within central European states raged for nearly forty years as Holy Roman Emperor Charles V tried to force the Lutheran genie back into the bottle.

In 1555, the exhausted Charles V gave up the fight. He agreed to allow the German princes the right to choose Lutheranism or Catholicism as the official religion within their domains (Calvinism was still outlawed). In 1556, he abdicated and divided his realm between his younger brother Ferdinand and his son Philip. Ferdinand (r. 1556–1564) became Holy Roman Emperor and the head of the Austrian Habsburg dynasty, which ruled the Austrian, German, and central European territories that straddled the Danube. Philip II (r. Spain 1556–1598)

St. Bartholomew's Day Massacre. *An important wedding between French Catholic and Huguenot families in Paris was scheduled for August 24, 1572, St. Bartholomew's Day. But instead of reconciliation, that day saw a massacre, as Catholics tried to stamp out Protestantism in France's capital city.*

received Spain, Belgium, the Netherlands, southern Italy, and the New World possessions. Philip also inherited the Portuguese throne (from his mother), giving his Spanish Habsburg house a monopoly on Atlantic commerce.

Charles V's concessions were supposed to enable the Catholic powers to suppress Protestantism and make peace on the continent. This strategy failed. Religious conflicts led to civil wars in France and a revolt against Spanish rule in the Netherlands, which finally ended, after nearly a hundred years of conflict, with Spain conceding the Calvinist Netherlands its independence. In 1588, the Spanish further embroiled themselves in conflict with Protestant powers by sending a mighty armada of 130 ships and almost 20,000 men into the English Channel in retaliation for English privateers' plundering of Spanish ships. But England amassed even more vessels and succeeded in handing the Spanish a humiliating and costly defeat. Spain's entanglement in these conflicts depleted the fortune it had made from New World silver mines, and its decline opened the way for the Dutch and English to extend their trading networks into Asia and the New World. By the middle of the seventeenth century the center of power in Europe had shifted decisively to the north—and to the non-European power in the eastern Mediterranean, the Ottoman Empire.

THE REVIVAL OF THE ASIAN ECONOMIES

By the time the Ottomans were seizing Constantinople, the economies clustered around the Indian Ocean and China Sea had begun a vigorous revival. This economic renewal would be linked to political developments as Asian empires expanded and consolidated their power. The Mughal ruler, Akbar, and the Ottoman sultan, Suleiman the Magnificent (see Chapter 11), were equally effective and esteemed rulers. The Ming dynasty's elegant manufactures enjoyed worldwide renown, and its ability to govern highly diverse peoples led outsiders to consider China the model imperial state. The Ming, like the Mughals, seemed unconcerned with the increasing appearance of foreigners, including Europeans bearing silver, although both regimes confined European traders to port cities. If anything, the arrival of European sailors and traders in the Indian Ocean strengthened trading ties across the region and enhanced the political power and expansionist interests of Asia's imperial regimes.

The Revival of the Ottoman Caravan Trade

Seaborne commerce eclipsed but did not eliminate overland caravan trading at this time. In fact, along some routes, overland commerce thrived. One well-trafficked route linked the Baltic Sea, Muscovy, the Caspian Sea, the central Asian oases, and

Akbar Hears a Petition. *In keeping with the multiethnic and multireligious character of Akbar's empire, the image reflects the diversity of peoples seeking to have their petitions heard by the Mughal emperor.*

China. Other land routes carried goods to the ports of China and the Indian Ocean; from there, they crossed to the Ottoman Empire's heartland and went by land farther into Europe.

Of the many entrepôts that sprang up, none enjoyed more spectacular success than Aleppo, in Syria. Located at the end of caravan routes from India and Baghdad, Aleppo soon overshadowed its Syrian rivals, Damascus and Homs. A vital supply point for Anatolia and the Mediterranean cities, Aleppo by the late sixteenth century was the most important commercial center in southwest Asia. Here, successful merchants of the type celebrated in the stories of *The Thousand and One Nights* were revered. The caravans gathered on the city's edge, where animals were hired, tents sewn, and saddles and packs arranged. Large caravans involved 600 to 1,000 camels and up to 400 men;

smaller parties required no more than a dozen animals. A good leader was essential. Only someone who knew the difficult desert routes and enjoyed the confidence of nomadic Bedouin tribes (which provided safe passage for a fee) could hope to make the journey profitable.

Ottoman authorities took a keen interest in this trade, since it generated considerable tax revenue. To facilitate the caravans' movement, the government maintained refreshment and military stations along the route. But gathering so many traders, animals, and cargoes could also attract marauders, especially desert tribesmen. To prevent raids, authorities and merchants offered cash payments to tribal chieftains as "protection money"—a small price to pay to protect the caravan trade, whose revenues ultimately supported imperial expansion.

Prosperity in Ming China

China's economic dynamism was the crucial ingredient in Afro-Eurasia's global economic revival following the devastation wrought by the Black Death. External trade revived and then expanded in the sixteenth century. But China's vast internal economy was also a mainspring of the country's economic expansion. Reconstruction of the Grand Canal opened a major artery that allowed food and riches from the economically vibrant Lower Yangzi area to reach the capital region of Beijing. Cities were hubs of economic activity, but periodic markets also proliferated in many rural areas, as commercialization gathered pace and increasingly shaped the everyday life of the inhabitants of Ming China. Urban manufacturing surged, but even more important was the spread of rural handicraft industries, where the majority of spinners and weavers were women.

Along China's elaborate trading networks flowed silk and cotton textiles, rice, porcelain ceramics, paper, and many other products. The Ming's initial concern about the potentially disruptive effects of trade did not dampen this activity, and efforts to curb overseas commerce (following Zheng He's voyages; see Chapter 11) were largely unsuccessful. Indeed, the prohibition of maritime trade was officially repealed in 1567, benefiting coastal regions in particular. (See Map 12.4.)

While Chinese silks and porcelain were esteemed across Afro-Eurasia, what did foreign buyers have to trade with the Chinese? The answer is silver, which became an important stimulant to the Ming economy and essential to the Ming monetary system. Whereas their predecessors had used paper money, Ming consumers and traders mistrusted anything other than silver or gold for commercial dealings. However, China did not produce sufficient silver for its growing needs—a situation that foreigners learned to exploit. Indeed, silver and other precious metals were about the only commodities for which the Chinese would trade their precious manufactures. Through most of the sixteenth century, China's main source of silver was Japan. After the 1570s, however, the Philippines, under the control of the Spanish, became a gateway for New World silver. According to one estimate, one-third of all silver mined in the Americas wound up in Chinese hands. This influx fueled China's phenomenal economic expansion, providing further impetus to its maritime trade. (See Primary Source: A Ming Official on Maritime Trade.)

One measure of greater prosperity under the Ming was its population surge. By the mid-seventeenth century, China's population probably accounted for more than one-third of the total world population. Although 90 percent of Chinese people lived in the countryside, large numbers filled the cities. Beijing, the capital, had perhaps a million inhabitants. Cities offered diversions ranging from literary and theatrical societies to schools of learning, religious societies, urban associations, and manufactures from all over the empire. The elegance and material prosperity of Chinese cities dazzled European visitors. One Jesuit missionary described Nanjing, the secondary capital, as surpassing all other cities "in beauty and grandeur. . . . It is literally filled with palaces and temples and towers and bridges. . . . There is a gaiety of spirit among the people who are well mannered and nicely spoken."

Urban prosperity fostered entertainment districts where people could indulge themselves anonymously. Some Ming women found a place here as refined entertainers and courtesans; others as midwives, poets, sorcerers, and matchmakers. Female painters, mostly from scholar-official families, emulated males who used the home and garden for creative pursuits. The expanding book trade also accommodated women, who were writers as well as readers, not to mention literary characters and archetypes (especially of Confucian virtues). But Chinese women made their greatest fortunes inside the emperor's Forbidden City as healers, consorts, and power brokers.

To be sure, Ming rule faced a variety of problems, from piracy along the coasts to ineptness in the state. Corruption and perceptions of social decay elicited even more criticism. Consider Wang Yangming, a government official and scholar of neo-Confucian thought who urged commitment to social action. Arguing for the unity of knowledge and action, he claimed that one's own thoughts and intuition, rather than observations and external principles (as earlier neo-Confucian thinkers had emphasized), could provide the answers to problems. His more radical followers suggested that women were equal to men intellectually and should receive a full education—a position that earned these radicals banishment from the elite establishment. But even as such new ideas and the state's weaknesses created discord, Ming society remained commercially vibrant. This vitality survived the dynasty's fall in 1644, laying the foundation for increased population growth and territorial expansion in subsequent centuries.

MAP 12.4 | Trade and Production in Ming China

The Ming Empire in the early seventeenth century was the world's most populous state and arguably its wealthiest.

- According to this map, what were the main items involved in China's export-import trade, and what were some of the regions that purchased its exports?

- In what way does the activity represented on this map indicate why China was the world's leading importer of silver at this time?

- Locate the major trading and shipbuilding centers, and then explain how important the export trade was to the Ming Empire's prosperity.

The Revival of Indian Ocean Trade

China's economic expansion occurred within the revival of Indian Ocean trade. In fact, many of the same merchants seeking trade with China developed a brisk commerce that tied the whole of the Indian Ocean together. As a result, ports in East Africa and the Red Sea again enjoyed links with coastal cities of

India, South Asia, and the Malay Peninsula. Muslims dominated this trade.

In dealing with China, Indian merchants faced the same problem as Europeans and West Asians: they had to pay with silver. So they became as dependent on gaining access to silver as others who were courting Chinese commerce. But unlike Chinese merchants, Islamic traders, including Indian Muslims,

PRIMARY SOURCE

A Ming Official on Maritime Trade

This text was written by a sixteenth-century Ming official whose family fortune benefited greatly from the textile industry. Despite his own family background, in this excerpt he reveals some degree of ambivalence, typical of the scholar-official elite, about the accumulation of mercantile wealth in Ming society. Also interesting, however, is the author's argument in favor of the expansion of maritime trade, which he saw as more of an opportunity than a threat, in contrast to many of his contemporaries. The commercial transactions along the southeast coast were distinctly different, he argued, from the overland trade with the country's northern neighbors. He also urged the government to avoid overtaxing the merchants.

Money and profit are of great importance to men. They seek profit, they suffer by it, yet they cannot forget it. They exhaust their bodies and spirits, run day and night, yet they still regard what they have gained as insufficient. Those who become merchants eat fine food and wear elegant clothes. They ride on beautifully caparisoned, double-harnessed horses—dust flying as they race through the streets and the horses' precious sweat falling like rain. Opportunistic persons attracted by their wealth offer to serve them. Pretty girls in beautiful long-sleeved dresses and delicate slippers play stringed and wind instruments for them and compete to please them. Merchants boast that their wisdom and ability are such as to give them a free hand in affairs. They believe that they know all the possible transformations in the universe and therefore can calculate all the changes in the human world, and that the rise and fall of prices are under their command. . . .

Some people say that the southeast sea foreigners have invaded us several times so they are not the kind of people with whom we should trade. But they should realize that the southeast sea foreigners need Chinese goods and the Chinese need their goods. If we prohibit the natural flow of this merchandise, how can we prevent them from invading us? I believe that if the sea trade was opened, the trouble with foreign pirates would cease. . . . Moreover, China's exports in the northwest trade come from the national treasury. Whereas the northwest foreign trade ensures only harm, the sea trade provides us with only gain. How could those in charge of the government fail to realize the distinction?

Turning to taxes levied on Chinese merchants, though these taxes are needed to fill the national treasury, excessive exploitation should be prohibited. Merchants from all areas are ordered to stop their carts and boats and have their bags and cases examined whenever they pass through a road or river checkpoint. Often the cargoes are overestimated and thus a falsely high duty is demanded. . . .

QUESTIONS FOR ANALYSIS

- According to this official, what are the benefits of maritime trade?
- What reservations does he have about increasing trade with foreigners?
- To what extent is this official in favor of China's adopting what we would call "free trade"?

Source: Chinese Civilization: A Sourcebook, 2nd ed., edited by Patricia Buckley Ebrey (New York: The Free Press, 1993), pp. 216–218.

in the region's commercial hubs did not obey one overarching political authority. This gave them considerable autonomy from political affairs and allowed them to occupy strategic positions in long-distance trade. Meanwhile, rulers all along the Indian Ocean enriched themselves with customs duties while flaunting their status with exotic goods. For glorifying sovereigns and worshipping deities, luxuries such as silks, porcelains, ivory, gold, silver, diamonds, spices, frankincense, myrrh, and incense were in high demand. Thus, the Indian Ocean trade connected a vast array of consumers and producers long before Europeans arrived on the scene.

Of the many port cities supporting Indian Ocean commerce, Melaka was key, located on the Malaysian Peninsula at a choke point between the Indian Ocean and the South China Sea. Lacking a hinterland of farmers to support it, Melaka thrived as an entrepôt for world traders, thousands of whom resided in the city or passed through it. Indeed, Melaka's merchants were a microcosm of the region's diverse commercial community. Arabs, Indians, Armenians, Jews, East Africans, Persians, and eventually western Europeans established themselves there to profit from the commerce that flowed in and out of the port.

India was the geographical and economic center of the trade routes connected by port cities. With a population expanding as rapidly as China's, its large cities (such as Agra, Delhi, and Lahore) each boasted nearly half a million residents. India's

Caravanserai. *As trade routes throughout the Ottoman Empire bustled with lucrative deals, roadside inns called caravanserais offered shrewd merchants and their helpers rest and refreshment. This illustration of a caravanserai comes from the 1581 travel journal of Venetian envoy Jacopo Soranzo.*

manufacturing center, Bengal, exported silk and cotton textiles and rice throughout South and Southeast Asia. Like China, India had a favorable trade balance with Europe and West Asia (they were exporting more than they were importing), exporting textiles and pepper (a spice that Europeans prized) in exchange for silver.

Mughal India and Commerce

The **Mughal Empire** ruled over the hub of the Indian Ocean trade in India. It became one of the world's wealthiest empires just when Europeans were establishing sustained connections with India. These connections, however, only touched the outer layer of Mughal India, one of Islam's greatest regimes. Established in 1526, it was a vigorous, centralized state whose political authority encompassed most of modern-day India. During the sixteenth century, it had a population of between 100 and 150 million.

The Mughals' strength rested on their military power (see Chapter 11). The dynasty's founder, Babur, had introduced horsemanship, artillery, and field cannons from central Asia, and gunpowder had secured his swift military victories over northern India. Under his grandson, Akbar (r. 1556–1605), the empire enjoyed expansion and consolidation that continued (under his own grandson, Aurangzeb) until it covered almost all of India. (See Map 12.5.) Known as the "Great Mughal," Akbar was skilled not only in military tactics but also in the art of alliance making. Deals with Hindu

chieftains through favors and intermarriage also undergirded his empire.

The Mughals derived their imperial power not only from military strength but also from their flexible attitude toward the realm's diverse peoples, especially in spiritual affairs. Akbar was a Muslim, but his regime did not rely on an Islamic sectarian ideology for its legitimation. He projected a new image of the emperor that stressed his earthly political and military prowess as much as his role as a guide in divine affairs. He was a philosopher-king. In keeping with this image, the imperial court welcomed advocates of different religions. Brahman, Jain, Zoroastrian, and Muslim scholars, along with Jesuit priests, who traveled from the new Portuguese settlements, gathered in his court for learned discussions. Akbar and his successor, Jahangir, believed that the universal truths of religion existed across traditions. Accordingly, their use of Islam and its symbols in imperial culture and architecture was never exclusionary; they coexisted with the subcontinent's diverse cultural and religious heritage. This tolerant imperial policy stood in stark contrast to the sharp religious conflict in contemporary Europe. But underlying the Mughals' pluralistic attitude was the history of Islam in India. It did not expand and spread as a religion of conquest. Rather, conversions occurred and an Indian Islam took shape gradually over centuries as the people of the subcontinent engaged creatively with the rulers' religion, interpreting it according to their own cultural traditions. In this sense, the erudite discussions on comparative religion in the Mughal court recognized the ground-level reality of India's plural religious and cultural context. This earned it widespread legitimacy.

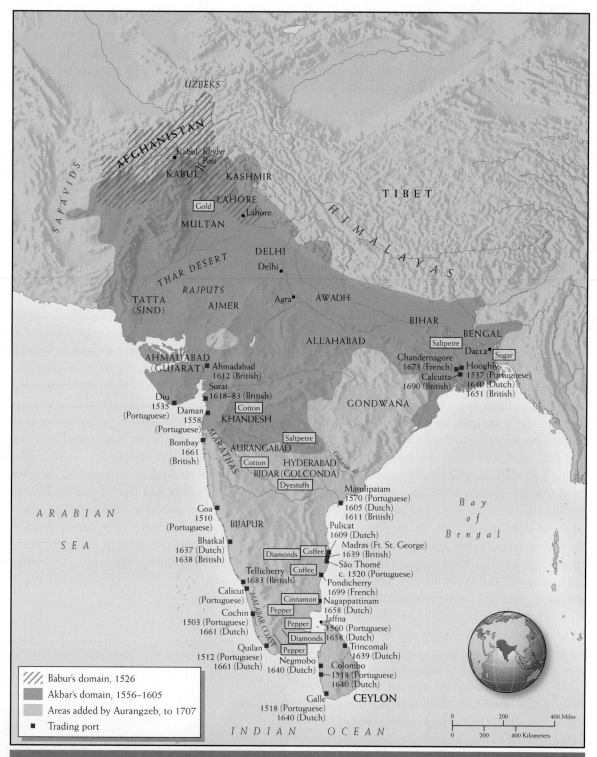

MAP 12.5 | Expansion of the Mughal Empire, 1556–1707

Under Akbar and Aurangzeb, the Mughal Empire expanded and dominated much of South Asia. Yet, by looking at the trading ports along the Indian coast, one can see the growing influence of Portuguese, Dutch, French, and English interests.

- Look at the dates for each port, and identify which traders came first and which came last.
- Compare this map with Map 12.2 (showing the earlier period 1420–1580). To what extent do the trading posts shown here reflect increased European influence in the region?
- How would these European outposts have affected Mughal policies?

Akbar's court benefited from commercial expansion in the Indian Ocean. Although the Mughals possessed no ocean navy, merchants from Mughal lands used overland routes and rivers to exchange Indian cottons, tobacco, saffron, betel leaf, sugar, and indigo for Iranian melons, dried fruits, nuts, silks, carpets, and precious metals or for Russian pelts, leathers, walrus tusks, saddles, and chain mail armor. Every year, Akbar ordered 1,000 new suits stitched of the most exquisite material. His harem preened in fine silks dripping with gold, brocades, and pearls. Carpets, mirrors, and precious metals adorned nobles' households and camps, while perfume and wine flowed freely. Soldiers, servants, and even horses and elephants sported elaborate attire.

During the sixteenth century, expanded trade with Europe brought more wealth to the Mughal polity, while the empire's strength limited European incursions. Although the Portuguese occupied Goa and Bombay on the Indian coast, they had little presence elsewhere and dared not antagonize the Mughal emperor. In 1578, Akbar recognized the credentials of a Portuguese ambassador and allowed a Jesuit missionary to enter his court. Thereafter, commercial ties between Mughals and Portuguese intensified, but merchants were still restricted to a handful of ports. In the 1580s and 1590s, the Mughals ended the Portuguese monopoly on trade with Europe by allowing Dutch and English merchantmen to dock in Indian ports.

Akbar used the commercial boom to overhaul his revenue system. Until the 1560s, the Mughal state relied on a network of decentralized tribute collectors called *zamindars*. These collectors possessed rights to claim a share of the harvest while earmarking part of their earnings for the emperor. But the Mughals did not always receive their agreed share and the peasants resented the high levies, so local populations resisted. As flourishing trade bolstered the money supply, Akbar's officials monetized the tax assessment system and curbed the *zamindars'* power. After other centralizing reforms, increased imperial revenues helped finance military expeditions and the extravagant beautification of Akbar's court.

Centered in northern India, the Mughal Empire used surrounding regions' wealth and resources—military, architectural, and artistic—to glorify the court. Over time, the enhanced wealth caused friction among Indian regions and even between merchants and rulers. Yet as long as merchants relied on rulers for their commercial gains, and as long as rulers balanced local and imperial interests, the realm remained unified and kept Europeans on the outskirts of society.

Asian Relations with Europe

As actors in the world of Asian commerce, Europeans were very much the newest, and weakest, kids on the block. Europeans'

overseas expansion had originally looked toward Asia in hopes of acquiring greater access to luxury goods such as silk and spices. It took some time for them to acquire access to these markets. But silver, followed by maritime and military advances and state-backed trading companies, offered Europeans the opportunity to gradually insert themselves into the Eurasian luxury trade.

The Portuguese blazed the way as collectors of customs duties from Asian traders and, after 1557, as transshippers of Chinese porcelain and silks from the coastal enclave of Macao (see again Map 12.4). The Portuguese also dominated the silver trade from Japan. Envying Portuguese profits, the Spanish, English, and Dutch also ventured into Asian waters. With its monopoly on American silver, Spain enjoyed a competitive advantage. In 1565, the first Spanish trading galleon reached the Philippines; in 1571, after capturing Manila and making it a colonial capital, the Spanish established a brisk trade with China. Each year, ships from Spain's colonies in the Americas crossed the Pacific to Manila, bearing cargoes of silver. They returned carrying porcelain and silks for well-to-do European consumers. Merchants in Manila also procured silks, tapestries, and feathers from the China seas for shipment to the Americas, where the mining elite eagerly awaited these imports.

The year 1571 was decisive in the history of the modern world, for in that year Spain inaugurated a trade circuit that made good on Magellan's earlier achievement of circumnavigating the globe. As Spanish ships circled the globe from the New World to China and from China back to Europe, the world became commercially interconnected. Silver solidified the linkage, being the only foreign commodity for which the Chinese had an insatiable demand. From the mother lodes of the Andes and Mesoamerica, silver made the commerce of the world go round.

Macao. *This Chinese painting depicts the Portuguese enclave of Macao, on the southern border of China, around 1800.*

Other Europeans, too, wanted their share of Asia's wealth. The English and the Dutch reached the South China Sea late in the sixteenth century. Captain James Lancaster made the first English voyage to the East Indies between 1591 and 1594. Five years later, 101 English subscribers pooled their funds and formed a joint-stock company (an association in which each member owns shares of capital). This English East India Company soon won a royal charter granting it exclusive rights to import East Indian goods. Soon the company displaced the Portuguese in the Arabian Sea and the Persian Gulf. Doing a brisk trade in indigo, saltpeter, pepper, and cotton textiles, the English East India Company eventually acquired control of ports on both coasts of India—Fort St. George (Madras; 1639), Bombay (1661), and Calcutta (1690).

Still, Europeans trading in Asia remained dependent on local power brokers and commercial traders. The number of European settlers was miniscule, their cultural inroads few. Trade in Asia continued, largely in Asian hands, and focused on older routes. Although Europeans came to control some small coastal enclaves, they did not have large colonial lands to rule. Things were very different in the Atlantic world, where conquest, settlement, and trade brought with it previously unknown plants, people, products—and pathogens.

COMMERCE AND COLONIZATION IN THE ATLANTIC WORLD

The Spanish, it was once said, came to the Americas for God, gold, and glory. Fittingly, gold (and silver) took precedence on this list. Those precious metals brought glory to conquistadors, enriched Spanish coffers, and helped to finance the spiritual conquests that Catholic missionaries undertook in the Americas. The products of American mines also soon found their way into global trading circuits, giving Europeans a commodity with which to purchase African slaves and Asian goods.

The flow of peoples to the Americas and products from the Americas transformed economies—and, even more, transformed environments—across the world. Those who came to the Americas carried devastating diseases that killed tens of millions of Amerindians. The newcomers also brought horses, cattle, pigs, wheat, grapevines, and sugarcane. In exchange, they learned about crops such as potatoes and corn that would fuel a population explosion across Afro-Eurasia. Historians call this hemispheric transfer of animals, plants, people, and pathogens in the wake of Columbus's voyages the **Columbian exchange**. Over time, these transfers would change the demography and the diets of both the New and the Old Worlds.

The Columbian Exchange

The first and most profound effect of the Columbian exchange was a destructive one: the decimation of the Amerindian population by European diseases. (See Analyzing Global Developments: The European Conquest of the Americas and Amerindian Mortality.) For millennia, the isolated populations of the Americas had been cut off from Afro-Eurasian microbe migrations. Africans, Europeans, and Asians had long interacted, sharing disease pools and gaining immunities; in this sense, the Amerindians were indeed "worlds apart."

Sickness spread from almost the moment the Spaniards arrived. Even Cortés took note. "Their excretions," he wrote to the Spanish emperor, "were the sort of filth that thin swine pass which have been fed on nothing but grass." Amerindian accounts of the fall of Tenochtitlán recalled the smallpox epidemic more vividly than the fighting. Even worse, no sooner had smallpox done its work than Indians faced a second pandemic: measles. Then came pneumonic plague and influenza. As each wave retreated, it left a population more emaciated than before, even less prepared for the next wave. The scale of death remains unprecedented: imported pathogens wiped out up to 90 percent of the Amerindian population. A century after smallpox arrived on Hispaniola in 1519, no more than 5 to 10 percent of the island's population were left alive. Diminished and weakened by disease, Amerindians could not resist European settlement and colonization of the Americas. Thus were Europeans the unintended beneficiaries of a horrifying catastrophe.

As time passed, all sides adopted new forms of agriculture from one another. Indians taught Europeans how to grow potatoes and corn, crops that would become staples all across Afro-Eurasia. The Chinese found that they could grow corn in areas too dry for rice and too wet for wheat, while corn replaced, at first by fits and starts, Africa's major food grains, sorghum, millet, and rice, to become the continent's principal food crop by the twentieth century. (See Current Trends in World History: Corn and the Rise of Slave-Supplying Kingdoms in West Africa.) Europeans also took away tomatoes, beans, cacao, peanuts, tobacco, and squash, while exporting livestock such as cattle, swine, and horses to the New World. The environmental effects of the introduction of livestock to the Americas were manifold. In the highland regions north of the valley of central Mexico (where Native Americans had once maintained irrigated, highly productive agricultural estates), Spanish settlers opened up large herding ranches. An area that had once produced corn and squash now supported herds of sheep and cattle. Without natural predators, these animals reproduced with lightning speed, destroying entire landscapes with their hoofs and their foraging.

As Europeans cleared trees and other vegetation for ranches, mines, or plantations, they undermined the habitats of many

The European Conquest of the Americas and Amerindian Mortality

I f the fourteenth century was an age of dying across Afro-Eurasia, the sixteenth century saw even higher mortality rates in the Americas. As a result of European conquest, the exposure to virulent diseases, and the hyperexploitation of their labor under miserable conditions, the Native American populations saw their numbers reduced by 85 percent. The numbers themselves, however, are highly controversial and have sparked intense debates. Some scholars believe that no reliable numbers can be found for the population of the Americas when Europeans first arrived. Others have used a range of methods and data sources to establish population figures, including European firsthand accounts from that period, archaeological and anthropological evidence, estimates of the maximum population size of people the land can contain indefinitely (carrying capacity), and projections built backward from more recent censuses. These estimates vary widely from as little as 8 million to as high as more than 100 million.

Area	Population in 1492	Later Populations	Mortality Rates
The Americas	53.9 m[a]	8 m in 1650	85%
The Caribbean			
Hispaniola	1.0 m	extinct by 1600	100%
The other islands	2.0 m	extinct by 1600	100%
Mexico	17.2 m	3.5 m in 1600	80%
The Andes	15.0 m	3.0 m in 1650	80%
Central America	5.63 m	1.12 m in 1700	80%
North America	3.79 m	1.5 m in 1700	60%
		250,000 in 1900	84%

[a] m = millions.

QUESTIONS FOR ANALYSIS

- Imagine yourself a historical demographer. How would you attempt to estimate the population of the Americas in 1492?

- What effect did European conquest and Amerindian dying have on the polities and religious beliefs of the Native Americans?

- Why do you think Native American population growth never recovered from the initial encounter with Europeans as Afro-Eurasian population growth eventually recovered from the Black Death?

Sources: Suzanne Austin Alchon, A Pest in the Land: New World Epidemics in a Global Perspective (2003); David Noble Cook, Born to Die: Disease and New World Conquest, 1492 to 1650 (1998); William M. Denevan, The Native Populations of the Americas in 1492 (1992); David Henige, Numbers from Nowhere: The Amerindian Contact Population Debate (1998); "La Catastrophe Demographique," L'Histoire, no. 322 (July–August 2007):17; Thornton, Russell, American Indian Holocaust: A Population History since 1492 (1987), p. xvii.

indigenous mammals and birds. On the islands of the West Indies, described by Columbus as "roses of the sea," the Spanish chopped down lush tropical and semitropical forests to make way for sugar plantations. Before long, nearly all of the islands' tall trees as well as many shrubs and ground plants were gone, and residents lamented the absence of birdsong. Over ensuing centuries, the flora and fauna of the Americas took on an increasingly European appearance—a process that the historian Alfred Crosby has called ecological imperialism. At the same time, the interactions between Europeans and Amerindians would continue to shape societies on both sides of the Atlantic.

Spain's Tributary Empire

Like the Europeans who sailed into the Indian Ocean to join existing commercial systems, the Spaniards sought to exploit the wealth of indigenous empires without fully dismantling them.

Those Native Americans who survived the original encounters could be harnessed as a means to siphon tribute payments to the new masters. Spain could thereby extract wealth without extensive settlement. In Mexico and Peru, conquistadors decapitated native communities but left much of their social and economic structure intact—including networks of tribute. But unlike the European penetration of the Indian Ocean, the occupation of the New World went beyond the control of commercial outposts. Instead, European colonialism in the Americas involved laying claim to large amounts of territory—and ultimately the entire landmass. (See Map 12.6.) We should be careful, however, not to mistake the expansive claims made by European empires in the Americas with actual control of the territory. Through the fifteenth and sixteenth centuries—and as we will see in Chapter 13, through the seventeenth and eighteenth—Amerindians still maintained their dominion over much of the Americas, even as disease continued to diminish their numbers.

MAP 12.6 | The Spanish and Portuguese Empires in the Americas, 1492–1750

This map examines the growth of the Spanish and Portuguese Empires in the Americas over two and a half centuries.

- Identify the natural resources that led the Spaniards and Portuguese to focus their empire building where they did.
- What were the major export commodities from these colonized areas?
- Looking back to Map 12.2, why do you think Spanish settlement covered so much more area than Portuguese settlement?
- According to your reading, how did the production and export of silver and sugar shape the labor systems that evolved in both empires?

CURRENT TRENDS IN WORLD HISTORY

Corn and the Rise of Slave-Supplying Kingdoms in West Africa

New World varieties of corn spread rapidly throughout the Afro-Eurasian landmass soon after the arrival of Columbus in the Americas. Its hardiness and fast ripening qualities made it more desirable than many of the Old World grain products. In communities that consumed large quantities of meat, it became the main product fed to livestock.

Corn's impact on Africa was as substantial as it was in the rest of Eurasia. Seeds made their way to western regions more quickly than regions south of the Sahara along two routes: via European merchants calling into ports along the coast and via West African Muslims returning across the Sahara after participating in the pilgrimage. The first evidence of corn cultivation in sub-Saharan Africa comes from a Portuguese navigator who identified the crop being grown on the island of Cape Verde

in 1540. By the early seventeenth century, corn was replacing millet and sorghum as the main grain being grown in many West African regions and was destined to transform the work routines and diets of the peoples living in the region's tropical rain forests all the way from present-day Sierra Leone in the east to Nigeria in the west. In many ways, this area, which saw the rise of a group of powerful slave-supplying kingdoms in the eighteenth century—notably, Asante, Dahomey, Oyo, and Benin—owed its prosperity to the cultivation of this New World crop. (See Chapter 14 for a fuller discussion of these states.)

The tropical rain forests of West and central Africa were thick with trees and ground cover in 1500. Clearing them so that they could support intensive agriculture was exhausting work, requiring enormous outlays of human energy and time. Corn, a crop first domesticated in central Mexico 7,000 years ago, made this task possible. It added much-needed carbohydrates to the carbon-deficient diets of

rain forest dwellers. In addition, as a crop that matured more quickly than those that were indigenous to the region (millet, sorghum, and rice) and required less labor, it yielded two harvests in a single year. Farmers also cultivated cassava, another New World native, which in turn provided households with more carbohydrate calories. Yet corn did more than produce more food per unit of land and labor. Households put every part of the plant to use: grain, leaves, stalks, tassels, and roots were all made to serve useful purposes.

Thus, at the very time that West African groups were moving southward into the rain forests, European navigators were arriving along the coast with new crops. Corn gave communities of cultivators the caloric energy to change their forest landscapes, expanding the arable areas. In a select few of these regions, enterprising clans emerged to dominate the political scene, creating centralized kingdoms like Asante, in present-day Ghana; Dahomey, in present-day Benin; and Oyo and Benin,

---

Within their colonial heartlands, Spanish masters fused traditional tribute taking with their own innovations to make villagers deliver goods and services. But because the Spanish authorities also bestowed *encomiendas*, those favored individuals could demand labor from their lands' Indian inhabitants—for mines, estates, and public works. Whereas Aztec and Inca rulers had used conscripted labor to build up their public wealth, the Spaniards did so for private gain.

Most Spanish migrants were men; very few were women. One, Inés Suárez, reached the Indies only to find her husband, who had arrived earlier, dead. She then became mistress of the conquistador Pedro de Valdivia, and the pair worked as a conquering team. Initially, she joined an expedition to conquer Chile as Valdivia's domestic servant, but she soon became much more—nurse, caretaker, adviser, and guard, having uncovered several plots to assassinate her lover. Suárez even served as a diplomat between warring Indians and Spaniards in an effort to secure the conquest. Later, she helped to rule Chile as the wife of Rodrigo de Quiroga,

governor of the province. Admittedly, hers was an exceptional story. More typical were women who foraged for food, tended wounded soldiers, and set up European-style settlements.

However, there were too few Spanish women to go around, so Spanish men consorted with local women—despite the crown's disapproval. From the onset of colonization, Spaniards also married into Indian families. After conquering the Incas, Pizarro himself wedded an Inca princess, thereby (or so he hoped) inheriting the mantle of local dynastic rule. As a result of intermarriages, mestizos became the fastest-growing segment of the population of Spanish America.

Spanish migrants and their progeny preferred towns to the countryside. Ports excepted, the major cities of Spanish America were the former centers of Indian empires. Mexico City took shape on the ruins of Tenochtitlán; Cuzco arose from the razed Inca capital. In their architecture, economy, and most intimate aspects, the Spanish colonies adopted as much as they transformed the worlds they encountered.

Corn Plantation. *This nineteenth-century engraving by famed Italian explorer Savorgnan de Brazza shows women of the West African tribe Bateke working in corn plantations. De Brazza would later serve as the governor general of the French colony in the Congo.*

in present-day Nigeria. These elites transformed what had once been thinly settled environments into densely populated states, with elaborate bureaucracies, big cities, and large and powerful standing armies.

There was much irony in the rise of these states, which owed so much of their strength to the linking of the Americas with Afro-Eurasia. The armies that they created and the increased populations that the new crops allowed were part and parcel of the Atlantic slave trade. That which the Americas gave with one hand (new crops), it took back with the other (warfare, captives, and New World slavery).

Portugal's New World Colony

No sooner did Europeans—starting with the Portuguese and Spanish—venture into the seas than they carved them up to prevent a free-for-all. The Treaty of Tordesillas of 1494, drawn up by the pope, had foreseen that the non-European world—the Americas, Africa, and Asia—would be divided into spheres of interest between Spain and Portugal. Yet the treaty was unenforceable. No less interested in immediate riches than the Spanish, the Portuguese were disappointed by the absence of tributary populations and precious metals in the areas set aside for them. What they did find in Brazil, however, was abundant, fertile land on which favored persons received massive royal grants. These estate owners governed their plantations like feudal lords (see Chapter 10).

COASTAL ENCLAVES Hemmed in along the coast, the Portuguese created enclaves. Unlike the Spanish, they rarely intermarried with Amerindians, most of whom had fled or had died from imported diseases. Failing to find established cities, the colonists remained in more dispersed settlements. By the late seventeenth century, Brazil's white population was 300,000.

The problem was where to find labor to work the rich lands. Lacking a centralized government to deal with the labor shortage, initially the Portuguese settlers tried to enlist the dispersed indigenous population; but when recruitment became increasingly coercive, Indians turned on the settlers, whom they perceived to be interlopers. Some fought. Others fled to the vast interior. Reluctant to pursue the Indians inland, the Portuguese hugged their beachheads, extracting brazilwood (the source of a beautiful red dye) and sugar from their enclaves.

African slaves became the solution to this labor problem. What had worked for the Portuguese on sugarcane plantations in the Azores and other Atlantic islands now found application on their Brazilian plantations. Especially in the northeast, in the Bay of All Saints, the Atlantic world's first sugar-producing commercial center appeared.

Mission São Miguel. *The Jesuits were avid missionaries in the Spanish and Portuguese Empires and often tried to shelter native peoples from conquistadors and labor recruiters. Missions, like this one, in the borderlands between Brazil and Spanish colonies were targets of attack from both sides.*

SUGAR PLANTATIONS Along with silver, sugar emerged as the most valuable export from the Americas. It also was decisive in rearranging relations between peoples around the Atlantic. Cultivation of sugarcane had originated in India, spread to the Mediterranean region, and then reached the coastal islands of West Africa. The Portuguese transported the West African model to Brazil, and other Europeans took it to the Caribbean. (See again Map 12.6.) By the early seventeenth century, sugar had become a major export from the New World. By the eighteenth century, its production required continuous and enormous transfers of labor from Africa, and its value surpassed that of silver as an export from the Americas to Europe.

At first, most Brazilian sugar plantations were fairly small, employing between 60 and 100 slaves. But they were efficient enough to create an alternative model of empire, one that resulted in full-scale colonization and dislocation of the existing population. The slaves lived in wretched conditions: their barracks were miserable, and their diets were insufficient to keep them alive under backbreaking work routines. Moreover, these slaves were disproportionately men. As they rapidly died off, the only way to ensure replenishment was to import more Africans. This model of settlement relied on the transatlantic flow of slaves.

Beginnings of the Transatlantic Slave Trade

As European demand for sugar increased, the slave trade expanded. Although African slaves were imported into the Americas starting in the fifteenth century, the first direct voyage carrying them from Africa to the Americas occurred in 1525. The transatlantic slave trade began modestly in support of one commodity, sugar. From the time of Columbus until 1820, more than five times as many Africans as Europeans moved to the Americas: approximately 2 million Europeans (voluntarily) and 12 million Africans (involuntarily) crossed the Atlantic—though the especially high mortality rate for Africans meant that only 10 million survived to reach New World shores.

First to master long-distance seafaring, the Portuguese also led the way in human cargo. Trade in slaves grew steadily throughout the sixteenth century, then surged in the seventeenth and eighteenth centuries (see Chapter 13). Initially, all European powers participated—Portuguese, Spanish, Dutch, English, and French. Eventually, New World merchants in both North and South America also established direct trade links with Africa.

Well before European merchants arrived off its western coast, Africa had known long-distance slave trading. In fact, the overall number of Africans sold into captivity in the Muslim world exceeded that of the Atlantic slave trade. Moreover, Africans maintained slaves themselves. African slavery, like its American counterpart, was a response to labor scarcities. In many parts of Africa, however, slaves did not face permanent servitude. Instead, they were assimilated into families, gradually losing their servile status and swelling the size and power of their adopted lineage-based groups.

With the additional European demand for slaves to work New World plantations alongside the ongoing Muslim slave trade, pressure on the supply of African slaves intensified. Only a narrow band stretching down the spine of the African landmass, from present-day Uganda and the highlands of Kenya to Zambia and Zimbabwe, escaped the impact of Asian and European slave traders.

Within Africa, the social and political consequences were not fully evident until the great age of the slave trade in the eighteenth century, but already some economic consequences were clear. The overwhelming trend was to further limit Africa's population. Indeed, African laborers fetched high enough prices to more than cover the costs of their capture and transportation across the Atlantic.

By the late sixteenth century, important pieces had fallen into place to create a new Atlantic world, one that could not have been imagined a century earlier. This was the three-cornered **Atlantic system**, with Africa supplying labor, the Americas land and minerals, and Europeans the technology and military power to hold the system together. If observers at the time counted the Ottomans or the Ming as the greatest world powers, in the longer run the wealth flows to Europe and the slave-based development of the Americas would tip the world balance of power in Europe's favor.

CONCLUSION

In this multicentered world of the fifteenth and sixteenth centuries, Europe was a poor cousin, embroiled in religious warfare. It was the Ottoman Empire that was on the rise. The Ottomans, like the Ming in China and the Mughals in India, built wealthy, multiethnic empires and thriving trade networks. But Ottoman inroads in the Mediterranean spurred European merchants and mariners to seek alternative routes to Asia. Breaking into the Indian Ocean trade, the Portuguese had some success; Spanish silver gave more Europeans access to these rich markets. But Asian empires did not lose their autonomy. On the contrary, they absorbed Europeans—and their silver—into their own networks.

But the incorporation into Afro-Eurasian history of a "New World" after Columbus's voyages was an event of monumental significance. In the Americas, Europeans found riches. Mountains of silver and rivers of gold helped them break into Asian markets. Europeans also found opportunities for conquest and colonization, which in turn transformed their own realm as rivals fought over the spoils.

Thus, two conquests characterize this age of increasing world interconnections. Ottoman expansionism drove Europeans to find new links to Asia, demonstrating Islam's pivotal role in shaping modern world history. In turn, the Spanish conquest of the Aztecs and the Incas gave Europeans access to silver, which bought them an increased presence in Asian trading networks. Yet this remained a world whose regions were not yet fully entangled, with many of its peoples still living in ecosystems little touched by these global developments.

Amerindians also played an important role, as Europeans sought to conquer their lands, exploit their labor, and confiscate their gold and silver. Sometimes local people worked with Europeans, sometimes under Europeans, sometimes against Europeans—and sometimes none were left to work at all. Then Europeans brought in African laborers, compounding the calamity of the encounter with the tragedy of slavery. Out of the catastrophe of contact, a new oceanic system arose to link Africa, America, and Europe. This was the Atlantic system. Unlike the tributary and trading orders of the Indian Ocean and China seas, the Atlantic Ocean supported a system of formal imperial control and settlement of distant colonies and profoundly transformed economies, agricultural practices, and environments across the globe. These catastrophes and exchanges would be foundational for the ways in which worlds connected and collided in the following centuries.

After You Read This Chapter

Go to iNQUIZITIVE to see what you know & learn what you've missed.

TRACING THE GLOBAL STORYLINES

FOCUS ON: *Regional Impacts of European Colonization and Trade*

Europe

- Portugal creates a trading empire in the Indian Ocean and the South China Sea.

- Spain and Portugal establish colonies in the Americas, discover silver, and establish export-oriented plantation economies.

- The Protestant Reformation breaks out in northern and western Europe, splitting the Catholic Church.

The Americas

- Millions of Amerindians, lacking immunity to European diseases, perish across the Americas.

- Spanish conquest and disease destroy the two greatest Native American empires in Mexico (the Aztecs) and Peru (the Incas).

Africa

- Trade in African captives fuels the Atlantic slave trade, which furnishes labor for European plantations in the Americas.

Asia

- Asian empires—the Mughals in India, the Ming in China, the Safavids in Iran, and the Ottomans in western Asia and the eastern Mediterranean—barely notice the Americas but profit economically from enhanced global trade.

CHRONOLOGY

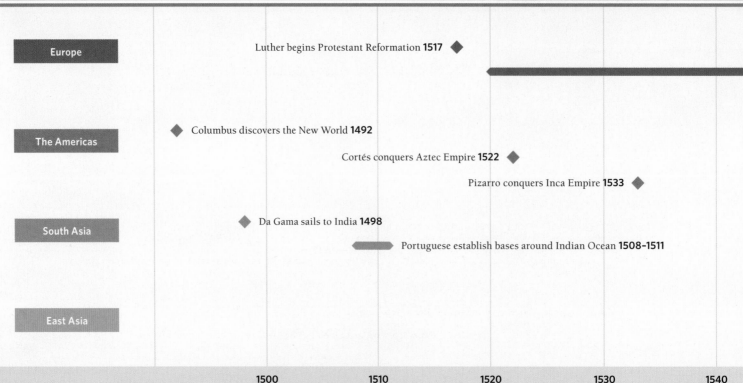

	1500	1510	1520	1530	1540
Europe			Luther begins Protestant Reformation **1517**		
The Americas	Columbus discovers the New World **1492**		Cortés conquers Aztec Empire **1522**	Pizarro conquers Inca Empire **1533**	
South Asia	Da Gama sails to India **1498**	Portuguese establish bases around Indian Ocean **1508–1511**			
East Asia					

STUDY QUESTIONS

1. **Identify** the broad patterns in world trade after 1450. **Compare** the major features of this trade in Asia, the Americas, Africa, and Europe.

2. **Identify** the factors that enabled Europeans to increase their trade relationships with Asian empires during this period, and **evaluate** the significance of each factor.

3. **Describe** the obstacles to consolidating power in the Aztec and Inca Empires before the arrival of European conquistadors.

4. **Compare** the practices and the impact of European explorers in Asia and the Americas.

5. **Explain** the role of silver in transforming global trade patterns during the sixteenth century. Which regions and dynasties benefited from the increased use of silver for monetary transactions?

6. **Describe** the types of social and political relationships that developed within Afro-Eurasian polities during this period, and **identify** the sources of conflict.

7. **Compare and contrast** political and commercial developments in the Mughal and Ming dynasties during the sixteenth century. How did the expansion of global commerce affect each region?

8. **Explain** the environmental consequences of the first contacts between Europeans and Amerindians. What consequences did the Columbian exchange have on regions both beyond the Atlantic world and within it?

9. **Compare and contrast** Spain's "tributary empire" in the Americas with Portugal's "seaborne empire" in the Indian Ocean. Why did these empires pursue such different strategies?

10. **Analyze** the ways in which European colonization of the Americas affected African and Amerindian peoples. **Discuss** how those groups responded.

11. **Explain** the transformation of the African slave trade during this period. What role did the growth of sugar plantations play?

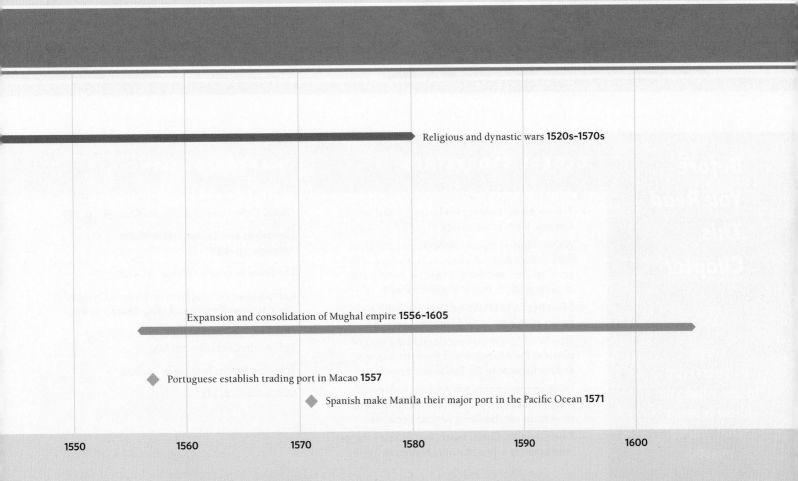

Religious and dynastic wars **1520s–1570s**

Expansion and consolidation of Mughal empire **1556–1605**

Portuguese establish trading port in Macao **1557**

Spanish make Manila their major port in the Pacific Ocean **1571**

| 1550 | 1560 | 1570 | 1580 | 1590 | 1600 |

13

Worlds Entangled, 1600–1750

FOCUS QUESTIONS

- What were the major steps in the integration of global trade networks in the seventeenth and eighteenth centuries?

- What effects did the Little Ice Age have on different parts of the world?

- How did the Atlantic slave trade change African societies socially and politically?

- What effect did New World silver and increased trade have on Asian empires?

- How was the impact of trade and religion on state power in various regions alike and different?

- What was the significance of European consumption of goods (like tobacco, textiles, and sugar) for the global economy?

The leading Ottoman intellectual of the sixteenth century, Mustafa Ali, was a gloomy man, convinced that the Ottoman Empire had slipped into an irreversible decline. He lived during difficult times. Islam was approaching its one-thousandth year (1000 After Hijra, AH, or 1591–1592 in the Julian calendar). Many *ulama* and high-level bureaucrats believed that the apocalypse was imminent, a day of judgment when those who were virtuous would be rewarded and those who were evil would be punished. Although Mustafa Ali did not believe that the end of the world was likely, he did think that the time was ripe for assessing not only the history of the Ottomans from their founding to the present but also the whole of human history. He began his magnum opus, *The Essence of History*, in the year when many thought that the world would end (1591). Indeed, the signs at the time were unfavorable for Ottoman success even though the first half of the century had witnessed the conquest of Egypt and the reign of Suleiman the Magnificent and the Lawgiver, arguably the most successful of the sultans. By century's end, however, the empire was losing territory to its main European adversaries, the Habsburgs, the Venetians, and the Russians; military rioting had occurred in protest against payments in debased

Stimulants, Sociability, and Coffeehouses

While armies, travelers, missionaries, and diseases have breached the world's main political and cultural barriers, commodities have been the least respectful of the lines that separate communities. It has been difficult for ruling elites to curtail the desire of their populations to dress themselves in fine garments, to possess jewelry, and to consume satisfying food and drink no matter where these products may originate. The history of commodities, thus, is a core area for world historical research, for products span cultural barriers and connect peoples over long distances. As the world's trading networks expanded in the seventeenth and eighteenth centuries, merchants in Europe, Asia, Africa, and the Americas distributed many new commodities. By far the most popular were a group of stimulants—coffee, cocoa, sugar, tobacco, and tea—all of which (except for sugar) were addictive

and also produced a sense of well-being. Previously, many of these products had been grown in isolated parts of the world: the coffee bean in Yemen, tobacco and cocoa in the New World, and sugar in Bengal. Yet, by the seventeenth century, in nearly every corner of the world, the well-to-do began to congregate in coffee-houses, consuming these new products and engaging in sociable activities.

Coffeehouses everywhere served as locations for social exchange, political discussions, and business activities. Yet they also varied from cultural area to cultural area, reflecting the values of the societies in which they arose.

The coffeehouse first appeared in Islamic lands late in the fifteenth century. As coffee consumption caught on among the wealthy and leisured classes in the Arabian Peninsula and the Ottoman Empire, local growers protected their

Coffee. *Coffee drinkers at an Ottoman banquet.*

silver coinage, a result of the import of vast quantities of New World silver; and uprisings against the empire were widespread in eastern Anatolia.

Historians now know that many of these problems stemmed from the cold spell that descended on the entire world at this time. Present-day scholars have labeled the seventeenth century the Little Ice Age. This sharp drop in global temperatures, lasting between 1620 and 1680, laid waste to agricultural and pastoral lands and spread hunger and famines worldwide. A double-edged global crisis ensued. Just as global empires ramped up their competition, they squeezed their peasants for resources to pay for warfare. At the same time, global cooling meant that peasants produced less food and surpluses. Across much of Afro-Eurasia, the result was a wave of suffering, peasant unrest, and political upheaval.

Mustafa Ali captured the sentiments of this age well: "Prosperity had turned to famine, the government careers had become confused, venality was rampant, and the military class was being overrun by *re'aya* [tax-paying subjects]" (Fleischer, p. 8). Even more apocalyptical were his poems. Here his view was that "in the social sphere the world is upside down; the *ulama* are no longer learned or pious; the pillars of the state are fiends

and lions; the truly learned are disdained and dismissed and government service now brings pain and poverty rather than pride and wealth. The plague destroying the world is moral as well as physical, for bribery and corruption are the order of the day" (p. 134).

In spite of the turmoil, the period 1600–1750 saw the world's oceans give way to booming sea-lanes for global trading networks. Sugar flowed from Brazil and the Caribbean, spices from Southeast Asia, cotton textiles from India, silks from China, and silver from Mesoamerica and the Andes. New World silver was crucial to these networks: it gave Europeans a commodity to exchange with Asians, and it tilted the balance of wealth and power in a westerly direction across Afro-Eurasia.

Imperial expansion and transoceanic trade, like climate change, spread across the entire globe. Europeans conquered and colonized more of the Americas, the demand for African slaves to work New World plantations leaped upward, and global trade intensified. Conquest, colonization, and commerce created riches for some but also provoked bitter rivalries. In the Americas, Spain and Portugal faced new competitors—primarily England and France. With religious tensions added to the mix, the stage was set for decades of bloody warfare in Europe and advantage by monopolizing its cultivation and sale and refusing to allow any seeds or cuttings from the coffee tree to be taken abroad.

Despite some religious opposition, coffee spread into Egypt and throughout the Ottoman Empire in the sixteenth century. Ottoman bureaucrats, merchants, and artists assembled in coffeehouses to trade stories, read, listen to poetry, and play chess and backgammon. Indeed, so deeply connected were coffeehouses with literary and artistic pursuits that people referred to them as schools of knowledge.

From the Ottoman territories, the culture of coffee drinking spread to western Europe. The first coffeehouse in London opened in 1652, and within sixty years the city claimed no fewer than 500 such establishments. In fact, the Fleet Street area of London had so many that the English essayist Charles Lamb commented, "The man must have a rare recipe for melancholy who can be dull in Fleet Street." Although coffeehouses attracted people from all levels of society, they especially appealed to the new mercantile and professional classes as locations where stimulating beverages like coffee, cocoa, and tea promoted lively conversation. Here, too, opponents claimed that excessive coffee drinking destabilized the thinking processes and even caused conversions to Islam. But against such opposition, the pleasures of coffee, tea, and cocoa prevailed. These bitter beverages in turn required liberal doses of the sweetener sugar. A smoke of tobacco topped off the experience. In this environment of pleasure, patrons of the coffeehouses indulged their addictions, engaged in gossip, conducted business, and talked politics.

QUESTIONS FOR ANALYSIS

- What factors drove the consumption of stimulants like coffee on a global scale?
- What other commodities from earlier in world history played a similar role? Were there differences in the underlying factors, such as scale of consumption, between the different periods?

Explore Further

Hattox, Ralph S. *Coffee and Coffeehouses: The Origins of a Social Beverage in the Medieval Near East* (1985).

the Americas. At the same time, rulers in India, China, and Japan enlarged their empires, while Russia's tsars incorporated Siberian territories into their domain. Meanwhile, the Ottoman, Safavid, and Mughal dynasties, though resisting most European intrusions, faced shocks from an increasingly entangled world.

GLOBAL COMMERCE AND CLIMATE CHANGE

In spite of the worldwide trauma brought on by the plunge in temperatures, global trade flourished during this period. Sugar, silver, and slaves were the primary items, promoted equally by merchant groups and the rulers and commoners of sponsoring nations. Increasing economic ties brought new products into world markets: furs from French North America, sugar from the Caribbean, tobacco from British colonies on the American mainland, coffee from Southeast and Southwest Asia, and slaves from West and central Africa. (See Current Trends in World History: Stimulants, Sociability, and Coffeehouses; see also Map 13.1.)

Closer economic contact enhanced the power of certain states and destabilized others. It bolstered the legitimacy of England and France, and it prompted strong local support of new rulers in Japan and parts of sub-Saharan Africa. With rising powers came rising competition, friction, and warfare. Governments had to squeeze more resources from trade and agriculture, a practice that spurred protest and open rebellions during the Little Ice Age, when civil wars and social unrest swept through much of the world. England, France, and Japan faced mass peasant uprisings. In the Ottoman state, rebellions almost brought the empire to its knees; the Safavid regime foundered and then collapsed; the Ming dynasty gave way to the Qing. In India, rivalries among princes and merchants eroded the Mughals' authority, compounding the instability caused by peasant uprisings.

Another result of the plunge in temperatures was a flight from marginal agricultural lands into the cities. The world had never experienced such massive urbanization: 2.5 million Japanese lived in cities, roughly 10 percent of the population, and in Holland, over 200,000 lived in ten cities close to Amsterdam. But city officials were ill equipped to deal with the influx. Disease swept through overcrowded houses, and fire ravaged whole districts. London had an excess of 228,000 deaths over births,

ALASKA

GREENLAND

ICELAND

DENMARK

NETHERLANDS

ENGLAND

Amsterdam
London

RUPERT'S
LAND

Paris

FRANCE

NEWFOUND-
LAND

Québec

NOVA
SCOTIA

NEW
FRANCE

Boston

New York
Philadelphia

THIRTEEN
COLONIES

LOUISIANA

PORTUGAL

SPAIN

Lisbon
Seville

Cadiz

From North America
and Caribbean

From South America

| Tobacco |
| Rice |
| Furs |
| Indigo |
| Meat |
| Timber |
| Grain |
| Taxes |

| Sugar |
| Gold |
| Hides |
| Coffee |
| Diamonds |
| Calico |
| Taxes |

Manufactures

| Silk |
| Spices |

VICEROYALTY
OF
NEW SPAIN

New Orleans

Zacatecas

MEXICO

Mexico City   Veracruz

Acapulco

| Sugar |
| Coffee |
| Indigo |
| Cotton |

| Sugar |
| Indigo |
| Hides |
| Taxes |

Timbuktu

ATLANTIC
OCEAN

CURAÇAO

Slaves

ASANTE

OYO

Accra   Lagos

FERNANDO PO

Cartagena

Panama

VICEROYALTY
OF
GRANADA

Quito

SURINAM

| Iron |
| Copper |
| Textiles |
| Cutlery |
| Firearms |

DUTCH
BRAZIL

Recife

Bahia

Slaves

PACIFIC
OCEAN

Lima

VICEROYALTY
OF BRAZIL

VICEROYALTY
OF PERU

Potosí

| Tobacco |
| Sugar |

Rio de Janeiro

Buenos Aires

Line of
Tordesillas
1494

| Pepper |
| Spices |
| Silk |
| Coffee |
| Tea |
| Teak |

Cape Town

Indonesia, Malaysia

Goa

Spices

Silk
Calico

China

| Silk |
| Calico |
| Coffee |
| Pepper |
| Indigo |
| Drugs |

India

MAP 13.1 | Trade in Silver and Other Commodities, 1650–1750

The seventeenth and eighteenth centuries were the first centuries of true global commerce. Silver was the one item that was traded all over the world.

- Can you trace the flows of silver from the Americas around the globe (by following the thick red arrows) and identify the commodities that silver was exchanged for in different parts of the world?

- Does the map provide enough information for you to conclude which of these global empires was the wealthiest and most powerful?

- According to this map, how did increased trade shape European states' territorial ambitions?

ARCTIC OCEAN

SWEDEN
St. Petersburg
Danzig
POLAND
TRIA

RUSSIAN EMPIRE

OTTOMAN EMPIRE
Aleppo
Alexandria
Suez
Baghdad
Isfahan
Basra
SAFAVID EMPIRE
Hormuz
ARABIA
Muscat

JAPAN

Silk
Spices

PACIFIC OCEAN

Delhi
Plassey
BENGAL
QING CHINA
MUGHAL EMPIRE
BIHAR
Diu
Calcutta
Guangzhou
Bombay
DECCAN PLATEAU
Goa
Rangoon
Da Nang
PHILIPPINES
Manila
Tellicherry
Madras
Pondicherry
Cochin
ANNAM (VIETNAM)
CEYLON
ETHIOPIA

Mogadishu
Malindi
Mombasa
ZANZIBAR
Luanda
Kilwa
Melaka
SUMATRA
Banten
MALUKU
BORNEO
NEW GUINEA

Mozambique
Sofala
MADAGASCAR
MAURITIUS
RÉUNION
INDIAN OCEAN
Batavia
JAVA
TIMOR
BANDA

Delagoa Bay

Cape Town
Cape of Good Hope

0   1000   2000 Miles
0 1000 2000 Kilometers

Spanish territory	Silver flow
Portuguese territory	Trade route
English territory	✕ Battle
French territory	Silk Commodity
Dutch territory	
Anglo-French contested area	

The Principles of Mercantilism

In 1757, a British commercial expert by the name of Malachy Postlethwayt published a commercial dictionary, **The Universal Dictionary of Trade and Commerce.** *Under the entry "trade," he set forth "some maxims relating to trade that should seem to be confirmed in the course of this work." The first five convey the economic philosophy of mercantilism and the importance that countries attached to the acquisition of precious metals.*

I. That the lasting prosperity of the landed interest depends upon foreign commerce.

II. That the increase of the wealth, splendour, and power of Great Britain and Ireland depends upon exporting more in value of our native produce and manufactures than we import of commodities from other nations and bringing thereby money into the kingdom by means of freight by shipping.

III. That domestic and foreign trade, as they are the means of increasing national treasure, of breeding seamen, and of augmenting our mercantile and royal navies they necessarily become the means of our permanent prosperity and of the safety and preservation of our happy constitution.

IV. That the constant security of the public credit and the payment of interest and principal of the public creditors depend upon the prosperous state of our trade and navigation.

V. That gold and silver is the measure of trade, and that silver is a commodity and may be exported, especially in foreign coin as well as any other commodity.

QUESTIONS FOR ANALYSIS

- According to this reading, whom does mercantilism serve?
- What are the key tenets of mercantilism?
- Why is silver more important than gold in trade?

Source: Malachy Postlethwayt, *The Universal Dictionary of Trade and Commerce,* vol. 2 (1757), p. 792.

---

yet continued to grow through in-migration. Hardly an escape from rural poverty, city dwellers had inordinately high mortality rates, what one scholar has called "the graveyard effect" (Parker, *Global Crisis*, p. 58).

Transformations in global relations began in the Atlantic, where the extraction and shipment of gold and silver siphoned wealth from the New World (the Americas) to the Old World (Afro-Eurasia). Mined mainly by coerced Amerindians and delivered into the hands of merchants and monarchs, silver from the Andes and Mesoamerica boosted the world's supply. In addition, a boom in gold production made Brazil the world's largest producer of that metal at this time.

American mining exports were so lucrative for Spain and Portugal that other European powers wanted a share in the bounty, so they, too, launched colonizing ventures in the New World. Although these latecomers found few precious minerals, they devised other ways to extract wealth, for the Americas had fertile lands on which to cultivate sugarcane, cotton, tobacco, indigo, and rice. The New World also had fur-bearing wildlife, whose pelts were prized in Europe. Better still from the colonizers' perspective, it was easy and inexpensive to produce and transport the New World crops and skins.

If silver quickened the pace of global trade, sugar transformed the European diet. First domesticated in Polynesia, sugar was not central to European diets before the New World plantations started exporting it. Previously, Europeans had used honey for sweetener, but they soon became insatiable consumers of sugar. Between 1690 and 1790, Europe imported 12 million tons of sugar—approximately 1 ton for every African enslaved in the Americas. Public tooth pulling became a popular entertainment (for spectators!) in cities like Paris, and tooth decay became a leading cause of death for Europeans.

No matter what products they supplied, colonies were supposed to provide wealth for their "mother countries"— according to exponents of mercantilism, the economic theory that drove European empire builders. **Mercantilism** saw the world's wealth as fixed: any one country's wealth came at the expense of other countries. The theory further assumed that overseas possessions existed solely to enrich European motherlands because it measured imperial power according to the hoard of treasure in the crown's coffers. To bulk up the treasury, motherlands were supposed to export more goods than they imported and thereby sustain trade surpluses. Thus, colonies should ship more "value" to the mother country than they received in return. (See Primary Source: The Principles of Mercantilism.) In addition, colonies were supposed to be closed to competitors, lest foreign traders drain precious resources from an empire's exclusive domain. As the mother country's monopoly over its colonies' trade generated wealth for royal treasuries, European states grew rich enough to wage almost unceasing wars against one another. Ultimately, mercantilists believed, as did the English philosopher Thomas Hobbes (1588–1679), that "wealth is power and power is wealth."

The mercantilist system required an alliance between the state and its merchants. Mercantilists understood economics and politics as interdependent, with the merchant needing the monarch to protect his interests and the monarch relying on the merchant's trade to enrich the state's treasury. **Chartered companies**, such as the Virginia Company (English) and the East India Companies (Dutch and English), were visible examples of the collaboration between the state and the merchant classes. European monarchs awarded these firms monopoly trading rights over vast areas. These policies and institutions of mercantilism augmented the competition among European empires for markets, colonies, and spoils, and this escalated the penetration into colonial interiors and wars between empires.

The Little Ice Age

Global cooling occurred unevenly around the world. In some places, the effect of falling temperatures, shorter growing seasons, and irregular precipitation patterns was felt as early as the fourteenth century. But the impact of the **Little Ice Age** reached further and deeper in the seventeenth century. What caused this climate change is a matter of debate. But a combination of low sunspot activity, changing ocean currents, and volcanic eruptions that filled the atmosphere with dust shocked an increasingly integrated world. While the seventeenth century was especially severe, the cold lasted well into the next century and in parts of North America into the nineteenth. The Thames River and Dutch canals froze over, which led to famous paintings of people skating on Dutch ponds and lakes. So did the waters separating Sweden from Denmark, which allowed Swedish armies to march right across to Copenhagen. In West Africa, colder and drier conditions saw an advance of the Sahara Desert, leading to repeated famines in the Senegambia region. In addition, Timbuktu and the region around the Niger bend suffered their greatest famines in the seventeenth century. It was still so cold in the early nineteenth century that the English novelist Mary Shelley and her husband spent their summer vacation indoors in Switzerland telling each other horror stories, which inspired Shelley to write *Frankenstein*. Climate change brought mass suffering because harvests failed. In China, the orange groves of Jiangxi Province had to be abandoned after constant and widespread freezing; rice fields, which need a wet spring, went dry. Famine spread across Afro-Eurasia.

There were also political consequences. As droughts, freezing, and famine spread across Afro-Eurasia, herding societies invaded settled societies. Starving peasants rose up against their lords and rulers. Political divides opened up. On the continent of Europe, the Thirty Years' War raged out of control, stoked by farmers' anger (see later in this chapter). Although the war was deeply influenced by religious and national conflicts, it owed much to the decline of food production. In the Americas, indigenous populations were already suffering grievously from the previous

Winter Landscape. *Hendrik Avercamp was one of the most prolific Dutch painters of the seventeenth century. He often painted skaters on frozen ponds, lakes, and canals. This painting is from around 1608, when the Little Ice Age was at its most intense, and shows skaters on one of the large frozen-over canals in Amsterdam.*

Woodlands Indians. *This late sixteenth-century drawing by John White, a pioneer settler on Roanoke Island, off the coast of North Carolina, depicts the Indian village of Secoton in eastern Virginia. In contrast to the great empires that the Spanish conquered in the Valley of Mexico and in the Andes, the Indians whom English, French, and Dutch colonizers encountered in the woodlands of eastern North America generally lived in villages that were politically autonomous entities.*

centuries' plagues. But the long cold snap brought more mayhem. Tensions between Iroquois and Huron rose in the Great Lakes region of North America. Civil war between Portugal and Spain in Europe wreaked havoc in Iberian colonies and led to invasion and panic. According to the bishop of Puebla, in Mexico, "the whole monarchy trembled and shook, since Portugal, Catalonia, the East Indies, the Azores and Brazil had rebelled." In the vice-regal capital of New Spain, "apprehension and panic" seized the city (Parker, *Global Crisis,* p. 461). The Ottomans faced a crippling revolt, while in China the powerful Ming regime could

not deal with the climate shock. It was invaded, as was so often the case when pastures turned to dust, by Manchurian peoples from beyond the Great Wall. They installed a new regime, the Qing dynasty. Indeed, Thomas Hobbes, England's notable political philosopher and author of a classic work of political theory, *Leviathan,* summed up the age: "Man's natural state, before they came together into society, was war; and not simply war, but the war of every man against every other man" (Parker, *Global Crisis,* p. 567). He went on to add famously that "the life of man (is) solitary, poor, nasty, brutish, and short" (p. xxiii)

The Little Ice Age had a devastating impact on populations. It is hard, however, to separate the victims of starvation from the victims of war, since warfare aggravated starvation and famine contributed to war. But in continental Europe, the Thirty Years' War carried off an estimated two-thirds of the total population, on a par with the impact of the Black Death (see Chapter 11). Elsewhere, estimates were closer to one-third. Not until the twentieth century did the world again witness such extensive warfare. For some Afro-Eurasian regimes, the global crisis led to collapse and decline; for others, it became an opportunity for renewal and reinvention.

EXCHANGES AND EXPANSIONS IN NORTH AMERICA

Freezing temperatures and warfare in Europe did not prevent England, France, and Holland from joining Spain and Portugal in the rush to reap riches from American colonies and to take a greater share of global commerce. As rulers in England, France, and Holland granted monopolies to merchant companies, they began to dominate the settlement and trade of new colonies in the Americas. (See Map 13.2.) Although the search for precious metals or water routes to Asia had initially spurred many of these enterprises, the new colonizers learned that only by exploiting other resources could their claims in the Americas generate profits. Also, differences among New World societies required rethinking the character of colonies within mercantilist regimes.

In their colonies along the Atlantic seaboard, the English established one model for new colonies in the Americas. Although these territories failed to yield precious metals or a waterway across the continent, they boasted land suitable for growing numerous crops. Within the English domain, different climates and soils made for very different agricultural possibilities: wheat, rye, barley, and oats from the Middle Colonies (Pennsylvania, New York, New Jersey, and Delaware), tobacco from Virginia and North Carolina, and rice and indigo from farther south. But all the English colonies shared a common feature: population growth led to greater demand for farmlands, which put pressure on Amerindian holdings. The Little

MAP 13.2 | Colonies in North America, 1607–1763

France, England, and Spain laid claim to much of North America at this time.

- Where was each of these colonial powers strongest before the outbreak of the Seven Years' War in 1756? (See p. 514 for a discussion of the Seven Years' War.)

- Which empire gained the most North American territory, and who lost the most at the end of the war in 1763?

- How do you think Native American peoples reacted to the territorial arrangements agreed to by Spain, France, and England at the Treaty of Paris, which ended the war?

Ice Age exacerbated the stress, because shorter growing seasons diminished harvests. Thus, more acreage had to be cultivated to support the colonies' surging population in North America, which meant more lands taken from Amerindians. The result: a souring of relations between Amerindians and colonists. In 1675, which colonists described as a "year without a summer," ferocious wars broke out between Amerindians and English colonists in Virginia and New England. Similar pressures ignited other conflicts throughout the seventeenth and eighteenth centuries and led to the dispossession of Amerindians from lands between the Atlantic Ocean and the Appalachian Mountains.

By contrast, Dutch and French colonies rested not on the expulsion of indigenous peoples, but on dependence on them. Holland's North American venture, however, proved short-lived, as the English took over New Netherland and renamed it New York in 1664. French claims were more enduring and extended across a vast swath of the continent, encompassing eastern Canada, the Great Lakes, and the Mississippi Valley.

Trade between Europeans and Amerindians

Crucial to the trade between Europeans and Amerindians in northern North America was the beaver, an animal for which Amerindian peoples previously had little use. In response to the Europeans' interest, one local Euro-American hunter heard an Amerindian say, "The beaver does everything perfectly well; it makes kettles, hatchets, swords, knives, bread; in short it makes everything." As long as there were beavers to be trapped, trade between the Europeans and their Indian partners flourished.

The distinctive aspect of the fur trade was the Europeans' utter dependence on Amerindian know-how. After all, trapping required familiarity with the beaver's habits and habitats, which Europeans lacked. This reliance especially forced French traders who ventured farther into the continent's interior to adapt to Indian ways. Responding to Amerindian desires to use trade as an instrument to cement familial bonds, the French gave gifts, participated in Amerindian diplomatic rituals, and even married into Indian families. As a result, *métis* (French-Amerindian offspring) played an important role in New France as interpreters, traders, and guides. Thus, the French colonization of the Americas—owing to their reliance on Amerindians as trading partners, military allies, and mates—rested more on cooperation than conquest, especially compared with the empires built by their Spanish and English rivals.

Over the long run, Europeans' trade in guns, alcohol, and trinkets gave them power advantages. It set off a crippling arms race between Amerindians and depletion of beaver stocks. But through the seventeenth and into the middle of the eighteenth century, the majority of lands in the interior of the North American continent remained firmly in Amerindian hands, despite the European empires' expansive claims. On the Great Plains in the center of North America, some Indian peoples lost ground to newcomers, but here the winners were other Indian groups. On the northern plains, the Lakotas, who had migrated westward onto the grasslands, emerged as the most successful expansionists. Coming eastward, the Comanches reigned across a vast swath of the southern plains. These and other invaders displaced existing indigenous societies from some lands, added to their ranks by capturing and often enslaving large

The Fur Trade. *For Europeans in northern North America, no commodity was as important as beaver skins. For the French especially, the fur trade determined the character of their colonial regime in North America. For Indians, it offered access to European goods, but overhunting depleted resources and provoked intertribal conflicts.*

numbers of people (especially females), and enriched themselves by their raiding and through their control over trading. The control that the Comanches asserted extended not only over other Amerindians whom they captured and whose horses they plundered, but also over would-be European colonizers. From the eastern Plains almost to the Pacific Ocean, with the exception of a few enclaves of European settlement, it was Amerindians who largely determined where Europeans could go, stay, and trade. Thus, while early eighteenth-century maps drawn by European empire makers divvied up North America principally among British, French, and Spanish realms, the reality on the ground mocked these imperial pretensions.

There was considerable irony in the fact that Spanish colonizers had empowered the Plains Amerindians. The Spanish, after all, had brought horses to the Americas, and it was the acquisition of these animals that revolutionized Amerindian life and enabled the expansions occurring on the Great Plains. Recognizing the role that horses played in their conquests, the Spanish had tried to keep them out of Indian hands. They failed. Raiders targeted horses. Once introduced into Amerindian circuits, the animals dispersed and flourished on the grasses of the Plains. So did the Indians who had greatest access to horses and who most decisively adapted to equestrianism. On horseback, Amerindians could kill bison much more effectively, which encouraged some groups to forsake farming for hunting and other groups, like the Lakotas and Comanches, to move onto the Plains in pursuit of buffalo. Astride horses, Amerindians also gained military superiority over more sedentary peoples, whose villages and cornfields were vulnerable to mobile forces.

Not all prospered, however, and certainly not all equally. The gains of nomadic equestrians often came at the expense of those who remained wedded to a mixture of horticulture and hunting. Within horse cultures, new inequalities materialized. More successful raiders and hunters not only earned greater honor but also acquired more horses. And with more horses usually came higher status and more wives. At the same time, the status of women generally declined in the transition from horticultural to hunting societies. Their burdens, however, did not, as there were now more buffalo waiting to be turned by women into the products that sustained Plains Amerindian life.

The Plantation Complex in the Caribbean

As late as 1670, the most populous English colony was not on the North American mainland, but on the Caribbean island of Barbados. Because sugar was so desirable, from the mid-seventeenth century onward the English- and French-controlled islands of the Caribbean replicated the Portuguese sugarcane plantations of Brazil; sugar became a quintessential mercantilist commodity.

Tobacco. *The cultivation of tobacco saved the Virginia colony from ruin and brought prosperity to increasing numbers of planters. The spread of tobacco plantations also pushed Indians off their lands and led planters to turn to Africa for a labor force.*

All was not sweet here, however. Because no colonial power held a monopoly, competition to control the region—and sugar production—was fierce. The resulting turbulence did not simply reflect imperial rivalry; it also reflected labor arrangements in the colonies. Because the indigenous populations had been wiped out in Columbus's wake (see Chapter 12), owners of Caribbean estates looked to Africa to obtain workers for their plantations.

Sugar was a killing crop. So deadly was the hot, humid environment in which sugarcane flourished (as fertile for disease as for sugarcane) that many sugar barons spent little time on their plantations. Management fell to overseers, who worked their slaves to death. Despite having immunity to yellow fever and malaria from their homeland's similar environment, Africans could not withstand the regimen. Inadequate food, atrocious living conditions, and filthy sanitation added to their miseries. Moreover, plantation managers treated their slaves as nonhumans: for example, on the first day all new slaves suffered branding with the planter's seal. One English gentleman commented that slaves were like cows, "as near as beasts may be, setting their souls aside."

Slaves Cutting Cane. *Sugar was the preeminent agricultural export from the New World for centuries. Owners of sugarcane plantations relied almost exclusively on African slaves to produce the sweetener. Labor in the fields was especially harsh, as slaves worked in the blistering sun from dawn until dusk. This image shows how women and men toiled side by side.*

More than disease and inadequate rations, the work itself was decimating. Average life expectancy was three years. Six days a week, slaves rose before dawn, labored until noon, ate a short lunch, and then worked until dusk. At harvest time, 16-hour days saw hundreds of men, women, and children bent over to cut the sugarcane and transport it to refineries, sometimes seven days per week. Under this brutal schedule, slaves occasionally dropped dead from exhaustion.

Amid disease and toil, the enslaved coped and resisted as they could. The most dramatic expression of resistance was violent revolt. A more common form was flight. Seeking refuge from overseers, thousands of slaves took to the hills—for example, to the remote highlands of Caribbean islands or to Brazil's vast interior. Those who remained on the plantations resisted via foot dragging, pilfering, and sabotage.

Caribbean settlements and slaveholdings were not restricted to any single European power. But it was the latecomers—the Dutch, the English, and especially the French—who concentrated on the West Indies and who grew wealthy and powerful. (See Map 13.3.) The English took Jamaica from the Spanish in 1655 and made it the premier site of Caribbean sugar by the 1740s. When the French seized half of Santo Domingo in the 1660s (renaming it Saint-Domingue, which is present-day Haiti), they created one of the wealthiest societies based on slavery of all time. This French colony's exports eclipsed those of all the Spanish and English Antilles combined. The capital, Port-au-Prince, was one of the richest cities in the Atlantic world. The colony's merchants and planters built immense mansions worthy of the highest European nobles. Thus, the Atlantic system benefited elite Europeans, who amassed new fortunes by exploiting the colonies' natural resources and the African slaves' labor. The American trade also laid the financial foundations and the heightened consumer demands that were crucial for Europe's late eighteenth- and early nineteenth-century industrial revolution (see Chapter 15).

THE SLAVE TRADE AND AFRICA

Although the slave trade began in the mid-fifteenth century, only in the seventeenth and eighteenth centuries did the numbers of human exports from Africa begin to soar and feed mercantilist regimes. (See Map 13.4.) By 1820, four slaves had crossed the Atlantic for every European. (See Analyzing Global Developments: The Atlantic Trade in Slaves from Africa (1501–1900).) At the same time, the departure of so many inhabitants depopulated and destabilized many parts of Africa.

Capturing and Shipping Slaves

Merchants in Europe and the Americas prospered as the slave trade soared, but their fortunes depended on trading and

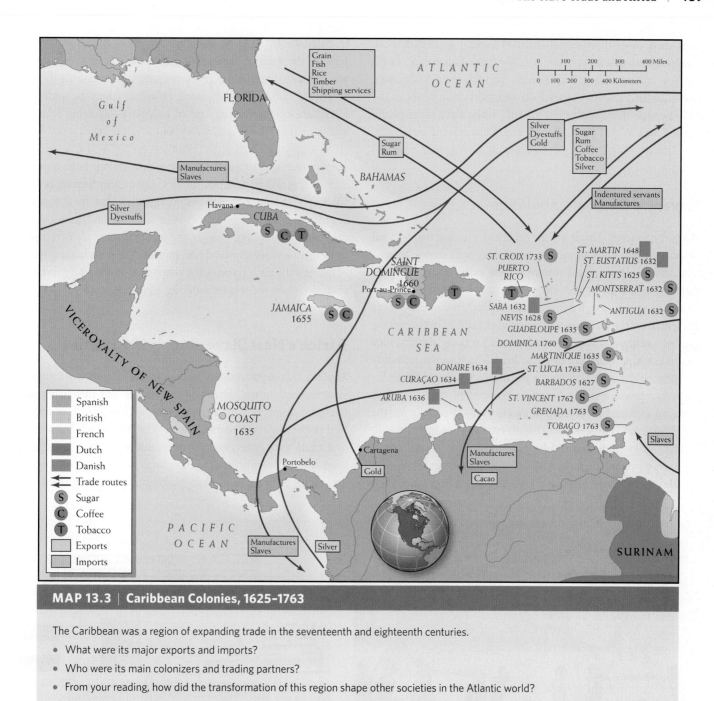

MAP 13.3 | Caribbean Colonies, 1625–1763

The Caribbean was a region of expanding trade in the seventeenth and eighteenth centuries.

- What were its major exports and imports?
- Who were its main colonizers and trading partners?
- From your reading, how did the transformation of this region shape other societies in the Atlantic world?

political networks in Africa. Because European slave traders feared African diseases, mainly malaria, they confined themselves to the coast, where they supplied powerful interior states with firearms with which to conquer other indigenous peoples and ship their defeated adversaries to the slavers.

Before the Europeans' arrival, Africa had an existing system of slave commerce, mainly flowing across the Sahara to North Africa and Egypt and eastward to the Red Sea and the Swahili coast of East Africa. From the Red Sea and Swahili coast destinations, Muslim and Hindu merchants shipped slaves to ports around the Indian Ocean. However, the number of these slaves could not match the volume destined for the Americas once plantation agriculture

began to spread. Indeed, 12.5 million Africans departed for forcible enslavement and shipment to Atlantic ports from the early fifteenth century until 1867, when the last voyage took place.

Now the slave ports along the African coast became gruesome entrepôts. Many captives perished before losing sight of Africa. Stuck in vast holding camps where disease and hunger were rampant, the slaves were then forced aboard vessels in cramped and wretched conditions. These ships waited for weeks to fill their holds while their human cargoes wasted away belowdecks. Crew members tossed dead Africans overboard as they loaded on other Africans from the shore. When the cargo was complete, the ships set sail. In their wake, crews continued to dump bodies.

Most died of gastrointestinal diseases leading to dehydration. Smallpox and dysentery were also scourges. Either way, death was slow and agonizing. Because high mortality led to lost profits, slavers learned to carry better food and more fresh water as the trade became more sophisticated. Still, when slave ships finally reached New World ports, they reeked of disease and excrement. (See Primary Source: Olaudah Equiano on the Atlantic Crossing.)

Slavery's Gender Imbalance

In moving so many Africans to the Americas, the slave trade played havoc with the ratios of men to women in both places because most slaves shipped to the Americas were males. European slave traders sought well-formed and strong males between the ages of 10 and 25, even though many plantation owners came to realize that females of the same age worked as hard as males. Although the numbers indicate Europeans' preferences for male laborers, they also reflect African slavers' desire to keep female slaves, primarily for household work. The gender imbalance made it difficult for slaves to reproduce in the Americas. So planters and slavers had to return to Africa to procure more captives—especially for the Caribbean islands, where slaves' death rates were so high.

Male slaves outnumbered females in the New World, but in the slave-supplying regions of Africa, women outnumbered men. Female captives were especially prized in Africa because of their traditional role in the production of grains, leathers, and cotton. Indeed, the Atlantic slave trade made the role of those women who remained in Africa even more essential for ensuring the subsistence of children and the aged. Moreover, the slave trade reinforced the traditional practice of polygyny—allowing relatively scarce men to take several wives. But in some states, notably the slave-supplying kingdom of Dahomey, on the West African coast, women managed to assert power because of their large numbers and heightened importance. In fact, Dahomean women became so deeply involved in succession disputes that their intrigues could make the difference between winning and losing political power. Ultimately, though, the fact that some women rose to power in a few societies did not diminish the destabilizing effects of the Atlantic slave trade or the chaos that slave raiding and slave trading had on the relations among African states.

Africa's New Slave-Supplying Polities

Africans did not passively let captives fall into the arms of European slave buyers; instead, local political leaders and merchants were energetic suppliers. This activity promoted the growth of centralized political systems, particularly in West African rain forest areas. The trade also shifted control of wealth away from households owning large herds or lands to those who profited from the capture and exchange of slaves—urban merchants and warrior elites.

The Slave Trade. Left: *Africans were captured in the interior and then bound and marched to the coast. Note that there is only one woman among the men (and a couple of children), reflecting the gender imbalance among those captured. Right: After reaching the coast, the captured Africans would be crammed into the holds of slave vessels, where they suffered grievously from overcrowding and unsanitary conditions. Long voyages were especially deadly. If the winds failed or ships had to travel longer distances than usual, many of the captives would die en route to the slave markets across the ocean.*

Olaudah Equiano on the Atlantic Crossing

The most compelling description of the horrifying conditions that captives endured on the African coast as they awaited the arrival of slaving ships and the perils of the Atlantic crossing came from the pen of a former slave, Olaudah Equiano (c. 1745–1797). After purchasing his freedom and becoming a skilled writer, Equiano published The Interesting Narrative of the Life of Olaudah Equiano, or Gustavus Vassa, the African, Written by Himself *(1789). An instantaneous best-seller, within ten years the book saw nine English editions and appeared in American, Dutch, German, Russian, and French editions. Although some critics have questioned the authenticity of Equiano's birth and early life in Africa, the scholarly consensus remains that he was indeed born in Igboland (in the eastern part of present-day Nigeria) and made the voyage across the Atlantic after his capture at age nine.*

The first object which saluted my eyes when I arrived on the coast was the sea, and a slave ship, which was then riding at anchor, and waiting for its cargo. These filled me with astonishment, which was soon converted into terror when I was carried on board. I was immediately handled and tossed up to see if I were sound by some of the crew; and I was now persuaded that I had gotten into a world of bad spirits, and that they were going to kill me. Their complexions too differing so much from ours, their long hair, and the language they spoke, (which was very different from any I had ever heard) united to confirm me in this belief. Indeed such were the horrors of my views and fears at the moment, that, if ten thousand worlds had been my own, I would have freely parted with them all to have exchanged my condition with that of the meanest slave in my own country. When I looked round the ship too and saw a large furnace or copper boiling, and a multitude of black people of every description chained together, every one of their countenances expressing dejection and sorrow, I no longer doubted of my fate; and, quite overpowered with horror and anguish, I fell motionless on the deck and fainted. When I recovered a little I found some black people about me, who I believed were some of those who brought me on board, and had been receiving their pay; they talked to me in order to cheer me, but all in vain. I asked them if we were not to be eaten by those white men with horrible looks, red faces, and loose hair. They told me I was not . . . .

In a little time after, amongst the poor chained men, I found some of my own nation, which in a small degree gave ease to my mind. I inquired of these what was to be done with us; they gave me to understand we were to be carried to these white people's country to work for them. I then was a little revived, and thought, if it were no worse than working, my situation was not so desperate: but still I feared I should be put to death, the white people looked and acted, as I thought, in so savage a manner; for I had never seen among any people such instances of brutal cruelty; and this not only shewn towards us blacks, but also to some of the whites themselves . . . .

At last, when the ship we were in had got in all her cargo, they made ready with many fearful noises, and we were all put under deck, so that we could not see how they managed the vessel. But this disappointment was the least of my sorrow. The stench of the hold while we were on the coast was so intolerably loathsome, that it was dangerous to remain there for any time, and some of us had been permitted to stay on the deck for the fresh air; but now that the whole ship's cargo were confined together, it became absolutely pestilential. The closeness of the place, and the heat of the climate, added to the number in the ship, which was so crowded that each had scarcely room to turn himself, almost suffocated us. This produced copious perspirations, so that the air soon became unfit for respiration, from a variety of loathsome smells, and brought on a sickness among the slaves, of which many died, thus falling victims to the improvident avarice, as I may call it, of their purchasers. This wretched situation was again aggravated by the galling of the chains, now become insupportable; and the filth of the necessary tubs [latrines], into which the children often fell, and were almost suffocated. The shrieks of the women, and the groans of the dying, rendered the whole a scene of horror almost inconceivable.

QUESTIONS FOR ANALYSIS

- The slave trade involved capturing Africans from various parts of the interior of the continent. Which lines in the reading give evidence of this?

- Equiano's book came out in 1789 in the midst of a campaign to abolish the slave trade. Considering the formality of his language, what type of audience do you suppose he was seeking to reach?

- Why would this book describing the horrors of the slave trade have appeared only in the late 1700s, even though such brutal conditions had been existing for more than two centuries?

Source: Olaudah Equiano, *The Interesting Narrative of the Life of Olaudah Equiano, or Gustavus Vassa, the African, Written by Himself,* A Norton Critical Edition, edited by Werner Sollors (New York: Norton, 2001), pp. 38–41.

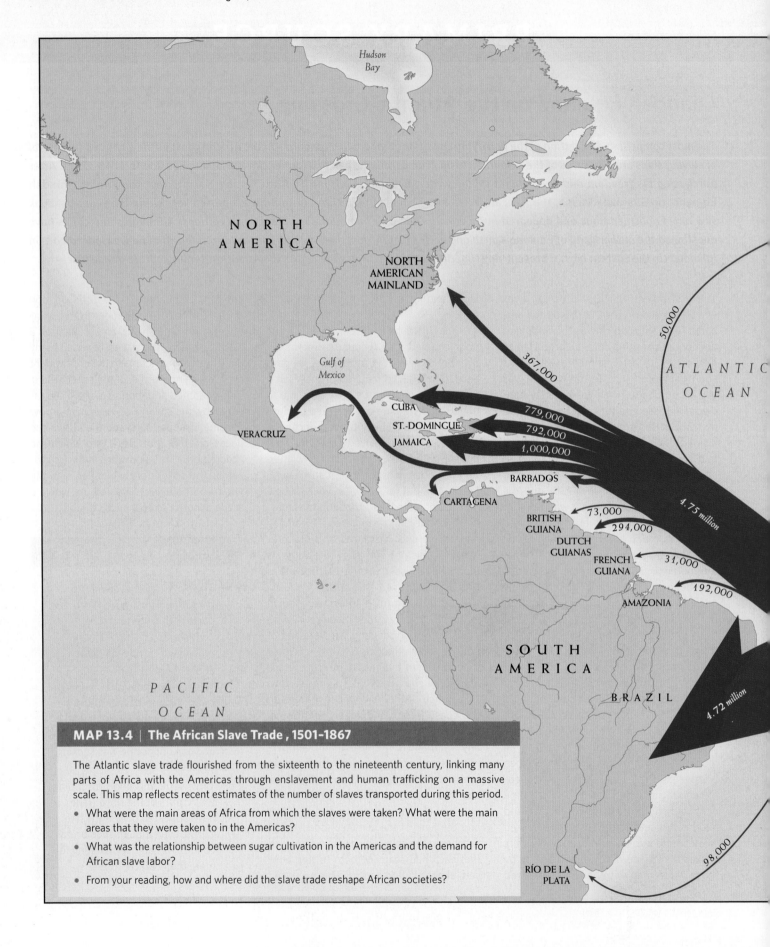

MAP 13.4 | The African Slave Trade , 1501–1867

The Atlantic slave trade flourished from the sixteenth to the nineteenth century, linking many parts of Africa with the Americas through enslavement and human trafficking on a massive scale. This map reflects recent estimates of the number of slaves transported during this period.

- What were the main areas of Africa from which the slaves were taken? What were the main areas that they were taken to in the Americas?

- What was the relationship between sugar cultivation in the Americas and the demand for African slave labor?

- From your reading, how and where did the slave trade reshape African societies?

NORTH SEA

EUROPE

BLACK SEA

CASPIAN SEA

ARAL SEA

ASIA

MEDITERRANEAN SEA

PERSIA

Persian Gulf

MOROCCO

ALGERIA   TUNISIA

LIBYA

EGYPT

RED SEA

ARABIA

2 million (1700-1900)

SAHARA

1.32 million

YEMEN

ARABIAN SEA

SENEGAMBIA

756,000

389,000

337,000

1.2 million

SIERRA LEONE

WINDWARD COAST

GOLD COAST

ASANTE

DAHOMEY

BIGHT OF BENIN

OYO

BIGHT OF BIAFRA

AFRICA

ETHIOPIA

892,000

280,000

533,000

1.99 million

1.6 million

AMERICAS
12.57 million
(1501-1867)

KONGO
WEST
CENTRAL
AFRICA

5.7 million

SWAHILI COAST

INDIAN OCEAN

SOUTHEAST AFRICA

200,000

MADAGASCAR

MASCARENE ISLANDS
359,000

0   500   1000   1500 Miles

0   500   1000   1500 Kilometers

ANALYZING GLOBAL DEVELOPMENTS

The Atlantic Trade in Slaves from Africa (1501–1900)

The world's leading slave traders were also the world's most important maritime powers during the period from 1501 to 1900. The following tables focus on which countries transported these slaves and where they ended up. The Spanish and Portuguese established the first European empires in the Americas and created the model for the early slave trade. But northern European powers like Great Britain and France, reflecting their growing strength in maritime commerce, dominated the Atlantic slave trade between 1642 and 1808. In the final phase of the Atlantic slave trade, 1808–1867, the northern European powers and the United States disengaged from the trade, allowing the Portuguese and the Spanish once again to dominate the trade now centered largely on Cuba and Brazil.

In recent decades, scholars of the Atlantic slave trade have created the Trans-Atlantic Slave Trade Database, which can be accessed at the Voyages Web site (www.slavevoyages.org). Constructed from nearly 35,000 documented voyages during this period, this database incorporates roughly 80 percent of the slave ventures that set out for Africa to obtain slaves from all around the Atlantic world during this era. Through painstaking research, historians have been able to reconstruct the Atlantic world slave trade and offer a clear insight into the experiences of all those involved and the impact of this trade on the global economy during four centuries.

QUESTIONS FOR ANALYSIS

- Which countries were the most heavily invested in the Atlantic slave trade based on the data in the first table? How do you know?
- What was the relationship between the slave-trading countries and the colonies in the New World based on the entries in both tables?
- Why is the total number of slaves traded different from the number of slaves that disembarked? Did you expect the differences between these two numbers to be greater than they are? If so, why?

Source: David Eltis and David Richardson, *Atlas of the Transatlantic Slave Trade* (2010).

Number of Slaves Taken from Africa to the Americas by Nationality of Vessels That Carried Them (1501–1867)

Vessel Nationality	Number of Slaves
Portugal/Brazil	5,849,300
Great Britain	3,259,900
France	1,380,970
Spain/Uruguay	1,060,900
Netherlands	555,300
United States	305,800
Baltic States	110,400
Total Atlantic World	**12,522,570**

Disembarkation of Slaves from Africa to the Americas (1501–1900)

Disembarking Country/Colony	Number of Slaves
Brazil (Portugal)	4,720,000
Smaller Caribbean islands (mix)	1,750,000
Jamaica (Spain then Great Britain)	1,000,000
Saint-Domingue (Spain then France)	792,000
Cuba (Spain)	779,000
Spanish Caribbean mainland	390,000
United States	389,000
Dutch Guiana	294,000
Amazonia	142,000
Total	**10,703,000**

THE KONGO KINGDOM In some parts of Africa, the booming slave trade wreaked havoc as local leaders feuded over control of the traffic; mercantilist rivalry along the African coast disrupted old states and produced new ones. In the Kongo kingdom, civil wars raged for over a century after 1665, and captured warriors were sold as slaves. As members of the royal family clashed, entire provinces saw their populations vanish. Most important to the conduct of war and the control of trade were firearms and gunpowder, which made the capturing of slaves highly efficient. Moreover, kidnapping became so prevalent that cultivators worked their fields bearing weapons, leaving their children behind in guarded stockades.

Some leaders of the Kongo kingdom fought back. Consider Queen Nzinga (1583–1663), a masterful diplomat and a shrewd military planner. Having converted to Christianity, she managed to keep Portuguese slavers at bay during her long reign. Even after Portuguese forces defeated her troops in battle, she conducted effective guerrilla warfare into her sixties.

The Port of Loango. *Partly as a result of the profits of the slave trade, African rulers and merchants were able to create large and prosperous port cities such as Loango (pictured here), which was on the western coast of south-central Africa.*

Consider also the Christian visionary Dona Beatriz Kimpa Vita. Born in the Kongo in 1684 and baptized as a Christian, at age twenty she claimed to have received visions from St. Anthony of Padua. She believed that she died every Friday and was transported to heaven to converse with God, returning to earth on Monday to broadcast God's commands to believers. Her message aimed to end the Kongo civil wars and re-create a unified kingdom. Although she gained a large following, she failed to win the support of leading political figures. In 1706, she was captured and burned at the stake.

OYO, ASANTE, AND OTHER GROUPS As some African merchants and warlords sold other Africans, their commercial success enabled them to consolidate political power and grow wealthy. Their wealth financed additional weapons, with which they subdued neighbors and extended political control. Among the most durable new polities was the Asante state, which arose in the West African tropical rain forest in 1701 and expanded through 1750. This state benefited from its access to gold, which it used to acquire firearms (from European traders) to raid nearby communities for servile workers. From its capital city at Kumasi, the state eventually encompassed almost all of present-day Ghana. Main roads spread out from the capital like spokes of a wheel, each approximately twenty days' travel from the center. Through the Asante trading networks, African traders bought, bartered, and sold slaves, who wound up in the hands of European merchants waiting in ports with vessels carrying manufactured products and weaponry.

Also active in the slave trade—and enriched by it—was the Oyo Empire. This territory, which straddled the main trade routes, linked tropical rain forests with interior markets of the northern savanna areas. The empire's strength rested on its impressive army brandishing weapons secured from trade with Europeans. Deploying cavalry units in the savanna and infantry units in the rain forest, the Oyo's military campaigns became annual events, only suspended so that warriors could return home for agricultural duties. Every dry season, Oyo armies marched on their neighbors to capture entire villages.

Slavery and the emergence of new political organizations enriched and empowered some Africans, but they cost Africa dearly. For the princes, warriors, and merchants who organized the slave trade, their business (like that of Amerindian fur suppliers) enabled them to obtain European goods—especially alcohol, tobacco, textiles, and guns. The Atlantic system also tilted wealth away from rural dwellers and village elders and increasingly toward port cities. Across the landmass, the slave trade thinned the population. True, Africa was spared a demographic catastrophe equal to the devastation of American Indians. The introduction of American food crops—notably maize and cassava, producing many more calories per acre than the old staples of millet and sorghum—blunted the trade's depopulating aspects. Yet some areas suffered grievously from three centuries of heavy involvement in the slave trade. The Atlantic trade enhanced the warrior class, who carried out raids for captives; the dislocations, internal power struggles, and economic hardships that followed precipitated the rise and fall of West African kingdoms.

Since the seventeenth century saw the deportation of 2 million African men, women, and children to the Americas, it is worth asking whether the Little Ice Age was a factor in the fate of these peoples. Unfortunately, information on sub-Saharan Africa is not as rich as it is for Europe and Asia. Nonetheless, what we do know, mainly from travelers' accounts, is that many of the areas from which slaves came—like Kongo, the interior of West Africa, and Senegambia—suffered from severe drought and witnessed a spike in the number of captives sold to slavers.

COMPARATIVE PERSPECTIVES ON CLIMATE CHANGE: THE OTTOMAN EMPIRE AND MING CHINA

The Little Ice Age tore asunder two of Afro-Eurasia's largest and most stable empires—the Ottoman Empire and Ming China—though in both cases other factors were also at work. One survived, and the other did not—although in both empires peasants and nomads, driven by severe famines, rose in rebellion, asserting that their rulers had failed to look after them.

The Ottomans Struggle to Maintain Power and Legitimacy

Hardest and earliest hit by climate change was the eastern Mediterranean. Here, fierce cold and endless drought brought famine and high mortality. In 1620, the Bosporus froze over, enabling residents of Istanbul to walk from the European side of the city into the Asian side. In Ottoman territories dependent on floodwaters for their well-being, such as Egypt and Iraq, food was in short supply and mortality rates skyrocketed. In addition, the import of New World silver led to high levels of inflation and a destabilized economy. Yet, in spite of the dire circumstances, the Ottomans continued their military campaigns against the Habsburgs. Banditry, nomadic invasions of settled lands, refusal to pay taxes, and ultimately outright revolt were the inevitable result.

THE CELALI REVOLT AND KÖPRÜLÜ REFORMS A revolt, begun in central Anatolia in the early sixteenth century, continued with fits and starts throughout the century and reached a crescendo at the beginning of the seventeenth century. This later full-blown uprising took its name from Sheikh Celali, who had led a rebellion in the early sixteenth century. Later rebels called themselves Celalis, looking to his life for inspiration. They united hordes of bandits and eventually challenged the sultan's authority. With a 30,000-strong army, the rebels turned much of Anatolia into a danger zone full of pillaging, looting, burning of villages, and killing. Large segments of the Ottoman population, many of whom were Shiites or turned to Shiism to express their opposition to Ottoman rule, joined the rebellion. Poised to assault Istanbul in 1607–1608, the rebels encountered the sultan's troops on the plains outside the capital and were trounced. The empire pulled back from the edge of collapse.

Although the Ottomans survived, they did so in a greatly weakened state. The empire's population, around 35 million in the 1590s, was still below that number when the first official census was carried out in 1830. Meanwhile, the European powers with access to New World colonies sprinted ahead of the Ottomans economically, militarily, and culturally.

The Ottomans did, however, experience a period of good governance in the mid- to late-seventeenth century in spite of Mustafa Ali's pessimistic predictions. New grand viziers from the Köprülü family spearheaded changes to revitalize the government. Known as the Köprülü reforms, the changes in administration reenergized the state and enabled the military to reacquire some of its lost possessions. Revenues again increased, and inflation decreased. Fired by revived expansionist ambitions, Istanbul decided to renew its assault on Christianity (see Chapter 11)—beginning with rekindled plans to seize Vienna. Although the Ottomans amassed an enormous force outside the Habsburg capital in 1683, both sides suffered heavy losses, but the Ottoman forces ultimately retreated. Under the treaty that ended the Austro-Ottoman war, the Ottomans lost major European territorial possessions, including Hungary.

Despite failing to take Vienna, the Ottoman state flourished in the first half of the eighteenth century. No event was more resplendent than the two weeks of feasting, parades, and entertainment that accompanied the circumcision of the sultan's sons in 1720. Istanbul also once again became a beehive of political activity, adorned with new palaces and mosques.

THE MAMLUKS IN OTTOMAN EGYPT A weakened Ottoman state prompted outlying provinces to assert their autonomy. Egypt led the way. Here, too, plummeting temperatures and monsoon failures leading to aridity and low Nile waters may have been factors. Egypt experienced extremely low Niles from 1641 to 1643, owing to catastrophic drought, and then such extreme cold that a Turkish traveler in the 1670s reported that everyone who could afford to wore fur-lined clothing.

In 1517, Egypt had become the Ottoman Empire's greatest conquest. The wealthiest Ottoman territory, it was an important source of revenue and initially was well governed by its Ottoman-appointed governors. Its payments to Istanbul exceeded those of any other Ottoman province. Yet, starting in the mid-seventeenth century, households modeled on the sultan's arose and increasingly asserted their independence from Istanbul. By the latter half of the eighteenth century, the dominant households were made up of **Mamluks** (Arabic for "owned" or "possessed"), military men who had ruled Egypt as an independent regime until the Ottoman conquest (see Chapter 10). Although the Ottoman forces had routed the Mamluks on the battlefield in 1517, Ottoman governors in Egypt allowed the Mamluks to reform themselves. By the second half of the eighteenth century, these military men were nearly as powerful as their ancestors had been in the fifteenth century when they ruled Egypt independently. Mamluk leaders also enhanced their power by aligning with Egyptian merchants and catering to the *ulama*. Turning the Ottoman governor in Egypt into a mere figurehead, this provincial elite kept much of the area's fiscal resources for themselves at the expense of the imperial coffers and the local peasantry.

Siege of Vienna. *This seventeenth-century painting depicts the Ottoman siege of Vienna, which began on July 14, 1683, and ended on September 12. The city might have fallen if the Polish king, John III, had not answered the pope's plea to defend Christendom and sent an army to assist German and Austrian troops in defeating the Ottomans.*

Although the Ottoman Empire survived the impact of the Little Ice Age (in contrast to the Ming dynasty in China), it emerged in a severely weakened condition. It was well on its way to becoming "the sick man of Europe," as the great European powers described the Ottoman state in the nineteenth century. The Celali revolts resulted in devastating population losses, while the repeated low Nile floods reduced food and tribute payments from Egypt to Istanbul, further weakening the Ottoman state. Not all the decline was associated with climate change, however. Heterodox and Sufi religious leaders challenged the Sunni orthodoxy of the clerical and bureaucratic classes. In Egypt and the other Arab provinces of the Ottoman Empire, local notables, notably Mamluks in Egypt and warlords and religious leaders in greater Syria, sought autonomy from Istanbul.

Ming China Succumbs to Manchu Rule

The Ming dynasty was less fortunate than the Ottomans. It did not survive. The Little Ice Age was not wholly responsible for the fall of the Ming, but it played a predominant role. Drought and freezing temperatures affected food production not only in China proper, where the Ming prevailed, but also throughout Inner China, where by the seventeenth century the Manchus of Manchuria were a rising power. The Ming capital of Beijing suffered grievously. An estimated 300,000 perished within the inner city in 1644, causing many Han Chinese to conclude that the Ming had lost the mandate of heaven.

THE MANCHUS FIND A VULNERABLE TARGET Unlike the Ottoman Empire, China's imperial state always had powerful enemies on its northern frontier, eager to take over the state apparatus and prosper by assuming control of a productive economy. By the early seventeenth century, a rising **Manchu** population, based in Inner China and unable to feed their people in Manchuria, were poised to breach the Great Wall in search of better lands. They found a Chinese government and its population in disarray from warfare and fiscal crisis. Peasant rebellions crippled central authorities. Outlaw armies swelled under charismatic leaders. The so-called "roving bands" wreaked havoc across the countryside. The most famous rebel leader, the "dashing prince," Li Zicheng, reached the outskirts of Beijing in 1644. Only a few companies of soldiers and a few thousand eunuchs stood to defend the capital's 21 miles of walls. Li Zicheng seized Beijing easily. Two days later, the emperor hanged himself. On the following day, the triumphant "dashing prince" rode into the capital and claimed the throne.

News of the fall of the Ming capital sent shock waves around the empire. One hundred and seventy miles to the northeast, where China meets Manchuria, the Ming's army's commander received the news within a matter of days.

MAP 13.5 | From Ming to Qing China, 1644–1760

Qing China under the Manchus expanded its territory significantly during this period.

- Find the Manchu homeland and then the area of Manchu expansion after 1644, when the Manchus established the Qing dynasty.
- Where did the Qing dynasty expand?
- Based on the map, why do you think the Qing dynasty expanded so aggressively during this period?
- What does the location of Manchuria tell you about the historical origins of the Qing?

Tasked to defend the Ming against their Manchu neighbors, the commander knew a precarious position when he saw one. Caught between an advancing rebel army on the one side and the Manchus on the other, he made a fateful decision: he made a pact with the Manchus for their cooperation to fight the "dashing prince." In return, his new allies got the "gold and treasure" in the capital. Thus, without shedding a drop of blood, the Manchus joined the Ming forces. After years of coveting the Ming Empire, the Manchus were finally marching on Beijing. (See Map 13.5.)

Other factors besides the Little Ice Age, including some that troubled the Ottoman Empire at this time, spelled the end of the Ming dynasty. As elsewhere, the influx of silver from the New World and Japan, while at first stimulating the Chinese economy, led to severe economic dislocations. As noted in Chapter 12, Europeans used New World silver to pay for their purchases of Chinese goods. Increasing monetization of the economy, which entailed silver becoming the primary medium of exchange, bolstered market activity and state revenues at the same time.

Yet the primacy of silver had differential impacts on the Ottomans and the Chinese. In the Ottoman Empire, the influx of New World silver undermined the Ottoman ambition to create an autonomous economy. In China, silver pressured peasants, who now needed that metal to pay their taxes and purchase goods. (See Primary Source: Huang Liuhong on Eliminating Authorized Silversmiths.) When silver supplies were abundant, the peasants faced inflationary prices. But when supplies became scant, as they did over the seventeenth century because of a decline in New World mining and rising silver demand in Europe, Chinese peasants could not meet their obligations to state officials and merchants. The frustrated masses

Silver. *This seventeenth-century helmet from the Ming (1368–1633) or Qing (1644–1911) dynasty features steel, gold, silver, and textiles, all of which were vital to the Chinese economy during this century. Silver was especially important, for its large influx from Japan and the Americas led to severe economic problems, political unrest, and the overthrow of the Ming dynasty.*

thus often seethed with resentment, which quickly turned to rebellion.

Although China had prospered in the sixteenth and seventeenth centuries, regional wealth undermined the central dynasty. Local power holders increasingly defied the Ming government. Moreover, because Ming rulers discouraged overseas commerce and forbade foreign travel, they did not reap the rewards of long-distance trade. Rather, these profits went to merchants and adventurers who evaded imperial edicts. All this happened as Beijing faced mounting defense costs. The combined result of climate shock, regional opposition, and fiscal crisis brought down the Ming dynasty in 1644.

THE QING DYNASTY ASSERTS CONTROL Despite their small numbers, the Manchus overcame early resistance to their rule and oversaw an impressive expansion of their realm. The Manchus were descendants of the Jurchens (see Chapter 10). They emerged as a force early in the seventeenth century, when their leader claimed the title of khan after securing the allegiance of various Mongol groups in northeastern Asia, paving the way for their eventual conquest of China.

When the Manchus defeated Li Zicheng and seized power in Beijing, they numbered around 1 million. Assuming control of a domain that included perhaps 250 million people, they were keenly aware of their minority status. Taking power was one thing; keeping it was another. But keep it they did. In fact, during the eighteenth century, the Manchu **Qing** ("pure") **dynasty** (1644–1911) incorporated new territories, experienced substantial population growth, and sustained significant economic growth. Despite coming to power at a time of political chaos, the Manchus established a stable and long-lived imperial system in contrast to the political and economic turmoil that rocked the societies of the Atlantic world.

The key to China's relatively stable economic and geographical expansion lay in its rulers' shrewd and flexible policies. The early Manchu emperors were able administrators who knew that to govern a diverse population, they had to adapt to local ways. To promote continuity, they respected Confucian codes and kept the classic texts as the basis of the prestigious civil service examinations (see Chapter 9). Social hierarchies of age, gender, and kin—indeed, the entire image of the family as the bedrock of social organization—endured. In some areas, like Taiwan, the Manchus added new territories to existing provinces. Elsewhere, they gave newly acquired territories, like Mongolia, Tibet, and Xinjiang, their own form of local administration. Imperial envoys in these regions administered through staffs of locals and relied on native institutions. Until the late nineteenth century, the Qing dynasty showed little interest in integrating those regions into "China proper."

At the same time, Qing rulers conveyed a clear sense of their own majesty and legitimacy. Rulers relentlessly promoted

Huang Liuhong on Eliminating Authorized Silversmiths

The influx of silver into China had profound effects on its economy and government. For instance, silver became the medium for assessing taxes. In his magistrate's manual from around 1694, Huang Liuhong (Huang Liu-hung) indicated the problems that arose from involving authorized silversmiths in the payment process. The situation demonstrates how silver had become an integral part of the lives of the Chinese people.

The purpose of using an authorized silversmith in the collection of tax money is twofold. First, the quality of the silver delivered by the taxpayers must be up to standard. The authorized silversmith is expected to reject any substandard silver. Second, when the silver is delivered to the provincial treasury, it should be melted and cast into ingots to avoid theft while in transit. But, to get his commission, the authorized silversmith has to pay a fee and arrange for a guarantor. In addition, he has to pay bribes to the clerks of the revenue section and to absorb the operating expenses of his shop—rent, food, coal, wages for his employees, and so on. If he does not impose a surcharge on the taxpayers, how can he maintain his business?

There are many ways for an authorized silversmith to defraud the taxpayers. First, he can declare that the quality of the silver is not up to standard and a larger amount is required. Second, he can insist that all small pieces of silver have to be melted and cast into ingots; hence there will be wastage in the process of melting. Third, he may demand that all ingots, no matter how small they are, be stamped with his seal, and of course charge a stamping fee. Fourth, he may require a fee for each melting as a legitimate charge for the service. Fifth, he can procrastinate until the taxpayer becomes impatient and is willing to double the melting fee. Last, if the taxpayer seems naive or simple minded, the smith can purposely upset the melting container and put the blame on the taxpayer. All these tricks are prevalent, and little can be done to thwart them.

When the silver ingots are delivered to the provincial treasury, few of them are up to standard. The authorized silversmith often blames the taxpayers for bringing in silver of inferior quality although it would be easy for him to reject them at the time of melting. Powerful official families and audacious licentiates often put poor quality silver in sealed envelopes, which the authorized silversmith is not empowered to examine. Therefore, the use of an authorized silversmith contributes very little to the business of tax collection; it only increases the burden of small taxpayers.

QUESTIONS FOR ANALYSIS

- What are the six ways that an authorized silversmith can defraud taxpayers?
- Why does the author suggest that the use of authorized silversmiths increases the burden of small taxpayers?
- What reasons would the Chinese state have for maintaining such a "flawed" system?

Source: Huang Liu-hung, *A Complete Book Concerning Happiness and Benevolence: A Manual for Local Magistrates in Seventeenth Century China* (Tucson: University of Arizona Press, 1984), pp. 190–91.

patriarchal values. Widows who remained "chaste" enjoyed public praise, and women in general were urged to lead a "virtuous" life serving male kin and family. To the majority Han population, the Manchu emperor represented himself as the worthy upholder of familial values and classical Chinese civilization; to the Tibetan Buddhists, the Manchu state offered imperial patronage. So, too, with Islamic subjects. Although the Islamic Uighurs, as well as other Muslim subjects, might have disliked the Manchus' easygoing religious attitude, they generally endorsed the emperor's claim to rule.

However, insinuating themselves into an existing order and appeasing subject peoples did not satisfy the Manchu yearning to leave their imprint. They also introduced measures that emphasized their authority, their distinctiveness, and the submission of their mostly Han Chinese subjects. For example, Qing officials composed or translated important documents into Manchu and banned intermarriage between Manchu and Han (although this was difficult to enforce). Other edicts imposed Manchu ways—for example, requiring all Han males to shave their forehead and braid their hair in a queue and to wear high collars and tight jackets instead of loose Ming-style clothes.

Nothing earned the regime's disapproval more than the urban elites' indulgence in sensual pleasure. The Qing court regarded the "decadence" of the late Ming, symbolized by its famous actresses, as one of the Ming's principal failings. In 1723, the Qing banned female performers from the court and then from commercial theaters, with young boys taking female roles onstage. The Qing also tried to regulate commercial theater by

Qing Theater with Female Impersonators. *The Qing court banned women from performing in theaters, which led to the practice of using young boys in female roles.*

excluding women from the audience. The popularity of female impersonators onstage, however, brought a new cachet to homosexual relationships. A gulf began to open between the government's aspirations and its ability to police society. For example, the urban public continued to flock to performances by female impersonators in defiance of the Qing's bans.

Manchu impositions fell mostly on the peasantry, for the Qing financed their administrative structure through taxes on peasant households. In response, the peasants sought new lands to cultivate in border areas, having lost much land during the Little Ice Age. On these estates, they planted New World crops that grew well in difficult soils. This move introduced an important change in the Chinese diet: while rice remained the staple diet of the wealthy, peasants increasingly subsisted on corn and sweet potatoes.

EXPANSION AND TRADE UNDER THE QING The Qing dynasty forged tributary relations with Korea, Vietnam, Burma, and Nepal, and its territorial expansion reached far into central Asia, Tibet, and Mongolia. In particular, the Manchus confronted the Junghars of western Mongolia, who controlled much of central Asia in the mid-seventeenth century and whose predecessors had once captured an early Ming emperor. Wary of a potential alliance between the Junghars and an emerging Russia on its northern frontiers, the Qing dynasty launched successive campaigns and defeated the Junghars by the mid-eighteenth century.

While officials redoubled their reliance on an agrarian base, trade and commerce flourished. Chinese merchants continued

to ply the waters stretching from Southeast Asia to Japan, exchanging textiles, ceramics, and medicine for spices and rice. Although initially the Qing state vacillated about permitting maritime trade with foreigners, it sought to regulate external commerce more formally as it consolidated its rule. In 1720, in Canton, a group of merchants formed a monopolistic guild to trade with Europeans. Although the guild disbanded in the face of opposition from other merchants, it revived after the Qing restricted European trade to Canton. The **Canton system**, established by imperial decree in 1759, required European traders to have guild merchants act as guarantors for their good behavior and payment of fees.

China, in sum, negotiated a century of climate change and political upheaval without dismantling established ways in politics and economics, much as the Ottomans did. Climate change was far from the only, or even the primary, factor in China's major political upheaval, the replacement of Ming rule with a long-lasting Qing dynasty. As in the Ottoman Empire, the influx of New World silver disrupted the economy, leading to a cycle of booms and busts. Even so, there was much continuity in the seventeenth and eighteenth centuries. At the heart of this continuity was the peasantry, who continued to practice popular faiths, cultivate crops, and stay close to fields and villages. Trade with the outside world remained marginal to overall commercial life; like the Ming, the Qing cared more about the agrarian than the commercial health of the empire, believing the former to be the foundation of prosperity and tranquility. As long as China's peasantry could keep the dynasty's coffers full,

Canton. *Not only were foreigners not allowed to trade with the Chinese outside of Canton, but they were also required to have Chinese guild members act as guarantors of their good behavior and payment of fees.*

the government was content to squeeze the merchants when it needed funds. Some historians view this practice as a failure to adapt to a changing world order, as it ultimately left China vulnerable to outsiders—especially Europeans. But this view puts the historical cart before the horse. By the mid-eighteenth century, Europe still needed China more than the other way around. For the majority of Chinese, no superior model of belief, politics, or economics was conceivable. Indeed, although the Qing had taken over a crumbling empire in 1644, a century later China was enjoying a new level of prosperity.

In both the Ottoman Empire and China, the Little Ice Age had severe effects. The Ottoman Empire barely survived, although its population losses were not recouped until well into the nineteenth century and its sense of power and legitimacy were badly shaken. In contrast, while the Ming dynasty lost out to a regime drawn from the much-despised Manchurian region, the new Qing dynasty created a stable political order, a prosperous economy, and a well-functioning social order—though one that favored those of Manchu descent. As noted previously, climate change was not the sole factor in causing these outcomes, but its role was significant.

OTHER PARTS OF ASIA IN THE SEVENTEENTH AND EIGHTEENTH CENTURIES

The other regions in Asia also experienced great difficulties brought on by the Little Ice Age. All had to cope with droughts, high winds, hailstorms, and earthquakes, but some weathered

the troubles better than others. In Iran, the Safavid regime came to an end in the seventeenth century, but here regime change was due more to ethnic diversity and ineffective rulers than to severe climatic conditions. A similar situation played out in India, which endured at least four lesser monsoons and a plethora of rebellions that led Shah Aurangzeb (r. 1658–1797) to carry out savage persecutions of non-Muslim groups. Nevertheless, Mughal monarchs, even Aurangzeb, dealt promptly and reasonably effectively with the famines, even the most severe one that ravaged the Gujarati region between 1630 and 1632. The Tokugawa regime in Japan, installed early in the sixteenth century, overcame the difficulties that the Little Ice Age presented. In fact, it experienced a century of increased agricultural productivity, rapid population growth, and impressive urbanization, mostly owing to the shrewd provincial administrators that the Tokugawa rulers appointed.

Global trading networks blossomed even more vigorously in Asia than in the Americas and Europe. China probably possessed one-fourth of the world's population and was still the wealthiest region in the world. In addition, the Europeans were less dominant in Asia than in the Americas and therefore had to content themselves as commercial intermediaries in Asia's brisk long-distance trade. They penetrated Asian markets with American silver largely because the Asians, especially the Chinese, regarded their trade goods as inferior. Nor could they conquer Asian empires or colonize vast portions of the region or enslave Asian peoples as they had Africans. The Mughal Empire continued to grow, and the Qing dynasty, which had wrested control from the Ming, significantly expanded China's borders. Still, in some places the balance of power was tilting in Europe's direction. Not only did the Ottomans' borders contract, but by the late eighteenth century, Europeans had established economic and military dominance in parts of India and much of Southeast Asia.

The Dutch in Southeast Asia

In Southeast Asia, the Dutch already enjoyed a dominant position by the seventeenth century. Although the Portuguese had seized the vibrant port city of Melaka in 1511 and the Spaniards had taken Manila in 1571, neither was able to monopolize the lucrative spice trade. To challenge them, the Dutch government persuaded its merchants to charter the Dutch East India Company (abbreviated as VOC) in 1602. Benefiting from Amsterdam's position as the most world's efficient money market with the lowest interest rates, the VOC raised ten times the capital of its English counterpart—the royal chartered English East India Company. The advantages of chartered companies were evident in the VOC's scale of operation: at its peak the company had 257 ships and employed 12,000 persons. Throughout two centuries it sent ships manned by a total of 1 million men to Asia.

Attack on Bantam. *This engraving depicts a Dutch attack on Bantam in the late seventeenth century as part of the VOC's effort to expand its empire in Southeast Asia.*

The VOC's main impact was in Southeast Asia, where spices, coffee, tea, and teak wood were key exports (see again Map 13.1). The company's objective was to secure a trade monopoly wherever it could, fix prices, and replace the indigenous population with Dutch planters. In 1619, under the leadership of Jan Pieterszoon Coen (who once said that trade could not be conducted without war nor war without trade), the Dutch swept into the Javanese port of Jakarta (renamed Batavia by the Dutch). In defiance of local rulers and English rivals, the Dutch burned all the houses, drove out the population, and constructed a fortress from which to control the Southeast Asian trade. Two years later, Coen's forces took over a cluster of nutmeg-producing islands known as Banda. The traditional chiefs and almost the entire population were killed outright, left to starve, or enslaved. Dutch planters and their slaves replaced the decimated local population and sent their produce to the VOC. The motive for such rapacious action was the huge profit to be made by buying nutmeg at a low price in the Bandanese Islands and selling it at many times that price in Europe.

With their monopoly of nutmeg secured, the Dutch went after the market in cloves. Their strategy was to control production in one region and then destroy the rest, which entailed, once again, wars against producers and traders in other areas. Portuguese Melaka soon fell to the Dutch and became a VOC outpost. Although this aggressive expansion met widespread resistance, by 1670 the Dutch controlled all of the lucrative spice trade from the Maluku islands.

Next, the VOC gained control of Bantam (present-day Banten), the largest pepper-exporting port. However, the Dutch had to share this commerce with Chinese and English competitors. Moreover, since there was no demand for European products in Asia, the Dutch had to participate more in inter-Asian trade as a way to reduce their need to make payments in precious metals. So they purchased, for example, calicoes (plain white cotton cloths) in India or copper in Japan for resale in Melaka and Java. They also diversified into trading silk, cotton, tea, and coffee, in addition to spices.

As a result of the Dutch enterprise, European outposts such as Dutch Batavia and Spanish Manila soon eclipsed old cosmopolitan cities such as Bantam. Indeed, as Europeans competed for supremacy in the borderlands of Southeast Asia, they made local societies serve their own ambitions and began replacing traditional networks with trade routes that primarily served European interests. The Dutch used Europe's traditional appetite for Southeast Asian spices like nutmeg, pepper, and cloves, to which they added coffee, tea, and teak wood, to integrate the islands of the Dutch East Indies into the global economy.

The Islamic Heartland

By the early seventeenth century, the three major Muslim empires of Afro-Eurasia, stretching from the Balkans and North Africa to South Asia, had a combined population of between 130 and 150 million. Yet, compared with Southeast Asia, they did not feel such direct effects of European intrusion. Here, trade was not as instrumental as in East Asia, and though the importation of silver was significant and destabilizing, it was not the powerful factor promoting large-scale trade with Europe that it was in China. The Islamic heartland did, however, face internal difficulties. While the Ottoman and Mughal Empires remained resilient, the Safavid Empire fell into chaos.

THE SAFAVID EMPIRE The Safavid Empire had always required a powerful, religiously inspired ruler to enforce Shiite religious orthodoxy and to hold together the realm's tribal, pastoral, mercantile, and agricultural factions. During its rise, charismatic political leadership and religious messianism had overcome the innate tendencies of the peoples living on the Iranian plateau to resist the authority of state power. The Iranian plateau consisted of vast semidesert and wooded areas surrounded by mountains and was inhabited by diverse, often hostile ethnic, linguistic, and religious communities. Moreover, a substantial percentage of the Safavid population of 8.5 million comprised nomadic peoples who bristled when confronted with centralized power. Abbas I (r. 1588–1629), the fifth Safavid shah, used the strength of his personality, his commitment to Shiism, and his talent for playing off one group against another to enhance the state's power (see Chapter 14). His successors were weaker and less charismatic, and the state foundered as eunuchs and harem women asserted their authority over that of the shahs and as tribal groups slipped away from control from the center.

By 1722, the state was under assault from within and without, and it collapsed abruptly at the hands of Afghan clansmen, who overran its inept and divided armies and besieged the capital at Isfahan (see again Map 13.1). As the city's inhabitants perished from hunger and disease, some desperate survivors ate the corpses of the deceased. After the shah abdicated, the invaders executed thousands of officials and members of the royal household. The empire limped along until 1773, when a revolt toppled the last ruler from the throne.

Even so, the Safavid period left an immense imprint on the peoples of the Iranian plateau. They continued their commitment to Shiism in a predominantly Sunni world and harkened back in admiration to their Persian historical traditions. (For a discussion of Safavid culture at its height, see Chapter 14.)

THE MUGHAL EMPIRE In contrast to the Ottomans' setbacks, the Mughal Empire reached its height in the 1600s. The period saw Mughal rulers extend their domain over almost all of India and enjoy increased domestic and international trade. But they eventually had problems governing dispersed and resistant provinces, where many villages retained traditional religions and cultures.

Before the Mughals, India had never had a single political authority. Akbar and his successors had conquered territory in the north (see Chapter 12, Map 12.5), so now the Mughals turned to the south and gained control over most of that region by 1689. As the new provinces provided additional resources, local lords, and warriors, the Mughal bureaucracy grew better at extracting services and taxes.

Indian Cotton. *European traders were drawn to India by its famed cotton textiles. This image from around 1800 shows a woman separating the cotton from the seeds; it captures the preindustrial technology of cotton production in India.*

Imperial stability and prosperity did not depend entirely on the Indian Ocean trading system. Indeed, although the Mughals profited from seaborne trade, they never undertook overseas expansion. The main source of their wealth was land rents, boosted via incentives to bring new land into cultivation. Here peasants planted, in part, New World crops like maize and tobacco. But the imperial economy also benefited from Europeans' increased demand for Indian goods and services—such as a sixfold rise in the English East India Company's textile purchases.

LOCAL AUTONOMY IN MUGHAL INDIA Eventually, Mughals were victims of their own success. More than a century of imperial expansion, commercial prosperity, and agricultural development placed substantial resources in the hands of local and regional authorities. As a result, local warrior elites became more autonomous. By the late seventeenth century, many regional leaders were well positioned to resist Mughal authority.

Thus, increased prosperity enabled distant provinces to challenge central rulers. When, under Aurangzeb (r. 1658–1707), the Mughals pushed deep into southern India, they encountered fierce opposition from the Marathas in the northwestern Deccan plateau (see again Map 13.1). To finance this expansion, Aurangzeb raised taxes on the peasants. As resentment spread, even the elite grew restive at the drain on imperial finances. Seeking support from the *ulama,* the monarch abandoned the toleration of heterodoxy and of non-Muslims that his predecessors had allowed. All this turmoil set the stage for successful peasant revolts.

Now the Indian peasants (like their counterparts in Ming China, Safavid Persia, and the Ottoman Empire) capitalized on weakening central authority to assert their independence. They, too, were feeling the effects of the Little Ice Age on their lands' productivity. Many rose in rebellions; others resorted to banditry. At this point the Mughal emperors had to accept diminished power over a loose unity of provincial "successor states." (For a discussion of Mughal culture at its height, see Chapter 14.) Most of these areas accepted Mughal control in name only, administering semiautonomous regimes through access to local resources. Yet India still flourished,

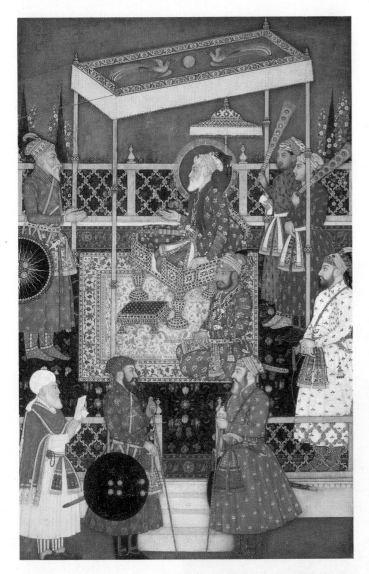

Aurangzeb. *The last powerful Mughal emperor, Aurangzeb continued the conquest of the Indian subcontinent. Pictured in his old age, he is shown here with his courtiers.*

and landed elites brought new territories into agrarian production. Cotton, for instance, supported a thriving textile industry as peasant households focused on weaving and cloth production. Much of their production was destined for export as the region deepened its integration into world trading systems.

PRIVATE COMMERCIAL ENTERPRISE The Mughals themselves paid scant attention to commercial matters, but local rulers welcomed Europeans into Indian ports, striking deals with merchants from Portugal, England, and Holland. Some Indian merchants formed trading companies of their own to control the sale of regional produce to competing Europeans; others established intricate trading networks that reached as far north as Russia.

One of these companies built a trading and banking empire that demonstrated how local prosperity could undercut imperial power. This was the House of Jagat Seth, which at first specialized in shipping Bengal cloth through Asian and European merchants. Increasingly, however, most of their business in the provinces of Bengal and Bihar was tax farming, whereby they collected taxes for the imperial coffers (see again Map 13.1). The Jagat Seths maintained their own retinue of agents to gather levies from farmers while pocketing substantial profits for themselves. In this way, they and other mercantile houses grew richer and gained greater political influence over financially strapped emperors. Thus, even as global commercial entanglements enriched some in India, the effects undercut the Mughal dynasty.

Tokugawa Japan

Integration with the Asian trading system exposed Japan to new external pressures, even as the islands grappled with internal turmoil. But the Japanese dealt with these pressures more successfully than the mainland Asian empires (Ottoman, Safavid, Mughal, and Ming), which saw political fragmentation and even the overthrow of ruling dynasties. In Japan, a single ruling family emerged. This dynastic state, the **Tokugawa shogunate**, accomplished something that most of the world's other regimes did not: it regulated foreign intrusion. While Japan played a modest role in the expanding global trade, it remained free of outside exploitation.

UNIFICATION OF JAPAN During the sixteenth century, Japan had endured political instability as banditry and civil strife disrupted the countryside. Regional ruling families, called *daimyos,* had commanded private armies of warriors known as samurai. The daimyos sometimes brought order to their domains, but no one family could establish preeminence over others. Although Japan had an emperor, his authority did not extend beyond the court in Kyoto.

Ultimately, several military leaders attempted to unify Japan. One general, who became the supreme minister, arranged marriages among the children of local authorities to solidify political bonds. Also, to coax cooperation from the daimyos, he ordered that their wives and children be kept as semihostages in the residences they were required to maintain in Edo. After the general died, one of the daimyos, Tokugawa Ieyasu, seized power. This was a decisive moment. In 1603, Ieyasu assumed the title of shogun (military ruler), retaining the emperor in name only while taking the reins of power himself. He also solved the problem of succession, declaring that rulership would be hereditary and that his family would be the ruling household. This hereditary Tokugawa shogunate lasted until 1867.

Now administrative authority shifted from Kyoto to the site of Ieyasu's domain headquarters: the castle town called Edo, later renamed Tokyo. (See Map 13.6.) The Tokugawa built Edo out of a small earthen fortification clinging to a coastal bluff. Behind Edo lay a village in a swampy plain. In a monumental work of engineering, the rulers ordered the swamp drained, the forest cleared, many of the hills leveled, canals dredged, bridges built, the seashore extended by landfill, and a new stone castle completed. By the time Ieyasu died, Edo had a population of 150,000.

The Tokugawa shoguns ensured a flow of resources from the working population to the rulers and from the provinces to the capital. Villages paid taxes to the daimyos, who transferred resources to the seat of shogunate authority. No longer engaged in constant warfare, the samurai became administrators. Peace brought prosperity. Agriculture thrived. Improved farming techniques and land reclamation projects enabled the country's population to triple between 1550 and 1700.

FOREIGN AFFAIRS AND FOREIGNERS Internal peace and prosperity did not insulate Japan from external challenges, especially the intrusion of Christian missionaries and European traders. Initially, Japanese officials welcomed these foreigners out of an eagerness to acquire muskets, gunpowder, and other new technology. But once the ranks of Christian converts swelled, Japanese authorities realized that Christians were intolerant of other faiths, believed Christ to be superior to any authority, and fought among themselves. Trying to stem the tide, the shoguns prohibited conversion to Christianity and attempted to ban its practice. After a rebellion by converted peasants protesting high rents and taxes, the government suppressed Christianity and drove European missionaries from the country.

Even more troublesome was the lure of trade with Europeans. The Tokugawa knew that trading at various Japanese ports would pull the commercial regions in various directions, away from the capital. When it became clear that European traders preferred the ports of Kyūshū (the southernmost island), the shogunate restricted Europeans to trade only in ports under Edo's direct rule in Honshū. Then Japanese authorities expelled all European competitors. Only the Protestant (and nonmissionizing) Dutch won permission to remain in Japan, confined to an island near Nagasaki. The Dutch were allowed to unload just one ship each year, under strict supervision by Japanese authorities.

These measures did not close Tokugawa Japan to the outside world, however. Trade with China and Korea flourished, and the shogun received missions from Korea and the Ryūkyū Islands. Edo also gathered information about the outside world from the resident Dutch and Chinese (who included monks, physicians,

Edo in the Rain. *This facsimile of an ukiyo-e ("floating world") print by Hiroshige (1797–1858) depicts one of several bridges in the bustling city of Edo (later Tokyo), with Mount Fuji in the background.*

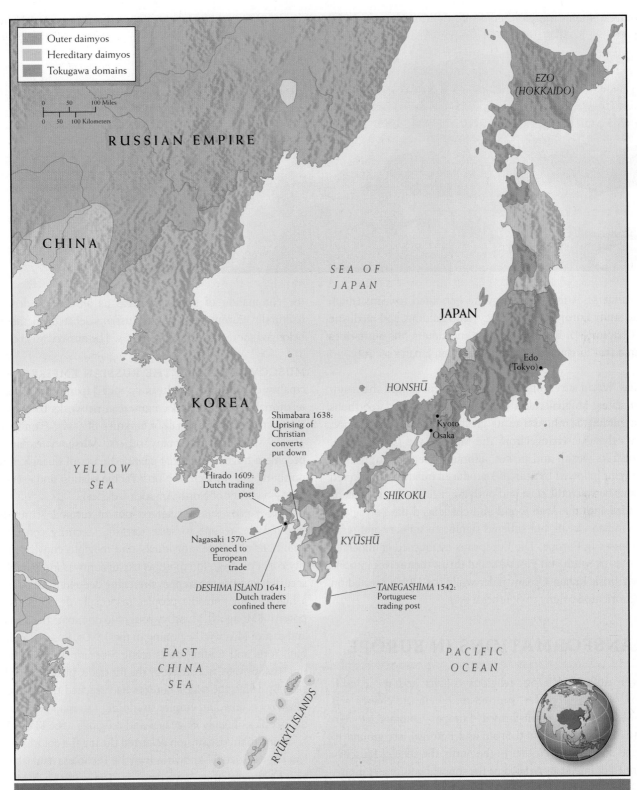

Outer daimyos
Hereditary daimyos
Tokugawa domains

0   50   100 Miles
0   50   100 Kilometers

RUSSIAN EMPIRE

CHINA

EZO
(HOKKAIDO)

SEA OF
JAPAN

JAPAN

Edo
(Tokyo)

HONSHŪ

KOREA

Kyoto
Osaka

Shimabara 1638:
Uprising of
Christian
converts
put down

Hirado 1609:
Dutch trading
post

YELLOW
SEA

SHIKOKU

Nagasaki 1570:
opened to
European
trade

KYŪSHŪ

DESHIMA ISLAND 1641:
Dutch traders
confined there

TANEGASHIMA 1542:
Portuguese
trading post

EAST
CHINA
SEA

PACIFIC
OCEAN

RYŪKYŪ ISLANDS

MAP 13.6 | Tokugawa Japan, 1603–1867

The Tokugawa shoguns created a strong central state in Japan at this time.

- According to this map, how extensive was their control?

- What foreign states were interested in trade with Japan?

- How did Tokugawa leaders attempt to control relations with foreign states and other entities?

Portuguese Arriving in Japan. *In the 1540s, the Portuguese arrival on the islands of Japan sparked a fascination with the strange costumes and the great ships of these "southern barbarians" (so called because they had approached Japan from the south). Silk-screen paintings depicted Portuguese prowess in exaggerated form, such as in the impossible height of the fore and aft of the vessel pictured here.*

and painters). A few Japanese were permitted to learn Dutch and to study European technology, shipbuilding, and medicine (see Chapter 14). By limiting such encounters, the authorities ensured that foreigners would not threaten Japan's security.

New World silver and climate change challenged the major Asian states. Mughal rulers dealt with famines and rebellions while guiding South Asia to its greatest power and influence. China's dynastic change from the Ming to the Qing did not diminish its wealth and power, although irregular supplies of silver (glut followed by scarcity) produced inflation and altered relations between the state and outlying regions. The Ottomans expanded into the Arab world and challenged the Portuguese in the Indian Ocean, but suffered significant military and territorial losses in Europe. The Europeans established commercial footholds in South and East Asia and thrust themselves into the already brisk Indian Ocean trade, while the Dutch created an export-oriented colony in Southeast Asia.

TRANSFORMATIONS IN EUROPE

Between 1600 and 1750, religious conflict and the consolidation of dynastic power, spurred on by climate change and long-distance trade, transformed Europe. Commercial centers shifted northward, and Spain and Portugal lost ground to England and France. Farther to the north, the state of Muscovy expanded dramatically to become the sprawling Russian Empire.

Expansion and Dynastic Change in Russia

During this period, the Russian Empire became the world's largest-ever state. It gained positions on the Baltic Sea and the Pacific Ocean, and it established political borders with both the Qing Empire and Japan. These momentous shifts involved

the elimination of steppe nomads as an independent force. Culturally, Europeans as well as Russians debated whether Russia belonged more to Europe or to Asia. The answer was both.

MUSCOVY BECOMES THE RUSSIAN EMPIRE The principality of Moscow, or Muscovy, like Japan and China, used territorial expansion and commercial networks to consolidate a powerful state. Originally a mixture of Slavs, Finnish tribes, Turkic speakers, and many others, **Muscovy** expanded to become a huge empire that spanned parts of Europe, much of northern Asia, numerous North Pacific islands, and even—for a time—a corner of North America (Alaska).

Like Japan, Russia emerged out of turmoil. Three factors inspired the regime to seize territory: security concerns, the ambitions of private individuals, and religious conviction. Security concerns were foremost, as expansion was inseparable from security. Because the steppe, stretching deep into Asia, remained a highway for nomadic peoples (especially descendants of the powerful Mongols), Muscovy sought to dominate the areas south and east of Moscow. Beginning in the 1590s, Russian authorities built forts and trading posts along Siberian rivers at the same time that privateers, enticed by the fur trade, pushed even farther east. By 1639, the state's borders had reached the Pacific. Now Muscovy claimed an empire straddling Eurasia and incorporating peoples of many languages and religions. (See Map 13.7.)

Much of this expansion occurred during the colorful and violent reign of Ivan IV, known as Ivan the Terrible, a name that could also be translated as "awesome" (r. 1547–1584). A Muscovite grand prince, he restyled himself "tsar of all of the Russias," ruling in the northern reaches of a European-Asian crossroads that lacked natural borders. The many invasions and counter-invasions that had taken place in the past persuaded Ivan that the only way to achieve security against hostile neighbors was to conquer them first and then rule in an autocratic fashion. Ivan's great military victory in 1552 over the powerful Tatar Khanate,

MAP 13.7 | Russian Expansion, 1462-1795

The state of Muscovy incorporated vast territories through overland expansion as it grew and became the Russian Empire. It did so in part because of its geographical position and its strategic needs.

- Using the map key, identify how many different expansions the Russian Empire underwent between 1462 and 1795 and in what directions generally.
- With what countries and cultures did the Russian Empire come into contact?
- What drove such dramatic expansion?

centered on the Volga River city of Kazan, began a transformation of his largely Orthodox, Christian, Russian-speaking realm through the incorporation of large Muslim, Turkic-speaking populations. Ivan also sponsored expeditions that led to the conquest of even vaster territories in the east, which came to be known as Siberia. His ambitions to expand in the south were blocked by the Ottoman Empire. In the northwest, despite twenty-four years of war against Sweden, Poland-Lithuania, and the Teutonic Knights of Livonia, he failed to conquer non-Russian territories on the Baltic Sea. His reign devolved into internal violence, and he even threatened to abdicate and become a monk. Ivan killed his son and heir in a violent argument, leaving the throne to

an enfeebled and childless son, so that the dynasty came to an end in 1598. Remarkably, in 1613, the various elite clans freely decided to restore autocratic rule, choosing the Romanov family.

Ivan's paradoxical reign, full of both dynamism and destruction, set Moscow on an expansionist course toward a transcontinental empire, a state of many religions, and a zealous commitment to strongly authoritarian rule. Like the Ottoman and Qing dynasts, Romanov tsars and their aristocratic supporters would retain power into the twentieth century.

ABSOLUTIST GOVERNMENT AND SERFDOM In the seventeenth and eighteenth centuries, the Romanovs created an absolutist system of government. Only the tsar had the right to make war, tax, judge, and coin money. The Romanovs also made the nobles serve as state officials. Now Russia became a despotic state that had no political assemblies for nobles or other groups, other than mere consultative bodies like the imperial senate. Indeed, away from Moscow, local aristocrats enjoyed nearly unlimited authority in exchange for loyalty and tribute to the tsar.

During this period, Russia's peasantry bore the burden of maintaining the wealth of the small nobility and the monarchy. Most peasant families gathered into communes, isolated rural worlds where people helped one another deal with plummeting Little Ice Age temperatures, severe landlords, and occasional poor harvests. Communes functioned like extended kin networks in that members reciprocated favors and chores. The typical peasant hut was a single chamber heated by a wood-burning stove with no chimney. Livestock and humans often shared the same quarters. In 1649, peasants were legally bound as serfs to the nobles and the tsar, meaning they had to perform obligatory services and deliver part of their produce to their lords. The lords essentially controlled all aspects of their serfs' lives.

IMPERIAL EXPANSION AND MIGRATION Three factors were key to Russia's becoming an empire: (1) the conquest of Siberia, which brought vast territory and riches in furs; (2) incorporation of the fertile southern steppes, known as Ukraine; and (3) victory in a prolonged war with Sweden. Peter the Great (r. 1682–1725) accomplished the victory in Sweden, after which he founded a new capital at St. Petersburg. Thereafter, Russia developed a formidable military-fiscal state bureaucracy, but the aristocracy remained predominant.

Nenets Hunters. *Hunters of the Nenets tribe in far North Asia's treeless tundra show off their warm animal-skin clothing and self-fashioned weapons, as depicted in a 1620 engraving by Theodore de Bry, one of the first Europeans to come into contact with them.*

Catherine the Great. *Catherine the Great styled herself an enlightened despot, furthering the Russian Empire's adaptation of European high culture.*

Under Peter's successors, including the hard-nosed Catherine the Great, Russia added even more territory. Catherine placed her former lover on the Polish throne and subsequently, together with the Austrians and Prussians, carved up the medieval state of Poland. Her victories against the Ottomans allowed Russia to annex Ukraine, the grain-growing "breadbasket" of eastern Europe. By the late eighteenth century, Russia's grasp extended from the Baltic Sea through the heart of Europe, Ukraine, and the Crimea on the Black Sea and into the ancient lands of Armenia and Georgia in the Caucasus Mountains.

The Russian Empire was a harsh but colossal space that induced the movement of peoples within it. Many people migrated eastward, into Siberia. Some were fleeing serfdom; others were being deported for having rejected changes in the state's official Eastern Orthodox religious services. Battling astoundingly harsh temperatures and frigid Arctic winds, these individuals traveled on horseback and trudged on foot to resettle in the east. But the difficulties of clearing forested lands or planting crops in boggy Siberian soils, combined with extraordinarily harsh winters, meant that many settlers died or tried to return. Isolation was a problem, too. There was no established land route back to Moscow until the 1770s, when exiles completed the Great Siberian Post Road through the swamps and peat bogs of western Siberia. The writer Anton Chekhov later called it "the longest and ugliest road in the whole world."

Economic and Political Fluctuations in Western Europe

During this period, the European economies became more commercialized. As in Asia, developments in distant parts of the world shaped the region's economic upturns and downturns. Compounding these pressures was the continuation of dynastic rivalries and religious conflicts.

Underlying the economic and political fluctuations taking place in Europe, especially the brutal warfare of the Thirty Years'

War, was the powerful impact of the Little Ice Age. Freezing temperatures shortened agricultural growing seasons by one to two months. The result was escalating prices for essential grain products, now in short supply. Famines and death from diseases because of malnourishment followed. Among the Europeans hardest hit at the end of the seventeenth century were the populations of France, Norway, and Sweden, where starvation took the lives of 10 percent of the population. Moreover, declining tax yields prevented European governments from offering vital services to their suffering citizens. The cooling had a few benefits, however, among which were the magnificent violins, still prized today, crafted by Antonio Stradivari (1644–1737) from the denser wood that freezing temperatures produced.

THE THIRTY YEARS' WAR For a century after Martin Luther broke with the Catholic Church (see Chapter 12), religious warfare raged in Europe. So did contests over territory, power, and trade. The **Thirty Years' War** (1618–1648) reflected all of these—a war between Protestant princes and the Catholic emperor for religious predominance in central Europe; a struggle for regional control among Catholic powers (the Spanish and Austrian Habsburgs and the French); and a bid for independence (from Spain) by the Dutch, who wanted to trade and worship as they liked.

The brutal conflict began as a struggle between Protestants and Catholics within the Habsburg Empire, but it soon became a war for preeminence in Europe. It took the lives of civilians as well as soldiers. In total, fighting, disease, and famine wiped out a third of the German states' urban population and two-fifths of their rural population. The war also depopulated Sweden and Poland. Ultimately, the Treaty of Westphalia (1648) stated, in essence, that as there was a rough balance of power between Protestant and Catholic states, they would simply have to put up with each other. The Dutch won their independence, but the war's enormous costs provoked severe discontent in Spain, France, and England. Central Europe did not recover in economic or demographic terms for more than a century.

The Thirty Years' War transformed war making. Whereas most medieval struggles had been sieges between nobles leading small armies, centralized states fielding standing armies now waged grand-scale campaigns. The war also changed the ranks of soldiers: as the conflict ground on, local enlisted men defending their king, country, and faith gave way to hired mercenaries or criminals doing forced service. Even officers, who previously obtained their stripes by purchase or royal decree, now had to earn them. Gunpowder, cannons, and handguns became standardized. By the eighteenth century, Europe's wars featured huge standing armies boasting a professional officer corps, deadly artillery, and long supply lines bringing food and ammunition to the front. The costs—material and human—of war began to soar and put added pressure on empires to expand and compete for overseas spoils.

WESTERN EUROPEAN ECONOMIES In spite of warfare's toll on economic activity, the European states enjoyed significant commercial expansion. Northern Europe gained more than did the south, however. Spain, for example, started losing ground to its rivals as the costs of defending its empire soared and merchants from northern Europe cut in on its trading networks. The weighty costs of its involvement in the Thirty Years' War dealt the Spanish economy a final, disastrous blow. Other previously robust economies also suffered under the pressures of greater economic connection and competition. Venice, for

The Thirty Years' War. *The mercenary armies of the Thirty Years' War were renowned for pillaging and tormenting the civilians of central Europe. In this engraving by Jacques Callot, the townsfolk exact revenge on some of these soldiers, hanging many, as an accompanying caption claims, "damned and infamous thieves, like bad fruit, from this tree."*

Amsterdam Stock Exchange. *The high concentration of merchants in Amsterdam naturally gave way to the world's first stock exchange in the seventeenth century. This diverse gathering of men trading stocks and preparing to participate in auctions, as depicted by renowned painter Emanuel de Witte, was a common sight throughout the Dutch Golden Age.*

example, which before the era of transoceanic shipping had been Europe's chief gateway to Asia, saw its economy decline.

As European commercial dynamism shifted northward, the Dutch led the way with innovative commercial practices and a new mercantile elite. They specialized in shipping and in financing regional and long-distance trade. Their famous *fluits-chips* carried heavy, bulky cargoes (like Baltic wood) with relatively small crews. Now shipping costs throughout the Atlantic world dropped as Dutch ships transported their own and other countries' goods. Amsterdam's merchants founded an exchange bank, established a rudimentary stock exchange, and pioneered systems of underwriting and insuring cargoes.

England and France also became commercial powerhouses, establishing aggressive policies to promote national business and drive out competitors. Consider the English Navigation Act of 1651. By stipulating that only English ships could carry goods between the mother country and its colonies, it protected English shippers and merchants—especially from the Dutch. The English subsequently launched several effective trade wars against Holland. The French, too, followed aggressive mercantilist policies and ultimately joined forces with England to invade Holland.

Economic development was not limited to port towns: the countryside, too, enjoyed breakthroughs in production. In northwestern Europe, investments in water drainage, larger livestock herds, and improved cultivation practices generated much greater yields. Also, a four-field crop rotation involving wheat, clover, barley, and turnips kept nutrients in the soil and provided year-round fodder for livestock. As a result (and as we have seen many times throughout history), increased output supported a growing urban population. By contrast, in Spain and Italy, agricultural change and population growth came more slowly.

Production rose most where the organization of rural property changed. In England, for example, in a movement known as **enclosure**, landowners took control of lands that traditionally had been common property serving local needs. Claiming exclusive rights to these lands, the landowners planted new crops or pastured sheep with the aim of selling the products in distant markets. The largest landowners put their farms in the hands of tenants, who hired wage laborers to till, plant, and harvest. Thus, in England, peasant agriculture gave way to farms run by wealthy families who exploited the marketplace to buy what they needed (including labor) and to sell what they produced. In this regard, England led the way in a Europe-wide process of commercializing the countryside.

DYNASTIC MONARCHIES: FRANCE AND ENGLAND

European monarchs had varying success with centralizing state power. In France, Louis XIII (r. 1610–1643) and especially his chief minister, Cardinal Richelieu, concentrated power in the hands of the king. After 1614, kings refused to convene the Estates-General, a medieval advisory body. Composed of representatives of three groups—the clergy (the First Estate, those who pray), the nobility (the Second Estate, those who fight), and the unprivileged remainder of the population (the Third Estate, those who work)—the Estates-General was an obstacle to the king's full empowerment. Instead of sharing power, the king and his counselors wanted him to rule free of external checks, to create—in the words of the age—an **absolute monarchy**. The ruler's authority was to be complete and his state free of bloody disorders. His rule would be lawful; but he, not his jurists, would dictate the last legal word. If the king made a mistake, only God could call him to account. Thus the French, like most Europeans, believed in the "divine right of kings," a political belief not greatly different from imperial China, where the emperor was thought to rule with the mandate of heaven.

In absolutist France, privileges and state offices flowed from the king's grace. All patronage networks ultimately linked to the king. The great palace Louis XIV built at Versailles teemed with nobles from all over France seeking favor, dressing according to the king's expensive fashion code, and attending the latest tragedies, comedies, and concerts. Just as the Japanese shogun monitored the daimyos by keeping their families in Edo, Louis XIV kept a watchful eye on the French nobility at Versailles.

The French dynastic monarchy provided a model of absolute rule for other European dynasts, like the Habsburgs of the Holy Roman Empire, the Hohenzollerns of Prussia, and the Romanovs of Muscovy. The king and his ministers controlled all public power, while other social groups, from the nobility to the peasantry, had no formal body to represent their interests. Nonetheless, French absolutist government was not as absolute as the king wished. Pockets of stalwart Protestants practiced their religion secretly in the plateau villages of central France. Peasant disturbances continued. Criticism of court life, wars, and religious policies filled anonymous pamphlets, jurists' notebooks, and courtiers' private journals. Members of the nobility also grumbled about their political misfortunes, but since the king would not call the Estates-General, they had no formal way to express their concerns.

England might also have evolved into an absolutist regime, but there were important differences between England and France. Queen Elizabeth (r. 1558–1603) and her successors used many policies similar to those of the French monarchy, such as control of patronage (to grant privileges) and elaborate court festivities. Also, refusing to share her power with a man, the "Virgin Queen" never married and exerted sole control over church, military, and aristocracy. However, the English Parliament remained an important force. Whereas the French kings did not need the consent of the Estates-General to enact taxes, the English monarchs had to convene Parliament to raise money.

Under Elizabeth's successors, fierce quarrels broke out over taxation, religion, and royal efforts to rule without parliamentary consent. Tensions ran high between Puritans (who preferred a simpler form of worship and more egalitarian church government) and Anglicans (who supported the state-sponsored, hierarchically organized Church of England headed by the king). Social and economic grievances led to civil war in the 1640s and an ultimate victory for the parliamentary army (largely Puritan)—and the beheading of King Charles I. Twelve years of government as a commonwealth without a king followed.

In 1660, the monarchy was restored, but without resolving issues of religious tolerance and the king's relation to Parliament. Charles II and his successor, James II, aroused opposition by their autocracy and secret efforts to bring England back into the Catholic fold. The conflict between an aspiring absolutist throne and Parliament's insistence on shared sovereignty and Protestant succession culminated in the Glorious Revolution of 1688–1689. In a bloodless upheaval, James II fled to France and Parliament offered the crown to William of Orange and his wife, Mary (a Protestant). The conflict's outcome established the principle that English monarchs must rule in conjunction with Parliament. Although the Church of England was reaffirmed as the official state church, Presbyterians and Jews were allowed to practice their religions. Catholic worship, still officially forbidden, was tolerated as long as the Catholics kept quiet. By 1700, then, England's nobility and merchant classes had a guaranteed

Versailles. *Louis XIV's Versailles, just southwest of Paris, was a hunting lodge that was converted at colossal cost in the 1660s–1670s into a grand royal chateau with expansive grounds. The image presented here was painted by the French artist Pierre Patel in 1688. Much envied and imitated across Europe, the palace became the epicenter of a luxurious court life that included entertainment such as plays and musical offerings, state receptions, royal hunts, boating, and gambling. Thousands of nobles at Versailles vied with each other for closer proximity to the king in the performance of court rituals.*

Queen Elizabeth of England. *This portrait (c. 1600, by the painter Robert Peake, the Elder) depicts an idealized Queen Elizabeth near the end of her long reign. The queen is pictured riding in a procession in the midst of an admiring crowd composed of the most important nobles of the realm.*

say in public affairs and assurance that state activity would privilege the properted classes as well as the ruler.

Events in France and England stimulated much political writing. In England, Thomas Hobbes published *Leviathan* (1651), a defense of the state's absolute power over all competing forces. John Locke published *Two Treatises of Civil Government* (1689), which argued not only for the natural rights to liberty and property but also for the rights of peoples to form a government and then to disband and re-form it when it did not live up to its contract. French theorists also proposed new ways of conducting politics and making law and debated the extent to which elites could check the king. As the eighteenth century unfolded, the question of where sovereignty lay grew more pressing.

MERCANTILIST WARS The rise of new powers in Europe intensified rivalries for control of the Atlantic system. As conflicts over colonies and sea-lanes replaced earlier religious and territorial struggles, commercial struggles became worldwide wars. Across the globe, European empires constantly skirmished over control of trade and territory. English and Dutch trading companies took aim at Portuguese outposts in Asia and the Americas and then at each other. Ports in India suffered repeated assaults and counterassaults. In response, European powers built huge navies to protect their colonies and trade routes and to attack their rivals. After 1715, mercantilist wars occurred mainly outside Europe, as empires feuded over colonial possessions. Each round of warfare ratcheted up the scale and cost of fighting.

The **Seven Years' War** (known as the French and Indian War in the United States) marked the culmination of this rivalry.

Fought from 1756 to 1763, it saw Native Americans, African slaves, Bengali princes, Filipino militiamen, and European foot soldiers dragged into a contest over imperial possessions and control of the seas. Some fleets, like the French at the Battle of Quiberon Bay, were dispatched to the bottom of the ocean. Some fortresses, like Spain's Havana and France's Quebec City, fell to invaders. What sparked the war was a skirmish of British colonial troops (featuring a lieutenant colonel named George Washington) allied with Seneca warriors against French soldiers in the Ohio Valley (see Map 13.2 for North American references). In India, the war had a decisive outcome, for here the East India Company trader Robert Clive rallied 850 European officers and 2,100 Indian recruits to defeat the French (there were but 40 French artillerymen) and their 50,000 Maratha allies at Plassey. The British seized the upper hand—over everyone—in India. Not only did the British drive off the French from the rich Bengali interior, but they also crippled Indian rulers' resistance against European intruders (see Map 12.4 for India references).

The Seven Years' War changed the balance of power around the world. Britain emerged as the foremost colonial empire. Its rivals took a pounding: France lost its North American colonies, and Spain lost Florida (though it gained the Louisiana Territory west of the Mississippi in a secret deal with France). In India, as well, the French were losers and had to acknowledge British supremacy in the wealthy provinces of Bihar and Bengal. But overwhelmingly, the biggest losers were indigenous peoples everywhere. With the rise of one empire over all others, it was harder for Native Americans to play the Europeans off against each other. Maratha princes faced the same problem. Clearly, as worlds became more entangled, the gaps between winners and losers grew more pronounced.

Wealth from long-distant trade and intense warfare led to the rise of militarily powerful, monarchical states in Europe. In the long run, beginning in the eighteenth century and coming to fulfillment in the nineteenth, the most dynamic of these states, notably Britain and France, ultimately joined by a newly unified Germany, were able to dominate the great states of Afro-Eurasia economically and militarily.

CONCLUSION

A radical decline in temperatures worldwide made the seventeenth century a time of famine, dying, epidemic disease, and political turmoil that produced regime change in China, Persia, and England and threatened the rulers of the Ottoman and Mughal Empires. Yet by the 1750s, the world's regions were more economically connected than ever. The process of integrating the resources of previous worlds apart that had begun with Columbus's voyages intensified during this period. Traders shipped a wider variety of commodities—from Baltic wood to Indian cotton, from New World silver and sugar to Chinese silks and porcelain—over longer distances. People increasingly wore clothes manufactured elsewhere, consumed beverages made from products cultivated in far-off locations, and used imported guns to settle local conflicts.

Everywhere, this integration and the consumer opportunities that it made possible came at a heavy price. Nowhere was it more costly than in the Americas, where colonization and exploitation led to the expulsion of Indians from their lands and the decimation of their numbers. The cost was also very high for the millions of Africans forced across the Atlantic to work New World plantations and for the millions more who did not survive the journey.

Along with sugar, silver was the product from the Americas that most transformed global trading networks and that showed how greater entanglements could both enrich and destabilize. Although Spanish colonizers mined New World silver and shipped it to western Europe and Asia, it was Spain's main competitors in Europe that gained the upper hand in the seventeenth and eighteenth centuries. Nearly one-third of the silver from the New World ended up in China as payment for products like porcelains and silks that consumers still regarded as the world's finest manufactures. But if China's economy remained vibrant, silver did play a part in the fall of one dynasty and the rise of another. For the Ottoman, Mughal, and Safavid Empires, the influx of silver created rampant inflation and undermined their previous economic autonomy.

Certain societies coped with climate change and increased commercial exchange more successfully than others. The Safavid and Ming dynasties could not withstand the pressures; both collapsed. The Spanish, Ottoman, and Mughal Empires managed to survive but faced increasing pressure from aggressive rivals. More than any other country, England survived the travails of climate change, but witnessed the execution of a monarch (Charles I) and an autocratic Puritan government under Oliver Cromwell. By century's end, England had a new empire, a strengthened parliament, and an energetic merchant class ready to dominate global markets. For newcomers to the integrating world, the opportunity to trade helped support new dynasties. Japan and Russia emerged on the world stage. But even in these newer regimes, commerce and competition did not erase conflict. To the contrary, while the world was more together economically than ever before, greater prosperity for some hardly translated into peace for most.

TRACING THE GLOBAL STORYLINES

After You Read This Chapter

Go to iNQUIZITIVE to see what you know & learn what you've missed.

FOCUS ON: *The Global Impact of the Little Ice Age and the Regional Impact of World Trade*

The Americas

- England, France, and Holland join Spain and Portugal as colonial powers in the Americas.

- The English and French colonies in the Caribbean become the world's major exporters of sugar.

Africa

- The Atlantic slave trade increases to record proportions, creating gender imbalances, impoverishing some regions, and elevating the power of slave-supplying states.

Southeast Asia

- The Dutch East India Company takes over the major islands of Southeast Asia.

The Islamic World

- World trade destabilizes the Safavid, Ottoman, and Mughal Empires.

- The Little Ice Age destabilizes the Ottoman state and leads to a powerful but ultimately unsuccessful rebellion, the Celali revolts.

East Asia

- The Ming dynasty in China, poorly administered and suffering from the effects of climate change, loses the mandate of heaven and is replaced by the Qing.

- The Tokugawa shogunate unifies Japan and limits the influence of Europeans in the country.

Europe

- Tsarist Russia expands toward the Baltic Sea and the Pacific Ocean and becomes the largest state in the world.

- The Thirty Years' War is partly the result of a dramatic cooling of the global climate and enmity between Protestant and Catholic countries.

- Europe recovers from the Thirty Years' War (1618-1648), with Holland, England, and France emerging as economic powerhouses.

CHRONOLOGY

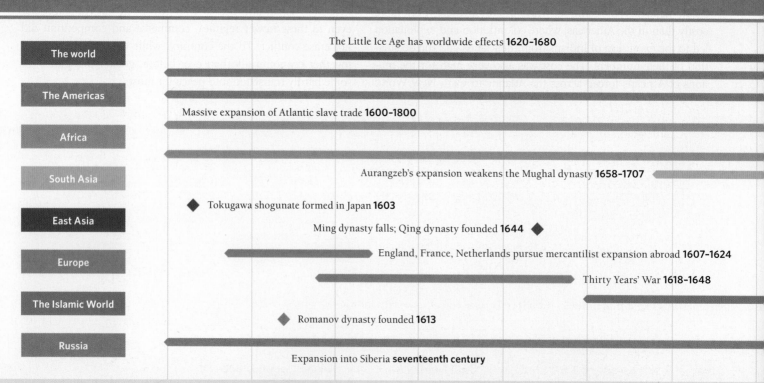

The world	The Little Ice Age has worldwide effects **1620-1680**
The Americas	
Africa	Massive expansion of Atlantic slave trade **1600-1800**
South Asia	Aurangzeb's expansion weakens the Mughal dynasty **1658-1707**
East Asia	Tokugawa shogunate formed in Japan **1603**
	Ming dynasty falls; Qing dynasty founded **1644**
Europe	England, France, Netherlands pursue mercantilist expansion abroad **1607-1624**
	Thirty Years' War **1618-1648**
The Islamic World	
Russia	Romanov dynasty founded **1613**
	Expansion into Siberia **seventeenth century**

1600   1650

1. **Identify** the main steps in the integration of global trade networks during this period, and **describe** some examples of resistance to this integration.

2. **Define** mercantilism, and **analyze** how mercantilist practices affected all regions of the Atlantic world between 1600 and 1750. Whose interests did mercantilism serve, and at whose expense?

3. **Explain** the global effects of the Little Ice Age.

4. **Describe** the plantation complex in the Caribbean. Why was it so valued by Europeans relative to other regions of the Americas?

5. **Analyze** how the Atlantic slave trade reshaped African societies socially and politically. Which regions and groups benefited from Africa's growing entanglements in global commerce?

6. **Discuss** the effect of New World silver and increased trade on Asian empires, and **compare** their different responses.

7. **Analyze** how global trade affected the Ottoman and Mughal Empires during this era. How did each regime respond to these growing entanglements?

8. **Analyze** to what extent the Tokugawa shogunate succeeded in creating a strong central government in Japan. How did it avoid the problems associated with expanding trade that many other dynasties faced at this time?

9. **Compare and contrast** the expansionist policies of the Russian state with those pursued by the British and French regimes during this period. How were they similar and how were they different?

10. **Compare and contrast** the impact of trade and religion on state power in various regions. In Europe and Asia, did certain dynasties hold an advantage over others in controlling commercial networks and using them to enrich their societies?

11. **Evaluate** how the European desire for consumer goods had an impact on the global economy at this time.

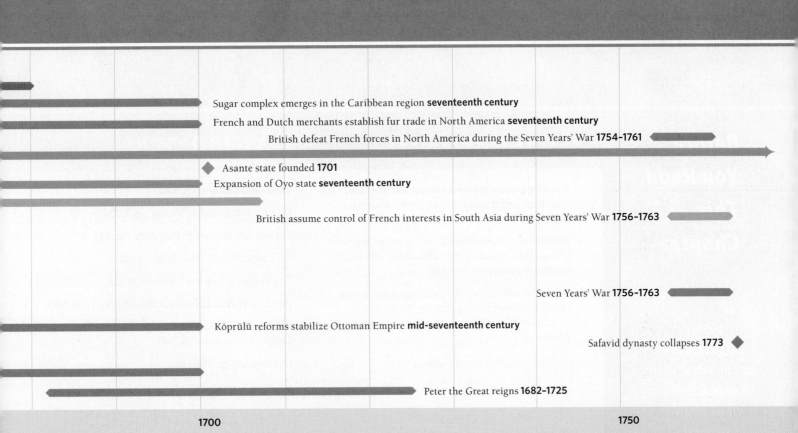

Sugar complex emerges in the Caribbean region **seventeenth century**

French and Dutch merchants establish fur trade in North America **seventeenth century**

British defeat French forces in North America during the Seven Years' War **1754–1761**

Asante state founded **1701**

Expansion of Oyo state **seventeenth century**

British assume control of French interests in South Asia during Seven Years' War **1756–1763**

Seven Years' War **1756–1763**

Köprülü reforms stabilize Ottoman Empire **mid-seventeenth century**

Safavid dynasty collapses **1773**

Peter the Great reigns **1682–1725**

1700   1750

Before You Read This Chapter

Go to inQuizitive to see what you know & learn what you've missed.

GLOBAL STORYLINES

- Growing global commerce enriches rulers and merchants, who express their power through patronage for the arts.

- Distinctive cultures flourish in the major regions of the world, blending new influences with local traditions to varying degrees.

- While the Islamic and Asian worlds confidently retain their own belief systems, the Americas and Oceania increasingly face European cultural pressures.

CHAPTER OUTLINE

14

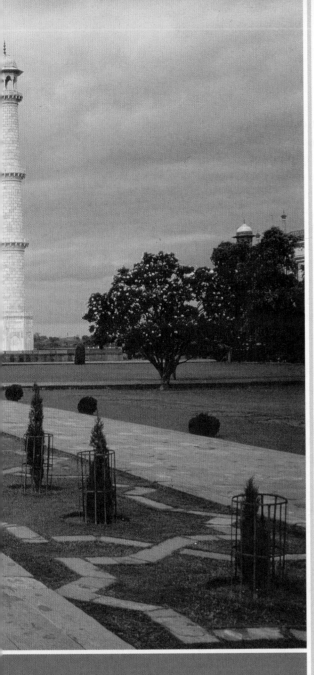

Cultures of Splendor and Power, 1500–1780

FOCUS QUESTIONS

- What were the connections between cultural growth and the creation of a global market?

- In what ways did each culture in this period reflect the ideas of the state in which it was produced? How were the various cultures alike and how were they different in this regard?

- What were the different responses to foreign cultures across Afro-Eurasia in the period 1500–1780? How were they similar and how were they different?

- How did hybrid cultures emerge in the Americas, and what was the connection between these cultures and Enlightenment ideology?

- In what ways did race and cultural differences play a role in the process of global integration?

In 1664, a sixteen-year-old girl from New Spain asked her parents for permission to attend the university in the capital. Although she had mastered Greek logic, taught Latin, and become a proficient mathematician, she had two strikes against her: she was a woman, and her thinking ran against the grain of the Catholic Church. So keen was she to pursue her studies that she proposed to disguise herself as a man. But her parents denied her requests, and instead of attending university she entered a convent in Mexico City, where she spent the rest of her life. Fortunately, the convent turned out to be a sanctuary for her. There she studied science and mathematics and composed remarkable poetry. Sor (Sister) Juana Inés de la Cruz was the bard of a new world where people mixed in faraway places, where new wealth created new customs, and where new ideas began to take hold. One of her poems, "You Men," begins: "Silly, you men—so very adept / at wrongly faulting woman-kind, not seeing you're alone to blame / for faults you plant in woman's mind." Her poetry illustrates how new discoveries and new knowledge challenged old ways. But her life story also reflects the fierce resistance to new ways. Sor Juana's poetry enraged church authorities, who forced her to recant her words and who burned her books. Only the intervention of the viceroy's wife prevented officials from torching the nun's complete works before she died of plague in 1695.

Sor Juana's story attests to the conflicts between new ideas and old orders that occurred once the entanglements of commerce and the consolidation of empires fostered knowledge of foreign ways. On the one hand, global commerce created riches that supported the arts, architecture, and scientific ventures. On the other, experimentations in new ways caused discomfort among defenders of the old order and provoked backlashes against innovation.

This chapter explores how global commerce enriched and reshaped cultures in the centuries after the Americas ceased to be worlds apart from Afro-Eurasia. Profiting from trade in New World commodities, many rulers and merchants displayed their power by commissioning fabulous works of art and majestic palaces and sprawling plazas. These cultural splendors were meant to impress. They also demonstrated the growing connections between distant societies, reflecting how exotic, borrowed influences could blend with domestic traditions. Book production and consumption soared, with some publications finding their way around the world. The spread of books and ideas and increasing cultural contact led to experiments in religious tolerance and helped foster cultural diversity. Yet even as Europeans, who were the greatest beneficiaries of New World riches, claimed to advance new universal truths, cultural productions worldwide still showed the resilience of local traditions.

Both Amerindians and Africans, for example, adapted to European missionizing by creating mixed forms of religious worship—but only because they were under pressure to do so. Europeans absorbed much from Native Americans and African slaves but did not share sovereignty or wealth in return.

Despite the unifying aspects of world trade, each society retained core aspects of its individuality. Ruling classes disseminated values based on cherished classical texts and long-established moral and religious principles. They used space in new ways to establish and project their power. (See Current Trends in World History: The Political Uses of Space.) They mapped geographies and wrote histories according to their traditional visions of the universe. Even as global trade drew their attention outward, societies celebrated their achievements in politics, economics, and culture with pride in their own heritages.

In 1500, the world's most dynamic cultures were in Asia, in areas profiting from the Indian Ocean and China Sea trades. It was in China and the Islamic world that the spice and luxury trades first flourished; here, too, rulers had successfully established political stability and centralized control of taxation, law making, and military force. This often involved recruiting people from diverse backgrounds and promoting secular (nonreligious) education. In the Ottoman, Ming, and Mughal Empires, for example, while older ways did not die out, both trade and empire building contributed to the spread of knowledge about distant people and foreign cultures.

TRADE AND CULTURE

For many groups, the period's global cultural flourishing owed much to burgeoning world trade, which allowed some rulers to consolidate wealth, administration, and military power. These rulers were eager to patronize the arts as a way to legitimize their power and reflect their cultural sophistication. In Europe, monarchs known as enlightened absolutists restricted the clergy and nobility and hired loyal bureaucrats who championed the knowledge of the new age. British monarchs, though not absolutists (because they shared power with Parliament), followed suit. Mughal emperors, Safavid shahs, and Ottoman sultans glorified their regimes by bringing artists and artisans from all over the world to give an Islamic flavor to their major cities and buildings. Rulers in China and Japan also looked to artists to extol their achievements. And in Africa, the wealth garnered from slave trading underwrote cultural productions of extraordinary merit.

Of course, some rulers and polities were more eager for change than others. Moreover, certain societies—in the Americas and the South Pacific, for example—found that contact, conquest, and commerce undermined indigenous cultural life. Although Europeans and native peoples often exchanged ideas and practices, these transfers were mediated by imbalances in power.

CULTURE IN THE ISLAMIC WORLD

For centuries, Muslim elites had generously funded cultural development. As the Ottoman, Safavid, and Mughal Empires gained greater expanses of territory in the sixteenth and seventeenth centuries, they acquired new resources to fund more such pursuits. Rulers supported new schools and building projects, and the elite produced books, artworks, and luxury goods. Cultural life reflected the politics of empire building, as emperors and elites sought greater prestige by patronizing intellectuals and artists.

Forged under different empires, Islamic cultural and intellectual life now reflected three distinct worlds. In place of an earlier Islamic cosmopolitanism, unique cultural patterns prevailed within each empire. Although the Ottomans, the Safavids, and the Mughals shared a common faith, each developed a relatively autonomous form of Muslim culture.

The Ottoman Cultural Synthesis

By the sixteenth century, the Ottoman Empire was enjoying a remarkably rich culture that blended ethnic, religious, and linguistic elements exceeding those of previous Islamic empires.

The Ottomans' cultural synthesis accommodated both Sufis (mystics who stressed contemplation and ecstasy through poetry, music, and dance) and ultraorthodox *ulama* (Islamic jurists who stressed tradition and religious law). It also balanced the interests of military men and administrators with those of clerics. Finally, it allowed autonomy to the minority faiths of Christianity and Judaism.

LAW AND OTTOMAN CULTURAL UNITY The Ottoman world achieved cultural unity, above all, by an outstanding intellectual achievement—its system of administrative law. As the empire absorbed diverse cultures and territories, the sultans realized that the *sharia* (Islamic holy law) would not suffice because it was silent on many secular matters. Moreover, the Ottoman state needed comprehensive laws to bridge differences among the many social and legal systems under its rule. Mehmed II, conqueror of Constantinople, began the reform. By recruiting young boys, rather than noblemen, for training as bureaucrats or military men and making them accountable directly to the sultan, he fashioned a professional bureaucracy with unswerving loyalty to the ruler. Mehmed's successor, Suleiman the Magnificent and the Lawgiver, continued this work by compiling a comprehensive legal code. The code addressed subjects' rights and duties, proper clothing, and how Muslims were to relate to non-Muslims.

RELIGION AND EDUCATION A sophisticated educational system was crucial for the empire's religious and intellectual integration and for its cultural achievements. Here, too, the Ottomans tolerated difference. They encouraged three educational systems that produced three streams of talent—civil and military bureaucrats, *ulama*, and Sufi masters. The administrative elite attended hierarchically organized schools that culminated in the palace schools at Topkapi (see Chapter 11). In the religious sphere, an equally elaborate system took students from elementary schools (emphasizing reading, writing, and numbers) on to higher schools, or *madrasas* (emphasizing law, religious sciences, the Quran, and the regular sciences). These graduates became *ulama* who served as judges, experts in religious law, or teachers. Another set of schools, *tekkes*, taught the devotional strategies and religious knowledge for students to enter Sufi orders.

Each set of schools created lasting linkages between the ruling elite and the orthodox religious elite. The *tekkes*, especially, helped integrate Muslim peoples living under Ottoman rule. The value that the Ottomans placed on education was evident in the saying that "an hour of learning is worth more than a year of prayer"—and in the advances that those schooled in Ottoman institutions made in astronomy, physics, history, geography, and politics.

NEW IDEAS AND THE ARTS The Ottomans combined inherited traditions with new elements in art as well. For

Islamic Scientists. *This fifteenth-century Persian miniature shows Islamic scholars working with sophisticated navigational and astronomical instruments and reflects the importance that the educated classes in the Islamic world attached to observing and recording the regularities in the natural world. Indeed, many of Europe's advances in sailing drew on knowledge from the Muslim world.*

example, portraiture became popular after the Italian painter Gentile Bellini visited Istanbul and composed a portrait of Mehmed II. In other areas, though, the Ottomans kept their own styles. Consider the magnificent architectural monuments of the sixteenth through eighteenth centuries, including mosques, gardens, tombs, forts, and palaces: these show scant western influence. Nor were the Ottomans interested in western literature or music. They generally believed that God had given the Islamic world a monopoly on truth and enlightenment and that their military successes proved his favor.

The elites' capacity to celebrate their well-being and prosperity spread to the broader public during the so-called Tulip Period during the first half of the eighteenth century. The elite had long admired the tulip's bold colors and graceful blooms, and for centuries the flower served as the sultans' symbol. In fact, both Mehmed the Conqueror and Suleiman the Magnificent grew tulips in the most prestigious courtyards at Topkapi Palace in Istanbul. And many Ottoman warriors heading into battle wore undergarments embroidered with tulips to ensure victory. By the early eighteenth century, tulip designs appeared on tiles, fabrics, and public buildings, and authorities sponsored elaborate tulip festivals.

Ottoman Court Women. *This eighteenth-century watercolor found in Topkapi Palace, in Istanbul, shows various musical instruments being played by court women, who were often called on to provide entertainment.*

Fascination with the tulip represented a widespread delight in worldly things. Commoners, too, now celebrated life's pleasures—in coffeehouses and taverns. Indeed, Ottoman demand for luxury goods grew so extensive (seeking lemons, soap, pepper, metal tools, coffee, and wine) that a well-traveled diplomat looked askance at the supposed wealth of Europe. He wrote, "In most of the provinces [of Europe], poverty is widespread, as a punishment for being infidels. Anyone who travels in these areas must confess that goodness and abundance are reserved for the Ottoman realms" (Mazower, p. 116). Thus, despite challenges from western Europe and foreboding that their best days were behind them, the Ottomans took some foreign elements into their culture while preserving inherited ways.

Safavid Culture

The Safavid Empire in Persia (modern-day Iran) was not as long-lived as the Ottoman Empire, but it was significant for giving Shiism a home base and a location for displaying Shiite culture. The brilliant culture that emerged during the Safavid period provided a unique blend of Shiism and Persia's distinctive historical identity. It found its highest expression in the city of Isfahan, capital of the Safavid state from its creation in 1598 until the empire's end in 1722.

THE SHIITE EMPHASIS The Safavids faced a critical dilemma when they seized power. They owed their rise to the support of Turkish-speaking tribesmen who followed a populist form of Islam. But to hold on to power, the Safavid shahs needed to cultivate powerful and conservative elements of Iranian society: Persian-speaking landowners and orthodox *ulama*. Thus, they turned away from the more popular Turkish-speaking Islamic brotherhoods with their mystical and Sufi qualities and instead built a mixed political and religious system that extolled a Shiite vision of law and society and drew on older Persian imperial traditions. Even after the Safavids lost power, Shiism remained the fundamental religion of the Iranian people.

The most effective architect of a cultural life based on Shiite religious principles and Persian royal absolutism was Shah Abbas I (r. 1587–1629). The location that he chose to display the wealth and royal power of his state, its Persian and Shiite heritages, and its artistic sensibility was the new capital city of Isfahan. For this purpose the shah hired skilled artists and architects to design a city that would dwarf even Delhi and Istanbul, the other showplaces of the Islamic world. The architectural goal was to create an earthly representation of heavenly paradise.

ARCHITECTURE AND THE ARTS The Safavid shahs were unique in seeking to project both absolute authority and accessibility. For example, their dwellings were unlike those of other Afro-Eurasian rulers—such as Topkapi Palace, in Istanbul; the Citadel, in Cairo; and the Red Forts of the Mughals. Those enclosed and fortified buildings enhanced rulers' power by concealing them from their subjects. In contrast, the buildings of Isfahan were open to the outside, demonstrating the Safavid rulers' desire to connect with their people.

Isfahan's centerpiece was the great plaza next to the royal palace and the royal mosque at the capital's heart. The plaza, surrounded by elaborate public and religious buildings, measured nearly 100,000 square yards, only slightly less than Tiananmen Square, in Beijing, and seven times bigger than the plaza of San Marco, in Venice. A suitably impressed seventeenth-century English visitor noted that the plaza was 1,000 paces from north to south and 200 from east to west—far larger than the largest urban squares in London and Paris. He added that it "is without

The Ottomans and the Tulip. *From the earliest times, the Ottomans admired the beauty of the tulip.* Left: *Sultan Mehmed II smelling a tulip, symbol of the Ottoman sultans.* Right: *The Ottomans used tulip motifs to decorate tiles in homes and mosques and to decorate pottery wares, as on the plate shown here.*

doubt as spacious, as pleasant, and aromatic a market as any in the universe" (Parker, p. 206).

Other aspects of intellectual life also reflected the elites' aspirations, wealth, and commitment to Shiite principles. Safavid artists perfected the illustrated book, the outstanding example being *The King's Book of Kings*, which contains 250 miniature illustrations demonstrating artists' mastery of three-dimensional representation and their ability to harmonize different colors. Weavers produced highly ornate and beautiful silks and carpets for trade throughout the world, and artisans painted tiles in vibrant colors and created mosaics that adorned mosques and other buildings. Moreover, the Safavids developed an elaborate calligraphy that was the envy of artists throughout the Islamic world. (See Primary Source: Islamic Views of the World.) All of these works celebrated Shiite visions of the sacred while reinforcing the authority and prestige of the empire's ruling elite.

Power and Culture under the Mughals

Like the Safavids and the Ottomans, the Mughals fostered a lavish high culture, supported primarily by taxes on agriculture but reliant on silver for its currency and, at its highpoint, open to global trade. Because they ruled over a large non-Muslim population, the culture that they developed was broad and open. So highly did it value art and learning that it welcomed non-Muslims into its circle. Thus, while Islamic traditions dominated the empire's political and judicial systems, Hindus shared with Muslims the flourishing of learning, music, painting, and architecture. In this arena, aesthetic refinement and philosophical sophistication could bridge religious differences.

RELIGION Mughal rulers were flexible toward their realm's diverse peoples, especially in spiritual affairs. Though its primary commitment to Islam stood firm, the imperial court also patronized other beliefs, displaying a tolerance that earned it widespread legitimacy. The contrast with Europe, where religious differences drove deep fractures within and between states, was stark.

The promise of an open Islamic high culture found its greatest fulfillment under the emperor Akbar (r. 1556–1605). This skillful military leader was also a popular ruler who allowed common people as well as nobles from all ethnic groups to converse with him at court. Unlike European monarchs, who tried to enforce religious uniformity, Akbar studied comparative religion and hosted regular debates among Hindu, Muslim, Jain, Parsi, and Christian theologians. His quest for universal truths outside the strict *sharia* led him to develop a religion of his own. Ultimately, he introduced at his court a "Divine Faith" (Dīn-i Ilāhī) that was a mix of Quranic, Hindu, Catholic, and other influences; it emphasized piety, prudence, gentleness, liberality, and a yearning for God.

A liberal religious attitude was not limited to Akbar's reign but remained an important feature of Mughal rule. Sufism was the most important expression of this attitude. Dara Shikoh, Emperor Shah Jahan's eldest son, for example, was an accomplished scholar of Sufism. He translated Sanskrit texts into Persian, including the Hindu text *Upanishads*, which, in turn, was translated into French and circulated in Europe. Dara Shikoh declared there was no fundamental difference between Islam and Hinduism. His open religious attitude drew the ire of the orthodox *ulama*, which pressed for the supremacy of Islamic law and upheld religious purity.

A debate between conservative and liberal attitudes also characterized Hinduism. Orthodox writers reiterated Brahman privileges and opposed the entry of women and the shudras (members of the lower caste) in the spiritual sphere. But saints of the Bhakti (devotional) sects offered a different vision. This movement, which had led to the establishment of Sikhism (see Chapter 11), swept through northern India between the fifteenth

Islamic Views of the World

Although maps give the impression of objectivity and geographical precision, they actually reveal the mapmaker's view of the world (via the way the world is arranged, names of locations, areas placed in the center or at the periphery, and accompanying text). In most cultures, official maps located their own major administrative and religious sites at the center of the universe and reflected local elites' ideas about how the world was organized.

The two maps shown here are from the Islamic world. The map of al-Idrisi, dating from the twelfth century, was a standard one of the period. Showing the world as Afro-Eurasian peoples knew it at that time, the map features only three landmasses: Africa, Asia, and Europe. The second map, made in Iran around 1700, was unabashedly Islamic: it offers a grid that measures the distance from any location in the Islamic world to the holy city of Mecca.

QUESTIONS FOR ANALYSIS

- What does each map reveal about the worldview of these Islamic societies?
- What do you think each map was used for?

Al-Idrisi map, twelfth century

Iranian map, seventeenth century

Sources: *Left:* Giraudon/Art Resource, NY. *Right:* Private Collection, courtesy of the owner and D. A. King, contributor; photo by Christie's of London.

and the seventeenth centuries. Devotion to the playful cowherd Krishna, rather than rituals officiated by Brahmans, gained popularity as the path to salvation. One famous Bhakti saint was Mirabai (1498–1547), a woman who was compelled to marry a warrior's son but preferred the company of Krishna's devotees. She composed many poems mocking marriage and asceticism. If Mirabai challenged the prohibition of women in the spiritual sphere, another Bhakti saint, Tukaram (1608–1649),

asserted the fundamental equality of human beings and challenged caste inequality. Yet another saint, Eknath (1533–1599), wrote poems that poked fun at both orthodox Hindus and Muslims and argued that true devotees of God were without caste or creed.

While Persian and Sanskrit functioned as languages of the court and the elite, the Bhakti movement addressed the common folk in regional languages. This promoted the development

Akbar Leading Religious Discussion. *This miniature painting from 1604 shows Akbar receiving Muslim theologians and Jesuits. The Jesuits (in the black robes on the left) hold a page relating, in Persian, the birth of Christ. A lively debate will follow the Jesuits' claims on behalf of Christianity.*

of Marathi, Hindi, Bengali, and other regional vernaculars. It also produced a lively engagement between Sufism and Hindu devotionalism—so much so that scholars cannot determine which tradition is the source of which particular poem. While Bhakti poetry narrated Krishna's story as a Sufi romance, some Sufi poetry began by invoking Allah before turning to Hindu imagery and themes. Sufism spread in popular culture with poetry and songs addressed to daily life, not just an esoteric union with God. Among these were songs for women, including one for those engaged in grinding food grains or spinning thread. These songs nurtured religious devotion and amplified the role of women in popular Islam. Women regularly visited Sufi shrines and prayed for divine intervention in their daily lives.

Religious life under the Mughals at both elite and popular levels presents a rich and diverse picture of dialogue and interaction between different religions, which is at odds with the image of Hindu-Muslim cultural separatism that some religious nationalists today hold.

ARCHITECTURE AND THE ARTS In architecture, too, the Mughals produced masterpieces that blended styles. This was already evident as builders combined Persian, Indian, and Ottoman elements in tombs and mosques under Akbar's predecessors. But Akbar enhanced this mixture in the elaborate city he built at Fatehpur Sikri, beginning in 1571. The buildings included residences for nobles (whose loyalty Akbar wanted), gardens, a drinking and gambling zone, and even an experimental school devoted to studying language acquisition in children. Building the huge complex took a decade, much less time than it took for construction of Louis XIV's comparable royal residence a century later at Versailles.

Akbar's descendant Shah Jahan also patronized architecture and the arts. In 1630, he ordered the building in Agra of a magnificent white marble tomb for his beloved wife, Mumtaz Mahal. Like many other women in the Mughal court, she had been an important political counselor. Designed by an Indian architect of Persian origin, this structure, the **Taj Mahal**, took twenty years and 20,000 workers to build. The 42-acre complex included a main gateway, a garden, minarets, and a mosque. The translucent marble mausoleum lay squarely in the middle of the structure, enclosed by four identical facades and crowned by a majestic central dome rising to 240 feet. The stone inlays of different types and hues, organized in geometric and floral patterns and featuring Quranic verses inscribed in Arabic calligraphy, gave the surface an appearance of delicacy and lightness. Blending Persian and Islamic design with Indian materials and motifs, this poetry in stone represents the most splendid example of Mughal high culture and the combining of cultural traditions. Like Shah Abbas's great plaza, the Taj Mahal gave a sense of refined grandeur to this empire's power and splendor. (See again Current Trends in World History: The Political Uses of Space.)

FOREIGN INFLUENCES VERSUS ISLAMIC CULTURE

Under later emperors, Mughal culture remained vibrant although not quite so brilliant. François Bernier, a seventeenth-century French traveler, wrote admiringly of the broad philosophical interests of Danishmand Khan, whom the emperor Aurangzeb had appointed as governor of Delhi. According to Bernier, Khan avidly read the works of the French philosophers Gassendi and Descartes and studied Sanskrit treatises to understand different philosophical traditions. But Aurangzeb, a pious Muslim, favored Islamic arts and sciences. He dismissed many of the court's painters and musicians and in 1669 ordered that all recently built non-Islamic places of worship be torn down. In his court, intellectuals debated whether metaphysics, astronomy, medicine, mathematics, and ethics were of use in the practice of Islam. Women, at least at court, apparently were allowed to pursue the arts, for two of Aurangzeb's daughters were accomplished poets.

Well into the eighteenth century, the Mughal nobility exuded confidence and lived in unrivaled luxury. The presence of foreign scholars and artists enhanced the courtly culture, and the elite eagerly consumed exotic goods from China and

CURRENT TRENDS IN WORLD HISTORY

The Political Uses of Space

The use of space for political purposes is a theme we can trace across world history. It has also allowed us to look at political history in new and different ways through a cultural lens by considering the ways rulers used symbols and space to convey this sense of power. In the early modern period, many kings and emperors opted to build grand palaces to create lavish power centers from which they could project their influence over their kingdoms; petitioners and potential rivals would have to come to *them* to ask for favors or to complete their business. Monarchs sculpted these environments, creating a series of spaces, each of them open to a smaller and smaller number of the king's favorites. Both palaces and their surrounding grounds were ornate and splendid, were expensive to construct, and involved the best craftsmen and artists available, which often meant borrowing ideas and designs from neighboring cultures. Palace complexes of this type, built in Beijing, in Istanbul, and just outside of Paris, used space to project the rulers' power and to show who was boss.

The **Forbidden City of Beijing** was the earliest of these impressive sites of royal power (see illustration on p. 427). Its construction took about four years—from 1416 to 1420—although the actual name "Forbidden City" did not appear until 1576. The entrance of the city was straddled by the Meridian Gate, the tallest structure of the entire complex, which towered over all other buildings at more than 115 feet above the ground. It was from this lofty position that the emperor extended his gaze toward his empire as he oversaw various court ceremonies, including the important annual proclamation of the calendar that governed the entire country's agricultural and ritual activities. Foreign emissaries received by the court were also often allowed to use one of the passageways through the gate, where they were expected to be duly awed. As for the officials' daily audience with the emperor, they had to line up outside the Meridian Gate around 3 A.M. before proceeding to the Hall of Supreme Harmony. It was typical of the entire construction project that this impressive hall with vermilion walls and golden tiles was built at considerable cost. For the columns of the hall, fragrant hardwood had to be found in the tiger-ridden forests of the remote southwest, while the mountain forests of the south and southwest were searched for other timbers that eventually made their way to the capital through the Grand Canal.

The **Topkapi Palace**, in Istanbul, capital of the Ottoman Empire, began to take shape in 1458 under Mehmed II and underwent steady expansion over the years (see illustration on p. 414). Topkapi projected royal authority in much the same way as the Forbidden City emphasized the power of Chinese emperors: governing officials worked enclosed within massive walls, and monarchs rarely went outside their inner domain.

More than two centuries later, in the 1670s and 1680s, the French monarch Louis XIV built the **Palace of Versailles** on the site of a royal hunting lodge 11 miles from Paris, the French capital (see illustration on p. 513). This enormously costly complex was built to house Louis's leading clergymen and nobles, who were obliged to visit at least twice a year. Louis hoped that by taking wealthy and powerful men and women away from their local power bases and diverting them with entertainments, he could keep them from plotting new forms of religious schism or challenging his right to rule. Going to Versailles also allowed him to escape the pressures and demands of the population of Paris. Many European monarchs—including Russia's Peter the Great—would build palace complexes modeled on Versailles.

If in China, the Ottoman Empire, and France emperors built what were essentially private spaces in which to conduct and dominate state business, Shah Abbas (r. 1587–1629), of the Safavid Empire, chose to create a great new public space

Europe. Foreign trade also brought in more silver, advancing the money economy and supporting the nobles' sumptuous lifestyles. In addition, the Mughals assimilated European military technology: they hired Europeans as gunners and military engineers in their armies, employed them to forge guns, and bought guns and cannons from them. However, Mughal appreciation for other European knowledge and technology was limited. Thus, when a representative of the English East India Company presented an edition of Mercator's *Maps of the World* to the emperor in 1617, the emperor returned it with the remark that no one could read or understand it. The Mughals, like the Ottomans, remained supremely confident of their own cultural world.

The Islamic world drew on intellectual currents that spanned the Eurasian–North African landmass, for its centers were in Istanbul, Cairo, Isfahan, and Delhi. From Islam's founding, Muslims had looked to India and China, not to Europe, for inspiration. By the eighteenth century, the increasing wealth and power of Christian kingdoms enriched by New World colonies made those cultures more imposing. Yet even as Muslims brought a few new European elements into their cultural mix, instead. In the early seventeenth century, Shah Abbas oversaw the construction of the **great plaza at Isfahan**, a structure that reflected his desire to bring trade, government, and religion together under the authority of the supreme political leader. An enormous public mosque, the Shah Abbas Mosque, dominated one end of the plaza, which measured 1,667 feet by 517 feet. At the other end were trading stalls and markets. Along one side sat government offices; the other side offered the exquisite Mosque of Shaykh Lutfollah. If the other rulers of this era devoted their (considerable) income to creating rich *private* spaces, Shah Abbas used the vast open space of the plaza to open up his city to all comers, keeping only the Mosque of Shaykh Lutfollah for his personal use.

The royal use of space says a great deal about how monarchs in this era wished to be seen and remembered and about how they wanted to rule. While some wanted to retreat from the rest of society, Shah Abbas wanted to create an open space for trade and the exchange of ideas. World history is full of palaces and plazas (the Piazza San Marco, in Venice, might be compared to the royal plaza at Isfahan); we can still visit and admire them. But when we do, we should also remember that architecture that either opens up to the public or sets aside privileged spaces has always had political as well as cultural functions.

Isfahan. *On the great plaza at Isfahan, markets and government offices operated in close proximity to the public Shah Abbas Mosque, shown here, and the shah's private mosque. The design of this plaza represented Shah Abbas's desire to unite control of trade, government, and religion under one leader.*

QUESTIONS FOR ANALYSIS

- Choose one of the places discussed in this feature. How did the architectural layout shape the political power exercised by that space?
- How did private spaces, like the palace at Versailles, differ from public spaces, like the great plaza at Isfahan? What political goals could be accomplished by each?

Explore Further

Babaie, Sussan. *Isfahan and Its Palaces: Statecraft, Shi'ism and the Architecture of Conviviality in Early Modern Iran* (2008).

Necipoğlu, Gülru. *Architecture, Ceremonial, and Power: The Topkapi Palace in the Fifteenth and Sixteenth Centuries* (1991).

most still regarded Europeans as rude barbarians. More impressive in the eyes of elites in Persia, India, and the Ottoman Empire were the cultural splendors to be found to the east.

CULTURE AND POLITICS IN EAST ASIA

Like the Ottomans, Safavids, and Mughals, the Chinese did not need to prove the richness of their scholarly and artistic traditions. China had long been a renowned center of learning, with its emperors and elites supporting artists, poets, musicians, scientists, and teachers. But in late Ming and early Qing China, cultural flourishing owed more to a booming internal market, as the growing population and extensive commercial networks propelled the circulation of ideas as well as goods. As a result, China's cultural sphere expanded and diversified well before similar changes occurred elsewhere.

In Japan, too, prosperity promoted cultural dynamism. Because of Japan's giant neighbor across the sea, the Japanese people had always been aware of outside influences. Like the Chinese government, the Tokugawa shogunate tried to

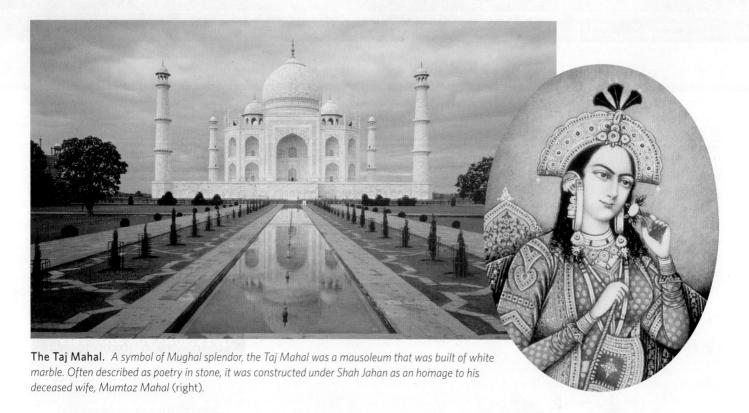

The Taj Mahal. *A symbol of Mughal splendor, the Taj Mahal was a mausoleum that was built of white marble. Often described as poetry in stone, it was constructed under Shah Jahan as an homage to his deceased wife, Mumtaz Mahal* (right).

promote Confucian notions of a social hierarchy organized on the basis of social position, age, gender, and kin. It also tried to shield the country from egalitarian ideas that would threaten the strict social hierarchy. But the forces that undermined government control of knowledge in China proved even stronger in Japan. Here, a decentralized political system enabled different cultural influences to spread, including European ideas and practices. By the eighteenth century, in struggling to define its own identity through these contending currents, the cultural scene in Japan was more lively, open, and varied than its counterpart in China.

China: The Challenge of Expansion and Diversity

In China, the circulation of books spread ideas among the literate, and religious rituals instilled cultural values among the broader population. Advances in cartography reflected the distinctive worldview of Chinese elites.

PUBLISHING AND THE TRANSMISSION OF IDEAS Broader circulation of ideas had more to do with the decentralization of book production than with technological innovations. After all, woodblock and movable type printing had been present in China for centuries. Initially, the state had spurred book production by printing Confucian texts; but before long, the economy's increasing commercialization

weakened government controls over what got printed. Even as officials clamped down on unorthodox texts, there was no centralized system of censorship, and unauthorized opinions circulated freely.

By the late Ming era, a burgeoning publishing sector catered to the diverse social, cultural, and religious needs of educated elites and urban populations. European visitors admired the vast collections of printed materials housed in Chinese libraries, describing them as "magnificently built" and "finely adorn'd." In fact, the late Ming was an age of collections of other sorts as well. Members of the increasingly affluent elite acquired objects for display (such as paintings, ceramics, and calligraphy) as a sign of their status and refinement. Consumers could build collections by purchasing from multiple sources—from roadside peddlers to monks to gentlemen dealers—because books and other luxury goods were now more affordable. Increasingly, publishers offered a mix of wares: guidebooks for patrons of the arts, travelers, or merchants; handbooks for performing rituals, choosing dates for ceremonies, or writing proper letters; almanacs and encyclopedias; morality books; and medical manuals.

Especially popular were study aids for the civil service examination, including models for the required, highly structured eight-part essay. In 1595, Beijing reeled with scandal over news that the second-place graduate had reproduced verbatim several model essays published by commercial printers. Just over twenty years later, the top graduate plagiarized a winning essay submitted years earlier. Ironically, then, the increased circulation of knowledge led critics to bemoan a decline in real learning. Instead of mastering the classics, they charged, examination candidates were simply memorizing the work of others.

Examination hopefuls were not the only beneficiaries of the book trade, for elite women also joined China's literary culture, penetrating the formerly male-only domain as readers, writers, and editors. Anthologies of women's poetry were especially popular, not only in the market, but also, when issued in limited circulation, to celebrate the refinement of the writer's family. Men of letters soon recognized the market potential of women's writings. Some also saw women's less regularized style (usually acquired through family channels rather than state-sponsored schools) as a means to challenge stifling stylistic conformity. A few women even served as publishers themselves.

Although elite women enjoyed success in the world of culture, the period brought increasing restrictions on their lives. Remarriage of widows and premarital sex might have met with disapproval in earlier times, but now they were utterly unthinkable for women from "good" families. Ironically, the thriving publishing sector indirectly promoted the stricter morality by printing plays and novels that echoed the government's conservative attitudes. Meanwhile, footbinding (which elite women first adopted around the late Tang-Song period) spread among common people, as small, delicate feet came to signify femininity and respectability.

Chinese Civil Service Exam. *This nineteenth-century photo shows a Chinese Civil Service Examination compound. Lining the compound were cells in which candidates sat for the examination. Other than three long boards—the highest served as a shelf, the middle one as a desk, and the lowest as a seat—the cell had neither furniture nor a door. Indeed, the cells were little more than spaces partitioned on three sides by brick walls and covered by a roof; the floors were packed dirt. Generations of candidates spent three days and two nights in succession in these cells as they strove to enter officialdom.*

POPULAR CULTURE AND RELIGION Important as the book trade was, it had only an indirect impact on most men and women in late Ming China. Those who could not read well or at all absorbed cultural values through oral communication, ritual performance, and daily practices. The Ming government tried to control these channels, too. It appointed village elders as guardians of local society and instituted "village compacts" to ensure shared responsibility for proper conduct and observation of the laws.

Still, the everyday life of rural and small-town dwellers went on outside these official networks. Apart from toiling in the field, villagers participated in various religious and cultural practices, such as honoring local guardian spirits, patronizing Buddhist and Daoist temples, or watching performances by touring theater groups. Furthermore, villagers often took group pilgrimages to religious sites and attended markets in nearby towns offering restaurants, brothels, and other types of entertainment. At the marketplaces the visitors gathered news and gossip or listened to itinerant storytellers and traveling monks; such open-ended cultural activities gave audiences opportunities to reinterpret official norms to serve their own purposes and to contest the government's rules. For example, commoners could take officially approved morality tales celebrating impartial officials and use them to challenge the real-life behavior of government bureaucrats.

Popular religions that mingled various traditions also reflected late Ming cultural flourishing. Here, at the grassroots level, there was little distinction among Buddhist, Daoist, and local cults. After all, the Chinese believed in cosmic unity; and although they venerated spiritual forces, they did not consider any of them to be a Supreme Being who favored one sect over another. They believed it was the emperor, rather than any religious group, who held the mandate of heaven; the enforcement of orthodox values was more a matter of political than of religious control. Unless sects posed an obvious threat, the emperor had no reason to regulate their spiritual practices. This situation promoted religious tolerance and avoided the sectarian warfare that plagued post-Reformation Europe.

TECHNOLOGY AND CARTOGRAPHY Belief in cosmic unity did not prevent the Chinese from devising technologies to master nature's operations in this world. For example, the magnetic compass, gunpowder, and the printing press were all Chinese inventions. Moreover, Chinese technicians had mastered iron casting and produced mechanical clocks centuries before Europeans did. Chinese astronomers also compiled accurate records of eclipses, comets, novae, and meteors. In part, the emperor's needs drove their interest in astronomy and calendrical science. After all, it was his job as the Son of Heaven, and thus mediator between heaven and earth, to determine the best dates for planting, holding festivities, scheduling mourning periods, and convening judicial court sessions. The

Footbinding. *Two images of bound feet: (left) as an emblem of feminine respectability when wrapped and concealed, as on this well-to-do Chinese woman; (right) as an object of curiosity and condemnation when exposed for the world to see.*

Chinese believed that the empire's stability depended on correct calculation of these dates.

In the realm of cartography, the Chinese demonstrated most clearly their understanding of the world. Their maps encompassed elements of history, literature, and art—not just technical detail. It was not that "scientific" techniques were lacking; a map made as early as 1136 reveals that Chinese cartographers could readily draw to scale. Yet, valuing written text over visual and other forms of representation, Chinese elites did not always treat geometric and mathematical precision as the main objective of cartography. Reflecting the elites' worldview, most maps placed the realm of the Chinese emperor, as the ruler of "All under Heaven," at the center, surrounded by foreign countries. Thus, the physical scale of China and distances to other lands were distorted. Still, some of the maps cover a vast expanse: one includes an area stretching from Japan to the Atlantic, encompassing Europe and Africa. (See Primary Source: Chinese Views of the World.)

CHINESE VIEWS OF EUROPEANS Before the nineteenth century, the Chinese had incomplete knowledge about foreign lands despite a long history of contact. The empire saw itself as superior to all others (a common feature of many cultures). A Ming geographical publication portrayed the Portuguese as men who are "seven feet tall, have eyes like a cat, a mouth like an oriole, an ash-white face, thick and curly beards like black gauze, and almost red hair" (quoted in Dikötter, p. 14). Qing authors in the eighteenth century confused France with the Portugal known during Ming times, and they characterized England and Sweden as dependencies

of Holland. During this period of cultural flourishing, in short, most Chinese did not feel compelled to revise their view of the world.

Cultural Identity and Tokugawa Japan

The culture that developed in Japan in this period drew on local traditions and, increasingly, foreign influences from China and Europe. Chinese cultural influence had long crossed the Sea of Japan, but under the Tokugawa shogunate there was also interest in European culture. This interest grew via the Dutch presence in Japan and via limited contact with Russians. At the same time, the study of Japanese traditions and culture surged. Thus, Tokugawa Japan engaged in a three-cornered conversation that included time-honored Chinese ways (transmitted via Korea), European teachings, and distinctly Japanese traditions.

NATIVE ARTS AND POPULAR CULTURE Until the sixteenth and seventeenth centuries, the main patrons of Japanese culture were the imperial court in Kyoto, the hereditary shogunate, religious institutions, and a small upper class. These groups developed an elite culture of theater and stylized painting. Samurai (former warriors turned bureaucrats) and daimyo (regional lords) favored a masked theater, called Noh and an elegant ritual for making tea and engaging in contemplation. In their gardens, the lords built teahouses with stages for Noh drama. These gave rise to hereditary schools of actors, tea masters, and flower arrangers. The elites also hired

Chinese Views of the World

The Chinese developed cartographical skills early in their history. A third-century map, no longer in existence, was designed to enable the emperors to "comprehend the four corners of the world without ever having to leave their imperial quarters." The *Huayi tu* (Map of Chinese and Foreign Lands) from 1136 depicted the whole world on a stone stele, including 500 place names and textual information on foreign lands. Chinese maps typically devoted more attention to textual explanations with moral and political messages than to locating places accurately. One such map, the Chinese wheel map from the 1760s, is full of textual explanations.

QUESTIONS FOR ANALYSIS

• Why do you think Chinese maps included messages that focused on moral and political themes?
• How are these maps similar to and different from the Islamic maps shown on p. 524?

The Huayi tu *map, 1136*

Chinese wheel map, 1760s

Sources: *Left:* The Needham Research Institute. *Right:* The British Library, London.

commoner-painters to decorate tea utensils and other fine articles and to paint the brilliant interiors and standing screens in grand stone castles. Some upper-class men did their own painting, which conveyed philosophical thoughts. Calligraphy was proof of refinement.

Alongside the elite culture arose a rougher urban one. Here, artisans and merchants could purchase, for example, works of fiction and colorful prints (often risqué) made from carved woodblocks and could enjoy the company of female entertainers known as geisha who were skilled (*gei*) in playing the three-stringed instrument (*shamisen*), storytelling, and performing;

some were also prostitutes. Kabuki—a type of theater that combined song, dance, and skillful staging to dramatize conflicts between duty and passion—became wildly popular. This art form featured dazzling acting, brilliant makeup, and sumptuous costumes.

Much popular entertainment chronicled the world of the common people rather than politics or high society. The urbanites' pleasure-oriented culture was known as "the floating world" (*ukiyo*), and the woodblock prints depicting it as *ukiyo-e* (*e* meaning "picture"). Here, the social order was temporarily turned upside down. Those usually considered inferior—actors,

Artist and Geisha at Tea. *The erotic, luxuriant atmosphere of Japan's urban pleasure quarters was captured in a new art form, the ukiyo-e, or "pictures from a floating world." In this image set in Tokyo's celebrated Yoshiwara district, several geisha flutter about a male artist.*

musicians, courtesans, and others seen as possessing low morals—became idols. Even some upper-class samurai partook of this "lower" culture. But to enter the pleasure quarters, they had to leave behind their swords, a mark of rank.

Literacy in Japan now surged, especially among men. The most popular novels sold 10,000 to 12,000 copies. In the late eighteenth century, Edo had some sixty booksellers and hundreds of book lenders. In fact, the presence of so many lenders allowed books to spread to a wider public that previously could not afford to buy them. By the late eighteenth century, as more books circulated and some of them criticized the government, officials tried to censor certain publications. The government's response testified to the uncommon power wielded by people of modest means and the relative significance of popular culture in Japan.

RELIGION AND CHINESE INFLUENCE In the realm of higher culture, China loomed large in the Tokugawa world. Japanese scholars wrote imperial histories of Japan in the Chinese style,

and Chinese law codes and other books attracted a significant readership. Some Japanese traveled south to Nagasaki to meet Zen Buddhist masters and Chinese residents there. A few Chinese monks won permission to found monasteries outside Nagasaki and to give lectures and construct temples in Kyoto and Edo.

Although Buddhist temples grew in number, they did not displace the native Japanese practice of venerating ancestors and worshipping gods in nature. Later called Shintō ("the way of the gods"), this practice boasted a network of shrines throughout the country. Shintō developed from time-honored beliefs in spirits, or *kami*, who were associated with places (mountains, rivers, waterfalls, rocks, the moon) and activities (harvest, fertility). Seeking healing or other assistance, adherents appealed to these spirits in nature and daily life through incantations and offerings. Some women under Shintō served as *mikos*, a kind of shaman with special divinatory powers.

Shintō rituals competed with a powerful strain of neo-Confucianism that issued moral and behavioral guidelines. For example, in 1762, "Greater Learning for Females" appeared—an influential text that made Confucian teachings understandable for nonscholars. In particular, it outlined social roles that stressed hierarchy based on age and gender as a way to ensure order. At the same time, merit became important in determining one's place in the social hierarchy. Doing the right thing (propriety) and being virtuous were key.

By the early eighteenth century, neo-Confucian teachings of filial piety and loyalty to superiors had become the official state creed. This philosophy legitimated the social hierarchy and the absolutism of political authorities, but it also instructed the shogun and the upper class to provide "benevolent administration" for the people's benefit. That meant taking into account petitioners' complaints and requests, whether for improved irrigation and roads or for punishment of unfair officials. Thus did Japanese culture shape state structure—and vice versa.

Reacting to the influence of Chinese Buddhism and desiring to honor their own country's greatness, some thinkers promoted intellectual traditions from Japan's past. These efforts stressed "native learning," Japanese texts, and Japanese uniqueness. In so doing, they formalized a Japanese religious and cultural tradition and denounced Confucianism and Buddhism as foreign contaminants.

EUROPEAN INFLUENCES Chinese thought was not the only outside influence to compete with revived native learning. By the late seventeenth century, Japan was also tapping other sources of knowledge. By 1670, a guild of Japanese interpreters in Nagasaki who could speak and read Dutch accompanied Dutch merchants on trips to Edo. As European knowledge spread to high circles in Edo, in 1720 the shogunate lifted its ban on foreign books. Thereafter, European ideas, called "Dutch learning," circulated more openly. Scientific, geographical, and medical texts

Kabuki Theater. *Kabuki originated among dance troupes in the environs of temples and shrines in Kyoto in the late sixteenth and early seventeenth centuries. As kabuki spread to the urban centers of Japan, the theater designs enabled the actors to enter and exit from many directions and to step out into the audience, lending the skillful, raucous shows great intimacy.*

appeared in Japanese translations and in some cases displaced Chinese texts. A Japanese-Dutch dictionary appeared in 1745, and the first official school of Dutch learning followed. Students of Dutch or European teachings remained a limited segment of Japanese society, but the demand for translations intensified.

Japan's internal debates about what to borrow from the Europeans and the Chinese illustrate the changes that the world had undergone in recent centuries. A few hundred years earlier, products and ideas generally did not travel beyond coastal regions and had only a limited effect (especially inland) on local cultural practices. By the eighteenth century, though, expanded networks of exchange and new prosperity made the integration of foreign ideas feasible and, sometimes, desirable. The Japanese did not consider the embracing of outside influences as a mark of inferiority or subordination, particularly when they could put those influences to good use. This was not the case for the great Asian land-based empires, which were eager lenders but hesitant borrowers.

Japanese Map of the World. *Japanese maps underwent a shift as a result of encounters with the Dutch. Here, in a map dated 1671, much information is incorporated about distant lands, both cartographically on the globe and pictorially, to the left, in two-person images representing various peoples of the world in their purported typical costumes.*

AFRICAN CULTURAL FLOURISHING

The wealth that spurred artistic achievement and displays of power in the three major Islamic states and China and Japan did not bypass African states. The slave trade enriched African upper classes who sold their captives to European slavers and used their wealth to fund cultural activities and invigorate centuries-old artisanal and artistic traditions. As in the Islamic world and East Asia, African artisans maintained local forms of cultural production, such as wood carving, weaving, and metal working.

Cultural traditions in Africa varied from kingdom to kingdom, but there were patterns among them. For example, all West African elites encouraged craftsmen to produce carvings, statues, masks, and other objects that glorified the rulers' power and achievements. (Royal patrons in Europe, Asia, and the Islamic world did the same with architecture and painting.) There was also a widespread belief that rulers and their families had the gods' blessing, much as was the case in Ottoman, Safavid, Mughal, Chinese, and Japanese societies at this time. But African arts and crafts not only celebrated royal power; they also captured the energy of a universe that people believed was filled with spiritual beings. Starting in the 1500s and continuing through the eighteenth century when the slave trade reached its peak, African rulers had even more reason—and means—to support cultural pursuits. After all, as destructive as the slave trade was for African peoples, it made the slave-trading states wealthy and powerful.

The Asante, Oyo, and Benin Cultural Traditions

The kingdom of Asante led the way in cultural attainments, and the Oyo Empire and Benin also promoted rich artistic traditions. The Asante kingdom's access to gold and the revenues that it derived from selling captives undergirded its prosperity, making it the richest state in West Africa—perhaps even in the whole of sub-Saharan Africa. So deeply imbued with a desire to achieve economic success were the citizens of Asante that they accorded the highest respect to entrepreneurs who made money and surrounded themselves with retainers and slaves. The adages of the age were inevitably about becoming rich: "Money is king," "Nothing is as important as money." People who had wealth displayed it ostentatiously, wearing special garments signaling that they were persons of wealth and power. Those who could command the services of at least 1,000 subjects were entitled to wear a special cloth and to have a horsetail switch borne in front of them. Even more coveted was the right to carry the elephant-tail whip, which denoted an esteemed title.

Artisans celebrated these traditions through the crafting of magnificent seats or stools coated with gold as symbols of authority; the most ornate were reserved for the head of the Asante federation, the Asantehene, who ruled this far-flung empire from the capital city of Kumasi. By the eighteenth century, these monarchs ventured out from the secluded royal palace only on ceremonial and feast days, when they wore sumptuous silk garments featuring many dazzling colors and geometric patterns in interwoven strips. Known as Kente cloth, this fabric was worn at first only by rulers, but later on wealthy individuals were permitted to garb themselves with it. Kings also had the golden elephant tail carried in front of them, a symbol of the greatest wealth. Held aloft on these celebratory occasions were maces, spears, staffs, and other symbols of power fashioned from the kingdom's abundant gold supplies. These reminded the common people of the Asantehene's connection to the gods.

Equally resplendent were rulers of the Oyo Empire and Benin, located in the territory that now constitutes Nigeria. Elegant, refined metalwork in the form of West African bronzes reflects these rulers' awesome power and their peoples' highest esteem. The bronze heads of Ife, capital city of the Yoruba Oyo Empire, are among the world's most sophisticated artworks. According to one commentator, "Little that Italy or Greece or Egypt ever produced could be finer, and the appeal of their beauty is immediate and universal" (Tignor, p. 428). Artisans fashioned the best known of these works in the thirteenth century (before the slave trade era), but the tradition continued and became more elaborate in the seventeenth and eighteenth centuries.

Kente Cloth. *Kente cloth originated among the Asante people and spread to other parts of West Africa. Threads of silk and cotton were interwoven to produce patterns with dazzling colors and geometric shapes. The colors represented different meanings important to the Asante peoples. Gray stood for healing and gold for royalty. Red was said to engender spiritual moods.*

Bronzes from Benin, too, displayed exquisite craftsmanship. Although historical records have portrayed Benin as one of Africa's most brutal slave-trading regimes, it also produced art of the highest order. Whether Benin's reputation for brutality was deserved or simply part of Europeans' later desire to label African rulers as "savage" in order to justify their conquest of the landmass, it cannot detract from the splendor of its artisans' creations.

Wealth acquired from the slave trade fostered cultural flourishing in Africa, notably though not exclusively in West Africa. Here, as in the Islamic world and East Asia, artisans and craftspersons drew on their own traditions. But the African artistic tradition, unlike Islamic and East Asian traditions, was little influenced by other cultures, even at a time when Africa was being drawn into global networks of exchange and political domination.

Ife Bronzes. *An Ife bronze from the Yoruba peoples of present-day Nigeria. This magnificent work, one of a collection of fifteen pieces, was crafted sometime between the eleventh and fifteenth centuries and discovered by an American researcher in 1939.*

THE ENLIGHTENMENT IN EUROPE

An extraordinary cultural flowering also occurred in Europe during the seventeenth and eighteenth centuries. Ironically, its origins lay in the period of the Little Ice Age, a time of devastating religious and civil wars, events that provoked many European thinkers to turn their backs on religious strife and to develop useful ways for understanding and improving *this* world. First came "the new science," a search for stable, testable, and objective knowledge, especially in physics and astronomy. From its findings and inspiration a wider movement, the **Enlightenment**, was born. Often defined purely in intellectual terms as the spreading of faith in reason and in universal rights and laws, this era encompassed broader developments, such as the expansion of literacy, the spread of critical thinking, the improvement of agricultural productivity, and the decline of religious persecution. As literate, middle- and upper-class men and women gained confidence in being able to reason for themselves, to understand the world without calling on traditional authorities, and to publicly criticize what they found distasteful or wrong, they embraced an increasingly "enlightened" age.

Quarrels and competition between European states and increasing contact between Europe and the wider world after the sixteenth century contributed to the shaping of Enlightenment culture. Conflict at home and competition between states pushed Europeans overseas, where they became eager consumers of other peoples' goods and practices, including Amerindian trapping methods and Chinese methods of making porcelain. The European states' aspirations to modernize and build their armies generated new patronage and support for ideas that sometimes troubled religious authorities and grew increasingly dynamic and radical as they spread downward to new social groups. But the more they learned in their interactions with others, and the more they succeeded in secularizing and spreading

Brass Oba Head. *The brass head of an Oba, or king, of Benin. The kingdom's brass and bronze work was among the finest in all of Africa.*

their ideas at home, the more European intellectuals became convinced not only that their culture was superior—for that was hardly rare—but that they had discovered a set of universal laws that applied to everyone, everywhere around the globe. (See Primary Source: European Views of the World.)

The New Science

The search for new, testable knowledge began centuries before the Enlightenment in the efforts of Nicolaus Copernicus (1473–1543) and Galileo Galilei (1564–1642) to understand the

European Views of the World

As Europeans became world travelers and traders, they needed accurate information on places and distances so they could get home as well as return to the sites they had visited. Europe's first printed map of the New World, the Waldseemüller map (produced in 1507), portrayed the Americas as a long and narrow strip of land. Asia and Africa dwarf its unexplored landmass. By the mid-seventeenth century, European maps were seemingly more objective, yet they still grouped the rest of the world around the European countries. Moreover, the effort to make world maps that served navigational purposes led to distortions (like the stretching of polar zones in the 1569 Mercator projection) that made Europe seem disproportionately large and central.

ESTIONS FOR ANALYSIS

- What are the most striking differences between the two maps?
- How are these European maps similar to and different from the Islamic and Chinese ones shown on pp. 524 and 531 respectively?

Waldseemüller map, 1507

Mercator projection, 1569

Sources: Top: Courtesy Wychwood Editions. *Bottom:* Rare Books Division, The New York Public Library, Astor, Lenox and Tilden Foundations.

Galileo. *Worried that the new science would undermine the Christian faith, the Catholic Church put Italian scientist Galileo on trial in 1633 for espousing heretical beliefs and condemned him to house arrest until his death in 1642.*

behavior of the heavens. These men were both astronomers and mathematicians. Making their own mathematical calculations and observations of the stars and planets, these scholars came to conclusions that contradicted age-old assumptions. By no means was trusting one's own work rather than the accepted authorities easy or without risk: when Galileo confirmed Copernicus's claims that the earth revolved around the sun, he was put on trial for heresy.

In the seventeenth century, a small but influential group of scholars committed themselves, similarly, to experimentation, calculation, and observation. They adopted a method for "scientific" inquiry laid out by the philosopher Sir Francis Bacon (1561–1626), who claimed that real science entailed the formulation of hypotheses that could be tested in carefully controlled experiments. Bacon believed that traditional authorities could never be trusted; only by conducting experiments could humans begin to comprehend the workings of nature. Bacon was chiefly wary of classical and medieval authorities, but his principle also applied to traditional knowledge that European scientists were encountering in the rest of the world. Confident of their calculations performed according to the new **scientific method**, scientists like Isaac Newton (1642–1727) defined what they believed were universal laws that applied to all matter and motion; they criticized older conceptions of nature (from Aristotelian ideas to folkloric and foreign ones) as absurd and obsolete. Thus, in his *Principia Mathematica*, Newton set forth the laws of motion—including the famous law of gravitation, which simultaneously explained falling bodies on earth and planetary motion.

It is no longer fashionable to call these changes a scientific revolution, for European thinking did not change overnight. Only gradually did thinkers come to see the natural world as operating according to inviolable laws such as gravity and inertia. But by the late seventeenth century, many rulers had developed a new interest in science's discoveries, and they established royal academies of science to encourage local endeavors. This patronage, of course, had a political function. By incorporating the British Royal Society in 1662, for example, Charles II hoped to show not only that the crown backed scientific progress but also that England's great minds backed the crown. Similar reasoning lay behind Louis XIV's founding of the French Academy of Sciences. As other rulers followed suit, the church's power over European culture—already weakened and divided by the Reformation—waned.

The new science was, at least at first, heavily theoretical. But this does not mean it lacked practical applications or appeal to wider audiences. The new math was useful for the science of ballistics, and the new astronomy for building better clocks and navigational devices, such as the chronometer. More technical sophistication necessitated, in turn, the establishment of military schools, which increasingly stressed engineering methods, made advances in surveying and mapping, and introduced a culture of meritocracy into the previously noble-dominated armies. In rural areas, landowners began to read books about crop rotation and formed societies to discuss the latest methods of animal breeding. In Italy, numerous female natural philosophers emerged, and the genre of scientific literature for "ladies" took hold. By about 1750, even artisans and journalists were applying Newtonian mechanics to their practical problems and inventions. A consensus emerged among proponents of the new science that useful knowledge came from collecting data and organizing them into universally valid systems, rather than from studying revered classical texts.

By the eighteenth century, the spread of the new science, together with expanding commerce and the relaxation, in some places, of censorship, began to give reform-minded Europeans hope that they were living in a *siècle des lumières*, or "century of light." In many places, this was still more hope than reality, as literacy was far from universal, peasants still suffered under arbitrary systems of taxation, and judicial regimes remained harsh. Most people still understood their relationship with God, nature, and other humans via Christian doctrines and local customs. But many thinkers could now hope that Thomas Hobbes's pessimism, formed in the midst of the Little Ice Age and the terrors of the seventeenth century (see Chapter 13), had been wrong and that human societies, along with the sciences, could be improved. That hope launched the movement we now call the Enlightenment.

Enlightened Thought and Its Spread

Enlightenment thinkers, called **philosophes** in France, built on the achievements of the new science, insisting that scientific reasoning could and should be used to understand human societies as well as the natural world. Thinkers such as the English scientist and political writer John Locke (1712–1704), the French writers Voltaire (1694–1778) and Denis Diderot (1713–1784), and the Scottish economist Adam Smith (1723–1790) believed in the power of human reason to criticize and improve existing institutions and practices. They claimed that oppressive governments, religious superstition, and irrational social inequalities were not ills people simply had to accept. Human beings could use their reason, Locke believed, to combat the human-made evils of intolerance and superstition. Similarly, Voltaire criticized the torture of criminals, Diderot denounced the despotic tendencies of the French kings Louis XIV and Louis XV, and Smith exposed the inefficiencies of mercantilism. Very few of these writers were political radicals or atheists (people who do not believe in any god), but their belief that Europe and the world could be improved by the universal application of law and reason made their ideas highly appealing to modernizing reformers and radical critics alike.

In general, Enlightenment thinkers distrusted institutions and conventions and argued that societies should be governed by applying reason and natural laws rather than by following traditions. The application of reason to history, Locke claimed, showed that divine-right monarchies were a myth. Early peoples had voluntarily *made* their political institutions, binding themselves to their rulers according to a "social contract." When a government became tyrannical, it violated that contract, and the people had the right to rebel and create a new contract. All men were born equal in God's eyes, Locke argued, and were equally endowed by nature with the facility to flourish; hence, they must be equal under human law. Similarly, Jean-Jacques Rousseau (1712–1778) reversed the pessimistic principle that humankind was inherently sinful and in need of a master. "Man is born good," he countered. "It is society that corrupts him." Other Enlightenment thinkers, similarly, believed that the only true inequalities among men were those produced by natural talents and education, and they criticized the European social

Colbert Presents French Scientists to Louis XIV.
In founding the Académie des Sciences in 1666, King Louis XIV hoped to show his support for the new science and win scientists' endorsement for his still rather fragile regime. Here his chief minister (and the inventor of mercantile policies), Jean-Baptiste Colbert, presents the scholars to the king. The central presence of maps and globes in the image tells us how much exploration of the world and conquest of colonies were part of this collaborative endeavor.

order in which status was based on birth rather than on merit. Voltaire ridiculed the nobility and clergy for their stupidity, greed, and injustice. In *The Wealth of Nations,* Smith remarked that there was little difference (other than education) between a philosopher and a street porter: both were born, he claimed, with the ability to reason, and both were (or should be) free to rise in society according to their talents. Yet, Locke, Rousseau, and Voltaire did not believe that women could act as independent, rational individuals in the same way that all men, presumably, could. Although educated women like Mary Wollstonecraft and Olympe de Gouges took up the pen to protest these inequities (see Chapter 15 for further discussion), the Enlightenment did little to change women's subordinate status in European society.

The Enlightenment touched all of Europe, but to varying extents. In the Netherlands, France, and Britain, where population density and urbanization were greatest, enlightened learning spread widely; in Spain, Poland, and Russia, enlightened circles were small and barely influenced the general population. Enlightened thought flourished in commercial centers such as Amsterdam and Edinburgh and in colonial ports such as Philadelphia and Boston. As education and literacy levels rose in these cities, book sales and newspaper circulation surged. Religious literature and bibles were still the best sellers, but the widening market increasingly put scientific treatises, scandalous novels, and even pornography into readers' hands.

POPULAR CULTURE The expanding reading public grew increasingly omnivorous and increasingly difficult to police. In England, the Netherlands, and Switzerland, authorities essentially gave up censoring, and radical books and pamphlets printed there were smuggled into other markets, where they found readers of many sorts. Some of the most popular works were not from high intellectuals but from more sensationalist essayists. Pamphlets charging widespread corruption, fraudulent stock speculation, and insider trading circulated widely. Sex, too, sold well. Works like *Venus in the Cloister or the Nun in a Nightgown* racked up as many sales as the now-classic works of the Enlightenment. Bawdy and irreligious, these vulgar

best-sellers exploited consumer demand—but they also seized the opportunity to mock authority figures, such as nuns and priests. Some even dared to go after the royal family, portraying Marie Antoinette as having sex with her court confessor. In these cases, pornography—some of it even philosophical—spilled into the literary marketplace for political satire. Such works displayed the seamier side of the Enlightenment, but they also revealed a willingness (on the part of high and low intellectuals alike) to challenge established beliefs and institutions and to undermine royal and clerical authority.

New readerships generated new cultural institutions and practices. In Britain and Germany, book clubs and coffeehouses sprang up to cater to sober men of business and learning; here, aristocrats and well-to-do commoners could read news sheets or discuss stock prices, political affairs, and technological novelties. Similar noncourtly socializing occurred in Parisian salons, where aristocratic women presided. Speaking their minds more openly in these private settings than at court or at public assemblies, women here freely exchanged ideas with men. The number of female readers and writers soared, and the relatively new genre of the novel, as well as specialized women's journals, appealed especially to them.

SEEKING UNIVERSAL LAWS Inspired by the new science, many thinkers sought to discover the "laws" of human behavior, an endeavor linked with criticism of existing governments. Explaining the laws of economic relations was chiefly the work of Adam Smith, whose book *The Wealth of Nations* described universal economic laws. It became one of the most influential and long-lived of enlightened works. Smith claimed that unregulated markets in a laissez-faire economy best suited humankind because they allowed the individual's "trucking and bartering" nature to express itself fully. (Laissez-faire expresses the concept that the economy works best when it is left alone—that is, when the state does not regulate or interfere with the workings of the market.) In Smith's view, the "invisible hand" of the market, rather than government regulations, would lead to prosperity and social peace. Smith recognized growing economic gaps between "civilized and thriving" nations and "savage" ones; the latter were so miserably poor that, Smith claimed, they were reduced to infanticide, starvation, and euthanasia. Yet, he believed that until these nations learned to play by what he called nature's laws, they could not expect a happy fate. Smith was just one of many writers who felt that non-Europeans had no other choice but to follow the Enlightenment's "universal" laws.

The French *Encyclopédie* was perhaps the Enlightenment's most characteristic attempt to encompass universal knowledge. Edited by the brilliant and irreverent writer Denis Diderot, it ultimately comprised twenty-eight volumes containing essays by more than 130 intellectuals. It was extremely popular among the elite despite its political, religious, and

Chronometer. *In the 1760s, the English clockmaker John Harrison perfected the chronometer, a timepiece mariners could use to reckon longitude while at sea. Although the Royal Society initially refused to believe that Harrison had solved this long-standing problem, Harrison's instrument made navigation so much safer and more predictable that it became standard equipment on European ships.*

Salon of Madame Geoffrin. *Much of the important work—and wit—of the Enlightenment was the product of private gatherings known as salons. Often hosted, like the one depicted here, by aristocratic women, these salons also welcomed down-at-the-heels writers and artists, offering everyone, at least in theory, the opportunity to discuss the sciences, the arts, politics, and the idiocies of their fellow humans on an equal basis.*

intellectual radicalism. Its purpose was "to collect all the knowledge scattered over the face of the earth" and to make it useful to men and women in the present and future. Indeed, the *Encyclopédie* offered a wealth of information about all manner of things, including detailed descriptions and illustrations showing how to make pins and bind books. It also described the virtues of peace and the evils of tyrannical governance, the principles of geometry, and the latest advances in painting. Although it covered all parts of the world, it generally treated the non-European world as historically important and interesting, but also as unmodern and in need of an Enlightenment only known to Europeans. (See Analyzing Global Developments: How Can We Measure the Impact of an Idea?)

Consequences of the Enlightenment

The Enlightenment—or, more properly, Enlightenments, as there was much variation across Europe—was a movement with numerous ambivalent consequences, both for religious and political institutions and for Europe's relationship with the rest of the world.

RELIGION AND THE ENLIGHTENMENT Although few Enlightenment thinkers were atheists, most criticized what they perceived to be the irrational rituals, superstitions, persecutions, and expenditures defended by clergy. The Scottish philosopher and historian David Hume attacked biblical miracles, and Voltaire underscored the bloodiness of the Crusades. They insisted that the use of reason, rather than force or rote repetition of formulas,

was the best way to create a community of believers and morally good people. Their critiques of church authorities and practices were highly controversial. Some governments bowed to clerical pressure and censored the most radical books or exiled writers, but many absolutist monarchs saw an advantage in reducing the church's power and introducing at least some measure of tolerance of religious minorities into their realms.

Tolerance did not mean full civil rights—for Catholics in England, for example, or for Jews anywhere in Europe. Tolerance simply meant a loosening of religious uniformity, and the population as a whole often resented even this. Few Europeans entirely lost their faith as a result of the spread of enlightened ideas and critiques. But it is unquestionably the case that the Enlightenment succeeded in spreading the suspicion of religious authorities and the distaste for religious persecution, and it did create new forms of religious belief and practice. At the level of institutions, the Enlightenment was instrumental in laying the foundation for revolutionaries' attacks on the church and for the evolution of secular states and societies in Europe in the nineteenth century.

The application of enlightened ideas to non-European religions had ambivalent effects. On the one hand, enlightened thinkers sought information about other religions and wrote books discussing similarities between Christian and non-Christian practices and beliefs. But their imposition of enlightened categories and principles often resulted in severe misunderstandings, as differences were increasingly explained as others' "backward" refusal to evolve along European lines. For example, authors of the *Encyclopédie* portrayed Islam with

The single most important work of the European Enlightenment, which set out to provide an objective compendium of all human knowledge, Denis Diderot's *Encyclopédie* was very French. Of its more than 130 authors, only sixteen were foreign, and, of those sixteen, seven came from the French-speaking city of Geneva, just across the border. All of them were men. Within France, the authors came primarily from the north, especially from Paris. Noble and clerical authors weighed more heavily on the list of authors than in society at large (this had to do with literacy rates, which were much higher among the elite); most of Diderot's authors came from the Third Estate. None of those bourgeois authors had much to do with capitalism, nor did the aristocratic authors have much to do with feudalism. There were large contingents of doctors, lawyers, government officials, and skilled artisans.

We know very little about the production and diffusion of the first edition of the *Encyclopédie*, produced from 1751 to 1772 under Diderot's direction. The first four editions, in fact, were expensive luxury items, relatively unimportant in terms of diffusion. The *Encyclopédie* that circulated in prerevolutionary Europe came from cut-rate smaller format editions published between 1777 and 1782, when the final, revised version, the *Encyclopédie méthodique*, began to appear. For these later editions, thorough records have survived, raising far-reaching questions about how ideas circulated and where during the Enlightenment, at least within Europe. (We know very little about the circulation of the *Encyclopédie* beyond Europe.) Where did the writers come from, where did their ideas go, and how, if at all, did their origins influence the content and ultimate significance of their project? We include a table of key words and their classification in thematic categories from the original edition, to give a sense of its contents and priorities.

Terms	# of Appearances	Principal Categories
Commerce	5,713	Commerce, geography
Science	2,095	[Multiple categories]
Christ	1,821	Theology, holy scripture
Africa	1,772	Geography, history, natural history, botany
Slavery	238	Natural law, ethics, religion, ancient history
African slavery (*La traite des nègres*)	15	Commerce
Negro	536	Natural history, commerce
Saint-Domingue	96	Geography, botany
China	957	Agriculture, chemistry, history, natural history, geography, metaphysics, tapestry
Turk or Turkey	701	Geography, history
Muhammad	356	Theology, history, philosophy

QUESTIONS FOR ANALYSIS

- What does the diffusion of the *Encyclopédie* within France and across Europe tell us about its influence? How should we evaluate the influence of a book?
- Do you think the *Encyclopédie*'s local origins compromise its universal ambitions?
- How do you think the social origins of the contributors shaped the kinds of topics covered by the *Encyclopédie*?

Source: Robert Darnton, *The Business of Enlightenment: A Publishing History of the Encyclopédie, 1775–1800* (1979).

the same ill will that they applied to other organized religions, condemning Muhammad as an imposter and the Quran as a book stuffed with barbaric and ignorant ideas that contradicted the laws of physics. The application of these enlightened tests to non-European religions often substituted new prejudices against "backward" religions and cultures for old prejudices against non-Christians destined for hell.

THE ENLIGHTENMENT AND POLITICS Absolutist governments did not entirely reject enlightened ideas, which included ideas that were in most cases reformist or critical of religious authorities rather than directly political. Rulers, like astronomers, recognized the virtues of universality (as in a universally applicable system of taxation) and precision (as in a well-drilled army). Also, social mobility allowed more skilled bureaucrats to rise through the ranks, while commerce provided the state with new riches. The idea of collecting knowledge, too, appealed to states that wanted greater control over their subjects and to extend their reach overseas. Consider Louis XIV, who was persuaded to establish a census (though he never carried it out)

The Encyclopédie. *Originally published in 1751, the Encyclopédie was the most comprehensive work of learning of the French Enlightenment. Left: The title page features an image of light and reason being dispersed throughout the land. The title itself identifies the work as a dictionary, based on reason, that deals not just with the sciences but also with the arts and occupations. It identifies two of the leading men of letters (gens de lettres), Denis Diderot and Jean le Rond d'Alembert, as the primary authors of the work. Contributors to the Encyclopédie included craftsmen as well as intellectuals. Below: The detailed illustrations of a pin factory and the processes and machinery employed in pin making are from a plate in the fourth volume of the Encyclopédie and demonstrate its emphasis on practical information.*

so that he could "know with certitude in what consists his grandeur, his wealth, and his strength." Many enlightened princes supported innovations in the arts and agriculture or sent scientific missions out to explore the world and plant their flags. Like the philosophes, they were convinced that the improvement of trade, agriculture, and national productivity was the right way forward, even though some also were beholden to the older values of the nobility and clergy. Merit and religious tolerance could also be useful in attempts to make states more profitable and armies more efficient. In this way, cultural efflorescence and secular state building in Europe went hand in hand.

But ideas are powerful things and could not be contained within elite circles or prevented from becoming increasingly radical. If many philosophes were themselves uncomfortable with offering liberty and equality (not to mention sovereignty) to *all* people, this was doubly true of their rulers. The Enlightenment in itself was revolutionary only in thought: but thought, too, can be powerful. In the later eighteenth century, new readerships and institutions enabled the extensive spread of concepts such as freedom of conscience, religious tolerance, and equality before the law, even to women, lower-class men, and enslaved peoples whom European elites felt might not deserve it. This was perhaps the Enlightenment's most important, if unintended, legacy.

THE ENLIGHTENMENT AND THE ORIGINS OF RACIAL THOUGHT A darker side of the Enlightenment is evident in the ways in which the new science's insistence on classification and universal natural laws led to a transformation in the idea of "race." Previously, the word *race* referred to a swift current in a stream or a test of speed or a lineage (mainly that of a royal or noble family). By the late seventeenth century, a few writers were expanding the definition to designate a European ethnic lineage, identifying, for example, the indomitable spirit and freedom-loving ethos of the Anglo-Saxon race.

The Frenchman François Bernier, who had traveled in Asia, may have been the first European to attempt to classify the world's peoples. He used a variety of criteria, including those that were to become standard from the late eighteenth century down to the present, such as skin color, facial features, and hair texture. Bernier published this work in his *New Division of the Earth by the Different Groups or Races Who Inhabit It* (1684). Later, the Swedish naturalist Carolus Linnaeus (1707–1778), the French scholar Georges Louis LeClerc, the comte de Buffon (1707–1788), and the German anatomist Johann Friedrich Blumenbach (1752–1840) also used racial principles to classify humankind.

Enlightened Europeans were not the first to remark on other peoples' distinctive—and to them, unpleasing—physical features and to see themselves as superior. Chinese elites glorified their "white" complexions against the peasants' dark skin; against the black, wavy-haired "devils" of Southeast Asia; and against the Europeans' "ash-white" pallor. Amerindians commented critically on the hairiness of European invaders. What the Enlightenment added was the drive to classify all of humankind and impose a hierarchy, one that put white Europeans on top.

Although Bernier may have begun the process, Carolus Linnaeus decisively pushed forward the project of creating a racial classification of humankind. His *Systema Naturae* (1735) sought to classify all the world's plants and animals by giving each a binomial, or two-word, name. In subsequent editions, Linnaeus perfected his system, identifying five subspecies of the mammal he called *Homo sapiens*, or "wise man." Linnaeus gave each of the continents a subspecies: *Homo europaeus*, *Homo americanus*, *Homo afer*, and *Homo asiaticus*. He added a fifth category, *Homo monstrosus*, for "wild" men and "monstrous" types. Linnaeus's classifications were based on a combination of physical characteristics that included skin color and social qualities. He characterized Europeans as light skinned and governed by laws; Asians as "sooty" and governed by opinion; indigenous American peoples as copper skinned and governed by custom; and Africans (whom he consigned to the lowest rung of the human ladder) as ruled by personal whim. Later eighteenth-century natural historians dismissed Linnaeus's fifth category, which contained mythical monstrous races and people with mental and physical disabilities, but the habit of ranking "races" and lumping together physical and cultural characteristics persisted.

In inventorying the world's peoples and assigning each group a place on the ladder of human achievement, Europeans applied their reverence for classical sculpture. Those who most resembled Greek nudes were considered the most beautiful and the most civilized and suited for world power. In his *Natural History* (1750), the comte de Buffon insisted that classical sculptures had established the proper proportion for the human form. Having divided humans into distinct "races," he determined that white peoples were the most admirable and Africans the most contemptible. It is one of the paradoxes of the Enlightenment that a movement that generated a quest for universal knowledge and spread the idea of human liberty far and wide also introduced a new form of what would be considered "scientific" racism—one marked, too, by European biases.

The European Enlightenment in Global Perspective

Europe's new science and enlightened thought arose in reaction both to Europe's expanding interaction with the rest of the world and to the period's environmental, religious, and political

Linnaeus and Classification. *Linnaeus's famous system of plant and animal classifications, which depended on sexual forms (such as the stamen and pistil in plants), was in wide use by the end of the eighteenth century.*

even fundamentalist ways, reiterating the importance of the religious sciences, which included studies of the Quran, the sayings of the Prophet (*hadith*), the *sharia* (religious law), theology, poetry, and the Arabic language, and questioning the value of the foreign sciences and the study of the natural world. Occasional scholars were able to challenge the *ulama*'s monopoly on learning and to look outward for inspiration, but such efforts relied on reformist patrons, who were not in great abundance.

Consider Ibrahim Muteferrika, a Hungarian convert to Islam who set up a printing press in Istanbul in 1729. Under the patronage of a reformist grand vizier, Muteferrika published works on science, geography, and history that drew on western findings. Encouraged by his success, Turkish intellectuals translated and published some of Europe's most influential scientific works. When Muteferrika's patron was killed, however, the *ulama* reasserted their control over education and publications and closed off this promising avenue of contact with western learning. While in Europe a diverse set of quarreling and competing churches and patrons made possible the articulation of new and more secular sciences, in Ottoman lands the older authorities and ideas could not so easily be dislodged.

China's science suffered a fundamental disadvantage compared with Europe's. It was practical and empirical rather than theoretical. Its practitioners were less inclined to mathematize the study of the natural world. Nor did they fully understand the use of the experimental method; and unlike European scientists, who fostered a mathematical and mechanistic view of the natural world, they saw all of life and nature organically. Nonetheless, starting in the late sixteenth century, Jesuit missionaries found Chinese literati and the official classes extraordinarily receptive to European breakthroughs in astronomy and mathematics. Here, it seemed, was a fruitful bridge between Europe's new science and China's ruling elites.

The two first Jesuit missionaries to reach China, Michele Ruggieri (1543–1607) and Matteo Ricci (1552–1610), arrived in China in 1582 and 1583, respectively. As was the case with many Jesuits at this time, both were brilliantly educated not just in religious and theological matters but in Europe's evolving new science. Although the Catholic Church had banned the works of Copernicus and Galileo, both men were "closet Copernicans" and believed that presenting Europe's scientific achievements to the ruling classes at the emperor's court would win them favor and facilitate conversions of many Chinese to Christianity. At the time of their arrival, China was in the midst of debates over its solar calendar, which now was out of sync with the seasons and causing difficulties coordinating ceremonial rites and rituals. Thus, Chinese officials were eager to employ Jesuit knowledge of mathematics and astronomy—based on Copernican and Galileo heliocentrism—to assist them in bringing ceremonial dates and political and economic activities into a better relationship with

chaos. But why Europe? Why not China or the Islamic world? As we have seen, Chinese and Muslim scholars could boast rich traditions of scientific and technological development and literary production. Why, then, did Chinese literati and, perhaps more important, Muslim scholars, who still had the most advanced knowledge of the natural sciences even as late as the fourteenth century, let the Europeans assume the lead in understanding the natural world? Answers are difficult to provide, but some suggestions are now coming to light.

For Islam, the rise of Sufi orders and Sufi mysticism posed a challenge to the dominance that the *ulama* believed that they should have over all fields of thought and principles of belief. The *ulama* responded to this threat in conservative, the seasons. For their part, the Jesuits participated in Confucian ceremonies, hoping to win favor with the emperor and arguing that the rites were compatible with Catholicism. But, to the Jesuits' great disappointment, the Chinese did not accept their religious and theological tenets, and the men made only a very small number of converts. When Pope Clement XI issued a papal bull in 1715 condemning the missionaries' participation in the rites, the project of cultural exchange broke down. Offended, the Jiangxi emperor, who had once been sympathetic to the Jesuits, banned Christian missionaries from practicing in China. His successor went even further, ordering the closing of all churches and the expulsion of Jesuits from China. Thus, starting in the mid-eighteenth century, the European window on China and the Chinese window on Europe were closed. China turned away from European contact, most notably Europe's new science that had once intrigued Chinese ruling classes.

Difficulties or disinterest in receiving and spreading foreign ideas in these two earlier scientific powerhouses made it impossible for them to keep pace with the European Enlightenment.

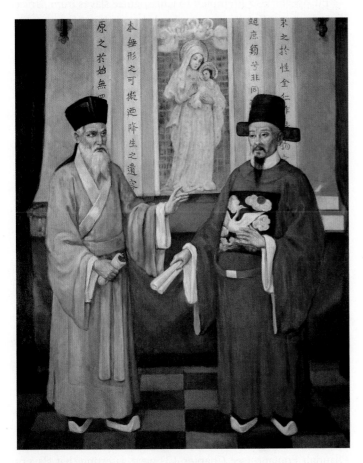

Matteo Ricci adapts to Chinese Culture. *This image depicts Jesuit father Matteo Ricci together with one of his most high-profile converts to Christianity, the scholar and official Xu Guangqi. Behind them stands a painting of the Madonna and baby Jesus with a text in literary Chinese, demonstrating Ricci's commitment to adapting Christianity and European culture to the text-oriented Chinese cultural world.*

Even more than the Ottomans, the Chinese remained a cultural world apart. The situation could not have been more different in the Americas.

CREATING HYBRID CULTURES IN THE AMERICAS

In the Americas, mingling between European colonizers and native peoples (as well as African slaves) produced hybrid cultures. But the cultural mixing grew increasingly unbalanced as Europeans imposed authority over more of the Americas. For Native Americans, the pressure to adapt their cultures to those of the colonists began from the start. Over time, Indians faced mounting pressure as Europeans insisted that their conquests were not simply military endeavors but also spiritual errands. In addition to guns and germs, all of Europe's colonizers brought Bibles, prayer books, and crucifixes with the intent of Christianizing and "civilizing" Indian and African populations in the Americas. Yet, missionary efforts produced uneven and often unpredictable outcomes. Even as Indians and African slaves adopted Christian beliefs and practices, they often retained older religious practices too.

European colonists likewise borrowed from the peoples they subjugated and enslaved. This was especially true in the sixteenth and seventeenth centuries, when the colonists' survival in the New World often depended on adapting. Before long, however, many American settlements had become stable and prosperous, and colonists preferred not to admit their past dependence on others. New hierarchies emerged, and elites in Latin America and North America increasingly followed the tastes and fashions of European aristocrats. Yet, even as they imitated Old World ways, these colonials forged identities that separated them from Europe.

Spiritual Encounters

Settlers in the New World had the military and economic power to impose their culture—especially their religion—on some indigenous peoples. While the Jesuits had little impact in China, Christian missionaries in the Americas had armies and officials to back up their insistence that Native Americans and African slaves abandon their own deities and spirits for Christ. Nonetheless, their attempts to force conversions were rarely a complete success, and some European settlers became interested in Amerindian culture.

FORCING CONVERSIONS European missionaries, especially Catholics, used numerous techniques to bring Indians within the Christian fold. Smashing idols, razing temples, and whipping backsliders all belonged to the missionaries' arsenal. Catholic orders (principally Dominicans, Jesuits, and Franciscans) also learned what they could about Indian beliefs and rituals— and then exploited that knowledge to make conversions to Christianity. For example, many missionaries demonized local gods, subverted indigenous spiritual leaders, and transformed Indian iconography into Christian symbols. But at the same time, the missionaries preserved much linguistic and ethnographic information about indigenous communities. In sixteenth-century Mexico, the Dominican friar Bernardino de Sahagún compiled an immense ethnography of Mexican ways and beliefs. In seventeenth-century Canada, French Jesuits prepared dictionaries and grammars of the Iroquoian and Algonquian languages and translated Christian hymns into Amerindian tongues.

Neither gentle persuasion nor violent coercion produced the results that missionaries desired. When conversions did occur, the resulting Christian practices were usually hybrid forms in which indigenous deities and rituals merged with Christian ones. Among Andean mountain people, for example, priestesses of local cults took the Christian name Maria to mask their secret worship of traditional deities. In other cases, indigenous communities turned their backs on Christianity and accused missionaries of bringing disease and death. Those who did convert often believed that Christian spiritual power supplemented, rather than supplanted, their own religions.

Indians Becoming Christians. *This image is from a colonial chronicle illustrated and narrated by indigenous scribes who had converted to Christianity. The picture of Indians before the conquest entering a house of prayer is intended to represent the Indians as proto-Christians.*

MIXING CULTURES More distressing to missionaries than the blending of beliefs or outright defiance were the Indians' successes in converting captured colonists, whom they often adopted (particularly women and children) as a way to replace lost kin. It deeply troubled the missionaries that many captured colonists accepted their adoptions and refused to return to colonial society when given the chance. Moreover, some other Europeans voluntarily chose to live among the Indians. Comparing the records of cultural conversion, one eighteenth-century colonist suggested that "thousands of Europeans are Indians," yet "we have no examples of even one of those Aborigines having from choice become European" (Crèvecoeur, p. 306). (Aborigines, or aboriginals, are original, native inhabitants of a region, as opposed to invaders, colonizers, or later peoples of mixed ancestry.) While this calculation may be exaggerated, it reflects the fact that Europeans who adopted Indian culture, like Christianized Indians, lived in a mixed cultural world. In fact, their familiarity with both Indian and European ways made them ideal intermediaries for diplomatic arrangements and economic exchanges.

Europeans also attempted to Christianize slaves from Africa, though many slave owners doubted the wisdom of converting persons they regarded as mere property. Sent forth with the pope's blessing, Catholic priests targeted slave populations in the American colonies of Portugal, Spain, and France. Applying many of the same techniques that missionaries used with Indian "heathens," these priests produced similarly mixed results. Often converts blended Islamic or traditional African religions with Catholicism. Converted slaves wove remembered practices and beliefs from their homeland into their American Christianity, transforming both along the way. In northeastern Brazil, for example, slaves combined the Yoruba faiths of their ancestors with Catholic beliefs, and they frequently attributed powers of African deities to Christian saints. Sometimes Christian and African faiths were practiced side by side. In Saint-Domingue, slaves and free blacks practiced *vodun* ("spirit" in the Dahomey tongue); in Cuba, *santería* ("cult of saints" in Spanish), a faith of similar origins.

Just as slaveholders feared, Christianity—especially in its hybrid forms—could inspire resistance, even revolt, among slaves. Indeed, a major runaway slave leader in mid-eighteenth-century Surinam was a Christian. Those held in bondage in the English colonies drew inspiration from Christian hymns that promised deliverance, and they embraced as their own the Old Testament story of Moses leading the Israelites out of Egypt. By the late eighteenth century, freed slaves like the Methodist Olaudah Equiano (see Chapter 13) were asserting that slavery was unjust and incompatible with Christian brotherhood.

INTERMARRIAGE AND CULTURAL MIXING Beyond the attractions of Indian cultures, Europeans mixed with Indians because there were many more men than women among the

Racial Mixing. Left: *This image shows racial mixing in colonial Mexico—the father is Spanish, the mother Indian, and the children mestizo. This is a well-to-do family, illustrating how Europeans married into the native aristocracy. Right: Here, too, we see a racially mixed family. The father is Spanish, the mother black or African, and the child a mulatto. Observe, however, the less aristocratic and markedly less peaceful nature of this family.*

colonists. Almost all the early European traders, missionaries, and settlers were men (although the British North American settlements saw more women arrive relatively early on). In response to the scarcity of women and as a way to help Amerindians accept the newcomers' culture, the Portuguese crown authorized intermarriage between Portuguese men and local women. These relations often amounted to little more than rape, but longer-lasting relationships developed in places where Indians kept their independence—as among French fur traders and Indian women in Canada, the Great Lakes region, and the Mississippi Valley. Whether by coercion or consent, sexual relations between European men and Indian women resulted in offspring of mixed ancestry. In fact, the mestizos of Spanish colonies and the métis of French outposts soon outnumbered settlers of wholly European descent.

The increasing numbers of African slaves in the Americas further complicated the mix of New World cultures. Unlike marriages between fur traders and Indian women, in which the women held considerable power because of their connections to Indian trading partners, sexual intercourse between European men and enslaved African women was almost always forced. Children born from such unions swelled the ranks of mixed-ancestry people in the colonial population. Again, however, unlike the offspring of European fur traders and Indian women, who generally found an equal place in their mothers' communities or gained power as intermediaries between their parents' cultures, the children of African women and European men generally became the enslaved property of their fathers.

Forming American Identities

Colonization of the Americas brought Europeans, Africans, and Indians into sustained contact, though the nature of the colonies and the character of the contact varied considerably. Where their dominance was strongest, European colonists imposed their ways on subjugated populations and imported what they took to be the chief attributes of the countries and cultures they had left behind. Yet Europeans were not immune to cultural influences from the groups they dispossessed and enslaved, and over time the colonists developed distinctive "American" identities. The cultures and identities of Indians and African slaves also underwent significant transformations, though often what Europeans imposed was only partially adopted.

CREOLE IDENTITIES In Spanish America, ethnic and cultural mixing produced a powerful new class, the **creoles**—persons of European descent born in the Americas. By the late eighteenth century, creoles increasingly resented the control that **peninsulars**—men and women born in Spain or Portugal but living in the Americas—had over colonial society. Creoles especially chafed under the peninsular rulers' exclusive privileges, like those that forbade creoles from trading with other colonial ports. Also, they disliked the fact that royal ministers gave most official posts to peninsulars.

In many cities of the Spanish and Portuguese Empires, reading clubs and salons hosted energetic discussions of fresh Enlightenment ideas and contributed to the growing creole identity. In one university in Peru, Catholic scholars taught their students that Spanish labor drafts and taxes on Andean natives not only violated divine justice but also offended the natural rights of free men. The Spanish crown, recognizing the role of printing presses in spreading troublesome ideas, strictly controlled the number and location of printers in the colonies. In Brazil, royal authorities banned them altogether. Nonetheless, books, pamphlets, and simple gossip allowed new notions of history and politics to circulate among literate creoles.

The global Enlightenment also inspired a quest for modern science as a basis for creole reform. The Spanish government sent Royal Botanical Expeditions composed of scientists and artists to Chile and Peru (1777–1788), New Granada (1783–1816), and New Spain (1787–1803). These campaigns collected and classified an astonishing array of flora; they also produced beautifully illustrated publications that launched an American style of natural painting, notable for documenting the richness of tropical habitats, and several new and marketable commodities that would change the shape of colonization forever.

Perhaps the most significant of these commodities was the one popularized by Celestino Mutis, a Spanish-born physician who had moved to New Granada as a young man. Mutis was fascinated by the medicinal properties of New World plants, and he oversaw the making of no less than 6,500 botanical illustrations from New Granada alone. He was especially interested in the cinchona plant, whose bark had been used by Amerindians and Jesuit missionaries for centuries to cure malaria. Mutis recognized that cinchona, or quinine, if scientifically cultivated, could be the commodity that allowed more Europeans to settle in the tropics. Committed both to the Enlightenment and to Spanish mercantilism, Mutis believed—rightly, it turned out—that his scientific efforts would improve the health of all of humanity *and* yield riches for Spanish colonies.

The botanical conquest of the New World added to the global warehouse of what Europeans and creoles knew about natural diversity. It also emboldened scientific and entrepreneurial activity in the tropics and gave Spanish American creoles a sense that they, too, were part of the "century of light" and on the side of reform and improvement.

ANGLICIZATION In one important sense, wealthy colonists in British America were similar to the creole elites in Iberian America: they, too, copied European ways. For example, they constructed "big houses" (in Virginia) modeled on the country estates of English gentlemen, imported opulent furnishings and fashions from the finest British stores, and exercised more control over colonial assemblies. Imitating the English also involved tightening patriarchal authority. In seventeenth-century Virginia, men had vastly outnumbered women, which gave women some power (widows, in particular, gained greater control over property and more choices when they remarried). During the

The Cinchona Plant. *The creole New Granada botanical expedition generated thousands of scientific illustrations of previously unknown tropical plants. One of the enlightened leaders of this expedition, Celestino Mutis, recommended the intensive cultivation of the cinchona plant, whose bark could be used to make the most effective antimalarial medicine of the day, quinine.*

eighteenth century, however, sex ratios became more equal, and women's property rights diminished as English customs took precedence. Overall, patriarchal authority was evident in family portraits, where husband-patriarchs sat or stood in front of their wives and children.

Intellectually, too, British Americans were linked to Europe. Importing enormous numbers of books and journals, these Americans played a significant role in the Enlightenment as producers and consumers of political pamphlets, scientific treatises, and social critiques. Indeed, drawing on the words of numerous Enlightenment thinkers, American intellectuals created the most famous of enlightened documents: the Declaration of Independence. It announced that all men were endowed with equal rights and were created to pursue worldly happiness. In this way, Anglicized Americans, like the creole elites of Latin America, showed themselves to be products of both European and New World encounters.

The Voyages of Captain James Cook. Left: *During his celebrated voyages to the South Pacific, Cook kept meticulous maps and diaries. Although he had little formal education, he became one of the great exemplars of enlightened learning through experience and experiment.* Right: *Kangaroos were unknown in the western world until Cook and his colleagues encountered (and ate) them on their first visit to Australia. This engraving of the animal (which unlike most animals, plants, and geographical features actually kept the name the Aborigines had given it) from Cook's 1773 travelogue,* A Voyage Round the World in the Years 1768–1771, *lovingly depicts the kangaroo's environs and even emotions.*

CAPTAIN COOK AND THE MAKING OF A NEO-EUROPEAN CULTURE IN OCEANIA

In the South Pacific, another kind of Anglicization was under way, one similarly shaped by imperialism and enlightened science. Here, even more than in Latin America, enlightened science, embodied in the voyages of Captain James Cook, had ecologically as well as culturally transformative consequences, creating replications of Europe in far distant parts of the world. The focus here is on Australia, but one could also analyze the English colonial territories of New Zealand or Canada in the same terms. Here the wiping out of local peoples and the resettlement by white Europeans—albeit many of them outcasts—created the basis for a variation on colonization marked by a greater degree of cultural transfer.

Until Europeans colonized it in the late eighteenth century, Australia was, like the Americas before Columbus, truly a world apart. Separated by water and sheer distance from other regions, Australia's main features were harsh natural conditions and a sparse population. At the time of the European colonization, the island was home to around 300,000 people, mostly hunter-gatherers. While Pacific seafarers may have ventured into the area in the past, there is little evidence that either Chinese or Muslim merchants had ever strayed that far south. Spices had drawn the Portuguese and Dutch into the South Pacific (see Chapter 13), and the Spanish, despite considerable resistance, had conquered Guam and the Mariana Islands by

1700. Both the Portuguese and the Dutch had seen the northern and western coasts of Australia, but they had found only sand, flies, and Aboriginals. Only after the scientific voyages of Captain James Cook (1728–1779) to the region in 1768–1779 did Europeans see Australia's more hospitable eastern coast and develop serious interest in colonization. Now the intrusion into **Oceania** (Australia, New Zealand, and the islands of the southwestern Pacific) presented Europeans with a previously unknown region that could serve as a laboratory for studying other peoples and geographical settings. (See Map 14.1.)

James Cook was a veteran sailor, a practitioner of the new science, and, as it turned out, an imperial transformer of worlds. Known to the Royal Society for his excellent maps and his successful attempts to combat scurvy, Cook was the ideal captain to guide the first of what would be three scholarly voyages to observe the movement of the planet Venus from the Southern Hemisphere. Besides Cook, the Royal Society sent along on this 1768 trip one of its members who was a botanist; a doctor and student of Carolus Linnaeus; and numerous artists and other scientists. The crew also carried sophisticated instruments and had instructions to keep detailed diaries. This grand data-collecting expedition returned in 1771 and was succeeded by two more. As in the case of Mutis's investigations in New Granada, Cook's voyages generated a flood of scholarly and popular publications. These featured approximately 3,000 drawings of Pacific plants, animals, birds, landscapes, and peoples never seen in Europe, all categorized according to Linnaeus's system, and most of them, with the exception of the kangaroo, given English, rather than Aboriginal, names.

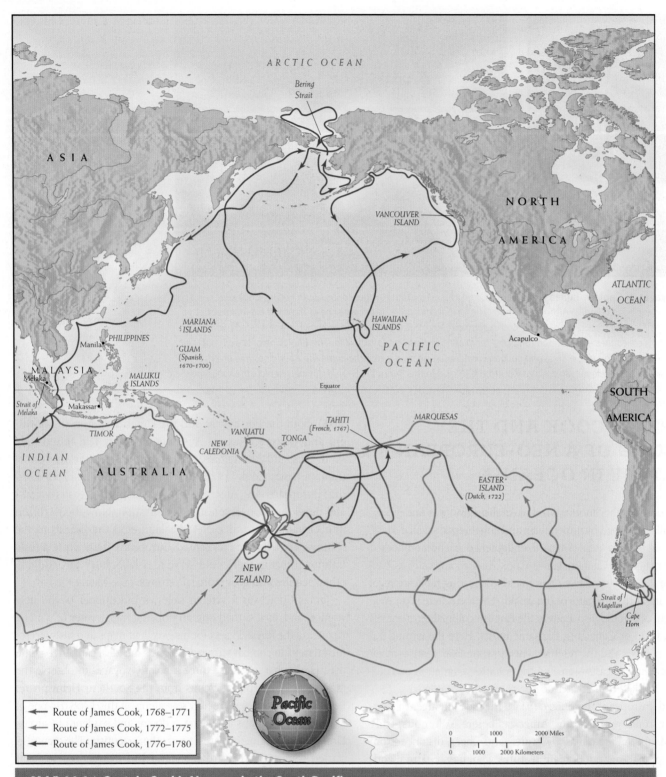

Route of James Cook, 1768–1771
Route of James Cook, 1772–1775
Route of James Cook, 1776–1780

MAP 14.1 | Captain Cook's Voyages in the South Pacific

Captain Cook's voyages throughout the Pacific Ocean symbolized a new era in European exploration of other societies.

- According to this map, how many voyages did Cook take?
- Where did Cook explore, and what peoples did he encounter?
- According to your reading, how did Cook's endeavors symbolize "scientific" imperialism?

Beyond the voyages' scientific purposes, however, the British government assigned Cook the secret mission of finding and claiming "the southern continent" for Britain. This he accomplished no less successfully than the project of scholarly data collection, discovering raw materials useful to Britain. Extracting those materials, however, required a labor force, and the Aboriginals of Australia, like the Indians of the Americas, perished in great numbers from imported diseases. Those who survived generally fled to escape control by British masters. Thus, to secure a labor force, plans arose for grand-scale conquest and resettlement by British colonists. On his third voyage, Cook brought an astonishing array of animals and plants with which to turn the South Pacific into a European-style garden. His lieutenant later brought apples, quinces, strawberries, and rosemary to Australia; the seventy sheep imported in 1788 laid the foundations for the region's wool-growing economy. In fact, the domestication of Australia arose from the Europeans' certainty about their superior know-how and a desire to make the entire landmass serve British interests.

In 1788, a British military expedition took official possession of the eastern half of Australia. The intent was, in part, to establish a prison colony far from home. This plan belonged to the realm of "enlightened" dreams: that of ridding "civilized" society of all evils by resettling lawbreakers among the "uncivilized." The intent was also to exploit Australia for its timber and flax and to use it as a strategic base against Dutch and French expansion. In the next decades, immigration—free and forced—increased the Anglo-Australian population from an original 1,000 to about 1.2 million by 1860. Importing their customs and their capital, British settlers turned Australia into a frontier version of home, just as they had done in British America. Yet, such large-scale immigration had disastrous consequences for the surviving Aboriginals. Like the Native Americans, the original inhabitants of Australia were decimated by disease and increasingly forced westward by European settlement, with European ideas and institutions simply replacing local ones. Thus was Oceania, even more than Latin America and far more than the major land empires of Afro-Eurasia, made over in Europe's image.

In their first encounters with Pacific Islanders, most notably in the French encounters in Tahiti that predated Cook's voyages, Europeans were often welcomed by aboriginals extending hospitality and willing to trade foodstuffs and luxury goods. Accordingly, Europeans often portrayed the islands as "tropical paradises" and their light-skinned inhabitants as direct descendants of Adam and Eve. They depicted Tahitians, Hawaiians, Australians, and New Zealanders as virtuous, uncorrupted people who fit the description of the "noble savage" popularized by Jean-Jacques Rousseau. But the more they sought to dominate and the more resistance they encountered, the more Europeans abandoned their romantic view of the South Sea Islanders. Declining appreciation for their innocence was clear after 1779, when

Cook himself was murdered by Hawaiians resentful of his contempt for their gods and his crew's less-than-friendly extraction of goods and treatment of local women. The news of Cook's death scandalized his homeland; the king himself, it is said, shed tears. Thereafter, Europeans began to emphasize the "savagery" of South Pacific cultures and insisted ever more urgently on the exportation of "civilized" European culture and forms of rule.

CONCLUSION

New wealth produced by commerce and state building created the conditions for a global cultural renaissance in the sixteenth, seventeenth, and eighteenth centuries. It began in the Chinese and Islamic empires and then stretched into Europe, Africa, and previous worlds apart in the Americas and Oceania. Experiments in religious tolerance encouraged cultural exchange; book production and consumption soared; grand new monuments took shape; luxury goods became available for wider enjoyment.

A striking aspect of this cultural renaissance was its unevenness. While elites and sometimes the middle classes benefited, the poor did not. They remained illiterate, undernourished, and often subjected to brutal treatment by rulers and landowners. Elite women in Europe and China increasingly joined literate society, but they gained no new rights. Urban areas also profited more from the new wealth than rural ones, so people seeking refinement flocked to the cities. Some former cultural centers, like the Italian Peninsula, lost their luster as new, more commercially and culturally dynamic centers took their place.

Among states, too, cultural inequalities were glaring. Although the Islamic and Chinese worlds confidently retained their own systems of knowing, believing, and representing, the Americas and Oceania increasingly faced European cultural pressures. Here, while hybrid practices became widespread by the late eighteenth century, European beliefs and habits predominated as the standards for judging degrees of "civilization." African cultures largely escaped this influence, though their homelands felt the impact of European expansionism through the slave trade.

From a commercial standpoint, the world was more integrated than ever before. But the exposure and cultural borrowing that global trade promoted largely reconfirmed established ways. The Chinese, for instance, still believed in the superiority of their traditional knowledge and customs. Muslim rulers, confident of Islam's primacy, allowed others to form subordinate cultural communities within their realm and adopted Europeans ideas only when doing so served their own imperial purposes. Meanwhile, the Europeans were constructing knowledge that they believed was both universal and objective, enabling mortals to master the world of nature and all its inhabitants. This view would prove consequential, as well as controversial, in the centuries to come.

After You Read This Chapter

Go to INQUIZITIVE to see what you know & learn what you've missed.

FOCUS ON: *The Flourishing of Regional Cultures*

The Islamic World

- The Ottomans' unique cultural synthesis accommodates not only mystical Sufis and ultraorthodox *ulama* but also military men, administrators, and clerics.

- The Safavid state proclaims the triumph of Shiism and Persian influences in the sumptuous new capital, Isfahan.

- Mughal courtly culture values art and learning and, at its high point, welcomes non-Muslim contributions.

East Asia

- China's cultural flourishing, coming from within, is evident in the broad circulation of traditional ideas, publishing, and mapmaking.

- Japan's imperial court at Kyoto develops an elite culture of theater, stylized painting, tea ceremonies, and flower arranging.

Europe

- Cultural flourishing known as the Enlightenment yields a faith in reason and a belief in humans' ability to fathom the laws of nature and human behavior.

- European thinkers articulate a belief in unending human progress.

- Europeans expand into Australia and the South Pacific.

Africa

- Slave-trading states such as Asante, Oyo, and Benin celebrate royal power and wealth through art.

The Americas

- Even as Euro-Americans participate in the Enlightenment, their culture reflects Native American and African influences.

CHRONOLOGY

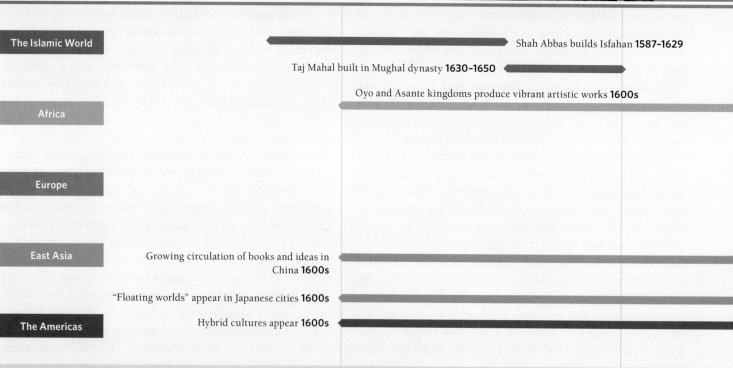

The Islamic World		Shah Abbas builds Isfahan **1587-1629**	
		Taj Mahal built in Mughal dynasty **1630-1650**	
		Oyo and Asante kingdoms produce vibrant artistic works **1600s**	
Africa			
Europe			
East Asia	Growing circulation of books and ideas in China **1600s**		
	"Floating worlds" appear in Japanese cities **1600s**		
The Americas	Hybrid cultures appear **1600s**		

1600   1650

KEY TERMS

creoles *p. 547*

Enlightenment p. 535

Forbidden City of Beijing
p. 526

great plaza at Isfahan p. 527

Oceania p. 549

Palace of Versailles p. 526

peninsulars *p. 547*

philosophes *p. 538*

scientific method p. 537

Taj Mahal p. 525

Topkapi Palace p. 526

STUDY QUESTIONS

1. **Explain** the connections between cultural growth and the creation of a global market.

2. **Discuss** the processes that brought forth cultural syntheses in the three Islamic dynasties during this era. To what extent did European culture influence each empire?

3. **Describe** Chinese and Japanese cultural achievements during this period. How did foreign influences affect each dynasty?

4. **Define** the term *Enlightenment* as it pertained to Europe. How did Enlightenment ideas shape European attitudes toward other cultures?

5. **Describe** how hybrid cultures emerged in the Americas during this era, and **explain** the connection between these cultures and Enlightenment ideology. Did the spread of this philosophy bring communities across the Atlantic together, or did it drive them apart?

6. **Analyze** the different responses to foreign cultures across Afro-Eurasia during this period, and **identify** their similarities and differences.

7. **Describe** and **compare** how each culture in this period reflected the ideas of the state in which it was produced.

8. **Compare and contrast** European exploration of Oceania in the eighteenth century with European exploration of the Americas in the sixteenth century (see Chapter 12). How did European exploration of Oceania transform European attitudes toward non-European groups around the world?

9. **Analyze** the role that race and cultural difference played in the process of global integration.

10. **Explore** the relationship between the scientific method, concepts of racial difference, and established social hierarchies. Pay particular attention to Cook's expeditions to Oceania.

11. **Evaluate** the extent to which dynastic rulers around the world were able to control cultural developments during this period. How did new cultural developments potentially undermine local governments?

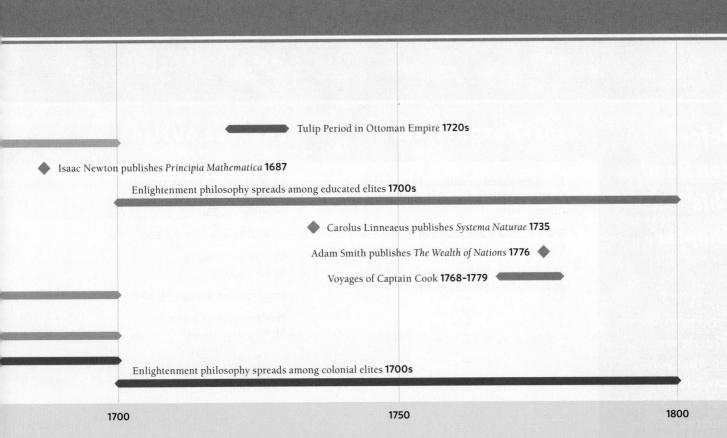

Tulip Period in Ottoman Empire **1720s**

Isaac Newton publishes *Principia Mathematica* **1687**

Enlightenment philosophy spreads among educated elites **1700s**

Carolus Linneaeus publishes *Systema Naturae* **1735**

Adam Smith publishes *The Wealth of Nations* **1776**

Voyages of Captain Cook **1768-1779**

Enlightenment philosophy spreads among colonial elites **1700s**

1700   1750   1800

15

Reordering the World, 1750–1850

FOCUS QUESTIONS

- What were the new ideas of freedom, and how did they differ from earlier understandings of this term?

- How did political and economic developments in the Atlantic world compare with those in regions elsewhere?

- What key developments constituted the industrial revolution? How did these changes alter the societies that began to industrialize during this time?

- What were the patterns of global trade and economic growth, and how did they relate to political changes?

- What were the similarities and differences between groups of people who held power in each region? What changes occurred in these societies?

In 1798, the French commander Napoleon Bonaparte invaded Egypt. At the time, Europeans regarded this territory as the cradle of a once-great culture, a land bridge to the Red Sea and trade with Asia, and an outpost of the Ottoman Empire. Occupying the country would allow Napoleon to introduce some of the principles of the French Revolution and to seize control of trade routes to Asia. Napoleon also hoped that by defeating the Ottomans, who ruled over Egypt, he would augment his and France's historic greatness. But events did not go as Napoleon planned, for his troops faced a resentful Egyptian population.

Although Napoleon soon returned to France and his dream of a French Egypt was short-lived, his invasion challenged Ottoman rule and threatened the balance of power in Europe. Indeed, the effect of Napoleon's actions in Africa, the Americas, and Europe, combined with the principles of the French Revolution, laid the foundations for a new era—one based on a radically new understanding of freedom as the absence of constraint, the opposition of privileges handed down by a lord or master.

The new idea of freedom first rang out across western Europe and the Americas and reverberated around the world. It destroyed the

American colonial domains of Spain, Portugal, Britain, and France, brought new nations to the stage, and challenged established elites everywhere. The impulse for change was a belief that governments should enact laws that apply to all peoples, though in practice there were exceptions (slaves, women, and colonial subjects). Free speech, free markets, and governments freely elected by freeborn men, it was thought, would benefit everyone. The idea of freedom also challenged systems like mercantilist control and chattel slavery that held empires together. In Europe and the Americas, though not elsewhere, the era also witnessed the emergence of the nation-state. This new form of political organization derived legitimacy from its inhabitants, often referred to as citizens, who, in theory if not always in practice, shared a common culture, language, and ethnicity.

Yet freedom in some corners of the globe set the stage for depriving people of freedom elsewhere and led inexorably to changes in the worldwide balance of power. Even as western Europeans lost their American colonies, they gained economic and military strength that further challenged Asian and African governments. In China, the ruling Manchus faced European pressure to permit expanded trade. In Egypt and the Ottoman Empire, reform-minded leaders tried to modernize. When the rise of Egypt threatened Europe's strategic interests in the eastern Mediterranean, the European states intervened to rein in that country's ambitions.

Underlying much of these political and social upheavals were major changes in the world economy. Countries began to produce goods less for their own population and more for people living in other places around the globe. This specialization for export markets further integrated the world. Regions in Europe began to build factories and harness new sources of energy, like coal, to make cheaper manufactured goods out of imported staples, like cotton, shipped from semitropical frontiers. But results were paradoxical. While the world became more integrated and economic growth took off, social disparities grew wider—both within and across countries. What is called "the industrial revolution" set in motion great divides between Europe and North America and the rest of the world and even within industrializing societies.

REVOLUTIONARY TRANSFORMATIONS AND NEW LANGUAGES OF FREEDOM

In the eighteenth century, the circulation of goods, people, and ideas created pressure for reform around the Atlantic world. As economies expanded, many people in Europe and the Americas felt that the restrictive mercantilist system prevented them from sharing in the new wealth and power. Similarly, an increasingly literate public called for their states to adopt just practices, including the abolition of torture and the accountability of rulers. Although elites resisted the demands for more freedom to trade and more influence in government, power holders could not stamp out these demands before they became—in several places—full-scale revolutions.

Reformers wanted to expand the franchise, to enable property holders to vote. Claims of **popular sovereignty**, the idea that political power depends on "the people," became rooted in the idea of the nation: people who share a common language, common culture, and common history. This, in turn, gave rise to the nation-state as a form of political organization. Over the course of the nineteenth century, political movements began to emphasize nationalism, the idea that peoples having a common identity and thus constituting a fully fledged nation should have states of their own, and democracy, the idea that the people, the *demos*, should choose their own representatives and be governed by them (see Chapter 16). In this chapter, we concentrate on first expressions of this new thinking in thirteen of Britain's North American colonies and in France. In both places, the "nation" and the "people" toppled their former rulers.

This chapter also concentrates on far-reaching economic developments that came in tandem with revolutionary political change. Economic reformers argued that unregulated economies would produce faster economic growth. Going well beyond the work of Adam Smith, they called for **free trade** (or **laissez-faire**), unencumbered by tariffs, quotas, and fees; free markets, which would be unregulated; and free labor, which meant using paid labor rather than slave labor. They insisted that these economic freedoms would yield more just and more efficient societies, ultimately benefiting everyone, everywhere in the world.

Yet the same elites who wanted a freer world often exploited slaves, denied women equal treatment, restricted colonial economies, and tried to forcibly open Asia's and Africa's markets to European trade and investment. In Africa, another corner of the Atlantic world, idealistic upheavals did not lead to free and sovereign peoples, but to greater enslavement.

POLITICAL REORDERINGS

Late in the eighteenth century, revolutionary ideas spread across the Atlantic world, following the trail of Enlightenment ideas about freedom and reason. (See Map 15.1.) As more newspapers, pamphlets, and books circulated in European countries and American colonies, readers began to discuss their societies' problems and to believe they had the right to participate in governance.

The slogans of independence, freedom, liberty, and equality seemed to promise an end to oppression, hardship, and inequities. In the North American colonies and in France, revolutions ultimately brought down monarchies and blossomed in republics. The examples of the United States and France soon encouraged others in the Caribbean and Central and South America to reject the rule of monarchs. In all of these revolutionary environments, new institutions—such as written constitutions and permanent parliaments—claimed to represent the people.

The North American War of Independence, 1776–1783

The American Revolution ended British rule in North America. It was the first in a series of revolutions to shake the Atlantic world, inspired by new ideas of freedom.

By the mid-eighteenth century, Britain's colonies in North America swelled with people and prosperity. Bustling port cities like Charleston, Philadelphia, New York, and Boston saw inflows of African slaves, European migrants, and manufactured goods, while agricultural staples flowed out. A "genteel" class of merchants and landowning planters dominated colonial affairs.

But with settlers arriving from Europe and slaves from Africa, land was a constant source of dispute. Large landowners struggled with independent farmers (yeomen). Sons and daughters of farmers, often unable to inherit or acquire land near their parents, moved westward, where they came into conflict with Amerindian peoples. To defend their lands, many Amerindians allied with Britain's rival, France. After losing the Seven Years' War (see Chapter 13), however, France ceded its Canadian colony to Britain to secure the return of its much more lucrative Caribbean colonies, especially Saint Domingue. This left many Amerindians no choice but to turn to Britain to help them resist the aggressive advances of land-hungry colonists. British officials did make some concessions to Indian interests, but they did not have the troops or financial strength to protect them.

ASSERTING INDEPENDENCE FROM BRITAIN Even as tensions simmered and sometimes boiled over into bloodshed on the western frontier of British North America, the situation of the British in North America still looked very strong in the mid-1760s. At that point, Britain stood supreme in the Atlantic world, with its greatest foes defeated and its empire expanding. Political revolution seemed unimaginable. And yet, a decade later, that is what occurred.

The spark came from the government of King George III, which insisted that colonists help pay for Britain's war with France and for the benefits of being subjects of the British Empire. It seemed only reasonable to King George and his ministers, faced with staggering war debts, that colonists contribute to the crown that protected them. Accordingly, the king's officials imposed taxes on a variety of commodities and tried to end the lucrative smuggling by which colonists had been evading the restrictions that mercantilism was supposed to impose on colonial trade. To the king's surprise and dismay, colonists raised vigorous objections to the new measures and protested having to pay taxes when they lacked political representation in the British Parliament. (See Primary Source: Declaring Independence.)

In 1775, resistance in the form of petitions and boycotts turned into open warfare between a colonial militia and British troops in Massachusetts. Once blood was spilled, more radical voices came to the fore. Previously, leaders of the resistance to taxation without representation had claimed to revere the British Empire while fearing its corruptions. Now calls for severing the ties to Britain became more prominent. Thomas Paine, a recent immigrant from England, captured the new mood in a pamphlet he published in 1776, arguing that it was "common sense" for people to govern themselves. Later that year, the Continental Congress (in which representatives from thirteen colonies gathered) adapted part of Payne's popular pamphlet for the Declaration of Independence.

Drawing on Enlightenment themes (see Chapter 14), the declaration written by Thomas Jefferson affirmed the people's natural rights to govern themselves. It also drew inspiration from the writings of British philosopher John Locke, notably the idea that governments should be based on a **social contract** in which the law binds both ruler and people. Locke had even

The Boston Massacre. *Paul Revere's idealized view of the Boston Massacre of March 5, 1770. In the years after the Seven Years' War, Bostonians grew increasingly disenchanted with British efforts to enforce imperial regulations. When British troops fired on and killed several members of an angry mob in what came to be called the "Boston Massacre," the resulting frenzy stirred revolutionary sentiments among the populace.*

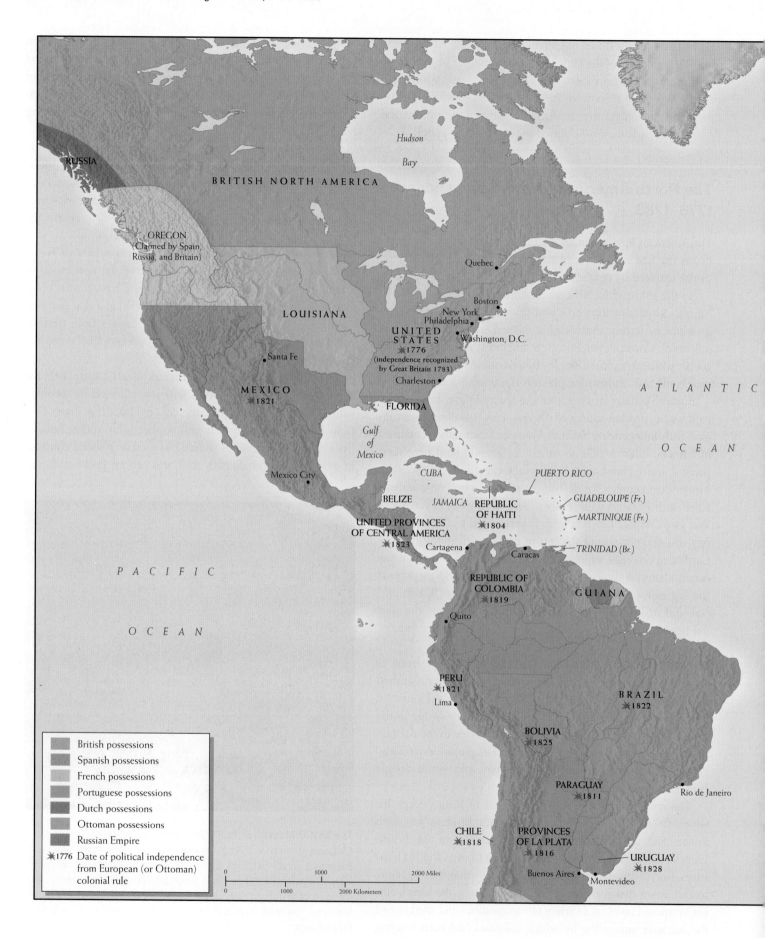

RUSSIA

*Hudson
Bay*

BRITISH NORTH AMERICA

OREGON
(Claimed by Spain,
Russia, and Britain)

Quebec

LOUISIANA

Boston
New York
Philadelphia
Washington, D.C.
UNITED
STATES
✳1776
(independence recognized
by Great Britain 1783)
Charleston

Santa Fe

MEXICO
✳1821

FLORIDA

ATLANTIC

*Gulf
of
Mexico*

OCEAN

Mexico City

CUBA

PUERTO RICO

BELIZE   *JAMAICA*   REPUBLIC
OF HAITI
✳1804

GUADELOUPE (Fr.)

MARTINIQUE (Fr.)

UNITED PROVINCES
OF CENTRAL AMERICA
✳1823   Cartagena

TRINIDAD (Br.)

Caracas

REPUBLIC OF
COLOMBIA
✳1819

GUIANA

PACIFIC

Quito

OCEAN

PERU
✳1821
Lima

BRAZIL
✳1822

BOLIVIA
✳1825

PARAGUAY
✳1811

Rio de Janeiro

CHILE
✳1818

PROVINCES
OF LA PLATA
✳1816

URUGUAY
✳1828

Buenos Aires
Montevideo

British possessions
Spanish possessions
French possessions
Portuguese possessions
Dutch possessions
Ottoman possessions
Russian Empire
✳1776 Date of political independence
from European (or Ottoman)
colonial rule

0   1000   2000 Miles
0   1000   2000 Kilometers

MAP 15.1 | Revolutions of National Independence in the Atlantic World, 1776–1829

Influenced by Enlightenment thinkers and the French Revolution, colonies gained independence from European powers (and in the case of Greece, from the Ottoman Empire) in the late eighteenth and early nineteenth centuries.

- Which European powers granted independence to their colonial possessions in the Americas during this period? What were the first two colonial territories to become independent in the Americas?

- Given that the second American republic arose from a violent slave revolt, why do you suppose the United States was reluctant to recognize its political independence?

- According to your reading, why did colonies in Spanish and Portuguese America obtain political independence decades after the United States won its independence?

written that the people had the right to rebel against their government if it broke the contract and infringed on their rights.

With the Declaration of Independence, the rebels announced their right to rid themselves of the English king and form their own government. But neither the Declaration of Independence nor Locke's writings explained how these colonists (now calling themselves Americans) should organize a nonmonarchical government—or how thirteen weakly connected colonies (now calling themselves states) might prevail against the world's most powerful empire. Nonetheless, the colonies soon became embroiled in a revolution that would turn the world upside down.

During their War of Independence, Americans designed new political arrangements. First, individual states elected delegates to state constitutional conventions, where they drafted written constitutions to govern the workings of their states. Second, by eliminating royal authority, the state constitutions gave extensive powers to legislative bodies, whose members "the people" would elect. But who constituted the people? That is, who had voting rights? Not women. Not slaves. Not Indians. Not even adult white men who owned no property.

Despite the limited extent of voting rights, the notion that all men are created equal overturned former social hierarchies. Thus, common men no longer automatically deferred to gentlemen of higher rank. Many women claimed that their contributions to the revolution's cause (by managing farms and shops in

their husbands' absence) earned them greater equality in marriage, including property rights. In letters to her husband, John Adams, who was a representative in the Continental Congress and a champion of American independence, Abigail Adams stopped referring to the family farm as "yours" and instead called it "ours." Most revolutionary of all, many slaves sided against the revolution, for it was the British who offered them freedom—most directly in exchange for military service.

Alas, their hopes for freedom were thwarted when Britain conceded the loss of its rebellious American colonies. That improbable outcome owed to a war in which British armies won most of the major battles but could not finish off the Continental Army under the command of General George Washington. Washington hung on and held his troops together long enough to convince the French that the American cause was not hopeless and that supporting it might be a way to settle a score against the British. This they did, and with the Treaty of Paris (1783), the United States gained its independence.

BUILDING A REPUBLICAN GOVERNMENT With independence, the former colonists had to build a new government. They generally agreed that theirs was not to be a monarchy. But what it *was* to be remained through the 1780s a source of much debate, involving heated words and sometimes heated action.

Amid the political revolution against monarchy, the prospect of a social revolution of women, slaves, and artisans generated a reaction against what American elites called the "excesses of democracy." Their fears increased after farmers in Massachusetts, led by Daniel Shays, interrupted court proceedings in which the state tried to foreclose on their properties for nonpayment of taxes. The farmers who joined in Shays's Rebellion in 1786 also denounced illegitimate taxation—this time, by their state's government. Acting in the interests of the fledgling government, Massachusetts militiamen defeated the rebel army. But to save the young nation from falling into "anarchy," propertied men convened the Constitutional Convention in Philadelphia a year later.

This gathering aimed to forge a document that would create a more powerful national government and a more unified nation. After fierce debate, the convention drafted a charter for a republican government in which power would rest with representatives of the people—not a king. When it went before the states for approval, the Constitution was controversial. Its critics, known as Anti-Federalists, feared the growth of a potentially tyrannical national government and insisted on including a Bill of Rights to protect individual liberties from abusive government intrusions. Ultimately, the Constitution won ratification, and it was soon amended by the Bill of Rights.

Ratification of the Constitution and the addition of the Bill of Rights did not end arguments about the scope and power of the national government of the United States. A question

Abigail Adams. *Abigail Adams was the wife of John Adams, a leader in the movement for American independence and later the second president of the United States. Abigail's letters to her husband testified to the ways in which revolutionary enthusiasm for liberty and equality began to reach into women's minds. In the spring of 1776, Abigail wrote to implore that the men in the Continental Congress "remember the ladies, and be more generous and favorable to them than your ancestors. . . . If particular care and attention is not paid to the Ladies we are determined to foment a Rebellion, and will not hold ourselves bound by any Laws in which we have no voice, or Representation."*

Declaring Independence

In July 1776, the Continental Congress issued a declaration of independence that announced the secession of the thirteen North American colonies from Great Britain. Principally authored by Thomas Jefferson, the document spelled out the American colonists' lengthy list of grievances against Britain that "impelled" their separation from the empire and that entitled them to international recognition. The Declaration's most famous sentence, however, addressed more universal aspirations based on natural rights: "We hold these Truths to be self-evident, that all men are created equal, that they are endowed by their Creator with certain unalienable Rights, that among these are Life, Liberty, and the pursuit of Happiness."

In the decades after 1776, the United States' declaration became a model for other colonies and provinces asserting their independence, as the documents excerpted here suggest.

The Venezuelan Declaration of Independence (July 5, 1811): It is contrary to order, impossible to the Government of Spain, and fatal to the welfare of America, that the latter, possessed of a range of country infinitely more extensive, and a population incomparably more numerous, should depend and be subject to a Peninsular Corner of the European Continent. . . . We, the Representatives of the United Provinces of Venezuela, calling on the SUPREME BEING to witness the justice of our proceedings and the rectitude of our intentions, do implore his divine and celestial help; and ratifying at the moment in which we are born to the dignity to which his Providence restores to us, the desire we have of living and dying free. . . . We, therefore, . . . DO declare solemnly to the world, that its united Provinces are, and ought to be, from the day, by act and right, Free, Sovereign, and Independent States. . . . And that this, our solemn Declaration may be held valid, firm, and durable, we hereby pledge our lives, fortunes, and sacred tie of our national honour.

The Unanimous Declaration of Independence made by the Delegates of the People of Texas (March 2, 1836): When, in consequence of such acts of malfeasance and abduction on the part of the government, anarchy prevails, and civil society is dissolved into its original elements, in such a crisis, the first law of nature, the right of self-preservation, the inherent and inalienable right of the people to appeal to first principles, and take their political affairs into their own hands in extreme cases, enjoins it as a right towards themselves, and a sacred obligation to their posterity, to abolish such government, and create another in its stead, calculated to rescue them from impending dangers, and to secure their welfare and happiness. . . . We, therefore, the delegates, with plenary powers, of the people of Texas, in solemn convention assembled, appealing to a candid world for the necessities of our condition, do hereby resolve and declare that our political connection with the Mexican nation has forever ended, and that the people of Texas do now constitute a free, sovereign, and independent republic, and are fully invested with the rights and attributes which properly belong to independent nations; and, conscious of the rectitude of our intentions, we fearlessly and confidently commit the issue to the decision of the supreme Arbiter of the destinies of nations.

A Declaration of Independence by the Representatives of the People of the Commonwealth of Liberia (July 16, 1847): We the representatives of the people of the Commonwealth of Liberia, in Convention assembled, invested with authority for forming a new government, relying upon the aid and protection of the Great Arbiter of human events, do hereby, . . . declare the said commonwealth a FREE, SOVEREIGN, AND INDEPENDENT STATE. . . . We recognize in all men, certain natural and inalienable rights: among these are life, liberty, and the right to acquire, possess, enjoy and defend property.

QUESTIONS FOR ANALYSIS

- What common elements can you identify in these declarations? Consider, in particular, the audiences at which they are aimed, the justifications for breaking free of colonial dependence they put forward, and the rights that they claim will be secured by national independence.

- What groups did the American Declaration of Independence overlook, and why?

Source: David Armitage, *The Declaration of Independence: A Global History* (Cambridge, MA: Harvard University Press, 2007), pp. 165, 199–207, 211–223.

that deeply troubled the new nation was slavery—specifically, whether a country that declared all men to be equal could tolerate a substantial slave population. Southern slaveholders, for whom slavery was a mainstay of the economy, answered that question unequivocally, and those individuals who would have preferred a different policy had to give way. In an uneasy truce, political leaders agreed not to let the debate over whether to abolish slavery escalate into a cause for disunion. As the frontier pushed westward, however, the question of which new states would or would not allow slavery sparked debates yet again. Initially, the existence of ample land postponed a confrontation. In 1800, Thomas Jefferson's election as the third president of the United States marked the triumph of a model of sending pioneers out to new lands in order to reduce conflict on old lands. In the same year, however, a Virginia slave named Gabriel Prosser raised an army of slaves to seize the state capital at Richmond and won support from white artisans and laborers for a more inclusive republic. His dream of an egalitarian revolution fell victim to white terror and black betrayal, though: twenty-seven slaves, including Prosser, went to the gallows. With them, for the moment, died the dream of a multiracial republic in which all men were truly created equal.

In a larger Atlantic world context, the American Revolution ushered in a new age based on ideas of freedom. The successful defiance of Europe's most powerful empire and the establishment of a nonmonarchical, republican form of government sent shock waves through the Americas and Europe and even into distant corners of Asia and Africa. It also helped pave the way for other revolts over the next several decades.

The French Revolution, 1789–1799

Partly inspired by the American Revolution, French men and women soon began to call for liberty, too—and the result profoundly shook Europe's dynasties and social hierarchies. Its impact, though, reached well beyond Europe, for the French Revolution, even more than the American, inspired rebels and terrified rulers around the globe.

ORIGINS AND OUTBREAK For decades, enlightened thinkers had attacked France's old regime—the court, the aristocracy, and the church—at the risk of imprisonment or exile. But by the mid-eighteenth century, discontent had spread beyond the educated few. In the countryside, peasants grumbled about having to pay taxes and tithes to the church, whereas nobles and clergy paid almost no taxes. Also, despite improved health and nutrition, peasants still suffered occasional deprivation. A combination of these pressures, as well as a fiscal crisis, unleashed the French Revolution of 1789.

The French king himself opened the door to revolution. Eager to weaken his rival, England, Louis XVI spent huge sums in support of the American rebels—and thereby overloaded the state's debt. To raise sufficient funds, Louis needed to change the structure of taxation; but to do so, he was forced to convene the Estates-General, a medieval advisory body that had not met since 1614. When the king reluctantly agreed to summon the Estates-General in 1788, his subjects rejoiced. The delegates of the clergy (the First Estate) and the aristocracy (the Second Estate) hoped to restore some of the privileges they had lost to the absolutist state. The delegates representing everyone else (the Third Estate), in contrast, believed that the time had come for taxation to be shared equally. The most forceful advocate for this position was a clergyman, Abbé Sieyès, who argued in January 1789 that the Third Estate, those who worked and paid taxes, *were* the nation; the privileged few were parasites. The terrible weather and poor harvest of 1788 also stoked discontent, as the price of bread—the foundation of the French diet—soared and many members of Sieyès's "nation" went hungry.

When the Estates-General finally assembled in late May 1789, but had not yet been convened, bread prices were painfully high. Afraid the king would crush the reform movement, delegates of the Third Estate declared themselves to be the "National Assembly," the body that should determine France's future. On July 14, 1789, a hungry and angry Parisian crowd took to the streets, looting bakeries and attacking the headquarters of the tax collectors. They stormed a medieval armory—the Bastille—that not only was an infamous prison for political prisoners but also held a large store of gunpowder. The crowd murdered the commanding officer, then cut off his head and paraded it through the streets of Paris. On this day (Bastille Day), the king made the fateful decision not to call out the army, and the capital city belonged to the crowd. As news spread to the countryside, peasants torched manor houses and destroyed municipal archives containing records of the hated feudal dues. Barely three weeks later, the French National Assembly abolished the feudal privileges of the nobility and the clergy. In the Declaration of the Rights of Man and of the Citizen, the assembly echoed the Americans' Declaration of Independence, but in more universal language.

REVOLUTIONARY CHANGES AND CONFLICTS The French Declaration laid out an array of enlightened principles that did indeed revolutionize French society and politics. It guaranteed all citizens of the French nation a new kind of liberty, defined not as a special privilege given by the king but as a freedom from constraint, including religious constraints. Against old regimes' legalized inequalities, it proclaimed equality under the law. It also ratified Sieyès's principle that sovereignty resides in the nation. These sweeping changes announced the coming

The "Tennis Court Oath."
Locked out of the chambers of the Estates-General, the deputies of the Third Estate reconvened at a nearby indoor tennis court in June 1789; there they swore an oath not to disband until the king recognized the sovereignty of a national assembly.

of a new era of liberty, equality, and fraternity that threatened to end dynastic and aristocratic rule in Europe.

Inspired by revolutionary rhetoric, some women argued that the new principles of citizenship should include women's rights as well. In 1791, a group of women demanded the right to bear arms to defend the revolution, but they stopped short of claiming equal rights for both sexes. In their view, women would become citizens by being good revolutionary wives and mothers, not because of any natural rights. In the same year, Olympe de Gouges composed the Declaration of the Rights of Woman and the Female Citizen, proposing rights to divorce, hold property in marriage, be educated, and have public careers.

The all-male assembly did not take up these issues, believing that a "fraternity" of free *men* composed the nation. (For a statement claiming similar rights for women in Britain, see Primary Source: Mary Wollstonecraft on the Rights of Women.)

As the revolution gained momentum, deep divisions emerged. In late 1790, all clergy had to take an oath of loyalty to the new state—an action that enraged Catholics. Meanwhile, the revolutionary ranks began to splinter, as men and women argued over the revolution's proper goals. Soon a new National Convention was elected by universal manhood suffrage, meaning that all adult males could vote—the first such election in Europe. In 1792, the first French Republic was proclaimed.

Women March on Versailles.
On October 5, 1789, a group of market women, many of them fishwives (traditionally regarded as leaders of the poor), marched on the Paris city hall to demand bread. Quickly, their numbers grew, and they redirected their march to Versailles, some 12 miles away and the symbol of the entire political order. In response to the women, the king finally appeared on the balcony and agreed to sign the revolutionary decree and return with the women to Paris.

Mary Wollstonecraft on the Rights of Women

As revolutionaries stressed the rights of "man" across the Atlantic world, Mary Wollstonecraft (1759-1797), an English writer, teacher, editor, and proponent of spreading education, resented her male colleagues' celebration of their newfound liberties. In **A Vindication of the Rights of Woman (1792),** *one of the founding works of modern feminism, she argued that the superiority of men was as arbitrary as the divine right of kings. For this, male progressives denounced her. The author is a "hyena in petticoats," noted one critic. In fact, she was arguing that women had the same rights to be reasonable creatures as men and that education should be available equally to both sexes.*

I love man as my fellow; but his sceptre, real or usurped, extends not to me, unless the reason of an individual demands my homage; and even then the submission is to reason, and not to man. In fact, the conduct of an accountable being must be regulated by the operations of its own reason; or on what foundation rests the throne of God?

It appears to me necessary to dwell on these obvious truths, because females have been insulated, as it were; and while they have been stripped of the virtues that should clothe humanity, they have been decked with artificial graces that enable them to exercise a short-lived tyranny. Love, in their bosoms, taking the place of every nobler passion, their sole ambition is to be fair, to raise emotion instead of inspiring respect; and this ignoble desire, like the servility in absolute monarchies, destroys all strength of character. Liberty is the mother of virtue, and if women be, by their very constitution, slaves, and not allowed to breathe the sharp invigorating air of freedom, they must ever languish like exotics, and be reckoned beautiful flaws in nature. Let it also be remembered, that they are the only flaw.

As to the argument respecting the subjection in which the sex has ever been held, it retorts on man. The many have always been enthralled by the few; and monsters, who scarcely have shown any discernment of human excellence, have tyrannized over thousands of their fellow-creatures. Why have men of superior endowments submitted to such degradation? For, is it not universally acknowledged that kings, viewed collectively, have ever been inferior, in abilities and virtue, to the same number of men taken from the common mass of mankind—yet have they not, and are they not still treated with a degree of reverence that is an insult to reason? China is not the only country where a living man has been made a God. *Men* have submitted to superior strength to enjoy with impunity the pleasure of the moment; *women* have only done the same, and therefore till it is proved that the courtier, who servilely resigns the birthright of a man, is not a moral agent, it cannot be demonstrated that woman is essentially inferior to man because she has always been subjugated.

QUESTIONS FOR ANALYSIS

- Wollstonecraft compares men to kings and women to slaves. What are her criticisms of kings, and why does she call them "monsters"?
- In what ways are Wollstonecraft's ideas an outgrowth of Enlightenment thinking?
- Do you find Wollstonecraft's arguments compelling? Explain why or why not.

Source: Mary Wollstonecraft, *A Vindication of the Rights of Woman,* edited by Miriam Brody (New York: Penguin Books, 1792/1993), pp. 122-123.

The radicals believed that to sweep away traditional forms of inequality and oppression, they would need to destroy the old regime's entire system of thinking and ways of speaking. So they changed street names to honor revolutionary heroes, destroyed monuments to the royal family, adopted a new flag, and insisted that everyone be addressed as "citizen." They were so exhilarated by the new world they were creating that they changed time itself. Now they proclaimed time not from the birth of Christ but from the moment that the French Republic was proclaimed. Thus, September 22, 1792, became day 1 of year 1 of the new age. A new calendar was created, and the new ten months were given the names of natural phenomena. For example, the month corresponding to our November was dubbed "Brumaire," the month of fog.

But these changes also produced opposition. As antirevolutionary armies began to mass on France's borders, radicals grew increasingly afraid that internal enemies, especially clergymen and aristocrats, were conspiring against the revolution. The radicals closed the churches and imprisoned all clergy members who would not swear the oath of loyalty to the revolutionary state. These measures were deeply unpopular and stoked counterrevolutionary opposition. Louis XVI himself was accused of conspiracy, and in January 1793 he lost his head to the guillotine.

FRUCTIDOR

Le Fructidor. *In 1792, radical French revolutionaries replaced France's traditional calendar, displacing saints and holy days, and renaming the months after natural phenomena. For example, the third month of the summer quarter (corresponding to the harvest months of August and early September) was renamed Le Fructidor, based on the Latin word fructus, meaning fruit. Almanacs such as this one offered French citizens visual representations of the new dating system.*

THE TERROR After the king's execution, radicals known as Jacobins, who wanted to extend the revolution beyond France's borders, instituted the first national draft to form, by 1794, the world's largest modern army of 800,000 soldiers. Led by the lawyer Maximilien Robespierre, the Jacobins also launched the Reign of Terror to purge the nation of its internal enemies. These included aristocrats but also those who hid priests, resisted the draft, or refused to hand their grain over to revolutionary troops. Some antirevolutionary Catholics, peasants, and draft dodgers took up arms, creating civil war conditions in several parts of France. Jacobin leaders oversaw the execution of as many as 40,000 of these so-called enemies of the people.

By mid-1794, enthusiasm for Robespierre's measures had lost popular support, and Robespierre himself went to the guillotine on 9 Thermidor (July 28, 1794). His execution marked the end of the Terror. Several years later, following more political turmoil, a coup d'état brought to power a thirty-year-old general from the recently annexed Mediterranean island of Corsica.

The general, **Napoleon Bonaparte** (1769–1821), put security and order ahead of social reform. True, his regime retained many of the revolutionary changes, especially those associated with more efficient state government; but retreating from the Jacobins' anti-Catholicism, he allowed religion to be freely practiced again in France. Determined not only to reform France but also to prevail over its enemies, he retreated from republican principles. Napoleon first was a member of a three-man consulate; then he became first consul; finally, he proclaimed himself emperor. Most important, he created a civil legal code—the Napoleonic Code—that applied throughout all of France (and the French colonies, including the Louisiana Territory). By designing a law code applicable to the nation as a whole, Napoleon created a model that would be widely imitated by emerging nation-states in Europe and the Americas in the century to come.

The Napoleonic Era, 1799–1815

Determined to extend the reach of French influence, Napoleon had his armies trumpet the principles of liberty, equality, and fraternity wherever they went. Many local populations actually embraced the French, regarding them as liberators from the old order—as indeed in many cases they proved to be. Inspired by his leadership, many non-Frenchmen, including many Poles, volunteered to fight in the army. Napoleon was not surprised to face resistance from aristocrats commanding foreign armies, but he so believed that he was the great liberator that he was shocked when ordinary people rebelled against the French, as was the case in Egypt. After defeating Mamluk troops there in 1798, Napoleon soon faced a rebellious local Egyptian population.

In Portugal, Spain, and Russia, French troops also faced fierce popular resistance. Portuguese and Spanish soldiers and peasants formed bands of resisters called guerrillas, and British troops joined them to fight the French in the Peninsular War (1808–1813). In Germany and Italy, as local inhabitants grew tired of hearing that the French occupiers' ways were superior, many looked to their past for inspiration to oppose the French. Now they discovered something they had barely recognized before: *national* traditions and borders.

In Europe, Napoleon extended his empire from the Iberian Peninsula to the Austrian and Prussian borders. (See Map 15.2.) In 1812, he invaded Russia and marched his now multinational army all the way to Moscow. His forces, however, were overstretched, undersupplied, and outmaneuvered by wily Russian troops. Soon, the French were forced to retreat through battle-scarred territory, suffering grievously from Russian harassment and the harsh winter. As Napoleon fled westward, all of the major European powers united against him and

MAP 15.2 | Napoleon's Empire, 1812

Early in the first decade of the nineteenth century, Napoleon controlled almost all of Europe.

- What major states were under French control? What countries were allied to France?
- Compare this map with the European part of Map 15.1, and explain how Napoleon redrew the map of Europe. What major country was not under French control?
- According to the reading, how was Napoleon able to control and build alliances with so many states and kingdoms?

decimated what was left of his army. Forced to capitulate in 1814, Napoleon was sent into exile, but he managed to escape soon after to lead his troops one last time. At the Battle of Waterloo in Belgium in 1815, armies from Prussia, Austria, Russia, and Britain crushed his troops as they made their last stand.

In 1815, delegates from the victorious states met at the Congress of Vienna. They agreed to respect one another's borders and to cooperate in preventing future revolutions and war. They restored thrones to monarchs deposed by the French under Napoleon, and they returned France itself to the care of a new Bourbon king.

The impact of the French Revolution and Napoleon's conquests, however, was far-reaching. The stage was now set for a

century-long struggle between those who wanted to restore monarchies and hierarchies as they existed before the French Revolution and those who wanted to guarantee a more liberal order based on individual rights, limited government, and free trade.

Revolution in Saint Domingue (Haiti)

The thirteen colonies in North America were not the only ones to secede from European masters. France also saw colonies break away in this age of new freedoms. This was the case in Saint Domingue, presently Haiti. Unlike most of British North

Battle of the Pyramids. *The French army invaded Egypt with grand ambitions and high hopes. Napoleon brought a large cadre of scholars along with his 36,000-man army, intending to win Egyptians to the cause of the French Revolution and to establish a French imperial presence on the banks of the Nile. This idealized portrait of the famous Battle of the Pyramids, fought on July 21, 1798, shows Napoleon and his forces crushing the Mamluk military forces.*

America, here the revolution came from the bottom rungs of the social ladder: slaves. In this Caribbean colony, freedom therefore meant not just liberation from Europe, but also emancipation from white planters. Saint Domingue therefore added a second, global dimension to the nineteenth-century struggle over personal liberties. It also posed very dramatically the question: How universal were these new rights?

The French Revolution sent shock waves through this highly prized French colony. At the time, the island's black slave population numbered 500,000, compared with 40,000 white French settlers and about 30,000 free "people of color" (individuals of mixed black and white ancestry as well as freed black slaves). Almost two-thirds of the slaves were relatively recent arrivals, brought to the colony to toil on its renowned sugar plantations, which were exceptional in their brutality. The slave population was an angry majority without local ties, producing wealth for rich absentee landlords of a different race.

The calling of the Estates-General in France in 1789 inspired white settlers in Saint Domingue, little realizing how small a minority they were and how deeply the vast slave population resented them, to demand self-government for themselves. The slaves, however, borrowed the French revolutionary slogan of liberty, equality, and fraternity to denounce their masters and to demand their freedom. Civil war erupted, and Dominican slaves fought French forces that had arrived to restore order. Finally, in 1793, the left wing of the National Convention in

Revolution in Saint Domingue. *In 1791, slaves and people of color rose up against white planters. This engraving was based on a German report on the uprising and depicts white fears of slave rebellion as much as the actual events themselves.*

Two Case Studies in Greed and Environmental Degradation

The Caribbean has four large islands, known as the Greater Antilles, each of which has a distinctive history—Cuba, Jamaica, Puerto Rico, and Hispaniola. Our discussion here is about the island of Hispaniola, which Columbus discovered in 1492 and which briefly became the center of Spain's New World empire. Later, in the seventeenth century, the French took over the smaller, western part of the island, and when political independence came to the Caribbean, the island evolved into the two present-day states of Haiti and the Dominican Republic. Although both are relatively poor countries, their present economic and social differences are markedly and surprisingly different, especially considering that they share a relatively small island.

Haiti is the poorest country in the Americas. It is 99 percent deforested, suffers from massive soil erosion, and has a government unable to provide even the most basic services of water, electricity, and education to its people. Right next door, the Dominican Republic, with a population roughly the same size as Haiti's, has five times as many cars and trucks, six times as many paved roads, seven times as many college and university graduates, and eight times as many physicians. Its citizens enjoy significantly longer life expectancy and lower infant mortality than their Haitian neighbors. The differences cry out for an explanation, and one can be found only by examining the radically different histories of the two lands.

Two hundred and fifty years ago, Haiti, which was under French colonial rule at that time and known as Saint Domingue, was the richest colony in the Americas, perhaps even the richest colony in the world, accounting for two-thirds of France's worldwide investment. In contrast, Spanish-ruled Santo Domingo, which had ceased to be of interest to the Spanish colonial elites, who had turned their attention to the more populous and resource-rich territories of Mexico and Peru, was a backwater colonial territory. Saint Domingue's extraordinary wealth came from large, white-owned sugar plantations that used a massive and highly coerced slave population. The slaves' lives were short and brutal, lasting on average only fifteen years; hence, the wealthy planter class had to replenish their labor supplies from Africa at frequent intervals.

White planters on the island were eager to amass quick fortunes so that they could sell out and return to France. Vastly outnumbered by enslaved Africans at a time when abolitionist sentiments were gaining ground in Europe and even

Toussaint L'Ouverture. *In the 1790s, Toussaint L'Ouverture led the slaves of the French colony of Saint Domingue in the world's largest and most successful slave insurrection. Toussaint embraced the principles of the French Revolution and demanded that universal rights be applied to people of African descent.*

France, more deeply committed to the ideal of equality, abolished slavery, though they also did so in an effort to restore order in the colony.

Once liberated, the former slaves took control of the island, but their struggles were not over. First they had to fight British and Spanish forces on the island. Then, after Napoleon took power in France, bringing with him a strong commitment to order and France's imperial ambitions, the French restored slavery and sent an army to suppress forces led by Toussaint L'Ouverture, a former slave. But before long, a combination of guerrilla fighters and yellow fever decimated the French army. In 1804, General Jean-Jacques Dessalines declared "Haiti" independent. (See Current Trends in World History: Two Case Studies in Greed and Environmental Degradation.)

The specter of a free country ruled by former slaves sent shudders across the Western Hemisphere and also in Britain and Spain, which had neighboring colonies with large slave populations. What if the revolt went viral? All around the Caribbean, news circulated about slave conspiracies. In Florida, fugitive slaves banded together with Seminole Indians to drive European settlers into the sea. The Haitian government contributed money and some troops to insurrectionists in South America. Charleston, South Carolina, went into a panic in 1793 when Dominican slaves were freed. As far away as Albany, New York, slaves were executed for arson. Jamaican rulers went on high alert. A version of martial law was declared in Venezuela. Thomas Jefferson, author of the Declaration of Independence and the U.S. president at the time, was also a holder of numerous slaves, and he refused circulating among slaves in the Americas, the planters' families knew that their prosperity was unlikely to last. They gave little thought to sustainable growth and were not troubled that they were destroying their environment.

Yet, the planters greeted the onset of the French Revolution in 1789 with enthusiasm. They saw an opportunity to assert their independence from France, to engage in wider trading contacts with North America and the rest of the world, and thus to become even richer. They ignored the possibility that the ideals of the French Revolution—especially its slogan of liberty, equality, and fraternity—could inspire the island's free blacks, free mulattoes, and slaves. Indeed, no sooner had the white planters thrown in their lot with the Third Estate in France than a slave rebellion broke out in Saint Domingue. From its beginnings in 1791, it led, after great loss of life to African slaves and French soldiers, to the proclamation of an independent state in Haiti in 1804, ruled by African Americans. Haiti became the Americas' second independent republican government.

Although the revolt brought political independence to its black population, it only intensified the land's environmental deterioration. Not only did sugarcane

fields become scorched battlefields, but freed slaves rushed to stake out independent plots on the old plantations and in wooded areas. In both places, the new peasant class energetically cleared the land. The small country became even more deforested, and intensive cultivation increased erosion and soil depletion. Haiti fell into a more vicious cycle of environmental degradation and poverty.

The second case study of greed leading to the destruction of the environment comes from the independent Brazilian state, where the ruling elite, having achieved autonomy from Portugal, expanded the agrarian frontier. Landowners oversaw the clearing of ancient hardwood forests so that slaves and squatters could plant coffee trees. The clearing process had begun with sugarcane in the coastal regions, but it accelerated with coffee plantings in the hilly regions of São Paulo. In fact, coffee was a worse threat to Brazil's forests than any other invader in the previous 300 years. Consider that coffee trees thrive on soils that are neither soggy nor overly dry. Therefore, planters razed the "virgin" forest, which contained a balanced variety of trees and undergrowth, and Brazil's once-fertile soil suffered rapid depletion by a single-crop industry. Within one generation, the

clear-cutting led to infertile soils and extensive erosion, which drove planters farther into the frontier to destroy even more forest and plant more coffee groves. The environmental impact was monumental: between 1788 and 1888, when slavery was abolished, Brazil produced about 10 million tons of coffee at the expense of 300 million tons of ancient forest biomass (the accumulated biological material from living organisms).

QUESTIONS FOR ANALYSIS

- Who intensified the deforestation and degradation in each story, and why did they do it?
- Why do you think deforestation increased in intensity after Haitians and Brazilians gained their autonomy/independence?

Explore Further

Diamond, Jared, and James A. Robinson (eds.). *Natural Experiments of History* (2010).

Geggus, David (ed.). *The Impact of the Haitian Revolution in the Atlantic World* (2001).

to recognize Haiti. Like other American slave owners, he worried that the example of a successful slave uprising might inspire similar revolts in the United States and elsewhere in the Americas.

The revolution in Saint Domingue therefore tilted the scales of campaigns for liberty far beyond the island. Fear of the contagion of slave revolt forced some governments to rethink the commitment to slavery altogether. The British government curtailed the expansion of plantation agriculture in Trinidad. One by one, European and American governments began to question the wisdom of importing more African slaves lest they lose control of their colonies. It was not just exalted ideals of liberty that fueled the abolitionist movement, but also the fear of what would happen if slaves rose up violently to claim rights given to other humans.

Revolutions in Spanish and Portuguese America

From North America and France, revolutionary enthusiasm spread through Spanish and Portuguese America. But unlike the colonists' war of independence that produced the United States, political upheaval in the rest of the Americas began first of all from subordinated people of color. (See Map 15.3.)

Even before the French Revolution, Andean Indians rebelled against Spanish colonial authority. In a spectacular uprising in the 1780s, they demanded freedom from forced labor and compulsory consumption of Spanish wares. After an army of 40,000 to 60,000 Andean Indians besieged the ancient capital of Cuzco and nearly vanquished Spanish

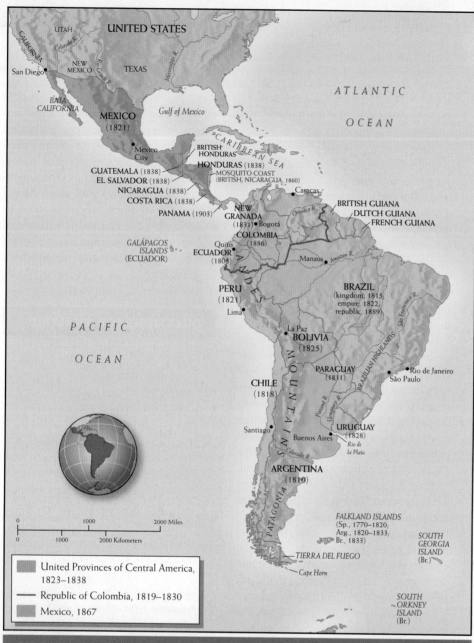

MAP 15.3 | Latin American Nation Building

Creating strong, unified nation-states proved difficult in Latin America. The map highlights this experience in Mexico, the United Provinces of Central America, and the Republic of Colombia. In each case, the governments' territorial and nation-building ambitions failed to some degree.

- During what period did a majority of the colonies in Latin America gain independence?
- Which European countries lost the most in Latin America during this period?
- According to the reading, why did all these colonies gain their independence during this time?

the independence-seeking Anglo-American colonists, lest they unleash a social revolution. Ultimately, however, the French Revolution and Napoleonic Wars shattered the ties between Spain and Portugal and their American colonies.

BRAZIL AND CONSTITUTIONAL MONARCHY Brazil was a prized Portuguese colony whose path to independence saw little political turmoil and no social revolution. In 1807, French troops stormed Lisbon, the capital of Portugal, but not before the royals and their associates fled to Rio de Janeiro, then the capital of Brazil. There they made reforms in administration, agriculture, and manufacturing, and they established schools, hospitals, and a library. In fact, the royals' migration prevented the need for colonial claims for autonomy, because with their presence Brazil was now the center of the Portuguese Empire. Furthermore, the royal family willingly shared power with the local planter aristocracy, so the economy prospered and slavery expanded.

In 1821, the exiled Portuguese king returned to Lisbon, instructing his son Pedro to preserve the family lineage in Rio de Janeiro. Soon, however, Brazilian elites rejected Portugal altogether. Fearing that colonists might topple the dynasty in Rio de Janeiro and spark regional disputes, in 1822 Pedro declared Brazil an independent empire. Shortly thereafter, he established a constitutional monarchy, which would last until the late nineteenth century. By the 1840s, Brazil had achieved a political stability unmatched in the Americas. Its socially controlled transition from colony to nation was unique in Latin America.

armies, it took Spanish forces many years to eliminate the insurgents.

After this uprising, Iberian American elites who feared their Indian or slave majorities renewed their loyalty to the Spanish or Portuguese crown. They hesitated to imitate

MEXICO'S INDEPENDENCE When Napoleon occupied Spain, he sparked a crisis in the Spanish Empire, spurring independence movements throughout the colonies. Because the ruling Spanish Bourbons fell captive to Napoleon in 1807, colonial elites in Buenos Aires (Argentina), Caracas (Venezuela), and Mexico City (Mexico) enjoyed self-rule without an emperor. Once the Bourbons returned to power in 1814 after Napoleon was crushed, creoles (American-born Spaniards) resented it when Spain reinstated peninsulars (colonial officials born in Spain). Creoles wanted to free themselves of these officials.

From 1810 to 1813, two rural priests in Mexico, Father Miguel Hidalgo and Father José María Morelos, galvanized an insurrection of peasants, Indians, and artisans. They sought an end to abuses by the elite, denounced bad government, and called for redistribution of wealth, return of land to the Indians, and respect for the Virgin of Guadalupe (who later became Mexico's patron saint). The rebellion nearly choked off Mexico City, the colony's capital, which horrified peninsulars and creoles alike and led them to support royal armies that eventually crushed the uprising.

Despite the military victory, Spain's hold on its colony weakened. Like the creoles of South America, those of Mexico identified themselves more as Mexicans and less as Spanish Americans. So when the Spanish king appeared unable to govern effectively abroad and even within Spain, the colonists considered home rule. Anarchy seemed to spread through Spain in 1820, and Mexican generals (with support of the creoles) proclaimed Mexican independence in 1821. Unlike in Brazil, Mexican secession did not lead to stability.

OTHER SOUTH AMERICAN REVOLUTIONS The loosening of Spain's grip on its colonies was more prolonged and militarized than Britain's separation from its American colonies. Venezuela's Simón Bolívar (1783–1830), the son of a merchant-planter family who was educated on Enlightenment texts, dreamed of a land governed by reason. He revered Napoleonic France as a model state built on military heroism and constitutional proclamations. So did the Argentine leader, General José de San Martín (1778–1850). Men like Bolívar, San Martín, and their many generals waged extended wars of independence against Spanish armies and their allies between 1810 and 1824. In some areas, like present-day Uruguay and Venezuela, the wars left entire provinces depopulated.

What started in South America as a political revolution against Spanish colonial authority escalated into a social struggle among Indians, mestizos, slaves, and whites. The militarized populace threatened the planters and merchants; rural folk battled against aristocratic creoles; Andean Indians fled the mines and occupied great estates. Provinces fought their neighbors. Popular armies, having defeated Spanish forces by the 1820s, fought civil wars over the new postcolonial order.

New states and collective identities of nationhood now emerged. However, a narrow elite led these political communities, and their guiding principles were contradictory. Simón Bolívar, for instance, urged his followers to become "American,"

Latin American Revolutionaries. Left: *At the center of this Juan O'Gorman mural is the Mexican priest and revolutionary Miguel Hidalgo y Costilla, who led—as O'Gorman portrays—a multiclass and multiethnic movement.* Right: *Simón Bolívar fought Spanish armies from Venezuela to Bolivia, securing the independence of five countries with the greater goal of transforming the former colonies into modern republics. Among his favorite models were George Washington and Napoleon Bonaparte, whose iconic portrait by Jacques-Louis David inspired this painting of Bolívar.*

to overcome their local identities. He wanted the liberated countries to form a Latin American confederation, urging Peru and Bolivia to join Venezuela, Ecuador, and Colombia in the "Gran Colombia." But local identities prevailed, giving way to unstable national republics. Bolívar died surrounded by enemies; San Martín died in exile. The real heirs to independence were local military chieftains, who often forged alliances with landowners. Thus, the legacy of the Spanish American revolutions was contradictory and echoed developments elsewhere around the world: the triumph of wealthy elites under a banner of liberty, yet often at the expense of poorer, nonwhite, and mixed populations.

CHANGE AND TRADE IN AFRICA

Africa also was swept up in revolutionary tides, as increased domestic and world trade—including the selling of African slaves—shifted the terms of state building across the continent. The main catalyst for Africa's political shake-up was the rapid growth and then the demise of the Atlantic slave trade. Here, in contrast to the Americas and Europe and even much of the rest of the world, ideals like liberty, equality, fraternity, and the pursuit of happiness had decidedly contrary effects. The abolition of the slave trade, which European reformers believed would lead to economic prosperity based on "legitimate trade," had the perverse effect of intensifying domestic slavery. As Africa became an exporter of raw materials rather than human beings, the hard work done on African farms and plantations—producing palm, palm kernels, peanuts, and gum for export—was done by slaves.

Abolition of the Slave Trade

Even as it enriched and empowered some Africans and many Europeans, the slave trade became a subject of fierce debate in the late eighteenth century. Some European and American revolutionaries argued that slave labor was inherently less productive than free wage labor and ought to be abolished. At the same time, another group favoring abolition of the slave trade insisted that traffic in slaves was immoral. In London they created committees, often led by Quakers, to lobby Parliament for an end to the slave trade. Quakers in Philadelphia did likewise. Pamphlets, reports, and personal narratives denounced the traffic in people. (See Primary Source: Frederick Douglass Asks, "What to the Slave Is the Fourth of July?")

In response to abolitionist efforts, North Atlantic powers moved to prohibit the slave trade. Denmark acted first in 1803, Great Britain followed in 1807, and the United States joined the campaign in 1808. Over time, the British persuaded the French and other European governments to do likewise. To enforce the ban, Britain posted a naval squadron off the coast of West Africa to prevent any slave trade above the equator and finally compelled Brazil and Cuba, the last countries to allow slavery after the end of the American Civil War, to end slave imports. After 1850, Atlantic slave shipping dropped sharply.

But up until the 1860s, even though the British had outlawed the slave trade and the Americans had agreed to cease importing slaves, slavers continued to buy and ship captives, often illegally. British squadrons that stopped these smugglers

Chasing Slave Dhows. *From being one of the major proponents of the Atlantic slave trade the British became its chief opponent, using their naval forces to suppress those European and African slave traders who attempted to subvert the injunction against slave trading. Here a British vessel chases an East African slave dhow trying to run slaves from the island of Zanzibar.*

Frederick Douglass Asks, "What to the Slave Is the Fourth of July?"

Frederick Douglass spent the first twenty years of his life as a slave. After running away in 1838, he toured the northern United States delivering speeches that attacked the institution of slavery. The publication of his autobiography in 1845 cemented his standing as a leading abolitionist. In the excerpt below, taken from an address delivered on July 5, 1852, Douglass contrasts the freedom and natural rights extolled in the Declaration of Independence and celebrated on the Fourth of July with the dehumanizing condition—and lack of freedom—of African American slaves.

Fellow-Citizens—pardon me, and allow me to ask, why am I called upon to speak here to-day? What have I, or those I represent, to do with your national independence? Are the great principles of political freedom and of natural justice, embodied in that Declaration of Independence, extended to us? and am I, therefore, called upon to bring our humble offering to the national altar, and to confess the benefits, and express devout gratitude for the blessings, resulting from your independence to us?...

But, such is not the state of the case. I say it with a sad sense of the disparity between us. I am not included within the pale of this glorious anniversary! Your high independence only reveals the immeasurable distance between us. The blessings in which you this day rejoice, are not enjoyed in common. The rich inheritance of justice, liberty, prosperity, and independence, bequeathed by your fathers, is shared by you, not by me. The sunlight that brought life and healing to you, has brought stripes and death to me. This Fourth of July is *yours*, not *mine*. *You* may rejoice, *I* must mourn. . . .

Must I undertake to prove that the slave is a man? That point is conceded already. Nobody doubts it. The slaveholders themselves acknowledge it in the enactment of laws for their government. They acknowledge it when they punish disobedience on the part of the slave. There are seventy-two crimes in the state of Virginia, which, if committed by a black man (no matter how ignorant he be) subject him to the punishment of death; while only two of these same crimes will subject a white man to the like punishment. What is this but the acknowledgment that the slave is a moral, intellectual, and responsible being. The manhood of the slave is conceded. It is admitted in the fact that southern statute books are covered with enactments forbidding, under severe fines and penalties, the teaching of the slave to read or write. When you can point to any such laws, in reference to the beasts of the field, then I may consent to argue the manhood of the slave. When the dogs in your streets, when the fowls of the air, when the cattle on your hills, when the fish of the sea, and the reptiles that crawl, shall be unable to distinguish the slave from a brute, then will I argue with you that the slave is a man!

QUESTIONS FOR ANALYSIS

- What examples does Douglass give of the disparity between slaves and free white Americans?
- How does Douglass suggest that slaves are human beings?
- What is the significance of the last sentence of the speech?

Source: David W. Blight (ed.), Narrative of the Life of Frederick Douglass: An American Slave, Written by Himself (Boston: Bedford Books, 1993), pp. 141–145.

took the freed captives to the British base at Sierra Leone and resettled them there. Liberia, too, became a territory for freed captives and for former slaves returning from the Americas.

New Trade with Africa

Even as the Atlantic slave trade died down, Europeans promoted commerce with Africa. Now they wanted Africans to export raw materials and to purchase European manufactures. What Europeans liked to call "legitimate" trade aimed to raise the Africans' standard of living by substituting trade in produce for trade in slaves. West Africans responded by exporting palm kernels and peanuts. The real bonanza was in vegetable oils to lubricate machinery and make candles and in palm oil to produce soap. Africa's palm and peanut plantations were less devastating to the environment than their predecessors in the West Indies had been. There, planters had felled forests to establish sugar estates (see Chapter 12). In West Africa, where palm products became crucial exports, the palm tree had always grown wild. Although intensive cultivation caused some deforestation, the results were not as extreme as in the Caribbean. Regardless of the environmental impact, European merchants argued that by becoming vibrant export societies, Africans would earn the wealth to profitably import European wares.

SUCCESS IN THE AGE OF LEGITIMATE COMMERCE
Emerging in the age of legitimate commerce, the new trade gave rise to a generation of successful West African merchants. There were many rags-to-riches stories, like that of King Jaja of Opobo (1821–1891). Kidnapped and sold into slavery as a youngster, he started out paddling canoes carrying palm oil to coastal ports. Ultimately becoming the head of a coastal canoe house, as a merchant-prince and chief he founded the port of Opobo and could summon a flotilla of war canoes on command. Another freed slave, a Yoruba, William Lewis, made his way back to Africa and settled in Sierra Leone in 1828. Starting with a few utensils and a small plot of land, he became a successful merchant who sent his son Samuel to England for his education. Samuel eventually became an important political leader in Sierra Leone.

EFFECTS IN AFRICA Just as the slave trade shaped African political communities, its demise brought sharp adjustments. For some, it was a welcome end to the constant drainage of people. For others, it was a disaster because it cut off income necessary to buy European arms and luxury goods. Many West African regimes, like the Yoruba kingdom, collapsed once chieftains could no longer use the slave trade to finance their retinues and armies.

The rise of free labor in the Atlantic world and the dwindling foreign slave trade had an unanticipated and perverse effect in Africa. It strengthened slavery there. In some areas, by the mid-nineteenth century, slaves accounted for more than half the population. No longer did they comfortably serve in domestic employment; instead, they toiled on palm oil plantations or, in East Africa, on clove plantations. They also served in the military forces, bore palm oil and ivory to markets as porters, or paddled cargo-carrying canoes along rivers leading to the coast. In 1850, northern Nigeria's ruling class had more slaves than independent Brazil and almost as many as the United States. No longer the world's supplier of slaves, Africa itself had become the world's largest slaveholding region.

ECONOMIC REORDERINGS

Behind the political and social upheavals, profound changes were occurring in the world economy. Until the middle of the eighteenth century, global trade touched only the edges of societies, most of which produced for their own subsistence. At that time, surpluses were confined to specialty goods such as porcelains and silks, which entered trade arteries but did not change the cultures that produced them. By the middle of the nineteenth century, however, global trade was experiencing

rapid growth. The export of silver and gold, mainly from the Americas, stimulated long-distance commercial exchanges, causing farmers to use their earnings to purchase the products of an increasing trade. Cities expanded as trade and industrialization brought new urban occupations into being.

Regional and Global Origins of Industrialization

Europeans were undergoing some basic changes, especially in northwestern Europe and British North America. Here, as elsewhere in the world, households had always produced mainly for themselves and made available for marketplaces only meager surpluses of goods and services. But dramatic changes occurred when family members, including wives and children, decided to work harder and longer in order to produce more for the market and purchase more in the market. In these locations, households devoted less time to leisure activities and more time to working, using the additional income from hard work to improve their standard of living. Scholars recently have come to call this change an **industrious revolution**. Beginning in the second half of the seventeenth century, it gained speed in the eighteenth century and laid the foundations for the industrial revolution of the late eighteenth and early nineteenth centuries.

MERGING SPHERES OF TRADE These local changes overlapped with the wider shifts in Europe's place in the world. The willingness to work more and an eagerness to eat more new foods, to wear better clothes, and to consume products that had once been available as luxuries only to the wealthy classes fueled regional and global trade. By the eighteenth century, separate trading spheres described in earlier chapters were merging into increasingly integrated circuits. Sugar and silver coming from the Americas were the pioneering products. By the eighteenth century, other staples joined the long-distance trading business. Tea, for instance, became a beverage of world trade. Its leaves came from China, the sugar to cut its bitterness from the Caribbean, the slaves to harvest the sweetener from Africa, and the ceramics from which to drink a proper cup from the English Midlands.

One of the most important imports to Europe and North America were cotton textiles, produced by skilled artisans in Bengal, Gujerat, and South India. These lightweight, brilliantly colorful, and easily washable textiles of an unusually high quality appealed to peoples all over the world, becoming a favorite of European populations. In addition, tobacco, raw cotton, rice, and sugar poured in from the Americas, originating mainly from large-scale slave plantations. These primary imports boosted the European standard of living and spurred institutions and industries connected to global trade, such as shipping and shipbuilding, and strong and diverse financial institutions, such as insurance companies, stock exchanges, and banks. These latter institutions were to serve the Europeans, especially the British, well during the industrial revolution. They became the instruments to channel more and more money into manufacturing enterprises.

So, Europe saw a double effect from increasing global trade: first, rising markets for cottons, linen, and silk; and second, institutions to pool capital for investment in other sectors. Cheap inputs and more efficient mass production soon gave new manufacturers the edge against Asian artisanal producers. European—and especially British—producers began to undercut Indians in their home market for textiles. In China, cheaper "Deftware" from the Netherlands and stoneware from England cut deeply into the market for Chinese porcelain. In this way, European industrialization resulted in the deindustrialization of Asia.

The state played an important role in nurturing European industries. States began to see the benefits of a strong merchant and manufacturing class: not only did manufacturing increase the wealth of nations, as Adam Smith had argued, but it created pools of money that the state could borrow in times of need. States also enacted new laws to defend the rights of private property owners and inventors, so they could reap rewards from patents and be encouraged to innovate further. If the state encouraged the making of money, it also agreed to protect those who loaned money. Capitalists could rely on the government to force debtors to honor their obligations, thus protecting lenders from risk. These measures formed a pact between merchants and the state that would make some parts of Europe and some colonies of Europe distinctive.

Nowhere was this new alliance clearer than in England. Critical for the takeoff of the English cotton manufacturing industry were tariffs against Indian textile imports. Here, the pressure came from the woolen and linen industries, which wanted to shut out their Indian competitors. The chief beneficiaries, however, would be cotton entrepreneurs. In 1701, the English Parliament passed a law against the importation of dyed or printed calicoes coming from China, India, and Persia. The state followed this act of Parliament by passing a law that fined anyone wearing printed or dyed calicoes, though Indian muslins were exempted.

SOCIAL AND POLITICAL CONSEQUENCES OF GLOBAL TRADE The expansion of global trade had important social and political consequences. Global trading now trickled its way down from elites to ordinary folk, especially in western Europe. Even ordinary people could purchase imported goods with their earnings. Thus, the poor began to enjoy—some would say became addicted to—coffee, tea, and sugar and eventually even felt the need to use soap. European artisans and farmers purchased tools, furnishings, and home decorations. Colonial laborers also used their meager earnings to buy imported cotton cloth made in Europe from the raw cotton they themselves had picked several seasons earlier.

As new goods flowed from ever more distant corners of the globe, immense fortunes grew. To support their enterprise, traders needed new services, in insurance, bookkeeping, and the recording of legal documents. Trade helped nurture the emergence of new classes of professionals—accountants and lawyers. The new cities of the commercial revolution, hubs like Bristol, Bombay, and Buenos Aires, provided the homes and flourishing neighborhoods for a class of men and women

New Farming Technologies. *Although new technologies only gradually transformed agriculture, the spread of more intensive cultivation led to increased yields.*

known as the **bourgeoisie**: urban businessmen, financiers, and other property owners without aristocratic origins.

As Europe moved to the center of this new global economic order, one class in particular moved to the top of the social ladder: the trader-financiers. Like the merchandiser, the financier did not have to emerge from the high and mighty of Eurasia's dynasties. Consider Mayer Amschel Rothschild (1744–1812): born the son of a money changer in the Jewish ghetto of Frankfurt, Rothschild progressed from coin dealing to money changing, then from trading textiles to lending funds to kings and governments. By the time of his death, he owned the world's biggest banking operation and his five sons were running powerful branches in London, Paris, Vienna, Naples, and Frankfurt.

By extending credit, families like the Rothschilds also enabled traders to ship goods across long distances without having to worry about immediate payment. All these financial changes implied world integration through the flow of goods as well as the flow of money. In the 1820s, sizable funds amassed in London flowed to Egypt, Mexico, and New York to support trade, public investment, and, of course, speculation.

The Industrial Revolution and the British Surge

Trade and finance repositioned western Europe's relationship with the rest of the world. So did the emergence of manufacturing—a big leap in output, as was taking place in agriculture, in this case of industrial commodities. The heart of this process was a gradual accumulation and diffusion of technical knowledge. Lots of little inventions, their applications, and their diffusion across the Atlantic world gradually built up a stock of technical knowledge and practice. Historians have traditionally called these changes the **industrial revolution**, a term first used by the British economic historian Arnold Toynbee in the late nineteenth century. Although the term suggests radical and rapid economic change, the reality was much more gradual and less dramatic than originally believed. Yet the term still has great validity, for the major economic changes that occurred in Britain, northwestern Europe, and North America catapulted these countries ahead of the rest of the world in industrial and agricultural output and standard of living.

MANUFACTURING AND THE COTTON TEXTILE INDUSTRY Nowhere was this industrial revolution more evident than in Britain. Britain had a few natural advantages, like large supplies of coal (for cheap carbon-based energy) and iron (for cheap and durable metal). It also had a political and social environment that allowed merchants and industrialists to invest heavily while also expanding their internal and international markets. But the cost of labor in Britain was relatively high, the result of the industrious revolution. For the British to outsell competitors in India and China, they would have to replace expensive workers with cheap energy and sufficient capital to purchase labor-saving machines.

In addition to its coal and iron reserves, by the eighteenth century Britain could boast an abundance of inventors and entrepreneurs. Few were university educated or conversant in the ideas of the Enlightenment, though some were. What was key to their success was their experimental and observational practices, a popularization of scientific methods to develop new technologies. This included intrepid young artisans, who were literate and numerate enough to lead the way in inventing laborsaving devices like steam engines and mechanical spinners, crucial inventions for the cotton textile industry.

The first problem tackled by these artisanal innovators was that of how to pump water out of coal mining shafts. Using steam to make smooth rotary power, they created a cheaper and more efficient energy source than a horse or river could provide. Coal and steam were also polluting and not renewable, which would create longer-term problems. But for the moment, they fueled the industrial revolution. Once rotary power was connected to spinning and weaving devices, the capacity to produce low-cost, high-volume cloth took off. Steam allowed factories to locate farther away from earlier energy sources and in swelling cities, where these units of production could grow in scale without driving up production costs. What followed was a cascade of smaller, but important, innovations. In this fashion, mechanical production eclipsed manual production that was the basis of textile production in the rest of the world.

A good example of how the alliance of the inventor with the investor furthered the industrial revolution was the advent of the steam engine. Such engines burned coal to boil water; the resulting steam drove mechanized devices. While several tinkerers worked on the device, the most famous was James Watt (1736–1819) of Scotland, who managed to separate steam condensers from piston cylinders. This enabled pistons to stay hot and run constantly. Watt joined forces with the industrialist Matthew Boulton, who marketed the steam engine and set up a laboratory where Watt could refine his device. The steam engine catalyzed a revolution in transportation. Steam-powered engines also improved sugar refining, pottery making, and other industrial processes, generating more products at lower cost than when workers had made them by hand.

In a dramatic way, cotton became Britain's dominant industry in the nineteenth century. Even in the middle of the eighteenth century, India's cotton textile industry had dwarfed Britain's. Factories in Bengal produced 85 million pounds of yarn per year compared with 3 million in England. At the time, cotton production was entirely a hand industry, but a series of macro inventions—James Hargreaves's spinning jenny, Richard Arkwright's water frame, and Samuel Crompton's combination

A Cotton Textile Mill in the 1830s. *The region of Lancashire became one of the major industrial hubs for textile production in the world. By the 1830s, mills had made the shift from artisanal work to highly mechanical mass production. Among the great breakthroughs was the discovery that cloth could be printed with designs, such as paisley or calico (as in this image), and marketed to middle-class consumers.*

of the jenny and the water frame into the "mule"—enabled the British to produce yarns that rivaled India's in durability, quality, and beauty. The difference? The British product was much cheaper because it relied on fewer workers. In contrast to India, where one person, usually a woman, produced yarn on a hand-held spinning wheel, in England and Scotland one person could operate a jenny, a water frame, and finally a mule and produce seventy times what a single hand-operated wheel could yield. Crompton's spectacular mule worked in pairs overseen by a single minder with the help of two boys to roll out fabric in large quantities. The largest carried up to 1,320 spindles and was as long as 150 feet. These macro inventions became the tools of the first industrial factories.

By the 1830s, Britain's dominance of world markets was unrivaled. In this decade, British cotton textile mills employed 425,000 workers and accounted for 16 percent of jobs in British manufacturing. To sustain the output of fabric, Britain's boom required imported raw cotton from Brazil, Egypt, India, and the United States. Most raw cotton for British factories had come from colonial India until 1793, when the American inventor Eli Whitney (1765–1825) patented a "cotton gin" that separated cotton seeds from fiber. After that, cotton farming spread so quickly in the southern United States that by the 1850s it was producing more than 80 percent of the world's cotton supply. In turn, every black slave in the Americas and many Indians in British India were wearing cheap, British-produced cotton shirts. In less than a century, India had gone from exporting fine textiles to Britain to exporting raw cotton, while imports of British cloth drove thousands of Bengali artisan weavers out of business. The Indian economy suffered doubly because even its cotton producers had to compete against new suppliers. Thus did the industrial revolution transform the balance of world economic power.

A NEW ECONOMIC ORDER It is important to note that the industrial revolution did not always result in the creation of large-scale industries. The large factory was rare in manufacturing. Indeed, the largest employers at the time were the slave plantations of the Americas that produced the staples for industrial consumption. Small-scale production remained the norm, mass production the exception. Small-scale production simply became more efficient through innovations in techniques and machinery. The silks of Lyon, cutlery of Solingen, calicoes of Alsace, and cottons of Pawtucket, Rhode Island, were all products of small firms in heavily industrialized belts.

One of the great mysteries of the industrial revolution was why China, the home of inventors of astronomical water clocks and gunpowder, did not become an epicenter of industrial production. There are three reasons. First, China did not foster experimental science of the kind that allowed Watt to stumble onto the possibility of steam or Hargreaves, Arkwright, and Crompton to invent spinning jennies. Chinese authorities discouraged the partnership of inventors and investors. Experimentation, testing, and the links between thinkers and investors were a distinctly Atlantic phenomenon. The Qing, like the Mughal and Ottoman dynasties, swept the great minds into the bureaucracy and reinforced the old agrarian system based on peasant exploitation and tribute. Second, unlike the Europeans, Chinese rulers saw little need to engage in overseas expansion or establish trading outposts in faraway lands in search of riches. The agrarian dynasties of China and India neither showered favors on local merchants nor effectively shut out interlopers. This made them vulnerable to cheap manufactured imports from European traders backed by their governments extolling the virtues of free trade. Third, China did not have ready access to cheap sources of fuel. China's coal deposits lay in the northwest, but merchants and trading hubs were in the southeast.

Cheap carbon gave British manufacturers a comparative advantage. And once ahead of the industrial game, British manufacturers could drive their Asian competitors out of business.

It is important to emphasize, however, that British inventions took hold elsewhere in Europe and in the British colonies. The British lead did not last forever. France and Belgium scrambled to catch up. By the end of the nineteenth century, German industrialists were eclipsing British leaders. The ability for Europeans and North Americans to close the British gap further underscores the importance of the political and economic obstacles faced by Chinese and other entrepreneurs in this age of fast-paced change.

The effects of British and then European and North American industrialization were profound. Historically, Europe had a trade imbalance with partners to the east—furs from Russia and spices and silks from Asia. It made up for this with silver from the Americas. But the new economic order meant that by the nineteenth century, western Europe not only had manufactures like textiles to export to the world; it also had capital. One of Europe's biggest debtors was none other than the sultan of the Ottoman Empire, whose tax system could not keep up with the daunting expenditures necessary to keep the realm together. More and more, Asian, African, and American governments found themselves borrowing from Europe's financiers just as their people were buying industrial products from Europe and selling their primary products to European consumers and producers.

Working and Living

The industrial revolution brought more demanding work routines—not only in the manufacturing economies of western Europe and North America but also on the farms and plantations of Asia and Africa. Although the European side of the story is better known, cultivators throughout the rest of the world toiled harder and for longer hours.

URBAN LIFE AND WORK ROUTINES Increasingly, Europe's workers made their living in cities. London, Europe's largest city in 1700, saw its population nearly double over the next century to almost 1 million. By the 1820s, population growth was even greater in the industrial hubs of Leeds, Glasgow, Birmingham, Liverpool, and Manchester. (See Map 15.4 and Analyzing Global Developments: Town and Countryside, Core and Periphery in the Nineteenth Century.) By contrast, in the Low Countries (Belgium and the Netherlands) and France, where small-scale, rural-based manufacturing flourished, the shift to cities was less extreme.

For most urban dwellers, cities were not healthy places. Water that powered the mills, along with chemicals used in dyeing, went directly back into waterways that provided drinking water. Overcrowded tenements shared just a few outhouses. Most European cities as late as 1850 had no running water, no garbage pickup, no underground sewer system. The result was widespread disease. (In fact, no European city at this time had as clean a water supply as the largest towns of the ancient Roman Empire once had.)

Often families were forced to send women and children outside the home to work. Their wages, usually less than half those paid to adult male workers, helped families survive but exposed these workers, too, to the dangers and hardships of working in factories or mines. Most worked shifts of 12 or more hours at a time, making it impossible for children to obtain the kind of education that might have made escape from the working class possible. Orphans and inhabitants of workhouses—places where debtors, drunks, or those accused of immoral behavior were sent—were treated essentially as slave labor.

Changes in work affected the understanding of time. Most farmers' workloads had followed seasonal rhythms, but after 1800, industrial settings imposed a rigid concept of work discipline and time. To keep the machinery operating, factory and mill owners installed huge clocks and used bells or horns to signify the workday's beginning and end. Employers also measured output per hour and compared workers' performance. Josiah Wedgwood, a maker of teacups and other porcelain, installed a Boulton & Watt steam engine in his manufacturing plant and made his workers use it efficiently. He rang a bell at 5:45 in the morning so employees could start work as day broke. At 8:30 the bell rang for breakfast, at 9:00 to call them back, and at 12:00 for a half-hour lunch; it last tolled when darkness put an end to the workday. Sometimes, though, factory clocks were turned back in the morning and forward at night, falsely extending the exhausted laborers' workday.

Despite higher production, industrialization imposed numbing work routines and paltry wages. Worse, however, was having no work at all. As families abandoned their farmland and depended on wages, being idle meant having no income. Periodic downturns in the economy put wage workers at risk, and many responded by organizing protests. In 1834, the British Parliament centralized the administration of all poor relief and deprived able-bodied workers of any relief unless they joined a workhouse, where working conditions resembled those of a prison.

SOCIAL PROTEST AND EMIGRATION While entrepreneurs accumulated private wealth, the effects of the industrial revolution on working-class families raised widespread concern. In the 1810s in England, groups of jobless craftsmen, called Luddites, smashed the machines that had left them unemployed. In 1849, the English novelist Charlotte Brontë

Legend:

— Railroads in 1850
□ Center of industry
• Iron ore deposit
• Coal and lignite deposits

Percent of Population Living in Cities of 100,000 or more
5 percent or less
6 to 10 percent
20 percent or more

MAP 15.4 | Industrial Europe around 1850

By 1850, much of western Europe was industrial and urban, with major cities linked to one another through a network of railroads.

- According to this map, what natural resources contributed to the growth of the industrial revolution? What effects did it have on urban population densities?

- Explain how the presence of an extensive railroad system helped to accelerate industrialization.

- According to your reading, why were the effects of the industrial revolution more rapidly apparent in Great Britain and in northwestern Europe?

The textile industry was by far the most dynamic sector of the world economy in the nineteenth century. It was dependent on cotton, whose production was labor-intensive but required relatively little capital investment and benefited little from economies of scale. In the first half of the century, cotton was primarily produced by slaves in the southern United States. By the late 1850s, the United States accounted for 77 percent of the cotton consumed in Britain, for 90 percent in France, and for about 92 percent in Russia. After the U.S. Civil War and subsequent slave emancipations, sharecroppers continued to produce the crop, though cotton production began to flourish in Brazil, Egypt, West Africa, and India.

Wheat, on the other hand, was the basic staple of European and Mediterranean diets well into the nineteenth century, and it remains vitally important. Before the advent of railroads, most wheat was consumed locally. In the second half of the century, however, vast quantities of wheat came onto world markets as railroads spread through the Midwest of the United States and the plains of central and eastern Europe. Grown on large, capital-intensive farms, that wheat—as well as rye, corn, millet,

and other grains—fed radically expanding European and American industrial cities and factory towns, linking them to rich agricultural hinterlands and contributing unwittingly to the economic volatility of the nineteenth century. Here we chart the fortunes of two of the most important commodities of the nineteenth-century world—cotton and wheat—against the growth of cities and railroads.

QUESTIONS FOR ANALYSIS

- Which countries appear to have been the most dynamic? Pay attention to relative change over time—not only in the biggest cities and most extensive rail networks but also in those growing the fastest.
- How did the growth of railroads and cities vary by country? What does this tell us about the relationship between economic core regions and their peripheries and about patterns of inequality more generally?
- How did the extension of railroads, along with the economic integration they fostered, influence patterns of inequality worldwide?

Population of Major Cities (in thousands)

	1800	1830	1850	1880	1900
Alexandria	15		60	231	320
Delhi		150	152	173	209
Rio de Janeiro	43	125	166	360	523
London	1,117		2,685	4,770	6,586
Paris	576		1,053	2,269	2,714
Moscow	250		365	748	989
New York City	60	161	340	847	1,478
Tokyo	457			824	1,819

Population Estimates (in thousands)

	1800	1825	1850	1875	1900
Egypt	3,854	4,541	4,752	6,961	10,186
India	255,000	257,000	285,000	306,000	
Brazil			7,678	9,930	17,438
England	8,893	12,000	17,928	22,712	32,528
France	27,349	30,462	35,783	36,906	38,451
Russia	35,500	52,300	68,500	90,200	132,900
America	5,297	11,252	23,261	45,073	76,094
Japan	25,622	26,602	27,201	25,037	44,359

Output of Cotton (in thousand metric tons)

	1800	1825	1850	1875	1900
Egypt				132	293
India			12	533	536
America	17	121	484	1,050	2,120

Wheat Production (in thousand metric tons)

	1825	1850	1875	1900
France	4,580	6,600	7,550	8,860
Russia			53	136
America		2,722	8,546	16,302

Length of Open Railway Lines (in kilometers)

	1825	1850	1875	1900
Egypt		1,184	1,410	2,237
India		32	10,527	39,834
Brazil		14	1,801	15,316
England	43	9,797	23,365	30,079
France	17	2,915	19,351	38,109
Russia	27	501	19,029	53,234
America	37	14,518	119,246	311,160
Japan		29	62	6,300

Source: S. Beckert, "Emancipation and Empire: Reconstructing the Worldwide Web of Cotton Production in the Age of the American Civil War," *The American Historical Review* 109, no. 5 (December 2004): 1405–1438; B. R. Mitchell, *International Historical Statistics: Africa, Asia, and Oceania, 1750–2005, International Historical Statistics: The Americas, 1750–2005,* and *International Historical Statistics: Europe, 1750–2005* (London: Palgrave Macmillan, 2007).

A Model Textile Mill. *Distressed by the terrible working conditions of nineteenth-century textile mills, Welsh industrialist and reformer Robert Owen sought to create humane factories. From maintaining the orderliness of the factory floor to posting work rules on the walls, Owen's reforms saw significant improvements in the health and morale of his workers. Nonetheless, he would continue to employ children in his factories, like most of his contemporaries.*

published a novel, *Shirley*, depicting the misfortunes caused by the power loom. Charles Dickens described a mythic Coketown to evoke pity for the working class in his 1854 classic *Hard Times*. Both Elizabeth Gaskell, in England, and Émile Zola, in France, described the hardships of women whose malnourished children were pressed into the workforce too early. Gaskell and Zola also highlighted the hunger, loneliness, and illness that prostitutes and widows endured. These social advocates sought protective legislation for workers, including curbing child labor, limiting the workday, and, in some countries, legalizing prostitution for the sake of monitoring the prostitutes' health.

Some people, however, could not wait for legislative reform. Thus, the period saw unprecedented emigration, as unemployed workers or peasants abandoned their homes to seek their fortunes in America, Canada, and Australia. During the Irish Potato Famine of 1845–1849, at least 1 million Irish citizens left their country (and a further million or so died) when fungi attacked their subsistence crop. Desperate to escape starvation, they booked cheap passage to North America on ships so notorious for disease and malnutrition that they earned the name "coffin ships." Those who did survive faced discrimination in their new land, for many Americans feared that the immigrants would drive down wages or create social unrest.

The industrial revolution produced wealth on an unprecedented scale, but that wealth was unevenly distributed. Inequalities existed both within societies and between them. Free trade had at first led to the creation of small firms, but over time, the most productive workshops expanded into massive, dynamic, creative, and unstable industrial corporations.

PERSISTENCE AND CHANGE IN AFRO-EURASIA

Western Europe's military might, its technological achievements, and its economic strength represented a threat to the remaining Afro-Eurasian empires. Across the continent, western European merchants and industrialists sought closer economic and (in some cases) political ties. They did so in the name of gaining "free" access to Asian markets and products. In response, Russian and Ottoman rulers modernized their military organizations and hoped to achieve similar economic strides while distancing themselves from the democratic principles of the French Revolution. The Chinese Empire remained outside the orbit of European power until the first Opium War of the early 1840s forced the Chinese to acknowledge their military weaknesses. Thus, changes in the Atlantic world unleashed new pressures around the globe, though with varying degrees of intensity.

Revamping the Russian Monarchy

Russian rulers responded to the pressures by strengthening their traditional authority through modest reforms and the suppression of domestic opposition. Tsar Alexander I (r. 1801–1825) was fortunate that Napoleon committed several blunders and lost his formidable army in the Russian snows. Yet the French Revolution and its massive, patriotic armies struck at the heart of Russian political institutions, which rested upon a huge peasant population laboring as serfs. The tsars could no longer easily justify their absolutism by claiming that enlightened despotism was the most advanced form of government, since a new model, rooted in popular sovereignty and the concept of the nation, had arisen.

In December 1825, when Alexander died unexpectedly and childless, there was a question over succession. Some of the Russian officers launched a patriotic revolt, hoping to convince Alexander's brother Constantine to take the throne and to guarantee a constitution in place of a more conservative brother, Nicholas. The Decembrists, as the proponents of Constantine were called, came primarily from elite families and were familiar with western European life and institutions. A few Decembrists wanted to establish a constitutional monarchy to replace Russia's despotism; others favored a tsar-less republic and the abolition of serfdom. But the officers' conspiracy failed to win over conservative landowners and bureaucrats, who believed in the tsar's divine right to rule and did not want to see serfdom abolished. As Constantine, too, supported Nicholas's claim to power, Nicholas (r. 1825–1855) became tsar and brutally suppressed the insurrectionists.

Russia's rulers and upper classes had always both feared and been inspired by western examples. They continued to borrow western technology and modes of administration but held at bay western ideas and practices of liberty through censorship and the promotion of a distinctly Russian identity. In trying to maintain absolutist rule, Nicholas and his successors portrayed the monarch's family as the ideal historical embodiment of the nation with direct ties to the people. Nicholas himself prevented rebellion by expanding the secret police, enforcing censorship, conducting impressive military exercises, and maintaining serfdom. And in the 1830s, he introduced a conservative ideology that stressed religious faith, hierarchy, and obedience. Although in 1861 a new tsar, Alexander II, would finally abolish serfdom, throughout the nineteenth century Russia remained the most conservative of the great powers.

Reforming Egypt and the Ottoman Empire

Unlike Russia, where Napoleon's army had reached Moscow, the Ottoman capital in Istanbul never faced a threat by French troops. Still, Napoleon's invasion of Egypt shook the Ottoman Empire. Even before this trauma, imperial authorities faced the challenge posed by increased trade with Europe and the greater presence of European merchants and missionaries. In addition, many non-Muslim religious communities in the sultan's empire wanted the European powers to advance their interests. In the wake of Napoleon, who had promised to remake Egyptian society, reformist energies swept from Egypt to the center of the Ottoman domain. (See Primary Source: An Egyptian Intellectual's Reaction to the French Occupation of Egypt.)

REFORMS IN EGYPT In Egypt, far-reaching changes came with **Muhammad Ali**, a skillful, modernizing ruler. After the French withdrawal in 1801, Muhammad Ali (r. 1805–1848) won a chaotic struggle for supreme power in Egypt and aligned himself with influential Egyptian families. Yet he looked to revolutionary France for a model of modern state building. As with Napoleon (and Simón Bolívar in Latin America), the key to his hold on power was the army. With the help of French advisers, the modernized Egyptian army became the most powerful fighting force in the Middle East.

Muhammad Ali also reformed education and agriculture. He established a school of engineering and opened the first modern medical school in Cairo under the supervision of a French military doctor. And his efforts in the countryside made Egypt one of the world's leading cotton exporters. A summer crop, cotton required steady watering when the Nile's irrigation waters were in short supply. So Muhammad Ali's public works department, advised by European engineers, deepened the irrigation canals

Decembrists in St. Petersburg. *Russians energetically participated in the coalition that defeated Napoleon, but the ideas of the French Revolution greatly appealed to the educated upper classes, including aristocrats of the officer corps. In December 1825, at the death of Tsar Alexander I, some regimental officers staged an uprising of about 3,000 men, demanding a constitution and the end of serfdom. But Nicholas I, the new tsar, called in loyal troops and brutally dispersed the "Decembrists," executing or exiling their leaders.*

An Egyptian Intellectual's Reaction to the French Occupation of Egypt

In the 1798 invasion of Egypt, Napoleon Bonaparte attempted to win rank-and-file Egyptian support against the country's Mamluks, who were the most powerful group in Egypt at the time, though the country was still under the authority of the Ottoman sultan. Bonaparte portrayed himself as a liberator and invoked the ideals of the French Revolution, as he had done with great success all over Europe. His Egyptian campaign did not succeed, however, and local opposition was bitter. The chronicler Abd al-Rahman al-Jabarti has left one of the most perceptive accounts of these years.

On Monday news arrived that the French had reached Damanhur and Rosetta [in the Nile Delta]. . . . They printed a large proclamation in Arabic, calling on the people to obey them. . . . In this proclamation were inducements, warnings, all manner of wiliness and stipulations. Some copies were sent from the provinces to Cairo and its text is:

In the name of God, the Merciful, the Compassionate. There is no God but God. He has no son nor has He an associate in His Dominion.

On behalf of the French Republic which is based upon the foundation of liberty and equality, General Bonaparte, Commander-in-Chief of the French armies makes known to all the Egyptian people that for a long time the Sanjaqs [its Mamluk rulers] who lorded it over Egypt have treated the French community basely and contemptuously and have persecuted its merchants with all manner of extortion and violence. Therefore the hour of punishment has now come.

Unfortunately, this group of Mamluks . . . have acted corruptly for ages in the fairest land that is to be found upon the face of the globe. However, the Lord of the Universe, the Almighty, has decreed the end of their power.

O ye Egyptians . . . I have not come to you except for the purpose of restoring your rights from the hands of the oppressors and that I more than the Mamluks serve God. . . .

And tell them also that all people are equal in the eyes of God and the only circumstances which distinguish one from the other are reason, virtue, and knowledge. . . . Formerly, in the lands of Egypt there were great cities, and wide canals and extensive commerce and nothing ruined all this but the avarice and the tyranny of the Mamluks.

[Al-Jabarti then challenged the arguments in the French proclamation and portrayed the French as godless invaders, inspired by false ideals.] They follow this rule: great and small, high and low, male and female are all equal. Sometimes they break this rule according to their whims and inclinations or reasoning. Their women do not veil themselves and have no modesty. . . . Whenever a Frenchman has to perform an act of nature he does so where he happens to be, even in full view of people, and he goes away as he is, without washing his private parts after defecation. . . .

His saying "[all people] are equal in the eyes of God" the Almighty is a lie and stupidity. How can this be when God has made some superior to others as is testified by the dwellers in the Heavens and on Earth? . . .

So those people are opposed to both Christians and Muslims, and do not hold fast to any religion. You see that they are materialists, who deny all God's attributes. . . . May God hurry misfortune and punishment upon them, may He strike their tongues with dumbness, may He scatter their hosts, and disperse them.

QUESTIONS FOR ANALYSIS

- When the proclamation speaks of "the fairest land that is to be found upon the face of the globe," what land is it referring to?
- Why do you think Napoleon's appeals to the ideals of the French Revolution failed with Egyptians?
- Why does al-Jabarti claim that the invaders are godless even though the proclamation clearly suggests otherwise?

Source: Abd al-Rahman al-Jabarti, *Al-Jabarti's Chronicle of the First Seven Months of the French Occupation of Egypt*, translated by S. Moreh (Leiden: E. J. Brill, 1975), pp. 39–40, 43, 46–47.

and constructed a series of dams across the Nile. These efforts transformed Egypt, making it the most powerful state in the eastern Mediterranean and alarming the Ottoman state and the great powers in Europe.

Muhammad Ali's modernizing reforms, however, disrupted the habits of the peasantry. After all, incorporation into the industrial world economy involved harder work (as English wage workers had discovered), often with little additional pay. Because irrigation improvements permitted year-round cultivation, Egyptian peasants now had to plant and harvest three crops instead of one or two. Moreover, the state controlled the prices of cultivated products, so peasants saw little profit from their extra efforts. Young men also faced conscription into the state's enlarged army, while whole families had to toil, unpaid, on public works projects. In addition, a state-sponsored program of industrialization aimed to put Egypt on a par with Europe: before long, textile and munitions factories employed 200,000 workers. But Egypt had few skilled laborers or cheap sources of energy, so by the time of Muhammad Ali's death in 1849, few of the factories survived.

External forces also limited Muhammad Ali's ambitious plans. At first, his new army enjoyed spectacular success. But Muhammad Ali overplayed his hand when he sent forces into Syria in the 1830s and later when he threatened Anatolia, the heart of the Ottoman state. Fearing that an Egyptian ruler might attempt to overthrow the Ottoman sultan and threaten the balance of power in the eastern Mediterranean region, the European powers compelled Egypt to withdraw from Anatolia and reduce its army.

Muhammad Ali. *The Middle Eastern ruler who most successfully assimilated the educational, technological, and economic advances of nineteenth-century Europe was Muhammad Ali, ruler of Egypt from 1805 until 1848.*

OTTOMAN REFORMS Under political and economic pressures like those facing Muhammad Ali in Egypt, Ottoman rulers also made reforms. Indeed, military defeats and humiliating treaties with Europe were painful reminders of the sultans' vulnerability. In 1805, Sultan Selim III tried to create a new infantry, trained by western European officers. But before he could bring this force up to fighting strength, the janissaries stormed the palace, killed its new officers, and deposed Selim in 1807. Over the next few decades, janissary military men and clerical scholars (*ulama*) cobbled together an alliance that continuously thwarted reformers.

Why did reform falter in the Ottoman state before it could be implemented? After all, in France and Spain the old regimes were also inefficient and burdened with debts and military losses. The French required a ferocious revolution to overturn the old order and to remove its supporters. But reform was possible only if the forces of restraint—especially old regime militaries—were weak or dismantled, as in France, where young officers like Napoleon Bonaparte emerged and reformers were strong and courageous. In the Ottoman Empire, the janissary class had grown powerful, providing the main resistance to change. Ottoman authority depended on clerical support, and the Muslim clergy also resisted change. Blocked at the top, Ottoman rulers were hesitant to appeal for popular support. Such an appeal, in the new age of popular sovereignty and national feeling, would be dangerous for an unelected dynast in a multiethnic and multireligious realm.

Mahmud II (r. 1808–1839), who acknowledged Europe's rising power, broke the political deadlock. He shrewdly manipulated his conservative opponents. Convincing some clerics that the janissaries neglected traditions of discipline and piety and promising that a new corps would pray fervently, the sultan won the *ulama*'s support and in 1826 established a European-style army corps. When the janissaries plotted their inevitable mutiny, Mahmud rallied clerics, students, and subjects. The schemers retreated to their barracks, only to be shelled by the sultan's artillery and then destroyed in flames. Thousands of other janissaries were rounded up and executed.

Like Muhammad Ali in Egypt, Mahmud brought in European officers to advise his forces. Here, too, military reform spilled over into nonmilitary areas. The Ottoman modernizers created a medical college and then a school of military sciences. To understand Europe better and to create a first-rate diplomatic corps, the Ottomans schooled their officials in European languages and had European classics translated into Turkish. As Mahmud's successors extended reforms into civilian life, this era—known as the Tanzimat, or reorganization period—saw legislation that guaranteed equality for all Ottoman subjects, regardless of religion.

The reforms, however, stopped well short of revolutionary change. For one thing, reform relied too much on the personal whim of rulers. Also, the bureaucratic and religious infrastructure remained committed to old ways. Moreover, any effort to reform the rural sector met resistance by the landed interests. Finally, the

Indian Resistance to Company Rule. *Tipu Sultan, the Mysore ruler, put up a determined resistance against the British. This painting by Robert Home shows Charles Cornwallis, the East India Company's governor, receiving Tipu's two sons as hostages after defeating him in the 1792 war. The boys remained in British custody for two years. Tipu returned to fighting the British and was killed in the war of 1799.*

merchant classes profited from business with a debt-ridden sultan. By preventing the empire's fiscal collapse through financial support to the state, bankers lessened the pressure for reform and removed the spark that had fired the revolutions in Europe. Together, these factors impeded reform in the Ottoman Empire.

Colonial Reordering in India

Europe's most important colonial possession in Asia between 1750 and 1850 was British India. Unlike in North America, the changes that the British fostered in Asia did not lead to political independence. Instead, India was increasingly dominated by the **East India Company**, which the crown had chartered in 1600. The company's control over India's imports and exports in the eighteenth and nineteenth centuries, however, contradicted British claims about their allegiance to a world economic system based on "free trade."

THE EAST INDIA COMPANY'S MONOPOLY Initially, the British, through the East India Company, tried to control India's commerce by establishing trading posts along the coast but without taking complete political control. After conquering the state of Bengal in 1757, the company began to fill its coffers and its officials began to amass personal fortunes. Even the British governor of Bengal pocketed a portion of the tax revenues. Such unbridled abuse of power caused the Bengal army, along with forces of the Mughal emperor and of the ruler of Awadh, to revolt. Although the rebels were unsuccessful, British officials left the emperor and most provincial leaders in place—as nominal rulers.

Nonetheless, the British secured the right for the East India Company to collect tax revenues in Bengal, Bihar, and Orissa and to trade free of duties throughout Mughal territory. In return, the Mughal emperor would receive a hefty annual pension. The company went on to annex other territories, bringing much of South Asia under its rule by the early 1800s. (See Map 15.5.)

To rule with minimal interference, however, required knowing the conquered society. This led to Orientalist scholarship: British scholar-officials wrote the first modern histories of South Asia, translated Sanskrit and Persian texts, identified philosophical writings, and compiled Hindu and Muslim law books. Through their efforts, the company state presented itself as a force for revitalizing authentic Hinduism and recovering India's literary and cultural treasures. Although the Orientalist scholars admired Sanskrit language and literature, they still supported English colonial rule and did not necessarily agree with local beliefs.

EFFECTS IN INDIA Maintaining a sizable military and civilian bureaucracy also required taxation. Indeed, taxes on land were the East India Company's largest source of revenue. From 1793 onward, land policies required large and small landowners alike to pay taxes to the company. As a result, large estate owners gained more power and joined with the company in determining who could own property. Whenever smaller proprietors defaulted on their taxes, the company put their properties up for auction, with the firm's own employees and large estate owners often obtaining title.

Company rule and booming trade altered India's urban geography as well. By the early nineteenth century, colonial cities

MAP 15.5 | The British in India, 1767–1857

Starting from locations in eastern and northeastern India, the British East India Company extended its authority over much of South Asia prior to the outbreak of the Indian Rebellion of 1857.

- What type of location did the British first acquire in India? How did the company expand into the interior of India and administer these possessions?

- Why did the British choose a strategy of direct rule over some areas and indirect rule over others within the larger region?

like Calcutta, Madras, and Bombay were the new centers at the expense of older Mughal cities like Agra, Delhi, Murshidabad, and Hyderabad. As the colonial cities attracted British merchants and Indian clerks, artisans, and laborers, their populations surged. Calcutta's reached 350,000 in 1820; Bombay's jumped to 200,000 by 1825. In these cities, Europeans lived close to the company's fort and trading stations, while migrants from the countryside clustered in crowded quarters called "black towns."

Back in Britain, the debts of rural Indians and the conditions of black towns generated little concern. Instead, calls for reform focused on the East India Company's monopoly: its sole access to Indian wealth and its protection of company shareholders and investors. In 1813, the British Parliament, responding to merchants' and traders' demands to participate in the Indian economy, abolished the company's monopoly over trade with India.

India now became an importer of British textiles and an exporter of raw cotton—a reversal of its traditional pattern of trade. In the past, India had been an important textile manufacturer, exporting fine cotton goods throughout the Indian Ocean and to Europe. But its elites could not resist the appeal of cheap

Calcutta. *Designated the capital of British India in 1772, Calcutta became vital to the British East India Company's activities as a main exporter of goods such as cotton and opium. The wealthy British merchants and Anglo-Indians that Calcutta attracted utterly transformed its landscape, as shown in this 1910 photograph of the Great Eastern Hotel, which was commonly hailed the "Jewel of the East." This street scene of wide paved roads, carriages, and Victorian architecture would be difficult to distinguish from one of turn-of-the-century London, were it not for the Indian figures in traditional dress.*

Packing Cotton Bales. *This 1864 engraving of the packing of cotton bales registers the shift in cotton trade between India and Britain: from being an exporter of cotton manufactures up to the eighteenth century, India became a source of raw cotton in the nineteenth century.*

British textiles. As a result, India's own industrialization stalled. In addition, the import of British manufactures caused unfavorable trade balances that changed India from a net importer of gold and silver to an exporter of these precious metals.

PROMOTING CULTURAL CHANGE Led by evangelical Christians and liberal reformers, the British did more than alter the Indian economy; they also advocated far-reaching changes in Indian culture so that its people would value British goods and culture. In 1817, James Mill, a philosopher and an employee of the East India Company, condemned what he saw as backward social practices and cultural traditions. He and his son, John Stuart Mill, argued that only dictatorial rule could bring good government and economic progress to India, whose people they considered unfit for self-rule or liberalism. (See Primary Source: James Mill on Indian Tradition.) The mood swung away from the Orientalists' respect for India's classical languages, philosophies, cultures, and texts. In 1835, the British poet, historian, and Liberal politician Lord Macaulay recommended that English replace Persian as the language of administration and that European education replace Oriental learning. This, he hoped, would produce a class that was Indian in blood and color but English in tastes and culture.

If British officials saw liberalism as an excuse for empire, Indian intellectuals saw in it a blueprint for reform. Thus, Ram Mohun Roy, an Indian reformer, locked horns with orthodox Hindus and took the lead in urging the British to abolish the practice of *sati*, by which women burned to death on the funeral pyres of their dead husbands. Roy also championed free press, unsuccessfully challenging its restriction in India by the British as a violation of universal liberal principles.

A new colonial order built with such contradictory application of liberalism was necessarily unstable. Most wealthy landowners resented the loss of their land and authority. Peasants, thrown to the mercy of the market, moneylenders, and landlords were in turmoil. Dispossessed artisans stirred up towns and cities. And merchants and industrialists chafed under the British-dominated economy. Even though India was part of a more interconnected world and thereby supported Europe's industrialization, it was doing so as a colony. As freedom expanded in Europe, exploitation expanded in India.

The Continuing Qing Empire

The Qing dynasty, which had taken power in 1644, was still enjoying prosperity and territorial expansion as the nineteenth century dawned. Its court elites accepted the dynasty's authority in spite of the fact that the Manchus were not Han Chinese but came originally from Manchuria. In this regard, Chinese upper classes were unlike most of the delegates called to the Estates-General in France in 1789, seething with resentment against the monarchy and the aristocracy.

Rice cultivation. *From hand-sowing seedlings to harvesting the grains in leech-infested waters, the process of rice cultivation was so labor-intensive that multigenerational households cropped up throughout imperial China to yield the necessary workforce.*

James Mill on Indian Tradition

James Mill was a Scottish political economist and philosopher who believed that according to the principles of utilitarianism, law and government are essential for maximizing a people's usefulness and happiness. Thus, his History of British India *(1818) criticized India's Hindu and Muslim cultures and attributed their so-called backwardness to the absence of a systematic form of law. Mill's critique was also an attack on earlier British Orientalists, whose close engagement with Indian culture and Indian texts led them to oppose interfering in traditional practices. A year after the book's publication, the East India Company appointed him as an official.*

The condition of the women is one of the most remarkable circumstances in the manners of nations. Among rude people, the women are generally degraded; among civilized people they are exalted.

• • •

Nothing can exceed the habitual contempt which the Hindus entertain for their women. Hardly are they ever mentioned in their laws, or other books, but as wretches of the most base and vicious inclinations, on whose natures no virtuous or useful qualities can be engrafted. "Their husbands," says the sacred code, "should be diligently careful in guarding them: though they well know the disposition with which the lord of creation formed them; Manu allotted to such women a love of their bed, of their seat, and of ornament, impure appetites, wrath, weak flexibility, desire of mischief, and bad conduct."

• • •

They are held, accordingly, in extreme degradation. They are not accounted worthy to partake of religious rites but in conjunction with their husbands. They are entirely excluded from the sacred books. . . .

• • •

They [the Hindus] are remarkably prone to flattery; the most prevailing mode of address from the weak to the strong, while men are still ignorant and unreflecting.

The Hindus are full of dissimulation and falsehood, the universal concomitants of oppression. The vices of falsehood, indeed, they carry to a height almost unexampled among other races of men. Judicial perjury is more than common; it is almost universal.

• • •

This religion has produced a practice, which has strongly engaged the curiosity of Europeans; a superstitious care of the life of the inferior animals. A Hindu lives in perpetual terror of killing even an insect; and hardly any crime can equal that of being unintentionally the cause of death to any animal of the more sacred species. This feeble circumstance, however, is counteracted by so many gloomy and malignant principles, that their religion, instead of humanizing the character, must have had no inconsiderable effect in fostering that disposition to revenge, that insensibility to the sufferings of others, and often that active cruelty, which lurks under the smiling exterior of the Hindu.

• • •

Few nations are surpassed by the Hindus, in the total want of physical purity, in their streets, houses, and persons. Mr. Forster, whose long residence in India, and knowledge of the country, render him an excellent witness, says of the narrow streets of Benares: "In addition to the pernicious effect which must proceed from a confined atmosphere, there is, in the hot season, an intolerable stench arising from the many pieces of stagnated water dispersed in different quarters of the town. The filth also which is indiscriminately thrown into the streets, and there left exposed, (for the Hindus possess but a small portion of general cleanliness) add to the compound of ill smells so offensive to the European inhabitants of this city."

• • •

The attachment with which the Hindus, in common with all ignorant nations, bear to astrology, is a part of their manners exerting a strong influence upon the train of their actions. "The Hindus of the present age," says a partial observer, "do not undertake any affair of consequence without consulting their astrologers, who are always Brahmans." The belief of witchcraft and sorcery continues universally prevalent.

QUESTIONS FOR ANALYSIS

- What did James Mill hold to be the chief indicator of a civilization's accomplishment?
- In what ways do Mill's views on India reflect a deep disagreement with British Orientalists?

Source: James Mill, *The History of British India* (New Delhi: Atlantic Publishers & Distributors, 1990), pp. 279, 281–282, 286–287, 288, 289, 297, 299.

EXPANDING BOUNDARIES The Qing had a talent for extending the empire's boundaries and settling frontier lands. Before 1750, they conquered Taiwan (the stronghold of remaining Ming forces), pushed westward into central Asia, and annexed Tibet. Qing troops then eliminated the threat of the powerful Junghars in western Mongolia and halted Russian efforts to take southern Siberia in the 1750s. To secure these territorial gains, the Qing encouraged settlement of frontier lands like Xinjiang. New crops from the Americas aided this process—especially corn and sweet potatoes, which grow well in less fertile soils.

Like their European counterparts, Chinese peasants were on the move. But migration occurred in Qing China for different reasons. The state-sponsored westward movement into Xinjiang, for example, aimed to secure a recently pacified frontier region through military colonization, after which civilians would follow. So peasants received promises of land, tools, seed, and the loan of silver and a horse—all with the dual objectives of producing enough food grain to supply the troops and relieve pressure on the poor and arid northwestern part of the country. These efforts brought so much land under cultivation by 1840 that the region's ecological and social landscape completely changed.

Other migrants were on the move by their own initiative. The ever-growing competition for land even drove them into areas where the Qing regime had tried to restrict migration (because of excessive administrative costs), such as Manchuria and Taiwan. As the migrants introduced their own agricultural techniques, they reshaped the environment through land reclamation and irrigation projects and sparked large population increases.

PROBLEMS OF THE EMPIRE Despite their success in expanding the empire, the Qing faced nagging problems. As a ruling minority, they took a conservative approach to innovation. And only late in the eighteenth century did they deal with rapid population growth. On the one hand, the tripling of China's population since 1300 demonstrated the realm's prosperity; on the other, a population of over 300 million severely strained resources—especially soil for growing crops and wood for fuel.

In spite of the difficulties that beset the Qing, European rulers and upper classes remained eager consumers of Chinese silks, teas, carved jade, tableware, jewelry, paper for covering walls, and ceramics. The Chinese, for their part, had little demand for most European manufactures. Trade with the Europeans continued, however, even though Emperor Qianlong famously wrote in 1793, in response to a request for more trade by Britain's king, that "as your ambassador can see for himself, we possess all things and have no use for your country's manufactures."

By the mid-nineteenth century, technological advances, such as steam-powered naval ships, strengthened European powers, and the Qing could no longer dismiss their increasing demands. The first clear evidence of an altered balance of power was a British-Chinese war over a narcotic. Indeed, the **Opium War** exposed China's vulnerability in a new era of European ascendancy.

THE OPIUM WAR AND THE "OPENING" OF CHINA Europeans had been selling staples and intoxicants in China for a long time. For example, tobacco, a New World crop, had become widely popular in China by the seventeenth century.

Opium. Left: *A common sight in late Qing China was establishments catering specifically to opium smoking. Taken from a volume condemning the practice, this picture shows opium smokers idling their day away.* Right: *Having established a monopoly in the 1770s over opium cultivation in India, the British greatly expanded their manufacture and export of opium to China to balance their rapidly growing import of Chinese tea and silk. This picture from the 1880s shows an opium warehouse in India where the commodity was stored before being transported to China.*

with tobacco. By the late eighteenth century, opium smokers with their long-stemmed pipes were conspicuous at every level of Chinese society.

Although the Qing banned opium imports in 1729, the Chinese continued to smoke the drug and import it illegally. Sensing its economic potential, the East India Company created an opium monopoly in India in 1773. The reason was a rapid growth in the company's purchase of tea. Because the Chinese showed little taste for British goods, the British had been financing their tea imports with exports of silver to China. But by the late eighteenth century, the company's tea purchases had become too large to finance with silver. Fortunately for the company, the Chinese were eager for Indian cotton and opium, and then mostly just opium.

Opium's impact on the balance of trade was devastating. In a reversal from earlier trends, silver began to flow out of instead of into China. Once silver shortages occurred, the peasants' tax burden grew heavier because they had to pay in silver (see Chapter 13). Consequently, long-simmering unrest in the countryside gained momentum. At the Qing court, some officials wanted to legalize the opium trade so as to eliminate corruption and boost revenues. (After all, as long as opium was an illegal substance, the government could not tax its traffic.) Others wanted stiffer prohibitions. In 1838, the emperor sent a special commissioner to Canton, the main center of the trade, to eradicate the influx of opium.

Though determined, the Chinese were no match for Britain's modern military technology. After a British fleet—including four steam-powered battleships—entered Chinese waters in June 1840, the warships bombarded coastal regions near Canton and sailed upriver for a short way. (See Map 15.6.) On land, Qing soldiers, some armed with imported matchlocks, fared badly against the modern artillery of British troops, many

MAP 15.6 | The Qing Empire and the Opium War

The Opium War demonstrated the superiority of British military technology. Their victory granted the British control of Hong Kong and established a series of treaty ports, which gave Europeans access to Chinese trade and which were subject to the laws of designated European countries.

- How many treaty ports were there after the Opium War? What was their significance?
- How did the Opium War change relations between China and the western powers?

Initially, few people would have predicted that tobacco smoking would lead to the widespread use of opium, previously used as a medicine or an aphrodisiac. But before long, people in Southeast Asia, Taiwan, and China were smoking crude opium mixed

Trade in Canton. *In this painting, we can see the hongs, the buildings that made up the factories, or establishments, where foreign merchants conducted their business in Canton. From the mid-eighteenth century to 1842, Canton was the only Chinese port open to European trade.*

of whom were Indians supplied with percussion cap rifles. Along the Yangzi River, outgunned Qing forces fought fiercely, but they were no match for British military technology. Many of the Qing soldiers killed their own wives and children before committing suicide.

FORCING MORE TRADE The Qing ruling elite capitulated, and with the 1842 Treaty of Nanjing, the British acquired the island of Hong Kong and the right to trade in five treaty ports. They also forced the Chinese to repay their costs for the war. Subsequent treaties guaranteed that the British and other foreign nationals would be tried in their own courts for crimes, rather than in Chinese courts, and would be exempt from Chinese law. Moreover, the British insisted that any privileges granted through treaties with other parties would also apply to them. Other western nations followed the British example in demanding the same right, and the arrangement thus guaranteed all Europeans and North Americans a privileged position in China.

Still, China did not become a formal colony. To the contrary, in the mid-nineteenth century, Europeans and North Americans were trading only on its outskirts. Most Chinese did not encounter the Europeans. Daily life for most people went on as it had before the Opium War. Only the political leaders and urban dwellers were beginning to feel the foreign presence and wondering what steps China might take to acquire European technologies, goods, and learning.

CONCLUSION

During the period 1750–1850, changes in politics, commerce, industry, and technology reverberated throughout the Atlantic world and, to varying degrees, elsewhere around the globe. By 1850, the world was more integrated economically, with Europe increasingly at the center.

In the Americas, colonial ties broke apart. In France, the people toppled the monarchy. Dissidents threatened the same in Russia. Such upheavals introduced a new public

vocabulary—the language of the nation—and made the idea of revolution empowering. In the Americas and parts of Europe, nation-states took shape around redefined hierarchies of class, gender, and color. Britain and France emerged from the political crises of the late eighteenth century determined to expand their borders. Their drive forced older empires such as Russia and the Ottoman state to make reforms.

As commerce and industrialization transformed economic and political power, European governments compelled others (including Egypt, India, and China) to expand their trade with European merchants. Ultimately, such countries had to participate in a European-centered economy as exporters of raw materials and importers of European manufactures. Trade underlay much of the fundamental political reorderings of this period. For North and South American colonists, having the right to trade freely in every market of the world intensified their demands for political freedom. The British fought a war with the Chinese to keep their ports open to all trade goods, including opium. European statesmen joined together to stymie Muhammad Ali's conquest of the Ottoman Empire in part because of their desire to keep eastern Mediterranean markets available to their merchants.

By the 1850s, many of the world's peoples became more industrious, producing less for themselves and more for distant markets. Through changes in manufacturing, some areas of the world also made more goods than ever before. With its emphasis on free trade, Europe began to force open new markets—even to the point of colonizing them. Gold and silver now flowed out of China and India to pay for European-dominated products like opium and textiles.

However, global reordering did not mean that Europe's rulers had uncontested control over other people or that the institutions and cultures of Asia and Africa ceased to be dynamic. Some countries became dependent on Europe commercially; others became colonies. China escaped colonial rule but was forced into unfavorable trade relations with the Europeans. In sum, dramatic changes combined to unsettle systems of rulership and to alter the economic and military balance between western Europe and the rest of the world.

After You Read This Chapter

Go to INQUIZITIVE to see what you know & learn what you've missed.

FOCUS ON: *The Global Effects of the "New Ideas"*

The Atlantic World

- North American colonists revolt against British rule and establish a nonmonarchical, republican form of government.

- In the wake of the American Revolution, the French citizenry proclaims a new era of liberty, equality, and fraternity and executes opponents of the revolution, notably the king and queen of France.

- Napoleon's French Empire extends many principles of the French Revolution throughout Europe.

- In the midst of the French Revolution, Haitian slaves throw off French rule, abolish slavery, and create an independent state.

- Napoleon's invasion of Iberia frees Portuguese and Spanish America from colonial rule.

- The British lead a successful campaign to abolish the Atlantic slave trade and promote new sources of trade with Africa.

- An industrial revolution spreads outward from Britain to a few other parts of the Atlantic world.

- The Russian monarchy strengthens its power through modest reforms and suppression of rebellion.

Africa, India, and Asia

- In Egypt, a military leader, Muhammad Ali, modernizes the country and threatens the political integrity of the Ottoman Empire.

- The British East India Company increasingly dominates the Indian subcontinent.

- The Qing Empire persists despite major European encroachments on its sovereignty.

CHRONOLOGY

	1750	1775
The Americas		The American Revolution **1776–1783**
		The Haitian Revolution **1791–1804**
Europe		James Watt invents the steam engine **1769**
		The French Revolution **1789–1799**
Africa		
Ottoman Empire		
South Asia	British East India Company rules India **1757–1858**	
East Asia		
Russia		

KEY TERMS

Ali, Muhammad p. 582

Bonaparte, Napoleon p. 565

bourgeoisie p. 576

East India Company p. 585

free trade p. 556

industrial revolution p. 576

industrious revolution p. 574

laissez-faire p. 556

Opium War p. 589

popular sovereignty p. 556

social contract p. 557

STUDY QUESTIONS

1. **Describe** the new ideas of freedom, and **explain** how they differed from earlier understandings of this term.

2. **Discuss** the political and social revolutions that occurred in the Atlantic world between 1750 and 1850. What ideas inspired these changes? How well did revolutionaries implement these changes?

3. **Compare and contrast** the way Latin American peoples achieved independence with the process in the United States. How similar were their goals? How well did they achieve these goals?

4. **Analyze** Napoleon's role in spreading the ideas of political and social revolution. How did his armies spread the concept of nationalism? How did Napoleon's military pursuits affect political and social ferment in the Americas?

5. **Explain** how the Atlantic world's political and social revolution led to the end of the Atlantic slave trade. What economic, social, and political consequences did this development have on sub-Saharan Africa?

6. **Compare** political and economic developments in the Atlantic world with those in regions elsewhere around the globe in the period 1750–1850.

7. **Explain** the relationship between industrialization and the "industrious revolution." Where did the industrial revolution begin? What other parts of the Atlantic world did it spread to during this time?

8. **Identify** and **explain** the key developments that constituted the industrial revolution. **Discuss** why some parts of Europe led the way.

9. **Explore** how industrialization altered the societies that began to industrialize during this time. What impact did this process have on the environment? How were gender roles and familial relationships altered?

10. **Analyze** how the two intertwined Atlantic revolutions (political and industrial) altered the global balance of power. How did the Russian, Mughal, Ottoman, and Qing dynasties respond to this change?

11. **Compare** the responses to European influence in Egypt under Muhammad Ali, in India under the rule of the East India Company, and in China during the Opium War.

12. **Describe** patterns of global trade and economic growth, and **connect** them to political changes during the period 1750–1850.

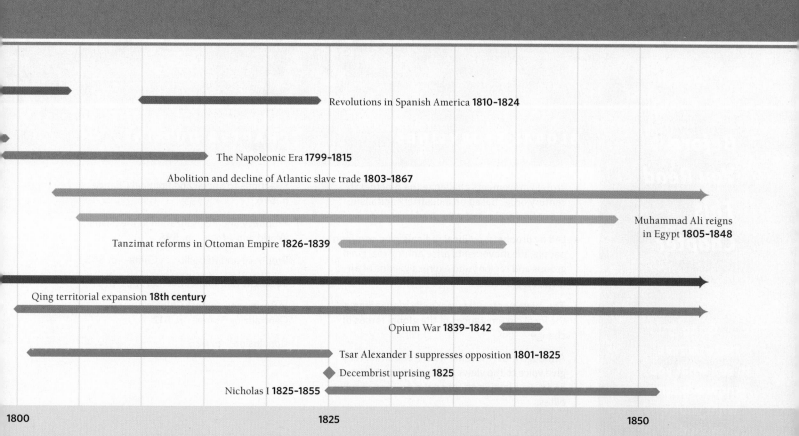

Revolutions in Spanish America **1810-1824**

The Napoleonic Era **1799-1815**

Abolition and decline of Atlantic slave trade **1803-1867**

Muhammad Ali reigns in Egypt **1805-1848**

Tanzimat reforms in Ottoman Empire **1826-1839**

Qing territorial expansion **18th century**

Opium War **1839-1842**

Tsar Alexander I suppresses opposition **1801-1825**

Decembrist uprising **1825**

Nicholas I **1825-1855**

1800   1825   1850

Before You Read This Chapter

Go to iNQuizitive to see what you know & learn what you've missed.

GLOBAL STORYLINES

- Protest movements challenge the nineteenth-century order based on industrial capitalism, the nation-state, and colonization.

- Led by prophets, political radicals, and common people, the movements arise among marginal groups and regions and express visions of an ideal, utopian future.

- The movements differ markedly, depending on the local circumstances of the global forces of change.

- Although most movements are defeated, they give voice to the views of peasants and workers and have a lasting effect on the policies of ruling elites.

CHAPTER OUTLINE

16

Alternative Visions of the Nineteenth Century

FOCUS QUESTIONS

- What alternative visions challenged the ideals of industrial capitalism, colonialism, and nation-states in this period?

- How similar were the utopian goals, immediate outcomes, and long-term influence of rebel movements around the world? How did they differ?

- How did an urge for social justice animate the alternative visions?

- What role did religion play in these alternative social visions?

B y the late nineteenth century, territorial expansion in the United States confined almost all Indians to reservations. The buffalo that once supported many tribes disappeared: white settlers built towns, farms, and railroads through the buffalo's natural habitat, and Native Americans overhunted the shrinking herds. Across the American West, many Indians fell into despair. One was a Paiute Indian named Wovoka. But in 1889, he had a vision of a much brighter future. In his dream, the "Supreme Being" told Wovoka that if Indians lived harmoniously, shunned white ways (especially alcohol), and performed the cleansing Ghost Dance, then the buffalo would return and Indians, including the dead, would be reborn to live in eternal happiness.

As word spread of Wovoka's vision, Indians from hundreds of miles around made pilgrimages to the lodge of this new prophet. Many proclaimed him the Indians' messiah or the "Red Man's Christ," an impression fostered by scars on his hands. Especially among the Shoshone, Arapaho, Cheyenne, and Sioux peoples of the northern Plains, Wovoka's message inspired new hope. Soon increasing numbers joined in the ritual Ghost Dance, hoping it would restore the good life that English colonialism in the Americas had extinguished. Among the hopefuls was

Sitting Bull, a revered Sioux chief who was himself famous for his visions. Yet, less than two years after Wovoka's vision, Sitting Bull died at the hands of police forces on a Sioux reservation. A few days later, on December 29, 1890, the U.S. Seventh Cavalry Regiment massacred Sioux Ghost Dancers at a South Dakota creek called Wounded Knee.

Though it failed, this movement was one of many prophetic crusades that challenged an emerging nineteenth-century order. The ideals of the French and American Revolutions, laissez-faire capitalism, the nation-state organization, new technologies, and industrial organizations now provided the dominant answers to age-old questions of who should govern and what beliefs should prevail. But these answers did not stamp out other views. A diverse assortment of political radicals, charismatic prophets, peasant rebels, and anticolonial insurgents put forward striking counterproposals to those that capitalists, colonial modernizers, and nation-state builders had developed. The people making these counterproposals were motivated by the impending loss of their existing worlds and were energized by visions of an ideal, utopian future.

This chapter attends to the voices and visions of those who opposed a nineteenth-century world in which capitalism, colonialism, and nation-states held sway. It puts the spotlight on challengers who shared a dislike of global capitalism and European (and North American) colonialism. Beyond that similarity, they differed in significant ways, for the alternatives they proposed reflected the local circumstances in which each of them developed. Although many of the leaders and movements they inspired suffered devastating defeats, like the Ghost Dancers at Wounded Knee, the dreams that aroused their fervor did not always die with them. Some of these alternative visions of the nineteenth century endured to propel the great transformations of the twentieth.

REACTIONS TO SOCIAL AND POLITICAL CHANGE

The transformations of the late eighteenth and early nineteenth centuries had upset polities and economies around the globe. In Europe, the tide of political and economic revolutions either swept aside or severely battered the old order. In North America, the newly independent United States began an expansion westward. Territorial growth led to the dispossession of hundreds of Indian tribes and the acquisition of nearly half of Mexico by conquest. In Latin America, fledgling nation-states that now replaced the Spanish Empire struggled to control their subject populations. And in Asia and Africa, rulers and common people alike confronted the growing might of western military and industrial power. At stake were issues of how to define and rule territories and what social and cultural visions they would embody.

The alternatives to the dominant trends varied considerably. Some rebels and dissidents called for the revitalization of traditional religions, and many reworked religious ideas in order to frame solutions to current social or political problems. Others wanted to strengthen village and communal bonds; still others imagined a society where there was no private property and where people shared goods equally. The actions of these dissenters depended on their local traditions and the degree of contact they had with the effects of industrial capitalism, European colonialism, and centralizing nation-states.

This era of rapid social change, when differing visions of power and justice vied with one another, offers unique opportunities to hear the voices of the lower orders—peasants, workers, women, religious minorities—whose perspectives the elites often ignored or suppressed and whose traditional historiography has been overlooked. While there are few written records that capture the views of the illiterate and the marginalized, we do have traditions of folklore, dreams, rumors, and prophecies. Handed down orally from generation to generation, these resources illuminate the visions of common folk.

The alternative visions that challenged the dominance of colonialism, capitalism, and nation-states differed markedly. In Europe and the Americas, the heartlands of industrial capitalism and the nation-state, radical thinkers dreamed of far-reaching changes. They sought nothing less than an end to private property and a socialist alternative to capitalism. In Africa, the Middle East, and China, regions not yet colonized by Europeans, dynamic religious prophets and charismatic military leaders emerged. Here, men (and sometimes women) revitalized traditional ways, rejuvenated destabilized communities, and reorganized societies in hopes of preventing the spread of unwelcome foreign ideas and institutions. Finally, in South Asia and the Americas, where indigenous groups had come under the domination of Europeans and peoples of European descent, rebellions targeted the authority of the state. Just as Wovoka inspired a revolt against the U.S. government, the Mayas similarly fought to defend their cultural and political autonomy against the power of the Mexican state. So, too, did Indian peasants and old elites join forces in a fierce revolt against their colonial masters in British India.

PROPHECY AND REVITALIZATION IN THE ISLAMIC WORLD AND AFRICA

By the end of the eighteenth century, the Islamic world and non-Islamic Africa had reached a crossroads. The Ottomans, Safavids, and Mughals had extended Muslim trading zones, facilitated cross-cultural communication, and promoted common knowledge over vast territories—but now their era of flowering had ended, and political and military declines had begun. Although much of this territory had not been colonized and was only partially involved with European-dominated trading networks, a sense of alarm intensified as Christian Europe's power spread. (See Current Trends in World History: Islam: An Enduring Alternative in Algeria.) In Egypt and the Ottoman Empire, leaders responded by attempting to modernize their states along European lines (see Chapter 15). Farther away from the main trade routes and political centers, however, this sense of alarm also bred religious revitalization movements that sought to recapture the glories of past traditions. Led by prophets who feared that Islam was in trouble, these movements spoke the language of revival and restoration as they sought to establish new religiously based governments across lands in which Muslims ruled and Islamic law prevailed.

Prophecy also exerted a strong influence in non-Islamic Africa, where long-distance trade and population growth were upending the social order. Just as Muslim clerics and political leaders sought solutions to unsettling changes by rereading Islamic classics, African communities looked to charismatic leaders who drew strength from their peoples' spiritual and magical traditions. Often uniting disparate groups behind their dynamic visions, prophetic leaders and other "big men" gained power because they were able to resolve local crises—mostly caused by drought, a shortage of arable land, or some other issue related to the harsh environment.

Islamic Revitalization

Movements to revitalize Islam took place on the peripheries—in areas that seemed immune from the potentially threatening repercussions of the world economy. Here, religious leaders rejected westernizing influences they felt were encroaching on their authority and way of life. (See Map 16.1.) Instead, revitalization movements looked back to Islamic traditions and modeled their revolts on the life of Muhammad. But even as they looked to the past, they attempted to establish something new: full-scale theocracies. These reformers conceived of the state as the primary instrument of God's will and as the vehicle for purifying Islamic culture.

WAHHABISM One of the most powerful reformist movements arose on the Arabian Peninsula, the birthplace of the Muslim faith. In the Najd region, an area surrounded by mountains and deserts, a religious cleric named Muhammad Ibn abd al-Wahhab (1703–1792) galvanized the population by attacking what he regarded as lax religious practices. His message found a ready response among local inhabitants, who felt threatened by the new commercial activities and fresh intellectual currents swirling around them. Abd al-Wahhab demanded a return to the pure Islam of Muhammad and the early caliphs.

Although Najd was far removed from the currents of the expanding world economy, abd al-Wahhab himself was not. Having been educated in Iraq, Iran, and the Hijaz (a region on the western end of modern Saudi Arabia, on the Red Sea), he was aware of the dramatic changes taking place around the world and feared that Islam was losing its vitality. No area seemed to have fallen into a more degraded and powerless state than its very birthplace, the Hijaz. Here, he railed against the polytheistic beliefs that had taken hold of the people, complaining that in defiance of Muhammad's tenets men and women were worshipping trees, stones, and tombs and making sacrifices to false images. Abd al-Wahhab's movement stressed the absolute oneness of Allah (hence his followers were called *Muwahhidin*, or Unitarians) and the need for Muslims to go back to what he considered the fundamental beliefs that had prevailed at the beginnings of Islam. He also severely criticized Sufi sects for extolling the lives of saints over the worship of God.

As **Wahhabism** swept across the Arabian Peninsula, the movement threatened the Ottomans' hold on the region. Wahhabism gained a powerful political ally in the Najdian House of Saud, a leading family whose followers, inspired by the Wahhabis' religious zeal, undertook a militant religious campaign. They sacked the Shiite shrines of Karbala in southern Iraq, and in 1803 they overran the holy cities of Mecca and Medina, damaging the tombs of the saints. Their assault on the Shiite sites reflected their commitment to Sunni Islam, while their destruction of the tombs of Sufi saints was an attack on the Sufi-inspired popular culture. It also stemmed from a belief that monuments to individuals whose beliefs were distant from the mainstream beliefs of Islam desecrated Islam's two holiest cities. Frightened by the Wahhabi challenge, the Ottoman sultan persuaded the provincial ruler of Egypt to send troops to the Arabian Peninsula to suppress the movement. The Egyptians defeated the Saudis in 1818, but Wahhabism and the House of Saud continued to represent a pure Islamic faith that attracted clerics and common folk throughout the Muslim world.

USMAN DAN FODIO AND THE FULANI In West Africa, Muslim revolts erupted from Senegal to Nigeria in the early nineteenth century, responding in part to increased trade with the outside world and the circulation of religious ideas from across the Sahara Desert. In this region, the Fulani people were decisive in religious uprisings that sought, like the Wahhabi movement, to re-create a supposedly purer Islamic past. The majority were cattle keepers, practicing a pastoral and nomadic way of life. But some were sedentary, living in settled communities, and people in this group converted to Islam, read the Islamic classics, and communicated with holy men of North Africa, Egypt, and the Arabian Peninsula. They concluded that West African peoples were violating Islamic beliefs and engaging in irreligious practices.

The most powerful of these reform movements flourished in what is today northern Nigeria. Its leader was a Fulani Muslim cleric, **Usman dan Fodio** (1754–1817), who ultimately created a vast Islamic empire. Dan Fodio's movement had all the trappings of the Islamic revolts of this period. It sought inspiration in the

Islam: An Enduring Alternative in Algeria

Many of the alternative movements featured in this chapter derived their impetus from deeply held religious beliefs. Religion played a role in the Indian mutiny and in the visions that spurred the Taiping rebels. In Muslim locations far from the main currents of western influence, like the Arabian Peninsula and northern Nigeria, it generated revivalist movements. But elsewhere it became a political force, and one that developed a palpably anti-European nature as well as the power to endure long beyond the victory of European invaders. World historians like to study political and social movements like these because they bring into relief the relationship between the colonizer and the colonized and, in the case of these alternative movements, the relationship between peoples living on the peripheries of empires and those living in the center who are part of the ruling elite, including indigenous elites.

This was the case in particular along the old Ottoman periphery, one of the major targets for European colonization. Strikingly, in the first decades of the nineteenth century, in the Ottomans' Balkan domains of Serbia and Greece, Christianity had linked together opponents against the empire. In the decades to follow, as Ottoman power receded, it left behind it Islamic groups who also used religion as the glue that bound together otherwise diverse peoples. The following example highlights the importance of Islam in galvanizing resistance to French imperialism in Algeria. But it would also be possible to cite examples from the Caucasus Mountains, another Ottoman periphery, where Islam linked together Chechen and other groups in opposition to Russian colonization in the 1840s and 1850s; and in the early twentieth century, Libyans attempted to oppose Italian colonization by rallying behind the green flag of the prophet. Unquestionably, the more Europeans sought to dominate lands inhabited by Muslims, the more they called forth in reaction Islamic alternatives and politicized forms of Islamic resistance.

In 1830, through a series of mishaps and miscalculations, the French found themselves in possession of the Regency of Algiers, a territory of 60,000 square miles where previously 10,000 Ottoman Turks had ruled over 3 million Arab and Berber tribespeople. The French invasion had been an ill-considered adventure, designed to divert attention from the fact that the backward-looking French king, Charles X, had lost his legitimacy at home. In 1830, Charles was toppled by the so-called July Revolution, but his successor, King Louis Philippe (r. 1830–1848), decided to pursue France's adventure abroad. This was a risky and in the long run costly plan, however, as the French controlled only a few coastal enclaves and the capital city of Algiers; in 1831, the European civilian population was a mere 3,228. Moreover, although the French had driven out the Turks, they had emboldened Arab tribes in the western part of the land to found their own independent state.

In seeking a leader to unite them, the Arab tribes turned to Abd al-Qadir (1807–1883), a charismatic and domineering personality, although he was only twenty-five years old. His father, head of the most important Sufi brotherhood in Algeria, had groomed his son to be a leader and taught him to despise the Ottoman overlords. Abd al-Qadir and his followers had already committed themselves to overthrowing the Ottomans; but once the French arrived, they were even more determined to rid the area of invaders they regarded as infidels who were intent on seizing their lands and imposing their way of life on them. In organizing resistance to the French, it mattered

life of Muhammad and demanded a return to early Islamic practices. It attacked false belief and heathenism and urged followers to wage holy war (*jihad*) against nonbelievers. Usman dan Fodio's adversaries were the old Hausa rulers (city-states that emerged between 1000 and 1200), who, in his view, were not sufficiently faithful to Islamic beliefs and practices. So dan Fodio withdrew from his original habitation in Konni and established a new community of believers at Gudu, citing the ancient precedent of Muhammad's withdrawal from Mecca to establish a community of true believers at Medina (see Chapter 9). The practice of withdrawal, called *hijra* in Muhammad's time, was yet another of the prophet's inspirations that religious reformers now invoked.

Dan Fodio was a member of the Qadiriyya, one of many Sufi brotherhoods that had helped spread Islam into West Africa. Sufism, the mystical and popular form of Islam, sought an emotional connection with God through a strict regimen of prayers, fasting, and religious exercises to obtain mystical states. Like Wovoka and Sitting Bull in North America, dan Fodio had visions that led him to challenge the West African ruling classes. In one vision, the founder of the Qadiriyya order instructed him to unsheathe the sword of truth against the enemies of Islam.

Dan Fodio blamed local leaders for what he saw as their failure to respect Islamic law. He won the support of devout Muslims in the area, who agreed that the people were not properly practicing Islam. He also gained the backing of his Fulani tribes and many of the Hausa peasantry, who had suffered under the rule of the Hausa landlord class. The revolt, initiated in 1804, resulted in the overthrow of the Hausa rulers and

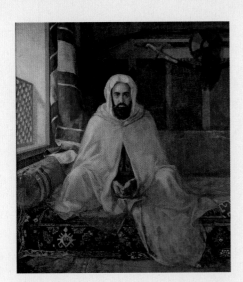

Abd al-Qadir. *Polish artist Stanislaw Chlebowski painted Abd al-Qadir in 1866 during his exile in Constantinople.*

greatly that Abd al-Qadir was also known as a holy man and a scholar, rather than as merely the head of one of the tribes. In preparation for battle, he called on his soldiers to follow him in a holy war (*jihad*) against Christian invaders, promising those who joined him in battle that "anyone of you who dies, will die a martyr; those of you who survive will gain glory and live happily." Tribes that might not have fought together, or fought together so long, did so because they were united by their loyalty to a religious as well as political leader. Abd al-Qadir succeeded in part because he was a forceful personality, but in part, too, because he stood for Islam, a powerful faith that the native Algerians shared, whatever their kinship ties or their loyalties to local leaders.

For fifteen years, Abd al-Qadir's forces held out, only surrendering to a massive French force of 108,000 men in 1847. Although often defeated in pitched battles, Abd al-Qadir used his superior knowledge of the terrain and his ability to wait in ambush for French columns to frustrate the French. The French government was finally compelled to send its most accomplished military man, Thomas-Robert Bugeaud, marshal of France, and to provide him with one-third of its entire military force to finish the job of "pacifying" Algeria.

France's conquest of Algeria marks one of the bloodiest episodes in the history of those two lands. No fewer than 300,000 Algerians perished during these years. Although the French portrayed Abd al-Qadir as a Muslim fanatic, determined to take his people back to a dark age, their message fell on deaf ears. The Algerians extolled him for resisting the French and later made him an iconic figure of the nationalist movement. One of the first acts carried out by the independent Algerian government in 1962 was to tear down the statue of Marshal Bugeaud and replace it with one of Abd al-Qadir. The religiously motivated resistance leader had prevailed over the secular political conquerors after all.

QUESTIONS FOR ANALYSIS

- What impact did Algeria's geographical location have in determining its role in these revolutionary events?
- How did the native Algerians view their former Ottoman rulers compared with the French Europeans? What was the Algerians' ultimate goal?

Explore Further

Clancy-Smith, Julia. *Rebel and Saint: Muslim Notables, Populist Protest, Colonial Encounter (Algeria and Tunisia, 1800–1904)* (1994).

Danziger, Raphael. *Abd al-Qadir: Resistance to the French and Internal Consolidation* (1977).

Ruedy, John. *Modern Algeria: The Origins and Development of a Nation* (2005).

the creation of a confederation of Islamic emirates, almost all of which were in the hands of the Fulani allies of dan Fodio.

Fulani women of northern Nigeria made critical contributions to the success of the religious revolt. Although dan Fodio and other male leaders of the purification movement expected women to obey the *sharia* (Islamic law), being modest in their dress and their association with men outside the family, they also expected women to support the community's military and religious endeavors. In this effort, they cited women's important role in the first days of Islam. The best known of the Muslim women leaders was Nana Asma'u (1793–1864), daughter of dan Fodio. Fulani women of the upper ranks acquired an Islamic education, and Asma'u was as astute a reader of Islamic texts as any of the learned men in her society. Like other Muslim Fulani devotees, she accompanied the warriors on their campaigns, encamped with them, prepared food for them, bound up their wounds, and provided daily encouragement. According to many accounts, Asma'u inspired the warriors at their most crucial battle, hurling a burning spear into the midst of the enemy army. Her poem "Song of the Circular Journey" celebrates the triumphs of military forces that trekked thousands of miles to bring a reformed Islam to the area. (For another poem by Asma'u, see Primary Source: A Female Muslim Voice in Africa.)

Usman dan Fodio considered himself a cleric first and a political and military man second. Although his political leadership was decisive in the revolt's success, thereafter he retired to a life of scholarship and writing. He delegated the political and administrative functions of the new empire to his brother

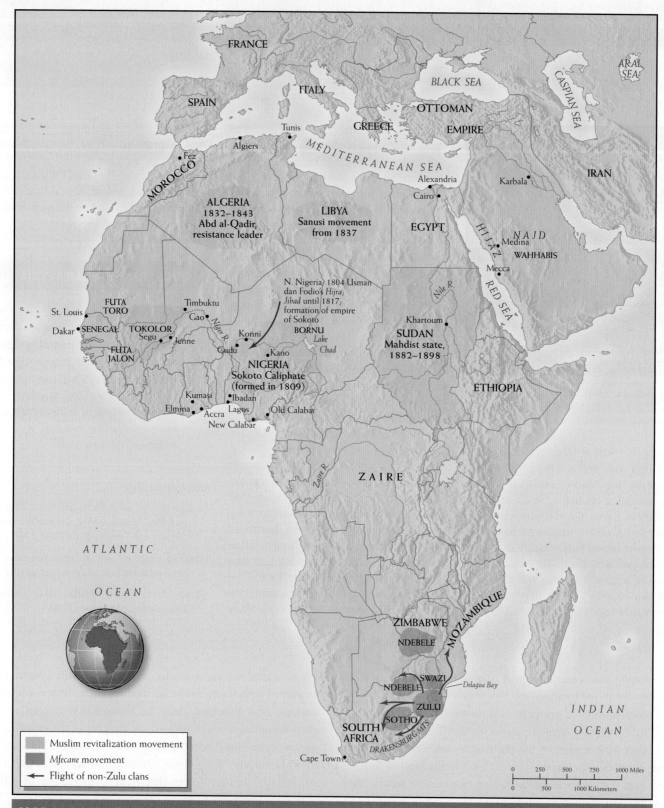

MAP 16.1 | Muslim Revitalization Movements in the Middle East and Africa, and the *Mfecane* Movement in Southern Africa

During the nineteenth century, a series of Muslim revitalization movements took place throughout the Middle East and North Africa.

- According to this map, in how many different areas did the revitalization movements occur?
- Based on their geographical locations within their larger regions, did these movements occur in central or peripheral areas?
- Based on your reading, were any of the same factors that led to Islamic revitalization involved in the *Mfecane* developments in southern Africa?

and his son. An enduring decentralized state structure, which became known as the Sokoto caliphate in 1809, developed into a stable empire that helped spread Islam through the region. A century later, the faith of a small minority of people living in northern Nigeria had become the religion of the vast majority.

Charismatic Military Men in Non-Islamic Africa

Non-Islamic Africa saw revolts, new states, and prophetic movements arise from the same combination of factors that influenced the rest of the world—particularly long-distance trade and population increase. Local communities here also looked to religious traditions and, as was so often the case in African history, expected charismatic clan leaders, known as "big men," to provide political leadership.

In southern Africa, early in the nineteenth century, a group of political revolts reordered the political map. Collectively known as the **Mfecane** ("the crushing" in Zulu) **movement**, its epicenter was a large tract of land lying east of the Drakensberg Mountains, an area where growing populations and land resources existed in a precarious balance (see again Map 16.1). Compounding this pressure, trade with the Portuguese in

Mozambique and with other Europeans at Delagoa Bay and the arrival of British colonists contesting both the earlier Dutch settlers and indigenous African communities disrupted the traditional social order. This set the stage for a political crisis for the northern Nguni (Bantu-speaking) peoples.

Many branches of Bantu-speaking peoples had inhabited the southern part of the African landmass for centuries. At the end of the eighteenth century, however, their political organizations still operated on a small scale, revolving around families and clans and modest chieftaincies. These tiny polities could not cope with the overpopulation and competition for land that now dominated southern Africa. A branch of the Nguni, the Zulus, produced a fierce war leader, Shaka (1787–1828), who created a ruthless warrior state. It drove other populations out of the region and forced a shift from small clan communities to large, centralized monarchies throughout southern and central Africa.

Shaka was the son of a minor chief who emerged victorious in the struggle for cattle-grazing and farming lands that arose during a severe drought. A muscular and physically imposing figure, Shaka was also a violent man who used terror to intimidate his subjects and to overawe his adversaries. His enemies knew that the price of opposition would be a massacre, even of women and children. Nor was he much kinder to his own people. Following the death of his beloved mother, for example, Shaka executed

Shaka and His Zulu Regiments. Left: *Though he is renowned for his reforms and infamous for his brutality, the only existing image of Shaka is this engraving by English trader Henry Francis Fynn, the first white settler in Natal, a British colony near the Zulu kingdom. Nonetheless, Shaka's awesome presence and strength is as obvious to modern viewers as it would have been to his young warriors, who were deeply loyal to him and superbly trained.* Right: *Shown here is a Zulu regimental camp; warrior huts were arranged in a circular pattern to surround a courtyard, where the warriors did their drills and practiced close combat.*

PRIMARY SOURCE

A Female Muslim Voice in Africa

The Islamic scholar, writer, and poet Nana Asma'u was the daughter of Usman dan Fodio, the leader of the Fulani revolt in northern Nigeria at the turn of the nineteenth century. Many of her poems conveyed religious inspiration and sought to demonstrate how much her father's revolt was inspired by the life and message of the Prophet Muhammad. She was also deeply attached to her brother, Muhammad Bello, who succeeded their father as head of the Sokoto caliphate. Muhammad Bello looked to his sister to promote traditional Muslim values among the female population in his empire, and she worked to extend education to rural women. Following is an elegy, written in poetic form, that Nana Asma'u composed in praise of her brother, underlining his commitment to an Islamic way of life.

I give thanks to the King of Heaven, the One God. I invoke blessings on the Prophet and set down my poem.

The Lord made Heaven and earth and created all things, sent prophets to enlighten mankind.

Believe in them for your own sake, learn from them and be saved, believe in and act upon their sayings.

I invoke blessings on the Prophet who brought the Book, the Qur'an: he brought the *hadith* to complete the enlightenment.

Muslim scholars have explained knowledge and used it, following in the footsteps of the Prophet.

It is my intention to set down Bello's characteristics and explain his ways.

For I wish to assuage my loneliness, requite my love, find peace of mind through my religion.

These are his characteristics: he was learned in all branches of knowledge and feared God in public and in private.

He obeyed religious injunctions and distanced himself from forbidden things: this is what is known about him.

He concentrated on understanding what is right to know about the Oneness of God.

He preached to people and instructed them about God: he caused them to long for Paradise.

He set an example in his focus on eternal values: he strove to end oppression and sin.

He upheld the *shari'a,* honored it, implemented it aright, that was his way, everyone knows.

And he made his views known to those who visited him: he said to them "Follow the *shari'a,* which is sacred."

He eschewed worldly things and discriminated against anything of ill repute; he was modest and a repository of useful knowledge.

He was exceedingly level-headed and generous, he enjoyed periods of quietude: but was energetic when he put his hand to things.

He was thoughtful, calm, a confident statesman, and quick-witted.

He honored people's status: he could sort out difficulties and advise those who sought his help.

those who were not properly contrite and did not weep profusely. Reportedly, it took 7,000 lives to assuage his grief.

Shaka built a new state around his own military and organizational skills and the fear that his personal ferocity produced. He drilled his men relentlessly in the use of short stabbing spears and in discipline under pressure. Like the Mongols, he had a remarkable ability to incorporate defeated communities into the state and to absorb young men into his ultradedicated warrior forces. His army of 40,000 men comprised regiments that lived, studied, and fought together. Forbidden from marrying until they were discharged from the army, Shaka's warriors developed an intense esprit de corps and regarded no sacrifice too great in the service of the state. So overpowering were these forces that other peoples of the region fled from their home areas, and Shaka claimed their estates for himself and his followers.

Thus did the Zulus under Shaka create a ruthless warrior state that conquered much territory in southern and central Africa, assimilating some peoples and forcing others to fashion their own similarly centralized polities. Shaka's defeated foes adopted many of the Zulu state's military innovations. They did so first to defend themselves and then to take over new land as they fled their old areas. The new states of the Ndebele in what later became Zimbabwe and of the Sotho of South Africa came into existence in the mid-nineteenth century in this way and proved long-lasting.

In turning southern Africa from a region of smaller polities into an area with larger and more powerful ones, Shaka seemed very much a man of the modern, nineteenth-century world. Yet he was, in his own unique way, a familiar kind of African leader, for he shared a charismatic and prophetic style with others who emerged during periods of acute social change. He was, in this sense, one of many big men to seek dominance. His new state built an enduring Zulu community and established its traditions against encroachments by outside, European forces.

He had nothing to do with worldly concerns, but tried to restore to a healthy state things which he could. These were his characteristics.

He never broke promises, but faithfully kept them: he sought out righteous things. Ask and you will hear.

He divorced himself entirely from bribery and was totally scrupulous: He flung back at the givers money offered for titles.

One day Garange [chief of Mafora] sent him a splendid gift, but Bello told the messenger Zitaro to take it back.

He said to the envoy who had brought the bribe, "Have nothing to do with forbidden things."

And furthermore he said, "Tell him that the gift was sent for unlawful purposes; it is wrong to respond to evil intent."

He was able to expedite matters: he facilitated learning, commerce, and defense, and encouraged everything good.

He propagated good relationships between different tribes and between kinsmen. He afforded protection; every-one knows this.

When strangers came he met them, and taught about religious matters, explaining things: he tried to enlighten them.

He lived in a state of preparedness, he had his affairs in order and had an excellent intelligence service.

He had nothing to do with double agents and said it was better to ignore them, for they pervert Islamic principles.

He was a very pleasant companion to friends and acquaintances: he was intelligent, with a lively mind.

He fulfilled promises and took care of affairs, but he did not act hastily.

He shouldered responsibilities and patiently endured adversities.

He was watchful and capable of restoring to good order matters which had gone wrong.

He was resourceful and could undo mischief, no matter how serious, because he was a man of ideas.

He was gracious to important people and was hospitable to all visitors, including non-Muslims.

He drew good people close to him and distanced himself from people of ill repute.

Those are his characteristics. I have recounted a few examples that are sufficient to provide a model for emulation and benefit.

May God forgive him and have mercy on him: May we be united with him in Paradise, the place we aspire to.

For the sake of the Prophet, the Compassionate, who was sent with mercy to mankind.

May God pour blessings on the Prophet and his kinsmen and all other followers.

May God accept this poem. I have concluded it in the year 1254 AH [after *hijra*, the Muslim dating system, equivalent to 1838 CE].

QUESTIONS FOR ANALYSIS

- In what ways does this description convey a sense of proper Muslim values?
- Identify at least ten ways in which Bello was exemplary, according to this poem.
- Why would Nana Asma'u feel compelled to write a poem in praise of her brother?

Source: Beverly B. Mack and Jean Boyd, *One Woman's Jihad: Nana Asma'u, Scholar and Scribe* (Bloomington: Indiana University Press, 2000) pp. 97–99.

PROPHECY AND REBELLION IN CHINA

In the mid-nineteenth century, China witnessed an explosive popular rebellion that incorporated Christian beliefs into its long tradition of peasant revolts. Even before 1842, European opium traders had conducted a brisk trade with the Chinese through Canton, the only port open to western commerce. After the Opium War, however, westerners forced Qing rulers to open up a number of other ports to trade. To be sure, the dynasty retained authority over almost the whole realm, and western influence remained confined to a small minority of merchants and missionaries. Nevertheless, foreign gunboats and extraterritorial rights reminded the Chinese of the looming power of the west.

As in the Islamic world and other parts of sub-Saharan Africa, population increases in China—from 250 million in 1644 to around 450 million by the 1850s—were putting considerable pressure on land and other resources. Moreover, the rising consumption of opium, grown in India and brought to China by English traders, was producing further social instability and financial crisis. As banditry and rebellions spread, the Qing dynasty turned to the gentry to maintain order in the countryside. But as the gentry raised its militia to suppress these troublemakers, it whittled away at the authority of the Qing Manchu rulers.

Searching for an alternative present and future, beginning in 1850 hundreds of thousands of disillusioned peasants joined what became known as the Taiping Rebellion. It put Qing China in a state of civil war for over a decade, costing some 20 to 30 million lives. The uprising drew on China's long history of peasant revolts. Traditionally, these rebellions ignited within popular religious sects whose visions were egalitarian or **millenarian** (convinced of the imminent coming of a just and ideal society). Moreover, in contrast to orthodox institutions, here women played important roles. Inspired by Daoists, who revered a past golden age before the world was corrupted by human conventions, or by Buddhist sources, these sects threatened the established order. In times of political breakdown, millenarian sects could transform local revolts into large-scale rebellions. Yet, the Christian influence on the Taiping and the fact that the rebellion was eventually defeated with the help of the British was a testament to the new global context. Qing China and the United States were the two largest international markets for the British. With the U.S. market lost to its civil war, the British felt compelled to intervene in China to protect its interests.

The Dream of Hong Xiuquan

The story of the rebellion begins with a complex dream that inspired its founding prophet, Hong Xiuquan (1813–1864). A native of Guangdong Province in the southernmost part of the country (see Map 16.2), Hong first encountered Christian missionaries in the 1830s. He was then trying, unsuccessfully, to pass the civil service examination, which would have won him entry into the elite and a potential career in the Qing bureaucracy. Disappointed by his poor showing, Hong began to have visions, including a dream in 1837 that led him to form the Society of God Worshippers and the Taiping Heavenly Kingdom.

In this dream, a ceremonial retinue of heavenly guards escorted Hong to heaven. The group included a cock-like figure that he later identified as Leigong, the Duke of Thunder, a familiar figure in Chinese mythology. When Hong reached heaven, his belly was slit open and his internal organs were replaced with new ones. As the operation for his renewal was completed, heavenly texts were unrolled for him to read. The "Heavenly Mother" then met and thoroughly cleansed him. She addressed him as "Son" before bringing him in front of the "Old Father." Although not part of the heavenly bureaucracy, Confucius and women generals from the Song dynasty were also present. Upon meeting Hong,

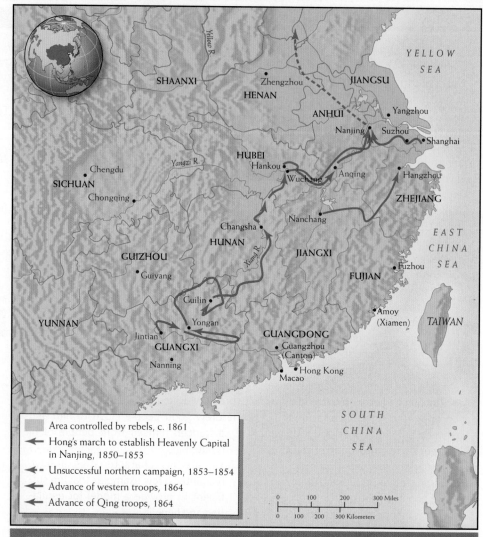

MAP 16.2 | The Taiping Rebellion in China, 1851–1864

Note that the Taiping Rebellion started in the southwestern part of the country. The rebels, however, went on to control much of the Lower Yangzi region and part of the coastal area.

- In which cities did the rebels' march start and end?
- Why do you think the Taiping rebels were so successful in southern China and not in northern regions?
- How did western powers react to the Taiping Rebellion?
- Would they have been as concerned if the rebellion took place farther to the north or west?

the "Old Father" complained that human beings had been led astray by demons, as demonstrated by the vanity of their shaven heads (a practice the Manchu Qing regime imposed), their consumption of opium, and other forms of debauchery. The "Old Father" even denounced Confucius, who, after being flogged and begging for mercy before Hong's heavenly "Elder Brother," was allowed to stay in heaven but forbidden to teach again. Still, the world was not yet free of demons. So the "Old Father" instructed Hong to leave his heavenly family behind and return to earth to rescue human beings from demons.

The Port of Canton. *Before the Opium Wars, the Canton (now Guangzhou) was the only Chinese port open to western traders. This image depicts the "factories" or trading stations operated by a number of different countries, including Denmark, Great Britain, Sweden, the United States, and the Netherlands.*

How much of this account has been embellished with hindsight scholars will probably never know. What we do know is that Hong, after failing the civil service exam for the third time, suffered a strange "illness" in which he had visions of combating demons. He also began proclaiming himself the Heavenly King. Relatives and neighbors thought he might have gone mad, but Hong gradually returned to his normal state. In 1843, after failing the exam for the fourth time, Hong immersed himself in a Christian tract entitled *Good Words for Exhorting the Age.* Reportedly, reading this tract enabled Hong to realize the full significance of his earlier dream. All the pieces suddenly fell into place. The "Old Father," he concluded, was the Lord Ye-huo-hua (a Chinese rendering of "Jehovah"), the creator of heaven and earth. Accordingly, the cleansing ritual foretold Hong's baptism. The "Elder Brother" was Jesus the Savior, the son of God. He, Hong Xiuquan, was the younger brother of Jesus—God's other son. Just as God had previously sent Jesus to save mankind, Hong thought that God was now sending *him* to rid the world of evil. What was once a dream was now a prophetic vision.

The Rebellion

Unlike earlier sectarian leaders whose plots for rebellion were secret before exploding onto the public arena, Hong chose a more audacious path. Once convinced of his vision, he began to preach his doctrines openly, baptizing converts and destroying Confucian idols and ancestral shrines. Such assaults on the establishment testified to his conviction that he was carrying out God's will. Hong's message of revitalization of a troubled land and restoration of the "heavenly kingdom," imagined as a just and egalitarian order, appealed to the subordinate classes caught in the flux of social change. Drawing on a largely rural social base and asserting allegiance to Christianity, the **Taiping** ("Great Peace") **Rebellion** of 1850–1864 claimed to herald a new era of economic and social justice.

Many early followers came from the margins of local society—those whose anger at social and economic dislocations caused by the Opium War was directed not at the Europeans, but at the Qing government. The Taiping identified the ruling Manchus as the "demons" and as the chief obstacle to realizing God's kingdom on earth. Taiping policies were strict: they prohibited the consumption of alcohol, the smoking of opium, or any indulgence in sensual pleasure. Men and women were segregated for administrative and residential purposes. (See Primary Source: The Taiping on the Principles of the Heavenly Nature.) At the same time, in a drastic departure from dynastic practice, women joined the army in segregated units. These female military units mostly comprised Hakka women. Hakka is an ethnic subgroup within the Han (to which Hong Xiuquan, the founder of the Taiping, belonged) with a distinct identity. An important part of their culture was that Hakka women did not bind their feet.

The Taiping on the Principles of the Heavenly Nature

In this excerpt from 1854, the Taiping leaders envision a radically new community based on values that challenge those of conventional Chinese society. Inspired by their understanding of Christianity, the Taiping leadership confronted the central role of the family and ancestral worship in Chinese society by urging all its followers to regard themselves as belonging to a single family. It also advocated the segregation of the sexes, despite striving to improve women's lives in some of its other policy proclamations.

We brothers and sisters, enjoying today the greatest mercy of our Heavenly Father, have become as one family and are able to enjoy true blessings; each of us must always be thankful. Speaking in terms of our ordinary human feelings, it is true that each has his own parents and there must be a distinction in family names; it is also true that as each has his own household, there must be a distinction between this boundary and that boundary.

Yet we must know that the ten thousand names derive from the one name, and the one name from one ancestor. Thus our origins are not different. Since our Heavenly Father gave us birth and nourishment, we are of one form though of separate bodies, and we breathe the same air though in different places. This is why we say, "All are brothers within the four seas." Now, basking in the profound mercy of Heaven, we are of one family. . . .

We brothers, our minds having been awakened by our Heavenly Father, joined the camp in the earlier days to support our Sovereign, many bringing parents, wives, uncles, brothers, and whole families. It is a matter of course that we should attend to our parents and look after our wives and children, but when one first creates a new rule, the state must come first and the family last, public interests first and private interests last.

Moreover, as it is advisable to avoid suspicion [of improper conduct] between the inner [female] and the outer [male] and to distinguish between male and female, so men must have male quarters and women must have female quarters; only thus can we be dignified and avoid confusion. There must be no common mixing of the male and female groups, which would cause debauchery and

violation of Heaven's commandments. Although to pay respects to parents and to visit wives and children occasionally are in keeping with human nature and not prohibited, yet it is only proper to converse before the door, stand a few steps apart and speak in a loud voice; one must not enter the sisters' camp or permit the mixing of men and women. Only thus, by complying with rules and commands, can we become sons and daughters of Heaven.

QUESTIONS FOR ANALYSIS

- What reasons do the Taiping leaders give for telling their followers "we are of one family"?
- Why do they insist that men and women have separate quarters?

Source: "The Principles of the Heavenly Nature," in *Sources of Chinese Tradition*, 2nd ed., Vol. 2, compiled by W. Theodore de Bary and Richard Lufrano (New York: Columbia University Press, 2000), pp. 229–230.

There were further challenges to established social and cultural norms. For example, women could serve in the Taiping bureaucracy. Also, examinations now focused on a translated version of the Bible and assorted religious and literary compositions by Hong. Finally, all land was to be divided among the families according to family size, with men and women receiving equal shares. Once each family met its own needs for sustenance, the communities would share the remaining surplus. These were all radical departures from Chinese traditions. But the Taiping opposition to the Manchus did not involve the formation of a modern nation-state. The rebellion remained caught between the modern and the traditional.

By 1850, Hong's movement had amassed a following of over 20,000, giving Qing rulers cause for concern. When they sent

troops to arrest Hong and other rebel leaders, Taiping forces repelled them and then took their turmoil beyond the southwestern part of the country. In 1851, Hong declared himself Heavenly King of the "Taiping Heavenly Kingdom" (or "Heavenly Kingdom of Great Peace"). By 1853, the rebels had captured major cities. Upon capturing Nanjing, the Taiping cleansed the city of "demons" by systematically killing all the Manchus they could find—men, women, and children. Then they established their own "heavenly" capital in the city.

But the rebels could not sustain their vision. Several factors contributed to the fall of the Heavenly Kingdom: struggles within the leadership, excessively rigid codes of conduct, and the rallying of Manchu and Han elites around the embattled dynasty. Disturbed by the Taiping's repudiation of Confucianism and

Taiping Rebellion. *The tens of thousands who had joined the "Heavenly King" became such a formidable force that they swiftly conquered and settled in many of the cities they encountered. Depicted in this mid-nineteenth-century painting are imperial Chinese troops driving the Taiping rebels from their stronghold in Tientsin.*

wanting to protect their property, landowning gentry led militias against the Taiping. Moreover, western governments also opposed the rebellion, claiming that its doctrines represented a perversion of Christianity. Thus did army units led by foreign officers take part in suppressing the rebellion. Hong himself perished as his heavenly capital fell in 1864. With the Qing victory imminent, few of the perhaps 100,000 rebels in Nanjing surrendered. Their slaughter prepared the stage for a determined attempt by imperial bureaucrats and elite intellectuals to rejuvenate the Qing state. Although the Taiping's millenarian vision vanished, the desire to reconstitute Chinese society and government did not. The rebellion, in that sense, continued to inspire reformers as well as future peasant uprisings.

Like their counterparts in the Islamic world and Africa, the Taiping rebels promised to restore lost harmony. Despite all the differences of cultural and historical background, what Abd al-Wahhab, dan Fodio, Shaka, and Hong had in common was the perception that the present world was unjust. Thus, they sought to reorganize their communities—an endeavor that involved confronting established authorities. In this regard, the language of revitalization used by prophets in Islamic areas and China was crucial, for it provided an alternative vocabulary of political and spiritual legitimacy. Although in non-Islamic Africa the impulse was not religious revitalization, it still was an appeal to tradition—to communal solidarity and to the familiar role of "big men" in stateless societies. By mobilizing masses eager to return to an imagined golden age, these prophets and charismatic leaders gave voice to those dispossessed by global change, while producing new, alternative ways of organizing society and politics.

SOCIALISTS AND RADICALS IN EUROPE

Europe and North America were the core areas of capitalist activity, nation-state building, and colonialism. But there, too, the main currents of thought and activity faced challenges. Prophets of all stripes—political, social, cultural, and religious—voiced antiestablishment values and dreamed of alternative arrangements. Radicals, liberals, utopian socialists, nationalists, abolitionists, and religious mavericks made plans for better worlds to come. They did so in the face of a new era dominated by conservative monarchies. This conservatism was pervasive in central Europe, where reestablished kings and aristocrats revived most of their former power and privileges. (See Map 16.3.) Restoration of the old regimes had occurred at the Congress of Vienna in 1815, at the end of the French Revolution and Napoleon's conquests (see Chapter 15). However, opposition to this arrangement was widespread, and radical voices confidently predicted the coming of a new day.

Congress of Vienna. *At the Congress of Vienna in 1815, the Austrian prime minister Clemens von Metternich took the lead in drafting a peace settlement that would balance power among the states of Europe.*

Legend:
- German Confederation
- ✳ Revolutionary activity

Foreign intervention to put down revolutions
- ← Austrian
- ← British
- ← Egyptian
- ← French
- ← Russian

MAP 16.3 | Civil Unrest and Revolutions in Europe, 1819–1848

Civil unrest and revolutions swept Europe after the Congress of Vienna established a peace settlement at the end of the French Revolution and Napoleon's conquests. Conservative governments had to fight off liberal rebellions and demands for change.

- How many sites of revolutionary activity can you locate on this map?
- What parts of Europe appear to have been politically stable and what parts rebellious?
- Drawing on what you have read in this chapter, can you explain the stability of some parts of Europe and the instability of others?

Restoration and Resistance

The social and political ferment of the efforts to restore the old order, known as the Restoration period (1815–1848), owed a great deal to the ambiguous legacies of the French Revolution and the Napoleonic Wars. Kings had been toppled and replaced by republics and then by Napoleon and his relatives; these breaks in traditional forms of rule meant that Restoration-era

states had political options to choose from. Most returned to monarchy, leaving, however, many of their citizens deeply dissatisfied and eager for reform of some kind. **Radicalism**—the conviction that real change was only possible by going to the root (in Latin, *radix*) of the problem—spread. We can identify several key groups of radicals in this period, including surviving Jacobins (see Chapter 15), convinced that the Revolution had not gone far enough and devoted to restoring republican governments, even if violent action had to be taken. Other radicals had become champions of nationalism in places where empires or princely city-states still dominated, such as the Metternich German Confederation and Italy. Yet another group of radicals looked farther back in time for inspiration, to sixteenth- and seventeenth-century religious radicals such as English Puritans and German Anabaptists, who had wanted to sweep away sinful communities and remake society from the ground up. Dubbed "utopian socialists," this group combined older religious fundamentalism with an attack on the evils of the new industrialism; but they hoped that by peacefully consenting to a reorganization of the workplace and the home, all of humankind could enjoy happiness on the earth.

But the radicals were by no means the only Europeans dissatisfied with the Restoration and eager to revive earlier ideas and models to effect change. The moderate reformers known as liberals did not wish to completely overthrow or overhaul Restoration regimes, but rather to work within them to establish a greater measure of liberty and equality. Liberals wanted their states to carry through the legal and political reforms envisioned in 1789—but not to attempt economic leveling in the manner of the radical Jacobins. Liberals were eager to curb the states' restrictions on trade, destroy the church's stranglehold on education, and give more people the right to vote—all the while preserving the free market, the Christian churches, and the rule of law. Proponents of **liberalism** insisted on equality under the law and on the individual's right to think, speak, act, and vote as he or she pleased, so long as no harm came to people or property. Liberals feared that powerful states would become corrupt or tyrannical and held that the proper role of government was to foster civil liberties and promote legal equality. Many of them also became proponents of nationalism over and against the reinstated privileges of the monarchies.

Self-conscious "reactionaries" also emerged at this time. Their crusade was not just to restore privileges to kings and nobles but also to reverse the religious and democratizing concessions that sovereigns had made during the revolutionary and Napoleonic periods. In Russia, for example, the Slavophiles touted what they regarded as "native" traditions and institutions against the excessively "westernizing" reforms introduced by Peter the Great and continued by his self-styled "enlightened despot" successors. Many Slavophiles were ardent monarchists. Their desire for a strong yet "traditional" Russia brought them into conflict with the conservative but modernizing tsarist state.

In sum, the reactionaries wanted a return to the traditionally ordered societies that existed prior to the French Revolution; the liberals wanted reforms that would limit the power of government and the church and promote the rights of individuals and free trade. For the most part, the reactionaries got their way in eastern, central, and southern Europe; but in Britain, France, and the Low Countries, liberals had greater sway. But neither group dominated fully, and the rivalry between these two groups continued to define the political landscape until at least the 1840s.

Radical Visions

What did it really mean to be a "radical" in the Restoration era? *Radicals* were men and women who favored the total reconfiguration of the old regime's state system: going to the root of the problem and continuing the revolution, not reversing it or stopping reform. In general, radicals shared a bitter hatred for the status quo and an insistence on popular sovereignty, but beyond this consensus there was much dissension in their ranks. If some radicals demanded the equalization or abolition of private property, others (like Serbian, Greek, Polish, and Italian nationalists) were primarily interested in throwing off the oppressive overlordship of the Ottoman, Russian, and Austrian Empires and creating their own nation-states. It was the radicals' threat of a return to revolution that ultimately reconciled both liberals and reactionaries to preserving the status quo.

NATIONALISTS In the period before 1848, nationalism was a cause dear to liberals and radicals and threatening to the conservative balance of power introduced into Europe at the Congress of Vienna in 1815. The age of revolutions had spread the idea of popular sovereignty (see Primary Source: Declaring Independence in Chapter 15), but the question remained: who exactly were "the people"? For radicals who longed for liberation from the multiethnic empires, "the people" encompassed all those who shared a common language and what was thought to be a common history, and each "people" deserved its own state.

Each fledgling nationalist movement—whether Polish, Czech, Greek, Italian, or German—had different contours, but they all drew backers from the liberal aristocracy and the well-educated and commercially active middle classes. University students were especially active in these movements. Most nationalist movements were at first weak and easily crushed, such as attempted Polish uprisings inside tsarist Russia in 1830–1831 and 1863–1864. Unable to win political power, the movements' leaders instead pursued educational and cultural programs to arouse and unite their nation for eventual statehood. The Greeks did manage to wrest independence from the Ottoman Turks—but only because the European powers intervened to help a cause that did not threaten to take territory away from any European state.

Other nationalist movements were suppressed or at least slowed down with little bloodshed. In places such as the German principalities, the Italian states, and the Hungarian parts of the Habsburg Empire, secret societies of young men—students and intellectuals—gathered to plan bright, republican futures. Regrettably for these patriots, however, organizations like Young Italy, founded in 1832 to promote national unification and renewal, had little popular or foreign support. Censorship and a few strategic executions suppressed them. Yet many of these movements would ultimately succeed in the century's second half, when conservatives and liberals alike in western Europe employed nationalist fervor to advance their own great power ambitions. However, in central Europe, nationalism pitted many claimants for the same territories against one another, like the Czechs, Serbs, Slovaks, Poles, and Ruthenians (Ukrainians). They did not understand why they could not have a nation-state too.

SOCIALISTS AND COMMUNISTS

Much more threatening to the ruling elite were the radicals who believed that the French Revolution had not gone far enough. They longed for a grander revolution that would sweep away the Restoration's political *and* economic order. Early socialists and communists (the terms were more or less interchangeable at the time) insisted that political reforms offered no effective answer to the more pressing "social question": What was to be done about the inequalities that industrial capitalism was introducing? The socialists worried in particular about two things. One was the growing gap between impoverished workers and newly wealthy employers. The other concern was that the division of labor—that is, the dividing up and simplifying of tasks so that each worker performs most efficiently—might make people into soulless, brainless machines. The socialists believed that the whole free market economy, not just the state, had to be transformed to save the human race from self-destruction. Liberty and equality, they insisted, could not be separated; aristocratic privilege along with capitalism belonged on history's ash heap.

No more than a handful of radical prophets hatched revolutionary plans in the years after 1815, but ordinary workers, artisans, domestic servants, and women employed in textile manufacturing joined them in staging strikes, riots, peasant uprisings, and protest meetings. A few socialists and feminists, such as the English thinker John Stuart Mill and his wife, Harriet Taylor Mill, campaigned for social and political equality of the sexes. In Britain in 1819, Manchester workers at St. Peter's Field demonstrated peacefully for increased representation in Parliament, but panicking guardsmen fired on the crowd, leaving 11 dead and 460 injured in an incident later dubbed the Peterloo Massacre. In 1839 and 1842, nearly half the adult population of Britain signed the People's Charter, which called for universal suffrage for all adult males, the secret ballot, equal electoral districts, and annual parliamentary elections. This mass movement, known as Chartism, like most such endeavors, ended in defeat. Parliament rejected the charter in 1839, 1842, and 1848.

FOURIER AND UTOPIAN SOCIALISM

Despite their many defeats, the radicals kept trying. Some sense of this age of revolutionary aspirations reveals itself in one European visionary who had big grievances and even bigger plans: Charles Fourier (1772–1837). Fourier's **utopian socialism** was perhaps the most visionary and influential of all Restoration-era alternative movements. He introduced planning, whereas the revolutionaries invoked violence, and he generally rejected the equalizing of conditions, fearing the suppression of diversity. Still, he and like-minded socialists dreamed of transforming states, workplaces, and human relations in a much more thorough way than their religious or political predecessors had done.

Fired by the egalitarian hopes and the cataclysmic failings of the French Revolution, Fourier believed himself to be the scientific prophet of the new world to come. He was a highly imaginative, self-taught man who earned his keep in the cloth trade, an occupation that gave him an intense hatred for merchants and intermediaries. Convinced that the division of labor and repressive moral conventions were destroying humankind's natural talents and passions, Fourier concluded that a revolution grander than that of 1789 was needed. But this utopian transformation of economic, social, and political conditions, he thought, could occur through organization, not through bloodshed. Indeed, by 1808, Fourier believed that the thoroughly corrupt world was on the brink of giving way to a new and harmonious age, of which he was the oracle.

The Phalanx. *The Phalanx, as one of Fourier's German followers envisioned it. In this rendering, the idealized home for the residents of the cooperative social system is represented as a building architecturally similar to the home of the French kings, the Louvre.*

First formulated in 1808, his "system" envisioned the reorganization of human communities into what he called phalanxes. In these harmonious collectives of 1,500 to 1,600 people and 810 personality types, diversity would be preserved but efficiency maintained; best of all, work would become enjoyable. All members of the phalanx, rich and poor, would work, though not necessarily at the same tasks. All would work in short spurts of no more than 2 hours, so as to make labor more interesting and sleep, idleness, and overindulgence less attractive. A typical rich man's day would begin at 3:30 A.M. for eating breakfast, reviewing the previous day, and participating in an industrial parade. At 5:30 he would hunt; at 7:00 he would turn to fishing. At 8:00 he would have lunch and read the newspapers (though what news there might be in this world is hard to fathom). At 9:00 he would meet with horticulturists, and at 10:00 he would go to Mass. At 10:30 he would meet with a pheasant breeder; later he would tend exotic plants, herd sheep, and attend a concert. Each man would cultivate what he wanted to eat and learn about what he wanted to know. As for unpleasant tasks, they would become less so because they would now occur in more comfortable settings, such as warmed barns and spotless factories. Truly undesirable jobs, like sweeping out stables or cleaning latrines, would fall to young adolescents, who, Fourier argued, actually liked mucking about in filth.

Fourier's phalanxes by no means constituted an Eden in which humankind lived without knowing what it was like to sweat; rather, it was a workers' paradise in which comforts and rewards made working enjoyable. However, this system of production and distribution would run without merchants. Fourier intentionally excluded intermediaries like himself from his plan for paradise. He believed that they corrupted civilization and introduced unnaturalness into the division of labor.

Fourier's writings gained popularity in the 1830s, appealing to radicals who supported a variety of causes. In France, women were particularly active in spreading his ideas. Longing for social and moral reforms that would address problems such as prostitution, poverty, illegitimacy, and the exploitation of workers (including women and children), some women saw in Fourierism a higher form of Christian communalism. By reshaping the phalanx to accommodate monogamous families and Christian values, women helped to make his work more respectable to middle-class readers. In Russia, Fourier's works fired the imaginations of the young writer Fyodor Dostoyevsky. He and fourteen others in the radical circle to which he belonged were sentenced to death for their views (though their executions were called off at the last minute). In 1835–1836, both the young Italian nationalist Giuseppe Mazzini and the Spanish republican Joaquín Abreu published important articles on Fourier's thought. The German thinker Karl Marx (1818–1883) read Fourier with great care, and there are many remnants of utopian thought in his work. In *The German Ideology*, Marx describes life in an ideal communist society; in a postrevolutionary world, he predicts that "nobody has one exclusive sphere of activity but each can become accomplished in any branch he wishes, society regulates the general production and thus makes it possible for me to do one thing today and another tomorrow, to hunt in the morning, fish in the afternoon, rear cattle in the evening, [and] criticize after dinner."

MARXISM Karl Marx fell in love with philosophy at university, but in the Restoration era, his socially radical and atheistic views prevented him from getting a job. To support his family, he took up a career in journalism in the Rhineland region, where he was exposed both to radical French ideas and to the plight of peasants being pushed off common land. Writing about legislative debates over property rights and taxation in Europe and America, he was forced to deal with economics. His understanding of *capitalism*, a term he was instrumental in popularizing, deepened through his collaboration with Friedrich Engels (1820–1895). Engels was a German-born radical who, after observing conditions in the factories owned by his wealthy father in Manchester, England, published a stinging indictment of industrial wage labor titled *The Condition of the Working Class in England* (1843).

Together, Marx and Engels developed what they called "scientific socialism," which they contrasted with the "utopian socialism" of others like Fourier. Scientific socialism was rooted, they argued, in a materialist theory of history: what mattered in history was the production of material goods and the ways in which society was organized into classes of producers and exploiters. History, they claimed, consisted of successive forms of exploitative production and rebellions against them. Capitalist exploitation of the wage worker was only the latest, and worst, version of class conflict, Marx and Engels contended. In industrialized societies, capitalists owned the means of production (the factories and machinery) and exploited the wage workers. Marx and Engels were confident that the clashes between industrial wage workers—or **proletarians**—and capitalists would end in a colossal transformation of human society and

Karl Marx. *The author (with Friedrich Engels) of* The Communist Manifesto, *Karl Marx argued that the exploitation of wage laborers would trigger a proletarian revolution and would lead to socialism supplanting capitalism.*

would usher in a new world of true liberty, equality, and fraternity. These beliefs constituted the fundamentals of **Marxism**. For Marx and Engels, history inevitably moved through stages: from feudalism to capitalism and then to communism.

From these fundamentals, Marx and Engels issued a comprehensive critique of post-1815 Europe. They identified a whole class of the exploited—the working class. They believed that more and more people would fall into this class as industrialization proceeded and that the masses would not share in the rising prosperity that capitalists monopolized. Marx and Engels predicted that there would be overproduction and underconsumption, which would lead to lower profits for capitalists and, consequently, lower wages or unemployment for workers—which would ultimately spark a proletarian revolution. This revolution would result in a "dictatorship of the proletariat" and the end of private property. With the destruction of capitalism, the men claimed, exploitation would cease and the state would wither away.

After a decade of hardship across Europe known as the hungry forties, in 1848 a series of revolutions shook the Restoration regimes. These were not proletarian revolutions. Modern industry had not developed beyond a few key locations, mostly in northern and western Europe. Instead, the revolutions were cross-class affairs made up of an uneasy coalition of liberal doctors, lawyers, students, urban artisans, wage workers, and social outcasts. As a group, they shared little more than a frustration with the old elites and a desire for an independent nation. But in 1848, that was enough to create a wave of uprisings in France, Austria, Russia, Italy, Hungary, and the German states. After hearing that revolution had broken out in France, Marx and Engels published *The Communist Manifesto,* calling on the workers of all nations to unite in overthrowing capitalism. (See Primary Source: "Bourgeoisie and Proletariat": From *The Communist Manifesto.*) But the men were sorely disappointed (not to mention exiled) by the reactionary crackdowns that followed the 1848 revolutions.

After 1850, Marx and Engels took up permanent residence in England, where they tried to organize an international workers' movement. In the doldrums of the midcentury, they turned to science, but they never abandoned the dream of total social reconfiguration. Nor would their many admirers and heirs. The failure of the 1848 revolutions did not doom prophecy itself or diminish commitment to alternative social landscapes.

INSURGENCIES AGAINST COLONIZING AND CENTRALIZING STATES

Outside Europe, for Native Americans and for Britain's colonial subjects in India, the greatest threat to traditional worlds was the colonizing process itself, not industrial capitalism and centralizing states. While European radicals looked back to revolutionary legacies in imagining a transformed society, Native American insurgents and rebels in British India drew on their traditional cultural and political resources to imagine local alternatives to foreign impositions. Like the peoples of China, Africa, and the Middle East, native groups in the Americas and India met the period's challenges with prophecy, charismatic leadership, and rebellion. Everywhere the insurgents spoke in languages of the past, but the new worlds they envisioned bore unmistakable marks of the present as well.

Native American Prophets

Like other native peoples threatened by imperial expansion, the Indians of North America dreamed of a world in which intrusive colonizers disappeared. Taking such dreams as prophecies, in 1805 many Indians in the Ohio Valley flocked to hear the revelations of a Shawnee Indian named Tenskwatawa. Facing a dark present and a darker future, they enthusiastically embraced the Shawnee Prophet's visions, which (like that of the Paiute prophet Wovoka nearly a century later) foretold how invaders would vanish if Indians returned to their customary ways and traditional rites.

EARLY CALLS FOR RESISTANCE AND A RETURN TO TRADITION Tenskwatawa's visions—and the anticolonial uprising they inspired—drew on a long tradition of visionary leaders. From the first encounters with Europeans, Indian seers had periodically encouraged native peoples to purge their worlds of colonial influences and to revitalize indigenous traditions. Often these prophets had aroused their followers not only to engage in cleansing ceremonies but also to cooperate in violent, anticolonial uprisings. In 1680, for example, previously divided Pueblo villagers in New Mexico had united behind the prophet Popé to chase Spanish missionaries, soldiers, and settlers out of that colony. After their victory, Popé's followers destroyed all things European: they torched wheat fields and fruit orchards, slaughtered livestock, and ransacked Catholic churches. For a dozen years the Indians of New Mexico reclaimed control over their lands, but soon divisions within native ranks prepared the way for Spanish reconquest in 1692.

Seventy years later and half a landmass away, the charismatic oratory of the Delaware shaman Neolin encouraged Indians of the Ohio Valley and Great Lakes to take up arms against the British, leading to the capture of several British military posts. Although the British put down the uprising, imperial officials learned a lesson from the conflict: they assumed a less arrogant posture toward Ohio Valley and Great Lakes Indians, and to preserve peace, they forbade colonists from trespassing on lands west of the Appalachian Mountains. The British, however, were

"Bourgeoisie and Proletariat": From *The Communist Manifesto*

In January 1848, Karl Marx and Friedrich Engels prepared a party program for the Communist League, a German working-man's association. Published in French as The Communist Manifesto, *the document foretold the inevitable overthrow of bourgeois-dominated capitalism by the working classes and the transition to socialism and ultimately to communism. The following excerpt demonstrates their certainty that history, driven by economic factors and class conflict, was moving unavoidably toward the revolution of the proletariat. Marx and Engels defined the bourgeoisie as capitalists, owners of the means of production and employers of wage laborers. They defined the proletariat as wage laborers who had to sell their labor to live.*

A spectre is haunting Europe—the spectre of Communism. . . .

The history of all hitherto existing society is the history of class struggles. . . .

The modern bourgeois society that has sprouted from the ruins of feudal society has not done away with class antagonisms. It has but established new classes, new conditions of oppression, new forms of struggle in place of the old ones.

Our epoch, the epoch of the bourgeoisie, possesses, however, this distinctive feature: it has simplified the class antagonisms: Society as a whole is more and more splitting up into two great hostile camps, into two great classes directly facing each other: Bourgeoisie and Proletariat. . . .

The bourgeoisie . . . has put an end to all feudal, patriarchal, idyllic relations. It has pitilessly torn asunder the motley feudal ties that bound man to his "natural superiors," and has left remaining no other nexus between man and man than naked self-interest, than callous "cash payment." . . .

The need of a constantly expanding market for its products chases the bourgeoisie over the whole surface of the globe. It must nestle everywhere, settle everywhere, establish connexions everywhere. . . .

The bourgeoisie, by the rapid improvement of all instruments of production, by the immensely facilitated means of communication, draws all, even the most barbarian, nations into civilisation. The cheap prices of its commodities are the heavy artillery with which it batters down all Chinese walls, with which it forces the barbarians' intensely obstinate hatred of foreigners to capitulate. . . .

The weapons with which the bourgeoisie felled feudalism to the ground are now turned against the bourgeoisie itself.

But not only has the bourgeoisie forged the weapons that bring death to itself; it has also called into existence the men who are to wield those weapons—the modern working class—the proletarians. . . . These labourers, who must sell themselves piece-meal, are a commodity, like every other article of commerce, and are consequently exposed to all the vicissitudes of competition, to all the fluctuations of the market. . . .

But with the development of industry the proletariat not only increases in number; it becomes concentrated in greater masses, its strength grows, and it feels that strength more. . . . Thereupon the workers begin to form combinations (Trades Unions) against the bourgeois;

they club together in order to keep up the rate of wages; they found permanent associations in order to make provision beforehand for these occasional revolts. Here and there the contest breaks out into riots.

Now and then the workers are victorious, but only for a time. The real fruit of their battles lies, not in the immediate result, but in the ever-expanding union of the workers. . . .

What the bourgeoisie, therefore, produces, above all, is its own grave-diggers. Its fall and the victory of the proletariat are equally inevitable.

QUESTIONS FOR ANALYSIS

- According to Marx and Engels, how does the bourgeoisie draw "all, even the most barbarian, nations into civilization"?
- How does the bourgeoisie contribute to its own downfall?
- Is the new social system supposed to arise automatically, or is human action required to bring it about?

Source: Karl Marx and Friedrich Engels, *The Communist Manifesto,* in *The Marx-Engels Reader,* 2nd ed., edited by Robert C. Tucker (New York: Norton, 1978), pp. 473–483, 490–491, 500.

incapable of restraining the flow of settlers across the mountains, and the problem became much worse for the Indians once the American Revolution ended. With the Ohio Valley transferred to the new United States, American settlers crossed the Appalachians and flooded into Kentucky and Tennessee.

Despite the settlers' considerable migration, much of the territory between the Appalachian Mountains and the Mississippi River, which Americans referred to as the "western country," remained an Indian country. North and south of Kentucky and Tennessee, Indian warriors more than held their own against

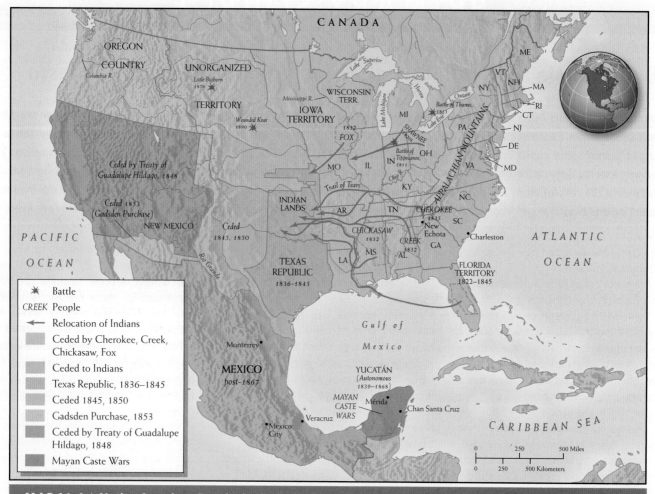

MAP 16.4 | Native American Revolts in the United States and Mexico

The new world order of expanding nation-states and industrial markets strongly affected indigenous peoples in North America.

- According to this map, where did the fiercest resistance to centralizing states and global market pressures occur?
- What regions of the United States were Indians forced to leave?
- According to your reading, to what extent, if any, did the natives' alternative visions create or preserve an alternative to the new emerging order?

American forces. As in previous anticolonial campaigns, the visions of various prophets bolstered the confidence and unity of Indian warriors, who twice joined together to rout invading American armies. But their confederation failed in a third encounter, in 1794, and their leaders had to surrender lands in what is now the state of Ohio to the United States. (See Map 16.4.)

TENSKWATAWA: THE SHAWNEE PROPHET The Shawnees, who lost most of their holdings, were among the most bitter—and bitterly divided—of Indian peoples living in the Ohio Valley. Some Shawnee leaders concluded that their people's survival now required that they cooperate with American officials and Christian missionaries. This strategy, they realized, entailed wrenching changes in Shawnee culture. European reformers,

after all, insisted that Indian men give up hunting and take up farming, an occupation that the Shawnees and their neighbors had always considered "women's work." Moreover, the Shawnees were pushed to abandon communal traditions in favor of private property rights. Of course, missionaries prodded Indians to quit their "heathen" beliefs and practices and become faithful, "civilized" Christians. For many Shawnees, these demands went too far; worse, they promised no immediate relief from the dispossession and impoverishment that now marked the Indians' daily lives. Young men especially grew angry and frustrated.

Among the demoralized Shawnees was **Tenskwatawa** (1775–1836), whose story of overcoming personal failures through religious visions and embracing a strict moral code has uncanny parallels with that of Hong Xiuquan, the Taiping leader. In his first thirty years, Tenskwatawa could claim few accomplishments. He had failed as a hunter and as a medicine man, had blinded himself in one eye, and had earned a reputation as an obnoxious braggart. All this changed in the spring of 1805, however, after he fell into a trance and experienced a vision, which he vividly recounted to one and all. In this dream, Tenskwatawa encountered a heaven where the virtuous enjoyed the traditional Shawnee way of life and a hell where evildoers suffered punishments. Additional revelations followed, and Tenskwatawa soon stitched these together into a new social gospel that urged disciples to abstain from alcohol and return to traditional customs.

Like other prophets, Tenskwatawa exhorted Indians to reduce their dependence on European trade goods and to sever their connections to Christian missionaries, even as his own vision of heaven and hell, like Wovoka's and Hong Xiuquan's, borrowed from the messages of those missionaries. Thus, he urged his audiences to replace imported cloth and metal tools with animal skins and implements fashioned from wood, stone, and bone. Livestock, too, was to be banished, as Indian men again gathered meat by hunting wild animals with bows and arrows, instead of guns and powder. If Indians obeyed these dictates, Tenskwatawa promised, the deer, which "were half a tree's length under the ground," would come back in abundant numbers to the earth's surface. Likewise, he claimed, Indians killed in conflict with colonial intruders would be resurrected, while evil Americans would depart from the country west of the Appalachians. (See Primary Source: Tenskwatawa's Vision.)

Like the Qing's response to Hong's visions, American officials initially dismissed Tenskwatawa as deluded but harmless; their concerns grew, however, as the Shawnee Prophet gathered more followers. These converts came not only from among the Shawnees but also from Delaware, Ottawa, Wyandot, Kickapoo, and Seneca villages. The spread of Tenskwatawa's message raised anew the specter of a pan-Indian confederacy. Hoping to undermine the Shawnee Prophet's claims to supernatural power, territorial governor William Henry Harrison challenged Tenskwatawa to make the sun stand still. But Tenskwatawa one-upped Harrison. Having learned of an impending eclipse from white astronomers, Tenskwatawa assembled his followers on June 16, 1806. Right on schedule, and as if on command, the sky darkened. Claiming credit for the eclipse, Tenskwatawa saw his standing soar, as did the ranks of his disciples. Now aware of the growing threat, American officials tried to bribe Tenskwatawa, hoping that cash payments might dim his vision and quiet his voice. Failing that, they wondered if one of the prophet's Indian adversaries might be encouraged to assassinate him.

In fact, Tenskwatawa had made plenty of enemies among his fellow Indians. His visions, after all, consigned drinkers to hell (where they would be forced to swallow molten metal) and singled out those who cooperated with colonial authorities for punishment in this world and the next. Indeed, Tenskwatawa condemned as witches those Indians who rejected his preaching in favor of the teachings of Christian missionaries and American authorities. (To be sure, Tenskwatawa's damnation of Christianized Indians was somewhat paradoxical, for missionary doctrines obviously influenced his vision of a burning hell for sinners and his crusade against alcohol.)

TECUMSEH AND THE WISH FOR NATIVE AMERICAN UNITY Although Tenskwatawa's accusations alienated some Indians, his prophecies gave heart to many more. This was particularly the case once his brother, Tecumseh (1768–1813),

Visions of American Indian Unification. Left: *A portrait of Tenskwatawa, the "Shawnee Prophet," whose visions stirred thousands of Indians in the Ohio Valley and Great Lakes to renounce dependence on colonial imports and resist the expansion of the United States. Right: A portrait of his brother, Tecumseh, who succeeded in building a significant pan-Indian confederation, although it unraveled following his death at the Battle of Thames in 1813.*

PRIMARY SOURCE

Tenskwatawa's Vision

In the first decade of the nineteenth century, the Shawnee Indian leader Tenskwatawa recalled an earlier, happier time for the Indian peoples of the Great Lakes and Ohio Valley. It was a time before the coming of the Europeans. In this oration, Tenskwatawa recounts how contact with the "white men's goods" contaminated and corrupted the Indians. He urges them to spurn the ways of white Americans and return to the pure ways of a precolonial past.

Our Creator put us on this wide, rich land, and told us we were free to go where the game was, where the soil was good for planting. That was our state of true happiness. We did not have to beg for anything. Our Creator had taught us how to find and make everything we needed, from trees and plants and animals and stone. We lived in bark, and we wore only the skins of animals.

Thus were we created. Thus we lived for a long time, proud and happy. We had never eaten pig meat, nor tasted the poison called whiskey, nor worn wool from sheep, nor struck fire or dug earth with steel, nor cooked in iron, nor hunted and fought with loud guns, nor ever had diseases which soured our blood or rotted our organs. We were pure, so we were strong and happy.

For many years we traded furs to the English or the French, for wool blankets and guns and iron things, for steel awls and needles and axes, for mirrors, for pretty things made of beads and silver. And for liquor. This was foolish, but we did not know it. We shut our ears to the Great Good Spirit. We did not want to hear that we were being foolish.

But now those things of the white men have corrupted us, and made us weak and needful. Our men forgot how to hunt without noisy guns. Our women don't want to make fire without steel, or cook without iron, or sew without metal awls and needles, or fish without steel hooks. Some look in those mirrors all the time, and no longer teach their daughters to make leather or render bear oil. We learned to need the white men's goods, and so now a People who never had to beg for anything must beg for everything! . . .

And that is why Our Creator purified me and sent me down to you full of the shining power, to make you what you were before!

No red man must ever drink liquor, or he will go and have the hot lead poured in his mouth! . . .

Do not eat any food that is raised or cooked by a white person. It is not good for us. Eat not their bread made of wheat, for Our Creator gave us corn for our bread. . . .

The Great Good Spirit wants our men to hunt and kill game as in the ancient days, with the silent arrow and the lance and the snare, and no longer with guns.

If we hunt in the old ways, we will not have to depend upon white men, for new guns and powder and lead, or go to them to have broken guns repaired. Remember it is the wish of the Great Good Spirit that we have no more commerce with white men! . . .

. . . Our Creator told me that all red men who refuse to obey these laws are bad people, or witches, and must be put to death. . . .

The Great Good Spirit will appoint a place to be our holy town, and at that place I will call all red men to come and share this shining power. For the People in all tribes are corrupt and miserable! In that holy town we will pray every morning and every night for the earth to be fruitful, and the game and fish to be plentiful again.

QUESTIONS FOR ANALYSIS

- Tenskwatawa mentions many commodities and habits that the Indians had been adopting from white men. Identify at least ten.
- According to Tenskwatawa, how has this dependency reduced a proud people to begging?
- What rules did "Our Creator" give Tenskwatawa to help him make his people "what you were before"?

Source: "Words of Tenskwatawa," in *Messages and Letters of William Henry Harrison*, edited by Logan Esarey (Indianapolis: Indiana Historical Commission, 1922). Retrieved from http://history.missouristate.edu/FTMiller/EarlyRepublic/tecandtensk.htm

helped circulate the message of Indian renaissance among Indian villages from the Great Lakes to the Gulf Coast. On his journeys after 1805, Tecumseh did more than spread his brother's visions; he also wed them to the idea of a renewed and enlarged Indian confederation. Moving around the Great Lakes and traveling across the southern half of the western country, Tecumseh preached the need for Indian unity. He repeatedly urged Indians to resist any American attempts to get them to sell more land. In response, thousands of followers renounced their ties to colonial ways and prepared to combat the expansion of the United States.

By 1810, Tecumseh had emerged, at least in the eyes of American officials, as even more dangerous than his brother. Impressed by Tecumseh's charismatic organizational talents, William Harrison warned that this new "Indian menace" was

Indian Removals after 1815.
After the failure of efforts to forge Native American solidarity, the American government forced Native Americans to relocate west of the Mississippi. Often these measures were extremely violent, as in the case of the removal of the Cherokee Nation from its southern lands to present-day Oklahoma, an event so traumatic for the Cherokee as to be known afterwards as "The Trail of Tears."

forming "an Empire that would rival in glory" that of the Aztecs and the Incas. In 1811, while Tecumseh was traveling among southern tribes, Harrison had his troops attack Tenskwatawa's village, Prophet's Town, on the Tippecanoe River in what is now the state of Indiana. The resulting battle was evenly fought, but the Indians eventually gave ground, and American forces burned Prophet's Town. That defeat discredited Tenskwatawa, who had promised his followers protection from destruction at American hands. Spurned by his former disciples, including his brother, Tenskwatawa fled to Canada.

Tecumseh soldiered on. Although he mistrusted the British, he recognized that only a British victory over the Americans in the War of 1812 could check further American expansion. So he aligned himself with the British. Commissioned as a brigadier general in the British army, Tecumseh recruited many Indians to the British cause, though his real aim remained the building of a pan-Indian union. But in 1813, with the war's outcome in doubt and the pan-Indian confederacy still fragile, Tecumseh perished at the Battle of the Thames, north of Lake Erie.

NATIVE AMERICAN REMOVALS The discrediting of Tenskwatawa and the death of Tecumseh damaged the cause of Indian unity; then British betrayal dealt it a fatal blow. Following the war's end in 1814, the British withdrew their support and left the Indians south of the Great Lakes to fend for themselves against land-hungry American settlers and the armies of the United States. By 1815, American citizens outnumbered Indians in the western country by a seven-to-one margin, and this gap dramatically widened in the next few years. Recognizing the hopelessness of military resistance, Indians south of the Great Lakes resigned themselves to relocation. During the 1820s, most of the peoples north of the Ohio River were

removed to lands west of the Mississippi River. During the 1830s, the southern tribes were cleared out, completing what amounted to an ethnic cleansing of Indian peoples from the region between the Appalachians and the Mississippi.

In the midst of these final removals, Tenskwatawa died, though his dream of an alternative to American expansion had faded for his people years earlier. Through the rest of the nineteenth century, however, other Indian prophets emerged, and their visions continued to inspire followers with the hope of an alternative to life under the colonial rule of the United States. In the restored world imagined by Native American seers, Indians maintained control of their homelands, retained traditional gender roles and identities in which men could hunt abundant game, and sustained communal customs at odds with the acquisitive individualism that American reformers, styling themselves "Friends of the Indian," had sought to impose on defeated native peoples. But like Wovoka and the Ghost Dancers in 1890, these dreams failed to halt the expansion of the United States and the contraction of Indian lands.

The Caste War of the Yucatán

As in North America, the Spanish establishment of an expansionist nation-state in Mexico sparked widespread revolts by indigenous peoples. The most protracted was the Maya revolt in the Yucatán. The revolt started in 1847, and its flames were not finally doused until the full occupation of the Yucatán by Mexican national troops in 1901.

EARLY MAYA AUTONOMY The strength and endurance of the Maya revolt stemmed in large measure from the unusual features of the Spanish conquest in southern Mesoamerica. Because this area was not a repository of precious metals or fertile lands, Spain and its rivals focused their efforts elsewhere—on central and northern Mexico and the Caribbean islands. As a result, the Maya Indians escaped forced recruitment for labor in silver mines or sugar plantations. This does not mean, however, that global processes sidestepped the Maya Indians. In fact, the production of dyes and foodstuffs for shipment to other regions drew the Yucatán into long-distance trading networks. Nonetheless, cultivation and commerce were much less disruptive to indigenous lives in the Yucatán than elsewhere in the New World.

The dismantling of the Spanish Empire early in the nineteenth century gave way to almost a century of political turmoil in Latin America. In the Yucatán, civil strife brought the region autonomy by default, allowing Maya ways to survive without much upheaval. Their villages still constituted the chief political domain, ruled by elders; ownership of their land was collective, the property of families and not individuals. Corn, a mere staple to white consumers, continued to enjoy sacred status in Maya culture.

GROWING PRESSURES FROM THE SUGAR TRADE Local developments, however, encroached on the Maya world. First, regional elites—mainly white, but often with the support of mestizo populations—bickered for supremacy so long as the central authority of Mexico City remained weak. Weaponry flowed freely through the peninsula, and some belligerents even appealed for Maya support. At the same time, regional and international trade spurred the spread of sugar estates, which threatened traditional corn cultivation. Over the decades, plantations encroached on Maya properties. Planters used several devices to lure independent Mayas to work, especially in the harvest. The most important device, debt peonage, involved giving small cash advances to Indian families, which obligated fathers and sons to work for meager wages to pay off the debts. In addition, Mexico's costly wars, culminating in a showdown with the United States in 1846, drove tax collectors and army recruiters into villages in search of revenues and soldiers.

The combination of spiritual, material, and physical threats was explosive. When a small band of Mayas, fed up with rising taxes and ebbing autonomy, used firearms to drive back white intruders in 1847, they sparked a war that took a half-century to complete. The rebels were primarily free Mayas who had not yet been absorbed into the sugar economy. They wanted to dismantle old definitions of Indians as a caste—a status that deprived the Indians of rights to defend their sovereignty on equal legal footing with whites and that also subjected the Indians to special taxes. Thus, local Maya leaders, like Jacinto Pat and Cecilio Chi, upheld a republican model in the name of formal equality of all political subjects and devotion to a spiritual order that did not distinguish between Christians and non-Christians. "If the Indians revolt," one Maya rebel explained, "it is because the

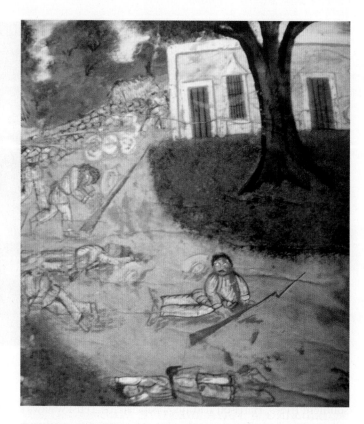

Caste War of the Yucatán. *The ruthless slaughter of Maya farmers by Mexican troops is captured in this 1850 painting. The intimacy of the bloodstained straw hats strewn on the road suggests that this work was an eyewitness account.*

whites gave them reason; because the whites say they do not believe in Jesus Christ, because they have burned the cornfield."

THE CASTE WAR Horrified, the local white elites reacted to the uprising with vicious repression and dubbed the ensuing conflict a caste war. In their view, the bloody conflict, which became known as the **Caste War of the Yucatán**, was a struggle between forward-looking liberals and backward-looking Indians. At first, whites and mestizos were no match for the determined Mayas, whose forces seized town after town, demolishing as they did so the whipping posts where Indians had endured public humiliation and punishment. By 1848, Indian armies controlled three-quarters of the peninsula and were poised to take the Yucatán's largest city, Mérida. Fear seized the embattled whites, who appealed for U.S. and British help, offering the peninsula for foreign annexation in return for military rescue from the Mayas.

In the end, fortune, not political savvy, saved the Yucatán's whites. The Maya farmers, who had taken up arms to defend their world, returned to their farms when planting season came, declaring that "the time has come for us to make our planting, for if we do not we shall have no Grace of God to fill the bellies of our children." Like many ordinary people, the farmers were unaware of international changes that had an impact on their situation. In 1848, the Mexican-American War ended with Washington paying the Mexican government $15 million for giving up its northern provinces. Thereafter, Mexico could spend freely to build up its southern armies. The Mexican government soon fielded a force of 17,000 soldiers and waged a scorched-earth campaign to drive back the depleted Maya forces.

By 1849, the confrontation had entered a new phase in which Mexican troops engaged in mass repression of the Mayas. Mexican armies set Indian fields and villages ablaze. Slaughtering Indians became a blood sport of barbaric proportions. Between 30 and 40 percent of the Maya population perished in the war and its repressive aftermath. The white governor even sold captured Indians into slavery to Cuban sugar planters. Indeed, the white formulation of the caste nature of the war eventually became a self-fulfilling prophecy. Entire Maya cities pulled up stakes and withdrew to isolated districts protected by fortified villages. War between armies degenerated into guerrilla warfare between an occupying Mexican army and mobile bands of Maya squadrons, inflicting a gruesome toll on the invaders. As years passed, the war ground to a stalemate, especially once the U.S. funds ran out and Mexican soldiers began deserting in droves.

RECLAIMING A MAYA IDENTITY Warfare prompted a spiritual transformation that reinforced a purely Maya identity against the Mexican invaders' efforts to create a strong, centralized state. Thus, a struggle that began with demands for legal equality and relative cultural autonomy became a crusade for spiritual salvation and the complete cultural separation of the Maya Indians. A particularly influential group under José María Barrera retreated to a hamlet called Chan Santa Cruz. There, at the site where he found a cross shape carved into a mahogany tree, Barrera had a vision of a divine encounter. Thereafter a swath of Yucatán villages refashioned themselves as moral communities orbiting around Chan Santa Cruz. Leaders created a polity, with soldiers, priests, and tax collectors pledging loyalty to the Speaking Cross. Villagers broke up landed estates and replaced them with a mixture of smallholding and communal lands to produce for families and local populations—not for the world market. As with the followers of Hong in China's Taiping Rebellion, Indian rebels forged an alternative religion: it blended Christian rituals, faiths, and icons with Maya legends and beliefs. At the center was a stone temple, Balam Na ("House of God"), 100 feet long and 60 feet wide. Through pious pilgrimages to Balam Na and the secular justice of Indian judges, the Mayas soon governed their autonomous domain in the Yucatán, almost completely cut off from the rest of Mexico.

This alternative to Latin American state formation, however, faced formidable hurdles. For example, disease ravaged the people of the Speaking Cross. Once counting 40,000 inhabitants, the villages dwindled to 10,000 by 1900. Also, a new crop, henequen, used to bind bales for North American farms and to stuff the seats of automobiles, began to spread across the Yucatán. In place of the peninsula's mixed agrarian societies, it now became a desiccated region producing a single crop, driving the people to seek refuge farther into the interior. As profits from henequen production rose, white landowners began turning the Yucatán into a giant plantation. But Maya villagers refused to give up their autonomy and rejected labor recruiters.

Finally, the Mexican oligarchy, having resolved its internal disputes, threw its weight behind the strong-arm ruler General Porfirio Díaz (r. 1876–1911). The general sent one of his veteran commanders, Ignacio Bravo, to do what no other Mexican could accomplish: defeat Chan Santa Cruz and drive Mayas into the henequen cash economy. When General Bravo finally entered the town, he found the once-imposing temple Balam Na covered in vegetation. Nature was reclaiming the territories of the Speaking Cross. Hunger and arms finally drove the Mayas to work on white Mexican plantations; the alternative vision was vanquished.

The Rebellion of 1857 in India

Like Native Americans, the peoples of nineteenth-century India had a long history of opposition to colonial domination. Armed revolts had occurred since the onset of rule by the English East India Company (see Chapter 15). Nonetheless, the uprising of 1857 was unprecedented in its scale, and it posed a greater threat than had any previous rebellion. (See Analyzing Global Developments: Alternative Movements in Asia and Africa.) Though led primarily by the old nobility and petty landlords, it was a popular uprising with strong support from the lower orders of Indian society. The rebels appealed to bonds of local and communal solidarity, invoked religious sentiments, and reimagined traditional hierarchies in egalitarian terms. They did this to pose alternatives to British rule and the deepening involvement of India in a network of capitalist relationships. Karl Marx, with his hope for revolution dashed in Europe, cast his eyes on the revolt in British India, eagerly following the events and commenting on them in daily columns for the *New-York Daily Tribune*.

INDIA UNDER COMPANY RULE When the revolt broke out in 1857, the East India Company's rule in India was a century old. During that time, the company had become an increasingly autocratic power whose reach encompassed the whole region. Mughal rule still existed in name, but the emperor lived in Delhi, all but forgotten and without any effective power. For a while, the existence of several princely states with which the British had entered into alliances prevented the British from exercising complete control over all of India. These princely domains enjoyed a measure of fiscal and judicial authority within the British Empire. They also contained landed aristocrats who held the right to shares in the produce and maintained their own militias.

ANALYZING GLOBAL DEVELOPMENTS

Alternative Movements in Asia and Africa

During the nineteenth century, five uprisings of global significance occurred in Africa and Asia. Two of these were carried out on a massive scale (the Taiping Rebellion and India's Great Rebellion); the other three involved much smaller numbers. The two large-scale uprisings did not last as long as the three movements in sub-Saharan Africa and the Arabian Peninsula and were put down with great loss of life. In contrast, the political and cultural successes of the Wahhabi Revolt in the Arabian Peninsula, Shaka's Zulu state in southern Africa, and the Fulani Revolt in northern Nigeria can be seen clearly even to this day.

- Although all five movements suffered stinging military defeats (the Fulani at the hands of the British in 1900, the Zulu state at the hands of the British in 1878, the Wahhabis at the hands of Egyptian troops at the beginning of the nineteenth century, the Taiping rebels at the hands of the Qing rulers, and the Indian rebels by British soldiers), were their long-term consequences markedly different?

- What holds these diverse movements together and allows us to represent them as alternatives to the main developments under way in western Europe and North America, the regions that had become dynamic centers of historical change?

QUESTIONS FOR ANALYSIS

- Why were Europeans involved in suppressing the larger-scale uprisings in China and India but not the smaller-scale ones in Africa and the Arabian Peninsula?

Movement/Leader	Short-Term Consequences	Long-Term Consequences
Smaller-Scale Uprisings		
FULANI REVOLT, NORTHERN NIGERIA (1804–1817) USMAN DAN FODIO (1754–1817)	• Created largest state in sub-Saharan Africa • Occupied two-thirds of present-day Nigeria • British conquered it in early twentieth century	• Gained independence in 1960 • Fulani elite families who worked with British now rule over present-day Nigeria
SHAKA'S ZULU STATE SHAKA (1787–1828)	• Created an army of 40,000 warriors • Created Zulu state covering 11,500 square miles in South Africa	• British conquered Zulu in 1878 • Zulu maintained their identity through apartheid • Population of 11 million today
WAHHABI REVOLT, ARABIAN PENINSULA (1744–1818) IBN ABD AL-WAHHAB (1703–1792)	• Ruled over much of the Arabian Peninsula • Defeated by Egyptian army in 1812	• Created the House of Saud, which rules over Saudi Arabia today • Retains commitment to Wahhab principles today
Larger-Scale Uprisings		
TAIPING REBELLION (1851–1864) HONG XIUQUAN (1813–1864)	• Accrued half a million members • Leader Hong and rebels ruled over central and southern China from Nanjing for eleven years	• Rebellion caused 20 million deaths by 1853 • Nearly toppled Qing dynasty; Mao Zedong viewed it as precursor to peasant-led communist movement; now viewed as threat to social order due to large-scale violence
GREAT REBELLION (1857–1858) GEOGRAPHICAL LEADERS, NO MONOLITHIC FIGURE	• Indian sepoys of East India Company started revolt • Sepoys pledged support to Mughal emperor • Revolt included sepoys, peasants, small landholders, and religious leaders across northern India	• British crown ended company rule after brutally suppressing rebellion • Laid the foundation for later Indian populist and nationalist resistance

Sources: William Dalrymple, *The Last Mughal: The Fall of a Dynasty: Delhi, 1857* (2007); Carolyn Hamilton (ed.), *The Mfecane Aftermath: Reconstructive Debates in Southern African History* (1995); Mervyn Hiskett, *The Sword of Truth: The Life and Times of the Shehu Usman dan Fodio* (1994); Jonathan Spence, *God's Chinese Son: The Taiping Heavenly Kingdom of Hong Xiuquan* (1996).

Rebellion of 1857. *Russian painter Vasili Vereshchagin depicts the cruel and unusual method in which British officers executed the Indian rebels—by strapping them to the mouths of cannons. The inhumanity of this practice was not soon forgotten by Europeans; this particular reproduction of the painting comes from Raubstaat England ("Robber State England"), an anti-British pamphlet published by the Nazis during World War II.*

Believing that the princely powers and landed aristocracies were out of date, the company instituted far-reaching changes in administration in the 1840s. These infuriated local peoples and laid the foundations for one of the world's most violent and concerted movements of protest against colonial authority. Lord Dalhousie, upon his appointment as governor-general in 1848, immediately began annexing what had been independent princely domains and stripping native aristocrats of their privileges. Swallowing one princely state after another, the British removed their former allies. The government also decided to collect taxes directly from peasants, displacing the landed nobles as intermediaries. In disarming the landed nobility, the British threw the retainers and militia of the notables into unemployment; and by demanding high taxes from peasants, the British forced them to rely on moneylenders, who could take ownership of land when peasant proprietors failed to pay. Meanwhile, the company transferred judicial authority to an administration that was insulated from the Indian social hierarchy.

The most prized object for annexation was the kingdom of Awadh in northern India. (See Map 16.5.) Founded in 1722 by an Iranian adventurer, it was one of the first successor states to have gained a measure of independence from the Mughal ruler in Delhi. With access to the fertile resources of the Ganges Plain, its opulent court in Lucknow was one place where Mughal splendor still survived. In 1765, the company imposed a treaty on Awadh under which the ruler paid an annual tribute for British troops stationed in his territory to "protect" his kingdom from internal and external enemies. The British constantly ratcheted up their demands for tribute and abused their position to monopolize the lucrative trade in cotton, indigo, textiles,

and other commodities. But the more successful they were in exploiting Awadh, the more they longed to annex it completely. Thus, Dalhousie declared in 1851 that Awadh was "a cherry which will drop into our mouths some day."

TREATY VIOLATIONS AND ANNEXATION In 1856, citing misgovernment and deterioration in law and order, the East India Company violated its treaty obligations and sent its troops to Lucknow to take control of the province. Nawab Wajid Ali Shah, the poet-king of Awadh, whom the British saw as effete and debauched, refused to sign the treaty of abdication. Instead, he came dressed in his mourning robes to meet with the British official charged to take over the province. After pleading unsuccessfully for his legal rights under the treaty, he handed over his turban to the official and then left for Calcutta to argue his case before Dalhousie. There was widespread distress at the treatment he received. Dirges were recited, and religious men rushed to Lucknow to denounce the annexation.

In fact, the annexation of princely domains and the abolition of feudal privileges formed part of the developing practices of European imperialism. To the policy of annexation, Dalhousie added an ambitious program of building railroads, telegraph lines, and a postal network to unify the disjointed territory into a single "network of iron sinew" under British control. Dalhousie saw these infrastructures as key to developing India into a productive colony—a supplier of raw materials for British industry and a market for its manufactures.

A year after Dalhousie's departure in 1856, India went up in flames. The spark that ignited the simmering discontent into a furious rebellion—the Rebellion of 1857 (Great Rebellion)—was the "greased cartridge" controversy. At the end of 1856, the British army, which consisted of hundreds of thousands of Hindu and Muslim recruits (sepoys) commanded by British officers, introduced the new Enfield rifle to replace the old-style musket. To load the rifle, soldiers had to bite the cartridge open. Although manufacturing instructions stated that linseed oil and beeswax be used to grease the cartridge, a rumor circulated that cow and pig fat had been used. But biting into cartridges greased with animal fat meant violating the Hindu and Muslim sepoys' religious traditions. The sepoys became convinced that there was a plot afoot to defile them and to compel their conversion to Christianity. So a wave of rebellion spread among the 270,000 Indian soldiers, who greatly outnumbered the 40,000 British soldiers employed to rule over 200 million Indians.

REBELLION BREAKS OUT The mutiny broke out on May 10, 1857, at the military barracks in Meerut. The previous day, the native soldiers had witnessed eighty-five of their comrades being manacled and shackled in irons and marched off to the prison for refusing to load their rifles. The next day, all three regiments at Meerut mutinied, killed their British officers, and marched 30 miles south to Delhi, where their comrades in regiments there welcomed them joyfully. Together, they "restored" the aging Bahadur Shah as the Mughal emperor, which lent legitimacy to the uprising. The Mughal capital quickly swarmed with rebel soldiers and religious leaders who gathered there from near and distant territories.

The revolt turned from a limited military mutiny into a widespread civil rebellion that involved peasants, artisans, day laborers, and religious leaders. While the insurgents did not eliminate the power of the East India Company, which managed to retain the loyalty of princes and landed aristocrats in some places, they did throw

MAP 16.5 | Indian Rebellion of 1857

The Indian Rebellion of 1857 broke out first among the Indian soldiers of the British army. Other groups soon joined the struggle.

- According to this map, how many centers of rebellion were located in British territory and how many in dependent states?
- Can you speculate on why the rebellion occurred in the interior of the subcontinent rather than along the coasts?
- In what way was the East India Company's expansion into formerly autonomous areas during the first half of the nineteenth century a factor in the rebellion?

the company into a crisis. Before long, the mutineers in Delhi issued a proclamation declaring that because the British were determined to destroy the religion of both Hindus and Muslims,

The Indian Sepoys. *Pictured here are Indian soldiers, or sepoys, who were armed, drilled, and commanded by British officers. The sepoys were drawn from indigenous groups that the British considered "martial races." This photograph shows the Sikhs, designated as one such "race."*

it was the duty of the wealthy and the privileged to support the rebellion. (See Primary Source: The Azamgarh Proclamation.) To promote Hindu-Muslim unity, rebel leaders asked Muslims to refrain from killing cows in deference to Hindu sentiments.

Triumphant in Delhi, the rebellion spread to other parts of India. In Awadh, proclamations in Hindi, Urdu, and Persian called on Hindus and Muslims to revolt. Troops at the garrison in Lucknow, Awadh's capital, did just that. Seizing control of the town, the rebels urged all classes to unite in expelling the British and succeeded in compelling the colonial forces to retreat.

Although the dispossessed aristocracy and petty landholders led the rebellion, leaders also appeared from the lower classes. Bakht Khan, who had been a junior noncommissioned officer in the British army, became commander in chief of the rebel forces in Delhi, replacing one of the Mughal emperor's sons. And Devi Singh, a wealthy peasant, set himself up as a peasant king. Dressed in yellow, the insignia of Hindu royalty, he constituted a government of his own, modeling it on the British administration. While his imitation of company rule showed his respect for the British bureaucracy, he defied British authority by leading an armed peasantry against the hated local moneylenders.

The call to popular forces also marked the rebel career of Maulavi Ahmadullah Shah, a Muslim theologian. He stood at the head of the rebel forces in Lucknow, leading an army composed primarily of ordinary soldiers and people from the lower orders. Claiming to be an "Incarnation of the Deity" and thus inspired by divine will, he emerged as a prophetic leader of the common people. He voiced his undying hatred of the British in religious terms, calling on Hindus and Muslims to destroy British rule and warning his followers against betrayal by landed authorities.

PARTICIPATION BY THE PEASANTRY The presence of popular leadership points to the important role of the lower classes as historical actors. Although feudal chieftains often brought them into the rebellion, the peasantry made it their own. The organizing principle of their uprising was the common experience of oppression. Thus, they destroyed anything that represented the authority of the company: prisons, factories, police posts, railway stations, European bungalows, and law courts. Equally significant, the peasantry attacked native moneylenders and local power holders who had purchased land at government auctions and were seen as benefiting from company rule.

Vigorous and militant as the popular rebellion was, it was limited in its territorial and ideological horizons. To begin with, the uprisings were local in scale and vision. Peasant rebels attacked the closest seats of administration and sought to settle scores with their most immediate and visible oppressors. They generally did not carry their action beyond the village or collection of villages. Their loyalties remained intensely local, based on village attachments and religious, caste, and clan ties. Nor did popular militants seek to undo traditional hierarchies of caste and religion.

THE BRITISH RESPONSE Convinced that the rebellion was the result of plotting by a few troublemakers, the British reacted with a brutal, vengeful counterinsurgent campaign. Villages were torched, and rebels were tied to cannons and blown to bits to teach Indians a lesson in power. Delhi fell in September 1857, Lucknow in March 1858. The British exiled the unfortunate Mughal emperor to Burma, where he died, and murdered his sons. Most of the other rebel leaders were either killed in battle or captured and executed. When, at the same time,

PRIMARY SOURCE

The Azamgarh Proclamation

The Indian leaders of the Rebellion of 1857 issued numerous proclamations. The Azamgarh Proclamation, excerpted below, is representative of these petitions. The emperor, Bahadur Shah, issued it in August 1857 on behalf of the mutineers who had seized the garrison town of Azamgarh, 60 miles north of Benares. Like other proclamations, it attacks the British for subverting Indian traditions and calls on its followers to restore the pre-British order—in this case, the Mughal Empire.

It is well known to all, that in this age the people of Hindoostan, both Hindoos and Mohammedans, are being ruined under the tyranny and oppression of the infidel and treacherous English. It is therefore the bounden duty of all the wealthy people of India, especially of those who have any sort of connection with any of the Mohammedan royal families, and are considered the pastors and masters of their people, to stake their lives and property for the well being of the public. . . .

Several of the Hindoo and Mussalman chiefs, who have long since quitted their homes for the preservation of their religion, and have been trying their best to root out the English in India, have presented themselves to me, and taken part in the reigning Indian crusade. . . . Parties anxious to participate in the common cause, but having no means to provide for themselves, shall receive their daily subsistence from me; and be it known to all, that the ancient works, both of the Hindoos and the Mohammedans, the writings of the miracle-workers and the calculations of the astrologers, pundits, and rammals, all agree in asserting that the English will no longer have any footing in India or elsewhere. . . .

Section I—Regarding Zemindars [large landholders, responsible for collecting land taxes for the government]. It is evident, that the British Government in making zemindary settlements have imposed exorbitant *Jumas* [revenue assessments], and have disgraced and ruined several zemindars. . . . Such extortions will have no manner of existence in the Badshahi Government; but on the contrary, the *Jumas* will be light, the dignity and honour of the zemindars safe, and every zemindar will have absolute rule in his own zemindary. . . .

Section II—Regarding Merchants. It is plain that the infidel and treacherous British Government have monopolized the trade of all the fine and valuable merchandise, such as indigo, cloth, and other articles of shipping, leaving only the trade of trifles to the people, and even in this they are not without their share of the profits, which they secure by means of customs and stamp fees, &c. in money suits, so that the people have merely a trade in name. . . . When the Badshahi Government is established, all these aforesaid fraudulent practices shall be dispensed with, and the trade of every article, without exception, both by land and water, shall be open to the native merchants of India. . . .

Section IV—Regarding Artisans. It is evident that the Europeans, by the introduction of English articles into India, have thrown the weavers, the cotton dressers, the carpenters, the blacksmiths, and the shoemakers, &c., out of employ, and have engrossed their occupations, so that every description of native artisan has been reduced to beggary. But under the Badshahi Government the native artisan will exclusively be employed in the services of the kings, the rajahs, and the rich. . . .

Section V—Regarding Pundits, Fakirs and other learned persons. The pundits and fakirs being the guardians of the Hindoo and Mohammedan religions respectively, and the Europeans being the enemies of both the religions, and as at present a war is raging against the English on account of religion, the pundits and fakirs are bound to present themselves to me, and take their share in the holy war.

QUESTIONS FOR ANALYSIS

- What are the main grievances against the English in India?
- How will the emperor's Badshahi Government alleviate these grievous conditions?
- What was the role of religion in the 1857 rebellion?

Source: "Proclamation of Emperor Bahadur Shah," in India in 1857: The Revolt against Foreign Rule, edited by Ainslie T. Embree (Delhi: Chanakya Publications, 1987), pp. 3–6.

the British also moved to annex the state of Jhansi in northern India, its female leader, Lakshmi Bai, mounted a counterattack. After a two-week siege, Jhansi fell to the British; but Lakshmi Bai escaped on horseback, only to die in the fighting for control of a nearby fortress. Her intelligence, bravery, and youth (she was twenty-eight) made her the subject of many popular Indian ballads in the decades to follow.

By July 1858, the vicious campaign to restore British control had achieved its goal. Yet, in August, the British Parliament abolished company rule and the company itself and

The Rani of Jhansi. *The Rani of Jhansi, who was deposed by the British, rose up during the revolt of 1857. In subsequent nationalist iconography, as this twentieth-century watercolor illustrates, she is remembered as a heroic rebel, all the more so because of her gender.*

CONCLUSION

The nineteenth century was a time of turmoil and transformation. While powerful forces reconfigured the world as a place for capitalism, colonialism, and nation-states, so, too, did prophets, charismatic leaders, radicals, peasant rebels, and anticolonial insurgents arise to offer alternatives. Reflecting local circumstances and traditions, the struggles of these men and women for a different future opened up spaces for the ideas and activities of subordinate classes.

Conventional historical accounts either neglect these struggles or fail to view them as a whole. These individuals were not just romantic, last-ditch resisters, as some scholars have argued. Even after defeat, their messages remained alive within their communities. Nor were their actions isolated and atypical events, for when viewed on a global scale, they bring to light a world that looks very different from the one that became dominant. To see the Wahhabi movement in the Arabian Peninsula together with the Shawnee Prophet in North America, the utopians and radicals in Europe with the peasant insurgents in British India, and the Taiping rebels with the Mayas in the Yucatán is to glimpse a world of marginalized regions and groups. It was a world that more powerful groups endeavored to suppress but could not erase.

In this world, prophets and rebel leaders usually cultivated power and prestige locally; the emergence of an alternative polity in one region did not impinge on communities and political organizations in others. As much as these individuals had in common, they envisioned widely different kinds of futures. Even Marx, who called the workers of the world to unite, was acutely aware that the call for a proletarian revolution applied only to the industrialized countries of Europe. Other dissenters had even more localized horizons. A world fashioned by movements for alternatives meant a world with multiple centers and different historical paths.

What gave force to a different mapping of the world was the fact that common people were at the center of these alternative visions, and their voices, however muted, gained a place on the historical stage. The quest for social justice in various forms defined efforts to reconstitute alternative worlds. In Islamic regions, the egalitarianism practiced by revitalization movements was evident in their mobilization of all Muslims, not just the elites. Likewise, charismatic military leaders in Africa, for all their use of raw power, used the framework of community to build new polities. The Taiping Rebellion distinguished itself by seeking to establish an equal society of men and women in service of the Heavenly Kingdom. Operating under very different conditions, the European radicals imagined a society free from aristocratic privileges and bourgeois property. Anticolonial rebels and insurgents depended on local solidarities and proposed alternative moral communities. In so doing, these movements compelled ruling elites to adjust the way they governed. The next chapter explores this challenge.

transferred responsibility for the governing of India to the crown. In November, Queen Victoria issued a proclamation guaranteeing religious toleration, promising improvements, and allowing Indians to serve in the government. She promised to honor the treaties and agreements with princes and chiefs and to refrain from interfering in religious matters. The insurgents had risen up not as a nation but as a multitude of communities acting independently, and their determination to find a new order shocked the British and threw them into a panic. Having crushed the uprising, the British resumed the work of transforming India into a modern colonial state and economy. But the desire for radical alternatives and traditions of popular insurgency, though vanquished, did not vanish.

After You Read This Chapter

Go to InQuizitive to see what you know & learn what you've missed.

FOCUS ON: *Regional Variations in Alternative Visions*

Europe

- European socialists and radicals envision a world free of exploitation and inequalities, while nationalists work to create new independent nation-states.

The Americas

- Native American prophets in the United States imagine a world restored to its customary ways and traditional rites.

- Mayas in the Yucatán defy the central Mexican government in a rebellion known as the Caste War.

The Islamic World and Africa

- Revivalist movements in the Arabian Peninsula and West Africa demand a return to traditional Islam.

- A charismatic warrior, Shaka, creates a powerful state in southern Africa.

Semicolonial China

- An inspired prophetic figure, Hong Xiuquan, leads the Taiping Rebellion against the Qing dynasty and European encroachment on China.

Colonial India

- Indian troops mutiny against the British and attempt to restore Mughal rule.

CHRONOLOGY

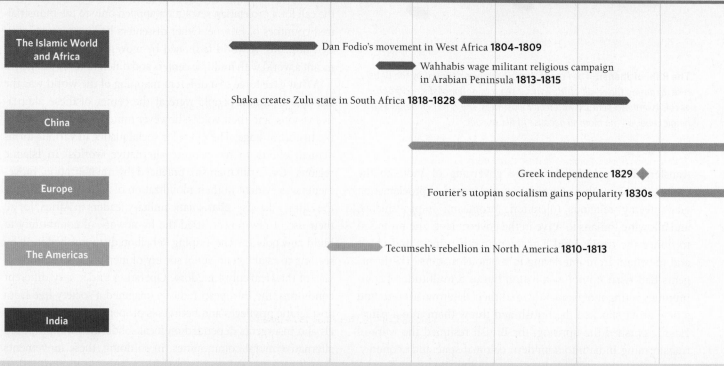

The Islamic World and Africa	Dan Fodio's movement in West Africa **1804–1809**	
	Wahhabis wage militant religious campaign in Arabian Peninsula **1813–1815**	
	Shaka creates Zulu state in South Africa **1818–1828**	
China		
Europe	Greek independence **1829**	
	Fourier's utopian socialism gains popularity **1830s**	
The Americas	Tecumseh's rebellion in North America **1810–1813**	
India		

1800   1825

KEY TERMS

STUDY QUESTIONS

Caste War of the Yucatán p. 618

dan Fodio, Usman p. 597

liberalism p. 609

Marxism p. 612

Mfecane movement p. 601

millenarian p. 603

proletarians p. 611

radicalism p. 608

Taiping Rebellion p. 605

Tenskwatawa p. 614

utopian socialism p. 610

Wahhabism p. 597

1. **Describe** the global order that emerged in the nineteenth century, and **identify** its core values.

2. **Identify** the challenges faced by the proponents of industrial capitalism, colonialism, and nation-states in this period.

3. **Compare and contrast** the utopian goals, immediate outcomes, and long-term influence of rebel movements around the world.

4. **Analyze** the connection between nineteenth-century protest movements and organized religion.

5. **Explain** the goals of Islamic revitalization movements such as Wahhabism in the Arabian Peninsula and dan Fodio's movement in West Africa. How were these regions affected by the new world order? What alternative did Islamic revitalization propose?

6. **Describe** Hong Xiuquan's vision for China during the Taiping Rebellion. How did he propose reordering Chinese society?

7. **Identify** the various alternative visions to the status quo that European radicals proposed in the nineteenth century. What traditions and beliefs did they reflect?

8. **Compare and contrast** the Shawnee rebellion in the United States and the Caste War in Mexico. How did they reflect tensions between Native Americans and European Americans?

9. **Explain** to what extent India's Great Rebellion of 1857 encouraged a new identity among its followers. What goals did participants in the rebellion share?

10. **Analyze** the role of religion in the alternate social visions explored in this chapter.

11. **Discuss** the role of women in promoting alternative visions around the world in the nineteenth century. Which of these movements proposed new roles for women in society?

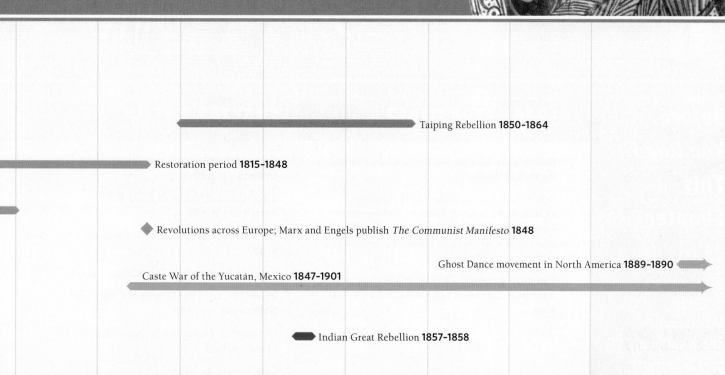

Taiping Rebellion **1850–1864**

Restoration period **1815–1848**

Revolutions across Europe; Marx and Engels publish *The Communist Manifesto* **1848**

Ghost Dance movement in North America **1889–1890**

Caste War of the Yucatán, Mexico **1847–1901**

Indian Great Rebellion **1857–1858**

1850

1875

Before You Read This Chapter

Go to
INQUIZITIVE
to see what you
know & learn
what you've
missed.

GLOBAL STORYLINES

- Nation-state building and imperialism change the map of the world.

- Industrialization, science, and technology enable states in North America and western Europe—and, to a lesser extent, Japan—to overpower other regions politically, militarily, and economically.

- European, American, and Japanese imperialists encounter significant opposition in Africa and Asia.

CHAPTER OUTLINE

Nations and Empires, 1850–1914

FOCUS QUESTIONS

- Which institutions enabled elites in western Europe, the Americas, and Japan to consolidate nation-states, and to what degree did they succeed during this period?

- How did industrialization, science, and technology affect the expansion of powerful states into the rest of the world?

- In what ways were the reactions to imperialism in Asia and Africa alike and in what ways different? How effective were these responses?

- To what extent did colonies contribute to the wealth and political strength of the nation-states that controlled them?

In 1895, the Cuban patriot José Martí launched a rebellion against the last Spanish holdings in the Americas. The anti-Spanish struggle continued until 1898, when Spain withdrew from Cuba and Puerto Rico. Martí hoped to bring freedom to a new Cuban nation and equality to all Cubans. But even as he helped secure freedom from the declining Spanish Empire, he could not prevent Cuba's military occupation and political domination by the world's newest imperial power, the United States.

Martí's hopes and frustrations found parallels around the world. After 1850, the building of nation-states and the expansion of their empires changed the map of the world, exhilarating some peoples and frustrating others. The communities that benefited most were Europeans and peoples of European descent. During these decades, the nation-states of Europe, now locked in intense political and economic rivalry, projected their power across the entire world. Much of the rivalry among European states intensified through disruptions in the European balance of power, caused by the unification of two new states (Italy and Germany). Across the Atlantic, the United States forsook its anticolonial origins and annexed overseas possessions. Yet, imperial expansion did not go unchallenged. It encountered fierce resistance from communities being incorporated into the new empires. In Asia and Africa, resisters struggled to repel their invaders, often demanding the right to govern themselves.

The second half of the nineteenth century witnessed the simultaneous—and entwined—advance of nationalism and imperialism. These decades also saw the further expansion of the industrial revolution. Taken together, the era's political and economic developments allowed western Europe and the United States to attain greater primacy in world affairs. But tensions inside these nations and their empires, as well as within other states, made the new world order anything but stable.

CONSOLIDATING NATIONS AND CONSTRUCTING EMPIRES

During the second half of the nineteenth century, the idea of building nation-states engulfed the globe. In the previous century, a series of wars, ending with the Napoleonic Wars, had made Europeans increasingly conscious of political and cultural borders and of the power of new bureaucracies. Enlightenment thinkers had emphasized the importance of nations, defined as peoples who share a common past, territory, culture, and tradition. To many people it seemed natural that once absolutist rulers had fallen, the state should draw its power and legitimacy from those who lived within its borders and that the body of institutions governing each territory should be uniquely concerned with promoting the welfare of that particular people. This seemed such a natural process that little thought was given to how nation-states arose; they were simply supposed to well up from the people's longing for liberty and togetherness.

Building Nationalism

In practice, nations did not usually well up from people's longings for liberty and togetherness. More often than not, ruling elites themselves created nations. They did so by compelling diverse groups of people and regions to accept a unified network of laws, a central administration, time zones, national markets, and a single regional dialect as the "national" language. To overcome strong regional identities, state administrators broadened public education in the national language and imposed universal military service to build a national army. These efforts nurtured the notion of a one-to-one correspondence between a "people" and a nation-state, and they radiated the values and institutions of dominant elites outward to regions throughout each nation-state and beyond their national borders.

The world's major nation-states of the late nineteenth century were not all alike, however. They took many forms. Some had been in existence for years, such as Japan, England, France, Spain, Portugal, and the United States; here, citizens widely embraced their national identities. Two nation-states (Germany and Italy) were entirely new, forged through strategic military conquests. Elsewhere, plans for nation-states in central Europe, the Balkans, Poland, and the Ukraine were chiefly the inventions of local elites; their plans displeased Russian, Austrian, and Ottoman monarchs and were of little interest to the multilingual, multiethnic peasantry in these areas. In many parts of the world, intellectuals were the primary agents agitating for new nation-states, often urging new states to break away from existing empires. That secessionist impulse posed a particularly thorny challenge to the rulers of multinational empires like Russia and Austria.

Expanding the Empires

In countries that became nation-states, the processes of nation building and the acquisition of new territories, often called **imperialism**, went hand in hand. Their rulers measured national strength not only by their people's unity and the possession of the most modern means of production, but also by the conquest of new territories. Thus, Germany, France, the United States, Russia, and Japan rivaled Britain by expanding and modernizing their industries and seizing nearby or far-off territories. By the century's end, gaining new territory had become so important that these states scrambled to colonize peoples from Africa to the Amazon, from California to Korea.

Never before had there been such a rapid reshuffling of peoples and resources. As transportation costs declined, workers left their homelands in search of better opportunities. Japanese moved to Brazil, Indians to South Africa and the Caribbean, Chinese to California, and Italians to New York and Buenos Aires. At the same time, American capitalists invested outside the United States, and British investors financed the construction of railroads in China and India. Raw materials from Africa and Southeast Asia flowed to the manufacturing nations of Europe and the Americas.

Imperial rule facilitated a widespread movement of labor, capital, commodities, and information. As scholars studied previously unknown tribes and races, new schools taught colonized peoples the languages, religions, scientific practices, and cultural traditions of their colonizers. Publications and products from the "mother country" circulated widely among indigenous elites. Yet empire builders did not extend to nonwhite inhabitants of their colonies the same rights that they gave to inhabitants of their own nations; here, nation and empire were incompatible. Not only were colonial subjects largely prohibited from participating in their own governments, but they were, with extremely modest exceptions, also not considered members of the nation at all. As a result, imperialism produced diametrically opposed reactions: exultation among the colonizers and bitterness among the colonized.

EXPANSION AND NATION BUILDING IN THE AMERICAS

Once freed from European control, the elites of the Americas set about creating political communities of their own. By the 1850s, they shared a desire both to create widespread loyalty to their political institutions and to expand territorial domains. This required refining the tools of government to include national laws and court systems, standardized money, and national political parties. It also meant finding ways to settle hinterlands that previously belonged to indigenous populations. Having once been European colonies, New World territories became vibrant nation-states based on growing prosperity and industrialization.

Although nation-states took shape throughout the world, the Americas saw the most complete assimilation of new possessions. Instead of treating outlying areas as colonial outposts, American nation-state builders turned them into new provinces. With the help of rifles, railroads, schools, and land surveys, frontiers became staging areas for the expanding populations of North and South American societies. For indigenous peoples, however, such national expansion meant the loss of traditional lands on a vast scale and many lost lives.

Not all national consolidations in the Americas were the same. The United States, Canada, and Brazil, for example, experienced different processes of nation building, territorial expansion, and economic development. Each one incorporated frontier regions into national polities and economies, although they used different techniques for subjugating indigenous peoples and administering their new holdings.

The United States

Military might, fortuitous diplomacy, and the power of numbers enabled the United States to claim territory that spanned the North American continent. (See Map 17.1.) At its independence, the new nation had been a barely united confederation of states. Indian resistance and Spanish and British rivalry hemmed in the "Americans" (as Americans of European descent came to call themselves). At the same time, the disunited states threatened to fracture into northern and southern polities, for questions of states' rights and slavery versus free labor intruded into national politics. Yet, rallying to the rhetoric of **Manifest Destiny**, a term first coined in 1845 that maintained it was God's will for the United States to "overspread" North America, Americans pushed their territorial claims and boundaries westward. They acquired territories via purchase agreements and treaties with France, Spain, and Britain and via warfare and treaties with diverse Native American nations and Mexico. (See Primary Source: Manifest Destiny.)

As part of the territories taken from Mexico after the Mexican-American War (1846–1848), the United States gained California, where the discovery of gold brought migration on an unprecedented scale. As news of the find spread, hopeful prospectors raced to stake their claims. In the next few years, over 100,000 Americans took to the overland trails and to the seas in quest of California's riches.

The California gold rush, however, was not only a great American migration; it also inspired tens of thousands of individuals from Latin America, Australia, Asia, and Europe to pour into California. What had just a few years earlier been a sparsely populated corner of northwestern Mexico was transformed almost overnight into the most cosmopolitan place on earth. In the 1850s, California was truly where worlds came together.

CIVIL WAR AND STATES' RIGHTS Ironically, California and the territories that the United States took from Mexico also spurred the coming apart of the American nation. The deeply divisive issue was whether these lands would be open to slavery or restricted to free labor. Following the 1860 election of Abraham Lincoln, who pledged to halt the expansion of slavery, the United States divided between North and South and plunged into a gruesome Civil War (1861–1865).

The bloody conflict led to the abolition of slavery, and the struggle to extend voting and citizenship rights to freed slaves qualified the Civil War as a second American Revolution. It gave the nation a new generation of heroes and martyrs, such as the assassinated president, Abraham Lincoln. Lincoln promised a new model of freedom for a nation reborn out of bloodshed. Its cornerstone would be the incorporation of freed slaves as citizens of the United States. Alas, the experiments in biracial democracy during the Reconstruction period (1867–1877) were short-lived. In the decades after the Civil War, counterrevolutionary pressure led to the denial of voting rights to African Americans and the restoration of (white) planter rule in the Southern states. This pressure was spearheaded by the terrorism of the Ku Klux Klan, a group of former Confederates that sought to undermine African Americans' legal and political gains and to restore white planters to power in the South.

Nonetheless, the war brought enduring changes across the United States. The defeat of the South established the preeminence of the national government. After the Civil War, Americans learned to speak of their nation in the singular ("the United States is" in contrast to "the United States are"). With an invigorated nationalism came an enlarged national government.

ECONOMIC AND INDUSTRIAL DEVELOPMENT Even more dizzying were social and economic changes. Within ten years of the war's end, the industrial output of the United States had climbed by 75 percent. Symbolizing this growth was the expansion of railroad lines. In 1865, the United States boasted 35,000 miles of track. By 1900, nearly 200,000 miles

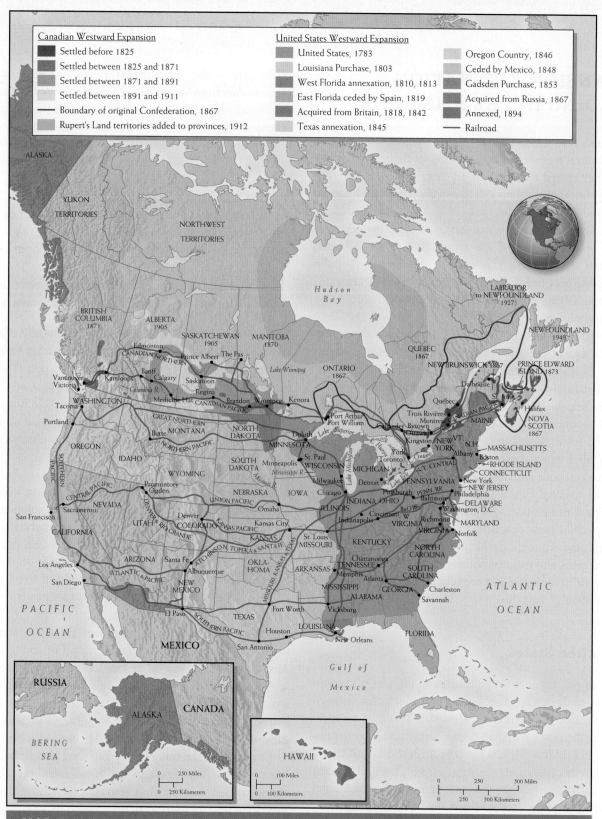

Canadian Westward Expansion
- Settled before 1825
- Settled between 1825 and 1871
- Settled between 1871 and 1891
- Settled between 1891 and 1911
- —— Boundary of original Confederation, 1867
- Rupert's Land territories added to provinces, 1912

United States Westward Expansion
- United States, 1783
- Louisiana Purchase, 1803
- West Florida annexation, 1810, 1813
- East Florida ceded by Spain, 1819
- Acquired from Britain, 1818, 1842
- Texas annexation, 1845
- Oregon Country, 1846
- Ceded by Mexico, 1848
- Gadsden Purchase, 1853
- Acquired from Russia, 1867
- Annexed, 1894
- —— Railroad

MAP 17.1 | U.S. and Canadian Westward Expansion, 1803–1912

Americans and Canadians expanded westward in the second half of the nineteenth century, aided greatly by railways.

- How many railroad lines ultimately reached the western borders of Canada and the United States?

- By what years were the territorial expansions of Canada and the United States complete? How did territorial expansion strengthen Canadian and American nationalism?

- What were the major events that led to the annexation of the western half of the United States?

PRIMARY SOURCE

Manifest Destiny

In July 1845, the New York newspaper editor John L. O'Sullivan coined the phrase Manifest Destiny *to explain how the "manifest design of Providence" supported the territorial expansion of the United States. In this excerpt, O'Sullivan outlines the reasons why the United States was justified in annexing Texas and why it must soon do the same in replacing Mexican rule in California. Claims of Manifest Destiny often accompanied American conquest and colonization of new territories.*

. . . Texas has been absorbed into the Union in the inevitable fulfilment of the general law which is rolling our population westward; the connexion of which with that ratio of growth in population which is destined within a hundred years to swell our numbers to the enormous population of *two hundred and fifty millions* (if not more), is too evident to leave us in doubt of the manifest design of Providence in regard to the occupation of this continent. It was disintegrated from Mexico in the natural course of events, by a process perfectly legitimate on its own part, blameless on ours; and in which all the censures due to wrong, perfidy and folly, rest on Mexico alone. And possessed as it was by a population which was in truth but a colonial detachment from our own, and which was still bound by myriad ties of the very heart strings to its old relations, domestic and political, their incorporation into the Union was not only inevitable, but the most natural, right and proper thing in the world. . . .

California will, probably, next fall away from the loose adhesion which, in such a country as Mexico, holds a remote province in a slight equivocal kind of dependence on the metropolis. Imbecile and distracted, Mexico never can exert any real governmental authority over such a country. The impotence of the one and the distance of the other, must make the relation one of virtual independence. . . . The Anglo-Saxon foot is already on its borders. Already the advance guard of the irresistible army of Anglo-Saxon emigration has begun to pour down upon it, armed with the plough and the rifle, and marking its trail with schools and colleges, courts and representative halls, mills and meeting-houses. A population will soon be in actual occupation of California, over which it will be idle for Mexico to dream of dominion. They will necessarily become independent.

QUESTIONS FOR ANALYSIS

- What is the main reason O'Sullivan gives for why the United States must expand westward?
- How does O'Sullivan justify the annexation of Texas by the United States?
- In terms of California, in what ways is "the Anglo-Saxon foot already on its borders"?
- Why does O'Sullivan think that the people of Texas and California will want to join the United States?

Source: John L. O'Sullivan, "Manifest Destiny," *Democratic Review* (July 1845), pp. 7–10, in *The American West: A Source Book*, edited by Clark C. Spence (New York: Thomas Y. Crowell Company, 1966), pp. 108–109.

of track connected the Atlantic to the Pacific and crisscrossed the American territory in between. Increasingly, steam-powered machines replaced human muscle as the engine of production, bringing dramatic improvements in output. Before the Civil War, it took 61 hours of labor to produce an acre of wheat; by 1900, new machinery cut the time to a little over 3 hours. Mechanization boosted production on farms and in factories, and rapid railroad transportation permitted the shipment of more goods at lower prices across greater distances. Americans made such impressive industrial gains that the United States soon joined Britain and Germany heading the list of economic giants.

A potent instrument of capital accumulation appeared at this time—the **limited-liability joint-stock company**. Firms such as Standard Oil and U.S. Steel mobilized capital from shareholders, who left the running of these enterprises to paid managers. Intermediaries, like J. Pierpont Morgan, the New York financial giant who became the world's wealthiest man, loaned money and brokered big deals on the New York Stock Exchange. So great were the fortunes amassed by leading financiers and industrialists that by 1890 the richest 1 percent of Americans owned nearly 90 percent of the nation's wealth.

As mechanized production churned out ever more goods, farms and factories produced more than Americans needed or could afford to purchase. In the 1890s, overproduction plunged the American economy into a harsh depression. Millions of urban workers lost their jobs; others suffered sharp cuts in wages. Soon radical labor leaders called for the dismantling of the industrial capitalist state, and strikes proliferated. In the

African American Gains and Losses. Above: *In the immediate aftermath of the American Civil War, "Radical Republicans" asserted political control by passing laws and constitutional amendments ending slavery, guaranteeing equal rights, and enfranchising freedmen. One result was the election of African Americans to the U.S. Congress. During the 1870s, however, white leaders retreated from the commitment to black rights, allowing ex-Confederates to reassert control over Southern politics. Right: The Ku Klux Klan terrorized African Americans in the post–Civil War South. Klan violence reversed many of the legal and political gains made by freedmen and helped restore planters to power in the South.*

countryside, declining prices and excessive railroad freight charges pushed countless farmers toward bankruptcy.

Meanwhile, Americans were continuing their migrations west. Joined by throngs of immigrants from Europe, they were attracted by homestead acts promising nearly free acreage to settlers and by the railroad's real estate promoters. (Railroad corporations had been given enormous land grants as a subsidy for building transcontinental lines.) The migrations sparked another round of wars with Amerindians, which resulted in their dispossession and concentration on reservations.

By now the United States had become a major world power. It boasted an economy that despite its troubles in the 1890s had expanded rapidly over the last decades of the nineteenth century. It also was a more integrated nation after the Civil War, with an amended constitution that claimed to uphold the equality of all members of the American nation. But there was no agreement on what that equality should involve or how the country would adjust to a new century in which the nation's "destiny" had already been fulfilled.

Canada

Canadians also built a new nation, enjoyed economic success, and followed an expansionist course. Like the United States, Canada had access to a vast frontier prairie for growing agricultural exports. And as in the United States, these lands became

the homes and farms of more European immigrants. However, whereas the United States had waged a war to gain independence, Canada's separation from Britain was peaceful. From the 1830s to the 1860s, Britain gradually passed authority to the colony, leaving Canadians to grapple with the task of creating a shared national community.

BUILDING A NATION Sharp internal divisions made that task especially difficult. For one thing, there was a well-established French population. It had remained after the British took control of France's northernmost North American colony in 1763. Wanting to keep their villages, their culture, their religion, and their language intact, these French Canadians did not feel integrated into the emerging Canadian national community. Nor were they eager to join the English-speaking population in settling new areas, lest such migration dilute their French Canadian presence.

The English speakers were equally unenthusiastic about creating an independent nation. Fear of being absorbed into the American republic reinforced these Canadians' loyalty to the British crown and made them content with colonial status. Indeed, when Canada finally gained its independence in 1867, it was by an Act of Parliament in London and not by revolution.

TERRITORIAL EXPANSION Lacking cultural and linguistic unity, not to mention an imperial overlord, Canadians used territorial expansion to build an integrated state. But their process

Oklahoma Land Rush. *This photograph captures the rush of homesteaders to claim lands on the "Cherokee Strip" on September 16, 1893. The opening of land that had previously been restricted to Indians set off several similar rushes in the Oklahoma Territory.*

differed from that of their neighbor to the south. In response to the U.S. purchase of Alaska from Russia and the movement of settlers onto the American plains, Canadian leaders realized that they had to incorporate their own western territories, lest these, too, fall into American hands. Pioneers seemed unwilling to venture to these prairies—it was far, it was cold, and the growing season was cruelly short. So the state lured emigrant farmers from Europe and the United States with subsidized railway rates and the promise of fortunes to be made. It also offered attractive terms to railway companies to connect agrarian hinterlands with Montreal and Toronto (see again Map 17.1) and *not* with commercial cities in the United States.

The Canadian state also faced friction with indigenous peoples. Frontier warfare threatened to drive away investors and settlers, who could always find property south of the border instead. To prevent the kind of bloodletting that characterized the United States' westward expansion, the Canadian government signed treaties with indigenous peoples to ensure strict separation between these communities and newcomers. It also created a special police force, the Royal Canadian Mounted Police, to patrol the territories.

Canadian expansion was hardly bloodless, however. Many indigenous and mixed-blood peoples (*métis*) resented the treaties. Moreover, the Canadian government was often less than honest in its dealings. As in the United States, the Canadian government sought to turn its indigenous peoples into farmers and then incorporate them into Canadian society—regardless of whether they wanted to become farmers or join the nation.

The need to accommodate resident French speakers, defensive expansionism, and a degree of legality in dealing with indigenous peoples gave the Canadian government a strong foundation. Indeed, it acquired significant powers to intervene, regulate, and mediate social conflict and relations. (These powers, in fact, were fuller than those of the U.S. government.) But even though the state was relatively strong, the sense of a national identity was comparatively weak. Expansionism helped Canada remain an autonomous state, but it did not solve the question of what it meant to belong to a Canadian nation.

Latin America

Latin American elites also engaged in nation-state building and expanded their territorial borders. But unlike the situation in the United States and Canada, expansion did not always create homesteader frontiers that could help expand democracy and forge national identities. Instead, civil conflict fractured certain countries in the region (see Chapters 15 and 16), although a few—most notably Mexico and Brazil—remained united.

Much of Latin America shared a common social history. Far more than in North America, the richest lands in Latin America went not to small farmers but to large estate holders producing exports such as sugar, coffee, or beef. The result: privileged elites monopolized power more than in North America's young democracies. Even though territorial expansion and strong economic growth were Latin American hallmarks, these processes sidelined the poor, the Native Americans, and the blacks.

CONSOLIDATION VERSUS FRAGMENTATION Amerindian and peasant uprisings were a major worry in new Latin American republics. Fearing insurrections, elites devised governing systems that protected private property and investments while limiting the political rights of the poor and the propertyless. Likewise, the specter of slave revolts, driven home not just by earlier, brutal events in Haiti (see Chapter 15) but also by daily rumors of rebellions, kept elites in a state of alarm. One Argentine writer, Domingo Faustino Sarmiento, echoed the concern about giving too much power to the masses, and he described the challenge of nation-state building in Latin America as a struggle between elitist "civilization" and popular "barbarism." Creating strong nations, it seemed to many Latin American elites, required excluding large groups of people from power.

BRAZIL: AN "EXCLUSIVE" NATION-STATE Brazil illustrates the process by which Latin American rulers built nation-states that excluded much of the population from both the "nation" and the "state." Through the nineteenth century, rulers in Rio de Janeiro defused political conflict by allowing planters to retain the reins of power. Moreover, although the Brazilian government officially abolished the slave trade in 1830, it allowed illegal slave imports to continue for another two decades (until British pressure compelled Brazil to enforce the ban).

The end of the slave trade, coupled with slave resistance, began to choke the planters' system by driving up the price of slaves within the region. Sensing that the system of forced labor was unraveling, slaves began to flee the sugar and coffee plantations, and army personnel refused to hunt them down. In the 1880s, even while laws still upheld slave labor, country roads in the state of São Paulo were filled with fugitive slaves looking for relatives or access to land. Finally, in 1888, the Brazilian emperor abolished slavery.

Thereafter, as in the United States, Brazilian elites followed two strategies in creating a new labor force for their estates. They retained some former slaves as gang-workers or sharecroppers, and they also imported new workers—especially from Italy, Spain, and Portugal. These laborers often came as seasonal migrant workers or indentured tenant farmers. Indeed, European and even Japanese migration to Brazil helped planters preserve their holdings in the post-slavery era. In all, 2 million Europeans and some 70,000 Japanese moved to Brazil.

The Brazilian state was deliberately exclusive. The constitution of 1891, which established a federal system and proclaimed Brazil a republic, separated those who could be trusted with power from the rest. After all, with the abolition of slavery, the sudden enfranchisement of millions of freedmen would have threatened to flood the electoral lists with propertyless, potentially uncontrollable voters. As in the United States, politicians responded by slapping severe restrictions on suffrage and by rigging rules to reduce political competition. However, given the greater share of the black population in Brazil, restrictions there excluded a larger share of the potential electorate than in the United States.

BRAZIL: EXPANSION AND ECONOMIC DEVELOPMENT Like Canada and the United States, the Brazilian state extended its reach to distant areas and incorporated them as provinces. The largest land grab occurred in the Amazon River basin, the world's largest drainage watershed and tropical forest. It had built up over millennia around the meandering tributaries that convey runoffs from the eastern slopes of the Andean Mountains all the way to the Atlantic Ocean. It was a massive yet delicate habitat of balanced biomass suspended by towering trees with a canopy of leaves and vines that kept the basin ecologically diverse. Here, the Brazilian state gave giant concessions to local capitalists to extract rubber latex. When combined with sulfur, rubber was a key raw material for tire manufacturing in European and North American bicycle and automobile industries.

As Brazil became the world's exclusive exporter of rubber, its planters, merchants, and workers prospered. Rich merchants became lenders and financiers, not only to workers but also to landowners themselves. The mercantile elite of Manaus, the capital of the Amazon region, designed and decorated their city to reflect their new fortune. Although the streets were still paved with mud, the town's elite built a replica of the Paris Opera House, and Manaus became a regular stopover for

Opera House in Manaus. *The turn-of-the-century rubber boom brought immense wealth to the Amazon jungle. As in many boom-and-bust cycles in Latin America, the proceeds flowed to a small elite and diminished when the rubber supply outstripped the demand. But the wealth produced was sufficient to prompt the local elite to build temples of modernity in the midst of the jungle. Pictured here is the Opera House in the rubber capital of Manaus. Like other works built by Latin American elites of the period, this one emulated the original in Paris.*

Rubber Plantation Workers. *Left: A worker harvests latex, a milky fluid that is secreted from a rubber tree via taps in its trunk. Right: The worker must work quickly to collect and process it into dry rubber before it coagulates.*

European opera singers on the circuit between Buenos Aires and New York. Rubber workers also benefited from the boom. Mostly either Amerindians or mixed-blood people, they sent their wages home to families elsewhere in the Amazon jungle or on the northeastern coast of Brazil.

But the Brazilian rubber boom soon went bust. One problem was the ecosystem: such a diversified biomass could not tolerate a regimented form of production that emphasized the cultivation of rubber trees at the expense of other vegetation and made the forest vulnerable to nonhuman predators. Leaf blight and ferocious ants destroyed all experiments at creating more sustainable rubber plantations. Moreover, it was expensive to haul the rubber latex out of the jungle all the way to the coast along the slow-moving Amazon River. Another problem was that Brazilian rubber faced severe competition after a British scientist smuggled rubber plant seeds out of Brazil in 1876. Following years of experimentation, British patrons transplanted a blight-resistant hybrid to the British colony of Ceylon (present-day Sri Lanka). As competition led to increased supplies and reduced prices, Brazilian producers went bankrupt. Merchants called in their loans, landowners forfeited their titles, and rubber workers returned to their subsistence economies. Tropical vines crept over the Manaus Opera House, and it gradually fell into disrepair.

Throughout the Americas, nineteenth-century elites adapted older models of politics while attempting to satisfy popular demands for inclusion. Although the ideal was to construct nation-states that could reconcile differences among their citizens and pave the way for economic prosperity, in fact political autonomy did not bring prosperity, or even the right to vote, to all. As each nation-state expanded its territorial boundaries, many new inhabitants were left out of the political realm.

CONSOLIDATION OF NATION-STATES IN EUROPE

In Europe, no "frontier" existed into which new nations could expand. Instead, nation-states took shape out of older monarchies and empires, and their borders were determined by diplomats or by battles between rival claimants. In the wake of the French Revolution, the idea caught on that "the people" should form the basis for the nation and that nations should be culturally homogeneous—but no one could agree on who "the people" should be. Yet, over the course of the nineteenth century, as literacy, the cities, industrial production, and the number and prosperity of property owners expanded, ruling elites had no choice but to share power with a wider group of citizens. These citizens, in turn, increasingly defined themselves as, say, Frenchmen or Germans, rather than as residents of Marseilles or subjects of the king of Bavaria.

Defining "The Nation"

For a very long time, in most places, "the nation" was understood to comprise kings, clergymen, nobles—and occasionally rich merchants or lawyers—and no one else. Although some peoples, such as the English and the Spanish, were already self-conscious about their unique histories, only in the late eighteenth century were the crucial building blocks of European nationalism put in place.

Enlightenment thinkers contributed key ideas to the ideological foundations of the nation. In 1776, Adam Smith (see Chapter 15) described the wealth of each nation as equivalent to the combined output of all its producers, not the sum in the king's treasury. Then, in 1789, the left-leaning French clergyman

Emmanuel Joseph Sieyès published a widely circulated pamphlet arguing that the nation consists of all of those who work to enrich it, and that those who are "parasites" (Sieyès meant the clergy and the aristocracy) do not belong. Sieyès's revolutionary "Declaration of the Rights of Man and of the Citizen," inspired by the American Declaration of Independence, declared that all men are equal under the law and insisted that "the principle of all sovereignty lies essentially in the nation." Thanks to the unpopularity of his occupation regimes, Napoleon inadvertently helped to strengthen German, Italian, and Spanish nationalism.

During the nineteenth century, a huge expansion of literacy and the periodical press made it possible for people all across Europe to read books and newspapers in their own languages. At the same time, the emerging industrial economy made merchants anxious to standardize laws, taxation policies, and weights and measures. States invested huge sums in building roads and then railroads, linking provincial towns with bigger cities and laying the foundations for a closer political integration.

But who were the people, and what constituted a viable nation-state? Neither Smith's treatise nor Sieyès's pamphlet clarified exactly who the communities were that belonged to a specific territory and shared cultural or religious traditions. For some people, the nation was a collection of all those who spoke one language; for others, it was all those who lived under a certain prince or who shared a religious heritage. This was a particularly acute problem in multiethnic central and southeastern Europe, where many people were multilingual, rich and poor alike. But some who shared the same language objected to being lumped into one nation-state. The Irish, for example, spoke English but were predominately Catholics and wanted to be free from Anglican rule.

The Europe-wide revolutions of 1848 (see Chapters 15 and 16) sought to put "the people" in power; in many cases, too, rebels sought to create unified nation-states, each of which would serve one particular cultural and linguistic group. (Examples include the Czechs and Italians, both of whom wanted states independent from the Habsburg Empire.) But the revolutions ran into difficulties defining who "the people" were and how to fashion new nations out of Europe's multiethnic empires. Deep divisions opened among ethnic groups and between middle-class liberals and radicals, some of whom wanted to share out the nation's wealth. Monarchs took advantage of the chaos and restored their regimes. The troubling questions continued to agitate Europe for many years to come. (See Primary Source: What Is a Nation?)

Unification in Germany and Italy

Two of Europe's fledgling nation-states came into being when the dynastic states of Prussia and Piedmont-Sardinia swallowed their smaller, linguistically related neighbors, creating the German and Italian nation-states. (See Map 17.2.) In both regions, conservative prime ministers—Count Otto von Bismarck of Prussia and Count Camillo di Cavour of Piedmont—exploited radical, and especially liberal, nationalist sentiment to rearrange the map of Europe.

BUILDING UNIFIED STATES The unification of Germany and Italy posed all the familiar problems of who the people were and who should be included in the new nation-states. To begin with, German speakers were spread all across central and eastern Europe; after 1815, many, but not all, resided in the Austrian-dominated German Confederation. They continued to live, as they had for centuries, in largely autonomous states of diverse size, wealth, and religious and ethnic makeup. Similarly, Italians had lived separately in city-states and small kingdoms on the Italian Peninsula and spoke a range of dialects. The historical experiences and economic developments had made Bavarian Germans (Catholic) quite different from Prussian Germans (Protestant); likewise, the Milanese (who lived in a wealthy urban industrial center) shared little with the typical Sardinian peasant. But liberal nationalists had made the case that their high culture—especially their musical and theatrical traditions—overrode all these differences, and emotional appeals by poets, composers, and orators convinced many people that this was indeed the case.

Ultimately, Bismarck and Cavour merged nationalist rhetoric with clever diplomacy to forge united German and Italian nations. But both had to go to war to accomplish their aims. In a famous address in 1862, Bismarck bellowed: "Not through speeches and majority decisions are the great questions of the day decided—that was the great mistake of 1848 and 1849—but through blood and iron." True to his word, Bismarck broke up the German Confederation and unified the northern German states under the Prussian crown by means of war: with Denmark in 1864, Austria in 1866, and France (over the western provinces of Alsace and Lorraine) in 1870–1871. Italy also was united under the banner of Piedmont-Sardinia through a series of small conflicts, many of them engineered to prevent the establishment of more radical republics.

INTERNAL CONFLICTS These "unified" states were favorable to liberal principles, but rejected democracy. In the new Italy, which was a constitutional monarchy, not a republic, less than 5 percent of the 25 million people could vote. The new German Empire (the Reich) did have an assembly elected by all adult males (the Reichstag), but it was ruled by a combination of aristocrats and bureaucrats under a monarch. Liberals dominated in many localities, but only the emperor (the kaiser) could depose the prime minister. In fact, Bismarck continued to dominate Prussian politics for twenty-eight years, until fired in 1890 by Kaiser Wilhelm II.

What Is a Nation?

The French linguist and historian of religion Ernest Renan explored the concept of nationhood in an 1882 essay titled "What Is a Nation?" Arguing with racial, religious, and language-based interpretations of nationhood, Renan offers an explicitly republican model.

. . . The principle of nations is our principle. But what, then, is a nation? . . . Why is Switzerland, with its three languages, its two religions, and three or four races, a nation, when Tuscany, for example, which is so homogeneous, is not? Why is Austria a state and not a nation? In what does the principle of nations differ from that of races? . . .

Ethnographic considerations have . . . played no part in the formation of modern nations. France is Celtic, Iberic, and Germanic. Germany is Germanic, Celtic, and Slav. Italy is the country in which ethnography finds its greatest difficulties. Here Gauls, Etruscans, Pelasgians, and Greeks are crossed in an unintelligible medley. The British Isles, taken as a whole, exhibit a mixture of Celtic and Germanic blood, the proportions of which are particularly difficult to define.

The truth is that no race is pure, and that to base politics on ethnographic analysis is tantamount to basing it on a chimera. . . .

What we have said about race, applies also to language. Language invites union, without, however, compelling it. The United States and England, as also Spanish America and Spain, speak the same language without forming a single nation. Switzerland, on the contrary, whose foundations are solid because they are based on the assent of the various parties, contains three or four languages. There exists in man a something which is above language: and that is his will. The will of Switzerland to be united, in spite of the variety of these forms of speech, is a much more important fact than a similarity of language, often attained by vexatious measures. . . .

Nor can religion provide a satisfactory basis for a modern nationality. . . . Nowadays . . . everyone believes and practices religion in his own way according to his capacities and wishes. State religion has ceased to exist; and a man can be a Frenchman, an Englishman, or a German, and at the same time a Catholic, a Protestant, or a Jew, or practice no form of worship at all.

A nation is a soul, a spiritual principle. Two things, which are really only one, go to make up this soul or spiritual principle. One of these things lies in the past, the other in the present. The one is the possession in common of a rich heritage of memories; and the other is actual agreement, the desire to live together, and the will to continue to make the most of the joint inheritance. . . . The nation, like the individual, is the fruit of a long past spent in toil, sacrifice, and devotion. . . . To share the glories of the past, and a common will in the present; to have done great deeds together, and to desire to do more— . . . These are things which are understood, in spite of differences in race and language.

. . . The existence of a nation is . . . a daily plebiscite. . . . A province means to us its inhabitants; and if anyone has a right to be consulted in the matter, it is the inhabitant. It is never to the true interest of a nation to annex or keep a country against its will. The people's wish is after all the only justifiable criterion, to which we must always come back.

QUESTIONS FOR ANALYSIS

- According to Renan, what are the two key ingredients needed to create a nation-state?
- What arguments does Renan offer against basing nationhood on a common race, religion, or language?

Source: Ernest Renan, "What Is a Nation?" in *The Nationalism Reader*, edited by Omar Dahbour and Micheline R. Ishay (Atlantic Highlands, NJ: Humanities Press, 1995), pp. 143–155.

The new states, and especially the Germans, enjoyed brisk economic growth, which simply highlighted the fact that they remained internally fragmented. In Italy, Piedmontese liberals in the north hoped that centralized rule would transform southern Italy into a prosperous, commercial, and industrial region like their own. The south was agricultural, isolated from modernizing impulses, and little attracted to northern customs. The north, industrialized and more fully developed economically, had important commercial links with Switzerland and France. In Germany, many non-Germans—Poles in Silesia, French in Alsace and Lorraine, Danes in the provinces of Schleswig-Holstein—became "national minorities" whose rights remained in question. In the 1870s, Bismarck branded both Catholics and socialists as traitors to the new state; both retaliated by forming powerful political movements. By the 1890s, too, colonial rivalries and conflicts in the Balkans combined to make nationalism more belligerent and potentially destabilizing, particularly in the continent's remaining multiethnic states: the Russian, Ottoman, and Habsburg Empires.

MAP 17.2 | Italian Unification and German Unification, 1815–1871

Italian unification and German unification altered the political map of Europe.

- What were the names of the two original states that grew to become Italy and Germany? Who were the big losers in these territorial transfers?

- According to your reading, what problems did the new Italian and German states face in creating strong national communities?

Nation Building and Ethnic Conflict in the Austro-Hungarian Empire

Bismarck's wars of unification came at the expense of Habsburg supremacy in central Europe and of French territory and influence in the west. Following Germany's swift victory over the Austrian army in 1866, the Hungarian nobles who controlled the eastern Habsburg Empire forced the weakened dynasts to grant them home rule. In the Compromise of 1867, the Habsburgs agreed that their state would officially be known as the Austro-Hungarian Empire. But this move did not solve Austria-Hungary's nationality problems. In both the Hungarian and the Austrian halves of the dual state, Czechs, Poles, and

other Slavs now began to clamor for their own power-sharing "compromise" or autonomous national homelands. The problems were only exacerbated after Austria-Hungary occupied the territory of Bosnia-Herzegovina in 1878 (annexed in 1908), a formerly Ottoman region where the Austrians now ruled over hundreds and thousands of discontented Serbs, Croatians, and Bosnian Muslims.

Domestic Discontents in France and Britain

Although already unified as nation-states, Britain and France, too, faced major difficulties. For the French, dealing with military defeat at the hands of the Germans was the primary national concern in the decades leading up to World War I. For the British, issues of Irish separatism, the rise of the working class, and feminists' demands troubled the political arena.

DESTABILIZATION IN FRANCE Bismarck launched the Franco-Prussian War of 1870–1871 to complete the unification of Germany; he did not intend to destabilize France. But the sound drubbing that the French troops received and the capture of Napoleon III early in the conflict proved embarrassing and upsetting. Even more catastrophic for France was the German siege of Paris, which lasted for more than three months. Having escaped the city by balloon so as to continue the war, the provisional government left Paris without leadership and without staples. Parisians had no food stocks and were compelled to eat all sorts of things, including two zoo elephants. Resistance collapsed in January 1871, when the government signed a humiliating peace treaty. Furious Parisians vented their rage and established a socialist commune proclaiming the city a utopia for workers. The leftist commune lasted until the provisional national government's predominantly peasant army stormed Paris a few months later. At least 25,000 Parisians died in the bloody mop-up that followed.

A "Third Republic" took the place of Napoleon III's empire, but its conservative leaders were wary of the socialists and workers. They also were determined to revenge themselves for their humiliation in 1871. For the French, the years to follow would bring two unsettling developments: increasingly sharp conflict between classes over the shape of the republic and rising anti-German nationalism. Some of this antagonism also radiated outward to target French colonial subjects, who now experienced more virulent forms of racism.

IRISH NATIONALISM IN GREAT BRITAIN The kingdom of England—which was composed of England, clearly the dominant state, and Wales—became the kingdom of Great Britain when it united with Scotland in 1707 and Ireland in 1801. Although the English had long thought of themselves as a nation, the idea that all Britons belonged in the same state was much more problematic. Great Britain was home to people whose historical experiences, religious backgrounds, and economic opportunities were very different. In the nineteenth century, British leaders wrestled in particular with lower-class agitation and demands for independence from Irish nationalists. Beginning in 1832, Britain responded to class conflict by extending political rights to most men but not women, then finally established universal suffrage for adult males after World War I. In 1918, roughly one-quarter of British women gained the right to vote and the rest a decade later.

Yet Ireland remained England's Achilles' heel. Although in 1836 Irish Catholics finally became equal to Protestants before the law, the two communities' political and economic conditions remained very uneven. English and Irish Protestants owned the vast majority of the land and attempted to squeeze Irish smallholders to give up their plots. Over the course of the early nineteenth century, more and more Irish peasants had planted energy-rich and easy-to-cultivate potatoes on their remaining rocky and sandy land. A relatively healthy diet of potatoes and milk had fueled population growth and put more pressure on the land. When a continent-wide potato blight ravaged the island's crops in 1845, this monoculture turned into a recipe for widespread famine. Although the blight continue to decimate harvests for the next four years, the English stuck

The Irish Potato Famine.
Many families in Ireland were left desperate and starving in the aftermath of the potato crop failure and were forced to find sustenance wherever they could. In this engraving from the late nineteenth century, a group of people by the coast collect limpets and seaweed to eat.

to their laissez-faire principles and were slow to send grain to relieve Irish suffering, resulting in the death of as many as a million and the emigration of about the same number. Many of these Irish emigrants made their way to England, seeking either passage to North America or work in the English mill towns. Like their Scottish brethren, they did not assimilate easily and often got the lowliest jobs. All of this, on top of 300 years of repressive English domination, spawned a mass movement for Irish home rule that continued into the twentieth century.

Born in opposition to the old monarchical regimes, European nationalism by the end of the nineteenth century had become a means used by liberal and conservative leaders alike to unite "the people" behind them. But this did not mean that everyone had equal access to power. Women, the poor, and minority ethnic and religious groups, in particular, did not have a just share. Moreover, by 1900, European nationalisms and bitterness, sowed by the wars of unification, were producing deeper enmities between states and within multinational empires. Nationalism had transformed Metternich's map and given more people a voice in political decision-making and a share in the cultural life than ever before. But it had made Europe a more volatile place.

INDUSTRY, SCIENCE, AND TECHNOLOGY

In addition to nationalist conceptions of "the people," nineteenth-century states in North America and western Europe were shaped by a powerful combination of industry, science, and technology. These forces also reordered the relationships between different parts of the world. One critical factor was that after 1850, western Europe and North America experienced a new phase of industrial development—essentially a second industrial revolution. Japan, too, joined the ranks of industrializing nations as its state-led program of industrial development started to pay dividends. These changes transformed the global economy and intensified rivalries among industrial societies. For example, Britain now had to contend with competition from the United States and Germany.

New Materials, Technologies, and Business Practices

New materials and new technologies were vital in late nineteenth-century economic development. The period witnessed major technological changes with the arrival of new organic sources of power (oil) and new ways to get old organic sources (like coal) to processing plants. These changes freed manufacturers from having to locate their plants close to their fuel sources.

Not only did the most important source of energy—electricity—permit factories to arise in areas with plenty of skilled workers, but it also slashed production costs. **Steel**, which was more malleable and stronger than iron, became essential for industries like shipbuilding and railways. The world output of steel shot up from half a million tons in 1870 to 28 million tons in 1900. The miracle of steel was celebrated through the construction of the Eiffel Tower in Paris (completed in 1889), an aggressively modern monument that loomed over the picturesque cityscape and was double the height of any other building in the world at the time. Steel was part of a bundle of innovations that included chemicals, oil, pharmaceuticals, and mass transportation vehicles like trolleys, buses, taxis, and trains. Scientific research, too, boosted industrial development. German companies led the way in creating laboratories where university-trained chemists and physicists conducted research to serve industrial production. The United States likewise wedded scientific research with capitalist enterprise: universities and corporate laboratories produced swelling ranks of engineers and scientists, as well as patents.

The breakthroughs of the second industrial revolution ushered in new business practices, especially mass production and

Eiffel Tower. *This 1890 photograph of an illuminated Eiffel Tower encapsulates the fact and spirit of early twentieth-century technological innovation, from the architectural breakthrough of the tower itself to the harnessing of electricity to truly render Paris its nickname—the City of Light.*

Railroad Workers. *The construction of railroad lines across the United States was dangerous work, much of it done by immigrant laborers, including large numbers of Chinese, such as those in this photograph taken in 1886.*

the giant integrated firm. No longer would modest investments suffice, as they had in Britain a century earlier. Now large banks were the major providers of funds. In Europe, limited-liability joint-stock companies were as wildly successful in raising capital on stock markets as they were in the United States. Companies like Standard Oil, U.S. Steel, and Siemens mobilized capital from a large number of investors, the shareholders. The scale of these firms was awesome. U.S. Steel alone produced over half the world's steel ingots, castings, rails, and heavy structural shapes—and nearly half of all its steel plates and sheets, which were vital in the construction of buildings, railroads, ships, and the like.

Integration of the World Economy

Not only did industrial change concentrate power in North Atlantic societies, but it also reinforced their power on the world economic stage and created a more integrated world economy. Of course, Europe and the United States increased their exports in new products; but at the same time, they grew eager to control the importation of tropical commodities such as cocoa and coffee. While the North Atlantic societies were still largely self-sufficient in coal, iron, cotton, wool, and wheat (the major commodities of the first industrial revolution), the second industrial revolution bred a need for rubber, copper, oil, and bauxite (an ore used to make aluminum), which were not available domestically. Equally important, large pools of money became available for investing overseas. London may have lost its industrial leadership, but it retained dominance over the world's financial operations. By 1913, the British had the huge sum of £4 billion invested overseas—funds that generated an annual income of £200 million, or one-tenth of Britain's national income.

MOVEMENTS OF LABOR AND TECHNOLOGY Because the more integrated world economy needed workers for fields, factories, and mines, vast movements of the laboring population took place. Indians moved thousands of miles to work on sugar plantations in the Caribbean, Mauritius, and Fiji, to labor in South American mines, and to build railroads in East Africa. Chinese workers constructed railroads in the western United States and toiled on sugar plantations in Cuba. The Irish, Poles, Jews, Italians, and Greeks flocked to North America to fill its burgeoning factories. Italians also moved to Argentina to harvest wheat and corn.

New technologies of warfare, transportation, and communication eased global economic integration—and strengthened European domination. With steam-powered gunboats and

Suez Canal. *The Suez Canal opened to world shipping in 1869 and reduced the time it took to sail between Europe and Asian ports. Although the French and the Egyptians supplied most of the money and the construction plans and Egyptians were the main workforce, British shipping dominated canal traffic from the outset.*

Charles Darwin. *Engraving of Darwin testing the speed of a tortoise in the Galápagos Islands. It was during his visit to these islands that Darwin developed many of the ideas that he would put forth in his 1859 Origin of Species.*

breech-loading rifles, Europeans opened new territories for trade and conquest. At home and in their colonial possessions, imperial powers constructed networks of railroads that carried people and goods from hinterlands to the coasts. From there, steamships bore them across the seas. Completion of the Suez Canal in 1869 shortened ship voyages between Europe and Asia and lowered the costs of interregional trade. Information moved even faster than cargoes, thanks to the laying of telegraph cables under the oceans, supplemented by overland telegraph lines.

CHARLES DARWIN AND NATURAL SELECTION
Although machines were the most visible evidence that humans could master the universe, perhaps the most momentous shift in the conception of nature derived from the travels of one British scientist: **Charles Darwin** (1809–1882). Longing to see exotic fauna, in 1831 he signed on for a four-year voyage on a surveying vessel bound for Latin America and the South Seas. As the ship's naturalist, Darwin collected large quantities of specimens and recorded observations daily. After returning to England, he became convinced that the species of organic life had evolved under the uniform pressure of natural laws, not by means of a special, one-time creation as described in the Bible.

Darwin's theory, articulated in his *On the Origin of Species* (1859), laid out the principles of **natural selection**. Inevitably, he claimed, populations grow faster than the food supply; this condition creates a "struggle for existence" among species. In later work he showed how the passing on of individual traits is also determined by what he called sexual selection—according to which the "best" mates are chosen for their strength, beauty, or talents. The outcome: the "fittest" survive to reproduce, while

the less adaptable do not. The "economy of nature" is, Darwin confessed, a painful reality: people would rather behold "nature's face bright with gladness" than recognize that some animals must be others' prey and that shortages are, ultimately, part of nature's "miraculous efficiency." Although Darwin's book dealt exclusively with nonhuman animals (and mostly with birds), his readers immediately wondered what his theory implied for humans. (See Primary Source: *On the Origin of Species*.)

A passionate debate began among scientists and laypeople, clerics and anthropologists. Some read Darwin's doctrine of the "survival of the fittest" to mean that it was natural for the strong nations to dominate the weak or justifiable to allow disabled persons to die—something Darwin explicitly refuted. As more groups (mis)interpreted Darwin's theory to suit their own objectives, a set of beliefs known as social Darwinism legitimated the suffering of the underclasses in industrial society: it was unnatural, social Darwinists claimed, to tamper with natural selection. In subsequent years, Europeans would repeatedly suggest that they had evolved more than Africans and Asians. Extending Darwinian ideas far beyond the scientist's intent, some Europeans came to believe that nature itself gave them the right to rule others.

IMPERIALISM AND THE ORIGINS OF ANTICOLONIAL NATIONALISM

Increasing rivalries among nations and social tensions within them produced an expansionist wave late in the nineteenth century. Although Africa became the primary focus of interest, a frenzy of territorial conquest overtook Asia as well. The period

On the Origin of Species

Charles Darwin's On the Origin of Species *(1859) was the product of his many years of studying animals and plants. In addressing the question "How and why are new species created?" the book describes the process of natural selection, according to which nature creates overabundance so that the "fittest" species survive and adapt themselves to their environments. Although Darwin's book says nothing about human beings, his contemporaries speculated on his theory's implications for the evolution of human beings.*

Again, it may be asked, how is it that varieties, which I have called incipient species, become ultimately converted into good and distinct species, which in most cases obviously differ from each other far more than do the varieties of the same species? How do those groups of species, which constitute what are called distinct genera, and which differ from each other more than do the species of the same genus, arise? All these results . . . follow inevitably from the struggle for life. Owing to this struggle for life, any variation, however slight and from whatever cause proceeding, if it be in any degree profitable to an individual of any species, in its infinitely complex relations to other organic beings and to external nature, will tend to the preservation of that individual, and will generally be inherited by its offspring. The offspring, also, will thus have a better chance of surviving, for, of the many individuals of any species which are periodically born, but a small number can survive. I have called this principle, by which each slight variation, if useful, is preserved, by the term of Natural Selection, in order to mark its relation to man's power of selection. We have seen that man by selection can certainly produce great results, and can adapt organic beings to his own uses, through the accumulation of slight but useful variations, given to him by the hand of Nature. But Natural Selection, as we shall hereafter see, is a power incessantly ready for action, and is as immeasurably superior to man's feeble efforts, as the works of Nature are to those of Art.

We will now discuss in a little more detail the struggle for existence. . . . I should premise that I use the term Struggle for Existence in a large and metaphorical sense, including dependence of one being on another, and including (which is more important) not only the life of the individual, but success in leaving progeny. Two canine animals in a time of dearth, may be truly said to struggle with each other which shall get food and live. But a plant on the edge of a desert is said to struggle for life against the drought, though more properly it should be said to be dependent on the moisture. . . .

A struggle for existence inevitably follows from the high rate at which all organic beings tend to increase. Every being, which during its natural lifetime produces several eggs or seeds, must suffer destruction during some period of its life, and during some season or occasional year, otherwise, on the principle of geometrical increase, its numbers would quickly become so inordinately great that no country could support the product. Hence, as more individuals are produced than can possibly survive, there must in every case be a struggle for existence, either one individual with another of the same species, or with the individuals of distinct species, or with the physical conditions of life. . . . Although some species may be now increasing, more or less rapidly, in numbers, all cannot do so, for the world would not hold them.

It may be said that natural selection is daily and hourly scrutinising, throughout the world, every variation, even the slightest; rejecting that which is bad, preserving and adding up all that is good; silently and insensibly working, whenever and wherever opportunity offers, at the improvement of each organic being in relation to its organic and inorganic conditions of life. We see nothing of these slow changes in progress, until the hand of time has marked the long lapses of ages, and then so imperfect is our view into long past geological ages, that we only see that the forms of life are now different from what they formerly were.

QUESTIONS FOR ANALYSIS

- How does Darwin explain the divergence of species?
- Why does Darwin think struggle is inevitable for all living beings?

Source: Charles Darwin, *On the Origin of Species*, Chapters 3 and 4.

witnessed the French occupation of Vietnam, Cambodia, and Laos and the British expansion in Malaya (present-day Malaysia). In China's territories, competition by foreign powers to establish spheres of influence heated up in the 1890s. And in India, imperial ambitions provoked the British to conquer Burma (present-day Myanmar). Moreover, Britain and Russia competed for preeminence from their respective outposts in Afghanistan and central Asia. In the Americas, expansion usually involved the incorporation of new territories as provinces, making them integral parts of the nation.

In Asia and Africa, however, European imperialism turned far-flung territories into colonial possessions. Here, inhabitants were usually designated as subjects of the empire without the rights and privileges of citizens. Britain's imperial regime in India provided lessons to a generation of European colonial officials in Africa and other parts of Asia. Yet, even as Europe's colonial administrators looked to earlier imperial practices in India and the Caribbean for use in Africa, they also regarded Africans as less economically and culturally developed than Asian communities. Hence, they believed that Africans would require an extended period of colonial tutelage.

The exponents of European and North American colonization argued that colonial rule produced benefits for both the colonial peoples and the colonizers. Economically, colonies would be drawn into and profit from an emerging world economy. They would export primary products in high demand in the industrialized parts of the global economy—most notably cocoa, tea, coffee, diamonds, gold, and copper from Africa; rubber from the Dutch East Indies; huge quantities of cotton from India and Egypt; and beginning mainly after World War I, oil from the Middle East to fuel industrial economies. In return, colonial peoples would import much-needed manufactured commodities—clothing made from their raw cotton; processed foods made from coffee, cocoa, and tea; railway engines; and oceangoing vessels. (See Primary Source: *The Dual Mandate in British Tropical Africa*.) But were the benefits truly evenly distributed, as some imperialist proponents claimed? A balance sheet of imperialism is difficult to construct, but the biggest beneficiaries were clearly not African and Asian peasant cultivators, as apologists asserted, or even the workers in western factories, whose wages, while rising, still remained low. Profits flowed mainly to European-run export-import firms, large global banks, and wealthy industrialists.

Not surprisingly, colonized peoples resisted the imposition of economic systems that destroyed older trading and agricultural systems and benefited only the colonial extractors. Resistance took different forms, including the demand for national self-determination. In many parts of colonial Asia, early forms of resistance, usually put down with savage reprisals, were followed by organized political protest and the formation of nationalist political parties. The African continent, the last to be colonized, at first went through an early phase of armed resistance to colonial rule, which was repressed with considerable bloodshed. After World War I, colonial critics followed in the footsteps of the Asian anticolonial nationalists. They, too, created anticolonial, mainly nonviolent, political organizations, seeking at first the redress of colonial grievances, such as lost lands. Many of these nations would have to wait until the post–World War II period to achieve full independence.

India and the Imperial Model

Having suppressed the Indian Rebellion of 1857 (see Chapter 16), authorities revamped the colonial administration and created what many British colonial officials regarded as a model system of imperial rule. Indians were not to be appeased—and certainly not brought into British public life. But they did have to be governed, and the economy had to be revived. So, after replacing East India Company rule by crown government in 1858, the British set out to make India into a more secure and productive colony. This period of British sovereignty was known as the **Raj** ("rule").

The most urgent tasks facing the British in India were those of modernizing its transportation and communication systems and transforming the country into an integrated colonial state. These changes had begun under the governor-general of the East India Company, Lord Dalhousie, who oversaw the development of India's modern infrastructure. When he left office in 1856, he boasted that he had harnessed India to the "great engines of social improvement—I mean Railways, uniform Postage, and the Electric Telegraph." A year later, northern India exploded in the 1857 rebellion. But the rebellion also demonstrated the military value of railroads and telegraphs, for these modern systems were useful tools for rushing British troops to severely affected regions. After the British suppressed the revolt, they took up the construction of public works with renewed vigor. Railways were a key element in this project, attracting approximately £150 million of British capital. (Though it came from British investors, Indian taxpayers paid off the debt through their taxes.) The first railway line opened in 1853, and by 1910 India had 30,627 miles of track in operation—the fourth largest railway system in the world.

Construction of other public works followed. Engineers built dams across rivers to tame their force and to irrigate lands; workers installed a grid of telegraph lines that opened communication between distant parts of the region. These public works served imperial and economic purposes: India was to become a consumer of British manufactures and a supplier of primary staples such as cotton, tea, wheat, vegetable oil seeds, and jute (used for making rope or burlap sacking). The control of India's massive rivers allowed farmers to cultivate the rich floodplains, transforming them into lucrative cotton-producing provinces. On the hillsides of the island of Ceylon and the northeastern plains of India, the British established vast plantations to grow tea—which was then marketed in England as a healthier alternative to Chinese green tea. India also became an important consumer of British manufactures, especially textiles, in an ironic turnaround to its centuries-old tradition of exporting its own cotton and silk textiles.

The reform efforts of the Raj made India into a unified territory and enabled its inhabitants to regard themselves as "Indians." These were the first steps to becoming a "nation" like Italy and the United States, but there were profound differences. Above all, as colonial subjects, Indians did not have basic civic and human rights. Other European powers, in parallel with the British example, tried to modernize and integrate their colonies economically without welcoming colonial peoples into the life of the nation.

PRIMARY SOURCE

The Dual Mandate in British Tropical Africa

Frederick Lugard, later Lord Lugard (1858–1945), was a military man, educated at the Royal Military Academy, Sandhurst, and an administrator of colonial territories. He was involved in the conquests of British East Africa and Nigeria, serving as high commissioner of Northern Nigeria from 1900 to 1906. He returned to Nigeria in 1912 and carried out the federation of Nigeria's northern and southern territories in 1914. He served as governor-general of Nigeria from 1914 to 1919. In 1922, following his retirement from colonial service, he published The Dual Mandate in British Tropical Africa, *a work that outlined his views on how European colonial powers should rule over African people. The excerpt presented here is from the conclusion to this book.*

Let it be admitted at the outset that European brains, capital, and energy have not been, and never will be, expended in developing the resources of Africa from motives of pure philanthropy; that Europe is in Africa for the mutual benefit of her own industrial classes, and of the native races in their progress to a higher plane; that the benefit can be made reciprocal, and that it is the aim and desire of civilised administration to fulfil this dual mandate.

By railways and roads, by reclamation of swamps and irrigation of deserts, and by a system of fair trade and competition, we have added to the prosperity and wealth of these lands, and checked famine and disease. We have put an end to the awful misery of the slave-trade and inter-tribal war, to human sacrifice and the ordeals of the witch-doctor. Where these things survive they are severely suppressed. We are endeavouring to teach the native races to conduct their own affairs with justice and humanity, and to educate them alike in letters and in industry.

. . .

As Roman imperialism laid the foundations of modern civilisation, and led the wild barbarians of these islands [the British Isles] along the path of progress, so in Africa to-day we are repaying the debt, and bringing to the dark places of the earth, the abode of barbarism and cruelty, the torch of culture and progress, while ministering to the material needs of our own civilisation. In this task the nations of Europe have pledged themselves to co-operation by a solemn covenant. Towards the common goal each will advance by the methods most consonant with its national genius. British methods have not perhaps in all cases produced ideal results, but I am profoundly convinced that there can be no question but that British rule has promoted the happiness and welfare of the primitive races. Let those who question it examine the results impartially. If there is unrest, and a desire for independence, as in India and Egypt, it is because we have taught the value of liberty and freedom, which for centuries these peoples had not known. Their very discontent is a measure of their progress.

We hold these countries because it is the genius of our race to colonise, to trade, and to govern. The task in which England is engaged in the tropics—alike in Africa and in the East—has become part of her tradition, and she has ever given of her best in the cause of liberty and civilisation. There will always be those who cry aloud that the task is being badly done, that it does not need doing, that we can get more profit by leaving others to do it, that it brings evil to subject races and breeds profiteers at home. These were not the principles which prompted our forefathers, and secured for us the place we hold in the world to-day in trust for those who shall come after us.

QUESTIONS FOR ANALYSIS

- What views does Lugard have of precolonial African peoples?
- Do you regard Lugard's views toward Africans as racist? If so, on what grounds does Lugard hold such views?
- How does Lugard think that European colonial rulers will improve African lives?
- In what ways does Lugard believe that Europeans will benefit as much as Africans from imperialism?

Source: The Right Hon. Sir F. D. Lugard, *The Dual Mandate in British Tropical Africa* (Edinburgh and London: William Blackwood and Sons, 1922), pp. 617, 618–619).

Dutch Colonial Rule in Indonesia

Decades before the British government took control of India away from the East India Company, Holland had terminated the rule of the Dutch East India Company over Indonesia. Beginning in the 1830s, the Dutch government took administrative responsibility over Indonesian affairs. Holland's new colonial officials envisioned a more regulated colonial economy than that of their British counterparts in India. For example, they ordered Indonesian villagers to allocate one-third of their

Sinews of the Raj. Bottom: *During the second half of the nineteenth century, the British built an extensive system of railroads to develop India as a profitable colony and to maintain military security. This engraving shows the East India Railway around 1863.* Top: *The British allowed several native princes to remain in power as long as they accepted imperial paramountcy. This photograph shows a road-building project in one such princely state. Officials of the Muslim princely ruler and British advisers supervise the workers.*

land for cultivating coffee beans, an important export. In return, the colonial government paid a set price (well below world market prices) and placed a ceiling on rents owed to landowners.

These policies had dreadful local consequences. For example, increased production of the export crops of coffee beans, sugar, and tobacco meant reduced food production for the local population. By the 1840s and 1850s, famine spread across Java; over 300,000 Indonesians perished from starvation. Surviving villagers voiced growing discontent, prompting harsh crackdowns by colonial forces. Back in Holland, the embarrassing spectacle of colonial oppression prompted calls for reform. Thus, in the 1860s the Dutch government introduced what it called an ethical policy for governing Asian colonies: it reduced governmental exploitation and encouraged Dutch settlement of the islands and more private enterprise. For Indonesians, however, the replacement of government agents with private merchants made little difference. In some areas, islanders put up fierce resistance. On the sprawling island of Sumatra, for instance, armed villagers fought off Dutch invaders. After decades of warfare, Sumatra was finally subdued in 1904. The shipping of Indonesian staples continued to enrich the Dutch.

Colonizing Africa

No region felt the impact of European colonialism more powerfully than Africa. In 1880, the only two large European colonial possessions in Africa were French Algeria and two British-ruled South African territories, the Cape Colony and Natal. But within a mere thirty years, seven European states had carved almost all of Africa into colonial possessions. (See Map 17.3.)

PARTITIONING THE AFRICAN LANDMASS A major moment in initiating the European scramble for African colonies occurred in 1882 when the British invaded and occupied Egypt. This action provoked the French, who had regarded Egypt as their special sphere of influence ever since Napoleon's 1798 invasion. Indeed, Britain's move not only intensified the two powers' rivalry to seize additional territories in Africa, but it also alarmed the other European states, fearful that they might be left behind. As these powers joined the scramble, Portugal called for an international conference to discuss claims to Africa. Meeting in Berlin between 1884 and 1885, delegates

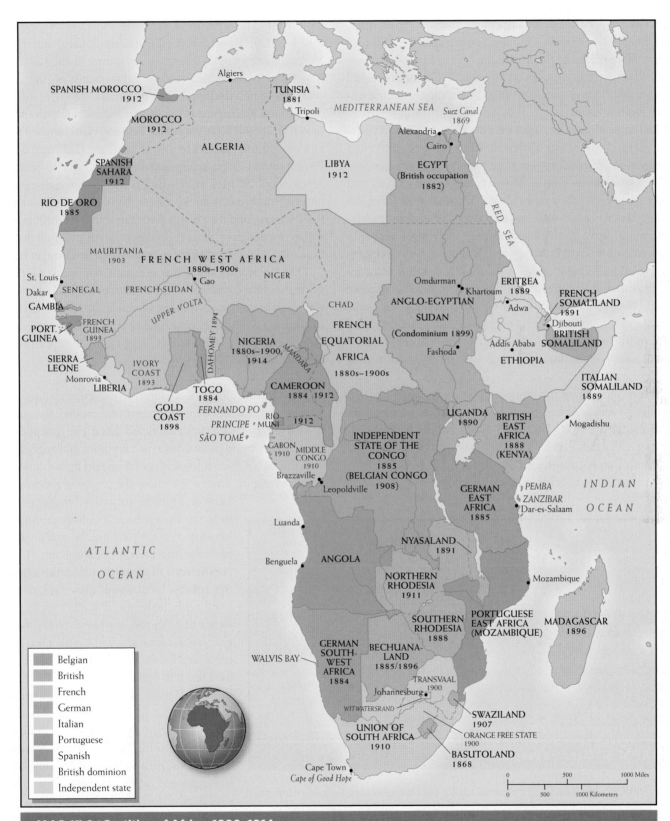

MAP 17.3 | Partition of Africa, 1880–1914

The partition of Africa took place between the early 1880s and the outbreak of World War I.

• Which two European powers gained the most territory in Africa? Which two African states managed to remain independent?

• Based on your reading, what kind of economic and political gain did Eueropean powers realize through the colonization of Africa? Did any of the European states fully realize their ambitions in Africa?

from Germany, Portugal, Britain, France, Belgium, Spain, Italy, the United States, and the Ottoman Empire agreed to carve up Africa and to recognize the acquisitions of any European power that had achieved occupation on the ground. Colonizers rushed to plant their flags as widely as possible, lest they be outmaneuvered by their rivals.

The consequences for Africa were devastating. Nearly 70 percent of the newly drawn borders failed to correspond to older demarcations of ethnicity, language, culture, and commerce—for Europeans knew little of the landmass beyond its coast and rivers. They based their new colonial boundaries on European trading centers rather than on the location of African population groups. In West Africa, for example, the Yoruba were split between the French in Dahomey and the British in southwestern Nigeria, and a segment of the very large and dynamic Mandara peoples came under British-ruled Nigeria, with another Mandara group being administered by the Germans in the Cameroons. (See Map 17.4.) In fact, Nigeria became an administrative nightmare, as the British attempted to integrate the politically centralized Muslim populations of the north with the city-state Yoruba dwellers and small tribes of the Ibos of the south.

Several motives led the European powers into their frenzied partition of Africa. Although European businesses were primarily interested in Egypt and South Africa, where their investments were lucrative, small-scale traders and investors harbored fantasies of great treasures locked in the vast uncharted interior. Politicians, publicists, and the reading public also took

an interest. The writings of explorers like David Livingstone (1813–1873), a Scottish doctor and missionary, and Henry Morton Stanley (1841–1904), an adventurer in the pay of the *New York Herald*, excited readers with accounts of Africa as a continent of unlimited economic potential.

The most determined of the African empire builders was Leopold II (r. 1865–1909), king of the Belgians. (See Current Trends in World History: Africa's Newest Hunters and Gatherers: Greed, Environmental Degradation, and Resistance.) But in southern Africa, Cecil Rhodes (1853–1902), the British champion of imperialism, brought the Rhodesias, Nyasaland, Bechuanaland, the Transvaal, and the Orange Free State into the British Empire as part of a design to have British territories stretching all the way from the Cape of Good Hope, in South Africa, to Cairo, in Egypt.

Other Europeans saw Africa as a grand opportunity for converting souls to Christianity. In fact, Europe's civilizing mission was an important motive in the scramble for African territory. In Uganda, northern Nigeria, and central Africa, missionaries went ahead of European armies, begging the European statesmen to follow their lead.

AFRICAN RESISTANCE Contrary to European assumptions, Africans did not welcome European "civilization." Resistance, however, was largely futile. Africans faced two unappealing options: they could capitulate to the Europeans and negotiate to limit the loss of their autonomy, or they could fight to preserve their sovereignty. Only a few chose the course of moderation.

Lat Dior, a Muslim warlord in Senegal, refused to let the French build a railway through his kingdom. "As long as I live, be well assured," he wrote the French commandant, "I shall oppose with all my might the construction of this railway. I will always answer no, no, and I will never make you any other reply. Even were I to go to rest, my horse, *Malay*, would give you the same answer." Conflict was inevitable, and Lat Dior lost his life in a battle with the French in 1886.

Only Menelik II of Ethiopia repulsed the Europeans, for he knew how to play rivals off one another. By doing so, he procured weapons from the French, British, Russians, and Italians. He also had a united, loyal, and well-equipped army. In 1896, his troops routed Italian forces at the Battle of Adwa, after which Adwa became a celebrated moment in African history. Its memory inspired many of Africa's later nationalist leaders.

Most resisters were ignorant of the disparity in military technology between Africans

MAP 17.4 | Mandara Peoples

The Mandara had established a powerful Islamic sultanate before the European partition of Africa, only to find their peoples divided between British and German colonial rulers.

- Why did the European colonizers divide so many African ethnic and religious communities?
- What problems do you suppose the divided communities faced when African states became independent?

and Europeans—especially the killing power of European breech-loading weapons and the Maxim machine gun. In addition, the European armies had better tactics and a more sustained appetite for battle. Africa's armies fought during the nonagricultural season, engaging in open battles so as to achieve quick and decisive results and then returning to their farms. Such military traditions were effective in fighting neighbors, but not well-equipped invaders.

Some African forces did adapt their military techniques to the European challenge. For example, Samori Touré (1830–1900) proved a stubborn foe for the French, employing guerrilla warfare and avoiding full-scale battles in the savanna lands of West Africa. From 1882 until 1898, Touré eluded the French. Dividing his 35,000-man army, Touré had one contingent take over territories not yet conquered by the French and there reestablish a fully autonomous domain. A smaller contingent conducted a scorched-earth campaign in the regions from which it was retreating, leaving the French with parched and wasted new possessions. But these tactics only delayed the inevitable. The French finally defeated and captured Touré and sent him into exile in Gabon, where he died in 1900.

COLONIAL ADMINISTRATIONS IN AFRICA Once the euphoria of partition and conquest had worn off, power fell to "men on the spot"—military adventurers, settlers, and entrepreneurs whose main goal was to get rich quick. As these individuals established near-fiefdoms in some areas, Africans (like Native Americans on the other side of the Atlantic) found themselves confined to territories where they could barely provide for themselves. To uphold such an invasive system at minimal expense, Europeans created permanent standing armies by equipping their African supporters, whom they either bribed or compelled to join their side. Such armies bullied local communities into doing the colonial authorities' bidding.

Eventually, these rough-and-ready systems led to violent revolts from aggrieved Africans, and in their aftermath the colonial rulers had to create more efficient administrations dedicated to providing health care and education for the colonized.

Europeans in Africa. Top: *Henry Morton Stanley was one of the most famous of the nineteenth-century explorers in Africa. He first made his reputation when he located the British missionary-explorer David Livingstone, feared dead, in the interior of Africa, uttering the famous words, "Dr. Livingstone, I presume." Stanley worked on behalf of King Leopold, establishing the Belgian king's claims to territories in the Congo and often using superior weaponry to cow African opponents. Bottom: The ardent British imperialist Cecil Rhodes endeavored to bring as much of Africa as he could under British colonial rule. He had an ambition to create a swath of British-controlled territory that would stretch from the Cape in South Africa to Cairo in Egypt, as this cartoon shows.*

Africa's Newest Hunters and Gatherers: Greed, Environmental Degradation, and Resistance

As we noted in Chapter 1, Africa was the birthplace of hunting and gathering. Ironically, although the European colonizers justified their partition of Africa on the grounds of bringing civilization to a benighted people, the first generation of colonizers, in their quest to enrich themselves, despoiled the continent, enslaved and killed huge numbers of people, and returned parts of the continent to a hunting and gathering mode of production. The most driven and greediest of these figures was Leopold II, king of the Belgians, who was determined, in spite of sweet-sounding rhetoric, to do whatever it took to line his pockets and make himself a formidable figure in European politics. King Leopold's story—and others like it—fascinates world historians because it conveys in the starkest detail the nature of the relationship between the rulers and the ruled. It also provides a strong point of comparison for the different models of ruling that each European power instituted in its colonies.

Even before ascending the throne in 1865, Leopold cast about for ways to become more than the constitutional monarch of a small, recently established, and neutral state. A voracious reader on colonialism, he was struck forcibly by one book: *How the Dutch Ruled Java*, published in 1861. By demonstrating how the Dutch colonial state had expropriated money from the East Indies (called Indonesia today) to spend on projects at home, the

book fired his imagination. Could he not do the same? Could he not stake out a colony, take money from it to swell his own exchequer, and use some of it on public works at home—to beautify the cities of Belgium the way Paris had been beautified in the 1850s and 1860s?

Fixing his gaze on central Africa, in the 1880s Leopold manipulated the other European states into recognizing him as the sovereign head of a "Congo Free State," in which he led a European effort to "civilize" (and especially to exploit) the Congo River basin. Leopold hired the world-famous explorer Henry Stanley to "pacify" the country and ready it for economic development.

But how to make these lands pay off? They were almost entirely unexplored and unsurveyed, and though in time they would yield some of the richest mineral deposits in the world, these prospects were initially unknown to Leopold and his administrators. What the rain forests of Africa had was wild products, especially rubber and ivory. But how to get Africans, who at that point hardly participated in world trade, to tap wild rubber vines and hunt elephants? The solution here and elsewhere in similar African environments was to create large standing armies (known in Leopold's state as the Force Publique), fix quotas for districts to procure, and compel villagers to bring in baskets of rubber and elephant tusks.

King Leopold. *Despite the inhumane ways in which he funded his vast array of public buildings, Leopold II is sometimes called, not unaffectionately, the "Builder King" by Belgians today.*

For Leopold the results were little short of astonishing. He extracted vast sums from the Congo, spending lavishly on himself and on Belgium. He sank millions of francs into making the seaside city of Ostend one of the finest resorts in the world. At Tervuren, while a choir sang the new Congo anthem, Leopold laid the foundation stone of a world college for overseas colonial administration. In Brussels he spent over $5 million renovating royal

As in India, colonial powers in Africa laid the foundations for future nation-state organizations. Once information trickling out of Africa revealed that the imperial governments were not realizing their goal of bringing "civilization" to the "uncivilized," each European power implemented a new form of colonial rule, stripping the strongman conquerors of their absolute powers, monitoring them more closely, and assuming greater responsibility for the conquered peoples.

However much the colonial systems of the European states differed, all had three similar goals. First, the colony was to pay for its own administration. Second, administrators on the spot had to preserve the peace; nothing brought swifter criticism from the mother country than a colonial rebellion. Third, colonial rule was to attract other European groups, such as missionaries, settlers, and merchants. Missionaries came to convert "heathens" to Christianity, convinced that they were writer Joseph Conrad took the Congo as his model of rapacious European imperialism in his novella *Heart of Darkness*. African villagers rebelled, though unsuccessfully, and by the first decade of the twentieth century, rumors and then detailed reports painted a stark picture of terror and environment degradation. In 1908, just a year before his death, Leopold was compelled, against his wishes, to turn the administration of the Congo over to the Belgian parliament.

Exploitation of the Congo. *Leopold II, king of the Belgians, gained wealth from a brutal exploitation of the Congo—wealth that he garnered from the killing of elephants for their ivory tusks and that he used to enhance his own personal riches and to beautify Belgian cities.*

QUESTIONS FOR ANALYSIS

- Why do you think King Leopold was able to rule over the Congo for as many years as he did unchecked by his own government? By the other governments in Europe?
- While the Congo story is arguably the most brutal of all stories of colonial exploitation and resistance, which other episodes in world history does it remind you of and why?

Explore Further

Herbst, Jeffrey, *States and Power in Africa: Comparative Lessons in Authority and Control* (2000).

Hochschild, Adam, *King Leopold's Ghost* (1998).

palaces and constructing parks, avenues, casinos, and racecourses.

For the Congolese, Leopold's state was nothing more than a reign of terror. Forced to roam farther and farther from their home villages in search of rubber and elephants to keep pace with ever-escalating quotas, villagers suffered an immense loss of life. Perhaps as many as 10 million Africans perished in a population that had been roughly 20 million before Leopold's agents arrived.

Leopold's brutality did not go unobserved, however. Already in 1899, the

---

battling with Islam for the soul of the continent. Settlers went only to those parts of Africa that had climatic conditions similar to those in Europe. They poured into Algeria and South Africa but only trickled into Kenya, Southern Rhodesia, Angola, and Mozambique, attracted by advertising at home that stressed comfortable living conditions and promised that these areas would someday become white man's territories. Moreover, colonial governments' promises to construct railroads, roads, and deep-water facilities persuaded European merchants and investors to take out bigger commercial stakes in Africa.

Eventually, stabilized colonies began to deliver on their economic promise. Whereas early imperialism in Africa had relied on the export of ivory and wild rubber, after these resources became depleted, the colonies pursued other exports. From the rain forests came cocoa, coffee, palm oil, and palm kernels. From the highlands of East Africa came tea, coffee, sisal (used

Battle of Adwa. *Portrait of King Menelik, who defeated the Italian forces at the Battle of Adwa in 1896, thus saving his country from European colonization.*

in cord and twine), and pyrethrum (a flower used to make insecticide). Another important commodity was long-staple, high-quality cotton, grown in Egypt and the Anglo-Egyptian Sudan. Indeed, tropical commodities from all across Africa (as from India and Latin America) flowed to industrializing societies. (See Analyzing Global Developments: Imperialism and the African Trade Revolution.)

Thus, European colonial administrators saw Africa as fitting into the world economy in the same way that British administrators viewed India—as an exporter of raw materials and an importer of manufactures. They expected Africa to profit from this role. But in truth, African workers gained little from

participating in colonial commerce, while the price they paid in disruption to traditional social and economic patterns was substantial.

Such disruptions were particularly acute in southern Africa, where mining operations lured African men thousands of miles from their homes. Meanwhile, women had to take care of subsistence and cash crop production in the home villages. By the turn of the century, the gold mines of Witwatersrand in South Africa required a workforce of 100,000, drawing miners from as far away as Mozambique, the Rhodesias, and Nyasaland, as well as from South Africa itself. Because work belowground was hazardous and health services were inadequate, workers often tried to flee. But armed guards and barbedwired compounds kept them in the mines. Companies made enormous profits for their European shareholders, while the workers toiled in dangerous conditions and barely eked out a living wage.

To observers, the European empires in Africa seemed solid and durable, but in fact, European colonial rule there was fragile. For all of British Africa, the only all-British force was 5,000 men garrisoned in Egypt. Elsewhere, European officers depended on African military and police forces. And prior to 1914, the number of British administrative officers available for the whole of northern Nigeria was less than 500. These were hardly strong foundations for statehood. It would not take much to destabilize the European order in Africa.

Diamond Mine. *The discovery of diamonds and gold in South Africa in the late nineteenth century led to the investment of large amounts of overseas capital, the mobilization of severely exploited African mine workers, and the Boer War of 1899–1902, which resulted in the incorporation of the Afrikaner states of the Transvaal and the Orange Free State into the Union of South Africa.*

Imperialism and the African Trade Revolution

The colonial period initiated a trade revolution in Africa, which, as we have seen, had been a supplier of human labor to the Americas from the fifteenth century until the middle of the nineteenth century (see Chapter 13). Even as the Europeans endeavored to eradicate the African institution of slavery and slave trading within the continent, they also promoted the reintegration of African economies into the world economy through the export of important, often new cash crops like cocoa from West Africa and significant minerals like gold and diamonds from South Africa and the import of European manufactures. To this end, the colonial powers financed railways and deepened harbors. Already by the outbreak of World War I, West Africa had become the leading exporter of cocoa, South Africa the leading exporter of diamonds and gold, and Egypt, along with the United States, the leading exporter of high-quality cotton.

QUESTIONS FOR ANALYSIS

- Is there a correlation between the increase in the number of railroads built and the amount of natural resources taken out of Africa? If so, how can you tell?
- During what period were the largest increases in the construction of the railroads and the largest exportation of cocoa and gold?
- Do you think the general trend toward increasing production continued well into the twentieth century, or do you think this was the high point? Explain your answer.

Length of Railway Line Opened (in kilometers)	
Year	Africa
1880	4,579
1885	6,813
1890	9,202
1895	11,962
1900	16,319
1905	25,574
1910	37,768
1915	47,624

Cocoa Exports from the Gold Coast and Nigeria (in tons)		
Year	Gold Coast	Nigeria
1900	536	202
1905	5,090	470
1910	22,600	2,932
1915	77,300	9,105
1920	125,000	17,155

Union of South Africa Gold (in ounces)		
Year	Total Output	Estimated % of World Output
1897	2,744	24%
1907	6,451	32.4%
1913	8,799	39.3%
1916	9,297	42.3%
1921	8,129	50.9%

Sources: B. R. Mitchell, *International Historical Statistics: Africa, Asia, and Oceania, 1750–2005* (2007); Polly Hill, *The Gold Coast Cocoa Farmer: A Preliminary Survey* (1965); Sara Berry, *Cocoa, Custom and Socio-Economic Change in Western Nigeria* (1975); S. Herbert Frankel, *Capital Investment in Africa: Its Course and Effects* (1938).

The American Empire

The United States, like Europe, was drawn into the mania of overseas expansion and empire building. Echoing the rhetoric of Manifest Destiny from the 1840s, the expansionists of the 1890s claimed that Americans still had a divine mission to spread their superior civilization and their Christian faith around the globe. However, America's new imperialists followed the European model of colonialism from Asia and Africa: colonies were to provide harbors for American vessels, supply raw materials to American industries, and purchase the surplus production of American farms and factories. These new territorial acquisitions were not intended for American settlement or statehood. Nor were their inhabitants to become American citizens, for nonwhite foreigners were considered unfit for incorporation into the American nation.

The pressure to expand came to a head in the late 1890s, when the United States declared war on Spain and invaded the Philippines, Puerto Rico, and Cuba. From 1895, Cuban patriots had been slowly pushing back Spanish troops and occupying

"That wicked man is going to gobble you up, my child!"

Uncle Sam Leading Cuba. *In the years before the Spanish-American War, cartoonists who wished to see the United States intervene on behalf of Cuba in the islanders' struggle for independence from Spain typically depicted Cuba as a white woman in distress. By contrast, in this and other cartoons following the Spanish-American War, Cubans were drawn as black and usually as infants or boys unable to care for themselves and in need of the benevolent paternal rule of the United States.*

sugar plantations—some of which belonged to American planters. Fearing social revolution off the shores of Florida, the American expansionists presented themselves as the saviors of Spanish colonials yearning for freedom, while at the same time safeguarding property for foreign interests during the Spanish-American War (1898). After defeating Spanish regulars in Cuba, American forces began disarming Cuban rebels and returning lands to their owners.

Although the Americans claimed that they were intervening to promote freedom in Spain's colonies, they quickly forgot their promises. The United States annexed Puerto Rico after minimal protest, but Cubans and Filipinos resisted becoming colonial subjects. Bitterness ran particularly high among Filipinos, to whom American leaders had promised independence if they joined in the war against Spain. Betrayed, Filipino rebels launched a war for independence in the name of a Filipino nation. In two years of fighting, over 5,000 Americans and perhaps 200,000 Filipinos perished. The outcome: the Philippines became a colony of the United States.

Colonies in the Philippines and Cuba laid the foundations for a revised model of U.S. expansionism. The earlier pattern had been to turn Native American lands into privately owned farmsteads and to extend the Atlantic market across the continent. But now, in this new era, the nation's largest corporations (with government support) aggressively intervened in the affairs of neighbors near and far. Following the Spanish-American War, the United States repeatedly sent troops to many Caribbean and Central American countries. The Americans preferred to turn these regimes into dependent client states, rather than making them part of the United States itself (as with Alaska and Hawaii) or converting them into formal colonies (as the Europeans had done in Africa and Asia). The entire world was an object for the powerful states to shape to their needs.

Imperialism and Culture

Europeans and Americans set out to bring "civilization" to the peoples of their colonies. At least since the Crusades, Europeans had regularly written and thought about other peoples. These images and ideas had grown more numerous and varied as commerce and colonialism in Asia and the Atlantic world increased; they served various purposes, including those of informing, entertaining, flattering, and criticizing European culture. As Europeans began to exert more control over various parts of the world, they found it easier to force open closed cultures and to carry away treasures. As Europeans and Americans grew more and more confident in their achievements, they became convinced that their arts and sciences were superior—and curiosity often turned to disdain. In time, Europeans presumed that the only true modern civilization was their own; other peoples might have reigned over great empires in antiquity but had since fallen into decadence and decline. In literature and painting, for example, a new genre known as Orientalism portrayed nonwestern peoples as exotic, sensuous, and economically backward. Rather than depicting Egyptian dock workers or middle-class Algerian women, these paintings featured snake charmers and inhabitants of the harem, thereby suggesting that the whole region was inhabited by people of these types, in contrast to a uniformly progressive Europe, inhabited by industrial workers and men of science.

Darwinism, and even Darwin himself, in his 1873 *Descent of Man*, ratified this view of "lower" and "higher" races, the former stuck in the past and the latter anointed by God (or, in Darwin's

The Women of Algiers in Their Apartment. *An oil painting by Eugène Delacroix (1798–1863) of Algerian women being attended by a black servant. European painters in the nineteenth century often used images of women to portray Arab Muslim society.*

case, by Nature itself) to define and dictate civilization's future. Europeans' relationship to others might now be one of condescending sympathy or of ruthless exploitation, but the bottom line was that it was up to white Europeans and Americans to create modern culture; the darker people, the cultural Darwinians argued, were not nearly as fully "evolved" as the Europeans and could not hope to catch up (or to offer a viable alternative model for poetry or painting, for example). At best, they could be taught European languages, sciences, and religions and perhaps be made to evolve more quickly. It is telling that French colonial subjects who did well at French schools were known as *evolués*, "the evolved ones."

CELEBRATING IMPERIALISM Especially in middle- and upper-class circles, Europeans celebrated their imperial triumphs. After the invention of photographic film and the Eastman Kodak camera in 1888, imperial images surfaced in popular forms such as postcards and advertisements. Imperial themes also decorated packaging materials; tins of coffee, tea, tobacco, and chocolates featured pictures highlighting the commodities' colonial origins. Cigarettes often had names like "Admiral," "Royal Navy," "Fighter," and "Grand Fleet." Some of this served as propaganda, produced by investors in imperial commodities or by colonial pressure groups.

Propaganda promoted imperialism abroad but also inspired changes at home. For example, champions of empire argued that if the British population did not grow fast enough to fill the world's sparsely settled regions, then the population of other nations would. Population was power, and the number of healthy children provided an accurate measure of global influence. "Empire cannot be built on rickety and flat-chested citizens," warned a British member of Parliament in 1905. In addition, writers for young audiences often invoked colonial settings and themes. Whereas girls' literature stressed domestic service, child rearing, and nurturing, boys' readings depicted exotic locales, devious Orientals and savage Africans, and daring colonial exploits.

It should be noted, however, that empire and imperial culture did not affect, or interest, all Europeans equally. In general, the extension and upkeep of colonies directly involved only a small minority of Europeans, and those who saw "Orientalist" paintings saw many other types of paintings too, including those of scantily clad Greeks and Romans. Nor were all students of Asian languages complicit in imperialist exploitation; some were truly curious about other peoples' histories and cultures and laid the foundations for studies of world history today. But even they were beneficiaries of imperialism, which made the world's cultures newly accessible to Europeans for the purposes of both exploiting others and learning more about them.

The Civilizing Mission. *This advertisement for Pears soap shamelessly tapped into the idea of Europeans bringing civilization to the people of their colonies. It said that use of Pears soap would teach the virtues of cleanliness to the "natives" and implied that it would even lighten their skin.*

PRESSURES OF EXPANSION IN JAPAN, RUSSIA, AND CHINA

The challenge of integrating political communities and extending territorial borders was a problem not just for western Europe and the United States. Other societies also aimed to overcome domestic dissent and establish larger domains. Japan, Russia, and China provide three contrasting models; their differing forms of expansion eventually led them to fight over possessions in East Asia.

Japan's Transformation and Expansion

Starting in the 1860s, Japanese rulers tried to recast their country less as an old dynasty and more like a modern nation-state. Since the early seventeenth century, the Tokugawa shogunate had kept outsiders within strict limits and thwarted internal unrest. But after an American naval officer, Commodore Matthew Perry, entered Edo Bay in 1853 with a fleet of steam-powered ships, other Americans, Russians, Dutch, and British followed in his wake. These outsiders forced the Tokugawa rulers to sign humiliating treaties that opened Japanese ports, slapped limits on Japanese tariffs, and exempted foreigners from Japanese laws. Younger Japanese, especially among the military (samurai) elites, felt that Japan should respond by adopting, not rejecting, western practices. They respected the power demonstrated by the intruding ships and weaponry; yet in adapting western technology, they expected to remain true to their own culture.

In 1868, a group of reformers toppled the Tokugawa shogunate and promised to return Japan to its mythic greatness. Then Emperor Mutsuhito—the Meiji ("Enlightened Rule") Emperor—became the symbol of a new Japan. His reign (1868–1912) was called the **Meiji Restoration**. By founding schools, initiating a propaganda campaign, and revamping the army to create a single "national" fighting force, the Meiji government promoted a political community that stressed linguistic and ethnic homogeneity as well as superiority compared with others. In this way, the Meiji leaders overcame age-old regional divisions, subdued local political authorities, and mobilized the country to face the threat from powerful Europeans.

ECONOMIC DEVELOPMENT One of the Meiji period's remarkable achievements was the nation's economic transformation. After 1871, when the government banned the feudal system and allowed peasants to become small landowners, farmers improved their agrarian techniques and saw their standard of living rise. The energetic new government unified the currency around the yen, created a postal system, introduced tax reforms, laid telegraph lines, formed compulsory foreign trade associations, launched campaigns to promote exports and personal savings, established an advanced civil service system, began to build railroads, and hired thousands of foreign consultants. In 1889, the Meiji government introduced a constitution (based largely on the German model). The following year, 450,000 people—about 1 percent of the population—elected Japan's first parliament, the Imperial Diet.

As the government sold valuable enterprises to the people it knew best, it created private economic dynasties. The new large companies (such as Sumitomo, Yasuda, Mitsubishi, and Mitsui) were family organizations. Fathers, sons, cousins, and uncles ran different parts of large integrated corporations—some in

Perry Arrives in Japan.
A Japanese woodblock print portraying the uninvited arrival into Edo (Tokyo) Bay on August 7, 1853, of a tall American ship, which was commanded by Matthew Perry. This arrival marked the end of Japan's ability to fully control the terms of its interactions with foreigners.

charge of banks, some running the trade wing, some overseeing factories. Women played a crucial role, not just as custodians of the home but also as cultivators of important family alliances, especially among potential marriage partners. In contrast to American limited-liability firms, which issued shares on stock markets to anonymous buyers, Japan's version of large-scale managerial capitalism was a personal affair.

CONFLICT WITH NEIGHBORS As in many other emerging nation-states, expansion was a tempting prospect. It offered the promise of more markets for selling goods and obtaining staples, and it was a way to burnish the image of national superiority and greatness. Japanese ventures abroad were initially spectacularly successful. The Meiji moved first to take over the kingdom of the Ryūkyūs, southwest of Japan. (See Map 17.5.) A small show of force, only 160 Japanese soldiers, was enough to establish the new Okinawa Prefecture there in 1879. The Japanese regarded the people of the Ryūkyūs as an ethnic minority and refused to incorporate them into the nation-state on equal terms. In contrast with the British in India or the Americans in Puerto Rico, the Japanese conquerors refused to train a native Ryūkyūs governing class. Meiji intellectuals insisted that the "backward" Okinawans were unfit for local self-rule and representation.

Even while incorporating surrounding territories into the state, the Japanese also engaged in imperial expansion. In 1876, the Japanese fixed upon Korea, which put their plans on a collision course with China's sphere of influence. In a formal treaty, the Japanese recognized Korea as an independent state, opened Korea to trade, and won extraterritorial rights. As a result, the Chinese worried that soon the Japanese would try to take over Korea. These fears were well founded, for Japanese designs on Korea eventually sparked the Sino-Japanese War of 1894–1895, in which the Chinese suffered a humiliating defeat.

The Sino-Japanese War accelerated Japan's rapid transformation to a nation-state and a colonial power with no peer in Asia. Having lost the war, China ceded the province of Taiwan to the Japanese. Japan also annexed Korea in 1910 and converted Taiwan and Korea into the twin jewels of its young empire. Like the British in India, the Japanese regarded their colonial subjects as racially inferior and unworthy of the privileges of citizenship. And like other imperial powers, the Japanese expected their possessions to serve the metropolitan center. Densely populated and short of land, Japan wanted these colonies to become granaries, sending rice to the mother country. Moreover, the Meiji regime exploited Taiwanese sugar exports to relieve a Japanese economy heavily dependent on imports.

Russian Transformation and Expansion

Russian expansion was motivated by both a civilizing mission and a need to defend against other countries expanding along its immense border. Facing an emerging Germany, a British presence in the Middle East and Persia, a consolidating China, and an ascendant Japan, Russia knew it would have to enlarge its already large territorial domain. So it established a number of

MAP 17.5 | Japanese Expansion, 1870–1910

Under the Meiji Restoration, the Japanese state built a strong national identity and competed with foreign powers for imperial advantage in East Asia.

- According to the map, what were the first areas that the Japanese Empire acquired as it started to expand?

- What two empires' spheres of influence were affected by Japan's aggressive attempts at expansion?

- Drawing from your reading, what were the new Japanese state's objectives? How were they similar to or different from European expansionism of the same period?

Economic Transformation of Japan. *During the Meiji period, the government transformed the economy by building railroads, laying telegraph lines, founding a postal system, and encouraging the formation of giant firms known as zaibatsu, which were family organizations consisting of factories, import-export businesses, and banks. Here we see a raw-silk-reeling factory that was run by one of the zaibatsu.*

expansionist fronts simultaneously: southwest to the Black Sea, south into the Caucasus and Turkestan, and east into Manchuria. (See Map 17.6.) Success depended on annexing territories and establishing protectorates over vulnerable conquered peoples.

Looking west and south, Russia invaded the Ottoman territories of Moldavia (present-day Moldova) and Walachia (present-day Romania) in 1853. The invasion provoked opposition from Britain and France, who joined with the Ottomans to defeat Russia in the Crimean War (1853–1856). By exposing Russia's lack of modern weapons and its problems in supplying troops without a railway system, the defeat spurred a course of aggressive modernization and expansion.

MODERNIZATION AND INTERNAL REFORM In the 1860s, Tsar Alexander II launched a wave of "Great Reforms" to make Russia more modern and to preserve its status as a great power. Autocratic rule continued, but officials reintegrated the society. In 1861, for example, a decree emancipated peasants from serfdom. Other changes included a sharp reduction in the duration of military service, a program of education for the conscripts, and the beginnings of a mass school system to teach children reading, writing, and Russian culture. Starting in the 1890s, as railroads and factories expanded, so did the steel, coal, and petroleum industries. But while the reforms strengthened the state, they did not enhance the lives of common people. Workers in Russia were brutally exploited, even by the standards of the industrial revolution. Also, large landowners had kept most of the empire's fertile land, and the peasants had

to pay substantial redemption fees for the poorer-quality plots they received.

The reforms revealed a fundamental problem: the rulers were eager to reform society, but not the basis of government (autocracy). This caused liberals, conservatives, and malcontents alike to question the state-led modernizing mission. Before long, in the press, courtrooms, and streets, men and women denounced the regime. Revolutionaries engaged in terror and assassination. In 1881, a terrorist bomb blew the tsar to pieces. In the 1890s, following another famine, the radical doctrines of Marxism (see Chapter 16) gained popularity in Russia. Even aristocratic intellectuals, such as the author of *War and Peace*, Count Leo Tolstoy, lamented their despotic government.

TERRITORIAL EXPANSION Yet the critics of internal reform did not hold back the Russian expansionists, who believed they had to take over certain lands to keep them out of rivals' hands. So they conquered the highland people of the Caucasus Mountains to prevent Ottomans and Persians from encroaching on Russia's southern flank. And they battled the British over areas between Turkestan and British India, such as Persia (Iran) and Afghanistan. Although some Russians emigrated to these lands, they never became a majority there. The new provinces were multiethnic, multireligious communities that were only partially integrated into the Russian nation. (See Primary Source: Two Faces of Empire.)

Perhaps the most impressive Russian expansion occurred in East Asia, where the underpopulated Amur River basin

MAP 17.6 | Russian Expansion, 1801–1914

The Russian state continued to expand in the nineteenth century.

- According to this map, what lands did Russia acquire during the period 1796–1855? What lands did it acquire next?
- Compare this map on Russian expansion with Map 13.7 (p. 509). How did the direction of Russia's expansion change in the nineteenth century? Which states did the expanding Russian Empire more resemble in this era, western Europe (such as Great Britain) or American states (such as the United States)?

boasted rich lands, mineral deposits, and access to the Pacific Ocean. The Chinese also wanted to colonize this area, which lay just north of Manchuria. After twenty years of struggle, Russia claimed the land north and south of the Amur River and in 1860 founded Vladivostok, a port on the Pacific Ocean whose name signified "Rule the East." Deciding to focus on these areas in Asia, the Russian government sold its one territory in North America (Alaska) to the United States. Then, to link the capital (Moscow) and the western part of the country to its East Asian spoils, the government began construction of the Trans-Siberian Railroad. When it was completed in 1903, the new railroad bridged the east and the west. Russia then began to eye the Korean Peninsula, on which Japan, too, had set its sights.

GOVERNING A DIVERSE NATION Russia was a huge empire whose rulers were only partially effective at integrating its diverse parts into a political community. In 1897, during the first complete population census, ethnographers struggled over what to call all the empire's peoples: nations or tribes. In the end, authorities chose the term *nationalities*, recognizing 104 of them, speaking 146 languages and dialects. Ethnic Russians accounted for slightly more than half the population.

Counting and categorizing peoples formed part of the state's attempts to figure out how to govern this diverse realm. As the United States did, Russia made conquered regions into full parts of the empire. But unlike the United States, Russia was suspicious of decentralized federalism, fearing it would lead groups to demand secession. Moreover, the tsars were terrified by the idea

Two Faces of Empire

Russification (forced assimilation) was one of the Russian Empire's responses to the challenge of the nation-state idea. In 1863, the tsar prohibited publication of the Bible in the Little Russian (Ukrainian) language, alienating many otherwise loyal Slavic subjects. By contrast, most non-Christians, such as the Muslims of newly annexed Turkestan (central Asia), were exempted from Russification because they were considered "aliens" who should be ruled separately. The first excerpt below presents an 1876 edict prohibiting the use of Ukrainian; the second excerpt is a celebration of colonialism by a member of the Russian governor-general's office in Turkestan.

RUSSIFICATION IN UKRAINE

In order to halt what is, from the state's point of view, the dangerous activity of the Ukrainophiles, it is appropriate to take the following measures immediately: 1. To prohibit the import into the empire of any books published abroad in the Little Russian dialect [Ukrainian], without the special permission of the Chief Press Administration. 2. To prohibit the printing inside of the empire of any original works or translations in this dialect, with the exception of historical documents. . . . 3. Equally to prohibit any dramatic productions, musical lyrics and public lectures (which at present have the charter of Ukrainophile demonstrations) in this dialect. . . . 6. To strengthen supervision by the local educational administration so as not to allow any subjects in primary schools be taught in the Little Russian dialect. . . . 7. To clear the libraries of all primary and secondary schools in the Little Russian provinces of books and pamphlets prohibited by paragraph 2. . . . 8. . . . To demand from the heads of these districts a list of teachers with a note as to their reliability in relation to Ukrainophile tendencies. Those noted as unreliable or doubtful should be transferred to Great Russian provinces.

COLONIALISM IN TURKESTAN

Our battalion arrived in Tashkent four years after Turkestan had been annexed to the empire. Tashkent at that time looked more like a military settlement than the chief city of the region, that is the capital of Russian Central Asia. The majority of the inhabitants were soldiers, either resting after some campaign or else about to go out on a new expedition. Civilians and women were a rarity. Now, thirty-six years later, looking proudly at the path we have followed, I can see the colossal results achieved by the Russian government, always humane to the vanquished, but insistently pursuing its civilising mission. Of course, there have been many mistakes, there have been abuses, but this has not halted the rational and expedient intentions of the government. We went into a region which had a population alien to us. . . . They had for many centuries been accustomed to submitting humbly to the barbaric and cruel despotism of their rulers, but they nevertheless came to terms with their position because their rulers were of their own faith. . . . The fanatical mullahs began rumours amongst the mass of the population that, instead of true believer khans, they were to be ruled by heathens who would convert them to Christianity, put crosses around their necks, send them to be soldiers, introduce their own laws, revoke the Sharia [the fundamental law of Islam] and make their wives and daughters uncover their faces.

. . . Frequent outbursts, uprisings and disorders took place and repression followed. But at the same time the natives saw that the very first steps of the first Governor-General proved the complete falseness of the mullahs. . . . It was announced solemnly everywhere to the local population, that as subjects of the Russian monarch, the population would keep its faith, its national customs, its courts and its judges, that all taxes demanded by the previous collectors were illegal and burdensome in the extreme and would be revoked, and that instead just taxes would be imposed, and that the position of women would remain inviolable. All this of course soon calmed the population and an industrious people settled down to a peaceful life.

Source: Martin McCauley and Peter Waldron, *The Emergence of the Modern Russian State, 1855–1881* (Totowa, NJ: Barnes and Noble Books, 1988), pp. 209, 211–212.

QUESTIONS FOR ANALYSIS

- Based on the "Russification in Ukraine" document, explain how important the arts and education can be in maintaining a people's identity—and in subverting a foreign power's authority.
- According to the "Colonialism in Turkestan" document, what steps did the Russians take to calm the Muslims' fears of colonial domination?

of popular sovereignty. Preferring the tried-and-true method of centralized autocracy, they divided most of the empire into governorships ruled by appointed civilian or military governors who were supposed to function like local tsars or autocrats.

Unlike the United States, which displaced or slaughtered native populations during its expansion across an entire continent, Russia tolerated and taxed the new peoples. In this daunting task, the state's approach ranged from outright

The Trans-Siberian Railroad. *Russia's decision to build a railway across Siberia to the Pacific Ocean derived from a desire to expand the empire's power in East Asia and to forestall British advances in Asia. The colossal undertaking, which claimed the lives of thousands of workers, reached completion just as Russia clashed militarily with Japan. The new railroad ferried Russian troops over long distances to battles, such as the one at Mukden, in Manchuria, which was then the largest land battle in the history of warfare.*

repression (of Poles and Jews) to favoritism (toward Baltic Germans and Finns), although the beneficiaries of favoritism often later lost favor if they became too strong. Further, unlike the United States, which managed to pacify borders with its weaker neighbors, Russia faced the constant suspicions of Persians and Ottomans and the menace of British troops in Afghanistan. And in East Asia, a clash with expansionist Japan loomed on the horizon.

China under Pressure

While the Russians and Japanese scrambled to copy European models of industrialism and imperialism, the Qing were slower to mobilize against threats from the west. Even as the European powers were dividing up China into spheres of influence, Qing officials were much more worried about internal revolts and threats from their northern borders. Into the 1850s and 1860s, many Qing officials still regarded the increasing European incursions and demands as a lesser danger by comparison.

ADOPTING WESTERN LEARNING AND SKILLS A growing number of Chinese officials, however, recognized the superior armaments and technology of rival powers and were deeply troubled by the threat posed by European military might. Starting in the 1860s, reformist bureaucrats sought to adopt elements of western learning and technological skills—but with the intention of keeping the core Chinese culture intact.

This so-called **Self-Strengthening movement** included a variety of new ventures: arsenals, shipyards, coal mines,

a steamship company to contest the foreign domination of coastal shipping, and schools for learning foreign ways and languages. Most interesting was the dispatch abroad of about 120 schoolboys under the charge of Yung Wing. The first Chinese graduate of an American college (Yale University, 1854), Yung believed that western education would greatly benefit Chinese students, so he took his charges to Connecticut in the 1870s to attend school and live with American families. Conservatives at the Qing court were soon dismayed by reports of the students' interest in Christianity and aptitude for baseball. In 1881, after the U.S. government refused to admit the boys into military academies, they summoned the students home.

Yung Wing's abortive educational mission was not the only setback for the Self-Strengthening movement, for skepticism about western technology was rife among conservative officials. Some insisted that the introduction of machinery would lead to unemployment; others worried that railways would facilitate western military maneuvers and lead to an invasion; still others complained that the crisscrossing tracks disturbed the harmony between humans and nature. The first short railway track ever laid in China was torn up in 1877 shortly after being built, and the country had only 288 kilometers of track prior to 1895.

Although they did not acknowledge the railroad's usefulness, the Chinese did adopt other new technologies to access a wider range of information. For example, by the early 1890s there were about a dozen Chinese-language newspapers (as distinct from the foreign-language press) published in major cities, with the largest ones having a circulation of 10,000 to 15,000. To avoid government intervention, these papers sidestepped political controversy; instead, they featured commercial news and literary contributions. In 1882, the newspaper *Shenbao* made use of a new telegraph line to publish dispatches within China.

INTERNAL REFORM EFFORTS China's defeat by Japan in the Sino-Japanese War (1894–1895), sparked by quarrels over Korea, prompted the first serious attempt at reform by the Qing. Known as the Hundred Days' Reform, the episode lasted only from June to September 1898. The force behind it was a thirty-seven-year-old scholar named Kang Youwei and his twenty-two-year-old student Liang Qichao. Citing rulers such as Peter the Great of Russia and Emperor Meiji of Japan as their inspiration, the reformers urged Chinese leaders to develop a railway network, a state banking system, a modern postal service, and institutions to foster the development of agriculture, industry, and commerce.

The reformers' opportunity to accelerate change came in the summer of 1898 when the twenty-seven-year-old Guangxu emperor decided to implement many of their ideas, including changes in the venerable civil service examination system. But the effort was short-lived, for conservative officials rallied behind Guangxu's aunt, the Empress Dowager Cixi, who emerged from retirement to overturn the reforms. The young emperor was put under house arrest. Kang and Liang fled for their lives and went into exile. It would take still more military defeats to finally jolt the Qing court into action, but by then it was too late to save the regime.

The reforms of the Self-Strengthening movement were ineffectual, too modest, and poorly implemented. Very few Chinese acquired new skills. Despite talk of modernizing, the civil service examination remained based on Confucian classics and still opened the only doors to government service. Governing elites were not yet ready to reinvent the principles of their political community, and they adhered instead to the traditional dynastic structure.

By the late nineteenth century, the success of the Qing regime in expanding its territories a century earlier seemed like a distant memory, as various powers repeatedly forced it to make economic and territorial concessions. Unlike Japan or Russia, however, the Qing government resisted any comprehensive social reforms (until after the turn of the twentieth century), and its policies left the country vulnerable to both external aggression and internal instability.

CONCLUSION

Between 1850 and 1914, empire and imperialism carried European, American, and, to a lesser extent, Japanese power and culture throughout the world. In terms of the size of populations that the peoples of European descent ruled, this era was the high point of European and Euro-American predominance. Although most of the world's people lived either in landed empires or under the authority of colonial rulers, the dominant political institution of Europeans, Euro-Americans, and the Japanese was the nation-state. This powerful political organization owed its full emergence in the nineteenth century to the inspiration of European and American reformers seeking a new political framework that expressed popular sentiments alongside the economic, cultural, and political interests of the ruling classes.

Although the ideal of "a people" united by territory, history, and culture grew increasingly popular worldwide, it was not easy to make it a reality. Official histories, national heroes, novels, poetry, and music helped, but central to the process of nation formation were the actions of bureaucrats. Asserting sovereignty over what it claimed as national territory, the state "nationalized" diverse populations by creating a unified system of law, education, military service, and government.

Colonization beyond borders was another part of nation building in many societies. In these efforts, territorial conquests took place under the banner of nationalist endeavors. In Europe, the Americas, Japan, and to some extent Russia, the intertwined processes of nation building and territorial expansion were most effective. The Amazon River basin, Okinawa, and especially the North American West became important provinces of integrated nation-states, populated with settlers who produced for national and international markets.

However, the integrating impulses of emerging nations did not wipe out local differences, mute class antagonisms, or eliminate gender inequalities. Even as Europeans and Americans came to see themselves as chosen—by God or by natural selection—to rule the rest, they suffered deep divisions. Not everyone identified with the nation-state or the empire or agreed on what it meant to belong or to conquer. But by the century's end, racist advocates and colonial lobbyists seem to have convinced many that their interests and destinies were bound up with their nations' unity, prosperity, and global clout.

Ironically, imperial expansion, based on the might of nation-states, had an unintended consequence, for self-determination could also apply to racial or ethnic minorities at home and in the colonies. Armed with the rhetoric of progress and uplift, colonial authorities tried to subjugate distant people, but colonial subjects themselves often asserted the language of "nation" and accused imperial overlords of betraying their own lofty principles. As the twentieth century opened, Filipino and Cuban rebels used Thomas Jefferson's Declaration of Independence to oppose American invaders, Koreans defined themselves as a nation crushed under Japanese heels, and Indian nationalists made colonial governors feel shame for violating English standards of "fair play."

After You Read This Chapter

Go to INQUIZITIVE to see what you know & learn what you've missed.

FOCUS ON: *Nationalism, Imperialism, and Technological Innovations*

The Americas and Europe: Consolidating Nations

- Residents of the United States claim territory across the North American continent after fighting a bloody civil war to preserve the union and abolish slavery.

- Canadians also build a new nation and expand across the continent.

- Brazilians create a prosperous nation-state that excludes much of the population from the privileges of belonging to the "nation" and the "state."

- The dynastic states of Prussia and Piedmont-Sardinia create German and Italian nation-states at the expense of France and the Austrian Empire.

Industry, Science, and Technology on a Global Scale

- Continued industrialization transforms the global economy.

- New technologies of warfare, transportation, and communication lead to greater global economic integration.

- Charles Darwin's *On the Origin of Species* overturns previous conceptions of nature, arguing that present-day life-forms evolved from simpler ones over long periods.

Empires

- After suppressing the Indian Rebellion of 1857, the British reorganize their rule in India, providing a model for other imperial powers.

- European powers partition the entire African continent (except for Ethiopia and Liberia) despite intense African resistance.

- Americans win the Spanish-American War, annex Puerto Rico, and establish colonial rule over the Philippines.

- The expansionist aims of Japan, Russia, and China lead to clashes over possessions in East Asia, with Russia gaining much territory and Japan defeating the Chinese.

- Colonial rule spurs nationalist sentiments among the colonized.

CHRONOLOGY

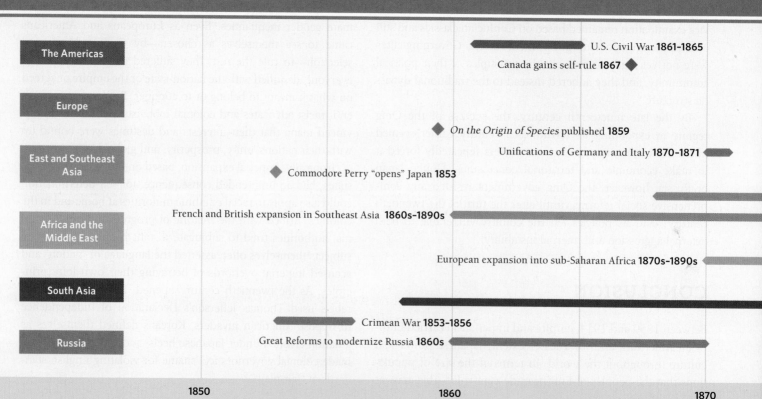

	1850	1860	1870
The Americas		U.S. Civil War **1861–1865** / Canada gains self-rule **1867** ◆	
Europe		*On the Origin of Species* published **1859** ◆	Unifications of Germany and Italy **1870–1871**
East and Southeast Asia	Commodore Perry "opens" Japan **1853** ◆	French and British expansion in Southeast Asia **1860s–1890s**	
Africa and the Middle East			European expansion into sub-Saharan Africa **1870s–1890s**
South Asia			
Russia	Crimean War **1853–1856** / Great Reforms to modernize Russia **1860s**		

KEY TERMS

KEY TERMS

Darwin, Charles p. 644

imperialism p. 630

limited-liability joint-stock company p. 633

Manifest Destiny p. 631

Meiji Restoration p. 658

natural selection p. 644

Raj p. 646

Self-Strengthening movement p. 664

steel p. 642

STUDY QUESTIONS

1. **Identify** the institutions that enabled elites in western Europe, the Americas, and Japan to consolidate their nation-states, and **analyze** the degree to which they succeeded.

2. **Identify** where strong nation-states emerged during this period. How did the nation-state idea challenge certain polities and other organized groups?

3. **Describe** the challenges that mass nationalism and economic expansion posed for the multiethnic, multireligious empires of Austria-Hungary and Russia.

4. **Explain** the role that industrialization, science, and technology played in the expansion of powerful states into the rest of the world.

5. **Define** imperialism. Why did state-directed efforts at nation building often lead to imperialist efforts and other forms of territorial expansion?

6. **List and explain** several major sources of the new wave of imperialism that occurred in the second half of the nineteenth century. To what extent did these ideas find support among the populations of imperialist states?

7. **Compare** Manifest Destiny in the United States with European imperialism in Africa. What common influences shaped both kinds of expansion? How did they differ?

8. **Analyze** to what extent different colonized societies resisted imperialist efforts. How successful were their actions?

9. **Describe** the policies that imperial powers used to govern their overseas colonies. What were the goals of imperial administrations, and how successful were they in achieving them?

10. **Analyze** the cultural impact of imperialist ambitions on imperialist nations themselves. How did colonization and territorial expansion shape notions of race and ethnicity there?

11. **Analyze** the extent to which colonies contributed to the wealth and political strength of the nation-states that controlled them.

12. **Compare** the Meiji Restoration with China's Self-Strengthening movement. What values did they share? What accounted for their differences?

13. **Explain** how nation-state building, territorial expansion, and imperialism reshaped the global economy. What was the relationship between industrial and non-industrial regions?

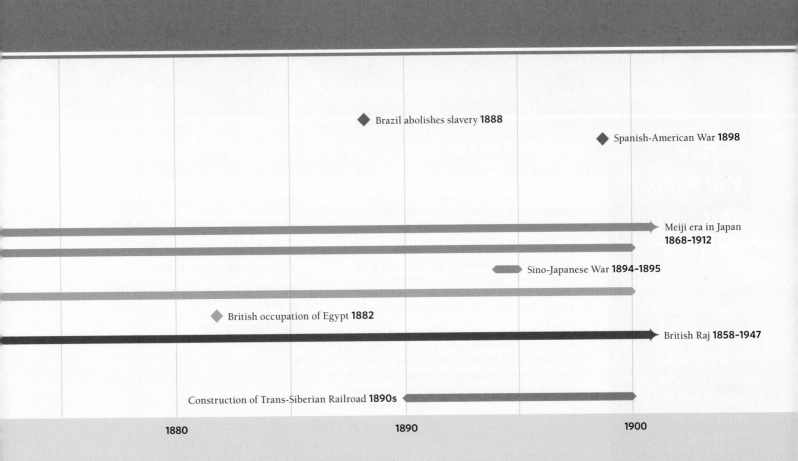

- Brazil abolishes slavery **1888**
- Spanish-American War **1898**
- Meiji era in Japan **1868-1912**
- Sino-Japanese War **1894-1895**
- British occupation of Egypt **1882**
- British Raj **1858-1947**
- Construction of Trans-Siberian Railroad **1890s**

1880 1890 1900

Before You Read This Chapter

Go to INQUIZITIVE to see what you know & learn what you've missed.

GLOBAL STORYLINES

- Numerous factors lead to global instability: vast population movements, worldwide financial crises, class conflict, the rise of women's consciousness, and hatred of colonial domination.

- Class conflict, economic instability, and great power rivalry within Europe combine with growing protest from overseas to undermine Europe's dominant position in world affairs.

- New forms of scientific thinking and artistic expression, known as cultural modernism, challenge the dominant western view of progress and open Europe and North America to the cultural achievements of nonwestern societies.

CHAPTER OUTLINE

An Unsettled World, 1890–1914

FOCUS QUESTIONS

- What was the connection between migration and the development of nationalism in this period?

- How did China's responses to imperialism compare with those in Africa?

- What political, economic, and social crises swept through the world in this period? What impact did they have on different regions of the world?

- How did new cultural forms at the turn of the century reflect challenges to the world order as it then existed?

- In what ways did race, nation, and religion unify populations but also make societies more difficult to govern and economies more difficult to manage?

In 1905, a young African man, Kinjikitile Ngwale, began to move among various ethnic groups in German East Africa, spreading a message of opposition to German colonial authorities. In the tradition of visionary prophets (see Chapter 16), Kinjikitile claimed that by anointing his followers with blessed water (*maji* in Swahili), he could protect them from European bullets and drive the Germans from East Africa. Kinjikitile's reputation spread rapidly, drawing followers from across 100,000 square miles of territory. Although German officials soon executed Kinjikitile, they could not prevent a broad uprising, called the Maji Maji Revolt. The Germans brutally suppressed the revolt, killing between 200,000 and 300,000 Africans.

The Maji Maji Revolt and its aftermath revealed the intensity of opposition to the world of nations and their empires. In Europe and North America, critics who felt deprived of the full benefits of industrializing nation-states—especially women, workers, and frustrated nationalists—demanded far-reaching reforms. In Asia, Africa, and Latin America, anticolonial critics and exploited classes protested European domination. Ironically, at the very moment when peoples of European descent seemed to have established preeminence in international affairs, they, too, began to feel that they had lost control over a world changing at an alarming rate. While continuing to trumpet the wonders of European civilization to the colonized abroad, at home the search began for new forms of social organization and cultural expression suitable to a deeply unsettled age.

This chapter tackles the anxieties and insecurities that unsettled the world around the turn of the twentieth century. It ties them in particular to three key factors: (1) the uprooting of millions of people from countryside to city and from one continent to another; (2) discontent with the poverty that many suffered even as economic production leaped upward; and (3) resentment of and resistance to European domination. Around the globe, this tumult caused a questioning of old ideas that led to a flowering of new thinking and fresh artistic expression under the label of "modernism." Championed by some and despised by others, modernism *meant* to be unsettling—to represent the world in shocking new ways—and thus tells us a great deal about the conflicts and crises that defined this era.

PROGRESS, UPHEAVAL, AND MOVEMENT

The decades leading up to 1914 were a time of unprecedented possibility for some and social disruption and economic frustration for others. They were also years of anxiety worldwide. Rapid economic progress brought challenges to the established order and the people in power. In Europe and the United States, radicals and middle-class reformers agitated for political and social change. In areas colonized by European countries and the United States, resentment focused on either colonial rulers or indigenous elites. Even in nations such as China, which had not been formally colonized but which faced repeated intrusions, popular discontent targeted domination by Europeans. In China, Mexico, and Russia, angry peasants and workers allied with frustrated reformers to topple autocratic regimes.

In the late nineteenth century, a larger concentration of capital made possible more intensive forms of agriculture and more mechanized forms of manufacturing, fueling economic growth. But advanced capitalism also spurred inequalities within industrial countries and, especially, between the world's industrial and nonindustrial regions. It also brought unwelcome changes in how and where people worked and lived. Rural folk flocked into the cities, hoping to escape the poverty that encumbered most people in the countryside. In the cities, even though public building projects produced sewer systems, museums, parks, and libraries, the poor had little access to them. Anxieties intensified when economic downturns left thousands out of work. This led, in some cases, to organized opposition to authoritarian regimes or to the free market system.

In Europe and North America, a generation of young artists, writers, and scientists broke with older conventions and sought new ways of seeing and describing the world. In Asia, Africa, and South America as well, many of these innovators were energized by the idea of moving beyond traditional forms of art, literature, music, and science. But this generation's exuberance worried those who were not ready to give up their cultural traditions and institutions.

Peoples in Motion

If the world was being *unsettled* by political, economic, and cultural changes, it was also being *resettled* by mass emigration. (See Map 18.1.) A "Caucasian tsunami," in the memorable words of historian Alfred Crosby, resulted in emigration of an unprecedented number of Europeans to North America, Australia, Argentina, Africa, and Cuba. This "tsunami" began after the Napoleonic Wars and gathered momentum in the 1840s, when the Irish fled their starving communities to seek better lives in North America. After 1870, the flow of Europeans became a torrent. The United States was the favored destination, with European migrants exceeding by sixfold the number of Europeans who migrated to Argentina (the second-place receiving country) between 1871 and 1920. The high point occurred between 1901 and 1910, when over 6 million Europeans entered the United States. This was nothing less than a demographic revolution.

EMIGRATION, IMMIGRATION, INTERNAL MIGRATION
Europeans were not the only peoples on the move. Between the 1840s and the 1940s, 29 million South Asians migrated into the Malay Peninsula and Burma (British colonies), the Dutch Indies (Indonesia), East Africa, and the Caribbean. Most were recruited to labor on plantations, railways, and mines in British-controlled territories. Merchants followed laborers, making the South Asian migrant populations more diverse. Meanwhile, the Chinese, too, emigrated in significant numbers. Between 1845 and 1900, forces such as population pressure, a shortage of cultivable land, and social turmoil drove 800,000 Chinese to seek new homes in North and South America, New Zealand, Hawaii, and the West Indies. Close to four times as many settled in Southeast Asia.

At the same time, industrial changes caused millions to migrate *within* their own countries or to neighboring ones, seeking employment in the burgeoning cities or other opportunities in frontier regions. In North America, hundreds of thousands headed west, while millions relocated from the countryside to the cities. In Asia, about 10 million Russians went east to Siberia and central Asia, and 2 million Koreans moved northwest to Manchuria. In Africa, small numbers of

South Africans moved north into Northern and Southern Rhodesia in search of arable land and precious metals. Across the world, gold rushes, silver rushes, copper rushes, and a diamond rush took people across landmasses and across oceans. Mostly men, these emigrants were hell-bent on profit and often willing to destroy the land in order to extract precious commodities as quickly as possible.

People traveled with varying credentials and goals. Some went as colonial officials or soldiers, some as missionaries or big-game hunters—most of these folks did not plan to stay. Merchants and traders were more likely to settle in for the long term. Several million East Asians (mostly Chinese) went to the Philippines and South Africa, California and Cuba, British Columbia and Singapore, Guyana and Trinidad, replacing freed slaves on plantations or doing construction. Japanese laborers migrated to Peru to mine guano for fertilizer and to Hawaii to harvest sugar.

Migrants took big risks. Travel was often hazardous, and leaving behind native cultures and kin groups was painful. Many experienced conflicts with resident populations, as did Chinese migrants who ventured into Taiwan and other frontier regions. In the cities, tensions mounted as migrant workers faced low wages, poor working and living conditions, and barriers to higher-paying positions. In China, women without male relatives to protect them sometimes suffered abuse or exploitation. And yet, the economic rewards were substantial enough that the risks of sending the men abroad seemed worth taking.

Until 1914, governments imposed almost no controls on immigration or emigration. In China, the Qing government tried to restrict emigration into the Manchus' northeastern homelands, but it failed. Eager to add both laborers and consumers to its expanding territory, the United States allowed entry to anyone who was not a prostitute, a convict, or a "lunatic"; but in 1882, racist reactions spurred legislation that barred entry to almost all Chinese. Travel within Europe required no passports or work permits; foreign-born criminals were subject to deportation, but that was the extent of immigration policy. (See Analyzing Global Developments: Migration and the Origin of Border Control Policies.)

URBAN LIFE AND CHANGING IDENTITIES Cities boomed, with both positive and negative repercussions. The population of Buenos Aires climbed from 180,000 in 1869 to 1.58 million in 1914, and London's passed 6.5 million. Local governments undertook massive rebuilding and beautification projects, but severe housing shortages remained. This was the era in which city planning came into its own—to widen and regularize thoroughfares for train and streetcar traffic and to make crowded city life attractive to new inhabitants. City governments in Paris, New York, Cairo, Buenos Aires, and Brussels spent lavishly on opera houses, libraries, sewers, and parks, hoping to ward off disease and crime and to impress others with their modernity.

Rebuilding medieval cities meant opening them up—to traffic, to consumption, to public enlightenment, to light and air—but it also meant reorganizing them along class lines. In Vienna, for example, medieval walls were replaced with a wide, circular boulevard, the *Ringstrasse*, which showcased a grand imperial theater, a neo-Renaissance opera house, and a neoclassical parliament. In Paris, fashionable new apartment houses and cafés took the place of centrally located but dilapidated and overcrowded workers' hovels; narrow and dark streets were replaced with wide, well-lighted avenues. The small, narrow streets of Tokyo, which reached 2 million inhabitants by 1905, escaped such engineering, but the city also acquired a new national museum in a city park. In theory the new public institutions were accessible to all, but in practice they mostly profited the elite, and in many cases poorer people were forced to leave their downtown dwellings and take up residence in shabby suburbs. For these urbanites, life continued to revolve around long hours at work, and they continued to inhabit overcrowded and unsanitary living conditions and to die from diseases such as cholera and tuberculosis.

Even the poorest, however, felt that the metropolis offered opportunities unavailable in small towns or in the countryside; here one could at least *hope* to change one's lot in life. For western women, in particular, the cities offered new possibilities. Some of those who had worked as domestic servants, textile workers, or agricultural laborers now took positions as shop girls, secretaries, or—thanks to educational opportunities—teachers; a very few became doctors, although their practices were largely limited to treating other women. Increasing female literacy and the falling price of books and magazines gave western women access to new models of acceptable behavior. In cities it became respectable, even fashionable, for women to be seen on the boulevards. The availability in some places of ready-made clothes and packaged goods changed the way wealthier women shopped and cooked. Yet, for most women, leisure time, professional work, and luxury consumption remained dreams rather than realities.

Increased population density made possible more collective action—and collective amusement—but did not necessarily lead to greater social harmony. The turn of the century was marked by the construction of new parks, soccer and baseball stadia, theaters, and pubs, but also by an increasing number of conflicts between workers and business owners or police. Social clubs, political organizations, and charitable associations met more and more frequently—but often battled with one another for members or influence. As cities grew, they often developed ethnically homogenous neighborhoods—"little Italies" or

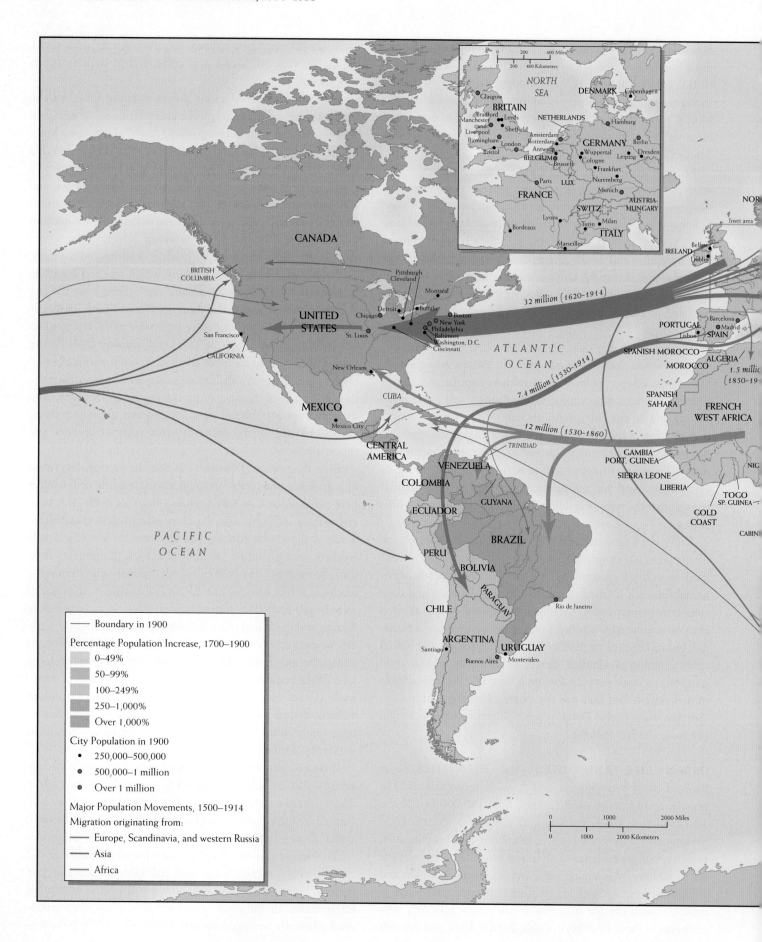

NORTH
SEA

DENMARK · Copenhagen

Glasgow

BRITAIN
Bradford   Leeds   NETHERLANDS
Manchester   Sheffield   · Hamburg
and
Liverpool   Amsterdam   GERMANY
Birmingham   Rotterdam   Wuppertal   · Berlin
London   Antwerp   Cologne   Leipzig   Dresden
Bristol   BELGIUM   Brussels   Frankfurt
Paris   LUX.   Nuremberg
FRANCE   Munich
SWITZ   AUSTRIA-
Lyons   Turin · Milan   HUNGARY
Bordeaux   ITALY
Marseilles

NOR

Inset area

0   200   400 Miles
0   200   400 Kilometers

CANADA

BRITISH
COLUMBIA

Pittsburgh
Cleveland

Montréal

Detroit · Buffalo · Boston
Chicago   New York
UNITED   Philadelphia
STATES   Baltimore
St. Louis   Washington, D.C.
Cincinnati

32 million (1620–1914)

ATLANTIC
OCEAN

IRELAND   Belfast
Dublin

PORTUGAL   Barcelona
Lisbon   SPAIN   Madrid

SPANISH MOROCCO
MOROCCO   ALGERIA

1.5 millic
(1850–19

San Francisco

CALIFORNIA

New Orleans

MEXICO

Mexico City

CUBA

7.4 million (1530–1914)

SPANISH
SAHARA

FRENCH
WEST AFRICA

12 million (1530–1860)

CENTRAL
AMERICA

TRINIDAD

GAMBIA
PORT. GUINEA

NIG

VENEZUELA

SIERRA LEONE

COLOMBIA

LIBERIA

TOGO
SP. GUINEA

GUYANA

GOLD
COAST

ECUADOR

CABIN

BRAZIL

PERU

BOLIVIA

PACIFIC
OCEAN

PARAGUAY

CHILE   Rio de Janeiro

ARGENTINA

Santiago ·   URUGUAY

Buenos Aires   Montevideo

— Boundary in 1900

Percentage Population Increase, 1700–1900

0–49%

50–99%

100–249%

250–1,000%

Over 1,000%

City Population in 1900

· 250,000–500,000

● 500,000–1 million

● Over 1 million

Major Population Movements, 1500–1914
Migration originating from:

— Europe, Scandinavia, and western Russia

— Asia

— Africa

0   1000   2000 Miles
0   1000   2000 Kilometers

ARCTIC OCEAN

SIBERIA

RUSSIAN

EMPIRE

DEN
Stockholm
St. Petersburg
10 million (1880–1914)
Riga
Moscow
2.2 million (1880–1914)
Warsaw
Lodz
Vienna
AUSTRO-
HUNGARIAN
EMPIRE
Budapest Bucharest
Odessa
Istanbul
OTTOMAN
EMPIRE

MONGOLIA
MANCHURIA

Beijing
2 million
NISIA
Alexandria
Cairo
RIPOLI
EGYPT
PERSIA
AFGHANISTAN
Tianjin
KOREA
Nagoya
Kyoto
JAPAN
Kobe
Tokyo
Yokohama
Osaka
1 million
(1880–1914)
CHINA
NEPAL BHUTAN
Wuhan
Chongqing
Shanghai
OMAN
INDIA
Lucknow
Calcutta
BURMA
Guangzhou
22 million
(1820–1914)
PHILIPPINES
8 million
(1900–1914)
PACIFIC
OCEAN
ANGLO-
EGYPTIAN
SUDAN
ERITREA
FRENCH
SOMALILAND
BRITISH
SOMALILAND
Bombay
Hyderabad
Madras
SIAM
Bangkok
FRENCH
INDOCHINA
FRENCH
EQUA-
TORIAL
AFRICA
ETHIOPIA
UGANDA
ITALIAN
SOMALILAND
BRITISH
EAST
AFRICA
3 million
(1850–1914)
MALAYA
BRUNEI
SARAWAK
N. BORNEO
BELGIAN
CONGO
GERMAN
EAST
AFRICA
4.3 million
(1500–1900)
Singapore
DUTCH EAST INDIES
KAISER
WILHELMSLAND
COLA
RHODESIA
MADAGASCAR
INDIAN
OCEAN
3 million
(1790–1914)
EAST
TIMOR
PAPUA
MAN
TH-
ST
ICA
MOZAMBIQUE
BECHUANALAND
AUSTRALIA
CAPE
COLONY
Sydney
Melbourne
NEW
ZEALAND

MAP 18.1 | Migrations, 1500–1914

European movement to the New World dates back to the time of Columbus's expeditions. But the nineteenth century witnessed a demographic revolution in terms of migration, urbanization patterns, and population growth. The world's population also rose from roughly 625 million in 1700 to 1.65 billion in 1900 (a two-and-a-half-fold increase).

- To what areas did most of the migrants from Europe go? What about the migrants from China, India, and Africa?
- What four areas saw the greatest population increase by 1900?
- How were migration flows and urbanization connected?
- What factor most accounted for this demographic trend, internal growth or external migration?

Migration and the Origin of Border Control Policies

The movement of large numbers of people within and across regions—namely, the spread of the Mongols, the Atlantic world slave trade, and nineteenth-century migrations from Europe and Asia to the Americas—is not a new phenomenon in world history. What is relatively more recent to world history is the effort over the last 150 years to increase border control and identity documentation of peoples on the move. Historian Adam McKeown has demonstrated that the origins of the effort to regulate and document border control go back to late nineteenth-century America and the efforts to substantially restrict the number of Asian immigrants trying to enter the United States. In contrast, earlier arguments held that modern-day border control grew out of long-standing sovereignty practices of states and countries dating back to even earlier centuries.

In the first table below, we see a comparison of the rates of population growth from 1850 to 1950 between the major regions of the world.

In the second table, we see more concretely the number of people on the move in terms of their points of origin and destinations.

Global Long-Distance Migration, 1840–1940

Destinations	Origins	Migrants (millions)	Auxiliary Origins
Americas	Europe	55–58	2.5 million from India, China, Japan, Africa
Southeast Asia, Indian Ocean Rim, Australasia	India, South China	48–52	5 million from Africa, Europe, Northeast Asia, Middle East
Manchuria, Siberia, central Asia, Japan	Northeast Asia, Russia	46–51	

These data were compiled from port and customs statistics at significant entry points to major countries. What we see in the data is that the "receiving" nations' populations grew by a factor of 4.0–5.5 during this 100-year period and that their overall growth was more than twice that of the "sending" regions during this time. Not only was the population growth rate of the receiving nations much more dramatic during this period, but the redistribution of the world's population was equally dramatic. In 1850, 10 percent of the world's population lived in the "receiving" areas; by 1950, nearly 25 percent of the world's population lived in those areas.

World Population Growth, 1850–1950

	1850 Population (millions)	1950 Population (millions)	Average Annual Growth (%)
Receiving			
Americas	59	325	1.72
North Asia	22	104	1.57
Southeast Asia	42	177	1.45
Sending			
Europe	265	515	0.67
South Asia	230	445	0.66
China	420	520	0.21
Africa	81	205	0.93
World	1,200	2,500	0.74

QUESTIONS FOR ANALYSIS

- The number of immigrants from Asia to the Americas was only about 3 percent of the total. Why do you think such a relatively small number of people would cause a dramatic change in border and identification control?
- Why do you think that during this period the populations in the sending areas also continued to grow at substantial rates?
- Why do you think so many people were on the move from South China and India to other parts of the Indian Ocean world? From northeast Asia to East Asia and Inner Asia?

Sources: Colin McEvedy and Richard Jones, *Atlas of World Population History* (1978); Adam McKeown, "Global Migration, 1846–1940," *Journal of World History* 15 (2004); McKeown, *Melancholy Order: Asian Migration and the Globalization of Borders* (2008).

"Chinatowns" in the United States, Jewish or Irish neighborhoods in England—where inhabitants kept to themselves and were sometimes feared and hated by their neighbors. Seeking to unify nations internally, many writers, artists, and political leaders created mythic histories that aimed to give diverse groups a common story of nationhood. Such inventions were crucial in nation building, but they also fueled conflict among nations that in 1914 erupted in the Great War, an event that would generate another huge wave of emigration and urban expansion—and hostility to "foreigners."

Urban Transportation. Left: *Streetcars in Tokyo, Japan's capital, are watched over by sword-bearing patrolmen in 1905, during the Russo-Japanese War. The first electric streetcar began running in Japan in 1895. Note the elevated electricity lines, which dated to the 1880s.* Right: *Heavy traffic in London, in about 1910, points to an urban population on the move. Note the many kinds of transportation—motor buses as well as horse-drawn wagons; the railings in the foreground mark the entrance to the underground, or subway.*

DISCONTENT WITH IMPERIALISM

In the decades before the Great War, opposition to European domination in Asia and Africa gathered strength. During the nineteenth century, as Europeans touted imperialism as a "civilizing mission," local prophets voiced alternative visions contesting European supremacy (see Chapter 16). While imperialists consolidated their hold, suppression of unrest in the colonies required ever more force and bloodshed. As the cycle of resistance and repression escalated, many Europeans back home questioned the harsh means of controlling their colonies. By 1914, these questions were intensifying as colonial subjects across Asia and Africa challenged imperial domination. In China, too, where Europeans were scrambling for trading opportunities without actually establishing formal colonial power, local populations resisted foreign influences.

Unrest in Africa

Africa witnessed many anticolonial uprisings in the first decades of colonial rule. (See Map 18.2.) Violent conflicts embroiled not only the Belgians and the Germans, who ruled autocratically, but also the British, whose colonial system left traditional African rulers in place. These uprisings made Europeans uneasy: why were Africans resisting regimes that had huge advantages in firepower and transport and that were bringing medical skills, literacy, and other fruits of European civilization? Some Europeans concluded that Africans were too stubborn or unsophisticated to appreciate Europe's generosity. Others, shocked by colonial cruelty, called for reform. A few radicals even demanded an end to imperialism.

African opposition was too spirited to ignore. Across the continent, organized armies and unorganized villagers rose up to challenge the European conquest. The resistance of villagers in the central highlands of British East Africa (Kenya) was so intense that the British mounted savage punitive expeditions to bring the area back under their control. Nonetheless, Africans continued to revolt against imperial authority—especially in areas where colonial rulers imposed forced labor, increased taxes, and appropriated land.

THE ANGLO-BOER WAR The continent's most devastating anticolonial uprising occurred in South Africa. This unique struggle pitted two white communities against each other: the British in the Cape Colony and Natal against the Afrikaners,

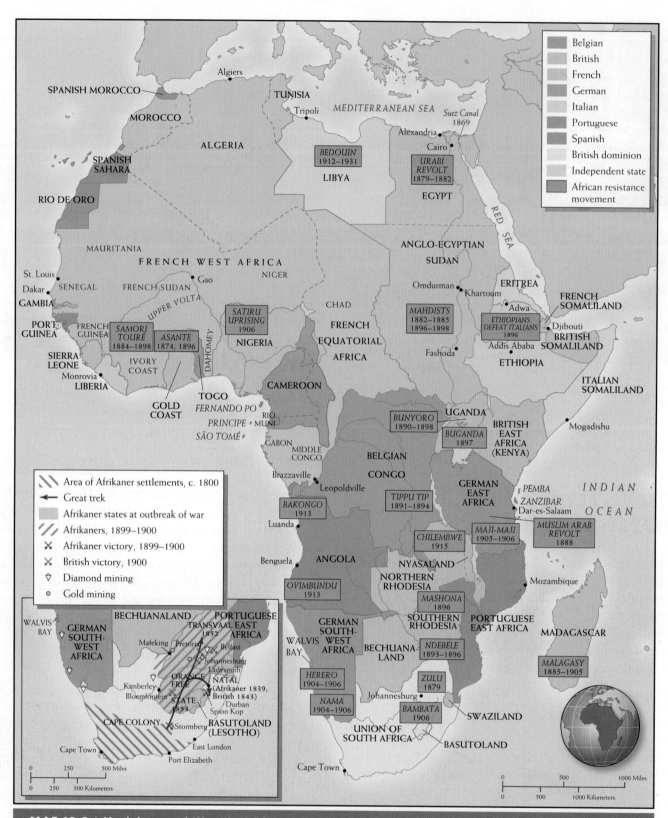

MAP 18.2 | Uprisings and Wars in Africa

The European partition and conquest of Africa were violent affairs.

• How many separate African resistance movements can you count on this map? • Where was resistance the most prolonged? • According to your reading, why were Ethiopians, who sustained their autonomy, able to do what other African opponents of European armies were not?

descendants of original Dutch settlers who lived in the Transvaal and the Orange Free State (see Map 18.2 inset). Although two white regimes were the main adversaries, the Anglo-Boer War (1899–1902) involved the area's 4 million black inhabitants as fully as its 1 million whites.

The war's origins lay in the discovery of gold in the Transvaal in the mid-1880s. As the area rapidly became Africa's richest state, the prospect that Afrikaner republics might become the powerhouse in southern Africa was more than British imperialists could accept. Joseph Chamberlain, colonial secretary in London, and Cecil Rhodes, the leading politician in the Cape Colony, found allies in the British population living in the Afrikaner republics. Lacking voting rights and experiencing other forms of discrimination, these outsiders protested the Afrikaner governments' policies and pressed the British government to intervene. For their part, Afrikaner leaders emphasized the rights of a free people to resist.

Fearing that war was inevitable, the president of the Transvaal launched a preemptive strike against the British. In late 1899, Afrikaner forces crossed into South Africa. Fighting a relentless guerrilla campaign, Afrikaners waged a war that would last three years and cost Britain 20,000 soldiers and £200 million. Britain's frustrated attempts to respond to the Afrikaner insurgency and to cut its soldiers off from the local civilian population led the British to institute a terrifying innovation: the concentration camp. At one moment in the war, at least 155,000 captured men, women, and children were held in camps surrounded by barbed wire. Nor were the camps restricted to Afrikaners. The British also rounded up Africans whom they feared would side with the "anticolonial" Dutch descendants. The suffering and loss in these camps were appalling; by the war's end, 28,000 Afrikaner women and children, as well as 14,000 black Africans, had perished there.

Thanks to a new sort of international actor, the war correspondent, newspaper reports and photographs brought the misery of the **Anglo-Boer War**, including reports of its atrocities, back to Europe. The horrors of the war traumatized the British, who were used to regarding themselves as Europe's most enlightened and efficient colonial rulers. They were scandalized, too, by how long it had taken for the "empire on which the sun never sets" to subdue such a ragtag opponent; but they did, eventually, win the war, bringing the Transvaal and the Orange Free State—with their vast gold reserves—into their empire.

OTHER STRUGGLES IN COLONIZED AFRICA The revulsion that the Anglo-Boer War aroused in western public opinion deepened after Germany's activities in Africa also went

The Anglo-Boer War. *The British sent a large contingent of troops to South Africa to deal with the resistance of the two Boer republics—the Orange Free State and the Transvaal. The loss of life and the cruelties inflicted on soldiers and civilians alike during the war, which lasted from 1899 to 1902, did much to undermine the British people's views of their imperial mission. Transvaal and the Orange Free State fought valiantly to keep from becoming part of the British Empire. In the end, they lost.*

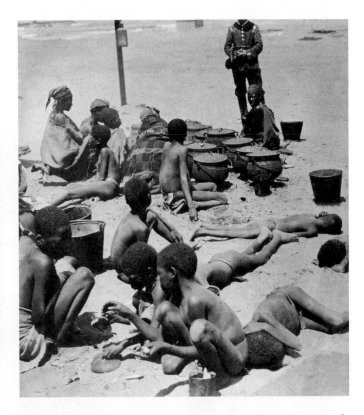

Extermination of the Herero. *The Germans carried out a campaign of near-extermination against the Herero population in German Southwest Africa in 1904–1905. Nearly 90 percent of the Herero were killed. In this 1906 photograph, a German soldier stands guard over Herero women and children in a prison camp.*

brutally wrong. Germany had established colonies in South West Africa (present-day Namibia), Cameroon, and Togo in 1884 and in East Africa in 1885. In German South West Africa, the Herero and San peoples resisted German settlers' attempts to seize their native pasturelands, and in German East Africa (modern-day Tanzania), the Muslim Arab peoples rebelled. Between 1904 and 1906, fighting in German South West Africa escalated to such an extent that the German commander issued a genocidal extermination order against the Herero population. Portraying Africans as either accepting subjects or childlike primitives—as in the Maji Maji Revolt in German East Africa, described at the beginning of this chapter—Europeans redoubled their efforts to impose colonial order. The problem, in their view, was not that empire building destroyed local ways of life, but that they had not yet succeeded in imposing civilization on a stubbornly "backward" world.

The Boxer Uprising in China

At the turn of the century, forces from within and without also unsettled China. Although not formally under colonial rule, but divided into spheres of influence, the Chinese, like the Africans, deeply resented European intrusions. As the population swelled to over half a billion and outstripped the country's resources, problems of landlessness, poverty, and peasant discontent (constants in China's modern history) led many to mourn the decay of political authority. In response, in 1898 the Qing emperor tried to modernize industry, agriculture, commerce, education,

and the military. But opponents blocked the emperor's designs. Before long, the emperor faced house arrest in the palace, while Empress Dowager Cixi, whom conservatives supported, actually ruled.

EXTERNAL FACTORS The breakdown of dynastic authority originated largely with foreign pressure. For one thing, China's defeat in the Sino-Japanese War of 1894–1895 (see Chapter 17) was deeply humiliating. Although Japan, which acquired Taiwan as its first major colony, was the immediate beneficiary of the war, Britain, France, Germany, and Russia quickly scrambled for additional concessions from China. They demanded that the Qing government grant them specific areas within China as their respective "spheres of influence." (See Map 18.3.) The United States also pushed the Qing to accept western norms of political and economic exchange. The Americans, however, were in favor of an "open-door" policy that would keep access available to all traders, while supporting missionary efforts to spread Christianity.

The most explosive reaction to these pressures, the **Boxer Uprising**, started within the peasantry. Like colonized peoples in Africa, the Boxers violently resisted European meddling in their communities. And like the Taiping Rebellion decades earlier (see Chapter 16), the story of the Boxers was tied to missionary activities. Whereas in earlier centuries Jesuit missionaries had sought to convert the court and the elites, by the mid-nineteenth century the missionary goal was to convert commoners. After the Taiping Rebellion, Christian missionaries had streamed into China, impatient to make new converts in the hinterlands and confident of their governments' backing.

Cixi's Allies. *The Empress Dowager Cixi emerged as the most powerful figure in the Qing court in the last decades of the dynasty, from the 1860s until her death in 1908. Highly able, she approved many of the early reforms of the Self-Strengthening movement, but her commitment to the preservation of the Manchu Qing dynasty made her suspicious of more fundamental and wide-ranging changes. Here she is shown surrounded by court eunuchs; Cixi relied upon them, especially as her relationships with orthodox officials were often ambivalent.*

MAP 18.3 | Foreign Spheres of Influence in China, 1842–1907

While technically independent, the Qing dynasty could not prevent foreign penetration and domination of its economy during the nineteenth century.

- Which five powers established spheres of influence in China?
- At what time was the greatest number of treaty ports established?
- According to your reading, what did the foreign powers hope to achieve within their spheres of influence?
- What kinds of local opposition did foreign attempts to exert influence inspire?

With the Qing dynasty in a weakened state, Christian missionaries became more aggressive.

An incident in 1897, in which Chinese residents killed two German missionaries in the northern province of Shandong, brought tensions to a boil. In retribution, the German government demanded the right to construct three cathedrals, to remove hostile local officials, and to seize the northeastern port of Jiaozhou. As tensions mounted, martial arts groups in the region began to attack the missionaries and converts, calling for an end to the Christians' privileges. In early 1899, several of these groups united under the name Boxers United in Righteousness and adopted the slogan "Support the Qing, destroy the foreign." Like the African followers of Kinjikitile, the Boxers believed that divine protection made them immune to all earthly weapons: "We requested the gods to attach themselves to our bodies. When they had done so, we became Spirit Boxers, after which we were invulnerable to swords and spears, our courage was enhanced, and in fighting we were unafraid to die and dared to charge straight ahead."

INTERNAL FACTORS The Boxer movement flourished especially where natural disasters and harsh economic conditions increased hardships. Shandong Province had suffered floods throughout much of the decade, followed by prolonged drought in the winter of 1898. Idle, restless, and often hungry, many peasants, boatmen, and peddlers turned to the Boxers for support. They also liked the Boxers' message that the gods were angry over the foreign presence in general and Christian activities in particular.

As these activists, many of them young men, swelled the Boxers' ranks, women also found a place in the movement. The so-called Red Lanterns were mostly teenage girls and unmarried women who announced their loyalty by wearing red garments. Although the Red Lanterns were segregated from the male Boxers—they worshipped at their own altars and practiced martial arts at separate boxing grounds—they were important to the movement in countering the influence of Christian women. Indeed, one of the Boxers' greatest fears was that cunning Christian women would use their guile to weaken the Boxers' spirits. The rebels believed that their invulnerability came from spirit possession and that the inherent polluting power of women threatened their "magic." However, they claimed that the "purity" of the Red Lanterns could counter this threat. The Red Lanterns were supposedly capable of incredible feats: they could walk on water or fly through the air. Belief in their magical powers provided critical assistance for the uprising.

As the movement gained momentum, the Qing vacillated between viewing the Boxers as a threat to order and embracing them as a force to check foreign intrusion. Early in 1900, Qing troops clashed with the Boxers in an escalating cycle of violence. By spring, however, the Qing could no longer control the tens of thousands of Boxers roaming the vicinities of Beijing and Tianjin. Embracing the Boxers' cause, the empress dowager declared war against the foreign powers in June 1900.

Acting without any discernible plan or leadership, the Boxers went after Christian and foreign symbols and persons. They harassed and sometimes killed Chinese Christians in parts of northern China, destroyed railroad tracks and telegraph lines, and attacked owners of foreign objects such as lamps and clocks. In Beijing, the Boxers besieged foreign embassy

The Boxer Uprising in China. *The Boxer Uprising was eventually suppressed by a foreign army made up of Japanese, European, and American troops that arrived in Beijing in August 1900. The picture here shows fighting between the foreign troops and the combined forces of Qing soldiers and the Boxers. After a period of vacillation, the Qing court, against the advice of some of its officials, finally threw its support behind the quixotic struggle of the Boxers against the foreign presence, laying the ground for the military intervention of the imperialist powers.*

compounds, where diplomats and their families cowered in fear. The Boxers also reduced the Southern Cathedral to ruins and then besieged the Northern Cathedral, where more than 3,000 Catholics and 40 French and Italian marines had sought refuge.

FOREIGN INVOLVEMENT AND AFTERMATH In August 1900, a foreign army of 20,000 troops crushed the Boxers. About half came from Japan; the rest came primarily from Russia, Britain, Germany, France, and the United States. Thereafter, the victors forced the Chinese to sign the punitive Boxer Protocol. Among other punishments, it required the regime to pay an exorbitant compensation in gold (about twice the empire's annual income) for damages to foreign life and property. The protocol also authorized western powers to station troops in Beijing. Furthermore, although the defeat prompted the Qing to make a last-ditch effort at reform, it dealt another blow to the dynasty's standing both internally and externally.

Even in defeat, the Boxers' anti-western uprising showed how much had changed in China since the Taiping Civil War. Although the Boxers were primarily peasants, even they had felt the unsettledness generated by European inroads into China. Indeed, the Europeans' commercial and spiritual reach, once confined to elites and port cities, had extended across much of China. Whereas the Taiping Rebellion had mobilized millions against the Qing, the Boxers remained loyal to the dynasty and focused their wrath on foreigners and Chinese Christians. The Boxer Uprising was, in many ways, like the Maji Maji Revolt in East Africa. Both were widespread protests against increased western influence. But whereas African protesters wanted to restore their precolonial societies, the Boxers sought to banish from their land all symbols and elements of a western way of life that angered their gods and ruined their world.

WORLDWIDE INSECURITIES

Protests against European intrusion in Africa and China were distant movements that most Europeans could disregard. News of unrest in the colonies and in China generally did not lead them to question their ways. Instead, it reinforced their belief in the inferiority of other cultures. In Africa, for example, unrest in a rival's empire was taken as a sign of poor management. Anxiety here reflected the difficulty of the "civilizing mission," although a few did begin to question imperial ethics. At the same time, however, conflicts closer to home tore at European and North American confidence. These included rivalries among western powers, the booms and busts of expanding industrial economies, new types of class conflict, challenges about the proper roles of women, and problems of uncontrolled urbanization (see again Map 18.1).

Imperial Rivalries at Home

The rise of a European-centered world deepened rivalries within Europe and promoted instability there. Numerous factors fostered conflict, including France's smoldering resentment at its defeat in the Franco-Prussian War (see Chapter 17), but tension increased as the European states competed for raw materials and colonial footholds. Even as these powers built up their supply of weapons, as well as ships and railroads to transport troops, not everyone supported the buildup. Many Europeans, for example, disapproved of spending on massive steam-powered warships. Others warned that the arms race would end in a devastating war.

Intra-European rivalry had powerful effects on Germany and Russia. In fact, the unifications of Germany and Italy at the expense of France and the Austrian Empire had smashed the old balance of power in Europe. New alliances began to crystallize after 1890, as German–French hostility persisted and German–Russian friendship broke down. This left Germany surrounded by foes: Britain and France to the west, Russia to the east. As ethnic nationalism spread among the Arabs, Turks, Czechs, and southern Slavs, the multinational Ottoman and Habsburg

Empires began to fragment; the Balkans in particular became a hotbed of interethnic violence. Roiled by internal conflicts, the two venerable empires looked likely to collapse, leaving power vacuums in central and southeastern Europe. Sensing conflict on the horizon, Britain, Germany, France, and Russia entered into a massive arms race.

FINANCIAL, INDUSTRIAL, AND TECHNOLOGICAL INSECURITIES Economic developments helped make powers "great," but they could also unsettle societies. Indeed, pride about wealth and growth coincided with laments about changes in national and international economies. To begin with, Americans and Europeans recognized that the small-scale, laissez-faire capitalism championed by Adam Smith (see Chapter 14) was giving way to an economic order dominated by huge, heavily capitalized firms. Gone, it seemed, was Smith's vision of many small producers in vigorous competition with one another, all benefiting from efficient—but not exploitative—divisions of labor.

Instead of smooth progress, the economy of the west in the nineteenth century bounced between booms and busts: long-term business cycles of rapid growth followed by stagnation. Late in the century, the pace of economic change accelerated. Large-scale steel production, railroad building, and textile manufacturing expanded at breakneck speed, while waves of bank closures, bankruptcies, and agricultural crises ruined many small property owners, including farmers. By the century's end, European and North American economies were dominated as never before by a few large firms, such as John D. Rockefeller's Standard Oil and the large banking institutions in France, Britain, Germany, and the United States. The same was true in Japan, where *zaibatsu*—large companies with banking subsidiaries for finance and industrial wings dominating different sectors of the market—like Sumitomo, Mitsui, and Mitsubishi were the engine of Japan's extraordinary economic growth.

GLOBAL FINANCIAL AND INDUSTRIAL INTEGRATION These were years of heady international financial integration. More and more countries joined the world system of borrowing and lending; more and more countries were linked financially because their national currencies were all backed by gold. At the hub of this world system were the banks of London, which since the Napoleonic Wars had been a major source of capital for international borrowers.

The rise of giant banks and huge industrial corporations caused alarm, for it seemed to signal an end to free markets and competitive capitalism. In the United States, an entire generation of journalists cut their teeth exposing the skullduggery (shady dealings) of financial and industrial giants. These "muckrakers" portrayed the captains of finance like J. P. Morgan and John D. Rockefeller as bent on amassing private power at the expense of working families and public authorities. In Europe, too, critics lamented a similar trend in which lack of competition created greater disparities of wealth between the owners of firms and the workforce.

Rather than longing for the return of truly free markets, many critics sought reforms that would protect people from economic instability. Indeed, starting in the 1890s, the reaction against economic competition gathered steam. Producers, big and small, grew unhappy with supply and demand mechanisms. To cope with an unruly market, farmers created cooperatives. For their part, big industrialists fashioned monopolies, or cartels, in the name of improving efficiency, correcting failures in the market, and heightening profits. At the same time, government officials and academic specialists worried that modern economies were inherently unstable, prone to overproduce, and vulnerable to bankruptcy and crisis. The solution, many economists thought, was for the state to manage the national economies.

FINANCIAL CRISES Banking especially seemed in need of closer government supervision. Many industrial societies already had central banks (banks that issued national currencies, fixed underlying interest rates, and in general controlled monetary policy), and London's Bank of England had long since overseen local and international money markets. But public institutions did not yet have the resources to protect all investments during times of economic crisis. Between 1890 and 1893, fully 550 American banks collapsed, and only the intervention of J. P. Morgan prevented the depletion of the nation's gold reserves.

The road to regulation, however, was hardly smooth. In 1907, a more serious crisis threatened, caused by a panic on Wall Street that led to a run on the banks. Once again, it fell to J. P. Morgan to rescue the American dollar from financial panic—by compelling financier after financier to commit unprecedented funds (eventually $35 million) to protect banks and trusts against depositors' panic. Morgan himself lost $21 million and emerged from the bank panic convinced that some sort of public oversight was needed. By 1913, the U.S. Congress ratified the Federal Reserve Act, creating boards to monitor the supply and demand of the nation's money.

The crisis of 1907 showed how national financial matters could quickly become international affairs. The sell-off of the shares of banks and trusts in the United States also led American investors to withdraw their funds from other countries that relied on American capital. As a result, Canada, for instance, suffered a bank crisis of its own. Countries like Egypt and Mexico, far apart geographically yet linked through international capital, also suffered either withdrawal of investors' funds or a suspension of new investments and a string of bankruptcies.

Although the head of Mexico's government, General Porfirio Díaz, tried to regain investors' confidence and their funds, Mexico fell into a severe recession as U.S. capital dried up. In turn, Mexicans lost faith in their own economic—and political—system. Unemployed and suffering new hardships, many Mexicans flocked to Díaz's political opponents, who eventually raised the flag of rebellion in 1910. A year later, the entire regime collapsed in revolution (discussed later).

INDUSTRIALIZATION AND THE MODERN ECONOMY
Just as financial circuits linked nations as never before, so did industrialization. Backed by big banks, industrialists could afford to extend their enterprises physically and geographically. So heavy industries now came to new places. In Russia, for example, industrial activity quickened. With loans from European (especially French, Belgian, and British) investors, Russia built railways, telegraph lines, and factories and developed coal, iron, steel, and petroleum industries. By 1900, Russia was producing half of the world's oil and a considerable amount of steel. Yet industrial development remained uneven: southern Europe and the American South continued to lag behind northern regions. The gap was even more pronounced in colonial territories, which contained few industrial enterprises aside from railroad building and mining.

By 1914, the factory and the railroad had become global symbols of the modern economy—and of its positive and negative effects. Everywhere, the coming of the railroad to one's town or village was a big event: for some, it represented an exhilarating leap into the modern world; for others, a terrifying abandonment of the past. Ocean liners, automobiles, and airplanes, likewise, could be both dazzling and disorienting.

For ordinary people, the new economy brought benefits and drawbacks. Factories produced cheaper goods, but they belched clouds of black smoke. Railways offered faster transport, but they ruined small towns unlucky enough to be left off the branch line. Machines (when operating properly) were more efficient than human and animal labor, but workers who used them felt reduced to machines themselves. Indeed, the American Frederick Winslow Taylor proposed a system of "scientific management" to make human bodies perform more like machines, maximizing the efficiency of workers' movements. But workers did not want to be managed or to cede control of the pace of production to employers. Labor's resistance to "Taylorization" led to numerous strikes. For strikers, as for conservatives, the course of progress had taken an unsettling turn.

The "Woman Question"

Complicating the struggle over social inequalities was the increasingly urgent issue of how women fit into the world's

Labor Disputes. *The late nineteenth century witnessed a surge in industrial strife, worker strikes, and violent suppression of labor movements. Left: One of the deadliest confrontations in the United States occurred in May 1892, when a strike against the Carnegie Steel Company escalated into a gunfight, which left ten dead and many more wounded. Here, a group of striking workers keeps watch over the steel mill in Homestead, Pennsylvania. Right: Striking dock workers rally in London's Trafalgar Square, 1911. By this time, residents of European cities were used to seeing crowds of protesters pressing for improved working conditions or political reform.*

rapidly changing economies and societies. Male advocates of empire, interestingly, had drawn attention early on to the hardships suffered by women in Asia and Africa; imposing reforms here was one way that imperial architects felt they could justify colonial regimes. At the same time, in the west, female advocates were demanding that women be given more rights as citizens, and more radical voices called for fundamental changes to the family and the larger society. In fact, none of the world's polities made significant progress in giving women opportunities or compensation equivalent to their male counterparts in this era. The most that could be said was that more people were now aware that the question of how society treated 50 percent of the population was a question worth asking.

Radical women met stiff repression wherever they challenged the established order. In 1903, China's Qiu Jin (1875–1907) left her husband and headed to Japan to study. There she befriended other radicals and made a name for herself by dressing in men's clothing, carrying a sword, and trying her hand at bomb making. Returning to China in 1906, she founded the *Chinese Women's Journal* (*Zhongguo nübao*) and wrote articles urging women to fight for their rights and to leave home if necessary. (See Primary Source: A Chinese Feminist Condemns Injustices to Women.) Qing authorities executed Qiu Jin after she participated in a failed attempt to topple the dynasty.

WOMEN'S STATUS IN THE COLONIES In the colonial world, the woman question was a contentious issue—but it was mainly argued among men. European authorities liked to boast that colonial rule improved women's status. Citing examples of traditional societies' subordination of women, they criticized as barbaric the veiling of women in Islamic societies, the binding of women's feet in China, widow burning (*sati*) in India, and female genital mutilation in Africa. Europeans believed that prohibiting such acts was a justification for colonial intervention.

And yet, for women in Africa, the Middle East, and India, colonialism added to their burdens. As male workers headed into the export economy, formerly shared agricultural work fell exclusively on women's shoulders. In Africa, for example, the opening of vast gold and diamond mines drew thousands of men away to work in the mines, leaving women to fend for themselves. Similarly, the rise of European-owned agricultural estates in Kenya and Southern Rhodesia depleted surrounding villages of male family members, who went to work on the estates. In these circumstances, women kept the local, food-producing economy afloat.

Nor did colonial "civilizing" rhetoric improve women's political or cultural circumstances. In fact, European missionaries preached a message of domesticity to Asian and African

A Chinese Feminist Condemns Injustices to Women

Although a small minority, Chinese feminists of the early twentieth century were vocal in condemning the injustices inflicted on women in China. In this essay from 1904, directed to her countrywomen, Qiu Jin compares the treatment of Chinese women to slavery. She also displays a strong nationalistic streak as she ties the future of Chinese women to the fate of the Chinese nation.

Alas! The greatest injustice in this world must be the injustice suffered by our female population of two hundred million. If a girl is lucky enough to have a good father, then her childhood is at least tolerable. But if by chance her father is an ill-tempered and unreasonable man, he may curse her birth: "What rotten luck: another useless thing." Some men go as far as killing baby girls while most hold the opinion that "girls are eventually someone else's property" and treat them with coldness and disdain. In a few years, without thinking about whether it is right or wrong, he forcibly binds his daughter's soft, white feet with white cloth so that even in her sleep she cannot find comfort and relief until the flesh becomes rotten and the bones broken. What is all this misery for? Is it just so that on the girl's wedding day friends and neighbors will compliment him, saying, "Your daughter's feet are really small"? Is that what the pain is for?

But that is not the worst of it. When the time for marriage comes, a girl's future life is placed in the hands of a couple of shameless matchmakers and a family seeking rich and powerful in-laws. A match can be made without anyone ever inquiring whether the prospective bridegroom is honest, kind, or educated. On the day of the marriage the girl is forced into a red and green bridal sedan chair, and all this time she is not allowed to breathe one word about her future. . . .

When Heaven created people it never intended such injustice because if the world is without women, how can men be born? Why is there no justice for women? We constantly hear men say, "The human mind is just and we must treat people with fairness and equality." Then why do they greet women like black slaves from Africa?

How did inequality and injustice reach this state? . . .

I hope that we all shall put aside the past and work hard for the future. Let us all put aside our former selves and be resurrected as complete human beings. Those of you who are old, do not call yourselves old and useless. If your husbands want to open schools, don't stop them; if your good sons want to study abroad, don't hold them back. Those among us who are middle-aged, don't hold back your husbands lest they lose their ambition and spirit and fail in their work. After your sons are born, send them to schools. You must do the same for your daughters and, whatever you do, don't bind their feet. As for you young girls among us, go to school if you can. If not, read and study at home. Those of you who are rich, persuade your husbands to open schools, build factories, and contribute to charitable organizations. Those of you who are poor, work hard and help your husbands. Don't be lazy, don't eat idle rice. These are what I hope for you. You must know that when a country is near destruction, women cannot rely on the men any more because they aren't even able to protect themselves. If we don't take heart now and shape up, it will be too late when China is destroyed.

Sisters, we must follow through on these ideas!

QUESTIONS FOR ANALYSIS

- Identify at least three ways in which Chinese women suffer injustice, according to Qiu Jin.
- In what way does the Qiu Jin's comparison of Chinese women to "black slaves from Africa" reveal a growing global awareness within the Chinese population?
- Why is nationalism an important part of Qiu Jin's message?

Source: Qiu Jin, "An Address to Two Hundred Million Fellow Countrywomen," in *Chinese Civilization: A Sourcebook* (Second Edition, revised and expanded) edited by Patricia Buckley Ebrey (New York: The Free Press, 1993), pp. 342–44.

families, emphasizing that a woman's place was in the home raising children and that women's education should be different from men's. Thus, males overwhelmingly dominated the new schools that Europeans built. Moreover, customary law in colonial Africa, as interpreted by chiefs who collaborated with colonial officials, favored men. As a result, African women often lost landholding and other rights that they had enjoyed before the Europeans' arrival. (See Primary Source: Industrialization and Women's Freedom in Egypt.)

WOMEN'S ISSUES IN THE WEST In western countries, for most of the nineteenth century, a belief in "separate spheres" had supposedly confined women to domestic matters, while leaving men in charge of public life and economic undertakings.

PRIMARY SOURCE

Industrialization and Women's Freedom in Egypt

In this selection, taken from a 1909 lecture in Cairo open only to women, an educated upper-class Egyptian woman insists that female confinement is unnatural and absurd. She demands a place for women in the workplace. The writer, Bahithat al-Badiya, criticizes the effect of traditional religious practices on women's freedom and blames men for not allowing women to enter the professions and enjoy the freedoms that men take for granted.

Men say when we become educated we shall push them out of work and abandon the role for which God created us. But isn't it rather men who have pushed women out of work? Before, women used to spin and to weave cloth for clothes for themselves and their children, but men invented machines for spinning and weaving and put women out of work. . . . Since male inventors and workers have taken away a lot of our work should we waste our time in idleness or seek other work to occupy us? Of course, we should do the latter. . . . Obviously, I am not urging women to neglect their home and children to go out and become lawyers or judges or railway engineers. But if any of us wish to work in such professions our personal freedom should not be infringed. . . .

Men say to us categorically, "You women have been created for the house and we have been created to be bread-winners." Is this a God-given dictate? How are we to know this since no holy book has spelled it out? Political economy calls for a division of labor but if women enter the learned professions it does not upset the system. The division of labor is merely a human creation. . . . If men say to us that we have been created weak we say to them, "No it is you who made us weak through the path you made us follow." After long centuries of enslavement by men, our minds rusted and our bodies weakened. . . .

Men criticize the way we dress in the street. They have a point because we have exceeded the bounds of custom and propriety. . . . [But] veiling should not prevent us from breathing fresh air or going out to buy what we need if no one can buy it for us. It must not prevent us from gaining an education nor cause our health to deteriorate.

When we have finished our work and feel restless and if our house does not have a spacious garden why shouldn't we go to the outskirts of the city and take the fresh air that God has created for everyone and not just put in boxes exclusively for men?

QUESTIONS FOR ANALYSIS

- How has al-Badiya's Muslim faith influenced her views on the role of women in society? Find two places in the reading where these influences are apparent.

- How have western influences affected her views on the role of women in society? Find at least two places in the reading where these influences are evident.

Source: Bahithat al-Badiya, "A Public Lecture for Women Only in the Club of the Umma Party," in *Opening the Gates: A Century of Arab Feminist Writing*, edited by Margot Badran and Miriam Cooke (translated by Ali Badran and Margot Badran) (Indianapolis: Indiana University Press, 1990), pp. 228–38.

(In practice, only women from middle- and upper-class families avoided working outside the home for wages.) Men did not mind having women work for their charities or churches or educate their daughters at home. But most men as well as most women continued to think that higher education and public activism were not suitable for "ladies"—and, if possible, these "ladies," too, should not have to labor outside the home or acquire a profession. Urbanization and advancing capitalism did begin to change this picture, especially in western Europe and America. Some women who craved new opportunities increasingly found work as teachers, secretaries, typists, department store clerks, social workers, and telephone operators. These jobs offered greater economic and social independence, at least for a few. But women in eastern and southern Europe and in Latin America were largely left out of these developments and remained subordinate members of their communities.

Advances toward political equality for women came even more slowly. By midcentury, several women's suffrage movements had appeared, but these campaigns bore little immediate fruit. In 1868, women received the right to vote in local elections in Britain. Within a few years, Finland, Sweden, and some American states allowed single, property-owning women the right to cast ballots—again, only in local elections. Women obtained the right to vote in national elections in New Zealand in 1893, in Australia in 1902, in Finland in 1906, and in Norway in 1913. Despite these modest gains, male alarmists portrayed women's suffrage and women's rights as the beginning of civilization's end.

Quietly, and without conferring with one another, many women began to take charge of their lives in another way, and that was to assert control over reproduction. Although in numerous countries the use of contraceptive devices was illegal,

Woman Suffrage in Finland. *The British and then the French introduced the concept of citizenship with universal rhetoric, but in practice the category of citizen was generally restricted to property-holding males. Finland granted its women the right to vote in 1906, earlier than most countries. In this photograph, a Finnish woman casts her ballot in the election of 1906.*

women still found ways to limit the number of children they bore. The French birthrate fell so precipitously in the second half of the nineteenth century that commentators began to worry about France's "degeneration." Declining birthrates, along with improved medicine, also meant that fewer women died in childbirth and more would see their children reach adulthood. Even in the first years of the twentieth century, these demographic changes, together with urbanization, resulted in much greater changes in women's lives than did political movements.

Social Conflict in a New Key

Capitalism's volatility shook confidence in free market economies and sharpened conflicts between classes; the tone of political debates was transformed as new, more strident voices called for radical change. Although living conditions for European and North American workers improved over time, widening inequalities in income and the slow pace of reform led to frustration. Most workers remained committed to peaceful agitation, but some radicals turned to violence. Often, especially in eastern Europe and Russia, the closed character of political systems fueled frustration—and radicalism. This was also the case in Latin America, where even the middle classes were largely shut out of politics until new parties offered fresh opportunities for political expression. In Argentina, for example, urban workers found outlets for protest within movements known as

syndicalism (the organization of workplace associations that included unskilled laborers), socialism, and **anarchism** (the belief that society should be a free association of members, not subject to government, laws, or police).

STRIKES AND REVOLTS In the Americas and in Europe, radicals adopted numerous tactics for asserting the interests of the working class. In Europe, the franchise was gradually expanded in hopes that the lower classes would prefer voting to revolution—and indeed, most of the new political parties that catered to workers had no desire to overthrow the state. But conservatives feared them anyway, especially as they gained electoral clout. The Labour Party, founded in Britain in 1900, quickly boasted a large share of the vote. By 1912, the German Social Democratic Party was the largest party in the Reichstag. But it was not the legally sanctioned parties that sparked violent street protests and strikes. A whole array of syndicalists, anarchists, radical royalists, and revolutionary socialists sprang up in this period, making work stoppages everyday affairs.

Although the United States did not have similarly radical factions or successful labor parties, American workers were also organizing. The labor movement's power burst forth dramatically in 1894 when the American Railway Union launched a strike that spread across the nation. Spawned by wage cuts and firings following an economic downturn, the Pullman Strike (directed against the maker of railway sleeping cars, George Pullman) involved approximately 3 million workers. The strike's conclusion, however, revealed the enduring power of the status quo. After hiring replacement workers to break the strike, Pullman requested federal troops to protect his operation. When the troops arrived, infuriated strikers reacted with violence—which led to a further crackdown by the government against the union. After its leaders were jailed, the strike collapsed. Although strikes and protests in the United States often failed to achieve their immediate goals, they worried those in power and ultimately led to important changes.

A few upheavals from below did succeed, at least briefly. In 1905, in the wake of the Russo-Japanese War (in which the Russians lost to the Japanese), revolt briefly shook the tsarist state and yielded a fledgling form of representative government. The revolutionaries tried some new forms, most notably workers' soviets, which were groups of delegates representing particular industries. Ultimately, however, the army put down both urban and rural unrest. Autocracy was reestablished. Both liberals and radicals were excluded from power.

REVOLUTION IN MEXICO Perhaps the most successful revolution of the prewar era occurred in Mexico. A peasant uprising, it thoroughly transformed the country. Fueled by the unequal distribution of land and by disgruntled workers, the **Mexican Revolution** erupted in 1910 when political elites split

The Mexican Revolution. Left: *By 1915, Mexican peasants, workers, and farmers had destroyed much of the old elitist system. This was the first popular, peasant revolution of the twentieth century. Among the most famous leaders were Pancho Villa and Emiliano Zapata. They are pictured here in the presidential office in the capital. Villa took the president's chair jokingly. Zapata, carrying the broad hat typical of his people, refused to wear military gear and glowered at the camera suspiciously. Right: By the 1920s, Mexican artists and writers were putting recent events into images and words. Pictured here is a detail from a mural by Diego Rivera. Notice the nationalist interpretation: Porfirio Díaz's troops defend foreign oil companies and white aristocrats against middle-class and peasant (and darker-skinned) reformers who call for a "social revolution." Observe also the absence of women in this epic mural.*

over the succession of General Porfirio Díaz after decades of his strong-arm rule. Dissidents balked when Díaz refused to step down, and peasants and workers rallied to the call to arms.

What destroyed the Díaz regime and its powerful army was the swelling flood of peasants, farmers, cattlemen, and rural workers who were desperate for a change in the social order. From the north (led by the charismatic Pancho Villa) to the south (under the legendary Emiliano Zapata), rural folk helped topple the Díaz regime. In the name of providing land for farmers and ending oligarchic rule, peasant armies defeated Díaz's troops and then proceeded to destroy many large estates. The fighting lasted for ten brutal years, during which almost 10 percent of the country's population perished.

Thereafter, political leaders had to accept popular demands for democracy, respect for the sovereignty of peasant communities, and land reform. As a result, the Constitution of 1917 incorporated widespread reform, and by 1920 an emerging generation of politicians recognized the power of a militarized peasantry and initiated deep-seated changes in Mexico's social structure. These leaders also realized that their new regime had to appeal ideologically to common folk. Revolutionaries gave trade unions sweeping rights to organize, paving the way for nationalizing the country's mines and oil industries. But perhaps the radicals' most lasting legacy was the creation of rural communes for Mexico's peasantry. These communal village holdings, called *ejidos*, sought to revive a precolonial way of life. The revolution thus spawned a set of new national myths, based

on the heroism of rural peoples, Mexican nationalism, and a celebration of the Aztec past.

PRESERVING ESTABLISHED ORDERS Although the Mexican Revolution succeeded in toppling the old elite, elsewhere in Latin America the ruling establishment remained united against assaults from below. Already in 1897, the Brazilian army had mercilessly suppressed a peasant movement in the northeastern part of the country. Moreover, in Cuba, the Spanish and then the American armies crushed tenant farmers' efforts to reclaim land from sugar estates. In Guatemala, Maya Indians lost land to coffee barons.

Much the same occurred in Europe and the United States, where the preservation of established orders did not rest on repression alone. Here, too, elites grudgingly agreed to gradual change. Indeed, by the end of the nineteenth century, left-wing agitators, muckraking reporters, and middle-class reformers began to win meaningful social improvements. Unable to suppress the socialist movement, Otto von Bismarck, the German chancellor, defused the appeal of socialism by enacting social welfare measures in 1883–1884 (as did France in 1904 and England in 1906). He enacted legislation insuring workers against illness, accidents, and old age and establishing maximum working hours. In the United States, it took lurid journalistic accounts of unsanitary practices in Chicago slaughterhouses, a series of bank failures (discussed earlier), and anxieties about the ill effects of the **"closing of the frontier"** in the

American West to spur the federal government into action. In 1906, President Theodore Roosevelt signed the Federal Meat Inspection Act, which provided for government supervision of meatpacking operations. In other cases (banking, steel production, railroads), the federal government's enhanced supervisory authority served corporate interests as well.

These consumer and family protection measures reflected a broader reform movement, one dedicated to creating a more efficient society and correcting the undesirable consequences of urbanization and industrialization. At local and state levels, **progressive reformers** attacked corrupt city governments that had allegedly fallen into the hands of immigrant-dominated "political machines." The progressives also attacked other vices, such as gambling, drinking, and prostitution—all associated with industrialized, urban settings. The creation of city parks preoccupied urban planners, who hoped parks' green spaces would serve as the city's "lungs" and offer healthier forms of entertainment than houses of prostitution, gambling dens, and bars. From Scandinavia to California, the proponents of old-age pensions and public ownership of utilities put pressure on lawmakers. Thousands of associations took shape against capitalism's excesses, and they occasionally succeeded in changing state policies. Intervening in the market and supporting the poor, the aged, the unemployed, and the sick in ways never dreamed of in classical liberal philosophy, progressive reform movements laid the foundations for the modern welfare state.

The period leading up to World War I was one of rapid social changes and of new social conflicts. Women and workers pressed for new rights, strikes disrupted industrial output, and revolutions broke out in Mexico and Russia. As financial crises reverberated across the globe, European elites were forced to make reforms, though they tended to be limited, especially in the colonial world.

CULTURAL MODERNISM

As revolutionaries and reformers wrestled with increasing social and economic tensions, the intellectuals, artists, and scientists began to recognize that a new cultural world, along with a new century, was dawning. What we call **modernism**—the sense of having broken with tradition—came to prominence in many fields, from physics to architecture, from painting to the social sciences. The experimental thinking of this era was shaped by turn-of-the-century anxieties and opportunities; its leaders sought not to please the public or make slight changes to older scientific theories but to question all the old rules and test the limits of the arts and sciences. Often older Enlightenment ideals of rationality and clarity were challenged in favor of the exploration of more primitive and darker sources of meaning and inspiration; in the sciences, probabilities replaced certainties.

Pablo Picasso. *The Franco-Spanish artist Pablo Picasso was one of the first to incorporate "primitive" artistic forms into his work, as displayed in his breakthrough canvas* Les Demoiselles d'Avignon (The Courtesans of Avignon, 1907), *which was inspired by the artist's study of African sculpture and masks.*

Emblematic of the new ideas was the work of Pablo Picasso (1881–1973), a Spanish painter who spent much of his life in Paris: inspired by African masks in Paris's Ethnographic Museum, Picasso broke with the Renaissance style of representation in producing *Les Demoiselles d'Avignon* (1907). Shocking in its form, this painting also depicted a series of nude prostitutes, who confront the viewer and seem to say, "Go ahead and look at me and here see what really lies beneath your civilized exterior." No wonder modernism remained, throughout its existence, controversial: it meant to break the rules and sometimes to terrorize the rule makers.

Modernist movements were notably international. Egyptian social scientists read the works of European thinkers, while French and German painters flocked to museums to inspect artifacts from Africa and Oceania. The Mexican writer and later Minister of Education José Vasconcelos became an avid reader of the Indian intellectual Swami Vivekanandaa, popularizer of yoga and champion of Hinduism as one of the world's great religions. His spiritual nationalism helped shape Vasconcelos's and other Latin Americans' anticolonial reforms. Thanks to the efforts of the publisher Eugen Diederichs, Germans at the turn of the century could read translations of modernist works originally written in Swedish, English, Russian, and Chinese. As travel times decreased, students, scholars, artists, social reformers, and writers crossed oceans and inspired one another with new ideas.

Popular Culture Comes of Age

From the late eighteenth to the late nineteenth century, production and consumption of the arts, books, music, and sports changed dramatically. The change derived mainly from new urban settings, technological innovations, and increased leisure time. As education (especially in America and Europe) became nearly universal, there were many more readers and museumgoers. At the same time, cultural works now found their way down to nonelite members of society. Middle-class art lovers who could not afford original paintings eagerly purchased lithographs and mass-produced engravings; millions who could not attend operas and formal dress balls attended dance halls and vaudeville shows (entertainment by singers, dancers, and comedians). People flocked to hear lectures given by travelers, often accompanied by slide shows. For the first time, sports attracted mass followings. Soccer in Europe, baseball in the United States, and cricket in India had wildly devoted middle- and working-class fans. Thus did a truly **popular culture** emerge, delivering affordable and accessible forms of art and entertainment to "the masses."

By the century's close, the press constituted a major form of popular entertainment and information. This was partly because publishers were offering different wares to different classes of readers and partly because many more people could read, especially in Europe and the Americas. The "yellow press" was full of stories of murder and sensationalism that appealed to the urban masses. By now, the English *Daily Mail* and the French *Petit Parisien* boasted circulations of over 1 million. In the United States, urban dwellers, many of whom were immigrants, avidly read newspapers—some in English, others in their native languages. Here, too, banner headlines, sensational stories, and simple language drew in readers with little education or poor English skills. Books, too, proliferated and fell in price; penny novels about cowboys, murder, and romance became the rage.

By now the kind of culture one consumed had become a reflection of one's real (or desired) status in society, a central part of one's identity. For many Latin American workers, for example, reading one's own newspaper or comic strip was part of the business of being a worker. Argentina's socialist newspaper, *La Vanguardia*, was one of Buenos Aires's most prominent periodicals, read and debated at work and in the cafés of working-class neighborhoods. Anyone seen reading the bourgeois paper, *La Prensa*, faced heckling and ridicule by proletarian peers.

As the community of cultural consumers broadened and as ideas from across the globe flooded in, writers, artists, and scholars struggled to adapt. Their attempts to confront the brave new world in the making resulted in the remarkable innovations that characterize modernism—the breaking with tradition.

Díaz and the Liberal Party. *In this 1910 print, the Mexican satirist José Guadalupe Posada portrays the leaders of the popular Liberal Party as being literally under the feet of the elitist followers of General Porfirio Díaz.*

Modernism in European Culture

In intellectual and artistic terms, Europe at the turn of the twentieth century experienced perhaps its richest age since the Renaissance. Artists' work reflected their ambivalence about the modern, as represented by the railroad, the big city, and the factory. While the artists and writers of the mid-nineteenth century had largely celebrated progress, the painters and novelists of the century's end took a darker view. They turned away from enlightened clarity and descriptive prose, searching for more instinctual truths. Now the primitive came to symbolize both Europe's lost innocence and the forces that reason could not control, such as sexual drives, religious fervor, or brute strength. The painter who led the way in incorporating these themes into modern art was Paul Gauguin (1848–1903), who left Europe for Tahiti in 1891 and there found new forms of contentment and new ways of representing the world that he believed were less artificial than those practiced in Europe. In paintings such as *Where Do We Come From? What Are We? Where Are We Going?* (1897), Gauguin posed humankind's great questions and

Impressionism. *These two paintings, Claude Monet's* The Gare Saint-Lazare *(left) and Camille Pissarro's* Sunset over the Boieldieu Bridge at Rouen *(right), exemplify the impressionists' celebration of modern life.*

intimated that the Polynesians—despite European contempt for their religious rituals and lack of "progress"—might have more answers than did his "civilized" compatriots back home.

However, the arts alone did not undermine older views of the world. Even science, in which the Enlightenment had placed so much faith, worked a disenchanting magic on the midcentury bourgeois worldview. After the century's turn, pioneering physicists and mathematicians like Albert Einstein took apart the Enlightenment's conviction that humans could achieve full knowledge of, and control over, nature. In his later work, Einstein drew on the previously ridiculed work of the Indian physicist Satyendra Nath Bose (1894–1974), who understood light to be a gas composed of particles. These particles were too tiny to

be distinguished by any microscope, but their existence could be hypothesized through the application of statistics. The work of Einstein, Bose, and other scholars of their generation laid the foundations for today's quantum physics. In this modernist form of science, probabilities took the place of certainties.

In philosophy and the social sciences, some European modernists began to question rationality itself. From the time of the Enlightenment, Europeans had prided themselves on their "reason." To be rational was to be civilized and to master irrational urges; respectable middle-class nineteenth-century men were thought to embody these virtues. But in the late nineteenth century, faith in rationality began to falter. Perhaps reason was *not* humankind's highest attainment, said some; perhaps

Paul Gauguin's *Where Do We Come From? What Are We? Where Are We Going?* *In this large-scale painting, Gauguin used Tahitian rather than European biblical figures to pose some of humanity's deepest questions about the meaning of life, the relationship between humans and gods, and our destinies after death.*

Sigmund Freud, at Work in His Study in Vienna. *Freud surrounded himself not only with books but also with Egyptian figurines and African masks, expressions of universal artistic prowess—and irrational psychological drives.*

reason was too hard for mortal beings to sustain, said others. Friedrich Nietzsche (1844–1900) claimed that conventional European attempts to assert The Truth—including science and Judeo-Christian moral codes—were nothing more than life-destroying quests for power; individuals would do better to dispense with the old forms and invent new forms of truth to live by. In 1895, the French social psychologist Gustave Le Bon (1841–1931) wrote a treatise in which he equated the unconscious volatility of crowds (including crowds of striking workers) with the irrationality of women and "primitives." Le Bon's work became wildly popular, appealing to Benito Mussolini in Italy and Vladimir Lenin in Russia and inspiring the work of Sigmund Freud (1856–1939) on "the collective unconscious." By this time, Freud had already begun to excavate layers of the human subconscious, where irrational desires and fears lay buried. For Freud, human nature was not as simple as it had seemed to Enlightenment thinkers. Instead, he asserted, humans were driven by sexual longings and childhood traumas, some revealed only as neuroses, in dreams, or during extensive psychoanalysis.

Neither Nietzsche nor Freud was well loved among liberal elites. But in the new century, Nietzsche would become the prophet for many antiliberal, antirational causes, from nudism to Nazism; and Freud's dark vision would become central to the twentieth century's understanding of the self.

Cultural Modernism in China

What it meant to be modern sparked debate beyond western Europe. Europeans provided one set of answers; thinkers

elsewhere offered quite different answers. Chinese artists and scientists at the turn of the century selectively engaged western ideas and transformed them. Indeed, some scholars have described the late Qing period as a time of competing cultural modernities, in contrast to the post-Qing era, which pursued a single, western-oriented modernity. These forms of modernity involved critical reflection on Chinese traditions and mixed reactions to western culture.

As in the west, Chinese writers now had a wider readership. By the later nineteenth century, more than 170 presses in China were serving a potential readership of 2 to 4 million concentrated mostly in the urban areas. These cities were more economically and culturally vibrant than the hinterlands. Not only was there an expanding body of readers, but newly rich beneficiaries of the treaty-port economy now patronized the arts.

Painters from the Lower Yangzi region congregated in Shanghai. Collectively known as the Shanghai School, these classically trained painters appropriated western technical novelties into their artistic practice. Consider the self-portrait of the artist Ren Xiong (1820–1857): bareheaded and legs apart, he stands upright and stares straight at the viewer. Ren Xiong's work reflected the influence of photography, a new visual medium. Similarly, experimental writers drew on modern science, sometimes to explore the question of China's future relations with the west. The novel *New Era* (1908), for example, put its opening scenes in the year 1999, by which time, as the story envisioned, China would be a supreme world power and a constitutional monarchy. Depicting China at war with western powers, *New Era* celebrated military strength but also introduced inventions

Ren Xiong, Self-Portrait. *This famous self-portrait of Ren Xiong was most likely produced in the 1850s. Ren Xiong was probably familiar with the new practice of portrait photography in the treaty ports. Although his self-portrait reproduced some old conventions of Chinese scholarly art, such as the unity of the visual image with a lengthy self-composed inscription, it is also clear that through its rather unconventional pose and image, it reflects the trend of cultural modernism in China during this period.*

692 | CHAPTER 18 An Unsettled World, 1890–1914

such as electricity-repellent clothing and bulletproof satin. More visionary still was the *The Stone of Goddess Nüwa* (1905), whose male author imagined a technologically advanced feminist utopia. Its female residents studied subjects ranging from the arts to physics, drove electric cars, and ate purified liquid food extracts. Their mission was to save China by eliminating corrupt male officials. Such works, combining the fanciful with the critical, offered a new and provocative vision of China.

Yet the integration of western modes of knowledge into Chinese culture was an intellectual challenge. Did being modern mean giving up China's scholarly traditions and values? Many Chinese scholars, for example, recognized and promoted the usefulness of western science and technology, although most of them considered it as a way to acquire national wealth and power rather than as a way of understanding the world. Indeed, many of the elite in this period still insisted that Chinese learning remain the principal source of all knowledge. What kind of balance should exist between western thought and Chinese learning, or even whether the ancient classics should keep their fundamental role, was an issue that would haunt generations to come. In this respect, the Chinese dilemma reflected a worldwide challenge to accepting the impulses of modernism.

Modernism arose at a time when intellectuals began to question the values that had sustained Europe and North America throughout most of the nineteenth century. It reflected discontent with industrialization, income inequality, and colonial repression. Even though modernism had its origins and most profound impact in Europe, in many ways, especially in art, it drew upon nonwestern traditions and spread its influence throughout Asia and Africa among the educated classes.

RETHINKING RACE AND REIMAGINING NATIONS

Ironically, at this time of huge population transfers and shared technological modernization, individuals and nations became passionate defenders of the idea that identities were deeply rooted and unchangeable and were based on physical as well as cultural characteristics. Although physical characteristics had always played *some* role in identifying persons, by the late nineteenth century the Linnaean classifications (see Chapter 14) had become the means for ranking the worth of whole nations and for defining who could belong to the nation and enjoy its rights and privileges.

By the century's close, racial roots had become a crucial part of national identity. This was the era of ethnographic museums, folkloric collectors, national essence movements, and racial genealogies. People wanted to know who they (and their neighbors) were—especially in terms of *biological* ancestry. Now the idea of inheritance took on new weight, in both cultural and biological forms. Doctors, officials, and novelists described the genetic inheritance of madness, alcoholism, criminality, and even homosexuality; nationalists spoke of the uniqueness of the Slavic soul, the German mind, and the Hispanic race. They spoke of Hindu spirituality and of Islamic principles as if there were no variations or conflicts within these categories. The preoccupation with race reflected a worldwide longing for fixed roots in an age that seemed to be burning all its bridges to the past.

Nationalist and racial ideas were different in different parts of the world, and they produced a variety of nationalist or sometimes panethnic movements. In Europe and America, debates about race and national purity reflected several concerns: fear of losing individuality in a technological world, rising tensions among states, and fear of being overrun by the brown, black, and yellow peoples beyond the borders of "civilization." By contrast, in India these ideas were part of the anticolonial debate. This was also the case in China, Latin America, and the Islamic world, where discussions of identity went hand in hand with opposition to western domination and corrupt indigenous elites.

Racial nationalisms were not necessarily to the taste of political leaders. Panethnic movements such as pan-Germanism, for example, looked beyond the nation-state, envisioning a Germanic community whose formation would require the breakup of the Habsburg Empire and economic ruin in multiethnic cities such as Vienna and Prague. Pan-Islamic movements, too, threatened to cause havoc in the Ottoman as well as British Empires. Behind these movements was the notion that political communities should be built on racial purity or unsullied indigenous traditions; but it was unclear *which* traditions could actually claim any sort of purity. Racial language might unify some communities—such as white Americans—but it also threatened the existence of the multiethnic empires and flourishing metropolises.

Nation and Race in North America and Europe

In Europe and the United States, the changing mood was striking. Americans and Europeans greeted the end of the century with a combination of chest-beating pride and shoulder-slumping pessimism, and this mood influenced attitudes about national identity, race, and religion. In the early 1890s, for example, Americans flocked to extravagant commemorations of the 400th anniversary of Christopher Columbus's discovery. The largest was the Columbian Exposition in Chicago. Such events displayed the most modern machinery and celebrated the nation's marvelous destiny. Yet, at the same time, Americans—like many Europeans—feared for their future, viewing the 1890s not only as the last decade of the nineteenth century, but more broadly as the end of an era.

The Columbian Exposition. *More than 27 million people attended the Columbian Exposition in Chicago in 1893. Like many of the era's world's fairs, this one celebrated technological progress, including the spread of electricity, as evidenced by the General Electric Tower of Light.*

RESTRICTING IMMIGRATION For many white Americans, concerns about the end of an era triggered cultural alarms and political reforms. In his 1893 essay "The Significance of the Frontier in American History," which became one of the most enduring and influential interpretations of the American past, the historian Frederick Jackson Turner called attention to the U.S. Census Bureau's 1890 announcement that the "American frontier" had "closed." According to Turner, that closing threatened the future access to new lands that had long shaped the individualistic nature of the American people and the democratic character of their political institutions.

Such fears fueled the rise of nativist political movements that sought to curb immigration into the United States, which often involved discriminations based on race, ethnicity, or religion. Animosity toward Chinese workers was particularly fervent in the American West and led to the 1882 Exclusion Act, which prohibited almost all immigration from China. After the Spanish-American War brought the United States new colonies in the Pacific and the Caribbean, darker peoples from the Philippines, Puerto Rico, and Cuba became a focus for those who feared the loss of "white America." Even more threatening at the turn of the century because they numbered in the millions were "swarthy" immigrants from southern and eastern Europe. To many white Americans of northwestern European heritage, these newcomers from the other end of Europe were barely more "white" than immigrants from Asia and Latin America. Reducing the flow from southern and eastern Europe, if not halting it entirely, galvanized anti-immigration movements in the first decades of the twentieth century (and culminated in the passage of severe restrictions during the 1920s).

FACING NEW SOCIAL ISSUES Like Americans, Europeans also expressed concerns about trends at home. For example, intellectuals suggested that mechanization deprived men of their vitality. Darwinist theory provoked new anxieties about **degeneration**, the fear that inherited diseases and racial mixing were causing "civilized" people to become soft, weak, and sickly. Sexual relations between European colonizers and indigenous women—and their mixed offspring—had almost always been a part of European expansionism, but as racial identities hardened, many saw racial mixing as harmful to the supposedly superior white races and to the moral fiber of the whole nation. Talk of virility arose, partly provoked by doctors' and scientists' involvement in treating social problems. Before long, English and American schoolboys were encouraged to play sports, to avoid becoming too weak to defend the nation. In addition, medical attention focused on homosexuality, regarding it as a disease and a threat to Anglo-Saxon civilization. In France, the falling birthrate seemed to signal a period of decadence characterized by weak, sickly men and irrational women.

Some people tied degeneration to debates about whether Jews—defined by religious practice or, increasingly, by ethnicity—could be fully assimilated into European society. Even though Jews had gained rights as citizens in most European nations by the late nineteenth century, powerful prejudices persisted. In the 1880s and 1890s, violent pogroms, often involving police complicity, targeted the large Jewish populations in the Russian Empire's western territories and pushed the persecuted farther westward. These emigrants' presence, in turn, stirred up fear and resentment, especially in Austria, Germany, and France. Reactionaries began to talk about the "pollution" of the European races by mixing with Semites and to circulate rumors about Jewish bankers' conspiratorial powers. Perhaps because nothing else seemed stable and enduring, wealthy white male Europeans (like their American counterparts) promoted programs of racial purity to shore up the civilizations they saw coming apart at the seams.

PROTECTING THE ENVIRONMENT In addition to immigration restriction, the dawning recognition about limitations on new lands and other vital natural resources prompted a rethinking of attitudes and policies about the environment on both sides of the North Atlantic. In the United States, the near extinction of the buffalo by hunters, the dramatic reduction of timber stands by logging companies, the rapid depletion of grasslands from overgrazing, and the pressing need to find water to sustain agriculture on the often parched lands of the American West attested to the passing of the frontier. When Theodore Roosevelt became president of the United States in 1901, he translated concerns about protecting natural resources into government policy. The market, insisted Roosevelt and like-minded conservationists, could not be trusted to sustain

Adapting to the Environment: Russian Peasants Take on the Steppe

The Eurasian steppe extends for some 5,000 miles north of the Caucasus Mountains, from northern China and Mongolia to Hungary, and below the forest belt of original Muscovy. When historians mention these grasslands at all, it is generally to treat them as a military highway for armies of nomads that formed their own short-lived empires and harassed others. In this telling, when steppe warriors stood in the way of imperial Russian state expansion, they were wiped out or bribed to enter into bargains with the state. In the case of the powerful freebooters of the Don River basin, known as Cossacks, the Russian Empire offered grants of land and respect for Cossack self-government in exchange for the Cossacks' help in defending the empire's southern frontier. But there is another, lesser known environmental history of the steppe—one that tells of wheat fields and locusts, of snowstorms and boundless skies, and of the ways in which peasant migrants from northern, watered forests learned to adapt their farming methods to the land.

Russians first became aware of the environmental peculiarities of this region soon after Catherine the Great annexed a large swathe of the southern steppe, dubbing it "New Russia." The Tsarina had hoped to use this rich earth to feed Russians living on poorer northern lands. But already by the later eighteenth century, it was clear that increased farming was not yielding great increases in food production. Why not? Catherine sent officials to investigate, and at first they blamed the land, pointing to natural vegetation, recurring droughts, and other special qualities of the steppe environment. Over time, however, they realized that the problem lay in the farmers' practices, not in the land itself. The peasants were practicing farming as they had up north, grateful for the land but ignorant of it. Gradually, painfully, peasants as well as officials learned that because the steppe was different—hot and dry—it required different methods. The old implements did not work either: a new type of plow was needed to break the heavier-rooted plant life, especially steppe fescue (feather grass).

A breakthrough occurred when a Mennonite farmer observed topsoil blowing off his field. He planted a line of trees to break the wind and, in winter, to help retain snow for moisture. Similarly, an agronomist noticed that ravines near the river were widening and advised peasants to leave a band of steppe grasses in place as they plowed, since the grasses would help hold down the soil. At first, many peasants resisted sowing less of the land. Eventually, however, they discovered that the advice enabled them to increase crop production because of reduced erosion. In other words, environmental awareness spread—and made a difference.

The geologist Vasily Dokuchaev (1846-1903) turned the environmental awareness of the settlers and peasants into the first form of soil science. Dokuchaev's breakthrough idea was this: the problem with steppe farming was not the steppe, but the farmer. He made extensive studies across Russian regions, developed a theory of soil formation in relation to climate and human usage, and created the first soil classification system. He recommended

natural resources. Instead, federal action and regulation were necessary. This led in 1902 to the passage of the National Reclamation Act, which provided funding for large-scale dams and irrigation projects. Three years later, the Roosevelt administration orchestrated the establishment of the National Forest Service to manage the development of millions of acres of permanent public lands.

Similar worries and remedies were at work in Europe. In France, nostalgia about vanishing pastoral landscapes and anxieties about widespread deforestation provoked efforts to restore at least portions of the countryside. As in the United States, conservation efforts were spearheaded not by rural inhabitants but by urban bourgeoisie, with newly protected landscapes often becoming tourist destinations for city dwellers. In Russia, however, it was peasant farmers and local officials, seeking to make the steppe lands more productive, who laid the foundation for a new kind of soil science. (See Current Trends in World History: Adapting to the Environment: Russian Peasants Take on the Steppe.)

Race-Mixing and the Problem of Nationhood in Latin America

In Latin America, debates about identity chiefly addressed ethnic intermixing and the legacy of a system of government that, unlike much of the North Atlantic world, excluded rather than included the populace. After all, social hierarchies reaching back to the sixteenth century ranked white Iberians (whites born in Spain and Portugal) at the top, creole elites in the middle, and indigenous and African populations at the bottom. Thus, the higher on the social ladder, the more likely the people were to be white.

CONTESTED MIXTURES It is important to note that "mixing" did not lead to a shared heritage. Nor did it necessarily lead to homogeneity. In fact, the "racial" order did not stick, since some Iberians occupied the lower ranks, while a few people of color did manage to ascend the social ladder. Moreover, starting in the 1880s, the racial hierarchy saw further disruption by the deluge

Vladimir Orlovsky, *Harvest in the Ukraine* (1880). *This painting by Orlovsky shows Ukrainian peasants bringing in the rich harvest of the steppe.*

act as if they still lived in northern forests with endless supplies of timber), and the black-earth topsoil was significantly diminished. Later, this would spur the introduction of chemical fertilizers—which would increase crop yields but once again change the steppe ecosystem, adding pollutants to rivers. Like human history, the natural history of the steppe never stands still.

QUESTIONS FOR ANALYSIS

- How did the steppe lands' usefulness to the Russian Empire change during the period described above?
- How did peasants, officials, and scientists learn to think differently about steppe lands?

Explore Further

Moon, David. *The Plough That Broke the Steppes: Agriculture and Environment on Russia's Grasslands, 1700–1914* (2013).

crop rotations, longer fallow periods, and lighter plowing (to preserve topsoil). He wanted peasants to become stewards, not just exploiters, of the land.

By the latter part of the nineteenth century, agriculture in the steppe had taken off. Cossacks, too, had become successful farmers. New Russia, which was also called Ukraine, became a breadbasket (which it still is to a large extent). Imperial Russia became the world's leading agricultural exporter, feeding both Germany and Britain in the run-up to World War I.

Russia's environment was transformed. And yet, the agriculture of the steppe was not what we would call "sustainable." The minimal woods in the area were depleted (peasants continued to

of poor European immigrants; they were flooding into prospering Latin American countrysides or into booming cities like Buenos Aires in Argentina and São Paulo in Brazil. Latin American societies, then, did not easily become homogeneous "nations." Indeed, many Latin American observers wondered whether national identities could survive these transformations at all.

In an age of acute nationalism, the mixed racial composition of Latin Americans generated special anxieties. In the 1870s in Mexico, it was common to view Indians as obstacles to change. One demographer, Antonio García Cubas, considered indigenous people "decadent and degenerate." According to him, their presence deprived the republic of the right kind of citizens. In Cuba and Brazil, observers made the same claims about blacks. According to many modernizers, Latin America's own people were holding it back. The solution, argued some writers, was to attract white immigrants and to establish educational programs that would "uplift" Indians, blacks, and people of mixed descent. Thus, many intellectuals joined the crusade

to modernize and westernize their populations. In the effort to "whiten" their republics, many Latin American governments made especially strong pitches for northern European migrants, despite the mounting evidence that they often made inferior farmers and did not work well with others. So, even by 1900, some of the shine of "pure" white races was rubbing off, not least because European migrants did not live up to the propagandists' expectations.

PROMOTING NATIONHOOD BY CELEBRATING THE PAST For their part, Latin American leaders began to exalt bygone glories as a way to promote national identity and foster unity. Inventing successful myths could make a government seem more legitimate—as the heir to a rightful struggle of the past. Thus, in Mexico, General Díaz took the bell that Father Hidalgo had tolled on September 16, 1810, to mark the beginning of the war against Spain (see Chapter 15) and placed it in the National Palace in Mexico City. In the month of that centennial

Brazilian Modernization. *These photographs convey two aspects of Brazilians' drive to civilize. To the left is an image of the military leader Cândido Mariano da Silva Rondon, himself of mixed-blood descent, who was raised as an orphan in military schools—which was one of the important institutions for racial blending and modernization. He made a career surveying the Amazon for telegraph lines and would become a great defender of indigenous peoples. Here he is in 1910, posing as the civilizer-protector receiving gifts from indigenous people in the Guaporé River valley near the Bolivian border. Contrast the scene of peaceful uplift to the image at right, of Café do Rio, one of the elite hot spots in the capital of Rio de Janeiro in 1912. Cafés were the symbol of Europeanization and the spread of new customs of gentlemanly socializing among writers, politicians, and military leaders. The fashion of the day was to wear Panama hats, to sport bicolored shoes, and to drink local spirits. Note the absence of women. And there appears to be only one Afro-Brazilian customer, seated, with hat on, at the central table. For all its modernizing rhetoric, this elite culture was still highly exclusive.*

in 1910, grand processions wound through the capital. Many of the parades celebrated Aztec grandeur, thereby creating a mythic arc from the greatness of the Aztec past to the triumphal story of Mexican independence—and to the benevolence and progress of the Díaz regime. As the government glorified the Aztecs with pageants, statues, and pavilions, however, it continued to ignore modern Aztec descendants, who lived in squalor.

Some thinkers now began to celebrate ancient heritages as a basis for modern national identities. For example, in Mexico and eventually in the Andes, the pre-Spanish past became a crucial foundation stone of the nation-state. The young Mexican writer José Vasconcelos (1882–1959) grew disenchanted with the brutal rule of Díaz and his westernizing ambitions. Nonetheless, he endorsed Díaz's celebration of the Indian past, for he believed that Mexicans were capable of a superior form of civilization. He insisted that if they had fewer material concerns, their combined Aztec and Spanish Catholic origins could create a spiritual realm of even higher achievement. In Vasconcelos's view, Mexico's greatness flowed not in spite of, but because of, its mixed nature.

Sun Yat-sen and the Making of a Chinese Nation

Just as Latin Americans celebrated an authentic past, Chinese writers emphasized the power and depth of Chinese culture—in contrast to the Qing Empire's failing political and social strength. Here, writers used race to emphasize the superiority of the Han Chinese. Here, too, the pace of change generated a desire to trace one's roots back to secure foundations. Moreover, traditions were reinvented in the hope of saving "Chinese culture" threatened by modernity.

In China, as elsewhere, scholars and political mobilizers took up the challenge of redefining identities. By the century's end, prominent members of both groups had abandoned their commitment to preserving the old order but were not ready to fully adopt western practices. Their attempts at combining traditions and values from home and abroad gave rise to the modern Chinese intelligentsia and modern Chinese nationalism.

PROMOTING HAN NATIONALISM Symbolizing the challenge of nation building were the endeavors of Sun Yat-sen (1866–1925), who was part of an emerging generation of critics of the old regime. Like his European counterparts, Sun dreamed of a political community reshaped along national lines. Born into a modest rural household in southern China, he studied medicine in the British colony of Hong Kong and then turned to politics during the Sino-Japanese War. When the Qing government rejected his offer of service to the Chinese cause, he became convinced that China's rulers were out of touch with the times. Subsequently, he established an organization based in Hawaii to advocate the Qing downfall and the cause of republicanism.

Diego Rivera's *History of Mexico*. *This is one of the most famous works of Mexican art, a portrait of the history of Mexico by the radical nationalist painter Diego Rivera. In this chapter and in Chapter 12, we have shown details from this mural. In stepping back to view the whole work, which is in the National Palace in Mexico City, we can see how Rivera envisioned the history of his people generally. Completed in 1935, this work seeks to show a people fighting constantly against outside aggressors, from their glorious preconquest days (lower center), winding like a grand epic through the conquest, colonial exploitation, the revolution for independence, nineteenth-century invasions from France and the United States, to the popular 1910 Mexican Revolution. It culminates in an image of Karl Marx, framed by a "scientific sun"—pointing to a future of progress and prosperity for all, as if restoring a modern Tenochtitlán of the Aztecs. This work captured many Mexicans' efforts to return to the indigenous roots of the nation and to fuse them with modern scientific ideas.*

The cornerstone of his message was Chinese nationalism—specifically, Han (the majority of the population) nationalism.

Sun blasted the feeble rule by the non-Han "outsiders," the Manchus, and trumpeted a sovereign political community of "true" Chinese. No ruler, he argued, could enjoy legitimacy without the nation's consent. He envisioned a new China free of Manchu rule, building a democratic form of government and an economic system based on equalized land rights. In this fashion, Sun claimed, China would join the world of nation-states and have the power to defend its borders.

Sun's nationalism did not catch on immediately in China itself, partly because the Qing regime persecuted all dissenters. His ideas fared better among the hundreds of thousands of Chinese who had emigrated in the second half of the nineteenth century. Often facing discrimination in their adopted homelands, these overseas communities applauded Sun's racial nationalism and democratic ideas. In addition, Chinese students studying abroad found inspiration in his message.

REPLACING THE QING AND RECONSTITUTING A NATION Sun's nationalist and republican call resonated more powerfully as the Qing Empire grew weaker early in the twentieth century. Military defeat at the hands of neighboring Japan and the fiasco of the Boxer Uprising further shook the dynasty.

Realizing that reforms were necessary, the Manchu court began overhauling the administrative system and the military after the turn of the century. Yet these changes came too late. The old elites grumbled, and the new class of urban merchants, entrepreneurs, and professionals (who often benefited from business with westerners) regarded the government as outmoded. Moreover, peasants and laborers resented the high cost of the reforms, which seemed to help only the rulers.

A mutiny, sparked in part by the government's nationalization of railroads and its low compensation to native Chinese investors, broke out in the city of Wuchang in central China in 1911. It signaled the start of what became known as the 1911 Revolution as unrest spread to other parts of the country, and Sun Yat-sen hurried home from traveling in the United States. Few people rallied to the emperor's cause, and the Qing dynasty collapsed—an abrupt end to a dynastic tradition of more than 2,000 years.

China would soon be reconstituted, and Sun's ideas, especially those regarding race, would play a central role. The original flag of the republic, for example, consisted of five colors representing the citizenry's major racial groups: red for the Han, yellow for the Manchus, blue for the Mongols, white for the Tibetans, and black for the Muslims. But Sun had reservations about this multiracial flag, believing there should be only one

Sun Yat-sen. *Through the medium of clothing, these two images of Sun Yat-sen, the man generally known as the "father of the Chinese nation," epitomize the evolving cultural ambiguities of China in the late nineteenth and early twentieth centuries. Left: As a young man studying medicine in the British colony of Hong Kong in the late 1880s, Sun and his friends dressed in the conventional Qing garb of Chinese gentlemen. Right: Two decades later, in early 1912, Sun and the officials of the new republic appeared in public in full western-style jackets and ties. Clothing, like so many parts of the cultural arena in China during this period, had become a contested ground in the battle to forge a new nation's identity.*

Chinese race. The existence of different groups in China, he argued, was the result of incomplete assimilation—a problem that the modern nation now had to confront.

Nationalism and Invented Traditions in India

British imperial rule persisted in India, but the turn of the century saw cracks in its stranglehold. Four strands had woven the territory together: the consolidation of colonial administration, the establishment of railways and telegraphs, the growth of western education and ideas, and the development of colonial capitalism. Now it was possible to speak of India as a single unit. And it was also possible for anticolonial thinkers to imagine seizing and ruling India by themselves. Thus, a new form of resistance emerged, different from peasant rebellions of the past. Now, dissenters talked of Indians as "a people" who had both a national past and national traditions.

A MODERNIZING ELITE Leaders of the nationalist opposition were western-educated intellectuals from colonial cities and towns. Although a tiny minority of the Indian population, they gained influence through their access to the official world and their familiarity with European knowledge and history. This elite group used their knowledge to develop modern cultural forms. For example, they turned colloquial languages (such as Hindi, Urdu, Bengali, Tamil, and Malayalam) into standardized,

literary forms for writing novels and dramas. Now the publication of journals, magazines, newspapers, pamphlets, novels, and dramas surged, facilitating communication throughout British India.

Along with print culture came a growing public sphere where intellectuals debated social and political matters. By 1885, voluntary associations in big cities had united to establish a political party, the Indian National Congress. Lawyers, prominent merchants, and local notables dominated its early leadership. The congress demanded greater representation of Indians in administrative and legislative bodies, criticized the government's economic policies, and encouraged India's industrialization.

Underlying this political nationalism, embodied by the **Indian National Congress**, was cultural nationalism. The nationalists claimed that Indians might not be a single race but were at least a unified people because of their unique culture and common colonial history. Indeed, nationalism in India (unlike in Europe) developed with an acute awareness of Indians as colonial subjects. The critical question was: could India be a modern nation *and* hold on to its Indian identity?

BUILDING A MODERN IDENTITY ON REWRITTEN TRADITIONS The recovery of traditions became a way to establish a modern Indian identity without acknowledging the recent subjugation by British colonizers. So Indian intellectuals (like those in Latin America) turned to the past and rewrote the histories of ancient empires and kingdoms. In this way,

Indian intellectuals promoted the idea of the nation-state even though the region had no integrated, national history prior to colonization.

To portray Indians as a people with a unifying religious creed, intellectuals reconfigured Hinduism so that it resembled western religion. This was no easy task, for traditional Hinduism did not have a supreme textual authority, a monotheistic God, an organized church, or an established creed. Nonetheless, nationalist Hindu intellectuals combined various philosophical texts, cultural beliefs, social practices, and Hindu traditions into a mix that they labeled the authentic Hindu religion. Other Indian revivalists, too, explored the roots of a national culture. Some researched ancient Indian contributions to astronomy, mathematics, algebra, chemistry, and medicine and called for a national science. In the fine arts, intellectuals constructed an

Modern Indian Art. *Painter Raja Ravi Varma's 1889 portrait of Maharani Chimnabai incorporates elements typical to western art while retaining the palette, patterns, and figures of prominence that reach back to India's glorious past.*

imaginary line of continuity to the glorious past to promote a specifically Indian art and aesthetics (sense of beauty).

While fashioning hybrid forms, revivalists also narrowed the definition of Indian traditions. As Hindu intellectuals looked back, they identified Hindu traditions and the pre-Islamic past as the only sources of India's culture. Other contributors to the region's mosaic past were forgotten; the Muslim past, in particular, had no prominent role. However, the Muslims and other religious, ethnic, and linguistic groups also attempted to mobilize their communities for modern, secular purposes. The Indian National Muslim League, for example, which formed in 1906, advanced the *political* interests of Muslims, not the Islamic religion.

HINDU REVIVALISM Hindu revivalism became a powerful political force in the late nineteenth century, when the nationalist challenge to the colonial regime took a militant turn. New leaders rejected constitutionalism and called for militant agitation. The British decision to partition Bengal in 1905 into two provinces—one predominantly Muslim, the other Hindu—drew militants into the streets to urge the boycott of British goods. Rabindranath Tagore, a famous Bengali poet and future Nobel laureate, composed stirring nationalist poetry. Activists formed voluntary organizations, called Swadeshi ("one's own country") Samities ("societies"), that championed indigenous enterprises for manufacturing soap, cloth, medicine, iron, and paper, as well as schools for imparting nationalist education. Although few of these ventures succeeded, they asserted Indians' autonomy as a people. But the movement's Hindu revivalist flavor alienated the Muslims. Even Tagore, who had served as the poet laureate of the Swadeshi movement, was so troubled by its divisiveness that he went on to pen a novel, *Home and the World* (1916), that lamented the narrow-mindedness of nationalism.

Meanwhile, the Swadeshi movement swept aside the moderate leadership of the Indian National Congress and installed a radical leadership that broadened the nationalist agitation. Although the people did not topple the colonial regime, Indian mass mobilization was enough to alarm the British rulers, who turned to force to keep the colony intact. When the movement slipped into a campaign of terrorism in 1908, the government responded by imprisoning militant leaders. However, the colonial administrators annulled their partition of Bengal in 1911.

Late nineteenth-century Indian nationalism posed a kind of challenge to the British that was different from that of the suppressed 1857 rebellion. Back then, insurgents had wanted to preserve local identities against the encroaching modern state and colonial economy. Now, in contrast, nationalist leaders imagined a modern national community. Invoking religious and ethnic symbols, they formed modern political associations to operate in a national public arena. Unlike the insurgents of 1857, they did not seek a radical alternative to the colonial

Rabindranath Tagore. *The Bengali writer, philosopher, and teacher Rabindranath Tagore became the poet laureate of the Swadeshi Movement in Bengal in 1903–1908. The first Asian Nobel laureate, he became disenchanted with nationalism, viewing it as narrow and not universalistic. The photo shows Tagore reading to a group of his students in 1929.*

order; instead, they fought for the political rights of Indians as a national community. In these new nationalists, British rulers discovered an enemy not so different from themselves.

The Pan Movements

India and China were not the only places where activists dreamed of founding new states. Across the globe, groups had begun to imagine new communities based on ethnicity or, in some cases, religion. **Pan movements** (from the Greek *pan*, "all") sought to link people across state boundaries. The grand aspiration of all these movements—which included pan-Asianism, pan-Islamism, pan-Africanism, pan-Slavism, pan-Turkism, pan-Arabism, pan-Germanism, and Zionism—was the rearrangement of borders to unite dispersed communities. But such remappings posed a threat to rulers of the Russian, Austrian, and Ottoman Empires, as well as to overseers of the British and the French colonial empires.

PAN-ISLAMISM Within the Muslim world, intellectuals and political leaders begged their coreligionists to put aside sectarian and political differences so that they could unite under the banner of Islam in opposition to European incursions. The leading spokesman for pan-Islamism was the well-traveled Jamal al-Din al-Afghani (1839–1897). Born in Iran and given a Shiite upbringing, he nonetheless called on Muslims worldwide to overcome their Sunni and Shiite differences so that they could work together against the west. During a sojourn in Egypt, he

Sultan Abdul Hamid II Agrees to a Constitution. *In 1876, the new Ottoman Sultan, Abdul Hamid II, agreed to reign as a constitutional monarch. Thanks in part to war with Russia, which commenced the next year, and in part to the Sultan's own dictatorial instincts, within two years' time the Ottoman Empire had reverted to absolute monarchy, and the Sultan had begun to promote himself as a Muslim leader.*

joined with a young Egyptian reformer, Muhammad Abduh (1849–1905), to inspire an Islamic protest against Europe. Later, Afghani and Abduh (then living in Paris) published a pan-Islamic newspaper. Afghani subsequently made his way to Istanbul, where he supported the pan-Islamic ambitions of Sultan Abdul Hamid II, who promoted the defense of Islam as a way to thwart European schemes to divide up the Ottoman Empire.

The pan-Islamic appeal only added to Muslims' confusion as they confronted the west. Indeed, Arab Muslims living as Ottoman subjects had many calls on their loyalties. Should they support the Ottoman Empire to resist European encroachments? Or should they embrace the Islamism of Afghani? Most decided to work within the fledgling nation-states of the Islamic world, looking to a Syrian or Lebanese identity as the way to deal with the west and gain autonomy. But Afghani and his disciples had struck a chord in Muslim culture, and their Islamic message has long retained a powerful appeal. (See Primary Source: A Muslim Philosopher Describes Why Islam Has Become Weak.)

PRIMARY SOURCE

A Muslim Philosopher Describes Why Islam Has Become Weak

Jamal al-Din al-Afghani is one of the most perplexing and mysterious figures in modern Islamic history. Born in Iran and raised in its Shiite tradition, he claimed Afghani birth and traveled widely in the Sunni world. His early sojourn in India, almost immediately after the Rebellion of 1857, left him with an undying hatred of the British and a conviction to unite the Islamic world. Although he believed that Islam was capable of reform, he devoted most of his energies to convincing the intellectual and political leaders in Arab and Ottoman-ruled lands to put aside their many differences and draw on their shared commitment to Islam in order to ward off Europe's ambitions in their region.

At the height of his influence in Egypt between 1871 and 1879, he gathered around him young men of leadership potential, though he would soon be exiled for his radical ideas and watch Egypt fall under British colonial power.

The undated document below was probably written toward the end of Afghani's career, which he spent in the court of Abdul Hamid II, sultan of the Ottoman Empire (r. 1876–1909), who also shared Afghani's vision of Islamic unity. It contrasts past Muslim greatness with present-day decline and encourages united resistance to western dominance; these are themes that have reverberated throughout the Islamic world ever since.

"God changes not what is in a people, until they change what is in themselves." (13:11)

"That is because God would never change His favour that He conferred on a people until they change what was within themselves." (8:55)

These are verses of the Honourable Qur'an, the Admonitory Book which leads to the Right Path, and which calls [men] to the true religion. . . . The Qur'an is the Book of God which He has sent down for the guidance [of mankind] and what is necessary for his life in this world and the world to come. It is a cure for the disease of straying [from the right path] and a remedy for the disease of ignorance. . . .

God roused the Islamic *umma* with a small number of people and gave them the highest rank to the point that the Muslims trod upon the lofty mountains and shook them with awe. . . . Their astonishing advent frightened every soul and their extraordinary progress amazed every intellect. The inhabitants of the world bit their fingers in astonishment at the unbelievable progress which these people achieved in a short period of time. They wondered . . . how the brave nations of the world had fallen helpless in facing them; and how the

powerful states had been worn out under the hoofs of their horses. . . .

Let us now take a look at the present situation of the Muslims and compare it with their past and clarify their progress vis à vis their decline. The Muslim population in the world today is more than. . . two thousand times as large as the Muslim population at the time of their conquest of the territories of the world. The Islamic state extended from the shore of the Atlantic Ocean in West Africa to the heart of China. All these areas were independent and prosperous lands located in the best regions of the earth. . . .

In spite of this, the Islamic states today are unfortunately pillaged and their property stolen; their territory is occupied by foreigners and their wealth in the possession of others. There is no day in which foreigners do not grab a part of the Islamic lands, and there is no night in which foreigners do not make a group of Muslims obey their rule. They disgrace the Muslims and dissipate their pride. . . . Sometimes they call them savages and sometimes regard them as hard-hearted and cruel and finally consider them insane animals. What a disaster! What an affliction! . . .

What should be done then? Where can we find the cause? Where can we look for the reason and whom should we ask? [There is no answer to these questions] except to say that: "God changes not what is in a people, until they change what is in themselves."(13:11)

QUESTIONS FOR ANALYSIS

- What is Afghani suggesting about the quality of his fellow Muslims when he points to the origins of the Islamic *umma*?

- Explain why Afghani uses the landmass of the Islamic state as a measure of the devoutness of the Muslims within it.

- Following the fall of Egypt to British rule, Afghani argued that *jihad* obligated every individual to defend the remaining Muslim land from European domination. What is *jihad*? Do you think the introspective self-reform that Afghani calls for is at odds with *jihad*?

Source: Sayid Jamāl al-Dīn al Afghānī and Abdul-Hādī Hā'irī, "Afghānī on the Decline of Islam," in *Die Welt des Islams*, New Series, 13: 1/2 (1971): 121-125.

A Pan-German Leader Rails against the Rising Power of the Slavs and the Jews in the Austro-Hungarian Empire

Georg von Schönerer was a right-wing radical and member of the Austrian House of Deputies. A German of Austrian descent, he was one of the first to object vehemently to the rising aspirations of the Slavic peoples of the Austro-Hungarian Empire for rights equal to those of the German population. For Schönerer, any sharing of cultural or political power with the Slavs or Jews was a threat to the dominance of ethnic Germans in the empire. Claiming (falsely) that Jews were taking all of the good jobs in the empire, controlling the press, and manipulating financial markets, he aimed not just at keeping them out of the economy, but, as he states below, at eliminating Jewish influence "in all areas of the administration, law making, and public life as a whole."

Schönerer delivered the following speech on April 28, 1887, before the Austrian House of Deputies. His attempt to push through anti-Semitic legislation a month later was unsuccessful, but he continued to campaign for such pan-German causes for the rest of his life. Although they never met in person, Schönerer would become a hero to another Austrian pan-German and anti-Semite, Adolf Hitler.

This I must say in advance: we can only lament, that some Germans have set out on a false path and most sincerely believe that if the foreigner, whether he be a Jew, or a Negro, or a Chinese, or a Singhalese, learns to speak German and declares himself without a religion, or allows himself to be baptized Christian, then he can be welcomed with friendship as a German brother. . . . Today I have . . . set myself the task . . . of discussing the social question together first of all with respect to the Jewish nation. Now as a few days ago the highest imperial court has supported the community's right to free expression of its opinion, I must also hope that I, as a representative of the people in the Parliament also will not have this right taken away from me today (bravo, bravo, on the far left). . . . I must also today most decidedly take the opportunity to announce, from our German-national standpoint, the division of Bohemia that has been advocated and perhaps even planned by various parties. Such a division must, in our view, necessarily lead to the division of other territories, such as Carinthia or Steiermark or other partially linguistically-mixed regions, and materially damage not only the solidarity of all the Germans in Austria, but also the united character of the formerly German federal states of Austria. Thus together with my party members in the German national party and in agreement with those who are most closely sympathetic with our views outside this House, I have requested again to present our program publicly, and particularly to today present important parts of it which bear on the so vital reforms in the social and economic sector.

This proposed, and we believe, authentic, racially organic reform legislation, is also . . . of great significance for our national struggles. The foundations, however, of this social political reformist measures especially lie, in our view, *first in protections to be created against the falsification of public opinion by the press; and secondly, in the pushing out of Jewish influence in all areas of the administration, law making, and public life as a whole.*

Above all, I must, in the name of the German Nationals, stress the fact that we are proud to be members of a great people (*Volk*) and that as such we feel a holy duty to stand up for the welfare and the power, for the securing of national identity and for the protection of the national life of the German community in Austria at all times and incessantly. We Germans in Austria are certainly obliged to maintain ourselves in between the expanded power-positions of the Slavs, remembering that our German brothers in the Empire have repeatedly fought and bled for our nation against the enemy [the French] in the West. . . . We will also never forget, especially in the light of the unremitting, threatening influx of Slavdom into ancient German-language territory, that the German lands of Austria have for a long time formed part of Germany, and we see it as our national duty, to enduringly strengthen the existing alliances between Germany and Austria with legal and economic laws, in order that the existing union organically and permanently grows together.

QUESTIONS FOR ANALYSIS

- According to Schönerer, what characteristics must a person possess in order to be properly deemed a German?
- Why does Schönerer consider this pan-German cause a "holy duty"? What other "holy duties" have you encountered in this book that ultimately resulted in violent conflict?
- Outline the political, economic, and cultural changes that Schönerer proposes in this speech.

Source: *Fünf Reden der Reichsratabgeordneten Georg Ritter von Schönerer* (Horn: Ferdinand Berger, 1891), pp. 89–90. Translated by Suzanne Marchand.

PAN-GERMANISM AND PAN-SLAVISM Pan-Germanism found followers across central Europe, where it often competed with a pan-Slavic movement that sought to unite all Slavs against their Austrian, German, and Ottoman overlords. This area had traditionally been ruled by German-speaking elites, who owned the land farmed by Poles, Czechs, Russians, and other Slavs. German elites began to feel increasingly uneasy as Slavic nationalisms (spurred by the midcentury revivals of traditional Czech, Polish, Serbian, and Ukrainian languages and cultures) became more popular. Even more threatening was the fact that the Slavic populations were growing faster than the German. As pogroms in the Russian Empire's borderlands in the 1880s, as well as economic opportunities, drove crowds of eastern European Jews westward, German resentment toward these newcomers also increased.

What made pan-Germanism a movement, however, was the intervention of a former liberal, Georg von Schönerer (1842–1921). In 1882, Schönerer, outraged by the Habsburg Empire's failure to favor Germans, founded the League of German Nationalists. It comprised students, artisans, teachers, and small businessmen in the interests of uniting German Austrians with the Germans in Bismarck's Empire. Schönerer detested the Jews, defining them by their "racial characteristics" rather than by their religious practices. After his election to the Austrian upper house, he attempted to pass anti-Jewish legislation modeled on the American Chinese Exclusion Act of 1882. Although Schönerer's plans were too radical for most German Austrians, his anti-Semitism found echoes in a milder form by Viennese mayor Karl Lueger in the late 1890s and in a stronger form by Adolf Hitler after 1933. (See Primary Source: A Pan-German Leader Rails against the Rising Power of the Slavs and the Jews in the Austro-Hungarian Empire.)

The rhetoric of pan-Germanism motivated central Europeans to think of themselves as members of a German *race*, their identities determined by blood rather than defined by state boundaries. This, too, was the lesson of pan-Slavism. Both movements led fanatics to take actions that were dangerous to existing states. The organization of networks of radical southern Slavs, for example, unsettled Serbia and Herzegovina (annexed by the Austrians in 1908). Indeed, it was a Serbian proponent of plans to carve an independent Slav state out of Austrian territory in the Balkans who assassinated the heir to the Habsburg throne in June 1914. By August, the whole of Europe had descended into mass warfare, bringing much of the rest of the world directly or indirectly into the conflict as well. Eventually, the Great War would fulfill the pan-Slav, pan-German, and anti-Ottoman Muslim nationalist longing to tear down the Ottoman and Habsburg Empires.

Intellectuals articulated the pan movements, and aspiring political leaders and secret societies took up their ideologies, leaving Europe and much of Asia at the end of the nineteenth century boiling with ideas on how to create new political communities that could go beyond the nations and transcend the borders of the states.

CONCLUSION

Ever since the Enlightenment, Europeans had put their faith in "progress." Through the nineteenth century, educated elites took pride in their booming industries, bustling cities, and burgeoning colonial empires. Yet by the century's end, urbanization and industrialization seemed more disrupting than uplifting, more disorienting than reassuring. Moreover, colonized people's resistance to the "civilizing mission" fueled doubts about the course of progress.

Especially unsettling to the ruling elite was the realization that "the people" not only were against them but also were developing ways to unseat them. In colonial settings, nationalists learned how to mobilize large populations. In Europe, socialist and right-wing leaders challenged liberal political power. By contrast, old elites, whose politics relied on closed-door negotiations between "rational" gentlemen, were unprepared to deal with modern ideas and identities.

Nor were the elites able to control the scope of change, for the expansion of empires had drawn ever more people into an unbalanced global economy. Everywhere, disparities in wealth appeared—especially in Africa, Asia, and Latin America. Moreover, the size and power of industrial operations threatened small firms and made individuals seem insignificant. Even some cities seemed too big and too dangerous. All these social and economic challenges stretched the capacities of gentlemanly politics.

Yet anxieties stimulated creative energy and experimental thinking that found expression in a movement that became known as modernism. Western artists borrowed nonwestern images and vocabularies; noneastern intellectuals looked to the west for inspiration, even as they formulated anti-western ideas. The upheavals of modern experience propelled scholars to study the past and to fabricate utopian visions of the future.

Revivals and dislocations, as well as cultural and political movements, influenced the reformulating of identities. However, this was an incomplete process. For even as these changes unsettled the European-centered world, they intensified rivalries among Europe's powers themselves. Thus, this order was unstable at its center—Europe itself. And in the massive conflict that destroyed this era's faith in progress, Europe would ravage itself. The Great War would yield an age of even more rapid change—and even more violent consequences.

TRACING THE GLOBAL STORYLINES

After You Read This Chapter

Go to INQUIZITIVE to see what you know & learn what you've missed.

FOCUS ON: *Sources of Global Anxieties and Expressions of Cultural Modernism*

Global Trends
- Mass migrations and unprecedented urban expansion challenge national identities.

Africa and China: Anticolonialism
- The Anglo-Boer War and violent uprisings against colonial rule in Africa call Europe's imperializing mission into question.
- The Chinese rise up against European encroachments in the Boxer Rebellion.

Europe and North America: Mounting Tensions
- Intense political rivalries, financial insecurities and crises, rapid industrialization, feminism, and class conflict roil Europe and spread to the rest of the world.

Mexico: Resentment toward Elites
- The most widespread revolution from below takes place in Mexico.

Cultural Modernism
- Increased earning power gives workers in wealthy nations the leisure to enjoy music, vaudeville shows, sports, and other forms of popular culture and to read mass-circulation newspapers.
- Elite culture explores new forms in painting, architecture, music, literature, and science in order to break with the past and differentiate itself more dramatically from popular culture.
- New ideas of race emerge, as does a renewed emphasis on the nation-state and nationalism.

CHRONOLOGY

	1870	1880	1890
Africa			
The Americas			Jim Crow laws (United States) **1890s**
Europe			
South Asia		Indian National Congress founded **1885**	
East Asia			
Russia			

STUDY QUESTIONS

1. **Explain** the varying effects of economic progress on different parts of the world at the end of the nineteenth and beginning of the twentieth centuries. What were the sources of this progress?

2. **Discuss** the connections between migration and the development of nationalism during this period.

3. **Compare** the responses to imperialism in Africa and China during this era. How similar were these movements to other alternative visions to the new world order explored in Chapter 16?

4. **Identify and analyze** examples of worldwide anxieties that challenged the idea of progress during this time. Which groups protested the status quo?

5. **Describe** the political, economic, and social crises that swept through the world during this period. **Assess** their impact on different regions.

6. **Compare and contrast** revolutionary and reform movements in Latin America (especially the Mexican Revolution) and China (especially the Boxer Uprising) during this era. How were their goals and methods similar? How were they different?

7. **Analyze** how anxieties about progress shaped cultural developments around the world. **Discuss** the ways in which new cultural forms at the turn of the century reflected challenges to the world order as it then existed.

8. **Explain** what cultural modernism was and how it challenged traditional assumptions about art and science.

9. **Define** popular culture. Why did it become so powerful during this time, and how did it shape individuals' identity?

10. **Evaluate** to what extent new ideas of race and nation created tension within and between states. What new forms of nationalism emerged during this time?

11. **Compare** the challenges to the west posed by the pan movements and Sun Yat-sen.

12. **Discuss** the ways in which race, nation, and religion unified populations but also made societies more difficult to govern and economies more difficult to manage.

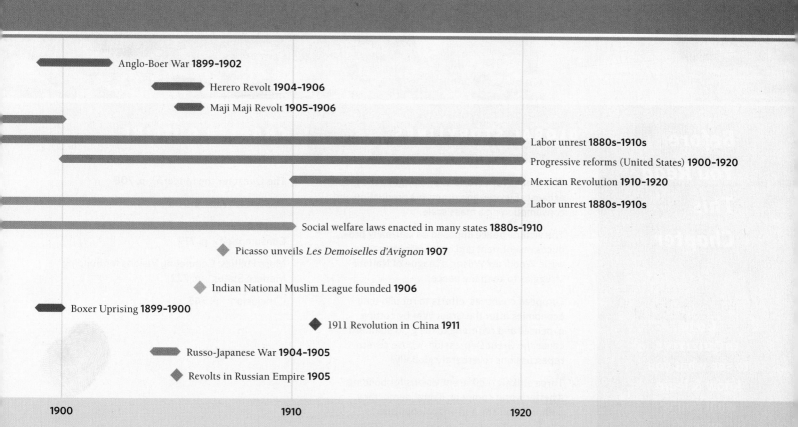

Anglo-Boer War **1899–1902**

Herero Revolt **1904–1906**

Maji Maji Revolt **1905–1906**

Labor unrest **1880s–1910s**

Progressive reforms (United States) **1900–1920**

Mexican Revolution **1910–1920**

Labor unrest **1880s–1910s**

Social welfare laws enacted in many states **1880s–1910**

Picasso unveils *Les Demoiselles d'Avignon* **1907**

Indian National Muslim League founded **1906**

Boxer Uprising **1899–1900**

1911 Revolution in China **1911**

Russo-Japanese War **1904–1905**

Revolts in Russian Empire **1905**

1900   1910   1920

19

Of Masses and Visions of the Modern, 1910–1939

FOCUS QUESTIONS

- What were the causes of World War I, and how did the war disrupt societies around the world?

- In what ways did the development of modern, mass societies cause the Great Depression? How were they affected by it?

- What were the ideologies of liberal democracy, authoritarianism, and anticolonialism? How were they alike, and how were they different? How successful was each during this period?

- In what ways did access to consumer goods and other aspects of mass society influence political conflict in Asia, Africa, and Latin America?

After millions were killed or wounded, overwhelmingly in Europe, the last guns of the Great War (World War I) fell silent in a remote corner of East Africa. It took a full day for news of the armistice to reach that region, where African soldiers, under British and German officers, were battling for control of German East Africa. Here, 10,000 German-led African soldiers used guerrilla tactics to thwart the efforts of over 300,000 British-led African soldiers. Thousands of African troops died in these battles, beyond the spotlight of international opinion. Campaigns bloodied the soil in sub-Saharan Africa, Egypt, Syria, and Turkey as well, and multitudes of African, Asian, and American soldiers were ferried across oceans to join the killing and maiming in Europe.

Raging from August 1914 to November 1918, World War I shook the foundations of the European-centered world. This was the first modern war, and its impact was thoroughly global. Its aftermath fostered notions of freedom and self-determination and a growing disillusionment with European rule in far-flung colonies. Elsewhere, nations grappled with competing postwar visions for building a dynamic, modern society amid ongoing international rivalries.

This chapter deals with the Great War and its global impact. First, because the war was fought between European countries, most of which had overseas empires, it brought in resources of a large part of the world. In the advanced countries it prompted production and consumption on a mass scale. Wartime leaders also used new media such as radio and film to promote national loyalties and to discredit enemies—and thereby helped to spread mass culture. Wartime practices of mobilization offered a new political model as well. Second, the terms of the peace settlement and the absence of international leadership unbalanced the global economy and laid the groundwork for the Great Depression. Third, political turmoil surrounding the war inflamed disputes over how to manage new mass societies and build a better world. To this end, three strikingly different visions arose: liberal democracy, authoritarianism, and anticolonialism. These ideologies competed for preeminence in the decades leading up to World War II as powerful countries pressed their preferred visions on others.

THE QUEST FOR THE MODERN

When people spoke of "being modern" in the 1920s and 1930s, they disagreed on what it meant. For culture and the arts (see Chapter 18), modernism meant breaking perceived conventions. In economic terms, the consensus was that modernity involved mass production and mass consumption. In the west, for example, the automobile, the gramophone (a record player), the cinema, and the radio reflected the benefits of economic and cultural modernism. In terms of political issues, being modern meant the involvement of the masses. Everywhere, many people favored strong leadership to reinvigorate their societies; some wanted more democracy to replace monarchical and colonial rule, while others favored more authoritarian solutions. Following the onset of the Great Depression in the early 1930s, these debates over how to build modern societies intensified and were accompanied by a surge in the popularity of authoritarianism and aggressive international behavior.

The first political vision of being or becoming modern—the *liberal democratic* one—confronted economic failings that beset this period, such as the Great Depression, without sacrificing market economies or parliamentary democracy. It did so through widened participation in governance but also gave greater power to regulatory bureaucracies. However, when the Great Depression spread hard times and unemployment, this predominantly American and western European model linking markets and democracy no longer seemed so promising. Around the world, people considered alternatives that might better deliver the promises of modernity. Although many countries rejected the parliamentary or liberal perspective, the system survived in the United States, parts of western Europe, and several Latin American nations.

For many observers, liberal democracies failed to match the astonishing dynamism of a second perspective—*authoritarianism*. Authoritarian regimes rejected parliamentary representation, subordinated the individual to the state, managed and, in the case of communism, owned most industries, used censorship and terror to enforce loyalty, and exalted an all-powerful leader. During this period, authoritarianism was evident in both right-wing dictatorships (fascist Italy, Nazi Germany, dictatorial Spain and Portugal, and militaristic Japan) and a left-wing dictatorship (the Soviet Union).

The third vision—*anticolonialism*—also questioned the liberal democratic order, primarily because of its connection to colonialism. However, most anticolonialists did not reject parliaments, private property, or free markets. Resentful of European rulers who preached democracy but practiced despotism, anticolonial leaders sought to oust their colonial rulers and find their own path to modernity. They generally favored mixing western ideas with indigenous traditions.

Authoritarian and anticolonial visions of modernity both embraced technology and economic dynamism. They sought to take advantage of economic growth and mass support and redefine what freedom meant, while rejecting what they considered the hypocrisy and weakness of liberal democracy. Yet they often produced their own hypocrisies.

THE GREAT WAR

Few events were more decisive in drawing men and women worldwide into national and international politics than the **Great War**. For over four years, millions of soldiers from Europe, its dominions, and its colonies killed and mutilated one another. Such carnage damaged European claims to civilized superiority and encouraged colonial subjects to break from imperial masters. Among Europeans, too, the war's effects shook the hierarchies of prewar society. Above all, the war made clear how much the power of the state now depended on the support of the people.

The war's causes were complex. Underlying European tensions were great-power rivalries, which pitted a rising Germany and a conflict-ridden Austria-Hungary against Britain, France, and Russia. Through most of the nineteenth century, Britain had been the preeminent power. By century's end, however, German industrial output had surpassed Britain's, and Germany had begun building a navy. For the British, who controlled the world's seas, the German navy was an affront; for the French, still seething from their defeat in the Franco-Prussian War of

1870–1871 (see Chapter 17), German military buildup seemed a threat to their very existence; for the Germans, it was a logical step in their expanding ambitions. British hawks, wielding their might in the international financial system, wanted to destroy German power. German hawks felt surrounded—by the French to the west, the Russians to the east—and argued for launching war before Russia grew too strong militarily. Germany joined Austria-Hungary to form the **Central Powers** (later adding the Ottoman Empire), and Britain affiliated itself with France and Russia in the Triple Entente (called the **Allied Powers** later, after Italy joined).

Well armed and secretly pledged to defend their partners, the rivals were provided with a spark in June 1914, when the heir to the Habsburg throne was assassinated in Sarajevo, the capital of Austrian-annexed Bosnia. The assassin, a teenage Bosnian Serb named Gavrilo Princip, hoped to trigger an independence movement that would unite South Slav territories in the Austro-Hungarian Empire (see Chapter 18) with independent Serbia. The Austro-Hungarian emperor decided to take a firm stand, and the German kaiser backed him; the Russians declared support for the Serbs in an effort to uphold state prestige and stifle domestic political opposition. The British and French were determined to prevent Germany and Austria from taking advantage of a possible Ottoman collapse and were keen to realize their own ambitions at German expense in the colonial world. Throughout July, diplomats sought to negotiate a deal, but no one managed to prevent the outbreak of a war that would devastate all of Europe and drag its colonies into the warfare, too.

Battle Fronts, Stalemate, and Carnage

Responsibility for the war was shared by Austria-Hungary, Serbia, Germany, Russia, Britain, and France. Despite many initial illusions about a swift resolution, the war became infamous for its duration and horrors. It began on July 29 with a massive Austrian bombardment of Serbian Belgrade, followed by the invasion of Austro-Hungarian troops who committed atrocities against civilians. The planned German offensive, a thrust through neutral Belgium into France, was slowed by French and Belgian resistance. German troops came close to Paris at the battle of the Marne in September 1914. (See Map 19.1.) A stalemate ensued. Instead of a quick war, vast land armies dug trenches along the Western Front—from the English Channel through Belgium and France to the Alps—installing barbed wire and setting up machine-gun posts.

Lord Kitchener—who had conquered Sudan in part by unleashing the machine gun on Sudanese warriors opposing conquest—had predicted to the British cabinet that the war in Europe "will not end until we have plumbed our manpower to the last military man" (Anderson, p. 69). In fact, soldierly life in the trenches, a combination of boredom, dampness, vermin, and disease, was punctuated by the terror of having to "go over the top" to attack the enemy's entrenched position. Doing so meant running across a "no man's land" in which machine guns mowed down almost all attackers

On the other side of Europe, Russian troops advanced into German East Prussia and Austria-Hungary along the Eastern Front. Although they defeated Austro-Hungarian troops in

Trenches in World War I.
The anticipated war of mobility turned out to be an illusion; instead, armies dug trenches and filled them with foot soldiers and machine guns. To advance entailed walking into a hail of machine-gun fire. Life in the trenches meant cold, dampness, rats, disease, and boredom.

MAP 19.1 | World War I: The European and Middle Eastern Theaters

Most of the fighting in World War I, despite its designation as a world war, occurred in Europe. Although millions of soldiers fought on both sides, the territorial advances were relatively small.
• Look at the maps above, and identify all the countries where Allies and Central Powers made advances. Which countries had to fight a two-front war? • Did the armies of the Central Powers or the Allies gain the most territory during the war? • According to your reading, how did this factor affect the war's outcome?

Galicia (between present-day Poland and Ukraine) and scored initial victories in eastern Germany, they suffered devastating reversals once the Germans threw in well-trained divisions that were better armed and better provisioned than the Russian troops.

By 1915, the war had ground to a gruesome standstill. Although neither the Allies nor the Central Powers could substantially advance, they refused to negotiate peace. At Ypres in 1915, the Germans tried to break the stalemate by introducing poison gas, but a countermove of equipping soldiers with gas masks nullified that advantage. In July 1916, the British launched an offensive along the Somme River in northeastern France. By November, when the futile attack halted, approximately 600,000 British and French and 500,000 Germans had perished. Yet the battle lines had hardly budged. Attempts to win by opening other fronts—in Turkey, the Middle East, and Africa—failed and added to the carnage. (See Map 19.2.)

Legacies of Mobilization

The stalemate and spiraling death toll forced governments to call up more men than ever before. More than 70 million men worldwide fought in the war, including almost all of Europe's young adult males. From 1914 to 1918, 13 million served in the German army; in Russia, some 15 million. The British Empire mobilized nearly 9 million soldiers. In France, around 8 million served, nearly 80 percent of the fifteen to forty-nine age-group.

More than half of the mobilized men died, were wounded or taken prisoner, or were reported missing in action. (See Analyzing Global Developments: Measuring Casualties in World War I.) Over four years, military deaths exceeded 9 million. Another 21 million soldiers were wounded. Vast numbers of survivors bore artificial limbs. Naval blockades and aerial bombardments had aggravated food shortages and left people susceptible to epidemics, like influenza. As demobilizing soldiers spread disease into their communities, influenza claimed perhaps 50 million people worldwide.

Mass mobilization changed expectations about the state. Civilian pressure forced many states to make promises they would have to fulfill after the war, such as welfare provisions, expanded suffrage, and pensions for widows and the wounded. Mass mobilization also undermined traditional gender boundaries. Tens of thousands of women served at or near the front as doctors, nurses, and technicians. Even more women mobilized on the "home front," taking on previously male occupations—especially in munitions plants. But women could also turn against the state. Particularly in central Europe and Russia, the war's demands for soldiers and supplies left farms untended and caused food shortages. Bread riots and peaceful protests by women trying to feed their children put states on notice that their citizens expected compensation for their sacrifices.

Women's War Effort. *With armies conscripting nearly every able-bodied man, women filled their places in factories, especially in those that manufactured war materials, such as the French plant pictured here in 1916.*

Military demobilization, meanwhile, hit societies hard, especially working women; when soldiers hobbled home, women faced layoffs from their wartime jobs. Still, their wartime roles helped women win the vote in Denmark (1915), the former Russian empire (1917), Britain (1918), Germany (1918), and the United States (1920). (France held out until 1944.) Young, unmarried women went out in public unescorted, dressed as they saw fit, and maintained their own apartments, to the shock of cultural conservatives.

Empire and War

The war's horrors spanned the world's regions (see again Map 19.2). The sprawling Ottoman Empire, which—almost three months after the war in Europe began—decided to side with the Central Powers, battled British- and Russian-led forces in Egypt, Iraq, Anatolia, and the Caucasus. In 1915–1916, Ottoman forces massacred or deported 1.3 million Armenians, accused en masse of collaborating with the Russians. Some analysts regard these attacks as the world's first genocide, the intentional elimination of a whole people.

The Ottoman decision to enter the war on the side of the Central Powers proved costly. It made inevitable that the British, French, and Russians, now enemies of the Ottomans, would draw up plans for dismembering the empire. Britain and France had long coveted Arab lands that remained under Ottoman control—what would later become Syria, Iraq, Lebanon, Jordan, and Palestine. Russia craved control of the Turkish Straits, which would provide its ships exporting grain with unfettered access to the Mediterranean. Although Germany was allied with the Ottomans, it, too, had designs

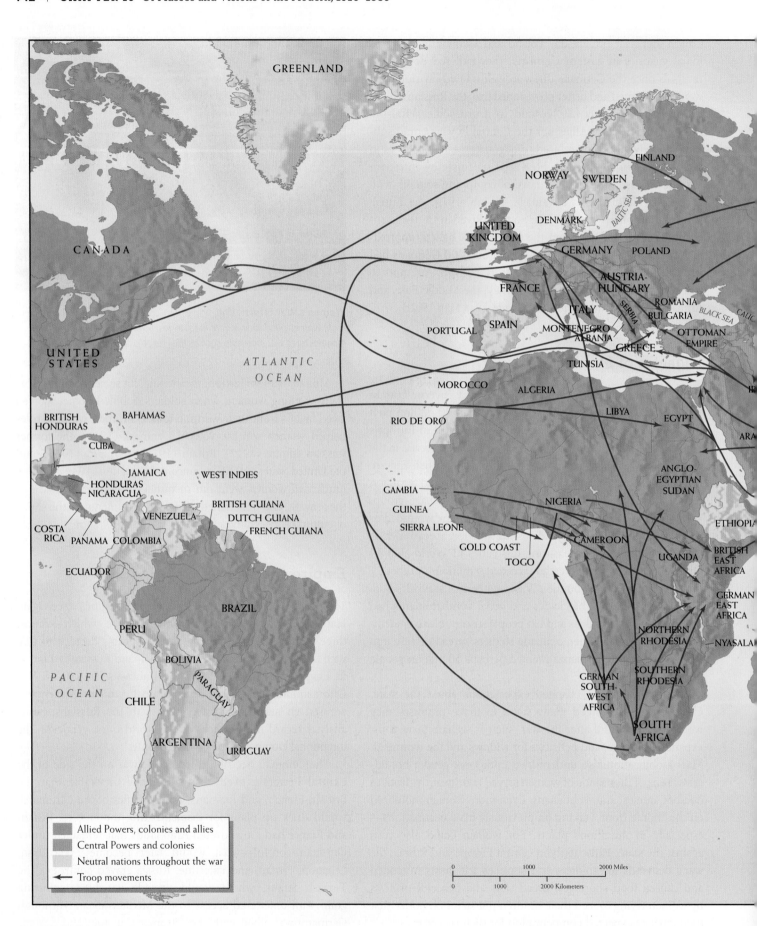

GREENLAND

FINLAND

NORWAY SWEDEN

DENMARK

BALTIC SEA

CANADA

UNITED
KINGDOM

GERMANY POLAND

FRANCE

AUSTRIA-
HUNGARY

ROMANIA

ITALY SERBIA

BLACK SEA

PORTUGAL SPAIN

MONTENEGRO
ALBANIA

BULGARIA

OTTOMAN
EMPIRE

UNITED
STATES

*ATLANTIC
OCEAN*

GREECE

CAUC

MOROCCO

ALGERIA

TUNISIA

LIBYA

EGYPT

BRITISH
HONDURAS

BAHAMAS

RIO DE ORO

ARA

CUBA

JAMAICA

HONDURAS
NICARAGUA

WEST INDIES

GAMBIA

NIGERIA

ANGLO-
EGYPTIAN
SUDAN

COSTA
RICA PANAMA COLOMBIA

VENEZUELA

BRITISH GUIANA
DUTCH GUIANA
FRENCH GUIANA

GUINEA

SIERRA LEONE

GOLD COAST

CAMEROON

ETHIOPIA

TOGO

ECUADOR

UGANDA

BRITISH
EAST
AFRICA

PERU

BRAZIL

GERMAN
EAST
AFRICA

BOLIVIA

NORTHERN
RHODESIA

NYASALA

PARAGUAY

*PACIFIC
OCEAN*

CHILE

SOUTHERN
RHODESIA

GERMAN
SOUTH-
WEST
AFRICA

ARGENTINA

URUGUAY

SOUTH
AFRICA

Allied Powers, colonies and allies
Central Powers and colonies
Neutral nations throughout the war
← Troop movements

0	1000	2000 Miles
0	1000	2000 Kilometers

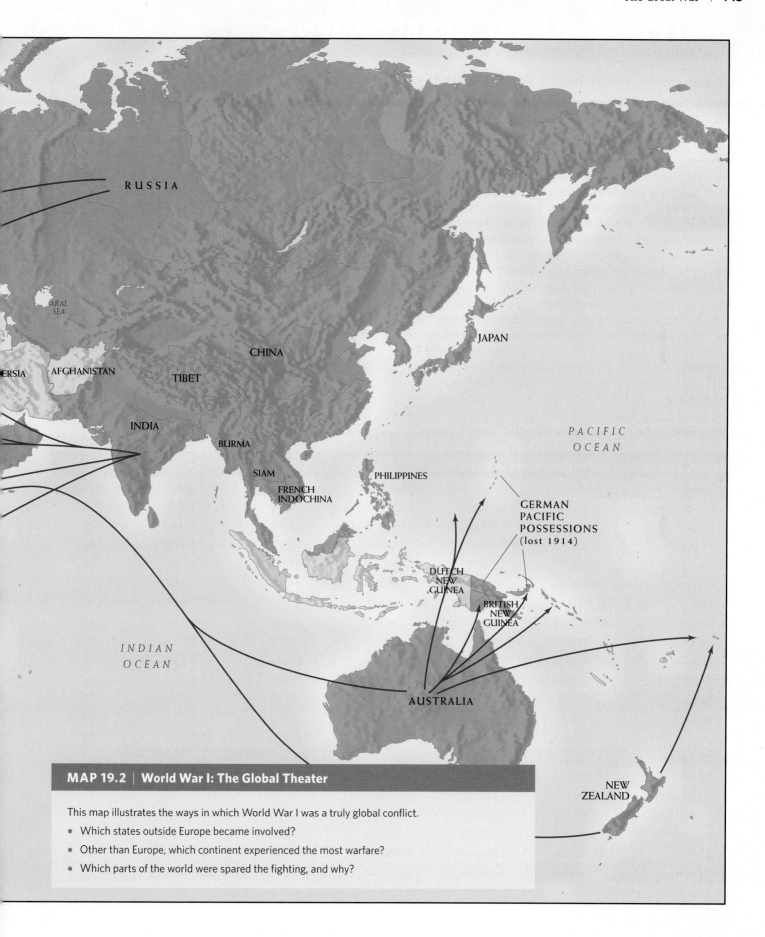

MAP 19.2 | World War I: The Global Theater

This map illustrates the ways in which World War I was a truly global conflict.

- Which states outside Europe became involved?
- Other than Europe, which continent experienced the most warfare?
- Which parts of the world were spared the fighting, and why?

ANALYZING GLOBAL DEVELOPMENTS

Measuring Casualties in World War I

You would think that tabulating historical data would be a fairly easy thing to do. At different points in this text, however, we have seen that it takes painstaking efforts on the part of historians and demographers first to figure out the best way to collect the data and then to accurately categorize and count them. Figuring out the number of Africans that left on slave ships and where they embarked and disembarked during the Atlantic slave trade is an obvious example of this kind of work. Historian Jay Winter and others have worked tirelessly for thirty years to come up with accurate death tolls for the soldiers and civilians in World War I. In a landmark book, *The Great War and the British People,* Winter used a range of archival sources from government agencies' data and mortality rate tables from major insurance companies to estimate and calculate the number of deaths among people in Britain and Ireland. While the carnage in World War I seems beyond measure, Winter, in one paradoxical finding, demonstrated that death rates among civilians actually went down during that war in Britain and Ireland. He suggests that the best explanation for this development was the efforts of the state to mobilize the civilian population and provide health insurance and, most important, to improve nutrition.

The table below builds on Winter's early efforts and shows the best estimates for the military death tolls across all the major participants in World War I.

QUESTIONS FOR ANALYSIS

- Based on data provided in the table, did the mobilization for the war have a greater impact on the Central Powers or the Allied Powers? Justify your answer.
- While the number of people mobilized was a factor of 1.5 greater for the Central Powers, why do you think the dead, wounded, and missing/POW rates were nearly twice as high as those of the Allied Powers?
- The United States played a major role in World War I, but why were its dead, wounded, and missing/POW rates so low compared with those of the other major combatants?

Military participation and military losses in World War I

Allied Powers	Mobilized	Dead	Wounded	POW/Missing	Total	% Casualties
Russia	15,798,000	1,800,000	4,950,000	2,500,000	9,250,000	59
France	7,891,000	1,375,800	4,266,000	537,000	6,178,800	78
GB, incl. empire	8,904,467	908,371	2,090,212	191,652	3,190,235	36
Italy	5,615,000	578,000	947,000	600,000	2,125,000	38
United States	4,273,000	114,000	234,000	4,526	352,526	8
Japan	800,000	300	907	3	1,210	0
Romania	1,000,000	250,706	120,000	80,000	450,706	45
Serbia	750,000	278,000	133,148	15,958	427,106	57
Belgium	365,000	38,716	44,686	34,659	118,061	32
Greece	353,000	26,000	21,000	1,000	48,000	14
Portugal	100,000	7,222	13,751	12,318	33,291	33
Montenegro	50,000	3,000	10,000	7,000	20,000	40
Total	**45,899,467**	**5,380,115**	**12,380,704**	**3,984,116**	**22,194,935**	**46**
Central Powers						
Germany	13,200,000	2,037,000	4,216,058	1,152,800	7,405,858	56
Austria-Hungary	9,000,000	1,100,000	3,620,000	2,200,000	6,920,000	77
Turkey	2,998,000	804,000	400,000	250,000	1,454,000	48
Bulgaria	400,000	87,500	152,390	27,029	266,919	67
Total	**25,598,000**	**4,028,500**	**8,388,448**	**3,629,829**	**16,046,777**	**63**
Grand Total	**71,497,467**	**9,408,615**	**21,219,152**	**7,613,945**	**38,241,712**	**53**

Sources: John Horne (ed.), *A Companion to World War I* (2010); Tucker Spencer (ed.), *The European Powers in the First World War: An Encyclopedia* (1996); J. M. Winter, *The Great War and the British People* (1985).

on the Straits and Ottoman-controlled Arab lands. In any event, the Ottoman Empire carved up by Europeans at war's end would provoke a reactive war by Turkish nationalists and much resentment by Arab nationalists. No one foresaw the full consequences of the hastily drawn-up postwar borders in places such as Iraq and Syria: they would remain in existence until the twenty-first century, then be exploded by emancipated Shiites as well as by radical Sunni Islamists—notably al-Qaeda and the Islamic State of Iraq and Syria (ISIS), also known as the Islamic caliphate.

To increase their forces, the British and the French conscripted colonial subjects: India provided 1 million soldiers; more than 1 million Africans fought in Africa and Europe for their colonial masters, and another 3 million transported war supplies. Even the sparsely populated British dominions of Australia, New Zealand, and Canada dispatched over 1 million young men to fight for the empire.

Despair and disillusionment at the prolonged, bloody war turned into revolt and revolution. In British-ruled Nyasaland, a mission-educated African, John Chilembwe, directed his compatriots to refuse British military demands and to stand up for "Africa for the Africans." Although the British suppressed the insurrection and executed the rebel leader, Chilembwe's death did not stop the growing desire to undo bonds to the imperial power.

The Russian Revolution

The war destroyed entire empires. The first to go was Romanov Russia. In February 1917, with its capital in revolt, Tsar Nicholas II stepped down under pressure from his generals. They wanted to quash the mass unrest in St. Petersburg, which, they believed, threatened the war effort along the Eastern Front. Some members of the suspended Russian parliament formed a "provisional" government; at the same time, grassroots councils (soviets) sprang up in factories and urban garrisons. The irony of what became known as the February Revolution, which ended the monarchy, was that the military and civilian elites had wanted to restore order. But with the tsar removed, millions of peasants seized land, soldiers and sailors abandoned the front, and borderland non-Russian groups declared autonomy from the crumbling empire.

Russia became free in a chaotic way. The unelected Provisional Government had no local organs of rule, while the grassroots soviets had no levers of national power. The despised tsarist police were disbanded, but public order deteriorated. The tsar's downfall incited widespread hopes that the hated war would now end, but the Provisional Government would not abandon its allies Britain and France by signing a separate peace with Germany and Austria-Hungary. In June 1917, the Provisional Government even decided to launch an offensive, which

The Russian Revolution. Right: *The July 1917 demonstrations in Petrograd were among the largest in the Russian Empire during that turbulent year of war and revolution. In this photo, marchers carry banners reading "Down with the Ministers-Capitalists" and "All Power to the Soviets of Worker, Soldier and Peasant Deputies."* Left: *Vladimir Lenin died just six years and three months after the October 1917 revolution, but he lived on in his writings and in images, such as this painting by Pavel Kuznetsov. Artists and propagandists helped make Lenin a ubiquitous icon of the new Soviet order.*

the elected leaders of the grassroots soviets supported, thereby infuriating rank-and-file soldiers, sailors, and workers.

In October, left-wing socialists calling themselves **Bolsheviks**, validating the peasants' land seizure and promising to end the war, seized power. Led by Vladimir Lenin and Leon Trotsky, the Bolsheviks drew support among the radicalized members of the soviets. Arresting Provisional Government members and claiming power in the name of the soviets, the Bolsheviks proclaimed a socialist revolution to overtake the February "bourgeois" revolution. In December, Soviet Russia held the then-largest free election in world history, with nearly 40 million men and women voting for delegates to a constitutional convention, or constituent assembly, but the Bolsheviks disbanded the body after one day. In March 1918, as the Russian army further disintegrated, Soviet Russia at Lenin's insistence signed the Treaty of Brest-Litovsk, acknowledging German victory on the Eastern Front and sacrificing vast territories to safeguard the socialist revolution. For additional protection, the Bolshevik leadership relocated the capital from St. Petersburg to Moscow, where they set about building a revolutionary dictatorship.

The Fall of the Central Powers

On April 2, 1917, the United States declared war on Germany. This occurred after German submarines sank several American merchant ships and after a secret telegram came to light in which German officials sought Mexican support by promising to help Mexico regain territories it had lost to the United States in 1848.

U.S. troops shifted the balance of military power in Europe. The Allies turned the tide at the Second Battle of the Marne in July 1918 and forced the Germans to retreat into Belgium. German troops then began to surrender en masse, and some went on strike in the face of raging hunger and influenza. Germany tottered on the edge of civil war as the Allied blockade caused starvation in the cities. German generals agreed to an armistice in November 1918. After Kaiser Wilhelm II fled into exile, the German Empire became a republic. The last Habsburg emperor also abdicated, and Austria-Hungary dissolved into several new states. With the collapse of the Ottoman Empire, the war claimed a fourth dynasty among its casualties.

The Peace Settlement and the Impact of the War

To decide the fate of vanquished empires and the future of the modern world, the victors convened five peace conferences, one for each of the Central Powers. Most important was the conference to negotiate peace with Germany, held at Versailles, France,

in January 1919. Delegates drew many of their ideas from American president Woodrow Wilson's "Fourteen Points," a blueprint he had issued in 1918 to counter Germany's occupation of eastern Europe. Wilson insisted that postwar borders be redrawn by following the principle of "self-determination of nations" and that an international **League of Nations** be established to negotiate future quarrels. Such high-minded ideas were appealing; but the French and Belgians, on whose territories so much of the devastation occurred, also wanted recompense and revenge. Ultimately, the Versailles treaty held the Germans solely responsible for the war, demanded that Germany pay reparations for the damages it had inflicted, and compelled the Germans to return Alsace and Lorraine, taken by Germany after the Franco-Prussian war of 1870–1871 (see Chapter 17), to France. The treaty also redistributed German colonies among the British, French, Belgians, and South Africans. Whereas Lenin expected nothing better from "the imperialists" at Versailles (Soviet Russia was excluded from the talks), Wilson professed horror at the treaty's harshness; but his own country backed away from the difficult task of making the peace last. When in 1920 a League of Nations was established, the United States refused to join.

Broken Promises and Political Turmoil

The war's hurricane of violence followed the invention of the Maxim gun and barbed wire (originally intended to hold livestock), pogroms in imperial Russian borderlands, British concentration camps in the Boer War, and Belgian horrors in the Congo, but still proved earth shattering in its scope. Home fronts suffered grim impoverishment as states failed the challenges of a total war their rulers had launched. Left-wing elements grew stronger even as they divided between moderate socialists and communists; the right underwent a radical and dangerous mutation toward fascism; and the center tried to accommodate itself to mass democracy. Violence became an enduring part of politics.

The American intervention in the war in 1917 provided the Allies with a powerful ideology—making the world safe for democracy and a war to end all wars. Yet although President Wilson had intended his ideology, especially his Fourteen Points, to apply principally to the ethnic minorities within the Russian and Austro-Hungarian Empires and to European peoples still under Ottoman rule, applying the principle of self-determination was exceedingly difficult in practice. Suddenly, 60 million people in central and eastern Europe emerged as inhabitants of new nation-states. (See Map 19.3.) Many were unhappy, as perhaps 25 million now lived in states in which they were ethnic minorities and vulnerable to persecution in the tumultuous years after the armistice.

Beyond Europe, the principle of self-determination galvanized anticolonial and nationalist sentiment, but these sentiments were

MAP 19.3 | Outcomes of World War I in Europe, North Africa, and Some of the Middle East

The political map of Europe and the Middle East changed greatly after the peace treaty of 1919.

- Comparing this map with Map 19.1, which shows the European and Middle Eastern theaters of war, identify the European countries that came into existence after the war.

- What happened to the Ottoman Empire, and what powers gained control over many territories of the Ottoman state?

- What states emerged from the Austro-Hungarian Empire?

almost entirely dashed by France's and Britain's imperial ambitions. The British after a long-drawn-out military campaign suppressed a 1919 rebellion in Egypt, albeit only after promising Egyptian nationalists a limited form of autonomy. The Syrians, too, did

not understand why they were less deserving of self-rule than the Czechoslovaks or Yugoslavs, but the French put down a Syrian nationalist revolt. In India, similarly inspired by Wilsonian ideals, a bloody confrontation between peaceful protestors, gathered in

MAP 19.4 | The Sykes-Picot Agreement

The Sykes-Picot Agreement was negotiated between British diplomat Mark Sykes and French diplomat François Georges-Picot in 1916. While the agreement reserved protectorates for the French in Syria and the British in Iraq, it also supported the creation of a politically independent Arab state or confederation of Arab states under an Arab chief.

- Why did the British and French governments want to divide up the Arab provinces of the Ottoman Empire?
- Compare the areas that were to be the Arab confederation, though dominated by the French and the British, with the map of ISIS that appears in the Epilogue. How similar are the territories in both maps?
- Why do you think that Arabs in particular and Muslims in general believe that this agreement was antithetical to their wishes and contributions to the war effort and continues to this day to provide powerful grievances against the west?

a garden in the city of Amritsar in the Punjab, resulted in the killing of 370 Indians and the wounding of 2,000 (although Indian eyewitnesses claimed that the dead totaled more than 1,000). In China, students, offended by the minor status accorded to their country at Versailles, launched a widespread protest in the name of Wilsonianism that solidified nationalist sentiment for this generation of students and later ones.

The bloodiest of all conflicts occurred in Iraq, where nearly 600,000 people—more than 20 percent of the population—rose up against British military efforts to force them into a colonial state. The rebellion's first stages were so successful that the Iraqis established an independent state in the Middle

Euphrates region, one that brought together Sunni and Shiite leaders and Arab officers and soldiers who had formerly served with the Ottoman army but desired an independent Iraqi state. Ultimately, British forces totaling 73,000, of whom 63,000 were Indian soldiers, were needed to crush the rebellion.

A final set of broken promises occurred in an Arab nationalist movement led by the emir of Mecca, Sharif Husayn. Believing that he had British military and political support to create an independent Arab state in Syria, parts of Palestine, Jordan, and Iraq, Sharif Husayn led a general Arab rebellion against the Ottoman Turks. He was disabused when the Bolsheviks published secret peace agreements that had been negotiated between the British and the French during the war. One of these was the Sykes-Picot Agreement (signed by Mark Sykes on behalf of the British and François Georges-Picot for the French), which divided the Arab east between Britain and France. (See Map 19.4.) A second promise, for a homeland for the Jews in Palestine, also angered Arab nationalists: the Balfour Declaration of November 2, 1917, took the form of a letter sent by the British foreign secretary, Arthur James Balfour, to Baron Rothschild, leader of the British Jewish community, and fulfilled a Zionist aspiration for a national homeland for the Jewish people in Palestine. The declaration did acknowledge the rights of the local residents, stating that it was "clearly understood that nothing shall be done which may prejudice the civil and religious rights of existing non-Jewish communities in Palestine, or the rights and political status enjoyed by Jews in any other country." Nonetheless, the declaration failed to reconcile competing claims, and it ultimately led to the creation of the state of Israel and numerous Arab-Israeli wars.

MASS SOCIETY: CULTURE, PRODUCTION, AND CONSUMPTION

The war also contributed to another modern phenomenon: mass societies. Even before World War I mobilized entire societies to produce shells, uniforms, and rations, democratic regimes had begun to extend the right to vote, in many cases making non–property holders and women eligible to cast ballots. Authoritarian regimes, meanwhile, had begun to mobilize the people via rallies and mass organizations. And new technologies, such as radio, were helping to create mass cultures that spanned geographical and class divides.

Mass Culture

Indicative of the modern world were new forms of mass communication and entertainment. In seeking to mobilize populations for total war, leaders had disseminated propaganda as never before—through public lectures, theatrical productions, musical compositions, and (censored) newspapers. Indeed, the war's impact had politicized cultural activities while broadening the audience for nationally oriented information and entertainment.

Postwar mass culture was distinctive. First, it differed from elite culture (opera, classical music, paintings, literature) because it reflected the tastes of the working and middle classes, who now had more time and money to spend on entertainment. Second, mass culture relied on new technologies, especially film and radio, which could reach an entire nation's population and consolidate their sense of being a single state.

RADIO Radio entered its golden age after World War I. Invented in the 1890s, it made little impact until the 1920s, when powerful transmitters permitted stations to reach larger audiences—often with nationally syndicated programs. Radio also was a way to mobilize the masses, especially in authoritarian regimes. For example, the Italian dictator Benito Mussolini pioneered the radio address to the nation. Later, Soviet and Nazi propagandists used this format with great effect. In Japan, too, radio promoted the right-wing government's goals. But even dictatorships could not exert total control over mass culture. Although the Soviets regarded jazz as "bourgeois," they could not prevent listeners from tuning in to foreign radio broadcasts or creating their own jazz bands.

FILM AND ADVERTISING Film, too, had profound effects. For traditionalists, Hollywood signified vulgarity and decadence because the silver screen prominently displayed modern sexual habits. But just like radio, film served political purposes. Here, again, antiliberal governments took the lead. Soviet film studios produced popular Hollywood-style musicals, such as

Triumph of the Will. *The shooting of* Triumph of the Will, *directed by Leni Riefenstahl, who made a series of films for the annual Nazi Party rallies in Nuremberg. This one, perhaps the greatest propaganda film ever, won gold medals in Venice in 1935 and at the World's Fair in 1937.*

Jolly Fellows (1934), with catchy songs sung by the whole country, alongside didactic pictures about socialist triumphs.

In market economies, radio and film became big businesses, and with expanded product advertising, they promoted other enterprises as well. Especially in the United States, advertising became a major industry, with radio commercials shaping national consumer tastes. Increasingly, too, American-produced entertainment, radio programs, and cinematic epics reached an international audience, and America and the world began to share mass-produced images and fantasies.

Mass Production and Mass Consumption

The same factors that promoted mass culture enhanced production and consumption on a mass scale. In fact, World War I paid perverse tribute to the power of industry, for machine technologies produced war materials with abundant and devastating effect.

Never before had armies had so much firepower at their disposal. Whereas in 1809 Napoleon's artillery had discharged 90,000 shells over two days during the largest battle waged in Europe to that point, by 1916 German guns were firing 100,000 rounds of shells per hour over the course of 12 hours in the Battle of Verdun. To sustain military production, millions of men and women worked in factories at home and in the colonies. Producing huge quantities of identical guns, gas masks, bandage rolls, and boots, these factories reflected the modern world's demands for greater volume, faster speed, reduced cost, and standardized output—key characteristics of mass production.

The war reshuffled the world's economic balance of power, further boosting the United States as an economic powerhouse. As its share of world industrial production climbed above one-third in 1929 (roughly equal to that of Britain, Germany, and Russia combined), people around the globe regarded the United States as a "working vision of modernity" in which not only production but also consumption boomed.

THE AUTOMOBILE ASSEMBLY LINE The most outstanding example of the relationship between mass production and consumption was the motor car, which symbolized American ingenuity. Before World War I, the automobile had been a rich man's toy. Then came Henry Ford, who founded the Ford Motor Company in 1903. Five years later, he began production of the Model T, a car that at $850 was within the reach of middle-class consumers. Soon popular demand outstripped supply. Seeking to make more cars faster and cheaper, Ford used mechanized conveyors to send the auto frame along a track, or assembly line, where each worker performed one simplified, repetitive task. By standardizing the manufacturing process, subdividing work, and substituting machinery for manual labor, Ford's assembly line vastly expanded output while lowering costs.

By the 1920s, a finished car rolled off Ford's assembly line every 10 seconds. Although workers complained about becoming "cogs" in a depersonalized labor process, Ford's factory near Detroit employed 68,000 workers—the largest factory in the world. In addition, millions of cars required millions of tons of steel alloys, as well as vast amounts of glass, rubber, textiles, and

Car Assembly Line. *Mass production was made possible by the invention of the electric motor in the 1880s, and it enacted three principles: the standardization of core aspects of products, the subdivision of work on assembly lines, and the replacement of manual labor by machinery as well as by reorganizing flow among shops. The greatest successes occurred in the auto plants of Henry Ford, shown here in 1930. With each worker along the line assigned a single task, millions of automobiles rolled off the Ford assembly line, and millions of Americans became owners of automobiles.*

PRIMARY SOURCE

Bruce Barton's Gospel of Mass Production

In 1925, the journalist (and, later, advertising executive) Bruce Barton published The Man Nobody Knows, *which became a best-seller. In the book, Barton interprets the life and teachings of Jesus as a gospel for success in modern business. In the excerpt below, Barton uses Henry Ford, whose Model T automobile reigned as the era's marvel of mass production, to show the profitable connections between religion and commerce.*

"If you're forever thinking about saving your life," Jesus said, "you'll lose it; but the man who loses his life shall find it."

Because he said it and he was a religious teacher, because it's printed in the Bible, the world has dismissed it as high minded ethics but not hard headed sense. But look again! . . .

What did Henry Ford mean, one spring morning, when he tipped a kitchen chair back against the whitewashed wall of his tractor plant and talked about his career?

"Have you ever noticed that the man who starts out in life with a determination to make money, never makes very much?" he asked. It was rather a startling question; and without waiting for my comment he went on to answer it: "He may gather together a competence, of course, a few tens of thousands or even hundreds of thousands, but he'll never amass a really great fortune. But let a man start out in life to build something better and sell it cheaper than it has ever been built or sold before—let him have *that* determination, and, give his whole self to it—and the money will roll in so fast that it will bury him if he doesn't look out.

"When we were building our original model, do you suppose that it was money we were thinking about? Of course we expected that it would be profitable, if it succeeded, but that wasn't in the front of our minds. We wanted to make a car so cheap that every family in the United States could afford to have one. So we worked morning, noon and night, until our muscles ached and our nerves were so ragged that it seemed as if we just couldn't stand it to hear anyone mention the word automobile again. One night, when we were almost at the breaking point I said to the boys, 'Well, there's one consolation,' I said, 'Nobody can take this business away from us unless he's willing to work harder than we've worked.' And so far," he concluded with a whimsical smile, "nobody has been willing to do that."

QUESTIONS FOR ANALYSIS

- What are the key ingredients to success, according to Ford?
- What was foremost on Ford's mind when he set out to build "our original model"?
- How do the lessons from the Bible and Henry Ford relate to each other? Do you think the indirect analogy is effective? Explain why or why not.

Source: Bruce Barton, *The Man Nobody Knows: A Discovery of the Real Jesus,* excerpted in *The Culture of the Twenties,* edited by Loren Baritz (Indianapolis: Bobbs-Merrill, 1970), pp. 241-242.

petroleum. Cars also needed roads and service stations. Altogether, nearly 4 million jobs related directly or indirectly to the automobile—an impressive total in a labor force of 45 million workers.

After World War I, automobile ownership became more common among Americans. By the 1920s, assembly-line production had dropped the Model T's price to $290. Ford further expanded the market for cars by paying his own workers $5 per day—approximately twice the nation's average manufacturing wage. He understood that without mass consumption, increased middle-class purchasing power, and appetite for goods, there could be no mass production. Whereas in 1920 Americans owned 8 million motor cars, a decade later they owned 23 million. The automobile's rapid spread seemed to demonstrate that mass production worked. (See Primary Source: Bruce Barton's Gospel of Mass Production.)

THE GREAT DEPRESSION Not all was easy listening or smooth motoring in countries where mass societies were taking root.

On October 24, 1929—Black Tuesday—the American stock market collapsed and revealed the rickety foundations of mass-market economies. The world economy had been experiencing underlying problems. For years, primary producers worldwide had seen their prices sink. Meanwhile, European borrowers had to pay off loans racked up to American creditors. In this delicate context, governments responded to the plunge in Wall Street share prices by relying on old gold standard orthodoxy while bankers called in their loans to struggling debtors. The result was a financial meltdown, plunging the

Stock Traders after the Crash. *On October 24, 1929, the American stock market crashed. Here traders are pictured congregating in the financial district of New York City on what came to be known as "Black Tuesday." As stock values plummeted, panic gripped Wall Street and soon spread across the nation. The market crash was followed by even more devastating bank runs as the Great Depression overtook the world.*

world into the **Great Depression**. Starting in central Europe, financial institutions began to fail, causing a tide of bank collapses from the Middle East to the American Midwest.

Financial turmoil undermined world trade. Striving to protect workers and investors from the influx of cheap foreign goods, governments raised tariff barriers against imports in tit-for-tat protectionism. Manufacturers cut back production, laid off millions of workers, and often went out of business. World prices for Argentine beef, Chilean nitrates, and Indonesian sugar all dropped sharply. Shrinking markets and drastic shortages of credit forced industries and farms worldwide into bankruptcy.

The Great Depression forced economists to rethink the core of laissez-faire liberalism (see Chapter 15), the idea that free markets regulate themselves and free trade leads to economic progress. By the late 1930s, the exuberant embrace of private mass production had ceded to a new conviction: state intervention to regulate the economy was critical to prevent disaster. In 1936, the British economist John Maynard Keynes published a landmark treatise, *The General Theory of Employment, Interest, and Money*. He argued that the market could not always adjust to its own failures and that sometimes the state had to stimulate it by increasing the money supply and creating jobs. Although the "Keynesian Revolution" took years to transform economic orthodoxy and to produce state policies designed to enhance citizens' lives, otherwise known as the welfare state, many governments had doubts whether capitalism could be saved. The Great Depression did more than any other event to challenge the belief that liberal democracy and capitalism were the best way to achieve political stability and economic progress.

MASS POLITICS: COMPETING VISIONS FOR BUILDING MODERN STATES

World War I and its aftermath upset class, gender, and colonial relations. On battlefronts and home fronts, workers, peasants, women, and colonial subjects had sacrificed and now expected to share in the fruits of peace as fully fledged citizens. Many, even in victorious nations, lost confidence in traditional authorities who had caused the cataclysm and allowed it to go on so long.

Politics, no longer contained in genteel chambers, shifted to the street. Everywhere except in the United States, variants of socialism gained throngs of new adherents. In the Soviet Union, Bolsheviks began to construct a society whose rules defied capitalist principles. Elsewhere, mass movements of paramilitaries sought to replace imperiled liberal democratic states, first in Italy, then in Germany and Spain. Liberal democratic empires, such as Britain and France, also faced challenges to square their rule over colonial subjects with their rhetoric of freedom. And a hybrid political order, mixing democratic and authoritarian institutions, emerged in Latin America. Then the Great Depression further undermined capitalism and parliaments. (See Current Trends in World History: Population Movements: Filling Up the Empty Spaces and Spreading Capitalism.)

Authoritarian solutions to problems like mass unemployment grew increasingly popular, especially as the communist Soviet Union, fascist Italy, Nazi Germany, dictatorial Portugal and Spain, and militaristic Japan projected images of national strength and pride. Outside Europe, liberal models could not cope with the scale and diversity of the new politics. Thus, by the late 1930s, the states that retained democracy and capitalism in some form appeared weak and vulnerable. Dictators seemed to be riding the wave of the future, and colonies were threatening to go their own separate ways.

Liberal Democracy under Pressure

Fighting a total war had offered European states the opportunity to experiment with illiberal policies. Indeed, the war brought both the suspension of parliamentary rule and democratic rights and an effort by governments to manage industry and distribution of goods and wealth. States on both sides of the conflict jailed many individuals who opposed the war. Governments regulated both production and, through rationing, consumption. Above all, the war revolutionized the size and scope of the state.

BRITISH AND FRENCH RESPONSES TO ECONOMIC CRISES Britain and France retained their parliamentary systems, but even here, old-fashioned liberal democracy was on the run. Strife rippled across the British Empire, and in the home isles, Britain gave independence to what became the Republic of Ireland in 1922. Britain's working-class Labour Party came to power twice between 1923 and 1931; but either alone or in coalition with Liberals and Conservatives, Labour could not lift the country out of its economic crisis.

Disorder was even more pronounced in France, which had lost 10 percent of its young men and seen destruction in vast territory. In 1932–1933, six government coalitions came and went over just nineteen months. Against the threat of a rightist coup, a coalition of the moderate and radical left, including the French Communist Party, formed the Popular Front government (1936–1939). It introduced the right of collective bargaining, a 40-hour workweek, two-week paid vacations, and a minimum wage.

THE AMERICAN NEW DEAL In the United States, too, markets and liberalism faced questions. When the Great Depression shattered the nation's fortunes, pressure intensified to create a more secure political and economic system.

In contrast to postwar Europe, where labor parties and socialist movements were surging, the 1920s saw a conservative tide engulf American politics in response to wartime government activism. The Republican Warren Harding won the presidency in 1920 with a resounding 60 percent of the popular vote. Four years later, Calvin Coolidge scored an even greater landslide, remarking that the "business of America is business" (and not government interference in free enterprise). Herbert

Hoover's election in 1928 continued Republicans' presidential triumphs. During these years of conservative ascendance, the United States adopted new laws to restrict mass immigration and a constitutional amendment to prohibit "the manufacture, sale, or transportation of intoxicating liquors." Prohibition, as the ban on alcohol came to be called, was a signature of the cultural reaction against modernity in the 1920s. To the proponents of Prohibition, mostly native-born Protestants living in rural America, alcoholic consumption was associated with immigrant populations in the cities and with the looser morals that prevailed there.

Along with immigrants, African Americans in the American South were targeted by the enforcers of Prohibition. Across the South, "Jim Crow" laws also enforced social segregation, economic inequality, and political disenfranchisement. Like rural

Josephine Baker. *The African American entertainer Josephine Baker, unable to perform in America because of her race, was a sensation on the stage in Paris after World War I. Many of her shows exoticized or even caricatured her African descent.*

Population Movements: Filling Up the Empty Spaces and Spreading Capitalism

As we have seen in Chapters 12 and 13, the European discovery of the Americas resulted in a vast movement of peoples across the Atlantic Ocean from Europe and Africa into the Western Hemisphere. These population movements, among the largest in world history to that point, pale when measured against the long-distance migrations that occurred in the hundred years between 1840 and 1940. During these years, 150 million individuals of European and Asian descent filled up the less populated parts of the world, moving from Europe, South Asia, and China into the Americas, Southeast Asia, and northern Asia in unprecedented numbers and spreading a capitalist mode of production wherever they moved. A great many of the migrants went as laborers in the factories and on the plains of the Americas and on

the rubber, sugar, tea, and coffee plantations springing up in the Dutch East Indies and eastern and southern Africa. They were as essential to the expansion of the capitalist system in these regions as the 12 million African captives transported to the Americas during the Atlantic slave trade were for the economic expansion of the Americas. Although the new watchword in economic relations was free labor, not all of the men and women who moved were in fact free workers. Indentured servitude—that is, agreeing to work for a certain number of years, usually between three and seven, in return for transportation to the region, food, housing, and clothing—was widely used with Chinese and Indian workers.

A good example of the movement and use of semi-coerced or indentured workers in developing regions comes from East Africa. There, the British and Germans were engaged in a furious political rivalry to extend their control over territories,

and British officials believed that constructing a railway from the coast of East Africa at the port of Mombasa to Kisumu at Lake Victoria would enhance their territorial ambitions in East Africa. They also concluded that they would be unable to recruit a sufficient supply of African workers to accomplish the task. Not surprisingly, they looked to the government of India to assist them in providing the necessary workforce.

The British government of India did more than help them. In all, it made available nearly 35,000 indentured South Asian workers on three-year contracts for the construction of what was known as the Uganda Railway, the track for which, covering a distance of 582 miles, was completed in a mere five years from 1896 to 1901. The work was arduous and the living conditions in the work camps were horrific; yet the British official overseeing the construction concluded that had it not been for this workforce, it is

"Jim Crow." *"Jim Crow" laws mandated the segregation of races in the American South, with African Americans forced to use separate, and usually unequal, facilities, including schools, hotels, and theaters, such as this one in Mississippi.*

Ugandan Railway *Indian workers cut rock for the Uganda Railway in this 1905 photograph, taken in British East Africa.*

QUESTIONS FOR ANALYSIS

- Why do you think that in some cases, like the building of the Uganda Railway, governments had to be involved in forcibly moving workers to where they were needed rather than letting market forces draw the workers to where work was available?
- What do you see as some of the similarities and differences between the way the African slaves were treated and the way the forced or indentured servants were treated during this period?

doubtful if the project could have been completed in under twenty years. The building of the Uganda Railway is one of many examples where we see significant numbers of people moving to new places and regions, sometimes by their own choosing and sometimes not, to play an important role in the expansion of the capitalist system and the rivalries between colonial powers.

Explore Further

McKeown, Adam. *Melancholy Order: Asian Migration and the Globalization of Border* (2008).

whites, millions of blacks quit the countryside and moved to northern cities such as New York and Chicago, finding some relief from the legal barriers to their opportunities and rights; but discrimination restricted their residences to urban ghettos. Still, within black neighborhoods, most famously New York City's Harlem, the New Negro movement, or Harlem Renaissance, showcased black novelists, poets, painters, and musicians, many of whom used their art to protest racial subordination.

With the Great Depression came deeper challenges to liberal modernity. By the end of 1930, more than 4 million American workers had lost their jobs. As President Hoover insisted that citizens' thrift and self-reliance, not government handouts, would restore prosperity, the economic situation worsened. By 1933, industrial production had dropped by a staggering 50 percent since 1929 as unemployment reached 25 percent. Hard times were even worse in the countryside, where farm income plummeted by two-thirds between 1929 and 1932.

In the 1932 presidential election, a Democrat, Franklin Delano Roosevelt, won by a landslide. He promptly launched what came to be called the **New Deal**, a set of programs and regulations that dramatically expanded the scope of the American national government and its role in the nation's economic life. In his first 100 days in office, Roosevelt obtained legislation to provide relief for the jobless and to rebuild the shattered economy. Among his administration's experiments were the Federal Deposit Insurance Corporation to guarantee bank deposits up to $5,000, the Securities and Exchange Commission to monitor the stock market, and the Federal Emergency Relief Administration to help states and local governments assist the needy. Subsequently, the Works Progress Administration put nearly 3 million people to work building roads, bridges, airports, and post offices. In addition, the Social Security Act inaugurated old-age pensions supported by the federal government.

Never before had the U.S. federal government expended so much on social welfare programs or intervened so directly in the national economy. Yet the Depression lingered, and unemployment again climbed—from 7 million in 1937 to 11 million in 1938, an increase of 19 percent.

The persistence of hard times opened the New Deal to attacks from both the left and the right. Emboldened labor leaders, resurgent radicals, and populist demagogues claimed that the New Deal was not addressing the problems of the poor and the unemployed. But Roosevelt refrained from substantially redistributing national income. Likewise, although his administration established public agencies to build dams and oversee the irrigation of arid lands and the electrification of rural districts, these were exceptions. Privately owned enterprises continued to dominate American society. Roosevelt's aim was not to destroy but to save capitalism. In this regard the New Deal succeeded, for it staved off authoritarian solutions to modern problems.

During the 1920s and 1930s, liberal democratic regimes respected elections and defended private property against challenges from labor movements and socialist critics. But they intervened in markets and regulated people's lives in ways that prewar governments would never have contemplated.

Stalin. *Joseph Stalin posing at the Allies' "Big Three" conference in Yalta, on Soviet soil, February 1945. Much had changed since Stalin had become leader of the Communist Party of the Soviet Union in 1922.*

Authoritarianism and Mass Mobilization

Like the liberal systems they challenged, authoritarian regimes came in various stripes. On the right arose dictatorships in Italy, Germany, and Japan. Although differing in important respects, all disliked the left-wing dictatorship of the Soviet Union. And the Soviets had no liking for the fascists. Yet all the postwar dictatorships were forged principally in opposition to the liberal democracies. In place of liberal inertia, these regimes touted their success in mobilizing the masses to create dynamic yet orderly societies. They also had charismatic leaders who personified the power and unity of the societies over which they ruled.

Although rejecting liberal democracy, post–World War I dictators insisted that they had their people's support. True, they treated their people as a mass conscript army that needed firm leadership to build new societies and guarantee well-being. But their demands, the leaders maintained, would yield robust economies, restore order, and renew pride. In addition, dictators gained support by embracing public welfare programs. They also vowed to deliver on all of modernity's promises (prosperity, national pride, technology) without having to endure any of its costs (class divisions, unemployment, urban-industrial squalor, moral breakdown). For a time, many of the globe's inhabitants believed them.

THE SOVIET UNION AND SOCIALISM The most dramatic blow against liberal capitalism occurred in Russia, where the radical Bolshevik Party seized power and established a socialist regime. Fearing the spread of socialist revolutions, Britain, France, Japan, and the United States sent armies to Russia to contain Bolshevism. But after executing Tsar Nicholas II and his family, the Bolsheviks rallied support by defending the

homeland against its invaders. They also mobilized people to fight and win a civil war (1918–1921) in the name of defending the socialist revolution. The conflict pitted an array of disunified forces (former tsarist supporters but also many social democrats and independent peasant armies) against the Bolshevik dictatorship and its supporters (many soldiers, sailors, workers, and state functionaries).

In the all-out mobilization against those whom they labeled the Whites, or counterrevolutionaries, the Bolsheviks, calling themselves the Reds, began to rebuild state institutions. Their forced requisitions of grain from the peasantry helped cause a severe famine between 1921 and 1923 in which some 7 to 10 million people died from hunger and disease.

To revive the economy, which had been devastated by war, revolution, and civil war, the Bolsheviks grudgingly legalized private trade in the countryside while retaining state control over most industries. In 1924, with the country still recovering from civil war, the leader of the revolution, Lenin, died. No one had done more to shape the institutions of the revolutionary regime, including creating expectations for a single ruler. After eliminating his rivals, **Joseph Stalin** (1878–1953) emerged as the new leader of the Communist Party and the country, which had become the Union of Soviet Socialist Republics (USSR), or Soviet Union.

Since socialism as a fully developed social and political order had never existed, no one was sure in the 1920s how the USSR would actually be built and work. Stalin resolved this dilemma by defining Soviet or revolutionary socialism in opposition to capitalism. Since many capitalist states had "bourgeois" parliaments, said to serve the interests of the rich, socialism would have soviets (councils) of worker and peasant deputies. Since capitalism had unregulated markets, said to lead to economic downturns and unemployment, socialism would have economic planning and full employment. And since capitalism relied on the "exploitation" of private ownership, socialism would outlaw private trade and private property. In short, socialism would eradicate capitalism and then invent socialist forms in housing, culture, values, dress, and even modes of reasoning.

To build a noncapitalist society, Stalin instigated class war, beginning in the heavily populated countryside. Rich peasants, derided as *kulaks*, were to be deported to remote areas. Villages had to fill quotas for deportation; often those selected were people who had slept with someone's wife rather than those who owned the most cows. Thus, "class warfare" was spurred by personal animosities, greed, and ambition. The remaining peasants, who lived in village communes, leasing the land together but working it individually (as households), were forced to combine their farms into larger units worked collectively and run by regime loyalists. Tens of thousands of urban activists, seeking to build a new world, led the drive to forcibly establish collective farms and compel farmers to sell their grain and livestock at state-run collection points for whatever price the state was willing to pay (often very little).

In protest, hundreds of thousands of peasants burned their crops, killed their livestock, and destroyed their farm implements. The government responded by deporting protesters to remote areas. But harvests again declined, and amid the regime-induced chaos in 1931–1933, a second famine claimed between 5 and 7 million lives. Grudgingly, the regime conceded small household plots to the collectivized peasants. Here they could grow their own food and take some of their produce to approved markets. But few escaped the collectives, which depended on the state for seed, fertilizers, and machinery.

The year 1928 saw the beginning of a frenzied Five-Year Plan to "catch and overtake" the leading capitalist countries. Millions of enthusiasts (as well as deported peasants) set about building a socialist urban utopia founded on advanced technology, most of it purchased from Depression-mired capitalist countries. Tens of millions of people helped build or rebuild thousands of factories, hospitals, and schools. Huge hydroelectric dams, automobile and tractor factories, and heavy-machine-building plants symbolized the promise of Soviet-style modernity, which entailed colossal waste but eliminated unemployment. While the capitalist world remained mired in the Depression, Soviet socialism and its promises gained adherents around the world.

Soviet authorities also promoted socialism in the borderlands. In 1922, the USSR joined the independent states of Ukraine, Belorussia (Belarus), and the Transcaucasian Federation with Soviet Russia to form a single federal state. The USSR also soon acquired several new republics, some from central Asia; eventually there were fifteen (see Map 19.5), all of which secured their own state institutions—but under centralized rule from Moscow. In the 1930s, collectivization and mass arrests

Collectivized Agriculture. *Soviet plans for the socialist village envisioned the formation of large collectives supplied with advanced machinery, thereby transforming peasant labor into an industrial process. The realities behind the images of smiling farmers—such as in this poster, exhorting "Give first priority to gathering the Soviet harvest!"—were low productivity, enormous waste, and often broken-down machinery.*

devastated the peasants and nomads as well as the officials of the republics, but industrialization and urbanization gave opportunities to new people and empowered new indigenous elites.

MASS TERROR AND STALIN'S DICTATORSHIP The Soviet political system became more despotic as the state expanded. Police power grew the most, partly from forcing peasants into collectives and organizing mass deportations. As the party's ranks swelled, ongoing loyalty verifications also led to the removal of party members, even when they professed absolute loyalty. From 1936 to 1938, more than 2 million supposedly treasonous "enemies of the people" were arrested, and more than 750,000 were executed; others faced long sentences in forced labor camps, collectively known as the Gulag. Such

MAP 19.5 | The Soviet Union

The Union of Soviet Socialist Republics (USSR) came into being after World War I.

- How did its boundaries compare with those of the older Russian Empire, as shown in Map 17.6 (p. 662)?
- What does the large number of Soviet republics suggest about the ethnic diversity within the Soviet Union?
- According to your reading, how did Soviet leaders govern non-Russian minorities within the new state?

purges decimated the loyal Soviet elite—party officials, state officials, intelligentsia, army officers, and even members of the police who had enforced the terror.

Lenin and Stalin secured a communist regime based in Russia but only through highly coercive methods. Nonetheless, Stalin's efforts at heavy industrialization were to pay off when Nazi Germany invaded the Soviet Union in World War II (see Chapter 20). Although Stalin initiated mass terror against the elite, his motives remain unclear. Neither he nor the regime was under threat. What is clear is that the political police, given sizable arrest quotas, often exceeded them. In addition, large numbers of ordinary people helped implement the terror. Some reluctantly turned in neighbors; some did so to try to save themselves; many showed fanatical zeal in fingering "enemies." In the end, the terror manifested highly petty motives as well as a desire to participate in the violent crusade of building socialism in a hostile world, full of internal and external enemies.

ITALIAN FASCISM The liberal model also faced a challenge from the right. Italy had been on the winning side of the Great War, but the outcome hardly seemed like a victory. Mass strikes, occupations of factories, and peasant land seizures swept the country in 1919 and 1920. Amid this disorder, rightists rose up in response. Their leader was **Benito Mussolini** (1883–1945), a former socialist journalist who in 1919 organized disaffected veterans and adventurers into a mass political movement called **fascism**.

Mussolini's early programs mixed aggressive nationalism with social radicalism and revealed a yearning to sweep away all the institutions discredited by the war. Fascist supporters demanded the annexation of "Italian" lands in the Alps (Austria) and on the Dalmatian coast (Yugoslavia) and called for female suffrage, an 8-hour workday, a share of factory control for workers, a tax on capital, and land redistribution.

Fascists attracted numerous followers. Their violence-prone shock troops wore black shirts and baggy trousers tucked into

Mussolini. *Benito Mussolini, known as Il Duce, liked to puff out his chest, particularly when appearing in public. He pioneered radio addresses to the people, and encouraged fascist versions of the mass spectacles that also became common in Soviet Russia.*

high black leather boots and saluted with a dagger thrust into the air. In 1920, the squads received money from landowners and factory owners to beat up socialist leaders, after which Italian fascism became fully identified with the right. Still, the fascists saw themselves as champions of the little guy, of peasants and (nonsocialist) workers, as well as of war veterans, students, and white-collar types—an all-class movement.

In 1922, Mussolini announced a march on Rome. The march was a bluff, yet it intimidated the king, who opposed fascist ruffians but feared bloodshed. So he withheld use of the army against the lightly armed marchers. When the Italian government resigned in protest, the monarch invited Mussolini to become prime minister, even though fascists had won only a small minority of seats in the 1921 elections. By 1924, taking advantage of disarray in the parliament, Mussolini began to outlaw other parties and force through a dictatorship.

Mussolini's dictatorship cut deals with big business and the church, thus falling short of a total social revolution. Nonetheless, it skillfully used parades, films, radio, and visions of recapturing Roman imperial grandeur to boost support during the troubled times of the Depression. The cult of the leader, Il Duce, also provided cohesion. As the first antiliberal, antisocialist alternative, the early phase of Italian fascism served as a model for other countries.

GERMAN NAZISM In Germany, too, fear of Bolshevism and anger over the war's outcome propelled the right to power. After a small workers' movement took shape in Munich, dedicated to winning workers over from socialism, the army high command ordered a young demobilized corporal to infiltrate the group. That corporal, **Adolf Hitler** (1889–1945), soon dominated the nationalist workers' movement, whose name he changed to the National Socialist German Workers' Party (*National-Sozialistische Arbeits-Partei,* or **Nazis**).

Unlike Mussolini, the young Hitler was never a socialist. The first Nazi Party platform, set forth in 1920, combined nationalism with a heavy dose of anticapitalism. It also called for the renunciation of the Treaty of Versailles and discrimination against Jews. It was an assertion of Germany's grievances against the world and of the small man's grievances against those whom the Nazis perceived as the rich. At first, Hitler and the Nazis were unsuccessful, and Hitler himself was arrested. Although sentenced to five years in prison for treason, he served less than a year. While in prison he wrote an autobiographical and fanatically anti-Semitic treatise called *Mein Kampf* (*My Struggle,* 1925), which was an initial flop but incorporated many of the ideas he would apply later as dictator.

What catapulted Hitler and the radical right to power was a combination of the Great Depression and the actions of traditional conservatives. Fearing popular support for the Communist and Socialist Parties and convinced that he could control Hitler, Germany's president appointed Hitler chancellor (prime minister) in January 1933, even though the Nazis had never won a majority of the vote and their share was declining. Traditional conservatives believed they could control Hitler while benefiting from his mass political base. Thus, like Mussolini, Hitler came to power peacefully and legally.

Hitler used fears of a communist conspiracy, crystallized by a mysterious fire at the German Reichstag, to repress the leftist parties and the free press, robbing opponents of the ability to criticize the regime publicly. Hitler then proposed legislation that would enable him to promulgate laws on his authority as chancellor without the parliament's approval.

By July 1933, the Nazis were the only legal party and Hitler was dictator of Germany. He aggressively curbed dissent and banned strikes, jailing political opponents and building the first concentration camps (initially to house political prisoners) when the jails overflowed. Like Mussolini, Hitler relied on choreographed mass rallies, new media like film and radio, and his personal charisma to mobilize a mass following.

Hitler also unleashed a campaign of persecution against the Jews, believing that assimilated Jews controlled the banks and that eastern Jewish emigrants carried disease. Like many other right-wing Germans, Hitler also believed that a Jewish-socialist conspiracy had stabbed the German army in the back, causing its surrender in World War I, and that intermarriage with Jews was destroying the supposed purity of the Aryan race (which included northern, white Europeans). Hitler and the Nazis did not believe that religious practice defined Jewishness; instead, they held, it was transmitted biologically from parents to children. In 1935, Hitler instituted legal measures, known as the Nuremberg Laws, that excluded Jews from the civil service and the professions, forced them to sell their property, deprived them of citizenship, and forbade them to marry or have sex with Aryans. Hitler also encouraged the use of terror against Jews, destroying their businesses, homes, and marriages with non-Jews and frightening them into leaving Germany, with the

Hitler. *Adolf Hitler and his advisers mastered the staging of mass rallies. These rallies and marches projected an image of dynamism and collective will, which Hitler claimed to embody.*

ultimate aim of eliminating all traces of Jewish life and culture in Nazi-dominated central Europe.

Although some Germans opposed Hitler's illiberal activism, the Nazis won popular support by reviving the economy and restoring national pride. In 1935, defying the Treaty of Versailles, Hitler announced a vigorous rearmament program. The state also financed public works, including reforestation, swamp drainage projects, and highway building that absorbed the unemployed; organized leisure, entertainment, travel, and vacations; and built public housing. Nazism mixed anti-Semitism with full employment and social welfare programs that privileged racially approved groups.

Germany reemerged as a great power with expansionist aspirations. Initially, Hitler called his state the Third Reich (the first being the Holy Roman Empire, or Reich, and the second the Reich created by Bismarck in 1871). He claimed that like the Holy Roman Empire, his empire would last 1,000 years. Hitler also harbored grand aspirations to impose racial purity and German power in Europe and perhaps beyond. (See Primary Source: Cult of the Dynamic Leader.)

DICTATORSHIPS IN SPAIN AND PORTUGAL As authoritarian regimes spread across Europe, the military instituted dictatorships in Spain and Portugal. Their effort to seize power in Spain provoked a brutal civil war from 1936 to 1939, which left 250,000 dead.

The Spanish civil war was, from the start, an international war. When the Spanish republican government introduced reforms to break the hold of the church and landlords on the state, the military launched a coup and received weapons, advisers, and other backing from fascist Italy and Nazi Germany. The Soviet Union supported the republic with weapons and advisers, and many volunteers fought in international brigades. Britain and France dithered, leading Stalin and many others to conclude that the democratic powers would not stand up to fascism. But the republic side became mired in bloody infighting among socialists, anarchists, and communists, and the purges in Spain reinforced the view in Britain and France that Stalin was not a desirable partner. The leader of the military coup, Generalissimo Francisco Franco (who had risen to prominence as an army officer in the campaign to establish a Spanish protectorate over what became Spanish Morocco), gained the upper hand in the civil war thanks to foreign support, his brutal tactics, and his forging of a broad political coalition of the traditional and radical right.

MILITARIST JAPAN Unlike authoritarian regimes in Europe, Japan's emerging right-wing movement did not suffer wounded power and pride during World War I. In fact, because wartime disruptions reduced European and American competition, Japan expanded production, exporting munitions, textiles, and consumer goods to Asian and western markets. During the war, the Japanese gross national product (GNP) grew 40 percent, and the country built the world's third-largest navy. After a devastating earthquake and fire in 1923, Tokyo was rebuilt with steel and reinforced concrete, symbolizing the new, modern Japan.

PRIMARY SOURCE

Cult of the Dynamic Leader

Nazi political theorists offered no apologies for dictatorship. On the contrary, they bragged about it as the best way of mobilizing the masses and directing the state. The Führer, or Leader, stood above the Nazi Party and all government institutions and embodied the supposed will of the German nation. He also decided who belonged, or did not belong, to the nation. The following excerpt, taken from the writings of Ernst Rudolf Huber, Germany's major constitutional expert of the 1930s, elaborated on the awesome powers being conferred on Hitler as Führer.

The office of Führer has developed out of the National Socialist movement. In its origins it is not a State office. This fact must never be forgotten if one wishes to understand the current political and legal position of the Führer. The office of Führer has grown out of the movement into the Reich, firstly through the Führer taking over the authority of the Reich Chancellor and then through his taking over the position of Head of State. Primary importance must be accorded to the position of "Führer of the movement"; it has absorbed the two highest functions of the political leadership of the Reich and thereby created the new office of "Führer of the Nation and of the Reich."...

The position of Führer combines in itself all sovereign power of the Reich; all public power in the State as in the movement is derived from the Führer power. If we wish to define political power in the Third Reich correctly, we must not speak of "State power" but of "Führer power." For it is not the State as an impersonal entity which is the source of political power but rather political power is given to the Führer as the executor of the nation's common will. Führer power is comprehensive and total; it unites within itself all means of creative political activity; it embraces all spheres of national life; it includes all national comrades who are bound to the Führer

in loyalty and obedience. Führer power is not restricted by safeguards and controls, by autonomous protected spheres, and by vested individual rights, but rather it is free and independent, exclusive and unlimited.

QUESTIONS FOR ANALYSIS

- How did the office of Führer arise, according to Huber?
- What are the source and scope of "Führer power"?

Source: Ernst Rudolf Huber, "Führergewalt," in *Nazism 1919–1945: A History in Documents and Eyewitness Accounts*, edited by J. Noakes and G. Pridham (Exeter, England: University of Exeter Press, 1984) pp. 198–99.

Initially, post–World War I Japan seemed headed down the liberal democratic road. When Japan's Meiji emperor died in 1912, his third son succeeded him and oversaw the rise of competing mass political parties. Suffrage expanded in 1925, increasing the electorate roughly fourfold. But along with democratization came repressive measures. Although the Meiji Constitution remained in effect, a new Peace Preservation Law specified up to ten years' hard labor for any member of an organization advocating change in the political system or abolition of private property. The law served as a club against the mass leftist parties.

Japan veered still further from the liberal democratic road after Emperor Hirohito came to power in 1926. Here, as in Germany, the Great Depression spurred the eventual shift to dictatorship. Japan's trade with the outside world had more than tripled between 1913 and 1929, but after 1929 China and the United States imposed barriers on Japanese exports in preference for domestic products. These measures contributed to a 50 percent decline in Japanese exports. Unemployment surged.

Hirohito. *A portrait of Crown Prince Hirohito of Japan in 1925, the year before he ascended the Japanese throne. Hirohito presided over Japan's war in Asia, beginning with the 1931 seizure of Manchuria and culminating in the 1945 surrender, but he remained emperor for another four decades. When he died in 1989, his wartime responsibility was still a difficult subject for many.*

Manchurian Incident. *Taken from among the throng of Japanese troops, this September 1931 photograph documents the Japanese invasion of Manchuria after the bombing of the South Manchurian Railroad, later known as the Manchurian Incident.*

Such turmoil invited calls for stronger leadership, which military commanders were eager to provide.

It was in the Japanese Empire that militarism and expansionism received a boost. In 1931, a group of army officers arranged an explosion on the Japanese-owned South Manchurian Railroad as a pretext for taking over Manchuria. In 1932, Japan added Manchuria to its Korean and Taiwanese colonies, proclaiming the puppet state of Manchukuo. (See Map 19.6.) Meanwhile, at home, "patriotic societies" waged a campaign of terror against uncooperative businessmen and critics of the military. Unlike Italian fascism and German Nazism, Japanese authoritarianism had an explicitly religious dimension. The state in Japan took on a sacred aura through the promotion of an official religion, Shinto, and through belief in Emperor Hirohito's divinity. By 1940, Hirohito and his closest advisers had merged all political parties into the Imperial Rule Association, ending even the semblance of democracy, and they advocated a form of racial purity. The Imperial Army divided Asian peoples into "master races," "friendly races," and "guest races," reserving a dominant position for the Japanese "Yamato Race."

COMMON FEATURES OF AUTHORITARIAN REGIMES

Despite important differences, the major authoritarian regimes—communist Soviet Union, fascist Italy, Nazi Germany, and militarist Japan—shared many traits. All rejected parliamentary rule and sought to revive their country's power through authoritarianism, violence, and a cult of the leader.

All claimed that modern economies required state direction. Japan's government fostered huge business conglomerates; Italy's encouraged big business to form cartels. The German state also regarded the private sector as the vehicle of economic growth, but it expected entrepreneurs to support the Nazis' racial, antidemocratic, and expansionist aims. The most thorough economic coordination occurred in the Soviet Union, which adopted American-style mass production while eliminating private enterprise. Instead, the Soviet state owned and managed all the country's industry.

Another common feature involved using mass organizations for state purposes. The Soviet Union, Italy, and Germany had single mass parties; Japan had various rightist groups until the 1940 merger. All promoted dynamic youth movements, such as the Hitler Youth and the Union of German Girls, the Soviet Communist Youth League, and the Italian squads marching to the anthem "Giovinezza" (Youth). State-organized labor forces replaced independent labor unions.

Three states adopted extensive social welfare policies. The Nazis emphasized full employment, built public housing, and provided assistance to needy Aryan families. The Italian National Agency for Maternity and Infancy provided services for unwed mothers and infant care. Soviet programs addressed maternity, disability, sickness, and old age. In fact, the Soviet state viewed welfare assistance as an ongoing program that distinguished socialism from capitalism. Although Japan did not enact innovative social welfare legislation, its Home Affairs Ministry enlisted helpmates among civic groups, seeking to raise savings rates and improve child-rearing practices.

All these regimes, except the Soviet Union, were ambivalent about women in public roles. Even the Soviets, who claimed to support gender equality, eventually restricted abortion and rewarded mothers who had many children. Officials sought to honor new mothers as a way to repair the loss of so many young men during the Great War. Yet many more women were also entering professional careers, and some were becoming their family's primary wage earners. In Italy, fascist authorities had to accept *la maschetta*—the new woman, or flapper, who wore short skirts, bobbed her hair, smoked cigarettes, and engaged in freer sex. In Japan, the *mogā* or *modangāru* ("modern girl") phenomenon provoked considerable negative comment, but authorities could not suppress it.

Finally, all the dictatorships used violence and terror as tools for remaking the sociopolitical order. The Italians and the Japanese openly arrested political opponents, particularly in their colonies. However, it was the Nazis and the Soviets who filled concentration and labor camps with alleged enemies of the state, whether Jews or supposed counterrevolutionaries.

Still, brutal as these regimes were, their successes in mastering the masses drew envious glances even from those following the liberal democratic road. They also attracted imitators. British and French fascists and communists, though never coming to power, formed national parties and proclaimed support for foreign models. Certain politicians, intellectuals, and labor

RUSSIA

AMUR
PROVINCE

SAKHALIN

SEA OF
OKHOTSK

KURILE ISLANDS

MANCHURIA
(MANCHUKUO, 1932)

OUTER
MONGOLIA

EZO
(HOKKAIDŌ)

INNER
MONGOLIA

JEHOL

Vladivostok

Mukden

Beijing

Dalian
Tianjin
Lüshun
(Port Arthur)
Weihaiwei

Seoul

SEA OF
JAPAN

JAPAN

Tokyo

HONSHŪ

Kyoto

Qingdao

KOREA

Pusan

Nanjing

CHINA

Shanghai

YELLOW
SEA

Nagasaki

SHIKOKU

KYŪSHŪ

RUSSIAN BALTIC FLEET

EAST
CHINA
SEA

PACIFIC
OCEAN

BONIN
ISLANDS

Fuzhou

OKINAWA

RYŪKYŪ ISLANDS

VOLCANO
ISLANDS

Xiamen
(Amoy)

TAIWAN

Guangzhou (Canton)

PESCADORES

Hong Kong
Macao

0   100   200   300 Miles

0   100   200   300 Kilometers

	Japanese acquisitions as of 1895
	Japanese acquisitions, 1905–1910
	Japanese area of influence before 1914
→	Japanese attack, 1914
	Extension of Japanese influence after 1918
	Occupied by Japan, 1920–1925
	Japan forms puppet state of Manchukuo, 1932
	Occupied by Japan, 1933

MAP 19.6 | **The Japanese Empire in Asia, 1933**

Hoping to become a great imperial power like the European states, Japan established numerous colonies and spheres of influence early in the twentieth century.

- What were the main territorial components of the Japanese Empire?

- How far did the Japanese succeed in extending their political influence throughout East Asia?

- According to your reading, what problems did the desire to extend Japanese influence in China present to Japanese leaders?

Hitler Youth. *Like the communists in the Soviet Union, the Nazis organized and indoctrinated boys and girls in the hopes of making them strong supporters of the regime. Pictured here are members of the Hitler Youth, about 1939.*

organizers in South and North America admired Hitler, Lenin, and Stalin. Many also hoped to use the methods of mass mobilization and mass violence for their own ends. This was particularly true of anticolonial movements.

The Hybrid Nature of Latin American Corporatism

Latin American nations felt the same pressures that produced liberal democratic and authoritarian responses in Europe, the Soviet Union, and Japan. However, Latin American leaders devised solutions that combined democratic and authoritarian elements. What they shared with European and Asian counterparts was the need to cope with the developing effects of the Depression and the breakdown of world trade and finance by shoring up domestic mass consumption and protecting native industries. As elsewhere, governments in Latin America turned inward. But they also aimed to integrate previously excluded and marginal peoples to bring legitimacy to the new order. So, with spreading mass consumption, new Latin American rulers expanded mass politics—which took democratic and autocratic forms. One such instance is called corporatism.

ECONOMIC TURMOIL Latin American countries had abstained from fighting in World War I, but their export economies had suffered. As trade plummeted, popular confidence in traditional oligarchic regimes fell, and radical agitation surged.

During the war years, trade unionists in Buenos Aires took control of the city's docks, and the women of São Paulo's needle trades inspired Brazil's first general strike. Bolivian tin miners, inspired by events in Russia, proclaimed a full-blown socialist revolution.

As in Europe, Latin American governments stepped in to manage volcanic economic markets. More than in any other region, the Depression battered Latin America's trading and financial systems because they were most dependent on the exports of basic staples, from sugar to wheat, and faced stiff protection or evaporating demand for their commodities. The region, in fact, suffered a double whammy because it had borrowed so much money to invest in infrastructure and expansion. When the world's major banks failed, creditors called in their loans from Latin America. This move drove borrowers to default. In response, Latin American governments—with backing from the middle classes, nationalist intellectuals, and urban workers—turned to their domestic rather than foreign markets as the main engine of growth. Here, too, the state took on a more interventionist role in market activity than it was expected to do under the model of classical liberalism.

After the war, Latin American elites confronted the age of mass politics by establishing mass parties and encouraging interest groups to associate with them. Collective bodies such as chambers of commerce, trade unions, peasant associations, and organizations for minorities like blacks and Indians all operated with state sponsorship. This form of modern politics, often labeled corporatist, used social groups to bridge the gap between ruling elites and the general population.

Getúlio Vargas. *This cartoon of Vargas, governor of the southern state of Rio Grande do Sul, portrays him as a country bumpkin even as he leads the way in overthrowing Brazil's Old Republic.*

CORPORATIST POLITICS IN BRAZIL Corporatist politics took hold especially in Brazil, where the Old Republic collapsed in 1930. In its place, a coalition led by the skilled politician Getúlio Vargas (1883–1954) cultivated a strong following by enacting socially popular reforms.

Dubbing himself the "father of the poor," Vargas encouraged workers to organize, erected monuments to national heroes, and supported the building of schools and the paving of roads. Striving to appeal to Brazilian blacks, who had been excluded from public life since the abolition of slavery, he legalized many previously forbidden Afro-Brazilian practices, such as the ritual *candomblé* dance, whose African and martial overtones seemed threatening to white elites. Vargas also supported samba schools, organizations that not only taught popular dances but also raised funds for public works. Moreover, Vargas addressed maternity and housing policies and enfranchised women (although they had to be able to read, as did male voters). Although he condemned the old elites for betraying the country to serve the interests of foreign consumers and investors, he arranged foreign funding and developed plans with foreign technical advisers to build steel mills and factories. However, he promoted domestic industry so that Brazil would not be so dependent on imports.

Ruling as a patriarch enabled Vargas to squelch dissent and build new lines of loyalty. When he revamped the constitution in 1937, he banned competitive political parties and created forms of national representation along corporatist lines. Each social sector, or class, would be represented by its function in society (for example, as workers, industrialists, or educators), and each would pledge allegiance to the all-powerful state. Although his opponents complained about losing democratic rights, Vargas also created rights for previously excluded groups like trade unions, who now could use their corporatist representatives to press for demands. One demand was to secure rights to basic economic needs, like food and shelter. To bolster the system, he employed a small army of modern propagandists using billboards, loudspeakers, and radio to broadcast the benevolence of "Father" Vargas. Among this campaign's

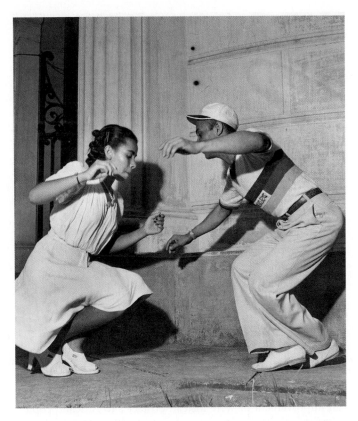

Samba dancers. *The dance started in the shanty towns of Rio de Janeiro and eventually became popular throughout the world, thanks to films, photographs, and long-playing records that featured samba music.*

objectives was the persecution of "speculators" and "oligarchs" that were believed to deprive Brazilian workers of their basic social rights. The "father of the poor" in turn protected national industries that produced manufactured goods for popular consumption. In this way, Vargas's corporatist aims created a new alliance of consuming commoners and new industrialists to eclipse the old rural order.

The Vargas appeal had echoes around a world struggling with economic depression and scarcity. Fueled by nationalism, policies protected domestic markets and tried to secure impoverished workers. The same kinds of claims were voiced in the colonial worlds of Africa and Asia. But here the fact that colonial peoples had no access to the instruments of a national government meant that their welfare demands went unanswered and heightened anticolonialism.

Anticolonial Visions of Modern Life

In both Africa and Asia, access to consumer goods and other aspects of mass society led to heightened inequalities and created tension between the privileged and the poor. Nationalist protest movements ensued. Mostly, the leading parties represented the aspirations of the educated and well-off, seeking a way of life like that of developed societies. But individuals like Gandhi and anticolonial socialists and communists championed the interests of the poor and spurned the desires of the middle classes.

Although World War I had ravaged Europe, it also yielded more colonies than ever before. Ottoman territories, in particular, wound up in Allied hands. Great Britain emerged with an empire that straddled one-quarter of the earth. Rechristened as the British Commonwealth of Nations, Britain conferred dominion status on white-settler colonies in Canada, Australia, and New Zealand. This meant independence in internal and external affairs in exchange for continuing loyalty to the crown. But no such privileges went to possessions in Africa or to India, where nonwhite peoples were the vast majority.

Debates over liberal democratic versus authoritarian models engaged the world's colonial and semicolonial regions. But here there was a larger concern: what to do about colonial authority? Throughout Asia, most educated people wanted to roll back the European and American imperial presence. Some Asians even accepted Japanese imperialism as an antidote, under the slogan "Asia for the Asians." In Africa, intellectuals questioned whether the British and the French were sincerely committed to African improvement or were instead obstacles to African peoples' well-being. (See again Current Trends in World History: Population Movements: Filling Up the Empty Spaces and Spreading Capitalism.)

In Africa as well as Asia, then, the search for the modern encompassed demands for power sharing or full political independence. Anticolonialism was the preeminent vision. To overcome the contradictions of European democratic liberalism, educated Asians and Africans proposed various forms of nationalism.

Behind the Asian and African nationalist movements were profound disagreements about how best to govern nations once they gained independence and how to define citizenship. For many intellectuals, the imperial powers' democratic ethos was appealing. Others liked the radical authoritarianism of fascism and communism, with their promises of a rapid leap to modernity. Whatever their political preferences, most literate colonials also regarded their own religious and cultural traditions as sources for political mobilization. Thus, Muslim, Hindu, Chinese, and African values were part of nationalist campaigns as leaders appealed for support from the rank and file. The colonial figures involved in political and intellectual movements insisted that the societies they sought to establish were going to be modern *and* at the same time retain their indigenous characteristics.

SUB-SAHARAN AFRICAN STIRRINGS Africa contained the most recent territories to come under the Europeans' control, so anticolonial nationalist movements there were quite young. After 1918, African peoples probed more deeply for the meaning of Europe's imperial presence.

In some regions, environmental degradation contributed to the resentment. In the peanut belt of Senegal, for example, African cultivators pushed into more arid regions, cutting down trees and eventually exhausting the soil. In Kenya, where African peoples were confined to specific locations so as to make land available to European settlers, Africans began to overgraze and overcultivate their lands. A severe problem occurred among the Kamba people living near Nairobi. Their herds had become so large that the government attempted to implement a forcible campaign of culling. Refusing to cooperate, the Kamba joined the chorus of African protesters against British authority.

There was some room (but not much) for voicing African interests under colonialism. The French had long sought to assimilate their colonial peoples into French culture. In France's primary West African colony, Senegal, four coastal cities had traditionally elected one delegate (of mixed African and European ancestry) to the French National Assembly. This practice lasted until 1914, when Blaise Diagne (1872–1934), an African candidate, ran for election to the Assembly and won, invoking his African origins and garnering the African vote. While the British allowed Africans to elect delegates to municipal bodies, they refused to permit colonial representatives to sit in Parliament. Committed to democracy at home, the European powers remained steadfastly against it in their colonies.

Excluded from representative bodies, Africans experimented with various forms of protest, but such opposition ran up against not only colonial administrators but also western-educated African elites. Yet, even this privileged group began reconsidering its relationship to colonial authorities. In Kenya, immediately after World War I, a contingent of mission-educated Africans called on the British to provide more and better schools and to return lands they claimed European settlers had stolen. The young nationalists

Blaise Diagne. *Diagne was the first African elected to the French National Assembly. He won the election to the French Parliament in 1914, beating white and mixed-race candidates by appealing to the majority black African population that lived in the four communes of Senegal.*

Facing Mount Kenya

Jomo Kenyatta, one of Kenya's leading nationalists, wrote a moving account of his own Kikuyu community in **Facing Mount Kenya** *(1937). The book demonstrated the cohesion and strong tribal bonds of precolonial Kikuyu society, as well as the destructive elements of the colonial assault on African traditions. The excerpt below is from the conclusion.*

And it is the culture which he inherits that gives a man his human dignity as well as his material prosperity. It teaches him his mental and moral values and makes him feel it worth while to work and fight for liberty.

But a culture has no meaning apart from the social organisation of life on which it is built. When the European comes to the Gikuyu country and robs the people of their land, he is taking away not only their livelihood, but the material symbol that holds family and tribe together. In doing this he gives one blow which cuts away the foundations from the whole of Gikuyu life, social, moral, and economic. When he explains, to his own satisfaction and after the most superficial glance at the issues involved, that he is doing this for the sake of the Africans, to "civilise" them, "teach them the disciplinary value of regular work," and "give them the benefit of European progressive ideas," he is adding insult to injury, and need expect to convince no one but himself.

There certainly are some progressive ideas among the Europeans. They include the ideas of material prosperity, of medicine, and hygiene, and literacy which enables people to take part in world culture. But so far the Europeans who visit Africa have not been conspicuously zealous in imparting these parts of their inheritance to the Africans, and seem to think that the only way to do it is by police discipline and armed force. They speak as if it was somehow beneficial to an African to work for them instead of for himself, and to make sure that he will receive this benefit they do their best to take away his land and leave him with no alternative. Along with his land they rob him of his government, condemn his religious ideas, and ignore his fundamental conceptions of justice and morals, all in the name of civilisation and progress.

If Africans were left in peace on their own lands, Europeans would have to offer them the benefits of white civilisation in real earnest before they could obtain the African labour which they want so much. They would have to offer the African a way of life which was really superior to the one his fathers lived before him, and a share in the prosperity given them by their command of science. They would have to let the African choose what parts of European culture would be beneficially transplanted, and how they could be adapted. He would probably not choose the gas bomb or the armed police force, but he might ask for some other things of which he does not get so much today. As it is, by driving him off his ancestral lands, the Europeans have robbed him of the material foundations of his culture, and reduced him to a state of serfdom incompatible with human happiness. The African is conditioned, by the cultural and social institutions of centuries, to a freedom of which Europe has little conception, and it is not in his nature to accept serfdom for ever. He realises that he must fight unceasingly for his own complete emancipation; for without this he is doomed to remain the prey of rival imperialisms, which in every successive year will drive their fangs more deeply into his vitality and strength.

QUESTIONS FOR ANALYSIS

- According to Kenyatta, why is it so devastating when European imperialists rob African people of their land?
- Why do you think the Europeans were not zealous in imparting "progressive ideas" to the Africans?
- Why does Kenyatta think the Africans would not choose to adopt "the gas bomb or the armed police force" from European culture?

Source: Jomo Kenyatta, *Facing Mount Kenya: The Tribal Life of the Gikuyu* (New York: Vintage Books, 1937) pp. 304–6.

drew important lessons from their confrontation with the authorities. Their new spokesperson, Jomo Kenyatta (1898–1978), invoked their precolonial Kikuyu traditions as a basis for resisting colonialism. (See Primary Source: Facing Mount Kenya.) These early anticolonial movements laid the foundations for more widespread resistance to colonial rule after World War II.

IMAGINING AN INDIAN NATION As Africans explored the use of modern politics against Europeans, in India opposition took a different form. World War I and its aftermath brought full-blown challenges to British rule. Indeed, the Indian nationalist challenge provided inspiration for other anticolonial movements.

For over a century, Indians had heard British authorities extol the virtues of parliamentary government, yet they were excluded from participation. In 1919, the British slightly enlarged the franchise in India and allowed more local self-government, but these moves did not satisfy Indians' nationalist longings. During the 1920s and 1930s, the nationalists, led by **Mohandas Karamchand (Mahatma) Gandhi (1869–1948)**, laid the foundations for an alternative, anticolonial movement.

GANDHI AND NONVIOLENT RESISTANCE Gandhi had studied law in England and had worked in South Africa on behalf of Indian immigrants before returning to India in 1915. Thereafter, he assumed leadership in local struggles and became the focus of the Indian nationalist movement. He also spelled out the moral and political philosophy of *satyagraha,* or **nonviolent resistance**, which he had developed while in South Africa. His message to Indians was simple: develop your own resources and inner strength and control the instincts and activities that encourage participation in colonial economy and government, and you shall achieve *swaraj* ("self-rule"). Faced with Indian self-reliance and self-control pursued nonviolently, Gandhi claimed, the British eventually would have to leave. (See Primary Source: India and Self-Government.)

The Amritsar massacre (discussed earlier in this chapter) and other conflicts spurred the nationalists to oppose cooperation with government officials, to boycott goods made in Britain, to refuse to send their children to British schools, and to withhold taxes. Gandhi added his voice, calling for an all-India *satyagraha*. He also formed an alliance with Muslim leaders and began turning the Indian National Congress from an elite organization of lawyers and merchants into a mass organization open to anyone who paid modest dues, including the illiterate and the poor.

When the Depression struck India in 1930, Gandhi singled out salt as a testing ground for his ideas on civil disobedience. Every Indian used salt, whose production was a heavily taxed government monopoly. Thus, salt symbolized the Indians' subjugation to a colonial government. To break that monopoly, Gandhi began a 240-mile march from western India to the coast to gather sea salt for free. Accompanying him were seventy-one followers representing different regions and religions of India. News wire services and mass circulation newspapers worldwide reported on the drama of the sixty-one-year-old Gandhi, wooden staff in hand, dressed in coarse homespun garments, leading the march. Thousands of people gathering en route were moved by the sight of the frail apostle of nonviolence encouraging them to seek independence from colonial rule. The air thickened with tension as observers speculated on the British reaction to Gandhi's arrival at the sea. After nearly three weeks of walking, Gandhi waded into the surf, picked up a lump of natural salt, held it high, confessed that he had broken the salt law, and invited every Indian to do the same.

Inspired by Gandhi's example, millions of Indians joined strikes, boycotted foreign goods, and substituted indigenous hand-woven cloth for imported textiles. Many Indian

Gandhi and the Road to Independence. Left: *Gandhi launched a civil disobedience movement in 1930 by defying the British government's tax on salt. Calling it "the most inhuman poll tax the ingenuity of man can devise," Gandhi, accompanied by his followers, set out on a month-long march on foot covering 240 miles to Dandi, on the Gujarat coast. The picture shows Gandhi arriving at the sea, where he and his followers broke the law by scooping up handfuls of salt. Right: Gandhi believed that India had been colonized by becoming enslaved to modern industrial civilization. Indians would achieve independence, he argued, when they became self-reliant. Thus, he made the spinning wheel a symbol of* swaraj *and handspun cloth the virtual uniform of the nation.*

India and Self-Government

The following excerpt is from Mohandas (Mahatma) Gandhi's Hind Swaraj, *a pamphlet that he wrote in 1909 to explain why India needed self-government. Gandhi wrote it as a dialogue between a newspaper editor and a reader. Taking the role of the editor, he criticized modernity as represented by modern western civilization, which was based on industry and materialism. In contrast, Gandhi's imagined civilization of India derived from religion and harmonious village life. According to Gandhi, India demanded modern nationhood (or self-rule,* swaraj*) so that it could restore the best elements of its age-old civilization.*

READER: . . . I would now like to know your views on Swaraj. . . .

EDITOR [GANDHI]: It is quite possible that we do not attach the same meaning to the term. You and I and all Indians are impatient to obtain Swaraj, but we are certainly not decided as to what it is. . . .

Why do we want to drive away the English?

READER: Because India has become impoverished by their Government. They take away our money from year to year. The most important posts are reserved for themselves. We are kept in a state of slavery. They behave insolently towards us, and disregard our feelings.

EDITOR: Supposing we get self-government similar to what the Canadians and the South Africans have, will it be good enough?

READER: . . . We must own our navy, our army, and we must have our own splendour, and then will India's voice ring through the world.

EDITOR: . . . In effect it means this: that we want English rule without the Englishman. You want the tiger's nature, but not the tiger; that is to say, you would make India English, and, when it becomes English, it will be called not Hindustan but Englistan. This is not the Swaraj that I want.

READER: Then from your statement I deduce that the Government of England is not desirable and not worth copying by us.

EDITOR: . . . If India copies England, it is my firm conviction that she will be ruined.

READER: To what do you ascribe this state of England?

EDITOR: It is not due to any peculiar fault of the English people, but the condition is due to modern civilisation. It is a civilisation only in name. Under it the nations of Europe are becoming degraded and ruined day by day.

READER: . . . I should like to know your views about the condition of our country.

EDITOR: . . . India is being ground down not under the English heel but under that of modern civilisation. It is groaning under the monster's terrible weight. . . . India is becoming irreligious. Here I am not thinking of the Hindu, the Mahomedan, or the Zoroastrian religion, but of that religion which underlies all religions. We are turning away from God.

READER: You have denounced railways, lawyers and doctors. I can see that you will discard all machinery. What, then, is civilisation?

EDITOR: . . . The tendency of Indian civilisation is to elevate the moral being, that of the Western civilisation is to propagate immorality. The latter is godless, the former is based on a belief in God. So understanding and so believing, it behooves every lover of India to cling to the old Indian civilisation even as a child clings to its mother's breast.

READER: . . . What, then, . . . would you suggest for freeing India?

EDITOR: . . . Those alone who have been affected by Western civilisation have become enslaved. . . . If we become free, India is free. And in this thought you have a definition of Swaraj. It is Swaraj when we learn to rule ourselves.

QUESTIONS FOR ANALYSIS

- What are Gandhi's complaints about English colonial rule?
- Why does Gandhi reject modern civilization?
- According to Gandhi, what are the best aspects of "the old Indian civilisation"?

Source: M. K. Gandhi, *Hind Swaraj and Other Writings,* edited by Anthony J. Parel (Cambridge, UK: Cambridge University Press, 1997), pp. 26–91

officials in the colonial administration resigned in solidarity. The colonizers were taken aback by the mass mobilization. Yet, British denunciations of Gandhi only added to his personal aura and to the anticolonial crusade. By insisting that Indians follow their conscience (always through nonviolent protest), by exciting the masses through his defiance of colonial power, and by using symbols like homespun cloth to counter foreign, machine-spun textiles, Gandhi instilled in the people a sense of pride, resourcefulness, and Indian national awareness.

A DIVIDED ANTICOLONIAL MOVEMENT Unlike the charismatic authoritarians who dominated Italy, Germany, and Russia, Gandhi did not aspire to dictatorial power. Moreover, his program met opposition from within, for not everyone shared his vision of a unified national community as the

PRIMARY SOURCE

Caste and Nation in India

The 1920s witnessed the emergence of B. R. Ambedkar as an eloquent and effective spokesperson for the stirrings for equality among the Dalit. An economist and a jurist, he went on to become the chief drafter of the Indian Constitution in 1950 and is revered today as one of modern India's most brilliant leaders.

Ambedkar argued that political freedom was inseparable from social freedom, and he identified the caste system and the authority it received from Hinduism as a fundamental obstacle to India's freedom. His radical stance on the incompatibility between caste and nation produced a clash with Gandhi. The two men squared off during 1930–1932 when, responding to Ambedkar's demands, the British granted the Dalits (called depressed classes) a separate electorate like other minorities, such as Muslims and Sikhs. Gandhi bitterly opposed this provision and went on a fast unto death in 1932. Not wishing to be held responsible for Gandhi's death, Ambedkar retreated from his demand for a separate electorate.

Underlying this conflict was a bedrock philosophical disagreement. Gandhi viewed caste discrimination as external to Hinduism and wished to address it by urging Hindus to treat the Dalits as Harijans (children of God). Ambedkar rejected this reform and scorned the plea that the Dalits should await a change of heart in upper-caste Hindus. He insisted that the caste system and its authority in Hindu scriptures (Shastras) had to be destroyed using politics.

In 1936, Ambedkar was invited to deliver a speech in Lahore on caste. But organizers withdrew the invitation when they read the advance copy with its attack on Hinduism. Ambedkar subsequently self-published the lecture, "Annihilation of Caste," which is a stinging indictment of the caste system and its origins in Hindu religion and sacred texts. In the piece, excerpted below, he outlines his views on how politics can transform society.

[The real key to destroying Caste is rejection of the Shastras]

[1:] There is no doubt, in my opinion, that unless you change your social order you can achieve little by way of progress. You cannot mobilize the community either for defence or for offence. You cannot build anything on the foundations of caste. You cannot build up a nation, you cannot build up a morality. Anything that you will build on the foundations of caste will crack, and will never be a whole.

[2:] The only question that remains to be considered is—*How to bring about the reform of the Hindu social order? How*

source of public life. Like elsewhere, the winds of modern social change were blowing in new ideologies and aspirations. Cambridge-educated Jawaharlal Nehru (1889–1964), for example, believed that only by embracing science and technology could India develop as a modern nation. And radical activists wanted revolution, not peaceful protest. These activists organized rural peasants and the growing industrial proletariat in the cities to overthrow colonial domination. Their stress on class conflict ran against Gandhi's ideals of national unity.

The era of mass politics brought lower castes and Dalits ("untouchables") onto the public stage, demanding an end to caste discrimination. This demand was articulated most powerfully by the brilliant Dalit leader B. R. Ambedkar. Born in 1891 to a poor family of the "untouchable" caste, Ambedkar graduated from Bombay University in 1912 and earned doctorates from Columbia University and the London School of Economics in the 1920s. On his return to India, he emerged as the most important Dalit leader and engaged Gandhi in a fierce debate over the relationship between caste and the nation. Gandhi argued that the unity of Hindu society, which included the Dalits, formed the bedrock of national unity. Ambedkar responded that the achievement of national unity demanded a rejection of Hinduism, which divided the society into castes and perpetuated social discrimination. Only social equality and democracy, not a caste-ridden Hindu society, could build nationhood, he claimed. The removal of Dalits' civil disabilities, such as untouchability and prohibition from entry into temples, that Gandhi proposed was not the answer. What was required, Ambedkar insisted, was the whole-scale destruction of the caste system. (See Primary Source: Caste and Nation in India.)

Religion, too, threatened to fracture Gandhi's hope for anticolonial unity. The Hindu-Muslim alliance crafted by nationalists in the early 1920s splintered over who represented them and how to ensure their political rights. The Muslim community found a leader in Muhammad Ali Jinnah, who set about making the Muslim League the sole representative organization *to abolish Caste?* This is a question of supreme importance. . . .

[9:] Caste may be bad. Caste may lead to conduct so gross as to be called man's inhumanity to man. All the same, it must be recognized that the Hindus observe Caste not because they are inhuman or wrong-headed. They observe Caste because they are deeply religious. People are not wrong in observing Caste. In my view, what is wrong is their religion, which has inculcated this notion of Caste. If this is correct, then obviously the enemy you must grapple with is not the people who observe Caste, but the Shastras which teach them this religion of Caste. Criticising and ridiculing people for not inter-dining or inter-marrying, or occasionally holding inter-caste dinners and celebrating inter-caste marriages, is a futile method of achieving the desired end. The real remedy is to destroy the belief in the sanctity of the Shastras.

[10:] How do you expect to succeed, if you allow the Shastras to continue to mould the beliefs and opinions of the people? Not to question the authority of the Shastras—to permit the people to believe in their sanctity and their sanctions, and then to blame the people and to criticise them for their acts as being irrational and inhuman—is an incongruous way of carrying on social reform. Reformers working for the removal of untouchability, including Mahatma Gandhi, do not seem to realize that the acts of the people are merely the results of their beliefs inculcated in their minds by the Shastras, and that people will not change their conduct until they cease to believe in the sanctity of the Shastras on which their conduct is founded.

[11:] No wonder that such efforts have not produced any results. You also seem to be erring in the same way as the reformers working in the cause of removing untouchability. To agitate for and to organise inter-caste dinners and inter-caste marriages is like forced feeding brought about by artificial means. Make every man and woman free from the thraldom of the Shastras, cleanse their minds of the pernicious notions founded on the Shastras, and he or she will inter-dine and inter-marry, without your telling him or her to do so.

[12:] It is no use seeking refuge in quibbles. It is no use telling people that the Shastras do not say what they are believed to say, if they are grammatically read or logically interpreted. What matters is how the Shastras have been understood by the people. You must take the stand that Buddha took. You must take the stand which Guru Nanak took. You must not only discard the Shastras, you must deny their authority, as did Buddha and Nanak. You must have courage to tell the Hindus that what is wrong with them is their religion—the religion which has produced in them this notion of the sacredness of Caste. Will you show that courage?

QUESTIONS FOR ANALYSIS

- Why does Ambedkar insist that social change is a prerequisite to a better political order?
- Why does Amebedkar not see caste as mere prejudice?
- How could religious practice and political freedoms be reconciled?

Source: Excerpted from *Annihilation of Caste* by B. R. Ambedkar (1891–1956), first published in 1936, based on the annotated edition published in 2014 by Navayana Publishing Pvt Ltd, New Delhi, India and by Verso, UK.

Gandhi and Nehru Sharing a Light Moment. *Despite their divergent views on modernity, Gandhi was personally close to Nehru, who was his chosen political heir.*

of the Muslim community. In 1940, the Muslim League passed a resolution demanding independent Muslim states in provinces where they constituted a majority, on the grounds that Muslims were not a religious minority of the Indian nation, but a nation themselves.

Hindus also sought a political role on the basis of religious identity. Leaders committed to revitalizing Hinduism began organizing Hindus as a religious nation. Hindu symbols and a Hindu ethos colored the fabric of Indian nationalism woven by Gandhi and the Indian National Congress Party.

A further challenge came from women. Long-standing efforts to "uplift" women now escalated into a demand for women's rights, including suffrage. Following the formation of the All India Women's Conference in 1927, activists addressed issues relating to women's work, health, employment, education, and literacy and demanded legislative seats for women. The Indian National Congress Party, however, elevated its nationalist agenda above women's demands, just as it had done in dealing with the lower castes and the relations between Hindus and Muslims.

In 1937, the British belatedly granted India provincial assemblies, a bicameral (two-chamber) national legislature, and a self-governing executive. By then, however, India's people were deeply politicized. The Indian Congress Party, which inspired the masses to overthrow British rule, struggled to incorporate divergent ideologies and new political institutions, such as labor unions, peasant associations, religious parties, and communal organizations. Seeking a path to economic modernization, Gandhi, on one side, envisioned independent India as an updated collection of village republics organized around the benevolent authority of male-dominated households. Nehru, on another side, hoped for a socioeconomic transformation powered by science and state-sponsored planning. Both believed that India's traditions of collective welfare and humane religious and philosophical practices set it apart from the modern west. By the outbreak of World War II, India was well on its way toward political independence, but British policies and India's divisions foretold a violent end to imperial rule (see Chapter 20).

CHINESE NATIONALISM Unlike India and Africa, China was never formally colonized. But foreign powers' "concession areas" on Chinese soil compromised its sovereignty. Indeed, foreign nationals living in China enjoyed many privileges, including immunity from Chinese law. Furthermore, unequal treaties imposed on the Qing government had robbed China of its customs and tariff autonomy. Thus, Chinese nationalists' vision of a modern alternative echoed that of Indian nationalists: ridding the nation of foreign domination was the initial condition of national fulfillment. For many, the 1911 Revolution (as the fall of the Qing dynasty

came to be known; see Chapter 18) symbolized the first step toward transforming a crumbling agrarian empire into a modern nation.

Despite high hopes, the new republic could not establish legitimacy. For one thing, factional and regional conflicts made the government little more than a loose alliance of gentry, merchants, and military leaders. Its intellectual inspiration came from the ideas of the nationalist leader Sun Yat-sen. In 1912, after the Qing emperor stepped down, a military strongman, Yuan Shikai, forced Sun Yat-sen to concede the presidency to him. Although Sun had organized his followers into a political party, the Guomindang, Yuan dismissed all efforts to further democracy and dissolved the parliament. Only Yuan's death in 1916 ended his attempt to establish a new personal dynasty.

The republic endured another blow when the Treaty of Versailles awarded Germany's old concession rights in the Shandong Peninsula to Japan. On May 4, 1919, thousands of Chinese students demonstrated in Beijing. As the protests spread to other cities, students appealed to workers and merchants to join their ranks. In what became known as the May Fourth movement, workers went on strike and merchants closed shops. Across the country, the Chinese boycotted Japanese goods.

As the Guomindang, still led by Sun Yat-sen, tried to rejuvenate itself, it looked to students and workers as well as the Russian Revolution for inspiration. In 1923, Sun reached an agreement with the Soviets and admitted Chinese Communists to the Guomindang as individual members, in exchange for Soviet military and financial assistance. Under the banner of anti-imperialism, the reorganized party sponsored mass organizations of workers' unions, peasant leagues, and women's associations.

In 1926, amid a renewed tide of antiforeign agitation, **Chiang Kai-shek** (1887–1975) seized control of the party following Sun's death. Chiang launched a partially successful military campaign to reunify the country and established a new national government with its capital in Nanjing. However, he broke with the Soviets and the Chinese Communists, whom he viewed as more threat than ally.

Chiang, like his Chinese Communist rivals, believed that the Chinese masses had to be mobilized in order for China to succeed as a modern nation and escape colonial rule. The New Life movement, launched with a torchlight parade in 1934 in Nanchang, exemplified his aspiration for a new Chinese national consciousness. Drawing on diverse ideas (from Confucian precepts to social Darwinism) and fascist practices such as the militarization of everyday life in the name of sacrificing for the nation, the movement aimed to instill discipline and moral purpose into a unified citizenry. It promoted dress codes for women, condemned casual

Chiang Kai-shek. *Riding the current of anti-imperialism, Chiang Kai-shek, shown here in 1924 in military dress, led the Guomindang on a military campaign in 1926–1928 and seized power, establishing a new national government based in Nanjing.*

sexual liaisons, and campaigned against spitting, urinating, or smoking in public.

PEASANT POPULISM IN CHINA: WHITE WOLF For many Guomindang leaders, the peasant population represented a backward class. Thus, the leadership failed to tap into the revolutionary potential of the countryside, which was alive with grassroots movements such as that of White Wolf.

From late 1913 to 1914, Chinese newspapers circulated reports about a roving band of armed men led by a mysterious figure known as White Wolf said to have almost magical power. It is unlikely that the band, rumored to have close to a million followers, had more than 20,000 members at its height. But the White Wolf movement's impact reverberated well beyond its physical presence.

Popular myth depicted White Wolf with the mission to rid the country of injustice. The band was known to raid major trade routes and market towns. It was said that once the band captured a town, "cash and notes were flung out to the poor." Such stories won the White Wolf army many followers in rural China. Although the army lacked the power to restore order to the countryside, its presence reflected the changing market forces that had come to China. For example, in the northwestern province of Shaanxi (Shensi), where the band made its most famous march, markets that formerly flourished with trade in Chinese cotton now awaited cotton bales shipped from Fall River, Massachusetts.

A POSTIMPERIAL TURKISH NATION Of all the postwar anticolonial movements, none was more successful or more committed to European models than that of **Mustafa Kemal Ataturk** (1881–1938), who helped forge the modern Turkish nation-state. Until 1914, the Ottoman Empire was a colonial power in its own right. But having fought on the losing German side, it saw its realm shrink to a part of Anatolia under the Treaty of Sèvres, which ended the war between the Allies and the Ottoman Empire.

Some of its former territories, such as those in southern Europe, became independent states; others, such as those in the Middle East, came under British and French administration as mandates of the League of Nations. Fearing that the rest of the empire would be colonized, Ottoman military leaders, many of whom had resisted Turkish nationalism, now embraced the cause. What made modern Turkish nationalism so successful was its ability to convert the mainstay of the old regime, the army, to the goal of creating a Turkish nation-state. These men, in turn, mobilized the masses and launched a state-led drive for modernity.

In 1920, an Ottoman army officer and military hero named Mustafa Kemal harnessed this groundswell of Turkish nationalism into opposition to Greek troops who had been sent to enforce the peace treaty. Rallying his own troops to defend the fledgling Turkish nation, Kemal reconquered most of Anatolia and the area around Istanbul and secured international recognition for the new state in 1923 at the Treaty of Lausanne. Thereafter, a forcible exchange of populations occurred. Approximately 1.2 million Greek Christians left Turkey to settle in Greece, and 400,000 Muslims relocated from Greece to Turkey.

With the Ottoman Empire gone, Kemal and his followers moved to build a state based on Turkish national consciousness. First they deposed the sultan. Then they abolished the Ottoman caliphate and proclaimed Turkey a republic, whose supreme authority would be an elected House of Assembly. Later, after Kemal insisted that the people adopt European-style surnames, the assembly conferred on Kemal the mythic name Ataturk, "father of the Turks."

Ataturk. *In the 1920s, Mustafa Kemal, known as Ataturk, introduced the Latin alphabet for the Turkish language as part of his campaign to modernize and secularize Turkey. He underscored his commitment to change by being photographed while giving instruction in the use of the new alphabet.*

In forging a Turkish nation, Kemal looked to construct a European-style secular state and to eliminate Islam's hold over civil and political affairs. The Turkish elite replaced Muslim religious law with the Swiss civil code, instituted the western (Christian) calendar, and abolished the once-powerful dervish religious orders. They also suppressed Arabic and Persian words from Turkish, substituted Roman script for Arabic letters, forbade polygamy, made wearing the fez (a brimless cap) a crime, and instructed Turks to wear European-style hats. The veil, though not outlawed, was denounced as a relic. In 1934, the government enfranchised Turkish women, granted them property rights in marriage and inheritance, and allowed them to enter the professions. Schools, too, were placed under state control and, along with military service, became the chief instrument for making the masses conscious of belonging to a Turkish nation. Yet, many villagers did not accept Ataturk's non-Islamic nationalism, remaining devoted to Islam and resentful of the prohibitions against dervish dancing.

In imitating Europe, Kemal borrowed many of its antidemocratic models. Inspired by the Soviets, he inaugurated a five-year plan for the economy emphasizing centralized coordination. Turkish nationalists also drew on Nazi examples by advocating racial theories that posited central Asian Turks

as the founders of all civilizations. In another authoritarian move, Kemal occasionally rigged parliamentary elections, while using the police and judiciary to silence his critics. The Kemalist revolution in Turkey was the most far-reaching and enduring transformation that had occurred outside Europe and the Americas up to that point. It offered an important model for the founding of secular, authoritarian states in the Islamic world.

NATIONALISM AND THE RISE OF THE MUSLIM BROTHERHOOD IN EGYPT Elsewhere in the Middle East, where France and Britain expanded their holdings at the Ottomans' expense, anticolonial movements borrowed from European models while putting their own stamp on nation-making and modernization campaigns. In Egypt, British occupation predated the fall of the Ottoman Empire, but here, too, World War I energized the forces of anticolonial nationalism.

When the war ended, Sa'd Zaghlul (1857–1927), an educated Egyptian patriot, pressed for an Egyptian delegation to attend the peace conference at Versailles. He hoped to present Egypt's case for national independence. Instead, British officials arrested and exiled him and his most vocal supporters. When news of this action came out, the country burst into revolt. Rural rebels broke away from the central government, proclaiming local republics. Villagers tore up railway lines and telegraph wires, the symbols of British authority.

After defusing the conflict, British authorities tried to mollify Egyptian sensibilities. In 1922, Britain proclaimed Egypt independent, though it retained the right to station British troops on Egyptian soil. Ostensibly, this provision would protect traffic through the Suez Canal and foreign populations residing in Egypt, but it also enabled the British to continue influencing Egyptian politics. Two years later, elections placed Zaghlul's nationalist party, the Wafd, in office. But the British prevented the Wafd from exercising real power.

This subversion of independence and democracy provided an opening for antiliberal variants of anticolonialism. During the Depression years, a fascist group, Young Egypt, garnered wide appeal. Much more influential and destined to have an enduring influence throughout the Arab world was an Islamic group, the Muslim Brotherhood, which attacked liberal democracy as a facade for middle-class, business, and landowning interests. The Muslim Brotherhood was anticolonial and anti-British, but its members considered mere political independence insufficient. Egyptians, they argued, must also renounce the lure of the west (whether liberal capitalism or "godless" communism) and return to a purified form of Islam. For the Muslim Brotherhood, Islam offered a complete way of life. A "return to Islam" through the nation-state created yet another model of modernity for colonial and semicolonial peoples.

CONCLUSION

The Great War and its aftermath accelerated both the trend toward mass society in a broad range of activities and the debate over how to define progress and organize the people. Because mass society meant production and consumption on a staggering scale, satisfying the populace became a pressing concern for rulers worldwide. Competing programs vied for ascendancy in the new, broader, public domain.

Most programs fell into one of three categories: liberal democratic, authoritarian, or anticolonial. Liberal democracy defined the political and economic systems in most of western Europe and the Americas in the decade following World War I. Resting on faith in free enterprise and representative democracy (with a restricted franchise), liberal regimes had already been unsettled before the Great War. Turn-of-the-century reforms broadened electorates and brought government oversight and regulation into private economic activity. But during the Great Depression, dissatisfaction again deepened. Only far-reaching reforms, introducing greater regulation and more aggressive government intervention to provide for the citizenry's welfare, saved capitalist economies and democratic political systems in Britain, France, and North America from collapse.

Through the 1930s, liberal democracy was in retreat. Authoritarianism seemed better positioned to satisfy the masses while representing the dynamism of modernity. While authoritarians differed about the faults of capitalism, they joined in the condemnation of electoral democracy. Authoritarians mobilized the masses to put the interests of the nation above the individual. That mobilization often involved brutal repression, yet it seemed also to restore pride and purpose to ordinary people.

Meanwhile, the colonial and semicolonial world searched for ways to escape European domination. In Asia and Africa, anticolonial leaders sought to eliminate foreign rule while turning colonies into nations and subjects into citizens. Some looked to the liberal democratic west for models of nation building, but others rejected liberalism because it was associated with colonial rule. Instead, socialism, fascism, and a return to religious traditions offered more promising paths.

The two decades after the end of World War I brought great political upheavals and deep economic dislocations. At times, powerful states stood behind the competition between liberal democracy, authoritarianism (both right and left), and anticolonial nationalism. Yet the traumas were tame compared with what followed with the outbreak in 1939 of World War II.

After You Read This Chapter

Go to INQUIZITIVE to see what you know & learn what you've missed.

FOCUS ON: *World War I and Its Aftermath*

The Great War

- The war destroys empires, starting with the Bolshevik Revolution against the tsarist regime in Russia, followed by the defeat and dissolution of the German, Austro-Hungarian, and Ottoman Empires.

- Mass mobilization sees almost 70 million men join the fighting, undermines traditional gender boundaries, and forces states to recognize their peoples' demands for compensation afterward.

- Mass culture spreads as leaders use the new media of radio and film to promote national loyalties and discredit enemies.

- Liberal democracies in France, Britain, and the United States survive the Great Depression by enacting far-reaching changes in their political systems and free market economies.

- Authoritarian (communist and fascist) dictatorships with many political similarities emerge in the Soviet Union, Italy, Germany, Spain, and Portugal.

- Latin American leaders devise hybrid solutions that combine democratic and authoritarian elements.

- Peoples living under colonial rule in Asia and Africa mobilize traditional values to oppose imperial rulers.

- Key individuals emerge in the struggle to define newly independent nations: Kenyatta, Gandhi, Chiang Kai-shek, and Ataturk.

CHRONOLOGY

	The Americas	Europe	Soviet Union	East Asia	South Asia	Middle East

U.S. enters World War I **1917** ◆

World War I **1914–1918**

Mussolini takes over Italy **1922** ◆

Bolshevik Revolution **1917** ◆
Russian civil war **1918–1921**

Mustafa Kemal creates modern Turkish nation-state **1923** ◆

1910   1915   1920

KEY TERMS

Allied Powers p. 709

Ataturk, Mustafa Kemal p. 743

Bolsheviks p. 716

Central Powers p. 709

Chiang Kai-shek p. 742

fascism p. 728

Gandhi, Mohandas Karamchand (Mahatma) p. 738

Great Depression p. 722

Great War p. 708

Hitler, Adolf p. 729

League of Nations p. 716

Mussolini, Benito p. 728

Nazis p. 729

New Deal p. 725

nonviolent resistance p. 738

Stalin, Joseph p. 726

STUDY QUESTIONS

1. **Analyze** the competing visions of modernity that emerged across the globe during the period covered in this chapter. How were they similar and how were they different?

2. **Identify** the causes of World War I, and **explain** the numerous ways in which it changed the world. How did it usher in a new age for diverse societies?

3. **How** did the Russian Revolution and socialism shape the course of the twentieth century?

4. **Discuss** how World War I helped to disperse the concepts of mass culture, mass production, and mass consumption across the world's cultures.

5. **Explore** the relationship between the development of modern, mass societies and the onset of the Great Depression. How were these modern societies affected by the Great Depression?

6. **Analyze** how the Great Depression challenged political establishments after World War I. How were the two events linked? What values and assumptions did the Great Depression challenge?

7. **Compare and contrast** the liberal democratic, authoritarian, and anticolonialist visions of modernity as epitomized by various states and regions. **Evaluate** the success of each during this period.

8. **Distinguish** fascism from traditional conservatism. **Compare** it with other political movements discussed in this chapter, especially Bolshevism.

9. **Explain** how authoritarian leaders (Stalin, Mussolini, and Hitler) defined progress. What elements did these leaders take from liberal democracy, and in what ways did they reject that tradition?

10. **List and explain** various anticolonial visions of modern life that emerged in the first half of the twentieth century. To what extent did they reflect borrowed developments versus native traditions and ideas?

11. **Describe** how Latin American societies adjusted to modern ideas at this time. How did visions of modernity affect states and societies in that region of the world?

12. **Analyze** the ways in which access to consumer goods and other aspects of mass society influenced political conflict in Asia, Africa, and Latin America.

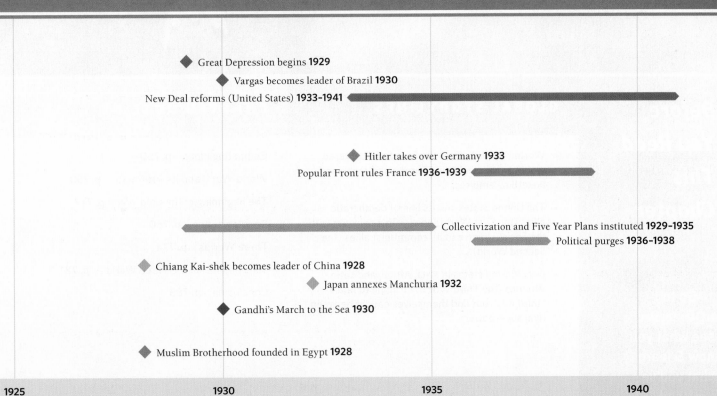

Great Depression begins **1929**

Vargas becomes leader of Brazil **1930**

New Deal reforms (United States) **1933-1941**

Hitler takes over Germany **1933**

Popular Front rules France **1936-1939**

Collectivization and Five Year Plans instituted **1929-1935**

Political purges **1936-1938**

Chiang Kai-shek becomes leader of China **1928**

Japan annexes Manchuria **1932**

Gandhi's March to the Sea **1930**

Muslim Brotherhood founded in Egypt **1928**

1925   1930   1935   1940

20

The Three-World Order, 1940–1975

FOCUS QUESTIONS

- How did World War II contribute to the creation of the three-world order after 1945?

- To what extent was World War II a global war?

- What roles did the United States and the Soviet Union play in the Cold War?

- What were the goals of Third World countries during this period, and to what degree were these goals achieved?

- How similar and different were civil rights issues in the First, Second, and Third worlds? In what ways did each "world" address these and other rights?

In February 1945, the three leaders of the World War II Allies—President Franklin Delano Roosevelt of the United States, Prime Minister Winston Churchill of Great Britain, and Premier Joseph Stalin of the Soviet Union—met to prepare for the postwar world. By then, Germany, Italy, and Japan were losing the war. But the world's reordering was a source of deep contention, for the three leaders had profoundly different visions. Roosevelt, who envisioned independent nation-states kept at peace by an international body, had no interest in restoring the old European empires. Churchill, however, resisted liquidation of the British Empire. Stalin's negotiations left no doubt that he intended to secure influence in eastern Europe and Asia and to weaken Germany so that it could never again menace the Soviet Union.

When the fighting finally stopped, it was clear that the European-centered order, shocked by World War I, had been shattered by World War II. Empires either lay in ruins or faced dismantling by colonial independence movements. Nation-states remained the prevailing form of political organization, and new ones emerged out of old empires. Moreover, the state's reach had expanded as it took on new functions related to postwar reconstruction. But internationally, states now organized themselves into three rough groupings, reflecting the unwillingness of all parties to find common ground. In this chapter, we will use the terms *First World*, *Second World*, and *Third World* for these groupings; those were the terms used at the time to describe a global geography in which a liberal capitalist ("First") world was opposed both by a communist ("Second") world and a ("Third") world made up largely of postcolonial nations that wanted to assert their right to stand apart from both of the Cold War's major geopolitical blocs.

This chapter explores the development of the three-world order in the wake of World War II. Heading the "First World" was the United States, which with its allies championed capitalism and democracy as the best way to bring unprecedented prosperity in the decades after 1945. Leading the "Second World" was the Soviet Union, the crucial ally of the United States during World War II, which became its chief adversary in the protracted Cold War that followed. As leader of the communist bloc, the Soviet Union contested capitalist societies' claims and trumpeted socialism's accomplishments. Caught in between (and sometimes literally caught in the crossfire when the Cold War turned hot) were formerly colonized and semicolonized people. Lumped together as the "Third World" by western intellectuals and by Asian and African leaders who embraced the idea of an alternative to the dominant blocs, these nations emerged from the war eager to seek their own ways forward.

COMPETING BLOCS

The roots of the world's division into three blocs lay in the breakup of Europe's empires and the demise of European world leadership. The destruction of Europe and the defeat of Japan left a power vacuum, which the United States and the Soviet Union rushed to fill. Both believed that their respective systems—capitalism and communism—had universal application. They were now superpowers because of the size of their economies and arsenals, the transcontinental reach of their political influence, and the fact that each embodied a model of civilization applicable to the whole world. As their spheres of influence expanded, they engaged in a bitter ideological rivalry known as the Cold War because no direct military conflict occurred between the superpowers, both of which after 1949 possessed the atomic bomb.

While the capitalist and communist blocs embarked on a cold war, conflicts in the Third World got very hot. In Asia and Africa, anticolonial leaders intensified their campaigns for independence. Winning popular support by mobilizing deep-seated desires for justice and autonomy, they swept away foreign rulers and asserted their claims for national independence. Latin American countries, too, sought progress and nationhood. But newfound political freedom did not easily translate into

economic development or social equity. Moreover, as the two superpowers looked for allies and client states, they militarized rival states and factions within the Third World.

Each superpower also faced internal problems. Even as the United States maintained that its booming industrial economy, abundant consumer goods, liberal democracy, and vibrant popular culture were proof of capitalism's superiority, the nation also wrestled with racism and became involved in unpopular wars to stop the spread of communism—most notably in Vietnam. The Soviet Union celebrated its own economic prowess and social welfare policies, but it continued to imprison and persecute reformers and dissenters and to operate a command economy, oriented to heavy industrial products and armaments. By the 1960s, the USSR's use of military force to crush socialist reform efforts within the Soviet bloc was undermining communism's allure.

By the 1960s and the early 1970s, tensions were simmering in the three-world order. The United States and the Soviet Union faced discontent within their societies and opposition within their respective blocs. At the same time, the rising economic might of Japan and the other Pacific economies, the emerging clout of oil-rich states, and the specter of radical revolution in Africa, Asia, and Latin America suggested a shift in the balance of wealth and power away from the First and Second Worlds.

WORLD WAR II AND ITS AFTERMATH

Especially for Europeans, the Great War (1914–1918) resulted in a horrific loss of life, economic devastation, and the shattering of multinational empires. Afterward, many hoped that it would be "the war to end all wars." But making peace turned out to be very hard, and the harsh provisions and controversial state boundaries set out in the post-1918 treaties, in particular, bred resentments that created interwar chaos and political radicalizations, paving the way for the outbreak of a second—and even more devastating and global—world war in 1939. The Great War, now, would be renamed the First World War.

World War II, then, grew out of the bitter experiences of both World War I and the failures of the peace. It also resulted from the aggressive ambitions and racial theories of Germany and Japan. Both states sought to impose racial hierarchies of master and inferior races through conquest and coerced labor. By the late 1930s, German and Japanese ambitions to become colonial powers brought these conservative dictatorships (which along with Italy constituted the **Axis Powers**) into conflict with France, Britain, the Soviet Union, and eventually the United States (the **Allied Powers**).

Fighting occurred in Europe, Africa, and Asia, the Atlantic and the Pacific Oceans, and the Northern and Southern Hemispheres as the warring nations mobilized millions of people, including the colonized, into armed forces and placed enormous demands on civilians. Noncombatants in places such as India and Greece, Yugoslavia and Korea, Poland and the Philippines suffered terrible hardships, including famines, reprisal killings, and deportations in the course of this war without mercy. Moreover, as aerial bombardment of cities caused colossal civilian casualties, the total war erased the old distinction between soldiers and civilians. Women— as victims and as collaborators, as volunteers and as forced laborers, as workers behind the scenes and as witnesses to the conflict—were involved as never before. They, together with children, the infirm, and the elderly, also swelled the enormous population of refugees seeking safety in the midst of worldwide chaos.

World War II also completed the decline of European world dominance that World War I had set in motion. The unspeakable acts of barbarism perpetrated during the Second World War, including the Nazi genocides directed against Jews and others, robbed Europe of its lingering claims as a superior civilization. In the war's wake, anticolonial movements demanded national self-determination from battered and morally bankrupted European powers.

The War in Europe

World War II began in September 1939 with Germany's invasion of Poland and the British and French decision to oppose it. Before it was all over in 1945, much of Europe, including Germany, had been leveled.

BLITZKRIEG AND TOTAL WAR Germany's early success was staggering. After signing a nonaggression pact with the Soviet Union in August 1939, Nazi troops overran western Poland; the Soviets invaded from the east and occupied Poland's eastern half. Thousands of Poles were murdered or deported by both sides. Hitler then attacked to the west, swiftly defeating and occupying France, Norway, Denmark, Luxembourg, Belgium, and Holland. Within less than two years, the Germans controlled virtually all of Europe from the English Channel to the Soviet border. (See Map 20.1.) Only Britain escaped Axis control, although Nazi bombers pulverized British cities. Hitler waited to strike to the east until June 1941, when Germany broke its pact and invaded the Soviet Union with 170 divisions, 3,000 tanks, and 3.2 million men— an invasion force of a size unmatched before or since. Here, as elsewhere, the Germans fought a *blitzkrieg* ("lightning war") of tank-led assaults followed by motorized infantrymen and then foot soldiers.

The Soviet response was a massive counteroffensive, as Stalin threw everything he had into the war. It took a full two years of terrible bloodletting before the Soviets could begin to drive Hitler's army slowly westward. At the Battle of Stalingrad, the German army and its allies suffered 1.5 million men killed, wounded, or captured against 75,000 Soviet troops suffering the same fate. Only six months later, at the Battle of Kursk, the largest tank battle in history, the Germans, boasting a tank force of 2,000, lost out to a Soviet tank force twice its size. Before 1944, the Soviets bore the brunt of the fighting, causing more than 85 percent of all German casualties, although the British attacked the Nazis in the air and on the sea and, along with American troops, stopped a German advance across North Africa into Egypt. The spectacular D-Day landing of western Allied forces in Normandy on June 6, 1944 (when the Germans had a mere 15 divisions in France, against more than 300 divisions on the Eastern Front), brought the Germans face to face with American and British troops who were determined to fight their way to Germany. On April 30, 1945, as Soviet and Anglo-American forces converged on Berlin, Hitler committed suicide. Days later, Germany surrendered unconditionally. At last, the devastating war in Europe—more "total" than any before—was over.

Kent, 1940. *During the Battle of Britain in 1940–1941, English civilians often had to take cover from Nazi bombers at a moment's notice. In this image, originally published in* Life Magazine, *the children of hops farmers in the southeastern English county of Kent anxiously watch the skies from a hastily dug air-raid trench.*

MAP 20.1 | World War II: The European Theater

The Axis armies enjoyed great success during the early stages of World War II.

- Which states were within the Axis territory when World War II began in September 1939? What were the territorial boundaries when the Axis Powers reached their greatest extent?

- When did the military balance begin to turn against Germany and Italy?

RACIAL WAR AND THE HOLOCAUST The Nazi war was not just a grab for land and raw materials; it was also a crusade for a new order based on race. Hitler considered Slavic peoples subhumans and was prepared to kill or starve them to make room for German Aryans. But his most powerful racial hatred was directed at Europe's Jewish population. Hitler had long talked of "freeing" Europe of all Jews. At the war's outset, the Nazis herded Jews into ghettos and labor camps and then seized their property. As the German army moved eastward, more and more Jews came under their control. At first the Nazi bureaucrats contemplated deportation, but then ruled out transporting "subhumans" as too costly and so settled for starving them and crowding them together in unsanitary ghettos. By the summer of 1941, special troops operating behind the army on the Eastern Front had begun mass shootings of communists and Jewish civilians, and by fall 1941, Hitler and the SS (the *Schutzstaffel*, or

Leningrad, Winter 1941–1942. *Surrounded by German forces for more than 900 days, the city of Leningrad experienced terrible hunger and cold. Here two women brave the bitter cold to collect the remains of a horse that has died in the street—probably from exhaustion and hunger.*

The Ovens at Auschwitz (Reconstruction). *One of the most horrifying aspects of Nazi behavior during World War II was the attempt to make mass killing efficient, scientific, and hygienic. At Auschwitz, the most deadly of the extermination camps, more than 1 million Jews and other racial and political "enemies" of the regime were murdered according to carefully designed plans. Many of bodies were then burned in specially built ovens like these in order to save the Nazis from having to dig potentially unhygienic mass graves and in order to hide the evidence that genocide was being committed. Still, prisoners and guards at the camp reported having to endure the terrible smell of burning flesh and the falling of ash containing fragments of human bones.*

special security forces) were building a series of killing centers. Cattle cars shipped Jews from all over Europe to extermination sites in the east where Nazis used the latest technology, including the cyanide-based poison gas Zyklon B, to kill men, women, and children. The largest facility, Auschwitz, combined an extermination center and work camp in a single complex.

The deliberate racial extermination of the Jews, known as the **Holocaust**, claimed around 6 million European Jews. About half of this number died in the gas chambers of concentration camps; the others perished in face-to-face executions or from starvation, disease, or exhaustion. The Nazis also turned their mass killing apparatus against gypsies, homosexuals, communists, and Slavs, with deportations to the death camps continuing to the very end of the war. Nazi genocides—enormous in scale and reliant on modern, "enlightened" administrative practices—stood as a powerful challenge to European claims that science, technology, and an efficient bureaucracy would make life better for everyone. Lamenting connections between European culture and the Holocaust, in 1949 the German philosopher Theodor Adorno wrote, "To write poetry after Auschwitz is barbaric."

COLLABORATION AND RESISTANCE Nazi occupation created massive social, economic, and political upheavals throughout Europe. Hitler established puppet governments that complied with deportation orders against Jews and dissidents. In occupied territories, most people simply struggled to survive and to take care of their families as best they could. A large number of collaborators, however, worked with the Germans, spurred by a mixture of ideology, opportunism, and fear. Hitler's giant police state also spawned resistance fighters, who opposed German occupiers for varying reasons. Among the resistance movements were both nationalists (who opposed

German domination) and communists (who wanted to defeat both fascism and capitalism), who would fight among themselves even after the war was won.

THE BITTER COSTS OF WAR The war in Europe had devastating human and material costs. This was particularly the case in eastern Europe, where German forces leveled more than 70,000 Soviet villages, obliterated one-third of the Soviet Union's wealth, and inflicted 7 million Soviet military deaths (by contrast, the Germans lost 3.5 million soldiers) and at least 20 million civilian deaths. German bombing of British cities, such as London, inflicted a heavy toll on civilians and buildings, as did Allied bombing of war plants and Axis cities like Dresden and Tokyo. Urban casualties were perhaps greatest in Leningrad, a city that was surrounded and besieged for 900 days; 900,000 people lost their lives during this struggle. By the war's end, Poland had lost 6 million people and Great Britain had lost 400,000. (See Analyzing Global Developments: World War II Casualties.)

World War II left much of Europe in ruins. Charred embers lay where great cities had once stood. Major bridges lay crumbled at the bottom of rivers; railway lines were twisted scrap; sunken ships blocked harbors. Scarcity and hunger were widespread. Millions had died; tens of millions more were wounded, displaced, widowed, and orphaned. "What is Europe now?" mused British prime minister Winston Churchill. "A rubble heap, a charnel house, a breeding ground of pestilence and hate."

ANALYZING GLOBAL DEVELOPMENTS

World War II Casualties

orld War II was the most destructive armed conflict in recorded history. It mobilized more than 120 million military personnel; more than 20 million died. The death toll of civilian populations was substantially greater. Civilian deaths directly caused by the war, including genocide, bombing, starvation, and disease, are now estimated to range from 30 million to 55 million, or slightly more than 60 percent of total losses; figures vary widely because of the difficulty of arriving at accurate numbers in places where loss of life was extremely high and chaos continued after the war, such as China, the USSR, and India. Historians now put the total human losses at roughly 60 million dead, including the 6 million Jews killed in the Holocaust, more than double the number killed in World War I.

QUESTIONS FOR ANALYSIS

- This chart lists the number mobilized, military deaths, and estimated total deaths during World War II for some of the countries and colonial regions where the loss of life was greatest. In many cases, civilian casualties are difficult to estimate because of the chaos that reigned both during and after the war.

- Which countries endured the greatest loss of life in World War II and why?

- Contrast civilian and military casualties in World War II, and explain why civilian casualty rates were so much higher than military losses. (To arrive at civilian casualty figures, subtract the military death toll from the estimated total casualty figures.) Why was this particularly the case in colonial territories such as India, the Dutch East Indies, and French Indochina?

- Compare and contrast the casualties for World Wars I and II. (See the Analyzing Global Developments feature in Chapter 19.)

- Many historians regard World War I as a greater turning point in European and western history than World War II, with its extraordinarily high loss of life. Why do you think historians would hold to this view? What is your view of the relative global importance of the two wars?

World War II Casualties				
Nation	**Population in 1939**	**Max. No. Mobilized**	**Military Deaths**	**Estimated Total Deaths**
USSR	108,377,000	12,500,000	8,800,000–10,700,000	27,000,000+
China	517,568,000	5,000,000	2,220,000	14–20,000,000
Germany	69,622,500	9,200,000	5,553,000	6,6–8,600,000
Poland	34,775,700	1,000,000	240,000	5,800,000

The Pacific War

Like the war in Europe, the conflict in the Pacific transformed the military and political landscape. (See Map 20.2.) The war broke out when Japan's ambitions to dominate Asia targeted American interests and might.

JAPAN'S EFFORTS TO EXPAND Japan's efforts to expand in Asia were already under way in the 1930s, but the outbreak of war in Europe opened opportunities for further expansion. Japan's military invaded and occupied Manchuria in 1931 and then launched an offensive against the rest of China in 1937. Although the Japanese did not achieve China's complete submission, the invaders exacted a terrible toll on the population. Most infamous was the so-called rape of Nanjing, in which Japanese aggressors slaughtered at least 100,000 civilians and raped thousands of women in the Chinese city between December 1937 and February 1938.

World War II Casualties (continued)

Nation	Population in 1939	Max. No. Mobilized	Military Deaths	Estimated Total Deaths
Dutch East Indies	69,435,000	N/A	N/A	3,500,000
Japan	71,380,000	6,095,000	2,120,000	2,600,000–3,100,000
India	311,820,000	2,150,000	87,000	1,500,000–2,500,000
Yugoslavia	5,510,100	500,000	305,000	1,505,000
French Indochina	24,568,000	N/A	N/A	1–1,500,000
Hungary	9,129,000	350,000	300,000	580,000
France	40,000,000	5,000,000	217,600	567,000
Greece	7,221,900	414,000	20–35,000	300–800,000
Italy	44,394,000	4,000,000	301,400	457,000
United Kingdom	47,760,000	4,683,000	383,400	450,700
United States	131,028,000	16,353,659	407,000	419,400
Philippines	16,000,300	105,000	N/A	118,000

Total WWII Deaths: 60 million (including 6 million Jews)

Sources: Data complied from: Alan Axelrod (ed.), *Encyclopedia of World War II*, vol. 1 (2007); Rana Mitter, *Forgotten Ally: China's World War II, 1937-1939* (2013); I. C. B. Dear, ed., *The Oxford Companion to World War II* (1995); The National WWII Museum, New Orleans. Note: casualty figures vary for most of these countries, in some cases widely. These are at best estimates.

After concluding a pact with Germany in 1940, the Japanese occupied French Indochina in 1941 and made demands on the Dutch East Indies for oil and rubber. Now the chief obstacle to further expansion in the Pacific was the United States, which already had imperial interests in places like China and the Philippines as well as other Pacific islands. Hoping to strike the United States before it was prepared for war, the Japanese launched a surprise air attack on the American naval base at Pearl Harbor, in Hawaii, on December 7, 1941.

Now Japan's expansion shifted into high gear. With French Indochina already under their control, the Japanese turned against the American colony of the Philippines and against the Dutch East Indies, both of which fell in 1942. By coordinating their army, naval, and air force units and using tactical surprise, the Japanese seized a huge swath of territory that included British-ruled Hong Kong, Singapore, Malaya, and Burma, while threatening the British Empire's hold on India as well.

MAP 20.2 | World War II: The Pacific Theater

Like Germany and Italy, Japan experienced stunning military successes in the war's early years.

- In what directions did the Japanese direct their military offensives? Analyzing this map, why do you think the Japanese were so concerned about an American presence in East Asia, when the United States was so geographically distant?

- According to your reading, how did the Allied strategies to defeat the Japanese Empire shape postwar relations in the region?

Japan justified its aggression on the grounds that it was anticolonial and pan-Asian; Japan promised to drive out the European imperialists and to build a new order reflecting "Asia for Asians." In practice, however, the Japanese made terrible demands on fellow Asians for resources, developed myths of Japanese racial purity and supremacy, and treated Chinese and Koreans with brutality. During the war, Japan put up to 4 million Koreans to work for its empire, forcibly imported another 700,000 Korean men as laborers, and pressed up to 200,000 young women into service as prostitutes for Japanese soldiers. (In a similar move, the Nazi war effort

Japanese Aggression. *The brutal Battle of Shanghai (August–November 1937) marked the beginning of what turned out to be World War II in Asia. Claiming to be "protecting" China from European imperialists and expecting a relatively easy victory, the Japanese instead met with stiff resistance from the Chinese troops under Chiang Kai-shek. Here we see Japanese marines parading through the streets of the city after they finally broke through Chinese defenses. About a quarter of a million Chinese soldiers, close to 60 percent of Chiang's best troops, were killed or wounded in the campaign, a blow from which Chiang's regime never recovered. The Japanese sustained more than 40,000 casualties.*

in Europe involved forcing 12 million foreign laborers—including 2 million prisoners of war—to settle and work in Germany.)

ALLIED ADVANCES AND THE ATOMIC BOMB Like the Germans in their war against Russia, the Japanese could not sustain their military successes against the United States. By mid-1943, U.S. forces had put the Japanese on the defensive. Fighting from island to island, American troops recaptured the Philippines, and a combined force of British, American, and Chinese troops returned Burma to Britain. The Allies then moved toward the Japanese mainland. By summer 1945, American bombers had all but devastated the major cities of Japan. Yet Japan did not surrender.

Anticipating that an invasion of Japan would cost hundreds of thousands of American lives, U.S. president Harry Truman unleashed the Americans' secret weapon. It was the work of a team of scientists who were predominantly European refugees. On August 6, 1945, an American plane dropped an atomic bomb on the city of Hiroshima, killing or maiming over 100,000 people and poisoning the air, soil, and groundwater for decades to come. Three days later, the Americans dropped a second atomic bomb on Nagasaki, and on Japan's western flank, the Russians made ready to invade. Within days, Emperor Hirohito announced Japan's surrender, bringing the war to an end. Japan's dreams of East Asian supremacy had been defeated, at the cost of millions displaced, wounded, widowed, and

orphaned. Asians, like Europeans, were relieved that six years of globalized horror had finally ended, but neither could guess what transformations the postwar world would bring.

THE BEGINNING OF THE COLD WAR

The destruction of Europe and the defeat of Japan left a power vacuum, which the United States and the Soviet Union rushed to fill. Avoiding direct warfare, the Americans and Soviets vied for influence in postwar Europe and around the globe.

Rebuilding Europe

In Europe, communism and liberal democracy offered competing approaches to rebuilding states and societies after World War II. Many of the interwar democracies had been corrupt or ineffectual, and supporters had to distance themselves from their discredited predecessors. By contrast, communism gained new appeal because its credo promised a clean slate. Many eastern Europeans, reacting to the horrors of fascism and not knowing the extent of Stalin's crimes, looked to the Soviets for answers.

Europe's leftward tilt alarmed U.S. policymakers. They feared that the Soviets would use their ideological influence and the territory taken over by the Red Army to spread communism. They also worried that Stalin might seize Europe's overseas possessions and create communist regimes outside Europe. But few wished to fight another "hot" war. As President Truman began advocating a policy of containment to prevent the further advance of communism, an American journalist popularized the term **Cold War** in 1946 to describe a new form of struggle in which both sides endeavored to avoid direct warfare.

Postwar Planning at Yalta. *The "Big Three" allies confer about the end of the war at the Black Sea resort of Yalta in February 1945. On the left is British prime minister Winston Churchill, at the center is American president Franklin Roosevelt, and on the right is Soviet premier Joseph Stalin.*

Truman's containment policy was tested when the Soviets attempted to seize control of Berlin. Like the rest of Germany, Berlin had been partitioned into British, French, American, and Soviet zones of occupation; but the city was an island within the Soviet zone. In 1948, the Soviets attempted to cut the city off from western access by blocking western routes to the capital. The U.S. and its western allies responded with the Berlin Airlift, which involved transporting supplies in planes to western Berlin to keep the population from capitulating to the Soviets. This crisis lasted for almost a year, until Stalin relented in May 1949, when trucks once again rolled through the eastern zone.

In that same year, occupied Germany was split into two hostile states: the democratic Federal Republic of Germany in the west and the communist German Democratic Republic in the east. In 1961, leaders in the German Democratic Republic built a wall around West Berlin to insulate the east from capitalist propaganda and to halt a flood of émigrés fleeing communism. The Berlin Wall became the great symbol of a divided Europe and of the Cold War.

U.S. policymakers wanted to shore up democratic governments in Europe, so Truman promised American military and economic aid. Containing the spread of communism meant securing a capitalist future for western Europe, a job that fell to Truman's secretary of state, General George C. Marshall. He launched the Marshall Plan, an ambitious program that provided over $13 billion in grants and credits to reconstruct Europe and facilitate an economic revival. U.S. policymakers hoped the aid would dim communism's appeal by fostering economic prosperity, muting class tensions, and integrating western European nations into an alliance of capitalist democracies.

Soviet troops had occupied eastern European nations at the war's end, and both communist and leftist members of other parties formed Soviet-backed coalition governments there. By tricking their moderate leftist allies and repressing their critics and opponents, the communists established dictatorships in Bulgaria, Romania, Hungary, and Czechoslovakia in 1948. The Americans offered Marshall Plan aid to eastern Europe, too, which Stalin saw as a threat to Soviet security. He felt the same about the formation in 1949 of the **North Atlantic Treaty Organization (NATO)**, a military alliance between countries in western Europe and North America. He believed that the Soviet Union, having sacrificed millions of people in the war against fascism, deserved to be dominant in eastern Europe. In 1955, the Soviets formally allied themselves with Europe's communist nations in the **Warsaw Pact**, a military alliance of their own. (See Map 20.3.) Each alliance concentrated military forces (and later atomic weapons) directly facing the other. The tense confrontations between NATO nations and Warsaw Pact nations in Europe and other parts of the world in the 1950s and 1960s brought the world to the brink of an atomic World War III.

War in the Nuclear Age: The Korean War

The dropping of the atomic bombs on Japan in 1945 changed military strategies and international relations forever. Spurred by the onset of the Cold War, the Soviets worked hard to catch up to the Americans and in 1949 tested their first nuclear bomb. Thereafter, each side rushed to stockpile nuclear weapons and

The Berlin Airlift. *In summer 1948, a new currency was issued for the united occupation zones of West Germany. It began to circulate in Berlin at more favorable exchange rates than the eastern zone's currency, and Berlin seemed poised to become an outpost of the west inside the Soviet occupation zone. The Soviets responded by blocking western traffic into Berlin; the west countered with an airlift, forcing the Soviets to back down in May 1949 but hastening the division of Germany into two countries.*

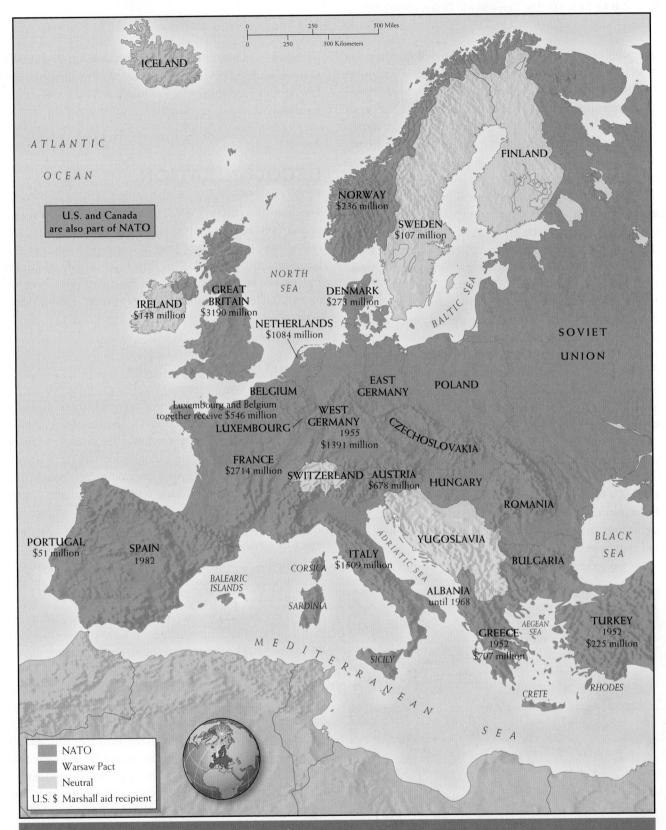

ICELAND

ATLANTIC
OCEAN

NORTH
SEA

NORWAY
$236 million

SWEDEN
$107 million

FINLAND

BALTIC SEA

SOVIET
UNION

U.S. and Canada
are also part of NATO

IRELAND
$148 million

GREAT
BRITAIN
$3190 million

DENMARK
$273 million

NETHERLANDS
$1084 million

BELGIUM
Luxembourg and Belgium
together receive $546 million

LUXEMBOURG

FRANCE
$2714 million

EAST
GERMANY

WEST
GERMANY
1955
$1391 million

POLAND

CZECHOSLOVAKIA

SWITZERLAND

AUSTRIA
$678 million

HUNGARY

ROMANIA

PORTUGAL
$51 million

SPAIN
1982

BALEARIC
ISLANDS

CORSICA

SARDINIA

ITALY
$1509 million

ADRIATIC SEA

YUGOSLAVIA

BLACK
SEA

BULGARIA

ALBANIA
until 1968

MEDITERRANEAN

SICILY

GREECE
1952
$707 million

AEGEAN
SEA

CRETE

TURKEY
1952
$225 million

RHODES

SEA

NATO
Warsaw Pact
Neutral
U.S. $ Marshall aid recipient

MAP 20.3 | NATO and Warsaw Pact Countries

The Cold War divided Europe into two competing blocs: those joined with the United States in the North Atlantic Treaty Organization
(NATO) and those linked to the Soviet Union under the Warsaw Pact.

- Which nations had borders with nations belonging to the opposite bloc?
- Comparing this map with Map 20.1, explain how combat patterns in World War II shaped the dividing line between the two blocs.
- According to the map, where would you expect Cold War tensions to be the most intense?

update its military technologies. By 1960, the explosive power of these weapons had increased so greatly that nuclear war might lead to the world's destruction without a single soldier firing a shot. This sobering realization changed the rules of the game. Each side now possessed the power to inflict total destruction on the other, a circumstance that inhibited direct confrontations but sparked smaller conflicts in parts of Asia where the postwar settlement was murky.

In 1950, North Korean troops backed by the Soviet Union invaded U.S.-backed South Korea, setting off the Korean War. (See Map 20.4.) Claiming this violated the Charter of the United Nations, which had been established in 1945 to safeguard world peace and protect human rights, President Truman ordered American troops to drive back the North Koreans. The U.N. Security Council, thanks to a Soviet boycott, also sent troops from fifteen nations to restore peace. Within a year, the invaders had been routed and were near collapse. When U.N. troops advanced to the Chinese border, however, Stalin maneuvered his communist Chinese allies into rescuing the communist regime in North Korea and driving the South Korean and U.N. forces back to the old boundary in the middle of the Korean Peninsula. Across the Korean isthmus, communist and American-led U.N. troops waged a seesaw war. The fighting continued until 1953, when an armistice divided the country at roughly the same spot as at the start of the war. Nothing had been gained. Losses, however, included 33,000 Americans, at least 250,000 Chinese, and up to 3 million Koreans.

The Korean War energized America's anticommunist commitments and spurred a rapid increase in NATO forces. The United States now saw Japan as a bulwark against communism and resolved to rebuild Japanese economic power. Like West

Atom Bomb Anxiety. *Schoolchildren taking shelter under their desks during an A-bomb drill in Brooklyn, New York, 1951. The Soviets had exploded their first test bomb in 1949. Underground bomb shelters were built in many American urban areas as places in which to survive a doomsday attack.*

Germany, Japan went from being the enemy in World War II to being a valued U.S. ally as the Cold War rivalry between the United States and the Soviet Union spurred both sides to shore up alliances around the globe.

DECOLONIZATION

The disastrous effects of WWII on all empires, including Japan's prewar and wartime empire and the longer-standing colonies belonging to the European powers, inspired colonial peoples to reconsider their political future. The process of **decolonization** and nation building followed four patterns: civil war; wars of independence; negotiated independence; and incomplete decolonization.

The Chinese Revolution

In China, the ousting of Japanese occupiers intensified a civil war that brought the communists to power. The communist movement in China had its origins in the struggle to free the country from western domination since the early twentieth century. Founded in 1921, the Communist Party sought power but was outgunned by Chiang Kai-shek's Nationalist regime and driven from China's cities; its members retreated into the interior, where they founded base camps. In 1934, under attack by Chiang's forces, the communists, led by **Mao Zedong** (1893–1976), abandoned their largest base and undertook an arduous 6,000-mile journey through rugged terrain of northwestern China. (See Map 20.5.) In the course of this great escape, glorified in communist lore as the Long March, fewer than 10,000 of the approximately 80,000 people who started the journey reached their destination. Fortunately for the communists, the Japanese invasion in 1937 diverted Nationalist troops and offered Mao and the survivors a chance to regroup.

The Japanese forces not only inflicted irreparable damage on the Nationalist military; they also further debilitated the capacity of Chiang's regime to govern areas that had not fallen to the invaders. Nationalist soldiers and citizens alike were often left to fend for themselves and became increasingly demoralized and disaffected. When the Japanese invaders seized China's major cities but were unable to control the countryside, the communists expanded their support among the vast peasantry.

Mao's followers cultivated popular support by advocating the lowering of taxes, cooperative farming, and policies aimed at women, such as the outlawing of arranged marriages and the legalization of divorce. Like many anticolonial reformers, Mao regarded women's emancipation as a key component in building a new nation, since he considered their oppression to be both unjust and an obstacle to progress.

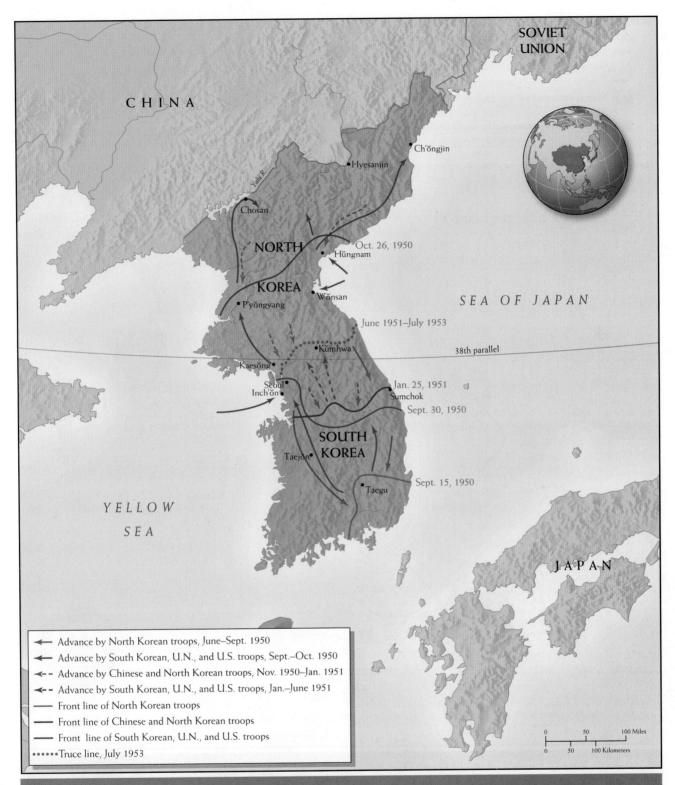

MAP 20.4 | The Korean War

The Korean War was an early confrontation between the capitalist and communist blocs during the Cold War era.

- What were the dates of each side's farthest advance into the other side's territory?
- Why was the Korean Peninsula strategically important?
- According to your reading, how did the outcome of the war shape political affairs in East Asia for the next several decades?

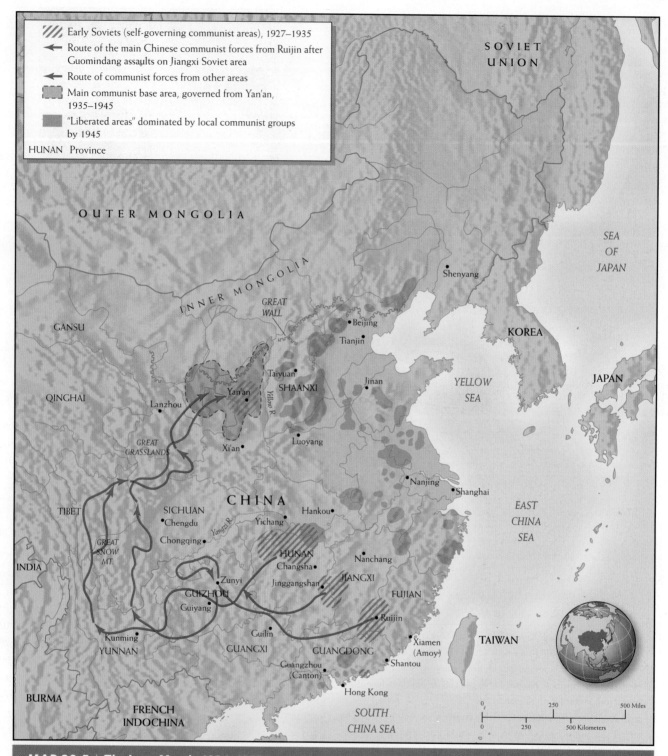

Legend:

//// Early Soviets (self-governing communist areas), 1927–1935

→ Route of the main Chinese communist forces from Ruijin after Guomindang assaults on Jiangxi Soviet area

→ Route of communist forces from other areas

⬚ Main communist base area, governed from Yan'an, 1935–1945

■ "Liberated areas" dominated by local communist groups by 1945

HUNAN Province

MAP 20.5 | The Long March, 1934–1935

During the Long March, which took place during the struggle for power between the Guomindang (Nationalists) and the communists within China, communist forces traveled over 6,000 miles to save their lives and their movement.

- What route did the communist forces take?

- Why did the communists take this particular route?

- How did this movement affect the outcome of this internal struggle in the long run?

The Long March. *In China, the Long March of 1934–1935 has been commemorated by the ruling communists as one of the most heroic episodes in the party's history. This photo shows communist partisans crossing the snow-covered mountains in the western province of Sichuan in 1935. Despite their efforts, the ranks of the party were decimated by the end of the 6,000-mile journey from the southeastern to the northwestern part of the country; fewer than one in eight reached their destination.*

The Founding of the People's Republic of China. *Mao Zedong speaks at a national flag raising ceremony at Shanghai, celebrating the founding of the People's Republic of China on October 1, 1949. Although most Chinese knew little about the communist party, many had high hopes for a new, independent, and liberated China.*

Negotiated Independence in India and Africa

In India and most of colonial Africa, gaining independence involved little bloodshed, although the aftermaths were often extremely violent. The British, realizing that they could no longer rule India without coercion, bowed to the inevitable and withdrew. Much the same happened in Africa, where nationalists also succeeded in negotiating independence from European empires, although, as we shall see, there were notable exceptions.

Communist expansion in the rural areas during World War II swelled the membership of the Communist Party from 40,000 in 1937 to over a million in 1945. After Japan's surrender, China's civil war between Nationalists and communists resumed. But communist forces now had the numbers, the guns (supplied by the Soviet Union and captured from the Nationalists), and the popular support to assault Nationalist strongholds and seize power. By contrast, although the Nationalist government had weapons and financing from the United States, as well as control of the cities, it had not recovered from its defeat at the hands of the Japanese. No match for the invigorated communists, the Nationalists fled to the island of Taiwan, where they established a rival Chinese state.

In 1949, Mao proclaimed that China had "stood up" to the world and had experienced a "great people's revolution." Subsequently, many of his ventures proved disastrous failures (see later in this chapter), but China's model of an ongoing people's revolution provided much hope in the Third World. (See Primary Source: Mao Zedong on "New Democracy.")

INDIA Unlike China, India achieved political independence without an insurrection. But it did veer dangerously close to civil war. As anticolonial elites in the Indian National Congress Party negotiated a peaceful transfer of power from British rule, they disagreed about what kind of state an independent India should have. Should it, as Gandhi wished, be a nonmodern utopia of self-governing village communities, or should it emulate western and Soviet models with the goal of establishing a modern nation-state? Even more pressing was the question of relations between a Hindu majority and the Muslim minority.

For the most part, the congress leadership retained tight control over the mass movement that it had mobilized in the 1920s and 1930s. Even Gandhi hesitated to leave the initiative to the common people, believing that they had not yet assimilated the doctrine of nonviolence. Accordingly, Gandhi and the leadership worked hard to convince the British that they, the middle-class leaders, spoke for the nation. At the same time, the threat of a mass peasant uprising with radical aims (as was occurring in China) encouraged the British to transfer power quickly.

PRIMARY SOURCE

Mao Zedong on "New Democracy"

Many twentieth-century Chinese political and intellectual leaders, including the communists, believed that the rejuvenation of China required changing its culture. The key question was what to embrace and what to discard. Here we find Mao in 1940 explaining the New-Democratic culture—nationalistic, scientific, and mass based—that he regarded as a transitional stage to communism. He cautions against the wholesale importation of western values and practices, including Marxism, and emphasizes instead the specific conditions of the Chinese Revolution.

New-Democratic culture is national. It opposes imperialist oppression and upholds the dignity and independence of the Chinese nation. . . . China should absorb on a large scale the progressive cultures of foreign countries as an ingredient for her own culture; in the past we did not do enough work of this kind. We must absorb whatever we today find useful, not only from the present socialist or New-Democratic cultures of other nations, but also from the older cultures of foreign countries, such as those of the various capitalist countries in the age of enlightenment. However, we must treat these foreign materials as we do our food, which should be chewed in the mouth, submitted to the working of the stomach and intestines, mixed with saliva, gastric juice, and intestinal secretions, and then separated into essence to be absorbed and waste matter to be discarded—only thus can food benefit our body; we should never swallow anything raw or absorb it uncritically.

So-called wholesale Westernization is a mistaken viewpoint. China has suffered a great deal in the past from the formalist absorption of foreign things. Likewise, in applying Marxism to China, Chinese Communists must fully and properly unite the universal truth of Marxism with the specific practice of the Chinese revolution; that is to say, the truth of Marxism must be integrated with the characteristics of the nation and given a definite national form before it can be useful; it must not be applied subjectively as a mere formula. . . .

Communists may form an anti-imperialist and anti-feudal united front for political action with certain idealists and even with religious followers, but we can never approve of their idealism or religious doctrines. A splendid ancient culture was created during the long period of China's feudal society. To clarify the process of development of this ancient culture, to throw away its feudal dross, and to absorb its democratic essence is a necessary condition for the development of our new national culture and for the increase of our national self-confidence; but we should never absorb anything and everything uncritically.

QUESTIONS FOR ANALYSIS

- How does Mao expect to integrate Marxism with the Chinese Revolution?
- What does Mao think of China's "splendid ancient culture"? In this regard, how does he differ from previous rulers of China?

Source: Mao Zedong, "Selected Works," in *Sources of Chinese Tradition,* 2nd ed., vol. 2, edited by William Theodore de Bary, Richard Lufrano, et al. (New York: Columbia University Press, 2000), pp. 422–423.

As negotiations moved forward, Hindu-Muslim unity deteriorated. Whose culture would define the new nation? The Indian nationalism that had existed in the late nineteenth century reflected the culture of the Hindu majority. Yet this movement masked the multiplicity of regional, linguistic, caste, and class differences *within* the Hindu community, just as Muslim movements that arose in reaction to Hindu-dominated Indian nationalism overlooked divisions within their own ranks. Now the prospect of defining "India" created a grand contest between newly self-conscious communities. Riots broke out between Hindus and Muslims in 1946, which increased the mutual distrust between congress and Muslim League leaders. The leader of the Muslim League demanded that British India be partitioned into separate Hindu and Muslim states if there were no constitutional guarantees for Muslims. The specter of civil war haunted the proceedings, as outgoing colonial rulers decided to divide the subcontinent into two states: India and Pakistan.

On August 14, 1947, Pakistan gained independence from Britain; a day later, India did the same. The euphoria of decolonization, however, drowned in a frenzy of brutality. Shortly after independence, up to 1 million Hindus and Muslims killed one another. Fearing further violence, 12 million Hindus and Muslims left their homes to relocate in the new countries where they would be in the majority. Distraught by the rampage, Gandhi fasted, refusing sustenance until the killings stopped. The violence abated. This was perhaps Gandhi's finest hour. But animosity and fanaticism remained. Less than six months later, a Hindu zealot shot Gandhi dead as he walked to a prayer meeting.

Jawaharlal Nehru. *Nehru, the leader of independent India, sought to create a "mixed economy" of private and public sectors with democracy to chart an independent path for India. This photo shows him speaking at the opening ceremonies for the Bhakra Dam in 1963.*

Had Gandhi lived, he would not have approved of the direction independent India took. He had already voiced disapproval of industrialization and of equipping the Indian state with an army and police forces. But Jawaharlal Nehru, India's first prime minister, and other leaders of the Indian National Congress Party were committed to building a strong state capable of modernizing India. Accordingly, they backed the Dalit leader B. R. Ambedkar, who drafted a constitution for a parliamentary democracy that guaranteed basic individual freedoms while equipping the state with substantial powers to foster social equality. Inspired by Soviet-style planned development but also committed to democracy, the new state under Nehru sought to build a "socialistic pattern of society" based on a mixed economy of public and private sectors. Declaring that he wanted to give India the "garb of modernity," Nehru asked Indians to consider hydroelectric dams and steel plants the temples of modern India. He made his watchwords "education" and "economic development," believing that these would loosen the hold of religion on Muslims and encourage them to join the national mainstream. He also hoped that the diminished role of religious traditions would improve the condition of women. Such a vision allowed Nehru, until his death in 1964, to guide Indian modernization along a third path. (See Primary Source: Nehru on Building a Modern Nation.)

AFRICA FOR AFRICANS Shortly after Indian independence, most African states also gained their sovereignty. Except for southern Africa, where minority white rule persisted, the old colonial states ceded to indigenous rulers. One reason for this rapid decolonization was the fact that nationalist movements had made gains during the interwar period. These years had taught a generation of nationalists to seek wider support for their political parties. World War II, then, swelled the ranks of anticolonial political parties, as many African soldiers expected tangible rewards for serving in imperial armies.

The postwar years also saw throngs of Africans flock to the cities in search of a better life. As expanding educational systems produced a wave of primary and secondary school graduates, these educated young people and other new urban dwellers became disgruntled when attractive employment opportunities were not forthcoming. The three groups—former servicemen, the urban unemployed or underemployed, and the educated—led the nationalist agitation that began in the late 1940s and early 1950s. (See Map 20.6.)

Faced with rising nationalist demands, and too much in debt themselves to invest more in pacifying the discontented, European powers agreed to decolonize. The new world powers, the Soviet Union and the United States, also favored decolonization. Thus, decolonization in most of Africa was a rapid and relatively sedate affair. In 1957, the Gold Coast (renamed Ghana), under Prime Minister Kwame Nkrumah, became tropical Africa's first independent state. Other British colonial territories followed in rapid succession, so that by 1963, all of British-ruled Africa except for Southern Rhodesia was independent. In these former colonial possessions, charismatic nationalist leaders became the authorities to whom the British ceded power. Many of the new rulers had obtained a western education but were committed to returning Africa to the Africans.

Decolonization in much of French-ruled Africa followed a similarly smooth path, although the French were initially resistant. Believing their own culture to be unrivaled, the French treated decolonization as assimilation: instead of negotiating independence, they tried first to accord fuller voting rights to their colonial subjects, even allowing Africans and Asians to send delegates to the French National Assembly. In the end, however, the French electorate had no desire to share the privileges of French citizenship with overseas populations. Nor did

Kwame Nkrumah. *West Africa's leading nationalist Kwame Nkrumah mobilized the peoples of the Gold Coast and, through electoral successes, convinced the British to confer independence on the Gold Coast, which was renamed Ghana in 1957.*

PRIMARY SOURCE

Nehru on Building a Modern Nation

The following excerpt, written by Jawaharlal Nehru in 1940, documents the centrality of planning in the desire to build a modern nation. Although the idea of planning derived from the Soviet experience, Nehru did not want India to adopt communism. He saw planned development as a scientific instrument for achieving rapid economic growth and fundamental social changes. Planning would avoid the excesses and inequalities of capitalism and provide a "third way"—equally distanced from both communism and capitalism.

The octopus of war grips and strangles the world and the energy of mankind is more and more directed to destroying what man has built up with infinite patience and labour. Yet it is clear that war by itself cannot solve any problem. It is by conscious, constructive and planned effort alone that national and international problems can be solved. In India many people thought, with reason, that it was premature to plan, so long as we did not have the power to give effect to our planning. The political and economic freedom of India was a prerequisite to any planning, and till this was achieved our national and international policy would continue to be governed, as heretofore, in the interests of the City of London and other vested interests. And yet we started, wisely I think, a National Planning Committee and we are trying, even in these days of world conflict and war, to draw up a picture of planned society in the free India of the future.

Our immediate problem is to attack the appalling poverty and unemployment of India and to raise the standards of our people. That means vastly greater production which must be allied to juster and more equitable distribution, so that the increased wealth may spread out among the people. That means a rapid growth of industry, scientific agriculture and the social services, all co-ordinated together, under more or less state control, and directed towards the betterment of the people as a whole. The resources of India are vast and if wisely used should yield rich results in the near future.

We do not believe in a rigid autarchy, but we do want to make India self-sufficient in regard to her needs as far as this is possible. We want to develop international trade, importing articles which we cannot easily produce and exporting such articles as the rest of the world wants from us. We do not propose to submit to the economic imperialism of any other country or to impose our own on others. We believe that nations of the world can co-operate together in building a world economy which is advantageous for all and in this work we shall gladly co-operate. But this economy cannot be based on the individual profit motive, nor can it subsist within the framework of an imperialist system. It means a new world order, both politically and economically, and free nations cooperating together for their own as well as the larger good.

QUESTIONS FOR ANALYSIS

- According to Nehru, what are the key problems that India faces?
- How does Nehru's vision of India compare with Gandhi's (see Chapter 19, p. 739)?

Source: Jawaharlal Nehru, "A Note to the Members of the National Planning Committee," May 1, 1940, in *Jawaharlal Nehru: An Anthology,* edited by Sarvepalli Gopal (Delhi: Oxford University Press, 1980), pp. 306–307.

African leaders wish to submerge their identities in a Greater France. Thus, France dissolved its political ties with French West Africa and French Equatorial Africa in 1960, having given protectorates in Morocco and Tunisia their independence in 1956. Algeria, always considered an integral part of France overseas, was a different matter. Its independence did not come quickly or easily (discussed shortly).

The leaders of African independence believed that Africa's precolonial traditions would enable the region to move from colonialism right into a special African form of socialism, escaping the ravages of capitalism. Without rejecting western culture completely, they extolled the so-called African personality, exemplified by the idea of "Negritude" developed by Senegal's first president, Léopold Sédar Senghor. Negritude, they claimed,

Léopold Sédar Senghor.
Senghor combined sharp intellect with political savvy. An accomplished poet and essayist and one of the founders of the Negritude movement among Francophone intellectuals, he became Senegal's first president when the country gained full independence in 1960.

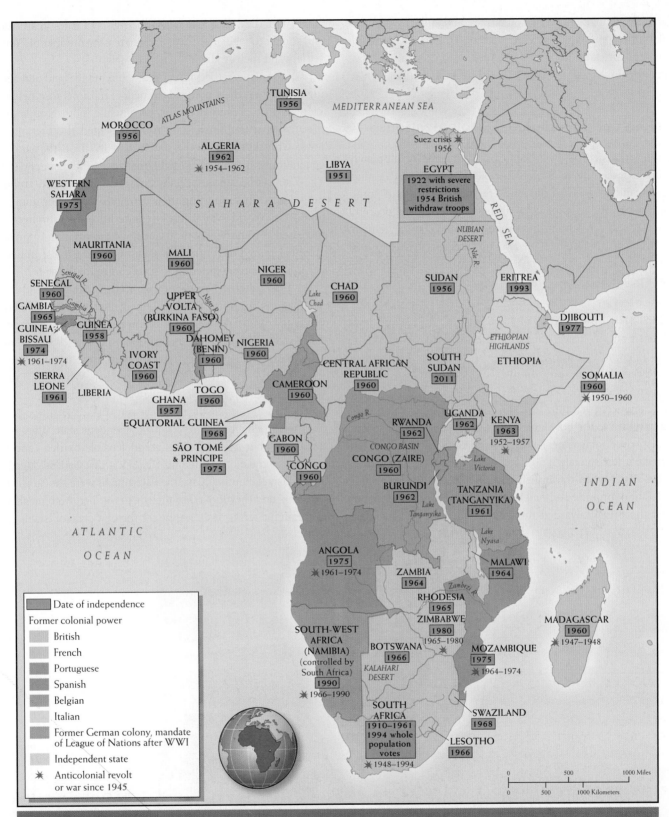

MAP 20.6 | Decolonization in Africa

African decolonization occurred after World War II, largely in the 1950s, 1960s, and 1970s.

- Find at least four areas that won independence in the 1950s, and identify which former colonial power had ruled each area.
- What areas took longer to gain independence?
- According to your reading, what problems and tensions contributed to this uneven process across Africa?

was steeped in communal solidarities and able to embrace social justice and equality, while rejecting the naked individualism that Africans felt lay at the core of European culture. (See Primary Source: Senghor's View of Political Independence.)

Violent and Incomplete Decolonizations

Although transfers of power in most of Africa and Asia ultimately occurred peacefully, there were notable exceptions. In Palestine, Algeria, and southern Africa, the presence of European immigrant groups created violent conflicts that aborted any peaceful transfer of power—or left the process incomplete. In Vietnam, the process was also violent and delayed, partly because of France's desire to reimpose colonial control and partly from the power politics of Cold War competition.

PALESTINE, ISRAEL, EGYPT In Palestine, Arabs and Jews had been on a collision course since the end of World War I. Before that war, a group of European Jews, known as Zionists, had argued that only an exodus from existing states to their place of origin in Palestine could lead to Jewish self-determination. **Zionism** combined a yearning to realize the ancient biblical injunction to return to the holy lands with a fear of anti-Semitism and anguish over increasing Jewish assimilation. Zionists wanted to create a Jewish state, and they won a crucial victory during World War I when the British government, under the Balfour Declaration, promised a homeland for the Jews in Palestine. But when the British awarded themselves Palestine as a mandate

after 1918, they also guaranteed the rights of Palestinian Arabs and sought to mediate between an increasing number of Zionist settlers and their Arab and Christian neighbors.

As more Jews settled in Palestine, buying up land and seeking to increase their political influence, tensions rose between Zionists and Palestinian Arabs. Meanwhile, both groups grew dissatisfied with British rule. Arabs resented the presence of Jews, who displaced farmers who had lived on the land for generations, and openly sought their own independent state. The Zionists became especially enraged when British authorities wavered in supporting their demands for greater immigration. After World War II, the pressure for Jewish immigration increased as hundreds of thousands of concentration camp survivors clamored for entry into Palestine, and Zionist militants began using force to attempt to gain control of the state.

In 1947, after the British announced that they would leave negotiations over the area's fate to the United Nations, that body voted to partition Palestine into Arab and Jewish territories. The Arab states rejected the partition, and the Jewish Agency, a nongovernmental agency that supported the immigration of Jews to Israel, only reluctantly accepted it. When the British withdrew their troops in 1948, a Jewish provisional government proclaimed the establishment of the state of Israel. Although the Jews were delighted to have an independent state, they were unhappy about its small size, its indefensible borders, and the fact that it did not include all the lands that had belonged to ancient Israel. For their part, the Palestinians were shocked at the partition, and they looked to their better-armed Arab neighbors to regain the territories set aside for the new state of Israel.

The Creation of the State of Israel. *Standing beneath a portrait of Theodore Herzl, the founder of the Zionist movement, David Ben Gurion, the first Israeli prime minister, proclaimed independence for the state of Israel in May 1948.*

PRIMARY SOURCE

Senghor's View of Political Independence

One of the most striking visions of African independence as a "third way" came from the pen of Léopold Sédar Senghor, a Senegalese nationalist leader who became the first president of Senegal. The first excerpt, drawn from an essay published in 1959, differentiates the socialism of Africa from Marxism. The second excerpt, taken from a 1961 speech titled "What is Negritude?", develops the idea of "Negritude," or black civilization, markedly different from but not inferior to European cultural forms.

AFRICAN SOCIALISM

In the respective programs of our former parties, all of us used to proclaim our attachment to socialism. This was a good thing, but it was not enough. Most of the time, we were satisfied with stereotyped formulas and vague aspirations, which we called scientific socialism—as if socialism did not mean a return to original sources. Above all, we need to make an effort to rethink the basic texts in the light of the Negro African realities. . . .

Can we integrate Negro African cultural values, especially religious values, into socialism? We must answer that question once and for all with an unequivocal "Yes.". . .

We are not Communists for a practical reason. The anxiety for human dignity, the need for freedom—man's freedom, the freedoms of collectivities—which animate Marx's thought and provide its revolutionary ferment—this anxiety and this need are unknown to Communism, whose major deviation is Stalinism. The "dictatorship of the proletariat," which was to be only temporary, becomes the dictatorship of the part and state by perpetuating itself. . . .

The paradox of socialistic construction in Communist countries—in the Soviet Union at least—is that it increasingly resembles capitalistic construction in the United States, the American way of life, with high salaries, refrigerators, washing machines, and television sets. And it has less art and freedom of thought. Nevertheless, we shall not be won over by a regime of liberal capitalism and free enterprise. We cannot close our eyes to segregation, although the government combats it; nor can we accept the elevation of material success to a way of life.

We stand for a middle course, for a *democratic socialism* which goes so far as to integrate spiritual values, a socialism which ties in with the old ethical current of the French socialists. . . . In so far as they are idealists, they fulfill the requirements of the Negro African soul, the requirements of men of all races and countries. . . .

A third revolution is taking place, as a reaction against capitalistic and Communistic materialism—one that will integrate moral, if not religious, values with the political and economic contributions of the two great revolutions. In this revolution, the colored peoples, including the Negro African, must play their part; they must bring their contribution to the construction of the new planetary civilization.

WHAT IS NEGRITUDE?

Assimilation was a failure; we could assimilate mathematics or the French language, but we could never strip off our black skins or root out black souls. And so we set out on a fervent quest for the "holy grail": our collective soul. And we came upon it. . . .

Negritude is the *whole complex of civilized values—cultural, economic, social, and political—which characterize the black peoples,* or, more precisely, the Negro-African world. All these values are essentially informed by intuitive reason, because this sentient reason, the reason which comes to grips, expresses itself emotionally, through that self-surrender, that coalescence of subject and object; through myths, by which I mean the archetypal images of the collective soul; and, above all, through primordial rhythms, synchronized with those of the cosmos. In other words, the sense of communion, the gift of mythmaking, the gift of rhythm, such are the essential elements of Negritude, which you will find indelibly stamped on all the works and activities of the black man.

QUESTIONS FOR ANALYSIS

- What is African socialism for Senghor?
- In what way, according to Senghor, does Negritude express Negro Africans' "collective soul"?

Source: Léopold Sédar Senghor, "African Socialism" and "What Is Negritude?" from *The Ideologies of the Developing Nations,* 2nd ed. edited by Paul Sigmund (New York: Frederick A. Praeger, 1972), pp. 242, 245-247, 250-251.

The ensuing Arab-Israeli War of 1948–1949 shattered the legitimacy of Arab ruling elites. Arab states entered the war poorly prepared to take on the well-run and enthusiastically supported Israeli Defense Force. By the time the United Nations finally negotiated a truce, Israel had extended its boundaries and more than 1 million Palestinians had become refugees in surrounding Arab countries.

Embittered by this defeat, a group of young officers in the Egyptian army plotted to overthrow a regime that they felt was corrupt and still under British influence. One of the officers,

The Anglo-Egyptian Treaty. *This photo shows Egyptian president Nasser signing the Anglo-Egyptian Treaty with the British minister of state in 1954. The agreement ended the stationing of British troops on Egyptian soil and called for the withdrawal of British troops stationed at the Suez Canal military base. But shortly after the last British soldiers left Egypt in early 1956, Britain invaded the country in a vain effort to block Nasser's nationalization of the Suez Canal Company and to remove the Egyptian leader from power.*

Gamal Abdel Nasser, became the head of a secret organization of junior military officers—the Free Officers Movement. These men had ties with communists and other dissident groups, including the Muslim Brotherhood, which favored a return to Islamic rule. They launched a successful coup in 1952, forcing the king to abdicate and leave the country. Then they enacted a land reform scheme that deprived large estate owners of lands in excess of 200 acres and redistributed these lands to the landless and smallholders, who instantly became ardent supporters of the new regime. The new regime also dissolved the parliament, banned political parties (including the communists and the Muslim Brotherhood), and stripped the old elite of its wealth.

In 1956, Nasser moved to nationalize the Suez Canal Company (an Egyptian company, mainly run by French businessmen and experts), inciting the Israelis, the British, and the French to invade Egypt and seize territory along the Suez Canal. Opposition by the United States and the Soviet Union forced them to withdraw, providing Nasser with a spectacular diplomatic triumph. As Egyptian forces reclaimed the canal, Nasser's reputation as leader of the Arab world soared. He became the chief symbol of a pan-Arab nationalism that swept across the Middle East and North Africa and especially through the camps of Palestinian refugees.

THE ALGERIAN WAR OF INDEPENDENCE The appeal of Arab nationalism was particularly strong in Algeria, where a sizable French settler population (the *colons*) of 1 million stood in the way of a complete and peaceful decolonization. Indeed,

French leaders claimed that Algeria was an integral part of France, an overseas department that was legally no different from Brittany or Normandy. Although the *colons* were a minority, they held the best land and lived in wealthy residential quarters in the major cities. And although all residents of Algeria were supposedly entitled to the same rights as the French citizenry, in fact the *colons*, mainly living in the country's coastal cities, controlled Algeria's finances and all of its public institutions.

As elsewhere, anticolonial nationalism in Algeria gathered force after World War II. The Front de Libération Nationale (FLN), the leading nationalist party, used violence to provoke its opponents and to make the local population choose between supporting the nationalist cause or the *colons*. The full-fledged revolt that erupted in 1954 pitted FLN troops and guerrillas against thousands of French troops. Atrocities and terrorist acts occurred on both sides.

The war dragged on for eight years, at a cost of perhaps 300,000 lives. On the French mainland, the war came as a terrible shock. Many French citizens had accepted the idea that Algeria was not a colonial territory but part of France itself. The *colons* insisted that they had emigrated to Algeria in response to their government's promises and that yielding power to the nationalists would be a betrayal. After an insurrection led by *colons* and army officers brought down the French government in 1958, the new French president, Charles de Gaulle, negotiated a peace accord.

Shortly after handing over power to FLN leaders, more than 300,000 *colons* left Algeria. By late 1962, over 90 percent of the European population had departed. At independence, then, Algeria had a population mix no different from that of the other North African countries.

EASTERN AND SOUTHERN AFRICA The bloody conflict in Algeria highlights a harsh reality of African decolonization: the presence of European settlers prevented the smooth transfer of power. Even in British-ruled Kenya, where the European settler population had never been large, a violent war of independence broke out between European settlers and African nationalists. Employing secrecy and intimidation, the Kikuyu peoples, Kenya's largest ethnic group, organized a revolt. This uprising, which began in 1952, forced the British to fly in troops to suppress it, but ultimately the British government conceded independence to Kenya in 1963. Decolonization proved even more difficult in the southern third of the continent, where Portuguese Angola, Portuguese Mozambique, and British Southern Rhodesia (present-day Zimbabwe) did not gain independence until the 1970s.

Women played vital roles in these decolonization struggles. In Egypt, for example, the leading nationalists were all men, but they gained crucial support from educated and modernizing women, many of whom organized impressive demonstrations on their behalf. The wife of Sa'd Zaghlul, Egypt's most dynamic nationalist figure after World War I, gained a large following

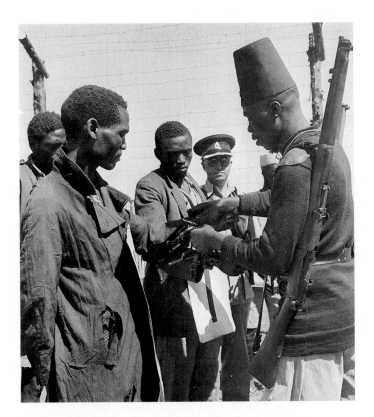

Mau Mau Rebellion. *A large segment of the Kikuyu population rose up against the British colonial occupation of Kenya. This revolt, which began in 1952, was finally suppressed by British arms and Kikuyu "loyalists." Nonetheless, the Mau Mau Uprising led to Kenya's independence from British rule.*

campaigned for an end to discriminatory legislation, was repeatedly harassed, detained, and tried by the government, even though he urged peaceful resistance. After the Sharpeville massacre in 1960, in which police killed demonstrators who were peacefully protesting the pass laws, Mandela and the ANC decided to oppose the apartheid regime with violence. Subsequently, the government announced a state of emergency, banned the ANC, and arrested those of its leaders who had not fled the country or gone underground. A South African court sentenced Mandela to life imprisonment. Other black leaders were tortured or beaten to death. Here, too, women kept resistance flames burning. The most dynamic of these individuals was Winnie Mandela, wife of the imprisoned Nelson Mandela. Unlike many of the ANC leaders, who opposed the regime from exile, she remained behind and openly and courageously spoke out against the apartheid government. Despite such human rights violations, the whites retained external support. Through the 1950s and 1960s, western powers (especially the United States) saw South Africa as a bulwark against the spread of communism in Africa.

VIETNAM The same concern to contain communism also drew the United States into support for a conservative and

and a reputation as mother of the nation. Moreover, during Kenya's battle against British colonial rule, women supplied the fighters with food, medical resources, and information about the British. Those who were caught ended up in concentration camps and suffered brutal treatment from their prison guards. Yet, once independence was achieved, most women reverted to their traditional subordinate status.

South Africa, which held the continent's largest and wealthiest settler population (a mixture of Afrikaans- and English-speaking peoples of European descent), defied black majority rule longer than other African states. After winning the elections of 1948, the white Afrikaner-dominated National Party enacted an extreme form of racial segregation known as **apartheid**. Under apartheid, laws stripped Africans, Indians, and colored persons (those of mixed descent) of their few political rights. Racial mixing of any kind was forbidden, and schools were strictly segregated. The Group Areas Act, passed in 1950, divided the country into separate racial and tribal areas and required Africans to live in their own racial areas, called homelands. Pass laws prohibited Africans from traveling outside their homelands without special work or travel passes.

The ruling party tolerated no protest. Nelson Mandela, one of the leaders of the African National Congress (ANC) who

Apartheid Protest. *In Johannesburg, South Africans march in the street to protest the new restrictions on African citizens, soon to be known worldwide as apartheid, implemented by the white minority government of Daniel Malan. During the Malan administration (1948–1954), informal discrimination was systematically made law, and all electoral, housing, civil, and employment rights of African citizens were dismantled.*

pro-western regime in Vietnam. Vietnam had come under French rule in the 1880s, and by the 1920s approximately 40,000 Europeans were living among and ruling over roughly 19 million Vietnamese. To promote an export economy of rice, mining, and rubber, the colonial rulers granted vast land concessions to French companies and local collaborators, while leaving large numbers of peasants landless.

The colonial system also generated a new intelligentsia. Primarily schooled in French and Franco-Vietnamese schools, educated Vietnamese worked as clerks, shopkeepers, teachers, and petty officials. Yet they had few opportunities for advancement in the French-dominated colonial system. Thus, discontented, they turned from the traditional ideology of Confucianism to modern nationalism. Vietnamese intellectuals overseas, notably Ho Chi Minh, took the lead in imagining a new Vietnamese nation-state.

Ho had left Vietnam at an early age and found his way to London and Paris. During the interwar period he read the writings of Marx, Engels, and Lenin, and he discovered not only an ideology for opposing French exploitation but also a vision for transforming the common people into a political force. He was a founding member of the French Communist Party and subsequently founded the Indochinese Communist Party. After the Japanese occupied Indochina, he traveled to China, embraced the idea of an agrarian revolution, and established the Viet Minh, a liberation force, in 1941. Back in Vietnam, the communist-led Viet Minh became a powerful nationalist organization as it mobilized the peasantry.

When the French tried to restore their rule in Vietnam after Japan's defeat in 1945, Ho led the resistance. War with France followed (1946–1954), featuring guerrilla tactics to undermine French positions. The Viet Minh were most successful in the north, but even in the south their campaign bled the French. Finally, in 1954, the anticolonial forces won a decisive military victory. At the Geneva Peace Conference, Vietnam (like Korea) was divided into two zones. Ho controlled the north, while a government with French and American support took charge in the south.

Although the French departed, decolonization in Vietnam was incomplete. North Vietnam supported the Viet Cong—communist guerrillas—who combined anti-imperialist nationalism with a land reform program that appealed greatly to the peasants. Determined to contain the spread of communism in Southeast Asia, the United States began smuggling arms to the regime in the south. During the early 1960s, U.S. involvement escalated. In 1965, large numbers of American troops entered the country to fight on behalf of South Vietnam, while communist North Vietnam turned to the Soviet Union for supplies. Over the next several years, the United States sent some 500,000 soldiers to fight the Vietnam War, but peasant support enabled the Viet Cong to continue fierce guerrilla fighting. Even the bombing of villages and the deployment of counterinsurgency forces

Ho Chi Minh. *Ho Chi Minh's formation of the League for the Independence of Vietnam, or Viet Minh, in 1941 set the stage for Ho's rise at the end of World War II. Here he attends a youth rally in October 1955, just over a year after the victory of his forces at Dien Bien Phu, which resulted in the ousting of the French from Vietnam.*

failed to prevent the spread of communism in Southeast Asia. In 1975, just two years after the final withdrawal of American troops, the South Vietnamese government collapsed.

Thus, the process of decolonization varied across regions. Although most of the lands in Asia and Africa had gained independence by the mid-1960s, there were significant exceptions in Africa (South Africa, Southern Rhodesia, and the Portuguese colonies) and in Asia (notably, Vietnam). Although the British and French realized that they no longer had the resources to stem the nationalist tide spreading through the Third World, they tried to use military might to regain control in areas with large European settlements, such as Kenya and Algeria. Here, too, however, local nationalists or communists eventually would seize control, ending direct imperial rule—but not western or Soviet attempts to interfere in the affairs of other states.

THREE WORLDS

World War II and postwar decolonization created a three-world order in which the liberal democratic and capitalist First World and the communist Second World competed for global influence, notably among the newly decolonized Third World states. Possessing nuclear weapons, superior armies, and industrial might, the Soviet Union and the United States had emerged from the war as the world's only superpowers. As decolonization spread, these Cold War belligerents offered new leaders their models for modernization. On one side, the United States, together with its western European allies and

Japan, had developed democratic forms of governance and a dynamic capitalist economy that produced immense quantities of affordable consumer goods. The Soviet Union, on the other side, trumpeted the Communist Party's egalitarian ideology and its rapid transition from being "backward" to highly industrialized. Both the First World and the Second World expected the decolonized Third World to adopt their models.

The decolonized, however, had their own ideas about how to modernize. Under Mao's leadership, China established full autonomy from the Cold War superpowers and implemented its own very radical form of modernization. Other postcolonial leaders, such as Nehru in India, developed unique mixtures of democracy and state planning. But in many decolonized nations in Asia and Africa, economies that had been exploited or left underdeveloped by colonial powers could not leap into industrial development, and they remained economically or politically dependent on western or Soviet states.

The First World

As the Cold War spread in the early 1950s, western Europe and North America became known as the First World, or "the free world." Later on, Japan joined this group. Following the principles of liberal modernism, First World states sought to organize the world on the basis of capitalism and democracy. Yet, in struggling against communism, the free world sometimes aligned with Third World dictators, thereby sacrificing its commitment to freedom and democracy for the sake of propping up pro-western regimes.

WESTERN EUROPE The reconstruction of western Europe after World War II was a spectacular success. By the late 1950s, most nations' economies there were thriving, thanks in part to massive American economic assistance. Improvements in agriculture were particularly impressive. With increased mechanization and the use of pesticides, fewer farmers were feeding more people. In 1950, for example, each French farmer had produced enough food for seven people; by 1962, one farmer could feed forty. And as industrial production boomed and wages rose, goods that had been luxuries before the war—refrigerators, telephones, automobiles, indoor plumbing—became commonplace. Prosperity and the dismantling of national military establishments allowed governments to expand social welfare systems, such that by the late 1950s, education and health care were within the reach of virtually all citizens.

In western Europe, the Cold War worked in various ways to prevent nations from joining the communist camp. Economic recovery blunted the appeal of socialist programs. The desire for stability over vengeance slowed down efforts to punish fascists, Nazis, and collaborators. Although war crimes trials brought the conviction of a number of prominent Nazis, the fear was that a complete purge of former Nazis would deprive Germany of political and economic leaders, leaving it susceptible to communist subversion.

THE UNITED STATES While Europe lay in ruins, the United States enjoyed economic expansion and a rising standard of living. The majority of Americans could afford more consumer goods than ever before—almost always U.S. manufactures. Home ownership became more common, especially in the burgeoning suburbs. Stimulating suburban development was a baby boom that reversed more than a century of declining birth rates. Indeed, in contrast to the gloomy 1930s, in the 1950s most Americans enjoyed unprecedented prosperity.

Yet, anxieties about the future of the Frist World abounded. Following the Soviet Union's explosion of an atomic bomb, the communist revolution in China, and the outbreak of the Korean War, fear of the communist threat prompted increasingly harsh rhetoric. In fact, anticommunist hysteria led the Republican senator from Wisconsin, Joseph McCarthy, to initiate a campaign to uncover closet communists in the State Department and in Hollywood. Televised congressional hearings broadcast his views to the entire nation, compelling elected officials to support a strong anticommunist foreign policy and a large military budget.

Postwar American prosperity did not benefit all citizens equally. During the 1950s, nearly a quarter of the American population lived in poverty. But many African Americans, a group disproportionately trapped below the poverty line,

Levittown. *In the decades after World War II, the American population shifted from the cities to the suburbs. To satisfy the demand for single-family homes, private developers, assisted by government policies, built thousands of new communities on the outskirts of urban centers. Places like Long Island's Levittown (pictured here), made affordable by the use of standard designs and construction, enabled many middle-class Americans to own their own home.*

Anticommunism. *As the Cold War heated up, anticommunist fervor swept the United States. Leading the charge against the "communist conspiracy" was Wisconsin senator Joseph McCarthy, pictured here with his aide, the attorney Roy Cohn.*

against injustices in the bus system of Montgomery, Alabama. Here and in subsequent campaigns against white supremacy, King borrowed his most effective weapon—the commitment to nonviolent protest and the appeal to conscience—from Gandhi. As the civil rights movement spread, the federal government gradually supported programs for racial equality.

THE JAPANESE "MIRACLE" Japan reemerged as an economic powerhouse in this period. The war had ended with Japan's unconditional surrender in 1945, its dreams of dominating East Asia dashed, and its homeland devastated. But after 1945, in an attempt to incorporate Japan into the First World, American military protection, investment, and transfers of technology helped to rebuild Japanese society. The Japanese government guided this economic development through directed investment, partnerships with private firms, and protectionist policies. By the mid-1970s, Japan, formerly a dictatorship, was a politically stable civilian regime with a thriving economy, enjoying considerable American guidance and the replacement of the emperor's power with a parliamentary system.

participated in a powerful movement for equal rights and the end of racial segregation. The National Association for the Advancement of Colored People (NAACP) won court victories that mandated the desegregation of schools. Boycotts, too, became a weapon of the growing **civil rights movement**, with Martin Luther King Jr. (1929–1968) leading a successful strike

The Second World

The Soviet Union and eastern European satellites, together with Mongolia and North Korea, constituted the communist Second World. The scourge of World War II and the shadow of the Cold War fell heavily on the Soviets. Having lost 70,000 Soviet

Civil Rights Movement. Left: *The 1955 arrest of Rosa Parks for refusing to relinquish her seat on a bus in Montgomery, Alabama, led to a boycott that brought Martin Luther King Jr. to prominence and galvanized the challenge to legal racial segregation in the American South.* Right: *Borrowing from Gandhi's tactics of nonviolent civil disobedience, protesters staged "sit-ins" across the southern United States in the 1950s and early 1960s, as in this photograph of black and white students seated together at a segregated lunch counter in Jackson, Mississippi.*

towns and villages, 32,000 factories, 82,000 schools, one-third of GDP, and 27 million people, the Soviet Union was determined to insulate itself from future aggression from the west. That meant turning eastern Europe, as well as parts of northeastern Asia, into a bloc of communist buffer states.

THE APPEAL OF THE SOVIET MODEL The Soviet model's egalitarian ideology and success with rapid industrialization made it seem a viable alternative to capitalism. Here there was no private property and thus, in Marxist terms, no exploitation. Workers "owned" the factories and worked for themselves. The Soviet state promised full employment, boasting that a state-run economy would be immune from upturns and downturns in business cycles. Freedom from exploitation, combined with security, was contrasted with the capitalist model of owners hoarding profits and suddenly firing loyal workers when they were not needed.

Soviet propaganda touted protections for workers, inexpensive mass transit, paid maternity leave, free health care, and universally available education. Whereas under the tsarist regime less than one-third of the Russian Empire's population had been literate, by the 1950s the literacy rate soared above 80 percent. True, Soviet policies did not provide material abundance of the sort that First World nations were enjoying. But if consumer goods were often scarce, in state stores they were cheap. Likewise, while it sometimes took ten years or more to obtain a small apartment through waiting lists at work, when one's turn finally came the apartment carried low annual rent and could be passed on to one's children.

Because of censorship, few inhabitants of the Soviet zone knew how people lived in the First World, so it was easy to believe in the advantages of the Soviet system. Yet, even when people learned about the prosperity of western Europe and the United States (usually from intercepting forbidden western TV and radio programs), many still contended that the Soviet Union was the more just society. Theirs, they believed, was a land with no racial or class divisions, no drive for foreign colonies, no imperialist wars over markets. If members of the Soviet elite lived in privileged circumstances, their luxurious lifestyles were often well concealed. Indeed, many of socialism's internal critics did not typically seek to overthrow the system and restore capitalism. Rather, they demanded that the Soviet regime introduce reforms that would create "socialism with a human face."

REPRESSION OF DISSENT Few outside the Soviet sphere knew just how inhuman Soviet communism was, and few within knew the extent of the brutality. Under Stalin, anyone suspected of opposing the regime risked imprisonment, forced labor, and often torture or execution. After the war, Stalin and the leadership tightened their grip. Surviving soldiers who had been prisoners of war in Germany and civilians who had survived being slave laborers for the Germans—and had therefore seen the better living conditions of the west—were sent to special screening camps. Many disappeared. By the time of Stalin's death in 1953, the vast gulag (labor camp complex) confined several million people, who dug for gold and uranium and survived on hunks of bread and gruel.

Stalin's successors had to face hard questions, including what to do with so many prisoners, many of whom were incarcerated for fabricated political crimes. This problem became acute when mass strikes rocked the camps in 1953 and 1954, forcing the regime's hand. In 1956, the new party leader, Nikita Khrushchev, delivered a speech at a closed session of the Communist Party Congress in which he attempted to separate Stalin's crimes from true communism. The speech was never published in the Soviet Union, but party members discussed it widely and it was leaked abroad. The extent of the arrests and executions under Stalin that Khrushchev revealed came as a terrible shock.

Repercussions were far-reaching. Eastern European leaders interpreted Khrushchev's speech as an endorsement for political liberation and economic experimentation. Right away, Polish intellectuals began a drive to break free from the communist ideological straitjacket. Soon Polish workers organized a general strike in Poznań—first over bread and wages, then against Soviet occupation. Emboldened by these events, Hungarian intellectuals and students held demonstrations demanding an uncensored press, free elections with genuine alternative parties, and the withdrawal of Soviet troops. The Hungarian Party leader, Imre Nagy, endorsed the campaign for reform and threatened to withdraw from the Warsaw Pact.

Soviet Model. *The rapid infrastructural development under Stalin was certainly a great feat, though it came at the cost of a great loss of human life. Displayed in this German poster is a map of new canals constructed in this period as part of Stalin's Five Year Plan.*

The Gulag. *The Soviet labor camp system was an integral part of the Soviet economy. At any given time, around 3 million prisoners labored in camps, like this one in Perm, Siberia, felling timber, building railroads, or digging for gold. Several million more were forced into exile in isolated locales. During World War II, the gulag population fell drastically, as inmates were sent to certain death at the front or perished from starvation. Between the war's end and Khrushchev's destalinization in the 1950s, the gulag system reached its peak, with German and Japanese POWs, the deportation of entire nations, and the Soviet internment of its own returnees from German camps.*

But the seeming liberalization promised by Khrushchev's speech proved short-lived. Rather than let eastern Europeans stray, the Soviet leadership crushed dissent. In Poland, the security police massacred strikers. In Hungary, tanks from the Soviet Union and other Warsaw Pact members invaded and installed a new government that aimed to smash all "counter-revolutionary" activities; Nagy was kidnapped, then murdered. After the revolts, Hungary and Poland did win some economic and cultural autonomy; but unquestionably, the Second World remained very much the dominion of the Soviet Union.

Despite the black eye it received from its crackdowns and arrests of nonconformists, the Soviet Union was undeniably a superpower. In fact, its status surged after the launching of Sputnik, the first satellite, into space in 1957. Students from Third World countries flocked to the Soviets' excellent education system for training as engineers, scientists, army commanders, and revolutionaries. The updated 1961 Communist Party program predicted euphorically that within twenty years the Soviet Union would surpass the United States and eclipse the First World, but the overwhelming emphasis on heavy industry left terrible scars both on the population and on the landscape. (See Current Trends in World History: Soviet Ecocide.)

The Third World

In the 1950s, French intellectuals coined the term **Third World** (*tiers monde*) to describe those countries that, like the "Third Estate" in the 1789 French Revolution, represented the majority of the population but were oppressed. By the early 1960s, the term characterized a large bloc of countries in Asia, Africa, and Latin America. All had experienced colonial domination and now aimed to create more just societies than those of the First

and Second Worlds. Their leaders believed that they could build strong democratic societies, like those in the west, and promote rapid economic development, as the Soviet Union had done. All this could occur, they felt, without the empty materialism of western capitalism or the state oppression of communist regimes.

The early 1960s were years of heady optimism in the Third World. Ghanaian prime minister Kwame Nkrumah trumpeted pan-Africanism as a way to increase the power of African nations in global politics. Egyptian president Gamal Abdel Nasser boasted that his democratic socialism was neither western nor Soviet and that Egypt would remain neutral in the Cold War struggle. Indian prime minister Jawaharlal Nehru blended democratic politics and vigorous state planning to promote India's quest for political independence and economic autonomy. Around Latin America, governments aggressively promoted industrialization and agrarian reform to break their dependence on exports and to break the grip of old elites.

LIMITS TO AUTONOMY Charting a third way proved difficult. Both the Soviets and the Americans saw the Third World as "underdeveloped" and as a place where they could showcase their competing virtues. Moscow championed central planning solutions, while Washington, D.C., sought to ensure that market structures and private property underlay modernization. Starting in the mid-1950s, institutions such as the **World Bank** funded loans for projects to lift societies out of poverty (such as providing electricity in India and building roads in Indonesia), while the **International Monetary Fund (IMF)** supported the new governments' monetary systems when they experienced economic woes (as in Chile, Ghana, Nigeria, and Egypt). Yet both institutions also intruded on these states' autonomy.

Another force that threatened Third World economic autonomy was the multinational corporation. In the rush to acquire advanced technology, Africans, Asians, and Latin Americans struck deals with multinationals to import their know-how. Owned primarily by American, European, and Japanese entrepreneurs, firms such as United Fruit, Firestone, and Volkswagen expanded cash cropping and plantation activities and established manufacturing branches worldwide. But such corporations impeded the growth of indigenous firms. Although the world's nations were more economically interdependent, the west still made the decisions—and reaped most of the profits.

Whether dealing with the west or the Soviet Union, Third World leaders had limited options because they faced pressure to choose one side or the other in the Cold War. To create more subservient client states, the Soviet Union backed communist insurgencies around the globe, while the United States supported almost all leaders who declared their anticommunism. Indeed, to contain communist expansion, the United States formed a number of military alliances. Following the 1949 creation of NATO, similar regional arrangements took shape in Southeast Asia (SEATO) and in the Middle East (the Baghdad Pact). These organizations brought many Third World nations into American-led alliances and allowed the United States to establish military bases in foreign territories. The Soviet Union countered by positioning its own forces in other Third World countries.

Nowhere was the militarization of Third World countries more threatening to economic development than in Africa. Whereas in the colonial era African states had spent little on military forces, this trend ended abruptly once the states became independent and were drawn into the Cold War. Civil wars, like the one that splintered Nigeria between 1967 and 1970, were opportunities for the great powers to wield influence. When the west refused to sell weapons to the Nigerian government so it could suppress the breakaway eastern province of Biafra, the Soviets supplied MIG aircraft and other vital weapons. A similar situation occurred in Egypt, a strategic region to both superpowers. After the founding of Israel, Egypt's new military rulers insisted that their country never again be caught militarily unprepared. Aware of the west's support for Israel, the Egyptians turned to the Soviet bloc. The resulting arms race between Egypt and Israel left the region bristling with modern weaponry.

Thus, Third World nations now confronted a situation that has been called **neocolonialism**. How were they to apply liberal or socialist models to their own situations? How were they to deal with economic structures and institutions that seemed to reduce their autonomy and limit their development? And how might they escape being puppets of the west or the Soviet Union? No wonder Third World nations grew frustrated about prospects for an alternative way to modernity.

By the late 1960s, as the euphoria of decolonization evaporated and new states became mired in debt and dependency, many Third World nations fell into dictatorship and authoritarian rule. Although some dictators still spoke about forging a third way, they did so mainly to justify their own corrupt regimes. They had forgotten the democratic commitments that were promised at independence. Most also had been drawn into the Cold War, the better to extract arms and assistance from one of the superpowers.

REVOLUTIONARIES AND RADICALS Against the background of bitterly disappointed expectations, Third World radicalism emerged as a powerful force. Revolutionary movements in the late 1950s and the 1960s sought to transform their societies. But while some radicals seized power, they, too, had trouble shaking the existing world order.

Third World revolutionaries drew on the pioneering writings of Frantz Fanon (1925–1961). While serving as a psychiatrist in French Algeria, Fanon (who was born in a French Caribbean colony) became aware of the psychological damage of European racism. He subsequently joined the Algerian revolution and became a radical theorist of liberation. His 1961 book *The Wretched of the Earth* urged Third World peoples to achieve catharsis through violence against their European oppressors.

THE MAOIST MODEL While Fanon moved people with his writings, others did so by building radical political organizations and undertaking revolutionary social experiments. One model was Mao Zedong. In 1958, Mao introduced the Great Leap Forward—an audacious attempt to unleash the people's energy. Mao's program organized China into 24,000 social and economic units, called communes. Peasants took up industrial production in their own backyards. The campaign aimed to catapult China past the developed countries, but the communes failed to feed the people and the industrial goods were inferior. Thus, China took an economic leap backward. As many as 45 million people may have subsequently perished from famine and malnutrition, forcing the government to abandon the experiment. The Great Leap also exacted a devastating environmental cost from the country. The drive for a dramatic—and unrealistic—increase in steel production, for example, led to widespread deforestation, as farmers everywhere made a mad dash to cut down trees for fuel for their backyard furnaces. In some areas, up to 80 percent of forestland disappeared, leading to severe problems of soil erosion and water loss.

Fearing that China's revolution was losing spirit, in 1966 Mao launched the Great Proletarian Cultural Revolution. This time Mao turned against his associates in the Communist Party and appealed to China's young people. They enthusiastically responded. Organized into "Red Guards," over 10 million of them journeyed to Beijing to participate in huge rallies. Chanting, crying, screaming, and waving the little red book of Mao's quotations, they pledged to cleanse the party of its corrupt elements and to thoroughly remake Chinese society.

CURRENT TRENDS IN WORLD HISTORY

Soviet Ecocide

Before the twentieth century, the spread of peasant agriculture, settlement in the steppe and forest zones, and the hunting of fur-bearing forest animals brought profound changes in the Russian environment, including soil degradation, deforestation, and depopulation of species. But the environmental impact of Soviet-era industrialization was staggering. No other industrial civilization poisoned its land, air, water, and people so systematically and over so long a time. Scholars have deemed the Soviet environmental catastrophe an "ecocide."

Soviet economic planners and propagandists celebrated the plumes of purple and orange smoke in their skies as evidence of their huge quantities of industrial production. Pollution control devices remained unheard of well after their 1950s introduction in Europe and the United States; even when installed in Soviet factories, they were rarely turned on so as not to depress output. Sulfur dioxide, hydrogen sulfide, and solid phenols in water, the food supply, and the air caused epidemic levels of respiratory and intestinal ailments, blood diseases, and birth defects. The giant steel plant at Magnitogorsk, once the pride of Stalin's industrial leap, became a zone of atmospheric and soil devastation 120 miles long and 40 miles wide; inside, chronic bronchitis, asthma, and cancers attacked the population.

In agriculture, the Soviet Union continued to use the pesticide DDT long after its 1972 banning in the United States. Despite the socialist country's overall development, in the 1970s Soviet life expectancy began to decline and infant mortality to rise. By 1989, Soviet men lived an average of 63.9 years, down from 66.1 in 1965. Infant mortality by the late 1980s rose to 25.4 per 1,000—roughly the same as in Malaysia, a developing country, and Harlem, in New York City. Alcoholism also contributed mightily to adverse health trends.

The April 1986 Chernobyl nuclear disaster exposed 20 million people in Ukraine and Belarus to excess radiation. Although there was no bomb concussion, the accident spewed more radioactive material into the atmosphere than had been released in the atomic bombs over Hiroshima and Nagasaki. The Chernobyl cleanup claimed around 7,000 lives. Soviet Uzbekistan, with twice the population of Soviet Belarus, was served by only one-third the number of hospitals.

Few symbols of Soviet ecocide surpassed the Aral Sea. Because of dams built for wasteful power plants and excess irrigation for cotton production, the Aral's volume shrank by two-thirds and gave way to huge white, lifeless salt marshes. Soviet cosmonauts looking down from space in 1975 were astonished to see immense storms of dust and salt over central Asia. Toxic salt rain wreaked enormous damage on human and animal lungs.

From the 1950s, Lake Baikal, the largest fresh body of water and once among the cleanest, suffered the construction

---

With help from the army, the Red Guards set out to rid society of the "four olds"—old customs, old habits, old culture, and old ideas. They ransacked homes, libraries, museums, and temples. They destroyed classical texts, artworks, and monuments. With its rhetoric of struggle against American imperialism and Soviet revisionism, the Cultural Revolution also targeted anything foreign. Knowledge of a foreign language was enough to compromise a person's revolutionary credentials. The Red Guards attacked government officials, party cadres, or just plain strangers in an escalating cycle of violence. Even family members and friends were pressured to denounce one another; all had to prove themselves faithful followers of Chairman Mao. As chaos mounted, in late 1967 the army moved in to quell the disorder and reestablish control. To forestall further disruption, the government created an entire "lost generation" when, between 1967 and 1976, it deprived some 17 million Red Guards and students of their formal education and relocated them to the countryside "to learn from the peasants."

Given the costs of the Great Leap Forward and the Cultural Revolution, many of Mao's revolutionary policies were hard to celebrate. But radicals in much of the Third World were unaware of these costs and found the style of rapid and massive—if deeply undemocratic—uplift of the populace attractive.

LATIN AMERICAN REVOLUTION Most Third World radicals did not go as far as Mao, but they still dreamed of overturning the social order. In Latin America, such dreams excited those who wished to throw off the influence of U.S.-owned multinational corporations and local elites.

Reform programs in Latin America addressed numerous concerns. Economic nationalists urged greater protection for domestic industries and sought to curb the multinationals. Liberal reformers wanted to democratize political systems and redistribute land, lest discontent erupt into full-blown revolutions like China's. But when liberals and nationalists joined forces, as in Guatemala in the 1950s, their reforms met resistance from local conservatives and from the United States. In Guatemala, the banana-producing American multinational United Fruit Company (which was the largest landowner and controlled the country's railroads and its major port) opposed land reform.

Aral Sea catastrophe. *What was once one of the largest lakes in the world shrank to less than 10 percent of its original size, due to the aggressive Soviet construction of irrigation canals in the 1960s to bolster cotton production. Here a shipping vessel is moored in the field of the former Aral Sea, in present-day Kazakhstan.*

meetings and signed their names to petitions to stop the damage and protect the environment.

Explore Further

Feshbach, Murray, and Alfred Friendly Jr. *Ecocide in the USSR: Health and Nation under Siege* (1992).

Wiener, Douglas R. *A Little Corner of Freedom: Russian Nature Protection from Stalin to Gorbachev* (2002).

of factories on its perimeter, especially a cellulose cord plant (for tires on Soviet bombers) and pulp plant (for paper). The threat to Baikal, as well as the Aral Sea catastrophe, sparked grassroots environmental groups in an otherwise tightly controlled Soviet society. Scientists led the way in breaking censorship taboos, and people from all walks of life turned up at unsanctioned

The Cultural Revolution in China. Left: *Young women were an important part of the Red Guards during the Cultural Revolution. Here female Red Guards, armed with their "little red books," march in the front row of a parade in the capital city of Beijing under a sign that reads "Rise." Right: In their campaign to cleanse the country of undesirable elements, the Red Guards often turned to public denunciation as a way to rally the crowd. Here a senior provincial party official is made to stand on a chair wearing a dunce cap while the young detractors chant slogans and wave their fists in the air.*

Still, the progressive and nationalist regime of Jacobo Arbenz persevered with plans for agrarian reform and proposed taking over uncultivated land owned by United Fruit. Despite Arbenz's intention of compensating the company for its land, the U.S. Central Intelligence Agency (CIA) plotted with sectors of the Guatemalan army to put an end to reform, culminating in a coup d'état. Through moves such as this, the United States warned other governments that Washington would not tolerate assaults on its national interests in what it deemed its backyard.

In Cuba, the failure to address political, social, and economic concerns spurred a revolution. Since the Spanish-American War of 1898, Cuba had been ruled by governments better known for their compliance with U.S. interests than with popular sentiment. In 1933, during the crisis resulting from the Great Depression, Sergeant Fulgencio Batista emerged as a strongman, and in 1952 he led a military coup that deposed a corrupt civilian government and made him dictator. Under the Batista dictatorship, sugar planters, casino operators, and North American investors prospered, but middle- and working-class Cubans did not. The latter demanded a voice in politics and a new moral bond between the people and their government. In 1953, a group composed heavily of university students launched a botched assault on a military garrison. One of the leaders, a law student named **Fidel Castro** (1926–2016), gave a stirring speech at the rebels' trial, which made him a national hero. After his release from prison in 1955, he fled to Mexico. Several years later, he returned and started organizing guerrilla raids from mountain jungles. In early 1959, his band of bearded rebels swept into the capital, Havana.

Castro then set about consolidating power, elbowing aside rivals and wresting control of the economy from the wealthy elite, who fled into exile. As his policies grew increasingly radical, American leaders began to plot his demise. When Castro announced a massive redistribution of land and the nationalization of foreign oil refineries, the United States ended all aid and sealed off the American market to Cuban sugar. Then, in 1961, the CIA mounted an invasion by Cuban exiles, landing at the Bay of Pigs. The invasion not only failed to overthrow Castro but further radicalized his ambitions for Cuba. He now declared himself a socialist and aligned himself with the Soviet Union. It was over Cuba and its radicalizing revolution that the world came closest to nuclear Armageddon in the Cuban Missile Crisis of 1962. To deter further U.S. attacks, Castro appealed to the Soviet Union to install nuclear weapons in Cuba—a mere 90 miles off the coast of Florida. When U.S. intelligence detected the weapons, President John F. Kennedy ordered a blockade of Cuba just as weapons-bearing Soviet ships were heading toward Havana. For several weeks, the world was paralyzed with anxiety as Kennedy, Khrushchev, and Castro matched threats. In the end, Kennedy succeeded in getting the Soviets to withdraw their nuclear missiles from Cuba.

Fidel Castro and Cuba's National Liberation. *The Cuban Revolution of 1958–1959 was a powerful model for many national liberation movements elsewhere in the world. No sooner did Cuban rebels force a break with the United States in 1959 than they discovered that they needed outside support to survive. The Soviet Union, eager to lay a toehold for communism close to the United States, began to provide economic and military subsidies to their Caribbean ally. Here Castro grasps the hand of Nikita Khrushchev atop the Lenin Mausoleum during Moscow's May Day parade in 1963.*

The Cuban Revolution was a turning point in the making of the Third World. By rejecting the power of capitalist industrial societies, Castro and his followers promoted revolution, not reform, as a way to achieve Third World liberation. The symbol of this new spirit was Castro's closest lieutenant, Ernesto "Che" Guevara (1928–1967). "El Che" grew up in Argentina and traveled widely around Latin America as a student. Shortly after receiving his medical degree in 1953, he arrived in Guatemala in time to witness the CIA-backed overthrow of the progressive Arbenz government. Thereafter, Guevara became increasingly bitter about American influences in Latin America. He joined Castro's forces and helped topple the pro-American regime of Fulgencio Batista in Cuba in 1958. After 1959, he held several posts in the Cuban government but grew restive for more action. Latin America, he felt, should challenge the world power of the United States. Soon his casual military uniform, his patchy beard, his cigar, and his moral energy became legendary symbols of revolt.

The idea of revolution as a way to overcome underdevelopment and to free Third World societies spread beyond Latin America. Che became Castro's envoy to world meetings and summits of Third World state leaders, where he celebrated the Cuban road to freedom. Returning to Latin America, Che set up his center of operations in highland Bolivia in 1966, among South America's most downtrodden Indians. "We have to create another Vietnam in the Americas with its center in Bolivia," he proclaimed. Guevara did not, however, know the local Indian language, and he had little logistical support. He and his two dozen fighters launched their regionwide war in absolute isolation. Thus, it took little time for the Bolivian army

Che Guevara. *Ernesto "Che" Guevara, shown here addressing a conference in Uruguay in 1961 at which he denounced U.S. interventions in Latin America, was a chief lieutenant to Cuba's Fidel Castro and a fierce champion of Third World radicalism.*

Latin American Human Rights. *By the early 1980s, human rights movements were gaining strength all over Latin America, even in Chile under the repressive General Pinochet. Here, a crowd of 400,000 demonstrates against his rule in November 1983.*

and CIA operators to capture the rebels. After a brief interrogation, Bolivian officers ordered that the guerrilla commander be killed on the spot.

To combat the germ of revolution, the Kennedy administration sent American advisers throughout Latin America to dole out aid, explain how to reform local land systems, and demonstrate the benefits of liberal capitalism. Working with American advisers, Latin American militaries were trained to root out radicalism. They learned that gaining the support of indigent civilians was the key to defeating the guerrillas. Even Salvador Allende's democratically elected socialist government in Chile was not spared; the CIA and U.S. policymakers aided General Augusto Pinochet's military coup against the regime in 1973 and looked the other way while political opponents were butchered. By 1975, rebel forces had been liquidated in Argentina, Uruguay, Brazil, Mexico, Bolivia, and Venezuela.

TENSIONS WITHIN THE THREE WORLDS

Third World radicalism did not alter the balance of global wealth and power, but it exposed vulnerabilities in the three-world order. So did the continuation of the Vietnam War, which opened fissures within the First World. As antiwar and civil rights movements mushroomed, the United States experienced social unrest on a scale not seen since the Great Depression. In the Second World, too, dissent challenged the Soviet Union's hold on world communism. Satellite states in eastern Europe

sought more flexible orbits, while Mao's China charted a course at odds with Soviet designs. Finally, in the 1970s, the rising fortunes of oil-producing nations and of Japan introduced new problems within and between worlds.

Tensions in the First World

Although the First World enjoyed great prosperity in the decades after World War II, a variety of issues created friction within these societies and between allies.

WOMEN'S ISSUES AND CIVIL RIGHTS In the First World, groups that believed they had been left behind in the surge of economic growth expressed deep unhappiness. One such group was women, whose economic and political opportunities remained severely restricted. In Italy, France, and Belgium, women did not obtain the right to vote until the end of World War II, and everywhere governance and high-paying jobs remained almost entirely in the hands of men. Although women made gains in employment outside the home, they still awaited a decrease in domestic responsibilities.

Another group, European students, expressed concerns about the deployment of nuclear weapons and about exclusive and unresponsive educational institutions that preserved the power and high culture of the elite few. Protests reached their peak in Paris in 1968 when workers joined with students in a general strike and clashed violently with police.

In the United States, a crescendo of protests against racial discrimination propelled the U.S. government to enact civil rights legislation and to promote programs designed to end poverty. The Civil Rights Act of 1964 banned segregation in public facilities and outlawed racial discrimination in employment, and

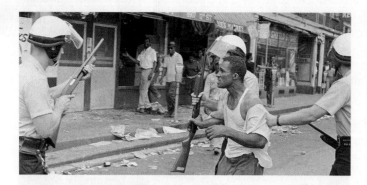

Urban Riots. *Racial tensions boiled over in a number of American cities during the 1960s. This photograph of a man being taken into custody was snapped on July 23, 1967, the first day of what turned out to be five days of rioting in Detroit. The unrest left 43 people dead, 467 injured, and more than 2,000 buildings burned down.*

the Voting Rights Act of 1965 gave millions of previously disenfranchised African Americans an opportunity to exercise equal political rights. The Lyndon Baines Johnson administration also supported programs bolstering social security, health, education, and assistance to the poor. Aided by impressive economic growth, the War on Poverty nearly halved the U.S. poverty rate.

But legacies of racism and inequality were not easy to overcome. In spite of Supreme Court decisions, most schools remained racially homogeneous not only in the South but across the United States, as "white flight" to the suburbs left inner-city neighborhoods and schools to minorities. Especially in Atlanta, Philadelphia, Detroit, Miami, and St. Louis, African Americans' frustration over discrimination and lack of jobs led to violence. Militant voices, like those of Malcolm X and the Black Panthers, became prominent. Instead of integration, these radicals advocated black separatism; instead of Americanism, they espoused pan-Africanism.

African American struggles inspired Native Americans, Mexican Americans, homosexuals, and women to initiate their own campaigns for equality and empowerment. Women now questioned a life built around taking care of home and family. In fact, the introduction of the birth control pill in 1960 and the publication of Betty Friedan's *The Feminine Mystique* in 1963 stand as watershed moments in American women's history. Because oral contraception allowed women to limit childbearing and to have sex with less fear of pregnancy, the resulting freedom helped unleash a sexual revolution. Moreover, Friedan blasted the myth of middle-class domestic contentment, describing the idealized 1950s suburban home as a "comfortable concentration camp" from which women must escape. Despite rising numbers of married women and college-educated women in the workforce, their compensation and opportunity for advancement lagged far behind those of men. (See Primary Source: Betty Friedan on "The Problem That Has No Name.")

ENVIRONMENTAL CONCERNS AND THE VIETNAM WAR A year before Friedan authored her challenge to the subordination of women, Rachel Carson published *Silent Spring*, a book that was equally revolutionary in its attack against long-held practices. In particular, Carson's book took on the use of synthetic pesticides such as dichlorodiphenyltrichloroethane (DDT), which she said caused cancer, devastated wildlife, and destroyed natural ecosystems. Although chemical manufacturers responded that pesticides had vastly multiplied agricultural yields, *Silent Spring* stirred opposition that ultimately led to the banning of DDT in the United States in 1972. More broadly, Carson's book spurred the development of an environmental movement that questioned many of the ideas about economic progress and material prosperity upon which the "American Dream" had rested.

The escalation of the war in Vietnam prompted many American college students to question the ideals of American

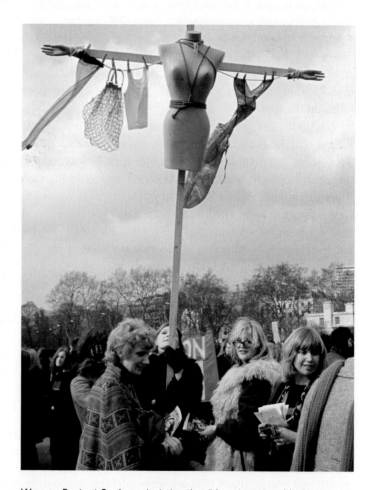

Women Protest Sexism. *Insisting that "the private is public," many women in the 1960s and 1970s argued that the problem of sexism went beyond equal rights and income equality: women's oppression began in the home, where they were treated merely as homemakers or as sex objects. At this 1971 rally in London, protesters suggested that women were being "crucified" by their association with these everyday objects: an apron, a net shopping bag, silk stockings, and an item of washing.*

PRIMARY SOURCE

Betty Friedan on "The Problem That Has No Name"

In 1963, Betty Friedan published The Feminine Mystique, *which challenged the idea that women found fulfillment solely by getting married, keeping house, and raising children. Friedan's book contributed to the rise of the women's movement in the United States. In this excerpt, Friedan writes about "the problem" that afflicted suburban housewives—a problem that, she suggested, was widely shared but as yet had "no name."*

The problem lay buried, unspoken, for many years in the minds of American women. It was a strange stirring, a sense of dissatisfaction, a yearning that women suffered in the middle of the twentieth century in the United States. Each suburban wife struggled with it alone. As she made the beds, shopped for groceries, matched slipcover material, ate peanut butter sandwiches with her children, chauffeured Cub Scouts and Brownies, lay beside her husband at night—she was afraid to ask even of herself the silent question—"Is this all?"

For over fifteen years there was no word of this yearning in the millions of words written about women, for women, in all the columns, books, and articles by experts telling women their role was to seek fulfillment as wives and mothers. Over and over women heard in voices of tradition and of Freudian sophistication that they could desire no greater destiny than to glory in their own femininity. Experts told them how to catch a man and keep him, how to breastfeed children and handle their toilet training, how to cope with sibling rivalry and adolescent rebellion; how to buy a dishwasher, bake bread, cook gourmet snails, and build a swimming pool with their own hands; how to dress, look, and act more feminine and make marriage more exciting; how to keep their husbands from dying young and their sons from growing into delinquents. They were taught to pity the neurotic, unfeminine, unhappy women who wanted to be poets or physicists or presidents. They learned that truly feminine women do not want careers, higher education, political rights—the independence and the opportunities that the old-fashioned feminists fought for.

Some women, in their forties and fifties, still remembered painfully giving up those dreams, but most of the younger women no longer even thought about them. A thousand expert voices applauded their femininity, their adjustment, their new maturity. All they had to do was devote their lives from earliest girlhood to finding a husband and bearing children.

By the end of the 1950s, the average marriage age of women in America dropped to 20, and was still dropping, into the teens. Fourteen million girls were engaged by 17. The proportion of women attending college in comparison with men dropped from 47 per cent in 1920 to 35 per cent in 1958. A century earlier, women had fought for higher education; now girls went to college to get a husband. By the mid-fifties, 60 per cent dropped out of college to marry, or because they were afraid too much education would be a marriage bar. Colleges built dormitories for "married students," but the students were almost always husbands. A new degree was instituted for the wives—"Ph.T." (Putting Husband through). . . .

The suburban housewife—she was the dream image of the young American women and the envy, it was said, of women all over the world. The American housewife—freed by science and labor-saving appliances from the drudgery, the dangers of childbirth, and the illnesses of her grandmother. She was healthy, beautiful, educated, concerned only about her husband, her children, her home. She had found true feminine fulfillment. As a housewife and mother, she was respected as a full and equal partner to man in his world. She was free to

choose automobiles, clothes, appliances, supermarkets; she had everything that women ever dreamed of. . . .

If a woman had a problem in the 1950s and 1960s, she knew that something must be wrong with her marriage, or with herself. Other women were satisfied with their lives, she thought. What kind of a woman was she if she did not feel this mysterious fulfillment waxing the kitchen floor? She was so ashamed to admit her dissatisfaction that she never knew how many other women shared it. If she tried to tell her husband, he didn't understand what she was talking about. She did not really understand it herself. . . .

If I am right, the problem that has no name stirring in the minds of so many American women today is not a matter of loss of femininity or too much education, or the demands of domesticity. It is far more important than anyone recognizes. It is the key to these other new and old problems which have been torturing women and their husbands and children, and puzzling their doctors and educators for years. It may well be the key to our future as a nation and a culture. We can no longer ignore that voice within women that says, "I want something more than my husband and my children and my home."

QUESTIONS FOR ANALYSIS

- What criticisms do you think were leveled at Friedan's book when it appeared in 1963?
- What criticisms have emerged in subsequent decades?

Source: Betty Friedan, Chapter 1, "The Problem That Has No Name," *The Feminine Mystique* (New York: Norton, 1963, 1974).

society. As the United States increased troop levels there in the 1960s, it conscripted more men. Tens of thousands of young Americans fled the country to escape the draft. Upward of 250,000 simply did not register; another 100,000 burned their draft cards. After President Richard Nixon sent American troops into Cambodia in 1970 to root out North Vietnamese soldiers, students at over 500 campuses occupied buildings and closed down universities. At Kent State University in Ohio, National Guardsmen attempting to stop the protests killed four students. One of the tactics used by the U.S. military was the spraying of the herbicide known as Agent Orange, used to destroy North Vietnamese crops and jungle hideouts. This chemical, which got its name from the orange barrels in which it was transported, gained notoriety as veterans and Vietnamese civilians claimed that this weaponized herbicide—more powerful than DDT—had caused severe damage to their health. The United States withdrew from Vietnam in 1973, but not before the divisions created by the war had strained the country almost to the breaking point.

Tensions in the Second World

The unity of the communist world also came under increasing pressure. As early as 1948, Yugoslavia had broken free of the Soviet yoke and embarked on its own road to building socialism. Other satellites within the Soviet bloc had more trouble freeing themselves. In 1956, Poland and Hungary had been forced back in line. Twelve years later, Czechoslovakia experienced the Prague Spring, in which communist authorities experimented with creating a democratic and pluralist socialist world. Workers and students rallied behind the reformist government of Alexander Dubček, calling for more freedom of expression, more autonomy for workers and consumers, and more debate within the ruling monopoly party. Once again, Soviet tanks crushed what they branded a "counterrevolutionary" movement. As the tanks rolled into Prague, the Czech capital, one desperate student doused himself with gasoline and lit a match—his public suicide a gesture of defiance against communist rule.

Thereafter, the Prague Spring served as a symbol for dissenters, who were divided between those who still wanted to reform socialism and those who wanted to overturn it. Underground reading groups proliferated throughout eastern Europe, and some Russians renewed their faith in Orthodox Christianity, their prerevolutionary religion. Many dissidents were exiled from the Soviet Union. Most famous by the early 1970s was the Russian novelist Alexander Solzhenitsyn. His masterwork, *The Gulag Archipelago*, repudiated the notion that socialism could be reformed by a turn away from Stalin's policies. Yet almost no one in the Soviet Union could obtain

Prague, Spring 1968. *In the spring of 1968, a movement demanding economic self-determination and freedom of speech took hold in Czechoslovakia, especially among students in its capital city, Prague. The Soviets allowed the movement to unfold for several months, but in late August they organized an invasion with troops and tanks from the USSR and several other Warsaw Pact countries. Although Czech students rallied to oppose the invaders—shouting "Ivan, go home!"—the Soviets suppressed the movement, afterward purging intellectuals from all leadership positions.*

copies of Solzhenitsyn's exposé, which had been published abroad and was a best-seller in the west. In 1974, the author himself was expelled from the USSR and took up residence in Vermont.

Still, there were important changes within the Second World. During the 1950s and 1960s, "national communism" became the rule throughout eastern Europe, even in countries that experienced Soviet invasions. National variations also arose within the Soviet Union, where Moscow conceded some autonomy to the Communist party machines of its fifteen republics—in exchange for fundamental loyalty. Dissidents were still persecuted, but by the 1970s, many fewer were executed or even arrested outright, and the population of the gulags declined.

Shared antipathy for the United States had created a Sino-Soviet alliance in the years just after the Chinese Revolution of 1949. By the late 1950s, the Soviet Union had contributed massive military and economic aid to China. But the Chinese increasingly sought to define their own brand of Marxism and criticized Khrushchev's efforts to distance himself from Stalin and reduce tensions with the United States and the west. Preferring to accentuate confrontation, the Chinese acquired their own nuclear weapons and began to tout themselves as a peasant-socialist alternative to the Soviet model of development, especially for Third World countries. The fissure raised China's profile throughout Asia and even in eastern Europe. Indeed, Romania achieved a measure of autonomy in foreign policy by playing off China and the Soviet Union. Albania declared its allegiance to China. African nations, interested in Soviet aid, increased their demands with subtle hints that they might consider deepening ties with China instead. In the 1970s, U.S. president Richard Nixon seized the opportunity offered by the Sino-Soviet split to woo Mao's China at Soviet expense.

Tensions in the Third World

In contrast to the First and Second Worlds, the Third World was never unified by economic, military, or political alliances. Despite a common history of domination and the shared search for a "third way," the Cold War polarized Third World nations. It pushed them to choose between alignment with the First World or the Second. Nonetheless, radicalism nourished new hopes for unifying and empowering the Third World.

One effort at collaboration was the formation in 1960 of a cartel of oil exporters. The Organization of Petroleum Exporting Countries (OPEC)—which included Algeria, Ecuador, Gabon, Indonesia, Iran, Iraq, Kuwait, Libya, Nigeria, Qatar, Saudi Arabia, the United Arab Emirates, and Venezuela—had little impact in raising oil revenues through the 1960s, even though several members nationalized their oil fields. But after the fourth major Arab-Israeli war broke out in 1973, OPEC's Arab members decided to pressure Israel's First World allies by halting oil exports to them. Overnight, the embargo raised oil prices more than threefold, a bonanza that enriched all oil producers and led to an oil crisis in the west. To many, the bulging treasuries of OPEC nations seemed like the Third World's revenge. Here were Saudi Arabian princes, Venezuelan magnates, and Indonesian ministers dictating world prices to industrial consumers.

But the realignment was not thorough. Third World producers of raw materials such as coffee and rubber tried unsuccessfully to duplicate OPEC's model, and OPEC itself had trouble controlling the world's oil market. During the 1970s, discoveries in the North Sea, Mexico, and Canada reduced pressures on the large oil-consuming states to be more fuel efficient. With supply up, prices fell. To compensate for lost revenue, various OPEC states raised their own production, putting further downward pressure on prices.

Nor did oil revenues help overcome poverty and dependency in the Third World as a whole. To the contrary, most revenue surpluses from OPEC simply flowed back to First World banks or boosted real-estate holdings in Europe and the United States. Some of it was in turn reloaned to the world's poorest countries in Africa, Asia, and Latin America, at high interest rates, to pay for more expensive imports—including oil! The biggest bonanza

went to multinational petroleum firms whose control over production, refining, and distribution yielded enormous profits.

For all the talk in the mid-1970s of changing the balance of international economic relations between the world's rich and poor countries, fundamental inequalities persisted. Those few Third World nations that appeared to break out of the cycle of poverty, like South Korea and Taiwan, did not achieve success through international markets. Rather, these states regulated markets, nurtured new industries, educated the populace, and required multinationals to work collaboratively with local firms. These were exceptions that proved the general rule: the international economy reinforced existing structures.

CONCLUSION

The three-world order arose on the ruins of European empires and their Japanese counterpart. World War II affirmed the nation-state rather than the empire as the primary form for organizing communities. In spite of the rhetoric of individualism and the free market, the war and postwar reconstruction also enhanced the reach and functions of the modern state. In the Third World, too, leaders of new nations saw the state as the primary instrument for promoting economic development.

The organization of the world into three blocs lasted into the mid-1970s. This arrangement fostered the economic recovery of western Europe and Japan from the wounds inflicted by war. These nations' recovery grew out of a Cold War alliance with the United States, where anticommunist hysteria accompanied an economic boom. The Cold War also cast a shadow over the citizens of the Soviet Union and eastern Europe. Gulags and political surveillance became widespread, while the Soviets and their satellite regimes mobilized resources for military purposes. The Third World, squeezed by its inability to reduce poverty, on the one hand, and superpower rivalry, on the other, struggled to pursue a "third way." While some states maintained democratic institutions and promoted economic development, many tumbled into dictatorships and authoritarian regimes and often suffered irreparable environmental damage.

In this context, Third World revolutionaries sought radical social and political transformation, seeking paths different from both western capitalism and Soviet communism. Though not successful, they energized considerable tensions in the three-world order. These tensions intensified in the late 1960s and early 1970s as Vietnamese communists defeated the United States, an oil crisis struck the west, and protests escalated in the First and Second Worlds. Thirty years after the war's end, the world order forged after 1945 was beginning to give way.

TRACING THE GLOBAL STORYLINES

After You Read This Chapter

Go to **INQUIZITIVE** to see what you know & learn what you've missed.

FOCUS ON: *World War II and a New Global Order*

WORLD WAR II

- World War II grows out of unresolved problems connected to World War I, especially the aggressive plans of Germany and Japan to expand their political and economic influence.

- The war brings huge human and material costs and ushers in an age of nuclear weapons.

- At war's end, the United States, fearing the spread of communism and Soviet influence, rebuilds war-torn Europe and Japan and creates military and political alliances to contain Soviet expansionist ambitions.

A NEW GLOBAL ORDER

- The Soviet Union and the United States become superpowers.

- Japan emerges as an economic powerhouse and a U.S. ally.

- A weakened Europe cannot resist demands for independence from Asian and African nationalists.

- Chinese communists engineer a revolution, while Indian nationalists and many African leaders achieve independence through negotiations.

- Elsewhere, especially in territories with large settler populations, decolonization is violent (Palestine, Israel, Egypt, Algeria, and Kenya) or incomplete (southern Africa).

- Actions by Latin American reformers and revolutionary insurgents spark counterinsurgency efforts by the United States and its regional allies.

- An insecure three-world order emerges after most Asian and African states achieve independence.

CHRONOLOGY

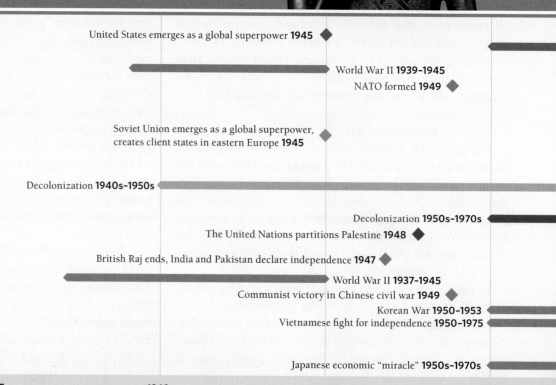

	1935	1940	1945	1950
The Americas			United States emerges as a global superpower **1945**	
Europe		World War II **1939–1945**	NATO formed **1949**	
Soviet Union			Soviet Union emerges as a global superpower, creates client states in eastern Europe **1945**	
Africa		Decolonization **1940s–1950s**		Decolonization **1950s–1970s**
Middle East			The United Nations partitions Palestine **1948**	
South Asia			British Raj ends, India and Pakistan declare independence **1947**	
East Asia		World War II **1937–1945**	Communist victory in Chinese civil war **1949** / Korean War **1950–1953** / Vietnamese fight for independence **1950–1975**	Japanese economic "miracle" **1950s–1970s**

KEY TERMS

STUDY QUESTIONS

1. **Explain** how World War II contributed to the development of the three-world order.

2. **Analyze** how World War II was a truly global war and why it led to the end of a European-dominated world. How did the war challenge the ideological justifications for imperialism?

3. **Define** the term *Cold War*, and **discuss** the roles played by the United States and the Soviet Union. How did the task of rebuilding Europe and Asia after World War II lead to the intense global rivalry between the two superpowers?

4. **Assess** the impact of nuclear weapons on state rivalries and superpower relations during the Cold War, and **evaluate** the role played by NATO and the Warsaw Pact.

5. **Discuss** the roles played by OPEC, the IMF, and the World Bank in postwar economic competition.

6. **Describe** decolonization, a process that dominated world affairs during these years. What forms did it take? **Analyze** where and why the process either turned violent or proceeded smoothly.

7. **List and explain** the tensions between the three worlds of the postwar era. How did Cold War rivalries affect the Third World?

8. **List and explain** the various goals, successes, and failures in the three competing worlds as they struggled to create "modern societies." What problems did the Third World face?

9. **Evaluate** the impact of Third World revolutionaries and radicals in transforming their societies. How successful were Mao Zedong and Fidel Castro in challenging the international status quo?

10. **Identify and compare** civil rights issues in the three worlds, and **describe** how each world addressed these and other rights.

11. **Describe** the tensions that emerged between 1945 and 1975 to challenge the three-world order. What challenges did they present for various states?

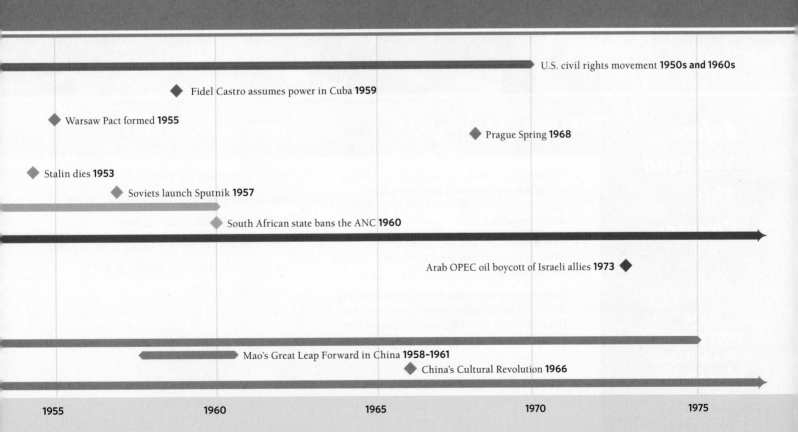

U.S. civil rights movement **1950s and 1960s**

Fidel Castro assumes power in Cuba **1959**

Warsaw Pact formed **1955**

Prague Spring **1968**

Stalin dies **1953**

Soviets launch Sputnik **1957**

South African state bans the ANC **1960**

Arab OPEC oil boycott of Israeli allies **1973**

Mao's Great Leap Forward in China **1958–1961**

China's Cultural Revolution **1966**

| 1955 | 1960 | 1965 | 1970 | 1975 |

Before You Read This Chapter

Go to INQUIZITIVE to see what you know & learn what you've missed.

GLOBAL STORYLINES

- Following the collapse of the three-world order, new global markets and communications networks integrate the world but also create deep inequalities.

- New technologies and vast population movements make global culture more homogeneous.

- Globalization, supranational organizations (like the World Bank, the European Union, and the United Nations), and religious fundamentalism erode the power of the nation-state.

CHAPTER OUTLINE

21

Globalization, 1970–2000

Consider the following comparison. In the thirteenth century, few people could imagine moving beyond their local region. Venetian explorer Marco Polo, who traveled through China, and Arab scholar Ibn Battuta, who traversed the Islamic world, were rare exceptions. In contrast, by the late twentieth century, people traversed in a matter of hours the distances that it took Marco Polo and Ibn Battuta years to cover. And many others staying at home could "travel" the world via the Internet, books, newspapers, and television.

But not all travelers moved about so comfortably. Many migrants—desperate to escape political chaos, religious persecution, or poverty—slipped across borders in the dark of night, traveled as human cargo inside containers, or used their own feet to flee their homeland. Billions of others still had no access to the global age's technological wonders and economic opportunities. Thus, while **globalization** (the development of integrated worldwide cultural and economic structures) created possibilities for some, it also caused deeper disparities.

Moreover, consider two different settings: a fishing village in the Amazon River basin and cosmopolitan Los Angeles. Picture an elderly Amazonian fisherman trying to teach his children their parents' tongue,

Cocama-Cocamilla, but to no avail. All his children speak Spanish instead. "I tried to teach them. It's like paddling against the current." Seven centuries ago, over 500 languages rang throughout the Amazon River basin. As of the year 2000, only 57 languages survived there. Evidently, one effect of globalization is to reduce diversity. But it can also increase local diversity. For example, Los Angeles, once the emblem of white, suburban America, became a cacophonous city with over 100 languages spoken in its public schools.

This chapter observes the impact of globalization in several ways: (1) the movement of families and groups, as well as goods and ideas, across boundaries that once divided religious, ethnic, and national communities; (2) the role of international financial organizations in addressing world financial issues; (3) the power of multinational corporations in transforming local markets into international ones; and (4) unexpected effects such as galvanizing discontent, sparking a revival of traditional religions (to counter secular and materialist influences) and driving deeper divisions among and within the world's regions—even while bringing them closer together.

GLOBAL INTEGRATION

The full impact of globalization remains unknown. Clearly, though, by the late twentieth century, the forces driving global integration—and inequality—were no longer the political empires of old. By the mid-twentieth century, the European empires had lost their sway. The Cold War and decolonization movements that had produced the three-world order had also lost their salience. Power structures in the First World, under such stress in the 1970s, did not crack. But those in the Second World did. Thus did the Cold War end with the implosion of the Soviet bloc. The Third World also splintered, with some areas becoming highly advanced and others falling into deep poverty; the term **developing world** obscured these differences. Now a new architecture of power organized the world into a unified marketplace with unhindered flows of capital, commerce, culture, and labor. By 2000, most societies had endorsed electoral systems and adopted some form of market economy.

Because the United States promoted these changes, globalization has looked to some like Americanization. The United States unquestionably stood as the world's most influential society, with its music, food, principles of representative government, and free markets spreading worldwide. Yet the process did not run one way. The world also came to America and shaped its society: people living in the United States—along with their inventions, sports stars, and musical inspirations—increasingly came from somewhere else.

Nor was the United States immune from transnational forces challenging the power of the nation-state itself. In the United States, as elsewhere, globalization functioned through networks of investment, trade, and migration that operated relatively independently of nation-states. In the process, globalization shook entrenched forms of political and social identification, including religious and military authority. Members of societies now often identified more with local, subnational, or international movements or cultures, rather than with nation-states. To be sure, nation-states remained essential for establishing democratic institutions and protecting human rights, but supranational institutions like the European Union and the International Monetary Fund (see later discussion) often impinged on their autonomy. As borders became more open, money, goods, and people flowed back and forth, further undermining the autonomy of nation-states.

REMOVING OBSTACLES TO GLOBALIZATION

In the mid-1970s, political practices and institutions associated with the three-world order started to deteriorate. By the late 1980s, the communist Second World was disintegrating. The collapse of the Soviet Union brought the Cold War to an end. At the same time, the capitalist First World gave up its last colonial possessions, and the remnants of white settler supremacy disintegrated. But as this occurred, the formerly colonized Third World's dream of a "third way" also vanished. As empires withdrew, they revealed a world integrated by markets for capital, labor, culture, and technology rather than by forced loyalties to imperial masters or other foreign powers.

Ending the Cold War

A world divided between two hostile factions limited the prospects for a global exchange of peoples, ideas, and resources. There was widespread exchange within the rival blocs—that is, among socialist countries and among capitalist countries—but for other countries the pressure from the Soviet Union and the United States to align with a superpower imposed limits to interaction, even with neighboring nations. A few countries, like Egypt, managed to switch sides (from the Soviets to the Americans), opening up some new global links while closing off others. Pushing against the Cold War superpower framework, however, were strong nationalist aspirations and religious movements, which the superpowers sought to control—or sought to inflame if they saw a chance to cripple their foe with a proxy war.

MOUNTING COSTS The many regional conflicts of the Cold War era (Vietnam, Afghanistan, Nicaragua) were deadly for countries caught in the ideological crossfire. Vietnam became a battleground for Russian, Chinese, and American ambitions. This war spilled over into Laos and Cambodia, dragging them to ruin along with Vietnam. China attracted several client states in the competition for influence in the Third World and within the communist bloc. In Afghanistan, Moscow propped up a puppet regime, only to fall into a bloody war against Islamic and tribal guerrillas financed and armed by the United States, Saudi Arabia, and Pakistan. In Central America, U.S. president Ronald Reagan and his advisers opposed the victory of the left-leaning Nicaraguan Sandinista coalition in 1979. During the 1980s the U.S. government pumped millions of dollars to the Contras (right-wing opponents of the left-wing Sandinistas) and lent military and monetary assistance to other Central American anti-communist forces. Thus, for much of the world, the Cold War was a real confrontation with tremendously high costs for local powers.

Rivalry was costly to the superpowers, too, for the 1970s and 1980s saw the largest peacetime accumulation of arms in history. Despite myriad treaties and summits, the United States and the Soviet Union stockpiled nuclear and conventional weaponry. Furthermore, in 1983 Reagan unveiled the Strategic Defense Initiative ("Star Wars"), a plan to use satellites and space missiles to insulate the United States from incoming nuclear bombs. For both sides, military spending sprees brought economic troubles. The U.S. national debt increased; Soviet life expectancy began to decline and infant mortality to rise.

Cracks on either side of the conflict appeared in the 1970s. The intelligence organizations of both the Soviet Union and the United States produced secret memos questioning whether the Soviet bloc could sustain its global position. As stalemate in Afghanistan undermined the image of the mighty Soviet armed forces, mothers of Soviet soldiers protested the regime's refusal to acknowledge the very fact of the war in which their sons were fighting and in some cases dying. The eastern European satellites became dependent on western European loans and consumer goods. At the same time, the western alliance itself faced internal tensions. In Europe and North America, the antinuclear movement rallied millions to the streets. Western industrialists worried about competition from Japan, which had been plowing money into rapid industrialization rather than arms. Political leaders also grappled with distressingly high unemployment rates. Thus, both sides shared a common crisis: fatigue from the Cold War and an economic challenge from East Asia.

THE SOVIET BLOC COLLAPSES In the end, the Soviet bloc collapsed. (See Map 21.1.) Even though planned economies employed the entire Soviet population, they failed to fill stores with sufficient consumer goods. Socialist health care and benefits lagged behind those of the capitalist welfare states. Authoritarian political structures relied on deception and coercion rather than elections and civic activism. Although the Communist Party had promised to beat capitalism by building socialism on

the way to achieving full communism, the latter paradise was nowhere on the horizon. The gap between socialism and capitalism was growing.

One catalyst in socialism's undoing was Poland. A critical event was the naming of a Polish archbishop as pope in 1978. The first non-Italian pope in 455 years, John Paul opposed the Soviet form of socialism. In 1979, he made a pilgrimage to his native Poland, holding enormous outdoor masses; in 1980, he supported mass strikes at the Gdansk shipyard, which led to the formation of the Soviet bloc's first independent trade union, Solidarity, led by a Polish nationalist and critic of Soviet control, Lech Walesa. As Communist Party members in Poland defected to its side, the union became a societywide movement; it aimed not to reform socialism (as in Czechoslovakia in 1968; see discussion of the Prague Spring in Chapter 20) but to overcome it. A crackdown by the Polish military and police put most of Solidarity's leadership in prison and drove the movement underground, but Soviet intelligence officials secretly worried that Solidarity could not be easily eradicated.

The most consequential factor in the collapse of the Soviet superpower was Mikhail Gorbachev, who became general secretary of the Soviet Communist Party in 1985 and launched an effort to reform the Soviet system. Under this effort (*perestroika*, "reconstruction"), Gorbachev permitted contested elections for a new Congress of Peoples' Deputies, relaxed censorship, sanctioned civic associations, legalized small nonstate businesses, granted autonomy to state firms, and encouraged the republics

Lech Walesa. *A Polish electrician from the Lenin Shipyard in the Baltic port city of Gdansk, Walesa spearheaded the formation of Solidarity, a mass independent trade union of workers who battled the communist regime that ruled in their name. He later was elected president of post-communist Poland.*

1989: Mass demonstrations, fall of the Berlin Wall
1990: Reunited with West Germany

1980 onward: Solidarity leads opposition
1981: Crackdown against Solidarity, driving it underground
1989: Solidarity wins 99 of the 100 seats in parliament that it is permitted to contest

1989: Mass demonstrations
1990: Multiparty elections
1993: Czechoslovakia splits into Czech Republic and Slovak Republic

1989: Removal of barbed wire on border with Austria allows East German tourists to cross westward
1990: Multiparty elections

1989: National uprising against Ceausescu
1992: First multiparty general election
1996: First noncommunist government

1990: Multiparty elections

1990: Multiparty elections
1991–1992: War between Croats and Serbs

1992: Fighting begins between Serbs and Bosnian Muslims
1995: Divided in two

1990: Multiparty elections
1991: Dissolved into warring states

1989: Loses autonomy from Serbia
1998–1999: Fighting between Serbs and ethnic Albanians
2000: First free elections

1989: Demonstrations
1990: Multiparty elections

1990: Multiparty elections
2001: Fighting erupts between Macedonians and ethnic Albanians

1990: Demonstrations, civil war
1991: Multiparty elections

✹ Civil unrest

MAP 21.1 | Collapse of the Communist Bloc in Europe

The Soviet Union's domination of eastern Europe ended precipitously in 1989. The political map of eastern and central Europe took on a different shape under European integration.

- What significant event in many communist countries signaled the collapse of communism?
- In what part of eastern and central Europe did the most political instability and conflict occur?
- According to your reading, why did the end of communist rule cause the reshuffling of political boundaries in the region?

to be responsible for their own affairs within the Soviet Union. These reforms were linked with dramatic arms control initiatives to ease the superpower burden on the Soviet Union. Gorbachev then began withdrawing troops from Afghanistan and informed

eastern European leaders that they could not count on Moscow's armed intervention to prop up their regimes.

Having set out to improve socialism, however, Gorbachev instead destabilized it. Civic groups called not for reform of the system, but for its liquidation. Eastern Europe declared its intention to leave the Soviet orbit, and some of the union republics began to push for independence. In response, disgruntled factions within the KGB (the main security agency of the Soviet Union from 1954 to 1991) and the Soviet military tried to preserve the destabilized old order by staging a coup attempt in 1991. However, the former Communist Party boss of Moscow, Boris Yeltsin, rallied the opposition, faced down the hardliners, and was elected president of the Russian republic in the Soviet's first democratic election in 1991. Under Yeltsin, Russia, like Ukraine and the other republics of the Soviet Union, became a refuge for beleaguered Soviet elites. Thereafter, they abandoned the cause of the Soviet Union and socialism and divided up state property among themselves.

When communist regimes collapsed, the European and Asian political maps changed dramatically. Old states disappeared, and new ones emerged. In Asia, although the division between North and South Korea remained, Vietnam was united and, along with China, welcomed western capitalism under Communist Party rule. In Europe, East Germany ceased to exist; West Germany absorbed its remnants after the Berlin Wall came down in 1989. (See Primary Source: Tidal Pull of the West: East Germany Disappears.) Soon after, Yeltsin and the leaders of Ukraine and Belarus formally dissolved the old USSR into independent states. (See Map 21.2.) But the end of Soviet-style socialism was not entirely peaceful. The worst carnage occurred in the former Yugoslavia, which suffered wars of dissolution as leaders exploited ethnic fears. Serbs and Croats, in particular, engaged in savage struggles over territories in the Balkans.

By historical standards the Cold War had been relatively brief, spanning four decades. But communism had played a major role in the military conflicts and the headlong modernization of Russia and China, and it exercised important influence on India and elsewhere in the Third World, where proxy wars were devastating. Communism, however, faced a trilemma: it could not keep up the Cold War *and* deliver the good life to its adherents *and* survive in a more competitive world economy. But ultimately, it was the inability to keep up with the consumption race more than the arms race that doomed the USSR and unleashed in the early 1990s economic and cultural energies that would buoy global integration.

Africa and the End of White Rule

Although the aftermath of World War II saw the dismantling of most of Europe's empires, remnants of colonial rule remained in southern Africa (see Map 20.6, on p. 767). Here, whites clung to centuries-old notions of their racial superiority over non-Europeans. Final decolonization meant that self-rule would return to all of Africa. The end of colonialism also set the stage for former colonies to find new trading and investment partners and to become more integrated with the wider world.

THE LAST HOLDOUTS The last fortresses under direct European control were the Portuguese colonies of southern and western Africa. However, by the mid-1970s, efforts to suppress African nationalist movements had exhausted Portugal's resources. As African nationalist demands led to a hurried Portuguese withdrawal from Guinea-Bissau, Angola, and Mozambique, formal European colonialism in Africa came to an end.

But white rule still prevailed elsewhere in Africa. In Rhodesia, a white minority resisted all international pressure to allow black rule. In the end, independent African neighbors helped support a liberation guerrilla movement under Robert Mugabe.

The Berlin Wall. *The breaching of the Berlin Wall in November 1989 spelled the end of the Soviet bloc. Decades of debate over whether communism could be reformed turned out to be moot. In the face of competition from the richer, consumer-oriented West, communism collapsed.*

PRIMARY SOURCE

Tidal Pull of the West: East Germany Disappears

After Soviet premier Mikhail Gorbachev instituted a series of reforms to save socialism, dissenters in eastern Europe saw their chance to throw off Russian dominance. The Berlin Wall (erected in 1961) was the most visible symbol of Soviet oppression. Here journalist Ann Tusa recalls the November 1989 press conference that accidentally led to the opening of the Berlin Wall. As both the wall and East Germany fell, Russia kept its nearly 400,000 troops that were on East German soil confined to their barracks.

At about 7 o'clock on the evening of November 9, 1989, some 300 journalists from all over the world are crammed into a room in East Berlin for a routine press conference.... For the first time since the foundation of a separate Communist East German state in 1946, the German Democratic Republic, there have been massive demonstrations against the regime....

East Germans, who have not known a free election since 1933, have been voting with their feet. From January to October 1989, some 200,000 people had left their country. By early November the figure was up to 250,000—and that was out of a total population of 16.7 million. At first, many East Germans went out on "holiday visas" to Iron Curtain countries [a term coined in 1946 to refer to the two-part division of Europe between the liberal democracies and the European states under Soviet domination], then claimed asylum in West German embassies in Warsaw, Budapest or Prague. Thousands more have driven or walked round the East German frontiers looking for an undefended crossing or a guard with a blind eye, wriggled across, then headed for Austria and a refugee camp....

The November 9 press conference is handled by Günter Schabowski.... This evening he feeds the press a startling hint that there might soon be free elections. Good story. Everyone wants to go out and file it. But then Schabowski turns up a sheet from the bottom of the pile of papers on his table. "This will be interesting for you." And in a style that suggests it is all news to him, slowly reads aloud: "Today the decision was taken to make it possible for all citizens to leave the country through the official border crossing points. All citizens of the GDR can now be issued with visas for the purposes of travel or visiting relatives in the West. This order is to take effect at once...."

The news is broadcast on an East German television bulletin at 7:30 P.M. The station's switchboard is immediately jammed with callers. "Is it true? I can't believe it." They always believed West German television, though, and it is soon flashing the announcement. A few East and West Berliners go to the Wall to see what is happening.... Then at 10:30 a discussion program on Sender Freies Berlin, the West Berlin television station, is interrupted by a live broadcast from the Wall. No preamble, just shots of a small crowd milling round a checkpoint, then a man runs toward the camera: "They've opened the crossing at Bornholmer Strasse." After that the news spreads like wildfire, by radio, television, telephone, shouts in the street. The trickle across the Wall swells to a flood. That weekend 2 million East Germans are reckoned to have stood in West Berlin. One reaction is common to them all: "We've seen the West on TV, of course. But this is real."

... The fatal piece of paper had been hurriedly swept up as he left for the press conference. It had never been intended for publication. It was a draft based on a recent Politburo decision: unable to control the tide of refugees, thrashing around for ways to quiet the demonstrators on the streets, they had decided that in their own good time they would ease travel restrictions, having first made arrangements for a limited issue of visas under carefully controlled circumstances.

QUESTIONS FOR ANALYSIS

- The Berlin Wall (and other border defenses) kept East Germans and West Germans apart for twenty-eight years. How did some East Germans try to circumvent the barriers during that time?

- Why didn't the 400,000 Soviet troops in East Germany intervene during the collapse of the Berlin Wall?

- What does this piece tell us about the state of mind of the East German government at this time?

Source: Ann Tusa, "A Fatal Error," in *Media Studies Journal,* Fall 1999, pp. 26–29.

Surrounded, Rhodesian whites finally capitulated. Mugabe swept to power with massive electoral support in 1979. The new constitutional government renamed the country Zimbabwe, erasing from Africa's map the name of the long-deceased British expansionist Cecil Rhodes (see Chapter 17). At first, President Mugabe worked well with the agriculturally and financially powerful former white ruling elite, but over time, under pressure from elements in his own party, he promoted land redistribution and turned against the white elite in ways that led to a steep economic decline and massive inflation.

MAP 21.2 | The Breakup of the Soviet Union

The Soviet Union broke apart in 1991. Compare this map with Map 17.6 (see p. 662), which illustrates Russian expansion in the nineteenth century.

- Which parts of the old Russian Empire remained under Russian rule, and which territories established their own states?
- In what areas did large migrations accompany the breakup, and for what reasons?
- According to your reading, how did the breakup of the Soviet Union change Russia's status in Europe and Asia?

SOUTH AFRICA AND NELSON MANDELA The final outpost of white rule was South Africa, where a European minority was larger, richer, and more entrenched than elsewhere in the region—and highly invulnerable to outside pressures. Although

powerful international firms operated there, they were reluctant to risk their investments by boycotting the racist regime. In addition, the U.S. government regarded South Africa's large army as a useful tool to fight Soviet allies elsewhere in southern

The End of Apartheid. *Nelson Mandela, running for president in 1994 as the candidate of the African National Congress, here casts a ballot in the first all-races election in South Africa. This election ended apartheid and saw the African National Congress take control of the Republic of South Africa.*

Africa. In any case, the ruling Afrikaner-led National Party used ruthless tactics against internal critics. Yet, in the countryside and cities, defiance of white rule was growing. Africans lobbed rocks and crude bombs (Molotov cocktails) at tanks and organized mass strikes in the multinational-owned mines.

At the same time, pressures from abroad to end the racist apartheid system were mounting. The International Olympic Committee banned South African athletes starting in 1970. American students insisted that their universities divest themselves of companies with investments in South Africa. As international pressures grew, foreign governments—even that of the United States, once South Africa's staunchest ally—applied economic sanctions against South Africa. A swelling worldwide chorus demanded that **Nelson Mandela**, the imprisoned leader of the African National Congress (ANC), be freed. The white political elite eventually realized that it was better to negotiate new arrangements than to endure international condemnation and years of internal warfare against a majority population. In 1990, President F. W. de Klerk (of the National Party) released Mandela from prison and legalized the ANC and the Communist Party of South Africa. Ensuing negotiations produced South Africa's first free, mass elections in 1994. These brought an overwhelming victory to the ANC, with Nelson Mandela elected as president. Majority rule had finally come to South Africa, and for the first time in centuries, Africans ruled over all of Africa.

In Nelson Mandela, South Africa's white rulers found a man of exceptional integrity and political savvy. He had spent more than two decades in prison, much of it at hard labor. But he looked beyond past injustices to ease the transition to full democracy. Besides, he was aware that with the country veering toward civil war, only a negotiated change would preserve South Africa's industries, wealth, and educational system.

The leaders of independent Africa faced immense problems in building stable political communities. Although they set out to destroy the vestiges of colonial political structures and to erect African-based public institutions, local contests for political power impeded this process. Ethnic and religious rivalries, held in check during the colonial period, now blazed forth. Civil wars erupted in many countries (most violently in Nigeria, Sudan, and Zaire), and military leaders were drawn into politics. Coups d'état were common. Nigeria, for instance, had six military coups between 1966 and 1999. By the 1990s, the continent was aflame with civil strife; armed conflicts that started with the Cold War endured well after it ended, even though white rule had finally come to an end throughout the entire continent.

UNLEASHING GLOBALIZATION

As obstacles to international integration began to dissolve, capital, commodities, people, and culture crossed borders with ever-greater freedom. Even though trade, foreign investment, migration, and cultural borrowing had long been hallmarks of modern history, the global age changed their scale. At the same time, never had there been such unequal access to the fruits of globalization. Several factors contributed to increasing integration and to new power arrangements: international banking, expanded international trade, population migrations, and technical breakthroughs in communications that facilitated the worldwide spread of cultural influences.

Finance and Trade

The increased international flow of goods and capital was well under way in the 1970s, but the end of the Cold War removed many impediments to globalization. During the 1990s, even the strongest nation-states felt the effects of economic globalization.

GLOBAL FINANCE AND DEREGULATED MARKETS

Major transformations occurred in the world's financial system in the 1970s. America's budget and trade deficits prompted President Richard Nixon to take the dollar off the gold standard, an action that enabled the yen, the lira, the pound, the franc, and other national currencies to cut their ties to the American dollar. Now international financiers enjoyed greater freedom from national regulators and found fresh business opportunities.

The primary agents of the heightened global financial activity were banks. Based mainly in London, New York, and Tokyo, big banks attracted large amounts of capital for lucrative ventures around the world. Revenues from oil producers provided a large infusion of cash into the global economy in the 1970s. At the same time, banks joined forces to issue mammoth loans to developing nations.

No international financial organization was more influential than the International Monetary Fund (IMF), which came into existence after World War II with a view to raising capital from all the participating states so as to be able to lend funds to states coping with balance-of-payments shortages. During the 1980s, it emerged as a central player, especially in response to a global debt crisis. This would be the first in a series of worldwide financial shocks that summoned new global actors above and beyond nation-states. Throughout the 1970s, European, Japanese, and North American banks had loaned money on very easy terms to cash-strapped Third World and eastern-bloc borrowers. But what was once good business soon turned sour. In 1982, a wave of defaults threatened to overrun Latin America in particular. South Korea, Egypt, and the Philippines also got hit. Throughout the 1980s, international banks and the IMF kept heavily indebted customers solvent. The IMF offered short-term loans to governments on strict conditions: balance budgets; compel civilian populations to give up subsidies on essential products, especially food products; slash imports; and boost exports. Latin Americans led the way in deregulating markets, reorganizing their finances, and promoting a return to a growth model based on exports and foreign markets. All across the world, tariffs and other barriers to foreign trade crumbled, state enterprises became private firms, and foreign banks and multinational companies took a greater interest in investing in these newly reformed economies. It was in developing countries, however, that the shift to globalism was most dramatic—and most destabilizing.

EFFECTS OF INTEGRATED NETWORKS

New technologies and institutions enabled many more financial investors and traders to participate in the integrated networks of world finance. The Internet and online trading accelerated the mobility—and volatility—of capital across borders. Volatility soon created problems, however. In the 1990s, currency devaluations in Mexico, in Russia, and across East Asia shocked financiers. When the Mexican economy became paralyzed in 1994, the crisis was so extreme that not even the IMF could bail it out; the U.S. Treasury had to issue the largest international loan in history to pull Mexico out of its economic tailspin. Despite acting as the lender in that instance, the United States emerged in the new financial order as the world's largest borrower, because it imported far more than it exported. Early in the new millennium, its net foreign debt soared past $2 trillion—a 700 percent increase since the early 1990s. Much of this debt was owed to China, which racked up huge trade surpluses with the United States.

Globalization deepened commercial, as well as financial, interdependence. The total value of world trade increased nearly tenfold between 1973 and 1998, and trade in Asia grew even faster. In 1960, trade accounted for 24 percent of the global gross domestic product (GDP; the total value of all goods and services produced in a country in a single year). By 1995, that share had almost doubled. Where an American would once have worn American-made clothes (Levi's), driven an American car (a Ford), and watched an American television (Zenith), such was rarely the case by century's end. Increasingly, consumers bought foreign goods and services and manufacturers sold a greater share of their own output abroad. This pattern had always been true of smaller regions like Central America and southern Africa. But in the 1980s, it intensified as countries with cheap and skilled labor, like China, India, and Brazil, could set up their own manufacturing capacity and outbid their competitors, who then entered a long cycle of what is called deindustrialization. It was in this fashion that globalization led to the worldwide spread of manufacturing.

International trade also shifted the international division of labor. After World War II, Europeans and North Americans dominated manufacturing, while Third World countries supplied raw materials. But by the 1990s, this was no longer the case. Brazil became a major airplane maker, South Korea exported millions of automobiles, and China emerged as the world's largest source of textiles, footwear, and electronics.

The most remarkable global shift involved East Asian industry and commerce. Manufactured goods, including high-technology products, now issued from the eastern fringe of Afro-Eurasia as often as from its western fringe. Japan blazed the Asian trail: between 1965 and 1990, its share of world trade doubled to almost 10 percent. China, too, flexed its economic muscle. When Deng Xiaoping took power in 1978, China was already a growing economy. Under Deng, China started to

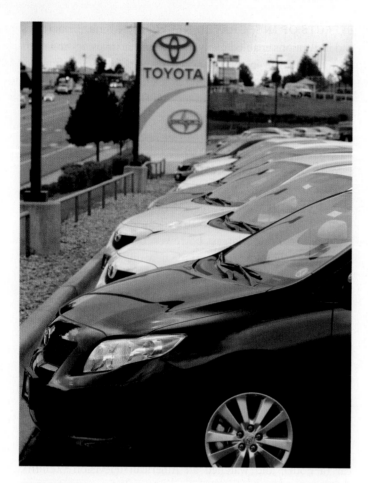

Globalization. *In the past, Americans mostly bought products, such as cars, that were manufactured domestically. Now Americans often buy products made abroad.*

become an economic powerhouse. For the next two decades, China chalked up astounding 10 percent annual growth rates, swelling its share of world GDP from 5 percent to 12 percent. Its share of world trade was even more astounding: China leaped from a meager 0.89 percent of world export shares in 1980 to 10 percent in 2011, muscling past the United States.

For East Asia as a whole, the share of world exports doubled in the same period, with smaller countries like Singapore, Taiwan, South Korea, and Hong Kong becoming mini-powerhouses. By the early 1990s, these countries and Japan were major investors abroad. As East Asia's share of world production quickly increased, the U.S. and European shares decreased.

REGIONAL TRADE BLOCS AND GROWING DISPARITIES Industrialization of previously less developed countries, combined with lower trade barriers, increased the pressures of world competition on national economies. Some areas responded by establishing regional trade blocs in an effort to create larger markets for themselves and stay competitive in an even more integrated world economy.

Meanwhile, the most complete regional integration occurred in Europe. Indeed, Europeans slashed trade barriers and harmonized their commercial policies toward the rest of the world. In 1993, the Maastricht Treaty established the **European Union (EU)** and what had been conceived as a trading and financial bloc began to evolve into a political union as well. In hopes of establishing permanent peace and prosperity, European states agreed to give up aspects of their sovereignty and allow European-wide legislative and judicial bodies (the European Parliament and the Court of Justice of the European Union) to make binding political and legal decisions. In 2002, a number of the European Union states deepened their economic interdependence by adopting a single currency, the euro. A few nations—most notably the United Kingdom—did not want to give up control of their own currency. By 2016, the European Union had twenty-eight members, with nineteen members using the euro.

Although international trade then increased, it also became increasingly unequal. High-technology and high-value goods now occupied an ever-greater share of the manufacturing and exports of the world's richest countries. For "rich" countries as a whole, about half of total GDP reflected the production and distribution of such goods and services, giving those countries a competitive advantage. In general, where global incomes were lower and people were less educated, the share of knowledge as a contributor to wealth was also lower. Poor nations remained, with few exceptions, locked in the production of low-tech goods and the export of raw materials. Increasingly, technology and knowledge now divided the world into affluent, technically sophisticated countries and poor, technically underdeveloped regions.

Migration

Migration, a constant feature of world history, became more pronounced in the twentieth century. (See Map 21.3.) After 1970, fewer Europeans were on the move, but many more Asians, Africans, and Latin Americans were chasing jobs in the richer countries. By 2000, there were 120 million migrants scattered across 152 countries, up from 75 million in 1965.

PATTERNS OF MIGRATION Migratory flows often followed the contours of past colonial and political ties. Where North America and Europe had had colonies or dependencies, their political withdrawal left tracks for migrants to follow. Indians and Pakistanis moved to Britain. Dominicans, Haitians, and Mexicans went to the United States. Algerians and Vietnamese moved to France. And where emerging rich societies cultivated close diplomatic ties, these relations opened migratory gates. This was true of Germany's relationship with Turkey, of Japan's with South Korea, and of Canada's with Hong Kong. In most cases, economic factors propelled migrants across national borders.

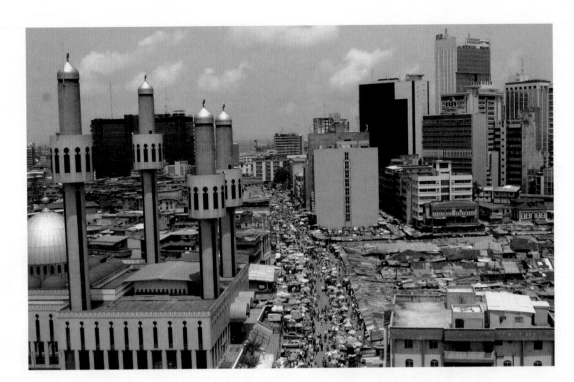

Lagos, Nigeria. *During the twentieth century, Lagos was one of the fastest-growing and most crowded cities in Africa.*

International migration was often an extension of regional and national migration from poorer, rural areas to urban centers. In Nigeria, for example, rural-urban migration intensified after 1970. In 1900, Nigeria's capital at the time, Lagos, had a population of 41,847. At the century's end, Lagos had more than 10 million people, with predictions that it would double by 2025. The key to Lagos's boom in the 1970s was the existence of large oil reserves inside the country and the high prices that oil fetched in international markets. When the Organization of Petroleum Exporting Countries (OPEC) sent oil prices soaring, money poured into Nigeria. The government kept most of it in its largest city. That, in turn, spurred people to move to Lagos. This rural-urban migration increased Lagos's population by 14 percent per year in the 1970s and 1980s. No government—least of all a new, weakly supported one like Nigeria's—could cope with such a huge influx. Electricity supplies failed regularly. There were never enough schools, teachers, or textbooks. But the city burst with the vitality of new arrivals, prompting one immigrant to exclaim: "It's a terrible place; I want to go there!"

One of the biggest changes in world migration patterns took place in the United States. Having all but closed its coastal borders on the Pacific in the late nineteenth century and on the Atlantic in the 1920s, the United States enacted a major immigration reform in 1965 that opened its gates to the world's migrants. By 2000, 27 million immigrants lived there, accounting for almost 10 percent of the population—double the share in 1970 and approaching levels not seen since the early twentieth century. The profile of migration also changed. In 1970, there were more Canadians or Germans living in the United States than Mexicans. Over the next thirty years, the Mexican influx rose tenfold and by 2000 accounted for almost one-third of immigrants in the United States. The numbers migrating from Asia also surged, accounting for over 40 percent of all immigrants to the United States in the 1990s.

TEMPORARY MIGRANTS Some migrants moved for temporary sojourns. At least that was the original intent. In the 1950s and 1960s, southern Europeans moved northward; but when Spain, Portugal, Greece, and Italy also became wealthy societies, not only did the exodus decline, but these countries became magnets for Middle Eastern, North African, South Asian, and then eastern European migrants. The economic downturn in Europe in the 1970s, however, resulted in high unemployment and made integration difficult. Most migrants from Asia and Africa went initially to Europe in search of temporary jobs as guest workers. With time, they and their families who followed them settled in their host countries, often living in dilapidated public housing projects, isolated from city centers and public services. The existence of welfare programs made them less likely to leave and return "home" than earlier generations of labor migrants.

In Japan, too, immigrants were not easily incorporated. Tokyo's policy in the 1970s resembled the European guest worker program. Discouraging permanent settlement and immigration, Japan encouraged mainly itinerant workers to move to the country, and yet its economy required increasing numbers of these sojourners. Indeed, Japan's deep reluctance to integrate migrants led to dire labor shortages.

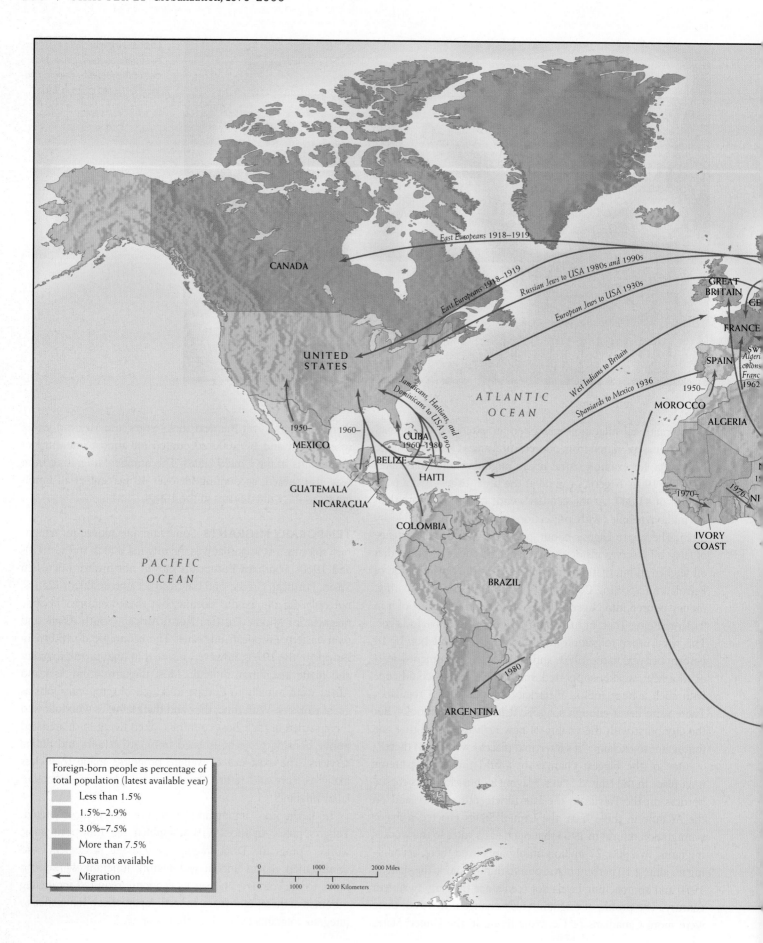

East Europeans 1918–1919

East Europeans 1918–1919

Russian Jews to USA 1980s and 1990s

European Jews to USA 1930s

West Indians to Britain

Spaniards to Mexico 1936

Jamaicans, Haitians and Dominicans to USA 1990s

CANADA

UNITED STATES

1950–

1960–

MEXICO

CUBA
1960–1980

BELIZE

HAITI

GUATEMALA

NICARAGUA

COLOMBIA

BRAZIL

1980

ARGENTINA

ATLANTIC OCEAN

PACIFIC OCEAN

GREAT BRITAIN

GE

FRANCE

SW

Algeri
colons
Franc
1962

SPAIN

1950–

MOROCCO

ALGERIA

N

1970–

1970– NI

IVORY COAST

Foreign-born people as percentage of
total population (latest available year)

Less than 1.5%

1.5%–2.9%

3.0%–7.5%

More than 7.5%

Data not available

→ Migration

0 — 1000 — 2000 Miles

0 — 1000 — 2000 Kilometers

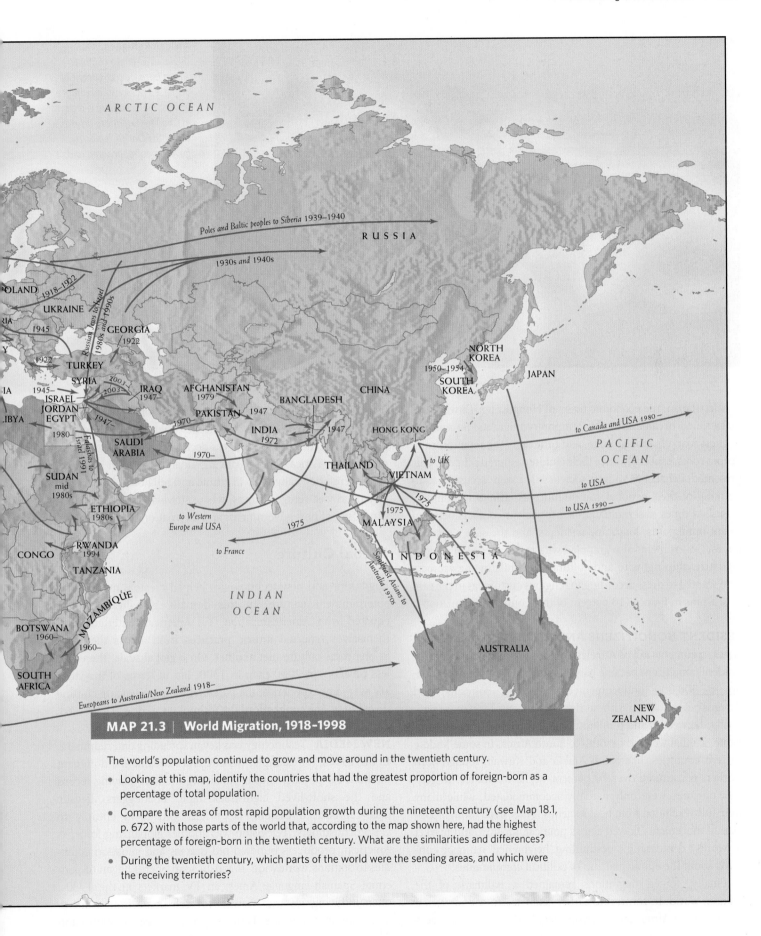

ARCTIC OCEAN

Poles and Baltic peoples to Siberia 1939–1940

RUSSIA

1930s and 1940s

POLAND

1918–1922

UKRAINE

Russian Jews to Israel 1980s and 1990s

1945

GEORGIA 1922

1922

TURKEY

SYRIA 2002 2003

IRAQ 1947

AFGHANISTAN 1979

BANGLADESH

CHINA

NORTH KOREA

1950–1954

SOUTH KOREA

JAPAN

1945–

ISRAEL JORDAN EGYPT

1947–

PAKISTAN 1947

1970–

INDIA 1972

1947

HONG KONG

to Canada and USA 1980 –

PACIFIC OCEAN

LIBYA

1980–

Falashas to Israel 1991

SAUDI ARABIA

1970–

THAILAND

VIETNAM

to UK

to USA

SUDAN mid 1980s

to Western Europe and USA

1975

1975

MALAYSIA

1975

to USA 1990 –

ETHIOPIA 1980s

1975

to France

INDONESIA

CONGO

RWANDA 1994

TANZANIA

Southeast Asians to Australia 1970s

INDIAN OCEAN

MOZAMBIQUE

BOTSWANA 1960–

1960–

AUSTRALIA

SOUTH AFRICA

Europeans to Australia/New Zealand 1918–

NEW ZEALAND

MAP 21.3 | World Migration, 1918–1998

The world's population continued to grow and move around in the twentieth century.

- Looking at this map, identify the countries that had the greatest proportion of foreign-born as a percentage of total population.

- Compare the areas of most rapid population growth during the nineteenth century (see Map 18.1, p. 672) with those parts of the world that, according to the map shown here, had the highest percentage of foreign-born in the twentieth century. What are the similarities and differences?

- During the twentieth century, which parts of the world were the sending areas, and which were the receiving territories?

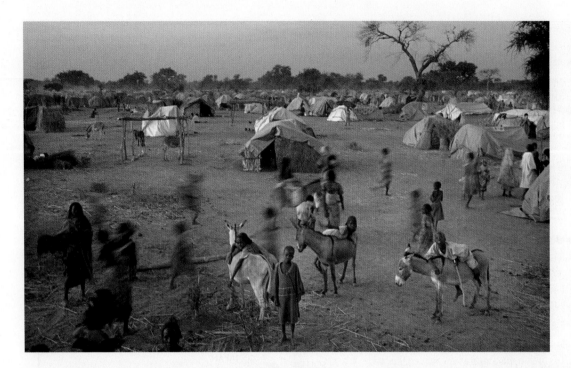

African Refugees. *During the late twentieth century, Africa became a continent of displaced persons and refugee camps. Pictured here is a camp in Chad for Sudanese driven out of the Darfur region by government-sponsored raids.*

After Japan, the economic tigers of Hong Kong, Taiwan, and Malaysia all became hosts for temporary migrants. So millions of guest workers moved there, and ultimately the migrants sank deeper roots, especially once their children entered schools. This presented a challenge to host societies that were accustomed to thinking of their national communities as ethnically homogeneous. At times, discrimination led to violent conflicts between recent immigrants, long-time residents, and the state's security forces. Governments also grappled with the challenge of extending citizenship rights to and culturally assimilating newcomers who wanted to dress according to religious custom, as in the case of Muslims in France (10 percent of that country's population).

RESIDENT NONCITIZENS AND REFUGEES In the United States, arguments in Los Angeles over schools and health care for resident noncitizens became part of a global debate. In Argentina, up to 500,000 undocumented Peruvians, Bolivians, and Paraguayans also lived without rights as citizens. Even more staggering, between 3 and 8 million migrants moved from Mozambique, Zimbabwe, and Lesotho to South Africa. In some Middle Eastern countries, like Saudi Arabia and Kuwait, foreign-born workers constituted over 70 percent of the workforce. In general, migrants were only partially accommodated, while many were fully excluded from host societies. Thus, even though population movements flowed across political, kinship, and market networks, demographic reshuffling heightened national concerns about the ethnic makeup of political communities.

Finally, forced migrations remained a hallmark of the modern world. In contrast to earlier centuries' forced migration of slaves from Africa, recent involuntary flows involved refugees

fleeing civil war and torture. Many suffered for weeks, months, or years in refugee camps on the periphery of violence. The greatest concentration of refugees occurred in the world's poorest region—Africa. Those Africans unable to reach wealthier areas were often caught up in ethnic and religious conflicts that generated vast refugee camps, where survival depended on the generosity of host governments and international contributions.

Global Culture

Migrations and new technologies helped create a more global entertainment culture. In this domain, globalization often equated with Americanization. Yet American entertainments themselves reflected artistic practices from across the globe as one mass culture met another. On a global scale, there was less diversity in 2000 than in 1300; but in terms of individuals' everyday experience, the potential for experiencing cultural diversity (if one could afford the technology to do so) increased.

NEW MEDIA Technology was key in spreading entertainment. In the 1970s, for example, cassette tapes became the dominant medium for popular music, sidelining the long-playing record and the short-lived eight-track tape. Bootleggers illegally mass-reproduced cassette tapes and sold them cheaply to young consumers. Television was another globalizing force, as American producers bundled old dramas and situation comedies to stations worldwide. Brazilian soap operas began to penetrate Spanish-language American TV markets in the 1980s, often inducing Mexican viewers to rush home from work to catch the latest episode. Latin American television shows and music were distributed in the United States in areas with large Spanish-speaking populations. Bombay also produced its fair share of programs for viewers of British television and today produces roughly twice as many films per year as Hollywood. (See Current Trends in World History: Urbanization as a Global Phenomenon: Transforming Bombay to Mumbai.) In terms of box office revenues, Hollywood remains the world's leading producer of films, helped in no small measure by its ability to export movies across borders and turn actors from around the world into global celebrities.

Television's globalizing effects were especially evident in sports. Soccer (known as football outside the United States) became an international passion, with devoted national followings for national teams. Indeed, by the 1980s, soccer was *the* world sport, with television ratings increasingly determining its schedule. Organizers of the 1986 World Cup in Mexico insisted that big soccer matches take place at midday so that games could be televised live at prime time in Europe, despite teams' having to play under the scorching sun. In many parts of the globe, major American sports made particularly deep inroads as more foreigners participated in them and as television broadcast American games in other countries. The National Basketball Association (and the athletic footwear firm Nike) was particularly successful in international marketing; in the process, it made Michael Jordan the world's best-known athlete in the late twentieth century.

CULTURAL EXCHANGES Technology was not the only driving force of world cultures, for migration and exchange were also important. For example, as people moved around, they brought their own musical tastes and borrowed others. Reggae, born in the 1960s among Jamaica's Rastafarians, became a hit sensation in London and Toronto, where large West Indian communities had migrated. Reggae lyrics and realist imagery invoked a black countercultural sensibility and a redemptive call for a return to African roots. Soon, Bob Marley and the Wailers, reggae's flagship band, played to audiences worldwide. In northeastern Brazil, where African culture emerged from decades of disdain, Bob Marley became a folk hero. In Soweto, South Africa, populated by black workers, he was a symbol of resistance.

Reggae propelled a shift in black American music. In broadcasting reggae, disc jockeys merged sounds and chanted lyrics over a beat, a "talkover" form that soon characterized rap music as well. This was a disruptive concept in the late 1970s, but within ten years rap had become mainstream. Rap lyrics emulated reggae realism by focusing on black problems, but they also opened a new domain of controversies involving gang worldviews. On the world stage, Latino rappers stressed multicultural themes, often in "Spanglish." Asian rap stressed the genre as a vehicle for cross-cultural sharing.

The effects of migration on global music were also evident in Latin American transformations of North American genres. Latin

Bob Marley. *In the 1970s, young Europeans and North Americans began to listen to music from the Third World. Among the most popular was Jamaican-based reggae, and its most renowned artist was Bob Marley. Marley's music combined rock and roll with African rhythms and lyrics about freedom and redemption for the downtrodden of the world.*

music came into its own thanks to Latin American migrants to the United States. In New York and New Jersey, Puerto Ricans and Dominicans popularized boogaloo, salsa, and merengue. In Los Angeles, Mexican *corridos* (ballads) became pop hits.

What reinforced cross-cultural borrowing was not just the medium of production and distribution of entertainment across borders, but also the message. Increasingly, world popular culture was youth culture—especially its message of generational opposition. Consider Egypt's popular TV serial *The School of Troublemakers*, which carried a resolutely antiestablishment message: it showed schoolboys challenging their teachers' authority and then reveling in the chaos that resulted. In Argentina, rock and roll was crucial to the counterculture during the military dictatorship of the 1970s and 1980s. Charlie García urged Buenos Aires audiences to defy authorities by daring to dream of a different order. Indeed, in countries where repressive regimes quashed public cultures, pop culture was usually counterculture.

The same globalizing effects influenced sports. Consider the staple of American identity, baseball, whose major league teams took on a more global cast. Beginning in the 1960s, the number of Latin Americans playing in North American professional leagues grew steadily. Notable in the 1980s was the Mexican pitcher Fernando Valenzuela, whose exploits as a member of the Los Angeles Dodgers made him a hero to that city's Mexican population and in his native land as well. The Dodgers also took the lead in reaching for Asian talent. In the 1990s, as Los Angeles experienced a growing Asian immigrant population, the Dodgers signed the Japanese pitcher Hideo Nomo. Meanwhile, in the Dominican Republic, baseball fans were riveted by their favorite players in the big leagues: slugger Sammy Sosa and ace pitcher Pedro Martínez. The emergence of so many Latin

Urbanization as a Global Phenomenon: Transforming Bombay to Mumbai

The city has played a pivotal role in world history since it first emerged thousands of years ago along the Tigris and Euphrates Rivers in Mesopotamia (modern-day Iraq). People have since flocked to cities for the social and economic advantages that these locations offer. By the end of the twentieth century, the proportion of people living in cities, usually defined as having populations over 5,000 or 10,000, exceeded 50 percent in the wealthiest countries and was approaching that proportion in the developing countries as well.

Of the burgeoning cities in the Southern Hemisphere, one of the most dynamic is Mumbai, in India. Acquired in the sixteenth century by the Portuguese, who then transferred its control to the British East India Company, Bombay (as it was named at that time) developed as a port city for colonial commerce. It profited from the cotton trade, developed a vibrant textile industry, attracted migrants, and acquired a cosmopolitan image. After India's independence in 1947, Bombay (renamed Mumbai in 1995) still epitomized the modern face of the nation, and its heterogeneous population symbolized the Indian melting pot.

Beginning in the 1980s, however, the nature of the city's relationship with the world economy started to change. The cotton textile industry, Bombay's economic backbone, went into a decline. Industrial employment fell sharply. Moreover, the share of informal household enterprises, small shops, petty subcontractors, and casual laborers rose, along with banking and insurance. Economic liberalization removed hurdles against foreign businesses and brought the city directly into the global economy.

Today, Mumbai occupies a strategic place in transnational geography. This is evident in the increasing presence of financial institutions, trading organizations, insurance companies, telecommunications corporations, and information technology enterprises with worldwide operations. Even the city's vibrant film industry addresses a global, not just national, audience; rather appropriately, Bombay cinema has acquired the nickname "Bollywood."

The city, however, still attracts a large number of poor migrants who live in slums or call the pavements their home. The gap between Mumbai's rich and poor has grown alarmingly. Millions who eke out a miserable living stand in stark contrast to a tiny elite enriched by the global economy.

Globalization has also affected its residents' identity. In the 1990s, the political party in power was the Shiv Sena,

---

American and Asian baseball players epitomized the ability of what were once purely American cultural forms to spread their influences and to bring peoples all over the world together.

Baseball Goes International. *The 1980s and 1990s saw an influx of ballplayers from Latin America and quite a few from Asia as well. Left: Boston Red Sox slugger David Ortiz hails from the Dominican Republic. Right: New York Yankees superstar Ichiro Suzuki is from Japan.*

LOCAL CULTURE World cultures may have become more integrated and homogeneous, but they did not completely replace national and local cultures. Indeed, technology and migration often reinforced the appeal of "national" cultural icons as national celebrities gained popularity among immigrant groups abroad. Inexpensive new technology introduced these stars to more and more people. In Egypt, the most popular singer of the Nasser years was Umm Kalthum, who became the favorite of the middle classes via radio. In 1975 she was given a state funeral, the likes of which had rarely been seen.

As the market for world cultures grew increasingly competitive and integrated, performers borrowed from one another and employed a wider variety of styles, with some becoming commercial sensations. The result was often a challenge to convention. Consider the Indian movie industry, which has become one of the world's behemoth entertainers. As long as Bombay's Hindi cinema was cut off from the world, it never developed new themes and forms. But now it did. In place of the time-worn East versus the West theme, it confidently embraced the global space with glamorous romance, breakout dancing, and chart-topping music. The local Hindi film became a

Bollywood. *Bombay cinema, or Bollywood, has an increasing global presence. This is the poster for Devdas, a 3-hour romance that won awards in India and around the world.*

a nativist regional party named after a seventeenth-century Maratha chieftain who opposed the Mughal Empire. As the industrial economy and trade unions gave way to the service sector and unorganized labor, the Shiv Sena utilized the social and political fluidity produced by globalization to win support for its nativist ideology. Mumbai's cosmopolitan image went up in smoke in 1992–1993, when the Shiv Sena led pogroms against the city's Muslim residents. In response, a Muslim underworld don engineered a series of bomb blasts in March 1993. Since then, the city has experienced episodes of violence, none more gruesome than the terrorist attacks on two luxury hotels, a crowded railway station, and a Jewish center in November 2006. Ironically, the terrorists chose to attack Mumbai for its reputation as a cosmopolitan city.

Mumbai today illustrates the uneven effects of globalization. The society is sharply divided, economic disparities are great, and the city's politics is a cauldron of conflicting identities. These are the local forms in which this vast and influential city experiences globalization.

QUESTIONS FOR ANALYSIS

- What similarities and differences emerge when you compare the vignette of Los Angeles in the chapter introduction with the decription of Mumbai given here?
- How does Mumbai fit into the larger theme of worlds together and worlds apart?

Explore Further

Mehta, Suketu. *Maximum City: Bombay Lost and Found* (2005).

Prakash, Gyan. *Mumbai Fables* (2010).

global Indian phenomenon, at home in London, Sydney, and New York, and sported a global lifestyle. Bombay cinema also acquired a new brand, Bollywood, which came to increasingly depend on revenues from the United States, Europe, and the Middle East, where South Asian migrants flocked to see the latest blockbusters.

Among the breakthroughs that have occurred since the 1970s was the triumph of black performers (Bob Marley, Whitney Houston, Michael Jackson), black athletes (Pelé, Michael Jordan, Carl Lewis), and black writers (Toni Morrison, Chinua Achebe). Competition also shattered some sexual biases. Female performers like Madonna became popular icons. So did gay performers, starting with the Village People, whose campy multicultural anthem "YMCA" created a place for a new generation of homosexual or bisexual artists. Of course, beyond Europe and North America, flirting with sexual conventions had its limits. In the Middle East, female video artists wore headscarves—but they still swung their hips. What were once relatively homogeneous national cultures, often dominated by men representing the ethnic majority, gave way to a wide variety of entertainers and artists who broke loose of confining local cultures.

Communications

Computer technology revolutionized global communications. In the late 1980s, while working in Switzerland, the British physicist Tim Berners-Lee devised a means to pool data stored on various computers. Whereas previous electronic links had existed only between major universities and research stations, Berners-Lee made data more accessible by creating the World Wide Web. With each use and each connection, and as people entered more data, however, the Web grew unmanageably crowded and difficult to navigate. The early 1990s saw the first commercial browsers used in navigating the so-called Internet. Suddenly people were communicating across global networks more easily than with neighbors and more inexpensively than with local phone calls.

The change created a new generation of wealth. CEOs of top companies like General Motors, Royal Dutch Shell, and Merck had less net worth than Michael Dell (hardware maker), Bill Gates (software maker), and Jeff Bezos (creator of Amazon.com). Shares of Internet firms, known as dot-coms, swept the world's stock markets. Money from these companies flowed globally as they

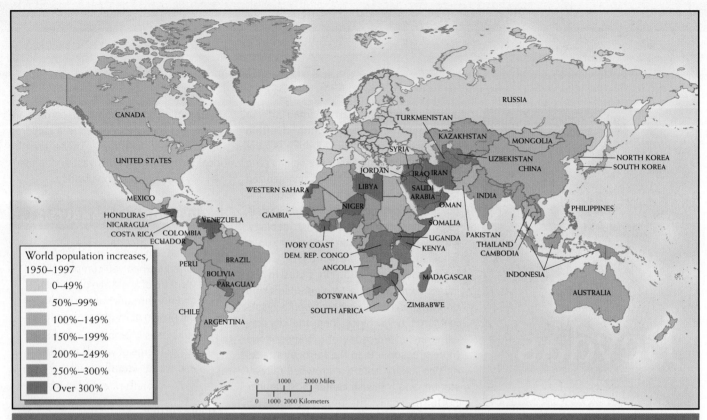

MAP 21.4 | World Population Increases, 1950–1997

The world's population more than doubled between 1950 and 1997, rising from approximately 2.5 billion to nearly 6 billion.

- Which countries had the largest population increases over these five decades? Why do you suppose these countries experienced such high population increases?

- According to your reading, why did western Europe and Russia have the lowest population increases?

established offices worldwide. Software and Internet technologies developed enormous economies of scale and thus became prone to monopolization as they took over small companies.

Hardware, software, and the Internet were not purely American innovations. Within a few years of their invention, personal computers were being made in Mexico and computer chips mass-produced in Taiwan. The brains behind the Internet were likely to be students from Indian institutes of technology. Originally engineering schools, these institutes trained a whole generation of pioneering computing engineers, many of whom resettled in California's Silicon Valley. By 1996, Indians held half of the 55,000 temporary work visas issued by the U.S. government for high-tech employees. Roughly half of Silicon Valley start-up companies in the late 1990s were the brainchildren of Indian entrepreneurs. Google, the biggest of them all, was founded by a couple of graduate students at Stanford. One of them, Sergey Brin, was a Jewish Russian fugitive. The current CEO of the giant firm is Sundar Pichai, who grew up in Chennai, India, before moving to the United States for graduate studies.

While the Internet revolution provided new means to share and sell information, it also reinforced hierarchies between haves and have-nots. Great swaths of the world's population living outside big cities had no access to the Internet. According to World Bank calculations, in the late 1990s countries with low-income economies had, on average, 26 phone lines per 1,000 people; countries with high-income economies had 550 lines per 1,000 people. The biggest losers were the billions living in rural areas or towns neglected by state and private communications providers. The have-nots were poor not just from lack of capital but from lack of access to knowledge and new media.

CHARACTERISTICS OF THE NEW GLOBAL ORDER

While providing access to an unimaginable array of goods and services, globalization also deepened world inequalities.

Family Planning in China. *To control China's burgeoning population, the government enacted the one-child policy in 1979, which restricted each household to one child. While the policy was generally effective, numerous cases of forced abortions by zealous party officials and overwhelming numbers of female orphans revealed the need for a less stringent approach to population control. This 1996 propaganda billboard in Wuhan reads: "Family planning is the need of mankind." It is no accident that the single child in the ideal family illustrated beneath the slogan is a girl.*

Families changed, and life spans increased. Education and good health determined one's status in society as never before. Populations expanded dramatically, requiring greater industrial and agricultural output from all parts of the world. While many regions consumed more than ever before, others struggled with famine; and as tropical rain forests were destroyed and the burning of fossil fuels increased, global warming threatened the world's population.

The Demography of Globalization

It took 160 years (1800–1960) for the world's population to increase from 1 billion to 3 billion; over the next 40 years (1960–2000), it jumped from 3 billion to over 6 billion. Behind this steepening curve were two important developments: a decline in mortality, especially among children, and a rise in life expectancy.

Population growth was hardly equal worldwide. (See Map 21.4 and Analyzing Global Developments: Globalization: One World or Many?) In Europe, population growth peaked around 1900, and it moved upward only gradually from 400 million to 730 million during the twentieth century, with little growth after the 1970s. North America's population quadrupled over the same period, mainly because of immigration. The population booms in the twentieth century occurred in Asia (400 percent), Africa (550 percent), and Latin America (700 percent). China and India each passed the billion-person mark. Increases were greatest in the cities. By the 1980s, the world's largest cities were Asian, African, and Latin American. Greater Tokyo-Yokohama had 30 million inhabitants; Mexico City, 20 million; São Paulo, 17 million; Cairo, 16 million; Calcutta, 15 million; and Jakarta, 12 million.

Population growth slowed most dramatically in richer societies. For some, like Italy, the growth rate declined to zero. More recently enriched societies like Korea, Taiwan, and Hong Kong also had fewer births. Societies that did not see their birthrates decline by the same rate (much of Africa, southern Asia, and impoverished parts of Latin America) had difficulty raising income levels. But even among poor nations, birthrates declined after the 1970s.

The most remarkable turnaround occurred in China, where the government instituted a "one-child family" policy with rewards for compliance and penalties for transgression. Inducements included cash subsidies, preferential access to nurseries and kindergartens, priority in medical care, and the promise of favored treatment in housing, education, and employment. The policy also prompted an imbalance in sex ratio at birth. The bias in favor of sons (long a feature of China's patrilineal system, which emphasized descent through the male line), together with the availability of ultrasound scanners, promoted the widespread—albeit illegal—practice of prenatal sex selection.

In general, however, declining family size resulted from choice. In rich countries, more women deferred having children as education, career prospects, and birth control devices provided incentives and methods to postpone starting a family. In addition, love became a precondition to marriage and family formation in societies that had traditionally emphasized arranged marriages.

FAMILIES In many countries, the legal definition of families became more fluid in this period. Here again, the change reflected women's choices and the relationship between love and

ANALYZING GLOBAL DEVELOPMENTS

Globalization: One World or Many?

People, funds, commodities, and information move around the world with lightning speed. This rapid mobility has contributed to radical changes in population growth rates from one country to the next and one continent to the next, and it has led to significant changes in the rate of economic growth worldwide. But do these kinds of changes dictate a growing uniformity in the world? In other words, is globalization creating a single world community? The following two tables reveal some striking demographic differences, by continent and country, with respect to rapid or not-so-rapid population growth rates, the age distribution of populations, and the gross national product (GNP) per person.

QUESTIONS FOR ANALYSIS

- Which of the continents is the fastest growing in terms of population, and why would this be the case?
- Although these tables do not provide data on the AIDS epidemic (see Map E.5 for that data), we know that Africa has been the most severely impacted continent. What impact is AIDS having on Africa's population growth rates? Why do you think that its effects are so muted?
- Three of the countries in Table 2, Russia, Germany, and Japan, have negative population growth rates. What would account for this situation, and what sorts of problems do you think these countries are likely to encounter?
- Japan and Germany are the only countries in Table 2 that have a smaller percentage of the population under the age of fifteen than over the age of sixty-five. On the other hand, the countries of sub-Saharan Africa have the largest proportion of their populations under the age of fifteen. What is the cause for these developments, and what problems are these countries likely to encounter as they move forward?
- Do these data suggest that the world is becoming more unified (more integrated)?

Table 1. Ten Most Populous Countries, 2012 and 2050

2012	Population in Millions	2050	Population in Millions
China	1,350	India	1,691
India	1,260	China	1,311
United States	314	United States	423
Indonesia	241	Nigeria	402
Brazil	194	Pakistan	314
Pakistan	180	Indonesia	309
Nigeria	170	Bangladesh	226
Bangladesh	153	Brazil	213
Russia	143	Democratic Republic of Congo	194
Japan	128	Ethiopia	166

marriage. First, couples chose to end their marriages at unprecedented rates. In the United States, for example, the divorce rate doubled between 1970 and 1998; by the century's end, one in two marriages ended in divorce. In Belgium and Britain late in the twentieth century, fewer than half of all marriages survived. China's divorce rate soared, too. In Beijing, by century's end it approached 25 percent—double the 1990 rate. As of 2000, women initiated more than 70 percent of divorces.

As marriages became shorter-lived, new forms of child-rearing proliferated. Europeans, including the supposedly more traditional Italians and Greeks, abandoned nuclear family conventions. In those European countries where divorce remained difficult, more couples lived together without getting married. In the United States, out-of-wedlock childbirths constituted one-third of all births in the late 1990s, with only about half of American children living in households with both parents (compared with nearly three-quarters of children in the early 1970s).

AGING Longer life spans also affected family fortunes, as more infants survived childhood and lived to be old. The population of industrial nations "grayed" considerably as the median age increased and the percentage over age sixty-five grew. In western

Table 2. World Population References for 2012 and Projection for 2050

Continents and Selected Countries	Population, 2012 (millions)	Annual Rate of Natural Increase (%)	Projected Population, 2050 (millions)	Percent of Population under age 15	Percent of Population over age 65	GNP per capita (US $)
World	7,058	+1.2	9,624	26	8	10,760
AFRICA	1,072	+2.5	2,339	41	3	2,630
Egypt	82.3	+2.0	135.6	32	4	5,760
Nigeria	170.1	+2.6	402.4	44	3	1,910
South Africa	51.1	+0.9	57.2	31	5	2,240
Democratic Republic of Congo	69.1	+2.8	194.2	46	3	320
THE AMERICAS	948	+1.0	1,212	25	9	23,870
United States	349	+0.5	471	20	13	47,310
Brazil	194.3	+1.0	213.4	24	7	11,000
Mexico	116.1	+1.5	143.9	29	6	14,400
Haiti	10.3	+1.8	14.2	36	4	1,180
ASIA	4,260	+1.1	5,284	25	7	6,860
China	1,350.4	+0.5	1,310.7	16	9	7,640
India	1,259.7	+1.5	1,691.1	31	5	3,430
Japan	127.6	−0.2	119.8	13	24	34,610
Indonesia	241.0	+1.3	309.4	27	6	4,200
EUROPE	740	0.0	732	16	16	27,080
United Kingdom	63.2	+0.4	79.6	18	17	35,840
France	63.6	+0.4	78.4	19	17	34,750
Germany	81.8	−0.2	71.5	13	21	38,100
Russia	143.2	−0.1	127.8	15	13	19,240

Source: Population Reference Bureau, 2012: World Population Data Sheet, Washington D.C., pp. 2, 6, 7, 8, and 9.

Europe and Japan, graying rates were even more marked. Japan's birthrate plummeted, and the citizenry aged at such a rate that the country began to depopulate. From a population of 127 million in 2000, estimates forecast a decline to 105 million by 2050.

The aging population presented new challenges for families. For centuries, being a parent meant providing for children until they could be self-sufficient. Old age, the years of relatively unproductive labor, was brief. Communities and households absorbed the cost of caring for the elderly. Household savings became family bequests to future, not older, generations. But as populations aged, retirees needed society's savings to survive. So public and private pension funds swelled to accumulate future pools of money for the retired. In Germany, over 30 percent of the government's social policy spending went into the state pension fund. Chinese demographers warned that the one-child policy might create an unbalanced population structure. In a society in which the family still largely provided the safety net, many people worried about having to support two parents and four grandparents.

In Africa, where publicly supported pension funds were rare, the aged faced bleaker futures. Whereas in earlier times the elderly were respected founts of wisdom, colonial rule and the postcolonial world elevated the young—especially those

Wedding Ceremonies. Left: *The union of bride and groom is symbolized in this Northern Indian Hindu ceremony by the knot between their garments.* Right: *South Korean martial artist Kim Jong-bok holds his bride, actress Song Hee-jung, during their 2005 wedding ceremony, held on the Tokto islets off the Korean Peninsula to protest Japan's claim of the territory.*

with western educations and lifestyles. Then, in the 1970s, as birthrates soared, the demand on family resources to care for infants and children rose at the very moment when society's resource base began to shrink. The elderly could no longer work, but neither could they rely on the household's support.

HEALTH The distribution of contagious diseases also reflected inequities in the globalized world. Although microbes have no respect for borders, the effects of public health regulations, antibiotics, and vaccination campaigns reduced the spread of contagions. By the late twentieth century, not only did nutrition and healthy habits count (as they always had), but access to medicines did, too.

What used to be universal afflictions in previous centuries (such as the Black Death) now just affected certain peoples. Water treatment and proper sewerage, for example, had banished cholera from most urban centers by the mid-twentieth century. More recently, however, its deadly grip again reached across Asia and into the eastern Mediterranean, parts of Latin America, and much of sub-Saharan Africa. From the 1970s, Africa suffered frequent outbreaks. The crucial cause of the respread of cholera was urban developers' failure to keep sanitation systems growing apace with the demand for water. Thus, diseases proliferated where urban squalor was most acute—in cities with the greatest post-1970s population growth.

AIDS Treatment and Education. Left: *At the Thirteenth International AIDS Conference in Durban, South Africa, in July 2000, AIDS activists express their displeasure at the high prices and unavailability of lifesaving drugs for most of those in the Third World who are affected by AIDS.* Right: *African governments did not tackle the problem of AIDS in their severely affected continent with the energy that it warrants. Pictured here, however, a doctor seeks to impress on the youth of a local community how they should conduct their social and sexual lives in light of the AIDS crisis.*

Adult prevalence rate

	0–0.09%
	0.1%–0.4%
	0.5%–0.9%
	1.0%–4.9%
	5%–14.9%
	15%–36%
	Data not available

MAP 21.5 | HIV Infection across the World, 1999

HIV, which leads to AIDS, spread across the whole world, providing further evidence of global interconnectedness. The outbreak began in Africa.

- Where in Africa have the highest rates of HIV infection occurred? Which countries *outside* the African continent have had the highest rates of infection, and why is this so?
- Why have Egypt, North Africa, and much of the rest of the Islamic world, despite their close connections with Africa below the Sahara, thus far been little affected?

In the 1970s, entirely new diseases began to devastate the world's population. Consider **AIDS (acquired immunodeficiency syndrome)**, which in its first two decades killed 12 million people. Transmitted through contact with the semen or blood of an infected person, AIDS compromises the ability of the infected person's immune system to ward off disease. First detected in 1981, AIDS was initially stigmatized as a "gay cancer" (it appeared primarily in homosexual men) and received little attention. But as it spread to heterosexuals and public awareness about it increased, a new campaign urged the practice of safe sex, control of blood supplies, and restrictions on sharing hypodermic needles. In Europe and North America,

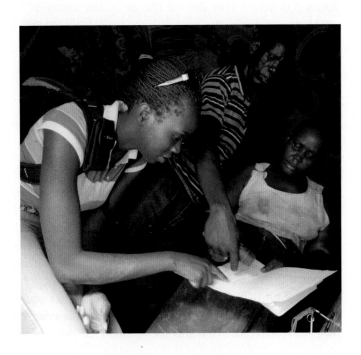

African Women and Education. *Though women's education lagged behind that of men in Africa, a number of women, like Stella Kenyi, pictured here (left), graduated from African high schools and attended universities at home or abroad. Kenyi taught business skills to men and women in Sudan after completing an undergraduate degree at Davidson College in North Carolina.*

astounding results. In the United States, by the late 1980s, more than half of all college degrees went to women (up from 38 percent in 1960). Chinese women made even greater strides, although roadblocks persisted. Ironically, with China's recent market reforms, women's access to basic education regressed, as families, particularly in rural areas, reverted to spending their limited resources on educating sons. Thus, in 2000, up to 70 percent of China's 140 million illiterates were female.

WORK Although more women held jobs outside the home, they lacked full equity at work. Limited by job discrimination and burdens of child-rearing, women's participation in the workforce reached a fairly stable level by the 1980s. The percentage of women at the top of the corporate pyramid was considerably smaller than their proportion in the labor force or their college graduation rates. In 1995, the Chinese government claimed that Chinese women had made better advances than their U.S. counterparts: there were more Chinese women (10 percent) than American women (3 percent) in senior managerial posts. Still, Chinese women graduates complained of discrimination in the job market. In 2000, some 60 percent of China's unemployed were women, and the number was growing. Women worldwide had difficulties breaking through the "glass ceiling"—a seemingly invisible barrier to women's advancement. Consequently, while income disparities between men and women narrowed, a significant gap persisted.

Working outside the home led to problems inside the home. Who would take care of the children? Changing gender norms in rich countries sparked major migration streams. Jamaican and Filipino women migrated by the thousands in the 1970s and 1980s to Canada and Australia to work as nannies to raise money to send back home, where they had often left their own children. In South Africa and Brazil, local women served as domestic servants and nannies. They were doing the jobs that once belonged to middle- and upper-class homemakers, women who now wanted the same rights as men: to parent *and* to work.

FEMINISM The deeply ingrained inequality between men and women prompted calls for change. Feminist movements arose mainly in Europe and North America in the 1960s and then become global in the 1970s. In 1975, the first truly international women's forum took place in Mexico City. But becoming global did not necessarily imply overturning local customs. What feminists called for was not the abolition of gender differences, but equal treatment—equal pay and equal opportunities for obtaining jobs and advancement. In general, then, in spite of rapid population growth, women's inequities between and within societies remained prominent in this period. The most glaring were between the rich and poor countries, although well-to-do classes of women emerged everywhere and tended to congregate in big cities.

Women took increasingly active stances against discrimination in government and in the workplace. Indeed, as economic integration intensified with regional trade pacts (usually negotiated by men in the interest of male-owned and male-run firms), women struggled to ensure that globalization did not cut them out of new opportunities. For instance, after Argentina, Uruguay, Paraguay, and Brazil negotiated the Mercosur free trade pact, traffic across South American borders soared. But as trade grew, so did government efforts to monitor illegal commerce and foster approved trade along new highways and bridges. Women were responsible for one kind of illicit commerce, because for generations they had transported goods across the river separating Argentina and Paraguay. When customs officers tried to stop this practice in the mid-1990s, Argentine and Paraguayan women locked arms to occupy the new bridge that male truckers used to ship Mercosur products, protesting the restrictions on their age-old enterprise.

The rising tide of global feminism culminated in a U.N. conference on Women in Beijing in 1995. Government delegates from more than 180 countries attended the Fourth World Conference on Women to produce "a platform for action" regarding women's rights in politics, business, education, and health. Alongside the official conference was a parallel conference for nearly 30,000 representatives at the NGO Forum for Women. These grassroots activists represented 2,000 nongovernmental organizations from every corner of the globe. Representatives planned strategies and coordinated programs on how to improve women's living and working conditions. What emerged from the conference were associations and groups that pledged to lobby for the rights of women and girls worldwide. One effect was to spotlight the ongoing shortage of opportunities for the advancement of women leaders worldwide.

Forum on Women. *Women representing different cultures of the world hold out a "peace torch" at the opening ceremony of the U.N. World Conference on Women in Beijing in 1995.*

Production and Consumption in the Global Economy

The growing world population, the desire for more education and better health, the entry of women into paid employment, and the promise of rising standards of living spurred unprecedented production and consumption of the world's resources. The most immediate challenge was how to feed so many people while developing sustainable practices that do not use up limited natural resources.

AGRICULTURAL PRODUCTION Changing agrarian practices made a huge difference in increasing food production. Starting in the 1950s, the "green revolution," largely involving nonfarm inputs such as chemical fertilizers, herbicides, and

pesticides, produced dramatically larger harvests. Then, in the 1970s, biologists began offering genetically engineered crops that multiplied yields at an even faster rate.

But these breakthroughs were not evenly distributed. American farmers, the biggest innovators, were the greatest beneficiaries. For example, by century's end they produced approximately one-ninth of the world's wheat and two-fifths of its corn. From this output, American exports accounted for about one-third of the world's international wheat trade and four-fifths of all corn exports. At the heart of the innovation was political power, for farmers had the clout to force officials to maintain roads, subsidize credit and prices, and mop up surplus supply. But Asian rice farmers made impressive innovations, too. In Taiwan and Korea, chemical and biological breakthroughs allowed rice yields to jump by 53 and 132 percent, respectively, between 1965 and 1985. And as Indian wheat farmers deployed chemical fertilizers, new seed varieties, and irrigation systems to double their output, the Ganges River basin supported an ever-larger urban population. The most miraculous transformation occurred in China. Beginning in the late 1970s, the Chinese government broke up some of the old collective farms and restored the individual household as the basic economic unit in rural areas. Thereafter, agricultural output surged by roughly 9 percent per year between 1978 and 1986.

Other agricultural producers also replied to world demand, but sometimes their added production was disruptive. While biology and chemistry allowed some farmers to get more out of their land, others simply opened up new lands to cultivation. Lacking access to credit, seed, and good land, small farmers

Saving the Amazon. *The rise of an international environmental movement in the 1970s led to alliances with local indigenous and environmental leaders, especially in the Amazon. Bottom: One of the most prominent advocates of the rights of indigenous people and the need to protect imperiled jungles was the British musician Sting. Here he is pictured alongside one of the Amazon's foremost Indian leaders, Bep Koroti Paiakan. Top: Farmers and ranchers cut and burned the Amazon at a ferocious rate in pursuit of frontier lands. In these remote regions, it was hard for local authorities to enforce conservation laws.*

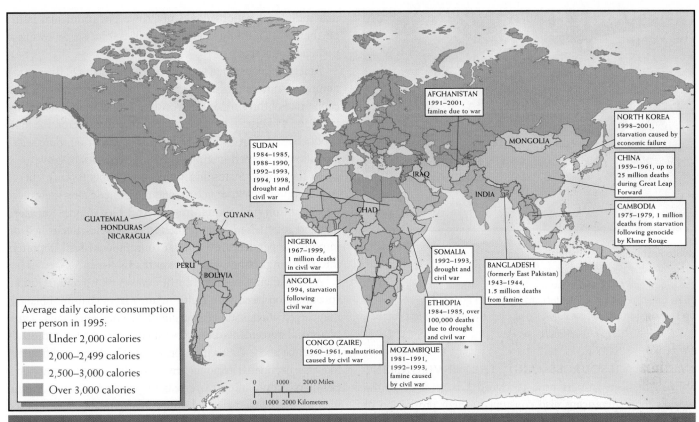

SUDAN
1984–1985,
1988–1990,
1992–1993,
1994, 1998,
drought and
civil war

AFGHANISTAN
1991–2001,
famine due to war

NORTH KOREA
1998–2001,
starvation caused by
economic failure

MONGOLIA

CHINA
1959–1961, up to
25 million deaths
during Great Leap
Forward

IRAQ

INDIA

CAMBODIA
1975–1979, 1 million
deaths from starvation
following genocide
by Khmer Rouge

GUATEMALA
HONDURAS
NICARAGUA

GUYANA

CHAD

NIGERIA
1967–1999,
1 million deaths
in civil war

SOMALIA
1992–1993,
drought and
civil war

BANGLADESH
(formerly East Pakistan)
1943–1944,
1.5 million deaths
from famine

PERU

BOLIVIA

ANGOLA
1994, starvation
following
civil war

ETHIOPIA
1984–1985, over
100,000 deaths
due to drought
and civil war

Average daily calorie consumption
per person in 1995:

Under 2,000 calories

2,000–2,499 calories

2,500–3,000 calories

Over 3,000 calories

CONGO (ZAIRE)
1960–1961, malnutrition
caused by civil war

MOZAMBIQUE
1981–1991,
1992–1993,
famine caused
by civil war

0   1000   2000 Miles
0   1000 2000 Kilometers

MAP 21.6 | Food Consumption and Famine since the 1940s

There is perhaps no better indicator of the division of the world into rich and poor, haves and have-nots, than this map on food consumption and famine.

- Which parts of the world have had the most difficulty in feeding their populations? What have been some of the causes of famine and malnourishment in these regions?
- How much have they been due to human agency, and how much to climate and other matters over which human beings have little control?

had to go where land was cheap. In Java, farmers cleared sloping woodland to make way for coffee plantings. In southern Colombia, peasants moved into semitropical woodlands to cultivate coca bushes (the source of cocaine) at profits that other cultivators could never realize.

The most notorious frontier expansion occurred in the Amazon River basin. Populations flocked to the Amazon frontier, largely from impoverished areas in northeastern Brazil. They cleared (by fire) cheap land, staked their claims, and, like nineteenth-century American homesteaders, tried to climb the social ladder by cultivating crops and raising livestock. But the promise of bounty failed: the soils were poor and easily eroded, and land titles provided little security, especially once large speculators moved into the area. So the dwellers on the frontier moved farther inland to repeat the cycle. By the 1980s, migrants to the Amazon River basin had burned away much of the jungle, contaminated the biosphere (the environment in which life exists), reduced the stock of diverse plant and animal life, and fostered social conflict in the Brazilian hinterland.

Nor were "breadbasket areas" always able to feed exploding populations. This was especially true in Africa from the 1970s onward, when domestic food production could not keep pace with population growth. (See Map 21.6.) Food shortages thereafter increased in frequency and duration, wiping out large numbers of sub-Saharan peoples. The protruding ribs on African children became a typical image of the region.

What explained Africa's famines? As the Indian Nobel Prize–winning economist Amartya Sen observed, famines—and their increasing frequency—are not natural disasters; they are human-made. Food shortages in Africa stemmed largely from governments that ignored the rural sector and its politically unorganized farmers. Unable to persuade their governments to raise prices for their crops, the farmers lacked incentives to expand production. Food shortages were also by-products of global inequities. African countries, earmarking hefty chunks of their economies to agrarian exports to repay debts incurred in the 1970s, could not produce enough foodstuffs domestically and thus became food importers.

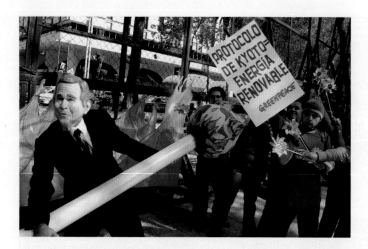

Kyoto Protocol. *That America would no longer participate in the Kyoto Protocol was especially infuriating to the global audience, as America is the largest emitter of carbon dioxide and other major greenhouse gases. Here, Greenpeace environmental activists look on as one of their cohorts, dressed as Bush, brandishes a flaming globe in a dramatic protest outside of the U.S. embassy in Mexico City.*

NATURAL RESOURCES AND THE ENVIRONMENT

While American farmers now produced a large share of the world's food, Americans also consumed a high proportion of its natural resources. Energy consumption presented a similar story, although America's enormous appetite for fossil fuels generated a domestic debate about reliance on foreign sources and pollution of the environment. In the 1970s, OPEC raised the price of crude oil (see Chapter 20). The cartel weakened in the 1980s, partly because new oil fields opened elsewhere in the world and partly because internal struggles divided the exporters.

The harshest conflict over oil occurred in the mid-1980s between Iran and Iraq, followed by the 1990 Iraqi invasion of Kuwait. Iraq was poised to become dominant in the area and thus to control oil policies. The conquest of Kuwait would have given Iraq control over about 7 percent of world oil supplies and nearly 20 percent of the world's known reserves. Only Iraq's neighbors, Saudi Arabia and Iran, would have been larger oil exporters, and Iraq would have been in a position to menace both. As the situation threatened to unsettle the regional balance of power, the U.S. government moved to restore it. Rallying a coalition of other nations, the Americans and their allies turned to the United Nations to gain approval for a military invasion called Operation Desert Storm. The ensuing Gulf War, which ended with Iraq's expulsion from Kuwait, restored an order in which the global distribution of power favored oil consumers over producers and preserved a regional balance of power.

The consumption of water, oil, and other natural resources became matters of international concern late in the twentieth century. So did pollution control and the disposal of waste products. Part of this internationalization reflected the recognition that individual nations could not solve environmental issues on their own. Air and water, after all, do not stop flowing at political boundaries.

Americans consumed a disproportionate share of the world's natural resources. By 2000, they were using water at a per capita rate of three times the world's average. Indeed, extensive irrigation was crucial to California's agricultural sector, the most productive and profitable in the world. Gathering more water also allowed a desert metropolis like Los Angeles to grow.

In the United States and Canada, attempts to curb energy consumption saw little success, and the United States grew more dependent on oil imports. In the late 1990s, North American demand for fuel-guzzling sport utility vehicles intensified oil imports. Dependence on foreign sources locked oil importers into recurring clashes with oil exporters.

As Canadians saw their northern lakes fill up with acid rain (precipitation laced with sulfur, mainly from coal-fired plants), they urged their southern neighbor to curb emissions. Thus, reciprocal agreements between Canada and the United States took shape in the 1980s. Europeans, also beset by acidification, likewise negotiated regional environmental treaties. But some polluters simply moved overseas to poorer and less powerful nations. As the west cleaned up its environment, the rest of the world paid the price.

Other problems crossed human-made borders as well, especially the growing problem of climate change. The world was now confronted with the greenhouse effect and **global warming** (worldwide rising temperatures caused in large part by the release into the air of human-made carbons), ocean pollution, and declining biological diversity. An increase in vehicles, factories, and air-conditioned homes—the general betterment of middle-class living—meant more combustion of coal, gas, and oil. Moreover, liberalizing world trade and industrializing Asia released 4 billion metric tons of carbon into the atmosphere in 1970; the figure by 2009 was 10 billion. Fully half of the fossil fuel–induced CO_2 emissions worldwide since 1750 took place after 1985.

People around the planet were emitting more carbon and at the same time were increasingly aware of the catastrophic risks. On June 26, 1974, *Time* magazine announced provocatively to the world that our "prolonged streak of exceptionally good climate has probably come to an end." But it took years to turn words and science into action plans. In 1992, Rio de Janeiro hosted a massive Earth Summit of state and NGO leaders, as well as scientists from around the world, that spotlighted the global threat of climate change. The follow-up in Kyoto, Japan, did lead to a major treaty that pledged countries to curb carbon emissions. But when President George W. Bush entered the White House in early 2001, he scrapped the Kyoto Treaty—to the dismay of many scientists, activists, and partner governments.

The response to environmental crises has been uneven at best. Where environmentalists acquired political power, they forced regulators to curb carbon emissions, a problem that grew with the rise of automobile traffic in cities like Tokyo, Mexico City, and Los Angeles. But control on fossil fuels depended on power and wealth, for it was hard to impose restrictions in societies where high energy use seemed a necessity of economic life. Even the Japanese, pioneers of clean fuel as early as the 1960s, were polluters in other spheres long thereafter. With increasing controls at home, Japanese industrialists went abroad to unload hazardous wastes. U.S. industrialists did the same, sending hazardous wastes to Mexico. Argentina and Canada sent their nuclear waste not abroad but to poor provinces desperate for jobs.

Environmental problems gained new urgency after the meltdown of a Soviet nuclear reactor in Chernobyl in 1986. Initially, communist authorities tried to cover up the disaster; but when the fallout reached Sweden, they had to accept responsibility. The delayed response was disastrous for Ukraine and Belarussia (present-day Belarus). Being relatively powerless under a centralized authoritarian regime, they had no political voice to cry out for help in addressing the contamination. As Chernobyl and

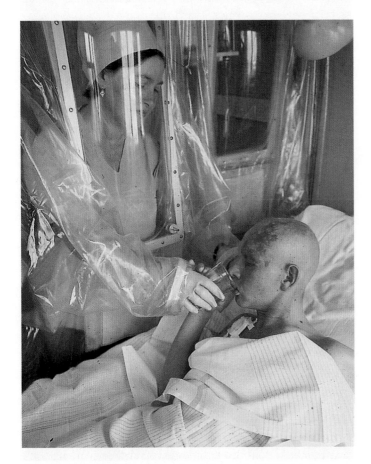

Chernobyl and Protest. *Among the victims of the 1986 explosion at the Chernobyl power plant, history's worst nuclear meltdown, were firefighters, such as the man pictured here, sent in to put out the blaze. Chernobyl turned Mikhail Gorbachev's glasnost, or openness, into more than a slogan, and it became a rallying cry for the populace, which hoped for political change and improvements in daily life.*

global warming demonstrated, environmental concerns do not observe boundary lines. Yet at the end of the twentieth century, global guidelines for regulating the impact of human activities on the environment had eluded the world's leaders.

CITIZENSHIP IN THE GLOBAL WORLD

Globalization distributed its benefits unequally. In general, people with access to better education and more opportunities profited from the border-crossing freedoms that the new order permitted. For most of the world's population, however, the new power structure was not so kind. Finding little opportunity in the globalized world, disadvantaged groups often invoked older religious and nationalist ideals. As globalization fostered human rights, environmental and labor standards, and women's rights worldwide, critics claimed that the language of international rights and standards was promoting neocolonial power in the form of a new "civilizing mission."

In particular, globalization posed massive problems for the nation-state. Since the nineteenth century, nation-states were supposed to be key in defining the rights of citizens. But now the rapid movement of ideas, goods, capital, and people across national boundaries undercut the authority of even the most powerful nations. Accordingly, other political spheres emerged to define and defend citizens. After the 1970s, people realized that international and supranational organizations often had more influence over their lives than did their own national governments. These organizations became increasingly important in shaping the meaning of citizenship. This was true especially in the Third World, where nation-states struggled hardest to accommodate globalization.

Supranational Organizations

New organizations with international responsibilities took shape after World War II for the purpose of facilitating global activities. These **supranational organizations** (organizations that transcend national boundaries) often successfully managed crisis situations, but they also impinged on the autonomy of all but the most powerful states.

Among the most prominent supranational organizations were the World Bank and the International Monetary Fund, which provided vital economic assistance to poorer nations. The World Bank, originally named the International Bank for Reconstruction and Development, was designed primarily to provide vital economic assistance for big development projects. In contrast, the International Monetary Fund provided funds and technical assistance to countries whose economies were in trouble. A good example of the World Bank's agenda was the financial support that it gave to the government of Ghana for the Volta River Project, which was intended to create an electrical grid for that country. Indeed, these international organizations financed and offered technical information for some of the largest development programs in the Third World. The World Bank also made available funds for a system of national parks in the Philippines to help indigenous people manage rain forests, coral reefs, and other threatened ecological zones. Nonetheless, the World Bank and the IMF required that recipient governments implement far-reaching economic reforms, such as devaluation of the currency and the privatization of public-sector companies. Many of these policies were deeply unpopular, leading to riots and charges that these international groups were agents of a new kind of imperialism.

Another set of supranational bodies, international nongovernmental organizations (NGOs), also stepped forward late in the twentieth century. Many championed human rights or highlighted environmental problems. Others, like the International Committee of the Red Cross, once dedicated to war relief, became more active in peacetime, sheltering the homeless or providing food for famine victims. What united NGOs was not so much their goals but the way they pursued them: autonomously from state power. NGOs created a layer of international forces that rivaled the political power of nation-states.

International NGOs reached a new level of influence in the 1970s because most nation-states at that time were still not democracies. Of the 121 countries in 1980, only 37 were democracies, accounting for only 35 percent of the world population. People found it difficult to rely on authoritarians to uphold their rights as citizens. Indeed, despite adopting a Universal Declaration of Human Rights in 1948, the United Nations (another international organization created after World War II and intended to provide a forum for settling international disputes) itself was a latecomer to enforcing human rights provisions, largely because many of its own members were the self-same authoritarians.

NGOs, then, took the lead in trying to make the language of human rights stick. The brutality of military regimes in Latin America inspired the emerging network of international human rights organizations to take action. After the overthrow of Chile's Salvador Allende in 1973, solidarity groups proliferated to protest the military junta's harsh repression. When the Argentine military began killing tens of thousands of innocent civilians in 1976 and news of their torture techniques leaked out, human rights movements again took action. Prominent among them was Amnesty International. Formed in 1961 to defend prisoners of conscience (detained for their beliefs, color, sex, ethnic origin, language, or religion), Amnesty International catalogued human rights violations worldwide. By 2000, an extensive network of associations was informing the public, lobbying governments, and pressuring U.N. member nations to live up to commitments to respect the rights of citizens.

Violence

International organizations and NGOs could play only a limited role in preserving peace and strengthening human rights. The end of the Cold War left entire regions in such turmoil that even the most effective humanitarian agencies could not prevent mass killings.

Consider the Balkans in the 1990s. In the territorial remains of Yugoslavia, groups of Serbs, Croats, Bosnians, ethnic Albanians, and others fought for control. Former neighbors, fueled by opportunistic leaders' rhetoric, no longer saw themselves as citizens of pluralistic political communities. Instead, demagogues trumpeted the superiority of ethnic Serbs. When international agencies moved in to try to bolster public authority, they failed as Yugoslavia's ethnic mosaic imploded into civil war. The Dayton Accords of 1995 ended the bloodshed by partitioning Bosnia

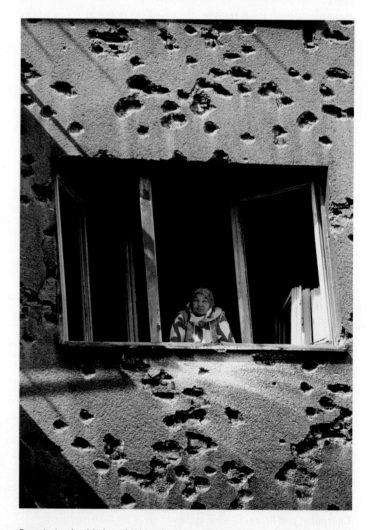

Bosnia in the Midst of War. *Despite extensive destruction and perpetual sniper fire, the multiethnic population of Sarajevo refused to abandon their city. With the help of U.N. soldiers and aid workers, they kept alive the hope for the peaceful coexistence of Muslims, Serbs, and Croats in Bosnia.*

and assigning several international organizations to maintain peace. But in 1999, Serbian president Slobodan Milosevic sent troops to suppress unrest in the province of Kosovo; only North Atlantic Treaty Organization (NATO) air strikes on Serbia's capital, Belgrade, convinced Milosevic to back down. Subsequently, Milosevic was indicted by the International Criminal Tribunal on sixty-six counts of war crimes and crimes against humanity, but he died of a heart attack before he could be found guilty.

Some of the most gruesome scenes of political violence occurred in Africa, where nation-states struggled to uphold the rule of law for all citizens. Here, tension often erupted in conflict between ethnic groups. The failure of African agriculture to sustain growing populations, as well as unequal access to resources like education, made ethnic rivalries worse. Droughts, famine, and corruption ignited the rivalries into riots and killings—even into bitter civil war and the breakdown of centralized authority.

Events in Rwanda reflected Africa's horrifying experience with political violence. Friction grew between the majority Hutus (agrarian people, often very poor) and the minority Tutsis (herders, better educated, wealthier, and chosen by the Belgians during the colonial period to rule over the Hutus) after the two peoples had intermarried and lived side by side for many generations. Some resentful Hutus blamed the Tutsis for all their woes. As tensions mounted, the United Nations dispatched peacekeeping troops. Moderate Hutus urged peaceful coexistence, only to be shouted down by government forces in command of radio stations and a mass propaganda machine. Although alerted to the impending problem, U.N. forces, fearing a clash and uncertain of their mandate, failed to prevent the violence.

The failure on the part of the international community, including the United States, which did not have troops on the ground and which had no clear policy toward Rwanda, gave the Hutu government an implicit green light to wipe out opponents. In 100 days of carnage in 1994, Hutu militias massacred 800,000 Tutsis and moderate Hutus. This was not, as many proclaimed, the militarization of ancient ethnic rivalries, for many Hutus were butchered as they tried to defend Tutsi friends, relatives, and neighbors. Meanwhile, the ensuing refugee crisis destabilized neighboring countries. The civil war in Rwanda sent riptides across eastern and central Africa, creating a whole new generation of conflicts.

Some societies, however, tried to put political violence behind them. In Argentina, El Salvador, Guatemala, and South Africa, the transition to democracy compelled elected rulers to establish inquiries into past rulers' human rights abuses. These **truth commissions** were vital for creating a new aura of legitimacy for democracies and for promising to uphold the rights of individuals. In South Africa, many blacks backed the new president, Nelson Mandela, but also demanded a reckoning with the punitive experience of the apartheid past. To avoid a backlash against the former white rulers, the South African leadership opted to record the past events rather than avenge them. Truth, the new leaders argued, would be powerful enough to heal old wounds. The Truth and Reconciliation Commission, chaired by Nobel Peace Prize winner and longtime opponent of apartheid Bishop Desmond Tutu, called on all who had been involved

Rwandan Refugees. *Perhaps as many as 800,000 Tutsis were killed in 1994 as the Hutus turned against the local Tutsi population while Rwanda was being invaded by a Tutsi-led army from Uganda. Not surprisingly, the massacre led to an enormous refugee crisis.*

in political crimes, whites as well as blacks, to come before its tribunal and speak the truth. Although the truth alone did not fully settle old scores, a more open discussion of basic liberties fostered new bonds between public authority and citizens.

The genocide in Rwanda represented the most egregious failure of the international community to deal with a severe humanitarian crisis. To some extent, the failure to respond was the result of the rapidity and ferocity with which the enmity toward the Tutsis exploded, catching off guard countries with the resources to deal with this level of violence. In other less politically charged crises, like famines, especially in Africa, international organizations like the Red Cross and Catholic Charities mobilized support and provided much relief.

Religious Foundations of Politics

Secular concerns for human rights and international peace were not the only foundations for politics after the Cold War. In many regions, people wanted religion to define the moral fabric of political communities. Very often, religion provided a way to reimagine the nation-state just as globalization was undermining national autonomy.

HINDU NATIONALISM In India, Hindu nationalism offered a communal identity for a country being rapidly transformed by globalization. In the 1980s, India freed market forces, privatized state firms, and withdrew from its role as welfare provider. Economic reforms under the ruling Congress Party sparked economic growth, thereby creating Asia's largest, best-educated, and most affluent middle class. But because these changes also widened the gap between rich and poor, lower classes and castes formed political parties to challenge the traditional elites. With established hierarchies and loyalties eroding, Hindu nationalists argued that religion could now fill the role once occupied by a secular state. Claiming that the ideology of Hindutva ("Hinduness") would bring the help that secular nationalism had failed to provide, Hindu militants trumpeted the idea of India as a nation of Hindus (the majority), with minorities relegated to a lesser status.

The chief beneficiary of the politics established by economic liberalization was a Hindu nationalist party, the Bhartiya Janata Party (BJP), or Indian People's Party. It was the political arm of an alliance of Hindu organizations devoted to establishing India as a Hindu state. By the late 1980s, the BJP and other like-minded parties were advancing an anti-minority (chiefly anti-Muslim) ideology. Claiming that the state had systematically appeased the minorities and trampled on the rights of the majority, they urged Hindus to overthrow "pseudo-secularism." This communal ideology was a winning formula, and by 1998, a BJP coalition came to power. Hindu nationalists sought to

transform the secular nation-state into a moral community, but without challenging the economic forces of globalization.

ISLAMIC CONSERVATISM In some cases, religion provided a way to resist seemingly American-dominated globalization. One of the most spirited challenges arose in the Islamic Middle East. Here, many people believed that modernizing and westernizing programs were leading their societies toward rampant materialism and unchecked individualism. Critics included traditional clerics and young western-educated elites whose job prospects seemed bleak and who felt that the promise of modernization had failed. Having criticized modernizing processes since the nineteenth century, Islamic conservatives flourished once more in the 1970s, as global markets and social dislocations undermined the moral foundations of secular leadership.

The most revolutionary Islamic movement arose in Iran, where clerics forced the shah from power in 1979. The revolt pitted a cadre of religious officials possessing only pamphlets, tracts, and tapes against the military arsenal and the vast intelligence apparatus of the Iranian state. Shah Mohammad Reza Pahlavi had enjoyed U.S. technical and military support since the Americans had helped place him on the throne in 1953. His

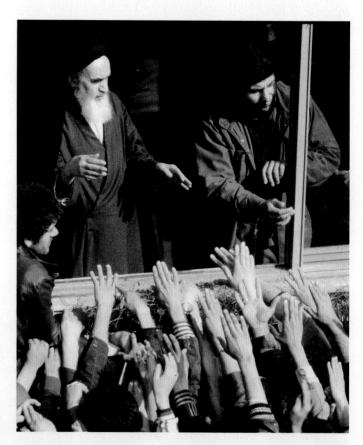

Ayatollah Khomeini. *After fifteen years of exile in France due to his outspoken opposition to the shah, Ayatollah Ruhollah Khomeini returned to Tehran in 1979 to the ardent welcome of his supporters.*

American Hostage Crisis in Iran. *The United States was stunned in 1979 by Iran's Islamic Revolution, which overthrew the shah and brought the exiled cleric Ayatollah Khomeini to power. After radical students captured the U.S. embassy, as well as fifty-three hostages, an American rescue raid failed, leading to celebration by Iranians, as shown here.*

bloated army and police force, as well as his brutally effective intelligence service, had crushed all challenges to his authority. The shah also had benefited from oil revenues, which soared after 1973. Yet the uneven distribution of income, the oppressive police state, and the royal family's ostentatious lifestyle fueled widespread discontent. As discontent rose, so did repression. And as repression intensified, so did the feeling that the government had abandoned the people.

The most vociferous critique came from the mullahs (Muslim scholars or religious teachers), who found in the Ayatollah Ruhollah Khomeini a courageous leader. Khomeini used his traditional Islamic education and his training in Muslim ethics to accuse the shah's government of gross violations of Islamic norms. He also identified the shah's ally, America, as the great Satan. With opposition mounting, the shah fled the country in 1979. In his wake, Khomeini established a theocratic state ruled by a council of Islamic clerics. Although some Iranians grumbled about aspects of this return to Islam (women's reduced status, leaders' arbitrariness, ruptured relations with the west, and the failure to institute democratic procedures), they prided themselves on having inspired a revolution based on principles other than those drawn from the west.

RELIGIOUS CONSERVATISM IN THE UNITED STATES
The search for moral foundations of politics in the global age reached beyond nonwestern societies. Indeed, in the United States, religion became a potent force after the 1970s as the membership and activism of conservative, fundamentalist Protestant churches eclipsed mainline denominations. Insisting

on literal interpretation of the Bible, Protestant fundamentalists railed against secularizing trends in American society. This traditionalist crusade took up a broad range of cultural and political issues. Religious conservatives (predominantly evangelical Protestants, but including some Catholics and Orthodox Jews) attacked many of the social changes that had emerged from liberation movements of the 1960s. Shifting sexual and familial relations were sore points, but the religious conservatives especially targeted public leaders who, they felt, had abandoned the moral purpose of authority by legalizing abortion and supporting secular values.

Acceptance of and Resistance to Democracy

New sources of power and new social movements drastically changed politics in the global age. Increasingly, international organizations were decisive in defining the conditions of democratic citizenship. Perhaps most remarkable was how much democracy spread toward the end of the twentieth century. In South Africa, Russia, and Guatemala, elections now decided politicians' fate. In this sense, the world's societies embraced the idea that people have a right to choose their own representatives. Nevertheless, democracy did not triumph everywhere.

An important holdout was China. Mao Zedong died in 1976, and within a few years his successor, Deng Xiaoping, opened the nation's economy to market forces. But Deng and other Chinese Communist Party leaders resisted multiparty competition. Instead of capitalism and western-style democracy, they maintained that China should follow its own path to modernity. By the late 1980s, economic reforms had produced spectacular increases in production and rising standards of living for most of China's people. But the widening gap between rich and poor, together with increasing public awareness of corruption within the party and the government, triggered popular discontent. Worker strikes and slowdowns, peasant unrest, and student activism spread.

On April 22, 1989, some 100,000 people gathered in **Tiananmen Square** at the heart of Beijing in silent defiance of a government ban on assembling. The following month brought a greater show of defiance when television cameras and world journalists converged on China to cover the historic visit of Soviet leader Mikhail Gorbachev. Several hundred students, flanked by thousands of supporters, began a hunger strike at the square to demand democratic reform. Tiananmen Square was now their stage and the world their audience. Within days, the strike spread to other cities. In Beijing, where well over a million people filled the city center, a carnivalesque atmosphere prevailed as the students sang and danced to rock songs and folk ballads.

The regime responded by declaring martial law. Two huge protest demonstrations followed, and residents erected barricades to defend the city against government troops. As the protest's momentum waned, a 28-foot icon, partly inspired by the Statue of Liberty, was unveiled at the square, capturing the imagination of the crowd and the attention of the cameras. But by then the government had assembled troops to crush the movement. In a night of terror that began at dusk on June 3, the People's Liberation Army turned their guns against the people. Most students in the square negotiated a safe passage; those who lost their lives—estimates vary from 2,000 to 7,000—were the nameless people who wielded Molotov cocktails, sticks, or bricks in a futile attempt to repel the troops.

The Chinese government weathered the storm. It continued to suppress unofficial social organizations; to control access to information, including that obtained over the Internet; and to crack down on dissidents. But it could not completely control the forces of globalization. Some organizations, like the quasi-religious group Falun Gong, eluded authorities and even used the Internet to enlist international support. At the dawn of the twenty-first century, signs of change were apparent. A visible urban entrepreneurial class had emerged, whose top echelon conducted its global businesses over nearly ubiquitous cellular phones. Rural dwellers paid what little they had to be smuggled abroad, at great risk and often with lethal consequences, so that they could make a better living in America

Tiananmen Square. *This white plaster and styrofoam statue, inspired in part by the Statue of Liberty and dubbed the Goddess of Democracy, was created by students in Beijing in the spring of 1989. It was brought to Tiananmen Square and unveiled at the end of May in an attempt to reinvigorate the democracy movement and the spirits of the protesters. For five days it captured worldwide attention, until it was toppled by a tank on June 4 and crushed as the Chinese People's Liberation Army cleared the square of its democracy advocates.*

or Europe. Within China, tens of millions of people lived a transient existence, with tens of thousands daily leaving the countryside for the cities. There they often suffered economic and social exploitation, as well as police and other government abuse. Existing at the margins of the new prosperity, they, too, served as reminders of the uneven effects of globalization.

In Mexico, democracy finally triumphed as the single party that had dominated the country for seventy-one years fell after the election of Vicente Fox in 2000. Until that time, Mexican rulers had combined patronage and rigged elections to stay in office. By the 1980s, corruption and abuse permeated the system. The abuse of democratic rights fell hardest on poor communities, especially those with large numbers of indigenous people.

PRIMARY SOURCE

Indigenous People in Mexico Speak Out

In late 1993, peasants of Chiapas rejected the false promises of the Mexican national government. Mostly Indians living in a jungle region, they had seen their land rights taken away and had tired of living under oppressive authorities. On January 1, 1994, they took up arms against the government, calling for a restoration of the principles of the Mexican Revolution: land for the hungry, democracy, and an end to centuries of neglect and oppression of Indians across the Americas. They formed the Zapatista Army for National Liberation (EZLN), mounted a brilliant public relations campaign, and enlisted massive international support. Here is an excerpt from their declaration of war against the Mexican government.

We are a product of 500 years of struggle: first against slavery, during the War of Independence against Spain led by the insurgents; afterward to avoid being absorbed by American imperialism; then to promulgate our constitution and expel the French Empire from our soil; and later the Porfirista dictatorship denied us just application of the Reform laws, and the people rebelled, forming their own leaders; . . . we have nothing, absolutely nothing, not even a decent roof over our heads, no land, no work, no health care, no food, or education; without the right to freely and democratically elect our authorities; without independence from foreigners, without peace or justice for ourselves and our children.

But TODAY WE SAY, ENOUGH! We are the heirs of those who truly forged our nationality. We the dispossessed are millions, and we call on our brothers to join in this call as the only path in order not to die of hunger in the face of the insatiable ambition of a dictatorship for more than 70 years led by a clique of traitors who represent the most conservative and sell-out groups in the country. They are the same as those who opposed Hidalgo and Morelos, who betrayed Vicente Guerrero, the same as those who sold over half our territory to the foreign invader, the same as those who brought a European prince to rule us, the same as those who formed the dictatorship of the Porfirista "scientists," the same as those who opposed the Oil Expropriation, the same as those who massacred the railroad workers in 1958 and the students in 1968, the same as those who today take everything from us, absolutely everything.

To prevent this, and as our last hope, after having tried everything to put into practice the legality based on our Magna Carta, we resort to it, to our Constitution, to apply Constitutional Article 39, which says:

"National sovereignty resides essentially and originally in the people. All public power emanates from the people and is instituted for the people's benefit. The people have, at all times, the unalienable right to alter or modify the form of their government."

Therefore, according to our Constitution, we issue this statement to the Mexican federal army, the basic pillar of the Mexican dictatorship that we suffer. . . .

In conformity with this Declaration of War, we ask the other branches of the Nation's government to meet to restore the legality and the stability of the Nation by deposing the dictator. . . .

PEOPLE OF MEXICO: We, upright and free men and women, are conscious that the war we declare is a last resort, but it is just. The dictators have been applying an undeclared genocidal war against our people for many years. Therefore we ask for your decided participation in support of this plan of the Mexican people in their struggle for work, land, housing, food, health care, education, independence, liberty, democracy, justice, and peace.

QUESTIONS FOR ANALYSIS

- In what other periods in this book have we encountered the ancestors of the Chiapas peasants?
- What does this declaration of war suggest about current and past Mexican governments?

Source: General Council of the EZLN, *Declaración de la Selva Lacandona*, 1993 (www.ezln.org, January 1, 1994).

Consider the state of Chiapas. An impoverished area with many Maya descendants, Chiapas had trouble coping with social and economic change in the 1980s. The president stripped Indians of their right to communal land and let the ruling party run Chiapas like a fiefdom. By the early 1990s, the province was demanding material betterment, cultural recognition of Indian rights, and local democracy. When one group of rebels, the Zapatistas, rose up in Mexico City against the government in 1994, the government prepared to crush the insurgents. (See Primary Source: Indigenous People in Mexico Speak Out.) But no one anticipated how supranational forces would play a role in helping local democracy: Cable News Network (CNN)

Protests in Mexico. Top: *Among the great Mexican muralists of the twentieth century, David Alfaro Siqueiros most advocated class struggle. In this 1957 mural image,* The People in Arms, *Siqueiros portrays Mexican peasants as they pick up arms in 1910 to fight for a new order. Paintings such as these provided inspiration for movements such as the Chiapas rebellion, depicted below. Bottom: After generations of oppression and exclusion, peasants of Chiapas, in southern Mexico, called for democracy and respect for their right to land. When Mexican authorities refused to bend, peasants took up arms. While they knew that they posed no military threat to the Mexican army, the Zapatista rebels used the world media and international organizations to embarrass the national political establishment into allowing reforms.*

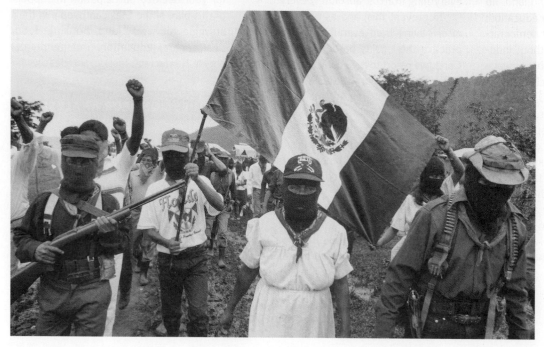

broadcast the clash worldwide, and the rebel leader created a Web site that drew thousands of "hits." Thereafter, international news media flooded Chiapas, filming Indians waving flags and pronouncing victory. Leaders in Mexico City, deeply embarrassed, asked local church authorities to negotiate peace and spearhead a commission to hear the villagers' concerns.

In 2000, national elections toppled the ruling party (including its representatives in Chiapas), and Mexico dismantled its one-party ruling system.

Mexico, South Africa, and China were powerful examples of how men and women in every corner of the earth yearned to choose their own leaders. In 1994, millions of previously disenfranchised South Africans lined up for hours to cast a vote for their new black African president, Nelson Mandela. In 2000, the Mexican electorate turned out the ruling party, while in China the ruling Communist Party had to call in the army to prevent regime change and democratic reforms.

With the fall of the Soviet Union, new political actors fueled by new social grievances led to a global wave of demands on governments for freedom, human and democratic rights and for welfare support to shelter the have-nots from the very forces unleashed by economic globalization. There were significant breakthroughs—as in South Africa and a number of other African states, many Latin American societies, and an eastern Europe released from the pall of the east-west divide. Even so, dictatorial regimes like those in China, parts of Africa, and parts of the Middle East held out against protest movements and maintained their autocracies.

CONCLUSION

In the thirteenth century (as long before), a few travelers like Ibn Battuta and Marco Polo ventured over long distances to trade, to explore, and to convert souls; yet communications technology was rudimentary, making long-distance mobility and exchange expensive, rare, and perilous. The world was much more a series of communities set apart than a world bound together by culture, capital, and communications networks.

By the late twentieth century, that balance had changed. Food, entertainment, clothing, and even family life were becoming more similar worldwide. To be sure, some local differences remained. In 2000, local cultures lived on and in some cases were revived through challenges to the authority of nation-states. No longer did the nation-state or any single level of community life define collective identities. At the same time, worldwide purveyors of cultural and commercial resources offered local communities the same kinds of products, from aspirin to Nike shoes. Exchanges across local and national boundaries became easier. For the first time, many of the world's peoples felt they belonged to a global culture.

New technologies, new methods of production and investment, and the greater importance of personal health and education for human betterment created new possibilities—and greater inequalities. Indeed, the disparities between haves and have-nots in 2000 were astonishing. For as humanity harnessed new technologies to accelerate exchanges across and within cultures, an ever-larger gulf separated those who participated in global networks from those who languished on the margins. This inequality produced a range of divergent political and cultural forms after the collapse of the three-world order. Thus, as the world became more integrated, it also grew apart along ever-deeper lines.

After You Read This Chapter

Go to INQUIZITIVE to see what you know & learn what you've missed.

TRACING THE GLOBAL STORYLINES

FOCUS ON: *Globalization*

Removing Obstacles to Globalization

- Communism's fall and the end of the Cold War improve prospects for global exchange of peoples, ideas, and resources.

- Final decolonization in Angola, Mozambique, and Guinea-Bissau and the end of apartheid in South Africa return self-rule throughout Africa.

Unleashing Globalization

- Financial deregulation and the end of gold and silver standards allow money to move freely across borders but lead to a Third World debt crisis.

- Widespread migrations occur as people in Africa, Asia, and Latin America move to Europe and America, following the tracks of their former colonizers.

- Revolutions in culture and communications make cultural diversity more possible for those who can afford it.

The New Global Order

- Globalization leads to dramatic population expansion, requiring greater agricultural and industrial output.

- Family structure changes, life spans increase, and more goods are available, yet inequalities deepen as education and good health determine social status as never before.

- As globalization erodes the power of the nation-state, greater violence occurs between and within states. Nongovernmental organizations (NGOs) and religion become resources for dealing with violence and inequality and for reimagining the nation-state.

CHRONOLOGY

	1975	1980	1985
The Americas			U.S. announces Strategic Defense Initiative (SDI) **1983** ◆
Europe			
Soviet Union			Gorbachev assumes power **1985** ◆ Chernobyl nuclear accident **1986** ◆
Africa			
The Middle East		◆ Khomeini establishes theocratic state in Iran **1979**	
South Asia			
East Asia			

AIDS (acquired immunodeficiency syndrome) *p. 811*

developing world *p. 790*

European Union (EU) *p. 798*

globalization *p. 789*

global warming *p. 816*

Mandela, Nelson *p. 796*

supranational organizations *p. 817*

Tiananmen Square *p. 822*

truth commissions *p. 819*

1. **Identify** the types of transnational forces that eroded the power of the nation-state in the last third of the twentieth century, and **explain** how they did so.

2. **Describe** to what extent the three-world order discussed in Chapter 20 did not exist by 1975. What architecture of power was replacing it?

3. **Discuss** the end of the Cold War. **Explore** how, and to what degree, U.S. containment policies contributed to the Soviet Union's demise.

4. **Describe** the process through which apartheid was dismantled in South Africa. Why was the process relatively nonviolent?

5. **Analyze** the role of the International Monetary Fund in the developing world. On what terms did it provide assistance? Who benefited, and what kind of sacrifices did it impose?

6. **Explore** the relationship between global migration, new technologies, and the spread of cultural influences during and after the Cold War.

7. **Discuss** how globalization transformed popular culture. To what extent does global popular culture reflect American culture?

8. **Explain** how globalization transformed world demography. What patterns emerged in terms of international migration?

9. **Identify** the ways in which globalization affected women. **Explore** how new patterns in trade, production, and finance helped or hindered opportunities for women worldwide.

10. **Examine** the ways in which globalization and population changes affected the environment, and vice versa. How effectively has the global community addressed new environmental concerns?

11. **Explain** the trends in agricultural production and natural resource consumption over the last several decades. Who produced the goods, and who consumed them?

12. **Consider** to what extent globalization changed societies. **Compare and contrast** globalization after the Cold War with earlier forms of globalization.

13. **Discuss** how globalization altered people's sense of identity. How did globalization challenge national identity and the idea of the nation-state?

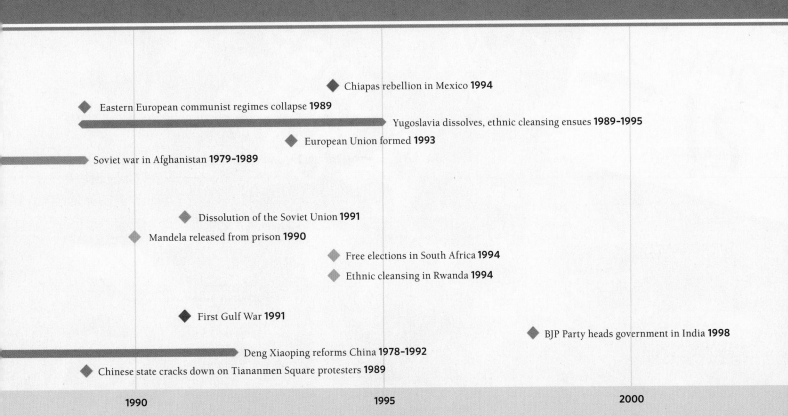

Chiapas rebellion in Mexico **1994**

Eastern European communist regimes collapse **1989**

Yugoslavia dissolves, ethnic cleansing ensues **1989–1995**

European Union formed **1993**

Soviet war in Afghanistan **1979–1989**

Dissolution of the Soviet Union **1991**

Mandela released from prison **1990**

Free elections in South Africa **1994**

Ethnic cleansing in Rwanda **1994**

First Gulf War **1991**

BJP Party heads government in India **1998**

Deng Xiaoping reforms China **1978–1992**

Chinese state cracks down on Tiananmen Square protesters **1989**

1990   1995   2000

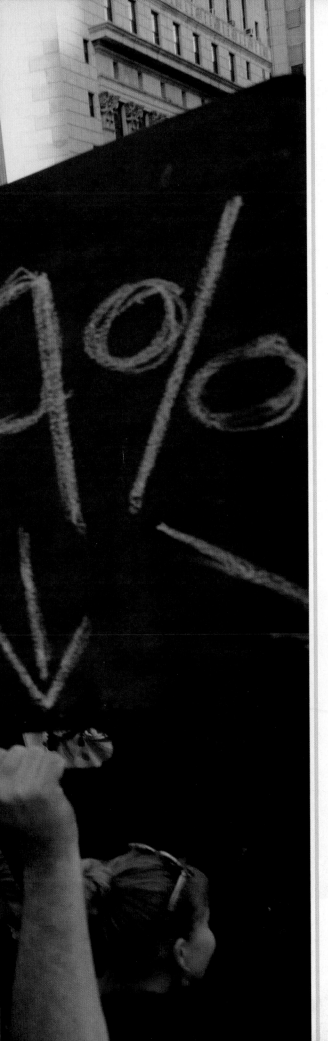

Epilogue

2001–The Present

The new millennium closed the chapter on the bloody wars and ideological rivalries of the twentieth century. Although the Cold War was over, and global integration seemed greater than ever before in human history, the twentieth-first century brought new explosive hostilities and fresh economic and political challenges.

On September 11, 2001, less than two years into the century, nineteen hijackers commandeered four commercial airplanes. The hijackers slammed two of the planes into the World Trade Center in New York City and a third into the Pentagon Building, home of the U.S. Department of Defense, in Washington, D.C. The fourth plane was deterred from its intended target—the White House or the Capitol—by the courageous actions of its passengers and crashed in a field in southwestern Pennsylvania. Television captured the event live for global viewers, recording the horrifying images of the Trade Center's twin towers engulfed in flames, then crumbling in a heap of ash and twisted metal. A still rather unknown Muslim militant organization, al-Qaeda, headed by an equally little known Saudi, Osama bin Laden, claimed responsibility for the attacks that took the lives of more than 3,000 Americans. What followed was a predictable and determined American military response—the invasions of Iraq, incorrectly blamed for engineering the attacks, and Afghanistan, where a fundamentalist Islamic government provided a haven for bin Laden and his al-Qaeda affiliates.

Economic turmoil added to the turbulence of terrorism and wars. The global economy and technologies had brought the world together as never before, but the benefits of integration were unequally distributed. Consequently, when an economic crisis broke out, as it did in 2008, its effects were felt globally but experienced unequally, causing despair and discontent. As people across the world came to grips with the shadow of mounting geopolitical and economic uncertainties, a populist politics of us versus them swept many parts of the world.

GLOBAL CHALLENGES

War on Terror

The terrorist attack of 9/11 created revulsion across the world. Anger focused on Osama bin Laden and al-Qaeda, the loosely organized militant networks of Islamist groups that had organized the attack. The militants claimed that it was a response to America's imperialist policies in the Middle East and retribution for American troops' presence in Saudi Arabia (during the first Iraq War). In the months and years that followed, countries grappled with a "war on terror," conflicts with militant Islamic groups, and a global economic crisis. George W. Bush, who had become president after a close and disputed election the year before, gained broad public support for his tough talk about bringing terrorists to justice and for his insistence that the events of September 11 had introduced a divide between the "pre-9/11 world" and the "post-9/11" one. Domestically, Bush pushed for security measures to curb future terrorist violence, protect freedom, and secure the American homeland.

Internationally, President Bush declared a "global war on terror." With the backing of the majority of the American people, as well as strong support from many nations, Bush unsuccessfully sent American forces to Afghanistan to hunt down bin Laden, destroy al-Qaeda training camps, and topple the Taliban government that had provided a haven for the terrorists. Expanding the battlefront of the war on terror, in 2003 the Bush administration ordered an invasion of Iraq, falsely charging its brutal dictator, Saddam Hussein, with abetting the terrorist assault of 9/11 and producing weapons of mass destruction. As in Afghanistan, the initial offensive went well; but defeating the Iraqi army and finding Hussein proved easier than restoring order to the country, improving living standards, and persuading the population to rally around the American vision of a democratic polity.

Moreover, the failure to find weapons of mass destruction or to uncover indisputable links between Hussein and al-Qaeda, together with mounting American losses from an ongoing insurgency, left many U.S. citizens questioning the wisdom of this war.

9/11. Left: *The North Tower already aflame, this photograph captures a second hijacked jet an instant before it crashed into the South Tower of New York's World Trade Center on September 11, 2001.* Right: *Firefighters search for survivors in the smoldering ruins.*

Iraqi Elections. *Iraqis voted on December 15, 2005, while the country was under American and allied military occupation. Voters' fingers were stained after voting so that they could not vote twice; many walked away from the polling booth showing their stained finger with pride.*

Although Bush won reelection in 2004, the national and global unity so evident right after September 11 seemed increasingly distant—as was the sense that the new century would be one of peace and prosperity under an American-led world order.

In Afghanistan, the situation shifted noticeably. U.S.-led coalition forces started to find themselves in a quagmire like the one that the Soviets had fallen into two decades earlier (see Chapter 21). Early successes to maintain stability became more challenging as local warlords exercised personal power toward achieving their own goals and as the revitalized Taliban were able to regroup in neighboring Pakistan.

While the campaigns in Iraq and Afghanistan faltered, the United States accelerated its campaign to hunt down terrorist leaders, and on May 2, 2011, under President Barack Obama, a daring operation in Pakistan ended with the death of Osama bin Laden. Even so, the American image suffered internationally with the exposés of its programs of extensive surveillance (including that of U.S. citizens), the use of coercive interrogation techniques, "rendition" of suspected militants to sites where they could be tortured to extract information, the inhumane treatment of Iraqi prisoners at the Abu Ghraib prison, and the harsh and indefinite detention of suspected terrorists at Guantanamo. The domestic support for the Bush administration also eroded.

Helped by a growing chorus of disapproval of the Iraq War, Barack Obama had secured the American presidency in 2008. Following his campaign promise, President Obama announced plans to end the Iraq War and refocus attention on Afghanistan. The Democratic president ended the Iraq occupation in 2011, and after promoting a surge of forces in Afghanistan, he reduced the number of American troops there.

Crisis and Inequality in the Global Economy

Beginning in 2007, the world economy fell into crisis. The problem began in the financial sector, the most globally interlinked of all. Seeking new sources of profits, investors from around the world poured their money into riskier and riskier investments—many of which were so complex that not even the regulators in charge of monitoring the financial sector could understand them.

One of the most enticing of these risky bets was real estate in the United States, where a frenzy of investment in the early 2000s created a "bubble" that drove real estate prices to an unsustainable level. The bubble eventually burst, leading to a plunge in property values. This meant not only that banks and financial agencies were stuck with increasingly worthless assets, but also that millions of homeowners could not afford to make their mortgage payments or sell their homes. Massive defaults on loans ripped through the world financial system and led to a seizure of credit. By the summer of 2008, there was a worldwide panic, and the banking system nearly collapsed. As it became more difficult to borrow money and consumers stopped spending, factories shut down and stores went bankrupt. Layoffs, higher taxes, and reduced consumption resulted in the contraction of developed economies and skyrocketing unemployment.

The financial crisis brought signs of gathering discontent. In Europe, where, at last, economic and political integration within the European Union had seemed to promise an end to conflict between states, the crisis created new tensions. In Greece, radical new parties arose to protest austerity measures or to take out frustrations on immigrants, and many blamed the richer nations, especially the Germans, for having profited from the creation of the Eurozone at the expense of the poorer nations. For the first time in decades, vehement nationalist slogans came into wide circulation, and some commentators

Global Financial Crisis. *When the major investment firm Lehman Brothers declared bankruptcy in September 2008, the world's increasingly integrated financial system teetered on the brink of collapse. Although massive government interventions kept the system afloat, they did not prevent a severe downturn and a sharply rising unemployment rate.*

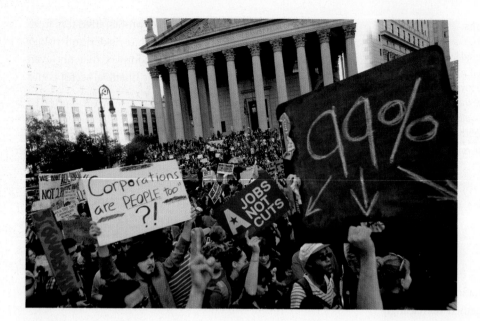

Occupy Wall Street. *Inspired by other stirrings around the world, this largely national movement was fueled by methods as novel as social media and as traditional as a sit-in. Here an Occupy Wall Street rally joins a labor union demonstration outside the New York County Courthouse in 2011.*

predicted that the common currency (the Euro)—and perhaps even the European Union—in its current form would not last.

Even as economies emerged from the crisis, economic inequality among individuals and between regions led to new challenges. The very same ongoing integration of the world economy that globalized the economic crisis also produced fresh wealth across the world. Brazil, Russia, China, India, Vietnam, Indonesia, and South Africa all became more prosperous than they were even just a decade before, leaving other states far behind economically. Capital, technology, and media brought the world together ever more closely. The movement of ideas and images across national borders accelerated. Social media like Facebook provided new lines of communication and connections, particularly among the young. New aspirations for employment, prosperity, consumption, and political expression appeared.

Juan Evo Morales came to power in Bolivia as the first president of Indian descent in 2005—and was reelected in 2009—on the basis of his activism as leader of peasants and working people. Thousands took to the streets in the Orange Revolution in Ukraine during 2004 and 2005, protesting electoral fraud and corruption. An upsurge against Vladimir Putin erupted in Russia in 2011, culminating in the dramatic protest staged in 2012 by Pussy Riot, a feminist punk rock band. The Arab Spring swept across the Middle East in 2011, offering new expressions of political transformation in sharp contrast to Islamic militancy. An anticorruption movement broke out in India in 2011, mobilizing people demanding transparency and accountability in politics. Barack Obama swept to power in 2008 as the first African American president. Even though his campaign of hope and change crashed at the shores of the economic crisis, he was reelected in 2012.

The global economic and political stirrings were full of paradoxes and contradictions. The growth of prosperity and wealth around the world was highly unequal and accompanied by an unprecedented rise in the power and influence of corporations and financial institutions. Even as a global middle class came into being, inequality deepened. This sparked protests, none more powerfully and dramatically than by Occupy Wall Street (OWS), a movement that started in September 2011 in New York and was organized by a Canadian anarchist group called Adbusters. It highlighted growing social and economic inequality and challenged the power of banks and corporations.

OWS was one among a wide range of emergent political upheavals around the world. Each one had a character specific to the region. Yet together they represented a new phenomenon. Almost all of them took shape outside conventional politics and ideological agendas. Expressing antiestablishment ideals and using social media to mobilize, the young took the lead in these new popular upsurges. We do not know if they will endure or what shapes they will take, but these global stirrings represent something new on the horizon.

Climate Change

Climate change has emerged as one of the most pressing issues for the new millennium. As the world population continues to grow and as more areas industrialize, the pressure on vital natural resources (especially oil and water) has inspired calls for greater conservation and more environmentally sustainable economic development. But the U.S. government's resistance to global regulations, as well as a rising demand for resources (especially by China and India), has made the future of the earth's environment uncertain.

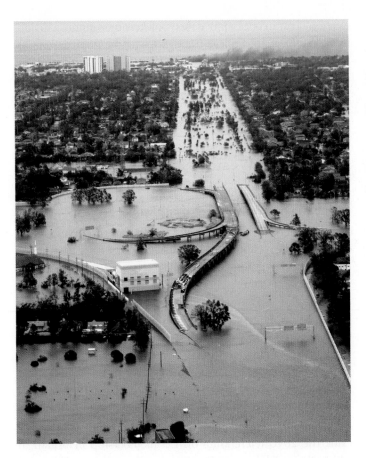

Hurricane Katrina. *As the hurricane dissipated in the tail end of August 2005, the U.S. Coast Guard surveyed the affected areas by aircraft and conducted damage assessment of what would be the costliest natural disaster in American history. This Coast Guard photograph captures New Orleans immediately after the passing of Katrina.*

Destruction by Hurricane Sandy on Ortley Beach, New Jersey. *Hurricane Sandy, moving ashore in New Jersey on October 29, 2012, was the second-costliest hurricane in U.S. history. Its high winds struck twenty-four states, including the entire eastern seaboard from Florida to Maine.*

Despite difficulties in achieving a consensus on actions, there is a broad agreement among scientists and environmental experts that the planet needs remedial action. Thus, when the Group of Eight (G8), a forum of leaders from Canada, France, Germany, Italy, Japan, Russia, the United Kingdom, and the United States, met in 2007, a key topic was climate change. It acknowledged that humankind is contributing to, if not causing, the emissions of greenhouse gases, which trap the sun's rays in the atmosphere. The result is warming temperatures, melting ice caps, drought in some parts, and more severe storms elsewhere. The effects on low-lying populations at sea level can be catastrophic. Hurricane Katrina in 2005, for example, left much of New Orleans and the Mississippi Gulf Coast in ruins. Hurricane Sandy had similar catastrophic effects on the shorelines of New Jersey and New York in 2013. Elsewhere, prolonged drought has led to agrarian crises and food shortages; this crept up on Syria over many years and led to an outburst of opposition to the despotic government of Bashar al-Assad. The resulting refugee crisis has spilled over into Turkey and Europe and widened the regional crisis.

Climate change demands shared solutions by the world's national governments. Yet there is no international agency with teeth to enforce a global accord. The result has been a series of often frustrating global summits, usually ending with countries deeply divided over solutions. With few exceptions, however, no country denies the causes: the reliance on fossil fuels for energy sources. But China objected that it would have to curb fossil fuel dependence when it has a much lower per capita income than, for instance, Germany. And the United States balked at the idea that it had to finance "poor countries'" adjustment to carbon reduction on the grounds that some of them, like China, were direct economic competitors. Meanwhile, climate change negotiators have scrambled to find a way forward, to coordinate a solution that is comprehensive yet allows each country to chart its own strategy. Moreover, two important shifts have taken place affecting public opinion in the world's two leading CO_2 emitters. In China, responsible for 20 percent of greenhouse gas emissions, life in most cities was becoming unbearable due to coal pollution. In the United States, responsible for 18 percent of CO_2 emissions, more and more citizens were growing angry about the slow pace of action on global warming; in fact, some states, like California, unilaterally imposed higher standards on vehicles, while cleaner natural gas began to replace "dirty" coal on a large scale.

A major breakthrough occurred in Paris in 2015 when, under the sponsorship of the United Nations Framework on Climate Change, most of the nations of the world gathered to hammer out an agreement that would limit the emission of greenhouse gases and hold the increase in global temperature to less than 2°C. The accord, scheduled to go into effect in 2020, has set a higher standard, aiming to achieve a less than 1.5°C increase in global temperature. No fewer than 194 countries signed the accord on December 12, 2015, and by the end of that year, 132 countries ratified the agreement. The two heaviest polluters, China and the United States, are crucial signatories. Yet the implementation of the agreement is reserved to the nations, each of which has to file reports with the United Nations. The new American president, Donald Trump, has threatened to repudiate American participation in the Paris accord and has even asserted that the entire science of climate change and global warming is a hoax.

THE UNITED STATES, THE EUROPEAN UNION, AND JAPAN

Although the global challenges of the twenty-first century touched virtually every corner of the world, countries and regions experienced specific local changes often related to globalizing forces.

The United States

In the United States, the Obama administration sought to cope with the economic crisis while introducing health care reform; it encountered a conservative backlash in the shape of the Tea Party movement, which espoused the ideals of small government and market freedom and contributed to a stinging defeat of the Democrats in the 2010 congressional elections. From the opposite side of the ideological spectrum arose the Occupy Wall Street movement in 2011. Claiming to speak on behalf of the 99 percent against the wealthy 1 percent, the Occupy activists, consisting largely of young people, railed against the banks and financial institutions that the federal government had rescued from bankruptcy by providing immense loans. Although the movement ran out of steam by the end of the year, it succeeded in inserting the growing inequality into political discussions. Partially helped by the focus on inequality brought about by the Occupy movement, Obama won reelection and his Democratic party fared better in the 2012 elections. But the political pendulum swung back toward the Republicans in the 2014 midterm elections.

More stunning was the 2016 election, in which Donald Trump, who had never held political office, inveighed against "inner-city" crime, immigrants, international trade, and long-standing American allies and foreign alliances. Although few pundits gave Trump much chance against a field of well-established and well-financed Republican opponents, his populist and nationalist platform resonated with primary voters and gained him the party's nomination. Facing Hillary Clinton in the general

election, Trump once more defied pollsters by winning a majority in the Electoral College (though losing the popular vote by nearly 3 million). Coming on the heels of the equally surprising election in which British voters narrowly chose to exit from the European Union, Trump's victory reflected the growing populist and nationalist tide against globalization.

A Changing Western Europe

The American invasion of Iraq created fractures in the alliance between the United States and western Europe. During the 1990s, the collapse of the Soviet Union and the development of the European Union (EU) had caused some rumblings about the future of NATO, but disagreements remained muted prior to the American military's entrance into Iraq. In fact, in the immediate wake of September 11, European allies rallied behind the United States. But before and after the invasion of Iraq, leaders in France and Germany sharply criticized U.S. foreign policy.

Far more serious divisions emerged over the fate of NATO and of the European Union, whose membership peaked at twenty-eight countries, including ten that formerly had been part of the Soviet bloc. Early warning signs included votes in France and the Netherlands rejecting the EU constitution. Then came the 2016 referendum on EU membership in Britain in which "Leave," known as Brexit, secured a majority. The trend toward expansion, whereby EU member states relinquished a significant degree of sovereignty as an answer to the legacies of war, ethnic cleansing, and genocide, was reversed over the issues of free integration within the union and the unlimited jurisdiction of the European Court of Justice.

Moreover, while the adoption of a single currency, the euro, by seventeen EU members had indeed facilitated commerce, it had also caused economic damage. Monetary integration, in the absence of corresponding fiscal integration, meant that countries with different economies could no longer adjust for imbalances and competitiveness by currency devaluations. Unemployment rose dramatically and remained high in Europe's southern tier, even as the northern tier did better. The calamity was most visible in Greece, where northern country debtors were protected at the expense of Greek jobs and the Greek standard of living, all in the name of preserving Greece's EU membership. The euro, which had promised prosperity, became a symbol of immiseration.

The combination of fears over unfettered immigration, crystallized by the war in Syria and resulting flow of desperate refugees into Europe, and the elite mismanagement of the euro and the economy created fertile ground for self-styled populist politics. The EU's signature identity, democratic institutions, experienced significant erosion beginning in Hungary and then Poland before spreading to much of the rest of the Continent. Europe's malaise put the long-term future of integration to the test.

British Voters Protest the Referendum to Leave the European Union. *In a hotly contested referendum in which 72 percent of registered voters cast ballots, 52 percent of the electorate chose to withdraw from the European Union.*

Demographic Issues

One threat to future peace and prosperity in Europe—and the United States and Japan as well—is the interlocking issues of aging and immigration. Women in the European Union would have to bear two children on average to maintain its population of 500 million, but women in the EU now average only 1.5 offspring. Adding to the demographic and labor pressures is the aging of the European population. With the percentage of elderly Europeans rising rapidly, sustaining the present workers-to-retirees ratio and paying for the region's burgeoning number of pensioners will require the European Union to attract around 15 million immigrants annually.

That number has not been reached. European populations have been boosted by millions of immigrants, many of them Muslims, but sustainable economic growth has proven elusive. Islam has become the fastest-growing religion in Europe. In France, the Muslim population exceeds 11 percent of the total. These immigrants often live in isolated and impoverished circumstances, and in many countries their status as guest workers (see Chapter 21) denies them the full benefits of citizenship. Their presence in Europe's larger cities threatens those who still equate Europe with Christendom and challenges those who believe that European integration requires complete assimilation of all inhabitants.

Europe is not alone in confronting the problems of an aging population and the integration of immigrants. As its baby boom generation ages, the United States faces a similar imbalance between retirees and workers that endangers its Social Security system. Likewise, the flood of immigrants, particularly from Asia and Latin America, continues to shift the nation's ethnic composition. According to the U.S. Census Bureau, in 2010 people

of Latin American descent in the United States numbered nearly 48 million (about 15.5 percent of the population). The presence of so many Spanish-speaking residents troubles those who think the United States should remain an English-only country, and the degree to which immigrants should be required to assimilate remains a contentious issue. More heated still are debates about illegal immigration, which Donald Trump, pledging to "build a wall" across the U.S.-Mexico border, made central to his campaign for the presidency in 2016. (For a global look at population growth and life expectancies, see Maps E.1 and E.2.)

In many respects, the dilemma of aging presses hardest today on Japan. Like Europeans and North Americans, the Japanese are marrying later and having fewer children. Japan's female population now averages barely 1.37 children, compared with nearly 3.7 in 1950. At the same time, Japanese life expectancy has reached eighty-five, the highest in the world, which further tilts the nation's age pyramid. In 1970, the elderly (those over age sixty-five) represented around 7 percent of the population; in 2005, they reached 20 percent and are expected to hit 40 percent by 2050. Analysts surmise that Japan's population peaked at around 128 million and might decline to perhaps 120 million by 2050, with a substantial number of those over the working age. Such a downturn bodes ill for Japan's dynamic economy, which is currently the world's third largest in terms of total GDP, China having moved into second place in 2012.

Like Europe and North America, Japan relies on immigrants to fill out its labor force. In the 1960s, the nation's booming economy experienced labor shortages, but neither the government nor major corporations chose to invite in foreign laborers. They preferred automation or recruitment of workers of Japanese descent from abroad. By the 1980s, however, deepening labor shortages and the yen's rising value led to an

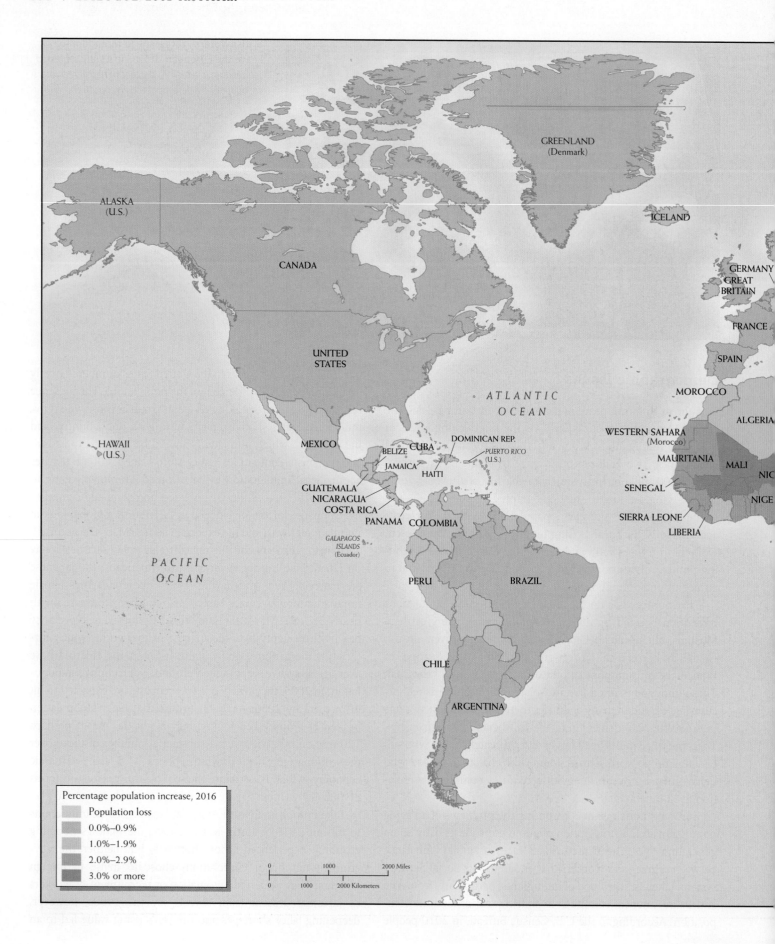

GREENLAND
(Denmark)

ALASKA
(U.S.)

ICELAND

CANADA

GERMANY
GREAT
BRITAIN

FRANCE

SPAIN

MOROCCO

UNITED
STATES

ATLANTIC
OCEAN

ALGERIA

WESTERN SAHARA
(Morocco)

HAWAII
(U.S.)

MEXICO

CUBA

DOMINICAN REP.

MAURITANIA

MALI

NIC

BELIZE

PUERTO RICO
(U.S.)

JAMAICA

HAITI

SENEGAL

NIGE

GUATEMALA

SIERRA LEONE

NICARAGUA

COSTA RICA

PANAMA

COLOMBIA

LIBERIA

GALAPAGOS
ISLANDS
(Ecuador)

PACIFIC
OCEAN

PERU

BRAZIL

CHILE

ARGENTINA

Percentage population increase, 2016

Population loss

0.0%–0.9%

1.0%–1.9%

2.0%–2.9%

3.0% or more

0	1000	2000 Miles
0	1000	2000 Kilometers

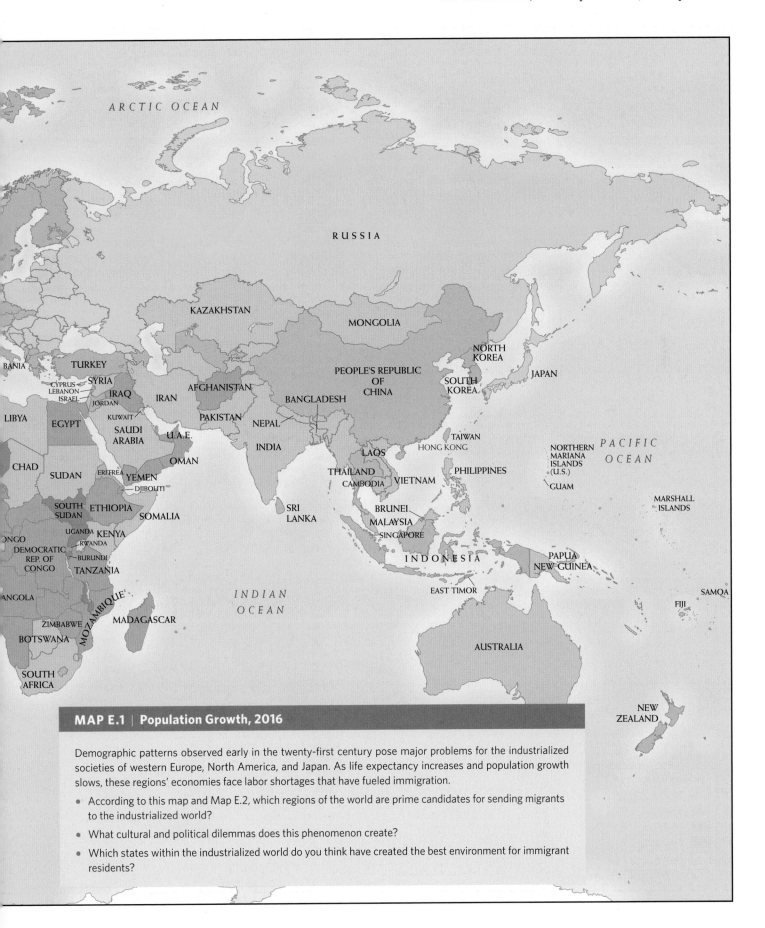

MAP E.1 | Population Growth, 2016

Demographic patterns observed early in the twenty-first century pose major problems for the industrialized societies of western Europe, North America, and Japan. As life expectancy increases and population growth slows, these regions' economies face labor shortages that have fueled immigration.

• According to this map and Map E.2, which regions of the world are prime candidates for sending migrants to the industrialized world?

• What cultural and political dilemmas does this phenomenon create?

• Which states within the industrialized world do you think have created the best environment for immigrant residents?

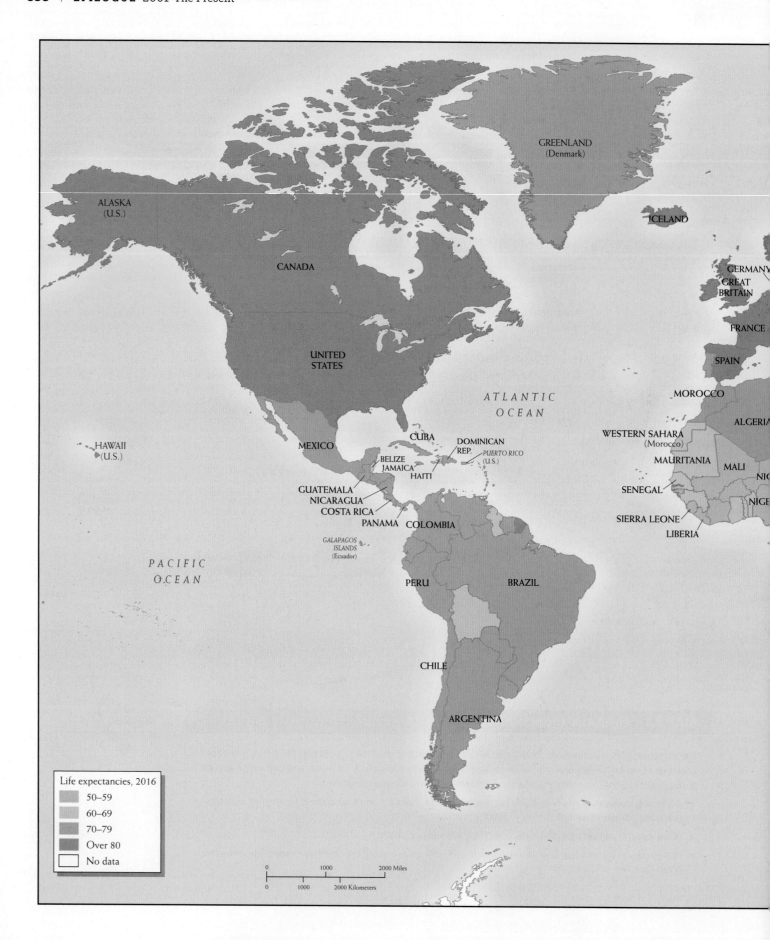

Life expectancies, 2016
50–59
60–69
70–79
Over 80
No data

GREENLAND
(Denmark)

ALASKA
(U.S.)

ICELAND

CANADA

GERMANY
GREAT
BRITAIN

FRANCE

SPAIN

UNITED
STATES

MOROCCO

ATLANTIC
OCEAN

WESTERN SAHARA
(Morocco)

ALGERIA

HAWAII
(U.S.)

CUBA

DOMINICAN
REP.

MAURITANIA

MALI

MEXICO

PUERTO RICO
(U.S.)

BELIZE
JAMAICA

SENEGAL

NIGER

HAITI

NIGE

GUATEMALA

SIERRA LEONE

NICARAGUA

COSTA RICA

LIBERIA

PANAMA

COLOMBIA

GALAPAGOS
ISLANDS
(Ecuador)

PACIFIC
OCEAN

PERU

BRAZIL

CHILE

ARGENTINA

0   1000   2000 Miles

0   1000   2000 Kilometers

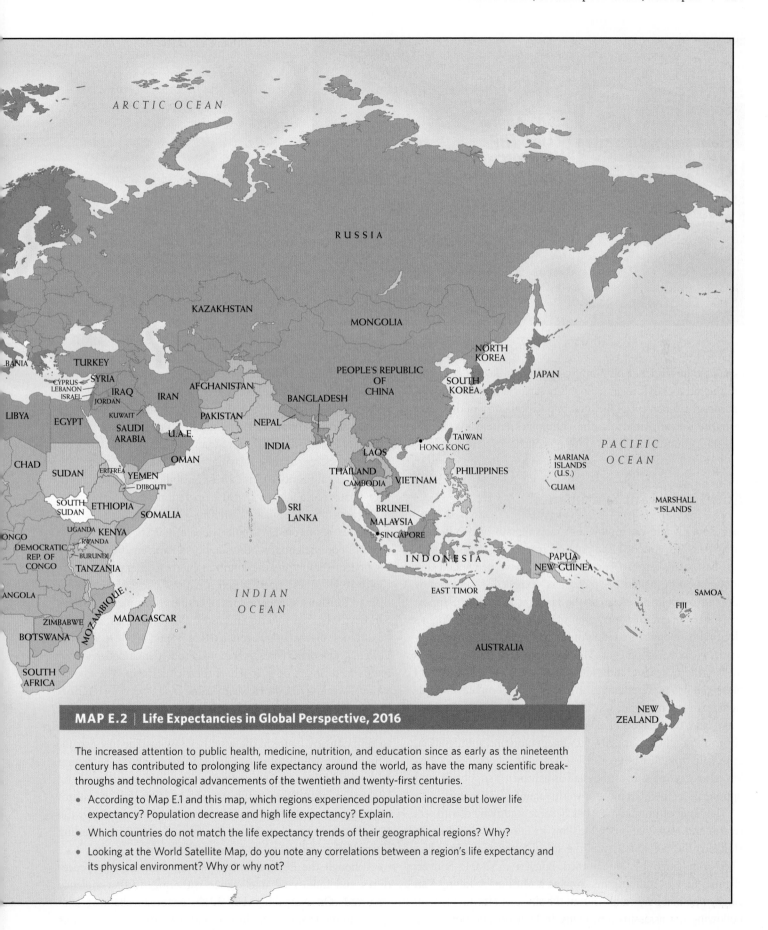

MAP E.2 | Life Expectancies in Global Perspective, 2016

The increased attention to public health, medicine, nutrition, and education since as early as the nineteenth century has contributed to prolonging life expectancy around the world, as have the many scientific breakthroughs and technological advancements of the twentieth and twenty-first centuries.

- According to Map E.1 and this map, which regions experienced population increase but lower life expectancy? Population decrease and high life expectancy? Explain.
- Which countries do not match the life expectancy trends of their geographical regions? Why?
- Looking at the World Satellite Map, do you note any correlations between a region's life expectancy and its physical environment? Why or why not?

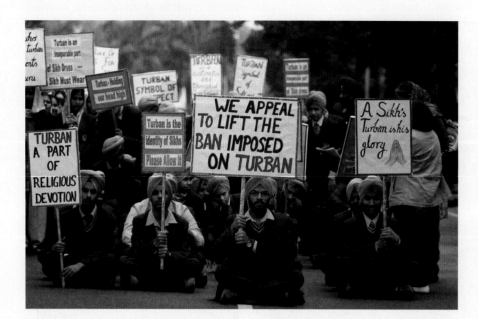

French Turban Ban. *During French President Sarkozy's state visit to India in 2010, Indian Sikh students held a demonstration in New Delhi calling for the lifting of the French ban on wearing the turban, a religious practice that dates back to the eighteenth century.*

expanded dependence on immigrant workers. Recent estimates put the number of foreign nationals in Japan at nearly 2 million, or around 1.5 percent of the total population. Most of them hail from the Korean Peninsula, the Philippines, Indochina, Brazil, and Iran, countries with a surplus of skilled workers.

Anti-Immigrant Sentiments

In Europe, where unemployment rates remain higher than in Japan or North America, the political reaction against immigration has been sharpest. Far right groups have demanded that immigration be halted or "foreigners" expelled, a stance now adopted by politicians across the far-right spectrum. Support levels vary in each country, but across Europe the far right's electoral base appears to be around 15 percent; in some countries it is above 25 percent. The Freedom Party in Austria and the Northern League and National Alliance in Italy regularly place cabinet representatives in coalition governments. Ultra-right forces such as France's National Front, Denmark's People's Party, and the League of Polish Families sometimes pressure governing coalitions to slow EU integration and immigration, especially from Muslim countries. The issue of accepting Muslim refugees from war-torn Syria has galvanized supporters and opponents in the EU's most powerful country, Germany.

The issue of immigration has become intertwined with terrorism and assimiliation of Muslims in European societies. In Holland, the precipitant was the grisly murder of filmmaker Theo Van Gogh by Mohammed Bouyeri in 2004. Bouyeri claimed he was fulfilling his duty as a Muslim by killing Van Gogh, who had made a film about the abuse of Muslim women. Following the assassination, many in Holland questioned the nation's traditional tolerance of diversity and expressed concern that Muslims were too alien in their values to ever fit in Dutch society. Several terrorist attacks further inflamed the debate. In 2004, a series of bombings of commuter trains in Madrid killed 191 people and wounded more than 2,000; in 2005, terrorists struck London's subways, leaving 52 dead and 700 injured. In both cases, authorities pinned responsibility on al-Qaeda. But investigators also alleged that the operations were the work of Muslim residents of Spain or Britain.

France confronted a similar debate after rioting rocked a series of poor neighborhoods, notably in Paris, in 2005, protesting police brutality and the country's failure to offer equal opportunity to all. These riots caused a nativist backlash that often blamed Muslims in general for the country's problems. Nicolas Sarkozy, who was interior minister at the time, ordered the deportation of immigrants convicted of rioting, while Jean-Marie Le Pen, leader of the far right National Front, demanded that even naturalized rioters be stripped of their citizenship. The French satirical weekly, *Charlie Hebdo*, became the target of two terrorist attacks after publishing deliberately irreverent depictions of Muhammad. The cartoonists aggressively defended their right to lampoon any figure in the way they saw fit. The first assault, a firebombing of the offices in 2011, followed an issue equating Islam and Muhammad with oppression of women under Sharia law; in the second assault, which came in 2015 after caricatures of the Prophet, two gunmen shouting "God is great" and the "Prophet is avenged" murdered twelve staff members, including the publisher and prominent cartoonists.

Although the Europeans stepped up their security procedures and intensified intelligence gathering, further violence occurred. On November 13, 2015, terrorists claiming allegiance to the Islamic State in Iraq and Syria carried out a series of coordinated attacks; while one group struck outside a Paris stadium where France was playing Germany in a football (soccer) match, others attacked restaurants and cafes. In all, 130 were killed and many more injured. Just a few months later, a Tunisian, Anis Amri, also asserting allegiance to the Islamic State, struck in a market in Berlin, killing twelve.

The United States, too, was trying to cope with the threat of terrorism and the challenge of immigration. Since September 11, 2001, the United States had not suffered another major attack, but smaller attacks raised the level of public alarm. And while Americans often described theirs as a nation of immigrants, anti-immigrant sentiments also gathered popular support, fueled by candidate Trump's campaign promises of curbing legal immigration, blocking illegal immigrants, and deporting undocumented foreigners, who, Trump maintained, were taking jobs from American citizens.

In just a few years, the mood of the world's most advanced industrial societies has shifted decisively. The triumphant atmosphere that ushered in the new millennium has given way to a pessimistic outlook. In the year 2000, talk of the blessings of global integration dominated the political and economic scene; now prognosticators warn about the dangers emanating from disaffected members of their societies and from radicals, especially Islamic radicals, willing and able to unleash terror anywhere in the world.

RUSSIA, CHINA, AND INDIA

Fueling anti-immigrant fires in Europe, Japan, and North America is the increasing number of jobs being "outsourced" to China, India, and other countries. In the past, businesses had turned to immigrants to fill low-wage positions (and to keep all wages down). But at the end of the twentieth and the beginning of the twenty-first centuries, it became more economical to relocate manufacturing to places where cheap labor is already available.

Economic Globalization and Political Effects

In the twenty-first century, business mobility is not limited to low-skilled and low-wage jobs. Technological advances—particularly in computers and communication—have enabled all sorts of enterprises to operate from almost any point on the globe. No longer do educated workers have to leave India and China for employment in Europe or North America, because it is increasingly cost-effective for corporations to shift certain operations to those countries. The playing field has been leveled in the globalized market economy, although countries with vast labor reserves such as China, India, and Russia still have a long

way to go to achieve the per capita income levels enjoyed in the older capitalist societies like the United States, Europe, and Japan. Nonetheless, Russia, China, and India have had healthy economic growth in the first years of the new century.

RUSSIA: ECONOMIC EXPANSION AND AGGRESSIVE NATIONALISM With the price of oil regularly topping $60 per barrel and spiking at $140 per barrel in 2008, Russia enjoyed windfall energy revenues that boosted budget and trade surpluses and expanded personal incomes. Between 1999 and 2008, Russia's gross domestic product climbed at an average rate of more than 7 percent per year—an impressive achievement after the steep economic decline that followed the Soviet Union's dissolution in 1991.

At the same time that Russia's economy was opening to the world, its political system seemed to be closing in on itself, with far-reaching economic consequences. In addressing the anarchy of the Yeltsin era (see Chapter 21), President Putin presided over a rebuilding of the central Russian state. This was widely welcomed in Russia. But the means used by Putin to reassert central state power led, once again, to personal rule. The president forcibly repossessed the two principal television stations from billionaires and reassigned other valuable private properties, especially oil and gas companies, to the state, to be run by his former colleagues from the Soviet-era KGB. He also eliminated elections for regional executives and restricted non-governmental organizations from receiving foreign financing. The result has been an authoritarian political system dominated by the executive, higher levels of corruption among runaway officials unchecked by the judiciary or press, economic stagnation, and a public sphere suffused with propaganda and outright lies.

The Gorbachev-Yeltsin era's promise of a real legislature, independent judiciary, and an end to arbitrary rule gave way, in the yearning for order and stability, to aggressive nationalism and mass emigration. President Putin, after his reelection to a third (nonconsecutive) term in 2012, seized the Crimean Peninsula in a short war in 2014, much to the delight of large numbers of Russians. The annexation of Crimea came after a brief war with Georgia in 2008 that resulted in Russian recognition of two breakaway enclaves, Abkhazia and North Ossetia, and it was followed by Russian promotion of a separatist war in the eastern Ukrainian territories bordering Russia. President Putin justified his actions by citing the expansion of NATO to Russia's borders and NATO's announcement of consideration of possible membership for Georgia and Ukraine. Russia also cited western involvement in the popular overthrow of the elected president of Ukraine, Viktor Yanukovych, who fled into exile in Russia.

CHINA: MARKET REFORMS AND SHIFTING FOREIGN POLICY The Chinese have followed a similar path, encouraging market economic reforms while quashing the possibilities

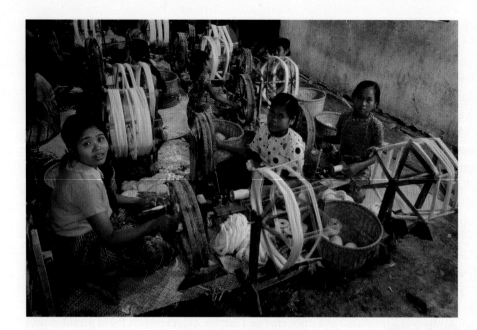

Child Labor. *Girls in a Javanese village work in a factory transferring bundles of cotton yarn to bobbins to be used in handlooms.*

for political liberalization. Their economic strategies seem to be successful. Over the last three decades, China's economy has maintained an average growth rate of over 9 percent annually, although it has shown signs of slowing down recently, with the rate dropping to under 7 percent in 2015 and 2016. Some analysts have suggested that the Chinese government is reluctant to reveal the "real" rate, which might be even lower. Still, it remains true that consumer goods made in China dominate so many markets that it is virtually impossible, as several newspaper reporters have found, to supply an American family's needs on a "China-free" diet. Indeed, the Chinese economy has been the second largest in the world since late 2010, and some projections suggest that China might have the world's largest economy by midcentury, even as its per capita income will still lag behind that of the United States.

In many ways, China's fortunes illustrate both the promises and the pitfalls of the economic reforms undertaken by many developing countries in the era of globalization. On the one hand, despite the continued monopoly of political power by the Chinese Communist Party at home, China's entry into the World Trade Organization (WTO) in 2001 signified its full integration into the global capitalist economy. On the other hand, the reforms have caused political, social, and environmental problems that defy easy solutions. The disparity between the relatively prosperous coastal areas and the poor interior of the country—a problem that the communist government pledged to redress after it came to power in 1949—has once again become a glaring challenge.

While the Chinese government insists that the gap between the rich and the poor has been closing, albeit at a modest rate, a 2016 report from Peking University, a leading Chinese academic institution, found that 1 percent of Chinese households controlled a third of the country's assets, with the poorest 25 percent of households owning just 1 percent of the country's wealth. A 2015 survey found that China had more dollar billionaires (596) than the United States (537). There are concerns, to be sure, both at home and abroad, about the environmental impact of China's economic development. China's homes and factories, for instance, use 40 percent more coal than those in the United States, and Chinese city dwellers suffer from some of the world's worst smog and air quality. But as its energy consumption and economy have soared, so has China's global standing.

In the period after 1949, China was the eager junior partner to the Soviet Union, following the Stalinist developmental model until the Sino-Soviet split of the 1960s (see Chapter 20). Subsequently, Richard Nixon and Henry Kissinger's courting of Mao in 1972 opened up a global option for China that Mao's successors have exploited. China's shift in foreign policy orientation from an alliance with the Soviet Union to a partnership with the United States has arguably been the most important geopolitical realignment in the contemporary world. However, a host of issues threaten to derail relationships between the two countries, especially after Donald Trump, with his strong anti-China rhetoric, assumed the presidency. A possible trade war aside, the Taiwan question remains unresolved, with the Chinese government always reserving its right to use force to reclaim the "province" and the United States, bound by the Taiwan Relations Act (1979), pledging to come to democratic Taiwan's aid.

CHINA AND THE PACIFIC RIM There are also potential conflicts regarding territorial disputes along the Pacific Rim, notably the recent escalation in hostility around the South China Sea, with many Asian nations looking to the United States as a counterweight to their giant neighbor flexing its newly found muscle. In addition, the Chinese government's increasing interference in Hong Kong—a major global financial

Chinese Environmental Concerns. *Despite its prosperity, Hong Kong, like other major Chinese cities, suffers from severe air pollution, which threatens its future as a hub of international commerce. This picture shows part of the city's waterfront shrouded in smog.*

center—despite its promise of a "one country, two systems" format to Hong Kong's governance, has raised eyebrows. While officially denied, its recent alleged abduction of a British passport holder and a Canadian passport holder—both of whom are of Chinese descent—from Hong Kong back to China, in open defiance of international laws, threatens to add fuel to the small but vocal Hong Kong independence movement and potentially to destabilize the region still further.

It is in China's own interest to ensure stability in the Pacific Rim—home to the world's second- and third-largest economies (China and Japan) and several other smaller but dynamic economic powers—and in the global arena. China has become the number one trading partner with almost every country in Asia, displacing the United States. It has even become the top trading partner with Brazil, as well as with many countries in Africa. China has also replaced the United States as the number one customer for Saudi Arabian oil. Chinese-Indian economic relations have strengthened, too. Moreover, the Chinese government has invested heavily in building an oceangoing navy. Although China faces numerous challenges, from environmental degradation to an aging population, it has regained the enormous global weight it held for centuries up until the eighteenth century.

INDIA: ECONOMIC LIBERALIZATION AND ITS EFFECTS

India has registered impressive economic growth in the new millennium. Building on economic reforms initiated in 1991, the Indian economy became increasingly open to the global economy in the twenty-first century. Under the Congress-led government, the growth rate topped 9 percent annually between 2004 and 2009, declining only to 7 percent during the next five years when it was affected by the global economic downturn. As

the state control over the economy loosened, over $20 billion in foreign investments poured in annually. The nation's information technology sector boomed, and India became a favorite destination for global corporations, utilizing the supply of a sizable English-speaking population. The state increased investments in infrastructure development, promoting public-private partnerships, to facilitate business development. Imports and exports grew, and agriculture registered an annual growth rate of over 2 percent each year. Per capita income rose by 20 percent annually, and poverty declined by an average of over 2 percent annually between 2004 and 2014.

Yet the benefits of economic liberalization were unequally experienced. High inflation hit the income of the salaried class hard. The government initiated several welfare schemes of rural employment to cushion economic distress, but problems of inequality and poverty remained acute. In an effort to boost capitalist economy, the government also declared an open season on land acquisition for real estate development, industrial parks, and mining, leading to the eviction of farmers and forest dwellers. The displaced people responded with armed insurgencies. Discontent mounted. High growth also created rising expectations and a drive for personal empowerment, and that stood at odds with the language of state patronage and welfare. Compounding the problem for the Congress government was that it became ensnared in a number of corruption scandals after 2012. A booming economy and new wealth had created opportunities for corrupt practices for which the government had failed to establish institutional controls. Riding on the widespread revulsion against corruption, the Bharatiya Janata Party (BJP), under Narendra Modi, swept the national elections and came to power in 2014.

844 | EPILOGUE 2001–The Present

Internal Divisions, External Rivalries

Internal divisions and external rivalries have threatened to undo many benefits of economic globalization in India, China, and Russia. In India, for example, the BJP, while advocating the free market, also aggressively championed *Hindutva* ("Hinduness") as the bedrock of Indian identity. Nowhere were the effects of this twin strategy of economic liberalism and Hindu nationalism more visible than in the western state of Gujarat. Home to merchant communities for centuries, Gujarat has been in the forefront of capitalist manufactures and commerce. While aggressively participating in the global economy, the state has also been a fertile ground for Hindu nationalism.

Violence erupted in February 2002 after sixty Hindus perished in a fire that consumed a train compartment. Although the circumstances of the fire remain disputed, a rumor immediately spread, authenticated by the BJP government in Gujarat, then under Narendra Modi, that Muslims and a "foreign hand" were responsible. For the next few months, Hindu mobs went on a rampage, burning Muslim homes and hacking the residents to death. Newspapers reported that government leaders and the police force assisted in this carnage or looked the other way as over 2,000 Muslims lost their lives. In the provincial elections of December 2002, the BJP aggressively projected itself as a Hindu nationalist and pro-business party. This strategy paid rich dividends, and the BJP was reelected to power with a commanding majority. It repeated its impressive electoral feat once again in the 2012 elections and finally triumphed in the national elections two years later.

The ongoing tension with neighboring Pakistan is yet another problem faced by India. Flexing its nationalist muscle, the Indian government exploded a nuclear device in 1998. Pakistan responded by exploding its own bombs, casting an ominous shadow over the two nations' unresolved conflict over Kashmir. In that contested province, terrorist violence repeatedly disturbed the peace and brought the nuclear-armed neighbors close to a potentially devastating war. The tension between the two countries escalated in 2008 when a small band of terrorists from Pakistan carried out raids in Mumbai, slaughtering many civilians and security personnel before being subdued.

Projecting recent trends into the future, many observers forecast a rearrangement of the world's economic order, with China and India especially moving to the fore during the twenty-first century. Yet China, India, and Russia, like other parts of the world, have not escaped from the past. These societies, too, struggle with widening internal divisions and potentially devastating external rivalries. (For a global look at hunger and disparities in income, see Maps E.3 and E.4.)

Hindu-Muslim Tensions. *In 2002, Gujarat was consumed by sectarian riots, set off by a train fire in which fifty-nine Hindu pilgrims died. Although an Indian government investigation concluded that the fire was accidental, the incident sparked an orgy of violence by Hindu mobs against Muslims. Shown here is an angry right-wing Hindu Party activist.*

THE MIDDLE EAST, AFRICA, AND LATIN AMERICA

In the Middle East, radical changes brought about by the Arab Spring and the growth of Islamic militancy have taken place, while more than a few countries in Africa have begun to achieve economic progress and gained political stability through democratic elections.

The Arab Spring

The trigger for what became known as the Arab Spring occurred on December 17, 2010, with the seemingly futile act of a twenty-six-year-old Tunisian vegetable vendor and father of eight who set himself on fire outside a provincial office to protest constant police harassment. This singular act aroused the entire population of Tunisia against the ruling elite. Not only had the police confiscated Mohammed Bouazizi's vegetable stand (and not for the first time), but a policewoman had slapped him in the face. In explaining his decision to take his

Arab Spring. *Day and night, Cairo's Tahrir Square swarmed with Egyptians of all ages to protest the ongoing military rule after the ousting of Mubarak. Here protestors burn the midnight oil to decry the dissolution of Parliament by Egypt's Supreme Constitutional Court, a move to consolidate power in the hands of military generals. Note the man documenting the heated demonstration with his video camera (bottom left), whose footage would likely have found its way to the wide array of social media sites for discussion and further dissemination.*

life, his sister exclaimed, "[I]n Sidi Bouzidi [where he resided] those with no connections and no money for bribes are humiliated and insulted and not allowed to live." As the story circulated through the country, large numbers poured out into the streets, demanding an end to the long-term dictatorship of Zine al-Abidine Ben Ali, who had taken over from Habib Bourguiba, Tunisia's president from independence in 1956 until 1978. Ben Ali was an easy target for reproach. Not only had he ruled with an iron fist, but his second wife, Leila Trabelsi, was a notoriously corrupt person, a former hairdresser who lived in splendor and spent lavishly on herself and her prominent European and Arab guests. Ben Ali's promises to change his behavior convinced no one. The catchword of the protesters was *degage*, "get out." With the army refusing to suppress the dissenters and the security police overwhelmed, Ben Ali departed for Saudi Arabia on January 14, 2011.

Young Egyptian radicals watched events in Tunisia with growing interest. After all, if the Tunisians could get rid of their dictator, why not the Egyptians? On January 25, 2011, ironically a holiday to honor Egypt's police forces, by now an object of people's hatred, Egyptians of all backgrounds and ages—Copts and Muslims, workers and professionals, men and women—assembled in Cairo's major plaza, Midan al-Tahrir, or Liberation Square, to let Egypt's president, Hosni Mubarak, in office since 1981, know that he was no longer wanted. Their watchword, *irhal*, meaning "scram" in Arabic, expressed the protesters' utter contempt for him and his rule. On February 11, 2011, just three weeks after the first mass demonstration, Hosni Mubarak left office, turning the reins of power over to the Supreme Command of the Armed Forces, a small group of officers whom the president had chosen to lead Egypt's army.

The ouster of Ben Ali and Mubarak sent shock waves of excitement throughout the Arab world. Decades of pent-up rage could no longer be contained. An outpouring of protests occurred in all of the Arab world's major cities. The demands were consistent—the end of repression, the establishment of democratic institutions, and the ousting of rulers who had stayed in power too long and who did not represent the will of the people. The results were astonishing. Monarchs in Jordan and Morocco promised new constitutions; they said that going forward they would rule, not reign. Bahraini Shiites exacted a new constitution from their Sunni king, and Ali Saleh, ruler of Yemen since 1978, fled the country. Even Muammar Qaddafi, the Libyan strongman, in power since ousting King Idris in 1969, felt the sting of protest, though his ouster and eventual execution on October 20, 2011, in the city of Sirte, owed as much to a United Nations–approved use of NATO air power as it did to the rebel army that rose up to unseat him.

CONTRIBUTING FACTORS Although much of the world had misunderstood the causes of these uprisings, they were not hard to discern after the fact. In the first place, Arab populations, 60 percent of whom were under thirty years of age and had known no other rulers, resented the fact that the wave of democratic reforms that had swept through Russia, much of eastern and central Europe, and large parts of sub-Saharan Africa had passed them by. They saw no reason why they, too, should not have leaders who represented their wishes rather than rigged elections and fraudulent referendums that supported the wishes of the ruling elites. The young came to be known as the generation in waiting—waiting for jobs that never seemed to appear; waiting to have enough money to move out of their parents' homes;

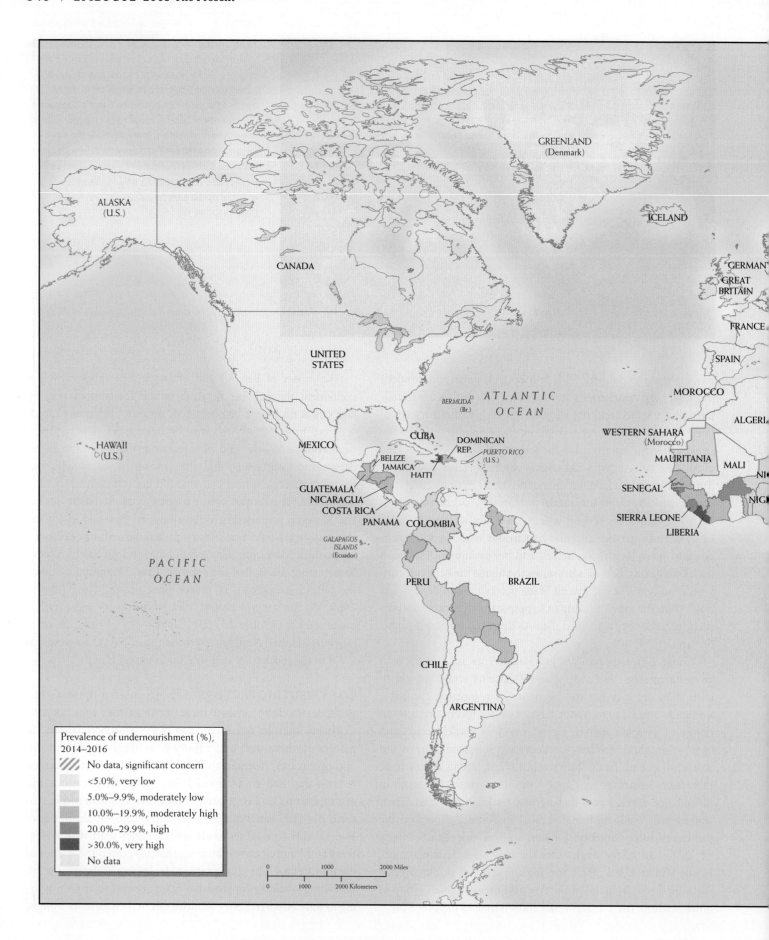

Prevalence of undernourishment (%), 2014–2016

- No data, significant concern
- <5.0%, very low
- 5.0%–9.9%, moderately low
- 10.0%–19.9%, moderately high
- 20.0%–29.9%, high
- >30.0%, very high
- No data

0   1000   2000 Miles

0   1000   2000 Kilometers

MAP E.3 | Hunger Is a Global Problem

Despite much optimism on the part of world leaders, globalization has not yet met the basic human needs of the entire world population.

- According to this map, in which regions is undernourishment very high?

- Comparing this map with Map E.4, identify at least twelve countries where undernourishment is very high *and* per capita income is low ($1,025 or less). What other characteristics do these regions share?

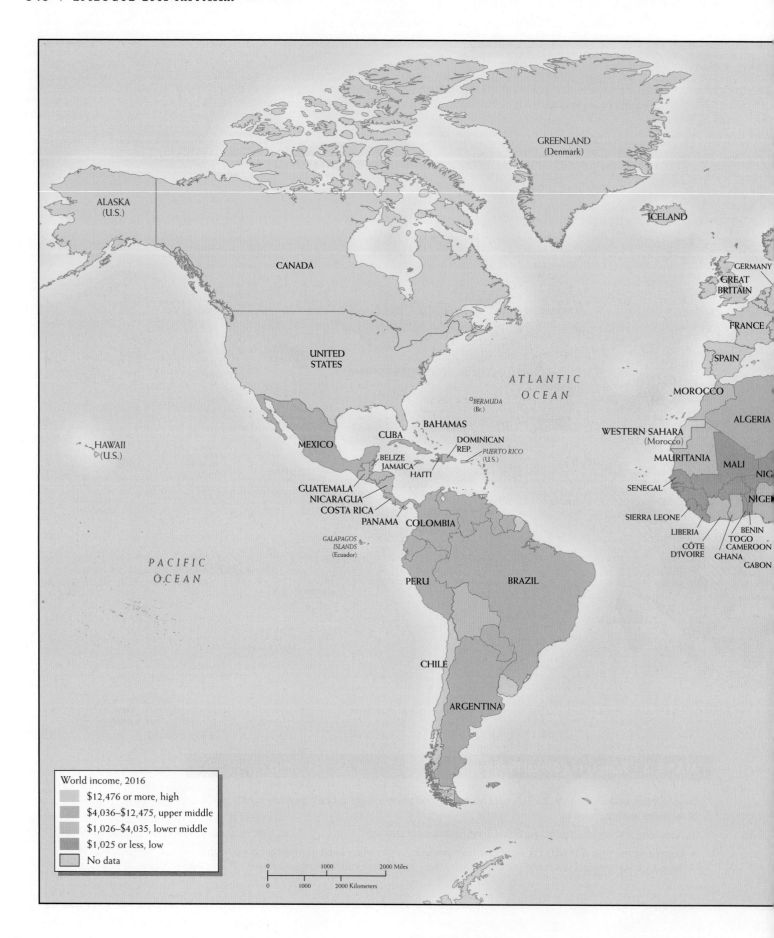

GREENLAND
(Denmark)

ICELAND

ALASKA
(U.S.)

CANADA

UNITED
STATES

GERMANY

GREAT
BRITAIN

FRANCE

SPAIN

MOROCCO

*ATLANTIC
OCEAN*

°*BERMUDA*
(Br.)

ALGERIA

WESTERN SAHARA
(Morocco)

HAWAII
(U.S.)

CUBA

BAHAMAS

DOMINICAN
REP.

MAURITANIA

MALI

NIG

MEXICO

PUERTO RICO
(U.S.)

SENEGAL

NIGE

BELIZE
JAMAICA

HAITI

SIERRA LEONE

GUATEMALA
NICARAGUA
COSTA RICA
PANAMA

COLOMBIA

LIBERIA

CÔTE
D'IVOIRE

BENIN
TOGO
CAMEROON

GHANA

GABON

*GALAPAGOS
ISLANDS
(Ecuador)*

*PACIFIC
OCEAN*

PERU

BRAZIL

CHILE

ARGENTINA

World income, 2016

$12,476 or more, high

$4,036–$12,475, upper middle

$1,026–$4,035, lower middle

$1,025 or less, low

No data

0   1000   2000 Miles

0   1000   2000 Kilometers

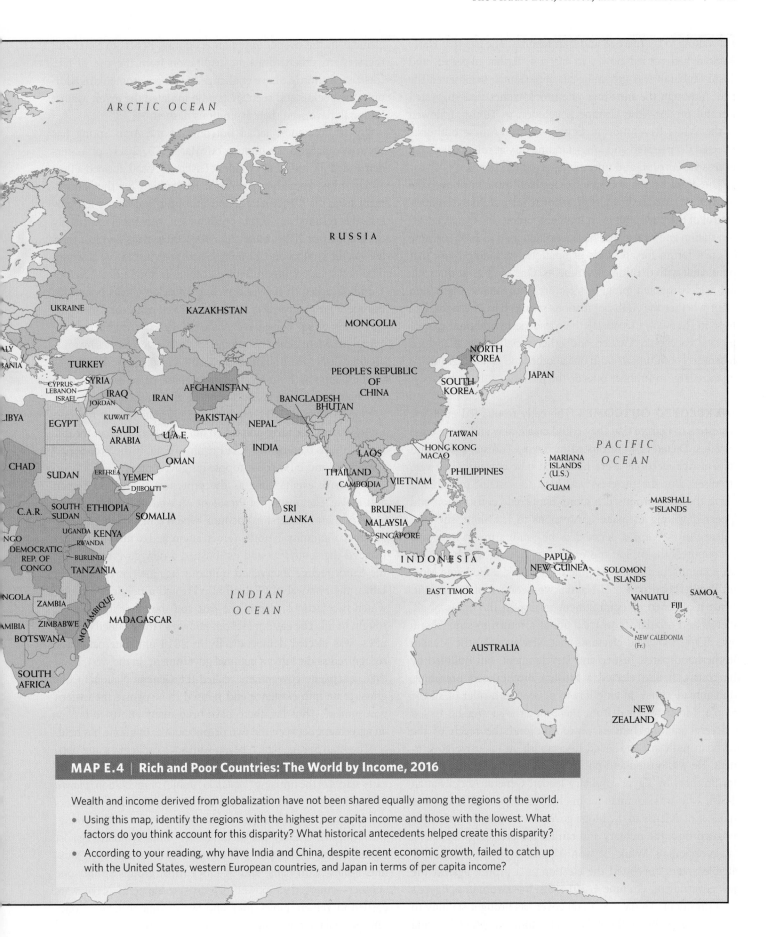

MAP E.4 | Rich and Poor Countries: The World by Income, 2016

Wealth and income derived from globalization have not been shared equally among the regions of the world.

- Using this map, identify the regions with the highest per capita income and those with the lowest. What factors do you think account for this disparity? What historical antecedents helped create this disparity?
- According to your reading, why have India and China, despite recent economic growth, failed to catch up with the United States, western European countries, and Japan in terms of per capita income?

and waiting to get married and start families. The fact that Hafez al-Assad had passed power to his son, Bashar al-Assad, and Hosni Mubarak was grooming his son, Gamal, heightened the rage. Although the uprisings often took names that suggested peaceful protest—the Jasmine Revolution in Tunisia followed by the White Revolution in Egypt—in reality these outbursts reflected deep-seated and long-standing fury at rulers who were repressive, corrupt, and unresponsive to their people.

The dictatorships and monarchies had lost control over the media. CNN was the first global station to intrude on the regimes' control of the news; but even more important, the Qatari television station and newspaper Al-Jazeera, founded in 1995, became an open forum for all kinds of opinions, including those that found fault with existing governments. One of its most dramatic and widely quoted programs featured an intense discussion about whether the Arab populations should have the right, like those in the west, to criticize their leaders. In addition, mobile phones, Facebook, Twitter, and other social media all helped dissenters communicate with one another and enabled groups to organize large assemblies outside the purview of the state.

UNEXPECTED OUTCOMES The early results led euphoric protesters to believe that they could create new and more open societies. Dictators were ousted in Egypt, Tunisia, Libya, and Yemen; free elections were held; and new constitutions were promised. But the progress was hard to sustain. In Bahrain, where the king promised a more democratic constitution and appeared willing to make concessions to his Shiite subjects, violence in the capital persuaded the Saudi army to intervene and suppress the protest movement. In Tunisia, which thus far has accomplished more than the other states, a moderate Muslim Brotherhood party, Al-Nahda, won control of Parliament. While it affirmed its commitment to respect the rights of all, liberals and secularists worried about a return to strict *sharia* law. Egypt, too, held elections that were won by the Muslim Brotherhood party, Justice and Development, but nullified by the courts. It also elected a Muslim Brotherhood president, Muhammad Morsi. In an effort to be seen as a ruler of all the people, Morsi resigned from the Brotherhood. Yet he issued a decree granting himself powers beyond the reach of the Egyptian judiciary and failed to establish an inclusive government. He was ousted and put in prison along with many Muslim Brothers by Egypt's military leader, General Abdel Fattah al-Sisi, who was commander-in-chief of the armed forces and minister of defense in the Morsi government. In early 2014, Sisi resigned from the military and ran for the presidency against a single opponent. While he won 96 percent of the vote, many eligible voters boycotted the election as a protest against the new government. On June 4, 2014, Sisi was sworn in as Egypt's sixth president. To date, Sisi's takeover has brought stability to much of Egypt, but without a revival of tourism, which is a vital element in the overall Egyptian economy. Rebels in Sinai and the western desert, drawing inspiration from the rise of ISIS (discussed shortly), have challenged Sisi's government; in addition, the liberals and secularists who initiated the revolt against Mubarak have seen their aspirations dashed.

By far, the most lethal outcome of the Arab Spring has occurred in Syria. Beginning on March 15, 2011, protesters demanded the ouster of President Bashar al-Assad, formed a Free Syrian army, gained international recognition for their movement from the United States and European states, and led protests that resulted in violent confrontation with Assad's forces. By the summer of 2014, more than 400,000 Syrians had lost their lives in the conflict and 12 million had been displaced, of whom 5 million sought refuge in Turkey, Lebanon, and Jordan. Another 1 million risked their lives traveling on rickety boats bound for Europe at great expense to themselves. Even while the Americans and many others considered Assad's days to be numbered, the Syrian president defied the protesters and western critics by gaining financial aid from Iran and crucial—indeed, regime-saving—military support from Hezbollah (a Shiite party established in Lebanon) and Russia. Assad's retaking of the rebel stronghold of Aleppo in January 2017 marked a significant military triumph for the Syrian president and called into question whether the different groups battling the Assad regime (notably the Free Syrian opposition and ISIS) could topple his government.

Nor have events gone as the protesters wanted in Yemen and Libya. The ousting of President Ali Abdullah Saleh created a political and leadership vacuum, which a marginalized Shiite Houthi community in north Yemen attempted to fill. Their forces invaded the southwest and established a new government, but the Saudi regime intervened militarily against the Houthis. In Libya, the removal of Qaddafi also created a political vacuum, which two factions, one in the east and the other in the west, sought to fill. The eastern faction, known as the Council of Deputies, was elected democratically in 2014 and internationally recognized as the Libyan national government. In the west, however, a separate government, called the General National Congress, came into existence and refused to recognize the eastern government. Thus far, there have been many efforts to broker an agreement between the two organizations, but none has held.

The Arab Spring, which began with such excitement and optimism, has failed in most Arab states to deliver on its promises. The early stages of the uprising (*inqilab* in Arabic) or revolution (*thawra* in Arabic)—the term that most Arab intellectuals and protesters employed in the early stages of the revolt—were led by young, well-educated liberals; but sectarianism—notably Shiites against Sunnis; Arabs against non-Arabs, especially the Kurds; even Muslims against Christians; and in Libya tribal groups against one another—emerged as powerfully divisive elements. Civil wars ensued in Yemen, Libya, Iraq, and Syria, while in Egypt a one-time general took over the reins of power, an obvious extension of the three previous military dictators who dominated the political system—Nasser, Sadat, and Mubarak. Only Tunisia has thus far overcome sectarianism and has thus far, with many bumps in the road, created a democratic and inclusive government.

Islamic Militancy

Islamic militancy, dominated by al-Qaeda in the 1990s and the first decade of the twenty-first century, changed significantly with the emergence of ISIS (the Islamic State of Iraq and Syria) in the early 2000s. As the Americans clipped the power of al-Qaeda, killing many of its important leaders, including Osama bin Laden, ISIS rose to take its place, becoming an even more formidable opponent of the United States and western influence in the Middle East. Islamic militancy has deep historical roots, its advocates looking back with favor on early Muslim warriors who carried out their conquests inspired by the doctrine of jihad. In the twentieth century, some Muslim intellectuals urged Muslims to embrace this earlier form of jihad, promoting the use violence to challenge the west and to create a powerful Islamic state. One of the most influential of these individuals was Sayyid Qutb, an Egyptian Muslim Brother who argued that the Quran sanctioned the use of force against corrupt and repressive Muslim rulers. In his influential book *Milestones*—written while Qutb was in prison, smuggled out, published in 1964, and circulated widely in Muslim societies—he argued that "the West has lost its vitality and Marxism has failed. At this crucial and bewildering juncture, the time of Islam and the Muslim community has arrived" (Wright, *Looming Towers*, p. 4).

Al-Qaeda's agenda of challenging the west was based on the belief that the west, and especially the Americans, was the main force standing in the way of Islam's rise. Thus, the first order of business was to challenge American power: hence the attack on the Twin Towers and the Pentagon. The leaders of al-Qaeda (notably the Saudi bin Laden and the Egyptian Ayman al-Zawahiri) came from elite families and were gradualists in their vision of liberating the Muslim world from western influence, believing that an Islamic state could emerge only after American power had been eroded. They were also extremely uncomfortable with the kinds of violence that more radical Islamists, like the founders of ISIS, urged upon their followers, such as beheadings and burning opponents of their state in prison cells. Their movement was explicitly transnational, always seeking to create branches in other Islamic countries. Early on, they succeeded in gaining the allegiance of militant Sunni Islamic movements in Somalia (al-Shabab), Nigeria (Boko Haram), Mali, Iraq, Yemen, and Saudi Arabia. Nonetheless, al-Qaeda, lacking a state structure, required the protection of the Taliban in Afghanistan to provide them a base from which to organize their attacks on the west. Once they lost this protection, as they did because of the American invasion in 2001, the leaders had to take refuge wherever they could. U.S. Navy Seals killed Osama bin Laden, hiding out, though really in plain sight, in Abbottabad, Pakistan; but the United States has yet to find Zawahiri in spite of offering $25 million for information concerning his whereabouts.

The founder of ISIS, Abu Musab al-Zarqawi, was an unlikely leader. A heavy drinker, a brawler, and a high school dropout, little more than a thug, he found religion, in his case militant

ISIS Warriors. *ISIS assembled a powerful group of soldiers, many from foreign countries (including the United States and Europe), and created a territorial state in western Syria and northern Iraq.*

Islam, as his salvation and the purpose of his life. Imprisoned by Jordan's King Hussein in 1992 in the fortress al-Jali in the eastern desert of Jordan (called by one inmate "a warning of what hell is like"; Warwick, p. 15), al-Zarqawi and other political prisoners were released by the new Jordanian king, Abdullah, in 1999 as a token of a new, more liberal regime. Al-Zarqawi made his way to Afghanistan, where he had fought the Soviets in the late 1980s, on this occasion to meet Osama bin Laden, whom he idolized. His meetings with bin Laden did not generate much enthusiasm for al-Zarqawi, probably because al-Qaeda's leadership considered him too violent and hotheaded. Nonetheless, some high-ranking members of al-Qaeda accepted him into their ranks because they wanted an al-Qaeda branch in Jordan. The Americans chased al-Zarqawi out of Afghanistan; eventually, he made his way to Iraq, anticipating that the Americans would invade and that he could put his form of radical and militant Islam into action there.

The American invasion, the failure of the Arab Spring in most Arab countries, the dismantling of the Iraqi army and civil bureaucracy, and the rise of Shiite dominance in Iraq catapulted al-Zarqawi's vision of a violent, jihadi world to prominence in Iraq. Here, because of his willingness to employ violence of a particularly repulsive nature, including beheadings and burning prisoners alive, he earned the nickname "the Sheikh of the Slaughterers" (Weiss and Hassan, p. 20). Although his hatred of the Americans was boundless, his rage against Iraqi Shiites was even more intense. In a country where the Sunnis had exercised power for centuries, in spite of being a minority to the Shiites, the dominance of Shiites in the new government of Nuri al-Maliki, a determined Shiite who refused to share power with any other group, enraged al-Zarqawi and his Sunni followers. In a letter addressed to bin Laden and intercepted by the Kurds in January 2004, al-Zarqawi wrote that the Shiite communities were "the insurmountable obstacle, the lurking snake, the crafty and malicious scorpion, the spying enemy, and the penetrating venom" (Weiss and Hassan, pp. 28–29). Many other Sunni Iraqis also looked favorably on the branch of al-Qaeda that al-Zarqawi had established in Iraq, believing that the use of heavy-handed violence was the only way to challenge the Shiite takeover of the government. Eventually, even bin Laden endorsed al-Zarqawi, calling him "the emir of al-Qaeda for the Jihad Organization in the Land of the two Rivers" (Warwick, p. 174).

Al-Zarqawi's rise to prominence proved short-lived, however. American troops tracked him to a safe house just outside Baghdad. The plan was to capture him alive, but the helicopter carrying American soldiers encountered engine problems. Forced to send in fighter jets to bomb the house, they killed al-Zarqawi on June 7, 2006. With his death, al-Qaeda in Iraq went into steep decline. The next two leaders were incompetent individuals, prompting Hayden White, director of the CIA, to consider al-Qaeda in Iraq to be moribund. President Obama went even

further, claiming that al-Qaeda in Iraq was "amateurish" and likening it to "a junior varsity team that puts on Lakers uniforms," but adding "that doesn't make them Kobe Bryant" (Gerges, p. 2).

The American president and the director of the CIA underestimated the capabilities of al-Qaeda in Iraq to resurrect itself, now having taken the name ISIS because of a rupture with the parent body. Its new leader, Abu Bakr al-Baghdadi, was as unlikely a man to rally the organization as al-Zarqawi was to be its founder. Baghdadi had neither military nor bureaucratic experience when he assumed leadership of ISIS in May 2010. He was an Islamic scholar, trained in some of the minor Iraqi Muslim schools, eventually gaining his doctorate by writing an exegesis of the Quran. Like so many of the members of ISIS, he had been imprisoned by the American military in Camp Bucca in Iraq, called "the Qaeda School" because strong anti-American and anti-Shiite discussions took place among the inmates. But he had something that the parent organization, al-Qaeda, lacked: a territorial state, based originally in northern and central Iraq, that became even more formidable following the departure of American forces from the country. Drawing on Iraqi Baathist bureaucrats dismissed by the Americans and discharged Iraqi army officers, his state surrounded itself with experienced military officers and bureaucrats. After moving into war-torn Syria and conquering Mosul in northern Iraq in 2014, ISIS also took the name the Islamic Caliphate, and Baghdadi announced to the world that he was the new Islamic State's first caliph.

The conquest of Mosul meant that ISIS controlled territories in central Syria and northern Iraq as large as those constituting the United Kingdom. It also had a population of between 6 and

TABLE E.1	Population of Shia Muslims, 2009	
	ESTIMATED 2009 SHIA POPULATION	APPROXIMATE PERCENTAGE OF MUSLIM POPULATION THAT IS SHIA
Iran	66–70 million	90–95
Iraq	19–22 million	65–70
Yemen	8–10 million	35–40
Azerbaijan	5–7 million	65–75
Syria	3–4 million	15–20
Lebanon	1–2 million	45–55
Kuwait	500,000–700,000	20–25
Bahrain	400,000–500,000	65–75
World total	154–200 million	10–13

Source: "Mapping the Global Muslim Population," Pew Research Center. October 7, 2009.

9 million; an army of 30,000; a capital city, Raqqa, in Syria; and large financial resources, amassed though oil revenues, looting, and taxes. (For a look at the territory held by the Islamic State and the population of Shia Muslims in the Middle East, see Map E.5 and the accompanying table.) In addition, it benefited from intellectuals who promoted Baghdadi's vision of a territorial state that they believed would capture the imagination of Muslims around the world. One of the most widely read individuals of this group was Abu Bakr al-Naji, whose manifesto,

The Management of Savagery, appeared on the Internet in 2004. In it, Naji contended that "it is naught but violence, crudeness, terrorism, frightening others, and massacres" that would strike fear in enemies and rally supporters and near-supporters to ISIS's causes (McCants, p. 83).

Whether ISIS can realize its ambition to found an Islamic state in Southwest Asia and extend its influence throughout the Muslim world seems doubtful. Its enemies are legion. Shiite Iran opposes it, as do Russia, the United States, the Assad

MAP E.5 | **Warring Factions in Iraq and Syria, March 27, 2017**

This map shows the territories held by the Kurdish fighters, ISIS, rebel Syrian fighters, and the Iraqi and Syrian governments.

- Compare the territories held by ISIS with the map of the Sykes-Picot agreement in Chapter 19 (Map 19.4). Are the territories that ISIS holds roughly similar to those that Sykes-Picot reserved for an Arab confederation?

- ISIS contends that the British-French agreements for the division of the Arab world after World War I need to be abolished. Why does ISIS hold these views, and is their state proof that they have succeeded, at least at this point?

- Why would the Turkish, Iraqi, and Syrian governments be dismayed that the Kurds have become the strongest militia against ISIS?

Abu Bakr al-Baghdadi, Caliph of the Islamic State. *Al-Baghdadi assumed control of ISIS in 2010 and was proclaimed caliph of the state in 2014.*

regime, and Kurdish fighters from northern Iraq, who have joined with the Iraqi army to liberate the city of Mosul as of March 2017. But what cannot be denied is that radical, militant Sunni Islam is here to stay. Not only does it have deep historical roots in the writings of many earlier and now modern Muslim theoreticians, but its appeal to marginalized Muslim groups all over the Muslim world—and even more powerfully to marginalized Muslims living in the west itself—makes it a force to be reckoned with for years to come.

The Iranian Nuclear Deal

In mid-June 2015, Iran and the United States, Russia, China, Britain, France, Germany, and the European Union reached an agreement on an issue that has troubled Iran's relations with the outside world for more than a decade and that resulted in the placing of severe economic sanctions on Iran. The agreement dealt with Iran's nuclear program, which the Iranians claimed was entirely for civil use; but the United States and many other countries believed that the Iranians were seeking to create nuclear weapon capability. The 2013 elections in Iran placed the government in the hands of moderate politicians, many of whom, like President Hassan Rouhani, believed that the sanctions placed on Iran by the west were undermining the country's standard of living and turning the state into an international pariah. The U.S. government, led by Secretary of State John Kerry, took full advantage of the situation and, along with five other states, negotiated a nuclear agreement that was to run for ten years and would allow inspections of the

Iranian nuclear facilities while permitting the Iranians to enrich uranium for civil but not military uses. The negotiating foreign powers agreed to lift the financial and economic sanctions, thus permitting Iran to engage in trade with the rest of the world and to gain access to its substantial financial resources, tied up in western banks. Not everyone was pleased with the agreement. Benjamin Netanyahu, the Israeli prime minister, was a severe critic, arguing that the Iranians would subvert the treaty and build nuclear weapons. As of early 2017, the newly elected American president, Donald Trump, opined that this agreement was the worst agreement ever signed and threatened to pull out of the deal; but at this early stage in his presidency, he has not taken any action.

Poverty, Disease, Genocide

In much of the developing world, poverty, disease, and violence persist. The new millennium did not begin auspiciously for the peoples of Africa. The region remained the poorest in the world and suffered the uncontrolled and uncontrollable spread of HIV/AIDS. Of the thirty-eight sub-Saharan African countries surveyed in the World Bank Development Report for 2009, all but seven were low-income countries. The poorest of the poor (Burundi, the Republic of the Congo, and Liberia) reported per capita incomes of $150 or less. Botswana, which enjoyed the second-highest per capita income level at $6,120 (behind only mineral-rich Gabon), was so devastated by HIV/AIDS that life expectancy, once the highest in Africa at close to seventy years, had tumbled to fifty-one years in 2007 and was one of the lowest in the world. (For a global look at HIV incidence, see Map E.6.)

There are nonetheless promising signs of political and economic progress. Ghana embraced parliamentary and presidential elections. Civil strife ended in Mozambique and Angola. South Africa convened a Truth and Reconciliation Commission to put the trauma of apartheid behind it and to stay on the course of parliamentary democracy while addressing the gross disparities of income between whites and blacks that were legacies of the twentieth century. Rwanda has made a spectacular comeback from the genocide of 2008 to achieve high levels of economic growth and educational achievement. In Kenya, Nigeria, South Africa, and many other African countries, in spite of glaring income inequalities, an emerging middle class has taken shape. Recently, Gambia democratically elected a new president, sending the country's dictator for more than two decades into exile.

Elsewhere, however, political instability wrought misery and devastation. Many of West Africa's countries (Liberia, Sierra Leone, Mali, the Ivory Coast, and the Central African Republic) were torn asunder because of ethnic and personal rivalries and required foreign intervention. Nigeria finally rid

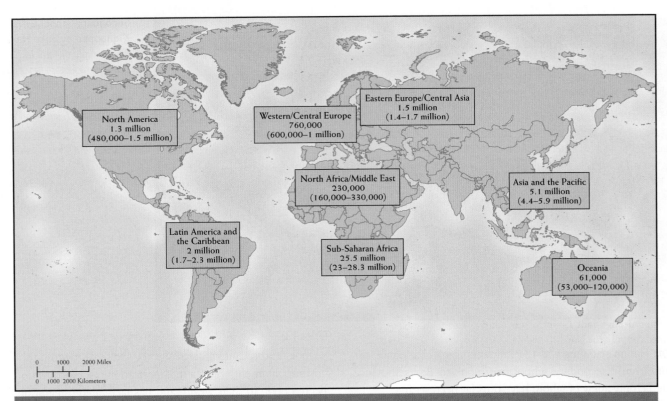

MAP E.6 | The Number of HIV-Positive People Worldwide, 2016

The spread of HIV threatens the development of human capital in the twenty-first century.

- According to this map, which region has the highest rate of HIV infection?
- Using Maps E.3 and E.4 as reference, what connections do you see between poverty and HIV prevalence?
- How does the spread of HIV compromise economic development in poorer regions of the world?

itself of unwanted military dictatorial control and moved to a civil, parliamentary system. But Nigeria's democratically elected presidents have barely been able to hold the country together. The peoples of the Niger delta in the south continue to rebel and demand a larger share of the oil wealth that is produced in their region, while in the impoverished northeast a Muslim group calling itself Boko Haram (meaning "no western learning") has carried out shocking violence. The most notorious of

AIDS Awareness. Left: *A Gambian health worker offers AIDS awareness literature.* Right: *Due, in part, to the high cost of medicines, AIDS has taken a deadly toll on Africans, prompting this memorial in the Netherlands on December 1, 2009, which was designated World AIDS Day. The crosses represented the millions of Africans unable to gain access to AIDS medications.*

Secondary School Girls Kidnapped by Boko Haram. *On the night of April 14, 2014, Boko Haram descended on a secondary school in northeastern Nigeria and kidnapped 276 girls, only a few of whom have thus far escaped or been rescued.*

Boko Haram's actions was the kidnapping of 276 female students from a secondary school in Chibok in Boma Province, Nigeria, only a few of whom have thus far been set free.

In 2011, just when Africa's longest-running civil war, pitting the animist and Christian southern Sudanese against the northern Muslim peoples, had seemingly been resolved through the creation of a new state carved out of Sudan and known as South Sudan, an ongoing dispute in western Sudan kept the Sudanese government in civil strife. In the region of Darfur, the state allowed local horse-riding, nomadic tribesmen to carry out ethnic cleansing campaigns against settled agriculturalists. This has led to one of Africa's worst cases of displaced peoples. Over 2 million refugees fled government terror and civil war to huddle in vast, miserable camps. As in Rwanda in the 1990s (see Chapter 21), genocide has once more visited Africa. But there is some hope. In the West African country of Liberia, after years of pitiless civil war, the belligerents agreed to put down their guns in 2004. In 2005, remarkable elections swept Ellen Johnson-Sirleaf into office to become Africa's first woman president.

Deepening Inequalities

Globalization has contributed to economic inequality in some of the poorest parts of the world. Compared with sub-Saharan Africa, Latin America's situation is not so bleak. Across the region, the divide between haves and have-nots has widened what has historically been the world's most unequal region. The very rich in Buenos Aires live like the very rich in Boston; magnates of Mexico City drive the same cars, eat the same food, read the same books, and vacation in the same spots as their social cousins from New York. They send their children to private

schools in the United States and the United Kingdom to join a cosmopolitan elite. To Latin American elites, globalization has been a boon to their wealth and has facilitated integration into the international circulation of goods, ideas, and people. Many, in fact, identify less and less with a particular place in the world.

Some of the same features hold for the social bottom. Being disadvantaged and poor in southern Mexico looks a lot like being on the losing end in southern Africa: people cling to tiny

Liberia's President. *Ellen Johnson-Sirleaf after her inauguration at the Capitol Building in Monrovia on January 16, 2006. Johnson-Sirleaf is Africa's first elected woman president; she enjoys strong U.S. support and has vowed to fight graft and rebuild her country after years of war.*

São Paulo, Brazil. *An aerial view of one of São Paulo's biggest slums, Favela Morumbi; Favela Morumbi borders one of the city's richest neighborhoods, also called Morumbi.*

parcels of land, migrate long distances for seasonal jobs, and fight against insensitive authorities for their basic needs. Globalization has offered few opportunities to make it at home. Old factories closed in Rosario, Argentina, when faced with competition from Japan; maize farmers in Mexico have to contend with imports from Iowa. In many cases, thanks to globalization, the main solution to the problem is to leave—to move to the city or across borders in search of opportunities elsewhere.

Latin Americans have responded to these challenges in many ways. One sweeping trend is for voters to elect left-wing governments. Most of these are not like the rebel firebrands of the 1960s. Instead, in Brazil, Chile, Argentina, and Uruguay, left-wing governments offer policies designed to soften the blows

Anti-Globalization. *Anti-globalists target annual summits of the leaders of the eight most industrialized countries. This photo shows riot police driving back protesters during the June 2007 summit in Germany. Notice the New York Yankees baseball cap on one of the protesters.*

of globalization and meet basic needs for land, schools, and decent housing. Here the same pressures of globalization that contribute to leftist electoral triumphs limit what these fledgling governments can do. Elsewhere, a more nationalist and populist brand of politics has emerged, one that decries globalization altogether. Rather than softening its effects, leaders here promise to reverse them. In Venezuela, Ecuador, and Bolivia, presidents criticize imperialism and challenge American influence. Their message is that Latin America is better off being a world apart; being together, especially if it means cozying up to the United States, implies a future of subservience and impoverishment. But while many of these leaders stifle criticism at home, being apart does not ensure empowerment and prosperity for all.

The appeal of anti-globalist politics is not limited to Latin America or even to the developing nations. In the most advanced industrial societies, as well as in rapidly rising nations like China and India, programs to check globalization or buffer people from its destabilizing effects have found receptive audiences. Still, opposition to deeper global integration continues to be greatest in the poorest parts of the world, where globalization's benefits are least apparent and its costs are often lethal.

POPULIST POLITICS AND AUTHORITARIAN REGIMES

Beginning with the financial crisis of 2008, groups that have felt marginalized by economic inequality and political powerlessness have asserted themselves all over the world. Successful efforts to rescue the big banks and biggest investors of the global financial system, many of whom had caused the crisis, while ordinary people largely became its victims, led to widespread anger that was initially ignored—until political entrepreneurs perceived an opportunity. The last decade has experienced a resurgence of populist political sentiments that pit "the people" against its enemies. This politics of us versus them directs discontent and anger against the illegitimate "others"—elites, immigrants, ethnic and religious minorities—that are portrayed as enemies of the nation. This kind of populism took many forms. In some countries, it was highly autocratic. In democracies like Britain, continental Europe, and the United States, it saw the rise of ethnic nationalists and the election or emergence of strong right-wing parties. In Britain, it also fueled the winning vote to leave the European Union.

National sentiment will always be majoritarian in any given country, but what populism does is to pit national sentiment against internationalism in a zero-sum fashion. Populism is also often a politics not of opportunity, economic or otherwise, but of resentment and grievance, division and polarization. However real the anger and the injustices, populism's ability to deliver for its angry constituents is never as strong as its ability to mobilize them. Populism, moreover, only succeeds in gaining office with the collaboration of establishment political parties, which perceive the populist fervor either as a threat to their viability, requiring cooperation, or as an opportunity to enact at least part of their agenda in volatile coalition.

Nowhere did this dynamic play out more dramatically than in the United States with the election of Donald Trump, an heir to a real estate fortune who became the world's number one celebrity thanks to television and new media, such as Twitter (in effect, a personal television network equivalent). Even as he lost the popular vote, 65 million to 63 million, Trump won the U.S. presidency in 2016 by a majority of 77,000 combined votes in three hotly contested states, Pennsylvania, Michigan, and Wisconsin, which delivered his majority in the decisive Electoral College. Trump campaigned against immigration and free trade, both of which he and his supporters blamed for the country's stagnant incomes and social immobility. Most fundamental, supporters of Trump felt ignored in the national conversation, their plight overlooked by the mainstream media and political establishment. Trump's surprise victory revealed the power of a white identity political faction that felt marginalized by the identity politics practiced by minority groups such as blacks, Hispanics, the LBGTQ community, and others.

In many ways, Trump's campaign to "Make America Great Again" mirrored developments in Russia, even beyond the American president's profuse admiration for Russia's strongman leader. In Russia, too, a powerful sense of aggrieved nationalism, accusations of western media falsehood, contempt for any limits on executive power, and charges that the open, rules-based international order was rigged galvanized a wide

Prime Minister Modi, of India, Meeting with President Erdogan, of Turkey. *President Recep Tayyip Erdogan (right), of Turkey, met with the Indian Prime Minister, Shri Narendra Modi, on November 16, 2015. Both men have used religion to enhance their popularity and the parties that they head: Erdogan fostering Islamism, and Modi Hinduism.*

following. The difference is that whereas Russia has always called into question the liberal world system, America has been that system's creator and defender. The diminishment or even disintegration of the west—which the 2008 financial crisis, the creation of monetary integration (the euro) without fiscal integration, and unlimited immigration all helped put into play, and which both Putin and Trump have openly stressed—have raised the stakes for this populist moment.

In India, Prime Minister Modi rose to become that nation's strongman, claiming to embody the interests of the nation. With opposition parties dispirited and weak, he skillfully used social media to portray himself as a leader working tirelessly to advance India's interests against its foreign and domestic enemies. Taking a cue from their leader's aggressive nationalism, BJP politicians and Hindu vigilante groups targeted minorities, particularly Muslims. Critics of the government's policies toward Muslims and Dalits were tarred as anti-national. In November 2016, Modi's government demonetized high currency notes, claiming the policy to be a measure directed against unaccounted wealth, the underground economy, and counterfeit money. This move shocked the financial system and caused grave distress to a significant section of the economy that is based on cash transactions. However, Modi successfully framed demonetization as a nationalist act; those opposed to it were labeled as anti-national and pro-"black money."

In Turkey, similar religious and autocratic tendencies emerged under the presidency of Recep Tayyip Erdogan. Having founded the Justice and Development Party (AKP) in 2001, Erdogan served as prime minister from 2003 until 2014 and then as president from 2014 to the present, championing a party and movement that won an overwhelming majority in the parliamentary election in its first effort in 2001 and has been in control of Turkey's politics ever since. Erdogan was brought up in a conservative Muslim household and imprisoned for four months in 1997 for reading a poem by a Turkish nationalist and Islamist, Ziya Gökalp, for which he was charged with inciting violence and racial and religious hatred. Yet as mayor of Istanbul from 1994 to l998 and then as prime minister, he promoted liberal and democratic policies, even making concessions to the powerful Kurdish minority community and clipping the wings of leading Kemalists in the armed forces, men who believed that any politician who failed to uphold the secularist politics of Mustafa Kemal, or Ataturk (see Chapter 19), should be removed from office.

Yet in the later years of his prime ministership, and especially after he became president, Erdogan embraced Islamist and authoritarian policies, intimidating journalists and intellectuals who opposed his efforts and curtailing freedom of speech, the press, and assembly. On July 15, 2016, a segment of the military carried out a failed coup d'état against the government, emboldening Erdogan to purge the country of those individuals who favored liberal, secular policies. Detained were more than 40,000 individuals, including 10,000 soldiers, many teachers, and judges, all charged with having supported the coup. An additional 100,000 teachers, intellectuals, and bureaucrats were removed from their positions. Although Erdogan's Turkey is not an Islamic theocracy like Iran or a militant state like the Taliban in Afghanistan and has joined the battle against ISIS, its shift toward Islamism and authoritarianism has been notable and has rendered its once-desired admission to the European Union unviable.

CONCLUSION—GLOBALIZATION AND ITS DISCONTENTS

Globalization has had a transforming effect, much of it decidedly good for large segments of the world's population, but some of it unsettling. Freer markets and international trade have created a global middle class, pulling nearly half a million Chinese out of poverty and equally huge proportions of the poor in India, Southeast Asia, Egypt, Nigeria, South Africa, and many other communities around the world. Members of the new international middle class communicate with one another, read the same newspapers and journals, see the same films, wear the same clothes, and eat the same foods. Nor is everything made in America, as the Nobel Prizes in Literature, the leading film actors in the world, and the major commentators on increasingly international television and radio networks demonstrate. The extremely high economic growth rates enjoyed by states once regarded as part of the developing world but now seen as economic powerhouses—countries like China, India, Indonesia, South Korea, Kenya, South Africa, and Mozambique, among others—could not have been achieved without international trade networks and significant free trade agreements.

Nonetheless, the negative impacts of globalization have been much in evidence, especially since the financial crisis of 2008. While major banks and large multinational corporations were bailed out, the less well-off populace, the so-called residents of Main Street, suffered grievously. Homes were foreclosed, and workers lost good-paying jobs. In America, the hardest hit were white workers between the ages of forty-five and fifty-four who lack a high school education. Their death rates were alarmingly high, the result of suicide, drug addiction and overdosing, and alcoholism, bringing about for the first time an overall decline in the average life span of white males. The marginalized no longer remain silent, however. They have entered the political arena with a vengeance. They voted overwhelmingly for Brexit (Britain's departure from the European Union) and contributed to the rise of Islamic militancy, Hindu nationalism, Turkey's turn toward Islamism and authoritarianism, and the increasing popularity of right-wing, ethnic nationalist parties in Europe, many of which oppose immigrant communities and balk at allowing refugees into their countries. America's marginalized segment embraced candidate Trump's campaign promises to keep Muslims out of the country and expel illegal entrants from Mexico. In short, globalization has drawn the world more closely together, enhancing the life prospects for many but threatening those groups who, through a lack in education and skills, are ill equipped to take advantage of globalism's opportunities.

CHAPTER 1

Alley, Richard B., and Michael L. Bender. "Greenland Ice Cores: Frozen in Time." *Scientific American* 278 (February 1998): 80–85. A study that describes the pioneering work that astronomers and climatologists have carried out in the twentieth century to enhance our knowledge of climate change and its impact on plants and animals, including human beings.

Arsuaga, Juan Luis. *The Neanderthal's Necklace: In Search of the First Thinkers*, translated by Anthony Klatt (2002). A stimulating overview of prehistory that focuses on the Neanderthals and compares them with *Homo sapiens.*

Barham, Lawrence, and Peter Mitchell. *The First Africans: African Archaeology from the Earliest Toolmakers to Most Recent Foragers* (2008). New findings on the evolution of hominins in Africa.

Barker, Graeme. *Agricultural Revolution in Prehistory: Why Did Foragers Become Farmers?* (2006). The most recent, truly global, and up-to-date study of this momentous event in world history.

Bellwood, Peter. *First Farmers: The Origins of Agricultural Societies* (2005). A state-of-the-art global history of the origins of agriculture, including recent archaeological, linguistic, and microbiological data.

Bender, Michael L. *Paleoclimate* (2013). A definitive overview of the world's climate over the entire life of our universe, written by a renowned geoclimatologist.

Bogucki, Peter. *The Origins of Human Society* (1999). An authoritative overview of prehistory.

Brooke, John L. *Climate Change and the Course of Global History: A Rough Journey* (2014). An excellent overview of the impact of climate on history, particularly useful for the hominin period and the emergence of *Homo sapiens.*

Cauvin, Jacques. *The Birth of the Gods and the Origins of Agriculture*, translated by Trevor Watkins from the original 1994 French publication (2000). An important work on the agricultural revolution of Southwest Asia and the evolution of symbolic thinking at this time.

Cavalli-Sforza, Luigi Luca. *Genes, Peoples, and Languages*, translated by Mark Selestad from the original 1996 French publication (2000). An expert's introduction to the use of gene research for revealing new information about the evolution of human beings in the distant past.

Childe, V. Gordon. *What Happened in History* (1964). A classic work by one of the pioneers in studying the early history and evolution of human beings. Though superseded in many respects, it is still an important place to start one's reading and a work of great power and emotion.

Christian, David. *Maps of Time: An Introduction to Big History* (2004). A definitive historical work on the origins of our universe and the emergence of plant and animal life, including the hominin populations. The work synthesizes discoveries since the end of World War II that have transformed our knowledge of the universe and its peopling.

Clark, J. Desmond, and Steven A. Brandt (eds.). *From Hunters to Farmers: The Causes and Consequences of Food Production in Africa* (1984). Excellent essays on the agricultural revolution.

Coon, Carleton Stevens. *The Story of Man; from the First Human to Primitive Culture and Beyond*, 2nd ed. (1962). An important early work on the evolution of humans, emphasizing the distinctiveness of "races" around the world.

Cunliffe, Barry (ed.). *The Oxford Illustrated Prehistory of Europe* (1994). The definitive work on early European history.

Ehrenberg, Margaret. *Women in Prehistory* (1989). What was the role of women in hunting and gathering societies, and how greatly were women affected by the agricultural revolution? The author offers a number of stimulating generalizations.

Ehret, Christopher. *The Civilizations of Africa: A History to 1800* (2002). Although this is a general history of Africa, the author, a linguist and an expert on early African history, offers new information and new overviews of African peoples in very ancient times.

Fagan, Brian. *People of the Earth: An Introduction to World Prehistory* (1989). An authoritative overview of early history, widely used in classrooms.

Fage, J. D., and Roland Oliver (eds.). *The Cambridge History of Africa*, 8 vols. (1975–1984). A pioneering work of synthesis by two of the first and foremost scholars of the history of Africa. Volume 1 deals with African prehistory.

Frison, George C. *Survival by Hunting: Prehistoric Human Predators and Animal Prey* (2004). An archaeologist applies his knowledge of animal habitats, behavior, and hunting strategies to an examination of prehistoric hunting practices in the North American Great Plains and Rocky Mountains.

Gebauer, Anne Birgitte, and T. Douglas Price (eds.) *Transition to Agriculture in Prehistory* (1992). Excellent essays on the agricultural revolution, especially those written by the two editors.

Harari, Yuval Noah. *Sapiens: A Brief History of Humankind* (2015). A largely successful overview of human history from the hominins to the present.

Imbrie, John, and Katherine Palmer Imbrie. *Ice Ages and Solving the Mystery* (1979). A readable overview of the work done by geologists and climatologists on the earth's temperatures, written by two scholars who contributed to these breakthroughs.

"Inter-Group Violence among the Early Holocene Hunter-Gatherers of West Turkana, Kenya." *Nature* 529 (January 21, 2016): 394–398. Describes a spectacular discovery of the remains of hunter-gatherers who engaged in warfare.

Johnson, Donald, Lenora Johnson, and Blake Edgar. *Ancestors: In Search of Human Origins* (1999). A good overview of human evolution, with insightful essays on *Homo erectus* and *Homo sapiens.*

Jones, Steve, Robert Martin, and David Pilbeam (eds.). *The Cambridge Encyclopedia of Human Evolution* (1992). A superb guide to a wide range of subjects, crammed with up-to-date information on the most controversial and obscure topics of human evolution and early history.

Ki-Zerbo, J. (ed.). *Methodology and African Prehistory*, vol. 1 of the UNESCO *General*

History of Africa (1981). A general history of Africa, written for the most part by scholars of African descent.

Klein, Richard G., and Blake Edger. *The Dawn of Human Culture* (2002). A fine and reliable guide to the tangled history of human evolution.

Leakey, Richard. *The Origin of Humankind* (1994). A readable and exciting account of human evolution, written by the son of the pioneering archaeologists Louis and Mary Leakey, a scholar of equal stature to his parents.

Lewin, Roger. *The Origin of Modern Humans* (1993). Yet another good overview of human evolution, with useful chapters on early art and the use of symbols.

Loewe, Michael, and Edward Shaughnessy (eds.). *The Cambridge History of Ancient China: From the Origins of Civilization to 221 B.C.* (1999). A good review of the archaeology of ancient China.

Mellaart, James. *Çatal Höyük: A Neolithic Town in Anatolia* (1967). A detailed description of one of the first towns associated with the agricultural revolution in Southwest Asia.

Meredith, Martin. *Born in Africa: The Quest for Human Origins* (2011). A well-written and authoritative overview of the evolution of humankind from the earliest hominins to *Homo sapiens*.

Mithen, Steven. *The Prehistory of the Mind: The Cognitive Origins of Art and Science* (1996). A stimulating discussion of the impact of biological and cultural evolution on the cognitive structure of the human mind.

Olson, Steve. *Mapping Human History: Genes, Race, and Our Common Origins* (2003). Using the findings of genetics and attacking the racial thinking of an earlier generation of archaeologists, the author writes powerfully about the unity of all human beings.

Price, T. Douglas (ed.). *Europe's First Farmers* (2000). A discussion of the agricultural revolution in Europe.

Price, T. Douglas, and Anne Birgitte Gebauer (eds.). *Last Hunters, First Farmers: New Perspectives on the Prehistoric Transition to Agriculture* (1996). An exciting collection of essays by some of the leading scholars in the field studying the transition from hunting and gathering to settled agriculture.

Reich, David, et al. "Genome-Wide Patterns of Selection in 230 Ancient Eurasians." *Nature*, November 23, 2015, Vol. 522, published online, November 23, 2015.

New DNA research on the skeletons of 230 West-Eurasians who lived between 6500 and 300 BCE shows the three waves of migrations into Europe in its distant past. These migrations came from Africa via Southwest Asia, Anatolia, and the Russian steppes.

Ruddiman, William F. *Plows, Plagues, and Petroleum: How Humans Took Control of Climate* (2005). An excellent study of how energy sources have changed over the very long run.

Sahlins, Marshall. "Notes on the Original Affluent Society." In *Man the Hunter*, edited by Richard B. Lee and Irven DeVore (1968), pp. 85–89. Sahlins coined the widely used and now famous expression "affluent society" for hunter-gatherers.

Scarre, Chris (ed.). *The Human Past: World Prehistory and the Development of Human Societies* (2005). An encyclopedia and an overview rolled up into one mammoth volume, written by leading figures in the field of early human history.

Shaw, Thurstan, Paul Sinclair, Bassey Andah, and Alex Okpoko (eds.). *The Archaeology of Africa: Food, Metals, and Towns* (1993). Research on the earliest history of human beings in Africa.

Shreeve, James. "Mystery Man." *National Geographic* 228 (October 2015): 30–57. An authoritative and up-to-date account of the extraordinary discovery of fossil remains of a hominid species, now named *Homo naledi*.

Smith, Bruce D. *The Emergence of Agriculture* (1995). How early humans domesticated wild animals and plants.

Stringer, Christopher, and Robin McKie. *African Exodus: The Origins of Modern Humanity* (1996). Detailed data on why Africa was the source of human origins and why *Homo sapiens* is a recent wanderer out of Africa.

Tattersall, Ian. *The Fossil Trail: How We Know What We Think We Know about Human Evolution* (1995). A passionately written book about early archaeological discoveries and the centrality of Africa in human evolution.

Tattersall, Ian. *The World from Beginnings to 4000 BCE* (2008). A brief up-to-date overview of humanity's early history by a leading authority.

Tattersall, Ian. *Masters of the Planet: The Search for Our Human Origins* (2012). The most recent survey of human evolution.

Van Oosterzee, Penny. *Dragon Bones: The Story of Peking Man* (2000). Describes

how the late nineteenth-century unearthing of sites in China containing fossils of animals used for medicinal purposes led to the discovery of Peking Man.

Weiss, Mark L., and Alan E. Mann. *Human Biology and Behavior: An Anthropological Perspective* (1996). The authors stress the contribution that biological research has made and continues to make to unravel the mystery of human evolution.

Wrangham, Richard. *Catching Fire: How Cooking Made Us Human* (2009). The author shows how fire made it possible for humans to have a more varied and richer diet but also one that provided energy for the one organ—the brain—that consumes the most energy.

CHAPTER 2

Adams, Robert McCormick. *The Evolution of Urban Society* (1966). A classic study of the social, political, and economic processes that led to the development of the first urban civilizations.

Algaze, Guillermo. *Ancient Mesopotamia at the Dawn of Civilization* (2008). A compelling analysis of the complex environmental and social factors underlying the rise of the world's first urban culture in southern Mesopotamia.

Andrews, Carol. *Egyptian Mummies* (1998). An illustrated summary of Egyptian mummification and burial practices.

Bagley, Robert. *Ancient Sichuan: Treasures from a Lost Civilization* (2001). Describes the remarkable findings in Southwest China, particularly at Sanxingdui, which have challenged earlier accounts of the Shang dynasty's central role in the rise of early Chinese culture.

Bar-Yosef, Ofar, and Anatoly Khazanov (eds.). *Pastoralism in the Levant: Archaeological Materials in Anthropological Perspectives* (1992). Classic study of the role of nomads in the development of societies in the Levant during the Neolithic period.

Bruhns, Karen Olsen. *Ancient South America* (1994). The best basic text on pre-Columbian South American cultures.

Butzer, Karl W. *Early Hydraulic Civilization in Egypt: A Study of Cultural Ecology* (1976). The best work on how the Egyptians dealt with the Nile floods and the influence that these arrangements had on the overall organization of society.

Cunliffe, Barry. *Europe between the Oceans, 9000 BC–AD 1000* (2008). A very up-to-date and spectacularly illustrated account of early Europe.

Feng, Li. *Early China: A Social and Cultural History* (2013). An important new study on the origins of Chinese culture.

Fukuyama, Francis. *The Origins of Political Order: From Prehistoric Times to the French Revolution* (2011). A superb overview of the powerful political elements that were behind the great river-basin societies in ancient times.

Habu, Junko. *Ancient Jomon of Japan* (2004). Study of prehistoric Jomon hunter-gatherers on the Japanese archipelago that incorporates several different aspects of anthropological studies, including hunter-gatherer archaeology, settlement archaeology, and pottery analysis.

Jacobsen, Thorkild. *The Treasures of Darkness: A History of Mesopotamian Religion* (1976). Best introduction to the religious and philosophical thought of ancient Mesopotamia.

Kemp, Barry J. *Ancient Egypt: Anatomy of a Civilization* (1989). An overview of the culture of the pharaohs.

Kramer, Samuel Noah. *The Sumerians: Their History, Culture and Character* (1963). Classic study of the Sumerians and their culture by a pioneer in Sumerian studies.

Pollock, Susan. *Ancient Mesopotamia: The Eden That Never Was* (1999). An analysis of the social and economic development of Mesopotamia from the beginnings of settlement until the reign of Hammurapi.

Possehl, Gregory L. *Indus Age: The Beginnings* (1999). The second of four volumes analyzing the history of the Indus Valley civilization.

Postgate, J. N. *Early Mesopotamia: Society and Economy at the Dawn of History* (1992). A study of the economic and political development of the Sumerian civilization.

Preziosi, Donald, and L. A. Hitchcock. *Aegean Art and Architecture* (1999). One of the best general guides to the figurative and decorative art produced by the Minoans and Mycenaeans and by related early societies in the region of the Aegean.

Ratnagar, Shereen. *Understanding Harappa: Civilization in the Greater Indus Valley* (2001). Harappan site archaeological data of the last century organized into a historical narrative comprehensible to the general audience.

Ratnagar, Shereen. *Trading Encounters: From the Euphrates to the Indus in the Bronze Age,* 2nd ed. (2004). A comprehensive presentation of the evidence for the relationship between the Indus Valley and its western neighbors.

Rice, Michael. *Egypt's Legacy: The Archetypes of Western Civilization, 3000–300 BC* (1997). The author argues for the decisive influence of Egyptian culture on the whole of the Mediterranean and its later historical development.

Roaf, Michael. *Cultural Atlas of Mesopotamia and the Ancient Near East* (1990). A comprehensive compendium of the historical and cultural development of the Mesopotamian culture from the Neolithic background through the Persian Empire.

Shaw, Ian (ed.). *The Oxford History of Ancient Egypt* (2000). The most up-to-date and comprehensive account of the history of Egypt down to the Greek invasion.

Thapar, Romila. *Early India: From the Origins to AD 1300* (2002). The standard work on this period in Indian history by India's leading historian.

Thorp, Robert. *The Chinese Neolithic: Trajectories to Early States* (2005). Uses the latest archaeological evidence to describe the development of early Bronze Age cultures in North and Northwest China from about 2000 BCE.

Tignor, Robert L. *Egypt: A Short History* (2011). An overview of the history of Egypt from the rise of the pharaohs to the present.

Van de Mieroop, Marc. *The Ancient Mesopotamian City* (1997). A highly readable presentation of the earliest cities in the world.

Van de Mieroop, Marc. *A History of the Ancient Near East, ca. 3000–323 BC* (2004). An overview of the Near East in its period of historical prominence, written by an expert historian and archaeologist.

Wright, Rita P. *The Ancient Indus: Urbanism, Economy, and Society* (2010). A reconstruction of the Indus society with updated archaeological data.

CHAPTER 3

Allan, Sarah. *The Shape of the Turtle: Myth, Art and Cosmos in Early China* (1991). Explains the roles of divination and sacrifice in artistic representations of the Shang cosmology.

Allen, James P. *Middle Egyptian: An Introduction to the Language and Culture of Hieroglyphs* (2000). An introduction to the system of writing and its use in ancient Egypt.

Anthony, David W. *The Horse, the Wheel, and Language: How Bronze-Age Riders from the Eurasian Steppes Shaped the Modern World* (2007). A superb analysis of the origins and spread of the Indo-European peoples.

Arnold, Dieter. *Building in Ancient Egypt: Pharaonic Stone Masonry* (1996). Details the complex construction of monumental stone architecture in ancient Egypt.

Baines, John, and Jaromir Málek. *Atlas of Ancient Egypt* (1980). Useful compilation of information on ancient Egyptian society, religion, history, and geography.

Beal, Richard H. *The Organization of the Hittite Military* (1992). A detailed study based on textual sources of the world's first chariot-based army.

Behringer, Wolfgang. *A Cultural History of Climate* (2010). A general history of the impact of climate on many different societies.

Bell, Barbara. "The Dark Ages in Ancient History. I. The First Dark Age in Egypt," *American Journal of Archaeology,* 75 (January 1971): 1–26. An environmental analysis of the decline of the Old Kingdom and the emergence of the First Intermediate Period.

Bogucki, Peter, and Pam J. Crabtree (eds.). *Ancient Europe 8000 BC–AD 1000: Encyclopedia of the Barbarian World,* 2 vols. (2004). An indispensable handbook on the economic, social, artistic, and religious life in Europe during this period.

Bruhns, Karen Olsen. *Ancient South America* (1994). The best basic text on pre-Columbian South American cultures.

Bryant, Edwin. *The Quest for the Origins of Vedic Culture: The Indo-Aryan Migration Debate* (2001). Insight into the highly charged debate on who the Indo-European speakers were, where they originated, and where they migrated to.

Castleden, Rodney. *The Mycenaeans* (2005). One of the best current surveys of all aspects of the Mycenaean Greeks.

Chadwick, John. *The Decipherment of Linear B,* 2nd ed. (1968). Not only a retelling of the story of the decipherment of the Linear B script, but also an introduction to the actual content and function of the tablets themselves.

Cline, E. H. *Sailing the Wine-Dark Sea: International Trade and the Late Bronze Age Aegean* (1994). An excellent account of the trade and contacts between the

Aegean and other areas of the Mediterranean, Europe, and the Near East during the late Bronze Age.

Cunliffe, Barry. *Facing the Ocean: The Atlantic and Its Peoples, 8000 BC–AD 1500* (2001). An in-depth, highly useful treatment of western Europe during this period.

Cunliffe, Barry (ed.). *Prehistoric Europe: An Illustrated History* (1997). A state-of-the-art treatment of first farmers, agricultural developments, and material culture in prehistoric Europe.

Curry, Andrew. "Slaughter at the Bridge," *Science* 351 (March 25, 2016): 1384–1389. New information on a battle among hunter-gatherer warriors in northern Europe in the thirteenth century BCE.

Davis, W. V., and L. Schofield. *Egypt, the Aegean and the Levant: Interconnections in the Second Millennium BC* (1995). A discussion of the complex interactions in the eastern Mediterranean during the "international age."

Doumas, Christos. *Thera: Pompeii of the Ancient Aegean* (1983). A study of the tremendous volcanic eruption and explosion that destroyed the Minoan settlement on the island of Thera.

Drews, Robert. *Coming of the Greeks: Indo-European Conquests in the Aegean and the Near East* (1988). A good survey of the evidence for the "invasions" or "movements of peoples" that reconfigured the world of the eastern Mediterranean and Near East.

Finley, M. I. *The World of Odysseus*, 2nd rev. ed. (1977; reprint, 2002). The classic work that describes what might be recovered about the social values and behaviors of men and women in the period of the so-called Dark Ages of early Greek history.

Frankfort, Henri. *Ancient Egyptian Religion: An Interpretation* (1948; reprint, 2000). A classic study of Egyptian religion and culture during the pharaonic period.

Frayne, Douglas. *Old Babylonia Period, 2003–1595 B.C.* (1990). A standard and still useful study of this period in Babylonian history.

Jamison, Stephanie W. *Sacrificed Wife, Sacrificer's Wife: Women, Ritual, and Hospitality in Ancient India* (1996). A linguistic analysis of gender roles in Vedic literature.

Keightley, David N. *The Ancestral Landscape: Time, Space, and Community in Late Shang China, ca. 1200–1045 BC* (2000). Provides insights into the nature of royal kinship that undergirded the Shang court and its regional domains.

Kemp, Barry J. *Ancient Egypt: Anatomy of a Civilization* (2006). A definitive presentation of the history, culture, and religion of ancient Egypt.

Klein, Jacob. "The Marriage of Martu: The Urbanization of 'Barbaric' Nomads." In Meir Malul (ed.), *Mutual Influences of Peoples and Cultures in the Ancient Near East* (1996). A collection of essays written by scholars of the ancient Near East.

Kristiansen, Kristian. *Europe before History* (1998). The finest recent survey of all the major developmental phases of European prehistory.

Kuhrt, Amelie. *The Ancient Near East, c. 3000 BCE–300 CE*, 2 vols. (1995). A fundamental treatment of Egypt and Southwest Asia during these three millennia by a top scholar.

Leick, Gwendolyn (ed.). *The Babylonian World* (2007). Comprehensive presentation of the Babylonian world based on archaeology, texts, and works of art.

McIntosh, Jane. *Handbook to Life in Prehistoric Europe* (2006). Highlights the archaeological evidence that enables us to re-create the day-to-day life of different prehistoric communities in Europe.

Pines, Yuri. *The Everlasting Empire: The Political Culture of Ancient China and Its Imperial Legacy* (2012). How imperial unity became the norm in ancient China.

Preziosi, Donald, and L. A. Hitchcock. *Aegean Art and Architecture* (1999). One of the best general guides to the figurative and decorative art produced by both the Minoans and the Mycenaeans and by related early societies in the region of the Aegean.

Quirke, Stephen. *Ancient Egyptian Religion* (1992). A highly readable presentation of ancient Egyptian religion that summarizes the roles and attributions of the many Egyptian gods.

The Rigveda, the Earliest Religious Poetry of India, translated by Stephanie W. Jamison and Joel P. Bereton (2014). A new translation of the earliest literature of South Asia, correcting errors made in earlier translations.

Robins, Gay. *Women in Ancient Egypt* (1993). An interesting survey of the place of women in ancient Egyptian society.

Robins, Gay. *The Art of Ancient Egypt* (1997). The most comprehensive survey to date of the art of pharaonic Egypt.

Romer, John. *Ancient Lives: Daily Life in Egypt of the Pharaohs* (1990). A discussion of the economic and social lives of everyday ancient Egyptians.

Roth, Martha. *Law Collections from Mesopotamia and Asia Minor* (1985). An assemblage of law codes from Southwest Asia, including Hammurapi's famous legal edicts.

Sandars, N. K. *The Sea Peoples: Warriors of the Ancient Mediterranean* (1985). A readable discussion of a very complex period of Levantine history.

Simpson, William Kelly (ed.). *The Literature of Ancient Egypt: An Anthology of Stories, Instructions, and Poetry* (1972). A compilation of the most important works of literature from ancient Egypt.

Thapar, Romila. *The Past before Us: Historical Tradition of Early North India* (2013). A comprehensive evaluation of ancient Indian literature.

Thorp, Robert L. *China in the Early Bronze Age: Shang Civilization* (2005). Reviews the archaeological discoveries near Anyang, site of two capitals of the Shang kings.

Warren, Peter. *The Aegean Civilizations: From Ancient Crete to Mycenae*, 2nd ed. (1989). An excellent textual and pictorial guide to all the basic aspects of the Minoan and Mycenaean societies.

Wilson, John A. *The Culture of Ancient Egypt* (1951). A classic study of the history and culture of pharaonic Egypt.

Yadin, Yigael. *The Art of Warfare in Biblical Lands in the Light of Archaeological Discovery* (1963). A well-illustrated presentation of the machinery of war in the second and first millennia BCE.

Yoffee, Norman (ed.). *The Cambridge World History*, Vol. 3, *Early Cities in Comparative Perspective* (2014). One of nine volumes that trace world history through individual articles written by experts.

CHAPTER 4

Ahlström, Gosta W. *The History of Ancient Palestine from the Paleolithic Period to Alexander's Conquests* (1993). An excellent survey of the history of the region by a renowned expert, with good attention to the recent archaeological evidence.

Astour, Michael. "New Evidence on the Last Days of Ugarit," *American Journal of Archaeology* 69 (1965). An early and important article on the destruction of important cities in the Levant in the twelfth century BCE.

Aubet, Maria Eugenia. *The Phoenicians and the West*, 2nd ed. (2001). The basic survey of the Phoenician colonization of the western Mediterranean and Atlantic, with special attention to recent archaeological discoveries.

Behringer, Wolfgang. *A Cultural History of Climate*, translated by Patrick Camiller (2010). A summary view of the place of climate in historical change, written by an expert in historical climatology.

Benjamin, Craig (ed.). *The Cambridge World History*, Vol 4: *A World with States, Empires, and Networks, 1200 BCE–900 CE* (2015). An important overview of developments in the world, with individual chapters written by experts.

Briant, Pierre. *From Cyrus to Alexander: A History of the Persian Empire*, translated by Peter T. Daniels (2002). A complex and comprehensive history of the Persian Empire by its finest modern scholar.

Bright, John. *A History of Israel*, 4th ed. (2000). An updated version of a classic and still very useful overview of the whole history of the Israelite people down to the end of the period covered in this chapter.

Cook, John M. *The Persian Empire* (1983). An older but still useful and highly readable standard history of the Persian Empire.

Fagan, Brian. *The Long Summer: How Climate Changed Civilization* (2004). An accessible overview of the role of climate in historical change, written by one of the leading historians of ancient history and an individual who has brought together considerable evidence about climatic change and historical development.

Falkenhausen, Lothar von. *Chinese Society in the Age of Confucius (1000–250 BC): The Archaeological Evidence* (2006). A timely reassessment of early Chinese history that compares the literary texts on which it has traditionally been based with the new archaeological evidence.

Fukuyama, Francis. *The Origins of Political Order: From Prehuman Times to the French Revolution* (2011). Argues that the first real kings in Chinese history and the first real states and dynasties did not appear until the Qin and Han.

Grayson, A. Kirk. "Assyrian Civilization." In *Cambridge Ancient History*, Vol. 3, pt. 2 (1992), pp. 194–228. Examines the Assyrian and Babylonian Empires and other states of Southwest Asia from the eighth to the sixth centuries BCE.

Hornung, Erik. *Akhenaten and the Religion of Light*, translated from the German by David Lorton (1999). A brief but important biography of Egypt's most controversial pharaoh.

Hornung, Erik. *History of Ancient Egypt: An Introduction*, translated from the German by David Lorton (1999). An accessible overview of the history of ancient Egypt by a leading Egyptologist.

Isserlin, Benedikt J. *The Israelites* (1998). A well-written illustrated history of all aspects of life in the regions of the Levant inhabited by the Israelites.

Keay, John. *India: A History* (2010). A useful, readable overview of the sweep of Indian history.

Lancel, Serge. *Carthage: A History*, translated by Antonia Nevill (1997). By far the best single-volume history of the most important Phoenician colony in the Mediterranean. (The first three chapters are especially relevant to materials covered in this chapter.)

Lemche, Niels Peter. *Ancient Israel: A New History of Israelite Society* (1988). A quick, readable, and still up-to-date summary of the main phases and themes.

Lewis, Mark Edward. *Writing and Authority in Early China* (1999). A work that traces the changing uses of writing to command assent and obedience in early China.

Liverani, Mario. *The Ancient Near East: History, Society and Economy* (2014). Parts 5 and 6 are especially relevant to the materials covered in this chapter.

Liu, Guozhong. *Introduction to the Tsinghua Bamboo-Strip Manuscripts*, translated by Christopher J. Foster and William N. French (2016). An important essay on the implications of these texts for our understanding of early Western Zhou history.

Markoe, Glenn E. *Phoenicians* (2000). A thorough survey of the Phoenicians and their society as it first developed in the Levant and then expanded over the Mediterranean, with excellent illustrations of the diverse archaeological sites.

Matthews, Victor H., and Don C. Benjamin. *Social World of Ancient Israel, 1350–587 BCE* (1993). A thematic overview of the main occupational groups and social roles that characterized ancient Israelite society.

Oates, Joan, and David Oates. *Nimrud: An Assyrian Imperial City Revealed* (2001). A fine and highly readable summary of the state of our knowledge of the Neo-Assyrian Empire from the perspective of the early capital of Assurnasirpal II.

Oded, Bustenay. *Mass Deportations and Deportees in the Neo-Assyrian Empire* (1979). A detailed textual examination of the deportation strategy of the Assyrian kings.

Potts, D. T. *The Archaeology of Elam: Formation and Transformation of an Ancient Iranian State* (1999). The definitive study of the archaeology of western Iran from the Neolithic period through the Persian Empire.

Quinn, Josephine C., and Nicholas C. Vella (eds.). *The Punic Mediterranean* (2014). A valuable and readable collection of chapters on various aspects of how the Phoenician colonization of the Mediterranean led to the formation of new cultural identities.

Radner, Karen. *Ancient Assyria: A Very Short Introduction* (2015). A highly readable and up-to-date survey of all the important aspects of Assyrian government and society.

Shaughnessy, Edward L. *Sources of Western Zhou History: Inscribed Bronze Vessels* (1992). Detailed work on the historiography and interpretation of the thousands of ritual bronze vessels discovered by China's archaeologists.

Stein, Burton. *A History of India*, 2nd ed., edited by David Arnold (2010). One of the standard general histories of India, brought up to date by a leading historian of the subcontinent.

Tanner, Harold M. *China: A History* (2009). A readable and up-to-date overview of the sweep of Chinese history.

Thapar, Romila. *From Lineage to State* (1984). The only book on early India that uses religious literature historically and analyzes major lineages to reveal the transition from tribal society to state institutions.

Thapar, Romila. *The Aryan. Recasting Constructs* (2011). On the rise of the theory of an Aryan race and the beginnings of Indian history.

Tignor, Robert L. *Egypt: A Short History* (2010). A succinct treatment of the entire history of Egypt from the pharaohs to the present, with three chapters on the ancient period.

Trautmann, Thomas. *India: Brief History of a Civilization* (2011). A highly readable survey of Indian history with emphasis on its early history.

Tubb, Jonathan N. *Canaanites* (1998). The best recent survey, well illustrated, of one of the main ethnic groups dominating the culture of the Levant.

CHAPTER 5

Adams, William Y. *Nubia: Corridor to Africa* (1977). The authoritative historical overview of Nubia, the area of present-day Sudan just south of Egypt and a geographical connecting point between the Mediterranean and sub-Saharan Africa.

Allan, Sarah. *Buried Ideas: Legends of Abdication and Ideal Government in Early Chinese Bamboo-Slip Manuscripts* (2016). Four recently discovered Warring States texts challenge long-standing ideas about Chinese intellectual history.

Armstrong, Karen. *Buddha* (2001). A readable and impressive account of the life of the Buddha.

Aubet, Maria Eugenia. *The Phoenicians and the West*, 2nd ed. (2001). The basic survey of the Phoenician colonization of the western Mediterranean and Atlantic, with special attention to recent archaeological discoveries.

Barker, Graeme, and Tom Rasmussen. *The Etruscans* (1998). The most up-to-date introduction to this important pre-Roman society in the Italian peninsula, with strong emphasis on broad social and material patterns of development as indicated by the archaeological evidence.

Benjamin, Craig (ed.). *The Cambridge World History*, Vol. 4: *A World with States, Empires, and Networks, 1200 BCE–900 CE* (2015). Essays by experts on these centuries in world history. Especially important for thinking about the Axial Age is the chapter by Bjorn Wittrock, "The Axial Age in World History," pp. 101–119.

Bresson, Alain. *The Making of the Ancient Greek Economy: Institutions, Markets, and Growth in the City-States*, translated by Steven Rendall (2015). The most conceptually sophisticated and factually up-to-date account of the economic regimes of the Greek city-states.

Burkert, Walter. *Greek Religion*, translated by John Raffan (1985). The best one-volume introduction to early Greek religion, placing the Greeks in their larger Mediterranean and Near Eastern contexts.

Burns, Karen Olsen. *Ancient South America* (1994). A very useful overview of recent debates and conclusions about pre-Columbian archaeology in South America, including both the Andes and the lowland and coastal regions.

Cartledge, Paul (ed.). *The Cambridge Illustrated History of Ancient Greece* (2002). An excellent history of the Greek city-states down to the time of Alexander the Great.

Chakravarti, Uma. *The Social Dimensions of Early Buddhism* (1987). A description of the life of Buddha drawn from early Buddhist texts.

Cho-yun, Hsu. *Ancient China in Transition* (1965). An account of the political, economic, social, and intellectual changes that occurred during the Warring States period.

Coarelli, Filippo (ed.). *Etruscan Cities* (1975). A brilliantly and lavishly illustrated guide to the material remains of the Etruscans: their cities, their magnificent tombs, and their architecture, painting, sculpture, and other art.

Coe, Michael, Richard A. Diehl, David A Freidel, et al. (eds.), *The Olmec World: Ritual and Rulership* (1996). A collection of field-synthesizing articles with important illustrations, based on one of the most comprehensive exhibitions of Olmec art in the world.

Confucius. *The Analects (Lun Yü)*, translated by D. C. Lau (1979). An outstanding translation of the words of Confucius as recorded by his major disciples. Includes valuable historical material needed to provide the context for Confucius's teachings.

Eisenstadt, S. N. (ed.). *The Origins and Diversity of Axial Age Civilizations* (1986). A set of essays that develops Jaspers's concept of the Axial Age cultures.

Elman, Benjamin A., and Martin Kern (eds.). *Statecraft and Classical Learning: The Rituals of Zhou in East Asian History* (2010). Traces the long-term political rise of classical learning and state rituals in East Asia from the decline of the Eastern Zhou kingdom to the rise of later imperial dynasties in China, Japan, and Korea.

Finley, M. I., and H. W. Pleket. *The Olympic Games: The First Thousand Years* (2005). A fine description of the most famous of the Greek games; it explains how they exemplify the competitive spirit that marked many aspects of the Greek city-states.

Garlan, Yvon. *War in the Ancient World: A Social History*, translated by Janet Lloyd (1976). A discussion of the emergence of the forms of warfare, including male citizens fighting in hoplite phalanxes and the development of siege warfare, that were typical of the Greek city-states.

Garlan, Yvon. *Slavery in Ancient Greece*, translated by Janet Lloyd (1988). A treatment of the emergence, development, and institutionalization of chattel slavery in the Greek city-states.

Iliffe, John. *Africans: The History of a Continent*, 2nd ed. (2007). A first-rate scholarly survey of Africa from its beginnings, with a strong emphasis on demography.

Jaspers, Karl. *The Origin and Goal of History* (1953). The book that first developed the idea of the Axial Age.

Lancel, Serge. *Carthage: A History*, translated by Antonia Nevill (1997). By far the best single-volume history of the most important Phoenician colony in the Mediterranean.

Lewis, Mark Edward. *Sanctioned Violence in Early China* (1990). An analysis of the use of sanctioned violence as an element of statecraft from the Warring States period to the formation of the Qin and Han Empires in the second half of the first millennium BCE.

Lewis, Mark Edward. *Writing and Authority in Early China* (1999). A revisionist account of the central role of writing and persuasion in models for the invention of a Chinese world empire.

Ling, Trevor. *The Buddha: Buddhist Civilization in India and Ceylon* (1972). An overview of Buddhism in India and Ceylon.

Lloyd, G. E. R. *Early Greek Science: Thales to Aristotle* (1970). An especially clear and concise introduction to the main developments and intellectuals that marked the emergence of critical secular thinking in the early Greek world.

Lloyd, G. E. R., and Nathan Sivin. *The Way and the Word: Science and Medicine in Early China and Greece* (2002). A comprehensive rethinking of the social and political settings in ancient China and city-state Greece that contributed to the different views of science and medicine that emerged in each place.

Mote, Frederick. *Intellectual Foundations of China* (1971). An early but still useful description of the seminal figures in China's early intellectual life.

Murray, Oswyn. *Early Greece*, 2nd ed. (1993). One of the best introductions to the emergence of the Greek city-states down to the end of the Archaic Age.

Ober, Josiah. *The Rise and Fall of Classical Greece* (2015). A compelling general interpretation of the rise of the Greek city-states in the sixth and fifth centuries BCE and their subsequent demise in the fourth century.

Osborne, Robin. *Archaic and Classical Greek Art* (1998). An outstanding book that clearly explains the main innovations in Greek art, setting them in their historical context.

Osborne, Robin. *Greece in the Making, 1200–479 BC* (1999). The standard history of the whole early period of the Greek city-states characterized by an especially fine and judicious mix of archaeological data and literary sources.

Pallottino, Massimo. *The Etruscans*, rev. ed., translated by J. Cremona (1975). A fairly traditional but still classic survey of all aspects of Etruscan history and political and social institutions.

Pines, Yuri, Paul R. Goldin, and Martin Kern (eds.). *Ideology of Power and Power of Ideology in Early China* (2015). A new assessment of state ideology and political legitimation under the Eastern Zhou dynasty during the Warring States era.

Redford, Donald B. *From Slave to Pharaoh: The Black Experience of Ancient Egypt* (2004). A description of Egypt's Twenty-fifth Dynasty, which was made up of Sudanese conquerors.

Schaberg, David. *A Patterned Past: Form and Thought in Early Chinese Historiography* (2002). A comprehensive study of the intellectual content of historical anecdotes by the followers of Confucius collected around the fourth century BCE.

Schaps, David. *The Invention of Coinage and the Monetization of Ancient Greece* (2004). A new analysis that offers a broad overview of the emergence of coined money in the Near East and the eastern Mediterranean and its effects on the spread of money-based markets.

Sharma, J. P. *Republics in Ancient India, c. 1500 B.C.–500 B.C.* (1968). Relying on information from early Buddhist texts, this book first revealed that South Asia had not only monarchies but also alternative polities.

Shaw, Thurston. *Nigeria: Its Archaeology and Early History* (1978). An important introduction to the early history of Nigeria by one of that country's leading archaeologists.

Shinnie, P. L. *Ancient Nubia* (1996). An excellent account of the history of the ancient Nubians, who, we are discovering, had great influence on Egypt and on the rest of tropical Africa.

Snodgrass, Anthony. *Archaic Greece: The Age of Experiment* (1981). A good introduction to the archaeological evidence of Archaic Greece.

Taylor, Christopher, Richard Hare, and Jonathan Barnes. *Greek Philosophers* (1999). A fine, succinct, one-volume introduction to the major aspects of the three big thinkers who dominated the high period of classical Greek philosophy: Socrates, Plato, and Aristotle.

Torok, Laszlo. *Meroe: Six Studies on the Cultural Identity of an Ancient African State* (1995). A good collection of essays on the most recent work on Meroe.

Von Falkenhausen, Lothar. *Chinese Society in the Age of Confucius (100–250 BC)* (2006). The larger Chinese society under the influence of Confucian thought.

Welsby, Derek. *The Kingdom of Kush: The Napatan and Meroitic Empires* (1996). A fine book on these two important Nubian kingdoms.

CHAPTER 6

Bradley, Keith. *Slavery and Rebellion in the Roman World, 140 B.C.–70 B.C.* (1989). A description of the rise of large-scale plantation slavery in Sicily and Italy and a detailed account of the three great slave wars.

Bresson, Alain. *The Making of the Ancient Greek Economy: Markets and Growth in the City-States*, translated by Steven Rendall (2015). An up-to-date and theoretically well-informed analysis of the market economics of the Greek city-states in the Hellenistic era.

Browning, Iain. *Palmyra* (1979). A narrative of the history of the important desert city that linked eastern and western trade routes.

Casson, Lionel. *The Periplus Maris Erythraei* (1989). An introduction to a typical ancient sailing manual, this one of the Red Sea and Indian Ocean.

Casson, Lionel. *Ships and Seamanship in the Ancient World* (1995). The classic account of the ships and sailors that powered commerce and war on the high seas.

Colledge, Malcolm. *The Art of Palmyra* (1976). A well-illustrated introduction to the unusual art of Palmyra with its mixture of eastern and western elements.

Fowler, Barbara H. *The Hellenistic Aesthetic* (1989). How the artists in this new age saw and portrayed their world in new and different ways.

Green, Peter. *Alexander to Actium: The Historical Evolution of the Hellenistic Age* (1990). The best general guide to the whole period in all of its various aspects, and well illustrated.

Habicht, Christian. *Athens from Alexander to Antony*, translated by Deborah L. Schneider (1997). The authoritative account of what happened to the great city-state of Athens in this period.

Hansen, Valerie. *The Silk Road: A New History* (2012). The most recent work on the Silk Road; authoritative on the eastern terminus of this vital trade route.

Herodotus. *The Histories*, 4 volumes, translated by Tom Holland (2013). A basic work, which many scholars regard as the first world history. The translation given here was done by Brent Shaw and came from the original Greek.

Holt, Frank L. *Thundering Zeus: The Making of Hellenistic Bactria* (1999). A basic history of the most eastern of the kingdoms spawned by the conquests of Alexander the Great.

Hopkirk, Peter. *Foreign Devils on the Silk Road* (1984). A historiography of the explorations and researches on the central Asian Silk Road of the nineteenth and early twentieth centuries.

Juliano, Annette L., and Judith A. Lerner (eds.). *Nomads, Traders and Holy Men along China's Silk Road* (2003). A description of the travelers along the Silk Road in human terms, focusing on warfare, markets, and religion.

Keay, John. *India: A History* (2000). A well-written and well-researched overview of the entire history of South Asia.

Kosmin, Paul J. *The Land of the Elephant Kings: Space, Territory, and Ideology in the Seleucid Empire* (2014). The best current analysis of the relationships of Seleucid kings, both with their own subjects and, especially, with the Mauryan kingdom of India and the nomadic peoples of central Asia.

Kuzima, E. E. *The Prehistory of the Silk Road* (2008). Valuable information on the early history of the Silk Road.

Lane Fox, Robin. *Alexander the Great* (1973). Still the most readable and in many ways the sanest biography of the world conqueror.

Lewis, Naphtali. *Greeks in Ptolemaic Egypt* (1986). An account of the relationships between Greeks and Egyptians as seen through the lives of individual Greek settlers and colonists.

Liu, Xinru. *Ancient India and Ancient China* (1988). The first work to connect political and economic developments in India and China with the evolution and spread of Buddhism in the first half of the first millennium.

Liu, Xinru. *The Silk Road in World History* (2010). A study of the history of the great trade and communications route that connected the different regions of Afro-Eurasia between the third century BCE and the thirteenth century CE.

Long, Antony A. *Hellenistic Philosophy: Stoics, Epicureans, Sceptics*, 2nd ed. (1986). One of the clearest guides to the new trends in Greek philosophical thinking in the period.

Martin, Luther H. *Hellenistic Religions: An Introduction* (1987). An introduction to the principal new Hellenistic religions and cults that emerged in this period.

Mendels, Doron. *The Rise and Fall of Jewish Nationalism* (1992). A sophisticated account of the various phases of Jewish resistance in Judah to foreign domination.

Miller, James Innes. *The Spice Trade of the Roman Empire, 29 B.C. to A.D. 641* (1969). A first-rate study of the spice trade in the Roman Empire.

Pomeroy, Sarah B. *Women in Hellenistic Egypt: From Alexander to Cleopatra* (1990). A highly readable investigation of women and family in the best-documented region of the Hellenistic world.

Ray, Himanshu P. *The Wind of Change, Buddhism and the Maritime Links of Early South Asia* (1994). Ray's study of Buddhism and maritime trade stretches from the Arabian Sea to the navigations between South Asia and Southeast Asia.

Rosenfield, John. *The Dynastic Art of the Kushans* (1967). Instead of focusing on the Gandharan Buddhist art itself, Rosenfield selects sculptures of Kushan royals and those representing nomadic populations in religious shrines to display the central Asian aspect of artworks of the period.

Rostovtzeff, Michael Ivanovich. *Caravan Cities*, translated by D. and T. Talbot Rice (1932). Though published more than eight decades ago, this small volume contains accurate descriptions of the ruins of many caravan cities in modern Jordan and Syria.

Rostovtzeff, Michael Ivanovich. *The Social and Economic History of the Hellenistic World* (1941). A monumental achievement. One of the great works of history written in the twentieth century. An unsurpassed overview of all aspects of the politics and social and economic movements of the period. Despite its age, there is still nothing like it.

Schoff, Wilfred H. (ed. and trans.). *The Periplus of the Erythraean Sea* (1912). An invaluable tool for mapping the names and places from the Red Sea to Indian coastal areas during this period.

Shipley, Graham. *The Greek World after Alexander, 323–30 BC* (2000). A more up-to-date survey than Peter Green's work (above), with more emphasis on the historical detail in each period.

Thapar, Romila. *Aśoka and the Decline of the Mauryas* (1973). Using all available primary sources, including the edicts of Aśoka and Greek authors' accounts, Thapar gives the most authoritative analysis of the first (and most important) empire in Indian history.

Vainker, Shelagh. *Chinese Silk: A Cultural History* (2004). A work that traces the cultural history of silk in China from its early origins to the twentieth century and considers its relationship to the other decorative arts. The author draws on the most recent archaeological evidence to emphasize the role of silk in Chinese history, trade, religion, and literature.

Wood, Francis. *The Silk Road: Two Thousand Years in the Heart of Asia* (2004). Illustrated with drawings, manuscripts, paintings, and artifacts to trace the Silk Road to its origins as far back as Alexander the Great, with an emphasis on its importance to cultural and religious movements.

Young, Gary K. *Rome's Eastern Trade: International Commerce and Imperial Policy, 31 BC–AD 305* (2001). This study examines the taxation and profits of eastern trade from the perspective of the Roman government.

CHAPTER 7

Barbieri-Low, Anthony J., and Robin D. S. Yates. *Law, State, and Society in Early Imperial China (2 Vols): A Study with Critical Edition and Translation of the Legal Texts from Zhangjiashan Tomb No. 247* (2015). A new account of changes in Western (Former) Han dynasty law in terms of its moralization via instituting Confucianism.

Batty, Roger. *Rome and the Nomads: The Pontic-Danubian Realm in Antiquity* (2007). A comprehensive account of relations between the Roman Empire and the nomads of the western Eurasian steppelands.

Bodde, Derk. *China's First Unifier: A Study of the Ch'in Dynasty as Seen in the Life of Li Ssu (280?–208 B.C.)* (1938). A classic account of the key Legalist adviser, Li Si, who formulated the Qin policy to enhance its autocratic power.

Bowman, Alan K. *Life and Letters on the Roman Frontier: Vindolanda and Its Peoples* (1994). An introduction to the exciting discovery of writing tablets from a Roman army base in northern Britain.

Bradley, Keith. *Slavery and Society at Rome* (1994). An excellent overview of the major aspects of the slave system in the Roman Empire.

Chevallier, Raymond. *Roman Roads*, translated by N. H. Field (1976). A guide to the fundamentals of the construction, maintenance, administration, and mapping of Roman roads.

Coarelli, Fillipo (ed.). *Pompeii*, translated by Patricia Cockram (2006). A lavishly illustrated large volume that allows the reader to sense some of the wondrous wealth of the buried city of Pompeii.

Colledge, Malcolm A. R. *The Parthians* (1967). A bit dated but still a fundamental introduction to the Parthians, the major power on the eastern frontier of the Roman Empire.

Cornell, Tim. *The Beginnings of Rome: Italy and Rome from the Bronze Age to the Punic Wars, c. 2000 to 264 B.C.* (1995). The single best one-volume history of Rome through its early history to the first war with Carthage.

Cornell, Tim, and John Matthews. *Atlas of the Roman World* (1982). A history of the Roman world; much more than simply an atlas. It provides not only good maps and a gazetteer but also marvelous color illustrations and a text that guides the reader through the basics of Roman history.

Csikszentmihalyi, Mark. *Readings in Han Chinese Thought* (2006). A volume presenting a representative selection of primary sources to illustrate the growth of ideas in early imperial times; a useful introduction to the key strains of thought during this crucial period.

Dien, Albert E. "The Qin Army and Its Antecedents." In Liu Yang (ed.), *China's Terracotta Warriors: The First Emperor's Legacy* (2013). An account of the Qin army in light of its Warring States precedents.

Dixon, Suzanne. *The Roman Family* (1992). The best one-volume guide to the nature of the Roman family and family relations.

Elvin, Mark. *The Retreat of the Elephants: An Environmental History of China* (2004). A pioneering environmental history of China covering over 4,000 years of its history.

Garnsey, Peter, and Richard Saller. *The Roman Empire: Economy, Society, and Culture*, 2nd ed. (2014). A perceptive and critical introduction to three basic aspects of social life in the empire.

Giardina, Andrea (ed.). *The Romans*, translated by Lydia Cochrane (1993). Individual studies of important typical figures in Roman society, from the peasant and the bandit to the merchant and the soldier.

Goldsworthy, Adrian. *The Roman Army at War: 100 B.C.–A.D. 200* (1996). A summary history and analysis of the Roman army in action during the late Republic and early Roman Empire.

Harris, William. *Ancient Literacy* (1989). A basic survey of what is known about communication in the form of writing and books in the Roman Empire.

Hopkins, Keith. *Death and Renewal: Sociological Studies in Roman History*, vol. 2 (1983). Innovative studies in Roman history, including one of the best on gladiators and another on death and funerals.

Hopkins, Keith. *A World Full of Gods: Pagans, Jews and Christians in the Roman Empire* (1999). A somewhat unusual but interesting and provocative look at the world of religions in the Roman Empire.

Hughes, J. Donald. *Environmental Problems of the Greeks and Romans: Ecology in the Ancient Mediterranean*, 2nd ed. (2014). A much improved and expanded edition of a classic work on the environment in Greek and Roman antiquity and a state-of-the-art summary of our current knowledge.

Juliano, Annette L., and Judith A. Lerner (eds.). *Nomads, Traders and Holy Men along China's Silk Road* (2003). A description of the travelers along the Silk Road in human terms, focusing on warfare, markets, and religion.

Kern, Martin, and Michael Hunter (eds.). *The Analects. A Western Han Text?* (2013). Challenges the assumption that the Confucian *Analects* was compiled before the Han dynasty.

Knapp, Robert C. *Invisible Romans* (2011). A highly readable introduction to the lower orders of Roman imperial society: the poor, slaves, freedmen, prostitutes, gladiators, bandits, and pirates (among others).

Lewis, Mark. *The Early Chinese Empires: Qin and Han* (2007). A recent account of the rise of imperial China after the Warring States period.

Liang, Cai. *Witchcraft and the Rise of the First Confucian Empire* (2014). A new account of the rise of the Confucians at the Former (Western) Han court during the famous witchcraft trials circa 91–87 BCE.

Loewe, Michael. *The Government of the Qin and Han Empires: 221 BCE–220 CE* (2006). A useful overview of the government of the early empires of China. Topics include the structure of central government, provincial and local government, the armed forces, officials, government communications, the laws of the empire, and control of the people and the land.

Millar, Fergus. *The Emperor in the Roman World, 31 B.C.–A.D. 337* (1992). Everything you might want to know about the Roman emperor, with special emphasis on his role as the administrator of the empire.

Millar, Fergus. *The Crowd in the Late Republic* (1998). An innovative study of the democratic power of the citizens in the city of Rome itself.

Potter, David. *The Roman Empire at Bay: A.D. 180–395*, 2nd ed. (2014). A new basic text covering the later Roman Empire, including the critical transition to a Christian state.

Qian, Sima. *Records of the Grand Historian: Qin Dynasty*, 3rd ed., translated by Burton Watson (1995). The classic work of Chinese history in a readable translation. The Han dynasty's Grand Historian describes the slow rise and meteoric fall of the Qin dynasty from the point of view of the succeeding dynasty, which Sima Qian witnessed or heard of during his lifetime.

Southern, Pat. *The Roman Army: A Social and Institutional History* (2006). A guide to all aspects of the Roman army.

Vainker, Shelagh. *Chinese Silk: A Cultural History* (2004). A work that traces the cultural history of silk in China from its early origins to the twentieth century and considers its relationship to the other decorative arts. The author draws on recent archaeological evidence to emphasize the role of silk in Chinese history, trade, religion, and literature.

Wood, Francis. *The Silk Road: Two Thousand Years in the Heart of Asia* (2004). A work illustrated with drawings, manuscripts, paintings, and artifacts to trace the Silk Road to its origins as far back as Alexander the Great. The author stresses the importance of the Silk Road to cultural and religious movements.

Woolf, Greg (ed.). *The Cambridge Illustrated History of the Roman World* (2005). A good guide to various aspects of Roman history, culture, and provincial life.

Woolf, Greg. *Rome: An Empire's Story* (2012). An up-to-date narrative of the Roman empire, told according to major themes that are particularly relevant to world history.

CHAPTER 8

Bowersock, Glen W. *Empires in Collision in Late Antiquity* (2013). Brilliant, short studies of the relations between Ethiopia, Arabia, and Byzantium as a background to the origins of Islam.

Brown, Peter. *The World of Late Antiquity: From Marcus Aurelius to Muhammad, AD 150–750* (1989). A social, religious, and cultural history of the late Roman and Sasanian Empires, with illustrations and a time chart.

Brown, Peter. *The Rise of Western Christendom: Triumph and Diversity, A.D. 200–1000*, 2nd ed. (2003). The rise and spread of Christianity in Europe and Asia, with up-to-date bibliographies on all topics, maps, and time charts. Reprinted with a new introduction in 2013.

Brown, Peter. *Through the Eye of a Needle: Wealth, the Fall of Rome, and the Making of Christianity in the West, 350–550* (2012). Christianity and Roman society before and after the end of the empire.

Brown, Peter. "The Silk Road in Late Antquity." In V. H. Maier and J. Hickman (eds.), *Reconfiguring the Silk Road* (2014). Silk Road from the perspective of its western outlets and influences.

Brown, Peter. *Treasure in Heaven: The Holy Poor in Early Christianity* (2016). On the social role of early Christian monasticism in Syria and Egypt.

Bühler, G. (trans.). *The Laws of Manu* (1886). The classic translation of one of India's most important historical, legal, and religious texts.

Canepa, Matthew P. *The Two Eyes of the Earth: Art and Ritual of Kingship between Rome and Sasanian Iran* (2009). An interesting look at how two great global powers, Rome and Iran, shared images of rulership.

Coe, Michael D. *The Maya,* 6th ed. (1999). A work by the world's most famous Mayanologist, with recent evidence, analyses, and illustrations.

Cowgill, George L. "The Central Mexican Highlands and the Rise of Teotihuacan to the Decline of Tula." In Richard Adams and Murdo Macleod (eds.), *The Cambridge History of the Native Peoples of the Americas,* Vol. 2: *Mesoamerica, Part 1* (2000). A thorough review of findings about urban states in central Mexico.

Fash, William L. *Scribes, Warriors and Kings: The City of Copan and the Ancient Maya* (2001). A fascinating and comprehensive study of one of the most elaborate of the Mayan city-kingdoms.

Fisher, Greg. *Between Empires: Arabs, Romans, and Sasanians in Late Antiquity* (2011). Arab, Roman, and Sasanian empires compared.

Fisher, Greg (ed.). *Arabs and Empires before Islam* (2015). A collection of up-to-date studies on the relationships of various Arab groups with imperial powers, especially Rome and Persia.

Fowden, Elizabeth Key. *The Barbarian Plain: Saint Sergius between Rome and Iran* (1999). The study of a major Christian shrine and its relations to Romans, Persians, and Arabs.

Fowden, Garth. *Empire to Commonwealth: The Consequences of Monotheism in Late Antiquity* (1993). A study of the relation between empire and world religions in western Asia.

Gombrich, Richard F., and Sheldon Pollack (eds.). *Clay Sanskrit Library* (2005–2006). All major works from the Gupta and post-Gupta periods, in both Sanskrit and English versions. During the Gupta period, classical Sanskrit literature reached its apex, with abundant drama, poetry, and folk stories.

Gordon, Charles. *The Age of Attila* (1960). The last century of the Roman Empire in western Europe, vividly illustrated from contemporary sources.

Haldon, John. *The Empire That Would Not Die: The Paradox of Eastern Rome's Survival* (2010). Incorporates much new climatological evidence.

Hansen, Valerie. *The Silk Road: A New History* (2012). A detailed history of the Silk Road, based largely on Chinese sources.

Harper, Prudence. *The Royal Hunter: The Art of the Sasanian Empire* (1978). The

ideology of the Sasanian Empire as shown through excavated hoards of precious silverware.

Heather, Peter. *The Fall of the Roman Empire: A New History of Rome and the Barbarians* (2006). A military and political narrative based on up-to-date archaeological material.

Herrmann, Georgina. *Iranian Revival* (1977). The structure and horizons of the Sasanian Empire as revealed in its monuments.

Hillgarth, Jocelyn (ed.). *Christianity and Paganism, 350–750: The Conversion of Western Europe,* rev. ed. (1986). A collection of contemporary sources.

Holcombe, Charles. *In the Shadow of the Han: Literati Thought and Society at the Beginning of the Southern Dynasties* (1994). A clear and concise account of the evolution of thought in China after the fall of the Han dynasty in 220 CE. The book presents the rise of Buddhism and Daoism as popular religions as well as elite interest in classical learning in a time of political division and barbarian conquest in North and South China.

La Vaissière, Étienne de. *Sogdian Traders: A History,* translated by James Ward (2005). A summary of historical facts about the most important trading community and its commercial networks on the Silk Road, from the early centuries CE to its demise in the ninth century CE.

Little, Lester (ed.). *Plague and the End of Antiquity: The Pandemic of 541–750* (2008). A series of debates over the nature and impact of the first great pandemic attested in global history.

Liu, Xinru, and Lynda Norene Shaffer. *Connections across Eurasia: Transportation, Communication, and Cultural Exchanges on the Silk Roads* (2007). A survey of trade and religious activities on the Silk Road.

Lopez, Ariel G. *Shenoute of Atripe and the Uses of Poverty: Rural Patronage, Religious Conflict, and Monasticism in Late Antique Egypt* (2013). Places a leading Egyptian abbot in his full social context.

Maas, Michael. *Readings in Late Antiquity: A Source Book* (1999). Well-chosen extracts that illustrate the interrelation of Romans and non-Romans and of Christians, Jews, and pagans.

Maas, Michael. *The Age of Atilla: The Cambridge Companion to the Age of Attila* (2013). Essays on this important age in the late Antique period.

Maas, Michael (ed.). *The Cambridge Companion to the Age of Justinian* (2005). A survey of all aspects of the Eastern Roman Empire in the sixth century CE.

Moffett, Samuel. *A History of Christianity in Asia,* Vol. 1 (1993). Particularly valuable on Christians in China and India.

Munro-Hay, Stuart. *Aksum: An African Civilization of Late Antiquity* (1991). The origins of the Christian kingdom of Ethiopia.

Murdock, George P. *Africa: Its Peoples and Their History* (1959). A vital introduction to the peoples of Africa and their history.

Oliver, Roland. *The African Experience: From Olduvai Gorge to the Twenty-First Century* (1999). An important overview, written by one of the pioneering scholars of African history and one of the leading authorities on the Bantu migrations.

Payne, Richard. *A State of Mixture: Christians, Zoroastrians, and Iranian Political Culture in Late Antiquity* (2015). A new view of Christianity in Sasanian Iran.

Pourshariati, Parvaneh. *The Decline and Fall of the Sasanian Empire: The Sasanian-Parthian Confederacy and the Arab Conquest of Iran* (2008). An innovative perspective on the demise of the Sasanians and the relevance of their decline for the Arab conquest of Iran.

Pregadio, Fabrizio. *Great Clarity: Daoism and Alchemy in Early Medieval China* (2006). An examination of the religious aspects of Daoism. The book focuses on the relation of alchemy to the Daoist traditions of the third to sixth century CE and shows how alchemy was integrated into the elaborate body of doctrines and practices of Daoists at that time.

Tempels, Placide. *Bantu Philosophy* (1959). A highly influential effort to argue for the underlying cultural unity of all the Bantu peoples.

Vansina, Jan. *Paths in the Rainforests: Toward a History of Political Tradition in Equatorial Africa* (1990). The best work on Bantu history.

Walker, Joel. *The Legend of Mar Kardagh: Narrative and Christian Heroism in Late Antique Iraq* (2006). Christians and Zoroastrians in northern Iraq and in Iran.

Yarshater, Ehsan. *Encyclopedia Iranica* (1982+). This encyclopedia offers countless articles dealing with all aspects of the Sasanian Empire and religion and culture in the regions between Mesopotamia and central Asia.

Zhang, Xun, *Fian Zhuan Jiaozhu* (1985) The account of a Chinese Buddhist who traveled to India to learn more about Buddhism and to bring back to China copies of important texts. The text excerpted in this chapter was done by Xinru Liu.

Zürcher, E. *The Buddhist Conquest of China: The Spread and Adaptation of Buddhism in Early Medieval China*, 3rd ed. (2007). A reissue of the classic account of the assimilation of Buddhism in China during the medieval period, with particular focus on the religious and philosophical success of Buddhism among Chinese elites in South China.

CHAPTER 9

Ahmed, Leila. *Women and Gender in Islam* (1992). A superb overview of the relations between men and women throughout the history of Islam.

Aneirin. *Y Gododdin: Britain's Oldest Heroic Poem*, edited and translated by A. O. H. Jarman (1988). A sixth-century CE Welsh text that describes the battle of the last Britons against the invading Anglo-Saxons.

Arberry, Arthur J. (trans.). Introduction to *The Koran Interpreted: A Translation* (1986). One of the most eloquent appreciations of this classical work of religion.

Augustine. *The City of God,* translated by H. Bettenson (1976). An excellent translation of Augustine's monumental work of history, philosophy, and religion.

Berkey, Jonathan P. *The Formation of Islam: Religion and Society in the Near East, 600–1800* (2005). A recent overview of the history of Islam before the modern era. It is particularly sensitive to the influence of external elements on the history of the Muslim peoples.

Bol, Peter. *This Culture of Ours: Intellectual Transitions in T'ang and Sung China* (1994). A study tracing the transformation of the shared culture of the Chinese learned elite from the seventh to the twelfth centuries.

Bowersock, G. W. *The Throne of Adulis: Red Sea Wars on the Eve of Islam* (2013). A vital study of the kingdom of Himyar, in present-day Yemen, a center of Judaism and Christianity before the rise of Islam in the Arabian Peninsula.

Brooke, John L. *Climate Change and the Course of Global History: A Rough Journey* (2014). An overview of a changing climate and its impact on historical developments.

Brown, Peter. *The Rise of Western Christendom: Triumph and Diversity, AD 200–1000,* 2nd ed. (2003). A description of the changes in Christianity in northern Europe and the emergence of the new cultures and political structures that coincided with this development.

Bulliet, Richard W. *Conversion to Islam in the Medieval Period: An Essay in Quantitative History* (1979). A study of the rate at which the populations overrun by Arab conquerors in the seventh century CE embraced the religion of their rulers.

Bulliet, Richard W. *Cotton, Climate, and Camels in the Early Islamic State* (2009). A fascinating account of the economic development on the Iranian plateau, with an emphasis on climate.

Cook, David. *Understanding Jihad* (2005). An exploration of the meaning of Jihad, a significant Muslim concept in today's world, as understood in early Islam.

Cook, Michael. *Muhammad* (1983). A brief but careful life of the Prophet that takes full account of the prolific and often controversial preexisting scholarship.

Cook, Michael. *The Koran: A Very Short Introduction* (2000). A useful overview of Islam's holy book.

Creswell, K. A. C. *A Short Account of Early Muslim Architecture,* revised and supplemented by James W. Allan (1992). The definitive treatment of the subject.

Crone, Patricia, *The Nativist Prophets of Early Islam: Rural Revolt and Local Zoroastrianism* (2012). The rise of protest movements in Islam that led to the Abbasid takeover from the Umayyads.

Cross, S. H., and O. P. Sherbowitz-Westor (trans.). *The Russian Primary Chronicle* (1953). A vivid record of the Viking settlement of Kiev, the conversion of Kiev, and the princes of Kiev in the tenth and eleventh centuries.

Donner, Fred M. *The Early Islamic Conquests* (1981). The best account of the Arab conquests in the Persian and Byzantine Empires in the seventh century CE.

Donner, Fred M. *Muhammad and the Believers at the Origins of Islam* (2010). A richly detailed study of Muhammad's prophecy and the rise of Islam during the Umayyad period.

Duncan, John. *The Origins of the Chosŏn Dynasty* (2000). A historical account of the early Korean dynasties from 900 to 1400.

Elman, Benjamin. *Precocious China: Civil Examinations, 1400–1900* (2013). Summary of civil exams in China from medieval times.

Fage, J. D. *Ghana: A Historical Introduction* (1966). A brief but authoritative history of Ghana from earliest times to the mid-twentieth century.

Fisher, Humphrey J. *Slavery in the History of Muslim Black Africa* (2001). A general history of the relations between North Africa and black Africa, focusing on one of the most important aspects of contact—the slave trade.

Fowden, Garth. *Before and after Muhammad: The First Millennium Refocused* (2014). The author sets Islam in its larger Greek and Christianity setting, part of the work of the Late Antique scholarly community.

Graham-Campbell, James. *Cultural Atlas of the Viking World* (1994). A positioning of the Vikings against their wider background in both western and eastern Europe.

Haider, Najam. *The Origins of the Shi'a: Identity, Ritual, and Sacred Space in Eighth-Century Kufah* (2011). A definitive study on the origin of Shiism.

Hawting, G. R. *The First Dynasty of Islam: The Umayyad Caliphate, A.D. 661–750* (2000). The essential scholarly treatment of Islam's first dynasty.

Herrmann, Georgina. *Iranian Revival* (1977). The structure and horizons of the Sasanian Empire as revealed in its monuments.

Hillgarth, J. N. (ed.). *Christianity and Paganism, 350–750: The Conversion of Western Europe,* rev. ed. (1986). A collection of contemporary sources.

Hodges, Richard, and David Whitehouse. *Mohammed, Charlemagne, and the Origins of Europe* (1983). A spirited comparison of Islam and the rise of Europe.

Hodgson, Marshall G. S. *The Venture of Islam: Conscience and History in a World Civilization, 3 vols.* (1977). A magnificent history of the Islamic peoples. Its first volume, *The Classical Age of Islam,* is basic reading for anyone interested in the history of the Muslim world.

Holdsworth, May. *Women of the Tang Dynasty* (1999). An account of women's lives during the Tang dynasty.

Hourani, Albert. *History of the Arab Peoples* (2002). The best overview of Arab history.

Hoyland, Robert G. *In God's Path: The Arab Conquests and the Creation of the Islamic Empire* (2015). New work that draws on non-Arabic sources to fill in gaps in Islamic historiography.

Jones, Gwynn. *The Norse Atlantic Saga* (1986). The Viking discovery of America.

Kennedy, Hugh. *The Prophet and the Age of the Caliphate: The Islamic Near East from the Sixth to the Eleventh Century* (2004). A very good recent synthesis of the rise and spread of Islam.

Lee, Peter, et al. (eds.). *Sources of Korean Tradition,* vol. 1 (1996). A unique view of Korean history through the eyes and words of the participants or witnesses themselves, as provided in translations of official documents, letters, and policies.

Levtzion, Nehemia. *Ancient Ghana and Mali* (1980). The best introduction to the kingdoms of West Africa.

Levtzion, Nehemia, and Jay Spaulding. *Medieval West Africa: Views from Arab Scholars and Merchants* (2003). An indispensable source book on early West African history.

Levy-Rubin, Milka. *Non-Muslims in the Early Islamic Empire: From Surrender to Co-existence* (2011). The exploitation of non-Muslims in early Islam and their later conversion and rise to prominence.

Lewis, Bernard. *The Middle East: Two Thousand Years of History from the Rise of Christianity to the Present Day* (1995). A stimulating introduction to an area that has seen the emergence of three of the great world religions.

Lewis, Bernard (trans.). *Islam from the Prophet Muhammad to the Capture of Constantinople.* Vol. 2: *Religion and Society* (1974). A fine collection of original sources that portray various aspects of classical Islamic society.

Lewis, David Levering. *God's Crucible: Islam and the Making of Europe, 570-1215* (2008). An exciting and well-written overview of the high period of Islamic power and cultural attainments.

Middleton, John. *The Swahili: The Social Landscape of a Mercantile Community* (2000). An exciting synthesis of the Swahili culture of East Africa.

Miyazaki, Ichisada. *China's Examination Hell* (1981). A study of China's examination system.

Nurse, Derek, and Thomas Spear. *The Swahili: Reconstructing the History and Language of an African Society, 800-1500* (1984). A work that explores the history of the Muslim peoples who lived along the coast of East Africa.

Peters, F. E. *Muhammad and the Origins of Islam* (1994). A work that explores the early history of Islam and highlights the critical role that Muhammad played in promoting a new religion and a powerful Arab identity.

Pourshariati, Parveneh. *Decline and Fall of the Sasanian Empire* (2008). Fundamental analysis of the end of the Sasanian Empire and the reasons for the success of the Arab/Muslim invasions.

Robinson, Chase F. *The New Cambridge History of Islam,* Vol. 1: *The Formation of the Islamic World, Sixth to Eleventh Centuries* (2010). An authoritative and up-to-date six-volume overview of the history of Islam from the sixth century CE to the present.

Schirokauer, Conrad, et al. *A Brief History of Japanese Civilization,* 2nd ed. (2005). A balanced account; chapters focus on developments in art, religion, literature, and thought as well as on Japan's economic, political, and social history in medieval times.

Shoemaker, Stephen T. *The Death of a Prophet: The End of Muhammad's Life and the Beginnings of Islam* (2012). The use of non-Arabic sources to learn about Muhammad and the rise of Islam.

Smith, Julia. *Europe after Rome: A New Cultural History, 500-1000* (2005). A vivid analysis of society and culture in so-called Dark Age Europe.

Totman, Conrad. *History of Japan* (2004). A recent and readable summary of Japanese history from ancient to modern times.

Twitchett, Denis. *Financial Administration under the T'ang Dynasty* (1970). A pioneering account—based on rare Dunhuang documents that survived from medieval times in Buddhist grottoes in central Asia—of the political and economic system undergirding the Chinese imperial state.

Twitchett, Denis. *The Birth of the Chinese Meritocracy: Bureaucrats and Examinations in T'ang China* (1976). A description of the role of the written civil examinations that began during the Tang dynasty.

Whittow, Mark. *The Making of Byzantium, 600-1025* (1996). A study on the survival and revival of the Eastern Roman Empire as a major power in eastern Europe and Southwest Asia.

Wood, Ian. *The Missionary Life: Saints and the Evangelization of Europe, 400-1050* (2001). The horizons of Christians on the frontiers of Europe.

CHAPTER 10

Allsen, Thomas. *Commodity and Exchange in the Mongol Empire: A Cultural History of Islamic Textiles* (1997). A study that uses golden brocade, the textile most treasured by Mongol rulers, as a lens through which to analyze the vast commercial networks facilitated by the Mongol conquests and control.

Allsen, Thomas. *Culture and Conquest in Mongol Eurasia* (2001). A work that emphasizes the cultural and scientific exchanges that took place across Afro-Eurasia as a result of the Mongol conquest.

Bagge, Svere, Michael Gelting, and Thomas Lundkvist (eds.). *Feudalism: New Landscapes of Debate* (2011). A collection of essays on interpretations of feudalism by experts on the topic.

Bailey, Mark. *The English Manor, c. 1200-c. 1500* (2002). An important detailed study of English manorialism.

Bartlett, Robert. *The Making of Europe: Conquest, Colonization and Cultural Change, 950-1350* (1993). The modes of cultural, political, and demographic expansion of feudal Europe along its frontiers, especially in eastern Europe.

Bay, Edna G. *Wives of the Leopards: Gender, Politics, and Culture in the Kingdom of Dahomey* (1998). A work that stresses the role of women in an important West African society and dips into the early history of this area.

Beach, D. N. *Shona and Zimbabwe, 900-1850: An Outline of Shona History* (1980). A good place to start for exploring the history of Great Zimbabwe.

Bloch, Marc. *Feudal Society,* translated by L. A. Manyon (1961). The classic study of feudalism, now being criticized.

Brooks, George E. *Landlords and Strangers: Ecology, Society, and Trade in Western Africa, 1000-1630* (1993). A survey assembled from primary sources of early West African history that stresses transregional connections.

Bulliet, Richard W. *Cotton, Climate, and Camels in Early Islamic Iran* (2009). An analysis of the upswing of the Iranian plateau economy after the Muslim conquest and then its decline as a result of climate change.

Buzurg ibn Shahriyar of Ramhormuz. *The Book of the Wonders of India: Mainland, Sea and Islands,* edited and translated by G. S. P. Freeman-Greenville (1981). A collection of stories told by sailors, both true and fantastic; they help us imagine the lives of sailors of the era.

Chappell, Sally A. Kitt. *Cahokia: Mirror of the Cosmos* (2002). A thorough and vivid account of the "mound people"; it explores not just what we know of Cahokia but how we know it.

Christian, David. *A Short History of Russia, Central Asia, and Mongolia.* Vol. 1: *Inner Eurasia from Prehistory to the Mongol Empire* (1998). Essential reading for students interested in interconnections across the Afro-Eurasian landmass.

Curtin, Philip. *Cross-Cultural Trade in World History* (1984). A groundbreaking book on intercultural trade with a primary focus on Africa, especially the cross-Saharan trade and Swahili coastal trade.

Dawson, Christopher. *Mission to Asia* (1980). Accounts of China and the Mongol Empire brought back by Catholic missionaries and diplomats after 1240 CE.

Duby, Georges. *The Three Orders: Feudal Society Imagined,* translated by Arthur Goldhammer (1982). Another classic study of feudalism.

Ellenblum, Ronnie. *The Collapse of the Eastern Mediterranean: Climate Change and the Decline of the East, 950-1072* (2012). An analysis of the impact of freezing temperatures and drought on the societies of the eastern Mediterranean.

Flori, Jean. "Knightly Society." In David Luscombe and Jonathon Riley Smith (eds.), *The New Cambridge Medieval History,* Vol. 4, Part 1: *c. 1024-1198* (2004). A brilliant overview of knights in medieval times and an overview of the debate on feudalism with the author's own insightful conclusions. Other useful articles in this volume are by Susan Reynolds and by David Luscombe and Jonathon Riley Smith.

Foltz, Richard C. *Religions of the Silk Road: Overland Trade and Cultural Exchange from Antiquity to the Fifteenth Century* (1999). A study of the populations and the cities of the Silk Road as transmitters of culture across long distances.

Franklin, Simon, and Jonathan Shepherd. *The Emergence of Rus: 750-1200* (1996). The formation of medieval Russia between the Baltic and Black Seas.

Ganshof, F. L. *Feudalism,* translated by Philip Griersur (1952). Perhaps the work most often dealt with by critics of the term *feudalism.* Simple, straightforward, easily comprehended study of feudalism.

Gibb, Hamilton A. R. *Saladin: Studies in Islamic History,* edited by Yusuf Ibish (1974). A sympathetic portrait of one of Islam's leading political and military figures.

Goitein, S. D. "New Light on the Beginnings of the Karim Merchants." *Journal of the Economic and Social History of the Orient* 1 (1957): 175-184. Goitein's description of Egyptian trade.

Goitein, S. D. *Letters of Medieval Jewish Traders* (1973). The classic study of medieval Jewish trading communities based on the commercial papers deposited in the Cairo Geniza (a synagogue storeroom) during the tenth and eleventh centuries; it explores not only commercial activities but also the personal lives of the traders around the Indian Ocean basin.

Goitein, S. D. *A Mediterranean Society: An Abridgment in One Volume,* revised and edited by Jacob Lassner (1999). A portrait of the Jewish merchant community with ties across the Afro-Eurasian landmass, based largely on the documents from the Cairo Geniza (of which Goitein was the primary researcher and interpreter).

Harris, Joseph E. *The African Presence in Asia: Consequences of the East African Slave Trade* (1971). One of the few books that looks broadly at the impact of Africans and African slavery on the societies of Asia.

Hartwell, Robert. "Demographic, Political, and Social Transformations of China, 750-1550." *Harvard Journal of Asiatic Studies* 42 (1982): 365-442. A pioneering study of the demographic changes that overtook China during the Tang and Song dynasties, which are described in light of political reform movements and social changes in this crucial era.

Historical Relations across the Indian Ocean: Report and Papers of the Meeting of Experts Organized by UNESCO at Port Louis, Mauritius, from 15 to 19 July, 1974 (1980). Excellent essays on the connections of Africa with Asia across the Indian Ocean.

Hitti, Philip. *An Arab-Syrian Gentleman and Warrior in the Period of the Crusades: Memoirs of Usāmah ibn-Munqidh* (1929). The Crusaders seen through Muslim eyes.

Hodgson, Natasha. *Women, Crusading, and the Holy Land in Historical Narrative* (2007). A book dealing with the Crusades and focusing on the place of women in them.

Holt, P. M. *The Age of the Crusades: The Near East from the Eleventh Century to 1517* (1984). The Crusades period as seen from the eastern Mediterranean and through the lens of a leading British scholar of the area.

Huff, Toby E. *The Rise of Early Modern Science* (2009) A bold attempt to look at the rise of scientific work in the Islamic world, premodern China, and Europe, seeking to explain why the scientific revolution occurred in Europe rather than the Islamic world or China.

Hunter, Timothy (ed.). *The New Cambridge Medieval History,* Vol. 3: *c. 900-c. 1024* (1999). Comprehensive articles written by experts of this period.

Hymes, Robert, and Conrad Schirokauer (eds.). *Ordering the World: Approaches to State and Society in Sung Dynasty China* (1993). A collection of essays that traces the intellectual, social, and political movements that shaped the Song state and its elites.

Ibn Battuta. *The Travels of Ibn Battuta,* translated by H. A. R. Gibb (2002). A readable translation of the classic book, originally published in 1929.

Ibn Fadlan, Ahmad. *Ibn Fadlan's Journey to Russia: A Tenth Century Traveler from Baghdad to the Volga River,* translated with commentary by Richard Frye (2005). A coherent summary of the observations of an envoy who traveled from Baghdad to Russia.

Irwin, Robert. *The Middle East in the Middle Ages: The Early Mamluk Sultanate, 1250-1582* (1986). Egypt under Mamluk rule.

Jeppie, Shamil, and Souleymane Bachir Diagne (eds.). *The Meanings of Timbuktu* (2008). New materials on the ancient Muslim city of Timbuktu by scholars who have been preserving its manuscripts and writing about its historical importance.

Keay, John. *India: A History* (2000). A spirited and informative overview of the entire history of the South Asian subcontinent.

Lancaster, Lewis, Kikun Suh, and Chai-shin Yu (eds.). *Buddhism in Koryo: A Royal Religion* (1996). A description of Buddhism at its height in the Koryo period, when the religion made significant contributions to the development of Korean culture.

Levtzion, Nehemia, and Randall L. Pouwels (eds.). *The History of Islam in Africa* (2000). A useful general survey of the place of Islam in African history.

Lewis, Bernard (trans.). *Islam: From the Prophet Muhammad to the Capture of Constantinople* (1974). Vol. 2: *Religion and Society*. A fine collection of original sources that portray various aspects of classical Islamic society.

Lopez, Robert S. *The Commercial Revolution of the Middle Ages, 950–1350* (1976). An account focusing on the development around the Mediterranean of commercial practices such as the use of currency, accounting, and credit.

Lyons, Malcolm C., and D. E. P. Jackson. *Saladin: The Politics of the Holy War* (1984: reprint 2001). The fundamental revisionist work on one of the more important historical figures of the time.

Maalouf, Amin. *The Crusades through Muslim Eyes,* translated by Jon Rothschild (1984). The European Crusaders as seen by the Muslim world.

Marcus, Harold G. *A History of Ethiopia* (2002). An authoritative overview of the history of this great culture.

Mass, Jeffrey. *Yoritomo and the Founding of the First Bakufu: The Origins of Dual Government in Japan* (1999). A revisionist account of how the Kamakura military leader Minamoto Yoritomo established the "dual polity" of court and warrior government in Japan.

McDermott, Joseph. *A Social History of the Chinese Book: Books and Literati Culture in Late Imperial China* (2006). The history of the book in China since the Song dynasty, with comparisons to the book's role in other civilizations, particularly the European.

McEvitt, Christopher. *The Crusaders and the Christian World of the East: Rough Tolerance* (2008). Excellent work on the relations of religious groups in the Crusader kingdoms.

McIntosh, Roderik. *The Peoples of the Middle Niger: The Island of Gold* (1988). A historical survey of an area often omitted from other textbooks.

Moore, Jerry D. *Cultural Landscapes in the Ancient Andes: Archaeologies of Place* (2005). The most recent and up-to-date analysis of findings based on recent archaeological evidence, emphasizing the importance of local cultures and diversity in the Andes.

Mote, F. W. *Imperial China, 900–1800* (1999). Still the best general history of China, written by one of the world's leading Sinologists.

Niane, D. T. (ed.). *General History of Africa.* Vol. 4: *Africa from the Twelfth to the Sixteenth Century* (1984). The fourth volume of the UNESCO history of Africa with articles by experts on this period. The work features the scholarship of Africans.

Oliver, Roland (ed.). *From c. 1050 to c. 1600,* vol. 3 of *The Cambridge History of Africa,* edited by J. D. Fage and Roland Oliver (1977). Another general survey of African history. This volume draws heavily on the work of British scholars.

Peters, Edward. *The First Crusade* (1971). The Crusaders as seen through their own eyes.

Petry, Carl F. (ed.). *Islamic Egypt, 640–1517,* vol. 1 of *The Cambridge History of Egypt,* edited by M. W. Daly (1998). A solid overview of the history of Islamic Egypt up to the Ottoman conquest.

Polo, Marco. *The Travels of Marco Polo,* revised from Marsden's translation and edited by Manuel Komroff (1926). A solid translation of Marco Polo's famous account.

Popovic, Alexandre. *The Revolt of African Slaves in Iraq in the 3rd/9th Century,* translated by Leon King (1999). The account of a massive revolt against their slave masters by African slaves taken to labor in Iraq's mines and fields.

Reynolds, Susan. *Fiefs and Vassals: The Medieval Evidence Reinterpreted* (1994). The book that made the most determined attack on the concept of feudalism.

Sarris, Peter. "The Origins of the Manorial Economy: New Insights from Late Antiquity." *The English Historical Review* 119 (April 2004): 279–311. An original contribution on the origins of manorialism, based first on Egyptian papyri and extended to other parts of the Byzantine Empire and western Europe.

Scott, Robert. *Gothic Enterprise: A Guide to Understanding the Medieval Cathedral* (2003). The meaning and social function of religious building in medieval cities in northern Europe.

Shaffer, Lynda Norene. *Maritime Southeast Asia to 1500* (1996). A history of the peoples of the southeast fringe of the Eastern Hemisphere, up to the time that they became connected to the global commercial networks of the world.

Shimada, Izumi. "Evolution of Andean Diversity: Regional Formations (500 BCE–CE 600)." In Frank Salomon and Stuart Schwartz (eds.), *South America,* vol. 3 of *The Cambridge History of the Native Peoples of the Americas,* part 1, pp. 350–517 (1999). A splendid overview that contrasts the varieties of lowland and highland cultures.

Steinberg, David Joel, et al. *In Search of Southeast Asia: A Modern History* (1987). An account of the emergence of the modern Southeast Asian polities of Cambodia, Burma, Thailand, and Indonesia.

Tyerman, Christopher. *God's War: A New History of the Crusades* (2006). The balance of religious and nonreligious motivations in the Crusades.

Waley, Daniel. *The Italian City-Republics,* 3rd ed. (1988). The structures and culture of the new cities of medieval Italy.

Watson, Andrew. *Agricultural Innovation in the Early Islamic World: The Diffusion of Crops and Farming Techniques, 700–1100* (1983). An impressive study of the spread of new crops throughout the Muslim world.

West, Charles. *Reframing the Feudal Revolution: Political and Social Transformation between Marne and Moselle, c. 800–c. 1100* (2013). Big change seen through an intensely studied region.

Wickham, Chris. *Sleepwalking into a New World: The Emergence of Italian City Communes in the Twelfth Century* (2015). Origins of the city democracies of medieval Italy.

Williamson, Tom. *Shaping Medieval Landscapes: Settlement, Society, Environment* (2004). A study of the manorial system in England.

CHAPTER 11

Barkey, Karen. *Empire of Difference: The Ottomans in Comparative Perspective* (2008). A revisionist view of the rise and flourishing of the Ottoman Empire.

Benedictow, Ole J. *The Black Death, 1346–1351: The Complete History* (2004). An exhaustive statistical study of the mortality during the first years of the Black Death's arrival in Europe.

Bois, Guy. *The Crisis of Feudalism: Economy and Society in Eastern Normandy, c. 1300–1550* (1984). A good case study of a French region that illustrates the turmoil in fourteenth-century France.

Brook, Timothy. *Praying for Power: Buddhism and the Formation of Gentry Society in Late Ming China* (1994). An analysis of the role of a significant religious force in the political and social developments of the Ming.

Dardess, John. *A Ming Society: T'ai-ho County, Kiangsi, Fourteenth to Seventeenth Centuries* (1996). A work that covers the different changes and developments of a single locality in China through the centuries.

Dols, Michael W. *The Black Death in the Middle East* (1977). One of the few scholarly works to examine the Black Death outside Europe.

Dreyer, Edward. *Early Ming China: A Political History, 1355–1435* (1982). A useful account of the early years of the Ming dynasty.

Faroqhi, Suraiya N., and Kate Fleet (eds.). *The Cambridge History of Turkey*, Vol. 2: *The Ottoman Empire as a World Power, 1453–1603* (2013). An overview of this crucial period in Ottoman history, written by experts in the field.

Finkel, Caroline. *Osman's Dream: The Story of the Ottoman Empire, 1300–1923* (2005). The most authoritative overview of Ottoman history.

Hale, John. *The Civilization of Europe in the Renaissance* (1994). A beautifully crafted account of the politics, economics, and culture of the Renaissance period in western Europe.

He, Yuming. *Home and the World: Editing the "Glorious Ming" in Woodblock-Printed Books of the Sixteenth and Seventeenth Centuries* (2013). An insightful exploration of Ming society through a close look at its vibrant print culture and market for books.

Ho, Ping-ti. *Studies on the Population of China, 1368–1953* (1959). A useful overview of China's population from Ming times until the mid-twentieth century.

Hodgson, Marshall. *The Venture of Islam: Conscience and History in a World Civilization*, vol. 3 (1974). A good volume on the workings of the Ottoman state.

Hoffman, Philip T. *Why Did Europe Conquer the World?* (2015). Makes an interesting case for the importance of Europe's use of gunpowder technologies.

Itzkowitz, Norman. *Ottoman Empire and Islamic Tradition* (1972). Another good book on the Ottoman state.

Jackson, Peter. *The Delhi Sultanate* (1999). A meticulous, highly specialized political and military history.

Jackson, Peter, and Lawrence Lockhart (eds.). *The Cambridge History of Iran*, Vol. 6 (1986). A volume that deals with the Timurid and Safavid periods in Iran.

Jones, E. L. *The European Miracle* (1981). A provocative work on the economic and social recovery from the Black Death.

Kafadar, Cemal. *Between Two Worlds: The Construction of the Ottoman State* (1995). A thorough reconsideration of the origins of one of the world's great land empires.

Karamustafa, Ahmed. *God's Unruly Friends: Dervish Groups in the Islamic Later Middle Period, 1200–1550* (1994). A book that describes the unorthodox Islamic activities that were occurring in the Islamic world prior to and alongside the establishment of the Ottoman and Safavid Empires.

Levathes, Louise. *When China Ruled the Seas: The Treasure Fleet of the Dragon Throne, 1405–33* (1994). A book that provides a lively account of the Zheng He expeditions.

Lowry, Heath W. *The Nature of the Early Ottoman State* (2003). New perspectives on the rise of the Ottomans to prominence.

McNeill, William. *Plagues and Peoples* (1976). A pathbreaking work with a highly useful chapter on the spread of the Black Death throughout the Afro-Eurasian landmass.

Morgan, David. *Medieval Persia, 1040–1797* (1988). Contains an informative discussion of the Safavid state.

Peirce, Leslie. *The Imperial Harem: Women and Sovereignty in the Ottoman Empire* (1993). A work that describes the powerful place that imperial women had in political affairs.

Pirenne, Henri. *Economic and Social History of Medieval Europe* (1937). A classic study of the economic and social recovery from the Black Death.

Reid, James J. *Tribalism and Society in Islamic Iran, 1500–1629* (1983). A useful account of how the Mongols and other nomadic steppe peoples influenced Iran in the era when the Safavids were establishing their authority.

Savory, Roger. *Iran under the Safavids* (1980). A standard work on Safavid history and still useful.

Schäfer, Dagmar. *The Crafting of the 10,000 Things: Knowledge and Technology in Seventeenth-Century China* (2011). An innovative study of the philosophy of technology and crafts in the late Ming period with important implications for the global history of science.

Singman, Jeffrey L. (ed.). *Daily Life in Medieval Europe* (1999). An introductory description of the social and material world experienced by Europeans of different walks of life.

Tuchman, Barbara W. *A Distant Mirror: The Calamitous Fourteenth Century* (1978). A book that shows, in a vigorous way, how war, famine, and pestilence devastated Europeans in the fourteenth century.

Wittek, Paul. *The Rise of the Ottoman Empire* (1958). A work that contains vital insights on the emergence of the Ottoman state amid the political chaos in Anatolia.

CHAPTER 12

Axtell, James. *Beyond 1492: Encounters in Colonial North America* (1992). A wonderfully informed speculation about Indian reactions to Europeans.

Brady, Thomas A., et al. (eds.). *Handbook of European History 1400–1600: Late Middle Ages, Renaissance, and Reformation.* Vol. 1: *Structures and Assertions* (1996). A good synthetic survey of recent literature and historiographical debates.

Brook, Timothy. *Vermeer's Hat: The Seventeenth Century and the Dawn of the Global World* (2008). An interesting look at the connections forged across the globe through the works of a well-known European artist.

Burns, Bradford. *A History of Brazil* (1993). A comprehensive study of the long-term effects of the European colonization of Brazil.

Casale, Giancarlo. *The Ottoman Age of Exploration* (2010). The author places Ottoman exploration in a comparative context alongside European overseas expansion.

Cass, Victoria. *Dangerous Women: Warriors, Grannies, and Geishas of the Ming* (1999). An original study of Chinese female archetypes in memoirs, miscellanies, short stories, and novels.

Chaudhuri, K. N. *Trade and Civilisation in the Indian Ocean: An Economic History from the Rise of Islam to 1750* (1985). An excellent, comprehensive work that deals with the Indian Ocean economy and the appearance of European merchants there from the sixteenth century onward.

Clendinnen, Inga. *Aztecs: An Interpretation* (1991). Brilliantly reconstructs the culture of Tenochtitlán in the years before its conquest.

Cortés, Hernán. *Five Letters of Cortés to the Emperor, 1519–1526* (1991). Offers fascinating insights into the mind of the conqueror.

Crosby, Alfred W. *The Columbian Exchange: Biological and Cultural Consequences of 1492* (1972). A provocative discussion of the ecological consequences that followed the European "discovery" of the Americas.

Crosby, Alfred W. *Ecological Imperialism: The Biological Expansion of Europe, 900–1900* (1986). Another important work on the ecological consequences of European expansion.

Curtin, Philip. *Cross-Cultural Trade in World History* (1984). A work stressing the role of trade and commerce in establishing cross-cultural contacts.

Diamond, Jared. *Guns, Germs, and Steel: The Fates of Human Societies* (1997). An influential argument about the biological and technological determinants of how some societies took charge over others.

Díaz del Castillo, Bernal. *The Conquest of New Spain* (1963). The eyewitness account of a Spanish soldier who participated in the conquest of the Aztec Empire.

Faroqhi, Suraiya N. (ed.). *The Cambridge History of Turkey*, Vol. 3: *The Later Ottoman Empire, 1603–1839* (2008). Definitive articles on this important period in Ottoman history.

Faroqhi, Suraiya N., and Kate Fleet (eds.). *The Cambridge History of Turkey*, Vol. 2: *The Ottoman Empire as a World Power, 1453–1603* (2013). A collection of articles written by leading scholars of this crucial period in Ottoman history.

Febvre, Lucien. *The Problem of Unbelief in the Sixteenth Century: The Religion of Rabelais* (1982). A tour de force of intellectual history by the man who moved the study of the Reformation away from great men to the broader question of religious revival and mentalities.

Finkel, Caroline. *Osman's Dream: The History of the Ottoman Empire* (2005). A detailed and exhaustively researched history of the Ottomans from the origins of the Ottoman state at the end of the thirteen century to the dismantling of the empire after World War I.

Flynn, Dennis, and Arturo Giráldez (eds.). *Metals and Monies in an Emerging Global Economy* (1997). Contains several articles relating to silver and the Asian trade.

Frank, Andre Gunder. *ReOrient: Global Economy in the Asian Age* (1998). A reassessment of the role of Asia in the economic development of the world from around 1400 onward.

Glahn, Richard von. *The Economic History of China: From Antiquity to the Nineteenth Century* (2016). A masterful new survey of Chinese economic history.

Greenblatt, Stephen. *Marvelous Possessions: The Wonder of the New World* (1991). An insightful study of the ways in which Europe's encounters with the New World changed European culture.

Gruzinski, Serge. *The Conquest of Mexico* (1993). An important work on the conquest of Mexico.

Habib, Irfan. *The Agrarian System of Mughal India* (1963). One of the best studies on the subject.

Hall, Richard Seymour. *Empires of the Monsoon: A History of the Indian Ocean and Its Invaders* (1996). A very engaging journalistic account with fabulous details.

Hodgson, Marshall. *The Venture of Islam,* vols. 2 and 3 (1974). A magisterial work that includes the Indian subcontinent in its careful study of the political and cultural history of the whole Islamic world.

Hulme, Peter. *Colonial Encounters: Europe and the Native Caribbean, 1492–1797* (1986). Presents an interesting interpretation of the encounters of Europeans and Native Americans.

Lach, Donald F. *Asia in the Making of Europe,* 5 books in 3 vols. (1965–). Perhaps the single most comprehensive and innovative guide to the European voyages of discovery.

Las Casas, Bartolomé. *A Short Account of the Destruction of the Indies*, edited by Anthony Pagden (2004). The most famous book written about the conquest of the New World.

Lockhart, James, and Stuart Schwartz. *Early Latin America* (1983). One of the finest studies of European expansion in the late fifteenth century.

McCann, James. *Maize and Grace: Africa's Encounter with a New World Crop, 1500–2000* (2005). A significant study of how maize, a New World crop, became Africa's most widely grown grain.

Melville, Elinor G. K. *A Plague of Sheep: Environmental Consequences of the Conquest of Mexico* (1994). A history of the transformation of a valley in Mexico from the Aztec period to the era of Spanish rule.

Mignolo, Walter D. *The Darker Side of the Renaissance: Literacy, Territoriality, and Colonization* (1995). Uses literary theory and literary images to present provocative interpretations of the encounter of Europeans and Native Americans.

Ozbaran, Salih. *Ottoman Expansion toward the Indian Ocean in the 16th Century* (2009). An important treatment of the Ottoman entry into the Indian Ocean at a time when the Portuguese were also expanding there.

Pagden, Anthony. *European Encounters with the New World* (1993). A complex look at the deep and lasting imprint of the New World on its conquerors.

Phillips, William D., and Carla Rahn Phillips. *The World of Christopher Columbus* (1992). One of the finest studies of European expansion in the late fifteenth century.

Roper, Lyndal. *Martin Luther: Renegade and Prophet* (2016). A magisterial biography that demonstrates the ways in which Luther was a rebel but also a man of his time.

Russell-Wood, A. J. R. *The Portuguese Empire, 1415–1808* (1992). An important survey of early Portuguese exploration.

Salmon, W. H. *An Account of the Ottoman Conquest of Egypt in the Year A.H. 932 (A.D. 1516), Translated from the Third Volume of the Arabic Chronicle of Muhammad Ahmed Ibn Iyas, an Eyewitness of the Scenes He Describes* (1921). An evocative primary source on the Ottoman-Mamluk conflict.

Von Glahn, Richard. *Fountain of Fortune: Money and Monetary Policy in China, 1000–1700* (1996). Includes an excellent analysis of the history of silver in Ming China.

CHAPTER 13

Alam, Muzaffar. *The Crisis of Empire in Mughal North India* (1993). Represents the best of the scholarly interpretations on the subject.

Bay, Edna. *Wives of the Leopard: Gender, Politics, and Culture in the Kingdom of Dahomey* (1998). A useful treatment of gender issues in Dahomey.

Blackburn, Robin. *The Making of New World Slavery: From the Baroque to the Modern, 1492–1800* (1997). A good place to begin when studying African slavery and the Atlantic slave trade, it compares the early expansion of the plantation systems across the Atlantic and throughout the Americas.

Blanning, Tim. *The Pursuit of Glory: Europe, 1648–1815* (2007). An elegantly written and deeply insightful overview of European political history from the Thirty Years' War to the fall of Napoleon.

Bushkovitch, Paul. *Peter the Great* (2016). An updated version of a standard work, offering a concise overview of one of Russia's most celebrated and energetic rulers.

Calloway, Colin G. *One Vast Winter Count: The Native American West before Lewis and Clark* (2003). A sweeping survey of North American Indian histories prior to the nineteenth century.

Crossley, Pamela. *A Translucent Mirror: History and Identity in Qing Imperial Ideology* (1999). The author deals with the formation of identities such as "Manchu" and "Chinese" during the Qing period.

Dale, Stephen F. *The Muslim Empires of the Ottomans, Safavids, and Mughals* (2010). A comparative overview of Islam's three most powerful empires of the sixteenth and seventeenth centuries.

Eaton, Richard. *Essays on Islam and Indian History* (2000). A wide-ranging account that pays particular attention to Islam's social history in the subcontinent.

Eltis, David, and Richardson, David. *Atlas of the Transatlantic Slave Trade* (2010). This work contains the most up-to-date data on the Atlantic slave trade, the numbers transported, where the captives came from, and where they landed.

Fleischer, Cornell H. *Bureaucrat and Intellectual in the Ottoman Empire (1542–1600)* (1986). A probing study into Mustafa Ali, the Ottoman Empire's leading sixteenth-century intellectual.

Flynn, Dennis O., and Arturo Giraldez (eds.). *Metals and Money in an Emerging World Economy* (1997). A collection of articles about the place of silver in the world economy.

Forsyth, James. *A History of the Peoples of Siberia: Russia's North Asian Colony 1581–1990* (1992). A narrative overview of a violent history reminiscent of the western expansion of the United States.

Glahn, Richard von. *Fountains of Fortune: Money and Monetary Policy in China, 1000–1700* (1996). A discussion of the place of silver in the Chinese economy.

Halperin, Charles J. *Russia and the Golden Horde: The Mongol Impact on Medieval Russian History* (1985). A book on the rise of Muscovy, forebear of the Russian Empire, from within the Mongol realm.

Hämäläinen, Pekka. *The Comanche Empire* (2008). A book that inverts the conventional history of empires in North America by arguing that the Comanches were the most successful expansionist power in the middle of the continent during the eighteenth century.

Hartley, Janet. *Siberia: A History of the People* (2014). A vivid portrait of diverse conquerors—fur traders, Cossack adventurers, political criminals—of a region larger than almost all continents.

Hattox, Ralph S. *Coffee and Coffeehouses: The Origins of a Social Beverage in the Medieval Near East* (1985). This work shows how widespread and popular coffee consumption and coffeehouses were around the world.

Herzog, Tamar. *Frontiers of Possession: Spain and Portugal in Europe and the Americas* (2015). An exploration of how Spanish and Portuguese rulers carved up the New World, less by military action and diplomatic treaties and more by quarrels over land settlement and rights to trade and travel.

Huang, Ray. *1587, a Year of No Significance: The Ming Dynasty in Decline* (1981). An insightful analysis of the problems confronting the late Ming.

Lensen, George. *The Russian Push Toward Japan: Russo-Japanese Relations 1697–1875* (1959). A discussion of why and how Japan established its first border with another state and how Russia pursued its ambitions in the Pacific.

Lockhart, James. *The Nahuas after the Conquest* (1992). A landmark study of the social reorganization of Mesoamerican societies under Spanish rule.

Lovejoy, Paul. *Transformations in Slavery: A History of Slavery in Africa* (1983). An excellent discussion of African slavery.

Mathee, Rudi. *Persia in Crisis, Safavid Decline, and the Fall of Isfahan* (2012). A study of the disintegration of the Safavid state.

Mikhail, Alan. *Nature and Empire in Ottoman Egypt: An Environmental History* (2011). An important study of the impact of the environment on Egypt in the eighteenth century.

Monahan, Erika. *The Merchants of Siberia: Trade in Early Modern Eurasia* (2016). A stirring account of entrepreneurs battling the harshest imaginable conditions

to establish trading networks connecting the far-flung territories north of the ancient Silk Road.

Moon, David. *The Plough That Broke the Steppes: Agriculture and Environment in Russia's Grasslands, 1700–1913* (2013). A bold incorporation of environmental aspects to retell the epic story of Russia's most numerous social group.

Nakane, Chie, and Shinzaburo Oishi (eds.). *Tokugawa Japan: The Social and Economic Antecedents of Modern Japan* (1990). First-rate essays on Japanese village society, urban life, literacy, and culture.

Nwokeji, G. Uko. *The Slave Trade and Culture in the Bight of Biafra: An African Society in the Atlantic World* (2010). A study of the Aro peoples of southeastern Nigeria and their use of their commercial powers to promote a vigorous trade with European slavers on the coast.

Pamuk, Sevket. *A Monetary History of the Ottoman Empire* (2000). A discussion of the place of silver in the Ottoman Empire.

Parker, Geoffrey. *Global Crisis: War, Climate Change, and Catastrophe in the Seventeenth Century* (2013). A comprehensive and exhaustively researched study of the effects of the Little Ice Age on the governments and societies of the entire world in the seventeenth century.

Parker, Geoffrey (ed.). *The Thirty Years' War* (1997). The standard account of the conflict and its outcomes.

Perdue, Peter C. *China Marches West: The Qing Conquest of Central Asia* (2005). This volume chronicles the expansion of the Qing Empire to its northwest, drawing comparisons to other colonial empires and their legacies.

Platonov, S. F. *Ivan the Terrible* (1986). Covers the controversies over Russia's infamous tsar.

Rawski, Evelyn. *The Last Emperors: A Social History of Qing Imperial Institutions* (1998). This volume explores the mechanisms and processes through which the Qing court negotiated its Manchu identity.

Reid, Anthony. *Charting the Shape of Early Modern Southeast Asia* (1999). A collection of articles by a leading historian of Southeast Asia.

Spence, Jonathan, and John Wills (eds.). *From Ming to Ch'ing: Conquest, Region, and Continuity in Seventeenth-Century China* (1979). Covers the various aspects of a tumultuous period of dynastic transition.

Subramanyam, Sanjay. *From the Tigris to the Ganges, Explorations in Connected History* (2012). A study that demonstrates that Afro-Eurasia in the seventeenth and eighteenth centuries contained a porous network of empires, cultures, and economies.

Subramanyam, Sanjay, and Muzaffar Alam. *Indo-Persian Travels in the Age of Discoveries, 1400–1800* (2012). A lively portrait of cultural exchanges between Persia, central Asia, and India as seen in travel literature.

Taylor, Alan. *American Colonies: The Settling of North America* (2001). Brings together British, French, and Spanish colonial histories and shows how the fortunes of each were entangled with one another and with those of diverse Native American peoples.

Thornton, John K. *Africa and Africans in the Making of the Atlantic World, 1400–1800* (1998). A wonderful discussion of how African slaves played a large role in the formation of the Atlantic world.

Thornton, John K. *The Kongolese Saint Anthony: Dona Beatriz Kimpa Vita and the Antonian Movement, 1684–1706* (1998). An excellent monograph on religious movements in the Kongo.

Toby, Ronald P. *State and Diplomacy in Early Modern Japan: Asia in the Development of the Tokugawa Bakufu* (1984). The author shows that the Japanese, far from being isolated from the outside world, engaged in vigorous and successful diplomacy.

Van Dusen, Nancy E. *Global Indios: The Indigenous Struggle for Justice in Sixteenth-Century Spain* (2015). A remarkable study of the ways that Spanish rulers enslaved Amerindians in the Americas and even exported them back to Europe.

Vilar, Pierre. *A History of Gold and Money* (1991). An excellent study of the development of the early silver and gold economies.

CHAPTER 14

Axtell, James. *The Invasion of America: The Contest of Cultures in Colonial North America* (1985). Discusses the strategies of Christian missionaries in converting the Indians, as well as the success of Indians in converting Europeans.

Babaie, Sussan. *Isfahan and Its Palaces: Statecraft, Shi'ism and the Architecture of Conviviality in Early Modern Iran* (2008). An overview of the city of Isfahan, as the capital of the Safavid state.

Barmé, Geremie R. *The Forbidden City* (2008). A concise introduction to the history of one of the most important physical emblems of Chinese imperial power.

Berlin, Ira. *Many Thousands Gone: The First Two Centuries of Slavery in North America* (1998). Surveys the development of African American culture in colonial North America.

Bleichmar, Daniela. *Visible Empire: Botanical Expeditions and Visual Culture in the Hispanic Enlightenment* (2012). A fascinating and beautifully illustrated history of creole botanical expeditions in the eighteenth century.

Brockey, Liam. *Journey to the East: The Jesuit Mission to China, 1579–1724* (2007). A detailed and definitive treatment of the Jesuits in China up to 1724, the year when Jesuit influence began to decline.

Brook, Timothy. *The Confusions of Pleasure: Commerce and Culture in Ming China* (1999). An insightful survey of Ming society.

Clunas, Craig. *Superfluous Things: Material Culture and Social Status in Early Modern China* (1991). A good account of the late Ming elite's growing passion for material things.

Collcutt, Martin, Marius Jansen, and Isao Kumakura. *A Cultural Atlas of Japan* (1988). A sweeping look at the many different forms of Japanese cultural expression over the centuries, including the flourishing urban culture of Edo.

Crèvecoeur, Hector St. John de. *Letters from an American Farmer*, reprinted from the orginal edition, with a prefatory note by W. P. Trent and an introduction by Ludwig Lewisohn (New York: Fox, Duffield, 1904). Powerful and informative letters of a French settler in the Americas in the eighteenth century.

Darnton, Robert. *The Business of the Enlightenment: A Publishing History of the Encyclopédie, 1775–1800* (1979). The classic study of Europe's first great compendium of knowledge.

Dash, Mike. *Tulipomania: The Story of the World's Most Coveted Flower and the Extraordinary Passions It Aroused* (1999). A global perspective on and lively account of the spread of the tulip around the world as a flower signifying both beauty and status.

Dikötter, Frank. *The Discourse of Race in Modern China* (1992). A good survey of Chinese discussions of race in the modern era.

Doniger, Wendy. *The Hindus: An Alternative History* (2009). A deeply scholarly yet accessibly written history of Hinduism that takes into account both texts and popular practices and contains a lively account of dissenting traditions.

Eaton, Richard. *Essays on Islam and Indian History* (2000). A wide-ranging account that pays particular attention to Islam's social history in the subcontinent.

Elman, Benjamin A. *On Their Own Terms: Science in China, 1550–1900* (2005). A study of the development of "native" Chinese science and how the process interacted with the introduction of western science to China over the course of three and a half centuries.

Eze, Emmanuel Chukwudi (ed.). *Race and the Enlightenment: A Reader* (1997). Readings examining the idea of race in the context of the Enlightenment.

Fleischer, Cornell. *Bureaucrat and Intellectual in the Ottoman Empire: The Historian Mustafa Ali (1540–1600)* (1986). Offers good insight into the world of culture and intellectual vitality in the Ottoman Empire.

Grafton, Anthony, April Shelford, and Nancy Siraisi. *New Worlds, Ancient Texts: The Power of Tradition and the Shock of Discovery* (1995). A concise discussion of the impact of the New World on European thought.

Gutierrez, Ramon. *When Jesus Came, the Corn Mothers Went Away: Marriage, Sexuality, and Power in New Mexico, 1500–1846* (1991). A provocative dissection of the spiritual dimensions of European colonialism in the Americas.

Harley, J. B., and David Woodward (eds.). *The History of Cartography.* Vol. 2, Book 2: *Cartography in the Traditional East and Southeast Asian Societies* (1994). An authoritative treatment of the subject.

Hart, Roger. *Imagined Civilizations: China, the West, and Their First Encounter* (2013). A treatment of the Jesuit mission to China as the first contact between Chinese and European cultures.

Horton, Robin. *Patterns of Thought in Africa and the West: Essays on Magic, Religion, and Science* (1993). Reflections on African patterns of thought and attitudes toward nature, which can help us understand African American religious beliefs and resistance movements.

Huff, Toby. *The Rise of Early Modern Science* (2003).

Huff, Toby. *Intellectual Curiosity and the Scientific Revolution: A Comparative Perspective* (2011). Huff's two books represent a sustained effort to deal with Europe's scientific revolution comparatively, asking the question why Europe and not China or the Islamic world.

Kai, Ho Yi. *Science in China, 1600–1900: Essays by Benjamin Elman* (2015). Elman, an expert on Chinese science, offers his latest word on China's scientific achievements in a context of Europe's transmission of science through the Jesuit mission.

Keene, Donald. *The Japanese Discovery of Europe: Honda Toshiaki and Other Discoverers, 1720–1798* (1952). A study of the ways Japan managed to incorporate knowledge from the outside world with the development of national traditions.

Ko, Dorothy. *Teachers of the Inner Chambers: Women and Culture in Seventeenth-Century China* (1994). Explores the lives of elite women in late Ming and early Qing China.

Lewis, Bernard. *Race and Color in Islam* (1979). Examines the Islamic attitude toward race and color.

Mazower, Mark. *Salonica, City of Ghosts: Christians, Muslims and Jews, 1430–1900* (2006). An overview of one of the most important cities of the Ottoman Empire.

Morgan, Philip D. *Slave Counterpoint: Black Culture in the Eighteenth-Century Chesapeake and Lowcountry* (1998). Describes the development of African American culture in colonial North America.

Munck, Thomas. *The Enlightenment: A Comparative Social History, 1721–1794* (2000). A wonderful survey, with unusual examples from the periphery, especially from Scandinavia and the Habsburg Empire.

Necipoglu, Gulru. *Architecture, Ceremonial, and Power: The Topkapi Palace in the Fifteenth and Sixteenth Centuries* (1991). A magnificently illustrated book that shows the enormous artistic talent that the Ottoman rulers poured into their imperial structure.

Needham, Joseph "Mathematics and Science in China and the West." In *Science and Civilisation in China*, Vol. 3, pp. 150–168 (1954). An important section of Needham's exhaustive multivolume treatment of Chinese science.

This section deals with what Needham considered the fundamental difference between Chinese and European science at the time of the scientific revolution, namely, Europe's mathematization of the natural world.

Needham, Joseph. *The Grand Tritation: Science and Society in East and West* (1969). Along with his three other entries here, Joseph Needham's efforts to understand Chinese science in relationship to Europe's new science.

Needham, Joseph. "The Evolution of Oecumenical Science: The Role of Europe and China." *Journal of Interdisciplinary Science* 1 (1976): 202–214. More from Needham on European and Chinese science.

Needham, Joseph. *Science in Traditional China: A Comparative Perspective* (1981). Needham's thoughts on Chinese science after the publication of his monumental *Science and Civilisation in China*.

Parker, Kenneth. *Early Modern Tales of the Orient: A Critical Anthology* (1999). A collection of travelers' accounts of the Near East.

Publishing and the Print Culture in Late Imperial China (Special Issue). *Late Imperial China* 17:1 (June 1996). A collection of important articles with a foreword by the French cultural historian Roger Chartier.

Qaisar, Ahsan Jan. *The Indian Response to European Technology, AD 1498–1707* (1998). A meticulous, scholarly work on this little-studied subject.

Rizvi, Athar Abbas. *The Wonder That Was India*. Vol. 2: *A Survey of the History and Culture of the Indian Sub-Continent from the Coming of the Muslims to the British Conquest, 1200–1700* (1987). A deeply learned work in intellectual history.

Safier, Neil. *Measuring the New World: Enlightenment Science and South America* (2008). Examines the ways in which European, and especially Parisian, surveyors set about gauging the curvature of the earth, starting in Quito, Ecuador. Along the way, they learned much more about local natural history, which flowed back to Paris to inform the Enlightenment.

Shapiro, Steven. *The Scientific Revolution* (1996). Still one of the most authoritative overviews of Europe's new science.

Sivan, Nathan. "Why the Scientific Revolution Did Not Take Place in China—or Didn't It?" The author questions the value of asking why China did not have

a scientific revolution even while arguing that the Chinese, in fact, did.

Smith, Bernard. *European Vision and the South Pacific* (1985). An excellent cultural history of Cook's voyages.

Smith, Richard J. *Chinese Maps: Images of "All under Heaven"* (1996). Provides a good introduction to the history of cartography in China.

Sorkin, David. *The Religious Enlightenment: Protestants, Jews, and Catholics from London to Vienna* (2008). Discusses a wide range of thinkers who were able to reconcile Enlightenment thought with religious belief.

Tignor, Robert L. "W. R. Bascom and the Ife Bronzes." *Africa: Journal of the International African Institute* 60, no. 3 (1990): 425–434. Explores controversies over issues of where antiquities of great artistic value like the Ife bronzes should reside.

Welch, Anthony. *Shah Abbas and the Arts of Isfahan* (1973). Describes the astonishing architectural and artistic renaissance of the city of Isfahan under the Safavid ruler Shah Abbas.

Whitfield, Peter. *The Image of the World: Twenty Centuries of World Maps* (1994). A good introduction to the history of cartography in different parts of the world.

Wilks, Ivor. *Forests of Gold: Essays on the Akan and the Kingdom of Asante* (1993). A study that focuses on the Asante's drive for wealth.

Zilfi, Madeline C. *The Politics of Piety: The Ottoman Ulema in the Post-Classical Age (1600–1800)* (1988). Explores the cultural flourishing that took place within the Islamic world in this period.

CHAPTER 15

Allen, Robert C. *The British Industrial Revolution in Global Perspective* (2009). The most recent and authoritative study of the industrial revolution in Britain and its implications around the world.

Anderson, Fred. *Crucible of War: The Seven Years' War and the Fate of Empire in British North America, 1754–1766* (2000). The best synthesis of the "great war for empire" that set the stage for the American Revolution.

Bayly, C. A. *Indian Society and the Making of the British Empire* (1998). A useful work on the early history of the British conquest of India.

Blackburn, Robin. *The Overthrow of Colonial Slavery, 1776–1848* (1988). Places the abolition of the Atlantic slave trade and colonial slavery in a large historical context.

Brown, Harold G. *Ending the French Revolution: Violence, Justice, and Repression from the Terror to Napoleon* (2007). Describes how the Directory and Napoleon imposed stability on France in the wake of the revolution.

Cambridge History of Egypt: Modern Egypt from 1517 to the End of the Twentieth Century, Vol. 2 (1998). Volume 2 contains authoritative essays on all aspects of modern Egyptian history, including the impact of the French invasion and the rule of Muhammad Ali.

Cassel, Par Kristoffer. *Grounds of Judgement: Extraterritoriality and Imperial Powers in Ninetheenth-Century China and Japan* (2012). A study of the idea and practice of extraterritoriality within the context of the triangular relationship between China, Japan, and the West.

Chaudhuri, K. N. *The Trading World of Asia and the East India Company, 1660–1760* (1978). An authoritative economic history of the East India Company's operations.

Crafts, N. F. R. *British Economic Growth during the Industrial Revolution* (1985). A pioneering study that emphasizes a long-term, more gradual process of adaptation to new institutional and social circumstances.

de Vries, Jan. *The Industrious Revolution: Consumer Behavior and the Household Economy, 1650 to the Present* (2008). A book on the lead-up to the industrial revolution, written by the leading economic historian who coined the term *industrious revolution.*

Diamond, Jared, and James A. Robinson (eds.). *Natural Experiments of History* (2010). This book consists of eight comparative studies drawn from history, archaeology, economics, economic history, geography, and political science, covering a spectrum of approaches, ranging from a nonquantitative narrative style to quantitative statistical analyses.

Doyle, William. *The Oxford History of the French Revolution* (1990). A highly detailed discussion of the course of events.

Drescher, Seymour. *Abolition: A History of Slavery and Anti-Slavery* (2009). A recent and authoritative overview of slavery and its opponents.

Elvin, Mark. *The Retreat of the Elephants: An Environmental History of China* (2004). A study of the different ways in which China's natural environment was shaped.

Fick, Carolyn E. *The Making of Haiti: The Saint Domingue Revolution from Below* (1990). Provides a detailed account of the factors that led to the great slave rebellion on the island of Haiti at the end of the eighteenth century.

Findley, Carter. *Bureaucratic Reform in the Ottoman Empire: The Sublime Porte, 1789–1922* (1980). A useful guide to Ottoman reform efforts in the nineteenth century.

Geggus, David (ed.). *The Impact of the Haitian Revolution in the Atlantic World* (2001). A lively effort to disentangle the effects of the Haitian Revolution from those of the French Revolution.

Hevia, James. *Cherishing Men from Afar: Qing Guest Ritual and the Macartney Embassy of 1793* (1995). Offers a definitive interpretation of the nature of Sino-British conflict in the Qing period.

Hobsbawm, Eric. *Nations and Nationalism since 1780* (1990). An important overview of the rise of the nation-state and nationalism around the world.

Howe, Daniel Walker. *What Hath God Wrought: The Transformation of America, 1815–1848* (2007). A Pulitzer Prize–winning interpretation of how new technologies and new ideas reshaped the economy, society, culture, and politics of the United States in the first half of the nineteenth century.

Hunt, Lynn. *Politics, Culture and Class in the French Revolution* (1984). Examines the influence of sociocultural shifts as causes and consequences of the French Revolution, emphasizing the symbols and practice of politics invented during the revolution.

Inikori, Joseph. *Africans and the Industrial Revolution in England* (2002). Demonstrates the important role that Africa and Africans played in facilitating the industrial revolution.

Isset, Christopher Mills. *State, Peasant, and Merchant in Qing Manchuria, 1644–1862* (2007). A study of the relationships between the sociopolitical structures and peasant lives in a key region during the Qing.

James, C. L. R. *The Black Jacobins: Toussaint L'Ouverture and the San Domingo Revolution* (1938). A classic chronicle of the only successful slave revolt in history, and providing a critical portrait of their leader, Toussaint L'Ouverture.

Jones, E. L. *Growth Recurring* (1988). Discusses the controversy over why the industrial revolution took place in Europe, stressing the unique ecological setting that encouraged long-term investment.

Kinsbruner, Jay. *Independence in Spanish America* (1994). A fine study of the Latin American revolutions that argues that the struggle was as much a civil war as a fight for national independence.

Landers, Jane. *Atlantic Creoles in the Age of Revolutions* (2011). A collection of fascinating and unique portraits of Atlantic world creoles who managed to move freely and purposefully through French, Spanish, and English colonies and through Indian territory in the unstable century between 1750 and 1850.

Lieven, Dominic. *Russia Against Napoleon* (2010). Explains how outnumbered Russian forces were able to defeat the massive army that Napoleon assembled for his conquest of Russia.

Mayer, Arno J. *The Furies: Violence and Terror in the French and Russian Revolutions* (2000). A stimulating and provocative essay comparing the French and Russian Revolutions.

Mokyr, Joel. *The Lever of Riches* (1990). An important study of the causes of the industrial revolution that emphasizes the role of small technological and organizational breakthroughs.

Mokyr, Joel. *Enlightened Economy: An Economic History of Britain, 1700–1850* (2009). Perspectives on the evolution of the British economy in the era that produced the industrial revolution.

Naquin, Susan, and Evelyn Rawski. *Chinese Society in the Eighteenth Century* (1987). A survey of mid-Qing society.

Neal, Larry. *The Rise of Financial Capitalism* (1990). An important study of the making of financial markets.

Nikitenko, Aleksandr. *Up from Serfdom: My Childhood and Youth in Russia, 1804–1824* (2001). One of the very few recorded life stories of a Russian serf.

Parthasarathi, Prasannan. *Why Europe Grew Rich and Asia Did Not: Global Economic Divergence, 1600–1800* (2011). A work that places the British industrial revolution in a global context, with much emphasis on India's textile manufacturing before being superseded by British manufacturers.

Pomeranz, Kenneth. *The Great Divergence: Europe, China, and the Making of the Modern World Economy* (2000). Offers explanations of why Europe and not some other place in the world, like parts of China or India, forged ahead economically in the nineteenth century.

Rudé, George. *Europe in the Eighteenth Century* (1972). Emphasizes the rise of a new class, the bourgeoisie, against the old aristocracy as a cause of the French Revolution.

Taylor, Alan. *American Revolutions: A Continental History, 1750–1804* (2016). A sweeping interpretation of the founding of the United States that places the War of Independence in a North American perspective, bringing together the diverse revolutions that transformed societies and borders across the continent.

Wong, R. Bin. *China Transformed: Historical Change and the Limits of European Experience* (2000). Draws attention to the relative autonomy of merchant capitalists in the European dynastic states in comparison with China.

Wood, Gordon S. *Empire of Liberty: A History of the Early Republic, 1789–1815* (2009). An excellent synthesis of the history of the United States in the tumultuous years between the ratification of the Constitution and the War of 1812.

Wortman, Richard. *Scenarios of Power: Myth and Ceremony in Russian Monarchy*, 2 vols. (1995–2000). Examines how dynastic Russia confronted the challenges of the revolutionary epoch.

CHAPTER 16

Anderson, David M. *Revealing Prophets: Prophets in Eastern African History* (1995). Good discussion of the prophets in eastern Africa.

Beecher, Jonathan. *The Utopian Vision of Charles Fourier* (1983). A fine biography of this important thinker.

Boyd, Jean. *The Caliph's Sister: Nana Asma'u, 1793–1865, Teacher, Poet, and Islamic Leader* (1988). A study of the most powerful female Muslim leader in the Fulani religious revolt.

Clancy-Smith, Julia. *Rebel and Saint: Muslim Notables, Populist Protest, Colonial Encounter (Algeria and Tunisia, 1800–1904)* (1994). Examines Islamic protest movements against western encroachments in North Africa.

Clogg, Richard. *A Concise History of Greece* (1997). A good introduction to the history of Greece in its European context.

Dalrymple, William. *The Last Mughal: The Fall of a Dynasty: Delhi, 1857* (2007). A deeply researched and riveting account of Delhi during the 1857 revolt.

Danziger, Raphael. *Abd al-Qadir: Resistance to the French and Internal Consolidation* (1977). Still the indispensable work on this important Algerian Muslim leader.

Dowd, Gregory E. *A Spirited Resistance: The North American Indian Struggle for Unity, 1745–1815* (1992). Emphasizes the importance of prophets like Tenskwatawa in the building of pan-Indian confederations in the era between the Seven Years' War and the War of 1812.

Earle, Rebecca. *The Return of the Native: Indians and Myth Making in Spanish America, 1810–1930* (2007). Examines how Indian resistance and the memory of struggles over sovereignty and land shaped emerging national identities, especially in Mexico and the Andes.

Guha, Ranajit. *Elementary Aspects of Peasant Insurgency in Colonial India* (1983). Not specifically on the Great Rebellion of 1857 but includes it in its pioneering "subalternist" interpretation of South Asian history.

Hamilton, Carolyn (ed.). *The Mfecane Aftermath: Reconstructive Debates in Southern African History* (1995). Debates on Shaka's *Mfecane* movement and its impact on southern Africa.

Hiskett, Mervyn. *The Sword of Truth: The Life and Times of the Shehu Usman dan Fodio* (1994). An authoritative study of the Fulani revolt in northern Nigeria.

Johnson, Douglas H. *Nuer Prophets: A History of Prophecy from the Upper Nile in the Nineteenth and Twentieth Centuries* (1994). Deals with African prophetic and charismatic movements in eastern Africa.

Keddie, Nikki. *An Islamic Response to Imperialism: Political and Religious Writings of Sayyid Jamal ad-Din "al-Afghani"* (1968). Definitive information on the Afghani's life and influence, coupled with a translation of one of his most important essays.

Laven, David, and Lucy Riall (eds.). *Napoleon's Legacy: Problems of Government in Restoration Europe* (2000). Excellent collection of essays on Restoration politics in various states.

Mukherjee, Rudrangshu. *Awadh in Revolt 1857–58* (1984). A careful case study of the Indian Rebellion.

Omer-Cooper, J. D. *The Zulu Aftermath: A Nineteenth-Century Revolution in Bantu Africa* (1966). A good place to start in studying Shaka's *Mfecane* movement, which greatly rearranged the political and ethnic makeup of southern Africa.

Ostler, Jeffrey. *The Plains Sioux and U.S. Colonialism from Lewis and Clark to Wounded Knee* (2004). Uses the lens of colonial theory to track relations between the Sioux and the United States, offering fresh insights about the Ghost Dance movement.

Peires, J. B. (ed.). *Before and After Shaka* (1981). Discusses elements in the debate over Shaka's *Mfecane* movement.

Pilbeam, Pamela. *French Socialists Before Marx: Workers, Women and the Social Question in France* (2001). Describes the development of a variety of socialist ideas in early nineteenth-century France.

Platt, Stephen R. *Autumn in the Heavenly Kingdom: China, the West, and the Epic Story of the Taiping Civil War* (2012). A study of the Taiping from a global perspective.

Reed, Nelson. *The Caste War of Yucatan* (1964). A classic narrative of the Caste War of the Yucatán.

Restall, Matthew. *The Maya World* (1997). Describes in economic and social terms the origins of the Yucatán upheaval in southern Mexico.

Ruedy, John. *Modern Algeria: The Origins and Development of a Nation* (2005). Still the best overview of the modern political history of Algeria.

Rugeley, Terry. *Rebellion Now and Forever: Mayans, Hispanics, and Caste War Violence in Yucatán, 1800–1880* (2009). Explains the combination of economic and cultural pressures that drove the Mayas in the Yucatán to revolt in the Caste War.

Spence, Jonathan. *God's Chinese Son: The Taiping Heavenly Kingdom of Hong Xiuquan* (1996). A fascinating portrayal of the Taiping through the prism of its founder.

Sperber, Jonathan. *Karl Marx: A Nineteenth-Century Life* (2013). An engaging and authoritative biography of Marx that emphasizes his role as a radical journalist.

Stedman Jones, Gareth. *Karl Marx: Greatness and Illusion* (2016). Now the authoritative biography of the founder of communism, showing Marx's own ambivalence about what he had created.

Wagner, Rudolf. *Reenacting the Heavenly Vision: The Role of Religion in the Taiping Rebellion* (1982). A brief but insightful analysis of the religious elements in the Taiping's doctrines.

White, Richard. *The Middle Ground: Indians, Empires, and Republics in the Great Lakes Region, 1650-1815* (1991). A pathbreaking exploration of intercultural relations in North America that offers a provocative interpretation of the visions of Tenskwatawa and the efforts of Tecumseh to resist the expansion of the United States.

CHAPTER 17

Berry, Sara. *Cocoa, Custom and Socio-Economic Change in Western Nigeria* (1975). Innovative study based on interviews with local farmers that suggests that farmer enterprise and microeconomic theory better explain the spectacular growth in cocoa production than grand economic theory.

Cain, P. A., and A. G. Hopkins. *British Imperialism: Innovation and Expansion, 1688-1914* (1993). An excellent discussion of British imperialism, especially British expansion into Africa.

Clark, Christopher. *Iron Kingdom: The Rise and Downfall of Prussia, 1600-1947* (2009). Includes an excellent discussion of the rise of German nationalism and Prussian power.

Cronon, William. *Nature's Metropolis: Chicago and the Great West* (1991). Makes connections between territorial expansion, industrialization, and urban development.

Davis, John. *Conflict and Control: Law and Order in Nineteenth-Century Italy* (1988). A superb study of the north-south and other rifts after Italian political unification.

Frankel, S. Herbert. *Capital Investment in Africa: Its Course and Effects* (1938). A careful study based on a mass of detailed figures and statistics on the general economic development of states in sub-Saharan Africa.

Friesen, Gerald. *The Canadian Prairies* (1984). The most comprehensive account of Canadian westward expansion.

Gluck, Carol. *Japan's Modern Myths: Ideology in the Late Meiji Period* (1985). A study of how states fashion useful historical traditions to consolidate and legitimize their rule.

Goswami, Manu. *Producing India: From Colonial Economy to National Space* (2004). An excellent study of how political economy produced the space of India, which the nationalists claimed as a national space.

Headrick, Daniel R. *The Tools of Empire: Technology and European Imperialism in the Nineteenth Century* (1981). A useful general study of the relationship between imperialism and technology.

Herbst, Jeffrey. *States and Power in Africa: Comparative Lessons in Authority and Control* (2000). An overview of the impact of colonial rule on contemporary African states.

Heyia, James I. *English Lessons: The Pedagogy of Imperialism in Nineteenth-Century China* (2003). A study of British imperialism in Qing China as a pedagogical project and a cultural endeavor.

Hill, Polly. *The Gold Coast Cocoa Farmer: A Preliminary Survey* (1965). An early but still important study of the introduction and spread of cocoa farming in the Gold Coast.

Hine, Robert V., and John Mack Faragher. *The American West: A New Interpretive History* (2000). Presents an excellent synthesis of the conquests by which the United States expanded from the Atlantic to the Pacific.

Hobsbawm, Eric J. *Nations and Nationalism since 1780: Programme, Myth, Reality* (1993). An insightful survey of the origins and development of nationalist thought throughout Europe.

Hochschild, Adam. *King Leopold's Ghost* (1998). A full-scale, eminently readable study of Europe's most egregiously destructive colonial regime in Africa.

Judson, Peter. *The Habsburg Empire: A New History* (2016). An innovative history of the relationship between "the people" and the state in a multiethnic empire.

Lieven, Dominic. *Empire: The Russian Empire and Its Rivals* (2000). A comparison of the British, Ottoman, Habsburg, and Russian Empires.

Mackenzie, John M. *Propaganda and Empire* (1984). Contains a series of useful chapters showing the importance of the empire to Britain.

Mamdani, Mahmood. *Citizen and State: Contemporary Africa and the Legacy of Late Colonialism* (1996). A survey of the impact of European colonial powers on African political systems.

McClintock, Anne. *Imperial Leather: Race, Gender and Sexuality in the Colonial Contest* (1995). A study of the imperial relationship between Victorian Britain and South Africa from the point of view of cultural studies.

McNeil, William. *Europe's Steppe Frontier: 1500-1800* (1964). An excellent study of the definitive victory of Russia's agricultural empire over grazing nomads and independent frontier people.

Mitchell, B. R. *International Historical Statistics: Africa, Asia, and Oceania, 1750-2005* (2007). This comparative volume provides data from over two centuries for all principal areas of economic and social activity in both eastern and western Europe.

Mittler, Barbara. *A Newspaper for China? Power, Identity and Change in Shanghai's News Media, 1872-1942* (2004). An analysis of how the influential foreign-managed newspaper *Shenbao* succeeded in capturing its Chinese readership in the late Qing.

Montgomery, David. *The Fall of the House of Labor: The Workplace, the State, and American Labor Activism, 1865-1925* (1987). An excellent discussion of changes in work in the late nineteenth century.

Myers, Ramon, and Mark Peattie (eds.). *The Japanese Colonial Empire, 1895-1945* (1984). A collection of essays exploring different aspects of Japanese colonialism.

Needell, Jeffrey. *A Tropical Belle Epoque: Elite Culture and Society in Turn of the Century Rio de Janeiro* (1987). Shows the strength of the Brazilian elites at the turn of the century.

Porter, Bernard. *The Absent-Minded Imperialists: What the British Really Thought about Empire* (2004). A careful discussion of the ways in which empire changed the British—and did not.

Prakash, Gyan. *Another Reason: Science and the Imagination of Modern India* (1999). A study of how science and technology transformed the British imperial governance and unified India into a geographical unity.

Prasad, Ritika. *Tracks of Change: Railways and Everyday Life in Colonial India*

(2016). A detailed analysis of how railways transformed the everyday experience of Indians under colonial rule.

Stengers, Jean. *Combien le Congo a-t-il coûté à la Belgique?* (1957). A detailed financial accounting of how much Leopold put into the Congo and how much he took out, underscoring just how ruthlessly he exploited this possession.

Topik, Steven. *The Political Economy of the Brazilian State, 1889–1930* (1987). An excellent discussion of the Brazilian state, especially of its elites.

Walker, Mack, *German Home Towns: Community, State, and the General State, 1648–1871* (1971, 1998). A brilliant, street-level analysis of the Holy Roman Empire (the First Reich) and the run-up to the German unification of 1871 (the Second Reich).

Wasserman, Mark. *Everyday Life and Politics in Nineteenth-Century Mexico* (2000). Wonderfully captures the way in which people coped with social and economic dislocation in late nineteenth-century Mexico.

Weeks, Theodore R. *Nation and State in Late Imperial Russia: Nationalism and Russification on the Western Frontier, 1863–1914* (1996). A good discussion of the Russian Empire's responses to the concept of the nation-state.

White, Richard. *Railroaded: The Transcontinentals and the Making of Modern America* (2011). A seering exposé of the corruptions and a startling critique of the economic and environmental costs associated with the expansion of railroad lines across Canada, the United States, and Mexico.

Zarrow, Peter. *After Empire: The Conceptual Transformation of the Chinese State, 1885–1924* (2012). A history of the changing ideas regarding the Chinese state that eventually led to the abandonment of monarchical rule by the Chinese people.

CHAPTER 18

Bayly, C. A. *The Birth of the Modern World, 1780–1914: Global Connections and Comparisons* (2004). A general study of the key political, economic, social, and cultural features of the modern era in world history.

Bergère, Marie-Claire. *Sun Yat-sen* (1998). Originally published in French in 1994, this is a judicious biography of the man generally known as the father of the modern Chinese nation.

Chatterjee, Partha. *The Nation and Its Fragments* (1993). One of the most important works on Indian nationalism by a leading scholar of "Subaltern Studies."

Conrad, Joseph. *Heart of Darkness* (1899). First published in a magazine in 1899, this novella contains a searing critique of King Leopold's oppressive and exploitative policies in the Congo and was part of a growing concern for the effects that European empires were having around the world, especially in Africa.

Crosby, Alfred. *Ecological Imperialism: The Biological Expansion of Europe, 900–1900* (2nd ed., 2004). A fascinating biohistory of European imperialism.

Esherick, Joseph. *The Origins of the Boxer Uprising* (1987). The definitive account of the episode.

Esherick, Joseph. "How the Qing Became China." In Joseph W. Esherick, Hasan Kayali, and Eric Van Young (eds.), *Empire to Nation: Historical Perspectives on the Making of the Modern World* (2006). A study of the processes through which the Qing Empire became the nation-state of China.

Everdell, William R. *The First Moderns: Profiles in the Origins of Twentieth-Century Thought* (1997). A rich account of the many faces of modernism, focusing particularly on science and art.

Finnane, Antonia. *Changing Clothes in China: Fashion, History, Nation* (2008). An exploration of changing Chinese identities from the perspective of clothing.

Gay, Peter. *The Cultivation of Hatred* (1994). A provocative discussion of the violent passions of the immediate pre–Great War era.

Hochschild, Adam. *King Leopold's Ghost: A Story of Greed, Terror, and Heroism in Colonial Africa* (1998). A well-written account of the violent colonial history of the Belgian Congo under King Leopold in the late nineteenth century.

Judge, Joan. *The Precious Raft of History: The Past, the West, and the Woman Question in China* (2008). An insightful exploration of the "woman question" in China at the turn of the twentieth century.

Katz, Friedrich. *The Life and Times of Pancho Villa* (1998). An exploration of the Mexican Revolution that shows how Villa's armies destroyed the forces of Díaz and his followers.

Keddie, Nikki. *An Islamic Response to Imperialism: Political and Religious Writings of Sayyid Jamal ad-Din "al-Afghani"* (1968). Definitive information on Afghani's life and influence, coupled with a translation of one of his most important essays.

Kern, Stephen. *The Culture of Time and Space 1880–1918* (1986). A useful study of the enormous changes in the experience of time and space in the age of late industrialism in Europe and America.

Kuhn, Philip. *Chinese among Others: Emigration in Modern Times* (2008). An overview of the history of Chinese migration.

McKeown, Adam. *Melancholy Order: Asian Migration and the Globalization of Borders* (2008). An examination of global migration patterns since the mid-nineteenth century and how regulations designed to restrict Asian migration to other parts of the world led to the modern regime of migration control.

Meade, Teresa. *"Civilizing" Rio: Reform and Resistance in a Brazilian City, 1889–1930* (1997). A wonderful study of cultural and class conflict in Brazil.

Moon, David. *The Plough That Broke the Steppes: Agriculture and Environment on Russia's Grasslands, 1700–1914* (2013). An excellent environmental history of the Russian steppe.

Pick, Daniel. *Faces of Degeneration: A European Disorder, c. 1848–c. 1918* (1993). A study of Europe's fear of social and biological decline, particularly focusing on France and Italy.

Pretorius, Fransjohn (ed.). *Scorched Earth* (2001). A study of the Anglo-Boer War in terms of its environmental impact.

Saler, Michael (ed.). *The Fin de Siècle World* (2014). A comprehensive anthology of essays on turn-of-the-century politics and culture across the world.

Sarkar, Sumit. *The Swadeshi Movement in Bengal* (1973). A comprehensive study of an early militant movement against British rule.

Schorske, Carl E. *Fin-de-Siècle Vienna: Politics and Culture* (1980). The classic treatment of the birth of modern ideas and political movements in turn-of-the-century Austria.

Trachtenberg, Alan. *The Incorporation of America: Culture and Society in the Gilded Age* (1982). A provocative synthesis of changes in the American economy, society, and culture in the last decades of the nineteenth century.

Wang, David Der-wei. *Fin-de-Siècle Splendor: Repressed Modernities of Late Qing Fiction, 1849–1911* (1997). A fine work that attempts to locate the "modern" within the writings of the late Qing period.

Warren, Louis. *Buffalo Bill's America: William Cody and the Wild West Show* (2005). A superb portrait of William F. Cody, the person; of Buffalo Bill, the persona Cody (and others) created; and of the popular culture his Wild West shows brought to audiences in Europe and North America.

Warwick, Peter. *Black People and the South African War, 1899–1902* (1983). An important study that reminds readers of the crucial involvement of black South Africans in this bloody conflict.

Womack, John, Jr. *Zapata and the Mexican Revolution* (1968). A major work on the Mexican Revolution that discusses peasant struggles in the state of Morelos in great detail.

CHAPTER 19

Akcam, Taner. *The Young Turks' Crime Against Humanity: The Armenian Genocide and Ethnic Cleansing in the Ottoman Empire* (2012). An exhaustive examination of the factors that impelled the Turkish authorities to carry out ethnic cleansing against the Armenians during World War I.

Aksakal, Mustafa. *The Ottoman Road to War in 1914: The Ottoman Empire and the First World War* (2008). An important study of the personalities and factors that led the Ottomans to join with Germany and Austria-Hungary during World War I, a fateful decision that ultimately spelled the end of the Ottoman Empire.

Ambedkar, B. R. *Annihilation of Caste: The Annotated Critical Edition* (1936). Ambedkar's brilliant polemic against Gandhi on caste. With a new introduction by Arundhati Roy, this work is an essential reading for an understanding of Ambedkar's thoughts.

Anderson, Scott. *Lawrence in Arabia: War, Deceit, Imperial Folly, and the Making of the Middle East* (2013). A new and authoritative biography of T. E. Lawrence, with significant new material on British policies in the Middle East as seen through the eyes of a strong pro-Arab figure.

Bloxham, Donald. *The Great Game of Genocide: Imperialism, Nationalism, and the Destruction of the Ottoman Armenians* (2005). The definitive work on the Armenian genocide, set in a wide historical context.

Bosworth, R. J. B. *Mussolini's Italy: Life under the Dictatorship, 1915–1945* (2006). An eye-opening treatment of fascism in Italy beyond Mussolini.

Brown, Judith. *Gandhi: Prisoner of Hope* (1990). A biography of Gandhi as a political activist.

Clark, Christopher. *Sleepwalkers: How Europe Went to War* (2012). A reexamination of the crucial role of Austria-Hungary in triggering the world war.

De Grazia, Victoria, and Ellen Furlough (eds.). *The Sex of Things: Gender and Consumption in Historical Perspective* (1996). Path-breaking essays on how gender affects consumption.

Dumenil, Lynn. *The Modern Temper: America in the 1920s* (1995). A general discussion of American culture in the decade after World War I.

Fainsod, Merle. *Smolensk under Soviet Rule* (1989). The most accessible and sophisticated interpretation of the Stalin revolution in the village.

Gelvin, James. *Divided Loyalties: Nationalism and Mass Politics in Syria at the Close of Empire* (1998). Offers important insights into the development of nationalism in the Arab world.

Horne, John (ed.). *State, Society, and Mobilization during the First World War* (1997). Essays on what it took to wage total war among all the belligerents.

Horne, John (ed.). *A Companion to World War I* (2010). A collection of articles written by leading scholars of World War I; the most comprehensive and up-to-date work on this war.

Johnson, G. Wesley. *The Emergence of Black Politics in Senegal* (1971). A useful examination of the stirrings of African nationalism in Senegal.

Kennedy, David M. *Freedom from Fear: The American People in Depression and War, 1929–1945* (1999). A wonderful narrative of turbulent years.

Kershaw, Ian. *Hitler*, 2 vols. (1998–2000). A masterpiece combining biography and context.

Kimble, David. *A Political History of Ghana* (1963). An excellent discussion of the beginnings of African nationalism in Ghana.

Kotkin, Stephen. *Magnetic Mountain: Stalinism as a Civilization* (1995). Recaptures the atmosphere of a time when everything seemed possible, even creating a new world.

Kotkin, Stephen. *Stalin.* Vol. 1: *Paradoxes of Power* (2014). A sweeping history of the tsarist regime, world war, Russian Revolution, civil war, and rise of Stalin.

Lambert, Nicholas A. *Planning Armageddon: British Economic Warfare and the First World War* (2012). Mines new archives to show that the British had an aggressive plan before the war to destroy Germany financially, which the British government approved and began to enact until the United States forced them to back off.

LeMahieu, D. L. *A Culture for Democracy: Mass Communication and the Cultivated Mind in Britain between the Wars* (1988). One of the great works on mass culture.

Lyttelton, Adrian. *The Seizure of Power: Fascism in Italy, 1919–1929* (1961). Still the classic account.

Marchand, Roland. *Advertising the American Dream: Making Way for Modernity, 1920–1945* (1985). An excellent discussion of the force of mass production and mass consumption.

Mazower, Mark. *Dark Continent: Europe's Twentieth Century* (1999). A wide-ranging overview of Europe's tempestuous twentieth century.

McGirr, Lisa. *The War on Alcohol: Prohibition and the Rise of the American State* (2016). Emphasizes the power of cultural reaction against modernity that brought about Prohibition and the irony that its enforcement helped to expand the power of the modern state.

McKeown, Adam. *Melancholy Order: Asian Migration and the Globalization of Border* (2008). A major study of the vast movement of peoples around the globe between the middle of the nineteenth and middle of the twentieth centuries.

Morrow, John H., Jr. *The Great War: An Imperial History* (2004). Places World War I in the context of European imperialism.

Musgrove, Charles D. *China's Contested Capital: Architecture, Ritual, and Response in Nanjing* (2013). An exploration of how the Chinese Nationalist capital of Nanjing served as a focal point for the making of a nation and a new form of mass politics.

Nottingham, John, and Carl Rosberg. *The Myth of "Mau Mau": Nationalism in Kenya* (1966). Dispels the myths in describing the roots of nationalism in Kenya.

Pedersen, Susan. *The Guardians: the League of Nations and the Crisis of Empire* (2015). Skillfully reexamines the neglected effort to regulate the colonial world under a so-called mandate system.

Rutledge, Ian. *Enemy on the Euphrates: The British Occupation of Iraq and the Great Arab Revolt, 1914-1921* (2014). An impassioned investigation of Britain's effort to take control of the oil-rich territory of Iraq and the determined resistance of the Iraqi peoples.

Strand, David. *An Unfinished Republic: Leading by Word and Deed in Modern China* (2011). A study of how the need for popular support led to a new political culture characterized by public speaking and performance in early twentieth-century China.

Suny, Ronald Gregor. *"They can Live in the Desert but Nowhere Else": A History of the Armenian Genocide* (2015). A careful, document-based analysis of the Armenian genocide.

Taylor, Jay. *The Generalissimo: Chiang Kai-shek and the Struggle for Modern China* (2009). The first serious biographical study of Chiang Kai-shek in English, although its reliance on Chiang's own diary as a source does raise some questions of historical interpretation.

Thorp, Rosemary (ed.). *Latin America in the 1930s* (1984). An important collection of essays on Latin America's response to the shakeup of the interwar years.

Tsin, Michael. *Nation, Governance, and Modernity in China: Canton, 1900-1927* (1999). An analysis of the vision and social dynamics behind the Guomindang-led revolution of the 1920s.

Vianna, Hermano. *The Mystery of Samba* (1999). Discusses the history of samba, emphasizing its African heritage as well as its persistent popular content.

Wakeman, Frederic Jr. *Policing Shanghai, 1927-1937* (1995). An excellent account of Guomindang rule in China's largest city during the Nanjing decade.

Winter, J. M. *The Experience of World War* (1988). A comprehensive presentation of the many sides of the twentieth century.

Young, Louise. *Japan's Total Empire: Manchuria and the Culture of Wartime Imperialism* (1998). An innovative case study of Japanese imperialism and mass culture with broad implications.

Zuber, Terence. *Inventing the Schlieffen Plan: German War Planning, 1871-1914* (2002). Uses new archives to demonstrate definitively that the famed Schlieffen Plan is essentially a myth, and explains how that myth was created.

CHAPTER 20

Aburish, Said K. *Nasser: The Last Arab* (2004). A recent and impressive look at Egypt's most powerful political leader in the 1950s and 1960s.

Anderson, Jon Lee. *Che Guevara: A Revolutionary Life* (1997). A sweeping study of the radicalization of Latin American nationalism.

Austin, Granville. *The Indian Constitution: Cornerstone of a Nation*, 2nd ed. (1999). A classic study of constitution making in India.

Bayly, Christopher, and Tim Harper. *Forgotten Armies: Britain's Asian Empire and the War with Japan* (2004). A brilliant social and military history of World War II as fought and lived in South and Southeast Asia.

Chatterjee, Partha. *Nationalist Thought and the Colonial World: A Derivative Discourse* (1986). An influential interpretation of the ideological and political nature of Indian nationalism and the struggle for a postcolonial nation-state.

Cook, Alexander C. (ed.). *Mao's Little Red Book: A Global History* (2014). A look at the global impact of the Chinese Cultural Revolution through the lens of the iconic "little red book" of quotations from Mao.

Crampton, R. J. *Eastern Europe in the Twentieth Century and After*, 2nd ed. (1997). A comprehensive overview covering all Soviet-bloc countries.

Dikötter, Frank. *Mao's Great Famine: The History of China's Most Devastating Catastrophe, 1958-1962* (2010). A recent detailed account of one of the greatest human-made disasters in twentieth-century history.

Dower, John W. *Embracing Defeat: Japan in the Wake of World War II* (1999). A prize-winning study of the transformation of one of the war's vanquished.

Elkins, Caroline. *Imperial Reckoning: The Untold Story of Britain's Gulag in Kenya* (2005). A Pulitzer Prize–winning study of the brutal war to suppress the nationalist uprising in Kenya in the 1950s that ultimately led to independence for that country.

Feshbach, Murray, and Alfred Friendly Jr. *Ecocide in the USSR: Health and Nation under Siege* (1992). A crucial study of ecological disasters in the Soviet Union.

Gao Yuan. *Born Red: A Chronicle of the Cultural Revolution* (1987). A gripping personal account of the Cultural Revolution by a former Red Guard.

Gordon, Andrew (ed.). *Postwar Japan as History* (1993). Essays covering a wide range of topics on postwar Japan.

Hargreaves, John D. *Decolonization in Africa* (1996). A good place to start when exploring the history of African decolonization.

Hasan, Mushirul (ed.). *India's Partition: Process, Strategy and Mobilization* (1993). A useful anthology of scholarly articles, short stories, and primary documents on the partition of India.

Iriye, Akira. *Power and Culture: The Japanese-American War, 1941-1945* (1981). A discussion that goes beyond the military confrontation in Asia.

Jackson, Kenneth T. *Crabgrass Frontier: The Suburbanization of the United States* (1985). An insightful and influential consideration of the movement of the American population from cities to suburbs.

Jalal, Ayesha. *The Sole Spokesman: Jinnah, the Muslim League and the Demand for Pakistan* (1985). A study of the high politics leading to the violent partition of British India.

Keep, John L. H. *Last of the Empires: A History of the Soviet Union 1945-1991* (1995). A detailed overview of the core of the "Second World."

Morris, Benny. *Righteous Victims: A History of the Zionist-Arab Conflict, 1881-1999* (2000). On the Arab-Israeli War of 1948.

Pantsov, Alexander V. *Mao: The Real Story*, translated by Steven I. Levine (2012). A well-researched biography of Mao.

Patterson, James T. *Grand Expectations: The United States, 1945-1974* (1996). Synthesizes the American experience in the postwar decades.

Patterson, Thomas. *Contesting Castro* (1994). The best study of the tension between the United States and Cuba. Culminating in the Cuban Revolution, it explores the deep American misunderstanding of Cuban national aspirations.

Roberts, Geoffrey. *Stalin's Wars: From World War to Cold War, 1939-1953* (2007). A reassessment of Stalin's wartime leadership that conveys the vast scale of what took place.

Ruedy, John. *Modern Algeria: The Origins and Development of a Nation* (1992). Gives the history of the Algerian nationalist movements and provides an overview of the Algerian War of Independence.

Tignor, Robert L. *W. Arthur Lewis and the Birth of Development Economics* (2006). An intellectual biography of the Nobel Prize–winning, West Indian–born economist who proposed formulas to promote the economic development of less developed societies and then sought to implement them in Africa and the West Indies.

Wiener, Douglas R. *A Little Corner of Freedom: Russian Nature Protection from Stalin to Gorbachev* (2002). A groundbreaking book about Russian environmentalism.

Zatlin, Jonathan. *The Currency of Socialism: Money and Political Culture in East Germany* (2007). A fascinating description of how the economy of East Germany did—and did not—work.

Zubkova, Elena. *Russia after the War: Hopes, Illusions, and Disappointments, 1945-1957* (1998). Uses formerly secret archives to catalogue the devastation and difficult reconstruction of one of the war's victors.

CHAPTER 21

Collier, Paul. *The Bottom Billion: Why the Poorest Countries Fail and What Can Be Done about It* (2007). Shows that despite the world's advancing prosperity, more than a billion people have been left behind in abject poverty.

Davis, Deborah (ed.). *The Consumer Revolution in Urban China* (2000). A look at the different aspects of the recent profound social transformation of urban China.

Davis, Mike. *City of Quartz: Excavating the Future in Los Angeles* (1990). Offers provocative reflections on the recent history, current condition, and possible future of Los Angeles.

Dutton, Michael. *Streetlife China* (1999). A fascinating portrayal of the survival tactics of those inhabiting the margins of society in modern China.

Eichengreen, Barry. *Globalizing Capital: A History of the International Monetary System* (1996). An insightful analysis of how international capital markets changed in the period from 1945 to 1980.

Gourevitch, Philip. *We Wish to Inform You That Tomorrow We Will Be Killed with Our Families: Stories from Rwanda* (1999). A volume that reveals the hatreds that culminated in the Rwanda genocide.

Guillermoprieto, Alma. *Looking for History: Dispatches from Latin America* (2001). A collection of articles by the most important journalist reporting on Latin American affairs.

Han, Minzhu (ed.). *Cries for Democracy: Writings and Speeches from the 1989 Chinese Democracy Movement* (1990). A collection of documents from the events leading up to the incident in Tiananmen Square on June 4, 1989.

Herbst, Jeffrey. *States and Power in Africa: Comparative Lessons in Authority and Control* (2000). Explores the political dilemmas facing modern African polities.

Honig, Emily, and Gail Hershatter. *Personal Voices: Chinese Women in the 1980's* (1988). A record of Chinese women during a period of rapid social change.

Huang, Yasheng. *Capitalism with Chinese Characteristics: Entrepreneurship and the State* (2008). A sharp, unsentimental inside look at China's market economy and its future prospects.

Kavoori, Anandam P., and Aswin Punathambekar (eds.). *Global Bollywood* (2008). A collection of essays by leading film scholars on Indian cinema on different aspects of the processes by which the Hindi film industry became Bollywood.

Klitgaard, Robert. *Tropical Gangsters* (1990). On the intimate connections between corrupt native elites and international aid agencies.

Kotkin, Stephen. *Armageddon Averted: The Soviet Collapse, 1970-2000* (2001). Places the surprise fall of the Soviet Union in the context of the great shifts in the post–World War II order.

Macekura, Stephen. *Of Limits and Growth: The Rise of Global Sustainable Development in the Twentieth Century* (2016). Explores the rise of global environmental politics in the 1970s and 1980s and the debate about resources and climate change.

Mamdani, Mahmood. *When Victims Become Killers: Colonialism, Nativism, and the Genocide in Rwanda* (2001). Discusses the genocide in Rwanda in light of the legacy of colonialism.

Mehta, Suketu. *Maximum City: Bombay Lost and Found* (2005). Examines one of the great, and contradictory, cities in the era of globalization.

Miller, Chris. *The Struggle to Save the Soviet Economy: Mikhail Gorbachev and the Collapse of the USSR* (2016). An insightful analysis of internal debates in Moscow over rival directions for the Soviet economy and the response to Chinese reforms after 1978.

Mottahedeh, Roy. *The Mantle of the Prophet: Religion and Politics in Iran*, 2nd ed. (2008). Perhaps the best book on the 1979 Iranian Revolution and its aftermath.

Nathan, Andrew, and Perry Link. *The Tiananmen Papers* (2002). An inside look at the divisions within the Chinese elite in connection with the 1989 crackdown.

Portes, Alejandro, and Rubén G. Rumbaut. *Immigrant America*, 2nd ed. (1996). A good comparative study of how immigration has transformed the United States.

Prakash, Gyan. *Mumbai Fables* (2010). A spirited account of the rise of India's most modern city, a center of intellectual, commercial, and political vitality.

Prunier, Gerald. *Africa's World War: Congo, the Rwandan Genocide, and the Making of a Continental Catastrophe* (2009). A chilling discussion of the spillover effects of the Rwandan genocide on central, eastern, and southern Africa.

Punathambekar, Aswin. *From Bombay to Bollywood: The Making of a Global Media Industry* (2013). A study of the transformation of the Indian film industry that globalizes its content and reach.

Reinhart, Carmen, and Kenneth Rogoff. *This Time Is Different: Eight Centuries of Financial Folly* (2009). Explains the latest financial crash using historical perspective.

Ruggie, John Gerard. *Just Business: Multinational Corporations and Human Rights* (2013). Shows how even big business got into human rights advocacy.

Sikkink, Kathryn. *The Justice Cascade: How Human Rights Prosecutions Are Changing World Politics* (2011). Shows how new forms of global organizing and new social norms are changing the political rules across borders.

Stein, Judith. *Pivotal Decade: How the United States Traded Factories for Finance in the Seventies* (2010). A comprehensive study of the rise of American banking and the decline of heartland industries.

Ther, Philipp. *Europe since 1989: A History* (2016). A concise account of European integration and neoliberalism since the fall of the Berlin Wall.

Van Der Wee, Hermann. *Prosperity and Upheaval: The World Economy, 1945-1980* (1986). Describes very well the transformation and problems of the world economy, particularly from the 1960s onward.

Westad, Odd Arne. *The Global Cold War: Third World Interventions and the Making of Our Times* (2007). A genuinely global perspective on the Cold War and its consequences.

Winn, Peter. *Americas: The Changing Face of Latin America and the Caribbean* (1992). A useful portrayal of Latin America since the 1970s.

EPILOGUE

Achcar, Gilbert. *Morbid Symptoms: Relapse in the Arab Uprising* (2016). An up-to-date overview of the difficulties that the proponents of the Arab Spring encountered, with long and detailed treatments of Syria and Egypt.

Christensen, Thomas J. *The China Challenges: Shaping the Choices of a Rising Power* (2015). A survey of "China's Rise" and the challenges and choices the country faces in the contemporary world.

Cleveland, William L., and Martin Bunton. *A History of the Modern Middle East*, 6th ed. (2016). The sixth edition of an important textbook that covers the whole of the Middle East from 1800 to the present.

Cooper, Frederick. *Africa in the World: Capitalism, Empire, Nation-State* (2014). An overview of Africa's place in global history, based on the most recent scholarship.

Darwall, Rupert. *The Age of Global Warming: A History* (2013). An accessible narrative about how scientists became increasingly aware of the threat of climate change and the multinational effort to reduce carbon emissions.

Deaton, Angus. *The Great Escape: Health, Wealth, and the Origins of Inequality* (2013). An examination of the heightened degree of inequality by a Nobel Prize–winning authority who emphasizes that contemporary well-to-do individuals have largely failed to help those not so fortunate to achieve their potential.

Eichengreen, Barry. *Hall of Mirrors: The Great Depression, the Great Recessions and the Uses—and Misuses—of History* (2015). A chronicle of the financial upheaval of 2008–2009, comparing the policies and mindsets of major decision makers to the choices made in the 1930s.

Esposito, John L., Tamara Sonn, and John O. Voll. *Islam and Democracy after the Arab Spring* (2016). An analysis of the prospects of democracy in Muslim countries, with case studies of Tunisia, Egypt, and Turkey, among others.

Ferguson, James. "Seeing Like an Oil Company: Space, Security, and Global Capital in Neoliberal Africa." *American Anthropologist* 107 (2005): 377–382. A critique of James Scott's book *Seeing Like a State*, and a view of the role of oil and mining companies in Africa and their failure to promote economic growth there.

Ferguson, James. *Global Shadows: Africa in the Neo-Liberal World Order* (2006). Journal articles brought together in a book by one of the leading African anthropologists. They deal with contemporary African issues and dilemmas, placed in a global context.

Ferguson, James. *Give a Man a Fish: Reflections on the New Politics of Distribution* (2015). An analysis of social welfare programs in southern Africa, involving cash payments to the poorest members of societies, and their implications for neoliberal capitalism.

Franco, Jean. *Cruel Modernity* (2013). An examination of the cultural dimensions of Latin America's experience with recent neoliberal policies and the tensions and violence of relatively stateless societies.

Gerges, Fawaz A. *ISIS: A History* (2016). One of a series of books that explores the rise of ISIS and stresses the place of violence in building a new Islamic state.

Jaffrelot, Christophe. *Saffron Modernity in India: Narendra Modi and His Experiment with Gujarat* (2014). A political history of how Narendra Modi emerged dominant in Gujarat using anti-Muslim nationalist ideology, captured the leadership of the BJP, and built a personality cult that catapulted him as a national leader.

Judis, John. *The Populist Explosion: How the Great Recession Transformed American and European Politics* (2016). A book by a journalist and political analyst that argues that the contemporary populist upsurges on both the right and left are responses to neoliberal globalization.

Lacau, Ernest. *On Populist Reason* (2007). This dense but insightful study by a political theorist offers original philosophical views on the meaning of "the people" by examining historical examples of populism.

Lee, Soo im, and Stephen-Murphy-Shigematsu. *Japan's Diversity Dilemmas: Ethnicity, Citizenship, and Education* (2006). Still an important work that examines whether Japan can assimilate foreigners, crucial for its aging workforce, or is condemned to demographic and economic decline because of its extremely low birthrate and pride in ethnic purity.

Lepore, Jill. *The Whites of Their Eyes: The Tea Party's Revolution and the Battle over American History* (2011). A history of the American far right and the Tea Party and their imagination of a nostalgic American past.

Lynch, Marc. *The New Arab Wars: Uprisings and Anarchy in the Middle East* (2016). Brings the narrative of the Arab Spring and the ambitions of its diverse proponents up to the present.

McCants, William. *The ISIS Apocalypse: The History, Strategy, and Doomsday Vision of the Islamic State* (2015). An important study of ISIS, based on a wide reading of ISIS's publications.

Milankovic, Brian. *Global Inequality: A New Approach for the Age of Globalization* (2016). Using the most up-to-date data on worldwide incomes, the author shows how the last quarter-century has yielded a convergence in global income distribution across societies and the widening of a gap within societies.

Moubayed, Sami. *Under the Black Flag: At the Frontier of the New Jihad* (2015). A study of the rise of jihadism within the Arab world, with a concentration on Syria.

Muller, Jan-Werner. *What Is Populism?* (2016). The sharpest analysis yet of the nature and prospects of populism, especially its relations to political establishments, which it condemns but on which it depends.

Owen, Roger. *The Rise and Fall of Arab Presidents for Life, with a New Afterword* (2014). A study that examines the emergence of Arab leaders who endeavored to hold on to power for as long as they lived, with insights into the actions of those who brought many of the leaders down during the Arab Spring.

Pietz, David A. *The Yellow River: The Problem of Water in Modern China* (2015). A critical look at health and environmental issues in China today, from a historical perspective through the lens of one of its major rivers.

Radelet, Steven. *Emerging Africa: How Seventeen Countries Are Leading the Way* (2010). An Afro-optimist sees many African countries enjoying economic growth and political stability, proving that Africa can also join much of the rest of the world in achieving economic and political progress.

Radelet, Steven. *The Great Surge: The Ascent of the Developing World* (2015). An overview of the extraordinary progress that many of the countries in what once was called the Third World have achieved in economic and political successes.

Reid, Michael. *Forgotten Continent: The Battle for Latin America's Soul* (2009). A journalistic account of how Latin America grappled with market openings, new democratic forces, and the search for policies to close the gap between the haves and have-nots.

Shambaugh, David. *China Goes Global: The Partial Power* (2013). An analysis of China's role in the global arena and its impact, from economics to culture.

Trenin, Dmitri. *Should We Fear Russia?* (2016). A clear-eyed view of what contemporary Russia is and is not.

Warwick, John. *Black Flags Flying: The Rise of ISIS* (2015). A detailed account of the leadership groups within ISIS and its relationship to al-Qaeda.

Weiss, Michael, and Hassan Hassan. *ISIS: Inside the Army of Terror* (2015). An account based on interviews and wide reading of western and Arabic sources on the rise of ISIS.

Wright, Lawrence. *The Looming Tower: Al-Qaeda and the Road to 9/11* (2006). A Pulitzer Prize–winning study of the origins and evolution of al-Qaeda.

Wright, Lawrence. *The Terror Years: From al-Qaeda to ISIS* (2016). Primarily a study of the decline of the power of al-Qaeda, which created an opening for the more territorially based ISIS.

GLOSSARY

Abd al-Rahman III Islamic ruler in Spain who held a countercaliphate and reigned from 912 to 961 CE.

aborigines Original, native inhabitants of a region, as opposed to invaders, colonizers, or later peoples of mixed ancestry.

absolute monarchy Form of government where one body, usually the monarch, controls the right to tax, judge, make war, and coin money. The term *enlightened absolutists* was often used to refer to state monarchies in seventeenth- and eighteenth-century Europe.

acid rain Precipitation containing large amounts of sulfur, mainly from coal-fired plants.

adaptation Ability to alter behavior and to innovate; finding new ways of doing things.

African National Congress (ANC) Multiracial organization founded in 1912 in an effort to end racial discrimination in South Africa.

African sacred kingships Institutions that marked the centralized politics of East, West, and central Africa. The inhabitants of these kingships believed that their kings were descendants of the gods.

Afrikaners Descendants of the original Dutch settlers of South Africa; often referred to as Boers.

agones Athletic contests in ancient Greece.

Ahmosis Egyptian ruler in the southern part of the country who ruled from 1550 to 1525 BCE. Ahmosis used Hyksos weaponry—horse chariots in particular—to defeat the Hyksos themselves.

Ahura Mazda Supreme god of the Persians believed to have created the world and all that is good and to have appointed earthly kings.

AIDS (acquired immunodeficiency syndrome) Virus that compromises the ability of the infected person's immune system to ward off disease. First detected in 1981, AIDS was initially stigmatized as a "gay cancer," but as it spread to heterosexuals, public awareness about it increased. In its first two decades, AIDS killed 12 million people.

Akbarnamah Mughal intellectual Abulfazl's *Book of Akbar*, which attempted to reconcile the traditional Sufi interest in the inner life within the worldly context of a great empire.

Alaric II Visigothic king who issued a simplified code of innovative imperial law.

Alexander the Great (356–323 BCE) Leader who used novel tactics and new kinds of armed forces to conquer the Persian Empire, which extended from Egypt and the Mediterranean Sea to the interior of what is now Afghanistan and as far as the Indus River valley. Alexander's conquests broke down barriers between the Mediterranean world and Southwest Asia and transferred massive amounts of wealth and power to the Mediterranean, transforming it into a more unified world of economic and cultural exchange.

Alexandria Port city in Egypt named after Alexander the Great. Alexandria was a model city in the Hellenistic world. It was built up by a multiethnic population from around the Mediterranean world.

Al-Khwarizmi Scientist and mathematician who lived from 780 to 850 CE and is known for having modified Indian digits into Arabic numerals.

Allied Powers Name given to the alliance between Britain, France, Russia, and Italy, who fought against Germany, Austria-Hungary, and the Ottoman Empire (the Central Powers) in World War I. In World War II the name was used for the alliance between Britain, France, and America, who fought against the Axis Powers (Germany, Italy, and Japan).

allomothering System by which mothers rely on other women, including their own mothers, daughters, sisters, and friends, to help in the nurturing and protection of children.

alluvium Area of land created by river deposits.

alphabet A writing system in which each character ideally represents a single sound. The first full alphabet was developed by the Phoenicians in the mid-second millenium BCE and consists of 22 letters (all of them consonants).

American Railway Union Workers' union that initiated the Pullman Strike of 1894, which led to violence and ended in the leaders' arrest.

Amnesty International Nongovernmental organization formed to defend "prisoners of conscience"—those detained for their beliefs, race, sex, ethnic origin, language, or religion.

Amorites Name that Mesopotamian urbanites called the transhumant herders from the Arabian desert. Around 2300 BCE, the Amorites, along with the Elamites, were at the center of newly formed dynasties in southern Mesopotamia.

Amun Once insignificant Egyptian god elevated to higher status by Amenemhet (1991–1962 BCE). *Amun* means "hidden" in ancient Egyptian; the name was meant to convey the god's omnipresence.

Analects Texts that include the teachings and cultural ideals of Confucius.

anarchism Belief that society should be a free association of its members, not subject to government, laws, or police.

Anatolia Now mainly the area known as modern Turkey. In the sixth millennium BCE, people from Anatolia, Greece, and the Levant took to boats and populated the Aegean. Their small villages endured almost unchanged for two millennia.

ancestral worship Religious practice in which the living honor their dead ancestors through rituals, believing that the dead intervene with their powers on behalf of the living.

Angkor Wat Magnificent Khmer Vaishnavite temple that crowned the royal palace in Angkor. It had statues representing the Hindu pantheon of gods.

Anglo-Boer War (1899–1902) War in South Africa between the British and the Afrikaners over the gold-rich Transvaal. In response to the Afrikaners' guerrilla tactics and in order to contain the local population, the British instituted the first concentration camps. Ultimately, Britain won the conflict.

animal domestication Gradual process that occurred simultaneously with or just before the domestication of plants, depending on the region.

annals Historical records. Notable annals are the cuneiform inscriptions that record successful Assyrian military campaigns.

Anti-Federalists Critics of the U.S. Constitution who sought to defend the people against the power of the federal government and insisted on a bill of rights to protect individual liberties from government intrusion.

apartheid Racial segregation policy of the Afrikaner-dominated South African government. Legislated in 1948 by the Afrikaner National Party, it existed in South Africa for many years.

Arab-Israeli War of 1948–1949 Conflict between Israeli and Arab armies that arose in the wake of a UN vote to partition Palestine into Arab and Jewish territories. The war shattered the legitimacy of Arab ruling elites.

Aramaic Dialect of a Semitic language spoken in Southwest Asia; it became the lingua franca of the Persian Empire.

Aristotle (384–322 BCE) Philosopher who studied under Plato but came to different conclusions about nature and politics. Aristotle believed in collecting observations about nature and discerning patterns to ascertain how things worked.

Aryans Nomadic charioteers who spoke Indo-European languages and entered South Asia in 1500 BCE. The early Aryan settlers were herders.

Asante state State located in present-day Ghana, founded by Akan-speaking peoples at the end of the seventeenth century. It grew in power in the next century because of its access to gold and its involvement in the slave trade.

ascetic One who rejects material possessions and physical pleasures.

Asiatic Society Cultural organization founded by British Orientalists who supported native culture but still believed in colonial rule.

Aśoka Emperor of the Mauryan dynasty from 268 to 231 BCE. A great conqueror and unifier of India, he is said to have embraced Buddhism toward the end of his life.

Assur One of two cities on the upper reaches of the Tigris River that were the heart of Assyria proper (the other was Nineveh).

Aśvaghosa First known Sanskrit writer. He may have lived from 80 to 150 CE and may have composed a biography of the Buddha.

Ataturk, Mustafa Kemal (1881–1938) Ottoman army officer and military hero who helped forge the modern Turkish nation-state. He and his followers deposed the sultan, declared Turkey a republic, and constructed a European-like secular state, eliminating Islam's hold over civil and political affairs.

Atlantic system New system of trade and expansion that linked Europe, Africa, and the Americas. It emerged in the wake of European voyages across the Atlantic Ocean.

Atma Vedic term signifying the eternal self, represented by the trinity of deities.

Atman In the Upanishads, an eternal being who exists everywhere. The atman never perishes but is reborn or transmigrates into another life.

Attila Sole ruler of all Hunnish tribes from 433 to 453 CE. Harsh and much feared, he formed the first empire to oppose Rome in northern Europe.

Augustus Title meaning "Revered One," assumed in 27 BCE by the Roman ruler Octavian (63–14 BCE). This was one of many titles he assumed; others included *imperator*, *princeps*, and *caesar*.

australopithecines Hominin species that appeared 3 million years ago and, unlike other animals, walked on two legs. Their brain capacity was a little less than one-third that of a modern human's, or about the size of the brain capacity of today's African apes. Although not humans, they carried the genetic and biological material out of which modern humans would later emerge.

Austro-Hungarian Empire New configuration of the Austrian Empire in which Hungary received greater autonomy; established in 1867, it collapsed at the end of World War I.

authoritarianism Centralized and dictatorial form of government, proclaimed by its adherents to be superior to parliamentary democracy and especially effective at mobilizing the masses. This thinking was widely accepted in parts of the world during the 1930s.

Avesta Compilation of holy works transmitted orally by Zoroastrian priests for millennia and eventually recorded in the ninth century CE.

axial age Term often used to describe the pivotal period of the first millennium BCE, when radical thinkers across the "second-generation societies" of Afro-Eurasia—including the Greek philosophers of the Mediterranean, Zoroaster in Southwest Asia, Buddha in South Asia, and Confucius and Master Lao in East Asia—offered dramatically new ideas that challenged their times.

Axis Powers The three aggressor states in World War II: Germany, Japan, and Italy.

Aztec Empire Mesoamerican empire that originated with a league of three Mexica cities in 1430 and gradually expanded through the Central Valley of Mexico, uniting numerous small, independent states under a single monarch who ruled with the help of counselors, military leaders, and priests. By the late fifteenth century, the Aztec realm may have embraced 25 million people. In 1521, they were defeated by the conquistador Hernán Cortés.

baby boom Post–World War II upswing in U.S. birthrates; it reversed a century of decline.

Bactria A Hellenistic kingdom that broke away from the Seleucids around 200 BCE to establish a state in the Gandhara region of modern Pakistan, which served as a bridge between South Asia and the Mediterranean Greek world.

bactrian camel Two-humped animal domesticated in central Asia around 2500 BCE. The bactrian camel was heartier than the one-humped dromedary and became the animal of choice for the harsh and varied climates typical of Silk Road trade.

Baghdad Capital of the Islamic Empire under the Abbasid dynasty, founded in 762 CE (in modern-day Iraq). In the medieval period, it was a center of administration, scholarship, and cultural growth for what came to be known as the Golden Age of Islamic science.

Baghdad Pact (1955) Middle Eastern military alliance between countries friendly with America who were willing to align themselves with the western countries against the Soviet Union.

Balam Na Stone temple and place of pilgrimage for the Maya people of Mexico's Yucatán Peninsula.

Balfour Declaration Letter (November 2, 1917) by Lord Arthur J. Balfour, British foreign secretary, that promised a homeland for the Jews in Palestine.

Bamboo Annals Shang stories and foundation myths that were written on bamboo strips and later collected.

Bantu Language first spoken by people who lived in the southeastern area of modern Nigeria around 1000 CE.

Bantu migrations Waves of rapid population movement from West Africa into eastern and southern Africa during the first millennium CE that brought advanced agricultural practices to these regions and absorbed most of the preexisting hunting and gathering populations.

barbarian Originally a relatively neutral Greek term for non-Greek speakers, it evolved into a derogatory term used by other cultures to describe outsiders, often pastoral nomads, painting them as enemies of civilization.

barbarian invasions Violent migration of people in the late fourth and fifth centuries CE into Roman territory. These migrants had long been used as non-Roman soldiers.

basilicas Early church buildings, based on old royal audience halls.

Battle of Adwa (1896) Battle in which the Ethiopians defeated Italian colonial forces. It inspired many of Africa's later national leaders.

Battle of Wounded Knee (1890) Bloody massacre of Sioux Ghost Dancers by U.S. armed forces.

Bay of Pigs (1961) Unsuccessful invasion of Cuba by Cuban exiles supported by the U.S. government. The invaders intended to incite an insurrection in Cuba and overthrow the communist regime of Fidel Castro.

Bedouins Nomadic pastoralists in the deserts of the Middle East.

Beer Hall Putsch (1923) Failed Nazi attempt to capture Bavarian leaders in a Munich beer hall, a prelude to a planned seizure of power in Germany. Adolf Hitler was imprisoned for a year after the incident.

Beghards (1500s) Eccentric European group whose members claimed to be in a state of grace that allowed them to do as they pleased—from adultery, free love, and nudity to murder; also called Brethren of Free Speech.

bell beaker Ancient drinking vessel, an artifact from Europe, so named because its shape resembles an inverted bell.

Berenice of Egypt Egyptian "queen" who helped rule over the Kingdom of the Nile from 320 to 280 BCE.

Beringia Prehistoric thousand-mile-long land bridge that linked Siberia and North America (which had not been populated by hominins). About 18,000 years ago, *Homo sapiens* edged into this landmass.

Berlin Airlift (1948) Supply of vital necessities to West Berlin by air transport primarily under U.S. auspices. It was initiated in response to a land and water blockade of the city instituted by the Soviet Union in the hope that the Allies would be forced to abandon West Berlin.

Berlin Wall Wall built by the communists in Berlin in 1961 to prevent citizens of East Germany from fleeing to West Germany; torn down in 1989.

bhakti Religious practice that grew out of Hinduism and emphasizes personal devotion to gods.

Bhakti Hinduism Popular form of Hinduism that emerged in the seventh century. The religion stresses devotion (*bhakti*) to God and uses vernacular languages (not Sanskrit) spoken by the common people.

big men Leaders of the extended household communities that formed village settlements in African rain forests.

big whites French plantation owners in Saint Domingue (present-day Haiti) who created one of the wealthiest slave societies.

Bilad al-Sudan Arabic for "the land of the blacks"; it consisted of the land lying south of the Sahara.

bilharzia Debilitating waterborne illness. It was widespread in Egypt, where it infected peasants who worked in the irrigation canals.

Bill of Rights First ten amendments to the U.S. Constitution; ratified in 1791.

bipedalism Walking on two legs, thereby freeing hands and arms to carry objects such as weapons and tools; one of several traits that distinguish hominins.

Black Death Great epidemic of the bubonic plague that ravaged Europe, East Asia, and North Africa in the fourteenth century, killing large numbers, including perhaps as many as 65 percent of the European population.

Black Jacobins Name employed by a West Indian historian for the rebels in Saint Domingue, including Toussaint L'Ouverture, a former slave who led the slaves of this French colony in the world's largest and most successful slave insurrection.

Black Panthers Radical African American group in the 1960s and 1970s who advocated black separatism and pan-Africanism.

black shirts Fascist troops of Mussolini's regime. The squads received money from Italian landowners to attack socialist leaders.

Black Tuesday (October 29, 1929) Historic day when the U.S. stock market crashed, plunging the United States and international trading systems into crisis and leading the world into the Great Depression.

blitzkrieg "Lightning war"; type of warfare in which the Germans, during World War II, used coordinated aerial bombing campaigns along with tanks and infantrymen in motorized vehicles.

bodhisattvas In Mahayana Buddhism, enlightened demigods who were ready to reach *nirvana* but delayed so that they might help others attain it.

Bolívar, Simón (1783–1830) Venezuelan leader who urged his followers to become "American," to overcome their local identities. He wanted the liberated countries to form a Latin American confederation, urging Peru and Bolivia to join Venezuela, Ecuador, and Colombia in the "Gran Colombia."

Bolsheviks Former members of the Russian Social Democratic Party who advocated the destruction of capitalist political and economic institutions and overthrew the Provisional Government in the second phase of the Russian Revolution of 1917. In 1918, the Bolsheviks changed their name to the Russian Communist Party.

Bonaparte, Napoleon (1769–1821) French military leader who rose to power in a postrevolutionary coup d'état, eventually proclaiming himself emperor of France. He placed security and order ahead of social reform and created a civil legal code. Napoleon expanded his empire through military action, but after his disastrous Russian campaign, the united European powers defeated him and forced him into exile. Napoleon escaped and reassumed command of his army but was later defeated at the Battle of Waterloo.

Book of the Dead Ancient Egyptian funerary text that contains drawings and paintings as well as spells describing how to prepare the jewelry and amulets that were buried with a person in preparation for the afterlife.

bourgeoisie The middle class, defined not by birth or title, but by capital and property.

Boxer Protocol Written agreement between the victors of the Boxer Uprising and the Qing Empire in 1901 that placed western troops in Beijing and required the regime to pay exorbitant damages for foreign life and property.

Boxer Uprising (1899–1900) Chinese peasant movement that opposed foreign influence, especially that of Christian missionaries; it was put down after the Boxers were defeated by an army composed mostly of the Japanese, Russians, British, French, and Americans.

Brahma One of three major deities that form a trinity in Vedic religion. Brahma signifies birth. *See also* Vishnu *and* Siva.

Brahmans Vedic priests who performed rituals and communicated with the gods. Brahmans provided guidance on how to live in balance with the forces of nature as represented by the various deities. The codification of Vedic principles into codes of law took place at the hands of the Brahmans. They memorized Vedic works and compiled commentaries on them. They also developed their own set of rules and rituals, which developed into a full-scale theology. Originally memorized and passed on orally, these may have been written down sometime after the beginning of the Common Era. Brahmanism was reborn as Hinduism sometime during the first half of the first millennium CE.

British Commonwealth of Nations Union formed in 1926 that conferred "dominion status" on Britain's white settler colonies in Canada, Australia, and New Zealand.

British East India Company *See* East India Company.

bronze Alloy of copper and tin brought into Europe from Anatolia; used to make hard-edged weapons.

brown shirts Informal name for the men who joined the Nazi SA (Sturmabteilung); they participated in mass rallies and street brawls, persecuting Jews, communists, and others who opposed the Nazis.

bubonic plague Acute infectious disease caused by a bacterium that is transmitted to humans by fleas from infected rats; sometimes referred to as the "Black Death." It ravaged Europe and parts of Africa and Asia in the fourteenth century.

Buddha (Siddhartha Gautama; 563–483 BCE) Indian ascetic who founded Buddhism.

Buddhism Major South Asian religion that aims to end human suffering through the renunciation of desire, derived from the teachings of Siddhartha Gautama, the Buddha (563–483 BCE). Buddhists believe that removing the illusion of a separate identity will lead to a state of contentment (nirvana). These beliefs challenged the traditional Brahmanic teachings of the time and provided the peoples of South Asia with an alternative to established traditions.

bullion Uncoined gold or silver.

Byzantium Modern term for the eastern Roman Empire (lasting from the fourth to the fifteenth century), centered at its "new Rome," Constantinople (founded by emperor Constantine in 324 CE on the site of a Greek city, Byzantium).

Cahokia Commercial center for regional and long-distance trade in North America. Its hinterlands produced staples for urban consumers. In return, its crafts were exported inland by porters and to North American markets in canoes. *See also* "Mound people."

calaveras Allegorical skeleton drawings by the Mexican printmaker and artist José Guadalupe Posada. The works drew on popular themes of betrayal, death, and festivity.

caliphate Institution that arose as the successor to Muhammad's leadership and became both the political and religious head of the Islamic community. Although the caliphs exercised political authority over the Muslim community and were the head of the religious community, the *umma*, they did not inherit Muhammad's prophetic powers and were not authorities in religious doctrine.

Calvin, Jean (1509–1564) A French theologian during the Protestant Reformation. Calvin developed a Christianity that emphasized moral regeneration through church teachings, laid out a doctrine of predestination, and established Calvinist dominance in Geneva, Switzerland.

Candomblé Yoruba-based religion in northern Brazil; it interwove African practices and beliefs with Christianity.

Canton system System officially established by imperial decree in 1759 that required European traders to have Chinese guild merchants act as guarantors for their good behavior and payment of fees.

caravan city Commercial hub of long-distance trade, where groups of merchants could assemble during their journeys. Several of these developed into full-fledged cities, especially in the deserts of Arabia.

caravans Companies of men who transported and traded goods along overland routes in North Africa and central Asia. Large caravans consisted of 600 to 1,000 camels and as many as 400 men.

caravansarais Inns along major trade routes that accommodated large numbers of traders, their animals, and their wares.

caravel Sailing vessel suited for nosing in and out of estuaries and navigating in waters with unpredictable currents and winds.

carrack Ship used on open bodies of water, such as the Mediterranean.

Carthage City in what is modern-day Tunisia; emblematic of the trading aspirations and activities of merchants in the Mediterranean. Pottery and other archaeological remains demonstrate that Carthaginian trading contacts were as far-flung as Italy, Greece, France, Iberia, and West Africa.

cartography Mapmaking.

caste system Hierarchical social system of organizing people and distributing labor.

Caste War of the Yucatán (1847–1901) Conflict between Maya Indians and the Mexican state over Indian autonomy and legal equality, which resulted in the Mexican takeover of the Yucatán Peninsula.

Castro, Fidel (1926–2016) Cuban communist leader whose forces overthrew Batista's corrupt regime in early January 1959. Castro became increasingly radical as he consolidated power, announcing a massive redistribution of land and the nationalization of foreign oil refineries. He declared himself a socialist and aligned himself with the Soviet Union in the wake of the 1961 CIA-backed Bay of Pigs invasion.

Çatal Hüyük Site in Anatolia discovered in 1958. It was a dense honeycomb of settlements filled with rooms whose walls were covered with paintings of wild bulls, hunters, and pregnant women. Çatal Hüyük symbolizes an early transition into urban dwelling and dates to the eighth millennium BCE.

Cathedra Bishop's seat, or throne, in a church.

Catholic Church Unifying institution for Christians in western Europe after the collapse of the Roman Empire. Rome became the spiritual capital of western Europe, and the bishops of Rome emerged as popes, the supreme head of the church, who possessed great moral authority.

Cato the Elder (234–149 BCE) Roman statesman, often seen as emblematic of the transition from a Greek to a Roman world. Cato the Elder wrote a manual for the new economy of slave plantation agriculture, invested in shipping and trading, learned Greek rhetoric, and added the genre of history to Latin literature.

caudillos South American local military chieftains.

cave drawings Images on cave walls. The subjects are most often large game, although a few are images of humans. Other elements are impressions made by hands dipped in paint and pressed on a wall or abstract symbols and shapes.

Celali revolts (1595–1610) Peasant and artisan uprisings against the Ottoman state.

Central Powers Defined in World War I as Germany, Austria-Hungary, and the Ottoman Empire.

Chan Chan City founded between 850 and 900 CE by the Moche people in what is now modern-day Peru. It had a core population of 30,000 inhabitants.

Chandra Gupta II King who reigned in South Asia from 320 to 335 CE. He shared his name with Chandragupta, the founder of the Mauryan Empire.

Chandravamsha One of two main lineages (the lunar one) of Vedic society, each with its own creation myth, ancestors, language, and rituals. Each lineage included many clans. *See* Suryavanha.

Chan Santa Cruz Separate Maya community formed as part of a crusade for spiritual salvation and the complete cultural separation of the Maya Indians; means "little holy cross."

chapatis Flat, unleavened Indian bread.

chariots Horse-driven carriages brought by the pastoral nomadic warriors from the steppes that became the favored mode of warfare and transportation for an urban aristocratic warrior class and for other men of power in agriculture-based societies. Control of chariot forces was the foundation of the new balance of power across Afro-Eurasia during the second millennium BCE.

charismatic Person who uses personal strengths or virtues, often laced with a divine aura, to command followers.

Charlemagne King of the Franks from 768 CE, king of the Lombards from 774 CE, and emperor of the Romans from 800 CE until his death in 814 CE.

chartered companies Firms that were awarded monopoly trading rights over vast areas by European monarchs (e.g., Virginia Company, Dutch East India Company).

Chartism (1834–1848) Mass democratic movement to pass the Peoples' Charter in Britain, granting male suffrage, secret ballot, equal electoral districts, and annual parliaments and absolving the requirement of property ownership for members of the parliament.

chattel slavery Form of slavery that sold people as property, the rise of which coincided with the expansion of city-states. Chattel slavery was eschewed by the Spartans, who also rejected the innovation of coin money.

Chavín A people who lived in what is now northern Peru from 1400 to 200 BCE. They were united more by culture and faith than by a unified political system.

Chernobyl Site in the Soviet Union (in Ukraine) of the 1986 meltdown of a nuclear reactor.

Chiang Kai-shek (1887–1975) Leader of the Guomindang following Sun Yat-sen's death. Chiang mobilized the Chinese masses through the New Life movement. In 1949, he lost to the communists and moved his regime to Taiwan.

Chimú Empire South America's first empire; it developed during the first century of the second millennium in the Moche Valley on the Pacific coast.

chinampas Floating gardens used by the Aztecs in the 1300s and 1400s to grow crops.

China's Sorrow Name given to the Yellow River, which, when it changed course or flooded, could cause mass death and waves of migration.

chinoiserie Chinese silks, teas, tableware, jewelry, and paper, popular among Europeans in the seventeenth and eighteenth centuries.

Christendom Entire portion of the world in which Christianity prevailed.

Christianity Religion that originated at the height of the Roman Empire and in direct confrontation with Roman imperial authority, founded by Yeshua ben Yosef (Joshua son of Joseph, known today by the Greek form of his name, Jesus), whom the Romans condemned for sedition and crucified. In the fourth century CE, Christianity was officially recognized as the Roman state religion.

Church of England Official form of Christianity established in England when Henry VIII broke with Rome during the Reformation. The English monarch, not the pope, is the head of this church.

city Highly populated concentration of economic, religious, and political power. The first cities appeared in river basins, which could produce a surplus of agriculture. The abundance of food freed most city inhabitants from the need to produce their own food, which allowed them to work in specialized professions.

city-state Political organization based on the authority of a single, large city that controls outlying territories.

Civil Rights Act (1964) U.S. legislation that banned segregation in public facilities, outlawed racial discrimination in employment, and marked an important step in correcting legal inequality.

civil rights movement Powerful movement for equal rights and the end of racial segregation in the United States that began in the 1950s with nonviolent boycotts and court victories against school segregation.

civil service examinations The world's first written civil service examination system, instituted by the Tang dynasty to recruit officials and bureaucrats. Open to most males, the exams tested a candidate's literary skills and knowledge of the Confucian classics. They helped to unite the Chinese state by making knowledge of a specific language and Confucian classics the only route to power.

Civil War, American (1861–1865) Conflict between the northern and southern states of America, leading to the abolition of slavery in the United States.

clan A social group comprising many households claiming descent from a common ancestor.

clandestine presses Small printing operations, especially in Switzerland and the Netherlands, that published banned texts in the early modern era.

closing of the frontier In 1893, responding to the recent U.S. Census, the historian Frederick Jackson Turner popularized the idea that the western frontier—so long crucial to the making of American identity—had closed. His announcement spurred many to worry that having lost the manliness and self-reliance nurtured by the hard life on the frontier, Americans would grow soft and weak.

Clovis people Early humans in America who used basic chipped blades and pointed spears in pursuing prey. They extended the hunting traditions they had learned in Afro-Eurasia, such as establishing campsites and moving with their herds. They were known as Clovis people because the arrowhead point that they used was first found by archaeologists at a site near Clovis, New Mexico.

Code of Manu Part of the handiwork of Brahman priests; a representative code of law that incorporated social sanctions and practices and provided guidance for living within the caste system.

codex Early form of book, with separate pages bound together; it replaced the scroll as the main medium for written texts. The codex emerged around 300 CE.

cognitive skills Skills such as thought, memory, problem solving, and—ultimately—language. Hominins were able to use these skills and their hands to create new adaptations, like tools that helped them obtain food and avoid predators.

Cohong Chinese merchant guild that traded with Europeans under the Qing dynasty.

coins Form of money that replaced goods, which previously had been bartered for services and other products. Originally used mainly to hire mercenary soldiers, coins became the commonplace method of payment linking buyers and producers throughout the Mediterranean.

Cold War (1945–1990) Ideological conflict in which the Soviet Union and eastern Europe opposed the United States and western Europe.

colonies Regions under the political control of another country.

colons French settler population in Algeria.

Colosseum Huge amphitheater, originally begun by Flavian and completed by Titus, which was dedicated in 80 CE. The structure is named after a colossal statue of Nero that formerly stood beside it.

Columbian exchange Movement between Afro-Eurasia and the Americas of previously unknown plants, animals, people, diseases, and products that followed in the wake of Columbus's voyages.

commanderies Provinces. Shi Huangdi (First August Emperor) divided China into commanderies (*jun*) to enable the Qin dynasty to rule the massive state effectively. The thirty-six commanderies were then subdivided into counties (*xian*).

Communist Manifesto Pamphlet published by Karl Marx and Friedrich Engels in 1848 at a time when political revolutions were sweeping Europe. It called on the workers of all nations to unite in overthrowing capitalism.

compass Navigation instrument invented by the Chinese and used to determine directions with a magnetized needle, which always points to the north cardinal direction on the compass rose.

Compromise of 1867 Agreement between the Habsburgs and the Austrian Empire's Hungarian population that gave the Hungarian lands more autonomy; the empire was now renamed the Austro-Hungarian Empire.

concession areas Territories, usually ports, where Chinese emperors allowed European merchants to trade and European people to settle.

Confucian ideals The ideals of honoring tradition, emphasizing the responsibility of the emperor, and respect for the lessons of history, promoted by Confucius, which the Han dynasty made the official doctrine of the empire by 50 BCE.

Confucianism Ethics, beliefs, and practices stipulated by the Chinese philosopher Kong Qiu, or Confucius, which served as a guide for Chinese society up to modern times.

Confucius (551–479 BCE) Influential teacher, thinker, and leader in China who developed a set of principles for ethical living. He believed that coercive laws and punishment would not be needed to maintain order in society if men following his ethics ruled. He taught his philosophy to anyone who was intelligent and willing to work, which allowed men to gain entry into the ruling class through education.

Congo Free State Large colonial state in Africa created by Leopold II, king of Belgium, during the 1880s, and ruled by him alone. After rumors of mass slaughter and enslavement, the Belgian parliament took the land and formed a Belgian colony.

Congress of Vienna (1814–1815) International conference to reorganize Europe after the downfall of Napoleon. European monarchies agreed to respect each other's borders and to cooperate in guarding against future revolutions and war.

cong tube Ritual object crafted by the Liangzhu. A cong tube was made of jade and was used in divination practices.

conquistadors Spanish military leaders who led the conquest of the New World in the sixteenth century.

Constantine Roman emperor who converted to Christianity in 312 CE. In 313 CE, he issued a proclamation that gave Christians new freedoms in the empire. He also founded Constantinople (at first called "New Rome").

Constantinople Capital city, formerly known as Byzantium, which was founded as the New Rome by Constantine the Great.

Constitutional Convention (1787) Meeting to formulate the Constitution of the United States of America.

Contra rebels Opponents of the Sandinistas in Nicaragua. They were armed and financed by the United States and other anti-communist countries (1980).

Conversion of Constantine Inspired by a dream to arm his soldiers with shields bearing Christ's name, the Emperor Constantine won a decisive battle for Rome in 312 CE. Afterward, he issued a proclamation giving privileges to Christian bishops, which began the process of spreading Christianity throughout the Roman Empire.

conversos Jewish and Muslim converts to Christianity in the Iberian Peninsula and the New World.

Coptic Form of Christianity practiced in Egypt. It was doctrinally different from Christianity elsewhere, and Coptic Christians had their own views of Christology, or the nature of Christ.

Corn Laws Laws that imposed tariffs on grain imported to Great Britain, intended to protect British farming interests. The Corn Laws were abolished in 1846 as part of a British movement in favor of free trade.

cosmology Branch of metaphysics devoted to understanding the order of the universe.

cosmopolitans The inhabitants of the multiethnic cities that thrived in the Hellenistic world, literally meaning "citizens belonging to the whole world" as opposed to a particular city-state.

Council of Nicaea Church council convened in 325 CE by Constantine and presided over by him as well. At this council, a Christian creed was articulated and made into a formula that expressed the philosophical and technical elements of Christian belief.

Counter-Reformation Movement initiated by the Catholic Church at the Council of Trent in 1545 with the aim of countering the spread of the Reformation. The Catholic Church enacted reforms to attack clerical corruption and placed a greater emphasis on individual spirituality. During this time, the Jesuits were founded to help revive the Catholic Church.

coup d'état Overthrow of the established state by a group of conspirators, usually from the military.

creation narratives Various accounts of the creation of the universe and humankind's place in it, conceived by virtually all peoples.

creed Formal statement of faith or expression of a belief system. A Christian creed, or "credo," was formulated by the Council of Nicaea in 325 CE.

creoles Persons of full-blooded European descent who were born in the Spanish American colonies.

Crimean War (1853–1856) War waged by Russia against Great Britain and France. Spurred by Russia's encroachment on Ottoman territories, the conflict revealed Russia's military weakness when Russian forces fell to British and French troops.

crossbow Innovative weapon used at the end of the Warring States period that allowed archers to shoot their enemies with accuracy, even from a distance.

Crusades Wave of attacks launched in the late eleventh century by western Europeans. The First Crusade began in 1095, when Pope Urban II appealed to the warrior nobility of France to free Jerusalem from Muslim rule. Four subsequent Crusades were fought over the next two centuries.

Cuban Missile Crisis (1962) Diplomatic standoff between the United States and the Soviet Union that was provoked by the Soviet Union's attempt to base nuclear missiles in Cuba; it brought the world close to a nuclear war.

cult Religious movement, often based on the worship of a particular god or goddess.

cultigen Organism that has diverged from its ancestors through domestication or cultivation.

cuneiform Wedge-shaped form of writing, used primarily by the Sumerian, Assyrian, and Persian Empires. By impressing these signs into wet clay with the cut end of a reed, scribes engaged in cuneiform.

Cyrus the Great Founder of the Persian Empire. This sixth-century ruler (559–529 BCE) conquered the Medes and unified the Iranian kingdoms.

Daimyo Ruling lords who commanded private armies in pre-Meiji Japan.

dan Fodio, Usman (1754–1817) Fulani Muslim cleric whose visions led him to challenge the Hausa ruling classes, whom he believed were insufficiently faithful to Islamic beliefs and practices. His ideas gained support among those who had suffered under the Hausa landlords. In 1804, his supporters and allies overthrew the Hausa in what is today northern Nigeria.

Daoism School of thought developed at the end of the Warring States period that focused on the importance of following the Dao, or the natural way of the cosmos. Daoism emphasized the need to accept the world as it was rather than trying to change it through politics or the government. Unlike Confucianism, Daoism scorned rigid rituals and social hierarchies.

Dar al-Islam Arabic for "the House of Islam"; it describes the territories ruled by Muslims and is contrasted with *Dar al-Harb*, the land of war, not yet under Islamic rule.

Darius I (521–486 BCE) Leader who put the emerging unified Persian Empire on solid footing after Cyrus's death.

Darwin, Charles (1809–1882) British scientist who became convinced that the species of organic life had evolved under the uniform pressure of the laws of natural selection, not by means of a special, one-time creation as described in the Bible.

D-Day (June 6, 1944) Day of the Allied invasion of Normandy under General Dwight Eisenhower to liberate western Europe from German occupation.

Dear Boy Nickname of an early human remain (an almost totally intact skull) discovered in 1931 by archaeologists Mary and Louis Leakey. Other objects discovered with Dear Boy demonstrated that by the time of Dear Boy, early humans had begun to fashion tools and to use them for butchering animals and possibly for hunting and killing smaller animals.

Decembrists Russian army officers who were influenced by events in revolutionary France and formed secret societies that espoused liberal governance. They were put down by Nicholas I in December 1825.

Declaration of Independence U.S. document stating the theory of government on which the United States was founded.

Declaration of the Rights of Man and Citizen (1789) French charter of liberties formulated by the National Assembly that marked the end of dynastic and aristocratic rule. The seventeen articles later became the preamble to the new constitution, which the assembly finished in 1791.

decolonization End of empire and emergence of new independent states in Asia and Africa as a result of anticolonial nationalism, the weakening of the European colonial powers in World War II, and the rise of the United States and the USSR as superpowers after the war, both of whom favored ending imperial rule.

degeneration In the later 19th century, many Europeans began to fear that Darwin had been wrong: urbanization, technology, racial hybridity, the emergence of the "modern" woman, and over-refinement were causing Europeans not to progress as a species, but to degenerate. This fear was often combined with anxieties about colonialism, homosexuality, emigration, and/or the advancement of women.

Delhi Sultanate (1206–1526) Muslim Turkish regime of northern India. The regime strengthened the cultural diversity and tolerance that were a hallmark of the Indian social order, which allowed it to bring about political integration without enforcing cultural homogeneity.

democracy The idea that people, through membership in a nation, should choose their own representatives and be governed by them.

Democritus Thinker in ancient Greece who lived from 470 to 360 BCE. He deduced the existence of the atom, postulating that there was such a thing as an indivisible particle.

demotic writing The second of two basic forms of ancient Egyptian writing. Demotic was a cursive script written with ink on papyrus, on pottery, or on other absorbent objects. It was the most common and practical form of writing in Egypt and was used for administrative record keeping and in private or pseudo-private forms like letters and works of literature. *See also* hieroglyphs.

developing world Term applied to countries collectively called the Third World during the Cold War; countries seeking to develop viable nation-states and prosperous economies.

devshirme System of taking non-Muslim children in place of taxes in order to educate them in Ottoman Muslim ways and prepare them for service in the sultan's bureaucracy.

dhamma Moral code espoused by Aśoka in the Kalinga edict, which was meant to apply to all—Buddhists, Brahmans, and Greeks alike.

dhimma **system** Muslim law and practice that permitted followers of religions other than Islam, such as Christians, Jews, and Zoroastrians, and later Buddhists and Hindus, to choose their own religious leaders and to settle internal disputes within their religious communities as long as they accepted Islam's political dominion.

dhows Ships used by Arab seafarers. The dhow's large sails were rigged to maximize the capture of wind.

Dien Bien Phu (1954) Defining battle in the war between French colonialists and the Viet Minh that secured North Vietnam for Ho Chi Minh and his army and left the south to form its own government to be supported by France and the United States.

Din-I-llahi "House of worship" in which the Mughal emperor Akbar engaged in religious debate with Hindu, Muslim, Jain, Parsi, and Christian theologians.

Diogenes Greek philosopher who lived from 412 to 323 BCE and who espoused a doctrine of self-sufficiency and freedom from social laws and customs. He rejected cultural norms as out of tune with nature and therefore false.

Directory Temporary military committee that took over the affairs of the state of France in 1795 from the radicals and held control until the coup of Napoleon Bonaparte.

divination The interpretation of rituals used to communicate the wishes of gods or royal ancestors to foretell future events. Divination was used to legitimize royal authority and demand tribute.

Djoser Ancient Egyptian king who reigned from 2630 to 2611 BCE. He was the second king of the Third Dynasty and celebrated the Sed festival in his tomb complex at Saqqara.

domestication Bringing wild plants and animals under human control.

Dominion in the British Commonwealth Canadian promise to keep up the country's fealty to the British crown, even after its independence in 1867. It later applied to Australia and New Zealand.

Dong Zhongshu Emperor Wu's chief minister, who advocated a more powerful view of Confucius by promoting texts that focused on Confucius as a man who possessed aspects of divinity.

double-outrigger canoes Vessels used by early Austronesians to cross the Taiwan Straits and colonize islands in the Pacific. These sturdy canoes could cover over 120 miles per day.

Duma Russian parliament, first convened in 1906.

Dutch learning Broad term for European teachings that were strictly regulated by the shoguns inside Japan.

dynastic cycle Political narrative in which influential families vied for supremacy. Upon gaining power, they legitimated their authority by claiming to be the heirs of previous grand dynasts and by preserving or revitalizing the ancestors' virtuous governing

r >9

ways. This continuity conferred divine support.

dynasty Hereditary ruling family that passed control from one generation to the next.

Earth Summit (1992) Meeting in Rio de Janeiro between many of the world's governments in an effort to address international environmental problems.

Eastern Front Battlefront between Berlin and Moscow during World War I and World War II.

East India Company (1600–1858) British charter company created to outperform Portuguese and Spanish traders in the Far East; in the eighteenth century, the company became, in effect, the ruler of a large part of India.

Edict of Nantes (1598) Edict issued by Henry IV to end the French Wars of Religion. The edict declared France a Catholic country but tolerated some Protestant worship. It was revoked by Louis XIV in 1685.

Egyptian Middle Kingdom Period of Egyptian history lasting from about 2040 to 1640 BCE, characterized by a consolidation of power and building activity in Upper Egypt.

Eiffel Tower Steel monument completed in 1889 for the Paris Exposition. It was twice the height of any other building at the time.

eight-legged essay Highly structured essay form with eight parts, required on Chinese civil service examinations.

Ekklesia Church or early gathering committed to leaders chosen by God and fellow believers.

Ekpe Powerful slave trade institution that organized the supply and purchase of slaves inland from the Gulf of Guinea in West Africa.

Elamites A people with their capital in the upland valley of modern Fars who became a cohesive polity that incorporated transhumant people of the Zagros Mountains. A group of Elamites who migrated south and west into Mesopotamia helped conquer the Third Dynasty of Ur in 2400 BCE.

empire Group of states or different ethnic groups under a single sovereign power.

Enabling Act (1933) Emergency legislation, enacted just after Hitler became German chancellor (prime minister), that undermined parliamentary democracy in Germany by giving the chancellor the right to dictate legislation without the approval of the Reichstag (German parliament). This legislation paved the way for Hitler's dictatorship.

enclosure A movement in which landowners took control of lands that traditionally had been common property serving local needs.

encomenderos Commanders of the labor services of the colonized peoples in Spanish America.

encomiendas Grants from European Spanish governors to *encomenderos* control the labor services of colonized people.

Endeavor Ship of Captain James Cook, whose celebrated voyages to the South Pacific in the late eighteenth century supplied Europe with information about the plants, birds, landscapes, and people of this uncharted territory.

Engels, Friedrich (1820–1895) German social and political philosopher who collaborated with Karl Marx on many publications, including *The Communist Manifesto*.

English Navigation Act of 1651 Act stipulating that only English ships could carry goods between the mother country and its colonies.

English Peasants' Revolt (1381) Uprising of serfs and free farmworkers that began as a protest against a tax levied to raise money for a war on France. The revolt was suppressed but led to the gradual emergence of a free peasantry as labor shortages made it impossible to keep peasants bound to the soil.

enlightened absolutists Seventeenth- and eighteenth-century monarchs who claimed to rule rationally and in the best interests of their subjects and who hired loyal bureaucrats to enact enlightened policies.

Enlightenment Intellectual movement in late seventeenth- and eighteenth-century Europe stressing natural laws and reason as the basis of authority.

entrepôts Trading stations at the borders between communities, which made exchange possible among many different partners. Long-distance traders could also replenish their supplies at these stations.

Epicurus (341–279 BCE) Greek philosopher who espoused emphasis on the self. He founded a school in Athens called The Garden and stressed the importance of sensation, teaching that pleasurable sensations were good and painful sensations bad. Members of his school sought to find peace and relaxation by avoiding unpleasantness or suffering.

Estates-General French quasi-parliamentary body called in 1789 to deal with the financial problems that afflicted France. It had not met since 1614.

Etruscans A dominant people on the Italian Peninsula until the fourth century BCE. The Etruscan states were part of the foundation of the Roman Empire.

eunuchs Loyal and well-paid men who were surgically castrated as youths and remained in service to the caliph or emperor. Both Abbasid and Tang rulers relied for protection on a cadre of eunuchs.

Eurasia The combined area of Europe and Asia.

European Union (EU) Western European organization that evolved out of post-1945 efforts to prevent warfare in Europe, initially by forging closer economic cooperation.

evolution Process by which the different species of the world—its plants and animals—make changes in response to their environment that enable them to survive and increase in numbers.

Exclusion Act of 1882 U.S. congressional act prohibiting nearly all immigration from China to the United States; fueled by animosity toward Chinese workers in the American West.

Ezo Present-day Hokkaido, Japan's fourth main island.

fascism Mass political movement founded by Benito Mussolini that emphasized nationalism, militarism, and the omnipotence of the state.

fascists Radical right-wing groups of disaffected citizens, often veterans of World War I, that were opposed to democracy and favored rule by a single leader. Fascist movements triumphed in Italy, Germany, Spain, Japan, and several central European countries after World War I.

Fatehpur Sikri Mughal emperor Akbar's temporary capital near Agra.

Fatimids Shiite dynasty that ruled parts of the Islamic Empire beginning in the tenth century CE. The Fatimids arose in North Africa, where they conquered Egypt and founded the city of Cairo.

February Revolution (1917) The first of two uprisings of the Russian Revolution, which led to the end of the Romanov dynasty. It ended with the forming of a Provisional Government under Alexander Kerensky.

Federal Deposit Insurance Corporation (FDIC) Organization created in 1933 to guarantee all bank deposits up to $5,000 as part of the New Deal in the United States.

Federalists Supporters of the ratification of the U.S. Constitution, which was written to replace the Articles of Confederation.

Federal Republic of Germany (1949–1990) Country formed of the areas occupied by the Allies after World War II. Also known as West Germany, this country experienced rapid demilitarization, democratization, and integration into the world economy.

Federal Reserve Act (1913) U.S. legislation that created a series of boards to monitor the supply and demand of the nation's money.

feminist movements Movements that call for equal treatment for men and women—equal pay and equal opportunities for obtaining jobs and advancement. Feminism arose mainly in Europe and in North America in the 1960s and then became global in the 1970s.

Ferangi Word taken from the Arabic word for "Franks," but referring to Europeans in general and widely used to describe the European Crusaders.

Fertile Crescent Site of the world's first agricultural revolution; an area in Southwest Asia, bounded by the Mediterranean Sea in the west and the Zagros Mountains in the east.

feudalism System instituted in medieval Europe after the collapse of the Carolingian Empire (888 CE) whereby each peasant was under the authority of a lord and typically owed him fees and/or service in exchange for protection and the right to live and work on his lands.

fiefdoms Medieval economic and political units.

First World Term invented during the Cold War to refer to western Europe and North America (also known as the "free world" or the west); Japan later joined this group. Following the principles of liberal modernism, First World states sought to organize the world on the basis of capitalism and democracy.

five pillars of Islam The five tenets, or main aspects, of Islamic practice: testification, or bearing witness, that there is no God other than God (Allah, in Arabic) and that Muhammad is the messenger of God; praying five times a day; fasting from sunup to sundown every day during Ramadan (a month on the Islamic calendar); giving alms; and making a pilgrimage to Mecca.

Five-Year Plan Soviet effort launched under Stalin in 1928 to replace the market with a state-owned and state-managed economy, to promote rapid economic development over a five-year period of time and thereby "catch and overtake" the leading capitalist countries. The First Five-Year Plan was followed by the Second Five-Year Plan (1933–1937), and so on, until the collapse of the Soviet Union in 1991. Because of the seeming Soviet economic successes, five-year plans became popular in many developing countries as a way to promote economic growth.

Flagellants European social group that came into existence during the bubonic plague in the fourteenth century. They believed that the plague was the wrath of God.

floating population Poor migrant workers in China who supplied labor under Emperor Wu.

Fluitschips Dutch shipping vessels that could carry heavy bulky cargo with relatively small crews.

flying cash Letters of exchange—early predecessors of paper cash instead of coins—first developed by guilds in the northwestern Shanxi. By the thirteenth century, paper money had eclipsed coins.

fondûqs Complexes in caravan cities that included hostels, storage houses, offices, and temples.

Forbidden City of Beijing Palace city of the Ming and Qing dynasties.

Force Publique Colonial army used to maintain order in the Belgian Congo.

During the early stages of King Leopold's rule, it was responsible for bullying local communities.

Fourierism Form of utopian socialism based on the ideas of Charles Fourier (1772–1837). Fourier envisioned communes where work was made enjoyable and systems of production and distribution were run without merchants. His ideas appealed to middle-class readers, especially women, as a higher form of Christian communalism.

free labor Wage-paying rather than slave labor.

free markets Unregulated markets.

Free Officers Movement Secret organization of Egyptian junior military officers led by Gamal Abdel Nasser that came to power in a coup d'état in 1952, forced King Faruq to abdicate, and consolidated control through dissolving the parliament, banning opposing parties, and rewriting the constitution.

free trade Domestic and international trade unencumbered by tariff barriers, quotas, and fees.

Front de Libération Nationale (FLN) Algerian anticolonial, nationalist party that waged an eight-year war against French troops, beginning in 1854, that forced nearly all of the 1 million colonists to leave.

Fulani A widespread ethnic group in West Africa, some of whose members embraced Islam and carried out religious revolts at the end of the eighteenth and the beginning of the nineteenth centuries in an effort to return to the pure Islam of the past.

fur trade Trading of animal pelts (especially beaver skins) by Indians for European goods in North America.

Gandharan art Buddhist sculptures, particularly from the northern Kushan territory, that show a high degree of Greek and Roman influences.

Gandhi, Mohandas Karamchand (Mahatma) (1869–1948) Indian leader who led a nonviolent struggle for India's independence from Britain.

garrisons Military bases, often built inside cities and often used for political purposes, such as protecting rulers, putting down domestic revolts, or enforcing colonial rule.

garrison towns Stations for soldiers originally established in strategic locations to protect territorial acquisition. Eventually, they became towns. Alexander the Great's garrison towns evolved into cities that served as centers from which Hellenistic culture was spread to his easternmost territories.

gauchos Argentine, Brazilian, and Uruguayan cowboys who wanted a decentralized federation, with autonomy for their provinces and respect for their way of life.

Gdansk shipyard Site of mass strikes in Poland that led in 1980 to the formation of the first independent trade union, Solidarity, in the communist bloc.

gendered relations A relatively recent hypothesis that gender roles emerged only with the appearance of modern humans and perhaps Neanderthals. When humans began to think imaginatively and in complex symbolic ways and give voice to their insights, perhaps around 150,000 years ago, gender categories began to crystallize.

genealogy History of the descent of a person or family from a distant ancestor.

Geneva Peace Conference (1954) International conference to restore peace in Korea and Indochina. The chief participants were the United States, the Soviet Union, Great Britain, France, the People's Republic of China, North Korea, South Korea, Vietnam, the Viet Minh party, Laos, and Cambodia. The conference resulted in the division of North and South Vietnam.

Genoa One of two Italian cities (the other was Venice) that linked Europe, Africa, and Asia as nodes of commerce in 1300 CE. Genoese ships linked the Mediterranean to the coast of Flanders through consistent routes along the Atlantic coasts of Spain, Portugal, and France.

German Democratic Republic Nation founded from the Soviet zone of occupation of Germany after World War II; also known as East Germany.

German Social Democratic Party Founded in 1875, the most powerful socialist party in Europe before 1917.

Ghana The most celebrated medieval political kingdom in West Africa and later the name of the first independent black African state.

Ghost Dance American Indian ritual performed in the nineteenth century in the hope of restoring the world to precolonial conditions.

Gilgamesh Heroic narrative written in the Babylonian dialect of Semitic Akkadian. This story and others like it were meant to circulate and unify the kingdom.

Girondins Liberal revolutionary group that supported the creation of a constitutional monarchy during the early stages of the French Revolution.

globalization Development of integrated worldwide cultural and economic structures.

globalizing empires Empires, such as the Han and the Roman, that covered immense amounts of territory, included huge, diverse populations; exerted influence beyond their own borders; and worked to integrate conquered peoples.

global warming Worldwide rising temperatures caused in large part by the release into the air of human-made carbons.

Gold Coast Name that European mariners and merchants gave to that part of West Africa from which gold was exported. This area was conquered by the British in the nineteenth century and became a British colony; upon independence, it became Ghana.

Goths One of the groups of "barbarian" migrants into Roman territory in the fourth century CE.

government schools Schools founded by the Han dynasty to provide an adequate number of officials to fill positions in the administrative bureaucracy. The Imperial University had 30,000 members by the second century BCE.

Gracchus brothers Two tribunes, the brothers Tiberius and Gaius Gracchus, who in 133 and 123–121 BCE attempted to institute land reforms that would guarantee all of Rome's poor citizens a basic amount of land that would qualify them for army service. Both men were assassinated.

Grand Canal Created in 486 BCE, a thousand-mile-long connector between the Yellow and Yangzi Rivers, linking the north and south, respectively.

grand unity Guiding political idea embraced by Qin rulers and ministers, with an eye toward joining the states of the Central Plain into one empire and centralizing administration.

"greased cartridge" controversy Controversy spawned by the rumor that cow and pig fat had been used to grease the ammunition to be used by sepoy gunners in the British army in India. Believing that this was a British attempt to defile their religion and speed their conversion to Christianity, the sepoys mutinied against their British officers and led a widespread revolt against British rule in 1857.

Great Depression Worldwide depression following the U.S. stock market crash on October 29, 1929.

great divide The division between economically developed nations and less developed nations.

Great East Asia Co-Prosperity Sphere Term used by the Japanese during the 1930s and 1940s to refer to Hong Kong, Singapore, Malaya, Burma, and other states that they seized during their run for expansion.

Great Flood One of many traditional Mesopotamian stories that were transmitted orally from one generation to another before being recorded. The Sumerian King List refers to this crucial event in Sumerian memory and identity. The Great Flood was thought to have led to Uruk's demise as punishment by the gods.

Great Game Competition for economic or political control of areas such as Turkistan, Persia (present-day Iran), and Afghanistan. The British (in India) and the Russians believed that controlling these areas was crucial to preventing their enemies' expansion.

Great League of Peace and Power Iroquois Indian alliance that united previously warring communities.

Great Leap Forward (1958–1961) Plan devised by Mao Zedong to achieve rapid agricultural and industrial growth in China. The plan failed miserably, and more than 20 million people died.

great plaza at Isfahan The center of Safavid power in the seventeenth century created by Shah Abbas (r. 1587–1629) to represent the unification of trade, government, and religion under one supreme political authority.

Great Proletarian Cultural Revolution (1966–1976) Mass mobilization of urban Chinese youth inaugurated by Mao Zedong in an attempt to reinvigorate the Chinese Revolution and to prevent the development of a bureaucratized Soviet style of communism. With this movement, Mao turned against his longtime associates in the Communist Party.

Great Trek Afrikaner migration to the interiors of Africa after the British abolished slavery in the empire in 1833.

Great War (August 1914–November 1918) Also known as World War I. A total war involving the armies of Britain, France, and Russia (the Allies) against those of Germany, Austria-Hungary, and the Ottoman Empire (the Central Powers). Italy joined the Allies in 1915, and the United States joined them in 1917, helping tip the balance in favor of the Allies, who also drew on the populations and material of their colonial possessions.

Greek Orthodoxy Enduring form of Christianity that arose in the "Roman" state inherited from Constantine and Justinian and eventually split off from the Roman Catholic Church. The Greek Orthodox capital was Constantinople, and its spiritual empire included the Russian peoples, Baltic Slavs, and peoples living in southwest Asia.

Greek philosophers "Wisdom lovers" of the ancient Greek city-states, including Socrates, Plato, Aristotle, and others, who pondered such issues as self-knowledge, political engagement and withdrawal, and the order of the world.

Greenbacks Members of the American political party of the late nineteenth century that worked to advance the interest of farmers by promoting cheap money.

griots Counselors and other officials serving royal families in African kingdoms and also in small-scale states. They were also responsible for the preservation and transmission of oral histories and repositories of knowledge.

Group Areas Act (1950) Act that divided South Africa into separate racial and tribal areas and required Africans to live in their own separate communities, including the "homelands."

guerrillas Small groups engaged in irregular fighting against larger regular forces; after the French word *guerre*.

guest workers Migrants looking for temporary employment abroad.

gulag Administrative name for the forced labor and "reeducation" camps established first by the Soviet Union and then by other Soviet-style socialist countries. Penal labor was required of both ordinary criminals (rapists, murderers, thieves) and those accused of political crimes (counterrevolution, anti-Soviet agitation).

Gulf War (1991) Armed conflict between Iraq and a coalition of thirty-two nations, including the United States, Britain, Egypt, France, and Saudi Arabia. It was started by Iraq's invasion of Kuwait, which it had long claimed, on August 2, 1990.

gunpowder Explosive powder. By 1040, the first gunpowder recipes were being written down. Over the next 200 years, Song entrepreneurs invented several incendiary devices and techniques for controlling explosions.

gunpowder empires Muslim empires of the Ottomans, Safavids, and Mughals that used cannonry and gunpowder to advance their military causes.

Guomindang Nationalist party of China, founded just before World War I by Sun Yat-sen and later led by Chiang Kai-shek.

Habsburg dynasty Powerful medieval monarchs whose hereditary lands lay along the Danube River, but whose domains also included, for a time, Spain and the Low Countries. Habsburg princes were regularly elected Holy Roman Emperors. In 1556, Charles V abdicated and divided the empire, and the Habsburgs, into a Spanish branch and an Austrian branch. In 1867, the Austrian Empire was reorganized into the Austro-Hungarian Dual Monarchy, and in 1918 it collapsed.

Hadith Sayings attributed to the Prophet Muhammad and his early converts, used to guide the behavior of Muslim peoples.

Hagia Sophia Enormous and impressive church sponsored by Justinian and built starting in 532 CE. At the time, it was the largest church in the world.

hajj Pilgrimage to Mecca; an obligation for Muslims.

Hammurapi's Code Legal code created by Hammurapi, the most famous of the Mesopotamian rulers, who reigned from 1792 to 1750 BCE. Hammurapi sought to create social order by centralizing state authority and creating a grand legal structure that embodied paternal justice. The code was quite stratified, dividing society into three classes: free men, dependent men, and slaves, each with distinct rights and responsibilities.

Han agrarian ideal Guiding principle for the free peasantry that made up the base of Han society. In this system, peasants were honored for their labors, while merchants were subjected to a range of controls, including regulations on luxury consumption, and were belittled for not engaging in physical labor.

Han Chinese Inhabitants of China proper who considered others to be outsiders. They felt that they were the only authentic Chinese.

Han Fei Chinese state minister who lived from 280 to 223 BCE; he was a proponent and follower of Xunzi.

Hangzhou City and former provincial seaport that became the political center of the Chinese people in their ongoing struggles with northern steppe nomads. It was also one of China's gateways to the rest of the world by way of the South China Sea.

Han military Like its Roman counterpart, a ruthless military machine that expanded the empire and created stable conditions that permitted the safe transit of goods by caravan. Emperor Wu heavily influenced the transformation of the military forces and reinstituted a policy that made military service compulsory.

Hannibal Great Roman general from Carthage whose campaigns in the third century BCE swept from Spain toward the Italian Peninsula. He crossed the Pyrenees and the Alps mountain ranges with war elephants. He was unable, however, to defeat the Romans in 217 BCE.

Harappa One of two cities (the other was Mohenjo Daro) that, by 2500 BCE, began to take the place of villages throughout the Indus River valley. Each city covered an area of about 250 acres and probably housed 35,000 residents.

harem Secluded women's quarters in Muslim households.

Harlem Renaissance Cultural movement in the 1920s that was based in Harlem, a part of New York City with a large African American population; also referred to as the "New Negro Movement." The movement gave voice to black novelists, poets, painters, and musicians, many of whom used their art to protest racism.

harnesses Tools made from wood, bone, bronze, and iron for steering and controlling horses. Harnesses discovered by archaeologists reveal the evolution of headgear from simple mouth bits to full bridles with headpiece, mouthpiece, and reins.

Hatshepsut Ancient Egypt's most powerful woman ruler. Hatshepsut served as regent and pharaoh for her young son, Thutmosis III, whose reign began in 1479 BCE. She remained co-regent until her death.

Haussmannization Redevelopment and beautification of urban centers; named after the city planner who modernized mid-nineteenth-century Paris.

Heian period Period from 794 to 1185 CE, during which began the pattern of regents ruling Japan in the name of the sacred emperor.

Hellenism Process by which the individuality of the cultures of the earlier Greek city-states gave way to a uniform culture that stressed the common identity of all who embraced Greek ways. This culture emphasized the common denominators of language, style, and politics to which anyone anywhere in the Afro-Eurasian world could have access.

hieroglyphs One of two basic forms of Egyptian writing that were used in conjunction throughout antiquity. Hieroglyphs are pictorial symbols; the term derives from a Greek word meaning "sacred carving"—they were employed exclusively in temple, royal, and divine contexts. *See also* demotic writing.

Hijra Tradition of Islam whereby one withdraws from one's community to create another, more holy one. The practice is based on the Prophet Muhammad's withdrawal from the city of Mecca to Medina in 622 CE.

Hinayana (Lesser Vehicle) Buddhism Form of Buddhism that accepted the divinity of Buddha himself but not of demigods, or bodhisattvas.

Hinduism A refashioning of the ancient Brahmanic Vedic religion, bringing it in accord with rural life and agrarian values. It emerged as the dominant faith in Indian society in the third century CE. Believers became vegetarians and adopted rituals of self-sacrifice. Three major deities—Brahma, Vishnu, and Siva—formed a trinity representing the three phases of the universe (birth, existence, and destruction, respectively) and the three expressions of the eternal self, or *atma*.

Hindu revivalism Movement to reconfigure traditional Hinduism to be less diverse and more amenable to producing a narrowed version of Indian tradition.

Hiroshima Japanese port devastated by an atomic bomb on August 6, 1945.

Hitler, Adolf (1889–1945) German dictator and leader of the Nazi Party who seized power in Germany after its economic collapse in the Great Depression. Hitler and his Nazi regime started World War II in Europe and systematically murdered Jews and other non-Aryan groups in the name of racial purity.

Hittites One of the five great territorial states. The Hittites campaigned throughout Anatolia, then went east to northern Syria, though they eventually faced weaknesses in their own homeland. Their heyday was marked by the reign of the king Supiliulimua (1380 to 1345 BCE), who preserved the Hittites' influence on the balance of power in the region between Mesopotamia and the Nile.

Holocaust Deliberate racial extermination of the Jews by the Nazis that claimed the lives of approximately 6 million European Jews.

Holy Roman Empire Enormous confederation of polities that encompassed much of central Europe and aspired to be the Christian successor state to the Roman Empire. It was headed by a Holy Roman Emperor, usually a Habsburg prince, selected by elite lower-level sovereigns. Despite its size, the empire never effectively centralized power.

Holy Russia Name applied to Muscovy and then to the Russian Empire by Slavic Eastern Orthodox clerics who were appalled by the Muslim conquest in 1453 of Constantinople (the capital of Byzantium and of Eastern Christianity) and who were hopeful that Russia would become the new protector of the faith.

home charges Fees India was forced to pay to Britain as its colonial master. These fees included interest on railroad loans, salaries to colonial officers, and the maintenance of imperial troops outside India.

hominins Humanlike beings who walked erect and are represented today only by modern humans.

Homo Genus that includes modern ("true") humans and species of premodern hominins.

Homo caudatus "Tailed man," believed by some European Enlightenment thinkers to be an early species of humankind.

Homo erectus Species that emerged about 1.5 million years ago and had a large brain and walked truly upright. *Homo erectus* means "standing man."

Homo habilis Species name meaning "skillful man." Toolmaking ability made *Homo habilis* the forerunners, though very distant, of modern humans.

Homo sapiens The first humans; they emerged in a small region of Africa about 200,000 years ago and migrated out of Africa about 100,000 years ago. They had bigger brains and greater dexterity than previous hominin species, whom they eventually eclipsed. *Homo sapiens* means "wise man."

horses Animals used by full-scale nomadic communities to dominate the steppe lands in western Afro-Eurasia by the second millennium BCE. Horse-riding nomads moved their large herds across immense tracts of land within zones defined by rivers, mountains, and other natural geographical features. In the arid zones of central Eurasia, the nomadic economies made horses a crucial component of survival.

Huguenots French Protestants who endured severe persecution in the sixteenth and seventeenth centuries.

humanism The Renaissance aspiration to know more about the human experience beyond what the Christian scriptures offered by reaching back into ancient Greek and Roman texts.

Hundred Days' Reform (1898) Abortive modernizing reform program of the Qing government of China.

hunting and gathering Lifestyle in which food is acquired through hunting animals, fishing, and foraging for wild berries, nuts, fruit, and grains, rather than planting crops, vines, or trees. As late as 1500, as much as 15 percent of the world's population still obtained food by this method.

Hyksos A western Semitic-speaking people whose name means "Rulers of Foreign Lands"; they overthrew the unstable Thirteenth Dynasty in Egypt around 1640 BCE. The Hyksos had mastered the art of horse chariots, and with those chariots and their superior bronze axes and composite bows (made of wood, horn, and sinew), they were able to defeat the pharaoh's foot soldiers.

Ibn Sina Persian philosopher and physician who lived from 980 to 1037 CE. He was also schooled in the Quran, geometry, literature, and Indian and Euclidian mathematics. He was known in Europe as Avicenna.

ideology Dominant set of ideas of a widespread culture or movement.

Il Duce Term designating the fascist Italian leader Benito Mussolini.

Iliad Epic Greek poem about the Trojan War attributed to Homer and completed several centuries after the events it describes. It was based on oral tales passed down for generations.

Il-khanate Mongol-founded dynasty in the thirteenth century and based in Persia.

imam Muslim religious leader among Sunni Muslims. Shiites believe that imams are the rightful successors to the Prophet Muhammad through Ali, the son-in-law of Muhammad, and accord them much greater political and religious legitimacy than the Sunnis do.

imperialism Acquisition of new territories by a state and the incorporation of those territories into a political system as subordinate colonies.

Imperial University University founded in 136 BCE by Emperor Wu. Important discoveries and advances were made here, including rational diagnoses of the body's functions, the magnetic compass, and high-quality paper. The university was a mechanism by which the Han state inculcated Confucian thought into the elite.

imperium Latin word used to express Romans' power and command over their subjects. It is the basis of the English words *empire* and *imperialism.*

Inca Empire Empire of Quecha-speaking rulers in the Andean valley of Cuzco that encompassed a population of 4 to 6 million. The Incas lacked a clear inheritance system, causing an internal split that Pizarro's forces exploited in 1533.

Indian Institutes of Technology (IIT) Institutions originally designed as engineering schools to expand knowledge and to modernize India, which produced a whole generation of pioneering computer engineers, many of whom moved to the United States.

Indian National Congress Formed in 1885, an anticolonial party deeply committed to constitutional methods, nonviolent protest, and cultural nationalism.

Indian National Muslim League Founded in 1906, an organization dedicated to advancing the political interests of Muslims in India.

Indo-Greek Fusion of Indian and Greek culture in the area under the control of the Bactrians, in the northwestern region of India, around 200 BCE.

Indu What we would today call India. It was called "Indu" by Xuanzang, a Chinese Buddhist pilgrim who visited the area in the 630s and 640s CE.

indulgences Church-sponsored fund-raising mechanism that gave certification that one's sins had been forgiven in return for money.

industrial revolution Gradual accumulation and diffusion of old and new technical knowledge that led to major economic changes in Britain at the end of the eighteenth century and spread to northwestern Europe and North America in the nineteenth century. The industrial revolution catapulted these countries ahead of the rest of the world in manufacturing and agricultural output and standard of living.

industrious revolution Interpretation of seventeenth- and eighteenth-century economic change, developed by Jan de Vries, that attributes the origins of the industrial revolution to northern European householders' decisions to work harder and longer hours to produce more for the market, enabling them to increase their income and standard of living.

innovation Creation of a new method that allows humans to make better adaptations to their environment. Toolmaking was an important innovation.

Inquisition Tribunal of the Roman Catholic Church that enforced religious orthodoxy during the Protestant Reformation.

internal and external alchemy In Daoist ritual, use of trance and meditation (internal) or chemicals and drugs (external) to cause transformations in the self.

International Monetary Fund (IMF) Agency founded in 1944 to help restore financial order in Europe and the rest of the world, to revive international trade, and to support the financial concerns of Third World governments.

invisible hand As described in Adam Smith's *The Wealth of Nations,* the idea that the operations of a free market produce economic efficiency and economic benefits for all.

iron Malleable metal found in combined forms almost everywhere in the world. It became the most important and widely used metal in world history after the Bronze Age.

Iron Curtain Term popularized by Winston Churchill after World War II to refer to the political, economic, and ideological division within Europe between western Europe, under American influence, and eastern Europe, under the domination of the Soviet Union.

irrigation The supply of water, other than through rainfall, to land and crops, often by means of water sluices and channels in river floodplains, to increase agricultural production.

Islam A religion that dates to 610 CE, when Muhammad believed God came to him in a vision. Islam ("submission"—in this case, to the will of God) requires its followers to act righteously, to submit themselves to the one and only true God, and to care for the less fortunate. Muhammad's most insistent message was the oneness of God, a belief that has remained central to the Islamic faith ever since.

Jacobins Radical French political group that came into existence during the French Revolution and executed the French king and sought to remake French culture.

Jacquerie A general term for peasant revolts, taken from the 1358 French peasant revolt against nobles and their restrictions.

jade The most important precious substance in East Asia. Jade was associated with goodness, purity, luck, and virtue and was carved into such items as ceremonial knives, blade handles, religious objects, and elaborate jewelry.

Jagat Seths Enormous trading and banking empire in eastern India.

Jainism Along with Buddhism, one of the two systems of thought developed in the seventh century BCE that set themselves up against Brahmanism. Its founder, Vardhamana Mahavira, taught that the universe obeys its own everlasting rules that no god or other supernatural being could affect. The purpose of life was to purify one's soul in order to attain a state of permanent bliss, which could be accomplished through self-denial and the avoidance of harming other creatures.

Janissaries Corps of infantry soldiers recruited as children from the Christian provinces of the Ottoman Empire and brought up with intense loyalty to Islam, the Ottoman state, and its sultan. The Ottoman sultan used these forces to clip local autonomy and to serve as his personal bodyguards.

Jati Social groups as defined by Hinduism's caste system.

Jesuits Religious order founded by Ignatius Loyola in Spain in the middle of the sixteenth century to counter the inroads of the Protestant Reformation. The Jesuits, or the Society of Jesus, were active in politics, education, and missionary work.

jihad Literally, "striving" or "struggle." This word also connotes military efforts or "striving in the way of God." It also came to mean spiritual struggles against temptation or inner demons, especially in Sufi, or mystical, usage.

Jih-pen Chinese for "Japan."

Jim Crow laws Laws that codified racial segregation and inequality in the southern part of the United States after the Civil War.

jizya Special tax that non-Muslims were forced to pay to their Islamic rulers in return for which they were given security and property and granted cultural autonomy.

jong Large oceangoing vessels, built by Southeast Asians, which plied the regional trade routes from the fifteenth century to the early sixteenth century.

Judah The southern kingdom of David, which had been an Assyrian vassal until 612 BCE, when it became a vassal of Assyria's successor, Babylon, against whom the people of Judah rebelled, resulting in the destruction of Jerusalem in the sixth century BCE.

Julius Caesar (100–44 BCE) Formidable Roman general who was also a man of letters and a great orator. He incited a civil war in 49 BCE; victorious, he seized power and began a series of populist reforms. He was assassinated by Senators who feared he was becoming a dictator in 44 BCE.

junks Trusty seafaring vessels used in the South China Seas after 1000 CE. These vessels helped make shipping by sea less dangerous.

Justinian Roman (Byzantine) emperor who ascended to the throne in 527 CE. In addition to his many building projects and military expeditions, he issued a new law code.

Kabuki Theater performance that combines song, dance, and skillful staging to dramatize conflicts between duty and passion; originated in Tokogawa, Japan.

kamikaze Japanese for "divine winds" or typhoons, such as the storm that saved Japan from a Mongol attack. The term also was used for Japanese suicide bombers during World War II.

kanun Highly detailed system of Ottoman administrative law that jurists developed to deal with matters not treated in the religious law of Islam.

Karim Loose confederation of shippers banding together to protect convoys.

karma Literally, "fate" or "action" in Confucian thought; this is a universal principle of cause and effect.

Kassites Nomads who entered Mesopotamia from the eastern Zagros Mountains and the Iranian plateau as early as 2000 BCE. They gradually integrated into Babylonian society by officiating at temples. By 1745 BCE, they had asserted order over the region, and they controlled southern Mesopotamia for the next 350 years, creating one of the territorial states.

Keynesian Revolution Economic ideas developed by British economist John Maynard Keynes during the Great Depression, wherein the state took a greater role in managing the economy, stimulating it by increasing the money supply and creating jobs. These ideas were only adopted by state policymakers after World War II.

KGB Soviet political police and spy agency, formed as the Cheka soon after the Bolshevik coup in October 1917 and known during the Stalinist period as the NKVD. The KGB grew to more than 750,000 operatives with military rank by the 1980s.

khan Ruler who was acclaimed at an assembly of elites and supposedly descended from Chinggis Khan on the male line; those not descended from Chinggis continually faced challenges to their legitimacy.

Khanate Major political unit of the vast Mongol Empire. There were four Khanates, including the Yuan Empire in China, forged by Chinggis Khan's grandson Kubilai.

Kharijites Radical sect from the early days of Islam. The Kharijites seceded from the "party of Ali" (who themselves came to be known as the Shiites) because of disagreements over succession to the role of caliph. The Kharjites were known for their strict militant piety.

Khmers A people who created the most powerful empire in Southwest Asia between the tenth and thirteenth centuries in what is modern-day Cambodia.

Khomeini, Ayatollah Ruhollah (1902–1989) Iranian religious leader who used his traditional Islamic education and his training in Muslim ethics to accuse the shah's government of gross violations of Islamic norms. He also identified the shah's ally, America, as the Great Satan. The shah fled the country in 1979; in his wake, Khomeini established a theocratic state ruled by a council of Islamic clerics.

Khufu The second pharaoh of the Fourth Dynasty in ancient Egypt (2575–2465 BCE), who constructed the Great Pyramid, the largest stone structure in the world. The pyramid is located in an area called Giza, just outside modern-day Cairo.

Khusro I Anoshirwan Sasanian emperor who reigned from 530 to 579 CE. He was a model ruler and was seen as the personification of justice.

Kiev City that became one of the greatest cities of Europe after the eleventh century. It was built to be a small-scale Constantinople on the Dnieper River.

Kikuyu Kenya's largest ethnic group; organizers of a revolt against the British in the 1950s.

King, Martin Luther, Jr. (1929–1968) Civil rights leader who borrowed his most effective weapon—the commitment to nonviolent protest and the appeal to conscience—from Gandhi.

Kingdom of Awadh One of the most prized lands for annexation and the fertile, opulent, and traditional vestige of Mughal rule in India.

Kingdom of Jerusalem A Crusader state established in Palestine in 1099 CE after the First Crusade. The kingdom lasted until 1187, when it was destroyed by Saladin.

Kizilbash Mystical, Turkish-speaking tribesmen who facilitated the Safavid rise to power.

Knossos Area in Crete where, during the second millennium BCE, a primary palace town existed.

***Koine* Greek** Common form of Greek that became the international spoken and written language in the Hellenistic world. This was a simpler everyday form of the ancient Greek language.

Köprülü reforms Reforms named after two grand viziers who revitalized the Ottoman Empire in the seventeenth century through administrative and budget trimming as well as by rebuilding the military.

Korean War (1950–1953) Cold War conflict between Soviet-backed North Korea and U.S.- and UN-backed South Korea. The two sides seesawed back and forth over the same boundaries until 1953, when an armistice divided the country at roughly the same spot as at the start of the war. Nothing had been gained. Losses, however, included 33,000 Americans, at least 250,000 Chinese, and up to 3 million Koreans.

Koryo dynasty Leading dynasty of the northern-based Koryo kingdom in Korea. It is from this dynasty that the name Korea derives.

Kremlin Once synonymous with the Soviet government; refers to Moscow's walled city center.

Kshatriyas The military caste, one of the four Hindu castes, which was supposed to protect society by fighting in times of warfare and governing in times of peace.

Kubilai Khan (1215–1294) Mongol leader who seized southern China after 1260 and founded the Yuan dynasty.

Ku Klux Klan Racist organization that first emerged in the U.S. South after the Civil War and then gained national strength as a radically traditionalist movement during the 1920s.

kulak Originally a pejorative word used to designate better-off peasants, the term used in the late 1920s and early 1930s to refer to any peasant, rich or poor, perceived as an opponent of the Soviet regime; Russian for "fist."

Kumarajiva Renowned Buddhist scholar and missionary who lived from 344 to 413 CE. He was brought to China by Chinese regional forces from Kucha, modern-day Xinjiang.

Kushans Northern nomadic group that migrated into South Asia in 50 CE. They unified the tribes of the region and set up the Kushan dynasty. The Kushans' empire embraced a large and diverse territory and played a critical role in the formation of the Silk Road.

Labour Party Founded in Britain in 1900, a party that has drawn its support from workers and has espoused moderately socialist principles.

laissez-faire The concept that the economy works best when it is left alone—that is, when the state does not regulate or interfere with the workings of the market.

"Land under the Yoke of Ashur" Lands not in Assyria proper, but under its authority. The inhabitants had to make exorbitant tribute payments to the Assyrian Empire.

language families Related tongues with a common ancestral origin. Language families contain languages that diverged from one another but share grammatical features and a root vocabulary. More than a hundred language families exist.

Laozi Also known as Master Lao; perhaps a contemporary of Confucius and the person after whom Daoism is named. His thought was elaborated upon by generations of thinkers.

latifundia Broad estates that produced goods for large urban markets, including wheat, grapes, olives, cattle, and sheep.

Laws of Manu Part of the handiwork of Brahman priests; a representative code of law that incorporated social sanctions and practices and provided guidance for living within the caste system.

League of Nations Organization founded after World War I to solve international disputes through arbitration; it was dissolved in 1946, and its assets were transferred to the United Nations.

Legalism Also called Statism, a system of thought about how to live an ordered life. It was developed by Master Xun, or Xunzi (310–237 BCE). It is based on the principle that people, being inherently inclined toward evil, require authoritarian control to regulate their behavior.

Lenin, Vladimir (1870–1924) Leader of the Bolshevik Revolution in Russia and the first leader of the Soviet Union.

Liangzhu Culture spanning centuries from the fourth to the third millennium BCE that represented the last New Stone Age culture in the Yangzi River delta. One of the Ten Thousand States, it was highly stratified and is known for its jade objects.

liberalism Political and social theory that advocates representative government, individual rights, free trade, and freedom of speech and religion.

limited-liability joint-stock company Company that mobilizes capital from a large number of investors, called shareholders, who were not to be held personally liable for financial losses incurred by the company.

Linear A and B Two linear scripts first discovered on Crete in 1900. On the island of Crete and on the mainland areas of Greece, documents of the palace-centered societies were written on clay tablets in these two scripts. Linear A script, apparently written in Minoan, has not yet been deciphered. Linear B was first deciphered in the early 1950s.

"Little Europes" Urban landscapes between 1100 and 1200 CE composed of castles, churches, and towns in what are today Poland, the Czech Republic, Hungary, and the Baltic states.

Little Ice Age Period of global cooling beginning at the close of the Medieval Warm Period and lasting for centuries. The most extreme drop in temperature was in the 1600s.

Liu Bang Chinese emperor from 206 to 195 BCE. After declaring himself the prince of his home area of Han, in 202 BCE, Liu declared himself the first Han emperor.

llamas Animals similar in utility and function to camels in Afro-Eurasia. Llamas can carry heavy loads for long distances.

Long March (1934–1935) Trek of over 10,000 kilometers by Mao Zedong and his communist followers to establish a new base of operations in northwestern China.

Longshan peoples Peoples who lived in small agricultural and river-basin villages in East Asia at the end of the third millennium BCE. They set the stage for the Shang in terms of a centralized state, urban life, and a cohesive culture.

lord Privileged landowner who exercised authority over the people who lived on his land.

lost generation The 17 million former members of the Red Guard and other Chinese youth who were denied education from the late 1960s to the mid-1970s as part of the Chinese government's attempt to prevent political disruptions.

Louisiana Purchase (1803) American purchase of French territory from Napoleon, including much of the present-day United States between the Mississippi River and the Rocky Mountains.

Lucy Relatively intact skeleton of a young adult female australopithecine unearthed in the valley of the Awash River in 1974 and nicknamed Lucy. Lucy walked upright at least some of the time, and her jaw and teeth were humanlike. Until recently, Lucy was the oldest hominin skeleton ever discovered.

Luftwaffe German air force.

Luther, Martin (1483–1546) A German monk and theologian who sought to reform the Catholic Church. He believed in salvation through faith alone, the importance of reading Scripture, and the priesthood of all believers. His Ninety-Five Theses, written in 1517, enumerated the abuses by the Catholic Church and catalyzed a movement that became the Protestant Reformation.

Maastricht Treaty (1992) Treaty that formed the European Union, an integrated trading and financial bloc with its own bureaucracy and elected representatives.

Ma'at Term used in ancient Egypt to refer to stability or order, the achievement of which was the primary task of Egypt's ruling kings, the pharaohs.

Maccabees Leaders of a riot in Jerusalem in 166 BCE. The riot was a response to a Roman edict outlawing the practice of Judaism.

Madhyamika (Middle Way) Buddhism Chinese branch of Mahayana Buddhism established by Kumarajiva (344–413 CE) that used irony and paradox to show that reason is limited.

madrassas Higher schools of Muslim education that taught law, the Quran, religious sciences, and the foreign sciences.

Mahayana Buddhism School of Buddhist theology that believed that the Buddha was a deity, unlike previous groups that had considered him a wise human being.

Mahdi The "chosen one" in Islam whose appearance was supposed to foretell the end of the world and the final day of reckoning for all people.

maize A grain crop, also known as corn, that the settled agrarian communities across the Americas cultivated, along with legumes (beans) and tubers (potatoes).

Maji-Maji Revolt (early 1900s) Swahili insurrection against German colonialists, inspired by the belief that those who were anointed with specially blessed water (*maji*) would be immune to bullets. It resulted in 200,000 to 300,000 African deaths.

Mali Empire West African empire, founded by the legendary king Sundiata in the early thirteenth century and lasting until the beginning of the seventeenth century. It facilitated thriving commerce, with routes linking the Atlantic Ocean, the Sahara, and beyond.

Mamluks Military men who ruled Egypt as an independent regime from 1250 until the Ottoman conquest in 1517.

Manaus Opera House Opera house built in the interior of Brazil in a lucrative rubber-growing area at the turn of the twentieth century.

Manchukuo Japanese puppet state in Manchuria in the 1930s.

Manchus Descendants of the Jurchens, who helped the Ming army recapture Beijing in 1644 after its seizure by the outlaw Li Zicheng. The Manchus numbered around 1 million but controlled a domain that included perhaps 250 million people. Their rule lasted more than 250 years and became known as the Qing dynasty.

mandate of heaven Ideology established by Zhou dynasts to communicate the moral transfer of power. Originally a pact between the Zhou people and their supreme god, it evolved in the first century BCE into Chinese political doctrine.

Mande A people who lived in the area between the bend in the Senegal River and the bend in the Niger River east to west and from the Senegal River and Bandama River north to south. Also known as the Mandinka, their civilization emerged around 1100 CE, and their merchants were deeply involved in long-distances trade throughout the region.

Mandela, Nelson (1918–2013) Leader of the African National Congress (ANC) who was imprisoned for more than two decades by the apartheid regime in South Africa for his political beliefs. Worldwide protests led to his release in 1990. In 1994, Mandela won the presidency in South Africa's first free mass elections.

Manifest Destiny Belief that it was God's will for the American people to expand their economic and political dominion across the North American continent.

manorialism System in which the manor (a lord's home, its associated industry, and surrounding fields) served as the basic unit of economic power; an alternative to feudalism (a term primarily used to describe political and hierarchical relationships of king, lords, and peasantry) for thinking about the nature of power in western Europe, 1000–1300.

Mao Zedong (1893–1976) Chinese communist leader who rose to power during the Long March (1934). In 1949, he defeated the Nationalists and established a communist regime in China. Mao's efforts to transform China, such as the industrialization program of 1958 (known as the Great Leap Forward) and the Cultural Revolution of 1966, failed and brought great suffering to the people, but he has been credited with instilling China with a sense of purpose after decades of political and economic weakness.

maroon community Sanctuary for runaway slaves in the Americas.

Marshall Plan Economic aid package given by the United States to certain European nations after World War II in hopes of a rapid period of reconstruction and economic gain, thereby securing those countries from a communist takeover.

martyrs People executed by the Roman authorities for persisting in their Christian beliefs and refusing to submit to pagan ritual or belief.

Marx, Karl (1818–1883) German philosopher and economist who, together with Friedrich Engels, founded the first International Working Mens' Association and developed the economic and political theories we now call Marxism.

Marxism Form of scientific socialism created by Karl Marx and Friedrich Engels that was rooted in a materialist theory of history: what mattered in history was what ordinary people ate and how they lived and worked, not political events or philosophies. Marx believed that capitalism enslaved workers, and he predicted that eventually a revolution of the working classes would overthrow the capitalist order and create a classless society.

mass consumption Increased purchasing power in the early twentieth-century prosperous and mainly middle-class societies, stemming from mass production.

mass culture Distinctive form of popular culture that arose in the wake of World War I. It reflected the tastes of the working and the middle classes, who now had more time and money to spend on entertainment, and relied on new technologies, especially film and radio, which could reach an entire nation's population and consolidate their sense of being a single state.

mass production System in which factories were set up to produce huge quantities of identical products, reflecting the early twentieth-century world's demands for greater volume, faster speed, reduced cost, and standardized output.

mastaba Word meaning "bench" in Arabic; it refers to a huge flat structure identical to earlier royal tombs of ancient Egypt.

Mau Mau Revolt (1952–1957) Kenyan uprising orchestrated by a guerrilla movement of the Kikuyu peoples. This conflict forced the British to grant independence to the black majority in Kenya.

Mauryan Empire Dynasty extended by the Mauryans from 321 to 184 BCE, from the Indus Valley to the northwest areas of South Asia, in a region previously controlled by Persia. It was the first large-scale empire in South Asia and was to become the model for future Indian empires.

Mawali Non-Arab "clients" attached to Arab patrons in the early Islamic Empire. Because patronage was so much a part of the Arabian cultural system, non-Arabs who converted to Islam affiliated themselves with extended Muslim families and became clients of those groups.

Maxim gun European weapon capable of firing many bullets per second; it was used against Africans in the conquest of the continent.

Maya Civilization that ruled over large stretches of Mesoamerica, composed of a series of kingdoms, each built around ritual centers rather than cities. The Maya were not defined by a great ruler or one capital city, but by their shared religious beliefs.

McCarthyism Campaign by Republican senator Joseph McCarthy in the late 1940s and early 1950s to uncover closet communists, particularly in the State Department and in Hollywood.

Meat Inspection Act (1906) Legislation that provided for government supervision of meat-packing operations. It was part of the broader Progressive Movement dedicated to correcting the negative consequences of urbanization and industrialization in the United States.

Mecca Arabian city in which Muhammad was born. Mecca was a trading center and pilgrimage destination in the pre-Islamic and Islamic periods. Exiled in 622 CE because of resistance to his message, Muhammad returned to Mecca in 630 CE and claimed the city for Islam.

Medes Rivals of the Assyrians and the Persians. The Medes inhabited the area from the Zagros Mountains to the modern city of Tehran. Although expert horsemen and archers, they were eventually defeated by the Persians.

megaliths Literally, "great stones." The word *megalith* is used when describing a structure such as Stonehenge, a massive structure that is the result of cooperative planning and work.

megarons Large buildings found in Troy (level II) that are the predecessors of the classic Greek temple.

Meiji Empire Empire created under the leadership of Mutsuhito, emperor of Japan from 1868 until 1912. During the Meiji period, Japan became a world industrial and naval power.

Meiji Restoration Reign of the Meiji emperor, which was characterized by a new nationalist identity, economic advances, and political transformation.

Mencius Disciple of Confucius who lived from 372 to 289 BCE.

mercantilism Economic theory developed in Europe in the seventeenth century based on the idea that the world had a fixed amount of wealth, which meant that one country's wealth came at the expense of another's. Mercantilism encouraged the placing of tariffs on imports and the founding of colonies to enrich the mother countries and in this way drove European empire building.

Mercosur Free trade pact between the governments of Argentina, Brazil, Paraguay, and Uruguay.

meritocracy Rule by persons of talent.

Meroe Ancient kingdom in what is today Sudan. It flourished for nearly a thousand years, from the fifth century BCE to the fifth century CE.

mestizos Mixed-blood offspring of Spanish settlers and native Indians.

métis Mixed-blood offspring of French settlers and native Indians.

Mexican Revolution (1910) Conflict fueled by the unequal distribution of land and by disgruntled workers; it erupted when political elites split over the succession of General Porfirio Díaz after decades of his rule. The fight lasted over ten years and cost 1 million lives, but it resulted in widespread reform and a new constitution.

Mfecane **movement** African political revolts in the first half of the nineteenth century that were caused by the expansionist methods of King Shaka of the Zulu people.

microsocieties Small-scale communities that had little interaction with others. These communities were the norm for peoples living in the Americas and islanders in the Pacific and Aegean from 2000 to 1200 BCE.

migration Long-distance travel for the purpose of resettlement. In the case of early humans, the need to move was usually a response to an environmental shift, such as climate change during the Ice Age.

millenarian Convinced of the imminent coming of a just and ideal society.

millenarian movement Broad, popular upheaval calling for the restoration of a bygone moral age, often led by charismatic spiritual prophets.

millets Minority religious communities of the Ottoman Empire.

minaret Slender tower within a mosque from which Muslims are called to prayer.

minbar Pulpit inside a mosque from which Muslim religious speakers broadcast their message to the faithful.

Minoans A people who built a large number of elaborate, independent palace centers on Crete, at Knossos, and elsewhere around 2000 BCE. Named after the legendary King Minos, said to have ruled Crete at the time, they sailed throughout the Mediterranean and by 1600 BCE had planted colonies on many Aegean islands, which in turn became trading and mining centers.

mission civilisatrice Term French colonizers used to refer to France's form of "rationalized" colonial rule, which attempted to bring "civilization" to the "uncivilized."

mitochondrial DNA Form of DNA found outside the nucleus of cells, where it serves as cells' microscopic power packs. Examining mitochondrial DNA enables researchers to measure the genetic variation among living objects, including human beings.

Moche A people who extended their power and increased their wealth at the height of the Chimu Empire over several valleys in what is now modern-day Peru.

Model T First automobile, manufactured by the Ford Motor Company, to be priced reasonably enough to be sold to the masses.

modernism Term used to describe artistic, literary, and scientific movements of the late nineteenth and early twentieth centuries that self-consciously broke with traditional rules, practices, and forms of thought.

modernists A generation of exuberant young artists, writers, and scientists in the late nineteenth century who broke with older conventions and sought new ways of seeing and describing the world.

Mohism School of thought in ancient China, named after Mo Di, or Mozi, who lived from 479 to 438 BCE. It emphasized one's obligation to society as a whole, not just to one's immediate family or social circle.

monarchy Political system in which one individual holds supreme power and passes that power on to his or her next of kin.

monasticism Christian way of life that originated in Egypt and was practiced as early as 300 CE in the Mediterranean. The word comes from the Greek *monos*, referring to a person "living alone" without marriage or family.

monetization An economic shift from a barter-based economy to one dependent on coin.

Mongols Combination of nomadic forest and prairie peoples who lived by hunting and livestock herding and were expert horsemen. Beginning in 1206, the Mongols launched a series of conquests that brought far-flung parts of the world together under their rule. By incorporating conquered peoples and adapting some of their customs, the Mongols created an empire of four khanate states that stretched from the Pacific Ocean to the shores of the eastern Mediterranean and the southern steppes of Eurasia.

monotheism The belief in only one god.

Moors Term employed by Europeans in the medieval period to refer to Muslim occupants of North Africa, the western Sahara, and the Iberian Peninsula.

mosque Place of worship for the people of Islam.

"Mound people" Name for the people of Cahokia, since the landscape was dominated by earthen monuments in the shapes of mounds. The mounds were carefully maintained and were the loci from which Cahokians paid respect to spiritual forces. *See also* Cahokia.

Mu Chinese ruler (956–918 BCE) who put forth a formal bureaucratic system of governance, appointing officials, supervisors, and military captains to whom he was not related. He also instituted a formal legal code.

muckrakers Journalists who aimed to expose political and commercial corruption in late nineteenth- and early twentieth-century America.

muftis Experts on Muslim religious law.

Mughal Empire One of Islam's greatest regimes. Established in 1526, it was a vigorous, centralized state whose political authority encompassed most of modern-day India. During the sixteenth century, it had a population of between 100 and 150 million.

Muhammad (c. 570–632 CE) Prophet and founder of the Islamic faith. Born in Mecca in the Arabian Peninsula and orphaned when young, Muhammad lived under the protection of his uncle. His career as a prophet began around 610 CE, with his first experience of spiritual revelation.

Muhammad Ali Ruler of Egypt between 1805 and 1848. He initiated a set of modernizing reforms that sought to make Egypt competitive with the great powers.

mullahs Religious leaders in Iran who in the 1970s led a movement opposing Shah Reza Pahlavi and denounced American materialism and secularism.

multinational corporations Corporations based in many different countries that have global investment, trading, and distribution goals.

Muscovy The principality of Moscow. Originally a mixture of Slavs, Finnish tribes, Turkic speakers, and many others, Muscovy used territorial expansion and commercial networks to consolidate a powerful state and expanded to become the Russian Empire, a huge realm that spanned parts of Europe, much of northern Asia, numerous North Pacific islands, and even—for a time—a corner of North America (Alaska).

Muslim Brotherhood Egyptian organization founded in 1928 by Hassan al-Banna. It attacked liberal democracy as a cover for middle-class, business, and landowning interests and fought for a return to a purified Islam.

Muslim League National Muslim party of India.

Mussolini, Benito (1883–1945) Italian dictator and founder of the fascist movement in Italy. During World War II, he allied Italy with Germany and Japan.

Muwahhidin Term meaning "unitarians," or believers in one God, these were followers of the Wahhabi movement that emerged in the Arabian Peninsula in the eighteenth century.

Mycenaeans Mainland competitors of the Minoans; they took over Crete around 1400 BCE. Migrating to Greece from central Europe, they brought their Indo-European language, horse chariots, and metalworking skills, which they used to dominate until 1200 BCE.

Nagasaki Second Japanese city to be hit by an atomic bomb near the end of World War II.

Napoleonic Code Legal code drafted by Napoleon in 1804; it distilled different legal traditions to create one uniform law. The code confirmed the abolition of feudal privileges of all kinds and set the conditions for exercising property rights.

National Assembly of France Governing body of France that succeeded the Estates-General in 1789 during the French Revolution. It was composed of, and defined by, the delegates of the Third Estate.

National Association for the Advancement of Colored People (NAACP) Founded in 1910, the U.S. civil rights organization dedicated to ending inequality and segregation for black Americans.

nationalism The idea that members of a shared community called a "nation" should have sovereignty within the borders of their state.

National Recovery Administration (NRA) New Deal agency created in 1933 to prepare codes of fair administration and to plan for public works. It was later declared unconstitutional.

nation-state Form of political organization that derived legitimacy from its inhabitants, often referred to as citizens, who in theory, if not always in practice, shared a common language, culture, and history.

native learning Japanese movement to promote nativist intellectual traditions and the celebration of Japanese texts.

native paramountcy British form of "rationalized" colonial rule, which attempted to bring "civilization" to the "uncivilized" by proclaiming that when the interests of European settlers in Africa clashed with those of the African population, the latter should take precedence.

natural rights Belief that emerged in eighteenth-century western Europe and North America that rights fundamental to human nature are discernible to reason and should be affirmed in human-made law.

natural selection Charles Darwin's theory that populations grow faster than the food supply, creating a "struggle for existence" among species in which nature selects which individuals are "fittest" to survive and reproduce.

Nazis National Socialist German Workers Party; German organization founded after World War I and dedicated to winning workers over from socialism to nationalism. The first Nazi Party platform combined nationalism with anti-capitalism and anti-Semitism.

Neanderthals Members of an early wave of hominins from Africa who settled in western Afro-Eurasia, in an area reaching from present-day Uzbekistan and Iraq to Spain, approximately 150,000 years ago.

needle compass Chinese invention made available to navigators after 1000 CE that helped guide sailors on the high seas.

Negritos Hunter-gatherer inhabitants of the East Asian coastal islands who migrated there around 28,000 BCE but by 2000 BCE had been replaced by new migrants.

Negritude Statement of the virtues of the black identity and the validation of African culture and the African past, even in a westernizing world. This idea was shaped by African and African American intellectuals like Senegal's first president, Léopold Sédar Senghor.

Nehemiah Jewish eunuch of the Persian court who was given permission to rebuild the fortification walls around the city of Jerusalem from 440 to 437 BCE.

Neo-Assyrian Empire Afro-Eurasian empire that dominated around 950 BCE. The Neo-Assyrians extended their control over resources and people beyond their own borders, and their empire lasted for three centuries.

neocolonialism Contemporary geopolitical policy or practice in which a politically, economically, and often militarily superior nation asserts control over a country that remains nominally sovereign.

Nestorian Christians Denomination of Christians whose beliefs about Christ differed from those of the official Byzantine church. Named after Nestorius, former bishop of Constantinople, they emphasized the human aspects of Jesus.

New Deal President Franklin Delano Roosevelt's set of government reforms enacted during the 1930s to provide jobs for the unemployed, social welfare programs for the poor, and security to the financial markets.

New Economic Policy (NEP) Enacted decrees of the Bolsheviks between 1921 and 1927 that grudgingly sanctioned private trade and private property.

New Negro Movement *See* Harlem Renaissance.

New World Term applied to the Americas that reflected the Europeans' view that anything previously unknown to them was "new," even if it had existed and supported societies long before European explorers arrived on its shores.

nirvana Literally, nonexistence; the state of complete liberation from the concerns of worldly life, as in Buddhist thought.

Noble Eightfold Path Buddhist concept of a way of life by which people may rid themselves of individual desire to achieve nirvana. The path consists of wisdom, ethical behavior, and mental discipline.

Noh drama Masked theater favored by Japanese bureaucrats and regional lords during the Tokugawa period.

Nok culture Spectacular culture that arose in the sixth century BCE in what is today Nigeria. Iron smelting occurred there around 600 BCE. Thus, the Nok people made the transition from stone to iron materials.

nomads People who move across vast distances without settling permanently in a particular place. Pastoralists, nomads, and transhumant herders introduced new forms of chariot-based warfare that transformed the Afro-Eurasian world.

nongovernmental organizations (NGOs) Term used to refer to private organizations like the Red Cross that play a large role in international affairs.

nonviolent resistance *Satyagraha*; moral and political philosophy developed by Indian National Congress leader Mohandas Gandhi and taken up by other reformers, such as Martin Luther King Jr. Gandhi believed that if Indians pursued self-reliance and self-control in a nonviolent way, the British would eventually have to leave.

North American Free Trade Agreement (NAFTA) Treaty negotiated in the early 1990s to promote free trade between Canada, the United States, and Mexico.

North Atlantic Treaty Organization (NATO) International organization set up in 1949 to provide for the defense of western European countries and the United States from the perceived Soviet threat.

Northern Wei dynasty Regime founded in 386 CE by the Tuoba, a people originally from Inner Mongolia, that lasted one and a half centuries. The rulers of this dynasty adopted many practices of the earlier Chinese Han regime. At the same time, they struggled to consolidate authority over their own nomadic people. Ultimately, several decades of intense internal conflict led to the dynasty's downfall.

Northwest Passage Long-sought marine passageway between the Atlantic and Pacific Oceans.

Oceania Collective name for the lands of Australia and New Zealand and the islands of the southwestern Pacific Ocean.

Odyssey Composed in the eighth century BCE and attributed to Homer, an epic tale of the journey of Odysseus, who traveled the Mediterranean back to his home in Ithaca after the siege of Troy.

oikos The word for "small family unit" in ancient Greece, similar to *familia* in Rome. Its structure, with men as heads of household over women and children, embodied the fundamental power structure in Greek city-states.

oligarchy Clique of privileged rulers.

Olmecs A people who emerged around 1500 BCE and lived in Mesoamerica. The name means those who "lived in the land of the rubber." Olmec society was composed of decentralized villages. Its members spoke the same language and worshipped the same gods.

Open Door Policy Policy proposed by American Secretary of State John Hay in the late nineteenth century to make sure that the United States, along with other foreign nations, would have equal access to trade with China.

Opium War (1839–1842) War fought between the British and Qing China over British trade in opium. China's loss resulted in the granting to the British the right to trade in five different ports and the ceding of Hong Kong to the British.

oracle bones Animal bones used by Shang diviners. Diviners applied intense heat to the shoulder bones of cattle or to turtle shells, which caused them to crack. The diviners would then interpret the cracks as signs from the ancestors regarding royal plans and actions.

Organization of Petroleum Exporting Countries (OPEC) International association established in 1960 to coordinate price and supply policies of oil-producing states.

Orientalism Genre of literature and painting that portrayed the nonwestern peoples of North Africa and Asia as exotic, sensuous, and economically and culturally backward with respect to Europeans.

Orientalists Western scholars who specialized in the study of the East.

Orrorin tugenensis Predecessor to hominins that first appeared 6 million years ago.

Ottoman Empire Domain that encompassed Anatolia, the Arab world, and much of southern and eastern Europe in the early sixteenth century. Ottoman leaders transformed themselves from nomadic warriors who roamed the borderlands between Islamic and Christian worlds in Anatolia into sovereigns of a vast, bureaucratic empire. The Ottomans embraced a Sunni view of Islam. They adapted traditional Byzantine governmental practices but tried new ways of integrating the diverse peoples of their empire.

Pacific War (1879–1883) War between Chile and the alliance of Bolivia and Peru.

palace Official residence of the ruler, his family, and his entourage, first appearing around 2500 BCE. Eventually, palaces became defining landmarks of city life and sources of power rivaling temples.

Palace of Versailles The palace complex, 11 miles away from the French capital of Paris, built by Louis XIV in the 1670s and 1680s to house and entertain his leading clergymen and nobles, with the hopes of diverting them from plotting against him.

Palmyra Roman trading depot in what is modern-day Syria; part of a network of trading cities that connected various regions of Afro-Eurasia.

pan movements Movements that sought to link people across state boundaries in new communities based on ethnicity or, in some cases, religion (e.g., pan-Germanism, pan-Islamism, pan-Slavism).

papacy The institution of the pope; the Catholic spiritual leader in Rome.

papal Of, relating to, or issued by a pope.

Parthians Horse-riding people who pushed southward around the middle of the second century BCE and wiped out the Greek kingdoms in Iran. They then extended their power all the way to the Mediterranean, where they ran up against the Roman Empire in Anatolia and Mesopotamia.

pastoralism Herding and breeding of sheep and goats or other animals as a primary means of subsistence.

pastoral nomads Groups of people who moved their domesticated animals from place to place to meet the animals' demanding grazing requirements. Around 3500 BCE, western Afro-Eurasia witnessed the growth and spread of pastoral nomadic communities.

paterfamilias From the Latin for "father of the family," the foundation of the Roman social order.

patria Latin, meaning "fatherland."

patrons In the Roman system of patronage, men and women of wealth and high social status who protected dependents or "clients" of a lower class.

Pax Mongolica Term that refers to the political and especially the commercial stability that the vast Mongol Empire provided for the travelers and merchants of Eurasia during the thirteenth and fourteenth centuries.

Pax Romana Latin for "Roman Peace"; refers to the period between 25 BCE and 235 CE, during which conditions in the Roman Empire were settled and peaceful.

Pax Sinica Period of peace (149–87 BCE) during which agriculture, commerce, and industry flourished in East Asia under the rule of the Han.

Peace Preservation Act (1925) Act instituted in Japan that specified up to ten years' hard labor for any member of an organization advocating a basic change in the political system or the abolition of private property.

Pearl Harbor American naval base in Hawaii on which the Japanese launched a surprise attack on December 7, 1941, bringing the United States into World War II.

Peloponnesian War War fought between 431 and 404 BCE between two of Greece's most powerful city-states, Athens and Sparta.

peninsulars Spaniards who, although born in Spain, resided in the Spanish colonial territories. They regarded themselves as superior to Spaniards born in the colonies (creoles).

Peninsular War (1808–1814) Conflict in which the Portuguese and Spanish populations, supported by the British, resisted the French invasion of the Iberian Peninsula by Napoleon.

Peoples' Charter Document calling for universal suffrage for adult males, the secret ballot, electoral districts, and annual parliamentary elections. It was signed by over 3 million British between 1839 and 1842.

periplus Book that reflected sailing knowledge; in such books captains would record landing spots and ports. The word *periplus* literally means "sailing around."

Persepolis Darius I's capital city in the highlands of Fars; a ceremonial center and expression of imperial identity as well as an important administrative hub.

Peterloo Massacre (1819) The killing of 11 and wounding of 460 following a peaceful demonstration for political reform by workers in Manchester, England.

Petra City in modern-day Jordan that was the Nabataean capital. It profited greatly by supplying provisions and water to travelers and traders. Many of its houses and shrines were cut into the rocky mountains. *Petra* means "rock."

phalanx Military formation used by Philip II of Macedonia, whereby heavily armored infantry were closely arrayed in battle formation. Term also used by Charles Fourier to describe a well-ordered utopian community.

Philip II of Macedonia Father of Alexander the Great, under whose rule Macedonia developed into a large ethnic and territorial state. After unifying Macedonia, Philip went on to conquer neighboring states but was assassinated in 336 BCE at the age of 46.

philosophes Enlightenment thinkers who applied scientific reasoning to human interaction and society.

philosophia Literally, "love of wisdom." This system of thought originally included speculation by Greek thinkers on the nature of the cosmos, the environment, and human existence. It eventually came to include thought about the nature of humans and life in society.

Phoenicians Known as the Canaanites in the Bible, an ethnic group in the Levant under Assyrian rule in the seventh century BCE; they provided ships and sailors for battles in the Mediterranean. The name *Phoenician* means "purple people," referring to the purple dye they manufactured and widely traded, along with other commercial goods and services, throughout the Mediterranean. Their major contribution was the alphabet, first introduced in the second millennium BCE, which made far-reaching communication possible.

phonemes Primary and distinctive sounds that are characteristic of human language.

piety Strong sense of religious duty and devoutness, often inspiring extraordinary actions.

plant domestication Process of growing plants, harvesting their seeds, and saving some of the seeds for planting in subsequent growing cycles, resulting in a steady food supply. This process occurred as far back as 5000 BCE, when plants began to naturally retain their seeds. Plant domestication was practiced first in the southern Levant and spread from there into the rest of Southwest Asia.

Plato (427–347 BCE) Disciple of the great philosopher Socrates; his works are the only record we have of Socrates' teaching. He was also the author of formative philosophical works on ethics and politics.

plebs In ancient Rome, term that referred to the "common people." Their interests were protected by officials called tribunes.

pochteca Archaic term for merchants of the Mexicos.

polyglot communities Societies composed of diverse linguistic and ethnic groups.

popular culture Affordable and accessible forms of art and entertainment available to people at all levels of society.

popular sovereignty The idea that the power of the state resides in the people.

Populists Members of a political movement that supported U.S. farmers in late nineteenth-century America. The term is often used generically to refer to political groups who appeal to the majority of the population.

potassium-argon dating Major dating technique based on the changing chemical structure of nonliving objects over time. It is carried out by measuring the ratio of potassium to argon, since over time potassium decays into argon. This method makes possible the dating of objects up to a million years old.

potato famine (1840s) Severe famine in Ireland that led to the rise of radical political movements and the migration of large numbers of Irish to the United States.

potter's wheel Fast wheel that enabled people to mass-produce vessels in many different shapes. This advance, invented at the city of Uruk, enabled potters to make significant technical breakthroughs.

pottery Vessels made of mud and later clay that were used for storing and transporting food. The development of pottery was a major breakthrough.

Prague Spring (1968) Popular movement that strove to create a democratic and pluralist socialism in Czechoslovakia; suppressed by Russian intervention in early 1969.

predestination Belief of many sixteenth- and seventeenth-century Protestant groups that God had foreordained the lives of individuals, including their bad and good deeds.

primitivism Western art movement of the late nineteenth and early twentieth centuries that drew upon the so-called primitive art forms of Africa, Oceania, and pre-Columbian America.

progressive reformers Members of the U.S. reform movement in the early twentieth century that aimed to eliminate political corruption, improve working conditions, and regulate the power of large industrial and financial enterprises.

proletarians Industrial wage workers.

prophets Charismatic freelance religious men of power who found themselves in opposition to the formal power of the kings, bureaucrats, and priests.

Prophet's Town Indian village in Indiana that was burned down by American forces in the early nineteenth century.

Protestantism Division of Christianity that emerged in western Europe from the Protestant Reformation.

Protestant Reformation Religious movement initiated by Martin Luther, who openly criticized the corruption in the Catholic Church and voiced his belief that Christians could speak directly to God. His doctrines gained wide support, and those who followed this new view of Christianity rejected the authority of the papacy and the Catholic clergy, broke away from the Catholic Church, and called themselves "Protestants."

Proto-Indo-European The parent of all the languages in the Indo-European family, which includes, among many others, English, German, Norwegian, Portuguese, French, Russian, Persian, Hindi, and Bengali.

Pullman Strike (1894) American Railway Union strike in response to wage cuts and firings.

Punic Wars Three wars waged between the Romans and Carthage in the third and second centuries BCE that resulted in the defeat of the Carthaginian hegemony in the western Mediterranean and demonstrated the might of the Roman military (army and navy) and the beginnings of Rome's aggressive foreign imperialism.

puppet states Governments with little power in the international arena that follow the dictates of their more powerful neighbors or patrons.

Puritans Seventeenth-century reform group of the Church of England; also known as dissenters or nonconformists.

Qadiriyya Sufi order that facilitated the spread of Islam into West Africa.

qadis Judges in the Muslim societies.

qanats Underground water channels, vital for irrigation, that were used in Persia. Little evaporation occurred when water was being moved through qanats.

Qing dynasty (1644–1911) Minority Manchu rule over China that incorporated new territories, experienced substantial population growth, and sustained significant economic growth.

Questions of King Milinda (Milindapunha) Name of a second-century BCE text espousing the teachings of Buddhism as set forth by Menander, a Yavana king. It featured a discussion between the king and a sophisticated Buddhist sage named Nagasena.

Quetzalcoatl Ancient deity and legendary ruler of Native American peoples living in Mexico.

Quran The scripture of the Islamic faith. Originally a verbal recitation, the Quran was compiled into a book soon after the death of Muhammad in the order in which we have it today. According to traditional Islamic interpretation, the Quran was revealed to Muhammad by the angel Gabriel over a period of twenty-three years.

radicalism The conviction that real change is possible only by going to the root (in Latin, *radix*) of the problem and promoting complete political and social reform. Tendencies toward radicalism can be found in every culture that develops a complex set of institutions and hierarchies, but have been found most frequently in the west since 1789.

radicals Widely used term in nineteenth-century Europe that referred to those individuals and political organizations that favored the total reconfiguration of Europe's political and/or economic systems.

radiocarbon isotope C^{14} Isotope contained by all living things. When organisms die, the C^{14} isotope they contain begins to decay into a stable nonradioactive element, C^{12}. The rate of decay is regular and measurable, making it possible to ascertain the date of fossils that leave organic remains for ages of up to 40,000 years.

Raj British crown's administration of India following the end of the East India Company's rule after the Great Rebellion of 1857.

raja The Sanskrit word for "king," used in South and Southeast Asia. It could also refer to the head of a family, but in South Asian city-states indicated the person who had control of land and resources.

Ramadan Ninth month of the Muslim year, during which all Muslims must fast during daylight hours.

Rape of Nanjing Attack against the Chinese in which the Japanese slaughtered at least 100,000 civilians and raped thousands of women between December 1937 and February 1938.

Rashtriya Swayamsevak Sangh (RSS) (1925) Campaign to organize Hindus as a militant, modern community in India; translated in English as "National Volunteer Organization."

Rebellion of 1857 (Great Rebellion) Indian uprising against the East India Company to bring religious purification, an egalitarian society, local and communal solidarity, and a return of a Mughal to the throne without the interference of British rule.

rebus Probably originating in Uruk, a representation that transfers meaning from the name of a thing to the sound of that name. For example, a picture of a bee can represent the sound "b." Such pictures opened the door to writing, a technology of symbols that uses marks to represent specific discrete sounds.

Reconquista Spanish reconquest of territories lost to the Islamic Empire, beginning with Toledo in 1061.

Red Guards Chinese students who were the shock troops in the early phases of Mao's Cultural Revolution in 1966–1968.

Red Lanterns Female supporters of the Chinese Boxers who rebelled against foreign intrusions in China at the turn of the twentieth century. Most were teenage girls and unmarried women, and they dressed in red garments.

Reds Bolsheviks.

Red Turban Movement Diverse religious movement in China during the fourteenth century that spread the belief that the world was drawing to an end as Mongol rule was collapsing.

Reich German word for "realm." Hitler claimed to be creating the Third German Reich (after the Holy Roman Empire and the German Empire that had lasted from 1871 to 1919).

Reichstag The German parliament.

Reign of Terror Campaign at the height of the French Revolution in the early 1790s that used violence, including systematic execution of opponents of the revolution, to purge France of its enemies and to extend the revolution beyond its borders. Radicals executed as many as 40,000 persons who were judged enemies of the state.

Renaissance Term meaning "rebirth" that historians use to characterize the expanded cultural production of European nations between 1430 and 1550. The Renaissance emphasized a break from the church-centered medieval world and a new concept of humankind as the center of the world.

republican government Government in which power and rulership rest with representatives of the people—not a king.

res publica Literally, "public thing"; this referred to the Roman republic, in which policy and rules of behavior were determined by the Senate and by popular assemblies of the citizens.

Restoration period (1815–1848) European movement after the defeat of Napoleon to restore Europe to its pre–French Revolutionary status and to quash radical movements.

Rift Valley Area of northeastern Africa where some of the most important early discoveries of human fossils were found, especially one of an intact skull that is 1.8 million years old.

river basins Areas drained by a river, including all its tributaries. River basins were rich in fertile soil, water for irrigation, and plant and animal life, which made them attractive for human habitation. Cultivators were able to produce surplus agriculture to support the first cities.

Roman army Military force of the Roman Empire. The Romans devised a military draft that could draw from a huge population. In their encounter with Hannibal, they lost up to 80,000 men in three separate encounters and still won the war.

Roman Catholicism Branch of Christianity established by 1000 CE in western Europe and led by the Roman papacy. In contrast to ancient Greek Orthodoxy, Western Catholics believed that their church was destined to expand everywhere, and they set about converting the tribes of northern Europe. Western Catholics contemptuously called the East Romans "Greeks" and condemned them for their "Byzantine" cunning.

Roman law Roman legal system, under which disputes were brought to the public courts and decisions were made by judges and sometimes by large juries. Rome's legal system featured written law and institutions for settling legal disputes.

roving bandits Large bands of dispossessed and marginalized Chinese peasants who vented their anger at tax collectors in the waning years of the Ming dynasty.

Royal Road A 1,600-mile road of the ancient Persian Empire that went from Sardis in Anatolia to Susa in Iran. It was used by messengers, traders, the army, and those taking tribute to the king.

Russification Programs to assimilate people of over 146 dialects into the Russian Empire.

S.S. (*Schutzstaffel*) Hitler's security police force.

Sack of Constantinople Rampage in 1204 by the Frankish armies on the capital city of Constantinople.

Sahel region The Arabic word for "coast," used to describe the area that borders the southern region of the Sahara Desert. This vast expanse of land, stretching from the Atlantic Ocean to the Red Sea, was significantly wetter and more temperate than the desert, especially in the upland massifs and their foothills, where villages and towns were able to emerge.

Salt March (1930) A 240-mile trek to the sea in India, led by Mohandas Gandhi, to gather salt for free, thus breaking the British colonial monopoly on salt.

Samurai Japanese warriors who made up the private armies of Japanese daimyos.

Sandinista coalition Left-leaning Nicaraguan coalition of the 1970s and 1980s.

Sanskrit cosmopolis A cultural synthesis based on Hindu spiritual beliefs and articulated in the Sanskrit language that served to culturally unify South Asia in place of a centralized empire.

Santería African-based religion, blended with Christian influences, that was first practiced by slaves in Cuba.

Sargon the Great King of Akkad, a city-state near modern Baghdad. Reigning from 2334 to 2279 BCE, Sargon helped bring the competitive era of city-states to an end and sponsored monumental works of architecture, art, and literature.

Sasanian Empire Empire that succeeded the Parthians in the mid-220s CE in Inner Eurasia. The Sasanian Empire controlled the trade crossroads of Afro-Eurasia and possessed a strong armored cavalry, which made them a powerful rival to Rome. The Sasanians were also tolerant of Judaism and Christianity, which allowed Christians to flourish.

Sati Hindu practice whereby a woman was burned to death on the pyre of her dead husband.

satrapies Provinces in the Persian Empire governed by a satrap. Each satrap was a relative or intimate associate of the king.

Satyagraha *See* nonviolent resistance.

scientific method Method of inquiry based on experimentation rather than on the acceptance of older authorities. Many of its principles were first laid out by the philosopher Sir Francis Bacon (1561–1626), who claimed that real science entailed the formulation of hypotheses that could be tested in carefully controlled experiments.

Scramble for Africa European rush to colonize parts of Africa at the end of the nineteenth century.

scribes Those who wield writing tools. From the very beginning, they were at the top of the social ladder, under the major power brokers.

Scythian ethos Warrior ethos that embodied the extremes of aggressive mounted-horse culture, c. 1000 BCE. In part the Scythian ethos was the result of the constant struggle between settlers, hunter-gatherers, and nomads on the northern frontier of Europe.

Sea Peoples Migrants from north of the Mediterranean who invaded the cities of Egypt and the Levant in the second millennium BCE. Once settled along the coast of the Levant, they became known as the Philistines and considerably disrupted the settlements of the Canaanites.

SEATO (Southeast Asia Treaty Organization) Military alliance of pro-American, anticommunist states in Southeast Asia in 1954.

second-generation societies Societies that expanded old ideas and methods by incorporating new aspects of culture and grafting them onto, or using them in combination with, established norms.

Second World Term invented during the Cold War to refer to the communist countries, as opposed to the west (or First World) and the former colonies (or Third World).

Seleucus Nikator Successor of Alexander the Great who lived from 358 to 281 BCE. He controlled Mesopotamia, Syria, Persia, and parts of the Punjab.

Self-Strengthening movement In the latter half of the nineteenth century, a movement of reformist Chinese bureaucrats that attempted to adopt western elements of learning and technological skill while retaining their core Chinese culture.

Semu Term meaning "outsiders" or non-Chinese people—Mongols, Tanguts, Khitan, Jurchen, Muslims, Tibetans, Persians, Turks, Nestorians, Jews, and Armenians—who became a new ruling elite over a Han majority population in the late thirteenth century.

sepoys Hindu and Muslim recruits of the East India Company's military force.

serfs Peasants who farmed the land and paid fees to be protected by lords under a system of rule called feudalism.

settled agriculture Application of human labor and tools to a fixed plot of land for more than one growing cycle. It entails the changeover from a hunting and gathering lifestyle to one based on agriculture, which requires staying in one place until the soil has been exhausted.

Seven Years' War (1756–1763) Worldwide war that ended when Prussia defeated Austria, establishing itself as a European power, and when Britain gained control of India and many of France's colonies through the Treaty of Paris; known in North America as the French and Indians Wars.

sexual revolution Increased freedom in sexual behavior, resulting in part from advances in contraception, notably the introduction of oral contraception in 1960, which allowed men and women to limit childbearing and to have sex with less fear of pregnancy.

shah Traditional title of Persian rulers.

shamans Certain humans whose powers supposedly enabled them to commune with the supernatural and to transform themselves wholly or partly into animals.

shamisen Three-stringed instrument, often played by Japanese geisha.

Shandingdong Man A *Homo sapiens* whose fossil remains and relics can be dated to about 18,000 years ago. His physical characteristics were close to those of modern humans, and he had a similar brain size.

Shanghai School Late nineteenth-century style of Chinese painting characterized by an emphasis on spontaneous brushwork, feeling, and the incorporation of western influences into classical Chinese pieces.

Shang state Dynasty in northeastern China that ruled from 1600 to 1045 BCE. Though not as well defined by borders as the territorial states in the southwest of Asia, it did have a ruling lineage. Four fundamental elements of the Shang state were a metal industry based on copper, pottery making, standardized architectural forms and walled towns, and divination using animal bones.

sharecropping System of farming in which tenant farmers rented land and gave over a share of their crops to the land's owners. Sometimes seen as a cheap way for the state to conduct agricultural affairs, sharecropping often resulted in the impoverishment and marginalization of the underclass.

sharia Literally, "the way"; now used to indicate the philosophy and rulings of Islamic law.

Sharpeville Massacre (1960) Massacre of sixty-nine black Africans when police fired on a rally against the recently passed laws requiring nonwhite South Africans to carry identity papers.

Shawnees Native American tribe that inhabited the Ohio Valley during the eighteenth century.

Shays's Rebellion (1786) Uprising of armed farmers that broke out when the Massachusetts state government refused to offer them economic relief.

Shi Huangdi King during the Qin era who defeated what was left of the Warring States between 230 and 221 BCE. He assumed the mandate of heaven from the Zhou and declared himself First August Emperor, to distinguish himself from other kings.

Shiism One of the two main branches of Islam, practiced in the Fatimid and Safavid Empires. Always a minority sect in the Islamic world, the interpretations of theology and politics in Shiism differ from those in Sunni Islam.

Shiites Group of supporters of Ali, Muhammad's cousin and son-in-law, who wanted him to be the first caliph and believed that members of the Prophet's family deserved to rule. The leaders of the Shiite community are known as "imams," which means "leaders."

Shinto Japan's official religion; it promoted the state and the emperor's divinity. The term means "the way of the gods."

shoguns Japanese military commanders. From 1192 to 1333, the Kamakura shoguns served as military "protectors" of the ruler in the city of Heian.

Shotoku Prince in the early Japanese Yamoto state (574–622 CE) who is credited with having introduced Buddhism to Japan.

shudras Literally, "small ones"; workers and slaves from outside the Vedic lineage.

Siddhartha Gautama Another name for the Buddha, the most prominent opponent of the Brahman way of life. He lived from 563 to 483 BCE and developed methods for overcoming life's suffering and achieving a state of grace, or nirvana.

Sikhism Islamic-inspired religion that calls on its followers to renounce the caste system and to treat all believers as equal before God.

Silicon Valley Valley between the California cities of San Francisco and San Jose, known for its innovative computer and high-technology industries.

silk Luxury textile that became a vastly popular export from China (via the Silk Road) to the cities of the Roman world.

Silk Road A series of trade routes linking China with central Asia and the Mediterranean; it extended over 5,000 miles, land and sea included, and was so named because of the quantities of silk that were traded along it. The Silk Road was a major factor in the development of cultures in China, Egypt, Persia, India, and even Europe.

Silla One of three independent Korean states that may have emerged as early as the third century BCE. These states lasted until 668 CE, when Silla took control over the entire peninsula.

Silver Islands Term used by European merchants in the sixteenth century to refer to Japan because of its substantial trade in silver with China.

Sino-Japanese War (1894–1895) Conflict over the control of Korea in which China was forced to cede the province of Taiwan to Japan.

Sipahi The Persian word for "cavalryman." *Sipahis* were expected to provide military service to the Ottoman Empire.

Siva The third of three Vedic deities, signifying destruction. *See also* Brahma *and* Vishnu.

slave plantations System whereby enslaved labor was used for the cultivation of crops to be sold for profit. Slave plantations were a crucial part of the growth of the Mediterranean economy.

small seal script Unified script that was used to the exclusion of other scripts under the Qin, with the aim of centralizing administration. Its use led to a less complicated style of clerical writing than had been in use under the Han.

social contract The idea, drawn from the works of the English writer John Locke, that all governments come into existence through agreements made between rulers and peoples; if a ruler violates those agreements, Locke argued, the people have the right to rebel.

Social Darwinism Belief that Charles Darwin's theory of evolution is applicable to humans and justifies the right of the ruling classes or countries to dominate the weak.

social hierarchies Distinctions between the privileged and the less privileged.

socialism Political ideology that calls for a classless society with collective ownership of all property.

Social Security Act (1935) New Deal act that instituted old-age pensions and insurance for the unemployed.

Socrates (469–399 BCE) Philosopher in Athens who encouraged people to reflect on ethics and morality. He stressed the importance of honor and integrity as opposed to wealth and power. Plato was his student.

Sogdians A people who lived in central Asia's commercial centers and maintained the stability and accessibility of the Silk Road. They were crucial to the interconnectedness of the Afro-Eurasian landmass.

Solidarity The communist bloc's first independent trade union, established in Poland at the Gdansk shipyard in 1980.

Song dynasty Chinese dynasty that took over the mandate of heaven for three centuries starting in 976 CE. It ruled an era of many economic and political successes but eventually lost northern China to nomadic tribes.

Song porcelain Type of ceramics perfected during the Song period that was translucent and delicate but also durable.

South African War (1899–1902) Conflict between the British and Afrikaner colonists of South Africa that resulted in bringing two Afrikaner republics under the control of the British; often called the Boer War.

Soviet bloc International alliance that included the east European countries of the Warsaw Pact as well as the Soviet Union but also came to include Cuba.

Spanish-American War (1898) War between the United States and Spain in Cuba, Puerto Rico, and the Philippines. It ended with a treaty in which the United States took over the Philippines, Guam, and Puerto Rico; Cuba won partial independence.

speciation The formation of different species.

specie Money in coin.

species Group of animals or plants possessing one or more distinctive characteristics and able to exchange genes and interbreed.

Spring and Autumn period Period between the eighth and fifth centuries BCE, during which China was ruled by the feudal system. Considered an anarchic and turbulent time, there were 148 different tributary states in this period.

Stalin, Joseph (1878–1953) Leader of the Communist Party and the Soviet Union. Stalin sought to create "socialism in one country."

St. Bartholomew's Day Massacre (1572) Roman Catholic massacre of French Protestants in Paris.

steel A metal more malleable and stronger than iron that became essential for industries like shipbuilding and railways.

stoicism Widespread philosophical movement initiated by Zeno (334–262 BCE). Zeno and his followers sought to understand the role of people in relation to the cosmos. For the Stoics, everything was grounded in nature. Being in love with nature and living a good life required being in control of one's passions and thus indifferent to pleasure or pain.

St. Patrick Former slave brought to Ireland from Briton who later became a missionary. Known as the "Apostle of Ireland," he died in 470 CE.

Strait of Malacca Seagoing gateway to Southeast and East Asia.

Strategic Defense Initiative ("Star Wars") Master plan, championed by U.S. president Ronald Reagan in the 1980s, that envisions the deployment of satellites and space missiles to protect the United States from incoming nuclear bombs.

stupa Dome monument marking the burial site of relics of the Buddha.

Suez Canal Channel completed in 1869 across the Isthmus of Suez to connect the Mediterranean Sea with the Red Sea and to lower the costs of international trade.

Sufi brotherhoods Mystics within Islam who were responsible for the expansion of Islam into many regions of the world.

Sufism Emotional and mystical form of Islam that appealed to the common people.

sultan Islamic political leader. In the Ottoman Empire, the sultan combined a warrior ethos with an unwavering devotion to Islam.

Sumerian King List Text that recounts the making of Sumerian political dynasties. Recorded around 2000 BCE, it organizes the reigns of kings by dynasty, one city at a time.

Sumerian pantheon The Sumerian gods, each of whom had a home in a particular floodplain city. In the Sumerian belief system, both gods and the natural forces they controlled had to be revered.

Sumerian temples Homes of the gods and symbols of Sumerian imperial identity. Sumerian temples also represented the gods' ability to hoard wealth at sites where people exchanged goods and services. In addition, temples distinguished the urban from the rural world.

Sunnis The majority sect of Islam, Sunnis originally supported the succession of Abu Bakr over Ali and supported the rule of consensus rather than family

lineage for the succession to the Islamic caliphate. *See also* Shiites.

Sun Yat-sen (1866–1925) Chinese revolutionary and founder of the Nationalist Party in China.

superior man In the Confucian view, a person of perfected moral character, fit to be a leader.

superpowers Label applied to the United States and the Soviet Union after World War II because of their size, their possession of the atomic bomb, and the fact that each embodied a model of civilization (capitalism or communism) applicable to the whole world.

supranational organizations International organizations such as nongovernmental organizations (NGOs), the World Bank, and the International Monetary Fund (IMF).

survival of the fittest Charles Darwin's belief that as species grow and resources become scarce, a struggle for existence arises, the outcome of which is that only the "fittest" survive.

Suryavanha The second lineage of two (the solar one) in Vedic society. *See* Chandravamsha.

Swadeshi movement Voluntary organizations in India that championed the creation of indigenous manufacturing enterprises and schools of nationalist thought in order to gain autonomy from Britain.

syndicalism A political and economic system, elaborated by the French social philosopher Georges Sorel (1847–1922), that sought to replace capitalism with a workplace organization that included unskilled laborers.

tabula rasa Term used by John Locke to describe the human mind before it begins to acquire ideas from experience; Latin for "clean slate."

Taiping Heavenly Kingdom (Heavenly Kingdom of Great Peace) Religious sect established by the Chinese prophet Hong Xiuquan in the mid-nineteenth century. Hong Xiuquan believed that he was Jesus's younger brother. The group struggled to rid the world of evil and "restore" the heavenly kingdom, imagined as a just and egalitarian order.

Taiping Rebellion Rebellion by followers of Hong Xiuquan and the Taiping Heavenly Kingdom against the Qing

government over the economic and social turmoil caused by the Opium War. Despite an army of 100,000 rebels, the rebellion was crushed.

Taj Mahal Royal palace of the Mughal Empire, built by Shah Jahan in the seventeenth century in homage to his wife, Mumtaz Mahal.

Tale of Genji Japanese work written by Lady Murasaki that gives vivid accounts of Heian court life; Japan's first novel (early eleventh century).

talking cures Psychological practice developed by Sigmund Freud whereby the symptoms of neurotic and traumatized patients would decrease after regular periods of thoughtful discussion.

Talmud Huge volumes of oral commentary on Jewish law eventually compiled in two versions, the Palestinian and the Babylonian, in the fifth and sixth centuries BCE.

Talmud of Jerusalem Codified written volumes of the traditions of Judaism, produced by the rabbis of Galilee around 400 CE.

Tang dynasty (608–907 CE) Regime that promoted a cosmopolitan culture, turning China into the hub of East Asian cultural integration, while expanding the borders of their empire. To govern such a diverse empire, the Tang established a political culture and civil service based on Confucian teachings. Candidates for the civil service were required to take examinations, the first of their kind in the world.

Tanzimat Reorganization period of the Ottoman Empire in the mid-nineteenth century. Modernizing reforms affected the military, trade, foreign relations, and civilian life.

tappers Rubber workers in Brazil, mostly either Indian or mixed-blood people.

Tarascans Mesoamerican society of the 1400s, rivals to and sometimes subjects of the Aztecs.

Tecumseh (1768–1813) Shawnee who circulated Tenskwatawa's message of Indian renaissance among Indian villages from the Great Lakes to the Gulf Coast. He preached the need for Indian unity, insisting that Indians resist any American attempts to get them to sell more land. In response, thousands of followers renounced their ties to colonial ways and prepared to combat the expansion of the United States.

tekkes Schools that taught devotional strategies and the religious knowledge that students needed to enter Sufi orders and become masters of the brotherhood.

temple Building where believers worshipped their gods and goddesses and where some peoples believed the deities had earthly residence.

Tenskwatawa (1775–1836) Shawnee prophet who urged disciples to abstain from alcohol and return to traditional customs, reducing dependence on European trade goods and severing connections to Christian missionaries. His message spread to other tribes, raising the specter of a pan-Indian confederacy.

Teotihuacán City-state in a large, mountainous valley in what is modern-day Mexico; the first major community to emerge after the Olmecs.

territorial state Political form that emerged in the river-basin cities of Mesopotamia, which was overwhelmed by the displacement of nomadic peoples. These states were kingdoms organized around charismatic rulers who headed large households; each had a defined physical border.

Third Estate The French people minus the clergy and the aristocracy; this term was popularized after 1789 and used to claim power for nonelite people during the French Revolution.

Third Reich The German state from 1933 to 1945 under Adolf Hitler.

Third World Nations of the world, mostly in Asia, Latin America, and Africa, that were not highly industrialized like First World nations or tied to the Soviet bloc (the Second World).

Thirty Years' War (1618–1648) Conflict between Protestants and Catholics in the Holy Roman Empire that escalated into a general European war.

Tiananmen Square Largest public square in the world and site of the pro-democracy movement in 1989 that resulted in the killing of as many as a thousand protesters by the Chinese army.

tiers-monde Term meaning "Third World," coined by French intellectuals to describe countries seeking a "third way"

between Soviet communism and western capitalism.

Tiglath Pileser III Assyrian ruler from 745 to 728 BCE who introduced a standing army and instituted reforms that changed the administrative and social structure of the empire to make it more efficient.

Tiwanaku Another name for Tihuanaco, the first great Andean polity, on the shores of Lake Titicaca.

Tlaxcalans Mesoamerican society of the 1400s; these people were enemies of the powerful Aztec Empire.

Tokugawa shogunate Hereditary military administration founded in 1603 that ruled Japan while keeping the emperor as a figurehead; it was toppled in 1868 by reformers who felt that Japan should adopt, not reject, Western influences.

Toltecs A Mesoamerican people who, by 1000 CE, had filled the political vacuum created by the decline of the city of Teotihuacán.

tomb culture Warlike group from northeast Asia who arrived by sea in the middle of the third century CE and imposed their military and social power on southern Japan. These conquerors are known today as the "tomb culture" because of their elevated necropolises near present-day Osaka.

Topkapi Palace Political headquarters of the Ottoman Empire, located in Istanbul.

total war All-out war involving civilian populations as well as military forces, often used in reference to World War II.

transhumant herders Nomads who entered settled territories in the second millennium BCE and moved their herds seasonally when resources became scarce.

Trans-Siberian Railroad Railroad built over very difficult terrain between 1891 and 1903 and subsequently expanded. It created an overland bridge for troops, peasant settlers, and commodities to move between Europe and the Pacific.

Treaty of Brest-Litovsk (1918) Separate peace treaty between imperial Germany and the new Bolshevik regime in Russia. The treaty acknowledged the German victory on the Eastern Front and took Russia out of the war.

Treaty of Nanjing (1842) Treaty between China and Britain following the First Opium War; it called for indemnities, the opening of new ports, and the cession of Hong Kong to the British.

Treaty of Tordesillas (1494) Treaty in which the pope decreed that the non-European world would be divided into spheres of trade and missionary responsibility between Spain and Portugal.

trickle trade Also called "down the line trade," a method by which a good is passed from one village to another, as in the case of obsidian among early farming villages. The practice began around 7000 BCE.

Tripartite Pact (1940) Pact that stated that Germany, Italy, and Japan would act together in all future military ventures.

Triple Entente Alliance developed before World War I that eventually included Britain, France, and Russia.

Troy Important site founded around 3000 BCE in Anatolia, to the far west. Troy is legendary as the site of the war that was launched by the Greeks (the Achaeans) and that was recounted by Homer in the *Iliad*.

Truman Doctrine (1947) Declaration promising U.S. economic and military intervention, whenever and wherever needed, for the sake of preventing communist expansion.

Truth and Reconciliation Commission Quasi-judicial body established after the overthrow of the apartheid system in South Africa and the election of Nelson Mandela as the country's first black president in 1994. The commission was to gather evidence about crimes committed during the apartheid years. Those who showed remorse for their actions could appeal for clemency. The South African leaders believed that an airing of the grievances from this period would promote racial harmony and reconciliation. Other countries suffering from traumatic political, ethnic, and cultural events have adopted the South African experiment and established their own truth and reconciliation commissions.

truth commissions Elected officials' inquiries into human rights abuses by previous regimes. In Argentina, El Salvador, Guatemala, and South Africa, these commissions were vital for creating a new aura of legitimacy for democracies and for promising to uphold the rights of individuals.

tsar/czar Russian word derived from the Latin *Caesar* to refer to the Russian ruler of Kiev and eventually to all rulers in Russia.

Tula Toltec capital city, a commercial hub and political and ceremonial center.

Uitlanders British populations living in Afrikaner republics; they were denied voting rights and subject to other forms of discrimination in the late nineteenth century. The term means "outsiders."

ulama Arabic word that means "learned ones" or "scholars"; used for those who devoted themselves to knowledge of Islamic sciences.

Umayyads Family who founded the first dynasty in Islam. They established family rule and dynastic succession to the role of caliph. The first Umayyad caliph established Damascus as his capital and was named Mu'awiya ibn Abi Sufyan.

umma Arabic word for "community"; used to refer to the "Islamic people" or "Islamic community."

Universal Declaration of Human Rights (1948) UN declaration that laid out the rights to which all human beings are entitled.

universalizing religions Universal religions that are proselytized by energetic and charismatic missionaries, that foster a deep sense of community felt by their converts, and that are supported by powerful empires.

universal religions Religions that appeal to diverse populations, that are easily adaptable across various cultural and geographical areas, and that promote universal rules and principles to guide behavior that transcend place, time, and specific cultural practices.

universitas Term used from the end of the twelfth century to denote scholars who came together, first in Paris. The term is borrowed from the merchant communities, where it denoted the equivalent of the modern "union."

Untouchables Caste in the Indian system whose jobs, usually in the more unsanitary aspects of urban life, rendered them "ritually and spiritually" impure.

Upanishads Vedic wisdom literature collected in the first half of the first millennium BCE. It took the form of dialogues between disciples and a sage.

urban-rural divide Division between those living in cities and those living in rural areas. One of history's most durable worldwide distinctions, the urban-rural divide eventually encompassed the globe. Where cities arose, communities adopted lifestyles based on the large-scale production of goods and on specialized labor. Those living in the countryside remained close to nature, cultivating the land or tending livestock. They diversified their labor and exchanged their grains and animal products for necessities available in urban centers.

utopian socialism The most visionary of all Restoration-era movements. Utopian socialists like Charles Fourier dreamed of transforming states, workplaces, and human relations, not through bloody revolution but through the wholesale reorganization of society.

Vaishyas Householders or lesser clan members in Vedic society who worked the land and tended livestock.

Vardhamana Mahavira Advocate of Jainism who lived from 540 to 468 BCE; he emphasized interpretation of the Upanishads to govern and guide daily life.

varna Caste system established by the Vedas in 600 BCE.

vassal states Subordinate states that had to pay tribute in luxury goods, raw materials, and labor as part of a broad confederation of polities under the kings' protection.

Vedas Rhymes, hymns, and explanatory texts composed by Aryan priests; the Vedas became their most holy scripture and part of their religious rituals. The Vedas were initially passed down orally, in Sanskrit. Brahmans, priests of Vedic culture, incorporated the texts into ritual and society. The Vedas are considered the final authority of Hinduism.

Vedic people People who came from the steppes of Inner Asia around 1500 BCE and entered the fertile lowlands of the Indus River basin, gradually moving as far south as the Deccan plateau. They called themselves Aryan, which means

"respected ones," and spoke Sanskrit, an Indo-European language.

veiling Practice of modest dress, including covering the hair and much of the face, required of respectable women in the Assyrian Empire, introduced by Assyrian authorities in the thirteenth century BCE.

Venus figures Representations of the goddess of fertility drawn on the Chauvet Cave in southeastern France. Discovered in 1994, they are probably about 35,000 years old.

Versailles Conference (1919) International peace conference at the end of World War I intended to shape the future of the world after the war. Delegates decided on the principles that would shape the resultant five peace treaties, one for each of the Central Powers (the most well-known of these is the Treaty of Versailles, which forced Germany to pay reparations, admit responsibility for the war, and give up its colonies). The Soviet Union, which had already made peace with the Central Powers, was not invited to this conference.

Viet Cong Vietnamese communist group committed to overthrowing the government of South Vietnam and reunifying North and South Vietnam.

Viet Minh Group founded in 1941 by Ho Chi Minh to oppose the Japanese occupation of Indochina; it later fought the French colonial forces for independence. Also known as the Vietnamese Independent League.

Vietnam War (1955–1975) Conflict that resulted from concern over the spread of communism in Southeast Asia. The United States intervened on the side of South Vietnam in its struggle against peasant-supported Viet Cong guerrilla forces, who wanted to reunite Vietnam under a communist regime. Faced with antiwar opposition at home and ferocious resistance from the Vietnamese, American troops withdrew in 1973; the puppet South Vietnamese government collapsed two years later.

Vikings A people from Scandinavia who replaced the Franks as the dominant warrior class in northern Europe in the ninth century CE. They used their superior ships to loot other seagoing peoples and sailed up the rivers of central Russia to establish a trade route that connected

Scandinavia and the Baltic with Constantinople and Baghdad. The Vikings established settlements in Iceland and Greenland and, briefly, North America.

Vishnu The second of three Vedic deities, signifying existence. *See also* Brahma *and* Siva.

viziers Bureaucrats of the Ottoman Empire.

vodun Mixed religion of African and Christian customs practiced by slaves and free blacks in the colony of Saint Domingue.

Voting Rights Act (1965) Law that granted universal suffrage in the United States.

Wafd Nationalist party that came into existence during a rebellion in Egypt in 1919 and held power sporadically after Egypt was granted limited independence from Britain in 1922.

Wahhabism Eighteenth-century reform movement organized by Muhammad Ibn abd al-Wahhab, who preached the absolute oneness of Allah and a return to the pure Islam of Muhammad.

Wang Mang Han minister who usurped the throne in 9 CE because he believed that the Han had lost the mandate of heaven. He ruled until 23 CE.

war ethos Strong social commitment to a continuous state of war. The Roman army constantly drafted men and engaged in annual spring military campaigns. Soldiers were taught to embrace a sense of honor that did not allow them to accept defeat and, their leaders commended those who repeatedly threw themselves into battle.

War of 1812 Conflict between Britain and the United States arising from U.S. grievances over oppressive British maritime practices in the Napoleonic Wars.

War on Poverty President Lyndon Johnson's push for an increased range of social programs and increased spending on Social Security, health, education, and assistance for the disabled.

Warring States period Period extending from the fifth century BCE to 221 BCE, when the regional warring states were unified by the Qin dynasty.

Warsaw Pact (1955–1991) Military alliance between the Soviet Union and other communist states that was established in response to the creation of the NATO alliance.

Weimar Republic (1919–1933) Constitutional republic of Germany that was subverted by Hitler soon after he became chancellor.

Western Front Military front that stretched from the English Channel through Belgium and France to the Alps during World War I.

White and Blue Niles The two main branches of the Nile, rising out of central Africa and Ethiopia. They come together at the present-day capital city of Sudan, Khartoum.

White Lotus Rebellion Series of uprisings in northern China (1790–1800s) inspired by mystical beliefs in folk Buddhism and, at times, the idea of restoring the Ming dynasty.

Whites "Counterrevolutionaries" of the Bolshevik Revolution (1918–1921) who fought the Bolsheviks (the "Reds"); included former supporters of the tsar, Social Democrats, and large independent peasant armies.

White Wolf Mysterious militia leader, depicted in popular myth as a Chinese Robin Hood whose mission was to rid the country of the injustices of Yuan Shikai's government in the early years of the Chinese Republic (1910s).

wokou Supposedly Japanese pirates, many of whom were actually Chinese subjects of the Ming dynasty.

Works Progress Administration (WPA) New Deal program instituted in 1935 that put nearly 3 million people to work building roads, bridges, airports, and post offices.

World Bank International agency established in 1944 to provide economic assistance to war-torn and poor countries. Its formal title is the International Bank for Reconstruction and Development.

World War II (1939–1945) Worldwide war that began in September 1939 in Europe and pitted Britain, the United States, and the Soviet Union (the Allies) against Nazi Germany, Japan, and Italy (the Axis).

Wu or Wudi Chinese leader known as the "Martial Emperor" because of his many military campaigns during the Han dynasty. He reigned from 141 to 87 BCE.

Wu Zhao Chinese empress who lived from 626 to 706 CE. She began as a concubine in the court of Li Shimin and became the mother of his son's child. She eventually gained power equal to that of the emperor, and she named herself regent when she finagled a place for one of her own sons after their father's death.

Xiongnu The most powerful and intrusive of the nomadic peoples, originally pastoralists from the eastern part of the Asian steppe in what is modern-day Mongolia. They appeared along the frontier with China in the late Zhou dynasty and by the third century BCE had become the most powerful of all the pastoral communities in that area.

Xunzi Confucian moralist whose ideas were influential to Qin rulers. He lived from 310 to 237 BCE and believed that rational statecraft was more reliable than fickle human nature and that strict laws and severe punishments could create stability in society.

Yalta Accords Results of the meeting in February 1945 in the Crimean city of Yalta between President Roosevelt, Prime Minister Churchill, and Premier Stalin; the meeting was held to plan for the postwar order.

Yavana kings Sanskrit name for Greek rulers, derived from the Greek name for the area of western Asia Minor called Ionia, a term that then extended to anyone who spoke Greek or came from the Mediterranean.

yellow press Newspapers that seek a mass circulation by featuring sensationalist reporting.

Yellow Turbans One of several local Chinese religious movements that emerged across the empire, especially under Wang Mang's officials, who considered him a usurper. The Yellow Turbans, so called because of the yellow scarves they wore around their heads, were Daoist millenarians.

Yin City that became the capital of the Shang in 1350 BCE, ushering in a golden age.

Young Egypt Antiliberal, fascist group that gained a large following in Egypt during the 1930s.

Young Italy Nineteenth-century nationalist organization made up of young students and intellectuals, devoted to the unification and renewal of the Italian state.

Yuan dynasty Dynasty established by the Mongols after the defeat of the Song. The Yuan dynasty was strong from 1280 to 1368; its capital was at Dadu, or modern-day Beijing.

Yuan Mongols Mongol rulers of China who were overthrown by the Ming dynasty in 1368.

Yuezhi A Turkic nomadic people who roamed on pastoral lands to the west of the Xiongnu territory of central Mongolia. They had friendly relationships with the farming societies in China, but the Yuezhi detested the Xiongnu and had frequent armed clashes with them.

zaibatsu Large-scale, family-owned corporations in Japan consisting of factories, import-export businesses, and banks that dominated the Japanese economy until 1945.

zamindars Archaic tax system of the Mughal Empire, where decentralized lords collected tribute for the emperor from peasants working on their estates.

Zapatistas Group of indigenous rebels that rose up against the Mexican government in 1994 and drew inspiration from an earlier Mexican rebel, Emiliano Zapata.

Zheng King during the Qin era who defeated what was left of the Warring States between 230 and 221 BCE. He assumed the mandate of heaven from the Zhou and declared himself First August Emperor, to distinguish himself from other kings.

Zheng He (1371–1433) Ming naval leader who established tributary relations with Southeast Asia, Indian Ocean ports, the Persian Gulf, and the east coast of Africa.

Zhongguo Term originating in the ancient period and subsequently used to emphasize the central cultural and geographical location of China in the world; means "Middle Kingdom."

Zhong Shang Administrative central complex of the Shang.

ziggurat The stepped platform base of a Sumerian temple. By the end of the third millennium BCE, the elevated platform base had transformed into the stepped platform.

Zionism Movement advocating the reestablishment of a Jewish homeland in Palestine.

Zoroaster Greek name for the Persian religious reformer known as Zarathustra, thought to have been a teacher around 1000 BCE in eastern Iran and credited with having solidified the region's religious beliefs into a unified system that moved away from animistic nomadic beliefs. The main source for his teachings is a compilation called the Avesta.

Zoroastrianism Dominant religion of the Persian Empire, based on the teachings of Zoroaster.

Zulus African tribe that, under Shaka, created a ruthless warrior state in southern Africa in the early 1800s.

CREDITS

CHAPTER 10

Photo Credits Page 356: Ramon Manent/REX/Shutterstock; p. 358: Nik Wheeler/Corbis Documentary/Getty Images; p. 359: Granger, NYC—All rights reserved; p. 361: Wikimedia Commons; p. 364: Peter Guttman/Corbis Documentary/Getty Images; p. 367 (top): Keren Su/Corbis Documentary/Getty Images; p. 367 (bottom): Macduff Everton/Corbis Documentary/Getty Images; p. 368: Rogers Fund, 1918 © The Metropolitan Museum of Art; p. 371 (top): Tom Cockrem/Lonely Planet Images/Getty Images; p. 371 (bottom): Wikimedia Commons; p. 372: Granger, NYC—All rights reserved; p. 374 (top): akg-images/Werner Forman; p. 374 (bottom): Yann Arthus Bertrand/Getty Images; p. 377: Erich Lessing/Art Resource, NY; p. 378 (top): Hubert Stadler/Corbis Documentary/Getty Images; p. 378 (bottom): akg-images/Volker Kreidler; p. 380: Mondadori Portfolio/Universal Images Group/Getty Images; p. 381: © British Library Board/Robana/Art Resource, NY; p. 383: Snark/Art Resource, NY; p. 386: Ramon Manent/REX/Shutterstock; p. 387 (top): Gavin Hellier/Alamy Stock Photo; p. 387 (bottom): Kaku Suzuki/Sebun Photo/amana images RM/Getty Images; p. 388: Persian School/Getty Images; p. 390 (top): Beren Patterson/Alamy Stock Photo; p. 390 (middle): Kevin Schafer/Corbis Documentary/Getty Images; p. 390 (bottom): INTERFOTO/Alamy Stock Photo; p. 392: Michael S. Lewis/Corbis Documentary/Getty Images; p. 393: akg-images; p. 396: Bettmann/Getty Images; p. 399: Granger, NYC—All rights reserved.

Text Credits Page 362: "Writing from Alexandria after Arrival from the Muslim West," republished with the permission of Princeton University Press from *Letters of Medieval Jewish Traders*, translated by S.D. Goitein. © 1973 Princeton University Press; p. 373: "Tale of the Genji," translated by Arthur Waley. From *Sources of Japanese Tradition, Vol. 1*, compiled by Ryusaku Tsunoda, Wm. Theodore de Bary and Donald Keene, pp. 177-79. Copyright © 1958 Columbia University Press. Reprinted with permission of the publisher; p. 385: From *Sundiata: An Epic of Old Mali*, by D. T. Niane, English translation by by G.D. Pickett, pp. 40-41. Copyright © 1965 Longman Group. Originally published as *Soundjata ou l'épopée mandingue*. Copyright © 1960 Présence Africaine. Reprinted with permission of Pearson Education Limited and Présence Africaine.

CHAPTER 11

Photo Credits Page 402: Snark/Art Resource; p. 405: Sarin Images/Granger, NYC—All rights reserved; p. 411: Album/Art Resource, NY; p. 413: robertharding/Alamy Stock Photo; p. 414: View of the Inner Courtyard of the Seraglio, Topkapi Palace, Constantinople, engraved by Schroeder and Desmaisons, 1815 (aquatint), Melling, Anton Ignaz (1763-1831) (after)/Private Collection/The Stapleton Collection/Bridgeman Images; p. 415: A Janissary officer recruiting devsirme for Sultan Suleyman I (1495-1566), from the 'Suleymanname' (Mss Hazine. 1517 f.31v), 1558 (ink & gold leaf on vellum), Ali Amir Beg (fl. 1558)/Topkapi Palace Museum, Istanbul, Turkey/Bridgeman Images; p. 417: Timur's defeat of Amlu Khan and the capture of Delhi. A miniature painting from a sixteenth century manuscript of the Zafarnama./British Library, London, UK/© British Library Board. All Rights Reserved/Bridgeman Images; p. 422: Jam World Images/Alamy Stock Photo; p. 424 (left): Images Group/REX/Shutterstock; p. 424 (right): Scala/Ministero per i Beni e le Attività culturali/Art Resource, NY; p. 427: Granger, NYC—All rights reserved; p. 428: The Art Archive/REX/Shutterstock; p. 430: © RMN-Grand Palais/Art Resource, NY; p. 432: © RMN-Grand Palais/Art Resource, NY; p. 433: China: Detail from the painting 'Beauties in History', attributed to the Ming Dynasty artist Qiu Ying (c. 1492-1552)/Pictures from History/Bridgeman Images; p. 434: The Jan Adkins Studio.

Text Credits Page 410: Ahmet T. Karamustafa, from *God's Unruly Friends: Dervish Groups in the Islamic Later Middle Period*, pp. 6-7, © Ahmet T. Karamustafa 1994. Reprinted with the permission of University of Utah Press; p. 418: "Nanak and His Teaching," from *Sources of Indian Tradition Vol. 2*, compiled by Wm. Theodore de Bary, Stephen Hay, Royal Weiler, Andrew Yarrow, pp. 536-538. Copyright © 1958 Columbia University Press. Reprinted with permission of the publisher; p. 425: "To Bibolo Semproni" from *Laura Cereta: Collected Letters of a Renaissance Feminist*, transcribed, translated and edited by Diana Robin (Chicago: University of Chicago Press, 1997), pp. 74-79. © 1977 by The University of Chicago. Reprinted by permission of the University of Chicago Press; p. 429: "Proclamations of the Hongwu Emperor," from *Chinese Civilization: A Sourcebook*, *2nd Edition* by Patricia Buckley Ebrey. Copyright © 1981 by The Free Press, a Division of Simon & Schuster, Inc. Copyright © 1993 by Patricia Buckley Ebrey. Reprinted by permission of Simon & Schuster, Inc. All rights reserved.

CHAPTER 12

Photo Credits Page 438: Minnesota Geological Survey, University of Minnesota; p. 441 (top): The Lee and Juliet Folger Fund Accession No.2013.1.1/National Gallery of Art; p. 441 (bottom): Scala/Art Resource, NY; p. 443: Granger, NYC—All rights reserved; p. 444: Rigged model of a Portuguese caravela from c. 1535 (wood) English School/Science Museum, London, UK/Bridgeman Images; p. 449: bpk Bildagentur/Bildarchiv Preussischer Kulturbesitz/Art Resource, NY; p. 450: Sarin Images/Granger, NYC—All rights reserved; p. 451 (left): Granger, NYC—All rights reserved; p. 451 (right): Pictures from History/Granger, NYC—All rights reserved; p. 453 (left): Schalkwijk/Art Resource, NY. © 2017 Banco de México Diego Rivera Frida Kahlo Museums Trust, Mexico, D.F./Artists Rights Society (ARS), New York; p. 453 (right): Granger, NYC—All rights reserved; p. 453 (bottom): Sarin Images/Granger, NYC—All rights reserved; p. 454 (top): Dagli Orti/REX/Shutterstock; p. 454 (bottom): Sarin Images/Granger, NYC—All rights reserved; p. 457: akg-images; p. 459: St. Bartholomew's Day Massacre, c. 1572–84 (oil on panel), Dubois, Francois (1529–1584)/Musee Cantonal des Beaux-Arts de Lausanne, Switzerland/De Agostini Picture Library/G. Dagli Orti/Bridgeman Images; p. 460: © RMN-Grand Palais/Art Resource, NY; p. 464: akg-images/Cameraphoto; p. 466: Dagli Orti/REX/Shutterstock; p. 471: © François Guenet/Art Resource, NY; p. 472: Andre Dib/Shutterstock.

Text Credits Page 455: Bartolomé Arzáns de Orsúa y Vela. *Tales of Potosí.* Edited by Robert C. Padden and translated from the Spanish by Frances M. López-Morillas. Providence, RI: Brown University Press, 1975. © 1975 Brown University. Reprinted with permission of University of New England; p. 463: "Zhang Han's Essay on Merchants," from *Chinese Civilization: A Sourcebook, 2nd Edition* by Patricia Buckley Ebrey. Copyright © 1981 by The Free Press, a Division of Simon & Schuster, Inc. Copyright © 1993 by Patricia Buckley Ebrey. Reprinted by permission of Simon & Schuster, Inc. All rights reserved.

CHAPTER 13

Photo Credits Page 476: © RMN-Grand Palais/Art Resource, NY; p. 478: Ms 439 f.9r Banquet scene with men drinking coffee, guests of honour sitting in a recess, entertained by three musicians, while an old man is taken ill, from an album of painting and calligraphy (vellum), Ottoman School/The Trustees of the Chester Beatty Library, Dublin/Bridgeman Images; p. 483: Winter Landscape with Skaters. c. 1608 (oil on panel), Avercamp, Hendrik (1585–1634)/Rijksmuseum, Amsterdam, The Netherlands/Bridgeman Images; p. 484: Granger,

NYC—All rights reserved; p. 486: MPI/Getty Images; p. 487: MPI/Getty Images; p. 488: Sarin Images/Granger, NYC—All rights reserved; p. 490 (left): © North Wind Picture Archives; p. 490 (right): The Slave Ship 'Brookes' of Liverpool, pub. by J. Robertson, Edinburgh, 1791 (wood engraving and letterpress), English School, (18th century)/Private Collection/© Michael Graham-Stewart/Bridgeman Images; p. 495: The Newberry Library, Chicago; p. 497: Dagli Orti/REX/Shutterstock; p. 499: Purchase, Bashford Dean Memorial Collection, Funds from various donors, by exchange, 1997 © The Metropolitan Museum of Art; p. 501: Granger, NYC—All rights reserved; p. 502: © Sotheby's/akg-images; p. 503: © Mary Evans Picture Library/The Image Works; p. 504: © The British Library/The Image Works; p. 505: MS 34.7 Aurangzeb I (1658–1707) and courtiers, attributed to Bhawani Das, c. 1710, Mughal/The Trustees of the Chester Beatty Library, Dublin/Bridgeman Images; p. 506: Dagli Orti/REX/Shutterstock; p. 508: © RMN-Grand Palais/Art Resource, NY; p. 510 (top): Granger, NYC—All rights reserved; p. 510 (bottom): Chris Hellier/Corbis/Getty Images; p. 511: Snark/Art Resource, NY; p. 512: bpk Bildagentur/Museum Boijmans van Beuningen, Rotterdam, The Netherlands/Art Resource, NY; p. 513: View of the Chateau, Gardens and Park of Versailles from the Avenue de Paris, detail of the Chateau, 1668 (oil on canvas) (detail of 81242), Patel, Pierre (1605–76)/Château de Versailles, France/Peter Willi/Bridgeman Images; p. 514: Queen Elizabeth I (1533–1603) being carried in Procession (Eliza Triumphans) c. 1601 (oil on canvas), Peake, Robert (fl.1580–1626) (attr. to)/Private Collection/Bridgeman Images.

Text Credits Page 491: From *Interesting Narrative of the Life of Olaudiah Equiano, or Gustavus Vassa, the African, Written by Himself: Norton Critical Edition*, edited by Werner Sollors. Copyright © 2001 by W.W. Norton & Company, Inc. Used by permission of W.W. Norton & Company, Inc; p. 500: Huang Liu-Hung, "Elimination of Authorized Silversmiths" from *A Complete Book Concerning Happiness and Benevolence: A Manual for Local Magistrates in Seventeenth Century China,* translated and edited by Djang

Chu, pp. 190–191. © 1984 The Arizona Board of Regents. Reprinted by permission of the University of Arizona Press.

CHAPTER 14

Photo Credits Page 518: Scala/Art Resource, NY; p. 521: Art Resource, NY; p. 522: © RMN-Grand Palais/Art Resource, NY; p. 523 (left): Portrait of Sultan Mehmet II (1432–81) (w/c on paper), Turkish School (15th century)/Topkapi Palace Museum, Istanbul, Turkey/Bridgeman Images; p. 523 (right): V&A Images, London/Art Resource, NY; p. 524 (left): akg-images/Pictures From History; p. 524 (right): Private Collection, courtesy of the owner and D.A. King; photo by Christie's of London; p. 525: © The Trustees of the Chester Beatty Library, Dublin; p. 527: Forman Archive/REX/Shutterstock; p. 528 (left): Scala/Art Resource, NY; p. 528 (right): Granger, NYC—All rights reserved; p. 529: Wikimedia Commons; p. 530 (left): George Rinhart/Corbis/Getty Images; p. 530 (right): Underwood & Underwood/Library of Congress/Corbis/VCG/Getty Images; p. 531 (left): The Needham Research Institute; p. 531 (right): A Korean World Map/British Library, London, UK/© British Library Board. All Rights Reserved/Bridgeman Images; p. 532: P. 359–1945 Scene 12, Comparison of celebrated beauties and the loyal league, c. 1797 (colour woodblock print), Utamaro, Kitagawa (1753–1806)/Fitzwilliam Museum, University of Cambridge, UK/Bridgeman Images; p. 533 (top): © RMN-Grand Palais/Art Resource, NY; p. 533 (bottom): Map of the World, 1671 (woodblock print), Japanese School, (17th century)/Private Collection/Bridgeman Images; p. 534: Alan Tobey/Getty Images; p. 535 (top): © The Trustees of the British Museum/Art Resource, NY; p. 535 (bottom): The Michael C. Rockefeller Memorial Collection, Bequest of Nelson A. Rockefeller, 1979 © The Metropolitan Museum of Art; p. 536 (top): Minnesota Geological Survey, University of Minnesota; p. 536 (bottom): Euriskodata CDrom/Wikimedia Commons; p. 537: Trial of Galileo, 1633 (oil on canvas) (detail of 2344), Italian School, (17th century)/Private Collection/Bridgeman Images; p. 538: © RMN-Grand Palais/Art

CHAPTER 15

CHAPTER 16

CHAPTER 17

CHAPTER 18

CHAPTER 19

All rights reserved. And by permission of The Random House Group Ltd. and East African Educational Publishers Ltd.

CHAPTER 20

Photo Credits Page 748: F.D.R. Library; p. 751: John Topham/Paul Popper/Popperfoto/Getty Images; p. 753 (left): Universal History Archive/UIG via Getty Images; p. 753 (right): Patrizia Wyss/Alamy Stock Photo; p. 757 (left): Three Lions/Getty Images; p. 757 (right): F.D.R. Library; p. 758: NATO Photo/TRH Pictures/Cody Images; p. 760: Bettmann/Getty Images; p. 763 (left): Granger, NYC—All rights reserved; p. 763 (right): © Collection J.A. Fox/Magnum Photos; p. 765 (top): Bettmann/Getty Images; p. 765 (bottom): Bettmann/Getty Images; p. 766: Bettmann/Getty Images; p. 768: Keystone/Getty Images; p. 770: Hulton Archive/Getty Images; p. 771 (top): Stroud/Express/Getty Images; p. 771 (bottom): FPG/Getty Images; p. 772: Hulton Archive/Getty Images; p. 773: Bettmann/Getty Images; p. 774 (top): Bettmann/Getty Images; p. 774 (left): AP Photo/Montgomery County Sheriff's office; p. 774 (right): Fred Blackwell/State Historical Society of Wisconsin Visual Materials Archive; p. 775: akg-images; p. 776: Sovfoto/UIG via Getty Images; p. 779 (top): Wikimedia Commons; p. 779 (left): © Roger-Viollet/The Image Works; p. 779 (right): Li Zhensheng/Contact Press Images; p. 780: Sovfoto/UIG via Getty Images; p. 781 (left): AP Photo; p. 781 (right): Bettmann/Getty Images; p. 782 (top): AP Photo/Alvin Quinn; p. 782 (bottom): Rolls Press/Popperfoto/Getty Images; p. 784: Bettmann/Getty Images.

Text Credits Page 769: Léopold Sédar Senghor, excerpts from *African Socialism* (New York: American Society of African Culture, 1959), trans.

Mercer Cook. Reprinted by permission of Moorland-Spingarn Research Center, Howard University, Washington, DC; p. 783: "The Problem That Has No Name," from *The Feminine Mystique* by Betty Friedan. Copyright © 1983, 1974, 1973, 1963 by Betty Friedan. Used by permission of W.W. Norton & Company, Inc., Curtis Brown, Ltd. and Victor Gollancz, an imprint of The Orion Publishing Group Ltd.

CHAPTER 21

Photo Credits Page 788: AP Photo/Anat Givon; p. 791: Keystone/Getty Images; p. 793: REX/Shutterstock; p. 796: Peter Turnley/Corbis/VCG via Getty Images; p. 798: AP Photo/David Zalubowski, File; p. 799: GEORGE ESIRI/REUTERS/Newscom; p. 802: Uriel Sinai/Getty Images; p. 803: Michael Ochs Archives/Stringer/Getty Images; p. 804 (left): Nick Laham/Getty Images; p. 804 (right): Jim McIsaac/Getty Images; p. 805: © Eros International/Courtesy: Everett Collection; p. 807: Serge Attal/The LIFE Images Collection/Getty Images; p. 810 (top left): Mira/Alamy Stock Photo; p. 810 (top right): LEE JAE-WON/REUTERS/Newscom; p. 810 (bottom left): Gisele Wulfsohn/Panos Pictures; p. 810 (bottom right): © Chris Johnson/Panos Pictures; p. 811: Vanessa Vick/Redux; p. 813: AP Photo/Anat Givon; p. 814 (top): Susan I. Cunningham/Panos Pictures; p. 814 (bottom): Morley Read/Alamy Stock Photo; p. 816: AP Photo/Jose Luis Magana; p. 817: SPUTNIK/Alamy Stock Photo; p. 818: Tom Stoddart Archive/Getty Images; p. 819: Peter Turnley/Corbis/VCG via Getty Images; p. 820: GABRIEL DUVAL/AFP/Getty Images; p. 821: Bettmann/Getty Images; p. 822: AP Photo/Jeff Widener; p. 824 (top): Clive Shirley/Panos Pictures; p. 824 (bottom): Schalkwijk/Art Resource, NY, © 2017 Artists Rights

Society (ARS), New York/SOMAAP, Mexico City.

Text Credits Page 794: Ann Tusa, "A Fatal Error," from *Media Studies Journal*, Fall 1999, pp. 26–29. Published by Freedom Forum, 1999. Copyright © Ann Tusa. Reproduced by permission of the author c/o Rogers, Coleridge & White Ltd., 20 Powis Mews, London W11 1JN; p. 812: World Bank. 2001. *World Development Report 2000/2001: Attacking Poverty*. World Development Report; New York: Oxford University Press. © World Bank. https://openknowledge.worldbank.org/handle/10986/11856 License: CC BY 3.0 IGO.

EPILOGUE

Photo Credits Page 828: AP Photo/Jason DeCrow; p. 828 (left): AP Photo/Carmen Taylor, File; p. 828 (right): Matthew McDermott; p. 831 (top): PA Images/Alamy Stock Photo; p. 831 (bottom): AP Photo/Mary Altaffer; p. 832: AP Photo/Jason DeCrow; p. 833 (left): Kyle Niemi/U.S. Coast Guard via Getty Images; p. 833 (right): AP Photo/Rich Schultz; p. 835: Jane Campbell/Shutterstock; p. 840: AP Photo/Mustafa Quraishi; p. 842: Dean Conger/Corbis via Getty Images; p. 843: Timothy O'Rourke/Bloomberg via Getty Images; p. 844: SEBASTIAN D'SOUZA/AFP/Getty Images; p. 845: AP Photo/Pete Muller; p. 851: Handout/Alamy Stock Photo; p. 854: Al-Furqan Media/Anadolu Agency/Getty Images; p. 855 (left): Liba Taylor/Corbis Documentary/Getty Images; p. 855 (right): Herman Wouters/Hollandse Hoogte/Redux; p. 856 (top): Militant video/Site Institute via AP; p. 856 (bottom): JASON REED/REUTERS/Newscom; p. 857 (top): AP Photo/Alexandre Meneghini; p. 857 (bottom): Alexander Hassenstein/Getty Images; p. 858: Kayhan Ozer/Anadolu Agency/Getty Images.

INDEX

Italic page references indicate maps, illustrations, or chronology entries.

agriculture *(cont.)*
  and Columbian exchange, 467, 468
  in Egypt, 582, 583
  in Eurasian steppes, 694, 695
  in Europe, 512
  and globalization, 814–15
  and industrialization, *575*, 578
  and manorialism/feudalism, 377–78
  Mayan, 619
  in North American colonies, 484, 486
  in Qing dynasty, 501
  in Soviet Union, 727, *727*, 778
  in Western Europe, 773
ahimsa, 368
AIDS (acquired immunodeficiency syndrome), *810*, 811–12, 854, *855*
AIWC (All India Women's Conference), 742
Akbar (Mughal ruler)
  architecture under, 525
  commerce under, 464–66
  economy under, 460
  expansion of Empire by, *465*, 504
  petitioners of, *460*
  religion under, 523, *525*
AKP (Justice and Development Party), 858
Alaska, 635, 662
Albania and Albanians, 785, 818
Albany, New York, 568
alcohol, 723
Alembert, Jean le Rond d', *542*
Aleppo, Syria, 460, 850
Alexander I, tsar of Russia, 581, 582, *582*, 593
Alexander II, tsar of Russia, 582, 661
Alexander III the Great, king of Macedonia, *374*, 398
Alexandria, Egypt, 359, 580
Algeria
  colonial administration in, 653
  decolonization in, 766, 768, 772
  French in, 648
  Islam in, 598, 599
  migration from, 798
  in OPEC, 785
  War of Independence in, 770
Algiers, 598
Algonquin, 546
Ali (caliph), 416
Ali, Muhammad (Egyptian ruler), 582–84, *584*, 591, *593*
Ali, Mustafa, 477, 478
al-Idrisi, map of, 524
Al-Jazeera, 850
Allende, Salvador, 781, 818
Allied Powers
  in Great War, 709, *710*, *712–13*, 714, 736, 743
  in World War II, 750, *752*, *756*, 757
All India Women's Conference (AIWC), 742
al-Maliki, Nuri, 852
Al-Nahda party, 850
Alps, 728
al-Qaeda, 715, 829, 830, 840, 851–52
Alsace, 577, 638, 639, 716
al-Shabab, 851
alternative movements (19th century), 594–627
  in China, 603–7
  in Europe, 607–12
  insurgencies against colonizing forces as, 612–25
  in Islamic world and Africa, 596–603, 620
  Native American, 595–96
  as reaction to social and political change, 596
al-Zarqawi, Abu Musab, 851–52
al-Zawahiri, Ayman, 851
Amazon River basin, 665
  agricultural production in, *814*, 815
  Brazil in, 636–37

diversity in, 789–90
  slave trade in, 494
Ambedkar, B. R., 740, 765
American colonies
  between 1750–1850, 556
  Anglicization in, 548–49
  cultural identity in, 547–48
  and global commerce, 479
  war of independence in, 557, 560–62
Americanization, 790
American Railway Union, 686
American Revolution, 557, 560–62, *592*
"Americans," 631
Americas, 388–91, 399
  see also Atlantic world; Mesoamerica; North America; South America; *specific people, cities, regions and topics*
  between 1500–1780, 551
  between 1600–1750, 478, 479, 515
  between 1750–1850, 556, 591
  between 1910–1939, 745
  Afro-Eurasian contact with, 440, 467
  Amerindian mortality in, 468
  Andean states in, 388
  Chinese crops from, 589
  cultural achievements in, 545–48
  global commerce in, 482
  Little Ice Age in, 483–84
  mercantilist wars in, 514
  migration in, 358, 674, 724
  nation building in, 631–37
  revolutions in, 556–62, 566–72, *593*
  silver from, *499*
  in slave trade, 488–90
  Spanish and Portuguese Empires in, *469*
  trade with, 387–91, 466, 495, 520, 574, 578
Amerindians
  see also Native Americans; *specific nations and tribes*
  between 1600–1750, 515
  in American Revolution, 557
  and colonization, 473
  in culture of Americas, 545–47, *547*
  disease and decimation of, 445, 448, *453*, 467
  European conquest of, 449, 468
  first encounters with, 449
  forced conversions of, *546*
  and Latin American nation building, 635, 637, 695
  in mercantilist wars, 514
  and North American colonies, 484, 486
  Portuguese interactions with, 471
  racial thought by, 543
  silver mining by, 455–56, 482
  Spanish tribute from, 468
  and tobacco plantations, *487*
  trade with, *486*, 486–87, 520
Amnesty International, 818
Amri, Anis, 841
Amritsar massacre, 718, 738
Amsterdam, Netherlands, 479, *483*, 502, *512*, 539
Amur River basin, 661–62
Anabaptists, 609
anarchism, 686
Anatolia
  see also Ottoman Empire
  after Great War, 743
  Egyptian invasion of, 584
  Great War in, 711
  Ottoman Empire in, 408, 410, 411, 441
  Safavids in, 416, 443
  Sufism in, 365
  trade with, 460
  Turks in, 363
  uprisings against Ottomans in, 478, 496

of India, 843
and industrialization, 682
integration of world, 643–44
of Japan, 658–59, *661*
of Latin America, 734
market, 720
modernism in terms of, 708
politics and globalization of, 841–43
in Song dynasty, 368, 369
in Third World, 785
of United States, 631, 633–34
of Western Europe, 510–12
worldwide insecurities about, 681
Ecuador, 454, 572, 785
Edinburgh, Scotland, 539
Edo, 506, *506*, 512, 532
see also Tokyo, Japan
Edo Bay, 658, *659*
Edo in the Rain (Hiroshige), *506*
education
see also literacy; *specific nations and empires*
in China, 664–65
in Egypt, 582
equality in, *811*, 812–13
European protests about, 781
and nation building, 630
in Ottoman Empire, 521
and popular culture, 689
in Soviet Union, 776
Egypt, 359, 361
between 1750–1850, 555, 556, *593*
19th century reforms in, 582–84
between 1910–1939, 707
Jamal al-Din al-Afghani in, 700, 701
anticolonialism in, 717, 744
in Arab Spring, 845, *845*, 850, 851
autonomy in, 776
Black Death in, 405
British occupation of, *667*
coffeehouses in, 479
in Cold War, 790
economy in, 576
financial crisis in, 682
French occupation of, 565, *567*, 583
global and local culture in, 803, 804
and global finance, 797
globalization's effect on, 859
Great War in, 711
imperialism in, 646, 648, 650, 654
industrialization and women's freedom in, 685
in industrial revolution, 577
Islam in, 363, 597
Mamluks in, 496–97
merchants and trade networks, 362
militarization in, 777
and Mongol conquest, 397, 398
Muslim Brotherhood in, 744, *747*
Ottoman conquests in, 440–43, 477
population of, 580, 809
Qalandar dervish order in, 410
slaves and slave trade in, 386, 387, 489
in Third World, 776
violent decolonization in, 769–70
and World War II, 751
Eiffel Tower (Paris, France), 642, *642*
Einstein, Albert, 690
ejidos, 687
Eknath, 524
"Elder Brother," 604
Eleanor of Aquitaine, 381
elections
see also voting
in Africa, 854
and Arab Spring, 850
and democracy, 824–25
democratic, 821
Iraqi, *831*
in South Africa, 796, *827*
Electoral College, 834, 858
electricity, 642
elites
see also social organization
between 1750–1850, 556
between 1850–1914, 703
and black rule in Africa, 794
cultural achievements for, 551
in India, 698
in Latin America, 635–37, 734, 856
mass culture vs. culture for, 719
in Ottoman Empire, 441
in Song dynasty, 369, 370
in sub-Saharan Africa, 736
Elizabeth I, queen of England, 457, 513, *514*
El Salvador, 819
empire(s)
see also specific dynasties and empires
expansion of, 630
and Great War, 711, 715
and postwar decolonization, 760
in three-world order, 749
enclosure, 512
encomenderos, 449, 451
encomiendas, 449, 453, 470
Encyclopédie (Diderot), 539–41, *542*
Enfield rifle, 622
Engels, Friedrich, *611*, 611–13, *627*
England and English, *421*
see also Great Britain and British; United Kingdom
between 1600–1750, 508, 515, *516*, *517*
in Americas, 478, 484–88, *485*, *489*
Asian trade with, 466, 467
Chinese view of, 530
dynastic monarchies of, 513–14
economy of, 420, 421, 512
Enlightenment in, 537
exploration by, *446–47*
feudalism in, 420
and global commerce, 479, *480–81*
in Hundred Years' War, 423
immigrants in, 674
and Irish nationalism, 641–42
manorialism in, 377, 378
Marx and Engels in, 612
in mercantilist wars, 514–15
monarchy in, 422, 434
and Mughal Empire, 466, 505
nationalism in, 630, 637
Parliament in, 420
Peasants Revolt in, 420, *436*
political consolidation in, 423
population of, 409, 423, 580
Protestant Reformation in, 457
religious warfare in, 459, 460
Renaissance in, 423, 426
in Thirty Years' War, 511
in transatlantic slave trade, 472
Tudors in, *437*
English language, 420, 634, 835
Enlightenment (European), 535–45
and basis of new science, 535, 537–38
consequences of, 540–43
and cultural modernism, 688
and culture in Americas, 548
global perspective on, 543–45